AF207896

VOODOO RAINBOW

LES SECRETS DU VAUDOU

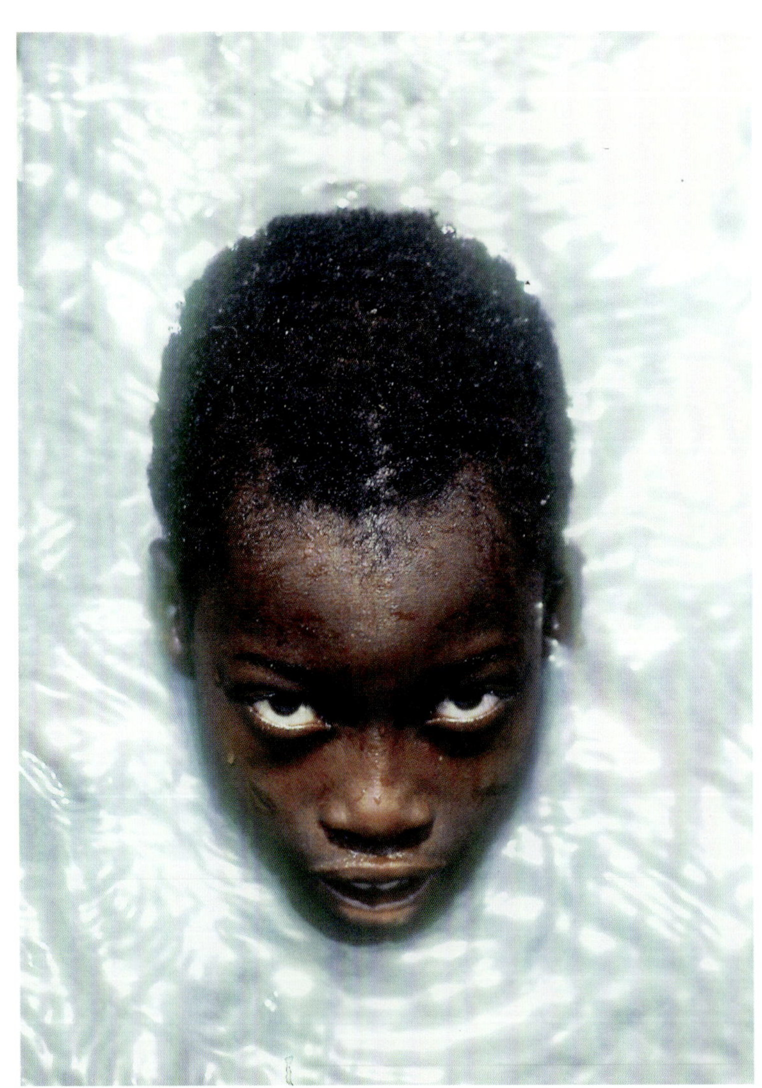

HENNING CHRISTOPH
MARKUS MATZEL
PHILIPP SCHIEMANN

VOODOO RAINBOW
LES SECRETS DU VAUDOU

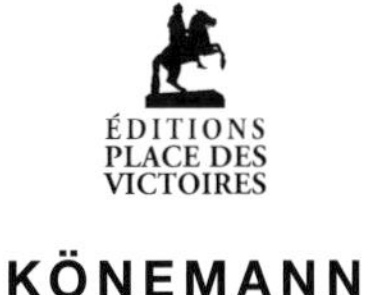

ÉDITIONS
PLACE DES
VICTOIRES

KÖNEMANN

Contents
Sommaire
Inhalt
Índice
Inhoud

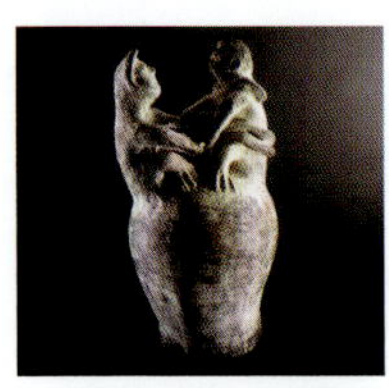

10 Introduction
Introduction
Einleitung
Observaciones preliminares
Observações introdutórias
Inleidende opmerkingen

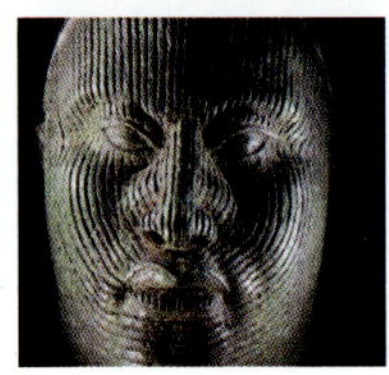

14 Bronze casting and the world of gods
Bronze coulé et monde des dieux
Bronzeguss und Götterwelt
La fundición en bronce y el mundo de los dioses
Fundição de bronze e o mundo dos deuses
Bronsgieten en godenwereld

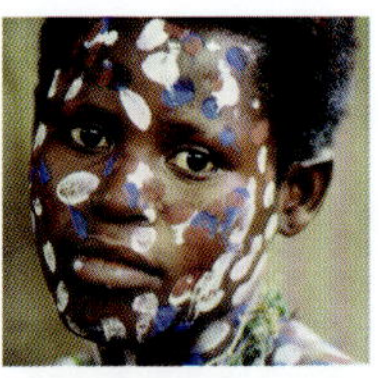

16 Sakpata, God of the bitter earth
Sakpata, dieu de la Terre amère
Sakpata, Gott der bitteren Erde
Sakpata, Dios de la tierra amarga
Sakpata, Deus da terra amarga
Sakpata, god van de bittere aarde

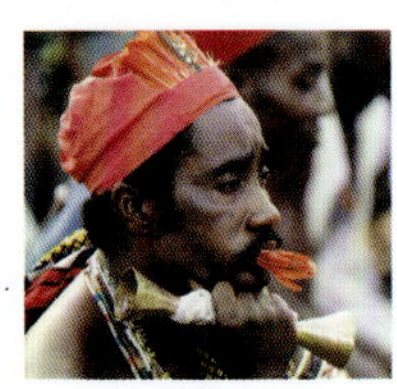

26 Shango, God of thunder and lightning
Shangô, dieu du tonnerre et des éclairs
Shango, Gott des Donners und Blitzes
Shango, Dios del trueno y del relámpago
Shango, Deus dos trovões e relâmpagos
Shango, god van donder en bliksem

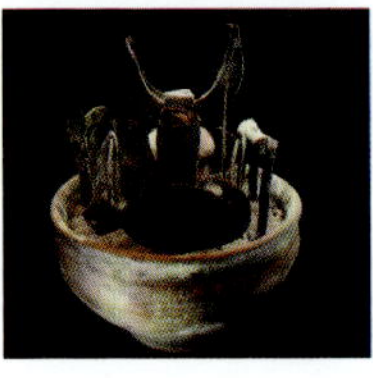

38 Gu, the Iron Warrior
Gu, le guerrier inébranlable
Gu, der eiserne Krieger
Gu, el guerrero de hierro
Gu, O Guerreiro de Ferro
Gu, de ijzeren krijger

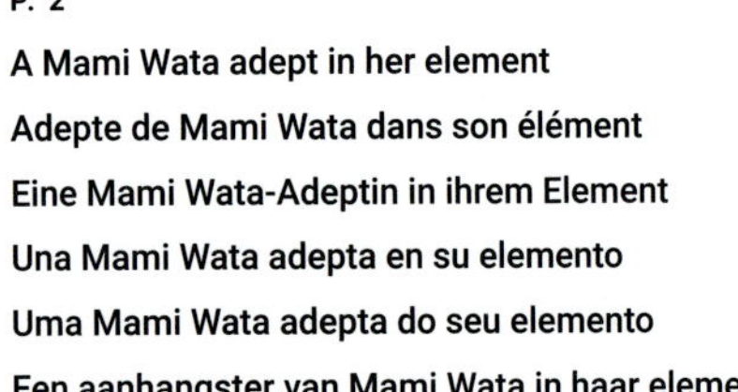

P. 2

A Mami Wata adept in her element

Adepte de Mami Wata dans son élément

Eine Mami Wata-Adeptin in ihrem Element

Una Mami Wata adepta en su elemento

Uma Mami Wata adepta do seu elemento

Een aanhangster van Mami Wata in haar element

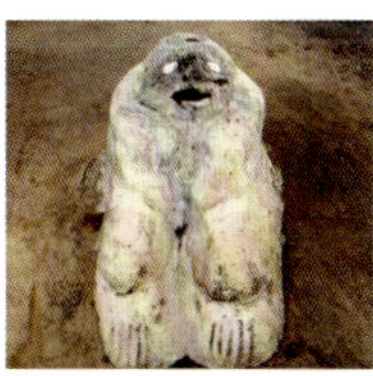

46 Legba, the mediator and joker
Legba, intermédiaire facétieux
Legba, der Vermittler und Joker
Legba, el mediador y guasón
Legba, O mediador e Joker
Legba, de bemiddelaar en joker

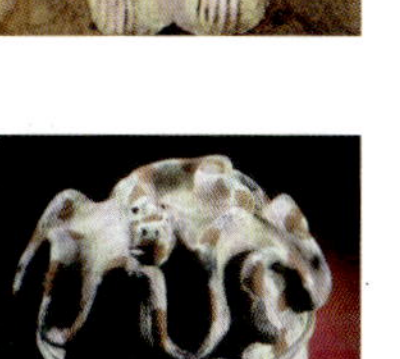

56 Dan—the snake of fate
Dan, le serpent du destin
Dan – die Schlange des Schicksals
Dan, la serpiente del destino
Dan – A cobra do destino
Dan, de slang van het lot

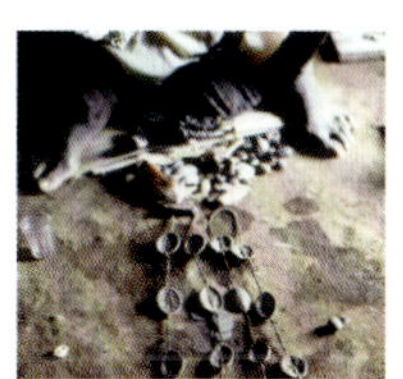

62 Ifa—Oracle and god
Ifa, oracle et divinité
Ifa – Orakel und Gottheit
Ifa– Oráculo y deidad
Ifa – Oráculo e Divindade
Ifa, orakel en godheid

72 Mami Wata

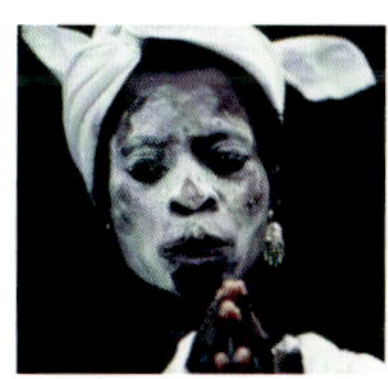

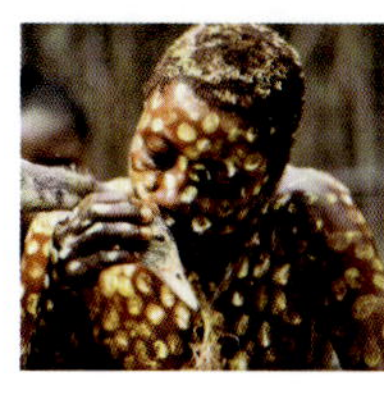

122 Sakpata – Healing with the Lord of Diseases
Sakpata, guérison par le seigneur des maladies
Sakpata – Heilung beim Herrn der Krankheiten
Sakpata– Curación con el señor de las enfermedades
Sakpata – Cura com o Senhor das Doenças
Sakpata, genezing door de heer over de ziekten

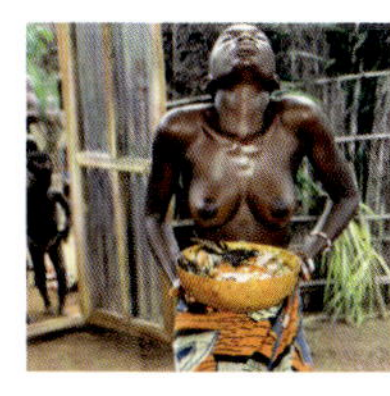

130 Lydwin's cure
La guérison de Lydwin
Lydwins Heilung
La cura de Lydwin
A cura de Lydwin
Lydwins genezing

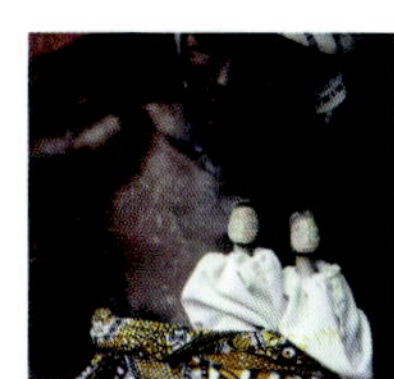

138 Twins—Remembrance in reverence
Jumeaux, mémoire respectueuse
Zwillinge – Gedenken in Ehrfurcht
Los gemelos– Recuerdos en reverencia
Gêmeos – Memória em reverência
Tweelingen – herdenken met eerbied

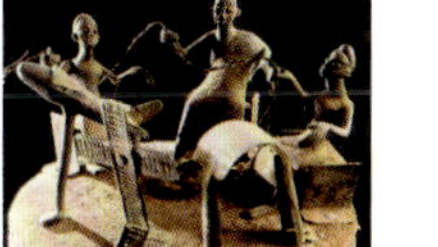

160 Asen—dwelling place for the spirits of the dead
Asen, les maisons des esprits des défunts
Asen – Wohnstätte für die Totengeister
Asen– Morada para los espíritus de los muertos
Asen – Lugar de morada para os espíritos dos mortos
Asen – thuis voor de geesten van de doden

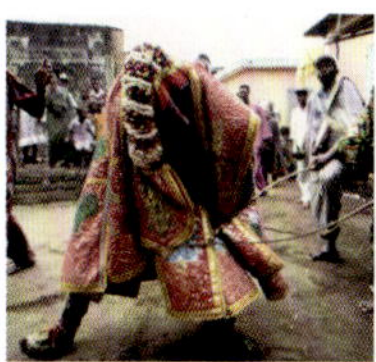

166 Egungun, the representatives of the ancestors
Egungun, les représentants des ancêtres
Egungun, die Vertreter der Ahnen
Egungun, los representantes de los ancestros
Egungun, Os representantes dos antepassados
Egungun, de vertegenwoordigers van de voorouders

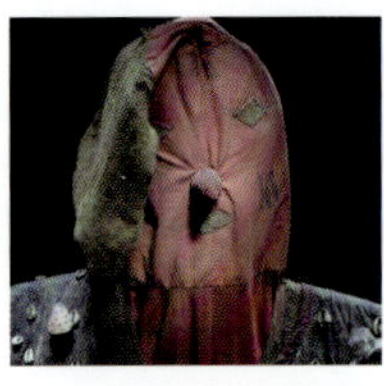

176 Egungun—The executioner
Egungun, le bourreau
Egungun – Der Scharfrichter
Egungun– El verdugo
Egungun – O carrasco
Egungun – de beul

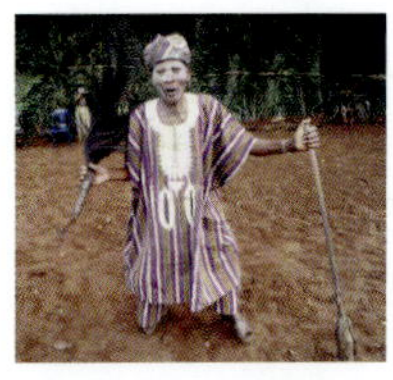

184 Gelede, the traditional theatre
Gèlèdé, le théâtre traditionnel
Gelede, das traditionelle Theater
Gelede, el teatro tradicional
Gelede, O teatro tradicional
Gelede, het traditionele theater

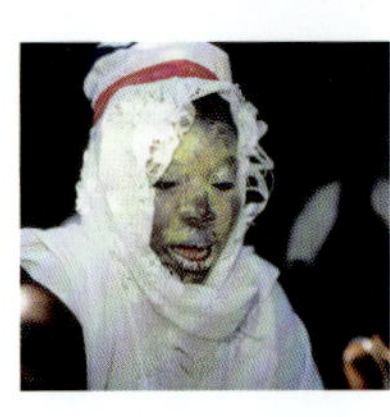

192 Oro, the buzzing woods guardian
Oro, les gardiens aux rhombes
Oro, die Schwirrholzwächter
Oro, el guardián churinga
Oro, O Guardião dos trovões.
Oro, de bromhoutwachter

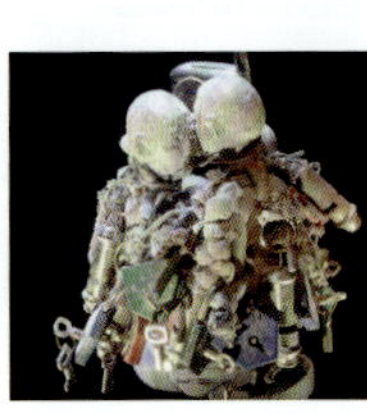

200 Tron—Warrior power against witchcraft
Tron, la force des guerriers contre la sorcellerie
Tron – Kriegerkraft gegen Hexerei
Tron– Poder guerrero contra la brujería
Tron – Poder guerreiro contra a bruxaria
Tron – krijgersmacht tegen hekserij

210 Bo and Bocio—Magic Objects
Bo et bocio, objets magiques
Bo und Bocio – Magische Objekte
Bo y Bocio– Objetos mágicos
Bo e Bocio – Objetos Mágicos
Bo en bocio, magische objecten

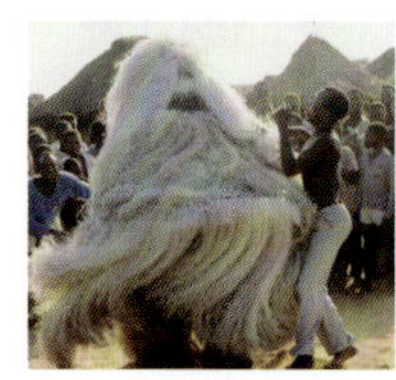

216 Zangbeto—the Police of the night
Zangbeto, la police de la nuit
Zangbeto – die Polizei der Nacht
Zangbeto– La policía de la noche
Zangbeto – A polícia da noite
Zangbeto – de politie van de nacht

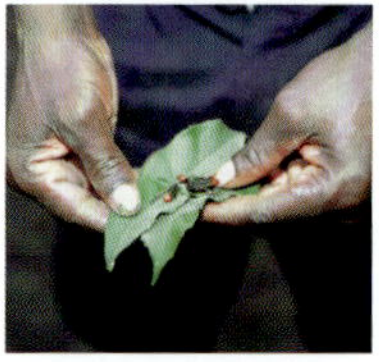

222 The Bush Spirits—Inhabitants of the Wild land
Les génies de brousse, habitants des terres sauvages
Die Buschgeister – Bewohner des Wildlandes
Los espíritus de Bush– Habitantes de la tierra salvaje
Os Espíritos Bush – Habitantes da Terra Selvagem
De bushgeesten – bewoners van het wilde land

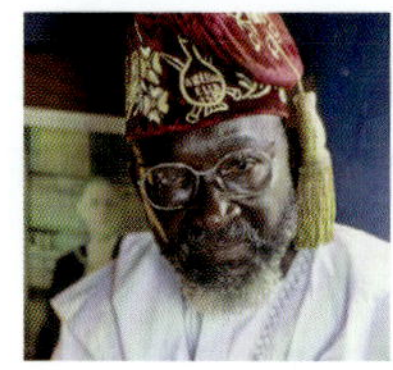

228 Tzakatou—healing from the African pistol
Le *tzakatou*, guérison contre le pistolet africain
Tzakatou – Heilung von der afrikanischen Pistole
Tzakatou– La curación de la pistola africana
Tzakatou – A cura da pistola africana
Tzakatou – genezing van het Afrikaanse pistool

238 Sergent Kiki—at the gods' command
Sergent Kiki, aux ordres des dieux
Sergent Kiki – den Göttern zu Befehl
Sargento Kiki, a las órdenes de los dioses
Sergent Kiki – Ao comando dos deuses
Sergeant Kiki – op bevel van de goden

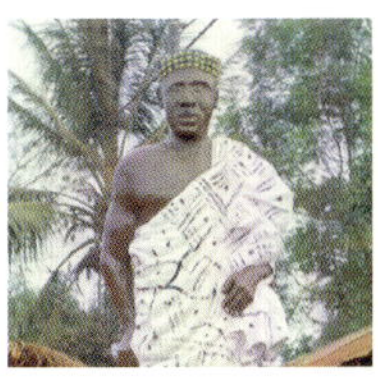

244 Last Honor for the Vodun Pope
Derniers honneurs pour le pape du
  vodun
Letzte Ehre für den Vodun–Papst
Última gloria al Papa Vudú
Última Glória ao Papa Vodu
Laatste eer voor de vodunpaus

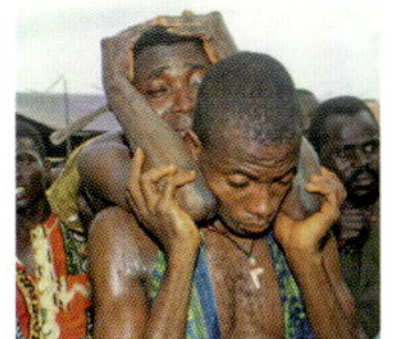

**256 Martial Witch Defense:
Ganbada and Kokou**
Défense martiale contre les sorciers,
  Ganbada et Kokou
Martialische Hexenabwehr:
  Ganbada und Kokou
Defensa de la bruja marcial:
  Ganbada y Kokou
Defesa das bruxas marciais:
  Ganbada e Kokou
Krijgshaftige heksenafweer:
  Ganbada en Kokou

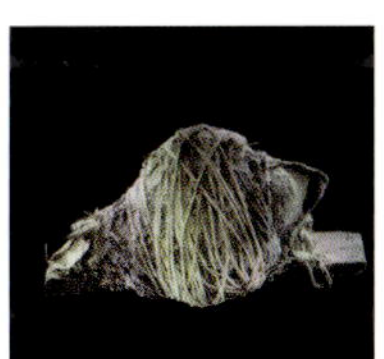

260 Magic, sorcery and witchcraft
Enchantement, magie et sorcellerie
Zauberei, Magie und Hexenwerk
Magia, hechicería y brujería
Magia, Feitiçaria e bruxaria
Magie, tovenarij en hekserij

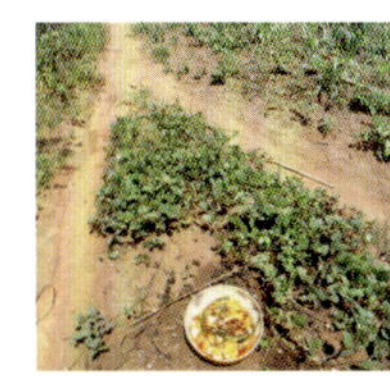

268 The Holi, the dreaded people
Les Holi, peuple redouté
Die Holi, das gefürchtete Volk
Los Holi, el pueblo temido
O Holi, As pessoas temidas
De Holi, het gevreesde volk

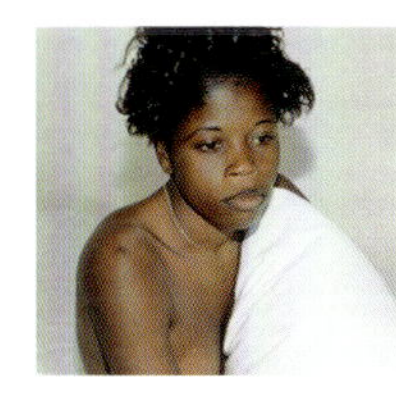

**292 Nightmares—Witches
come at night**
Cauchemars, les sorciers viennent
  la nuit
Albträume – Nachts kommen die
  Hexen
Pesadillas– Las brujas vienen de
  noche
Pesadelos – As bruxas vêm à noite
Nachtmerries – 's nachts komen de
  heksen

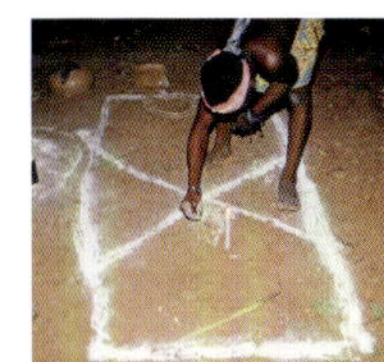

**294 Harmful spells—draconian
defense against the
greatest suffering**
Magie maléfique, méthodes
  draconiennes en cas d'urgence
Schadenzauber – drakonische
  Abwehr in höchster Not
Hechizo maligno– Defensa
  draconiana en los casos de
  máxima emergencia
Feitiço de dano – Defesa draconiana
  no mais alto nível de perigo
Zwarte magie – draconische
  verdediging in hoge nood

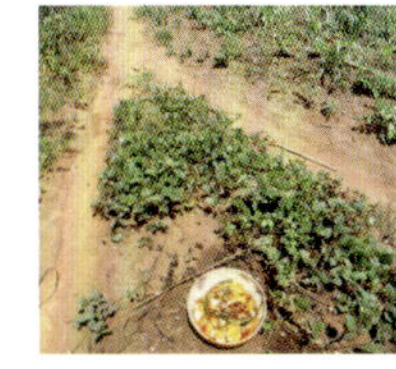

**304 Crossroads—The sacrifice
at the crossroads**
Sacrifices au croisement
Crossroads – Das Opfer an der
  Kreuzung
Crossroads– La víctima en el cruce
Crossroads – A vítima na
  encruzilhada
Crossroads – het offer op het
  kruispunt

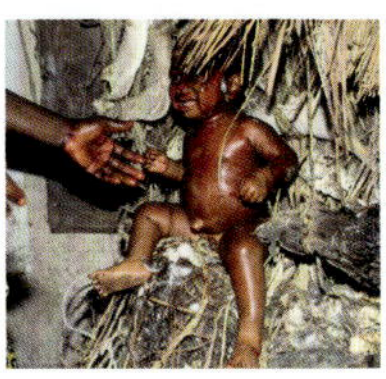

306 Witch protection for a baby
Protection d'un bébé contre les sorciers
Hexenschutz für ein Baby
Protección de las brujas para un bebé
Protecção de bruxas para um bebé
Bescherming tegen heksen voor baby's

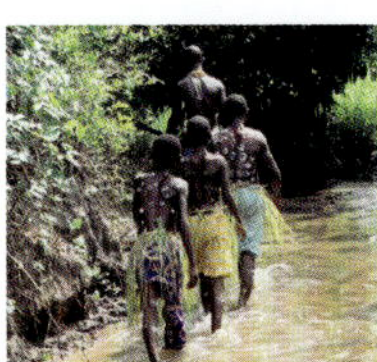

312 Healing three bewitched brothers
Guérison de trois frères envoûtés
Heilung drei verhexter Brüder
Sanando a tres hermanos maldecidos
Curando três irmãos enfeitiçados
Genezing van drie behekste broers

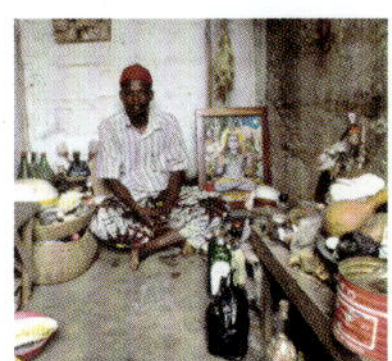

326 The youngest healer of Porto-Novo
Le plus jeune guérisseur de Porto-Novo
Der jüngste Heiler von Porto-Novo
El curandero más joven de Porto-Novo
O mais jovem curandeiro de Porto-Novo
De jongste genezer van Porto-Novo

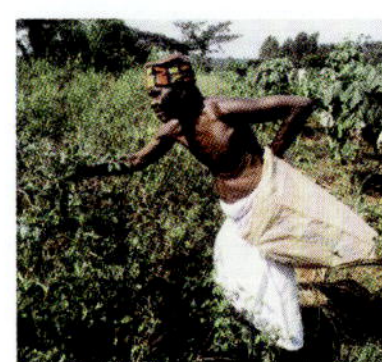

332 Medicine—image of divine powers
Médecine, à l'image de la puissance des dieux
Medizin – Abbild göttlicher Kräfte
Medicina– Imagen de los poderes divinos
Medicina – Imagem dos poderes divinos
Geneeskunde – beeld van goddelijke krachten

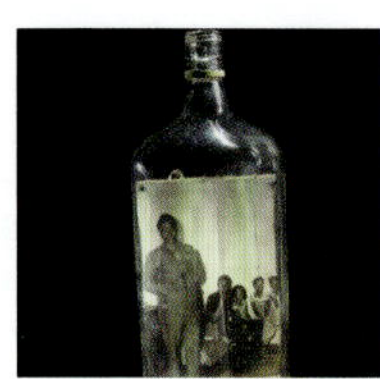

342 Bottles—objects of power
Les bouteilles, objets de puissance
Flaschen – Objekte der Kraft
Botellas– Objetos de poder
Garrafas – Objetos de poder
Flessen – objecten van macht

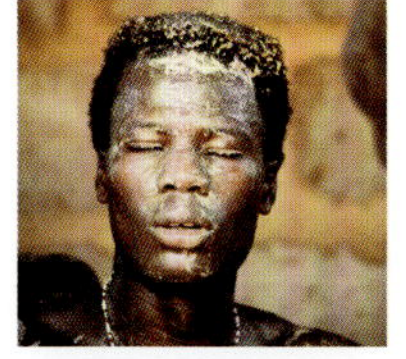

346 Nana Tongo, the god from the north
Nana Tongo, le dieu venu du nord
Nana Tongo, der Gott aus dem Norden
Nana Tongo, el Dios del Norte
Nana Tongo, o deus do norte
Nana Tongo, de god uit het noorden

354 Kokou—unleashed against the witches
Kokou, déchaîné contre les sorciers
Kokou – entfesselt gegen die Hexen
Kokou– desatado contra las brujas
Kokou – Libertado contra as bruxas
Kokou – ontketend tegen de heksen

372 Djagli—Wild as a bird
Djagli, sauvage comme un oiseau
Djagli – Wild wie ein Vogel
Djagli– Salvaje como un pájaro
Djagli – Jogo como um pássaro
Djagli – wild als een vogel

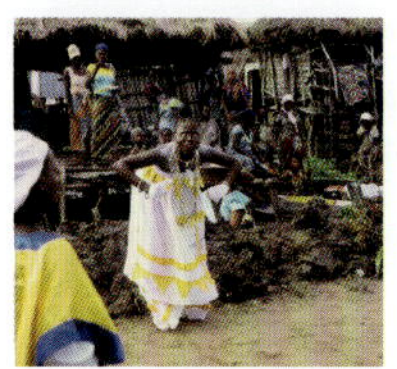

386 Attigali—Wild mixture against witches
Attigali, mélange sauvage contre les sorciers
Attigali – Wilde Mischung gegen Hexen
Attigali– Mezcla salvaje contra las brujas
Attigali – Mistura selvagem contra bruxas
Attigali – wilde mix tegen heksen

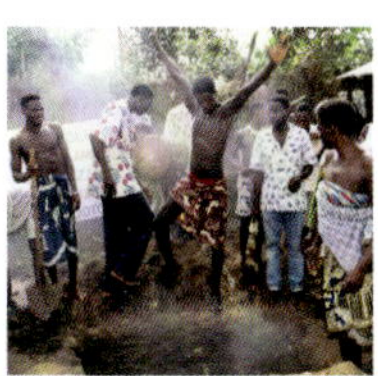

398 New Year—Funeral of Sin and Rebirth
Nouvelle année, enterrement des péchés et renaissance
Neujahr – Sündenbegräbnis und Wiedergeburt
Año Nuevo– El entierro del pecado y el renacimiento
Ano Novo – Funeral do Pecado e Renascimento
Nieuwjaar – begrafenis van zonden en wedergeboorte

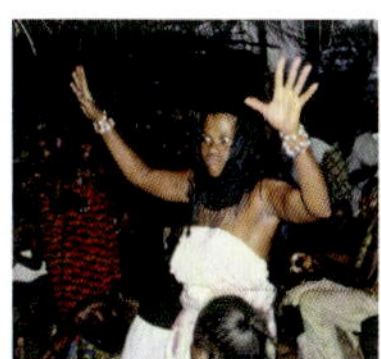

402 Delassi—unleashing par excellence
Delassi, déchaînement par excellence
Delassi – Entfesselung par excellence
Delassi– La liberación por excelencia
Delassi – Libertando por excelência
Delassi – ontketening bij uitstek

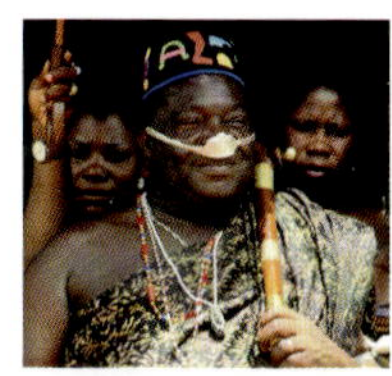

410 The King of Abomey
Le roi d'Abomey
Der König von Abomey
El Rey de Abomey
O Rei de Abomey
De koning van Abomey

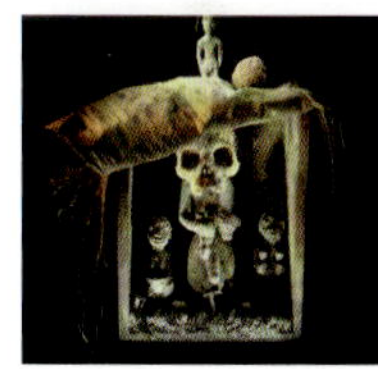

414 The Amazons—Dahomey's fearless women's army
Les Amazones, l'armée de femmes intrépides du Dahomey
Die Amazonen – Dahomeys furchtlose Frauenarmee
Las Amazonas– El ejército de mujeres intrépidas de Dahomey
As Amazonas – Dahomeys destemido exército de mulheres
De Amazones – het onverschrokken vrouwenleger van Dahomey

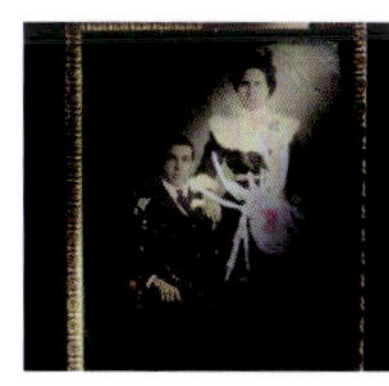

416 Slavery—The unpunished injustice
Esclavage, violente oppression
Sklaverei – Das ungesühnte Unrecht
Esclavitud– La injusticia impune
Escravidão – A injustiça impune
Slavernij – ongewroken onrecht

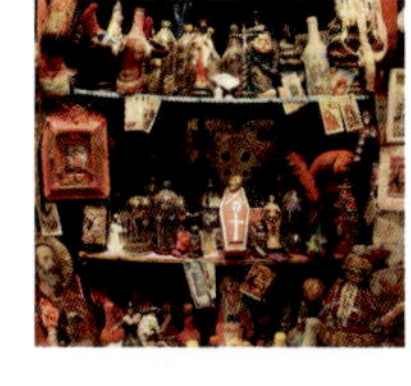

420 Haiti—Rada and Petro
Haïti, Rada et Petro
Haiti – Rada und Petro
Haití– Rada y Petro
Haiti – Rada e Petro
Haïti – rada en petro

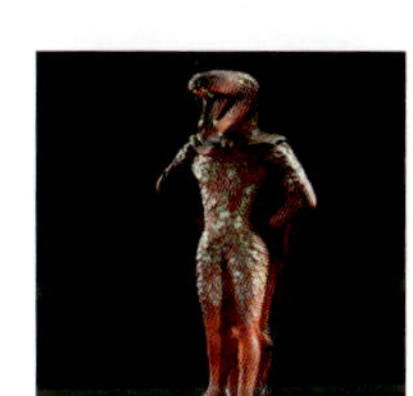

424 Palo—Congo in Cuba
Palo, Congo de Cuba
Palo – Kongo in Kuba
Palo– El Congo en Cuba
Palo – Congo em Cuba
Palo – Congo in Cuba

430 Quimbanda, a child of Macumba
Quimbanda, enfant de Macumba
Quimbanda, ein Kind Macumbas
Quimbanda, un hijo de Macumba
Quimbanda, uma criança de Macumba
Quimbanda, een kind van Macumba

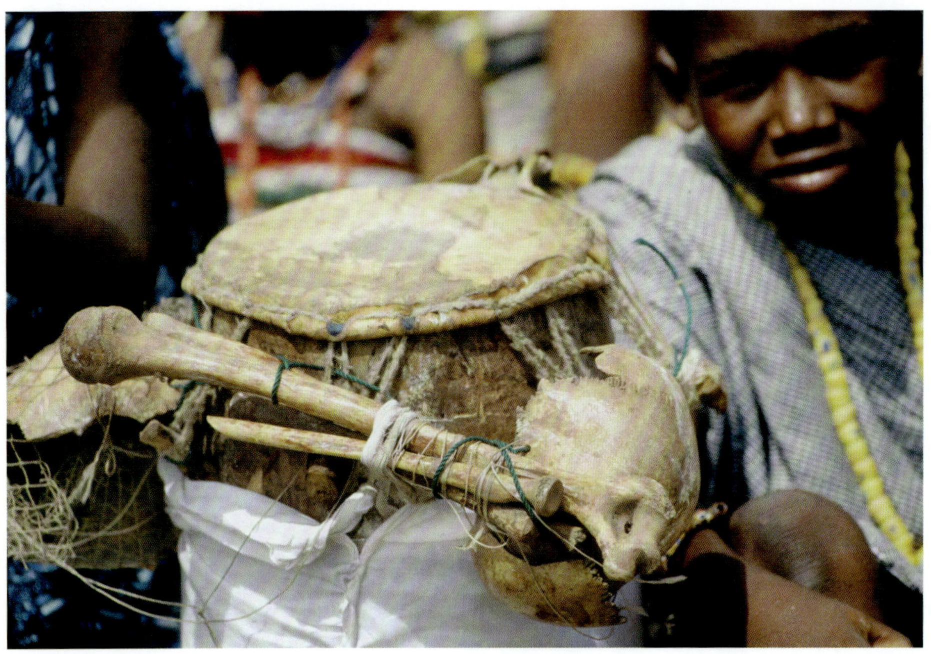

Introduction

There is hardly a religion in the world about which so many horror stories have been told as about Voodoo. The word itself, which comes from the language area of the Fon people in West African Benin and is actually called *Vodun,* means nothing more than "God" or "divine". The Vodun are the ancient gods of Benin, with whom in Africa and the Diaspora (in Haiti: *Vodou*) a wealth of fascinating beliefs and customs are connected.

Largely unnoticed by the western industrial nations, parallel worlds exist here in which effective solutions for all problems of human existence are found with traditional, ancient knowledge. Extensive secrets about medicinal plants and their application are inseparably linked with a world view in which every human being is part of a magical, spiritually significant whole.

The well-known ethnologist and photographer Henning Christoph has gained access to these areas and documented them in the course of many years of research trips.

Introduction

Peu de religions dans le monde ont autant été décriées que le vaudou. Pourtant, son nom, emprunté à la langue du peuple Fon du Bénin, ne signifie rien de plus que « dieu » ou « divin ». Le vaudou, ou plus exactement *vodun*, désigne ainsi les dieux anciens du Bénin (anciennement le Dahomey), auxquels sont associées de très nombreuses croyances et coutumes fascinantes en Afrique, mais également chez des peuples issus de la diaspora africaine (vaudou haïtien).

Dans ces régions, loin des nations industrielles occidentales, des mondes parallèles perdurent, et des connaissances traditionnelles ancestrales qui continuent d'être diffusées permettent aux hommes de trouver des solutions efficaces à tous leurs problèmes. Ces vastes savoirs secrets autour des plantes médicinales et de leur emploi sont directement liés à une vision du monde dans laquelle chaque humain fait partie d'un tout significatif spirituel et magique.

Au cours de nombreux voyages d'études s'étendant sur plusieurs années, le célèbre

Einleitung

Über kaum eine Religion auf der Welt sind so viele Schauermärchen erzählt worden wie über Voodoo. Dabei bedeutet das Wort selbst, das aus dem Sprachraum des Volkes der Fon im westafrikanischen Benin stammt und eigentlich *Vodun* heißt, nichts weiter als „Gott" oder „göttlich". Die Vodun, das sind die alten Götter Benins, mit denen in Afrika und der Diaspora (in Haiti: *Vodou*) eine Fülle faszinierender Glaubensvorstellungen und Gebräuche verbunden sind.

Weitgehend unbemerkt von den westlichen Industrienationen existieren hier Parallelwelten, in denen mit traditionellem, uraltem Wissen für alle Probleme menschlichen Seins effektive Lösungen gefunden werden. Umfangreiche Geheimnisse über Heilpflanzen und deren Anwendung sind hier untrennbar mit einer Weltsicht verbunden, in der jeder Mensch Teil eines magischen, spirituell bedeutsamen Ganzen ist.

Der bekannte Ethnologe und Fotograf Henning Christoph hat im Laufe jahrelanger

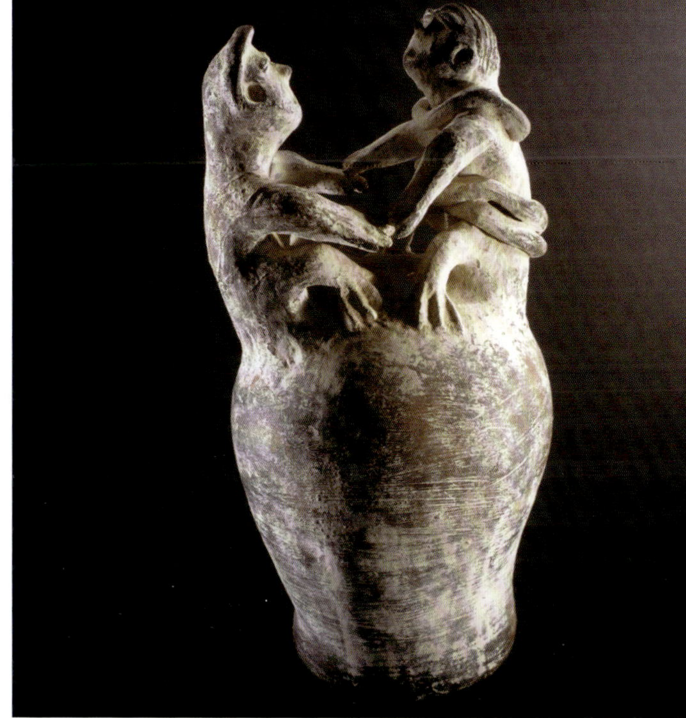

The figures stand for Mami Wata and her husband Nana Densu
Figures représentant Mami Wata et son époux Nana Densu
Die Figuren stehen für Mami Wata und ihren Ehemann Nana Densu
Las figuras corresponden a Mami Wata y su marido Nana Densu
As figuras representam Mami Wata e seu marido Nana Densu
De beelden staan voor Mami Wata en haar man Nana Densu

Observaciones preliminares

No hay ninguna religión en el mundo sobre la que se hayan contado tantas historias de horror como sobre el *Voodoo*. La palabra en sí, que proviene del área lingüística del pueblo Fon en el África Occidental de Benín y que en realidad se llama Vudú, no significa nada más que "Dios" o "divino". Los Vudú son los antiguos dioses de Benin, con los que en África y en la Diáspora (en Haití: *Vodou*) se relacionan un sinfín de creencias y costumbres fascinantes.

Los países industrializados occidentales pasan en gran medida desapercibidos, y aquí existen mundos paralelos en los que se encuentran soluciones eficaces para todos los problemas de la existencia humana gracias a los conocimientos tradicionales y antiguos. Extensos secretos sobre las plantas medicinales y su aplicación están inseparablemente ligados a una visión del mundo en la que cada ser humano es parte de un todo mágico y espiritualmente significativo.

El conocido etnólogo y fotógrafo Henning Christoph ha accedido a estas áreas y

Observações introdutórias

Dificilmente há uma religião no mundo sobre a qual tantas histórias de horror tenham sido contadas como sobre Voodoo. A palavra em si, que vem da área linguística do povo Fon no Benin da África Ocidental e é realmente chamada Vodun, não significa nada mais do que "Deus" ou "divino". O Vodun, estes são os antigos deuses do Benin, com quem na África e na diáspora (no Haiti: Vodou) uma riqueza de crenças e costumes fascinantes estão ligados.

Desapercebido largamente pelas nações industriais ocidentais, os mundos paralelos existem aqui em que as soluções eficazes para todos os problemas da existência humana são encontradas com o conhecimento tradicional, antigo. Segredos extensos sobre as plantas medicinais e sua aplicação estão inseparavelmente ligados a uma visão de mundo na qual cada ser humano é parte de um todo mágico e espiritualmente significativo.

O conhecido etnólogo e fotógrafo Henning Christoph ganhou acesso a estas

Inleiding

Er zijn weinig religies in de wereld waarover zoveel gruwelverhalen zijn verteld als over voodoo. Het woord zelf, dat afkomstig is uit het taalgebied van het Fon-volk in het West-Afrikaans Benin en eigenlijk *vodun* luidt, betekent niets meer dan 'god' of 'goddelijk'. De vodun zijn de oude goden van Benin, waarmee in Afrika en de diaspora (in Haïti: vodou) een schat aan fascinerende geloofsovertuigingen en gebruiken verbonden zijn.

Grotendeels onopgemerkt door de westerse industrielanden bestaan hier parallelle werelden waarin met oeroude traditionele kennis effectieve oplossingen worden gevonden voor alle problemen van het menselijk bestaan. Uitvoerige geheimen over geneeskrachtige planten en de toepassing ervan zijn onlosmakelijk verbonden met een wereldbeeld waarin ieder mens deel uitmaakt van een magisch, spiritueel belangrijk geheel.

De bekende etnoloog en fotograaf Henning Christoph kreeg toegang tot deze

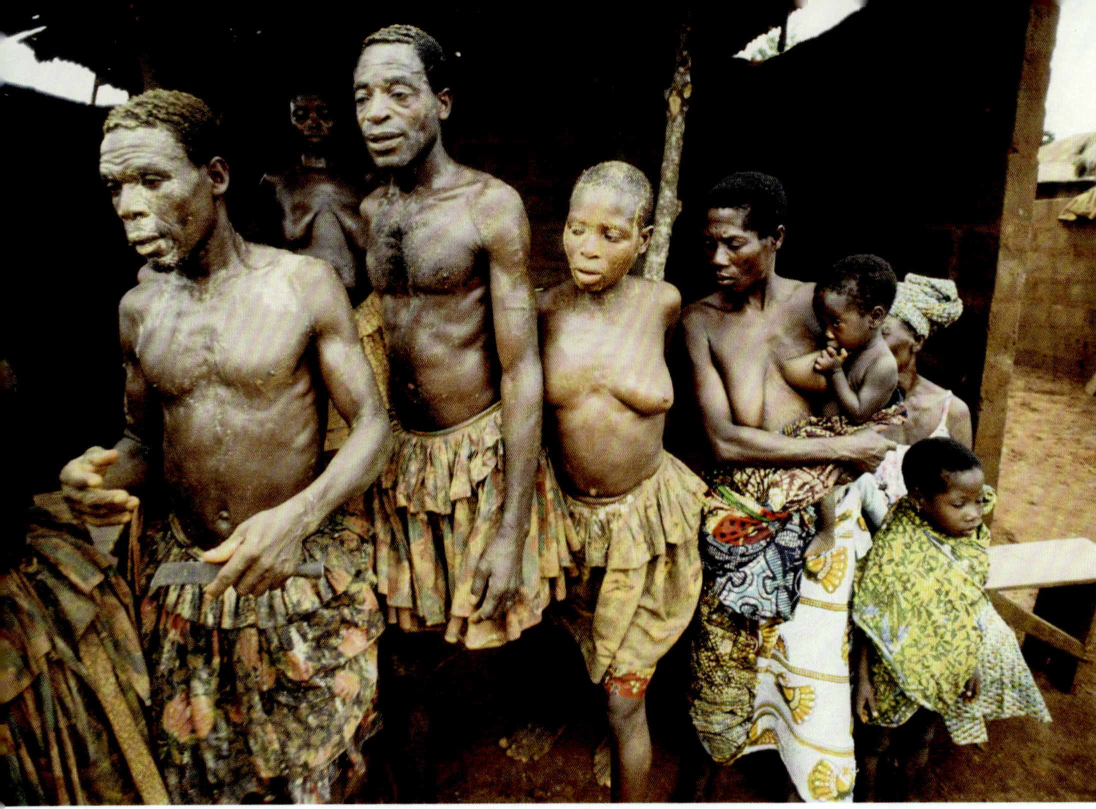

It often took many visits to the remotest areas until so much trust was built that he was allowed to participate in the events. In the course of this, events were photographed that had previously been taboo for outsiders, in some cases even considered extinct. They impressively bear witness to the fact that the scientific approach of facts and formulas is just one variant with which our existence can be described.

The images of rituals, gods and secret societies collected in this volume represent in this density a unique collection. Many of the ceremonies shown have never before been portrayed in an illustrated book and cast a new light on a misunderstood but nevertheless ancient genuine African religion: Vodun.

ethnologue et photographe Henning Christoph a pu pénétrer dans ces sphères et les documenter. Il lui a fallu plusieurs visites dans les régions les plus reculées, avant qu'une confiance mutuelle ne soit établie et qu'on le laisse prendre part aux événements. Il a alors pu photographier des cérémonies jusqu'ici restées taboues pour le monde extérieur, et dont certaines étaient considérées comme disparues. Ses images témoignent avec force que l'approche scientifique des faits n'est qu'une manière parmi d'autres de dépeindre notre existence et qu'une approche artistique n'est pas à négliger.

Les photographies de rituels, représentations divines et sociétés secrètes regroupées dans ce livre constituent une collection unique. Nombre de cérémonies n'avaient encore jamais été présentées dans un livre de photographies et apportent un éclairage nouveau sur une religion africaine mal comprise et pourtant ancestrale et authentique : le vodun.

Forschungsreisen Zugang zu diesen Bereichen bekommen und sie dokumentiert. Oftmals brauchte es dazu viele Besuche in entlegensten Gebieten, bis soviel Vertrauen entstanden war, dass man ihn am Geschehen teilhaben ließ. Im Zuge dessen wurden Ereignisse fotografiert, die für Außenstehende bislang tabu waren, teils sogar als ausgestorben galten. Eindrucksvoll legen sie Zeugnis darüber ab, dass der naturwissenschaftliche Ansatz der Fakten und Formeln eben nur eine Variante ist, mit der sich unsere Existenz beschreiben lässt.

Die im vorliegenden Band versammelten Bilder von Ritualen, Göttern und Geheimbünden stellen eine in dieser Dichte einmalige Sammlung dar. Viele der gezeigten Zeremonien wurden zuvor noch nie in einem Bildband portraitiert und werfen ein neues Licht auf eine missverstandene, aber gleichwohl uralte genuin afrikanische Religion: Vodun.

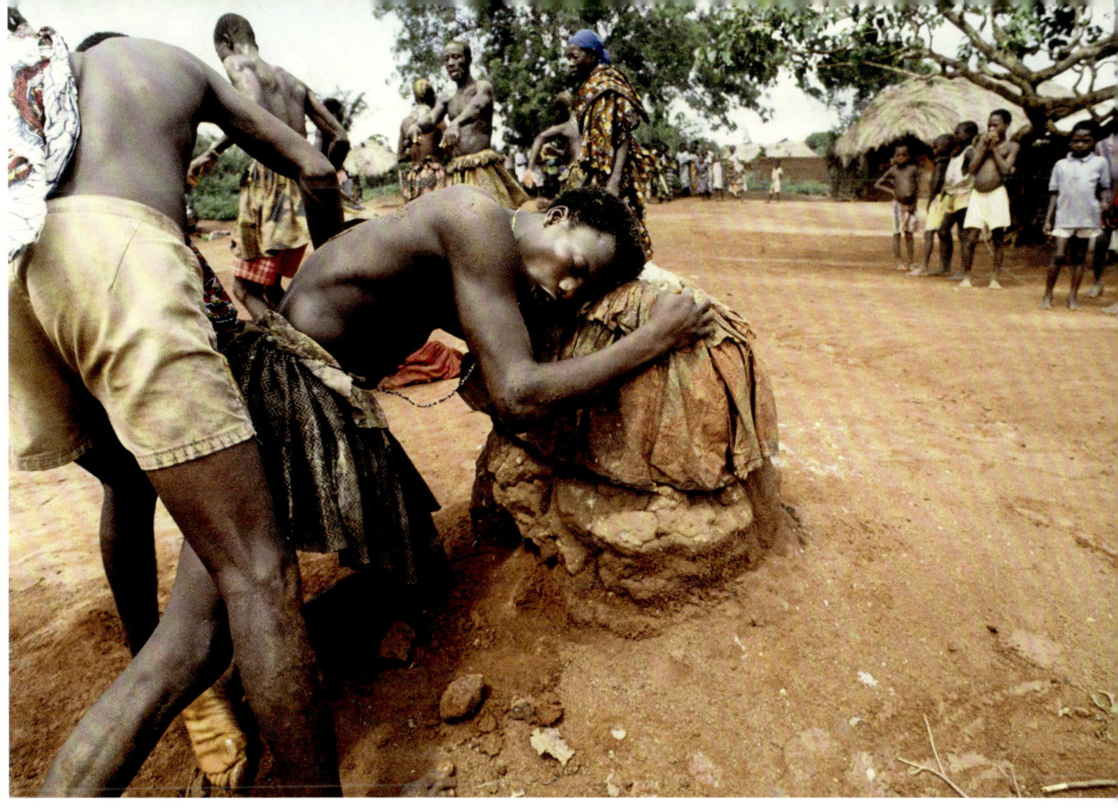

A follower of the Vodun Djagli in a trance embraces a Legba shrine

Un adepte du vodun Djagli en transe embrasse un autel dédié à Legba

Ein Anhänger des Voduns Djagli umarmt in Trance einen Legba-Schrein

Un seguidor del vudú Djagli abraza en trance un santuario de Legba

Um seguidor do vodu Djagli abraça em transe um santuário Legba

Een aanhanger van de vodun Djagli omarmt in trance een Legba-heiligdom

las ha documentado en el transcurso de muchos años de investigación. A menudo se necesitaban muchas visitas a las zonas más remotas hasta que se construyó tanta confianza que se le permitió participar en los eventos. En el transcurso de este proceso, se fotografiaron hechos que antes eran tabú para los forasteros, algunos de los cuales incluso se consideraban extintos. Son un testimonio impresionante del hecho de que el enfoque científico de los hechos y las fórmulas es sólo una de las variantes con las que se puede describir nuestra existencia.

Las imágenes de rituales, dioses y sociedades secretas recogidas en este volumen representan una colección única en esta densidad. Muchas de las ceremonias mostradas nunca antes han sido retratadas en un libro ilustrado y arrojan una nueva luz sobre una religión africana genuina incomprendida, pero sin embargo antigua: el Vudú.

áreas e documentou-as no decurso de muitos anos de investigação. Muitas vezes foram necessárias muitas visitas às áreas mais remotas até que se construiu tanta confiança que ele foi autorizado a participar nos eventos. No decorrer deste, foram fotografados eventos que anteriormente eram tabu para os forasteiros, alguns deles até considerados extintos. Eles testemunham de forma impressionante o fato de que a abordagem científica de fatos e fórmulas é apenas uma variante com a qual nossa existência pode ser descrita.

As imagens de rituais, deuses e sociedades secretas recolhidas neste volume representam uma colecção única nesta densidade. Muitas das cerimônias mostradas nunca antes foram retratadas em um livro ilustrado e lançaram uma nova luz sobre uma religião africana genuína e incompreendida, mas ainda assim antiga: Vodu.

terreinen en heeft ze in de loop van vele jaren van onderzoek gedocumenteerd. Hij moest vaak een flink aantal bezoeken afleggen aan de meest afgelegen gebieden om zoveel vertrouwen op te bouwen dat hij aan de evenementen mocht deelnemen. Daarbij werden gebeurtenissen gefotografeerd die tot dusver taboe waren voor buitenstaanders en deels zelfs als uitgestorven werden beschouwd. Ze getuigen op indrukwekkende wijze van het feit dat de wetenschappelijke benadering van feiten en formules slechts één variant is waarmee ons bestaan kan worden beschreven.

De foto's van rituelen, goden en geheime genootschappen die in dit boek bijeen zijn gebracht, vormen een unieke collectie. Veel van de getoonde ceremoniën zijn nooit eerder in een fotoboek afgebeeld en werpen een nieuw licht op een verkeerd begrepen, maar tegelijkertijd oude, echt Afrikaanse religie: vodun.

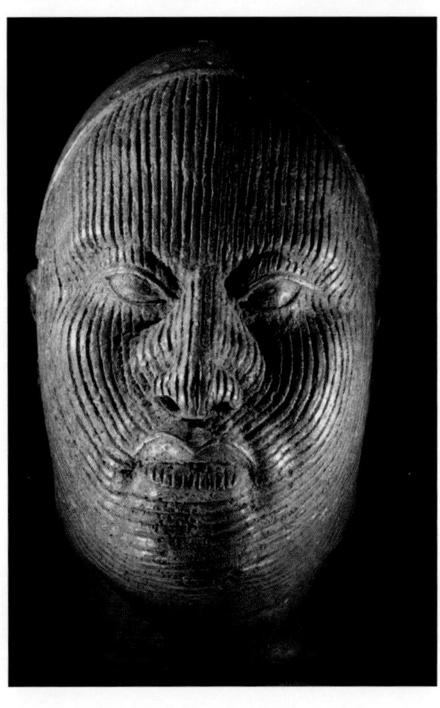

Head of an Ife Princess
Tête d'une princesse Ife
Kopf einer Ife-Prinzessin
Cabeza de una princesa de Ife
Cabeça de uma Princesa Ife
Hoofd van een Ife-prinses
12th century, Bronze, 110 × 35 cm

Boat with Vodun pantheon from Benin
Bateau avec le panthéon vodun, Bénin
Boot mit Vodunpantheon aus Benin
Barco con un panteón vudú de Benin
Barco com Vodunpantheon do Benin
Boot met het vodunpantheon uit Benin
Wood, bone, horn, metal, clay/Bois, os, corne, métal, argile

Bronze casting and the world of gods

The city of Ile-Ife in Nigeria was once the setting for the finest bronze casting. Countless masterpieces were created exclusively for the kings, and in the course of time the secrets of the casting techniques began to travel.

In this way, the Ifa Oracle, a highly complicated secret technique of divination, and with it the gods of the Yoruba, the *Orishas,* arrived in the western neighborhood of Dahomey. These were adapted and assimilated, and the number of Voduns grew steadily and still does today.

The Mina, for example, who live on both sides of the Mono River, build boats to keep the status of the gods up to date. These boats are used in a figurative sense to send their own gods to the other side of the river. In return, gods, who are known there, are sent back. In this way one expands the horizon and the heaven of the gods.

Bronze coulé et monde des dieux

La ville d'Ile-Ife au Nigeria était autrefois un haut lieu de la fonderie d'art en bronze. D'innombrables œuvres étaient fabriquées exclusivement pour les rois, puis au fil du temps, les secrets de cet artisanat se sont diffusés alentour.

C'est par la fonderie d'art que le royaume du Dahomey voisin découvrit la croyance Ifa, technique secrète de divination très complexe, et avec elle, les *orishas,* dieux des Yoruba. Progressivement adaptés et assimilés, ces *orishas,* appelés vodun au Dahomey, ne cesseront de croître et se développent toujours aujourd'hui.

Ainsi, le peuple Mina, qui vit sur les deux rives du fleuve Mono, construit des bateaux afin de préserver l'actualité de son panthéon de divinités. Ces bateaux servent, symboliquement, à envoyer les dieux de l'autre côté du fleuve. En retour, les dieux de l'autre rive sont également envoyés aux Mina. C'est ainsi que s'élargissent mutuellement leur horizon et leurs cieux.

Bronzeguss und Götterwelt

Die Stadt Ile-Ife in Nigeria war einst Schauplatz für feinsten Bronzeguss. Unzählige Meisterwerke entstanden exklusiv für die Könige, und im Laufe der Zeit gingen die Geheimnisse der Gusstechnik auf Reisen.

Beim westlichen Nachbarn Dahomey kam auf diese Weise auch das Ifa-Orakel an, eine hochkomplizierte Geheimtechnik der Divination, und mit ihm die Götter der Yoruba, die *Orishas*. Diese wurden adaptiert und assimiliert, und die Zahl der Vodun wuchs beständig und tut es noch heute.

Die Mina beispielsweise, die beidseitig am Monofluss leben, bauen Boote, um den Götterstand aktuell zu halten. Diese Boote nutzt man im übertragenen Sinne dazu, die eigenen Götter auf die andere Seite des Flusses zu schicken. Im Gegenzug werden Götter, die wiederum dort bekannt sind, zurückgeschickt. So erweitert man sich gegenseitig gleichsam Horizont und Götterhimmel.

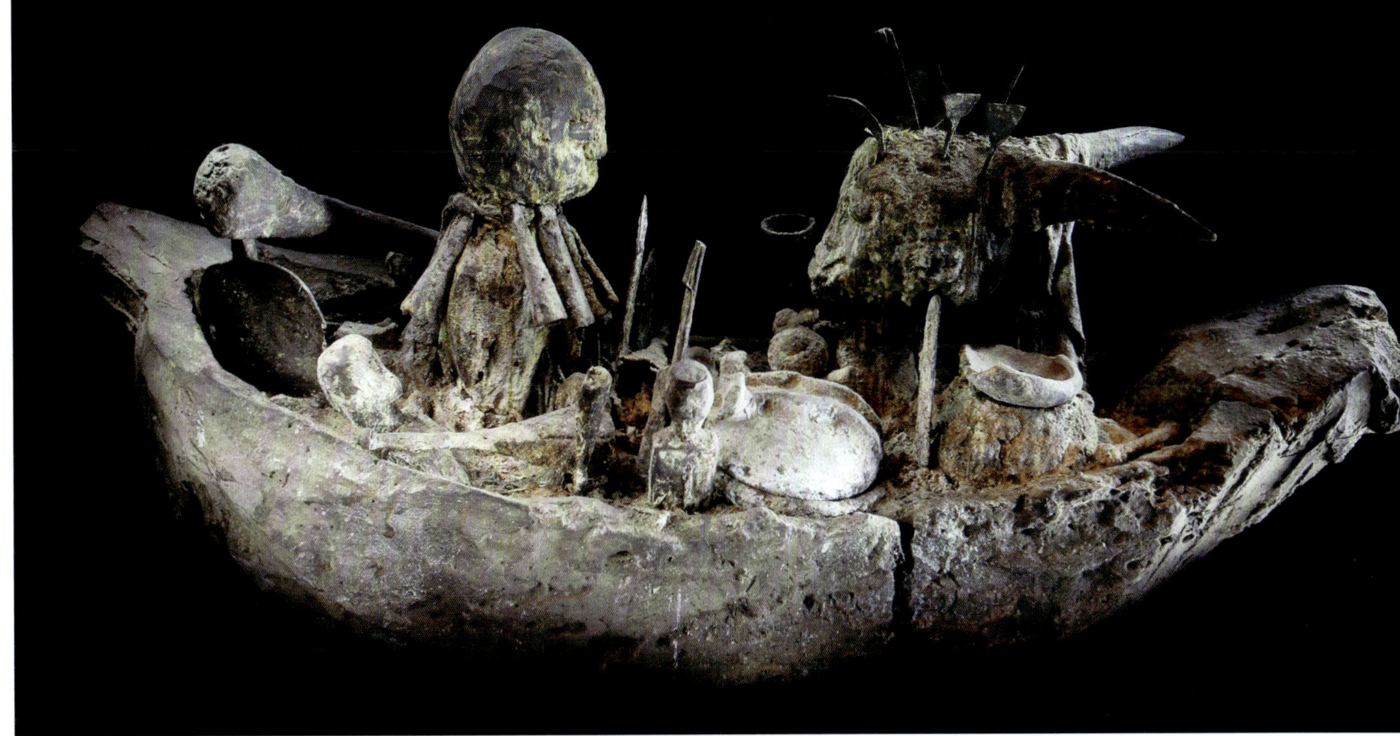

La fundición en bronce y el mundo de los dioses

La ciudad de Ile-Ife en Nigeria fue alguna vez el escenario de la mejor fundición de bronce. Innumerables obras maestras fueron creadas exclusivamente para los reyes, y con el paso del tiempo, los secretos de la tecnología de fundición se fueron de viaje.

De esta manera, el Oráculo de Ifá, una técnica secreta de adivinación muy complicada, y con él los dioses de los yoruba, los *Orishas,* llegaron al vecino occidental Dahomey. Esta técnica se fue adaptando y asimilando, y el número de vudúes empezó a crecer de manera constante y aún sigue creciendo hoy en día.

Los Mina, por ejemplo, que viven a ambos lados del río Mono, construyen barcos para mantener al día el estado de los dioses. Estos barcos se utilizan figurativamente para enviar a sus propios dioses al otro lado del río. A cambio, los dioses que son conocidos allí son enviados de vuelta. De esta manera se amplía el horizonte y el cielo de los dioses.

Fundição de bronze e o mundo dos deuses

A cidade de Ile-Ife, na Nigéria, já foi o cenário para a melhor seleção de bronze. Inúmeras obras-primas foram criadas exclusivamente para os reis, e com o passar do tempo os segredos da tecnologia de fundição foram em viagens.

Assim, o Oráculo Ifa, uma técnica secreta de adivinhação altamente complicada, e com ele os deuses dos iorubás, os orishas, chegaram ao vizinho ocidental Dahomey. Estes foram adaptados e assimilados, e o número de voduns cresceu constantemente e ainda hoje cresce.

A Mina, por exemplo, que vive em ambos os lados do rio mono, constrói barcos para manter o estado dos deuses atualizado. Estes barcos são usados figurativamente para enviar seus próprios deuses para o outro lado do rio. Em troca, os deuses que são conhecidos lá são enviados de volta. Desta forma, expande-se o horizonte e o céu dos deuses.

Bronsgieten en godenwereld

De stad Ile-Ife in Nigeria was ooit het toneel van het fraaiste bronsgietwerk. Ontelbare meesterwerken werden exclusief voor koningen gemaakt, maar in de loop van de tijd gingen de geheimen van de giettechniek op reis.

Zo belandde het Ifa-orakel, een uiterste gecompliceerde, geheime divinatietechniek, en daarmee ook de goden van de Yoruba, de orishas, bij de westelijke buurman Dahomey. Deze werden aangepast en geassimileerd, en het aantal vodun groeide gestaag en groeit nog steeds.

De Mina, bijvoorbeeld, die aan weerszijden van de rivier de Mono wonen, bouwen boten om de godenstand actueel te houden. Deze boten worden figuurlijk gebruikt om hun eigen goden naar de andere kant van de rivier te sturen. In ruil daarvoor worden de daar bekende goden teruggestuurd. Op deze manier verruimt men onderling de horizon en hemel van de goden.

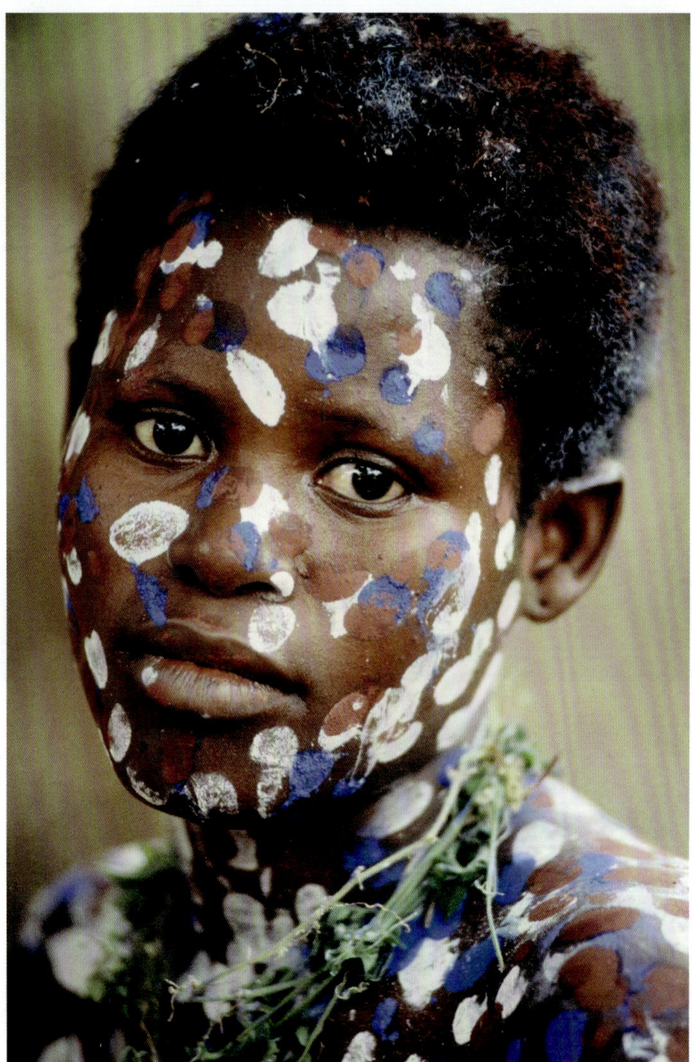

Dots symbolize smallpox, one of Sakpata's diseases
Les points symbolisent la variole, une des maladies de Sakpata
Punkte symbolisieren Pocken, eine der Krankheiten Sakpatas
Los puntos simbolizan la viruela, una de las enfermedades de Sakpata
Os pontos simbolizam a varíola, uma das doenças de Sakpata
Stippen symboliseren de pokken, een van de ziekten van Sakpata

Songs reconcile the soul of the sacrificed animal
Les chansons apaisent l'âme de l'animal sacrifié
Gesänge stimmen die Seele des geopferten Tieres versöhnlich
Las canciones reconcilian el alma del animal sacrificado
As canções reconciliam a alma do animal sacrificado
Gezangen stemmen de ziel van het geofferde dier vergevensgezind

Sakpata, God of the bitter earth

Sakpata is the first child of the creator deity Mawu-Lisa and brother of Shango, the thunder god. While Shango reigns in heaven, Sakpata is active on earth and is responsible for opposites such as disease/health and their balance.

Agriculture and factors influencing the harvest also belong to Sakpata's sphere of sovereignty, whereby the deity is often dependent here on the cooperation with Shango, because the latter, as the

Sakpata, dieu de la Terre amère

Sakpata est le premier enfant du dieu créateur Mawu-Lisa et le frère de Shangô, dieu du tonnerre. Alors que Shangô règne dans le ciel, Sakpata est actif sur terre et y est responsable d'états antagonistes tels que santé/maladie et de leur équilibre.

Les facteurs influant sur les cultures et les récoltes dépendent également de la souveraineté de Sakpata, même si, dans ce domaine, il est contraint de collaborer avec Shangô. En tant que représentant du ciel,

Sakpata, Gott der bitteren Erde

Sakpata ist das erste Kind der Schöpfergottheit Mawu-Lisa und Bruder Shangos, des Donnergottes. Während Shango im Himmel regiert, ist Sakpata auf Erden aktiv und dort für Gegensätze wie Krankheit/Gesundheit und deren Gleichgewicht zuständig.

Auch Landwirtschaft und die Ernte beeinflussende Faktoren gehören zum Hoheitsbereich Sakpatas, wobei die Gottheit hier oft auf die Zusammenarbeit mit Shango

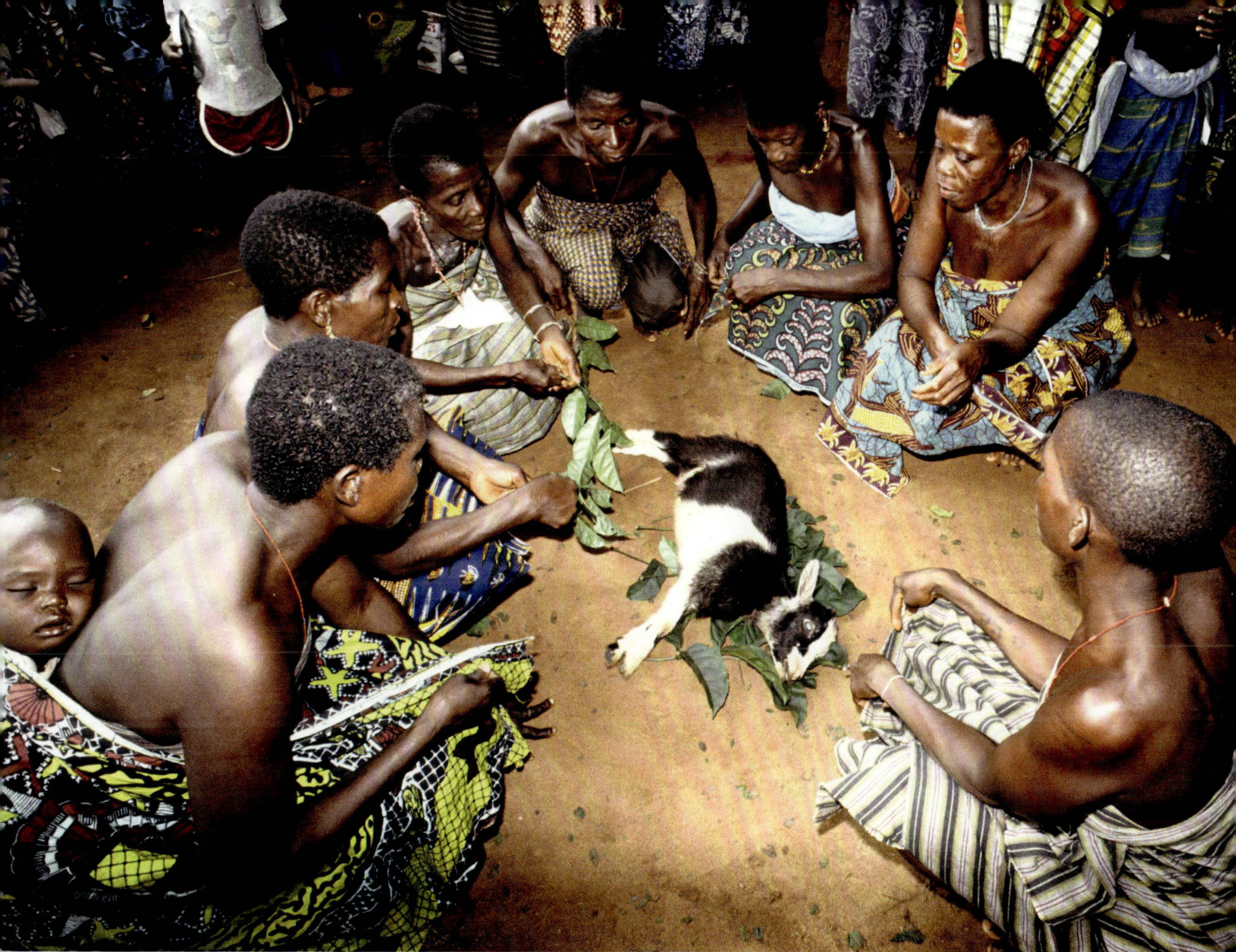

Sakpata, Dios de la tierra amarga

Sakpata es el primer hijo de la deidad creadora Mawu-Lisa y hermano de Shango, el dios del trueno. Mientras Shango reina en el cielo, Sakpata es activo en la tierra y es responsable de los opuestos como la enfermedad/salud y su equilibrio.

La agricultura y los factores que influyen en la cosecha también forman parte de la esfera de soberanía de Sakpata, donde la deidad depende a menudo de la cooperación con Shango, porque como representante

Sakpata, Deus da terra amarga

Sakpata é o primeiro filho da divindade criadora Mawu-Lisa e irmão de Shangos, o deus trovão. Enquanto Shango reina no céu, Sakpata é ativa na terra e é responsável por opostos como doença/saúde e seu equilíbrio.

A agricultura e os fatores que influenciam a colheita também fazem parte da esfera de soberania de Sakpata, onde a divindade aqui muitas vezes depende da cooperação com Shango, porque como

Sakpata, god van de bittere aarde

Sakpata is het eerste kind van de schepper-god Mawu-Lisa en de broer van Shango, de dondergod. Terwijl Shango over de hemel regeert, is Sakpata actief op aarde, waar hij verantwoordelijk is voor tegenpolen zoals ziekte/gezondheid en hun evenwicht.

De landbouw en alle factoren die van invloed zijn op de oogst, horen ook bij het territorium van Sakpata, waarbij de god hier vaak is aangewezen op de samenwerking met Shango, omdat die

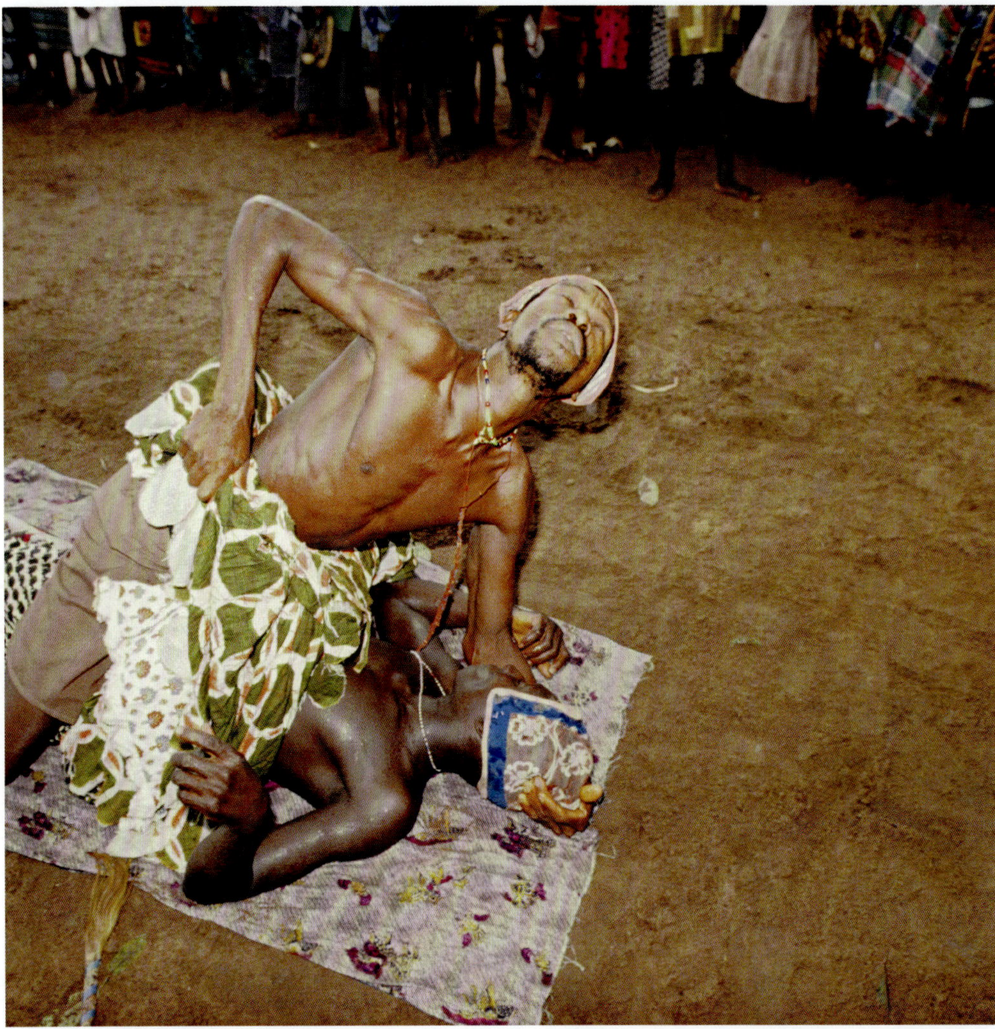

Symbolic sex act. Two Sakpata adepts mime coitus. This should remind the villagers of the danger of AIDS and warn them not to indulge in promiscuity.

Acte sexuel symbolique. Deux adeptes de Sakpata miment un rapport sexuel. Ils entendent ainsi rappeler aux villageois le risque du sida et les détourner des changements fréquents de partenaires.

Symbolischer Geschlechtsakt. Zwei Sakpata-Adepten mimen den Beischlaf. Dies soll die Dorfbewohner an die Gefahr von Aids erinnern und davor warnen, der Promiskuität zu fröhnen.

Acto sexual simbólico. Dos adeptos de Sakpata simbolizan el coito. Esto debería recordar a los aldeanos el peligro del SIDA y advertirles que no se dejen llevar por la promiscuidad.

Acto sexual simbólico. Dois adeptos de Sakpata mime coitus. Isto deveria recordar aos aldeões o perigo da SIDA e avisá-los para não se entregarem à promiscuidade.

Symbolische geslachtsdaad. Twee aanhangers van Sakpata imiteren de geslachtsgemeenschap. Die moet de dorpelingen herinneren aan het gevaar van aids en hen waarschuwen tegen promiscuïteit.

representative of heaven, is responsible for rainfall and moistening the earth.

Known to the Yoruba as "Sopona", Sakpata is probably the name most frequently called upon when it comes to fighting disease. One asks for a decline in infant mortality, but sometimes also for the reduction of envy, greed and jealousy, because these factors can destroy the sensitive social fabric. Of course, Sakpata can also help with cases of witchcraft.

celui-ci est en effet responsable des pluies et de l'approvisionnement en eau de la terre.

Connu chez les Yoruba sous le nom de Sopona, Sakpata est surtout appelé pour lutter contre la maladie. On le prie de diminuer la mortalité infantile, mais également parfois de supprimer l'envie, l'avidité et la jalousie, car ces sentiments peuvent détruire la structure sociale. Bien évidemment, Sakpata peut également apporter son aide dans les cas de sorcellerie.

angewiesen ist, weil dieser als Vertreter des Himmels für Niederschläge und die Tränkung der Erde verantwortlich zeichnet.

Bei den Yoruba als „Sopona" bekannt, wird Sakpata wohl am meisten angerufen, wenn es um die Bekämpfung von Krankheiten geht. Man erbittet die Senkung der Kindersterblichkeit, manchmal aber auch den Rückgang von Neid, Gier und Eifersucht, weil diese Faktoren das empfindliche soziale Gefüge zerstören können. Selbstverständlich kann Sakpata auch bei Fällen von Hexerei helfen.

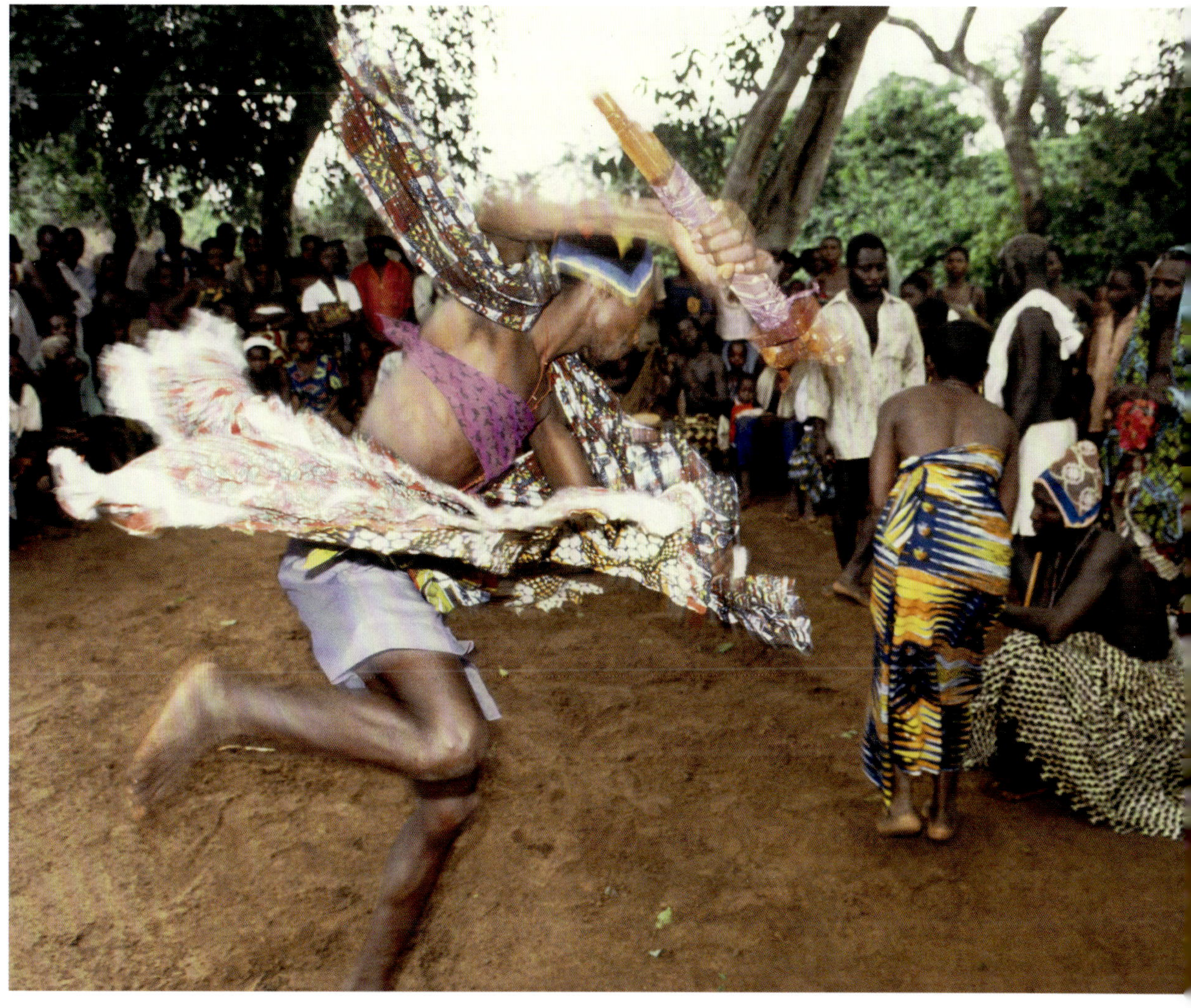

del cielo es responsable de las lluvias y de la impregnación de la tierra.

Conocida por los yoruba como "Sopona", Sakpata es probablemente el más invocado cuando se trata de combatir enfermedades. Se pide la reducción de la mortalidad infantil, pero a veces también la disminución de la envidia, la codicia y los celos, porque estos factores pueden destruir la sensible estructura social. Por supuesto, Sakpata también puede ayudar en casos de brujería.

representante do céu ele é responsável pela precipitação e impregnação da terra.

Conhecida pelos iorubás como "Sopona", Sakpata é provavelmente a mais chamada quando se trata de combater doenças. Pede-se a redução da mortalidade infantil, mas às vezes também a diminuição da inveja, da ganância e do ciúme, pois esses fatores podem destruir a estrutura social sensível. É claro que Sakpata também pode ajudar em casos de bruxaria.

als vertegenwoordiger van de hemel verantwoordelijk is voor de neerslag en het drenken van de aarde.

Sakpata, die bij de Yoruba bekend is als Sopona, wordt waarschijnlijk het meest genoemd als het gaat om het bestrijden van ziekten. Men vraagt hem om afname van de kindersterfte, maar soms ook om minder jaloezie, hebzucht en afgunst, omdat deze aspecten de gevoelige maatschappelijke structuur kunnen ondermijnen. Natuurlijk kan Sakpata ook helpen bij gevallen van hekserij.

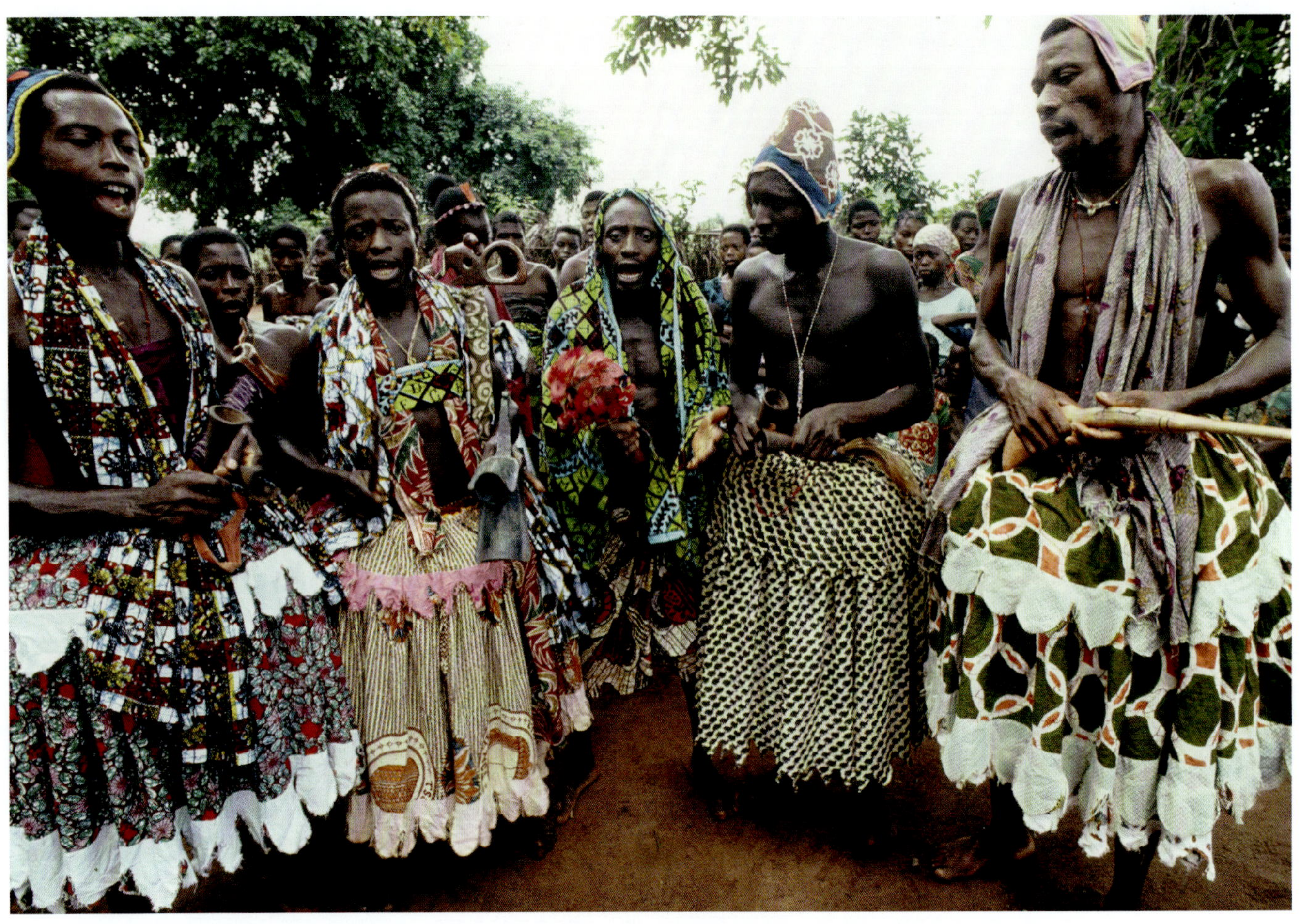

Sakpata adepts in magnificent robes

Adeptes de Sakpata habillés de magnifiques vêtements

Sakpata-Adepten in prächtigen Gewändern

Adeptos de Sakpata con magníficas túnicas

Os adeptos da Sakpata vestidos com vestes magníficas

Sakpata-adepten in prachtige gewaden

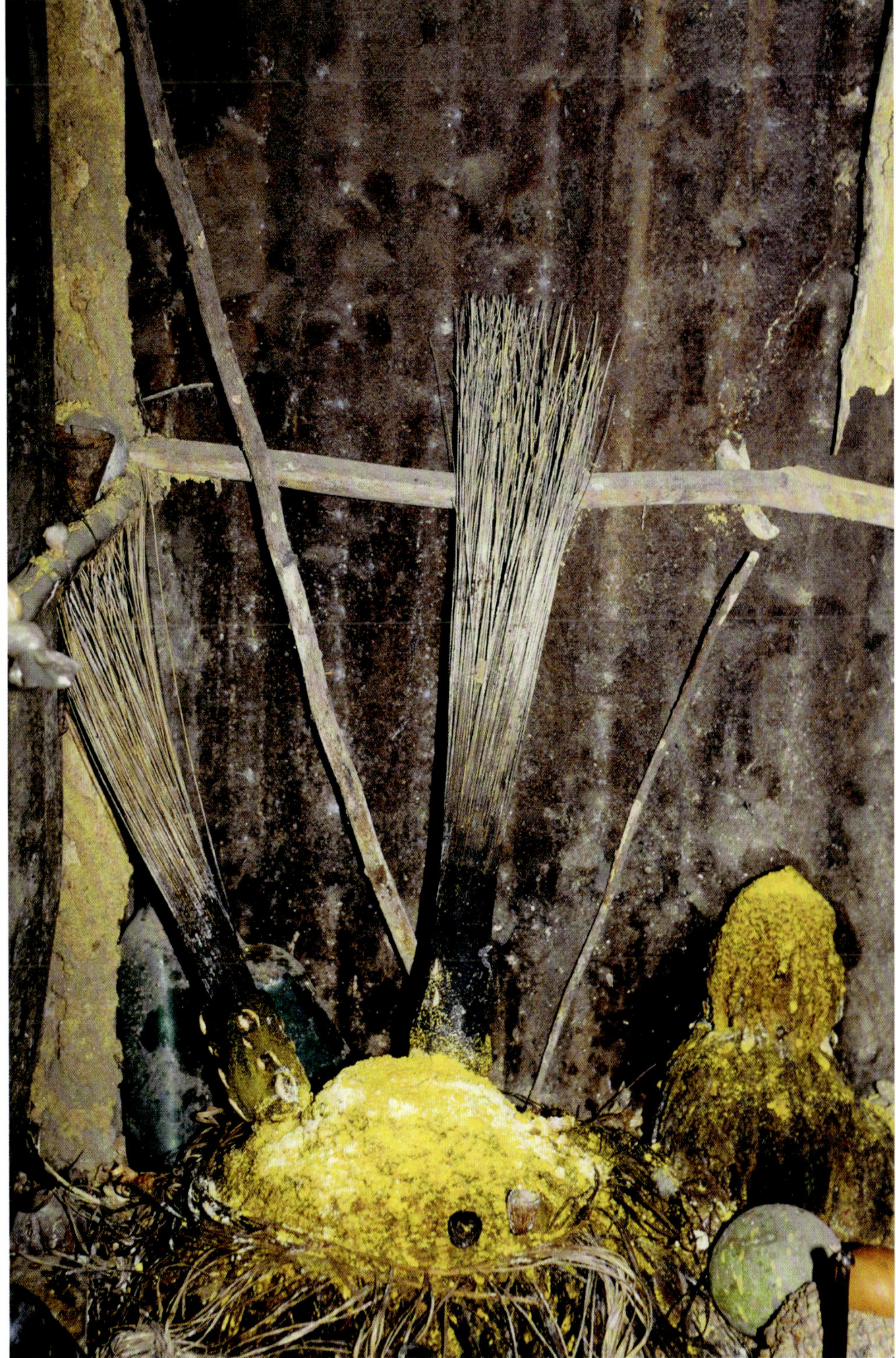

A small Sakpata shrine in Cotonou. The remains of past food sacrifices shine yellow, here it is probably palm oil.

Petit sanctuaire à Sakpata à Cotonou. Les restes jaune vif d'une offrande de nourriture, probablement de l'huile de palme.

Ein kleiner Sakpata-Schrein in Cotonou. Gelb leuchten die Überreste vergangener Speiseopfer, hier vermutlich Palmöl.

Un pequeño santuario de Sakpata en Cotonou. os restos de los sacrificios de comida del pasado brillan en amarillo, aquí probablemente aceite de palma.

Um pequeno santuário Sakpata em Cotonou. Os restos de sacrifícios de comida do passado brilham em amarelo, aqui provavelmente óleo de palma.

Een klein Sakpata-heiligdom in Cotonou. De overblijfselen van vroegere voedseloffers, hier waarschijnlijk palmolie, lichten geel op.

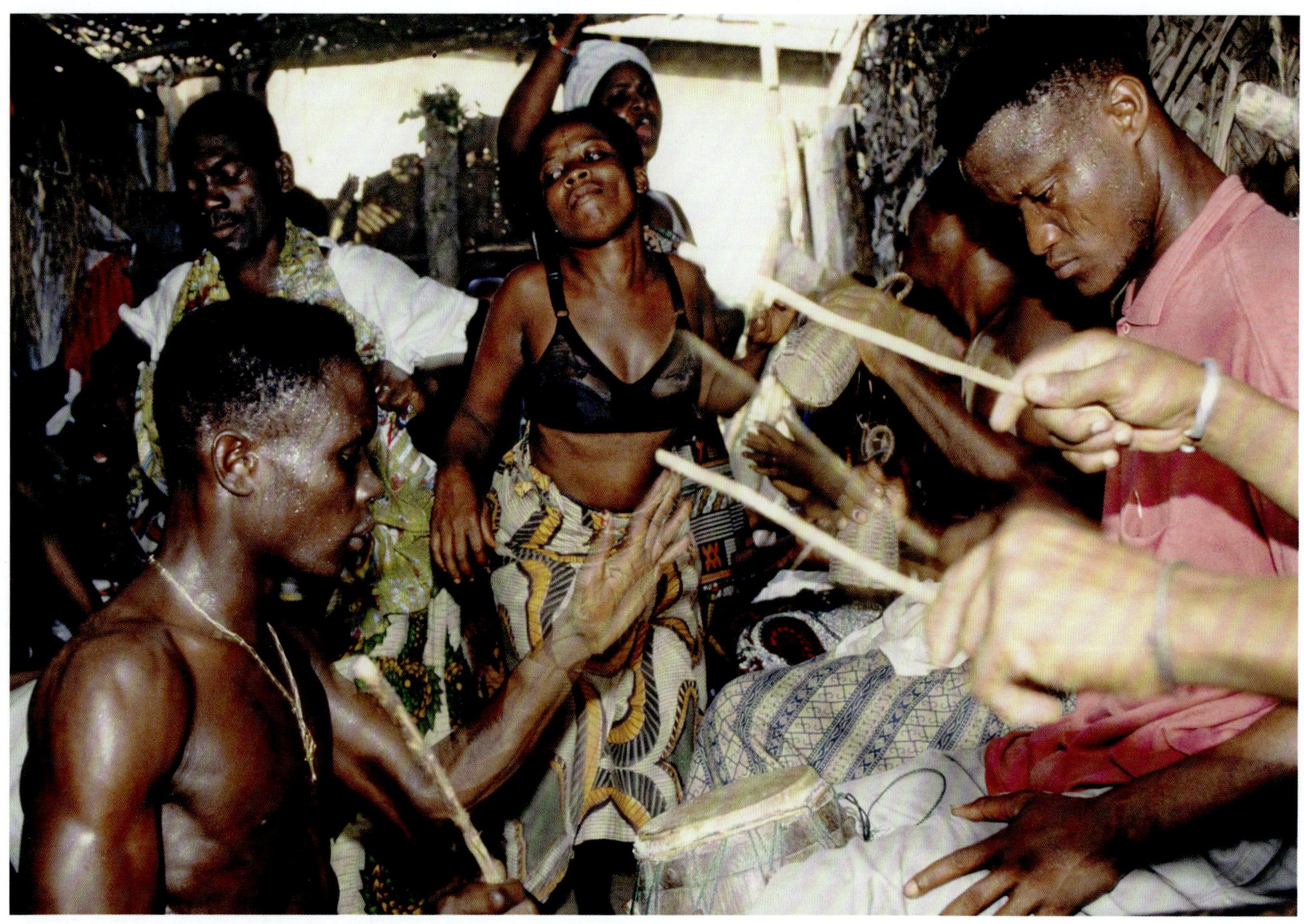

Drummers playing in front of Sakpata's shrine

Percussionnistes jouant devant le sanctuaire de Sakpata

Trommler spielen vor Sakpatas Schrein

Tambores tocando frente al santuario de Sakpata

Bateristas tocando em frente ao santuário de Sakpatas

Trommelaars spelen voor Sakpata's heiligdom

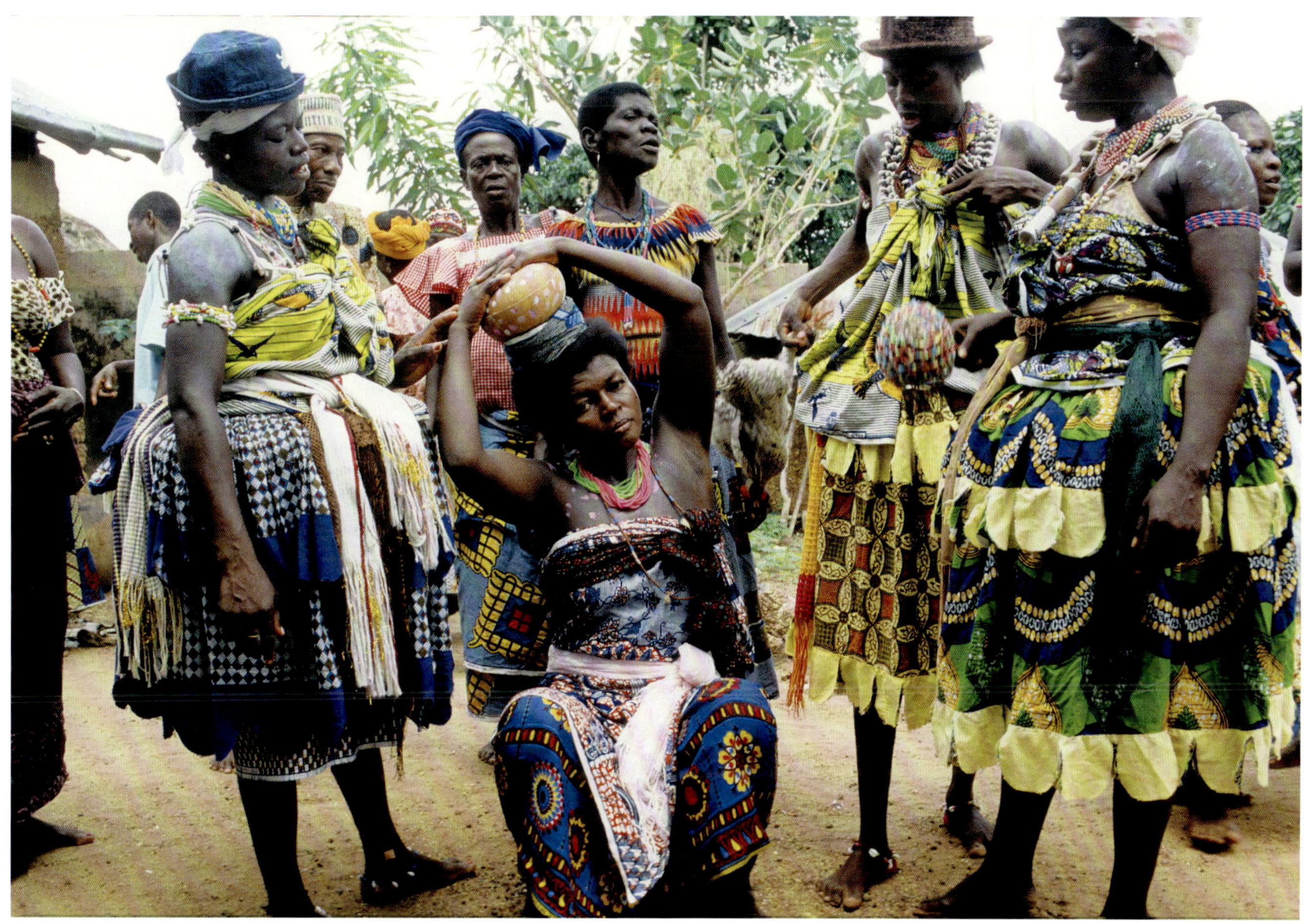

Healing in Dassa. In the village of Dassa a Sakpata ceremony is held for a woman whose legs are paralyzed. A pot with magical herbs on her head puts her in a trance.

Guérison à Dassa. Dans le village de Dassa, une cérémonie autour de Sakpata est organisée pour une femme dont les jambes sont paralysées. Un pot contenant des herbes magiques posé sur sa tête la fait entrer en transe.

Heilung in Dassa. In dem Dorf Dassa wird eine Sakpata-Zeremonie für eine Frau abgehalten, deren Beine gelähmt sind. Ein Topf mit magischen Kräutern auf ihrem Kopf versetzt sie in Trance.

Sanación en Dassa. En el pueblo de Dassa se celebra una ceremonia de Sakpata para una mujer con las piernas paralizadas. Una olla con hierbas mágicas en la cabeza la hace entrar en trance.

Cura em Dassa. Na aldeia de Dassa é realizada uma cerimónia Sakpata para uma mulher cujas pernas estão paralisadas. Uma panela com ervas mágicas na cabeça coloca-a em transe.

Genezing in Dassa. In het dorp Dassa wordt een Sakpata-ceremonie gehouden voor een vrouw met verlamde benen. Een pot met magische kruiden op haar hoofd brengt haar in trance.

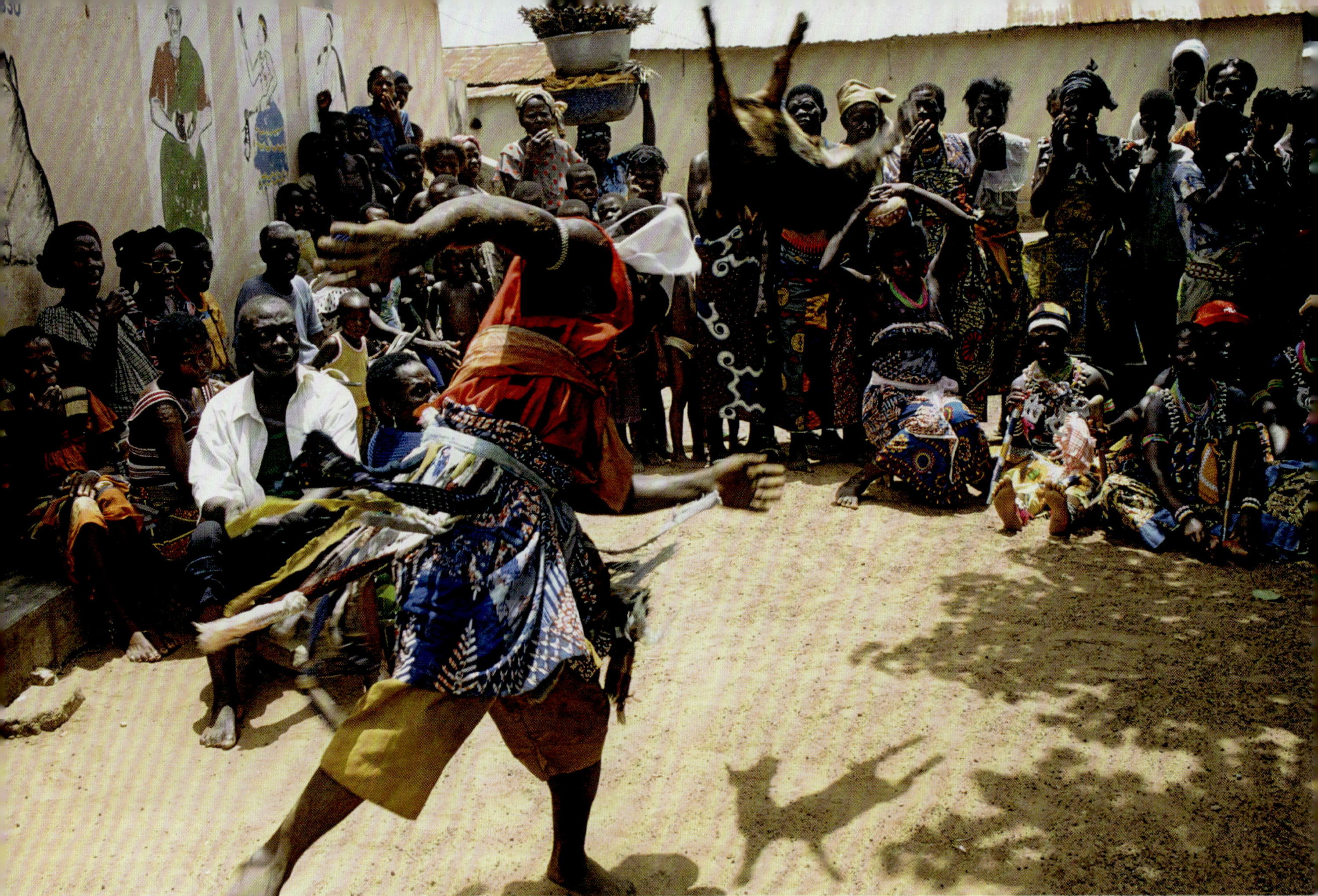

Demonstration of power. The assistant of the Sakpata priest grabs the animal sacrifice with his teeth and whirls it around without using his hands, which demonstrates the strength and wildness of the deity.

Démonstration de puissance. L'assistant du prêtre de Sakpata tient l'animal sacrifié entre ses dents et le fait tournoyer dans l'air afin de démontrer la puissance et la sauvagerie de la déité.

Machtdemonstration. Der Assistent des Sakpata-Priesters greift das Tieropfer mit den Zähnen und wirbelt es freihändig herum, was die Stärke und Wildheit der Gottheit demonstriert.

Demostración de poder. El asistente del sacerdote Sakpata agarra el sacrificio animal con sus dientes y lo hace girar libremente, lo que demuestra la fuerza y ferocidad de la deidad.

Demonstração de poder. O assistente do sacerdote Sakpata agarra o sacrifício animal com os dentes e gira-o livremente, o que demonstra a força e a ferocidade da divindade.

Machtsvertoon. De assistent van de Sakpata-priester grijpt het offerdier met zijn tanden en draait het zonder handen rond, wat de kracht en de woestheid van de god aantoont.

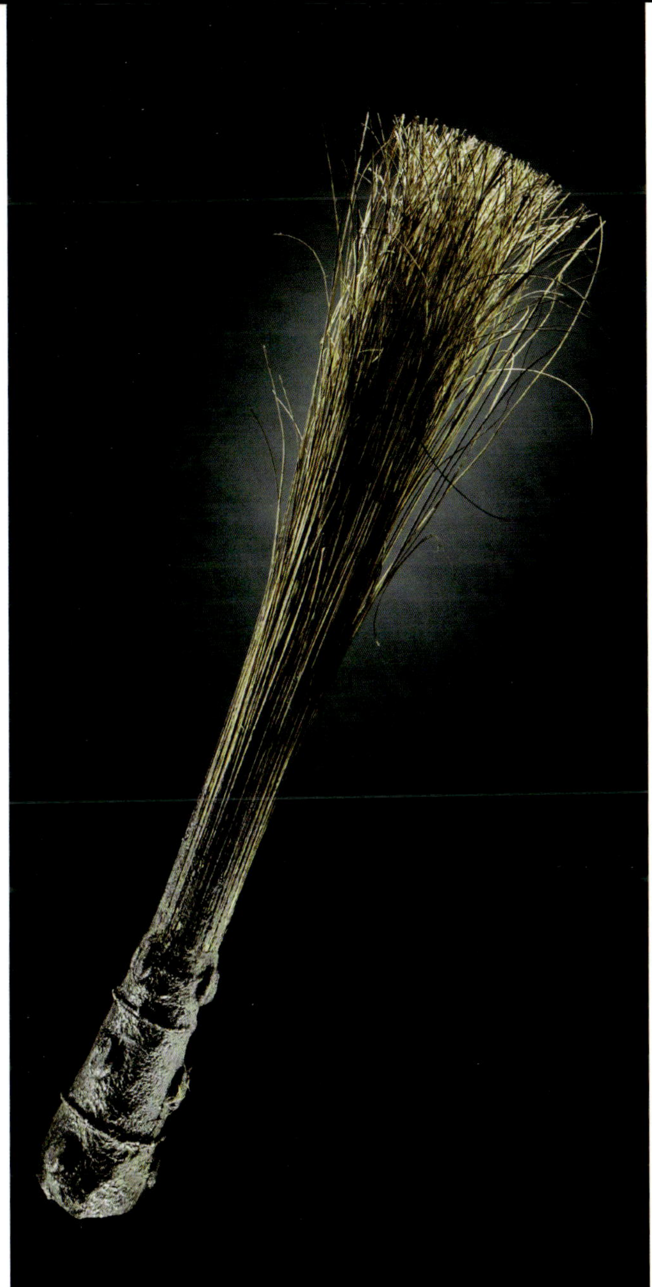

Sakpata's Broom

Balai de Sakpata

Sakpatas Besen

Escoba de Sakpata

Vassoura Sakpatas

Bezem van Sakpata

Brushwood, leather, cowrie shell, glass beads/Branchages, cuir, coquillages, perles de verre, 56 × 5 cm

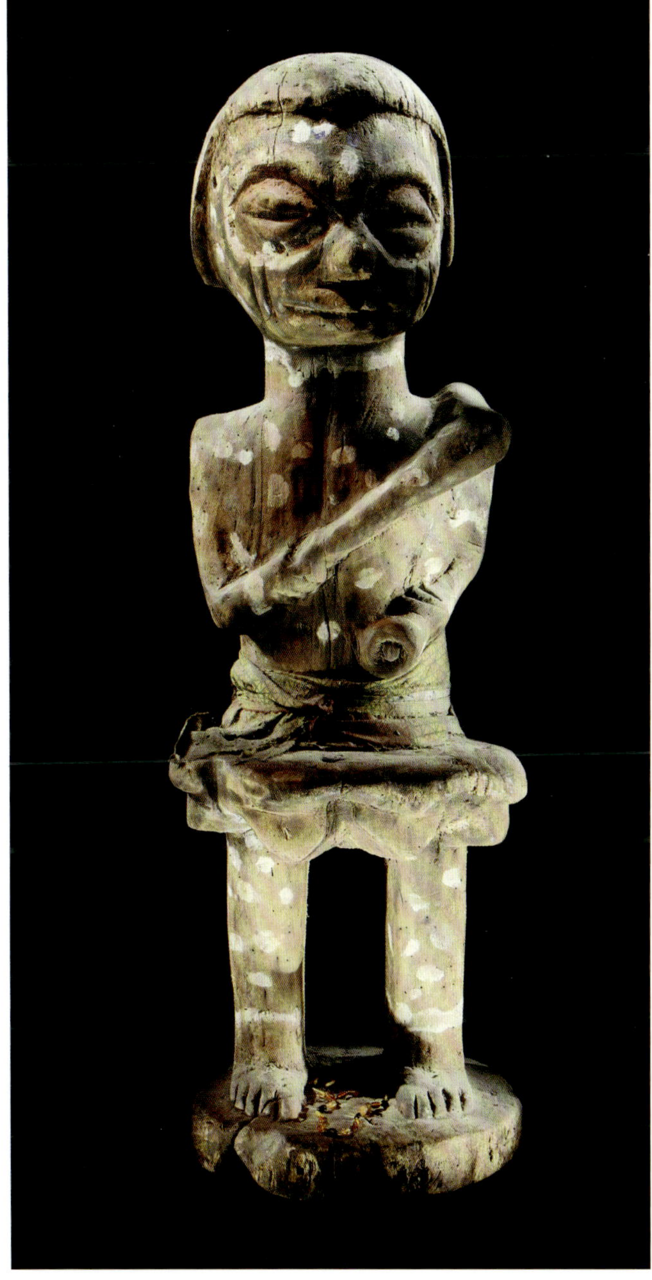

Sakpata figure

Figure de Sakpata

Sakpata-Figur

Figura de Sakpata

A figura de Sakpata

Sakpata-beeldje

Wood/Bois, 53 × 26 cm

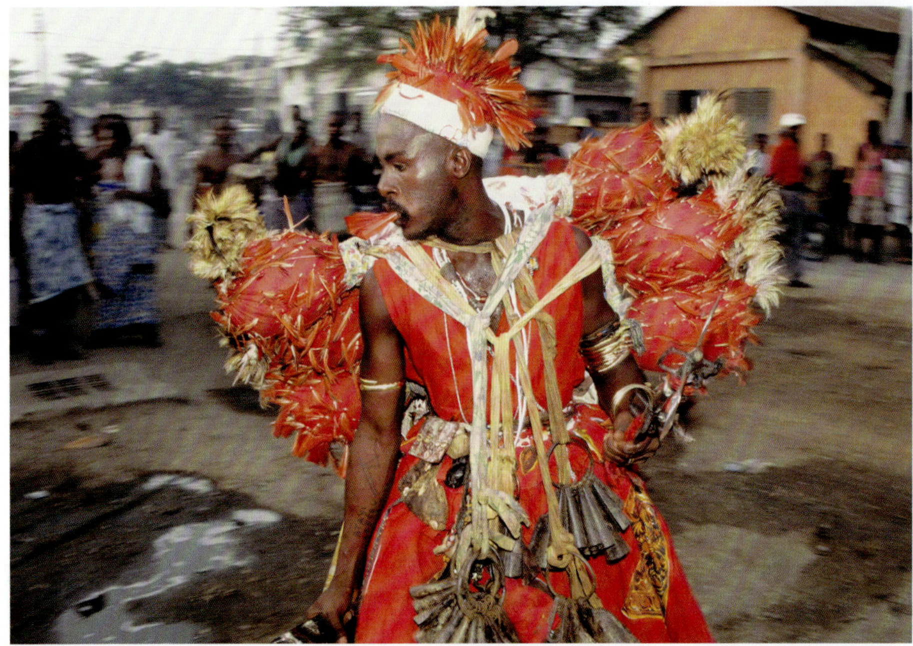

Shango, God of thunder and lightning

Shango is the god of thunder among the Yoruba people, who according to tradition once ruled as the fourth king in Oyo, today's West Nigeria. The Ewe and Fon in Benin know him as Xeviésó, where, according to myths in the city of Xevié, he replaced the thunderstorm god formerly known as Só (Sogbo).

There are many legends that describe Shango's close relationship with kings and their position of power. He is regarded as Ogun's brother and is considered to be a powerful moral judge and is revered accordingly.

It is up to him to punish liars, adulterers and thieves; the last he judges with his lightning strike. This is Shango's whip, thunder its bang. In the past, the people who had been convicted and judged, were quickly taken out of the villages, as well as all their possessions, for it was expected that Shango would be angry if the corpse of the wrongdoer was not ostracized and the village was not cleansed.

Shangô, dieu du tonnerre et des éclairs

Pour l'ethnie Yoruba, Shangô est le dieu du tonnerre. Selon une tradition, il fut le quatrième roi du royaume d'Oyo, aujourd'hui situé dans l'ouest du Nigeria. Pour les Éwé et les Fon du Bénin, il est Hêviosso qui, selon les mythes du village de Hêvié, remplaça le précédent dieu de la foudre Sô (Sogbo).

De nombreuses légendes décrivent une relation étroite entre Shangô, les rois et leur pouvoir. Frère d'Ogun, il est considéré comme un juge moral puissant et est loué en tant que tel.

C'est à lui que revient la tâche de punir les menteurs, les époux adultères et les voleurs ; il frappe ces derniers de la foudre symbolisée par son fouet et dont le tonnerre est le claquement. Les personnes jugées coupables de délit étaient autrefois rapidement emportées à l'extérieur des villages avec l'ensemble de leurs possessions, car on redoutait la colère de Shangô si le corps du malfaisant n'était pas banni et le village purifié.

Shango, Gott des Donners und Blitzes

Shango ist beim Volk der Yoruba der Donnergott, der nach einer Überlieferung einst als vierter König in Oyo, dem heutigen Westnigeria, herrschte. Die Ewe und Fon in Benin kennen ihn als Xeviésó, wo er laut Mythen in der Stadt Xevié den vormals unter dem Namen Só (Sogbo) bekannten Gewittergott ablöste.

Es gibt viele Sagen, die Shangos enge Beziehung mit Königen und ihrer Machtposition beschreiben. Er gilt als Bruder Oguns und wird als mächtiger moralischer Richter angesehen und entsprechend verehrt.

Es ist an ihm, Lügner, Ehebrecher und Diebe zu bestrafen; letzte richtet er mit seinem Blitzschlag. Dieser ist Shangos Peitsche, der Donner ihr Knall. Die so überführte wie gerichtete Person und ihr ganzer Besitz wurden in früheren Zeiten schnell aus den Dörfern herausgeschafft, denn man rechnete mit Shangos Zorn, wenn der Leichnam des Schädlings keine Ächtung und das Dorf keine Reinigung erfuhr.

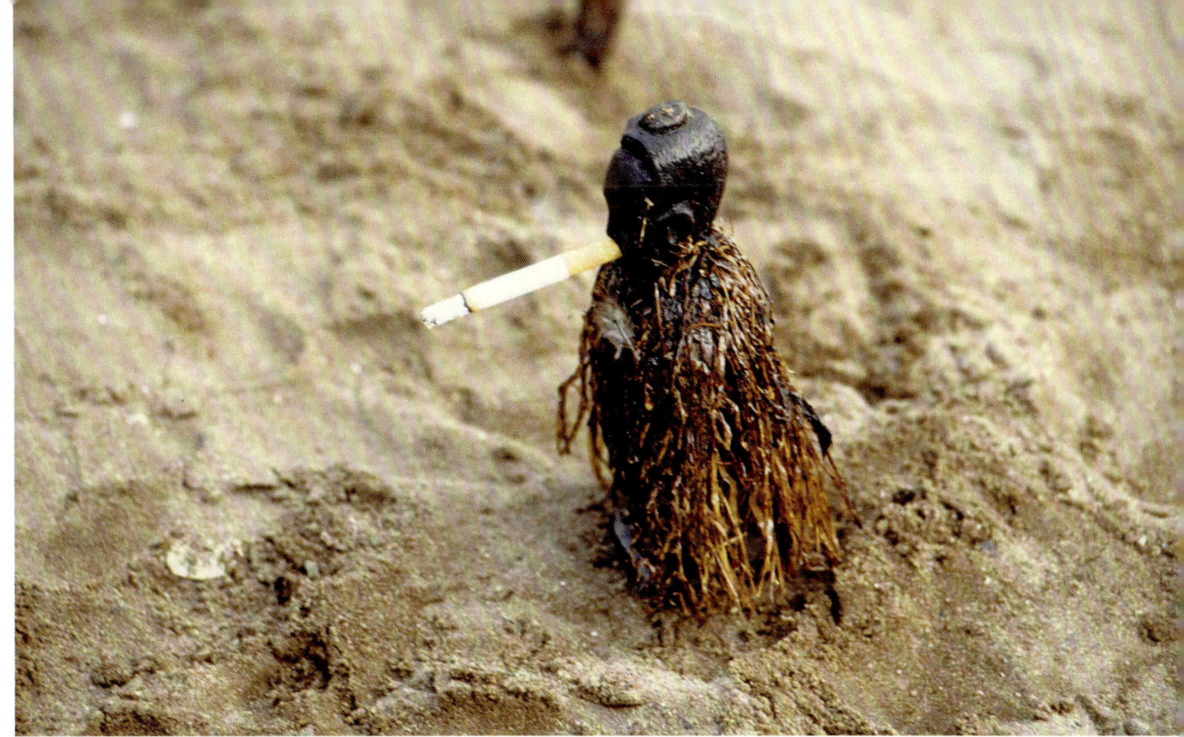

Tobacco sacrifice for a wooden figure charged with the power of Shango

Sacrifice de tabac pour une figurine en bois chargée du pouvoir du Shangô

Tabakopfer für eine mit der Kraft Shangos aufgeladene Holzfigur

Sacrificio de tabaco para una figura de madera cargada con el poder de Shangho

Sacrifício de tabaco por uma figura de madeira carregada com o poder de Shangho

Tabaksoffer voor een houten beeld dat geladen is met de kracht van Shangho

Shango, Dios del trueno y del relámpago

Shango es el dios del trueno entre el pueblo yoruba, que según la tradición alguna vez gobernó como el cuarto rey en Oyo, la actual Nigeria Occidental. El Ewe y el Fon en Benin lo conocen como Xeviésó, donde según los mitos de la ciudad de Xevié reemplazó al dios del trueno antes conocido como Só (Sogbo).

Hay muchas leyendas que describen la estrecha relación de Shango con los reyes y su posición de poder. Es el hermano de Ogun y se le considera un poderoso juez moral y se le venera en consecuencia.

A él le corresponde castigar a los mentirosos, adúlteros y ladrones; al éste último lo juzgacon su rayo. Este es el látigo de Shango, el trueno de su explosión. En épocas anteriores, se sacaba rápidamente de las aldeas junto con todas sus posesiones a la persona condenada, así como a lajuzgada, ya que se temíala ira de Shango si el cadáver de la plaga no era condenado al ostracismo y la aldea quedaba limpia.

Shango, Deus dos trovões e relâmpagos

Shango é o deus do trovão entre o povo iorubá, que segundo a tradição já governou como o quarto rei em Oyo, hoje o oeste da Nigéria. O Ewe e Fon em Benin conhece-o como Xeviésó, onde de acordo com mitos na cidade de Xevié ele substituiu o deus trovão anteriormente conhecido como Só (Sogbo).

Há muitas lendas que descrevem a estreita relação de Xangai com os reis e sua posição de poder. Ele é considerado o irmão de Ogun e é considerado um poderoso juiz moral e é reverenciado em conformidade.

Cabe-lhe a ele punir mentirosos, adúlteros e ladrões; o último julga com o seu golpe de relâmpago. Este é o chicote de Xangai, o trovão o seu estrondo. Nos primeiros tempos, a pessoa que foi condenada, bem como a pessoa que foi julgada e todos os seus bens foram rapidamente retirados das aldeias, pois foi contabilizado com a ira de Xangai se o cadáver da praga não fosse ostracizado e a aldeia não fosse limpa.

Shango, god van donder en bliksem

Shango is de god van de donder bij het Yoruba-volk, die naar verluidt ooit als vierde koning heerste in Oyo, het huidige West-Nigeria. De Ewe en Fon in Benin kennen hem als Xeviésó, waar hij volgens de mythen in de stad Xevié de destijds als Só (Sogbo) bekende dondergod afloste.

Er zijn veel legendes die de nauwe relatie van Shango met koningen en hun machtspositie beschrijven. Hij wordt beschouwd als de broer van Ogun en wordt gezien als een krachtige morele rechter en dienovereenkomstig vereerd.

Het is aan hem om leugenaars, echtbrekers en dieven te straffen; die hij beoordeelt met zijn bliksemflits. Die is Shangos' zweep, de donder zijn klap. Vroeger werden de voorgeleide en veroordeelde personen en al hun bezittingen snel uit de dorpen verdreven, omdat men rekening hield met de toorn van Shango als het lichaam van het gevaarlijke individu niet werd verbannen en het dorp niet werd gezuiverd.

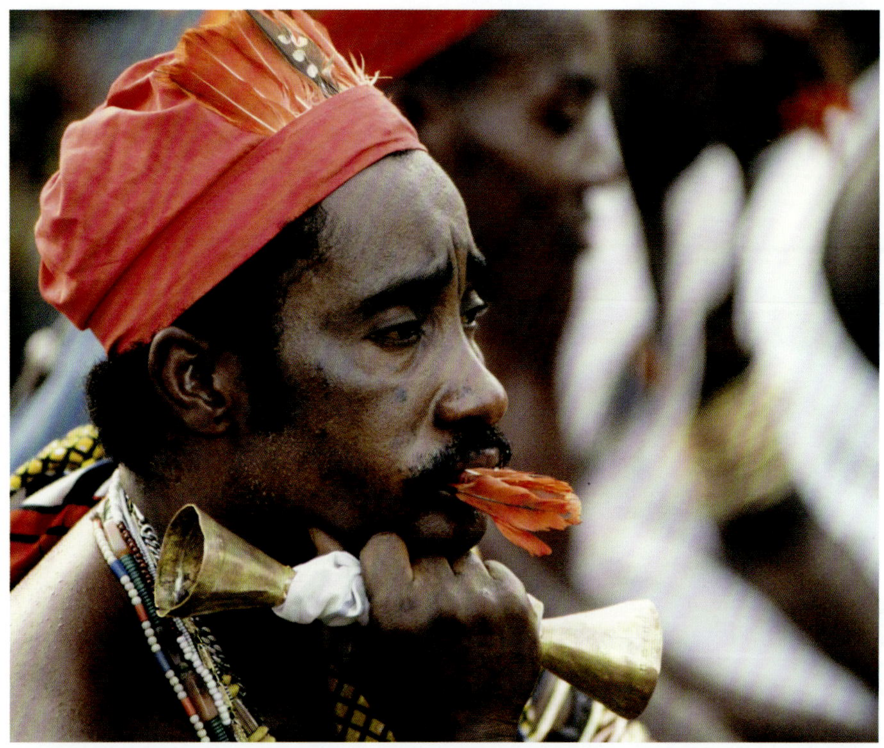
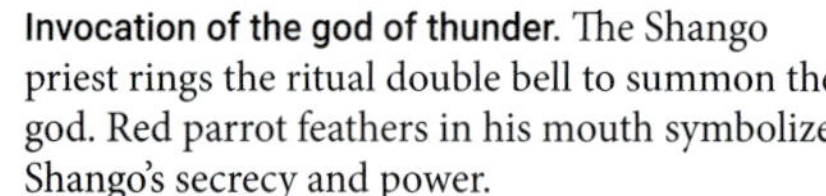

Invocation of the god of thunder. The Shango priest rings the ritual double bell to summon the god. Red parrot feathers in his mouth symbolize Shango's secrecy and power.

Invocation du dieu du tonnerre. Le prêtre de Shangô fait sonner la double cloche rituelle pour appeler le dieu. Les plumes de perroquets rouges dans sa bouche symbolisent le silence et la puissance de Shangô.

Anrufung des Donnergottes. Der Shangopriester läutet die rituelle Doppelglocke, um den Gott herbeizurufen. Rote Papageienfedern in seinem Mund symbolisieren Shangos Verschwiegenheit und Kraft.

Invocación del dios del trueno. El sacerdote Shango toca la doble campana ritual para llamar al Dios. Las plumas rojas de loro en su boca simbolizan el secreto y el poder de Shango.

Invocação do deus do trovão. O Shango padre toca o sino duplo ritual para invocar o Deus. Penas de papagaio vermelho na boca simbolizam o segredo e o poder de Shango.

Aanroeping van de dondergod. De Shango-priester luidt de rituele dubbele bel om de god op te roepen. Rode papegaaienveren in zijn mond symboliseren Shangho's zwijgzaamheid en kracht.

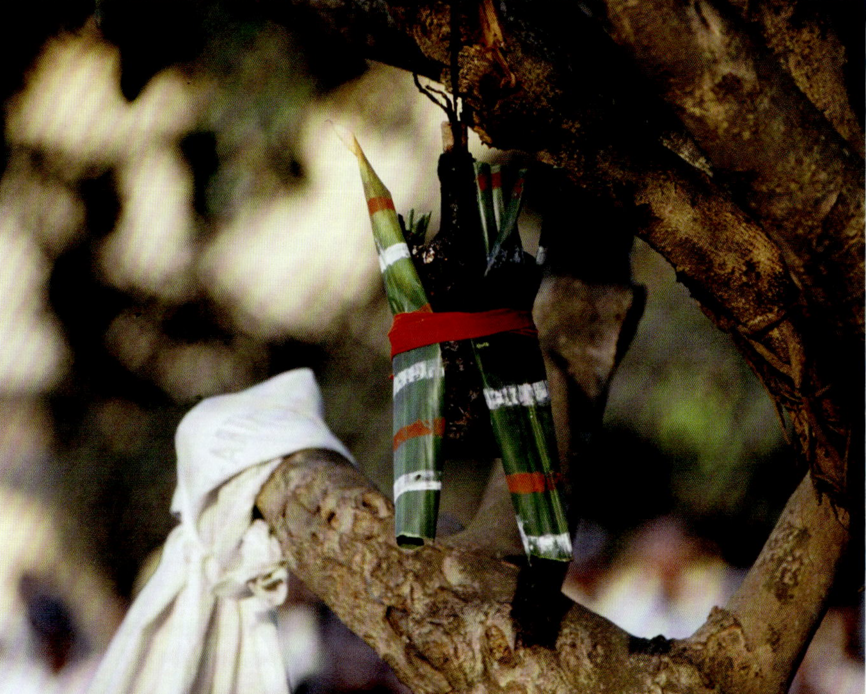

Protection from above. A bottle-Bo hangs in a tree above the ceremonial ground. With this magical power object, the scene is under Shango's protection.

Protection d'en haut. Une bouteille bo est suspendue à un arbre au-dessus d'un lieu de cérémonie. Grâce à cet objet magique, le site est placé sous la protection de Shangô.

Schutz von oben. Ein Flaschen-Bo hängt in einem Baum über dem Zeremoniengrund. Mit diesem magischen Kraftobjekt steht der Schauplatz unter Shangos Schutz.

Protección desde arriba. Una botella de Bo cuelga de un árbol sobre el suelo ceremonial. Con este objeto de poder mágico, la escena está bajo la protección de Shango.

Proteção de cima. Uma garrafa de Bo pendurada numa árvore acima do solo cerimonial. Com este objecto mágico de poder, a cena está sob a protecção de Shango.

Bescherming van bovenaf. Een fles-bo hangt in een boom boven de ceremoniële grond. Met dit magische object staat het tafereel onder Shango's bescherming.

Altar for Shango
Autel pour Shangô
Altar für Shango
Altar para Shango
Altar para Shango
Altaar voor Shango

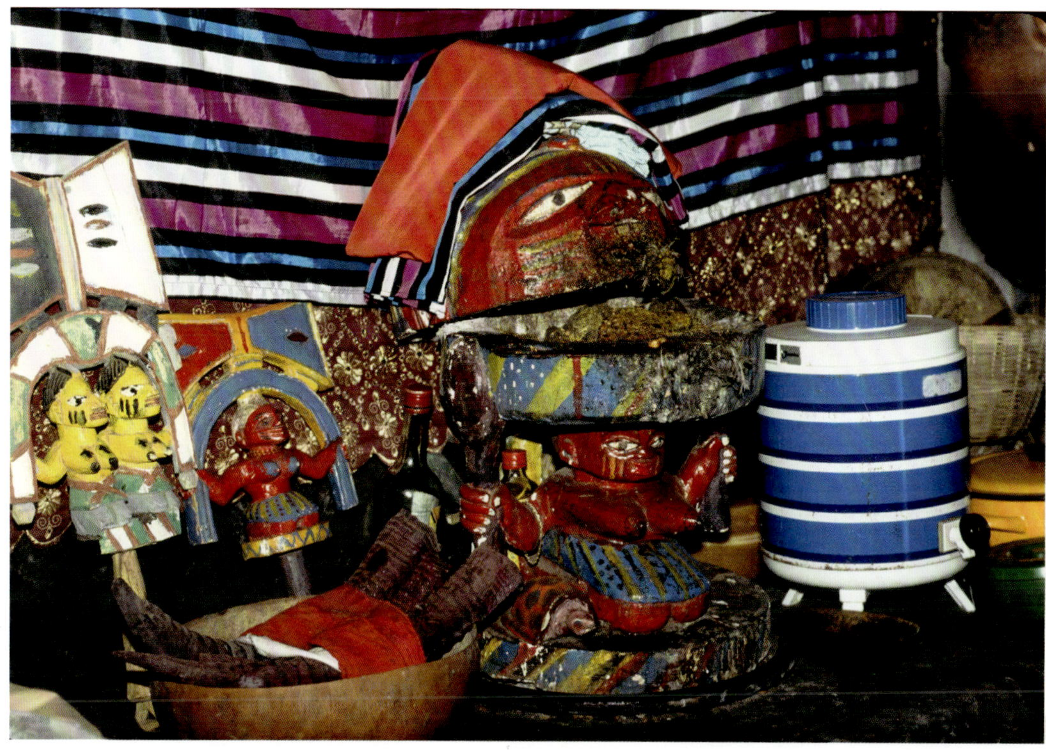

Place of honor for Shango
Shangô à l'honneur
Ehrenplatz für Shango
Lugar de honor para Shango
Lugar de honra para Shango
Aanbiddingsplaats
voor Shango

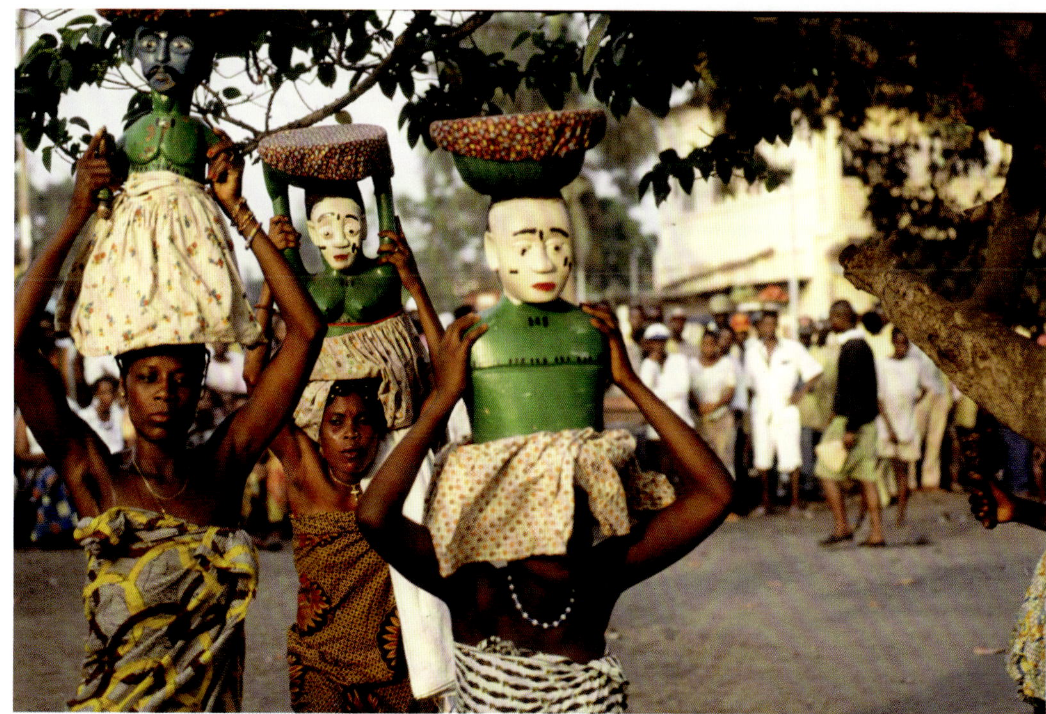

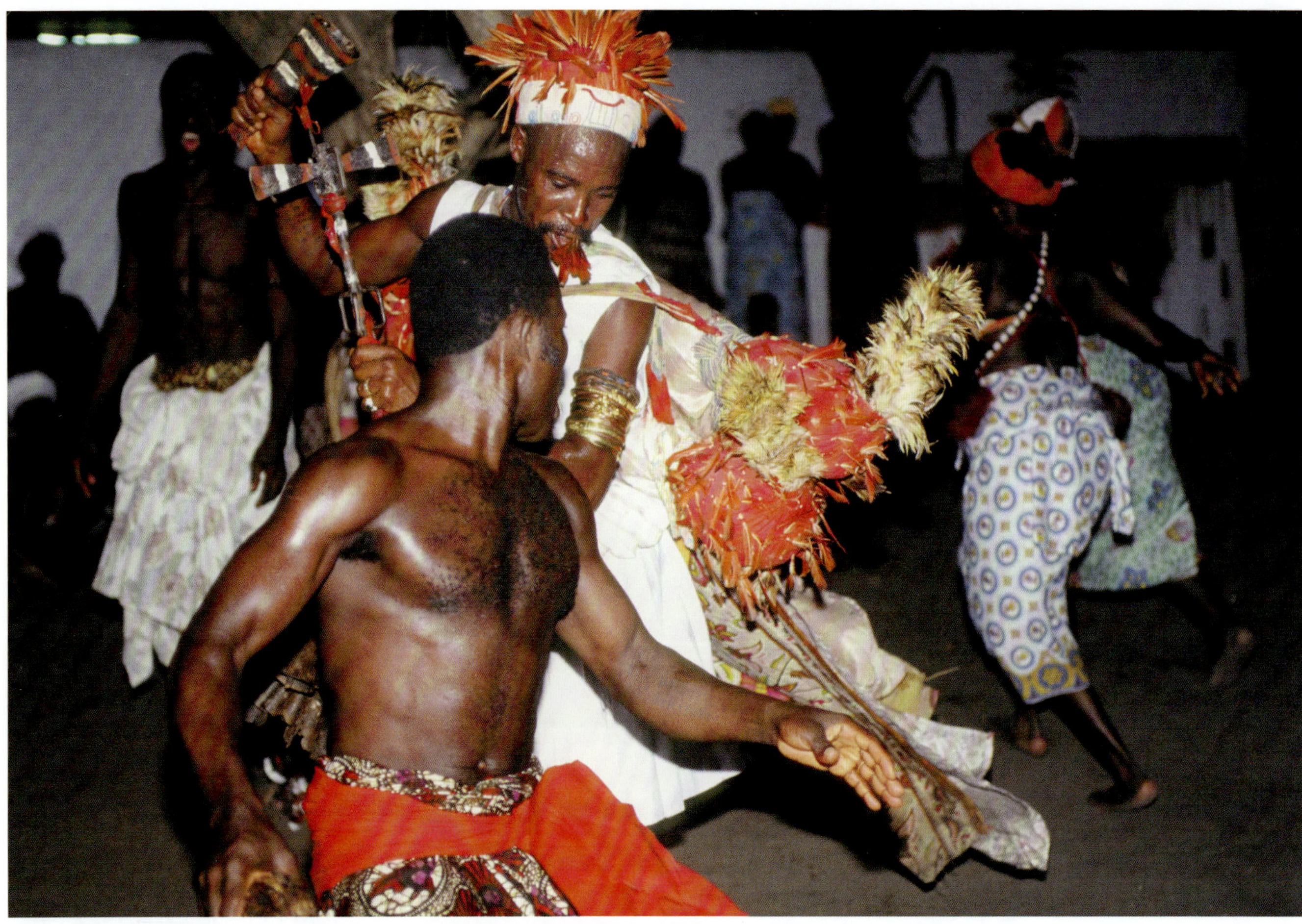

Shango priest shortly before the trance. Shortly before he falls into a trance, this white-robed priest carries the "Achina kpon", Shango's flint stones, demonstratively on his back to show his attachment to the deity.

Prêtre de Shangô, peu avant la transe. Peu avant d'entrer en transe, le prêtre vêtu de blanc parade en transportant ostensiblement sur son dos les *achina kpon*, pierres de Shangô, afin de prouver son lien à la déité.

Shangopriester kurz vor der Trance. Kurz bevor er in Trance fällt trägt dieser weißgewandete Priester die „Achina kpon", Shangos Feuersteine, demonstrativ auf seinem Rücken, um seine Verbundenheit mit der Gottheit zu demonstrieren.

Sacerdote Shango poco antes del trance. Poco antes de entrar en trance, este sacerdote de túnica blanca lleva el "Achina kpon", las piedras de sílex de Shango, sobre su espalda para demostrar su apego a la deidad.

Shango padre pouco antes do transe. Pouco antes de cair em transe, este sacerdote de vestes brancas carrega o "Achina kpon", as pedras de pedra de Xangai, demonstrativamente nas costas para demonstrar seu apego à divindade.

Shango-priester kort voor de trance. Kort voordat hij in trance raakt, draagt deze in het wit geklede priester de achina kpon, de vuurstenen van Shango, demonstratief op zijn rug om zijn verbondenheid met de god te tonen.

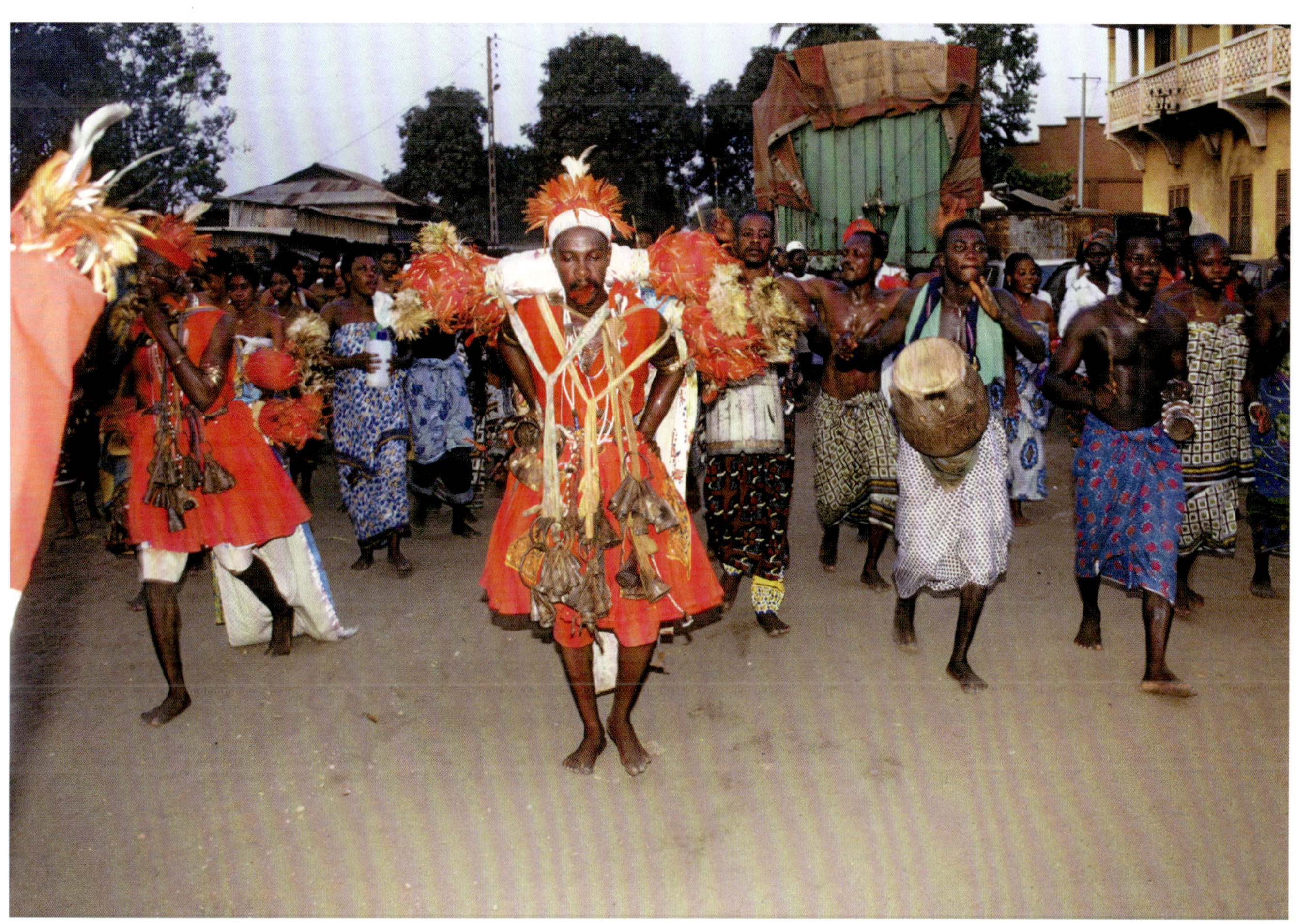

Shango in Cotonou

Shangô à Cotonou

Shango in Cotonou

Shango en Cotonou

Shango em Cotonou

Shango in Cotonou

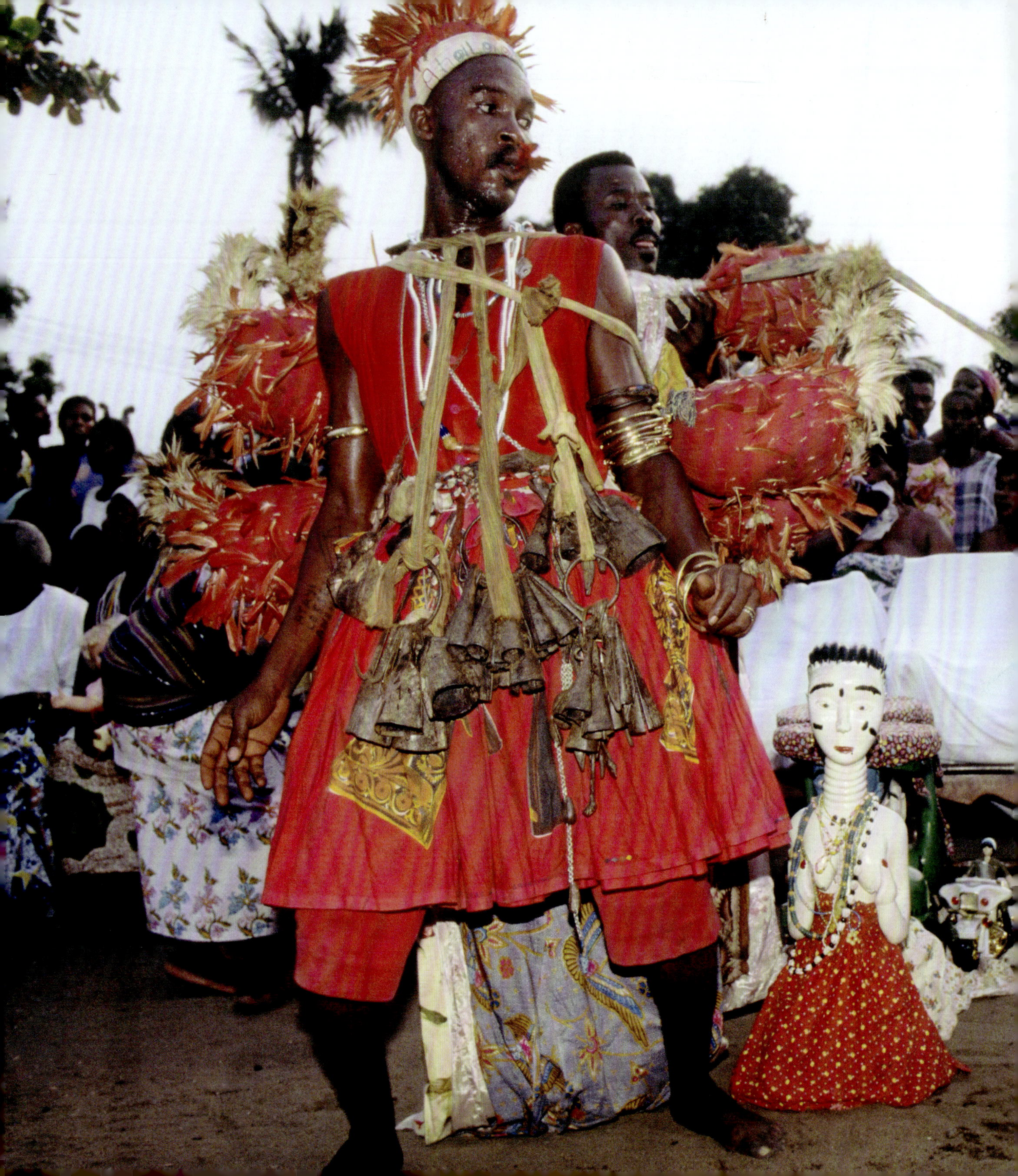

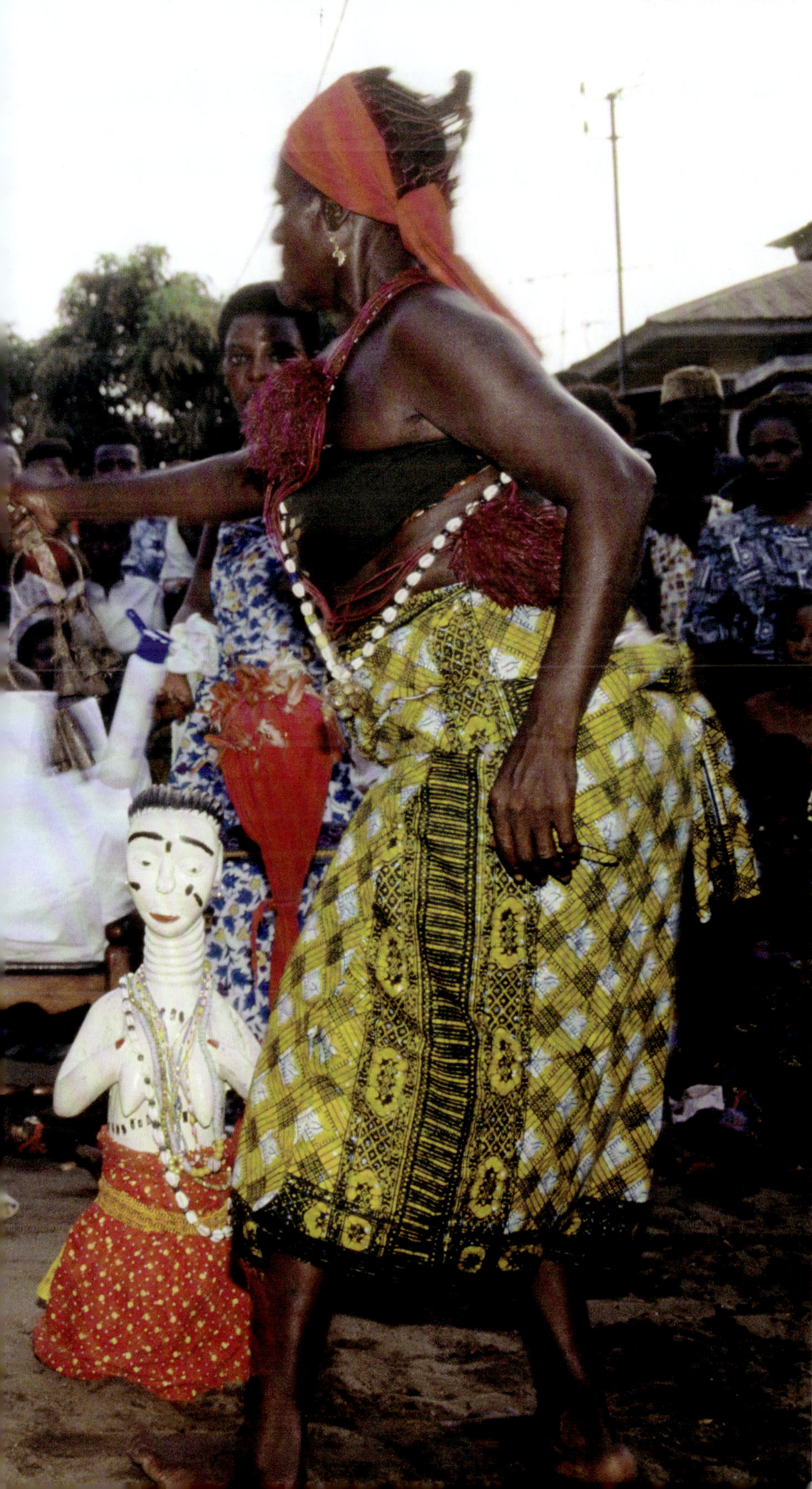

Ceremony for Shango. The Shango priest and an adept deliver a symbolic exchange of blows before the eyes of the spectators. At their centre are ritual figures in the red robes of the god of thunder.

Cérémonie pour Shangô. Sous les regards de la foule rassemblée, le prêtre de Shangô et une adepte se prêtent à une joute symbolique. Au centre sont installées des figurines rituelles vêtues de la tenue rouge du dieu du tonnerre.

Zeremonie für Shango. Vor den Augen der Versammelten liefern sich der Shangopriester und eine Adeptin einen symbolischen Schlagabtausch. In ihrer Mitte stehen rituelle Figuren in den roten Gewändern des Donnergottes.

Ceremonia para Shango. El sacerdote Shango y un adepto hacen un intercambio simbólico de golpes ante los ojos de los reunidos. En su centro hay figuras rituales con las rojas túnicas del dios del trueno.

Cerimônia para Shango. O Shangopriest e um adepto entregam uma troca simbólica de golpes diante dos olhos dos reunidos. No seu centro estão figuras rituais nas vestes vermelhas do deus do trovão.

Ceremonie voor Shango. De Shango-priester en een aanhangster leveren een symbolische slagenuitwisseling voor de ogen van de verzamelde mensen. In het midden staan rituele beelden in de rode gewaden van de dondergod.

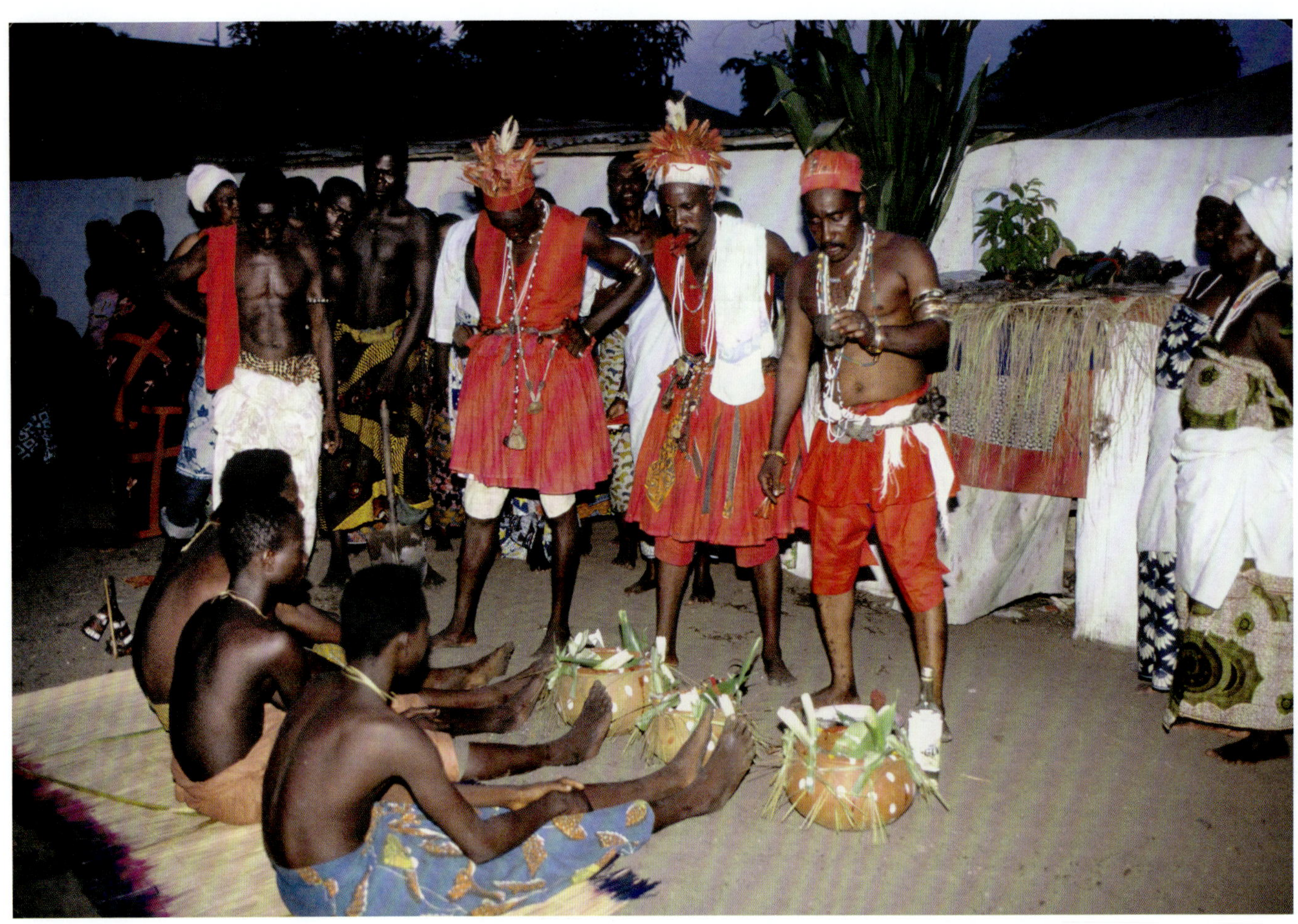

Ritual Cleaning

Nettoyage rituel

Rituelle Reinigung

Limpieza ritual

Limpeza Ritual

Rituele reiniging en bescherming

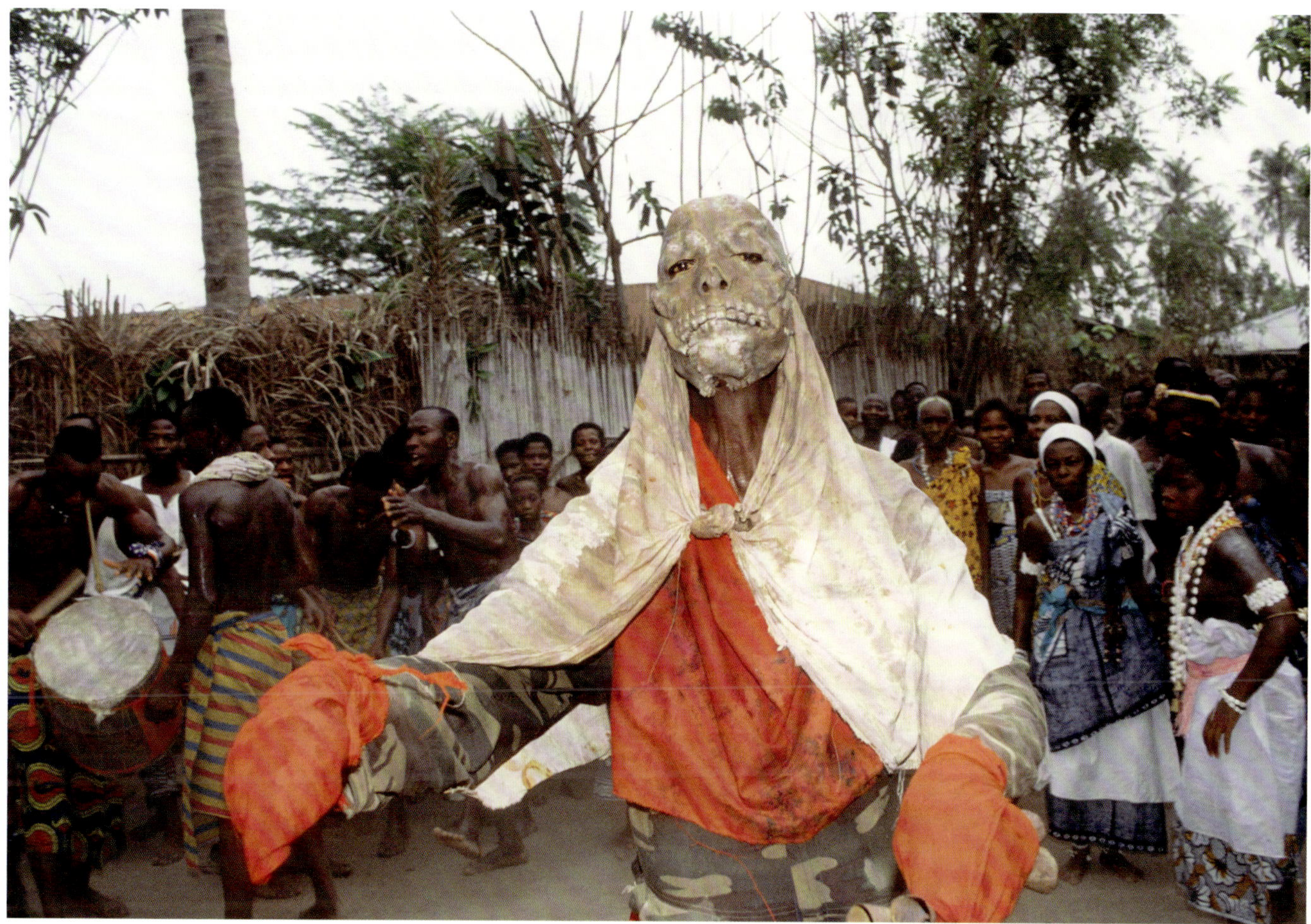

Death in Lokossa. Ceremonial appearance of a death mask of the thunder and thunderstorm god Shango in Lokossa, Benin

La Mort à Lokossa. Apparition cérémonielle d'un masque de mort du dieu du tonnerre et de l'orage, Shangô, à Lokossa.

Der Tod in Lokossa. Zeremonieller Auftritt einer Totenmaske des Donner- und Gewittergottes Shango in Lokossa, Benin

Muerte en Lokossa. Ceremonia de aparición de una máscara mortuoria del dios Shango en Lokossa, Benín.

Morte em Lokossa. Aparição cerimonial de uma máscara de morte do deus do trovão e da tempestade Shango em Lokossa, Benin

De dood in Lokossa. Ceremonieel optreden van een dodenmasker van de donder- en onweersgod Shango in Lokossa, Benin.

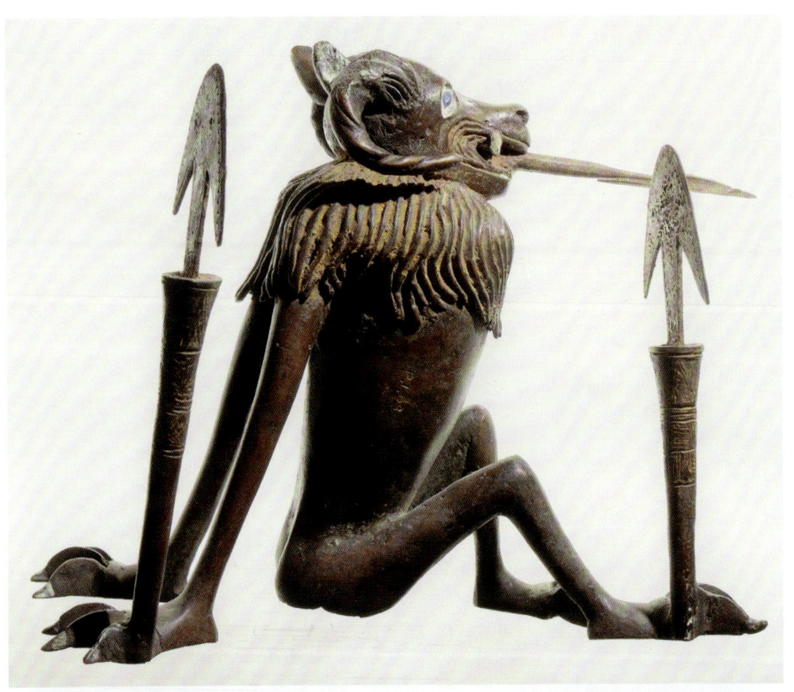

Classic symbol for Shango
Symbole classique de Shangô
Klassisches Symbol für Shango
Símbolo clásico de Shango
Símbolo clássico para Shango
Klassiek symbool voor Shango
Bronze, 25 × 30 cm

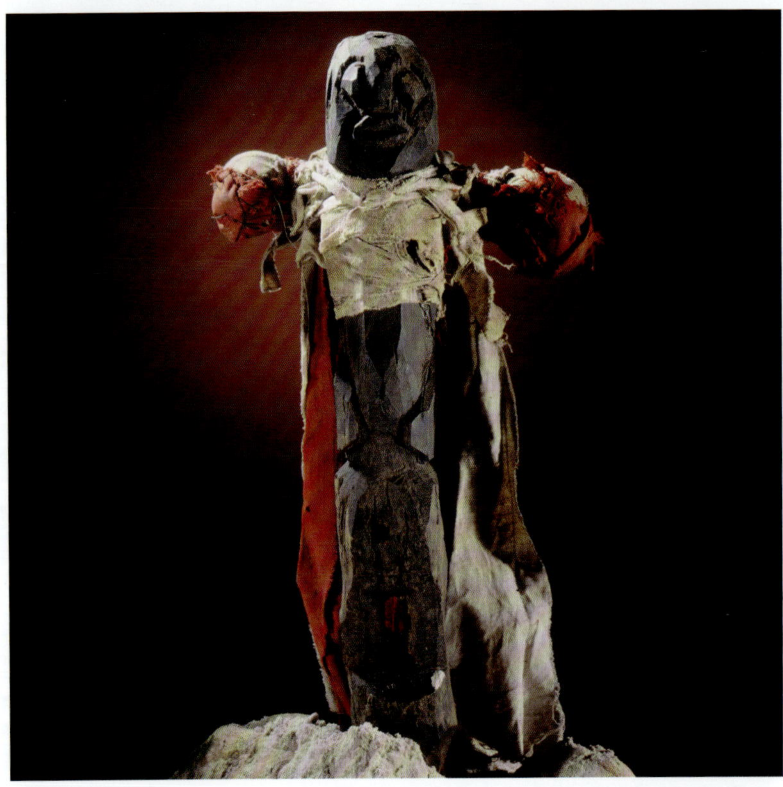

Figure from a Shango shrine
Figurine d'un sanctuaire de Shangô
Figur aus einem Shangoschrein
Figura de un santuario de Shango
Figura de um santuário Shangos
Beeld uit een heiligdom van Shango
Wood, textiles/Bois, textiles, 45 × 15 cm

Shango's Lightning rod.
There is gunpowder in the decorated calabashes, the thighbones come from convicted thieves. With this magical weapon the Shango priest can direct the lightning towards thieves still alive.

Paratonnerre de Shangô.
Les calebasses fixées à cet objet contiennent de la poudre à canon et les fémurs proviennent de voleurs exécutés. Cette arme magique aide le prêtre de Shangô à diriger la foudre sur des voleurs encore impunis.

Blitzlenker Shangos. In den applizierten Kalebassen ist Schießpulver, die Oberschenkelknochen stammen von überführten Dieben. Mit dieser magischen Waffe kann der Shangopriester den Blitz auf noch lebende Diebe lenken.

Pararrayos de Shango.
En las calabazas se aplica pólvora, los muslos provienen de ladrones convictos. Con esta arma mágica el sacerdote Shango puede dirigir el rayo hacia los ladrones que aún viven.

Pára-raios Shangos. Nas calabaças aplicadas é pólvora, os fémures vêm de ladrões condenados. Com esta arma mágica o Shangopriest pode dirigir o relâmpago a ladrões ainda vivos.

Bliksemafleider van Shango. In de geappliceerde kalebassen zit buskruit, de dijbeenbotten komen van veroordeelde dieven. Met dit magische wapen kan de Shango-priester de bliksem richten op nog levende dieven.

Human bone, calabashes/
Os humain, calebasses,
50 × 25 cm

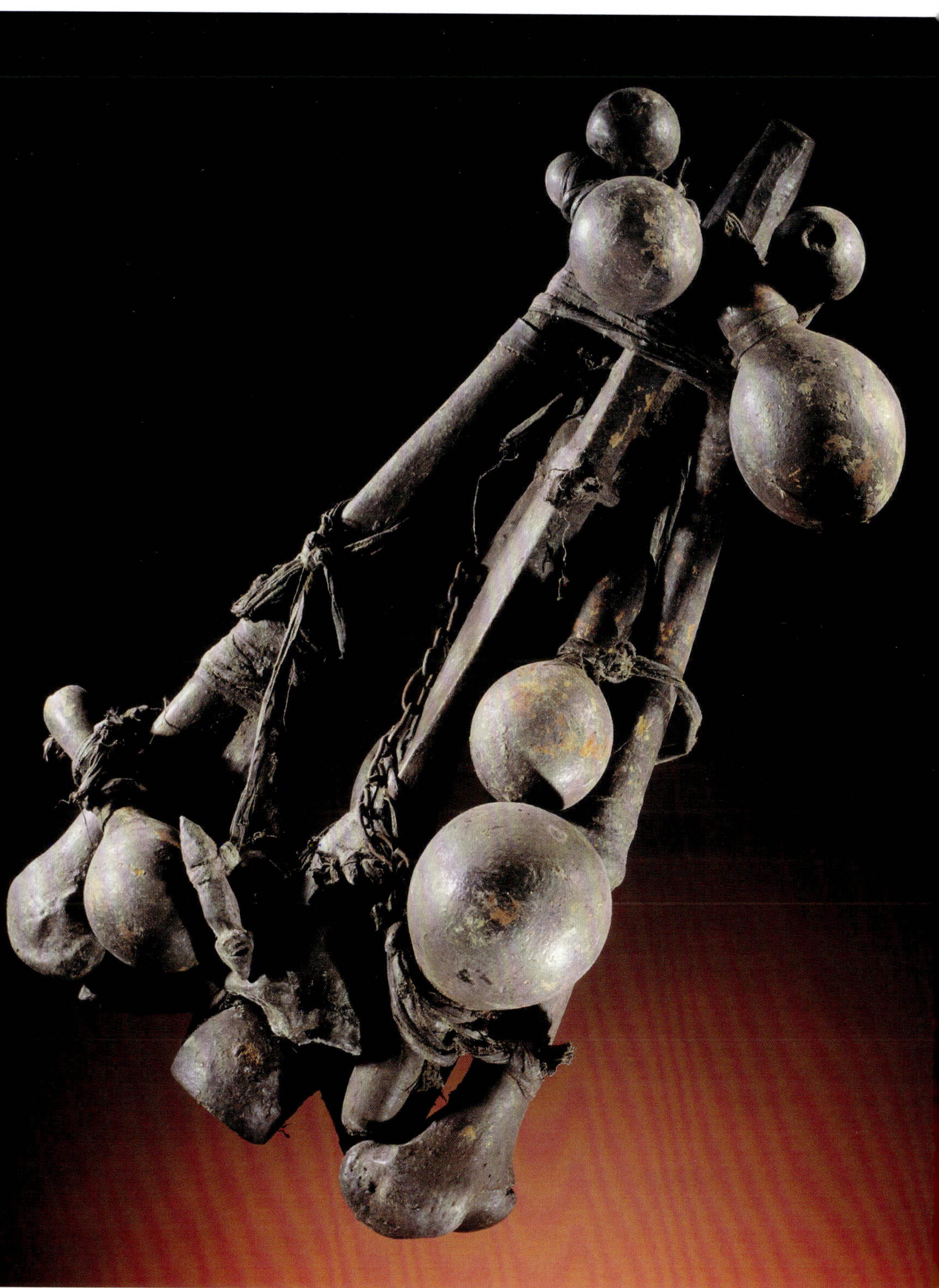

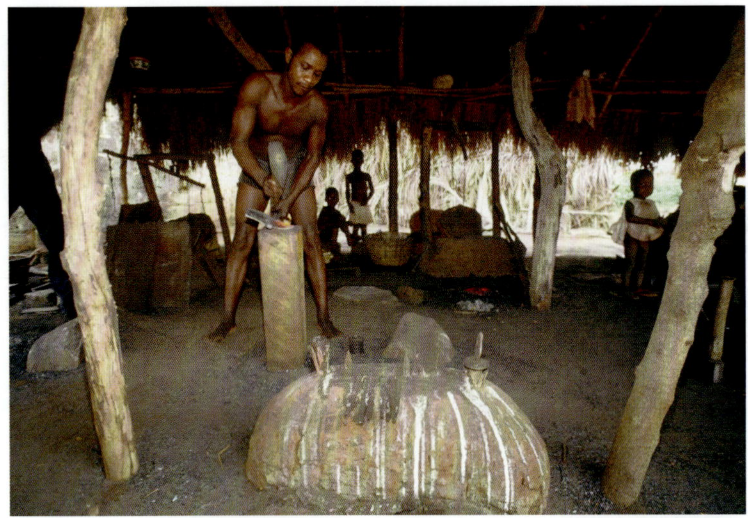

Blacksmith working on a shrine for Gu
Forgeron au travail et autel dédié à Gu
Schmied bei der Arbeit mit einem Schrein für Gu
Smith trabajando con un santuario para Gu
Ferreiro trabalhando com um santuário para Gu
Smid aan het werk met een heiligdom voor Gu

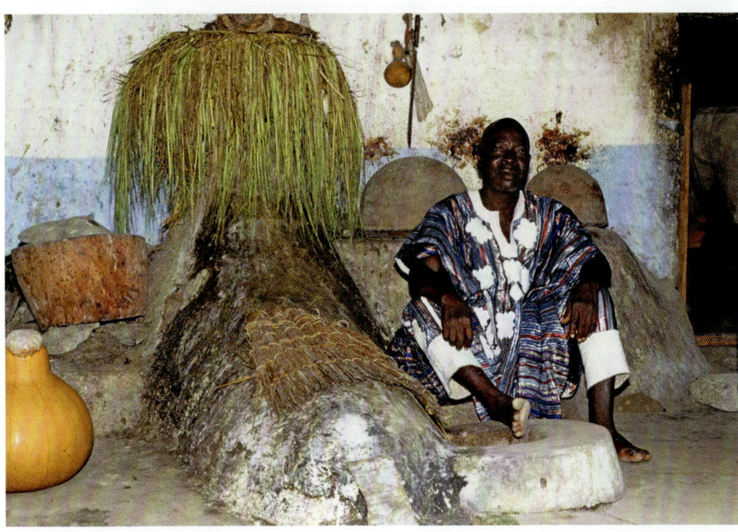

A shrine for Gu
Autel dédié à à Gu
Ein Schrein für Gu
Un santuario para Gu
Um santuário para Gu
Een heiligdom voor Gu

Adept with Gu force objects
Une adepte avec les objets de force de Gu
Adeptin mit Gu-Kraftobjekten
Adepta con objetos de fuerza Gu
Adeptin com objetos de força Gu
Aanhangster met krachtobjecten van Gu

Gu, the Iron Warrior

He is the epitome of the powerful warrior revered by the Fon in Benin as *Gu,* and by the Yoruba as *Ogun.* His domain is iron and the cultivation of land in the world.

Old myths say that Gu had cleared the way for the gods on their first visit to earth with the machete, which is why people in professions that have to do with metal and transport revere him. Blacksmiths, taxi drivers like to pay homage to him,

Gu, le guerrier inébranlable

Gu, vénéré par le peuple Fon du Bénin, est Ogun pour les Yoruba. Il est l'incarnation du guerrier puissant, dont les domaines sont le fer et le défrichement du monde.

Les mythes anciens racontent que, lors de son premier séjour sur terre, Gu aurait ouvert la voie aux dieux à coups de machette. Il est ainsi loué par les corporations associées au métal et aux voies de circulation : les forgerons, chauffeurs

Gu, der eiserne Krieger

Bei den Fon in Benin als *Gu*, bei den Yoruba als *Ogun* verehrt, ist er der Inbegriff des kraftvollen Kriegers. Seine Domäne ist das Eisen und die Urbarmachung der Welt.

Alte Mythen sagen, Gu hätte den Göttern bei ihrem ersten Erdbesuch den Weg mit der Machete freigemacht, weshalb man ihm gern in Berufszweigen huldigt, die mit Metall und Verkehrswegen zu tun haben. Schmiede, Taxifahrer, Mechaniker und

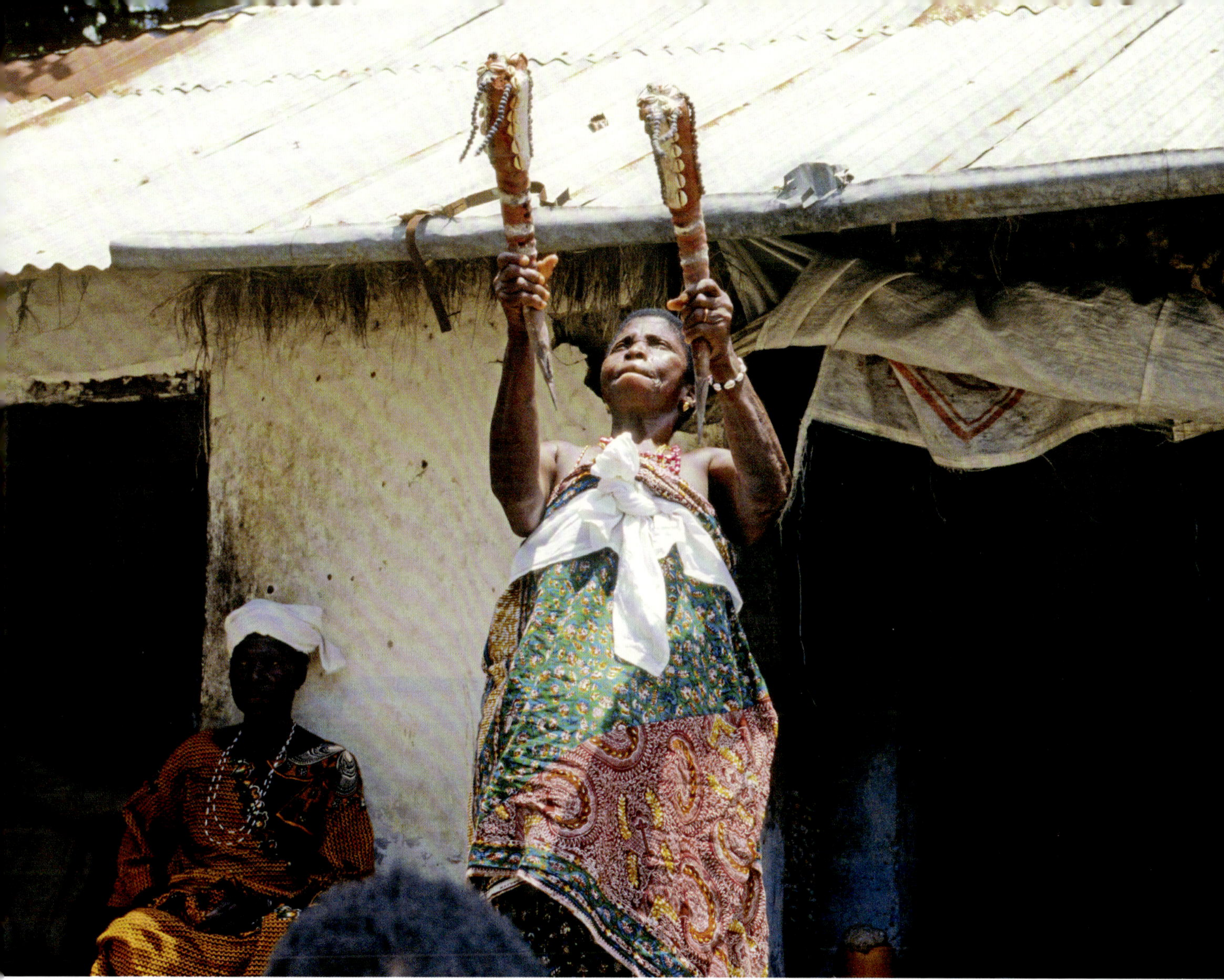

Gu, el guerrero de hierro

Es el epítome del poderoso guerrero del reino Fon en Benin como *Gu,* y del Yoruba como *Ogun.* Su dominio es el hierro y la recuperación de la tierra del mundo.

Los viejos mitos dicen que Gu abrió el camino a los dioses en su primera visita a la tierra con un machete, por lo que a la gente le gusta rendirle homenaje en profesiones que tienen que ver con el metal y las rutas de tráfico. Entre sus admiradores se encuentran

Gu, O Guerreiro de Ferro

Ele é a epítome do poderoso guerreiro no Fon em Benin como Gu, no Yoruba como Ogun. Seu domínio é o ferro e a recuperação da terra do mundo.

Mitos antigos dizem que Gu abriu o caminho para os deuses em sua primeira visita à terra com o facão, e é por isso que as pessoas gostam de prestar homenagem a ele em profissões que têm a ver com metal e rotas de tráfego. Ferreiros, taxistas,

Gu, de ijzeren krijger

De god die bij de Fon in Benin als Gu en bij de Yoruba als Ogun bekendstaat, is de belichaming van de machtige krijger. Zijn domein is het ijzer en de ontginning van de wereld.

Volgens oude mythen maakte Gu met een machete de weg vrij voor de goden tijdens hun eerste bezoek aan de aarde. Daarom brengen mensen in beroepen die te maken hebben met metaal en verkeerswegen

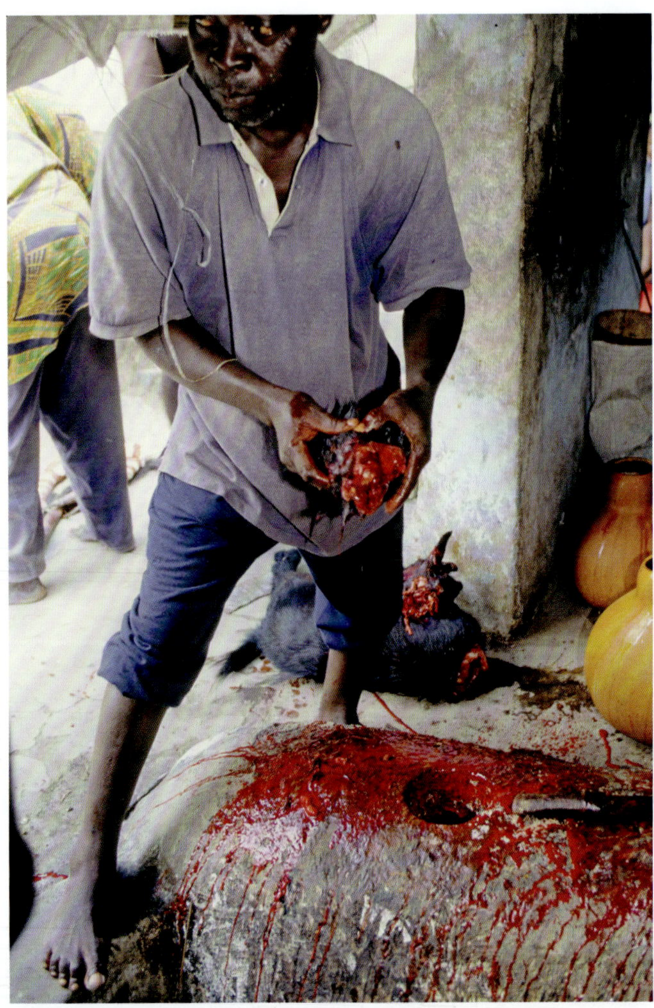

Blood for Gu. Gu, who as the god of war and iron is a violent god, demands blood sacrifices. Here his shrine is being soaked with the blood of a sacrificial animal.

Du sang pour Gu. Gu, divinité violente puisque responsable de la guerre et du fer, exige des offrandes de sang. Ici, le sang d'une victime sacrifiée vient tout juste d'être versé sur son autel.

Blut für Gu. Gu, der als Gott des Krieges und des Eisens ein gewalttätiger Gott ist, verlangt nach Blutopfern. Hier wird gerade sein Schrein mit dem Blut eines Opfertieres getränkt.

Sangre para Gu. Gu, dios violento de la guerra y del hierro, exige sacrificios de sangre. Aquí su santuario está siendo empapado con la sangre de un animal de sacrificio.

Sangue para Gu. Gu, que é um deus violento como deus da guerra e do ferro, exige sacrifícios de sangue. Aqui seu santuário está sendo encharcado com o sangue de um animal de sacrifício.

Bloed voor Gu. Gu, die als de god van oorlog en ijzer een gewelddadige god is, eist bloedoffers. Hier wordt zijn heiligdom doordrenkt met het bloed van een offerdier.

Blood distribution on the shrine
Distribution de sang sur l'autel
Blutverteilung auf dem Schrein
Distribución de sangre en el santuario
Distribuição de sangue no santuário
Verdeling van het bloed over het heiligdom

mechanics and soldiers are among his admirers, because the blessing of Gu is regarded as life insurance.

The divinity contains both the aspect of the ruthless, violent fighter and that of the virile, responsible man, for whom the safety of his own people goes above all else. Destruction and the creation of new things, symbolized in the smithy where the iron is melted and converted into a new form, are the insignia of Gu. He is one of the most important and oldest Vodun gods.

de taxi, mécaniciens et soldats comptent parmi ses adorateurs, car sa bénédiction est considérée comme une assurance-vie.

Cette divinité prend l'aspect d'un combattant puissant et impitoyable, mais aussi celui d'un homme viril et responsable, pour qui la sécurité des siens est primordiale. Les attributions de Gu sont la destruction et la création, symbolisées par la forge dans laquelle le fer est fondu puis modelé en une forme nouvelle. Il compte parmi les déités vodun les plus importantes et les plus anciennes.

Soldaten zählen zu seinen Verehrern, denn der Segen Gus gilt als Lebensversicherung.

Die Gottheit enthält sowohl den Aspekt des unbarmherzigen, gewalttätigen Kämpfers als auch den des virilen, verantwortungsvollen Mannes, dem die Sicherheit der Seinen über alles geht. Zerstörung und die Erschaffung von Neuem, versinnbildlicht in der Schmiede, in der das Eisen geschmolzen und in eine neue Form gebracht wird, sind die Insignien von Gu. Er gehört zu den wichtigsten und ältesten Vodungottheiten.

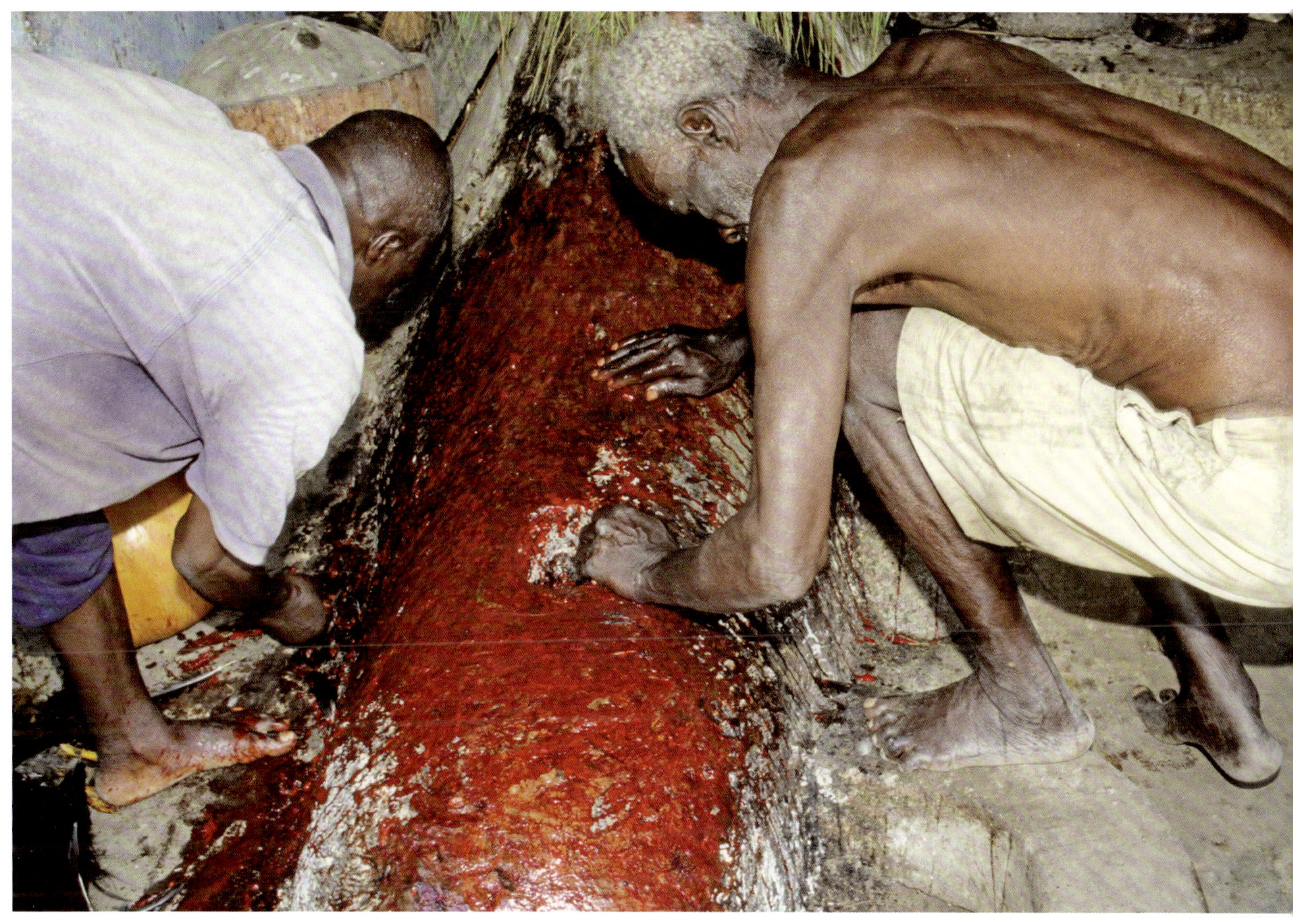

herreros, taxistas, mecánicos y soldados, porque la bendición de Gu es considerada como un seguro de vida.

La deidad contiene tanto el aspecto del luchador despiadado y violento como el del hombre viril y responsable, para quien la seguridad propia está por encima de todo. La destrucción y la creación de cosas nuevas, simbolizadas en la forja donde el hierro se funde y se transforma en una nueva forma, son la insignia de Gu. Es uno de los dioses vudú más importantes y antiguos.

mecânicos e soldados estão entre seus admiradores, pois a bênção de Gus é considerada um seguro de vida.

A divindade contém tanto o aspecto do lutador impiedoso e violento quanto o do homem viril e responsável, para quem a segurança do próprio homem está acima de tudo. A destruição e a criação de coisas novas, simbolizadas na forja onde o ferro é derretido e trazido para uma nova forma, são a insígnia de Gu. Ele é um dos vodungods mais importantes e mais antigos.

hem graag hulde. Smeden, taxichauffeurs, monteurs en soldaten behoren tot zijn aanbidders, want de zegen van Gu wordt gezien als een levensverzekering.

De godheid omvat zowel het aspect van de genadeloze, gewelddadige strijder als dat van de viriele, verantwoordelijke man, voor wie de veiligheid van de zijnen boven alles gaat. Vernietiging en creatie van nieuwe dingen, gesymboliseerd in de smederij waar het ijzer wordt gesmolten en in een nieuwe vorm wordt gebracht, zijn de insignes van Gu. Hij is een van de belangrijkste en oudste vodungoden.

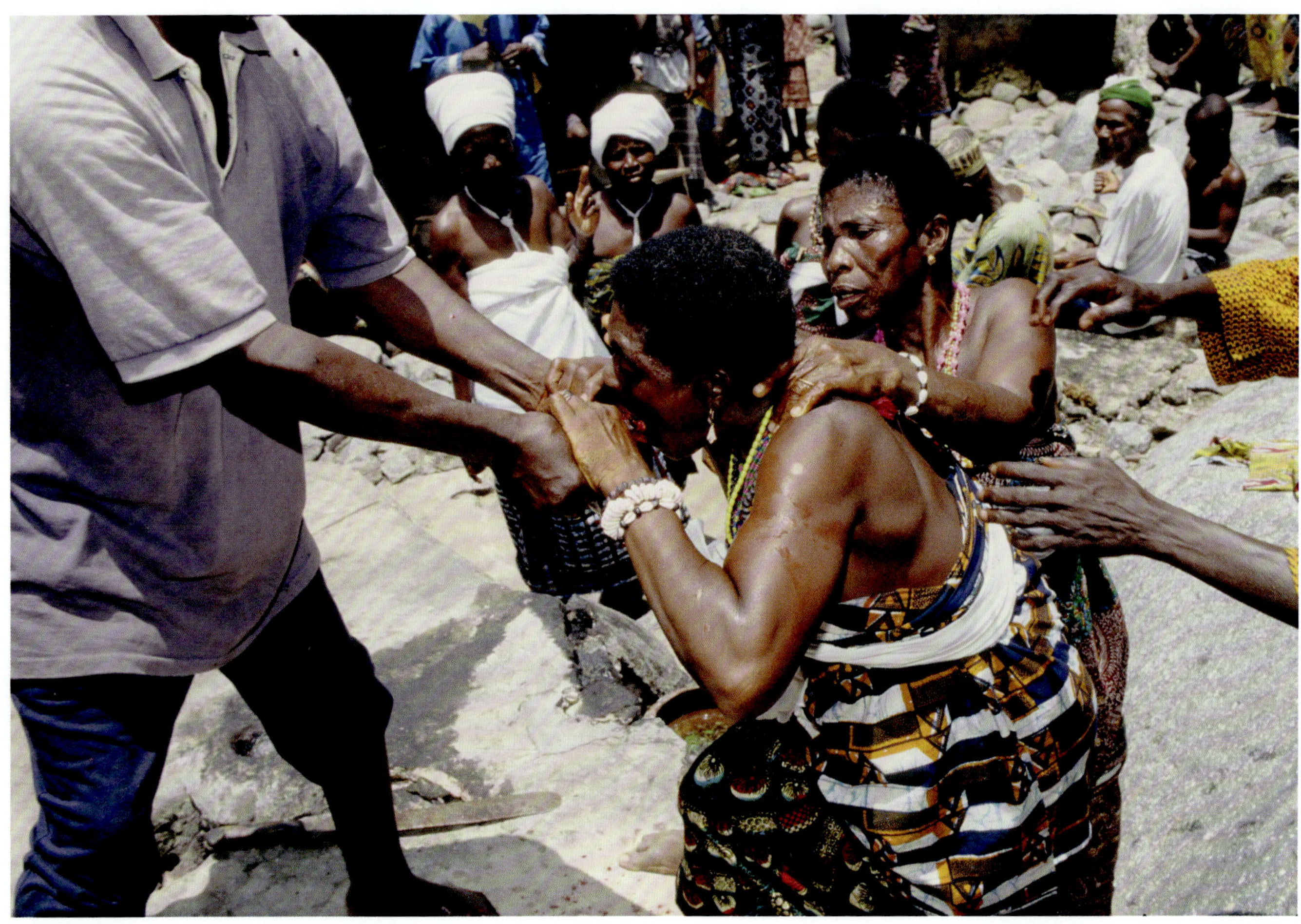

Potion of the Gods

Potion des Dieux

Trank der Götter

Poción de los dioses

Poção dos Deuses

Drank van de goden

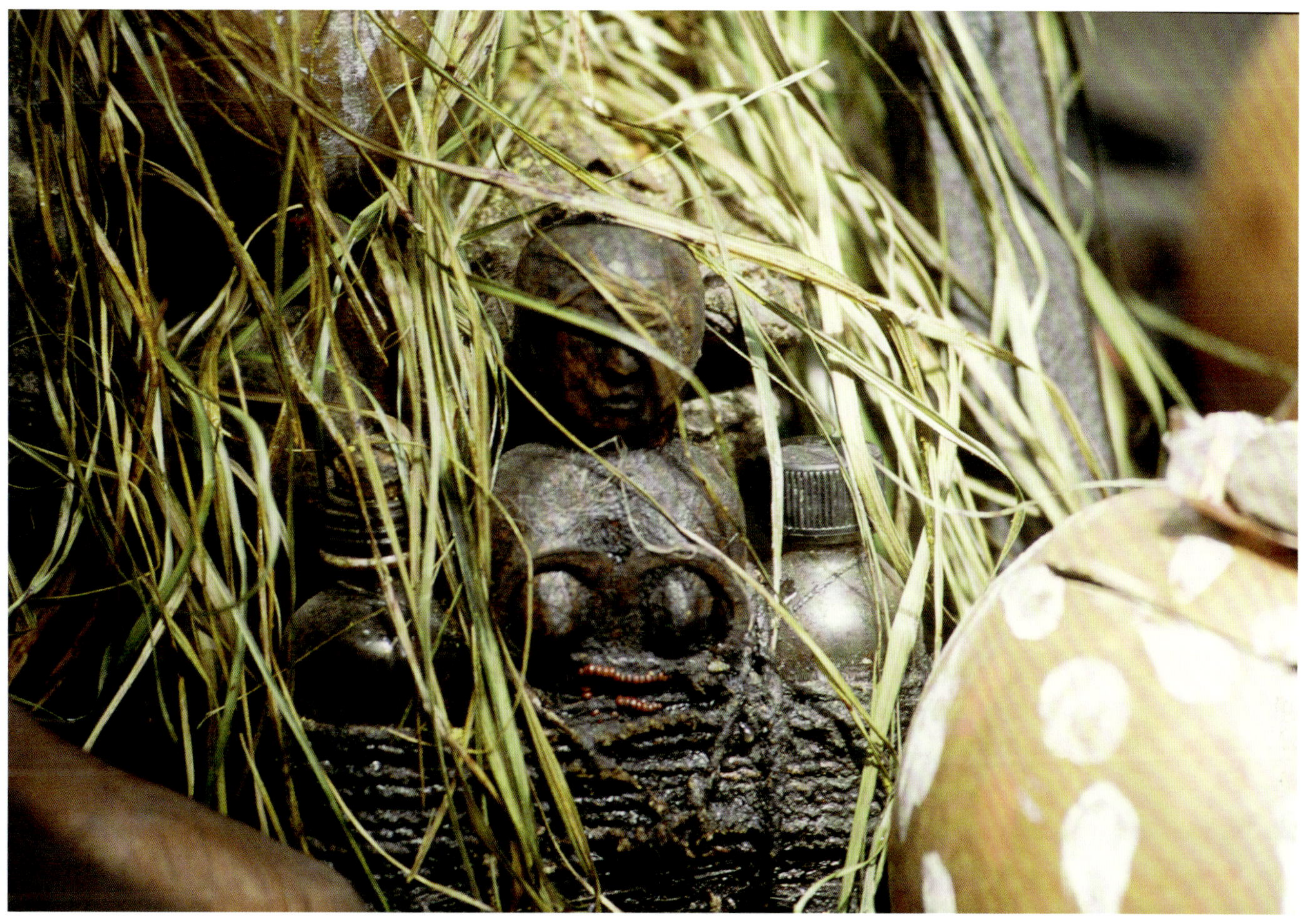

Ceremony at Dassa. A solemn ceremony is held for a deceased hunter. The setting is the rocks of Dassa, the mythological home of Gu in Benin.

Cérémonie à Dassa. Une cérémonie commémorative est organisée en mémoire d'un chasseur décédé. Elle se déroule sur les collines de Dassa, terre d'origine mythologique de Gu au Bénin.

Zeremonie bei Dassa. Für einen verstorbenen Jäger wird eine feierliche Zeremonie abgehalten. Der Schauplatz sind die Felsen von Dassa, der mythologischen Heimat von Gu in Benin.

Ceremonia en Dassa. Se celebra una ceremonia solemne para un cazador fallecido. El escenario son las rocas de Dassa, el hogar mitológico de Gu en Benin.

Cerimônia na Dassa. Uma cerimónia solene é realizada para um caçador falecido. O cenário são as rochas de Dassa, a casa mitológica de Gu em Benin.

Ceremonie bij Dassa. Hier wordt een plechtige ceremonie gehouden voor een overleden jager. Decor zijn de rotsen van Dassa, het mythologische thuisland van Gu in Benin.

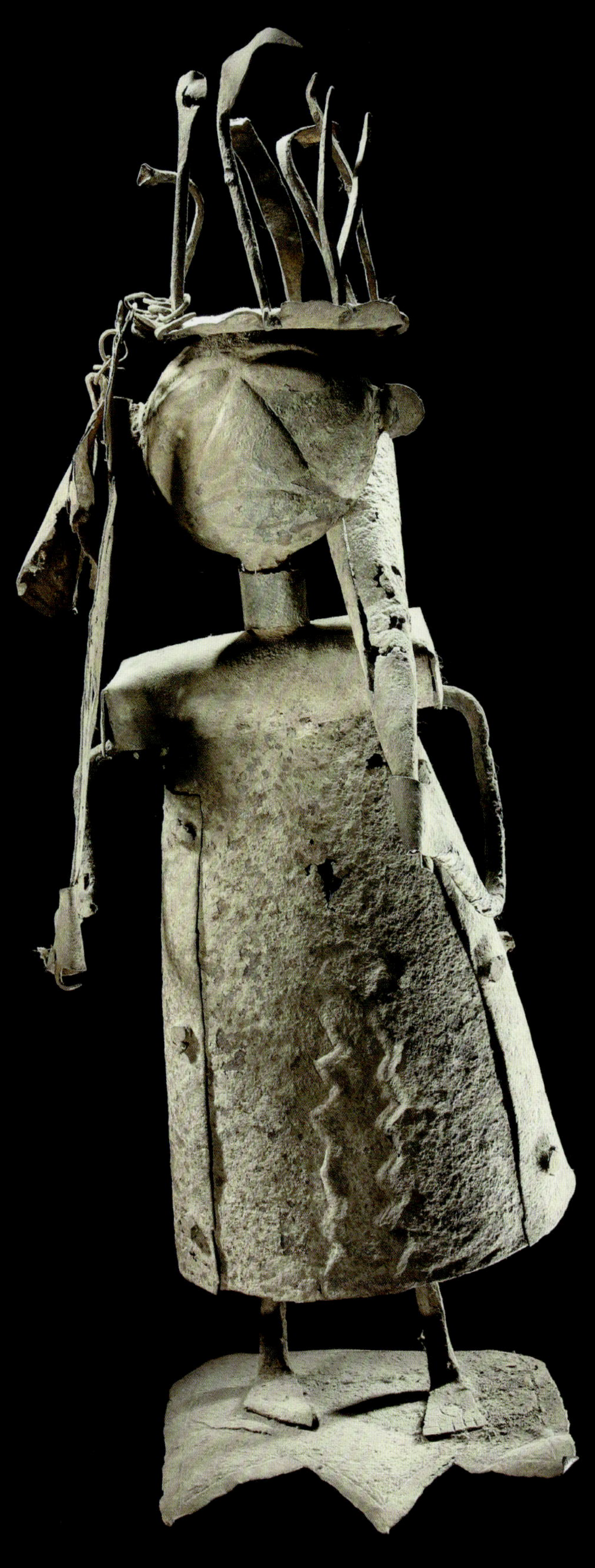

Gu, the god of iron. The figurative depiction of Gu as an "iron man" or warrior is as common in Benin today as it was in the past.

Gu, le dieu du fer. Les figurines représentant Gu en « homme du fer » ou en guerrier étaient autrefois courantes au Bénin, et le sont toujours.

Gu, der Gott des Eisens. Die figürliche Darstellung von Gu als „Eisenmann" oder Krieger findet man in Benin früher wie heute häufig.

Gu, el dios del hierro. La representación figurativa de Gu como "hombre de hierro" o guerrero es tan común en Benin hoy como en el pasado.

Gu, o deus do ferro. A representação figurativa de Gu como um "homem de ferro" ou guerreiro é tão comum em Benin hoje como era no passado.

Gu, de god van het ijzer. De figuratieve voorstelling van Gu als 'ijzeren man' of krijger is in Benin nog net zo gewoon als vroeger.

Metal/Métal, 49 × 18 cm

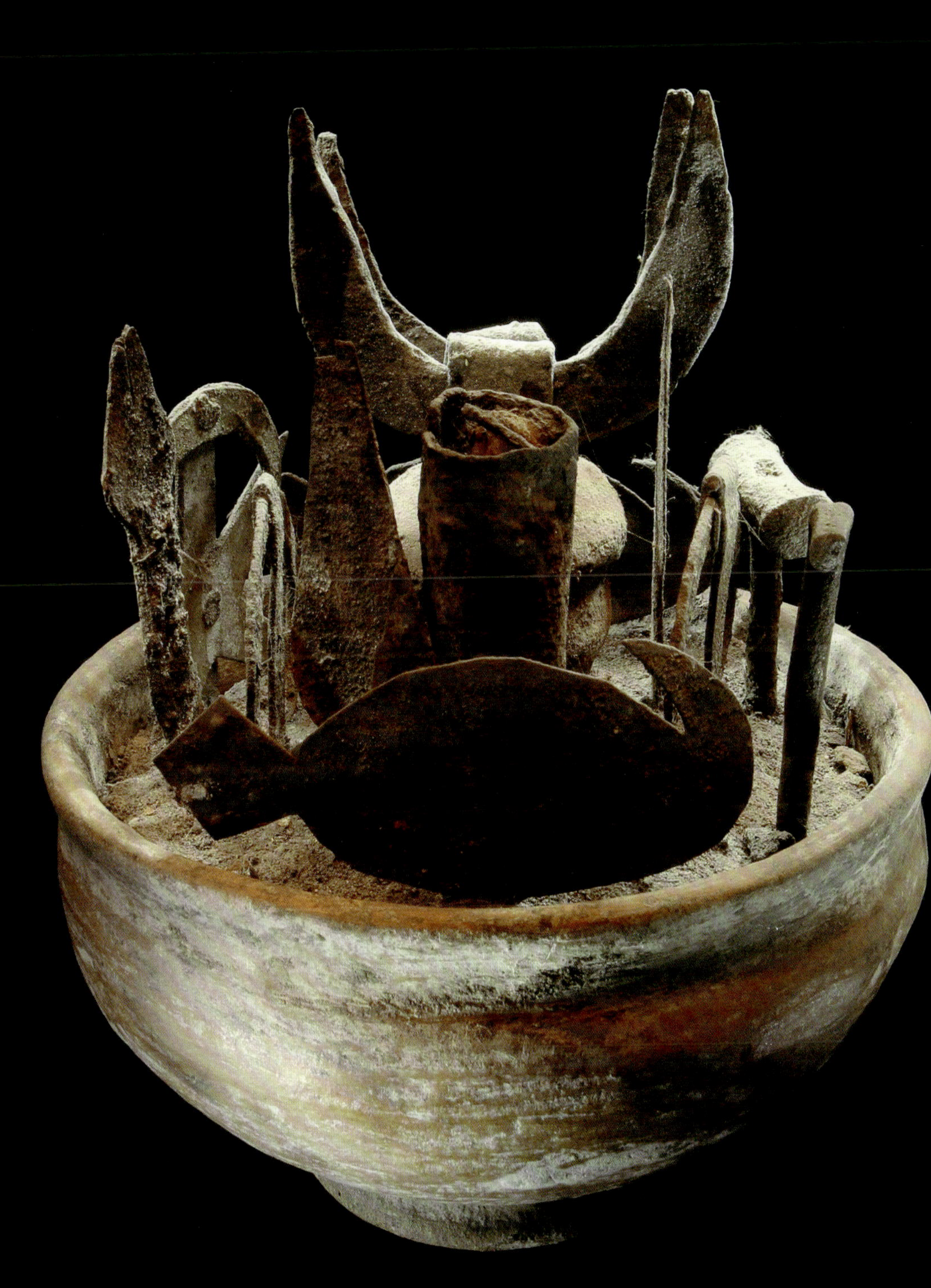

Cult bowl for Gu. This pot contains secret substances which are associated with the deity and which make him a carrier of magical powers. Typical insignia of the iron god protrude from the fetish substance.

Bol pour le culte de Gu. Ce pot contient des substances secrètes associées à la déité et devient ainsi porteur de puissances magiques. Les insignes habituels du dieu du fer émergent de la substance fétiche

Kultschale für Gu. Dieser Topf enthält geheime Substanzen, die mit der Gottheit assoziiert sind und die ihn zum Träger magischer Kräfte machen. Typische Insignien des Eisengottes ragen aus der Fetischsubstanz heraus.

Cuenco de culto para Gu. Este pote contiene sustancias secretas que están asociadas con la deidad y que lo hacen portador de poderes mágicos. Las insignias típicas del dios del hierro destacan de la sustancia fetiche.

Tigela de culto para Gu. Este vaso contém substâncias secretas que estão associadas com a divindade e que fazem dele um portador de poderes mágicos. A insígnia típica do deus de ferro destaca-se da substância fetiche.

Cultuskom voor Gu. Deze kom bevat geheime substanties die met de god geassocieerd worden en hem tot een drager van magische krachten maken. Typische insignes van de ijzergod steken boven de fetisjsubstantie uit.

Metal, mud, clay/Métal, boue, argile, 20 × 15 cm

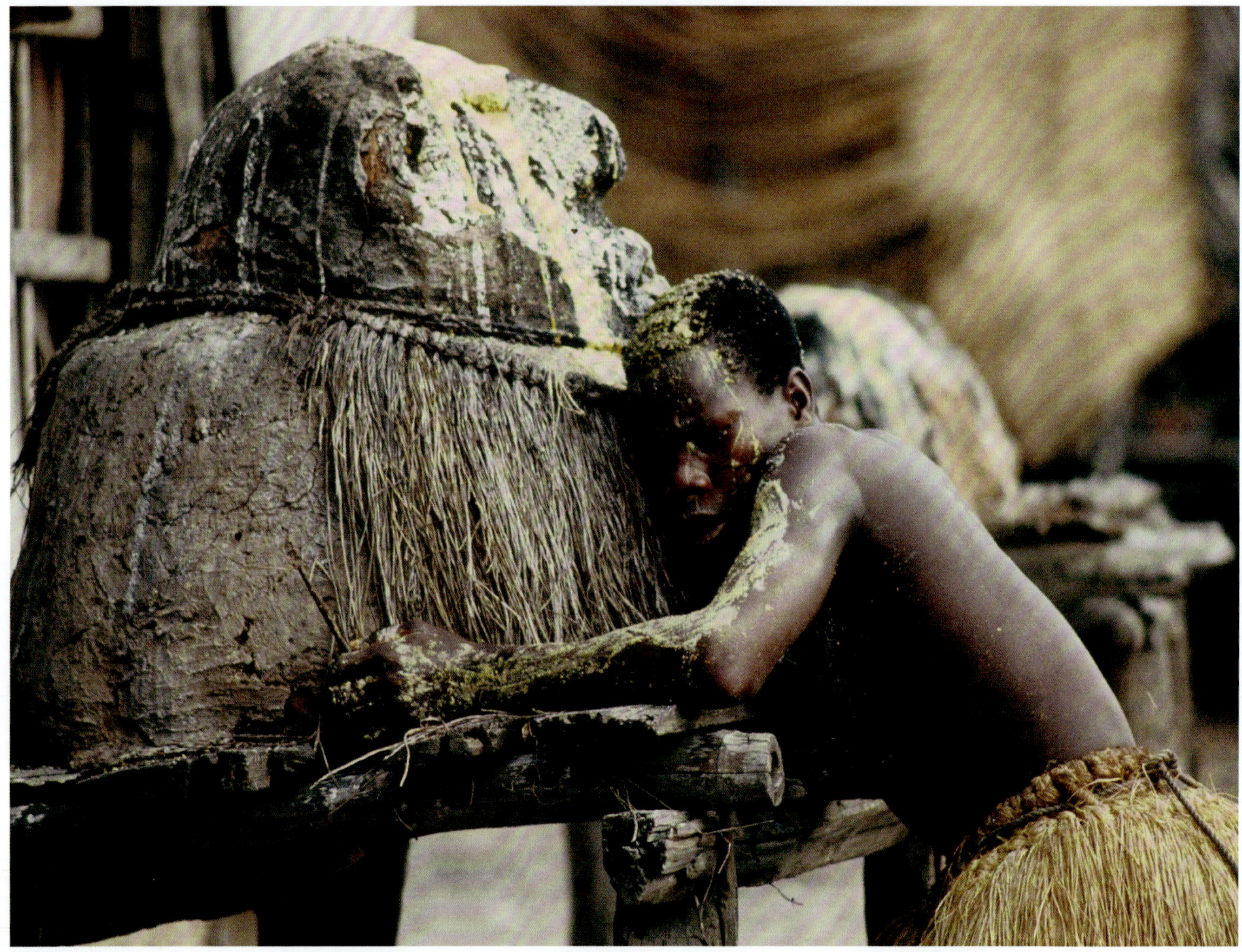

Refuge with Legba   Zuflucht bei Legba   Refúgio em Legba

Trouver refuge en Legba   Refugio en Legba   Toevlucht tot Legba

Legba, the mediator and joker

Legba is a god in the Pantheon of Vodun, who has special importance in the general communication between humans and gods. He makes the connection between the worlds and is therefore the first to be given sacrifices. Legba is considered a capricious companion; if he was not satisfied or if he considers it appropriate, he is happy to

Legba, intermédiaire facétieux

Dans le panthéon vodun, Legba joue un rôle particulièrement important dans la communication entre les hommes et les dieux. Il établit le lien entre ces deux mondes et devient ainsi le premier à recevoir des offrandes. Legba est cependant une entité lunatique. Lorsqu'il n'est pas satisfait, ou qu'il estime cela plus approprié, il transmet de

Legba, der Vermittler und Joker

Legba ist im Pantheon der Vodun ein Gott, dem besondere Bedeutung bei der generellen Kommunikation zwischen Menschen und Göttern zukommt. Er stellt die Verbindung zwischen den Welten her und ist daher der Erste, dem Opfergaben zuteil werden. Dabei gilt Legba als ein launischer Geselle; wenn er nicht zufriedengestellt wurde oder es für angebracht hält, übermittelt er Anfragen der

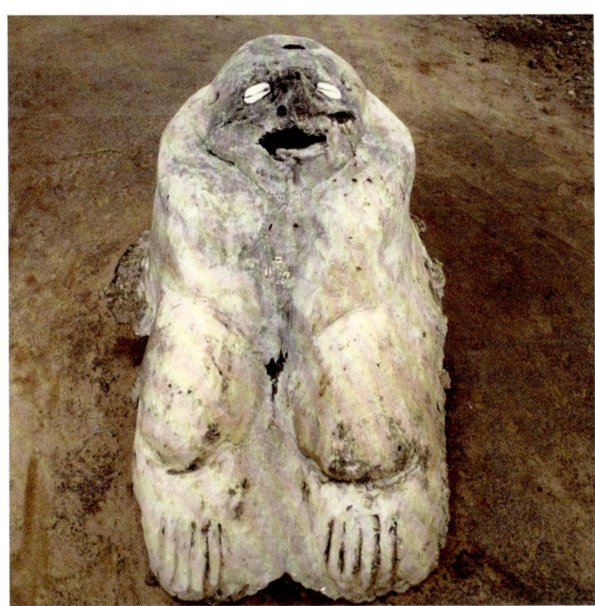

Typical representation of Legba in Benin
Représentation typique de Legba, Bénin
Typische Darstellung Legbas in Benin
Representación típica de Legba en Benín
Representação típica de Legbas no Benin
Typische weergave van Legba in Benin

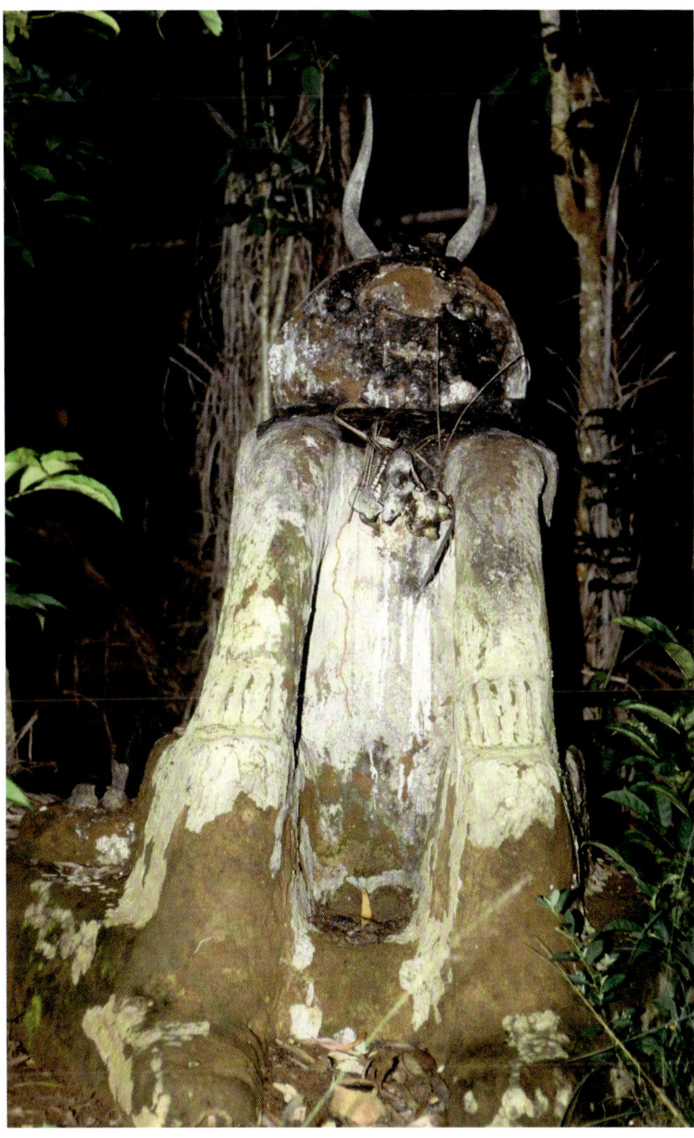

Impressive Legba figure
Imposante figure de Legba
Imposante Legbafigur
Impresionante figura de Legba
Impressionante figura Legba
Indrukwekkend Legba-beeld

Legba, el mediador y guasón

Legba es un dios en el Panteón de Vudú, que tiene especial importancia en la comunicación general entre humanos y dioses. Él establece la conexión entre los mundos y por lo tanto es el primero en recibir ofrendas. Legba es considerado un dios caprichoso; si no quedasatisfecho o si lo considera apropiado, le gusta transmitir incorrectamente las peticiones humanas a

Legba, O mediador e Joker

Legba é um deus no Panteão do Vodu, que tem especial importância na comunicação geral entre humanos e deuses. Ele estabelece a ligação entre os mundos e é, portanto, o primeiro a receber ofertas. Legba é considerado como um viajante caprichoso; se ele não estava satisfeito ou se ele o considera apropriado, ele está feliz em transmitir pedidos humanos aos outros

Legba, de bemiddelaar en joker

Legba is een god uit het vodunpantheon die van bijzondere betekenis is in de algemene communicatie tussen mens en goden. Hij legt de verbinding tussen de werelden en is daarom de eerste die offers krijgt aangeboden. Legba wordt beschouwd als een grillige metgezel; als hij niet tevreden is of iets niet gepast vindt, brengt hij de menselijke verzoeken graag foutief over aan

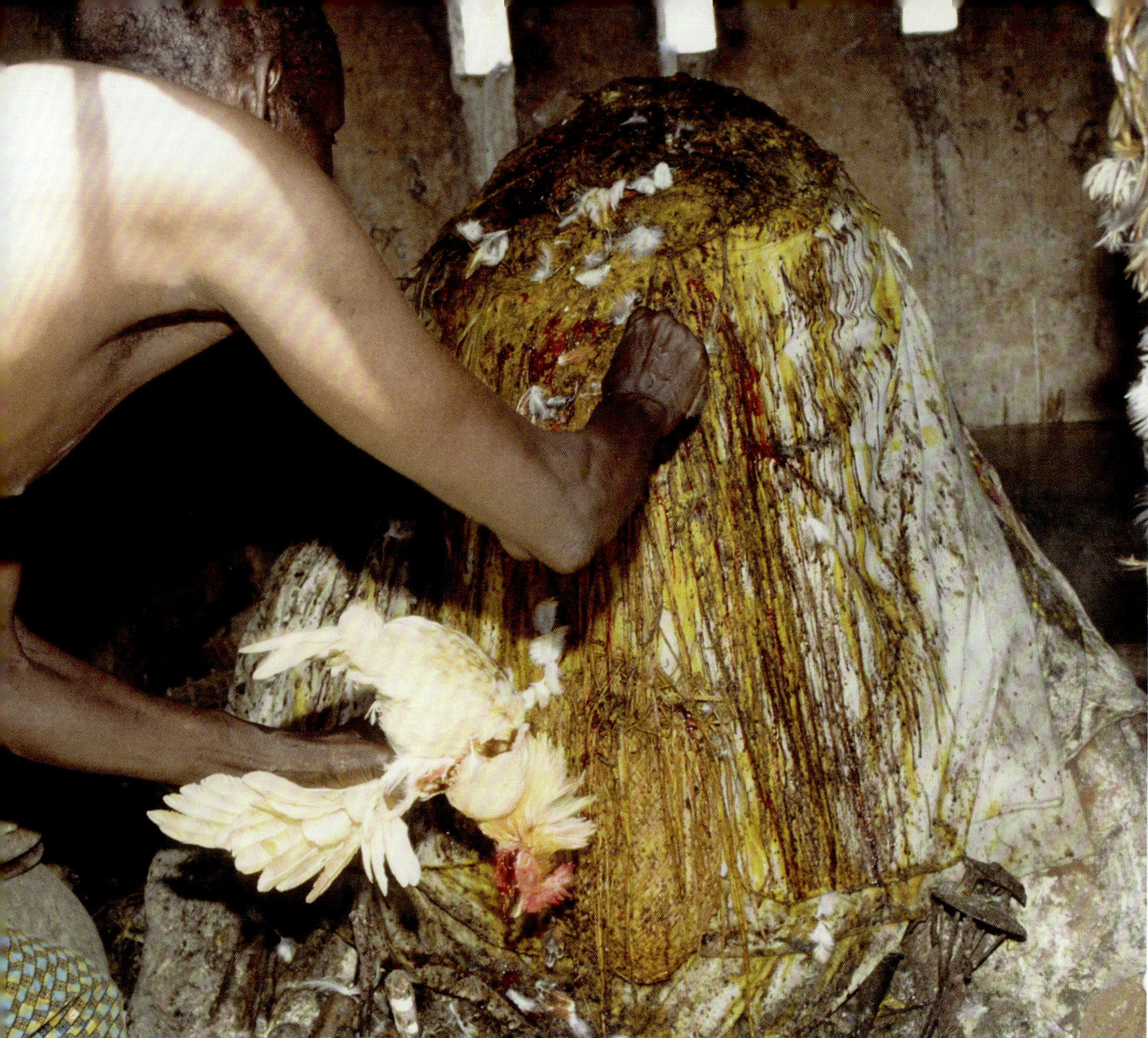

convey human requests to the other gods incorrectly. One is therefore always anxious not to annoy or ignore him.

Among the Fon people in Benin, Legba is the youngest child of the Mawu-Lisa couple, among the Yoruba the first servant of the creator god Olodumare. Legba representations can mostly be seen in front of farmsteads or at entrances to villages and towns, because Legba is also a guard.

Dogs are sacred to him, so sacrifices for Legba are sometimes also presented to dogs. If they eat the gift, the sacrifice is considered to have been accepted.

manière erronée les demandes des hommes aux autres dieux. On s'efforcera donc de ne jamais le contrarier ni de l'ignorer.

Pour les Fon du Bénin, Legba est le plus jeune enfant du couple divin Mawu-Lisa ; chez les Yoruba, il est le premier serviteur du dieu créateur Olodumare. On trouve de nombreuses représentations de Legba devant les fermes et les voies d'accès des localités, car il tient également le rôle de gardien.

Les chiens étant sacrés pour lui, les offrandes destinées à Legba sont parfois présentées à ces animaux. L'offrande est considérée comme acceptée lorsqu'elle est mangée.

Menschen an die anderen Götter gern einmal fehlerhaft. Man ist daher stets bemüht, ihn nicht zu verärgern oder zu übergehen.

Beim Volk der Fon in Benin ist Legba das jüngste Kind des Götterpaares Mawu-Lisa, bei den Yoruba erster Diener des Schöpfergottes Olodumare. Man sieht Legbadarstellungen meist vor Gehöften oder an Ortseingängen, denn Legba ist auch ein Wächter.

Hunde sind ihm heilig, daher werden Opfer für Legba manchmal auch Hunden vorgelegt. Wenn diese die Gabe fressen, gilt das Opfer als angenommen.

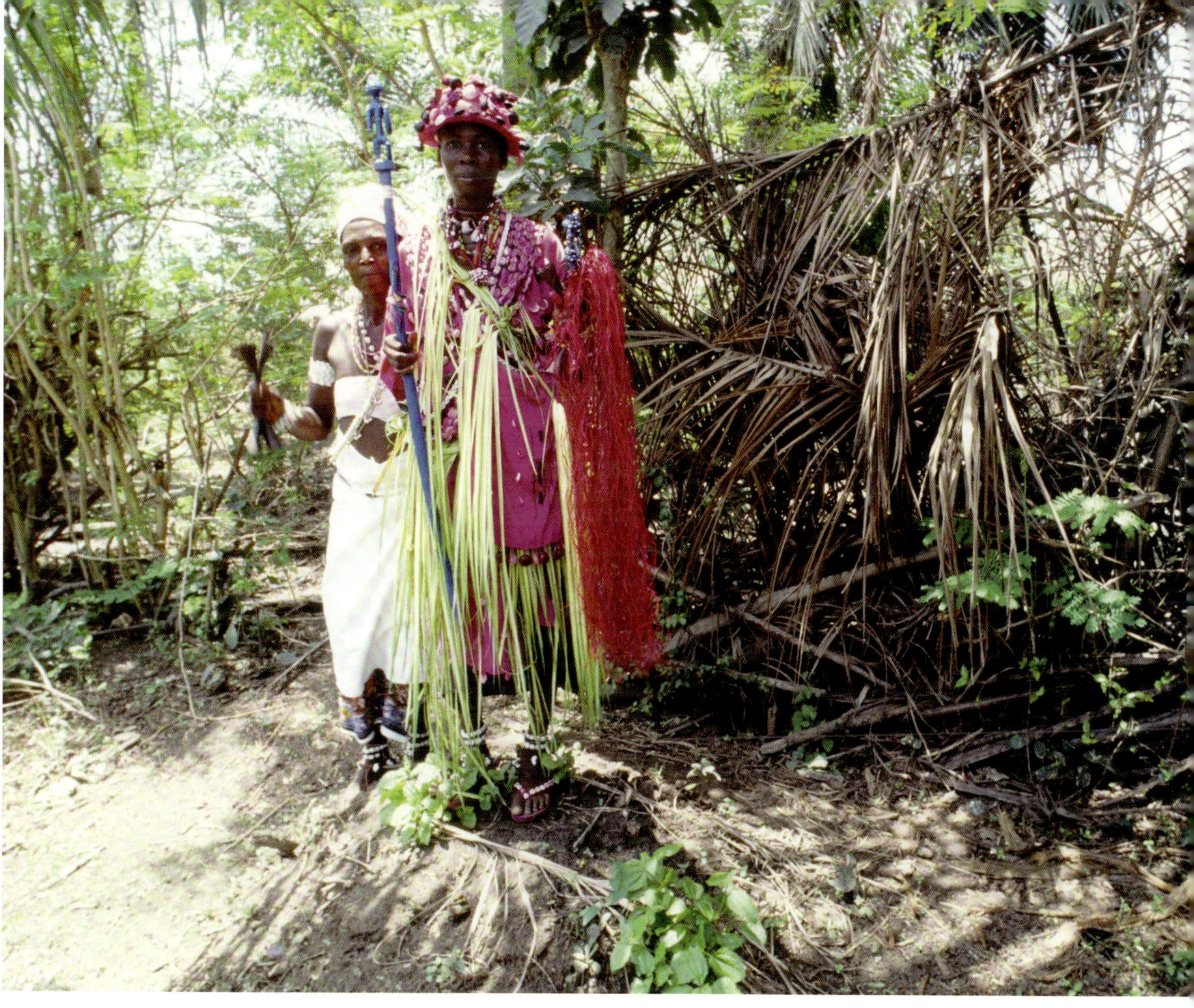

los otros dioses. Por lo tanto, uno siempre se esfuerza en no molestarle o ignorarle.

Entre los Fon de Benin, Legba es el hijo menor de los dioses Mawu-Lisa, entre los Yoruba el primer servidor del dios creador Olodumare. Las representaciones de Legba se suelen ver delante de los caseríos o en las entradas de los pueblos, ya que Legba también es un guardián.

Los perros son sagrados para él, por lo tanto en los sacrificios para Legba a veces también se presentan a los perros. Si éstos se comen la ofrenda, el sacrificio se considera aceptado.

deuses incorretamente. Por isso, estamos sempre ansiosos por não o incomodar ou ignorar.

Entre o povo Fon em Benin Legba está o filho mais novo dos deuses Mawu-Lisa, entre os iorubás o primeiro servo do deus criador Olodumare. As representações de Legba são geralmente vistas em frente às fazendas ou nas entradas das aldeias, porque Legba é também um guardião.

Os cães são sagrados para ele, por isso os sacrifícios pela Legba são por vezes também apresentados aos cães. Se estes comerem o presente, o sacrifício é considerado aceite.

de andere goden. Men is er daarom altijd op gebrand hem niet boos te maken of te negeren.

Bij de Fon in Benin is Legba het jongste kind van het godenpaar Mawu-Lisa, bij de Yoruba de eerste dienaar van de schepper-god Olodumare. Voorstellingen van Legba zijn meestal te zien voor boerderijen of bij dorpsingangen, omdat Legba ook een bewaker is.

Honden zijn heilig voor hem en daarom worden offers voor Legba soms ook aan honden gebracht. Als zij de offergaven opeten, geldt het offer als geaccepteerd.

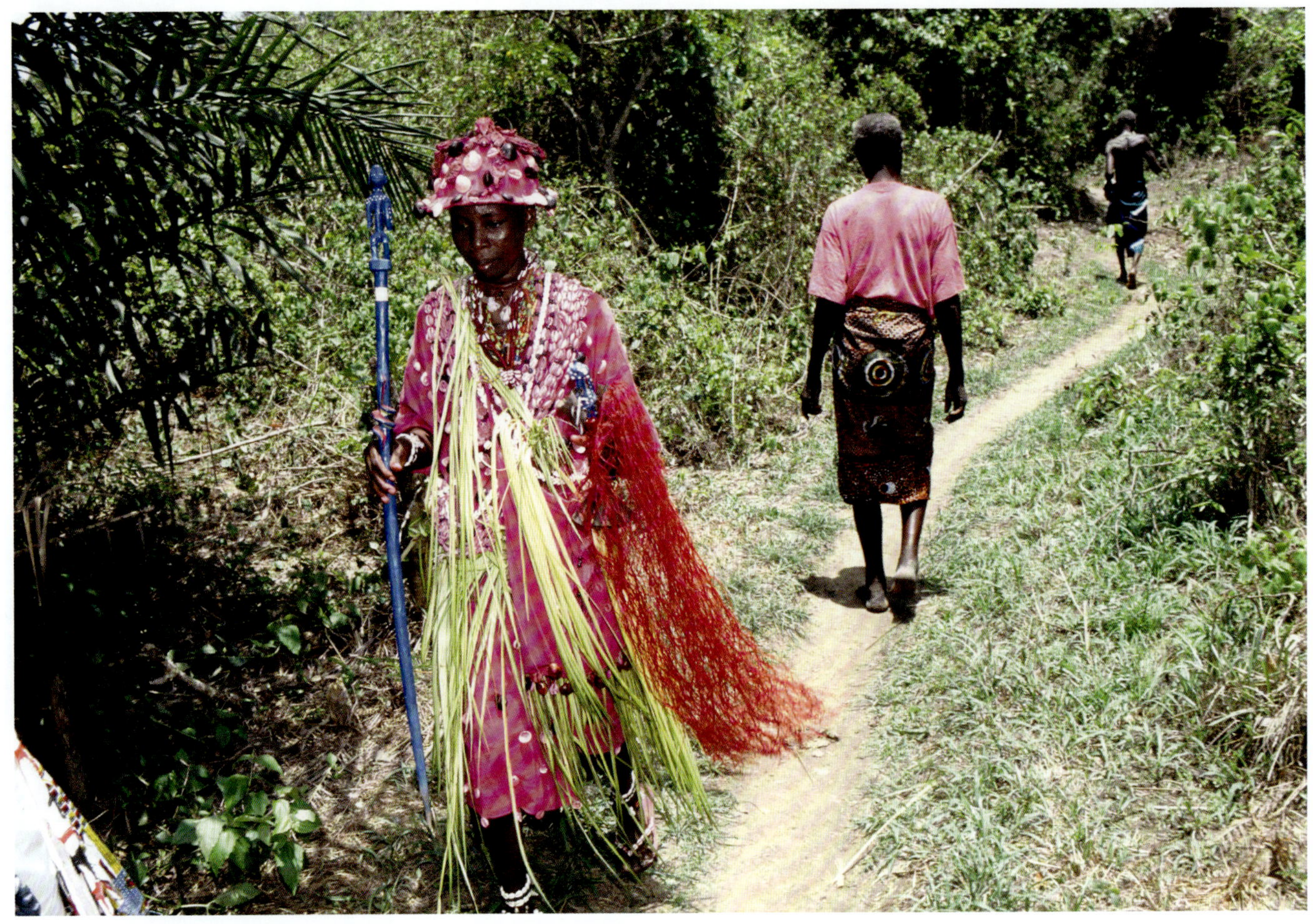

Legba follower in festive costume

Adepte de Legba en costume de fête

Legba-Anhängerin in Festkostüm

Colgante de Legba con traje de fiesta

Pingente Legba em traje festivo

Legba-aanhangster in feestkostuum

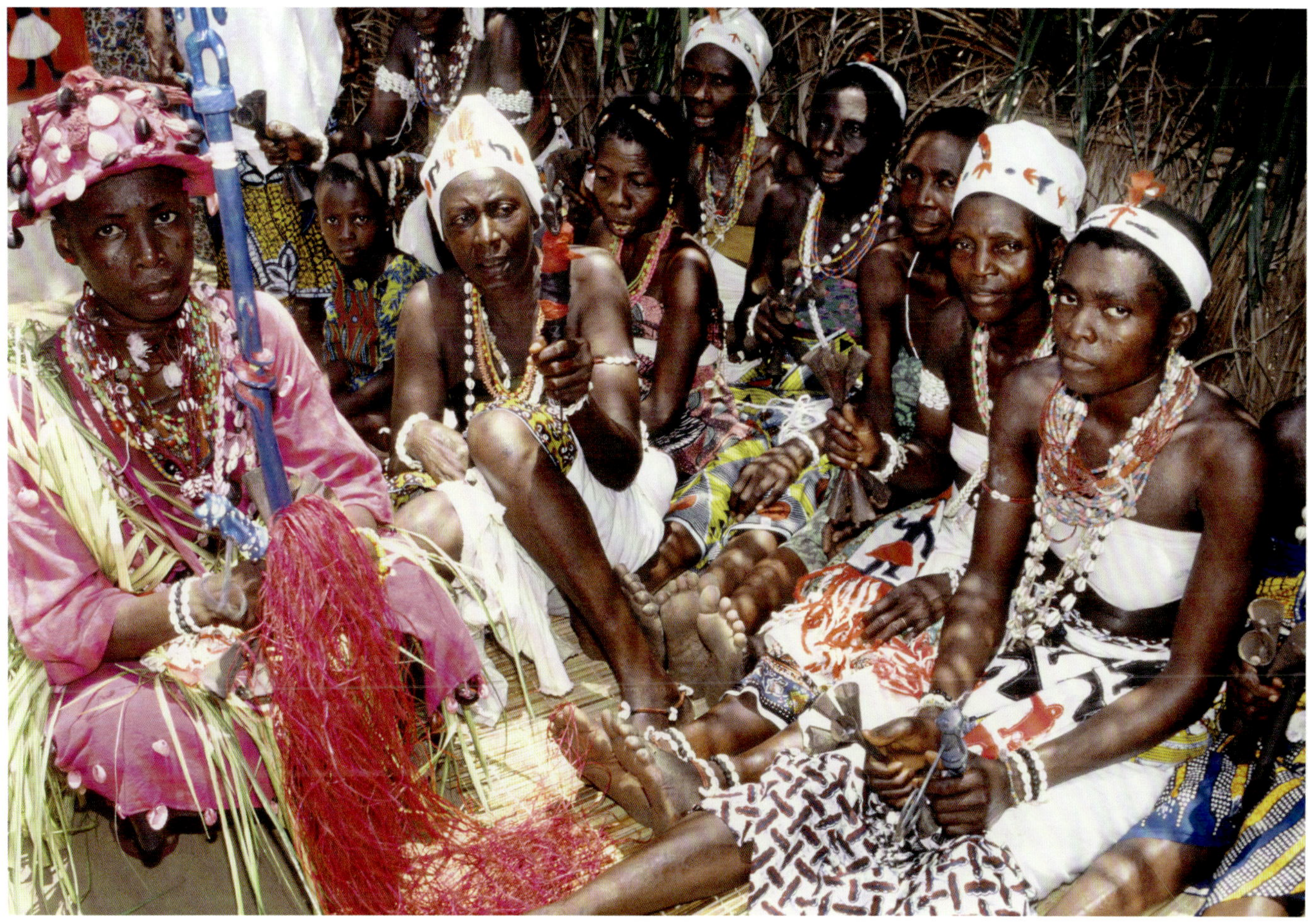

The followers of the gods. The newly initiated Legba adept in the company of adepts of other gods. The red parrot feathers in the headdress on the right refer to Shango.

Les adeptes des dieux. La toute nouvelle adepte de Legba se tient en compagnie de disciples d'autres dieux. Les plumes de perroquet rouges ornant la coiffe des femmes à droite symbolisent la dévotion à Shangô.

Die Gefolgschaft der Götter. Die frisch gebackene Legba-Adeptin in Gesellschaft von Adeptinnen anderer Götter. Die roten Papageienfedern im Kopfschmuck rechts weisen auf Shango hin.

El seguimiento de los dioses. La adepta de Legba recién horneada en compañía de las adeptas de otros dioses. Las plumas de loro rojas en el tocado de la derecha se refieren a Shango.

O seguinte dos . A Legba recém cozida, adepta da companhia de adeptos de outros deuses. As penas de papagaio vermelho no toucador à direita referem-se a Shango.

Het gevolg van de goden. De nieuwbakken Legba-aanhangster in het gezelschap van adepten van andere goden. De rode papegaaienveren in de hoofdtooi rechts verwijzen naar Shango.

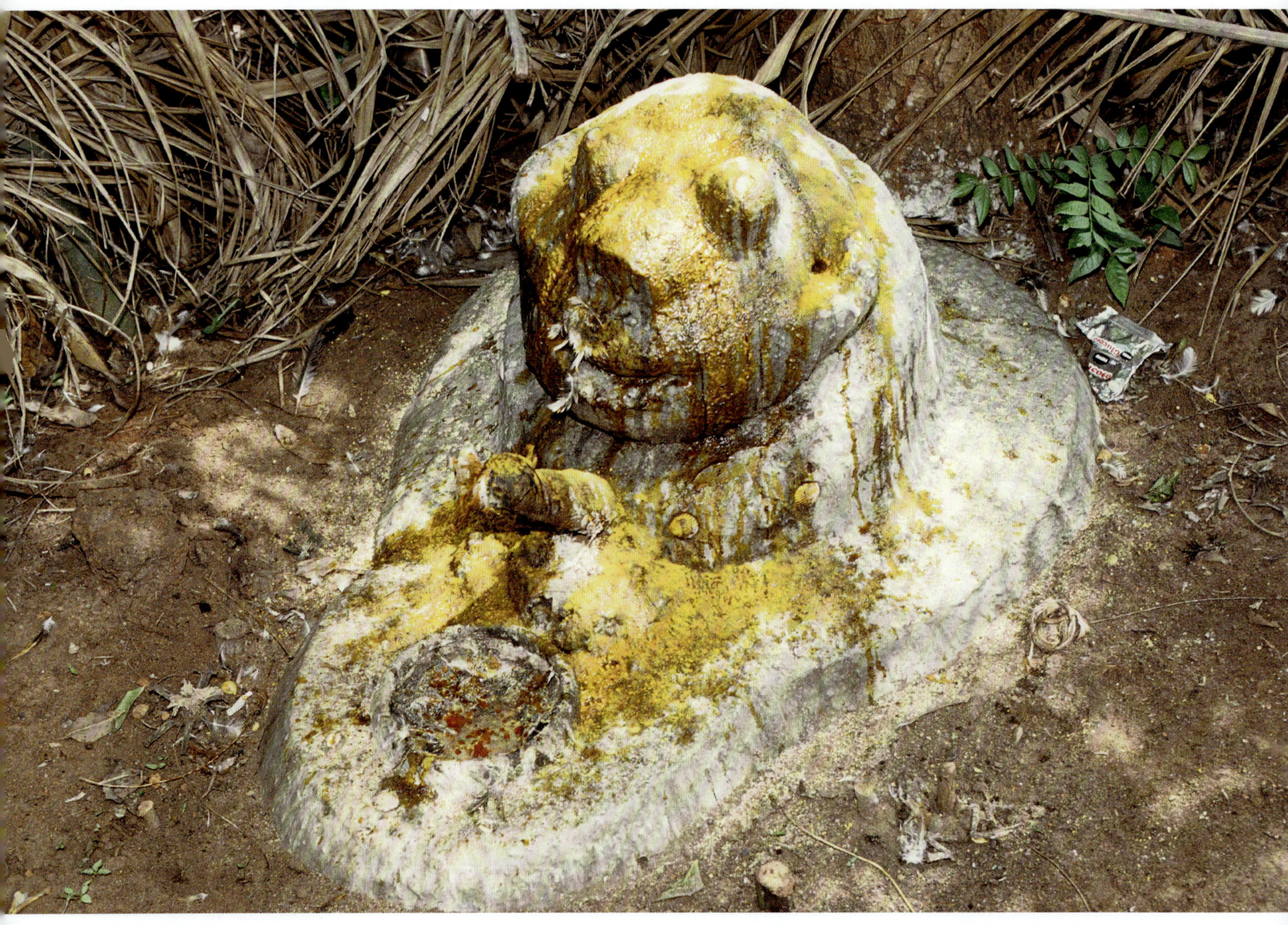

Shrine for Legba with palm oil

Autel dédié à Legba recouvert d'huile de palme

Schrein für Legba mit Palmölgabe

Santuario de Legba con aceite de palma

Santuário para Legba com óleo de palma

Heiligdom voor Legba met offer van palmolie

Legba Bocio.
Figurative representation of Legba with applied magic power pack in the abdominal area.

Bocio Legba. Figure représentant Legba portant, autour du ventre, des petits paquets magiques actifs.

Legba Bocio.
Figürliche Darstellung Legbas mit applizierter magischer Kraftpackung im Bauchbereich.

Bocio de Legba.
Representación figurativa de Legba con paquete de poder mágico en la zona abdominal.

Legba Bocio.
Representação figurativa de Legba com power pack mágico aplicado na área abdominal.

Legba-bocio.
Figuratieve weergave van Legba met applicatie van pakjes met magische kracht op de buik.

Wood, glass, metal, string/Bois, verre, métal, ficelle,
128 × 23 cm

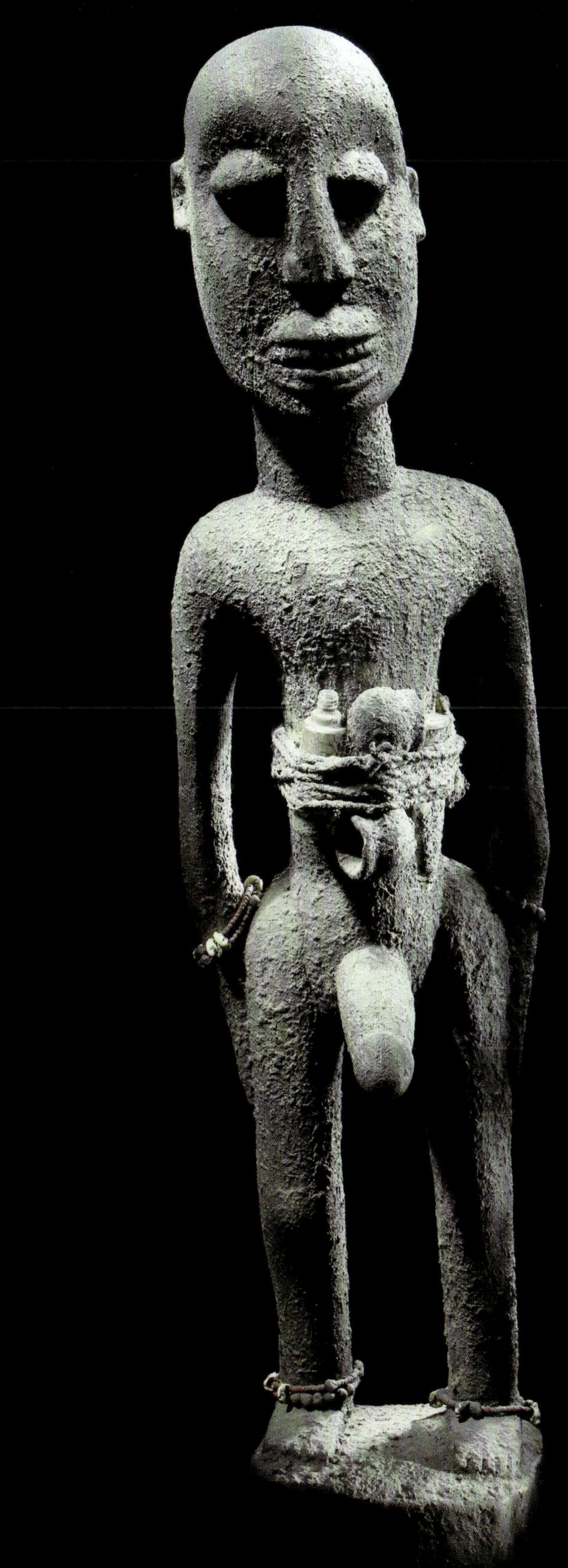

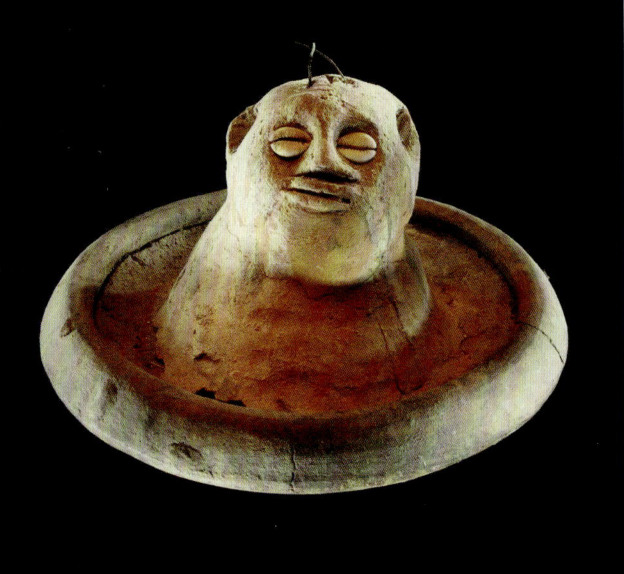

Legba Bowl
Coupe Legba
Legba Schale
Tazón de Legba
Tigela Legba
Legba-kom
Mud, clay/Boue, argile,
15 × 20 cm

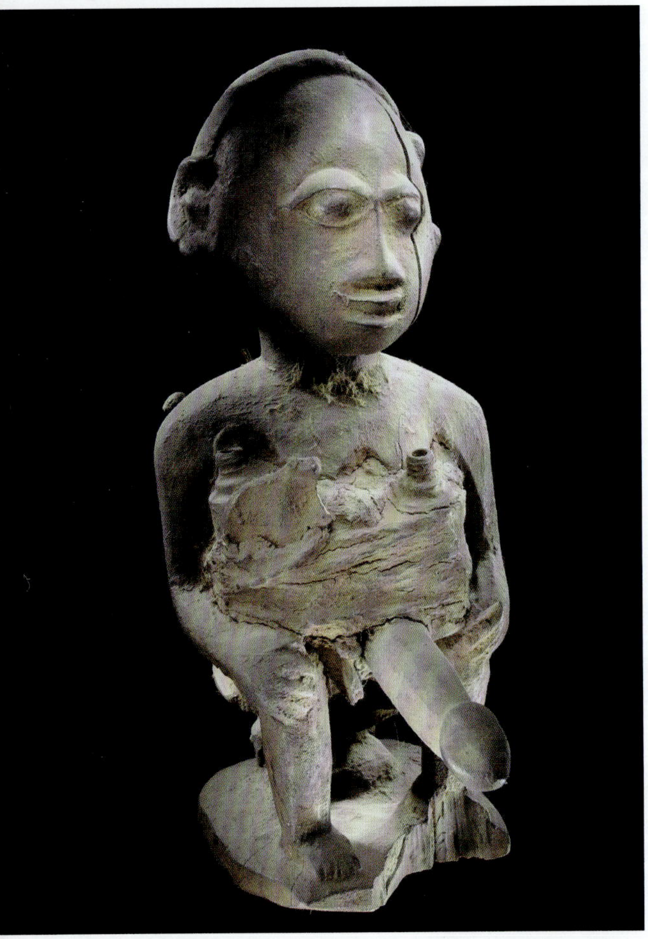

Legba Bocio
Bocio Legba
Legba Bocio
Bocio de Legba
Legba Bocio
Legba-bocio
Wood, bone, glass, metal/
Bois, os, verre, métal,
35 × 15 cm

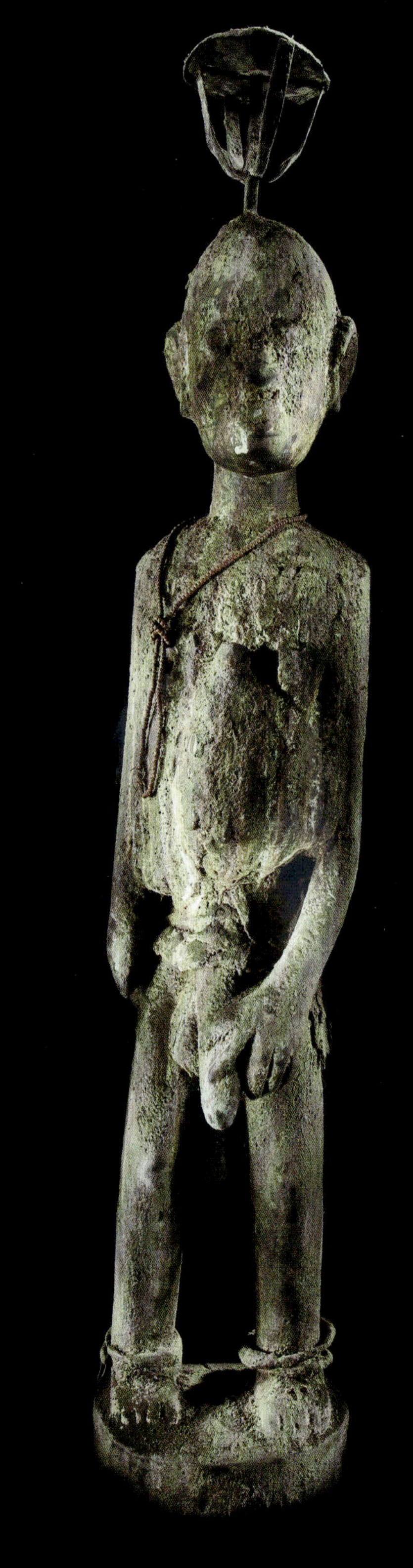

Legba Bocio
Bocio Legba
Legba Bocio
Bocio de Legba
Legba Bocio
Legba-bocio
Mud, clay, metal, plant
fibres/Boue, argile,
métal, fibres végétales,
20 × 15 cm

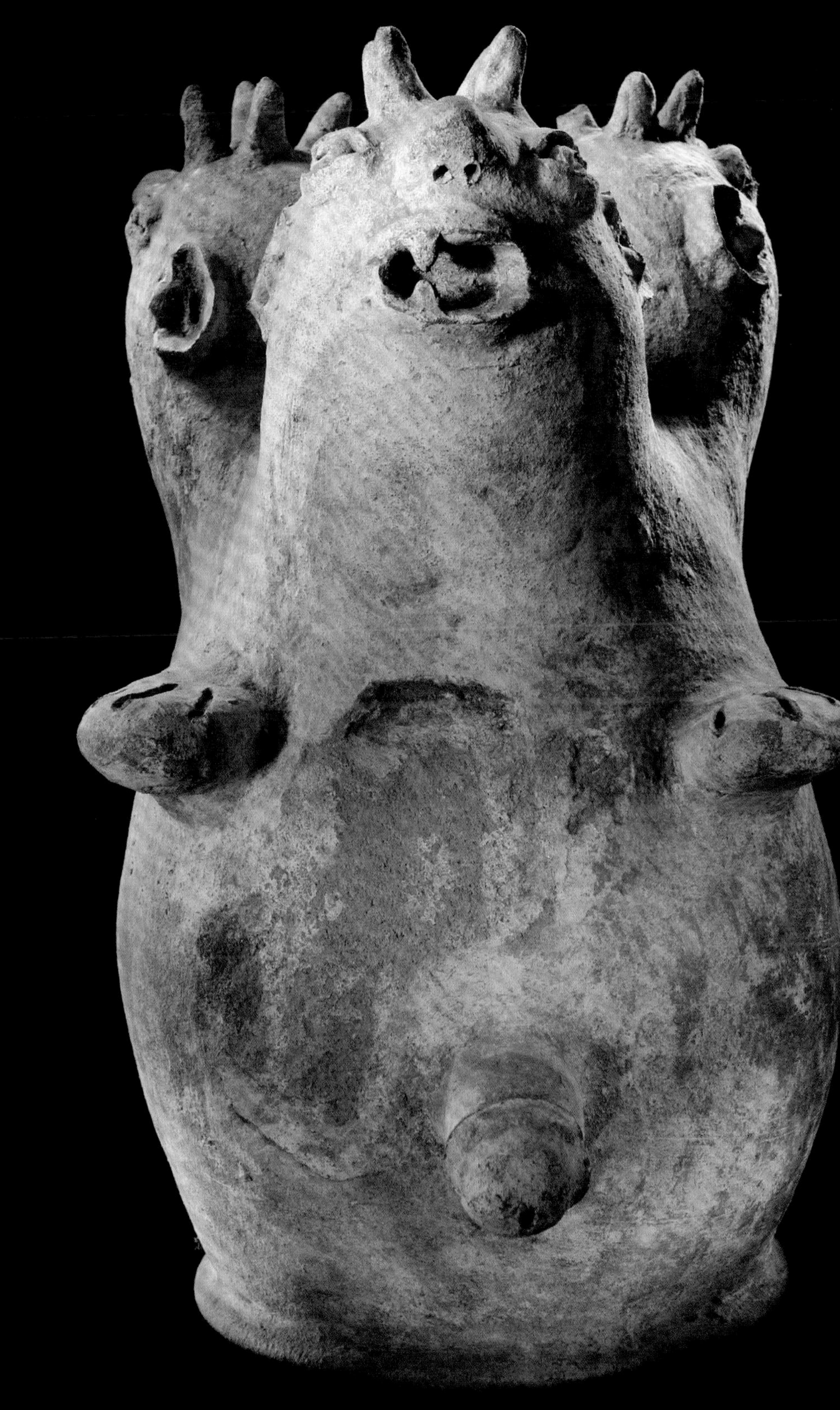

Legba Nana Densu Terracotta. In this sculpture, the three heads indicate that Nana Densu, a deity from the pantheon of the water gods, is involved. The symbolic language goes back to Hindu influences.

Nana Densu Legba en terracotta. Dans cette sculpture, les trois têtes témoignent de l'implication de Nana Densu, divinité appartenant au panthéon des dieux de l'eau. La langue symbolique remonte aux influences hindouistes.

Legba Nana Densu Terrakotte. Bei dieser Skulptur weisen die drei Köpfe darauf hin, dass Nana Densu, eine Gottheit aus dem Pantheon der Wassergötter, mit im Spiel ist. Die Symbolsprache geht auf hinduistische Einflüsse zurück.

Terrracota Legba Nana Densu. En esta escultura, las tres cabezas indican que Nana Densu, una deidad del panteón de los dioses del agua, está involucrada. El lenguaje simbólico se remonta a las influencias hindúes.

Legba Nana Densu Terracota. Nesta escultura, as três cabeças indicam que Nana Densu, uma divindade do panteão dos deuses da água, está envolvida. A linguagem simbólica remonta às influências hindus.

Terracotta Legba Nana Densu Densu. Bij dit beeld geven de drie hoofden aan dat Nana Densu, een god uit het pantheon van de watergoden, erbij betrokken is. De symbooltaal gaat terug op hindoeïstische invloeden.

Clay/Argile, 40 × 25 cm

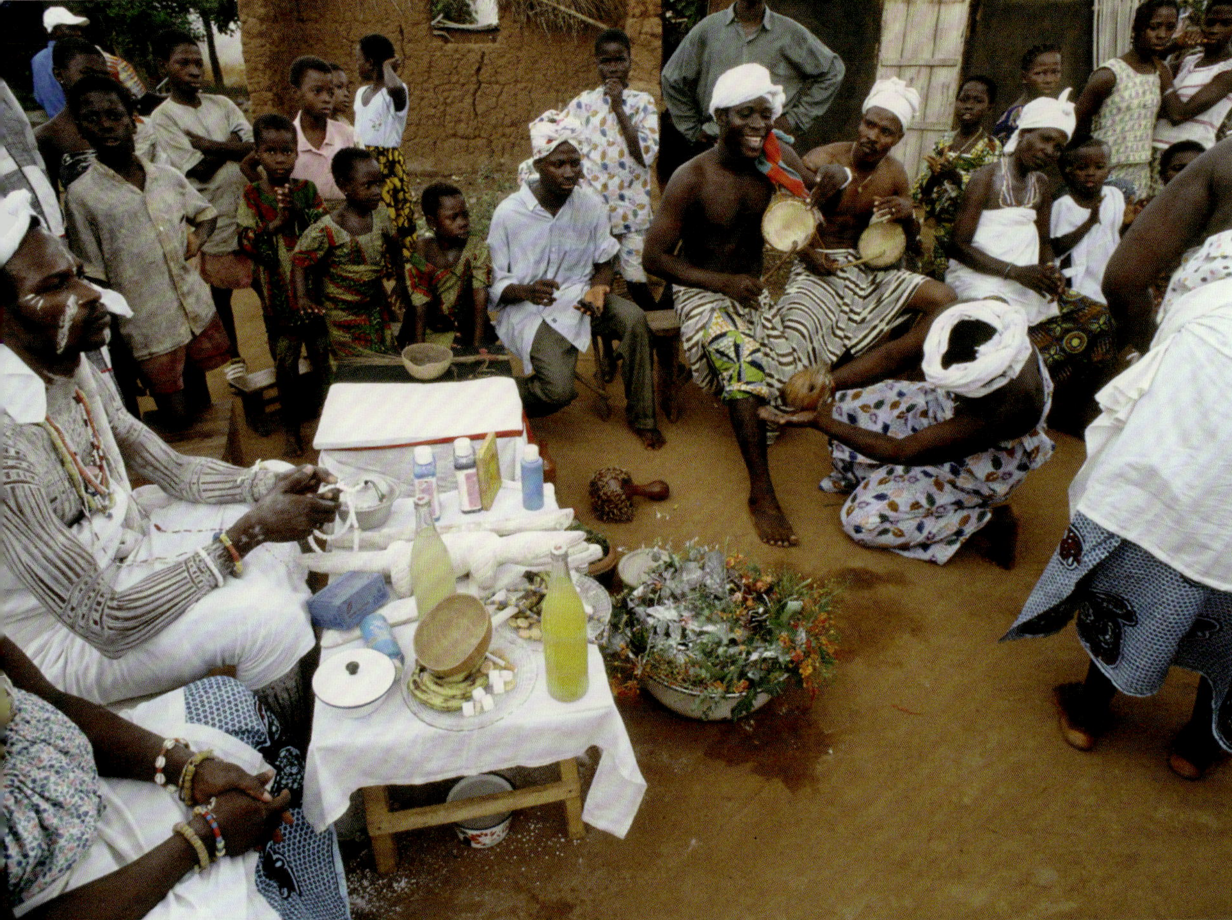

Dan—the snake of fate

At a simplified level, Dan is considered to be the protective deity of traders and market women. It is responsible for human happiness or "good skill", the attainment, continuance or increase of which can be significantly influenced by the worship of Dan.

In this sense, the deity also symbolizes unpredictability and transience. Any gain can be reversed if Dan moves away from the individual.

According to tradition, Dan is the creation of a pregodly primordial power, which it served as a helper when shaping the world in the beginning. The mythology

Dan, le serpent du destin

Pour simplifier, on peut dire que Dan est le dieu protecteur des négociants et des marchands. Il est responsable de la chance ou du « bon destin » des humains, dont les acquisitions, les possessions et l'enrichissement peuvent être considérablement influencés par son culte.

En ce sens, cette divinité symbolise également le caractère imprévisible et éphémère de la vie. Chaque profit peut se transformer en perte si Dan se détourne de l'individu.

Selon une tradition, Dan a été créé par une puissance originelle antérieure aux dieux, qu'il aurait assistée au cours de la

Dan – die Schlange des Schicksals

Auf einer vereinfachten Ebene gilt Dan als die Schutzgottheit der Händler und Marktfrauen. Sie zeichnet für das menschliche Glück oder „gutes Geschick" verantwortlich, dessen Erlangung, Bestand oder Mehrung durch die Verehrung Dans maßgeblich beeinflusst werden kann.

In diesem Sinne symbolisiert die Gottheit auch Unberechenbarkeit und Vergänglichkeit. Jeder Gewinn kann sich ins Gegenteil verkehren, wenn Dan sich vom Individuum entfernt.

Einer Überlieferung zufolge ist Dan die Schöpfung einer prägöttlichen Urkraft, der sie zu Anbeginn der Welt als Helfer bei

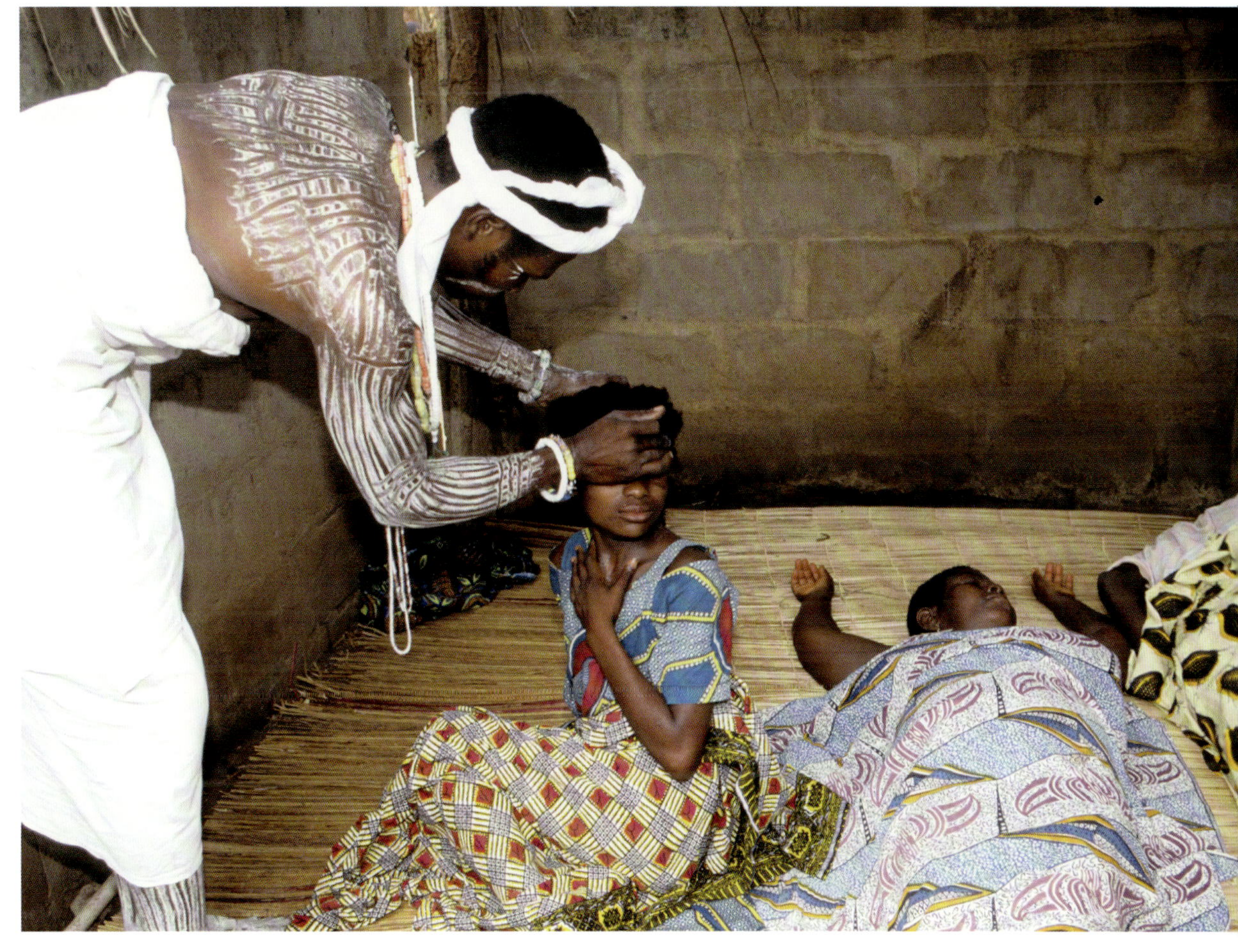

Dan, la serpiente del destino

En un nivel simplificado, se considera que Dan es la deidad protectora de los comerciantes y las mujeres del mercado. Ella es responsable de la felicidad humana o "buena suerte", cuyo logro, supervivencia o aumento puede ser influenciado significativamente por la adoración de Dan.

En este sentido, la deidad también simboliza la imprevisibilidad y la fugacidad. Cualquier ganancia puede ser revertida cuando Dan se aleja del individuo.

Según una tradición, Dan es la creación de un poder primordial predivino, que ella sirvió como ayudante para dar forma al principio del mundo. La mitología de

Dan – A cobra do destino

A um nível simplificado, Dan é considerado a divindade protetora dos comerciantes e das mulheres do mercado. Ela é responsável pela felicidade humana ou "boa habilidade", cujo alcance, sobrevivência ou aumento pode ser significativamente influenciado pela adoração de Dan.

Neste sentido, a divindade também simboliza a imprevisibilidade e a transitoriedade. Qualquer ganho pode ser revertido quando o Dan se afasta do indivíduo.

De acordo com uma tradição, Dan é a criação de um poder primordial pré-divino, que ela serviu como ajudante na

Dan, de slang van het lot

Op een vereenvoudigd niveau wordt Dan beschouwd als de beschermgod van handelaars en marktvrouwen. Zij is verantwoordelijk voor het menselijk geluk of het 'gunstige gesternte', waarvan het verkrijgen, voortbestaan of vergroten aanzienlijk kan worden beïnvloed door de verering van Dan.

In die zin staat de godheid ook symbool voor onberekenbaarheid en vergankelijkheid. Elk gewin kan worden teruggedraaid als Dan zich distantieert van een individu.

Volgens een traditie is Dan de schepping van een pregoddelijke oerkracht, die zij

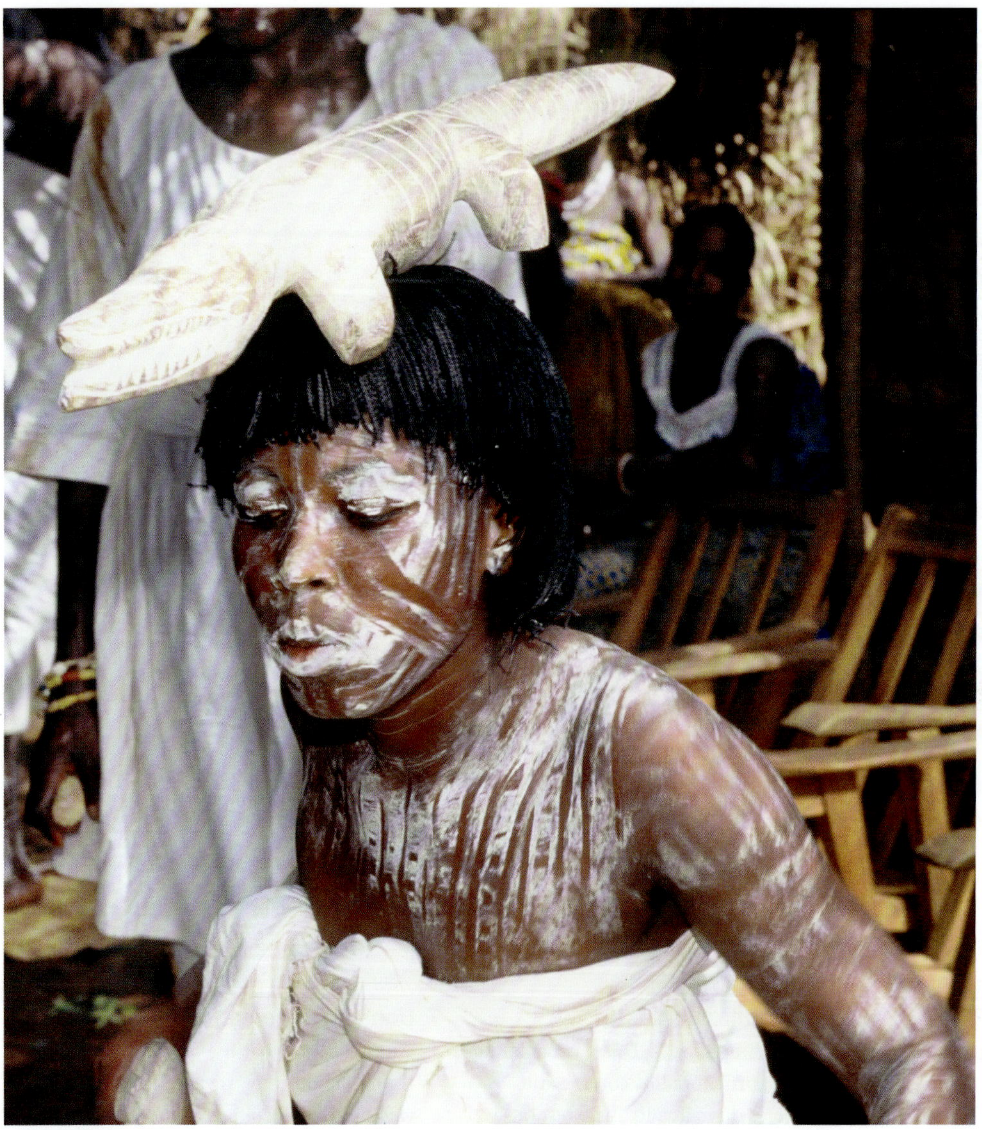

Guest appearance by Adzakpa. Adzakpa, the god of the crocodile, has made itself known on a metaphysical level during this trance of possession of a Dan devotee. It is at home on the land and in the water and is therefore close to Dan.

Apparition d'Adzakpa. À travers cette danse de possession d'une adepte de Dan, Adzakpa, dieu des crocodiles, s'est manifesté. Celui-ci est proche de Dan car c'est un animal présent sur terre et dans les eaux.

Gastauftritt Adzakpas. Bei dieser Besessenheitstrance einer Dan-Anhängerin hat sich auf metaphysischer Ebene Adzakpa, der Gott des Krokodils, gemeldet. Dieser ist auf dem Land und im Wasser zuhause und steht Dan daher nah.

Aparición como invitado de Adzakpa. Adzakpa, el dios del cocodrilo, se ha hecho oír a nivel metafísico en este trance de posesión de un devoto de Dan. Él está como en casa en la tierra y en el agua y por lo tanto está cerca de Dan.

Aparência do convidado Adzakpas. Adzakpa, o deus do crocodilo, fez-se ouvir a nível metafísico neste transe obsessivo de um devoto de Dan. Ele está em casa na terra e na água e, portanto, está perto de Dan.

Gastoptreden van Adzakpa. Adzakpa, de god van de krokodil, heeft zich op metafysisch niveau laten horen in deze bezeten trance van een Dan-aanhangster. Hij is thuis op het land en in het water en staat daarom dicht bij Dan.

of Dahomey, the ancient Benin, tells of this earliest known appearance of Dan as the gigantic snake "Aido Hwedo", whose task was to carry the Creator in its mouth over the primeval earth's surface.

The Python is regarded as the embodiment of Dan and is considered sacred.

formation du monde en tant que serviteur. La mythologie du royaume du Dahomey évoque cette apparition précoce de Dan sous la forme d'un immense serpent, Aido-Hwedo, dont la mission consistait à transporter le créateur dans sa gueule à la surface de la terre originelle.

Considéré comme l'incarnation de Dan, le python est sacré.

deren Gestaltung diente. Die Mythologie Dahomeys, des alten Benins, berichtet von dieser frühesten bekannten Erscheinung Dans als der gigantischen Schlange „Aido Hwedo", deren Aufgabe es war, den Schöpfer in ihrem Maul über die urweltliche Erdoberfläche zu tragen.

Die Python wird als Verkörperung Dans betrachtet und gilt als heilig.

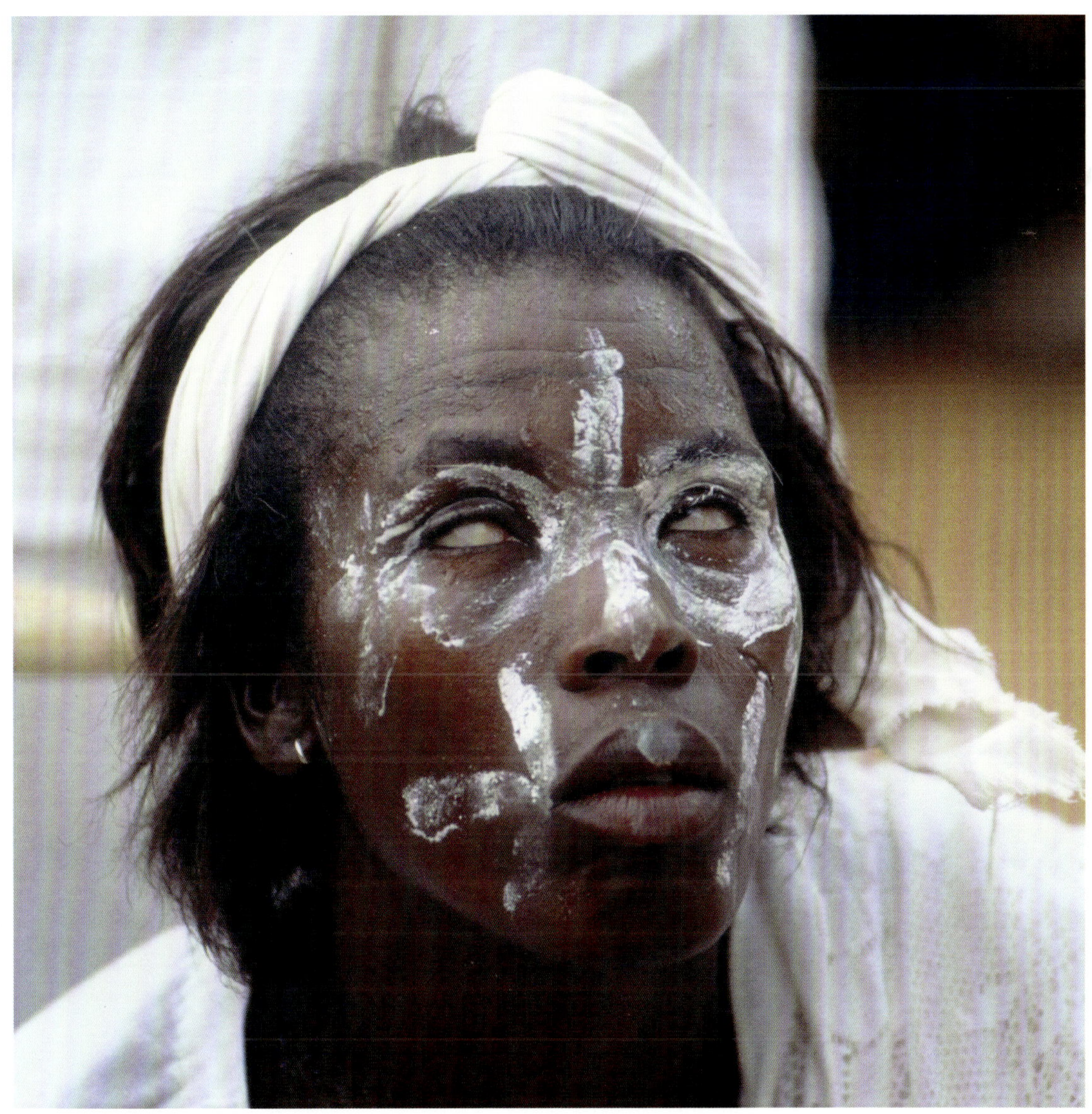

Dahomey, el antiguo Benín, habla de esta primera aparición conocida de Dan como la gigantesca serpiente "Aido Hwedo", cuya tarea era llevar al Creador en su boca sobre la superficie primitiva de la tierra.

La serpiente pitón es considerada como la encarnación de Dan y, por tanto, es sagrada.

formação do início do mundo. A mitologia de Dahomey, o antigo Benin, conta dessa primeira aparição conhecida de Dan como a gigantesca serpente "Aido Hwedo", cuja tarefa era levar o Criador em sua boca sobre a superfície primitiva da terra.

O Pitão é considerado como a encarnação de Dan e é considerado sagrado.

aan het begin van de wereld hielp bij de vormgeving ervan. De mythologie van Dahomey, het oude Benin, vertelt over deze vroegst bekende verschijning van Dan als de gigantische slang 'Aido Hwedo', wier taak het was om de schepper in haar bek over het voorwereldlijke aardoppervlak te dragen.

De python wordt gezien als de belichaming van Dan en als heilig beschouwd.

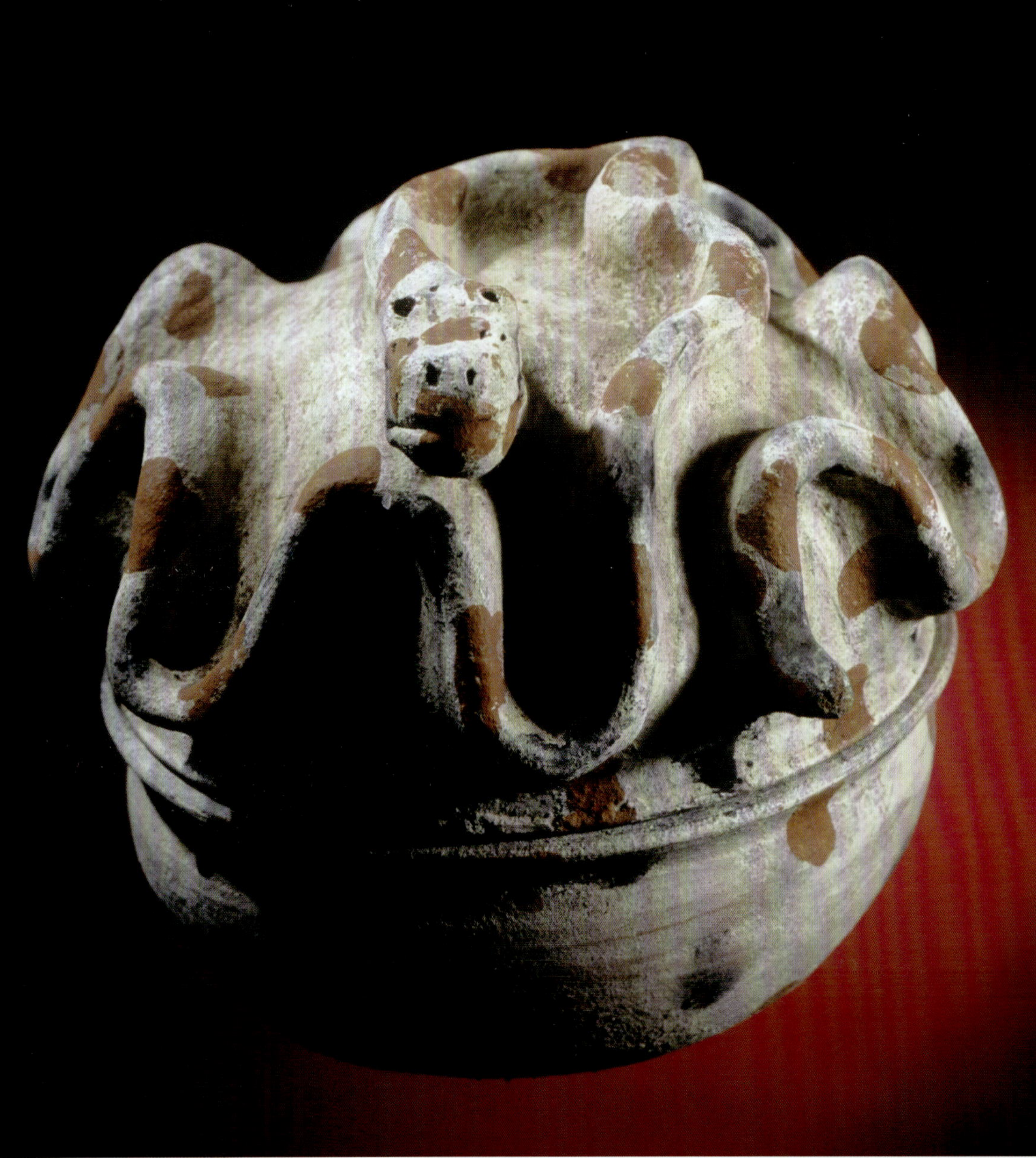

Terracotta for Dan. Richly decorated pottery for the Dan shrine of a high dignitary from the Mono region in Benin.

Terracotta pour Dan. Poterie richement décorée destinée à l'autel pour Dan d'un haut dignitaire de la région béninoise de Mono.

Terrakotte für Dan. Reich verzierte Töpferarbeit für den Dan-Schrein eines hohen Würdenträgers aus der Monoregion in Benin.

Terracota para Dan. Cerámica ricamente decorada para el santuario de Dan de un alto dignatario de la monoregión de Benin.

Terracota para Dan. Cerâmica ricamente decorada para o santuário Dan de um alto dignitário da monoregião de Benin.

Terracotta voor Dan. Rijk versierd aardewerk voor het Dan-heiligdom van een hoogwaardigheidsbekleder uit het departement Mono in Benin.

Clay/Argile, 26 × 16 cm

Terracotta for Dan. A typical ritual sculpture for the deity Dan is this bowl, which is clearly decorated with a snake, the animal symbol of Dan (Python).

Terracotta pour Dan. Ce couvercle est décoré selon la symbolique rituelle typique associée à la déité Dan. Il porte en effet un serpent (python), animal de Dan.

Terrakotte für Dan. Eine typische Ritualplastik für die Gottheit Dan ist diese Aufsatzschale, die deutlich von einer Schlange, dem Symboltier Dans (Python), geschmückt wird.

Terracota para Dan. Una escultura ritual típica para la deidad Dan es este cuenco, que está claramente decorado por una serpiente, el símbolo animal de Dan (Pitón).

Terracota para Dan. Uma escultura ritual típica para a divindade Dan é esta tigela, que é claramente decorada por uma cobra, o símbolo animal Dans (Python).

Terracotta voor Dan. Een typisch ritueel beeld voor de god Dan is deze schaal, die duidelijk versierd is met een slang, het symbooldier van Dan (python).

Clay/Argile, 16 × 16 cm

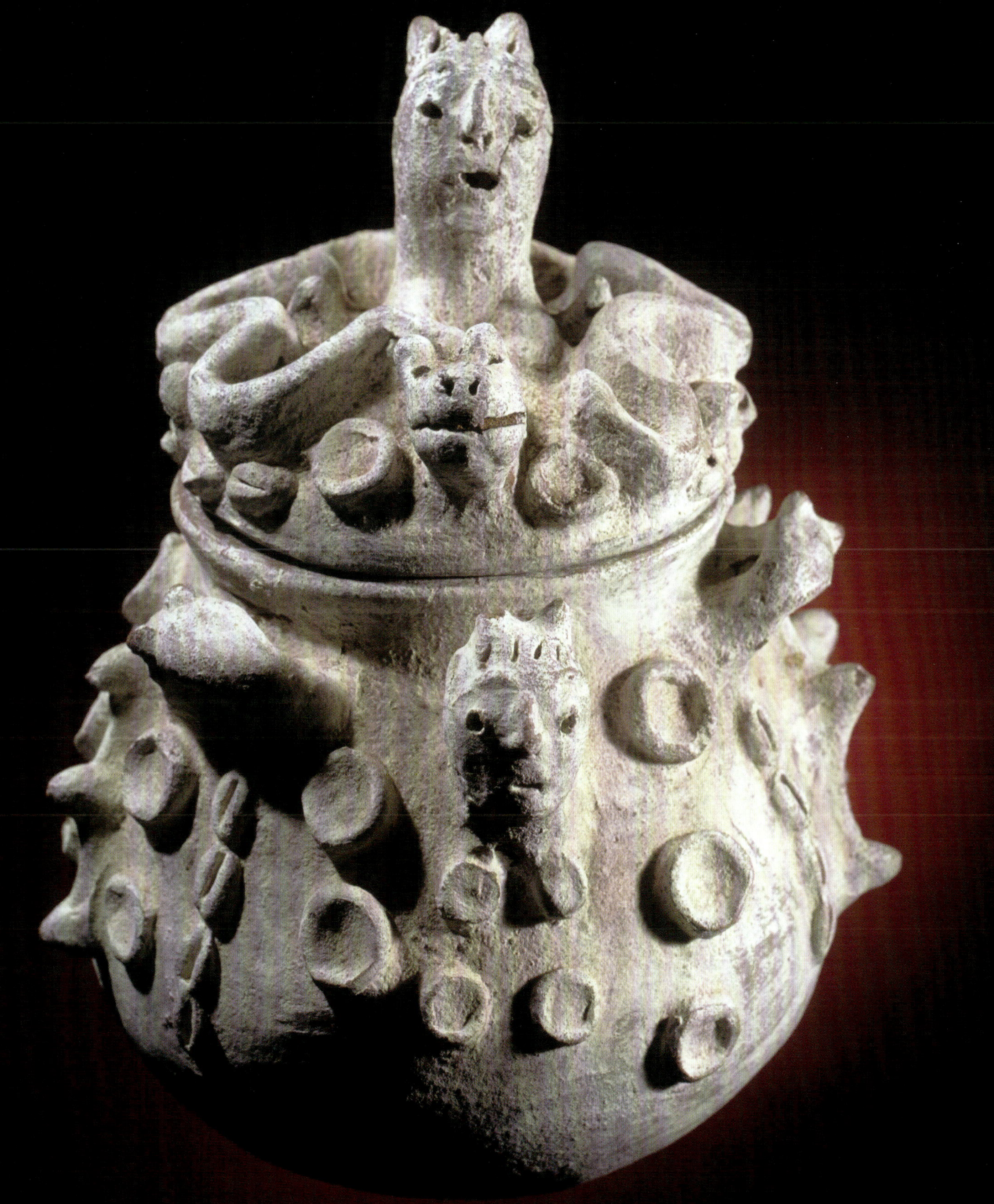

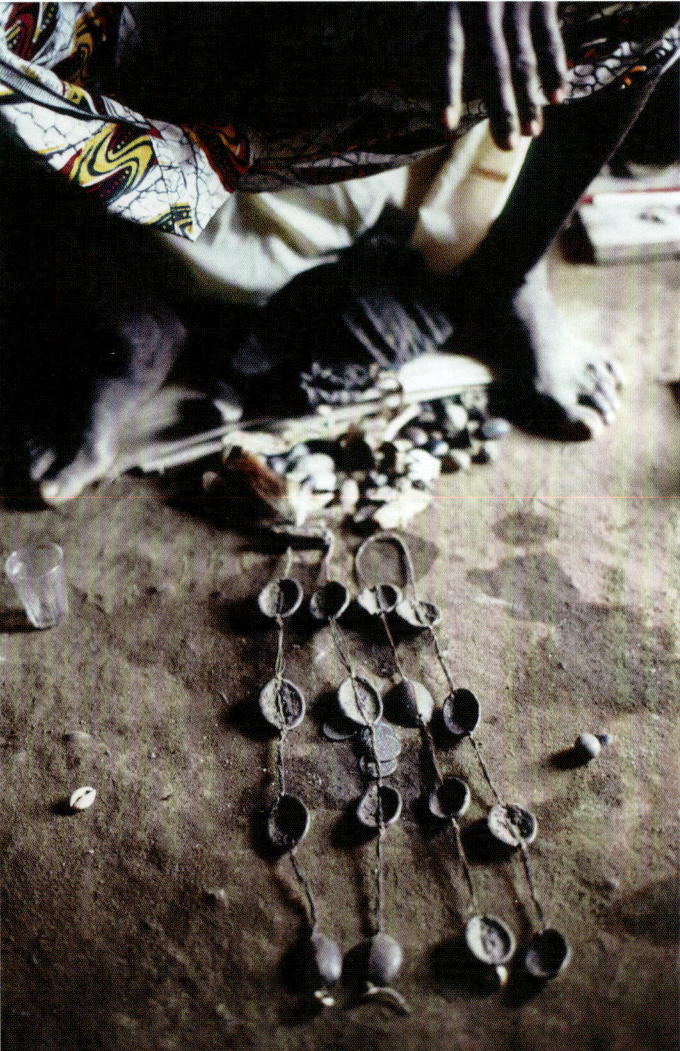

Ifa—Oracle and god

Among the Yoruba people, Ifa is an important god and a powerful oracle. There are very few experts left who can apply the highly complex system, in which the prophecies of the gods are determined by throwing palm kernels.

Because the holy traditions connected with the results of the casting are extremely extensive, the training to be a Babalawo, the "Father of the Mystery", can last up to seven years.

Ifa, oracle et divinité

Pour les Yoruba, Ifa est un dieu important et un oracle puissant. Un très petit nombre d'experts est encore capable de maîtriser son système complexe de communication, dans lequel les prophéties des dieux sont exprimées à travers le lancer de noix de palmes.

La formation du Babalawo, « père des secrets », peut durer sept années, car les traditions sacrées associées aux résultats du lancer sont extrêmement nombreuses.

Ifa – Orakel und Gottheit

Ifa ist beim Volk der Yoruba ein wichtiger Gott und ein mächtiges Orakel. Es gibt nur noch sehr wenige Experten für die Anwendung dieses hochkomplexen Systems, bei dem durch den Wurf von Palmkernen die Prophezeiungen der Götter ermittelt werden.

Weil die mit den Wurfergebnissen in Zusammenhang stehenden heiligen Überlieferungen äußerst umfangreich sind, kann die Ausbildung zum Babalawo, dem

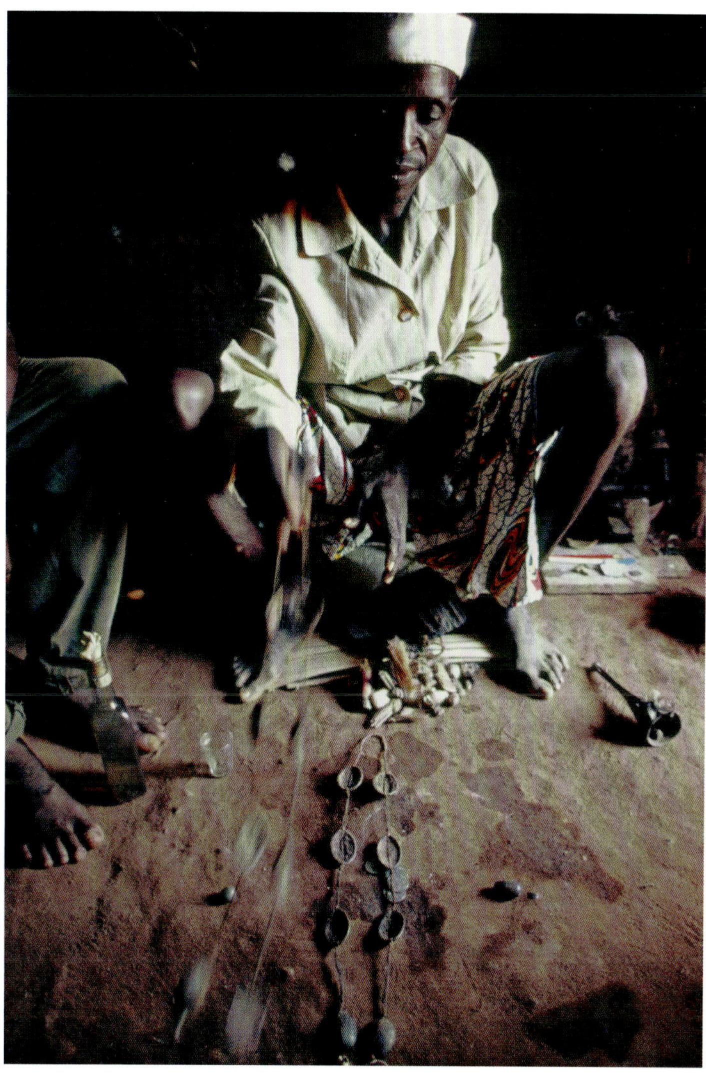

Ifa– Oráculo y deidad

Entre el pueblo yoruba, Ifa es un dios importante y un oráculo poderoso. Quedan muy pocos expertos para la aplicación de este sistema tan complejo, en el que las profecías de los dioses se determinan lanzando almendras de palma.

Debido a que las sagradas tradiciones relacionadas con los resultados de los lanzamientos son extremadamente extensas, el entrenamiento para el Babalawo, el "Padre del Secreto", puede durar hasta siete años.

Ifa – Oráculo e Divindade

Entre o povo iorubá, Ifa é um deus importante e um oráculo poderoso. Há muito poucos especialistas para a aplicação deste sistema altamente complexo, no qual as profecias dos deuses são determinadas pelo lançamento de amêndoas de palma.

Porque as tradições sagradas relacionadas com os resultados dos lançamentos são extremamente extensas, o treinamento para o Babalawo, o "Pai do Segredo", pode durar até sete anos.

Ifa, orakel en godheid

Bij de Yoruba is Ifa een belangrijke god en een krachtig orakel. Er zijn nog maar weinig experts die dit zeer complexe systeem kunnen toepassen, waarin de profetieën van de goden worden bepaald door palmpitten te werpen.

Omdat de heilige tradities met betrekking tot de worpresultaten zeer omvangrijk zijn, kan de opleiding tot babalawo, 'vader van het geheim', wel zeven jaar duren.

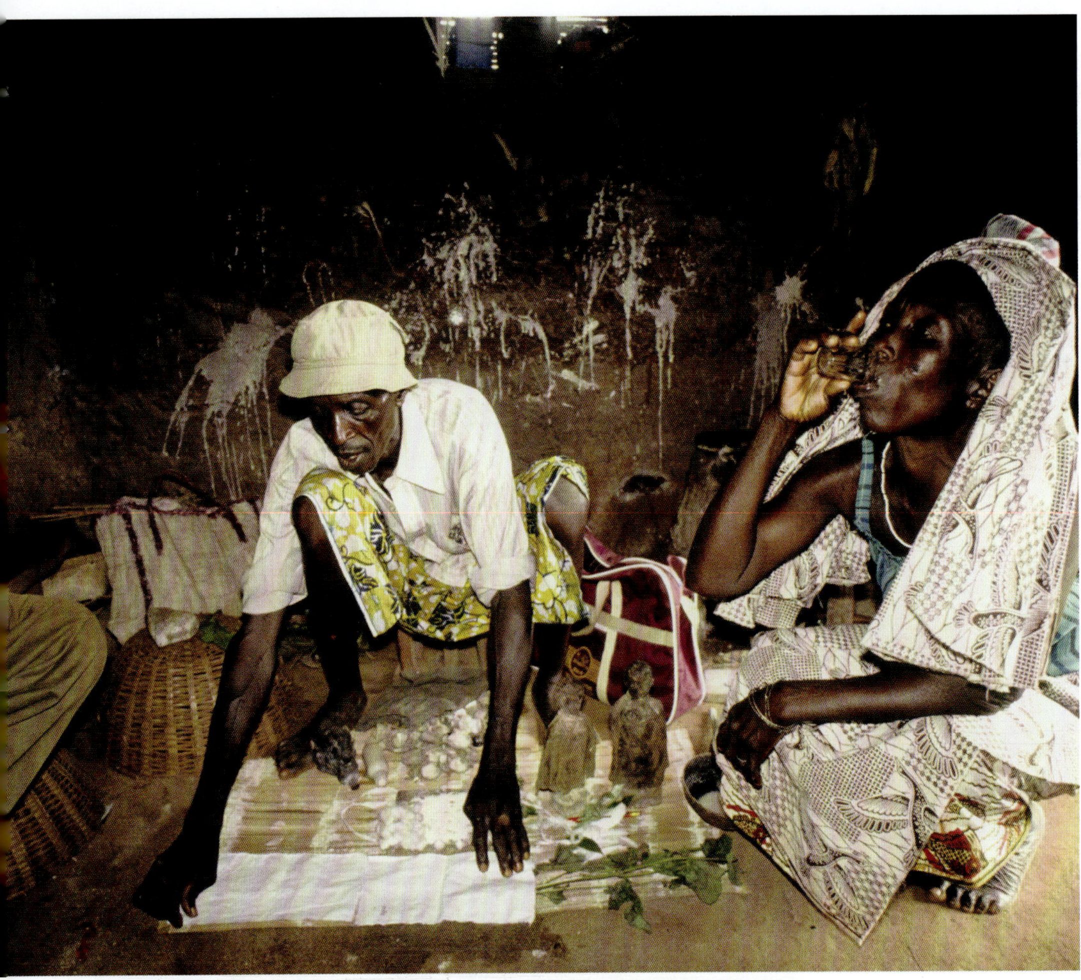

The centuries-old Ifa Oracle, which was adopted by the Fon people of Benin under the name "Fa", combines a multitude of essential truths and wisdom about man and nature. It takes time, competent leadership and a special aptitude, which the oracle is able to reveal, to learn to know and interpret these in an all-embracing way.

Similar to other ceremonies, offerings are also suitable here to appease the gods.

L'oracle Ifa multiséculaire, dénommé « Fa » par le peuple Fon, rassemble une multitude de vérités et de sagesses essentielles sur les hommes et la nature. Apprendre à les connaître parfaitement et à les interpréter nécessite beaucoup de temps, ainsi qu'un accompagnement compétent dévolu à un oracle qui a le pouvoir de les révéler et de bonnes prédispositions.

Comme dans d'autres cérémonies, les offrandes permettent également d'obtenir la clémence des dieux.

„Vater des Geheimnisses", bis zu sieben Jahre dauern.

Das Jahrhunderte alte Ifa-Orakel, das vom Volk der Fon in Benin unter dem Namen „Fa" übernommen wurde, bindet eine Vielzahl essentieller Wahrheiten und Weisheiten über den Menschen und die Natur. Diese tatsächlich allumfassend kennen und deuten zu lernen bedarf es Zeit, einer kompetenten Führung und zudem einer besonderen Eignung, welche das Orakel aber zu offenbaren vermag.

Ähnlich wie bei anderen Zeremonien sind auch hier Opfergaben geeignet, die Götter milde zu stimmen.

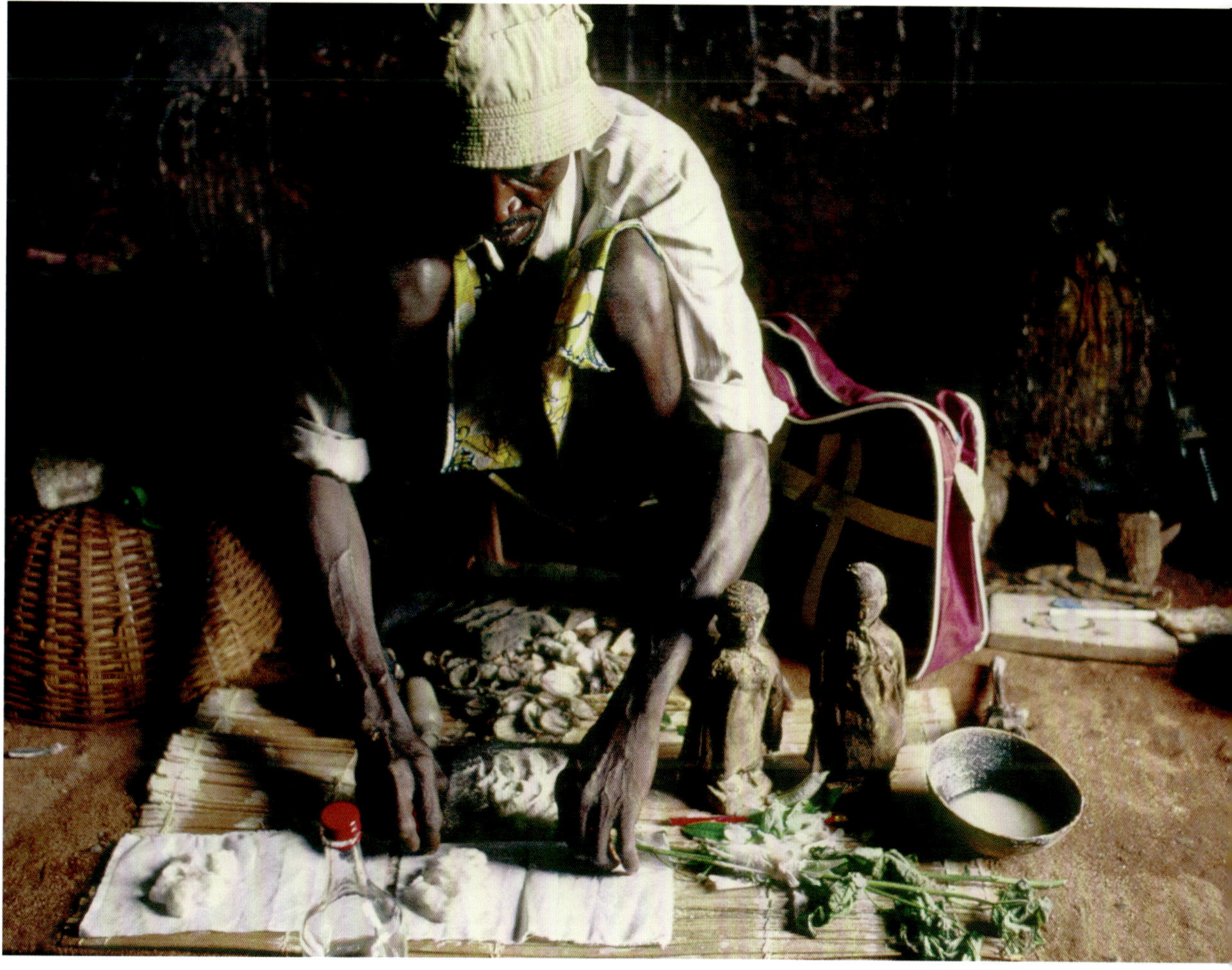

El oráculo de Ifa, de siglos de antigüedad, que fue adoptado por el pueblo Fon de Benin bajo el nombre de "Fa", aglutina una multitud de verdades y sabidurías esenciales sobre el hombre y la naturaleza. Se necesita tiempo, una guía competente y una aptitud especial, que el oráculo es capaz de revelar, para aprender a conocerlos e interpretarlos de una manera global.

Al igual que otras ceremonias, los sacrificios también son adecuados aquí para apaciguar a los dioses.

O Oráculo Ifa centenário, que foi adotado pelo povo Fon de Benin sob o nome de "Fa", une uma multidão de verdades e sabedorias essenciais sobre o homem e a natureza. É preciso tempo, orientação competente e uma aptidão especial, que o oráculo é capaz de revelar, para aprender a conhecê-los e interpretá-los de forma abrangente.

Semelhante a outras cerimônias, os sacrifícios também são adequados aqui para apaziguar os deuses.

Het eeuwenoude Ifa-orakel, dat door het Fon-volk in Benin werd overgenomen onder de naam Fa, bundelt allerlei essentiële waarheden en wijsheden over de mens en de natuur. Het kost tijd, bekwame begeleiding en een speciale aanleg om de onthullingen van het orakel daadwerkelijk op een allesomvattende manier te leren kennen en interpreteren.

Net als bij andere ceremoniën komen er hier ook offers aan te pas om de goden tevreden te stellen.

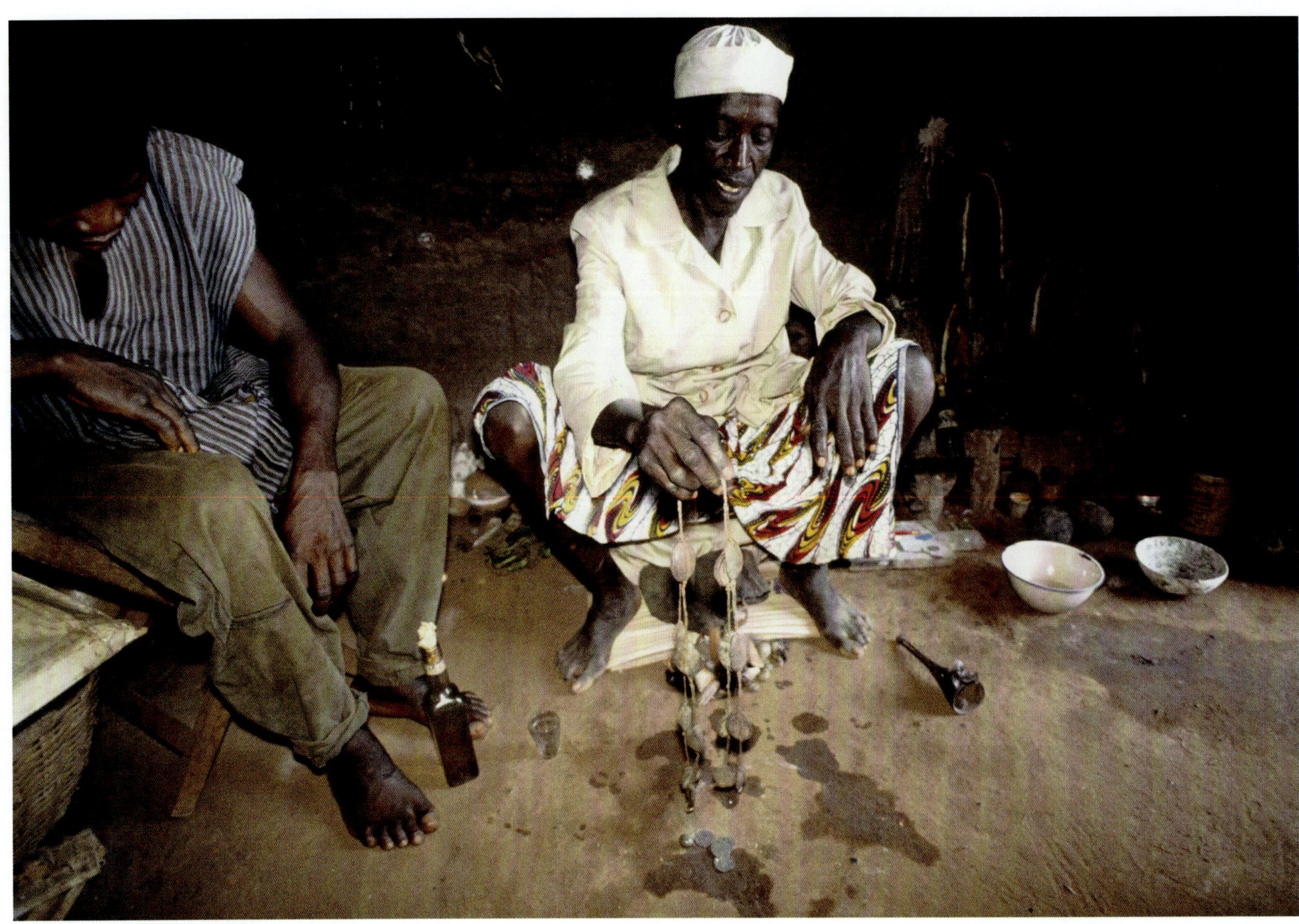

Oracle questioning for a client

Consultation des oracles pour un client

Orakelbefragung für einen Klienten

Consulta al oráculo para un cliente

Pesquisa de oráculos para um cliente

Ondervraging van een orakel voor een klant

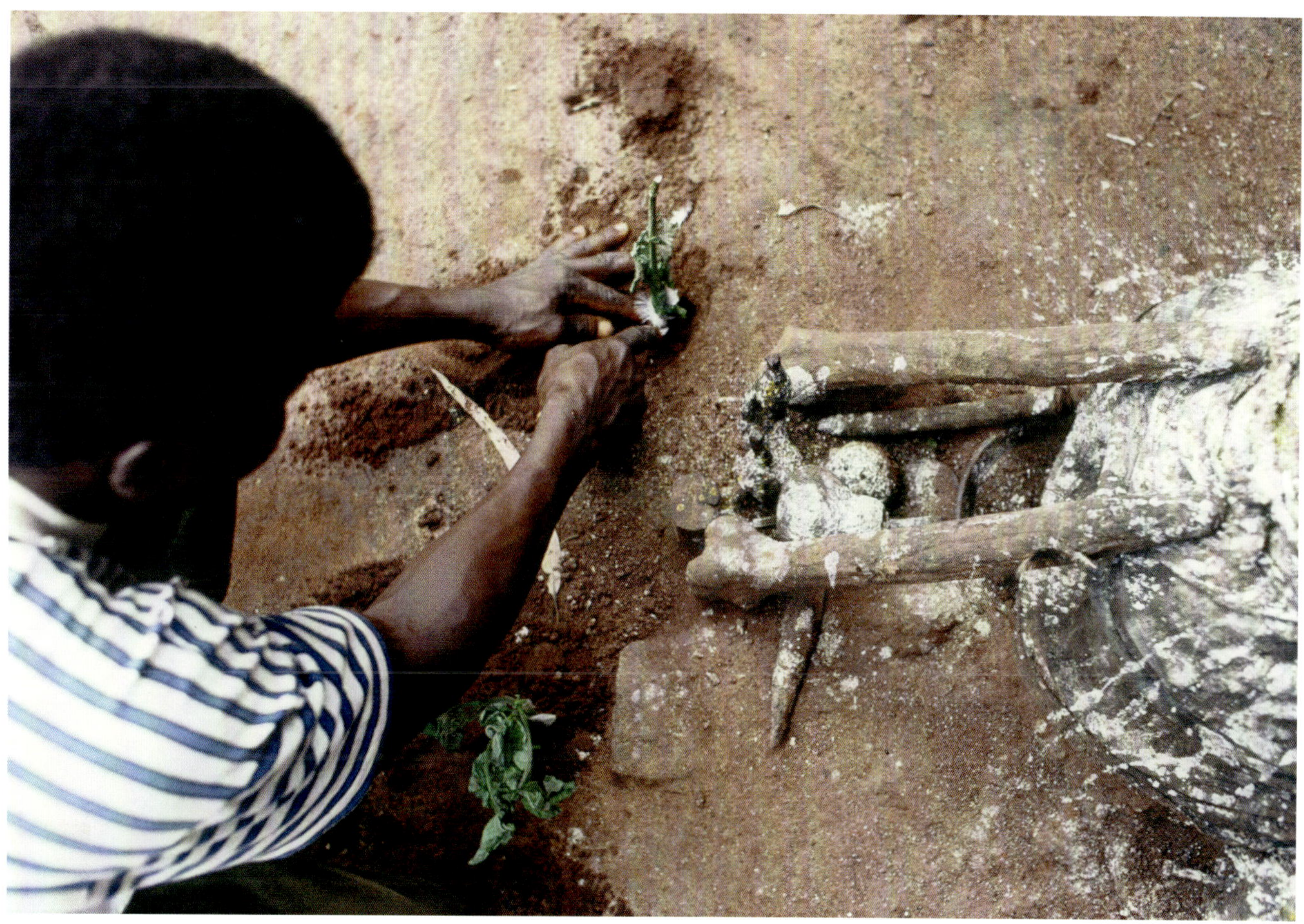

A call for help to the gods. A man persecuted by misfortune buries certain plants in a ritual setting in front of the shrine of the Fa oracle in order to change his fate.

Appel pour obtenir l'aide des dieux. Dans le cadre d'un rituel, un homme frappé de malchance enterre des plantes spécifiques devant l'autel de l'oracle Fa, afin de modifier son destin.

Hilferuf an die Götter. Ein vom Unglück verfolgter Mann vergräbt im rituellen Rahmen bestimmte Pflanzen vor dem Schrein des Fa-Orakels, um sein Schicksal zu wenden.

Llamada de ayuda a los dioses. Un hombre perseguido por la desgracia entierra ciertas plantas en un lugar ritual frente al oráculo del Santuario de la Ley para cambiar su destino.

Pede ajuda aos deuses. Um homem perseguido pelo infortúnio enterra certas plantas em um ambiente ritual diante do santuário do Fa oráculo para mudar seu destino.

Hulpoproep aan de goden. Een door ongeluk achtervolgde man begraaft bepaalde planten in een rituele setting voor het heiligdom van het Fa-orakel om zijn lot te veranderen.

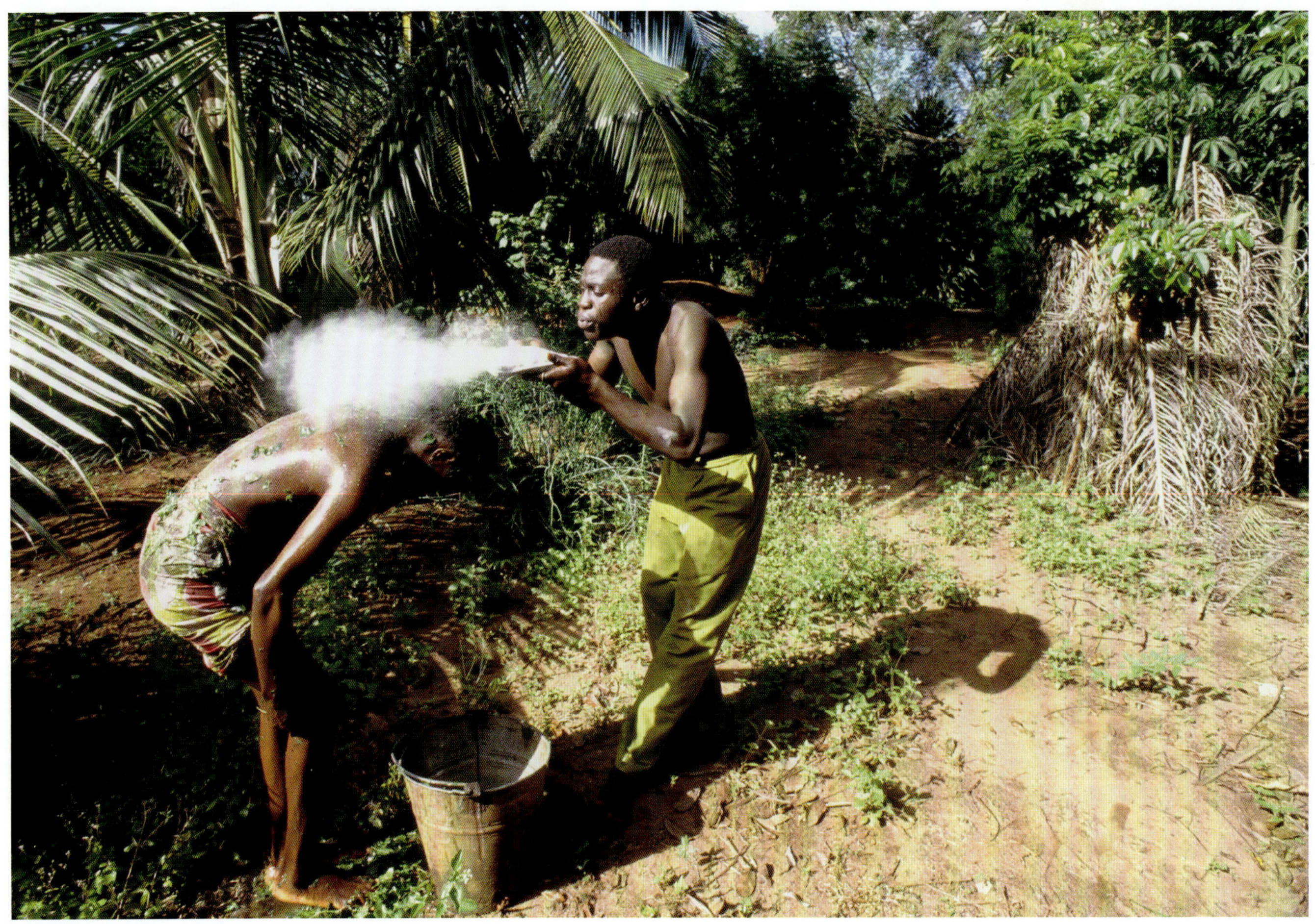

Ritual cleaning and protection
Nettoyage rituel et protection
Rituelle Reinigung und Schutz
Limpieza y protección de los rituales
Limpeza e protecção ritual
Rituele reiniging en bescherming

A female oracle skull of the Adja people from Benin
Crâne d'oracle féminin du peuple Adja, Bénin
Ein weiblicher Orakelschädel des Volks der Adja aus Benin
Un cráneo de oráculo femenino del pueblo Adja de Benin
Um crânio oráculo feminino do povo Adja do Benin
Een vrouwelijke orakelschedel van het Adja-volk uit Benin
Female human skull, cowrie shell, string/Crâne de femme, coquillages, ficelle, 16 × 10 cm

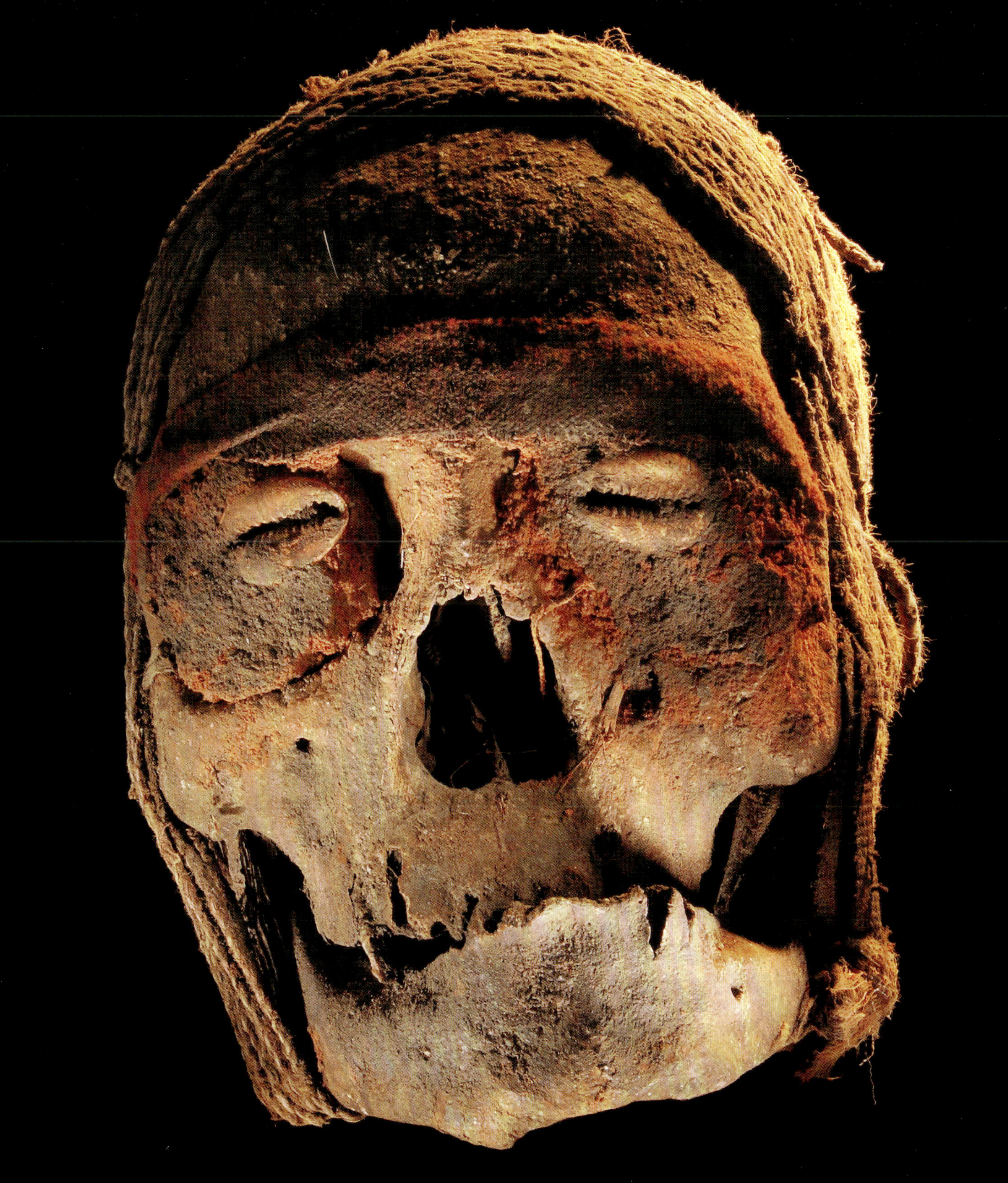

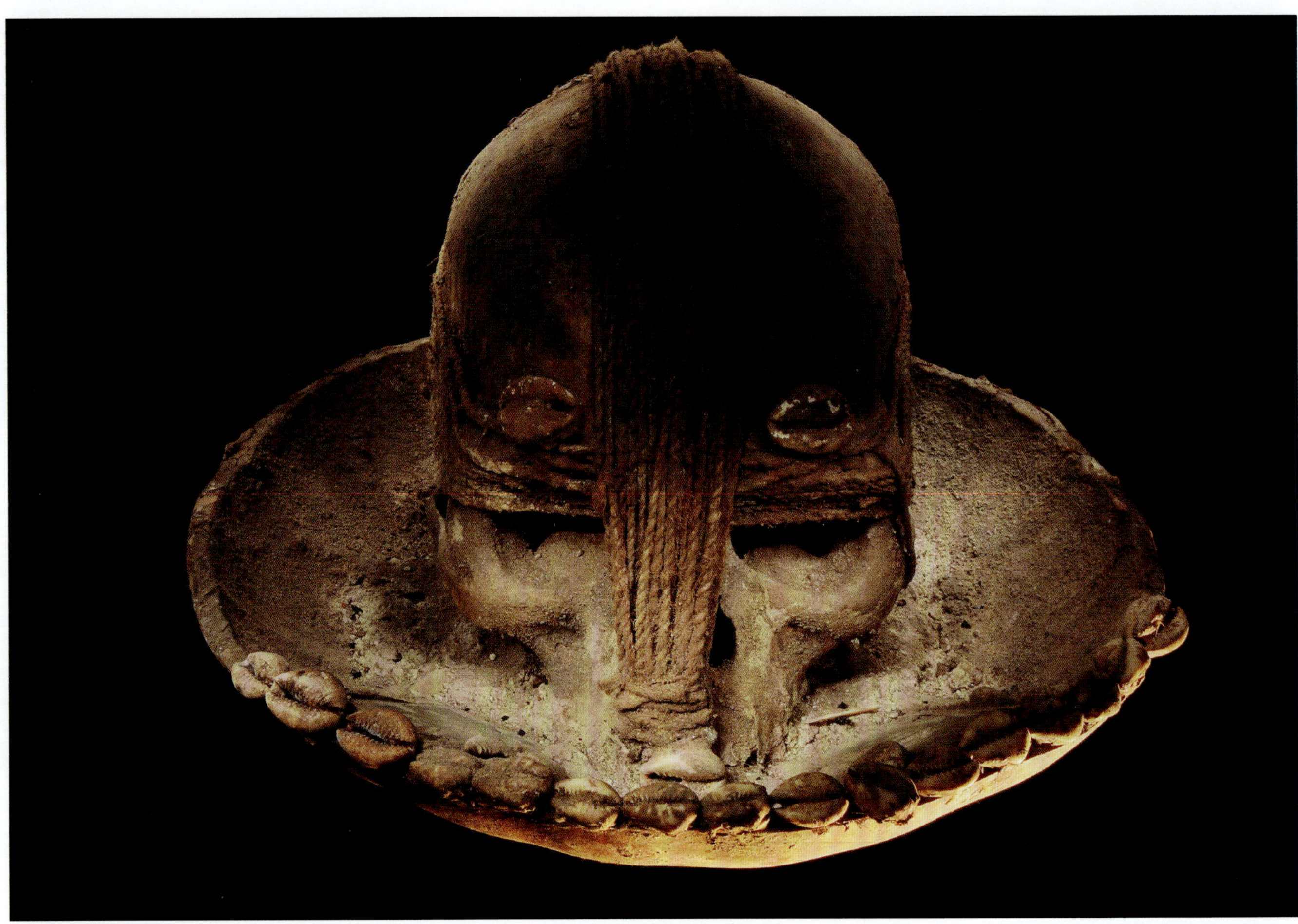

A male oracle skull of the Adja people from Benin

Crâne d'oracle masculin du peuple Adja, Bénin

Ein männlicher Orakelschädel des Volks der Adja aus Benin

Un cráneo de oráculo masculino del pueblo Adja de Benin

Um crânio oráculo masculino do povo Adja do Benin

Een mannelijke orakelschedel van het Adja-volk uit Benin

Male human skull, calabash, mirror, cowrie shell, string/Crâne d'homme, calebasses, miroir, coquillages, ficelle, 18 × 12 cm

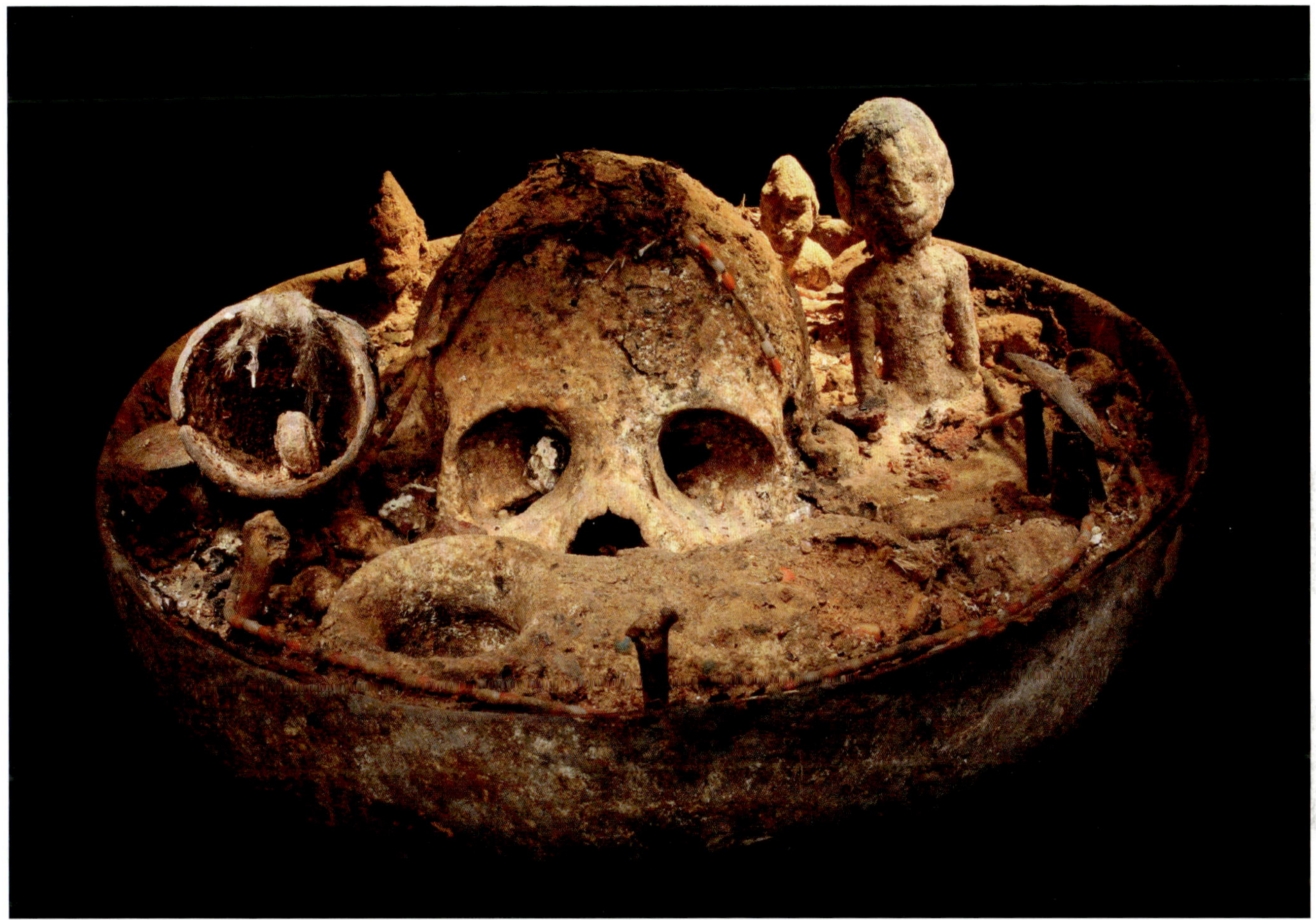

An oracle bowl of the Nago people

Bol d'oracle du peuple Nago

Eine Orakelschale des Nago-Volkes

Una concha de oráculo del pueblo Nago

Uma concha de oráculo do povo Nago

Een orakelkom van het Nago-volk

Human skull, calabash, clay, cowrie shell, metal, organic substances/Crâne humain, calebasses, argile, coquillages, métal, matières organiques, 22 × 33 cm

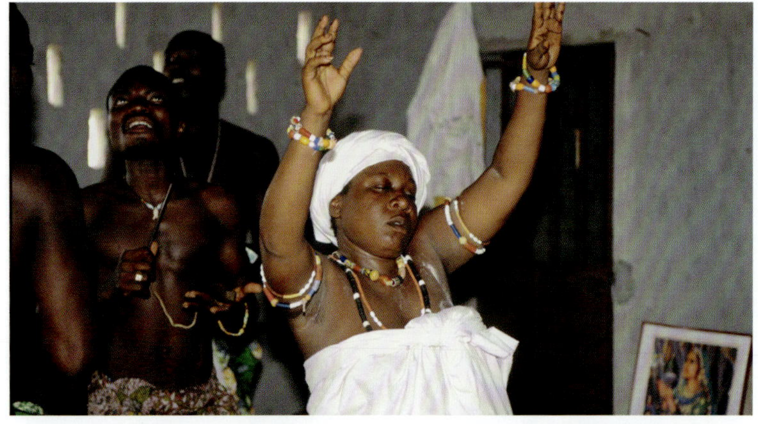

Mami Wata Cleansing Ceremony

Cérémonie de purification de Mami Wata

Mami Wata-Reinigungszeremonie

Ceremonia de limpieza de Mami Wata

Cerimônia de Limpeza Mami Wata

Reinigingsceremonie voor Mami Wata

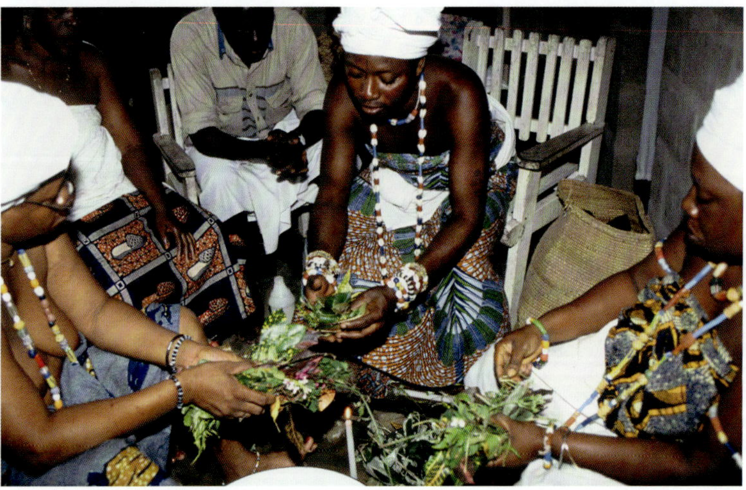

Mami Wata priestesses mix selected medicinal plants with consecrated water

Les prêtresses de Mami Wata mélangent des plantes médicinales qu'elles ont sélectionnées avec de l'eau sacrée

Mami Wata-Priesterinnen mischen ausgesuchte Heilpflanzen mit geweihtem Wasser

Sacerdotisas Mami Wata mezclan plantas medicinales seleccionadas con agua consagrada

Sacerdotisas Mami Wata misturam plantas medicinais selecionadas com água consagrada

Mami Wata-priesteressen mengen een selectie geneeskrachtige planten met gewijd water

Mami Wata—Prosperity, seduction and danger

In Africa, "Mami Wata" (mother water) has for a long time been a key term known in at least 14 countries. Strictly speaking, it designates countless regionally revered water deities and spirits. Nevertheless, the seductive figure of the mermaid, the attractive woman from the intermediate realm, whose favor, just like water, is constantly changing and in motion, usually stands in the foreground.

In some places, such as Cameroon, Mami Wata is feared as a witch. In Benin and Togo it is often believed that Mami Wata can

Mami Wata, prospérité, séduction et danger

En Afrique, Mami Wata (« mère des eaux ») est un concept clé connu dans au moins quatorze pays. Elle désigne à proprement parler les innombrables dieux et esprits de l'eau, régionalement vénérés. Si elle apparaît dans les rêves comme une sirène, Mami Wata rend visite aux humains sous les traits d'une femme séduisante et mystérieuse dont les bonnes grâces, tout comme l'eau, sont toujours en évolution et en mouvement.

Dans de nombreuses régions, notamment au Cameroun, Mami Wata est redoutée comme une sorcière. Au Bénin et au

Mami Wata – Wohlstand, Verführung und Gefahr

In Afrika ist „Mami Wata" (Mutter Wasser) längst zu einem Schlüsselbegriff geworden, der in mindestens 14 Ländern bekannt ist. Streng genommen bezeichnet es unzählige regional verehrte Wassergottheiten und -geister. Im Vordergrund steht dennoch meist die verführerische Figur der Nixe, der attraktiven Frau aus dem Zwischenreich, deren Gunst, genau wie das Wasser, ständig wechselt und in Bewegung ist.

Mancherorts, wie beispielsweise in Kamerun, ist Mami Wata als Hexe gefürchtet. In Benin und Togo glaubt man

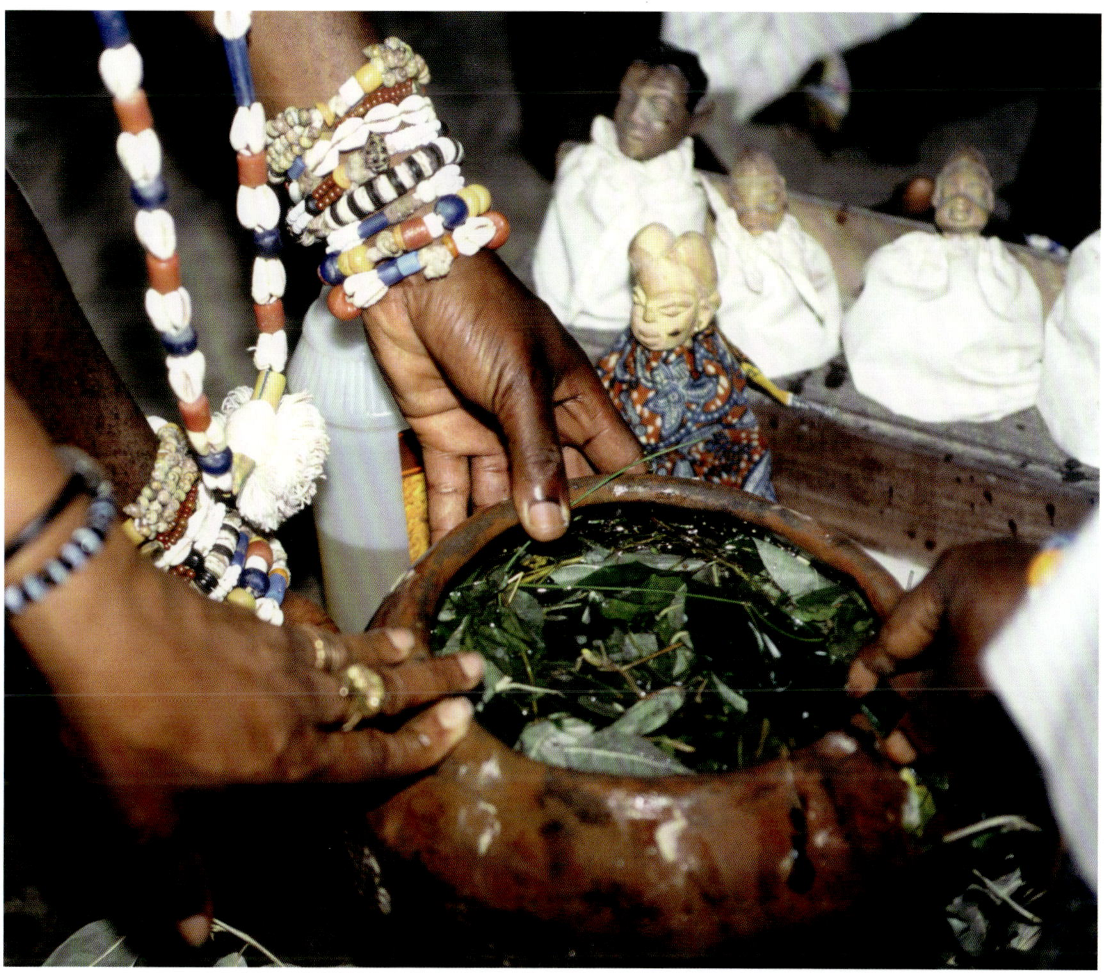

Mami Wata– Prosperidad, seducción y peligro

En África, "Mami Wata" (agua madre) se ha convertido desde hace mucho tiempo en un término clave conocido en al menos 14 países. Estrictamente hablando, se refiere a innumerables deidades y espíritus del agua venerados regionalmente. Sin embargo, la seductora figura de la sirena, la atractiva mujer del reino intermedio, cuyo favor, al igual que el agua, cambia constantemente y está en movimiento, suele estar en primer plano.

En algunos lugares, como Camerún, se teme que Mami Wata sea una bruja. En

Mami Wata – Prosperidade, sedução e perigo

Em África, o termo "Mami Wata" (água-mãe) há muito que se tornou um termo-chave conhecido em pelo menos 14 países. Estritamente falando, refere-se a incontáveis deidades e espíritos da água reverenciados regionalmente. No entanto, a figura sedutora da sereia, a mulher atraente do reino intermediário, cujo favor, assim como a água, muda constantemente e está em movimento, geralmente está em primeiro plano.

Em alguns lugares, como nos Camarões, Mami Wata é temida como uma bruxa.

Mami Wata – welvaart, verleiding en gevaar

In Afrika is Mami Wata ('moeder water') allang een begrip geworden dat in minstens veertien landen bekend is. Strikt genomen verwijst Mami Wata naar talloze regionaal vereerde watergoden en -geesten. Op de voorgrond staat echter meestal de verleidelijke figuur van de waternimf, de aantrekkelijke vrouw uit de tussenwereld, wier gunst, net als het water, voortdurend verandert en in beweging is.

Op sommige plaatsen, zoals in Kameroen, wordt Mami Wata gevreesd als een heks. In Benin en Togo geloven mensen

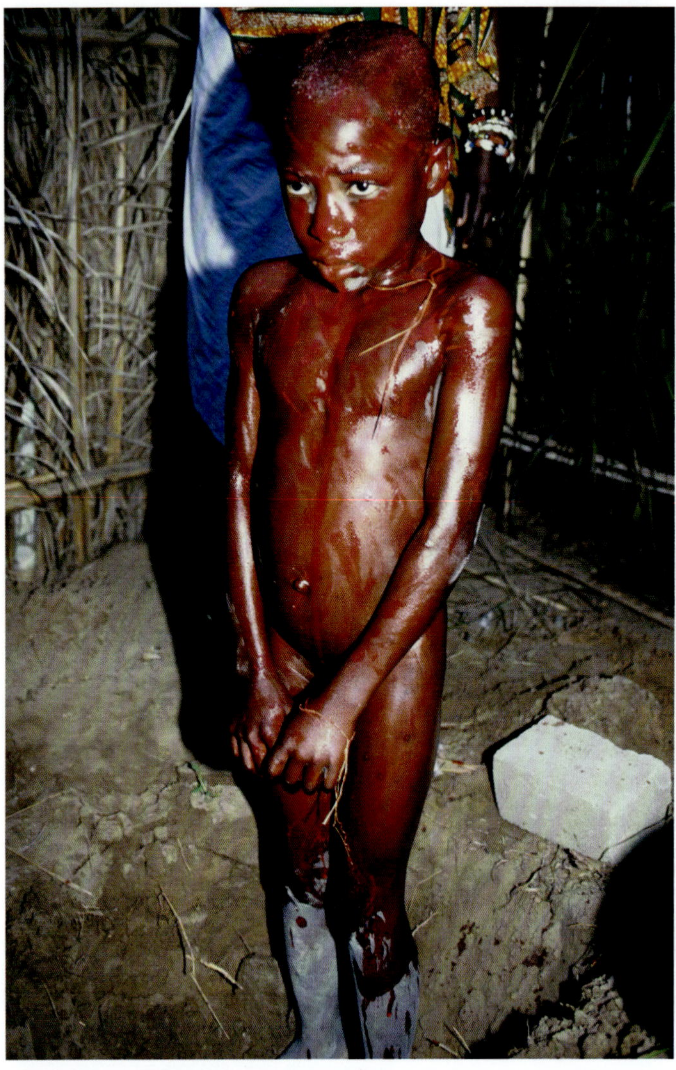

Covered with blood. The little patient receives a blood bath with the blood of the sacrificial animal, which was slaughtered for her during the Mami Wata healing ceremony.

Couvert de sang. On a douché la petite patiente avec le sang de l'animal qui a été sacrifié pour elle lors d'une cérémonie de guérison sous l'égide de Mami Wata.

Mit Blut bedeckt. Die kleine Patientin erhält ein Blutbad mit dem Blut des Opfertieres, das im Rahmen der Mami Wata-Heilzeremonie für sie geschlachtet wurde.

Cubierto de sangre. La pequeña paciente recibe un baño de sangre con la sangre del animal del sacrificio, que fue sacrificado por ella durante la ceremonia de sanación de Mami Wata.

Coberto de sangue. A pequena paciente recebe um banho de sangue com o sangue do animal do sacrifício, que foi abatido por ela durante a cerimônia de cura de Mami Wata.

Bedekt met bloed. De jonge patiënte krijgt een bloedbad met het bloed van het offerdier, dat voor haar werd geslacht in het kader van de Mami Wata-genezingsceremonie.

increase individual prosperity by remaining faithful to her and worshipping her alone.

Sometimes oracle questioning with sick people also show that Mami Wata must be ritually established in the person's life because they have had a bond with her since birth that has never been recognised. Giving a place to the goddess then usually ensures recovery.

Togo, on estime souvent qu'elle favorise la prospérité de celui qui lui reste dévoué et qui ne vénère qu'elle.

Pour certains malades, les consultations des oracles préconisent parfois l'établissement d'un culte à Mami Wata. Cela signifie que la relation avec la déité est établie depuis la naissance, mais qu'elle n'a jamais été prise en compte. Il suffit alors souvent de se tourner vers elle et de l'honorer pour guérir.

häufig, Mami Wata könne den individuellen Wohlstand vergrößern, wenn man ihr dafür nur treu bleibt und sie allein verehrt.

Manchmal zeigen die Orakelbefragungen bei Kranken auch, dass Mami Wata in ihrem Leben kultisch etabliert werden muss, weil eine seit Geburt bestehende, nie berücksichtigte Bindung an sie vorliegt. Der Göttin einen Platz einzuräumen sorgt dann meistens für Genesung.

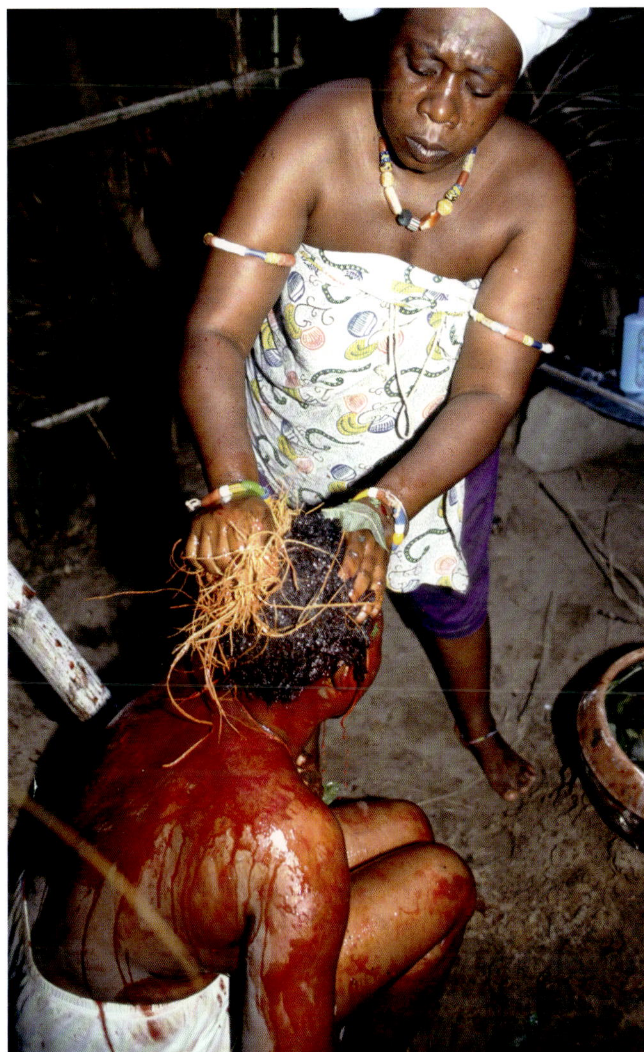

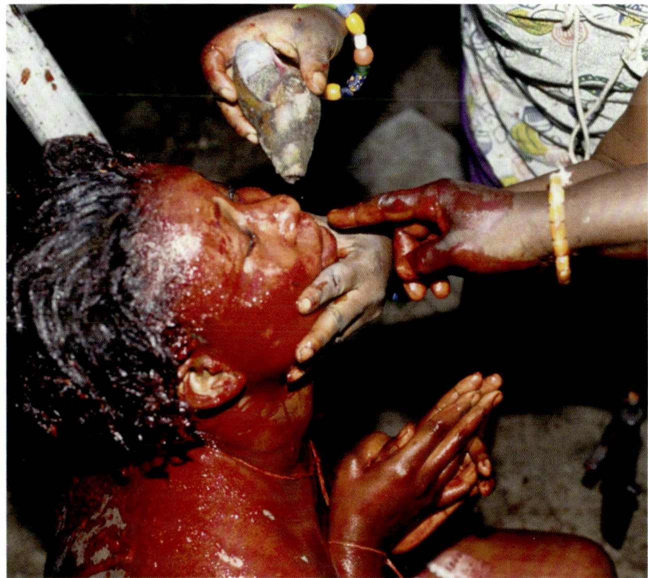

Washing the patient
Lavage riruel du patient
Waschung der Patientin
Lavado del paciente
Lavagem do paciente
Wassen van de patiënte

Drops for a clear view
Des gouttes pour une vue claire
Tropfen für die klare Sicht
Gotas para una visión clara
Gotas para uma visão clara
Druppels voor een goed zicht

Benin y Togo, la gente a menudo cree que Mami Wata puede aumentar la prosperidad individual si uno permanece fiel y solamente la adora a ella.

A veces, las entrevistas del oráculo con los enfermos también muestran que Mami Wata tiene que ser establecida cultualmente en su vida porque hay un vínculo con ella que ha existido desde su nacimiento y que nunca ha sido considerado. En estos casos, darle un lugar a la diosa normalmente asegura la recuperación.

Em Benin e Togo, as pessoas muitas vezes acreditam que Mami Wata pode aumentar a prosperidade individual se você permanecer fiel a ela e adorá-la sozinha.

Às vezes as entrevistas de oráculo com pessoas doentes também mostram que Mami Wata tem que ser estabelecida culticamente em sua vida porque há um vínculo com ela que existe desde o nascimento e nunca foi considerado. Dar um lugar à deusa normalmente garante a recuperação.

vaak dat Mami Wata de persoonlijke welvaart kan vergroten als je haar maar trouw blijft en alleen haar aanbidt.

Soms blijkt uit de orakelraadpleging bij zieke mensen ook dat Mami Wata cultisch moet zijn verankerd in hun leven, omdat er vanaf hun geboorte een band met haar bestaat waar nooit rekening mee is gehouden. Alsnog een plaats geven aan de godin zorgt dan meestal voor herstel.

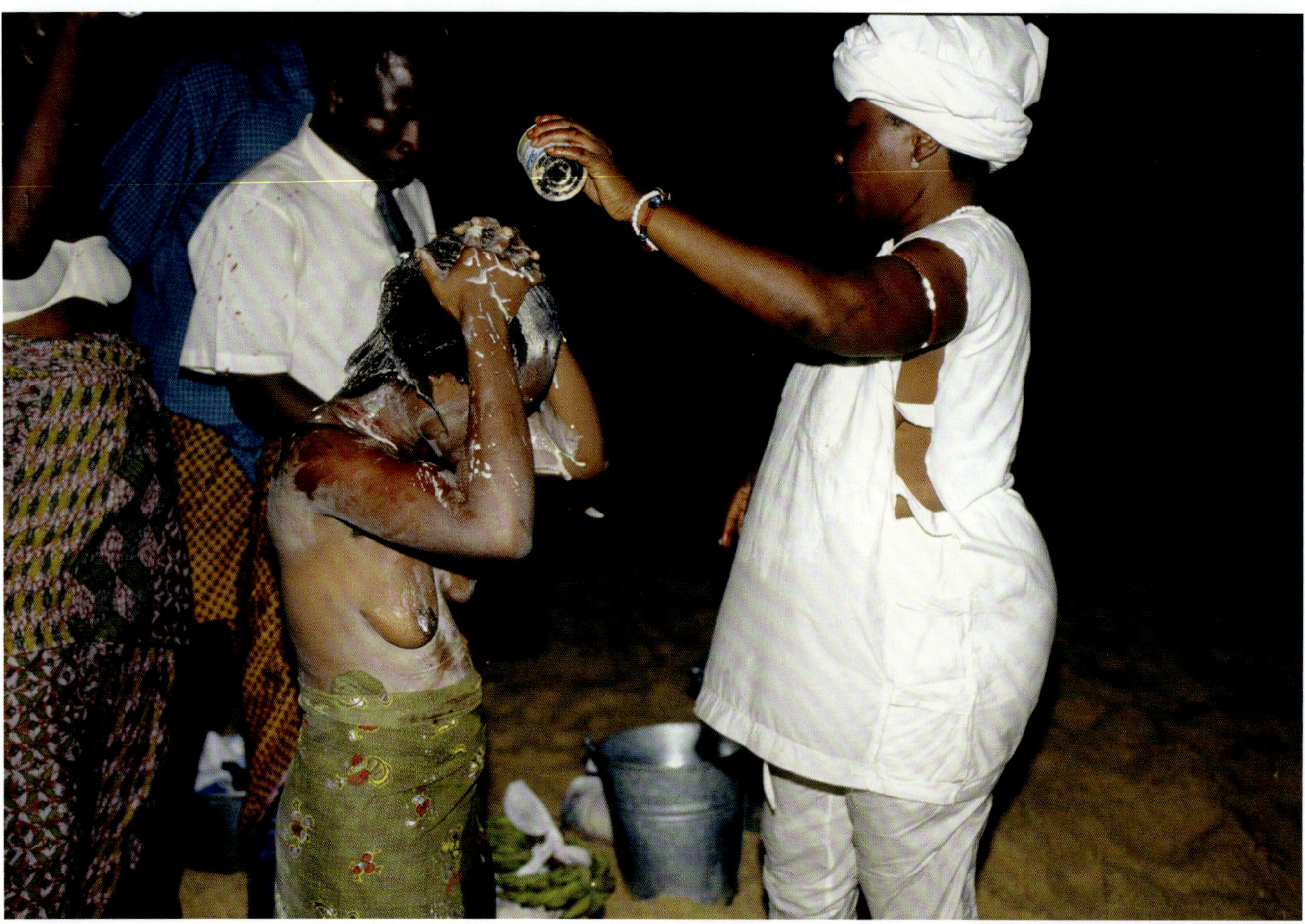

Beach ceremony. During the ritual, which takes place close to the sea, the clients are powdered and perfumed, because Mami Wata likes her subjects to smell good.

Cérémonie sur la plage. Au cours de ce rituel qui se déroule à proximité de l'océan, les clientes sont poudrées et parfumées car Mami Wata apprécie que ses protégées sentent bon.

Strandzeremonie. Bei dem Ritual in unmittelbarer Meeresnähe werden die Klienten gepudert und parfümiert, denn Mami Wata hat es gern, wenn ihre Schutzbefohlenen gut riechen.

Ceremonia en la playa. Durante el ritual, que tiene lugar cerca del mar, los clientes son empolvados y perfumados, porque a Mami Wata le gusta que sus súbditos huelan bien.

Cerimônia na praia. Durante o ritual, que acontece perto do mar, os clientes são pulverizados e perfumados, porque Mami Wata gosta que seus súditos cheirem bem.

Strandceremonie. Tijdens het ritueel, dat vlak bij zee plaatsvindt, worden de klanten gepoederd en geparfumeerd, want Mami Wata houdt ervan dat haar beschermelingen lekker ruiken.

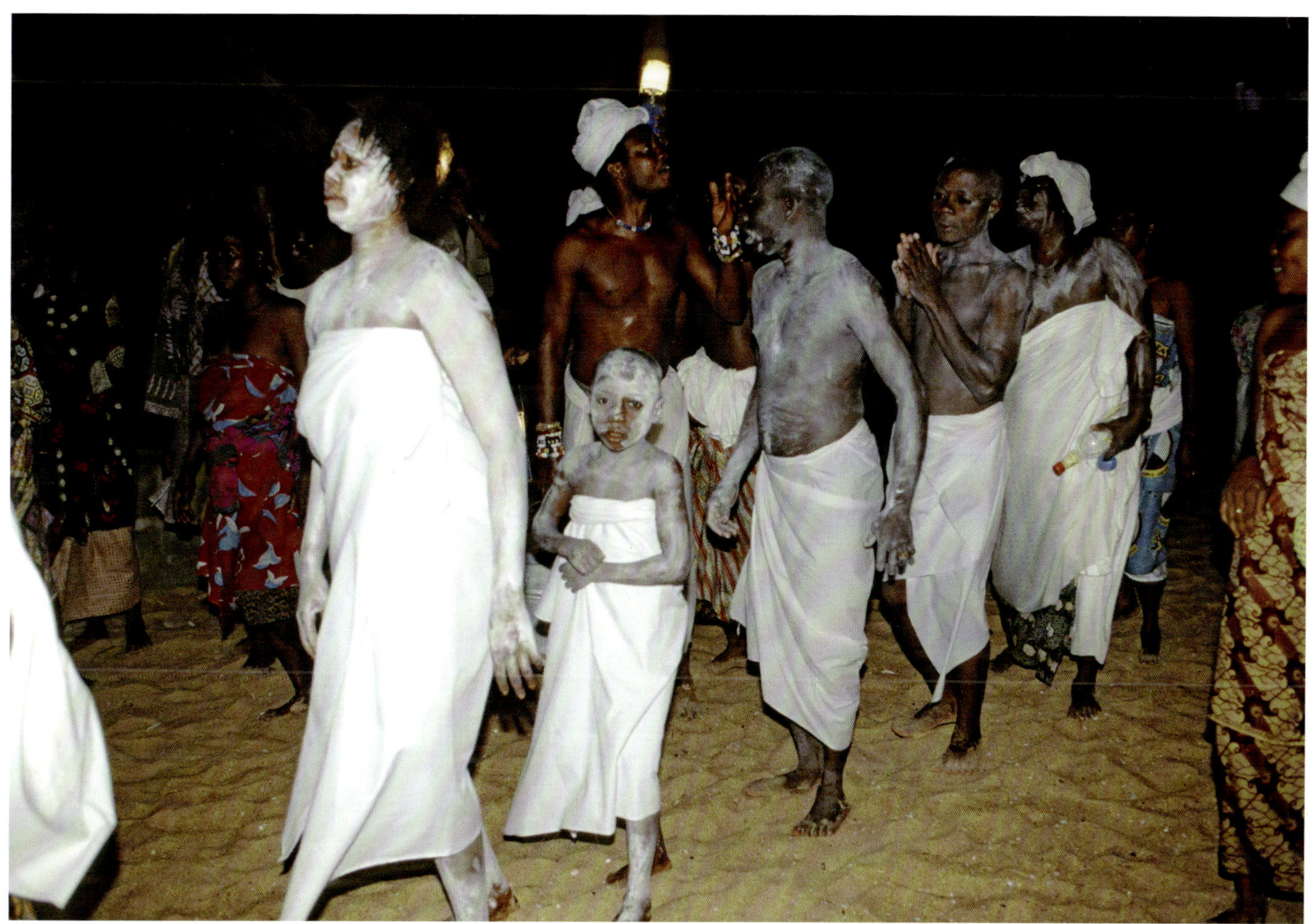

Procession into the city
Procession dans la ville
Prozession in die Stadt
Procesión a la ciudad
Procissão para a cidade
Optocht naar de stad

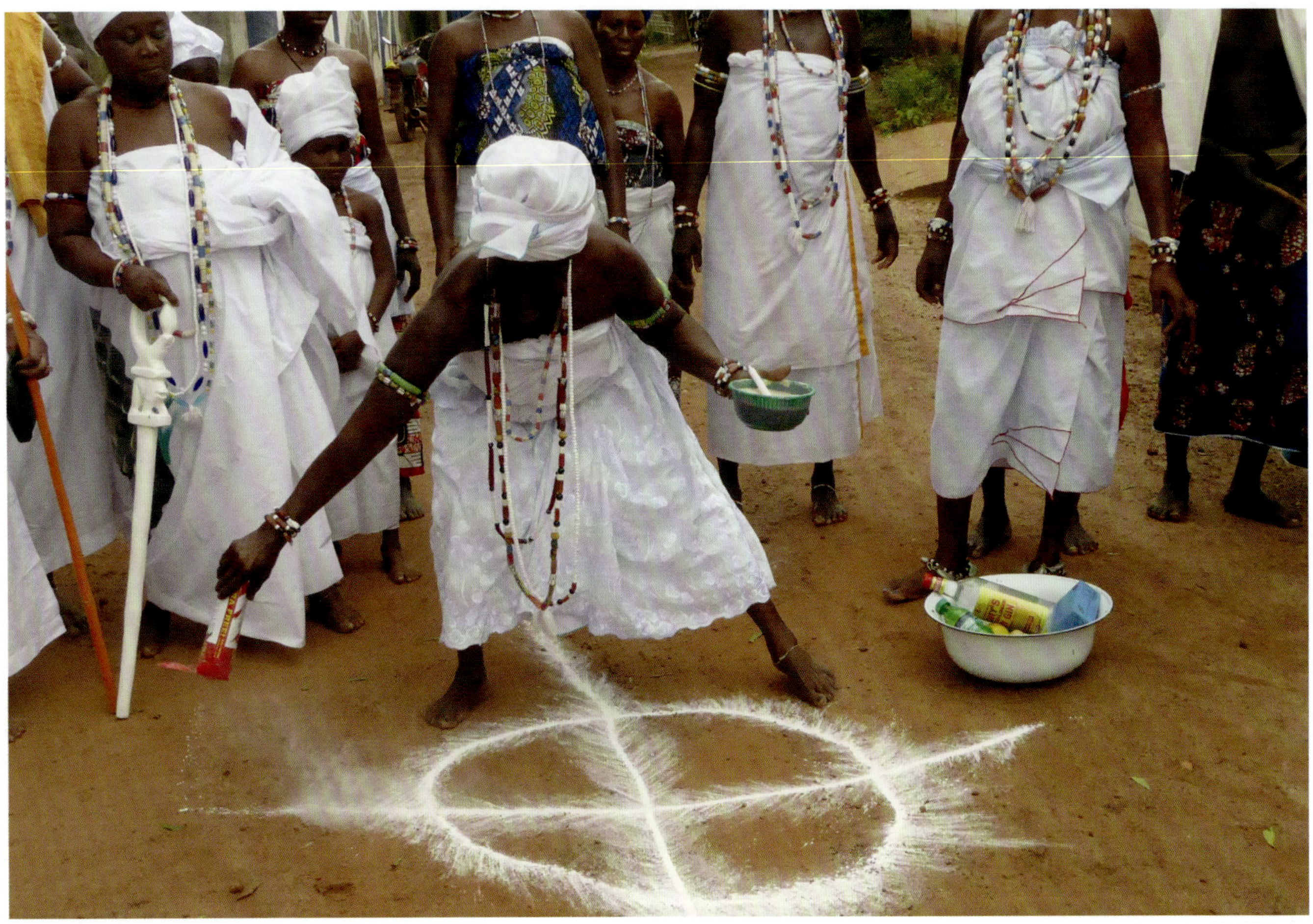

Summoning of the Gods

Invocation des dieux

Beschwörung der Götter

Invocación de los Dioses

Convocação dos Deuses

Oproep van de goden

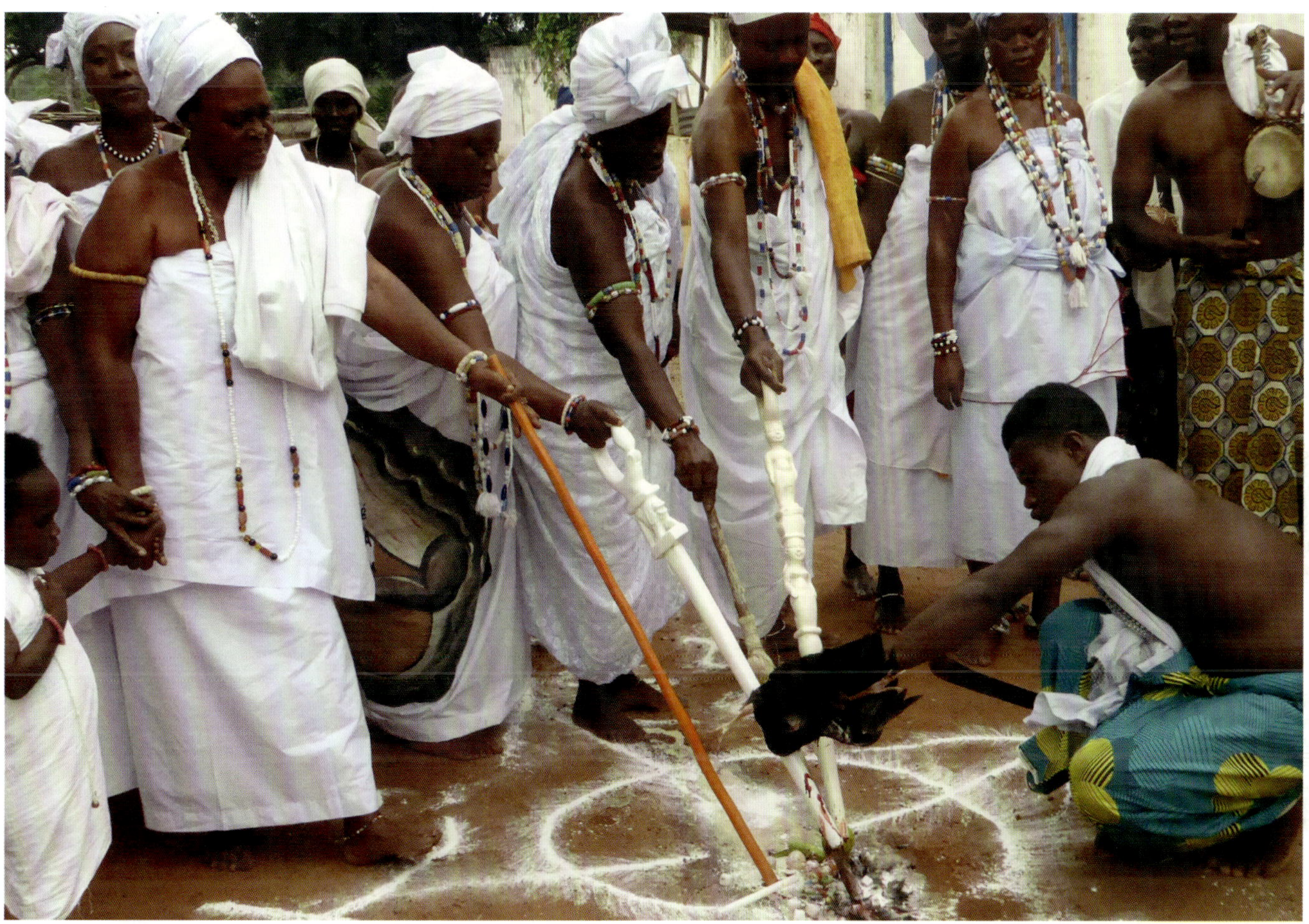

Summoning of the Gods. The symbols they draw serve to invoke certain gods and to integrate them into the ceremony. This is about Dan, symbolized by the closed circle.

Invocation des dieux. Les symboles tracés servent à appeler des dieux spécifiques pour les convier à la cérémonie. Sur cette photograhie, c'est à Dan que l'on s'adresse, symbolisé par un cercle fermé.

Beschwörung der Götter. Die gezeichneten Symbole dienen dazu, bestimmte Götter anzurufen und in die Zeremonie einzubinden. Hier geht es um Dan, symbolisiert durch den geschlossenen Kreis.

Invocación de los Dioses. Los símbolos dibujados sirven para llamar a ciertos dioses e integrarlos en la ceremonia. Se trata de Dan, simbolizado por el círculo cerrado.

Convocação dos Deuses. Os símbolos desenhados servem para chamar certos deuses e integrá-los na cerimônia. Isto é sobre o Dan, simbolizado pelo círculo fechado.

Oproep van de goden. De getekende symbolen dienen om bepaalde goden op te roepen en bij de ceremoniete betrekken. Hier gaat het om Dan, die gesymboliseerd wordt door de gesloten cirkel.

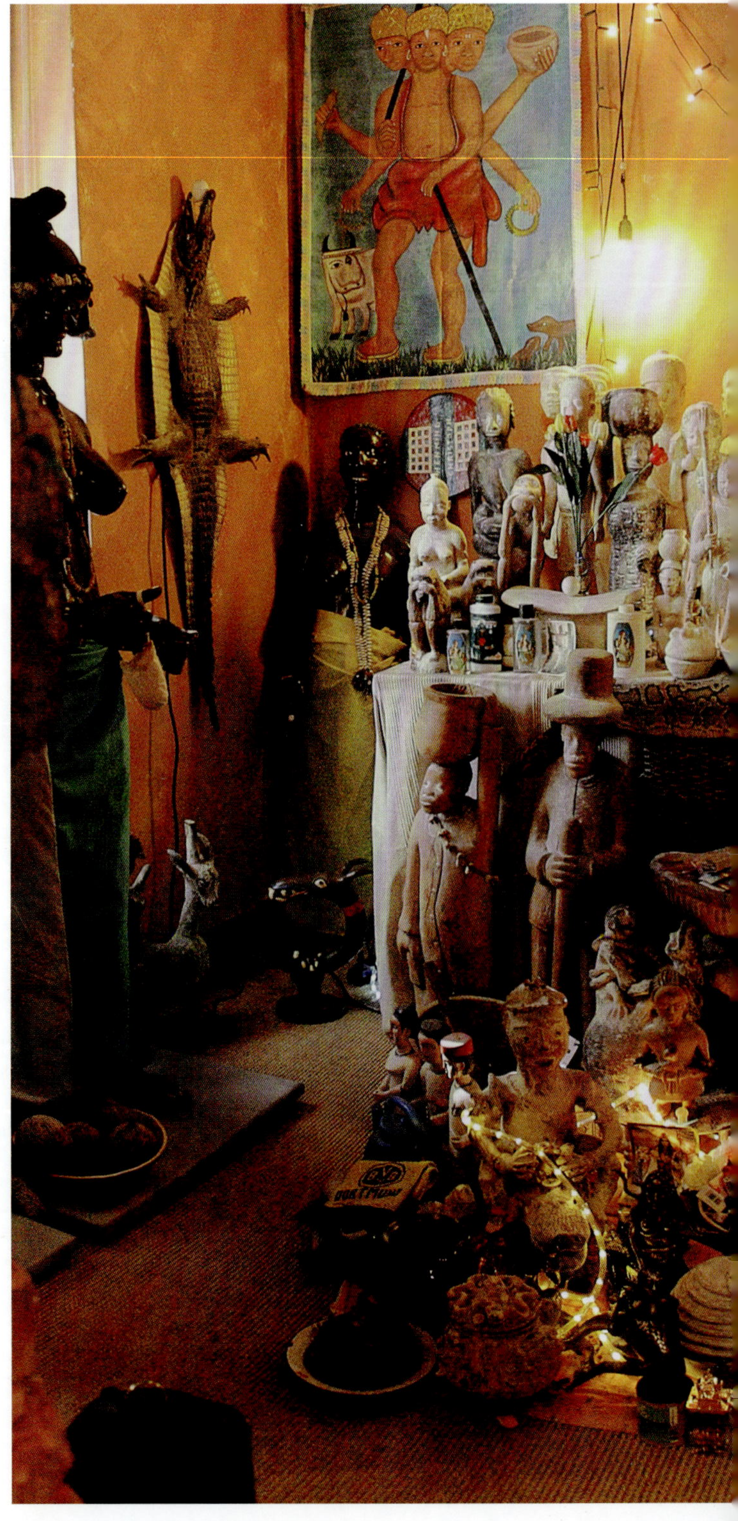

Mami Wata Altar. This Mami Wata altar is in the Soul of Africa Museum in Essen. Altars for Mami Wata are rarely so large, but can expand through added offerings and assistant spirits.

Autel à Mami Wata. Cet autel pour Mami Wata est installé dans le Soul of Africa Museum d'Essen en Allemagne. Les autels destinés à la déesse sont rarement aussi grands mais peuvent cependant s'étoffer à mesure que sont apportées des offrandes et que viennent s'ajouter des esprits auxiliaires.

Mami Wata-Altar. Dieser Mami Wata-Altar steht im Soul of Africa Museum in Essen. Altäre für Mami Wata sind selten so groß, können aber durch die Zugabe von Opfergaben und Addierung von Assistenzgeistern wachsen.

Altar Mami Wata. Este altar de Mami Wata se encuentra en el Museo Soul of Africa en Essen. Los altares para Mami Wata raramente son tan grandes, pero pueden crecer a través de la adición de ofrendas y espíritus asistentes.

Altar Mami Wata. Este altar Mami Wata está no Museu Soul of Africa em Essen. Os altares para Mami Wata raramente são tão grandes, mas podem crescer através da adição de oferendas e espíritos assistentes.

Altaar voor Mami Wata. Dit Mami Wata-altaar staat in het Soul of Africa Museum in Essen. Altaren voor Mami Wata zijn zelden zo groot, maar kunnen uitgroeien door de toevoeging van offers en hulpgeesten.

Wood, clay and other materials/Bois, argile et autres matériaux, 280 × 75 cm

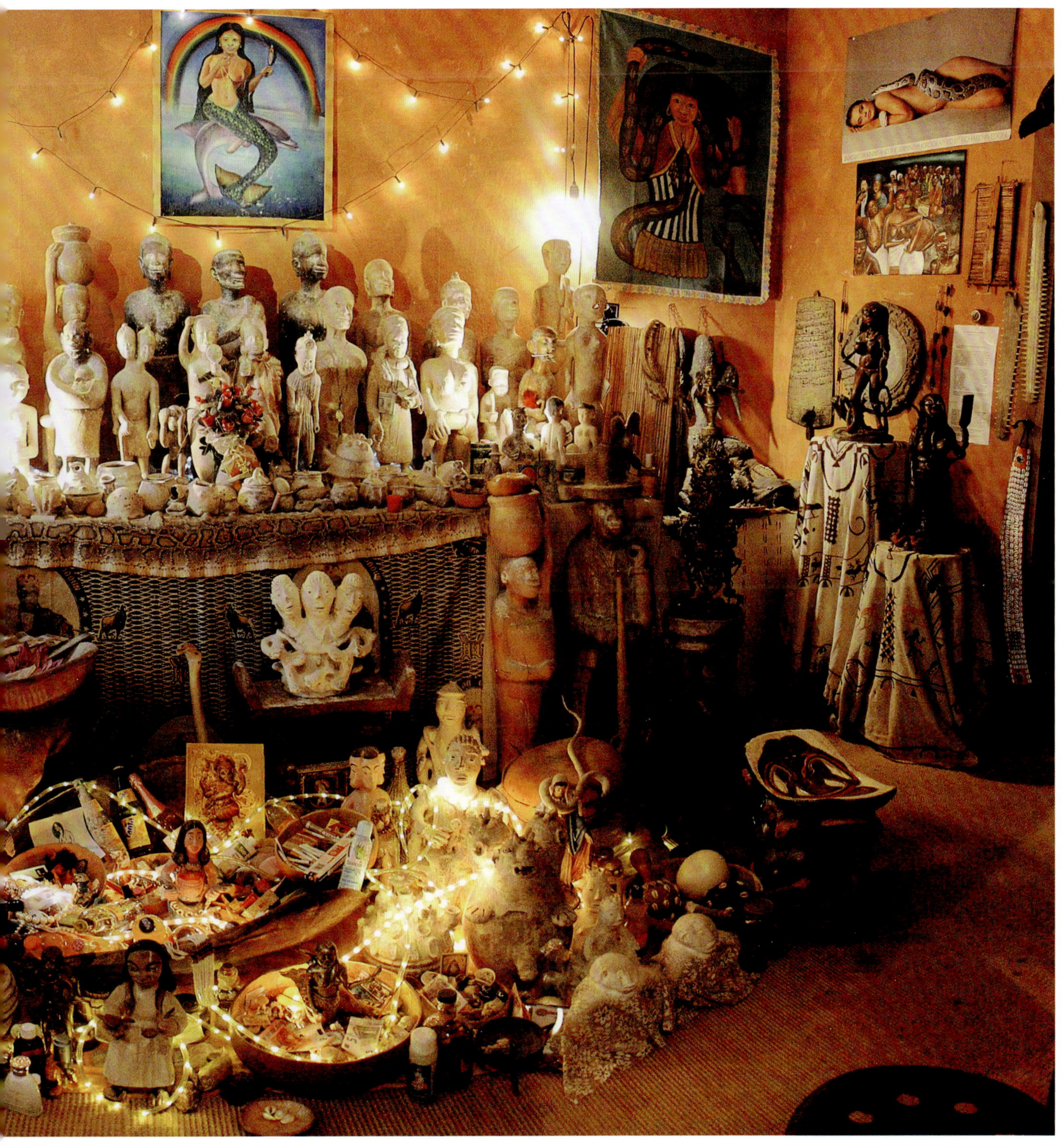

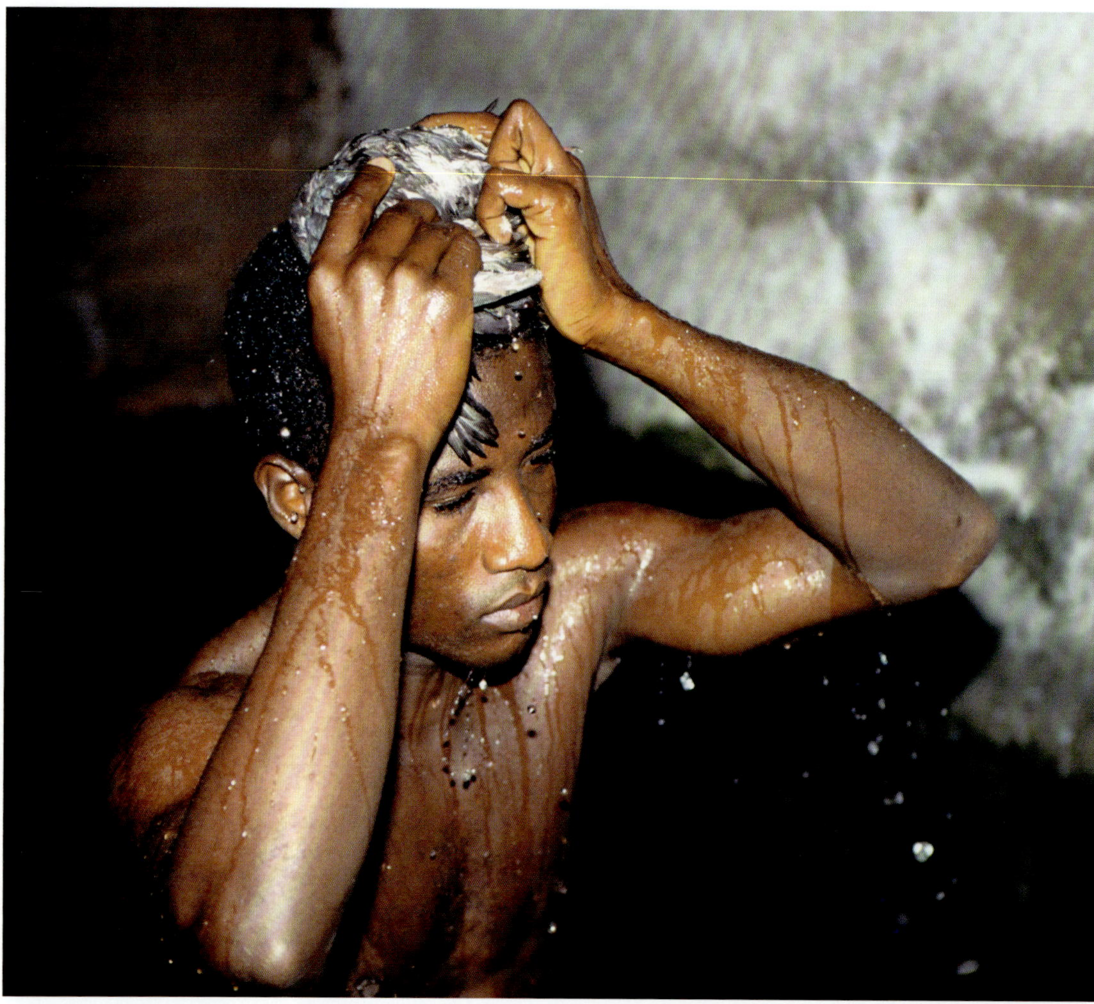

Wedding night with Mami Wata

Those who allow themselves to be initiated into the Mami Wata cult usually do so for good reason. Some people hope for a carefree life in which at least materially there is no shortage. In the case of women, it is often infertility that should be cured by joining the religious community.

Most likely, however, there are prenatal bonds that were unknown and have become virulent in the course of their lifetime, i.e. caused health problems due to their unrecognized existence. Recurring dreams with Mami Wata are a sign of this.

Nuit de noces avec Mami Wata

Une personne souhaitant s'initier au culte de Mami Wata le fait généralement pour de bonnes raisons. Nombreux sont ceux qui espèrent une vie sans souci, au moins débarrassée des difficultés matérielles. Chez les femmes, l'entrée dans la communauté religieuse vise souvent à lutter contre l'infertilité.

Autre cas courant, un lien prénatal ignoré s'est violemment manifesté à la personne en provoquant des problèmes de santé. Elle perçoit alors des signes à travers des rêves récurrents de Mami Wata.

Hochzeitsnacht mit Mami Wata

Wer sich in den Mami-Wata-Kult initiieren lässt, tut dies meist aus gutem Grund. Manch einer hofft auf ein sorgenfreies Leben, in dem zumindest materiell kein Mangel mehr aufkommt. Bei Frauen ist es häufig die Unfruchtbarkeit, die der Beitritt zur Glaubensgemeinschaft kurieren soll.

Am ehesten sind es jedoch vorgeburtliche Bindungen, die unerkannt waren und im Laufe des Lebens virulent wurden, das heißt aufgrund ihrer unberücksichtigten Existenz gesundheitliche Probleme erzeugten. Immer

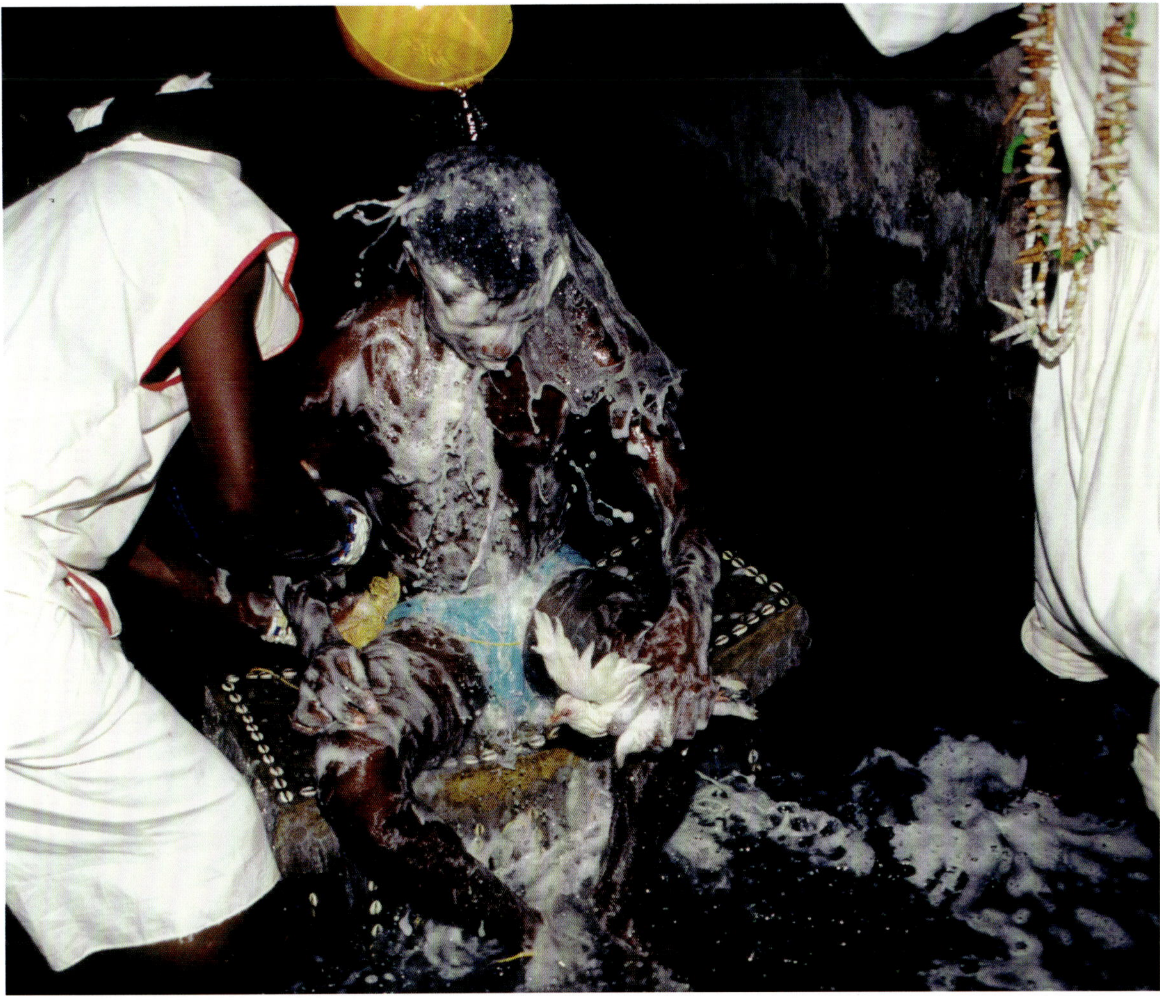

Noche de bodas con Mami Wata

Aquellos que se inician en el culto de Mami Wata usualmente lo hacen por una buena razón. Algunas personas esperan una vida despreocupada en la que al menos materialmente no haya escasez. En el caso de las mujeres, a menudo es la infertilidad la que debe curarse al unirse a la comunidad religiosa.

Sin embargo, lo más probable es que sean lazos prenatales que no fueron reconocidos y que se volvieron virulentos en el curso de la vida, es decir, que causaron problemas de salud debido a su existencia inconsiderada.

Noite de núpcias com Mami Wata

Aqueles que se permitem ser iniciados no culto Mami Wata geralmente o fazem por uma boa razão. Algumas pessoas esperam uma vida despreocupada, na qual pelo menos materialmente não há escassez. No caso das mulheres, é muitas vezes a infertilidade que deve ser curada através da adesão à comunidade religiosa.

O mais provável, no entanto, são os vínculos pré-natais que não foram reconhecidos e se tornaram virulentos ao longo da vida, ou seja, causaram problemas de saúde devido à sua existência

Huwelijksnacht met Mami Wata

Degenen die zich laten inwijden in de cultus van Mami Wata doen dat meestal met een goede reden. Sommige mensen hopen op een zorgeloos bestaan waarin er in elk geval materieel gezien nergens gebrek aan is. Bij vrouwen gaat het vaak om onvruchtbaarheid die moet genezen door toetreding tot de geloofsgemeenschap.

Waarschijnlijk zijn het echter vooral prenatale, niet-herkende banden die in de loop van het leven kwaadaardig zijn geworden, oftewel gezondheidsproblemen hebben veroorzaakt als gevolg van hun

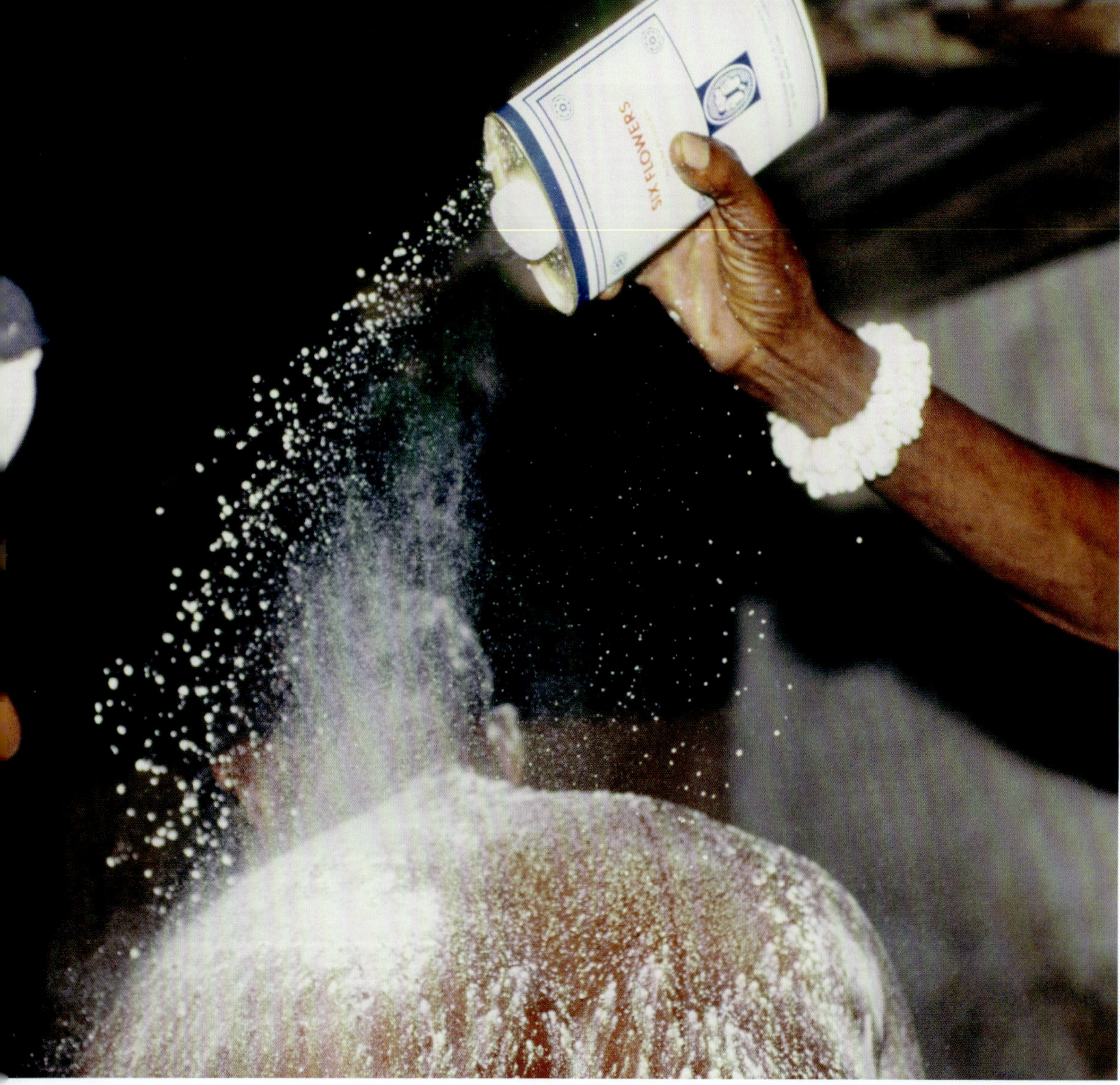

Applying powder to
a novice

Poudrage du novice

Puderung des
Novizen

Empolvamiento
del novicio

Pulverizando o noviço

Het poederen van
de novice

The initiation into the Mami Wata faith
community is accompanied by ceremonies
lasting several days during which the
aspirants are married to Mami Wata in a
ritual setting. These include white robes,
rituals with a white and a black dove,
washes, perfumes and a wedding night close
to the water.

L'initiation à la communauté religieuse
de Mami Wata s'effectue par des cérémonies
de plusieurs jours au cours desquelles le
postulant doit rituellement épouser Mami
Wata. Elles impliquent notamment des
rituels avec un pigeon noir et un pigeon
blanc, des ablutions, l'utilisation de parfums
et une nuit de noces à proximité immédiate
de l'eau.

wiederkehrende Träume mit Mami Wata
sind ein Zeichen dafür.

Die Initiation in die Mami-Wata-
Glaubensgemeinschaft geht mit mehrtägigen
Zeremonien einher, bei denen die Anwärter
im rituellen Rahmen mit Mami Wata
vermählt werden. Dazu gehören unter
anderem weiße Gewänder, Rituale mit
einer weißen und einer schwarzen Taube,
Waschungen, Parfümierungen und eine
Hochzeitsnacht in unmittelbarer Nähe
zum Wasser.

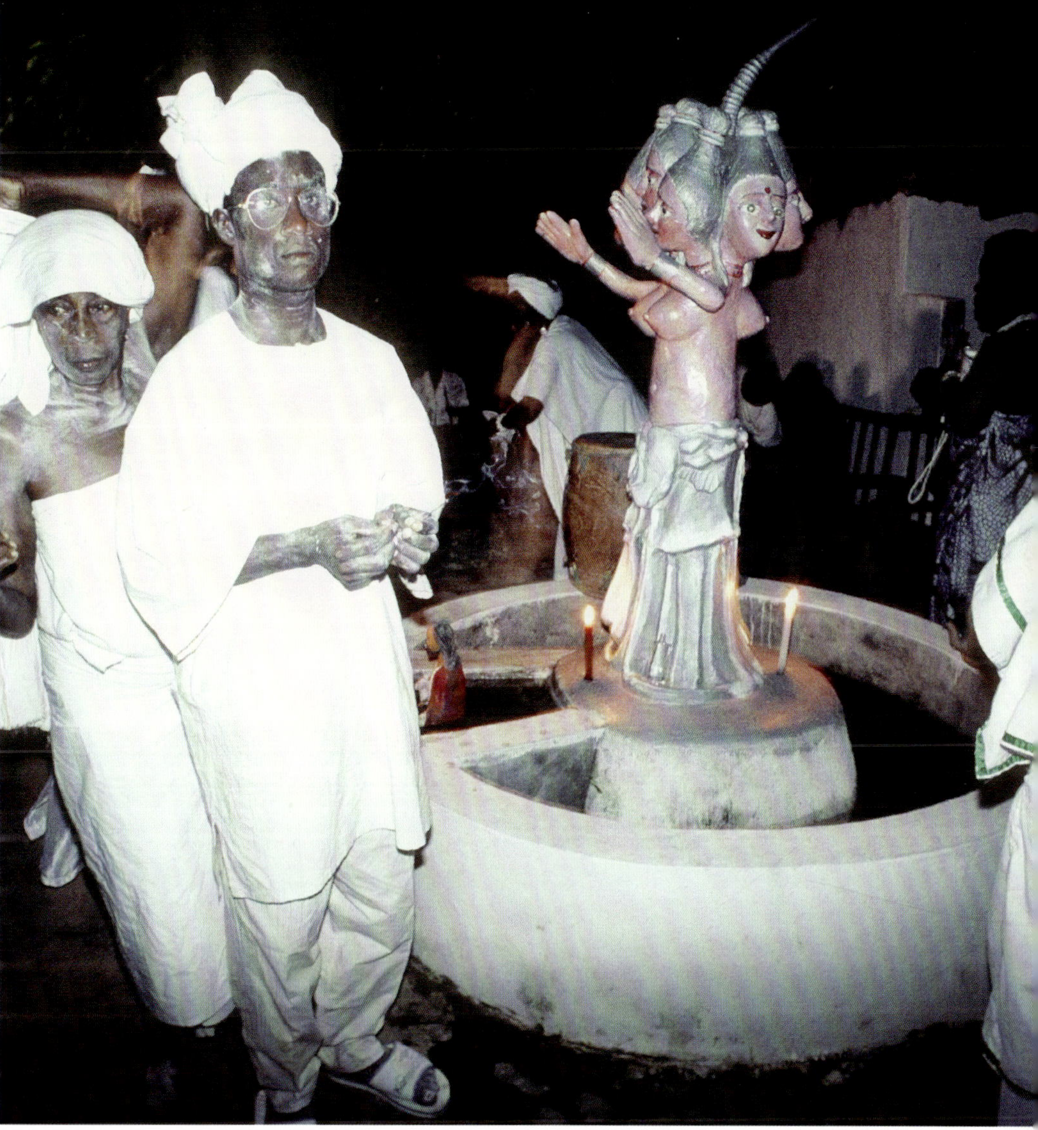

Los sueños recurrentes con Mami Wata son un signo de ello.

La iniciación en la comunidad de fe de Mami Wata se acompaña de ceremonias de varios días en las que los aspirantes se casan con Mami Wata en un marco ritual. Estos incluyen túnicas blancas, rituales con una paloma blanca y otra negra, lavados, perfumes y una noche de bodas muy cerca del agua.

inconsiderada. Sonhos recorrentes com a Mami Wata são um sinal disso.

A iniciação à comunidade de fé Mami Wata é acompanhada por cerimônias que duram vários dias, nas quais as aspirantes são casadas com Mami Wata em uma estrutura ritual. Estes incluem vestes brancas, rituais com uma pomba branca e uma pomba preta, lavagens, perfumes e uma noite de núpcias nas proximidades da água.

buiten beschouwing gebleven bestaan. Steeds terugkerende dromen met Mami Wata zijn daar een teken van.

De initiatie in de geloofsgemeenschap van Mami Wata gaat gepaard met ceremoniën die meerdere dagen duren en waarbij de aspiranten in een ritueel kader trouwen met Mami Wata. Daar horen onder andere witte gewaden, rituelen met een witte en een zwarte duif, wassingen, parfumering en een huwelijksnacht in de nabijheid van water bij.

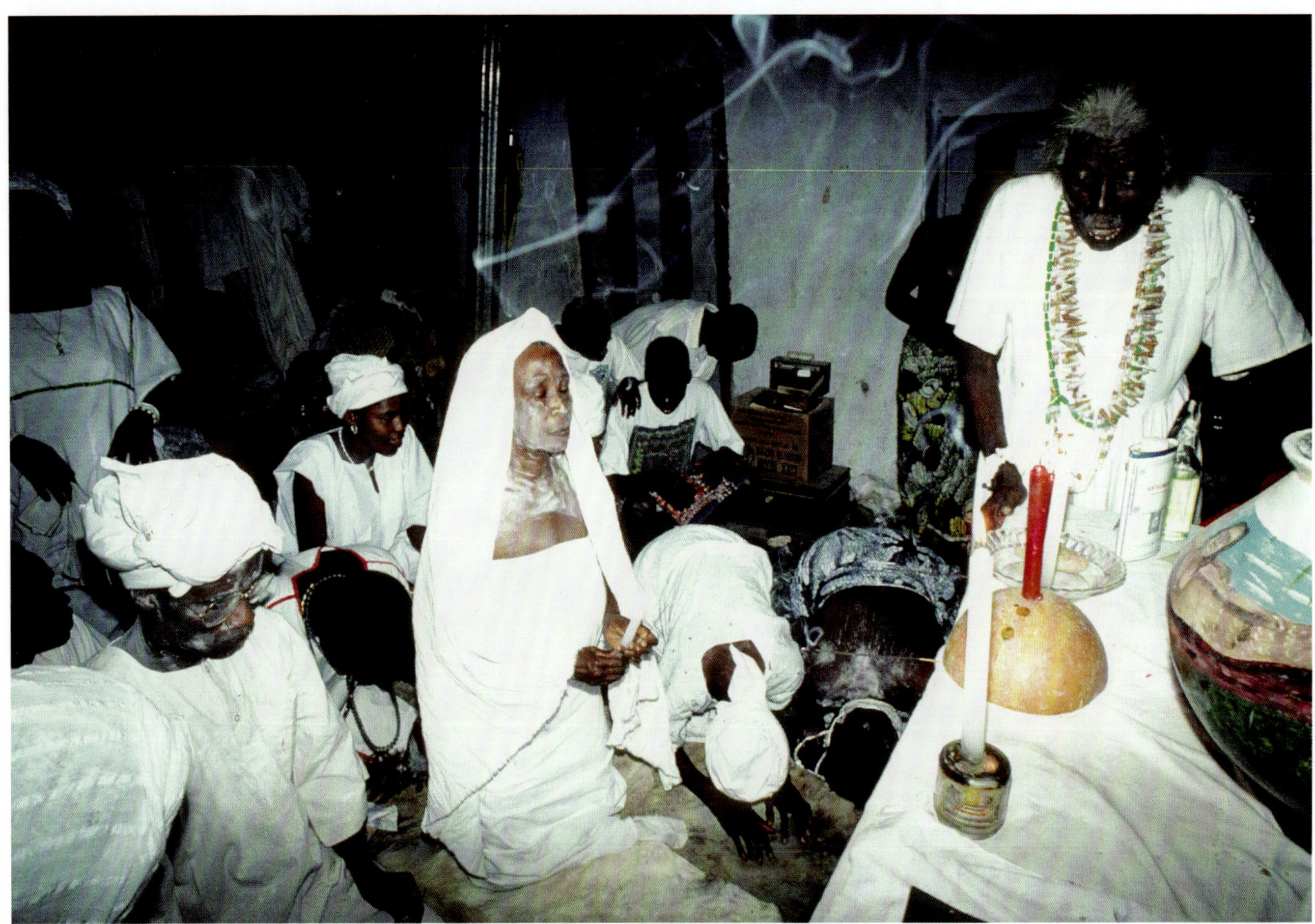

In front of the altar

Devant l'autel

Vor dem Altar

Delante del altar

Em frente ao altar

Voor het altaar

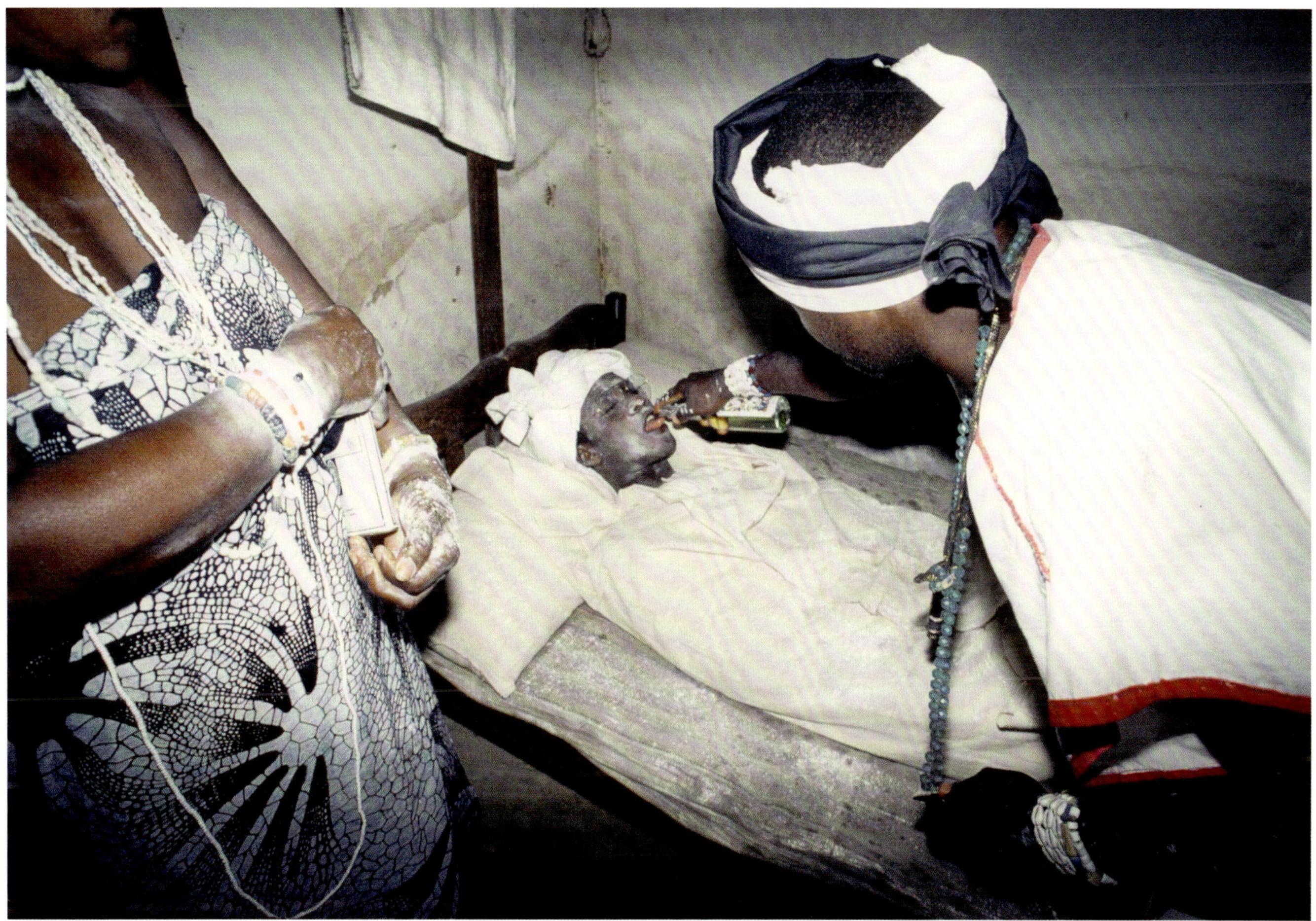

Wedding Nights with Mami. The novice is then taken to a hut on the banks of the river, where he will spend the next eight days and nights. In this phase his wedding with Mami Wata takes place.

Nuit de noces avec Mami. À la fin du rituel, le novice est amené dans une hutte installée à proximité de la rive du fleuve. Il devra y rester pendant les huit jours et les huit nuits à venir. Cette phase correspond à son mariage avec Mami Wata.

Hochzeitsnächte mit Mami. Anschließend wird der Novize in eine Hütte unmittelbar am Flussufer gebracht, wo er die nächsten acht Tage und Nächte zubringen wird. In dieser Phase vollzieht sich seine Hochzeit mit Mami Wata.

Noches de bodas con Mami. El novicio es llevado a una cabaña a orillas del río, donde pasará los próximos ocho días y noches. En esta fase tiene lugar su boda con Mami Wata.

Noites de casamento com a mamã. O noviço é então levado para uma cabana às margens do rio, onde passará os próximos oito dias e noites. Nesta fase, seu casamento com Mami Wata acontece.

Huwelijksnachten met Mami. De novice wordt aansluitend naar een hut op de rivieroever gebracht, waar hij de komende acht dagen en nachten zal verblijven. In deze fase vindt zijn bruiloft met Mami Wata plaats.

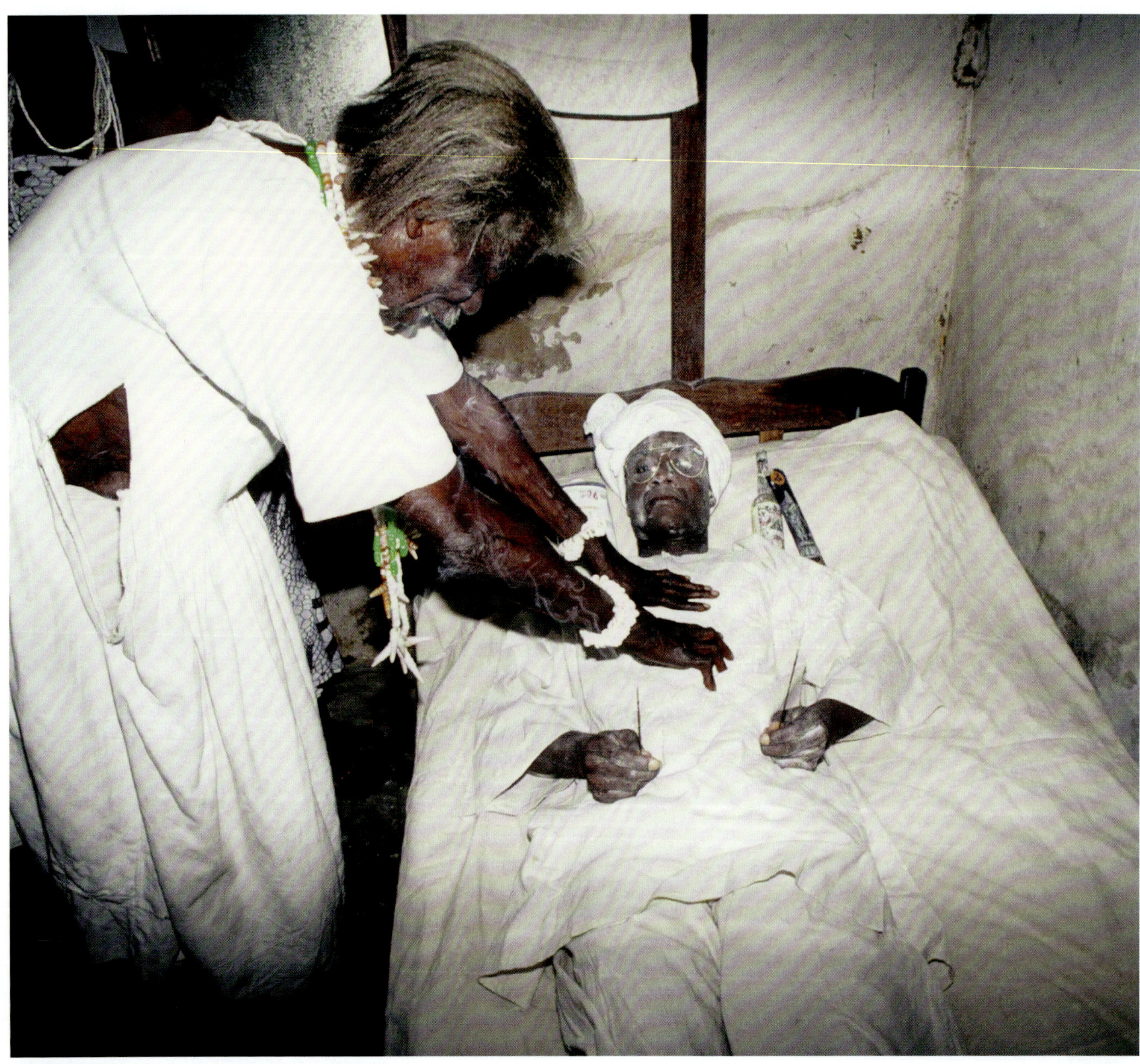

Final blessing

Bénédiction finale

Finale Segnung

Bendición final

Bênção final

Laatste zegen

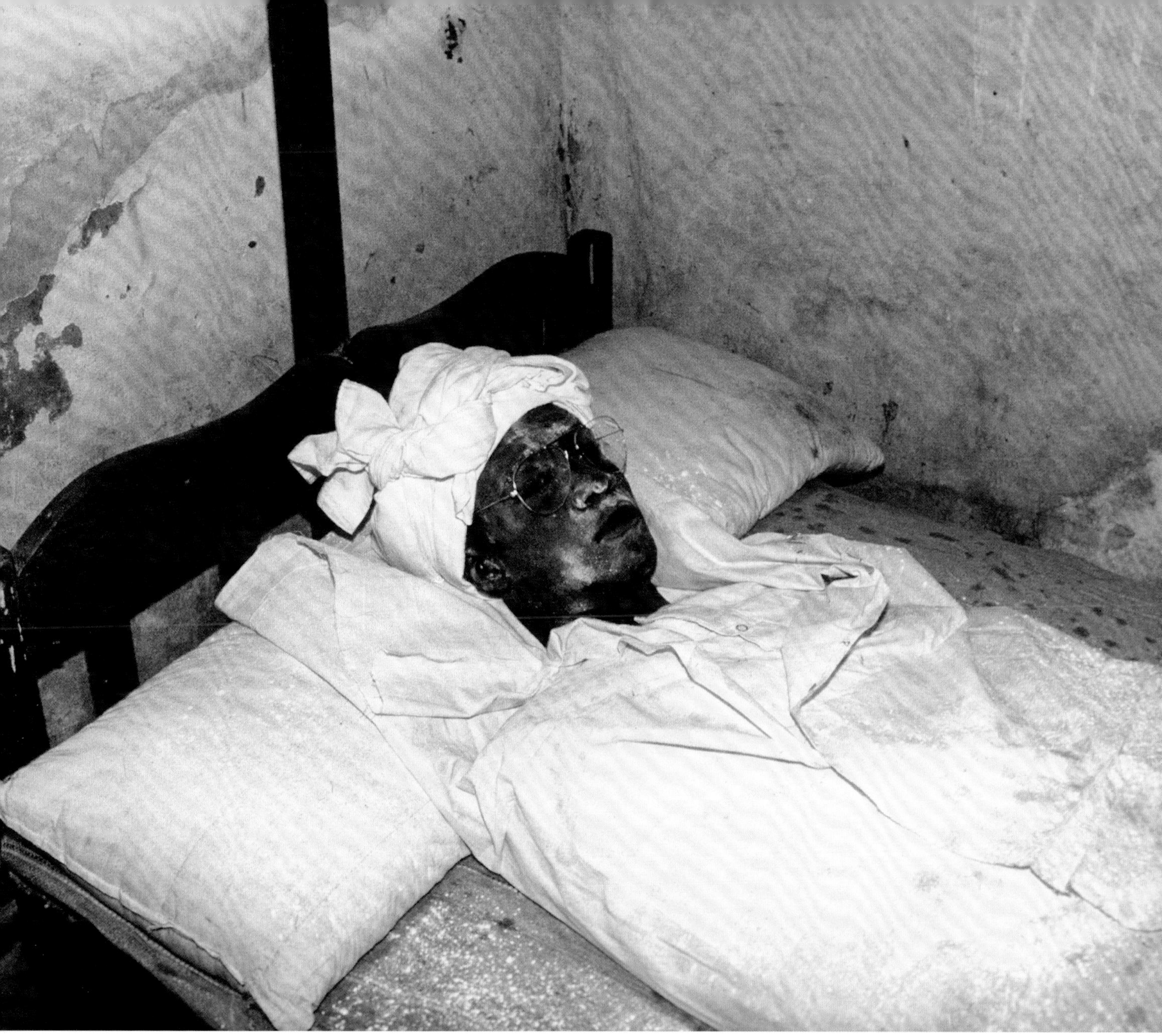

The journey to Mami Wata. In the dream the novice will now meet Mami, unite with her and live according to her commandments from now on.

Le voyage vers Mami Wata. Ce n'est qu'à ce moment que le novice va rencontrer en rêve Mami et s'unir à elle. Il vivra dorénavant selon ses commandements.

Die Reise zu Mami Wata. Im Traum wird der Novize nun Mami treffen, sich mit ihr vereinigen und fortan nach ihren Geboten leben.

El viaje a Mami Wata. En el sueño, el novicio se encontrará con Mami, se unirá a ella y vivirá de acuerdo a sus mandamientos.

A viagem a Mami Wata. No sonho, a noviça vai agora encontrar Mami, unir-se com ela e viver de acordo com os seus mandamentos.

De reis naar Mami Wata. In een droom zal de novice Mami ontmoeten, zich met haar verenigen en leven volgens haar geboden.

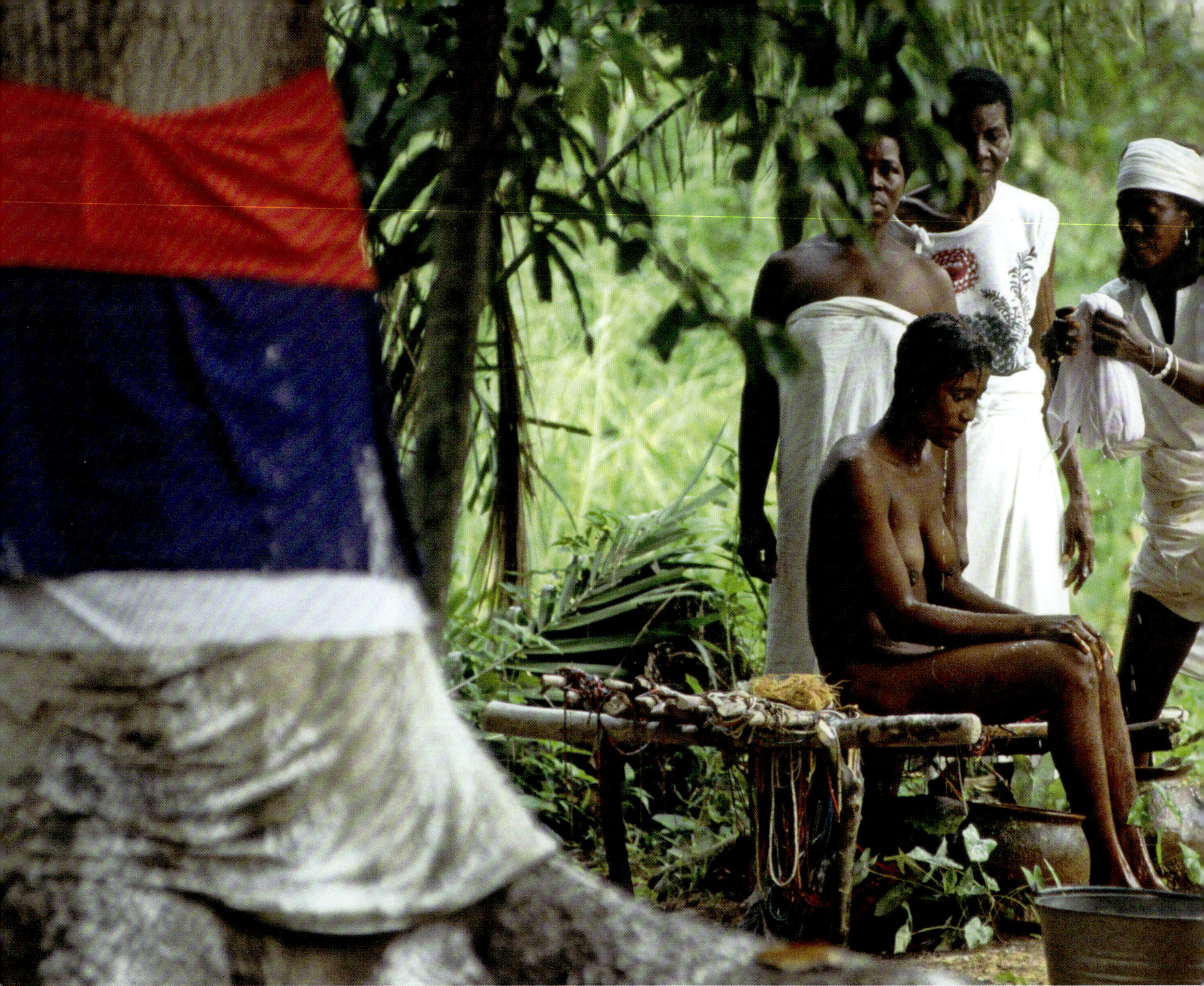

Mami Wata punishes the adulteress

A frequent offence in the social fabric
is adultery, which among her followers
results in Mami Wata depriving the guilty
person of her protection. It is enough
for dreams to arise in this direction or
for a woman to cook for someone other
than her husband. In these cases, the
punishment usually includes only shaving
the person's head and symbolic whip lashes

Mami Wata punit la femme adultère

Infraction courante aux structures sociales,
l'adultère entraîne chez les adeptes de
Mami Wata le retrait de sa protection sur
la personne fautive. Rêver d'un homme ou
cuisiner pour un autre homme que son mari
suffit. Dans ce cas, la punition implique
généralement uniquement un rasage de la
tête ou un fouettage symbolique avec un
rameau, avec des variations selon les régions.

Mami Wata straft die Ehebrecherin

Ein häufiges Vergehen im sozialen Gefüge
ist der Ehebruch, der bei den Anhängern
Mami Watas zur Folge hat, dass die Göttin
der schuldigen Person ihren Schutz entzieht.
Dabei reicht es schon, wenn Träume in
dieser Richtung auftreten oder eine Frau
für einen anderen als ihren Ehemann
kocht. In diesen Fällen beinhaltet die Strafe
meist nur ein Kahlscheren des Kopfes

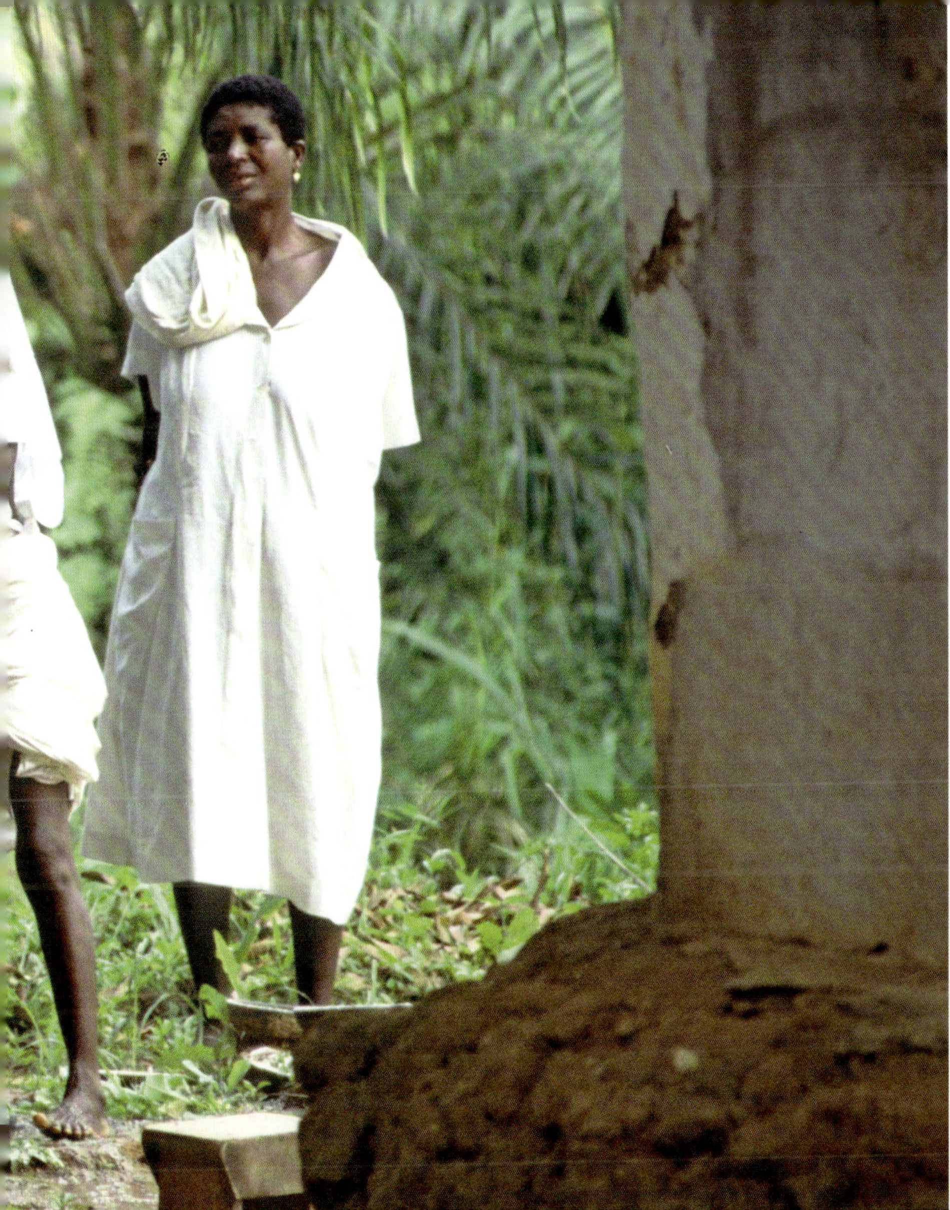

Ritual purification of a devotee who in a trance accused herself of adultery

Purification rituelle d'une adepte qui, en transe, s'est accusée d'adultère

Rituelle Reinigung einer Anhängerin, die sich in Trance selbst des Ehebruchs bezichtigt hat

Purificación ritual de una devota que en trance se acusa de adulterio

Purificação ritual de um devoto que, em transe, se acusou de adultério

Rituele zuivering van een aanhangster die zich in trance zelf beschuldigd heeft van overspel

Mami Wata castiga a la adúltera

Un delito frecuente en el tejido social es el adulterio, que hace que los seguidores de Mami Wata hagan que la diosa prive a la persona culpable de su protección. Basta con que los sueños surjan en esta dirección o que una mujer cocine para alguien que no sea su marido. En estos casos, el castigo suele incluir sólo un tijereteo de la cabeza y latigazos

Mami Wata castiga a adúltera

Uma ofensa frequente no tecido social é o adultério, que faz com que os seguidores de Mami Wata tenham a deusa de privar a pessoa culpada de sua proteção. Basta que os sonhos surjam nesta direcção ou que uma mulher cozinhe para alguém que não seja o seu marido. Nestes casos, a punição geralmente inclui apenas uma tesoura da cabeça e cílios chicote simbólico com

Mami Wata straft de echtbreekster

Een veelvoorkomende overtreding in het maatschappelijke stelsel is overspel, wat er bij de aanhangers van Mami Wata toe leidt dat de godin de schuldige niet langer beschermt. Het is genoeg als er dromen in deze richting opduiken of als een vrouw voor een man kookt die niet haar eigen man is. In deze gevallen omvat de straf meestal alleen het kaalscheren van het hoofd en

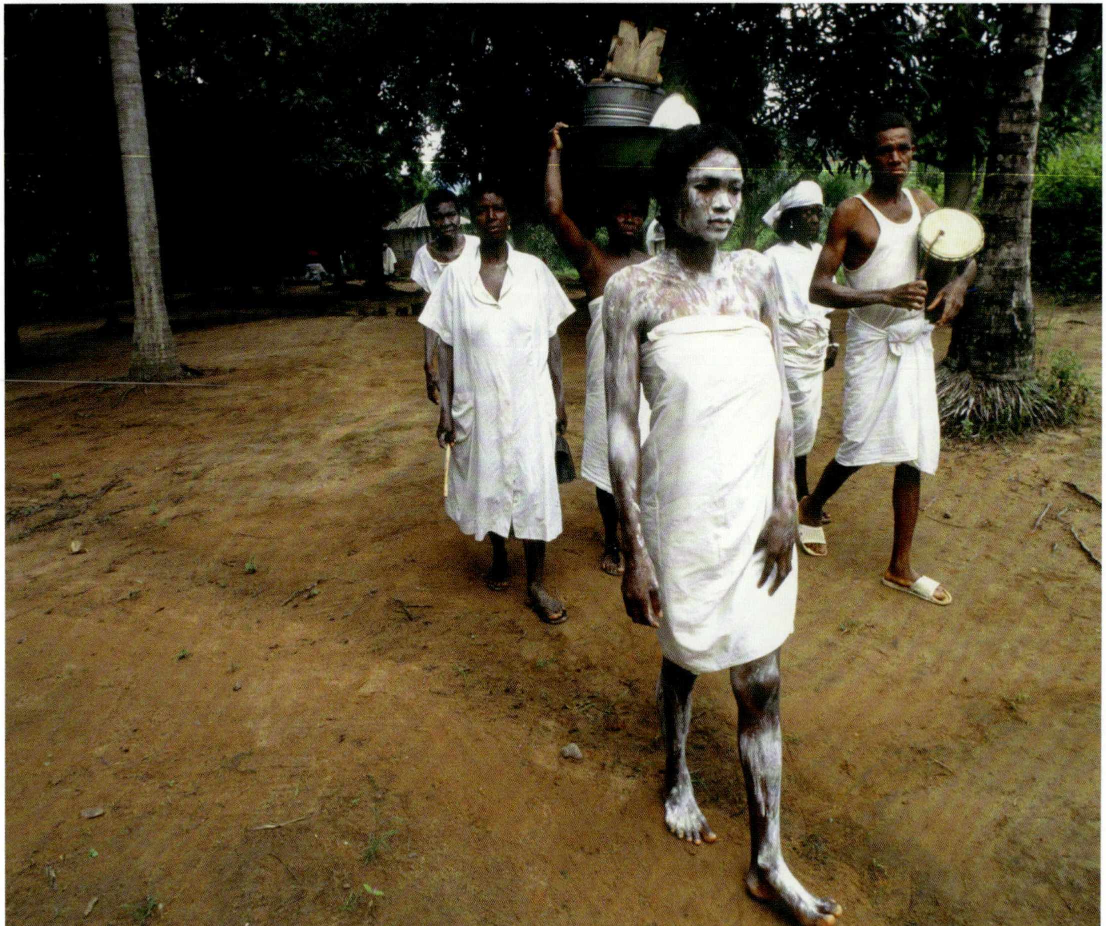

with a branch, but this can vary, depending on the region.

Often the goddess asks the adulteress to offer a ram as a blood sacrifice after a ritual purification. Precise instructions only arise when initiates of Mami Wata fall into a trance in a ceremonial setting and then, as the mouthpiece of the goddess, announce what is to be done in the individual case.

The convicted rival must also do penance: He pays a certain sum to the husband and for an animal sacrifice for the ancestors.

Souvent, la déesse réclame à la femme adultère un bélier qui, après un lavage rituel, est saigné en sacrifice. Les consignes précises sont données par la suite : lorsque les adeptes de Mami Wata tombent en transe dans le cadre cérémoniel, elles deviennent porte-parole de la déesse et expriment ce qui doit être fait dans ce cas précis.

Le rival condamné doit également se repentir : il paie à l'époux une somme spécifique et offre aux aïeux un animal sacrifié.

und symbolische Peitschenschläge mit einem Zweig, was aber je nach Region variieren kann.

Oft verlangt die Göttin von der Ehebrecherin einen Widder, der nach einer rituellen Reinigung als Blutopfer darzubringen ist. Genaue Anweisungen ergeben sich erst, wenn Adeptinnen Mami Watas im zeremoniellen Rahmen in Trance fallen und dann als Sprachrohr der Göttin verkünden, was im individuellen Fall zu tun ist.

Auch der überführte Nebenbuhler muss büßen: Er bezahlt eine bestimmte Summe an den Ehemann und ein Tieropfer für die Ahnen.

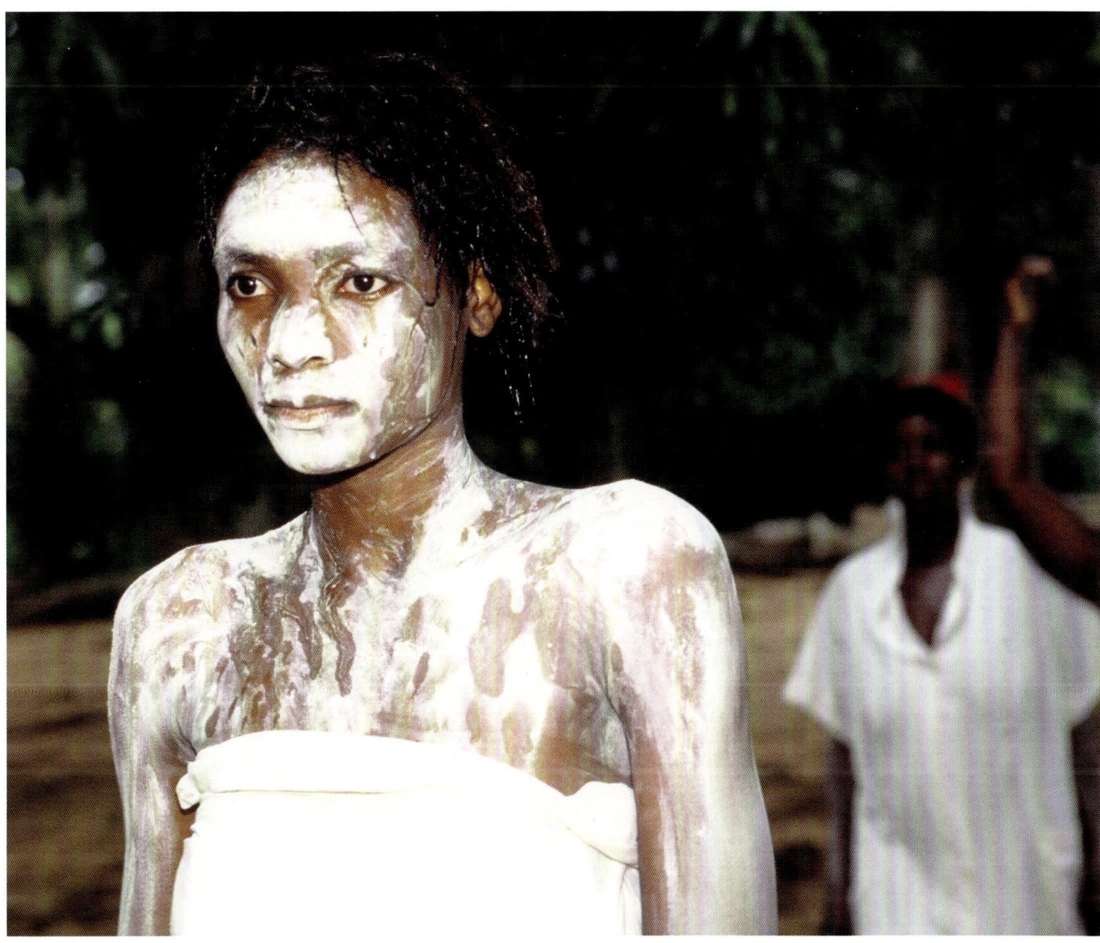

simbólicos con una rama, que pueden variar según la región.

A menudo la diosa le pide a la adúltera que ofrezca un carnero como sacrificio de sangre después de una purificación ritual. Sólo se dan instrucciones precisas cuando los adeptos de Mami Wata entran en trance en un ambiente ceremonial y luego anuncian como portavoz de la diosa lo que hay que hacer en el caso individual.

El rival también debe arrepentirse: paga una cierta suma al marido y un sacrificio de animales por los antepasados.

um ramo, que pode variar dependendo da região.

Muitas vezes a deusa pede à adúltera que ofereça um carneiro como sacrifício de sangue após uma purificação ritual. Instruções precisas só são dadas quando os adeptos Mami Watas caem em transe em um ambiente cerimonial e então anunciam como porta-voz da deusa o que deve ser feito no caso individual.

O rival transferido deve também arrepender-se: Ele paga uma certa quantia ao marido e um sacrifício animal pelos antepassados.

symbolische zweepslagen met een tak. Dit verschilt per regio.

Vaak verlangt de godin van de echtbreekster een ram, die na een rituele zuivering als bloedoffer wordt aangeboden. Exacte instructies worden pas gegeven als aanhangsters van Mami Wata in een ceremoniële setting in trance raken en dan als spreekbuis van de godin aankondigen wat er in het individuele geval moet gebeuren.

De voorgeleide medeminnaar moet ook boeten: hij betaalt een bepaald bedrag aan de echtgenoot en een dierlijk offer voor de voorouders.

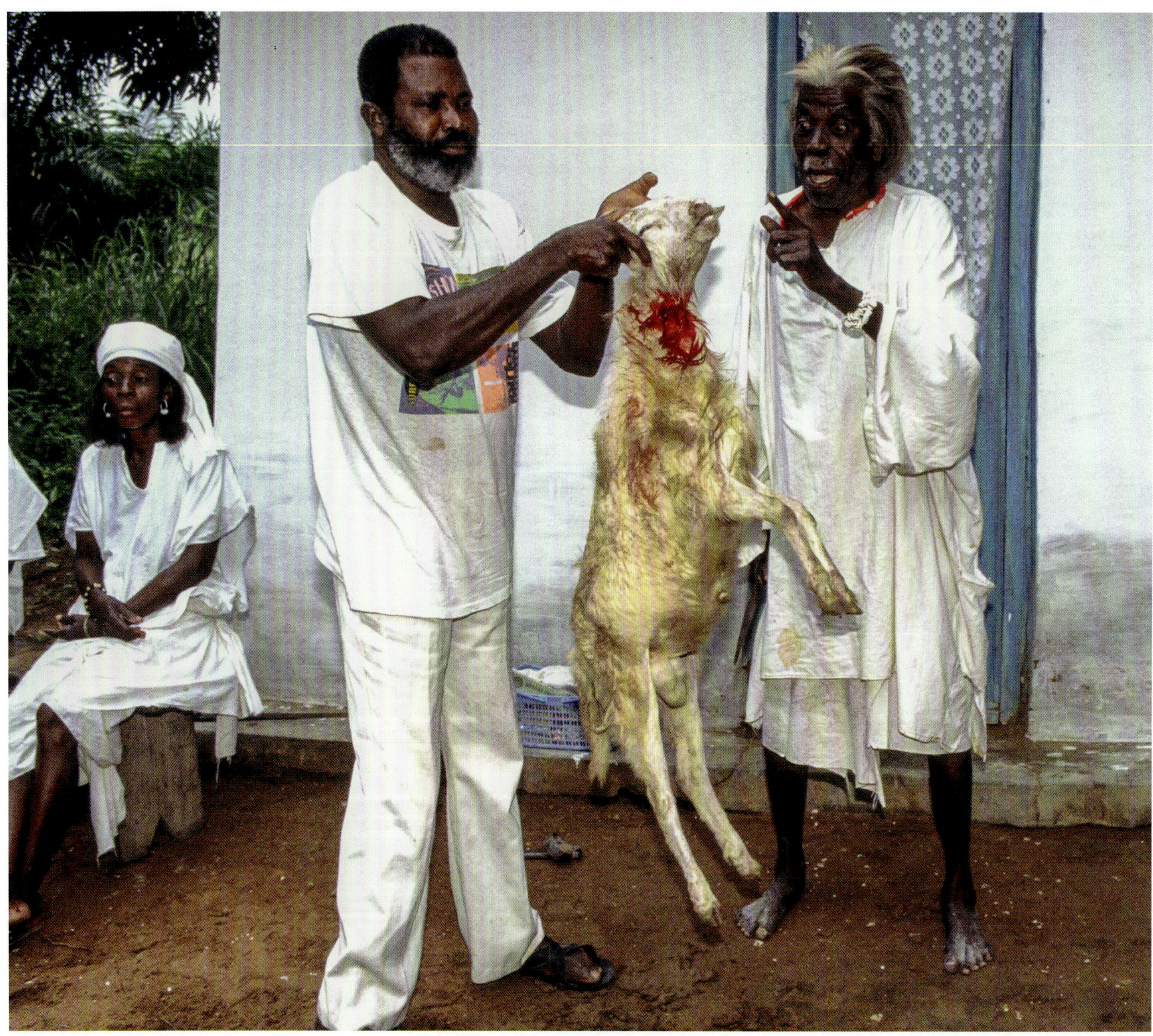

A sacrifice for reconciliation. To reconcile the goddess, the adulteress must donate a ram, which is ritually sacrificed by Abidjan Mami Wata. The priest asks the goddess for clemency with her daughter.

Victime de la réconciliation. Afin de se réconcilier avec la déesse, l'épouse adultère doit offrir un bélier, qui est sacrifié rituellement par Abidjan Mami Wata. Le prêtre demande à la déesse d'être indulgente envers sa protégée.

Das Versöhnungsopfer. Zur Versöhnung der Göttin muss die Ehebrecherin einen Widder stiften, der von Abidjan Mami Wata rituell geopfert wird. Der Priester bittet die Göttin um Milde mit ihrer Tochter.

La víctima de la reconciliación. Para reconciliar a la diosa, la adúltera debe donar un carnero, que es sacrificado ritualmente por Abidjan Mami Wata. El sacerdote le pide a la diosa clemencia con su hija.

A vítima da reconciliação. Para reconciliar a deusa, a adúltera deve doar um carneiro, que é ritualmente sacrificado por Abidjan Mami Wata. O padre pede clemência à deusa com a sua filha.

Het verzoeningsoffer. Om vrede te sluiten met de godin moet de echtbreekster een ram schenken, die ritueel wordt geofferd door Abidjan Mami Wata. De priester vraagt de godin om clementie met haar dochter.

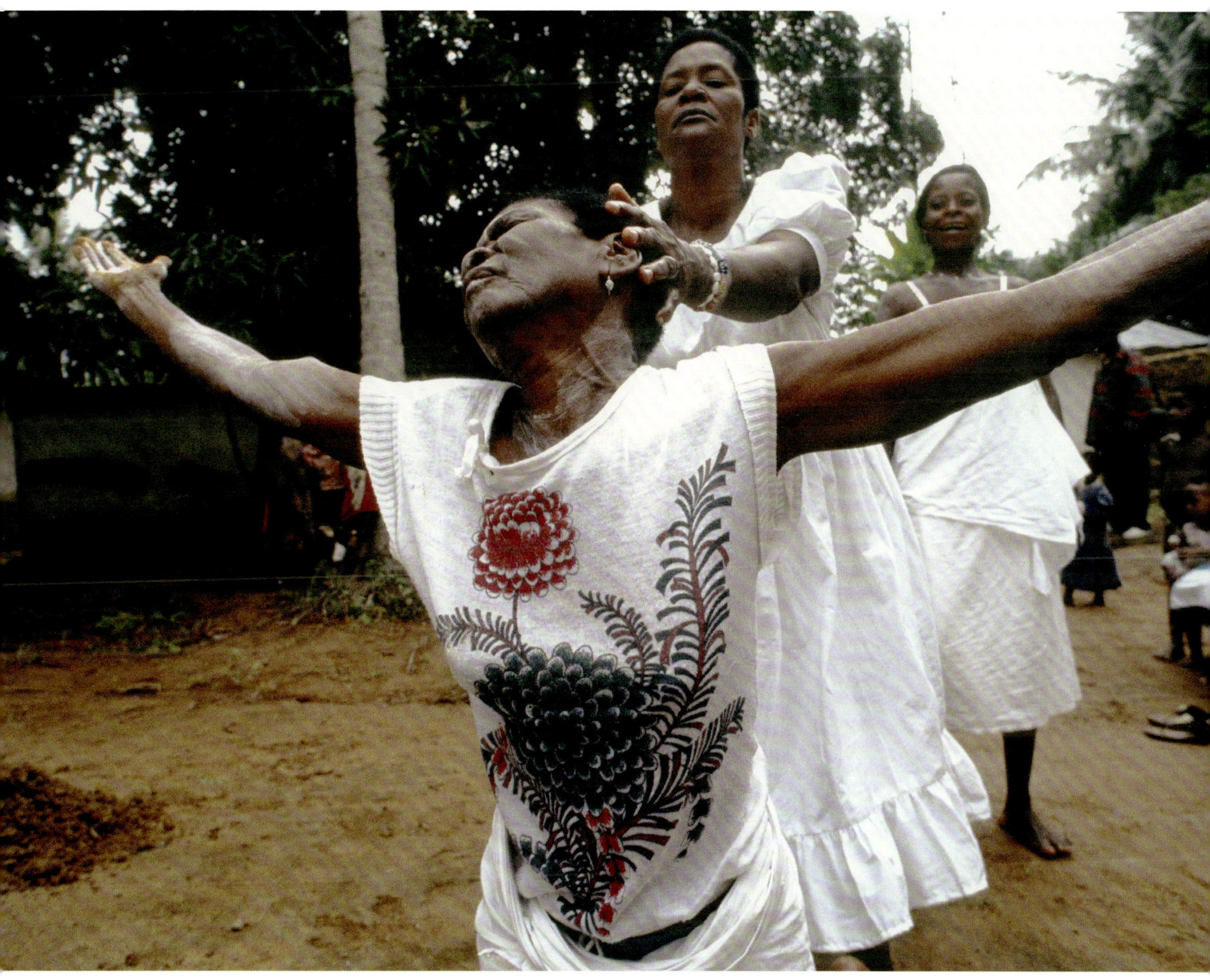

The medium speaks

Le médium parle

Das Medium spricht

El médium habla

O médium fala

Het medium spreekt

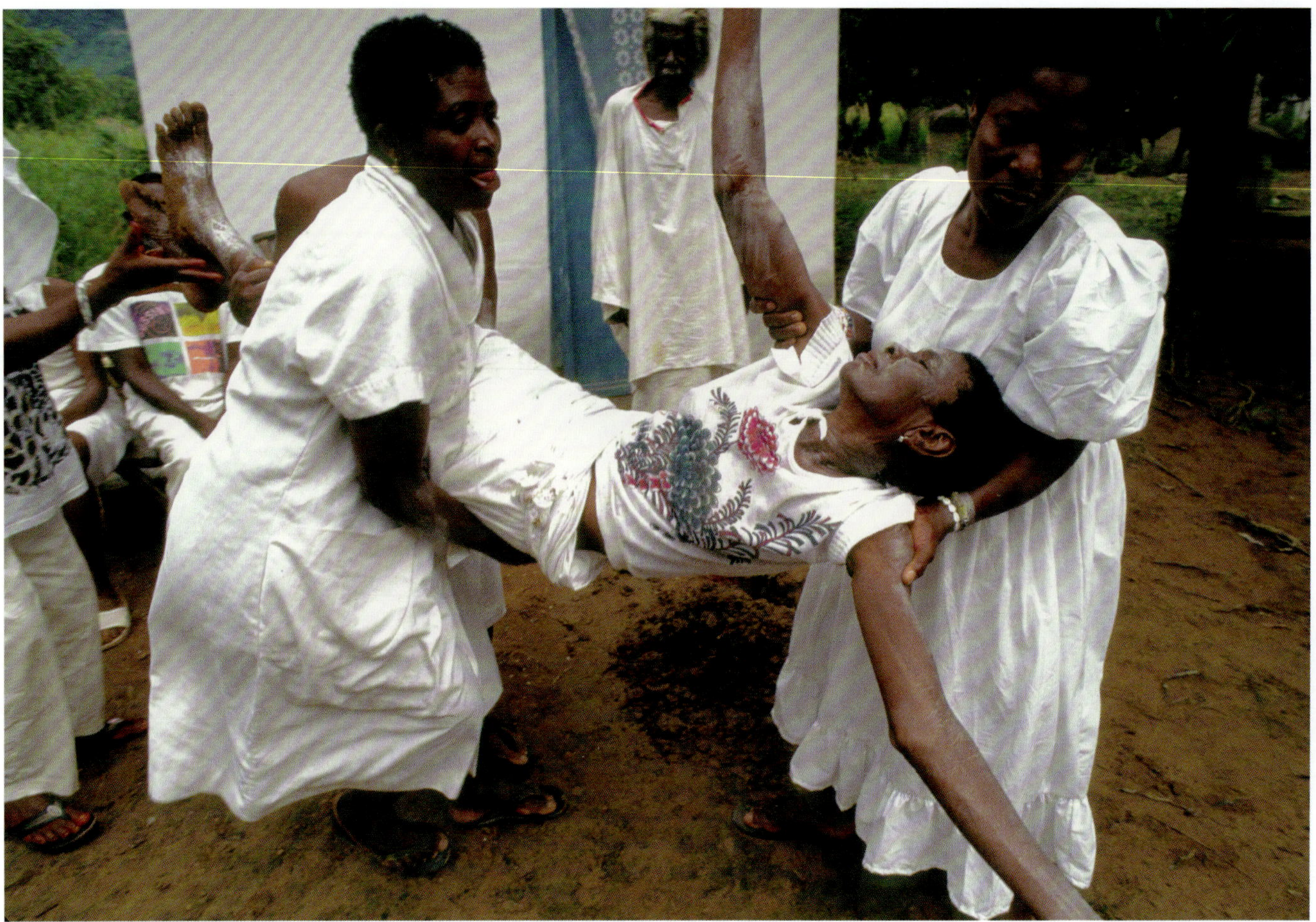

Collapsing from exhaustion. At the end of the trance, the medium who has made his body available to the goddess for the period of the trance, collapses exhausted.

Effondrement d'épuisement. La médium s'écroule de fatigue, car son corps a été mis à disposition de la déesse pendant le temps de la transe.

Erschöpfter Zusammenbruch. Am Ende der Trance bricht das Medium, das seinen Körper für den Zeitraum der Trance der Göttin zur Verfügung gestellt hat, erschöpft zusammen.

Colapso agotador. Al final del trance, el médium que ha puesto su cuerpo a disposición de la diosa durante el trance se descompone exhausto.

Colapso exausto. No final do transe, o médium que disponibilizou seu corpo para a deusa durante a duração do transe quebra-se exausto.

Uitgeput ineengezakt. Aan het einde van de trance stort het medium dat zijn lichaam voor de duur van de trance ter beschikking van de godin heeft gesteld, uitgeput neer.

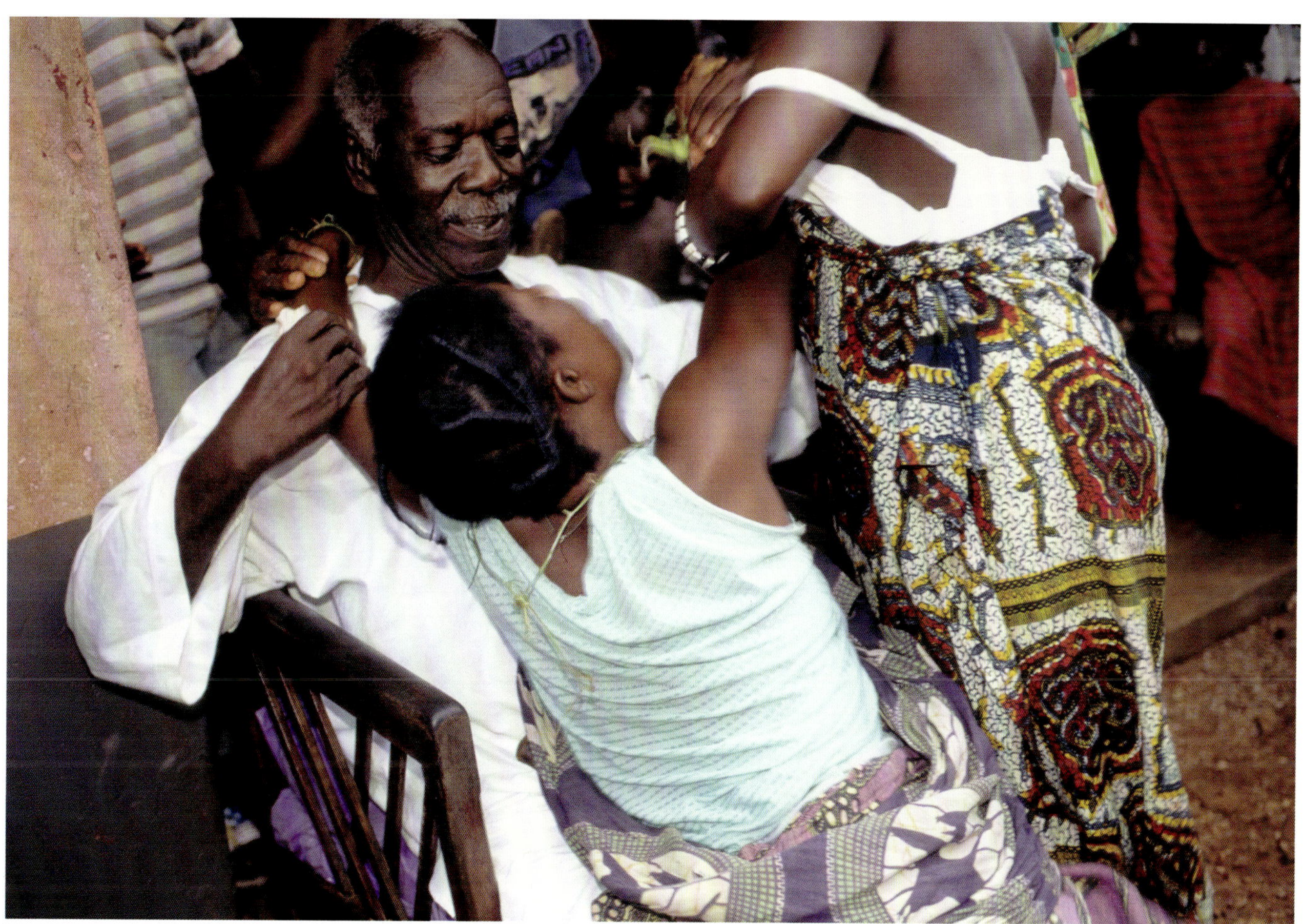

Medium in a trance

Médium en transe

Medium in Trance

Médium en trance

Médio em Trance

Medium in trance

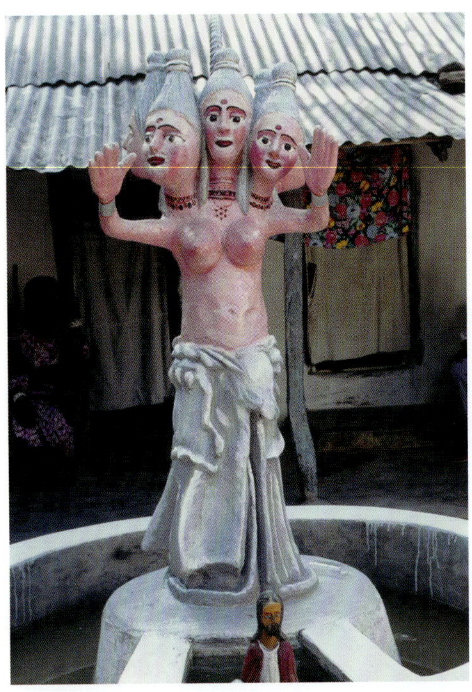

Abidjan Mami Wata

His birth name is just like his first life in the past—at that time, in the early eighties, Abidjan Mami Wata, a Vodun priest born in southern Ghana, was a simple laborer who often worked on the Ivory Coast.

One day, in Abidjan, the capital at that time, he experienced strong visions in which Mami Wata appeared to him and told him to become her faithful servant and follower. Should he follow this, the divine apparition proclaimed, he would be rewarded with the knowledge of secret medicinal plants and their application.

He quickly changed his name and went back to Ghana, where he built a place of worship for Mami Wata in his home village, which grew bigger and bigger over the years. In the end the village was called "Mami Wata Village" and the reputation of the priest Abidjan, a knowledgeable, learned healer, increased with each successful treatment.

Abidjan Mami Wata

Son nom de naissance est tombé dans l'oubli, tout comme sa première vie. Au début des années 1980, le prêtre vodun Abidjan Mami Wata, né au Sud-Ghana, était un simple ouvrier souvent employé en Côte d'Ivoire.

C'est là, dans l'ancienne capitale Abidjan, qu'il fut un jour frappé de puissantes visions dans lesquelles Mami Wata lui apparut et lui demanda de devenir un serviteur et adepte fidèle. En échange, l'apparition divine lui annonça qu'il serait récompensé par la connaissance des propriétés des plantes médicinales secrètes et de leur emploi.

L'homme changea rapidement de nom et revint au Ghana, dans son village natal, où il érigea un culte à Mami Wata, qui se développa au fil des ans. Finalement, le village fut surnommé le « village de Mami Wata » et la renommée du prêtre Abidjan, en tant que sage et guérisseur érudit, s'accrut à mesure que ses traitements réussissaient.

Abidjan Mami Wata

Sein Geburtsname liegt ebenso wie sein erstes Leben in der Vergangenheit – damals, in den frühen Achtzigerjahren, war der in Südghana gebürtige Vodunpriester Abidjan Mami Wata einfacher Hilfsarbeiter, der oft an der Elfenbeinküste arbeitet.

Dort bekam er in der damaligen Hauptstadt Abidjan eines Tages heftige Visionen, in denen ihm Mami Wata erschien und auftrug, ihr treuer Diener und Anhänger zu werden. Sollte er dem folgen, so verkündete die göttliche Erscheinung, würde er mit dem Wissen um geheime Heilpflanzen und deren Anwendung belohnt.

Er änderte kurzerhand seinen Namen und ging zurück nach Ghana, wo er in seinem Heimatdorf eine Kultstätte für Mami Wata errichtete, die mit den Jahren immer größer wurde. Am Ende hieß das Dorf „Mami Wata Village" und der Ruf des Priesters Abidjan, ein Wissender, ein gelehrter Heiler zu sein, potenzierte sich mit jeder erfolgreichen Behandlung.

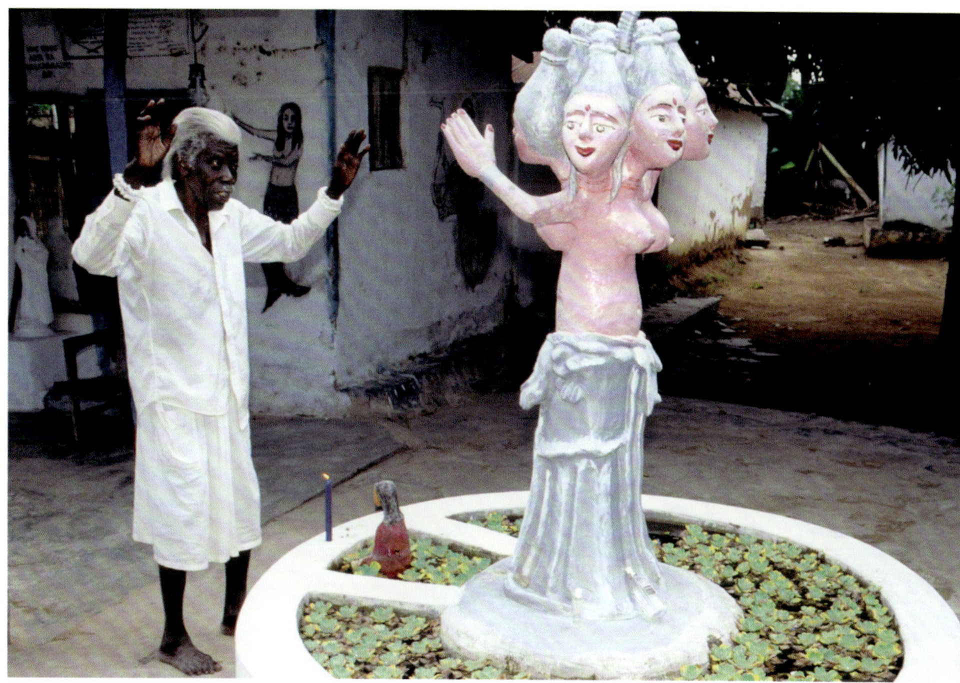

Abidjan Mami Wata

Su nombre de nacimiento es como su primera vida en el pasado– en esa época, a principios de los ochenta, Abidjan Mami Wata, un sacerdote vudú nacido en el sur de Ghana, era un simple trabajador que a menudo trabajaba en Costa de Marfil.

Un día, en Abidjan, la capital de Costa de Marfil en ese momento, tuvo visiones feroces en las que Mami Wata se le apareció y le dijo que se convirtiera en su fiel sirviente y seguidor. Si seguía sus instrucciones, se anunciaría la aparición divina y sería recompensado con el conocimiento de las plantas medicinales secretas y su aplicación.

Rápidamente cambió su nombre y regresó a Ghana, donde construyó un lugar de adoración para Mami Wata en su pueblo natal, que se hizo cada vez más grande con el paso de los años. Al final, la aldea fue llamada "Aldea Mami Wata" y la reputación del sacerdote Abidjan, un curandero culto y conocedor, aumentó con cada tratamiento exitoso.

Abidjan Mami Wata

O seu nome de nascimento é exactamente como a sua primeira vida no passado – nessa altura, no início dos anos oitenta, Abidjan Mami Wata, um padre vodu nascido no sul do Gana, era um simples trabalhador que trabalhava frequentemente na Costa do Marfim.

Um dia, em Abidjan, então capital da Costa do Marfim, ele teve visões ferozes, nas quais Mami Wata lhe apareceu e lhe disse para se tornar sua fiel serva e seguidora. Se ele seguir isto, a aparição divina anunciada, ele será recompensado com o conhecimento de plantas medicinais secretas e sua aplicação.

Ele rapidamente mudou seu nome e voltou para Gana, onde construiu um lugar de culto para Mami Wata em seu vilarejo natal, que cresceu cada vez mais e mais ao longo dos anos. No final, a aldeia foi chamada "Vila Mami Wata" e a reputação do padre Abidjan, um curandeiro conhecedor e instruído, aumentou com cada tratamento bem sucedido.

Abidjan Mami Wata

Zijn geboortenaam ligt net als zijn eerste leven in het verleden – in die tijd, begin jaren tachtig, was Abidjan Mami Wata, een in Zuid-Ghana geboren vodunpriester, een eenvoudige arbeider die vaak in Ivoorkust werkte.

Op een dag kreeg hij in Abidjan, de toenmalige hoofdstad van Ivoorkust, hevige visioenen waarin Mami Wata aan hem verscheen en hem opdroeg haar trouwe dienaar en volgeling te worden. Mocht hij haar volgen, zo kondigde de goddelijke verschijning aan, dan zou hij beloond worden met de kennis van geheime geneeskrachtige planten en hun toepassing.

Hij veranderde resoluut zijn naam en ging terug naar Ghana, waar hij een offerplaats voor Mami Wata oprichtte in zijn geboortedorp, die in de loop der jaren steeds groter werd. Uiteindelijk werd het dorp 'Mami Wata Village' genoemd en de reputatie van priester Abidjan als goed geïnformeerde, geleerde genezer nam met elke succesvolle behandeling toe.

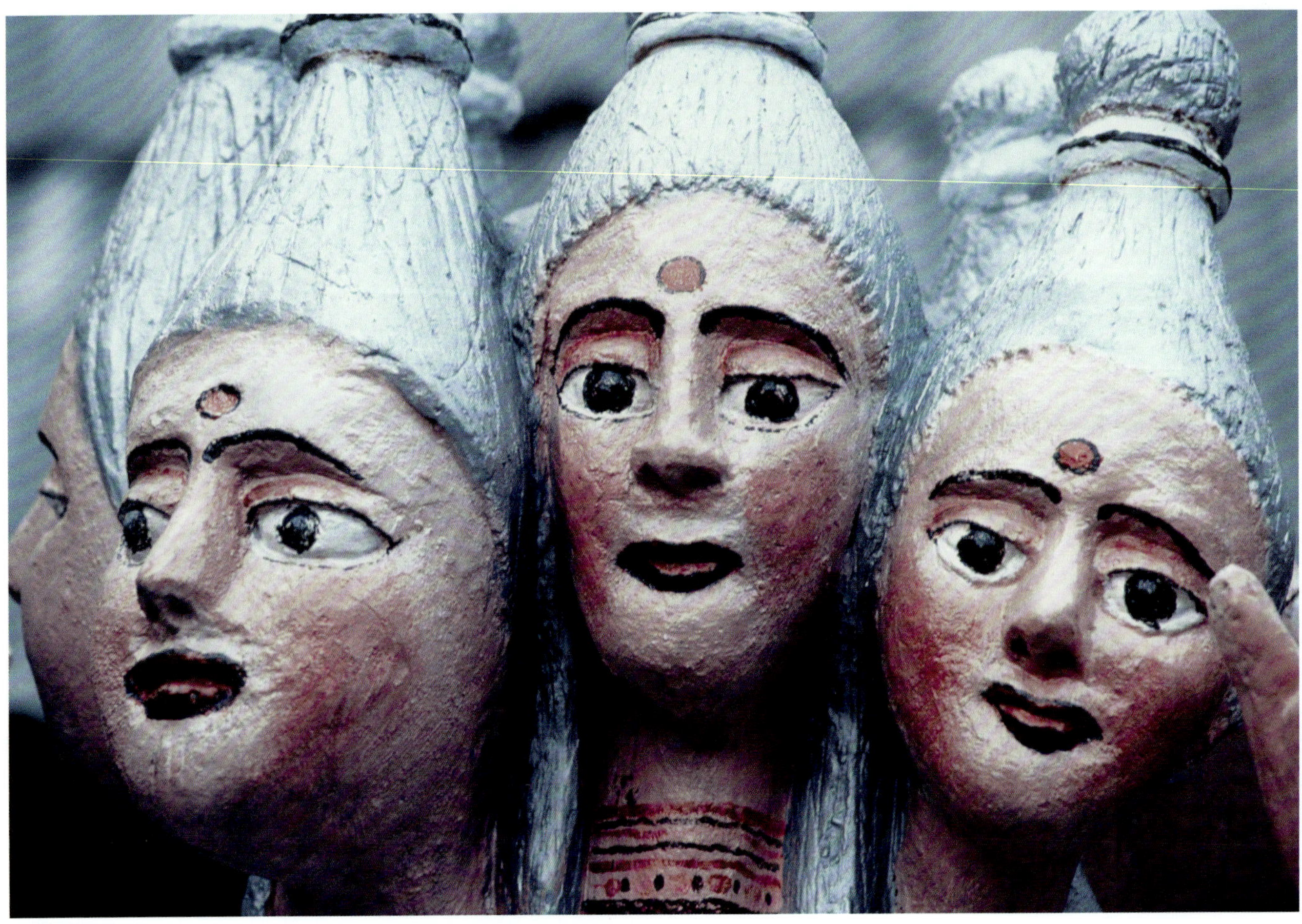

Mami Wata in cement. Indian foreign workers, who were employed by the colonial powers as track builders, brought portraits of their Hindu gods to Africa. These were integrated and regarded as a gain.

Mami Wata en ciment. Les travailleurs indiens employés par les colonisateurs à la construction des voies ferrées importèrent des représentations des divinités hindoues en Afrique. Elles furent intégrées à la culture locale.

Mami Wata in Zement. Indische Gastarbeiter, die von den Kolonialmächten als Gleisbauarbeiter eingesetzt wurden, brachten Bildnisse ihrer Hindugötter nach Afrika. Diese wurden integriert und als Zugewinn verstanden.

Mami Wata en cemento. Los trabajadores invitados indios, que fueron utilizados por las potencias coloniales como constructores de caminos, trajeron retratos de sus dioses hindúes a África. Éstos se integraron y se entendieron como una ganancia.

Mami Wata em cimento. Trabalhadores convidados indianos, que foram usados pelas potências coloniais como construtores de trilhos, trouxeram retratos de seus deuses hindus para a África. Estes foram integrados e entendidos como um ganho.

Mami Wata van cement. Indiase gastarbeiders, die door de koloniale mogendheden werden ingezet als spoorwegbouwers, brachten afbeeldingen van hun hindoegoden naar Afrika. Deze werden geïntegreerd en opgevat als aanwinst.

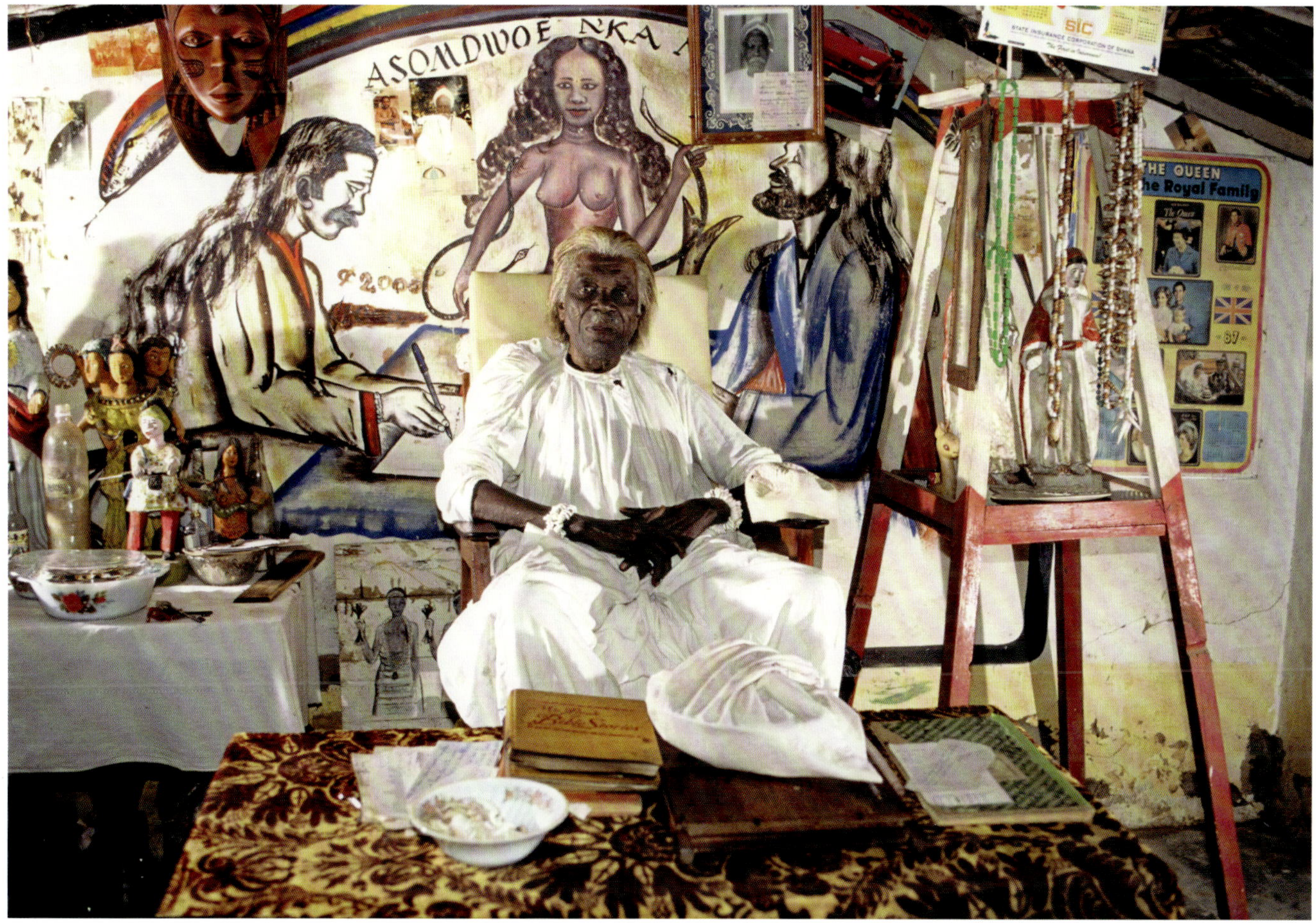

The priest Abidjan Mami Wata. The priest in his sanctuary. The wall behind him is richly decorated with images that have a direct relation to Mami Wata and the events in the monastery.

Le prêtre Abidjan Mami Wata. Le prêtre dans la salle de son autel. Les murs derrière lui sont richement ornés de représentations directement associées à Mami Wata et aux événements qui se déroulent dans le monastère.

Der Priester Abidjan Mami Wata. Der Priester in seinem Altarraum. Die Wand hinter ihm ist reich geschmückt mit Bildnissen, die einen unmittelbaren Bezug zu Mami Wata und dem Geschehen im Kloster haben.

El sacerdote Abidjan Mami Wata. El sacerdote en su santuario. La pared detrás de él está decorada con retratos que tienen una relación directa con Mami Wata y los acontecimientos del monasterio.

O sacerdote Abidjan Mami Wata. O padre no seu santuário. O muro atrás dele é ricamente decorado com retratos que têm uma relação direta com Mami Wata e os eventos no mosteiro.

De priester Abidjan Mami Wata. De priester in zijn altaarruimte. De muur achter hem is versierd met voorstellingen die een directe relatie hebben met Mami Wata en de gebeurtenissen in het klooster.

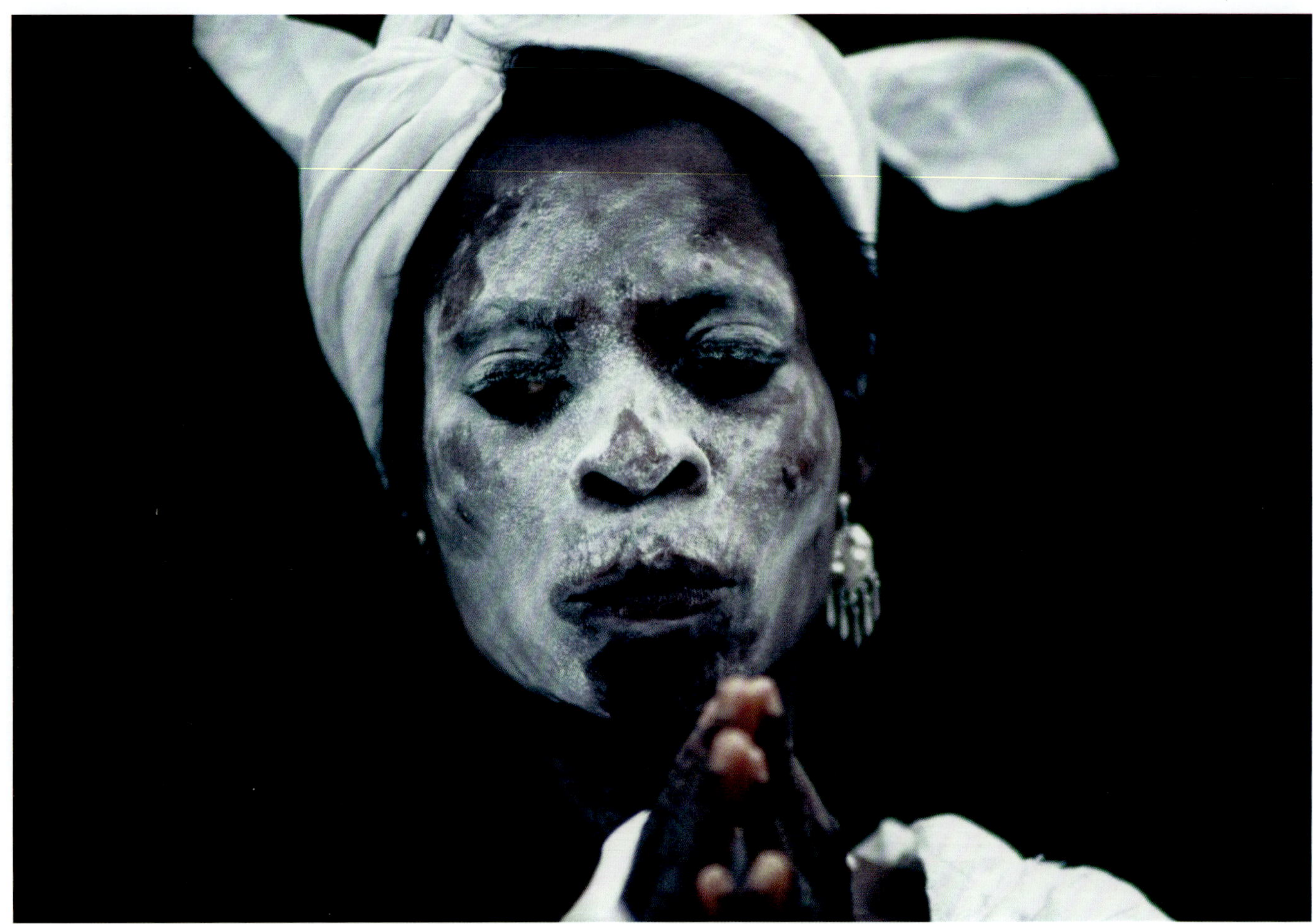

Mami Wata adept in a trance

Adepte de Mami Wata en transe

Mami Wata Adeptin in Trance

Adepta de Mami Wata en trance

Mami Wata Adeptin em Trance

Aanhangster van Mami Wata in trance

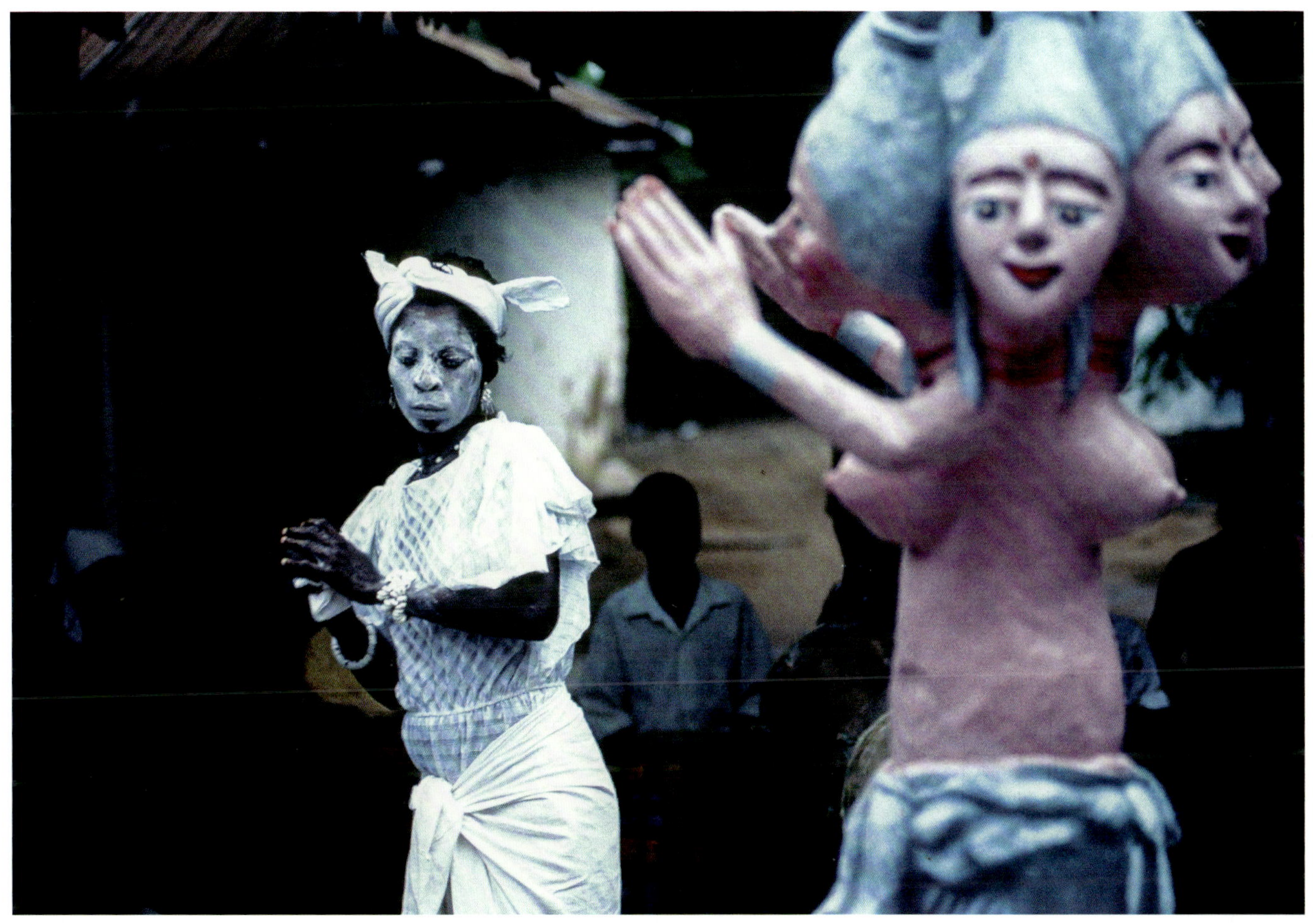

Mami Wata adept in a trance

Adepte de Mami Wata en transe

Mami Wata Adeptin in Trance

Adepta de Mami Wata en trance

Mami Wata Adeptin em Trance

Aanhangster van Mami Wata in trance

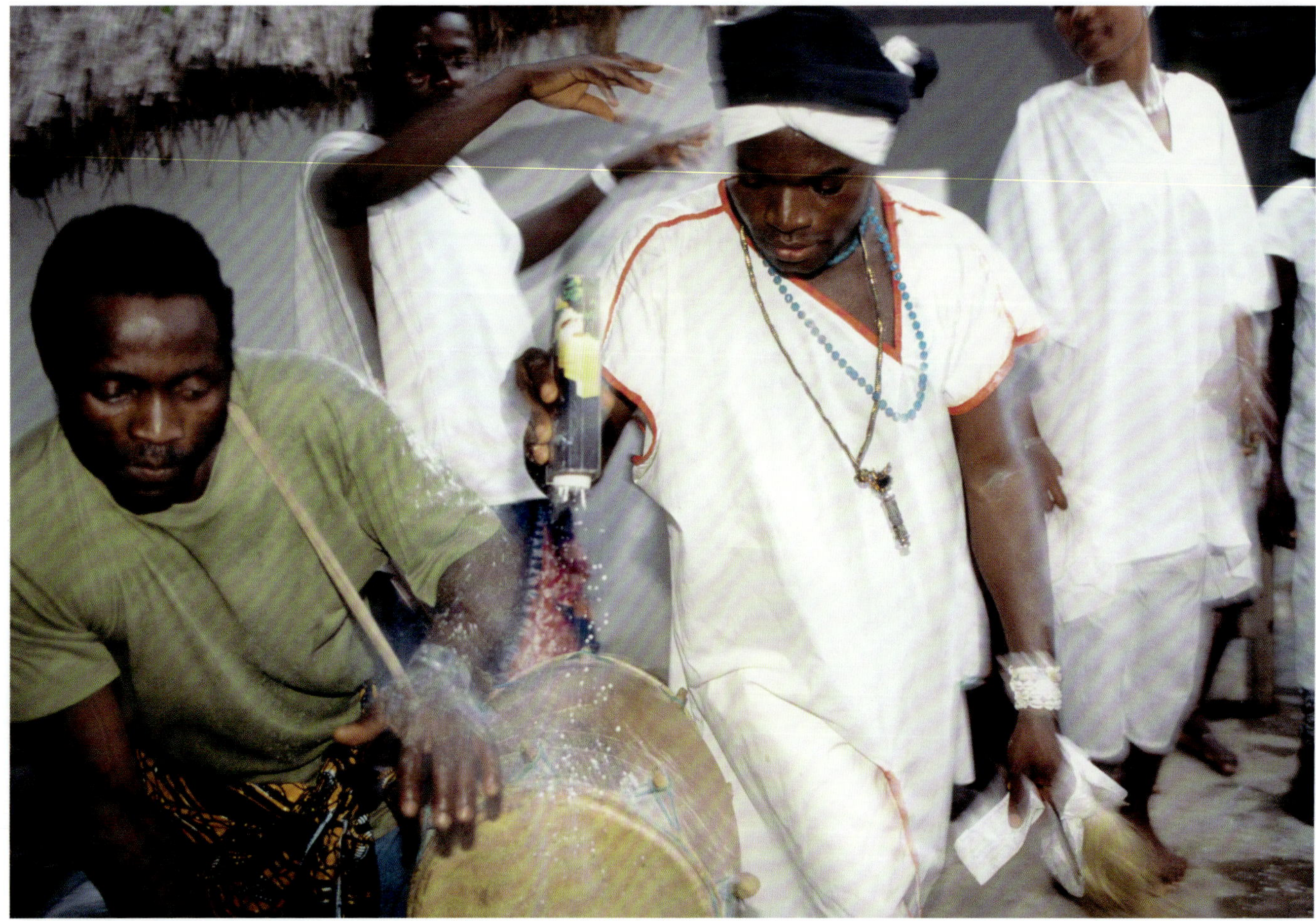

Applying powder to the drum. Mami Wata appreciates fragrances and fine accessories. An assistant of the priest therefore powders the ritual drum with perfumed talcum.

Poudrage du tambour. Mami Wata apprécie les parfums et les beaux accessoires. Un assistant du prêtre poudre le tambour du rituel de talc parfumé.

Pudern der Trommel. Mami Wata schätzt Wohlgerüche und feine Accessoires. Ein Gehilfe des Priesters pudert daher die Ritualtrommel mit parfümiertem Talkum.

Empolvando el tambor. Mami Wata aprecia las fragancias y los accesorios finos. Un asistente del sacerdote empolva el tambor del ritual con talco perfumado.

Pulverizando o tambor. Mami Wata aprecia fragrâncias e acessórios finos. Um assistente do padre pinta o tambor ritual com talco perfumado.

Poederen van de trommel. Mami Wata houdt van lekkere geuren en fijne accessoires. Een assistent van de priester bestrooit de rituele trommel daarom met geparfumeerd talkpoeder.

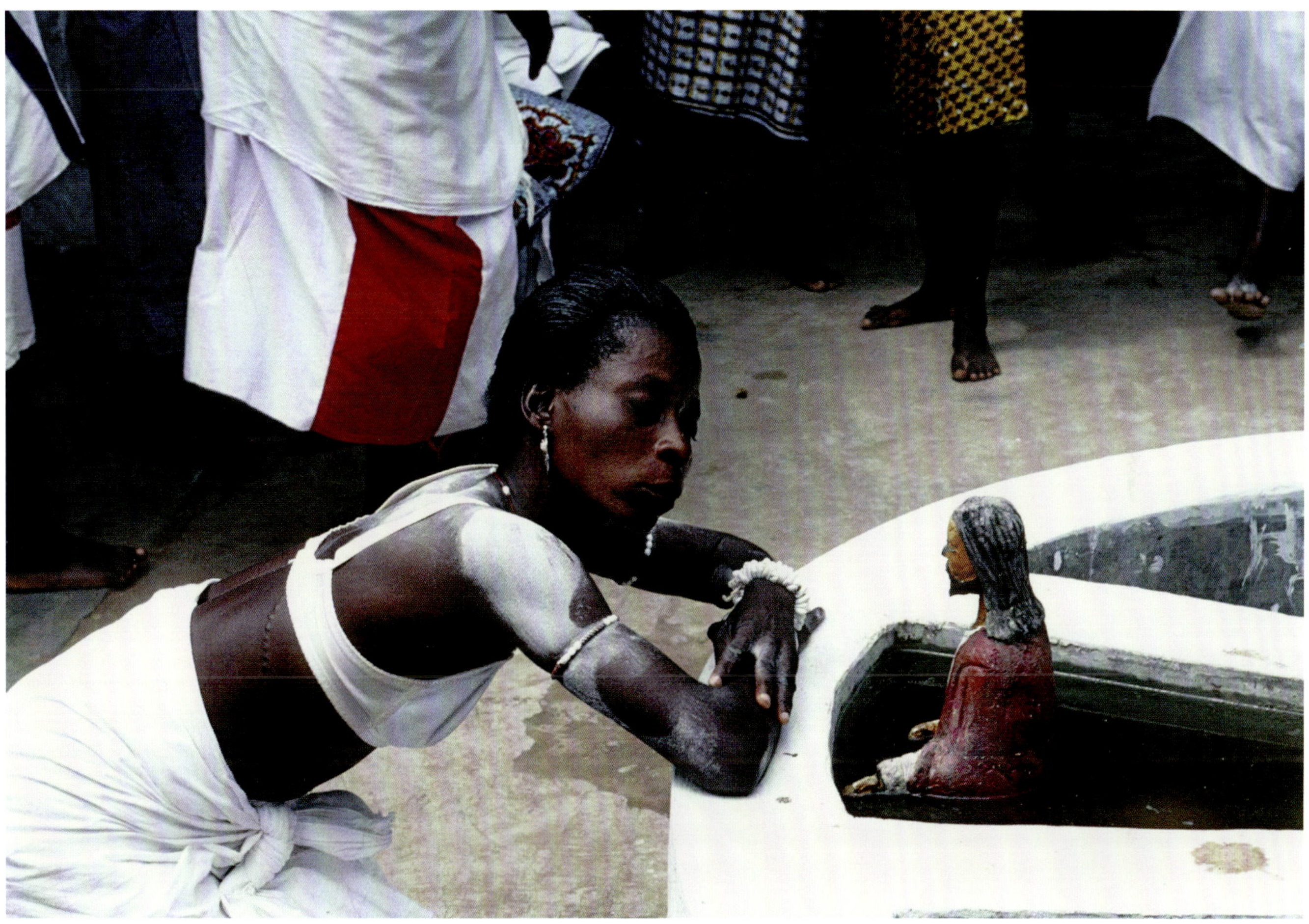

Dialog with the gods

Dialogue avec les dieux

Zwiegespräch mit den Göttern

Diálogo con los dioses

Diálogo com os Deuses

Dialoog met de goden

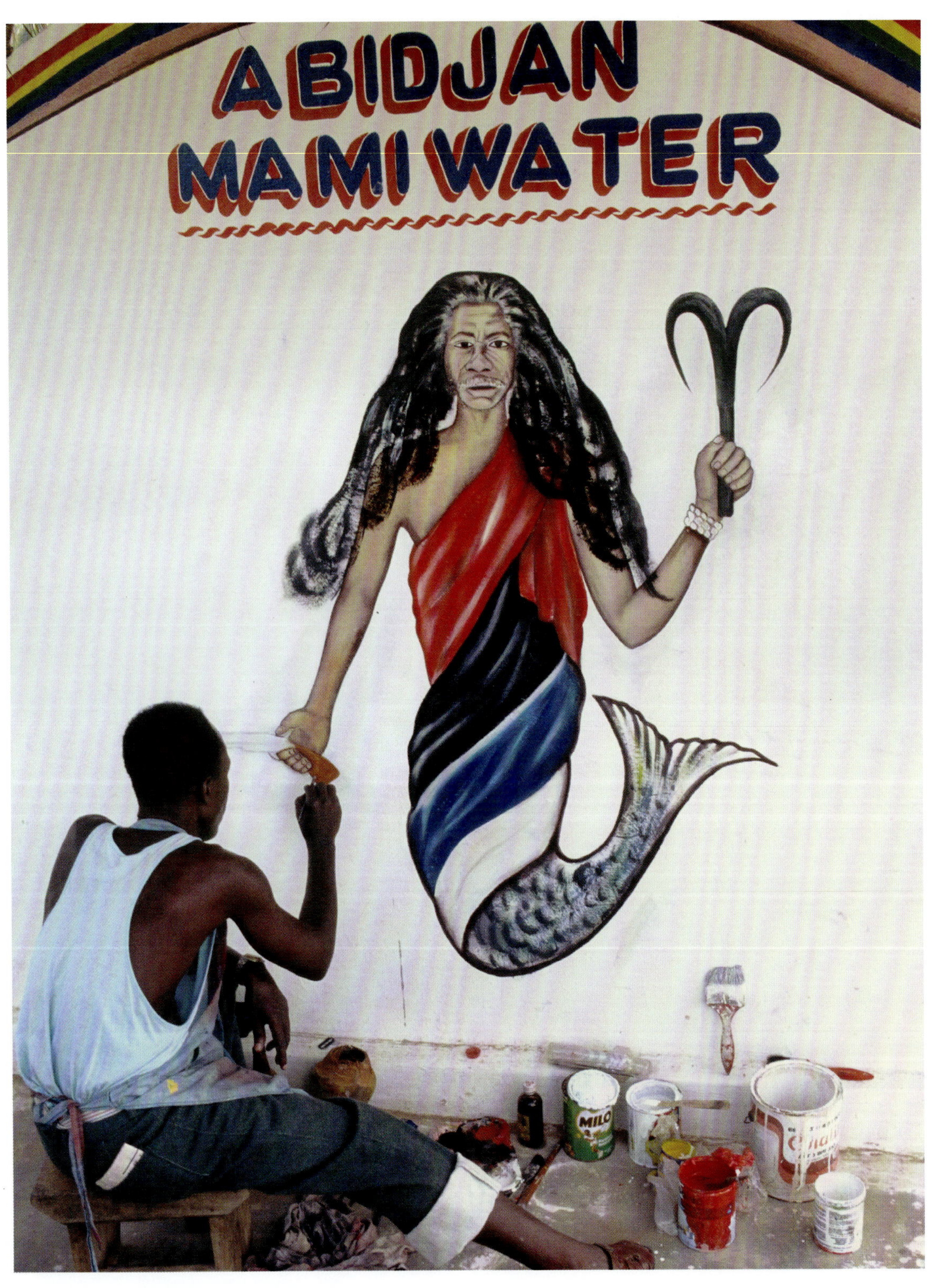

Wall painting in honor
of the priest

Peinture murale en
l'honneur du prêtre

Wandmalerei zu
Ehren des Priesters

Pintura mural en
honor al sacerdote

Pintura mural em
honra do sacerdote

Muurschildering ter
ere van de priester

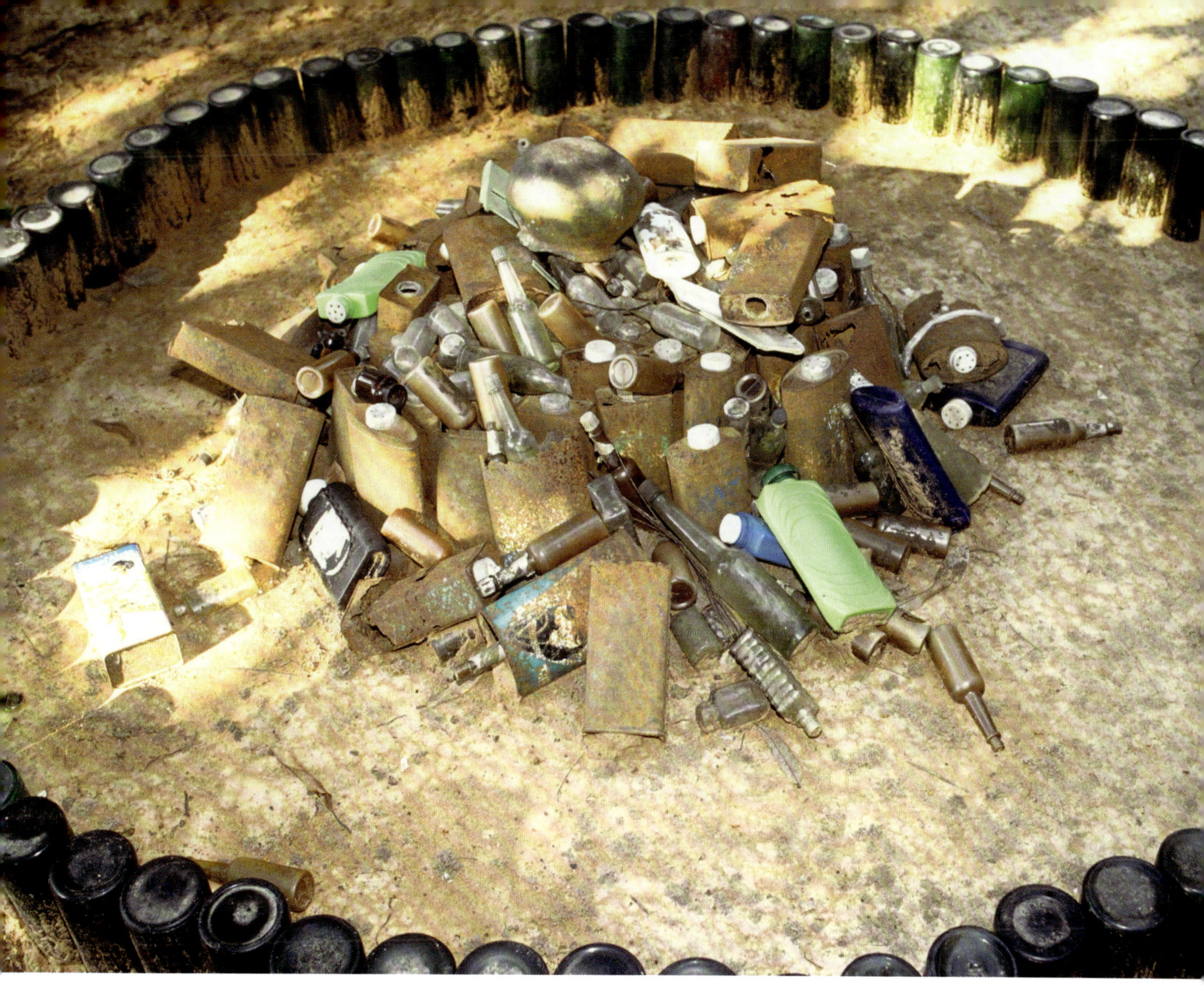

Memorial. The perfume bottles and tins of talcum of deceased cult followers are a reminder of all the dignitaries who belonged to the community in the past.

Commémoration. Les bouteilles de parfum et les boîtes de talc d'adeptes décédés évoquent tous les dignitaires passés ayant appartenu à la communauté.

Gedenkstätte. Die Parfümflaschen und Talkumdosen verstorbener Kultanhänger erinnern an all die Würdenträger, die der Gemeinde in der Vergangenheit angehörten.

Memorial. Los frascos de perfume y las latas de talco de los seguidores del culto fallecidos recuerdan a todos los dignatarios que pertenecieron a la congregación en el pasado.

Memorial. Os frascos de perfume e as latas de talco dos seguidores falecidos do culto fazem lembrar todos os dignitários que pertenceram à congregação no passado.

Gedenkplaats. De parfumflessen en talkpoederblikken van overleden cultusaanhangers herinneren aan alle hoogwaardigheidsbekleders die in het verleden tot de congregatie behoorden.

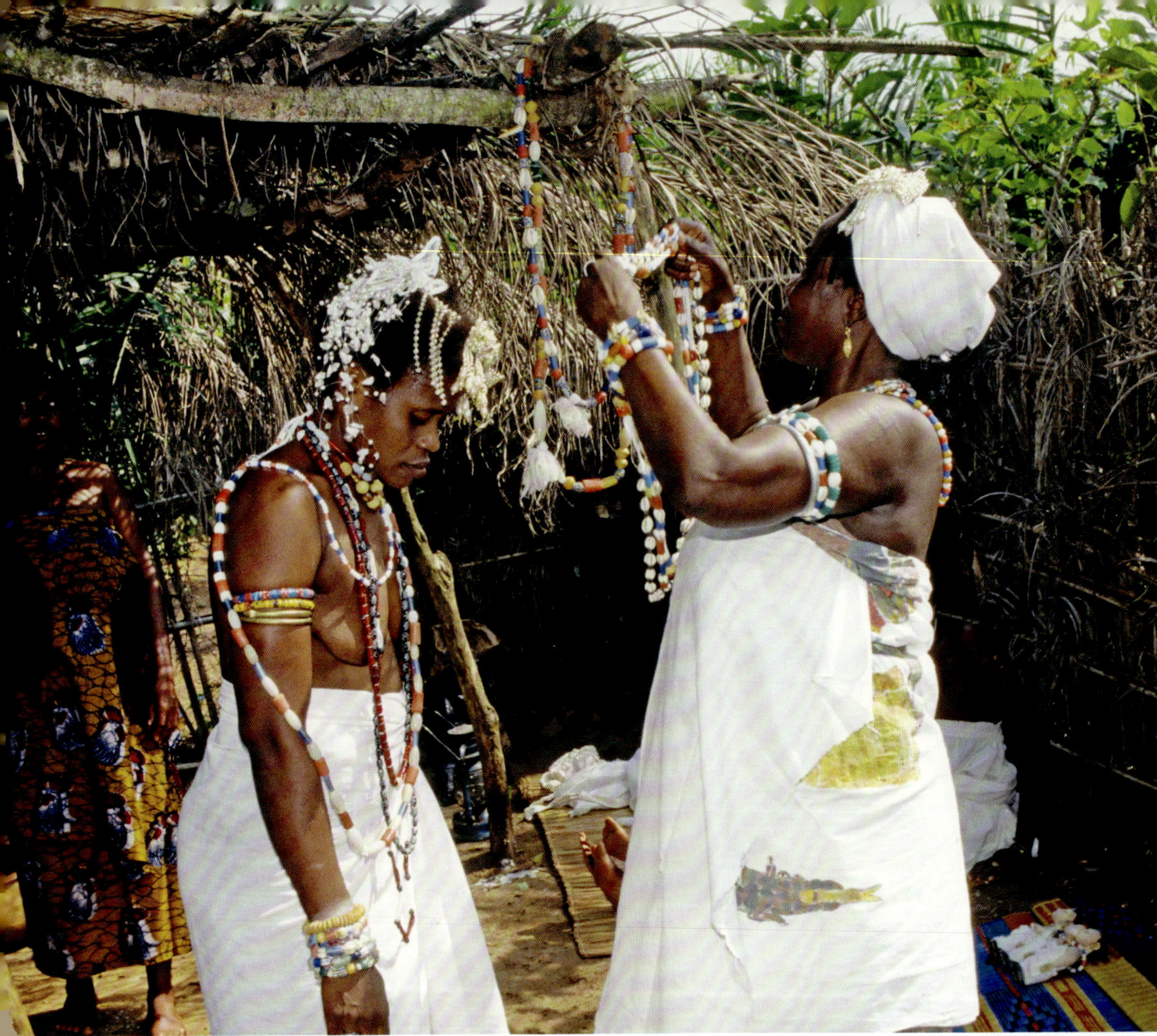

Mami Wata—how to become an Initiate

The reasons for joining a traditional faith community like Mami Wata are complex. As a rule, it is chronic diseases and existing but unconsidered attachments to certain gods that require initiation into the cult. The diagnosis in this respect is made by an experienced priest within the framework of an oracle questioning.

While short initiations have established themselves in cities where time is short, the classic path from novice to adept is much longer. It begins with ritual death and a farewell to the old way of life.

Mami Wata, le parcours de l'adepte

Diverses raisons peuvent amener à vouloir intégrer une communauté religieuse traditionnelle telle que celle de Mami Wata. Il s'agit en général de guérir des maladies chroniques ou de rétablir des liens avec cette déesse, préexistants mais ignorés, qui imposent une initiation à son culte. Le diagnostic est effectué par un prêtre expérimenté dans le cadre d'une consultation de l'oracle.

Alors que dans les villes, où le temps est précieux, des initiations courtes ont été instaurées, la voie classique permettant à la novice de devenir adepte est nettement plus

Mami Wata – der Weg zur Adeptin

Die Gründe, in eine traditionelle Glaubensgemeinschaft wie die Mami Watas einzutreten, sind vielschichtig. In der Regel sind es chronische Krankheiten und bestehende, aber unberücksichtigte Bindungen an bestimmte Götter, die eine Initiation in den Kult erforderlich machen. Die Diagnose diesbezüglich trifft ein erfahrener Priester im Rahmen einer Orakelbefragung.

Während sich in den Städten, in denen die Zeit knapp ist, Kurzinitiationen etabliert haben, ist der klassische Weg von der Novizin zur Adeptin deutlich länger. Er

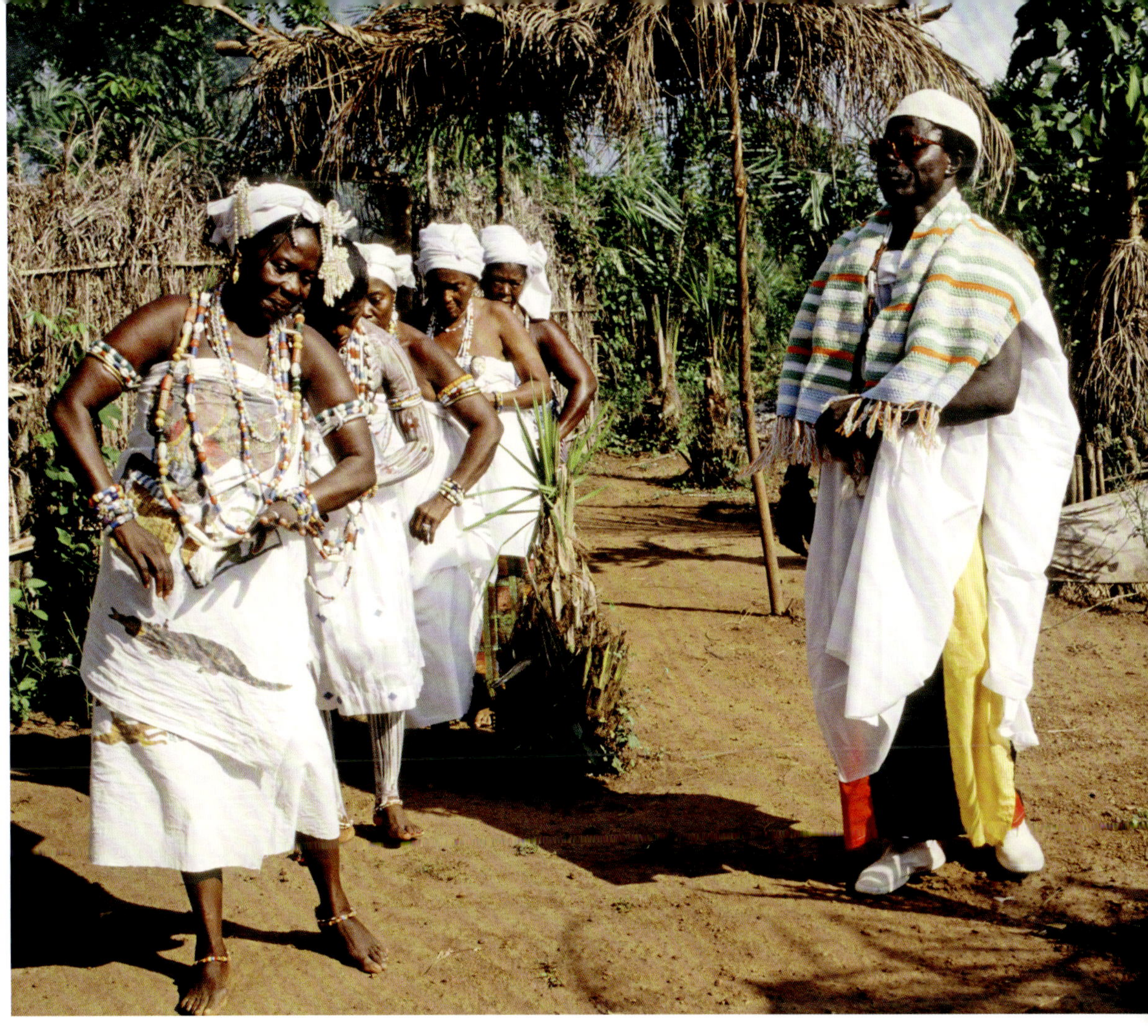

Mami Wata– El camino hacia convertirse en adepta

Las razones para unirse a una comunidad de fe tradicional como la de Mami Wata son complejas. Como regla general, son las enfermedades crónicas y los apegos existentes, pero no considerados, a ciertos dioses, los que requieren la iniciación en el culto. El diagnóstico a este respecto es realizado por un sacerdote experimentado en el marco de una consultaconsulta al oráculo.

Mientras que las iniciaciones cortas se han establecido en ciudades donde no hay mucho tiempo, el camino clásico de novicio

Mami Wata – O caminho para o Adeptin

As razões para aderir a uma comunidade de fé tradicional como Mami Watas são complexas. Como regra geral, são as doenças crônicas e os apegos existentes, mas inconsiderados, a certos deuses que requerem iniciação ao culto. O diagnóstico a este respeito é feito por um sacerdote experiente no quadro de um oráculo questionador.

Enquanto as iniciações curtas se estabeleceram em cidades onde o tempo é curto, o caminho clássico do novato ao adepto é muito mais longo. Começa com

Mami Wata – de weg tot aanhangster

De redenen om toe te treden tot een traditionele geloofsgemeenschap als die van Mami Wata zijn complex. In de regel zijn het chronische ziekten en bestaande, maar nog niet gehonoreerde banden met bepaalde goden die een inwijding in de cultus noodzakelijk maken. De diagnose in dit verband wordt gesteld door een ervaren priester in het kader van een orakelverhoor.

Terwijl korte inwijdingen gangbaar zijn geworden in de steden, waar tijd kostbaar is, is de klassieke weg van novice naar aanhangster veel langer. Die begint met

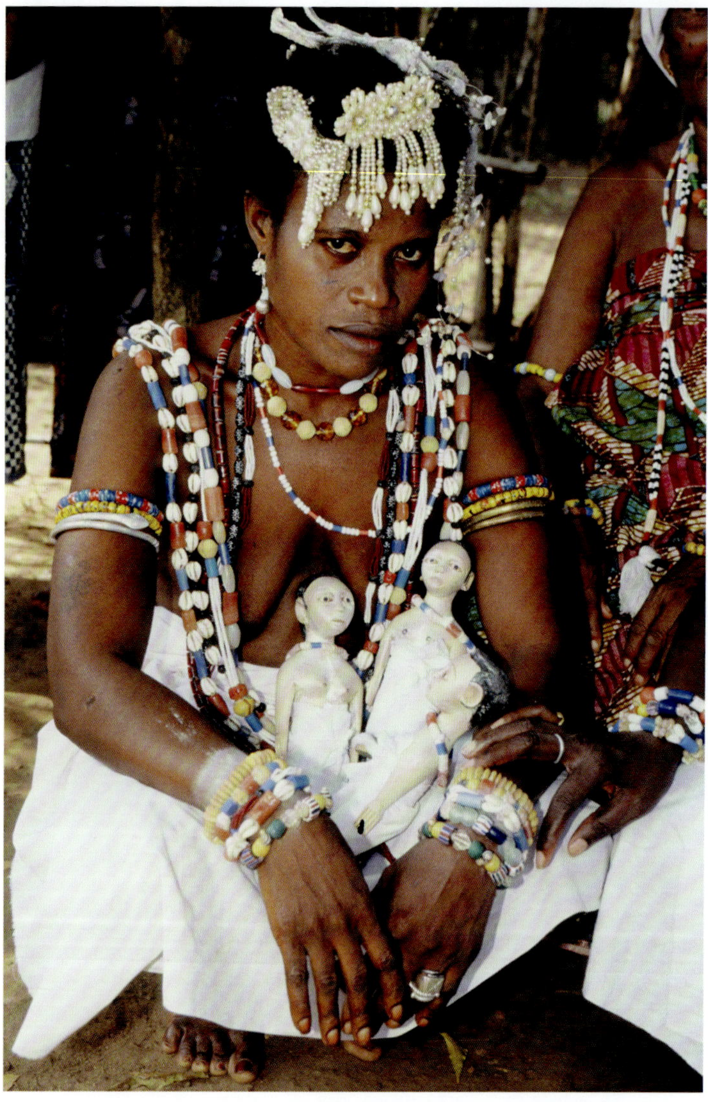

Inauguration of the Ceremonial Stool. The stool made and painted for the new adept is now on the dance floor and serves Ama as a throne. This event is one of the highlights of the ceremony.

Inauguration du tabouret de cérémonie. Le tabouret fabriqué et peint pour la nouvelle fidèle est installé sur la place des danses et sert de trône à Ama. Cet acte compte parmi les grands moments de la cérémonie

Einweihung des Zeremonienhockers. Der für die neue Adeptin angefertige und bemalte Schemel steht nun auf dem Tanzplatz und dient Ama als Thron. Dieser Akt gehört zu den Höhepunkten der Zeremonie.

Inauguración del taburete ceremonial. El taburete hecho y pintado para la nueva adepta ahora está en la pista de baile y sirve a Ama como trono. Este acto es uno de los momentos culminantes de la ceremonia.

Inauguração do Banco Cerimonial. O banco feito e pintado para o novo adepto está agora na pista de dança e serve de trono a Ama. Este ato é um dos destaques da cerimônia.

Inwijding van de ceremoniële kruk. De voor de nieuwe adept gemaakte en beschilderde kruk staat nu op de dansvloer en dient Ama als troon. Deze daad is een van de hoogtepunten van de ceremonie.

In the second step the secret, cult-specific customs are learned, which include dances, trance, costumes and other practices, as well as sometimes secret languages. In the end the rebirth as a cult member brings increased social status and a great celebration takes place.

longue. Elle débute par une mort rituelle et un adieu à l'ancien milieu de vie.

Dans un deuxième temps, la novice doit apprendre les usages secrets spécifiques au culte, qui impliquent danses, transes et autres coutumes, costumes particuliers voire une langue secrète. L'initiation se termine par une renaissance en tant que membre du culte qui se traduit par l'accès à un statut social élevé et l'organisation d'une grande fête.

beginnt mit dem rituellen Tod und einem Abschied vom alten Lebensmillieu.

Im zweiten Schritt werden die geheimen, kultspezifischen Gebräuche erlernt, was Tänze, Trance, Trachten und sonstige Gepflogenheiten, wie manchmal auch Geheimsprachen, miteinschließt. Am Ende steht die Neugeburt als Kultmitglied inklusive gestiegenem sozialen Status und großem Fest.

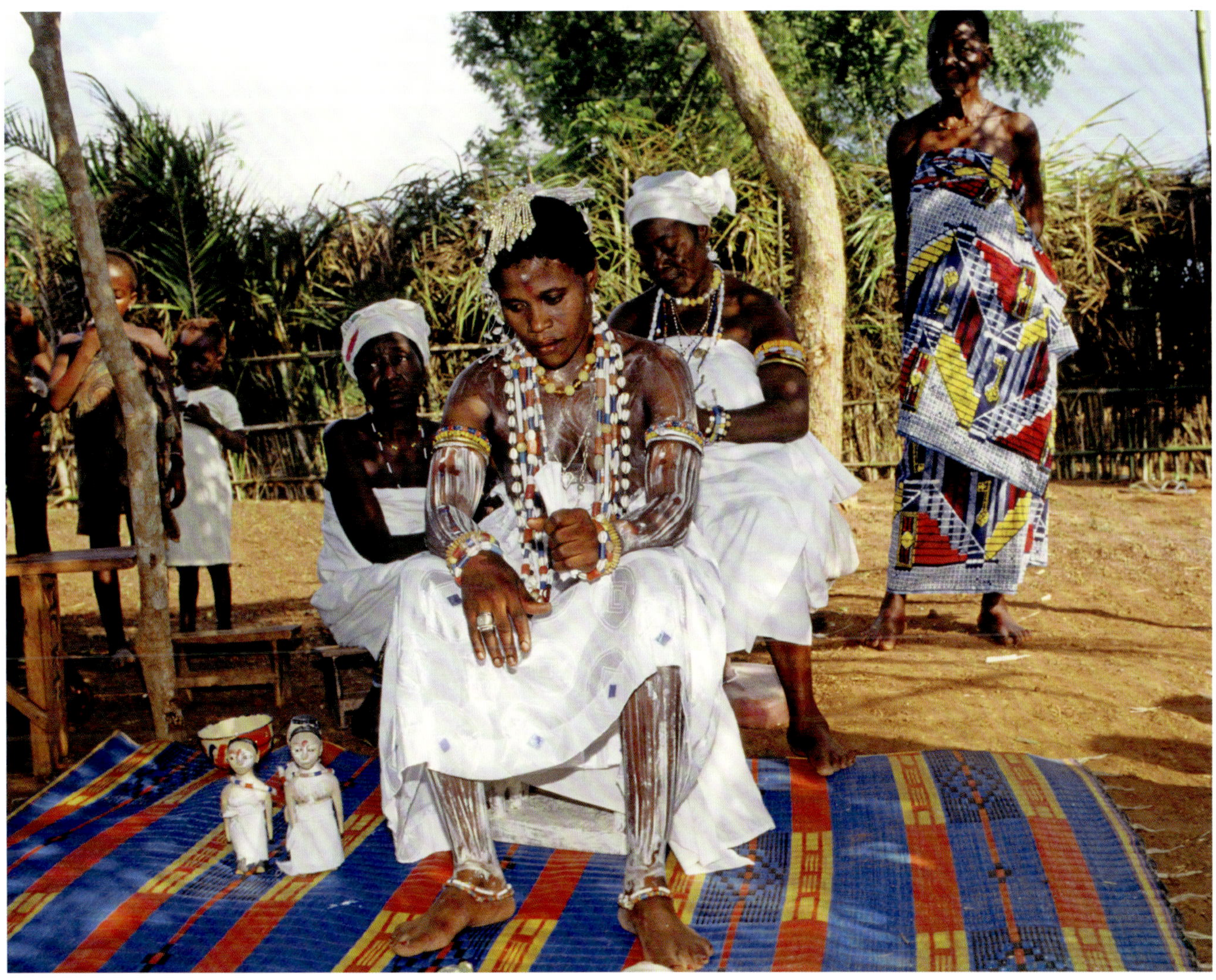

a adepto es mucho más largo. Comienza con la muerte ritual y la despedidadel antiguo ambiente o entorno.

En el segundo paso, se aprenden las costumbres secretas y específicas del culto, que incluyen bailes, trances, trajes tradicionales y otras costumbres, así como idiomas a veces secretos. Al final, el renacimiento como miembro de una secta incluye un aumento de estatus social y una gran celebración.

a morte ritual e uma despedida do velho millieu da vida.

Na segunda etapa, aprendem-se os costumes específicos do culto secreto, que incluem danças, transe, trajes tradicionais e outros costumes, bem como, por vezes, línguas secretas. No final, o renascimento como membro do culto, incluindo o aumento do status social e uma grande celebração.

de rituele dood en het afscheid van het oude levensmilieu.

In de tweede stap worden de geheime, cultusspecifieke gebruiken aangeleerd, waar dans, trance, klederdracht en andere gewoontes, maar soms ook geheime talen onder vallen. Aan het eind komt de wedergeboorte als cultuslid, inclusief een verhoogde sociale status en een groot feest

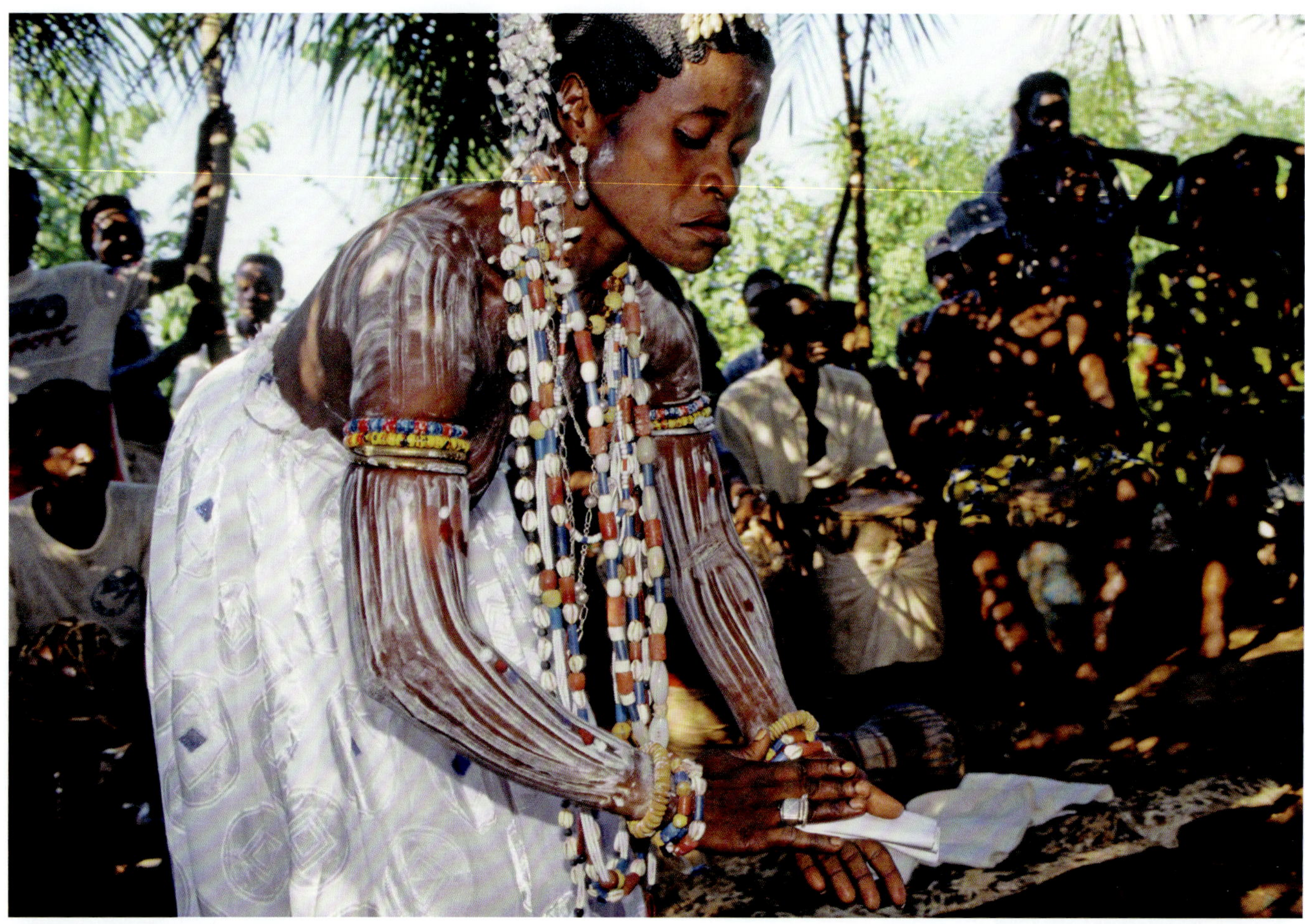

Ama dances in honor of the goddess

Ama danse en l'honneur de la déesse

Ama tanzt zu Ehren der Göttin

Ama baila en honor a la diosa

Ama dança em honra da deusa

Ama danst ter ere van de godin

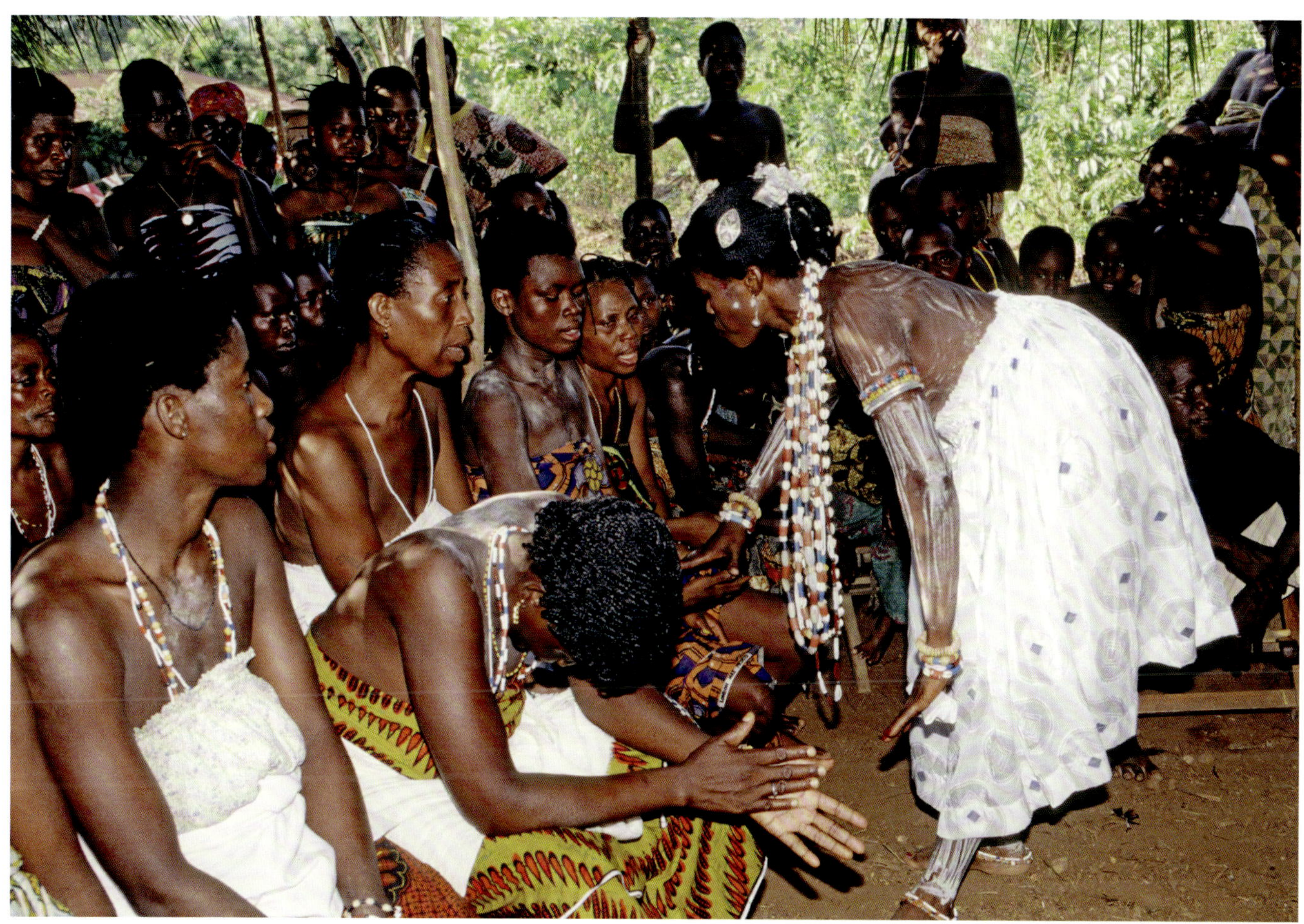

Greeting the other adepts

Salutation aux autres adeptes

Begrüßung der anderen Adeptinnen

Saludo de las otras adeptas

Saudação dos outros adeptos

Begroeting van de andere adepten

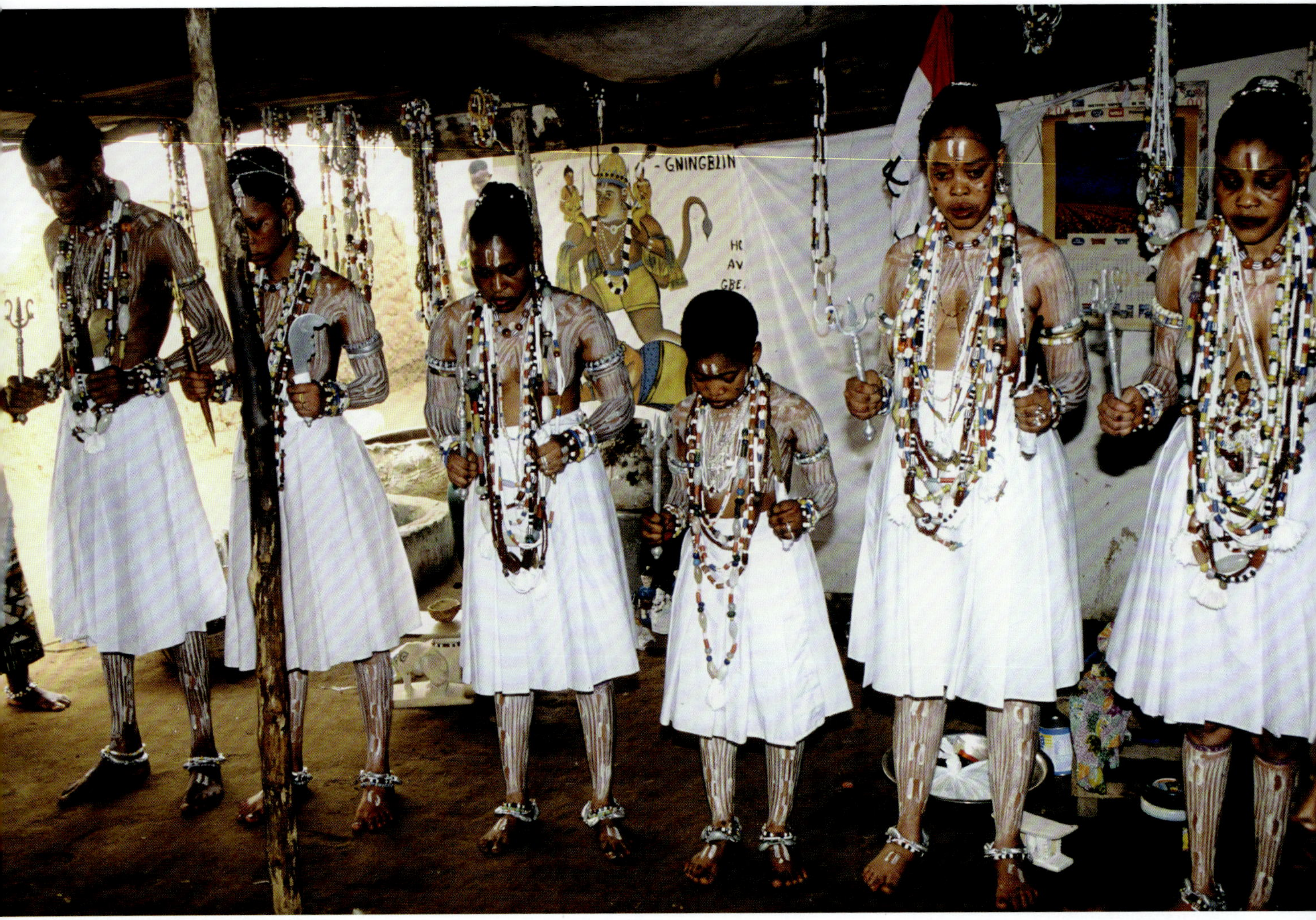

Mami Wata—the great initiation

In Benin, Togo and Ghana one finds faith communities for various different deities. All have in common that an initiation is required for accession, in the context of which the individual peculiarities relating to the respective deity must be learned. The process includes the symbolic end of the old life, the phase of formation and the resurrection as a new human being.

With Mami Wata these ceremonies are connected with extensive, spectacular festivities. The special dances, the snow-

Mami Wata, la longue initiation

Au Bénin, au Togo et au Ghana, diverses communautés religieuses se sont constituées pour honorer différentes divinités. Toutes ces communautés ont en commun une longue initiation au cours de laquelle les particularités du dieu concerné doivent être apprises. Le processus d'initiation implique l'achèvement symbolique de l'ancienne vie, une phase de formation et une renaissance en tant qu'individu nouveau.

Dans le culte de Mami Wata, ces cérémonies sont associées à de

Mami Wata – die große Initiation

In Benin, Togo und Ghana findet man Glaubensgemeinschaften für die unterschiedlichsten Gottheiten. Allen gemein ist, dass es zum Beitritt einer Initiation bedarf, im Rahmen derer die individuellen Besonderheiten rund um die jeweilige Gottheit erlernt werden müssen. Der Vorgang umfasst das symbolische Ende des alten Lebens, die Phase der Ausbildung und die Wiederauferstehung als neuer Mensch.

Bei Mami Wata sind diese Zeremonien mit umfangreichen, spektakulären

Six people solemnly become adepts of a Mami Wata cult in
Bopa, Benin

Entrée solennelle de six nouveaux adeptes du culte de Mami
Wata à Bopa, Bénin

Sechs Personen werden feierlich Adepten eines Mami Wata-
Kultes in Bopa, Benin

Seis personas se convierten solemnemente en adeptos de un
culto a Mami Wata en Bopa, Benin

Seis pessoas se tornam solenemente adeptas de um culto
Mami Wata em Bopa, Benin

Zes personen worden plechtig adepten van een Mami Wata-
cultus in Bopa, Benin

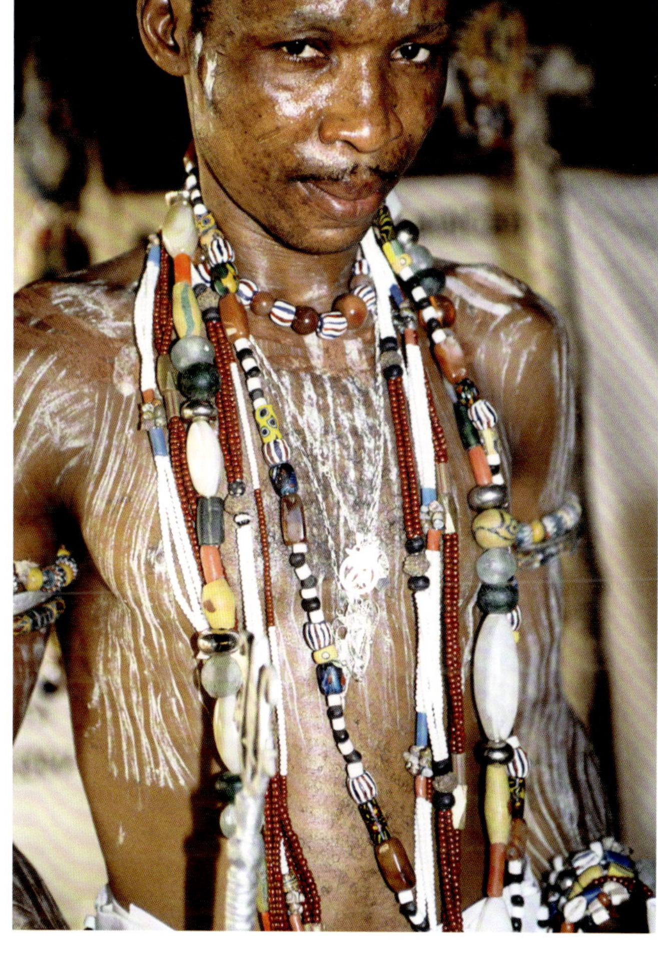

Men are in the minority with Mami Wata

Les hommes sont en minorité dans le culte de Mami Wata

Männer sind bei Mami Wata in der Minderheit

En el caso de Mami Wata, los hombres son minoría

Os homens estão em minoria com Mami Wata

Mannen zijn bij Mami Wata in de minderheid

Mami Wata– La gran iniciación

En Benin, Togo y Ghana se encuentran
comunidades de fe para las más diversas
deidades. Lo que todos tienen en común
es que unirlos requiere una iniciación en
la que deben aprenderse las peculiaridades
individuales en torno a la deidad respectiva.
El proceso incluye el fin simbólico de la
antigua vida, la fase de formación y la
resurrección como nuevo ser humano.

Con Mami Wata, estas ceremonias están
conectadas con extensas y espectaculares
festividades. Las danzas aprendidas, las

Mami Wata – A grande iniciação

Em Benin, Togo e Gana, encontram-se
comunidades de fé para as mais diferentes
divindades. O que todos têm em comum
é que unir-se a eles requer uma iniciação
na qual as peculiaridades individuais em
torno da respectiva divindade devem
ser aprendidas. O processo inclui o fim
simbólico da vida antiga, a fase de formação
e a ressurreição como novo ser humano.

Com Mami Wata, essas cerimônias
estão ligadas a festividades extensas e
espetaculares. As danças aprendidas, as

Mami Wata – de grote initiatie

In Benin, Togo en Ghana zijn er
geloofsgemeenschappen voor de meest
uiteenlopende godheden. Wat ze allemaal
gemeen hebben, is dat voor toetreding een
initiatie vereist is waarbij de afzonderlijke
eigenaardigheden van elke specifieke god
moeten worden geleerd. De procedure
omvat het symbolische einde van het
oude leven, de vormingsfase en de
wederopstanding als nieuw mens.

Bij Mami Wata zijn deze ceremoniën
verbonden met omvangrijke, spectaculaire

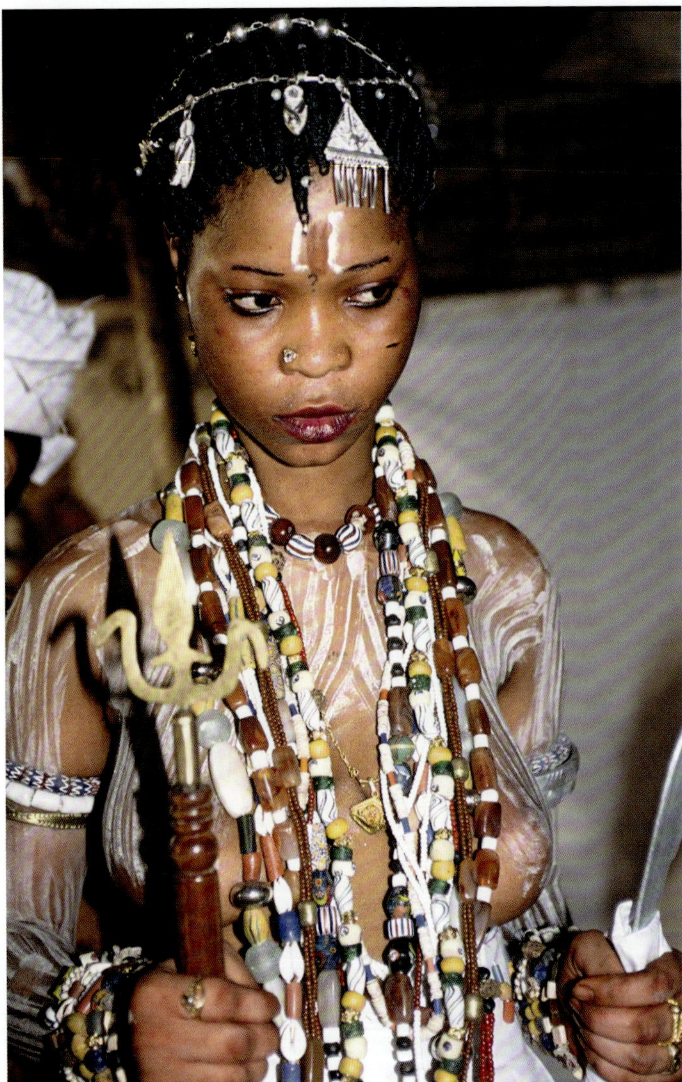

white robes and the specific, rich jewellery are proudly displayed and the whole village takes part in the events with wonder and reverence. Often, deceased twins are remembered, whose dead souls are represented by small, festively decorated wooden figures.

From time to time there are also men among the initiates.

spectaculaires festivités. Les danses apprises sont pratiquées en public, et les vêtements d'un blanc éclatant, agrémentés de riches ornementations, sont fièrement exposés. La totalité du village participe à l'événement, dans un mélange d'étonnement et de respect. On évoque également souvent des jumeaux décédés, dont les âmes sont représentées par de petites figurines de bois décorées.

Parmi les initiés se trouvent parfois quelques hommes.

Festivitäten verbunden. Die erlernten Tänze, die blütenweißen Gewänder und der dazugehörige, reiche Schmuck werden stolz zur Schau gestellt und das ganze Dorf nimmt staunend und ehrfurchtsvoll am Geschehen teil. Oft wird dabei auch verstorbener Zwillinge gedacht, für deren Totenseelen stellvertretend kleine, festlich geschmückte Holzfiguren stehen.

Ab und an finden sich auch Männer unter den Initianden.

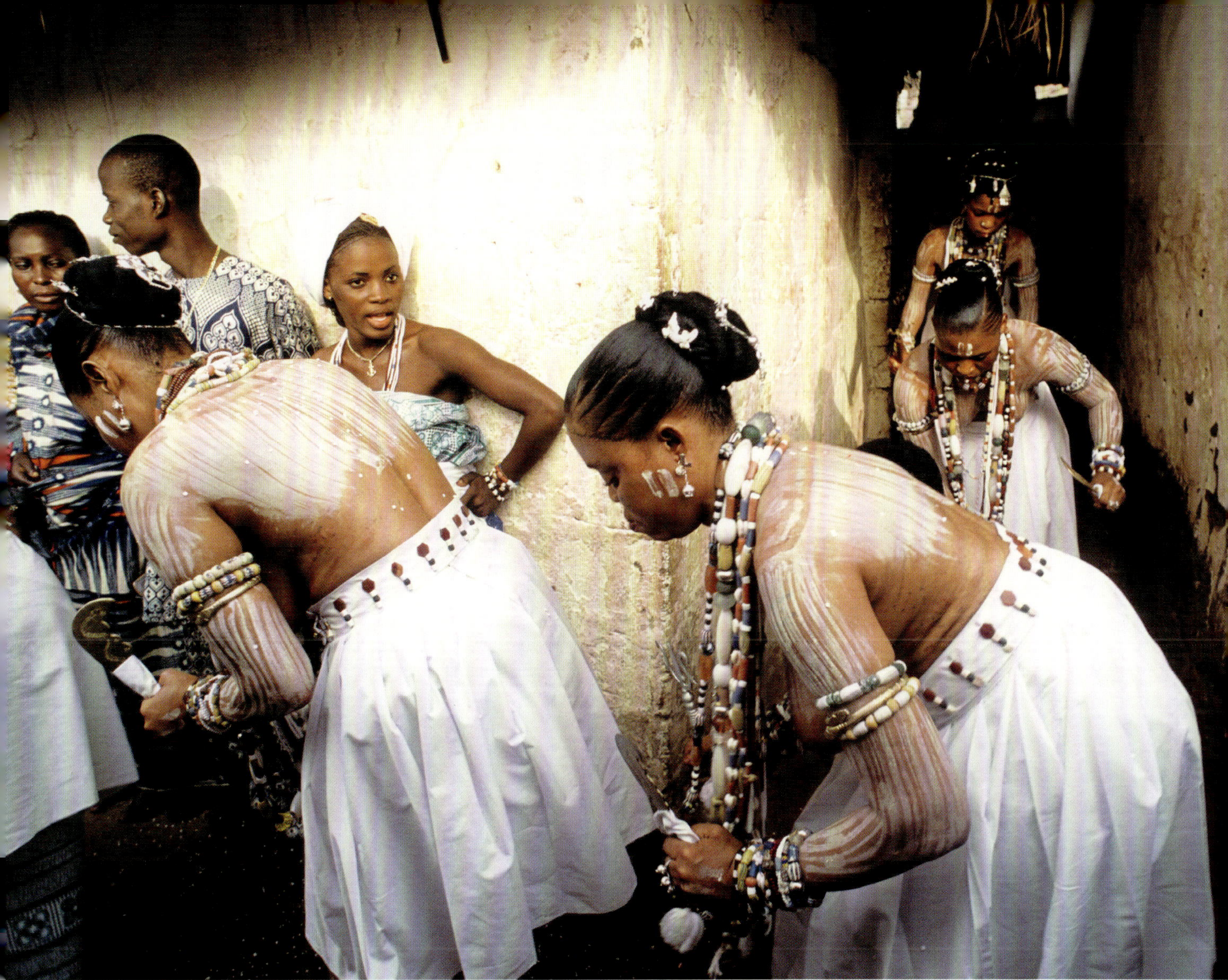

túnicas de flores blancas y las joyas ricas asociadas se exhiben con orgullo y todo el pueblo participa en los eventos con asombro y reverencia. También se recuerda a menudo a los gemelos muertos, cuyas almas muertas están representadas por pequeñas figuras de madera decoradas festivamente.

De vez en cuando hay también hombres entre los iniciados.

vestes brancas floridas e as jóias ricas associadas são orgulhosamente expostas e toda a aldeia participa nos eventos com espanto e reverência. Os gémeos mortos são também muitas vezes lembrados, cujas almas mortas são representadas por pequenas figuras de madeira decoradas festivamente.

De vez em quando também há homens entre os iniciados.

festiviteiten. De geleerde dansen, de zuiverwitte gewaden en de bijbehorende rijke opsmuk worden met trots tentoongespreid en het hele dorp neemt met verbazing en eerbied deel aan de evenementen. Vaak worden daarbij ook overleden tweelingen herdacht, wier dode zielen worden vertegenwoordigd door kleine, feestelijk versierde houten poppen.

Af en toe zijn er ook mannen onder de inwijdelingen.

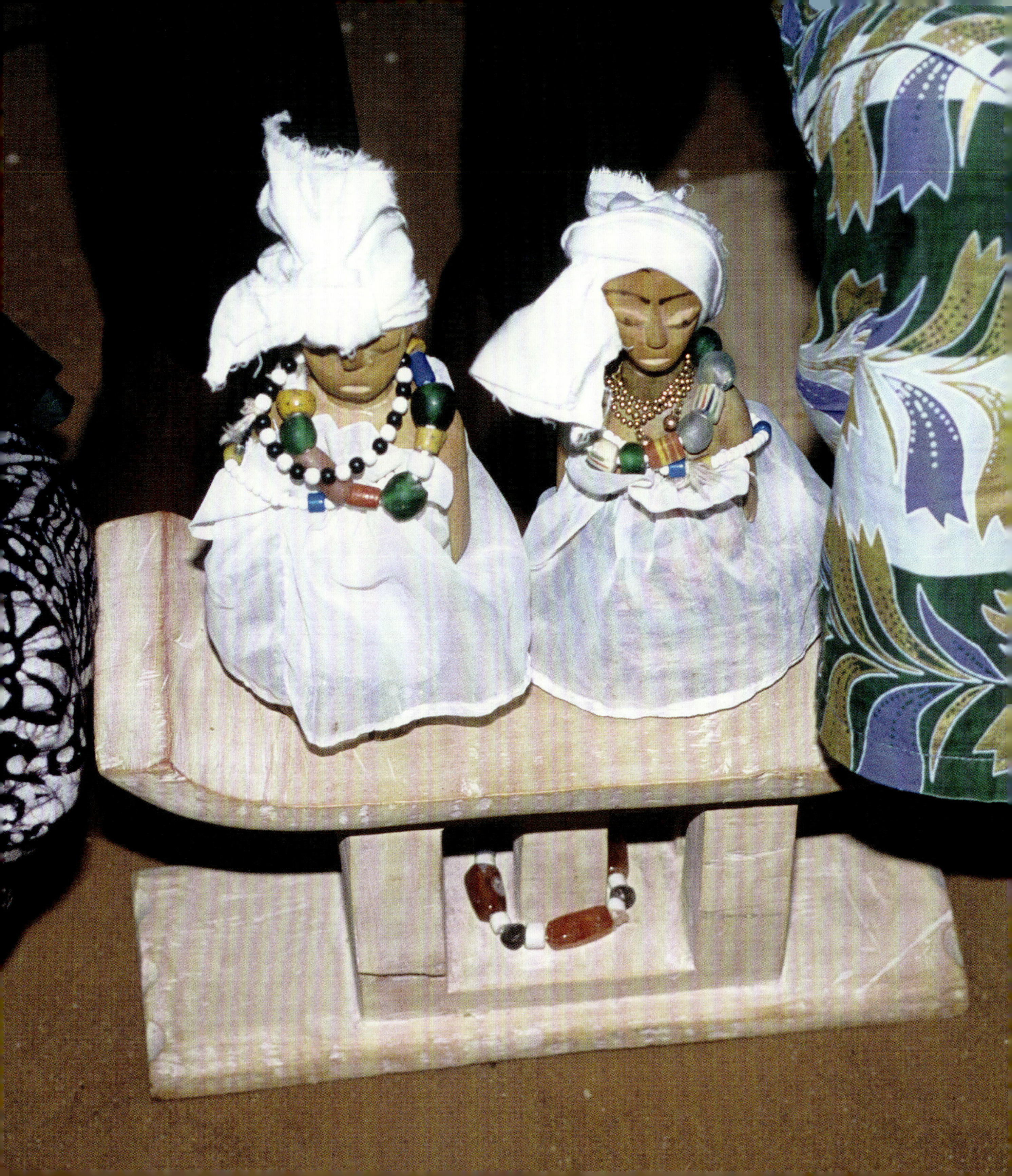

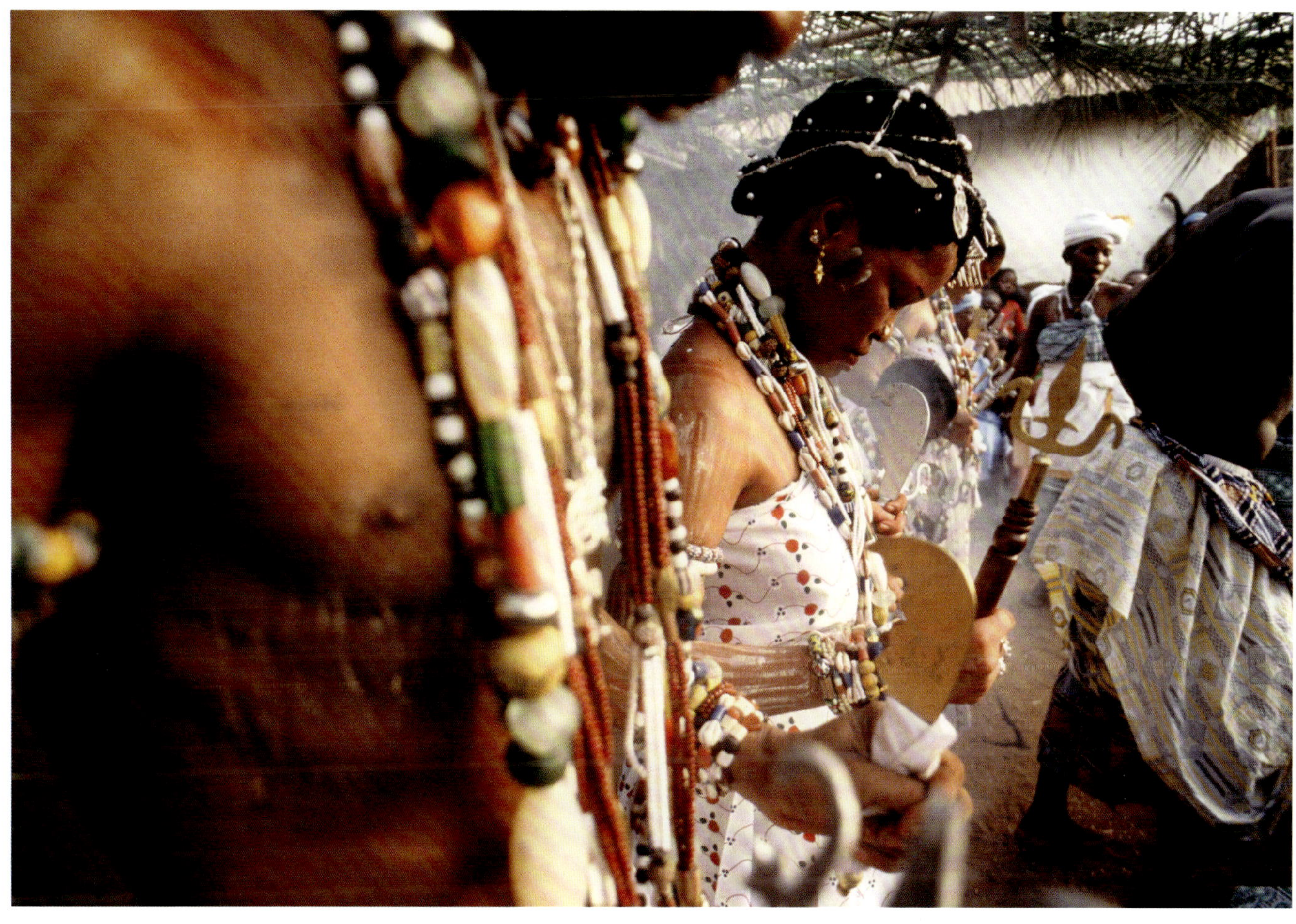

Stool with twins. The souls of the deceased twins are very close to Mami Wata. Here two of them take part in the ceremony. They have their own stool and are festively decorated.

Tabouret avec jumeaux. Les âmes des jumeaux décédés sont très proches de Mami Wata. Sur cette photographie, deux figurines participent à une cérémonie. Elles disposent de leur propre tabouret et portent des tenues de fête.

Schemel mit Zwillingen. Die Seelen der verstorbenen Zwillinge stehen Mami Wata sehr nah. Hier nehmen zwei von ihnen an der Zeremonie teil. Sie haben ihren eigenen Hocker und sind festlich geschmückt.

Taburete con gemelos. Las almas de los gemelos fallecidos están muy cerca de Mami Wata. Aquí dos de ellos participan en la ceremonia. Tienen su propio taburete y están decorados de forma festiva.

Banco com gémeos. As almas dos gémeos falecidos são muito próximas da Mami Wata. Aqui dois deles participam na cerimónia. Eles têm o seu próprio banco e são decorados festivamente.

Krukje met tweeling. De zielen van overleden tweelingen staan Mami Wata zeer na. Hier nemen twee ervan deel aan de ceremonie. Ze hebben hun eigen krukje en zijn feestelijk uitgedost.

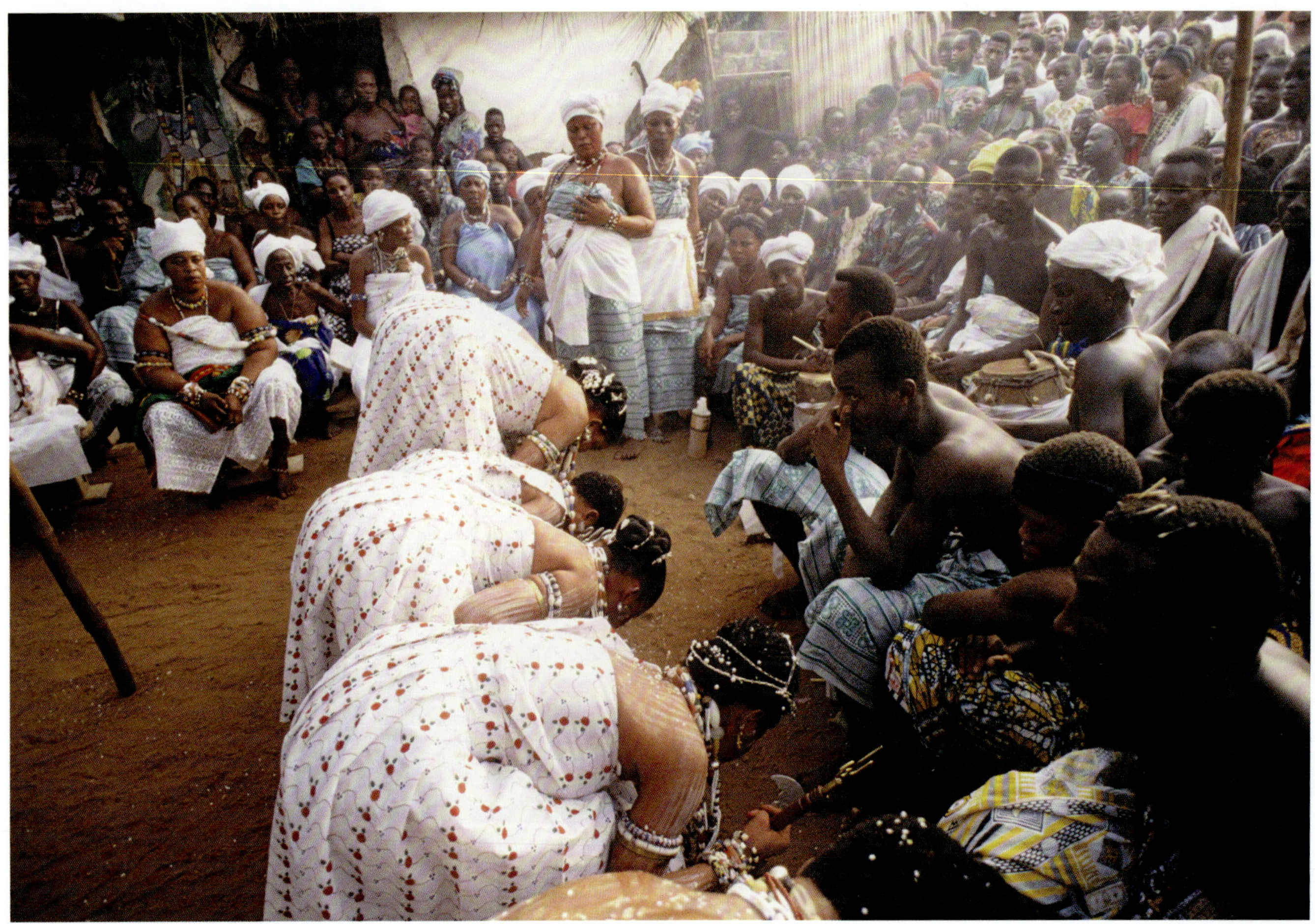

Welcoming the village community

Accueil de la communauté villageoise

Begrüßung der Dorfgemeinschaft

Bienvenida de la comunidad del pueblo

Boas-vindas da comunidade da aldeia

Begroeting door de dorpsgemeenschap

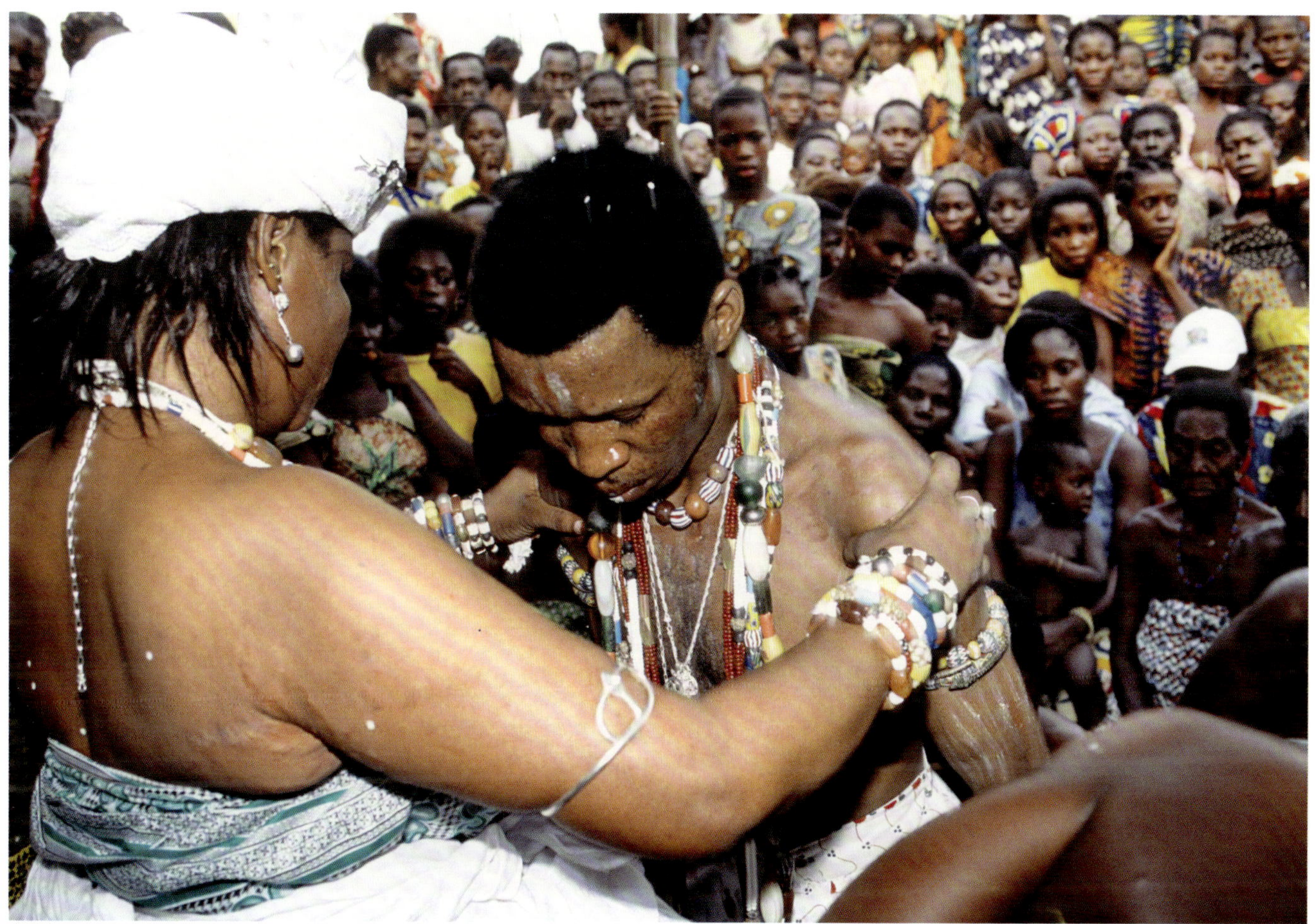

The big day. Now that the transformation from novice to adept and thus a full member of the Mami Wata community has been completed, the "newcomers" now enjoy special respect.

Le grand jour. Dès que les novices sont devenus des disciples de Mami Wata, et donc des membres à part entière de sa communauté, ils jouissent d'un respect particulier.

Der große Tag. Nun, da die Wandlung vom Novizen zum Adepten und somit vollwertigem Mitglied der Mami Wata Gemeinschaft vollzogen ist, genießen die „Neuen" ab sofort besonderen Respekt.

El gran día. Ahora que se ha completado la transformación de novicio a adepto y, por tanto, miembro de pleno derecho de la comunidad Mami Wata, los "recién llegados" gozan ahora de un respeto especial.

O grande dia. Agora que a transformação de noviço em adepto e, portanto, membro pleno da comunidade Mami Wata foi concluída, os "recém-chegados" agora gozam de um respeito especial.

De grote dag. Nu de transformatie van novice naar adept en daarmee volwaardig lidmaatschap van de Mami Wata-gemeenschap eropzit, genieten de nieuwkomers meteen veel respect.

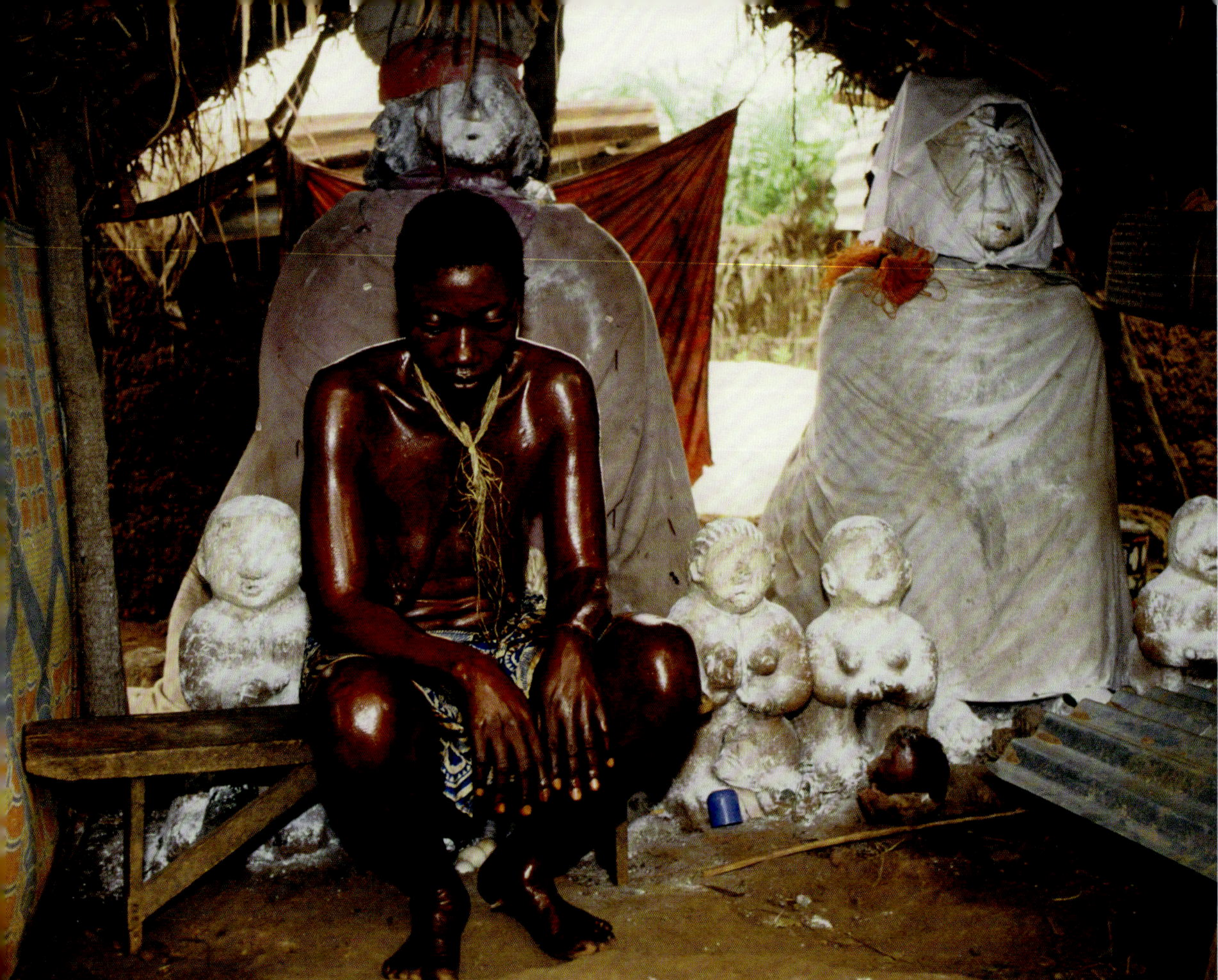

Sakpata—Healing with the Lord of Diseases

In Doutou in southern Benin, a long illness led a young woman to seek advice and help from a traditional healer. She diagnosed that the woman, who had previously been initiated into a Vodun cult, had violated the divine rules several times. The result was a complicated ceremony in which several gods had to be called upon and appeased.

Heviesso (Shango), the god of thunder, was first soothed with red palm oil, symbolic of the bloody mucus of a new birth. Later, Sakpata, the Lord of Diseases, played a leading role.

Painted all over the body with dots, the "smallpox of Sakpata", the sick person

Sakpata, guérison par le seigneur des maladies

À Doutou, dans le sud du Bénin, la longue maladie d'une jeune femme a conduit son entourage à rechercher l'aide et les conseils d'une guérisseuse traditionnelle. Celle-ci a diagnostiqué que la jeune femme, autrefois initiée à un culte vodun, avait à plusieurs reprises méprisé de manière impardonnable l'ensemble des règles divines. En conséquence, il fallut organiser une cérémonie complexe, au cours de laquelle plusieurs dieux devaient être conviés et apaisés.

Hêviosso (Shangô), dieu du tonnerre, fut tout d'abord calmé avec de l'huile de palme rouge, symbolisant les mucosités sanglantes

Sakpata – Heilung beim Herrn der Krankheiten

In Doutou im Süden Benins führte die lange Krankheit eine junge Frau dazu, Rat und Hilfe bei einer traditionellen Heilerin zu suchen. Diese diagnostizierte, dass die bereits vormals in einen Vodunkult initiierte Frau das göttliche Regelwerk einige Male sträflich missachtet hatte. Infolgedessen kam es zu einer komplizierten Zeremonie, bei der gleich mehrere Götter angerufen und beschwichtigt werden mussten.

Mit rotem Palmöl, symbolisch für den blutigen Schleim einer Neugeburt, wurde zunächst Heviesso (Shangô), der Donnergott, besänftigt. Im weiteren Verlauf spielte Sakpata, der Herr über Krankheiten, eine Hauptrolle.

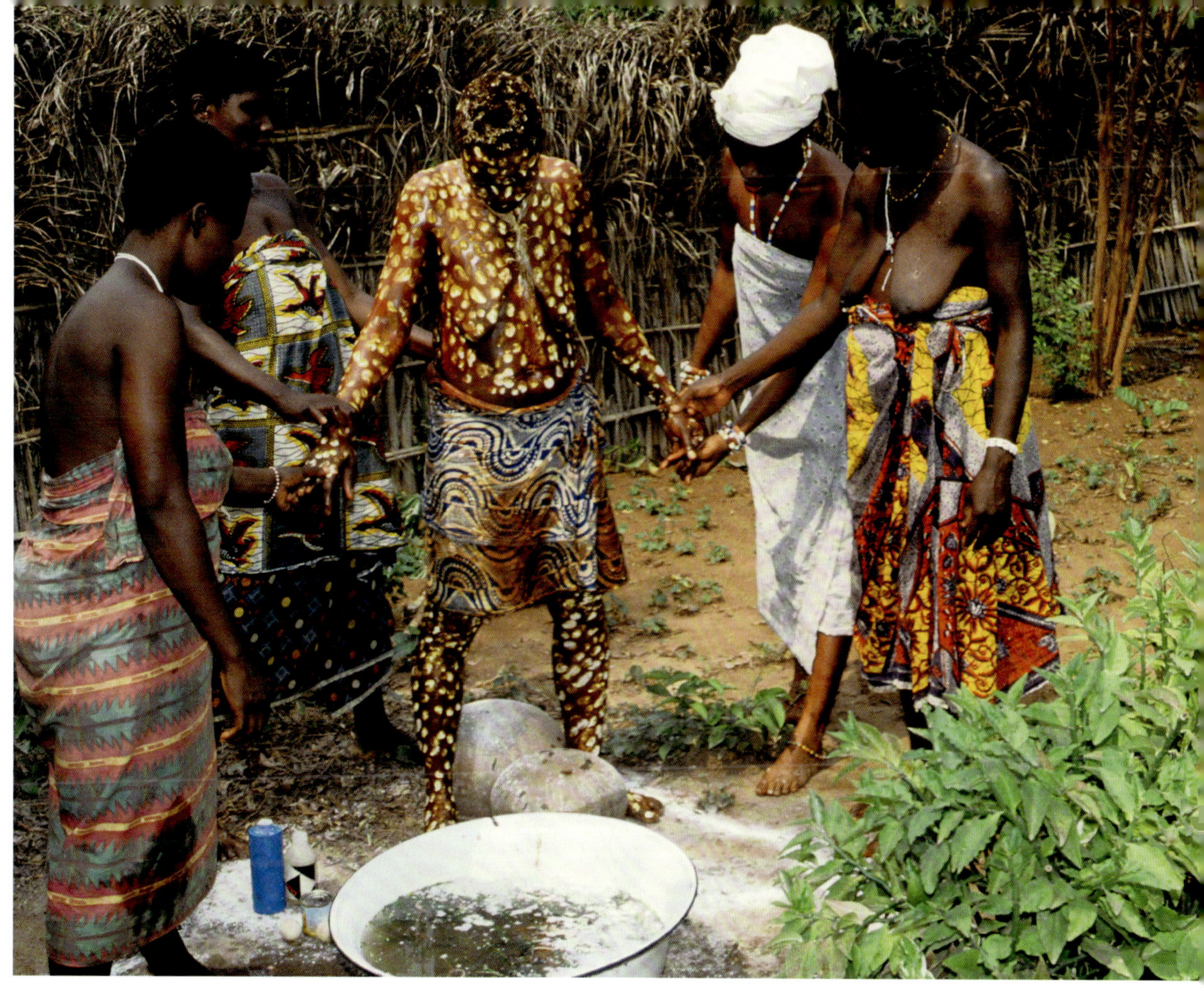

Sakpata - Curación con el señor de las enfermedades

En Doutou, en el sur de Benin, la larga enfermedad llevó a una joven a buscar consejo y ayuda de una curandera tradicional. Ésta diagnosticó que la mujer, que había sido iniciada previamente en un culto vudú, había violado las reglas divinas varias veces. El resultado fue una ceremonia complicada en la que varios dioses tuvieron que ser convocados y apaciguados.

Heviesso (Shango), el dios del trueno, fue calmado con aceite de palma roja, símbolo de la mucosidad sangrienta de un nuevo nacimiento. En el curso siguiente, Sakpata, el señor de las enfermedades, desempeñó un papel principal.

Sakpata - Cura com o Senhor das Doenças

Em Doutou, no sul do Benin, a longa doença levou uma jovem a procurar aconselhamento e ajuda de um curandeiro tradicional. Ela diagnosticou que a mulher, que havia sido previamente iniciada em um vodunkult, havia violado várias vezes as regras divinas. O resultado foi uma cerimônia complicada na qual vários deuses tiveram que ser convocados e apaziguados.

Heviesso (Shango), o deus do trovão, foi acalmado com óleo de palma vermelho, símbolo do muco sangrento de um novo nascimento. No curso seguinte, Sakpata, o senhor das doenças, desempenhou um papel de liderança.

Sakpata, genezing door de heer over de ziekten

In Doutou, in Zuid-Benin, bracht een langdurige ziekte een jonge vrouw ertoe advies en hulp in te roepen bij een traditionele genezeres. Die stelde vast dat de vrouw, die eerder was ingewijd in een voduncultus, de goddelijke regels meermaals onvergeeflijk had overtreden. Dientengevolge kwam het tot een gecompliceerde ceremonie waarbij verschillende goden tegelijk moesten worden opgeroepen en gesust.

Eerst werd Heviesso (Shango), de god van de donder, gekalmeerd met rode palmolie, symbool voor het bloedige slijm van een wedergeboorte. In het verdere verloop speelde Sakpata, de heer over de ziekten, een hoofdrol.

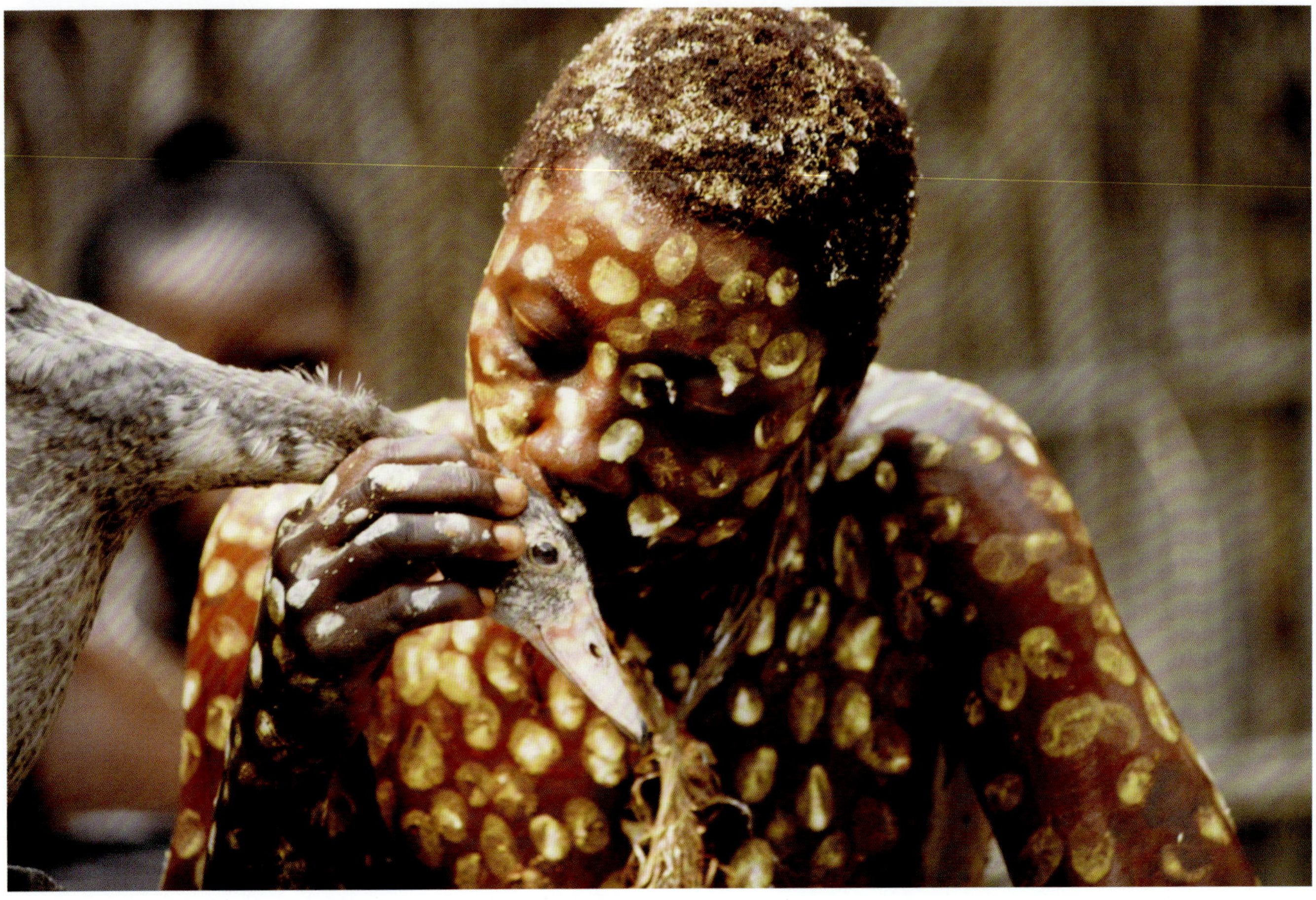

Message for the gods. The patient whispers her wishes and messages to the goose that is to be sacrificed for her. These are to be transmitted to the gods by the dead soul of the animal.

Message pour les dieux. La patiente chuchote ses souhaits et ses messages à l'oie qui doit être sacrifiée pour elle. Ses propos doivent être transmis aux dieux par l'âme de l'animal défunt.

Botschaft für die Götter. Die Patientin flüstert der Gans, die für sie geopfert wird, ihre Wünsche und Botschaften zu. Diese sollen den Göttern von der Totenseele des Tieres übermittelt werden.

Mensaje para los dioses. La paciente susurra sus deseos y mensajes al ganso que es sacrificado por ella. Estos deben ser transmitidos a los dioses por el alma muerta del animal.

Mensagem para os Deuses. A paciente sussurra seus desejos e mensagens ao ganso que é sacrificado por ela. Estes devem ser transmitidos aos deuses pela alma morta do animal.

Boodschap voor de goden. De patiënte fluistert de gans die voor haar wordt geofferd haar wensen en boodschappen in. Deze moeten door de dode ziel van het dier aan de goden worden doorgegeven.

underwent various baths, at the end of which an animal sacrifice was offered. This finally led to an intense trance, which proved that the gods had accepted the sacrifice.

d'une renaissance. Ensuite, Sakpata, seigneur des maladies, a tenu un rôle important.

Le corps entièrement recouvert de pois peints symbolisant la « variole de Sakpata », la malade fut baignée plusieurs fois, puis un animal fut sacrifié. La cérémonie se termina par une transe intense qui indiqua que les dieux avaient accepté l'offrande.

Am ganzen Körper mit Punkten, den „Pocken Sakpatas" gezeichnet, erhielt die Kranke verschiedene Bäder, an deren Ende ein Tieropfer dargebracht wurde. Dies führte schließlich zu einer heftigen Trance, die belegte, dass die Götter das Opfer angenommen hatten.

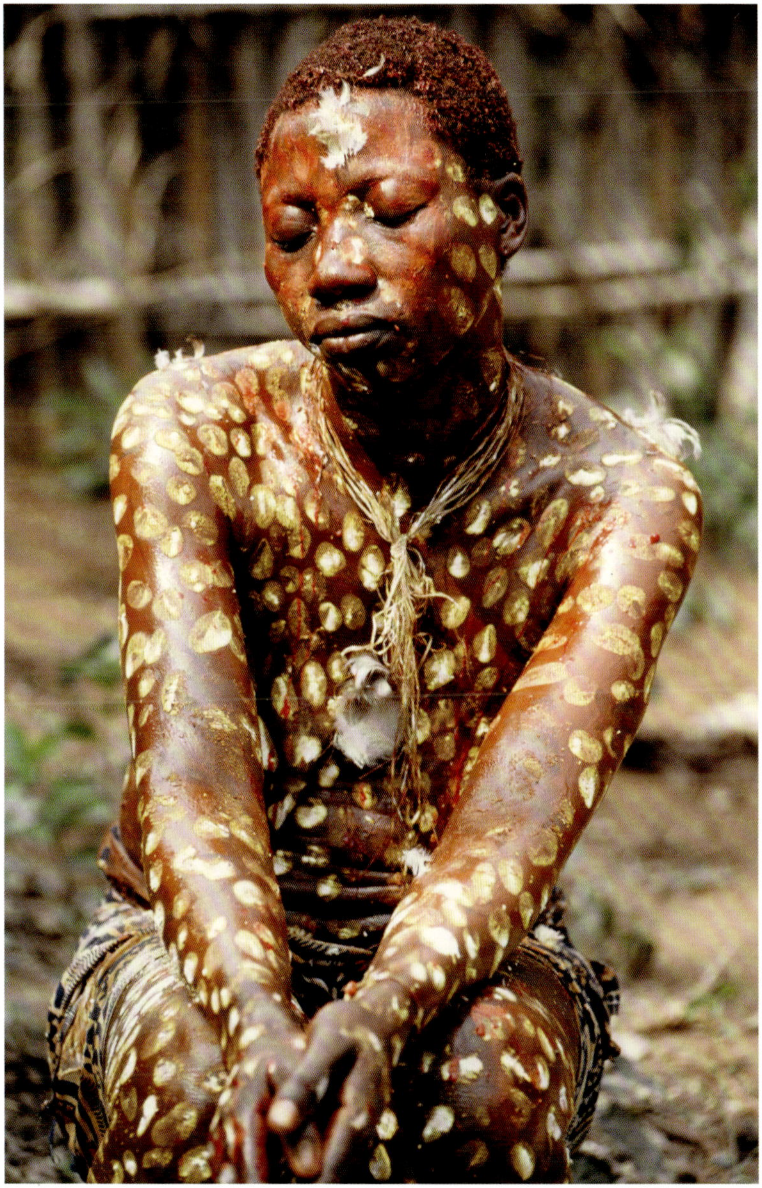

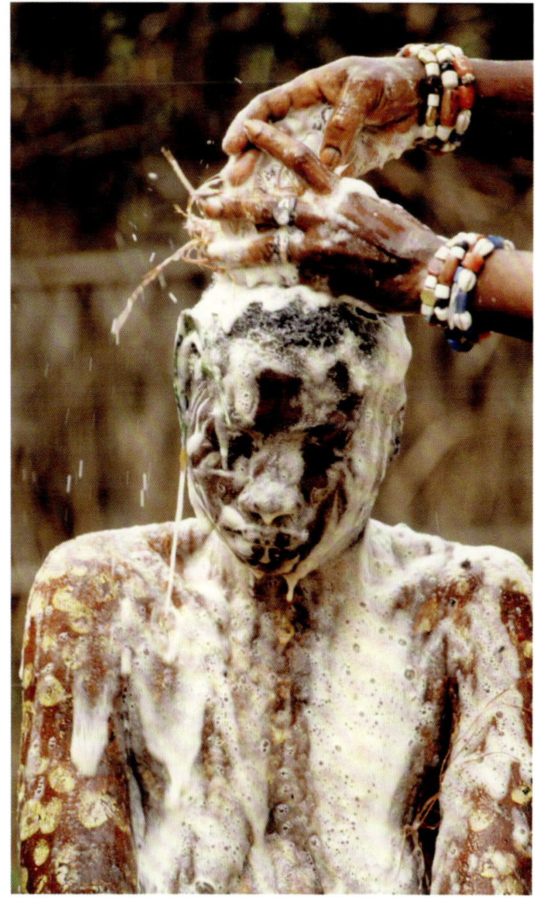

Con todo su cuerpo pintado de lunares, la "viruela de Sakpata", la enferma recibió varios baños, al final de los cuales se le ofreció un sacrificio animal. Esto finalmente condujo a un trance violento, que demostró que los dioses habían aceptado el sacrificio y eran reconciliadores.

Desenhada por todo o corpo com pontos, a "varíola de Sakpata", a doente recebeu vários banhos, no final dos quais foi oferecido um sacrifício animal. Isso finalmente levou a um transe violento, que provou que os deuses tinham aceitado o sacrifício e eram reconciliadores.

De 'pokken van Sakpata' werden over haar hele lichaam met stippen getckend en de zieke kreeg verschillende baden, waarna tot slot een dierenoffer werd gebracht. Dit leidde uiteindelijk tot een hevige trance, die bewees dat de goden het offer hadden aanvaard.

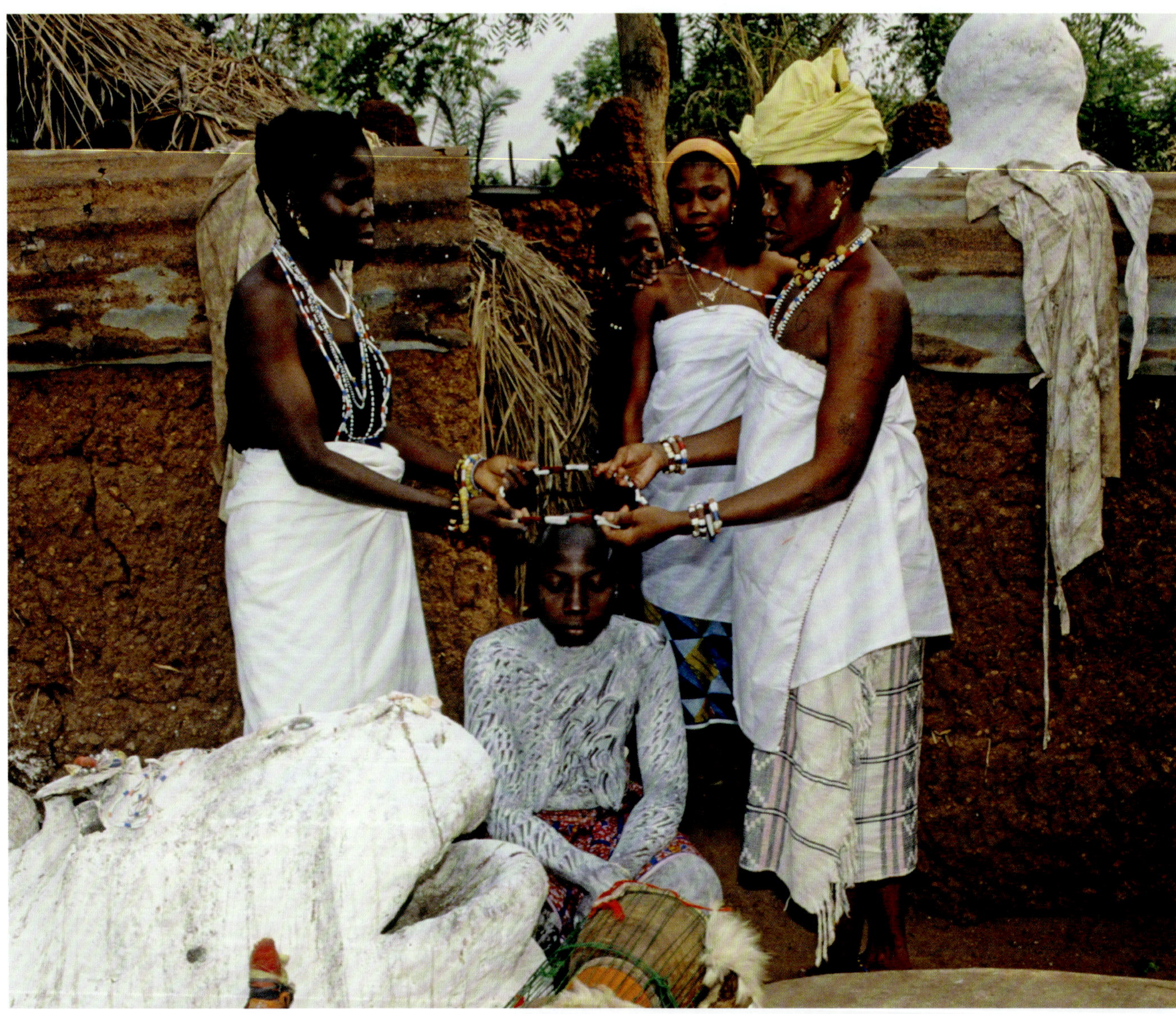

Rebirth in white. After the ritual cleansing bath, the patient is now painted white and decorated with pearls, which are mainly placed around the hip, as is the custom with newborns.

Renaissance en blanc. Après le bain rituel, la patiente est peinte en blanc et décorée de perles disposées essentiellement autour des hanches, comme le veut la coutume pour les nouveau-nés.

Neugeburt in Weiß. Nach dem rituellen Reinigungsbad wird die Patientin nun weiß angemalt und mit Perlen geschmückt, die vor allem um die Hüfte gelegt werden, wie es bei Neugeborenen der Brauch ist.

Renacimiento en blanco. Después del baño de limpieza ritual, la paciente es pintada de blanco y decorada con perlas, que se colocan principalmente alrededor de la cadera, como es costumbre en el caso de los recién nacidos.

Renascimento em branco. Após o banho de limpeza ritual, o paciente é agora pintado de branco e decorado com pérolas, que são colocadas principalmente em torno do quadril, como é costume com os recém-nascidos.

Wedergeboorte in het wit. Na het rituele reinigingsbad wordt de patiënte wit geschilderd en versierd met kralenkettingen, die vooral om de heupen worden gelegd, net zoals bij pasgeborenen gebruikelijk is.

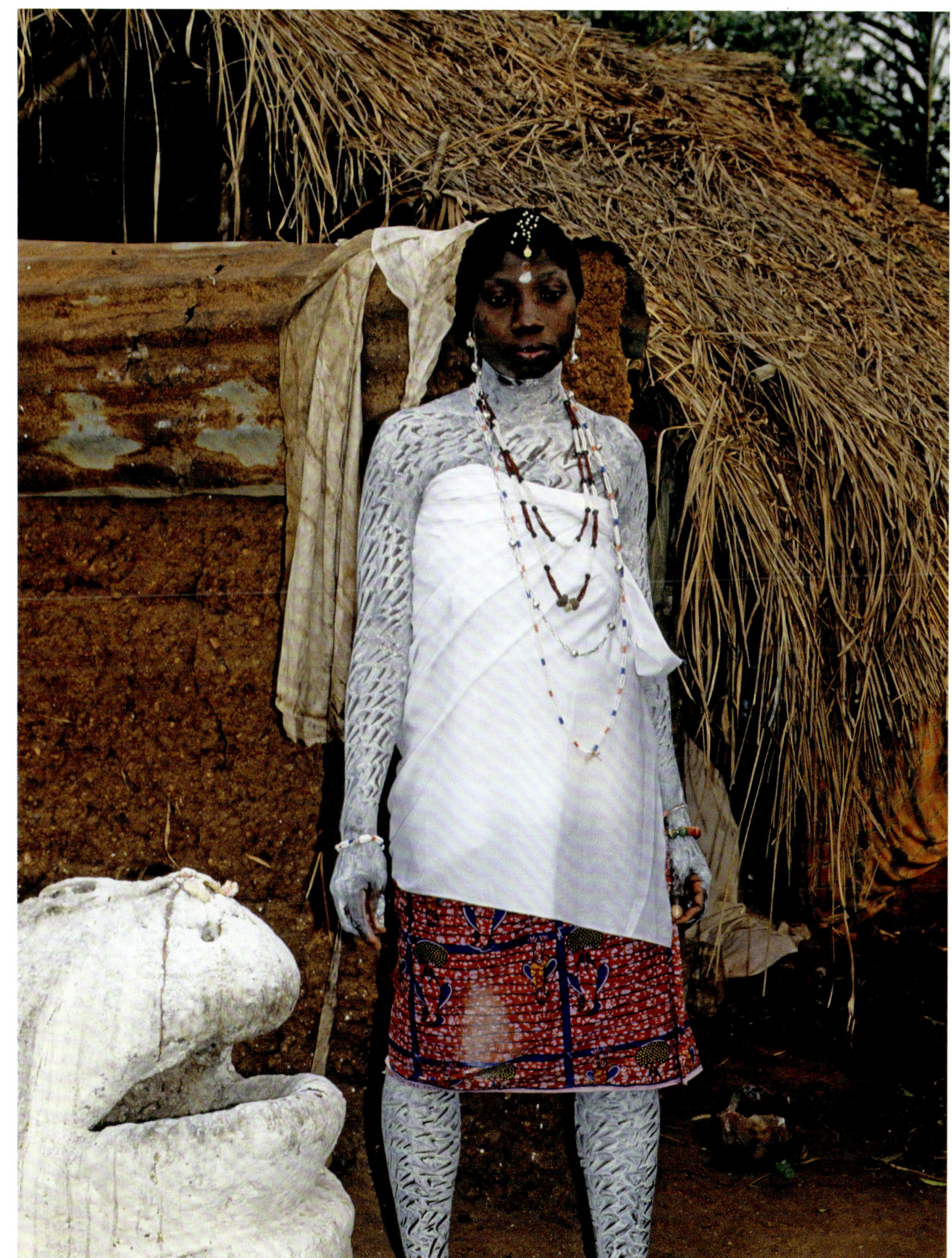

Cleansed from
misfortune

Purifiée du malheur

Vom Unglück
gereinigt

Limpios de
infortunios

Limpado do
infortúnio

Gezuiverd van
tegenslag

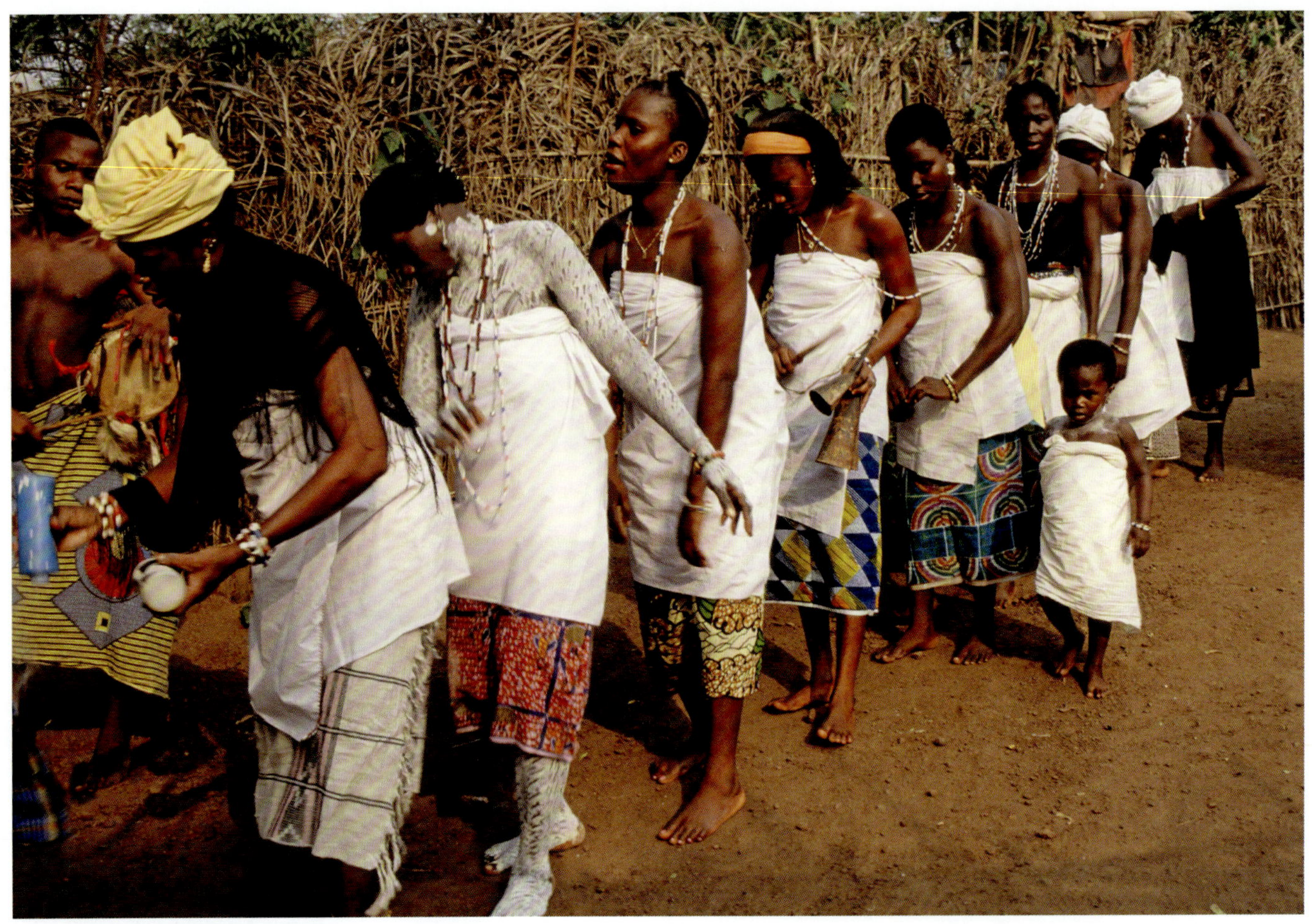

Procession to the Ceremonial Square

Procession vers le lieu de cérémonie

Prozession zum Zeremonialplatz

Procesión a la Plaza de la Ceremonia

Procissão para a Praça Cerimonial

Optocht naar het ceremonieplein

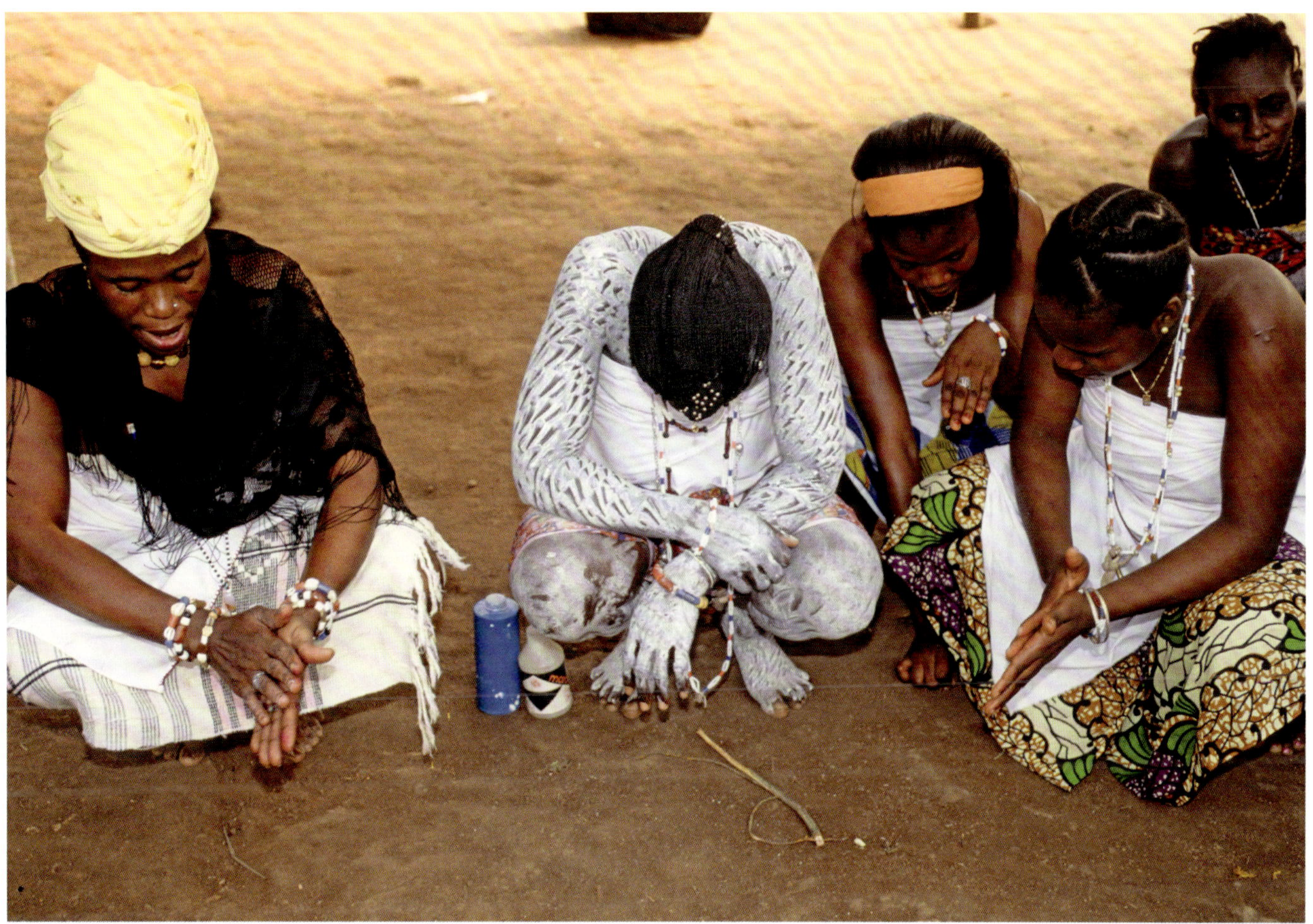

Reintegrated. After the healing ceremony the young woman kneels next to the priestess and other adepts. She is now reintegrated into the group and part of the community.

Réintégrée. À la fin de la cérémonie de guérison, la jeune femme s'accroupit au côté de la prêtresse et des autres adeptes. Elle est réintégrée dans le groupe et fait à nouveau partie de la communauté.

Wieder integriert. Nach der heilenden Zeremonie kniet die junge Frau neben der Priesterin und anderen Adepten. Sie ist nun wieder in die Gruppe integriert und Teil der Gemeinschaft.

Reintegrado. Después de la ceremonia de curación, la joven se arrodilla junto a la sacerdotisa y otros adeptos. Ahora está integrada de nuevo en el grupo y forma parte de la comunidad.

Reintegrado. Depois da cerimônia de cura, a jovem se ajoelha ao lado da sacerdotisa e de outros adeptos. Ela está agora integrada de volta ao grupo e parte da comunidade.

Gereïntegreerd. ie knielt de jonge vrouw naast de priesteres en andere adepten. Ze is nu weer geïntegreerd in de groep en maakt deel uit van de gemeenschap.

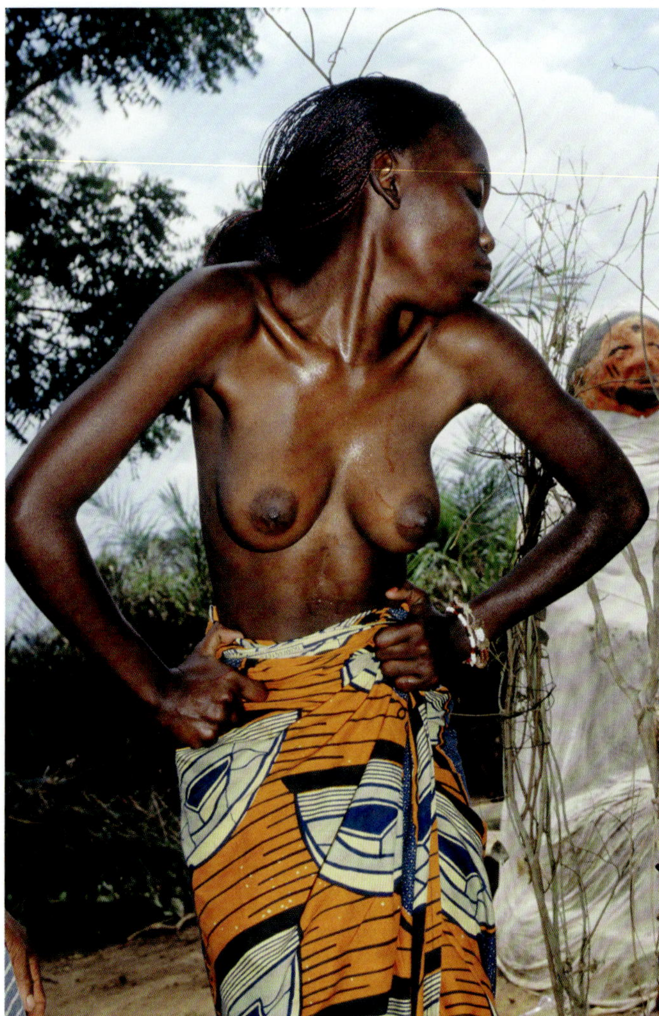

Lydwin dances in a trance
Lydwin danse en transe
Lydwin tanzt in Trance
Lydwin baila en trance
Lydwin dança em transe
Lydwin danst in trance

Lydwin's cure

Shortly after her 18th birthday, Lydwin, a young woman from Benin, collapsed and became unconscious. Malaria was diagnosed in the Cotonou clinic and she received the appropriate medication. The fever decreased, but afterwards she was suffering from insomnia, pain and fainting.

Six months later her mother brought her to Hounon Djalé, a well-known Vodun priest of the region. He diagnosed "disease by curse," which was the result of an unfortunate love affair involving Lydwin.

La guérison de Lydwin

Peu de temps après son 18e anniversaire, Lydwin, une jeune Béninoise, perdit connaissance. Conduite à la clinique de Cotonou, les médecins diagnostiquèrent la malaria et la traitèrent avec les médicaments adaptés. La fièvre tomba mais elle souffrait encore d'insomnies, de douleurs et de pertes de conscience.

Six mois plus tard, sa mère la conduisit auprès d'Hounon Djalé, prêtre vodun réputé de la région. Il découvrit une « maladie de malédiction », provoquée par une relation

Lydwins Heilung

Kurz nach Vollendung ihres 18. Geburtstages brach Lydwin, eine junge Frau aus Benin, bewusstlos zusammen. In der Klinik von Cotonou wurde Malaria diagnostiziert, und sie erhielt die entsprechenden Medikamente. Das Fieber war rückläufig, aber sie litt fortan an Schlaflosigkeit, Schmerzen und Ohnmachtsanfällen.

Ein halbes Jahr später brachte ihre Mutter sie zu Hounon Djalé, einem bekannten Vodunpriester der Region. Er diagnostizierte „Krankheit durch Fluch", was das Resultat

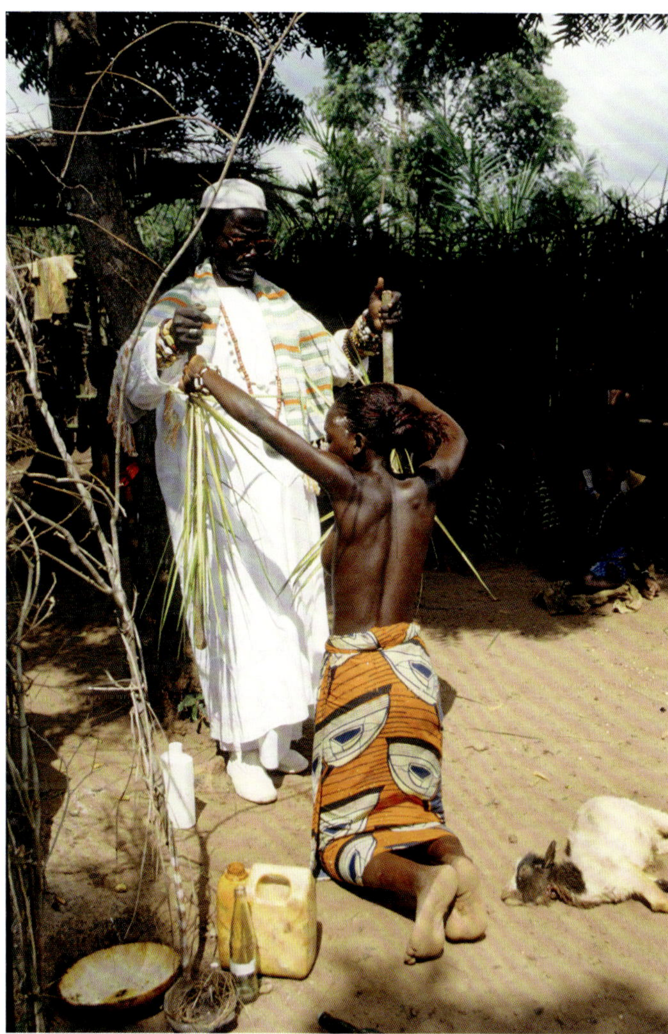

La cura de Lydwin

Poco después de cumplir 18 años, Lydwin, una joven de Benin, se desmayó. Le diagnosticaron malaria en la clínica de Cotonou y recibió la medicación adecuada. La fiebre disminuyó, pero ahora sufría de insomnio, dolor y desmayos.

Medio año después, su madre la llevó a Hounon Djalé, un conocido sacerdote vudú de la región, cl cual le diagnosticó "enfermedad por maldición", resultado de la infeliz historia de amor de Lydwin. Se le recomendaba la iniciación en la comunidad

A cura de Lydwin

Pouco depois do seu 18º aniversário, Lydwin, uma jovem do Benin, desmaiou inconsciente. A malária foi diagnosticada na clínica de Cotonou e ela recebeu a medicação apropriada. A febre estava diminuindo, mas ela agora sofria de insônia, dor e desmaio.

Meio ano depois, a mãe levou-a a Hounon Djalé, um conhecido vodueiro da região. Ele diagnosticou "doença por maldição", que foi o resultado do infeliz caso de amor de Lydwin. Agora, a iniciação

Lydwins genezing

Kort na haar achttiende verjaardag stortte Lydwin, een jonge vrouw uit Benin, bewusteloos in elkaar. In de Cotonou-kliniek werd malaria gediagnosticeerd en ze kreeg de bijbehorende medicatie. De koorts nam af, maar vanaf die tijd had ze last van slapeloosheid, pijn en flauwvallen.

Een halfjaar later nam haar moeder haar mee naar Hounon Djalé, een bekende vodunpriester uit de regio. Hij stelde de diagnose 'ziekte door vloek', als gevolg van Lydwins ongelukkige liefdesrelatie.

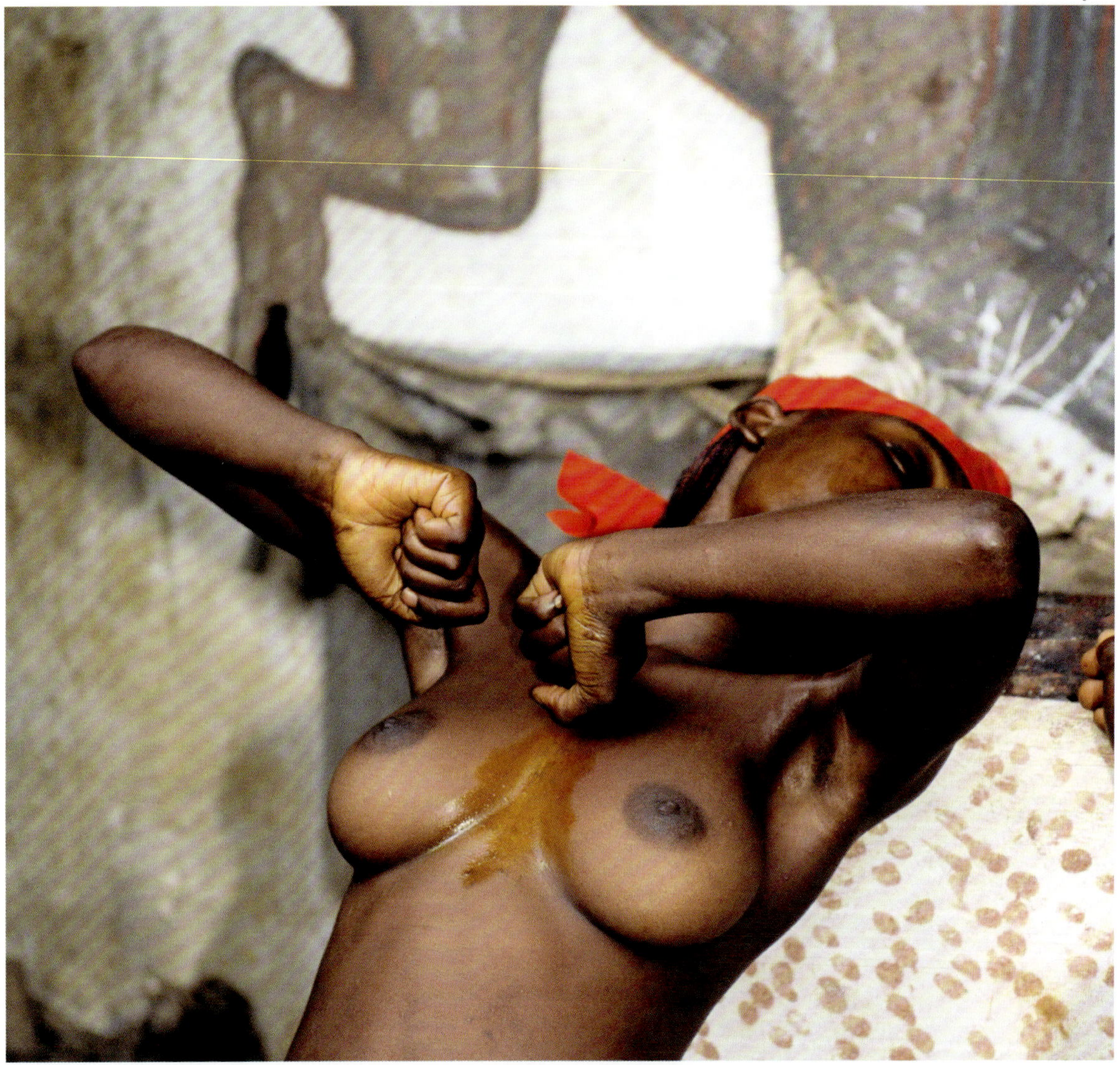

Now the initiation into the community of followers of a strong, warlike god was indicated, in order to help Lydwin to recover, give her protection and new self-confidence.

After long preparation in the monastery there were energetic ceremonies where she became the ward of Danou-Woto, a war god of the local Mami Wata cult.

amoureuse malheureuse. Il recommanda à Lydwin de suivre l'initiation d'une communauté religieuse dédiée à un dieu puissant et belliqueux, afin qu'il puisse lui apporter la guérison et la protection, et l'aider à retrouver confiance en elle.

Au terme d'une longue préparation dans un monastère, elle devint, au cours d'une cérémonie énergétique, la protégée de Danou-Woto, dieu de la guerre du culte local de Mami Wata.

einer unglücklichen Liebesbeziehung Lydwins war. Angezeigt war nun die Initiation in die Anhängergemeinschaft eines starken, kriegerischen Gottes, um Lydwin zu Genesung, Schutz und neuem Selbstbewusstsein zu verhelfen.

Nach langer Vorbereitung im Kloster wurde sie im Zuge energetischer Zeremonien Schutzbefohlene Danou-Wotos, eines Kriegsgotts des lokalen Mami Wata Kultes.

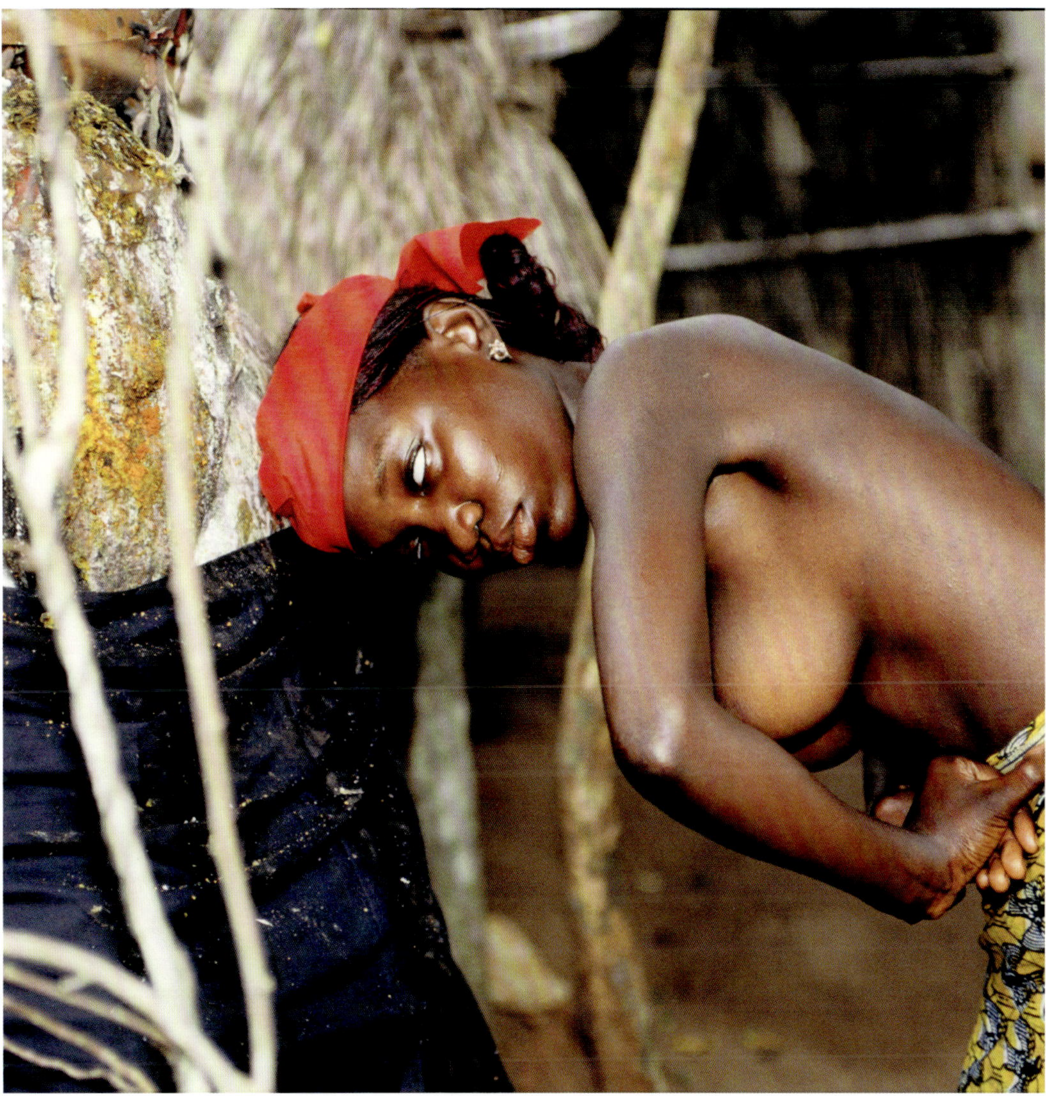

de seguidores de un Dios fuerte y guerrero para que ayudase a Lydwin a recuperarse, protegerse y a recuperar la confianza en sí misma.

Después de una larga preparación en el monasterio, se convirtió en la orden protegida Danou-Wotos, un dios de la guerra del culto local Mami Wata, en el curso de las ceremonias energéticas.

na comunidade de seguidores de um Deus forte e guerreiro foi indicada, a fim de ajudar Lydwin a recuperar, proteger e ter uma nova autoconfiança.

Depois de uma longa preparação no mosteiro, ela se tornou a Ordenada Protegida Danou-Wotos, um deus da guerra do culto local Mami Wata, no curso de cerimônias energéticas.

Aanbevolen werd de inwijding in de volgelingengemeenschap van een sterke, oorlogszuchtige god, om Lydwin te helpen bij haar herstel, haar te beschermen en nieuw zelfvertrouwen te geven.

Na een lange voorbereiding in het klooster werd ze na energetische ceremoniën beschermelinge van Danou-Woto, een oorlogsgod uit de plaatselijke Mami Wata-cultus.

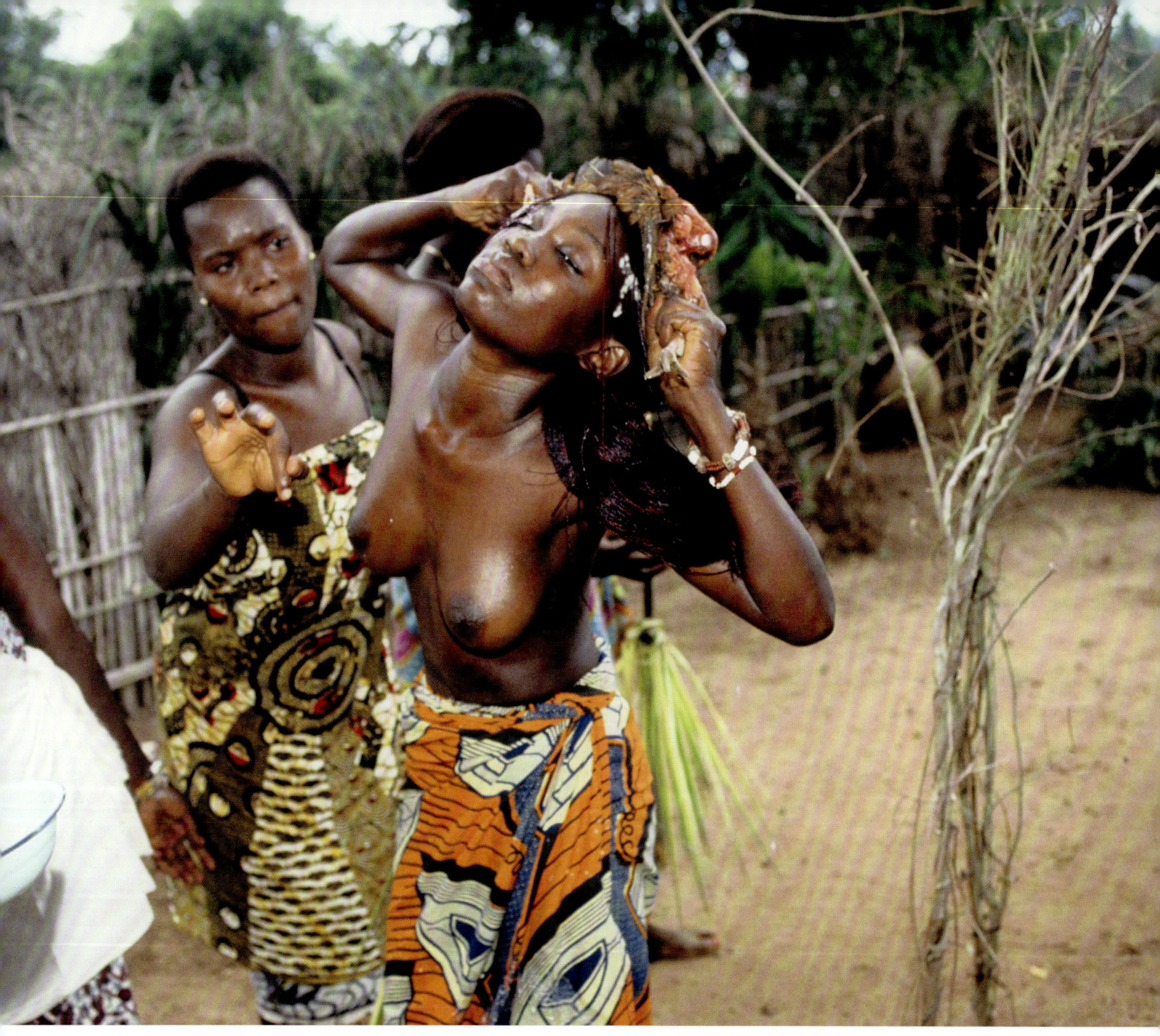

Lydwin in a state of trance. Since Lydwin's trance is violent and impulsive, some Mami Wata adepts stand nearby to protect Lydwin from injuries if necessary.

Lydwin en état de transe. La transe de Lydwin est tellement intense et impulsive que des fidèles de Mami Wata restent à proximité de la jeune femme pour éviter qu'elle ne se blesse.

Lydwin im Zustand der Trance. Da Lydwins Trance heftig und impulsiv ausfällt, stehen einige Mami Wata-Adeptinnen in der Nähe, um Lydwin nötigenfalls vor Verletzungen zu schützen.

Lydwin en estado de trance. Como el trance de Lydwin es violento e impulsivo, algunos adeptos de Mami Wata están cerca para proteger a Lydwin de lesiones si es necesario.

Lydwin em estado de transe. Como o transe de Lydwin é violento e impulsivo, alguns adeptos de Mami Wata ficam por perto para proteger Lydwin de lesões, se necessário.

Lydwin in trance. Aangezien Lydwins trance heftig en impulsief uitpakt, staan sommige Mami Wata-adepten in de buurt om Lydwin indien nodig te beschermen tegen verwondingen.

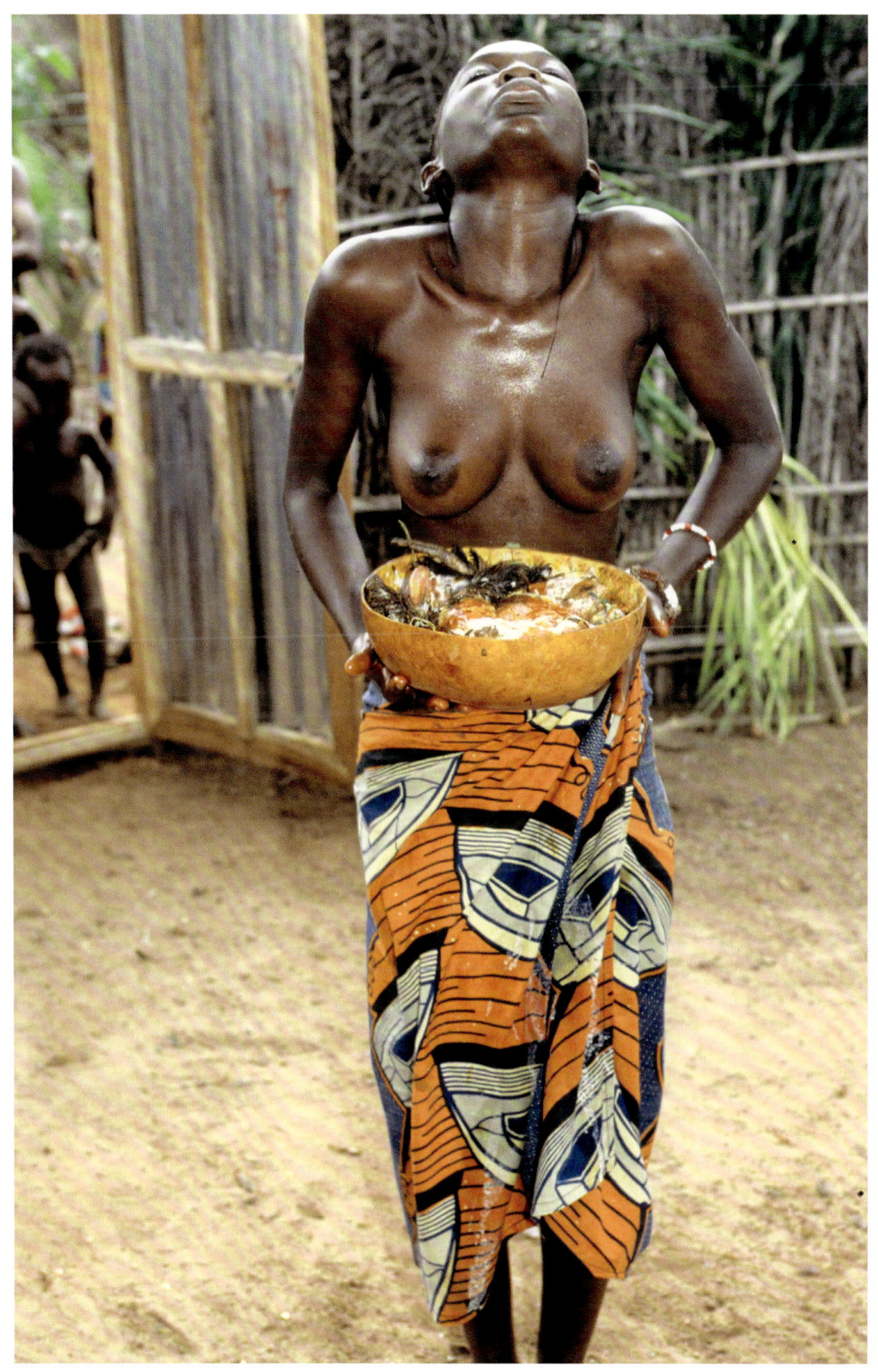

Lydwin in a state of trance
Lydwin en état de transe
Lydwin im Zustand der Trance
Lydwin en estado de trance
Lydwin em estado de transe
Lydwin in trance

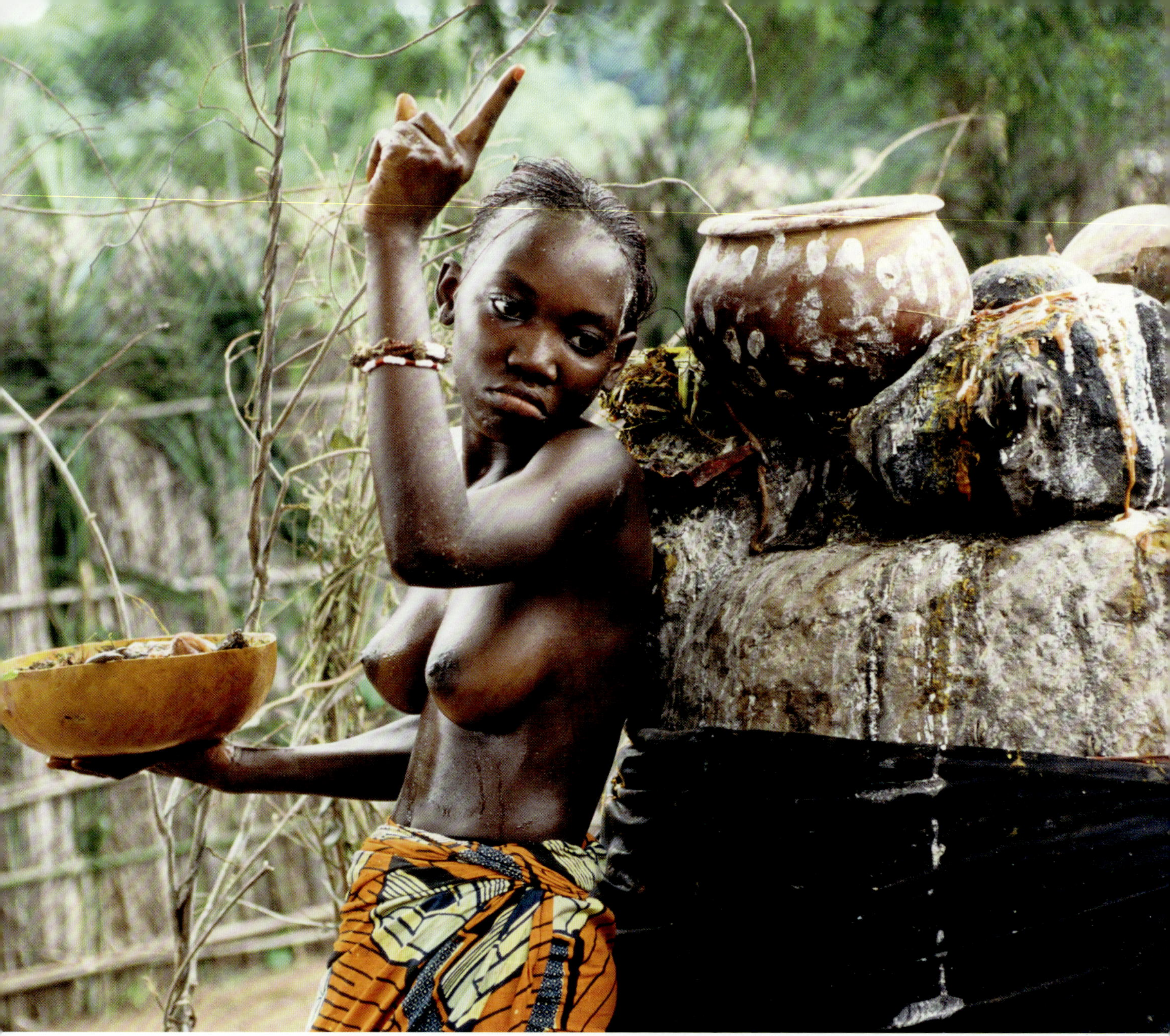

Lydwin in a state of trance. With new self-confidence and a sacrifice for the deity, Lydwin leans against Danou-Woto's shrine. She's under his protection from now on.

Lydwin en état de transe. Dotée d'une nouvelle conscience d'elle-même, Lydwin porte des offrandes à la divinité et s'appuie contre l'autel de Danou-Woto. À partir de cet instant, elle est sous sa protection.

Lydwin im Zustand der Trance. Mit neuem Selbstbewusstsein und einer Opfergabe für die Gottheit lehnt Lydwin an Danou-Wotos Schrein. Sie steht ab sofort unter seinem Schutz.

Lydwin en estado de trance. Con nueva confianza en sí misma y un sacrificio por la deidad, Lydwin se apoya en el santuario de Danou-Woto. Ahora está bajo su protección.

Lydwin em estado de transe. Com nova autoconfiança e um sacrifício pela divindade, Lydwin inclina-se contra o santuário de Danou-Woto. Ela está agora sob a protecção dele.

Lydwin in trance. Met nieuw zelfvertrouwen en een offer voor de god leunt Lydwin tegen het Danou-Woto-heiligdom. Ze staat nu onder zijn bescherming.

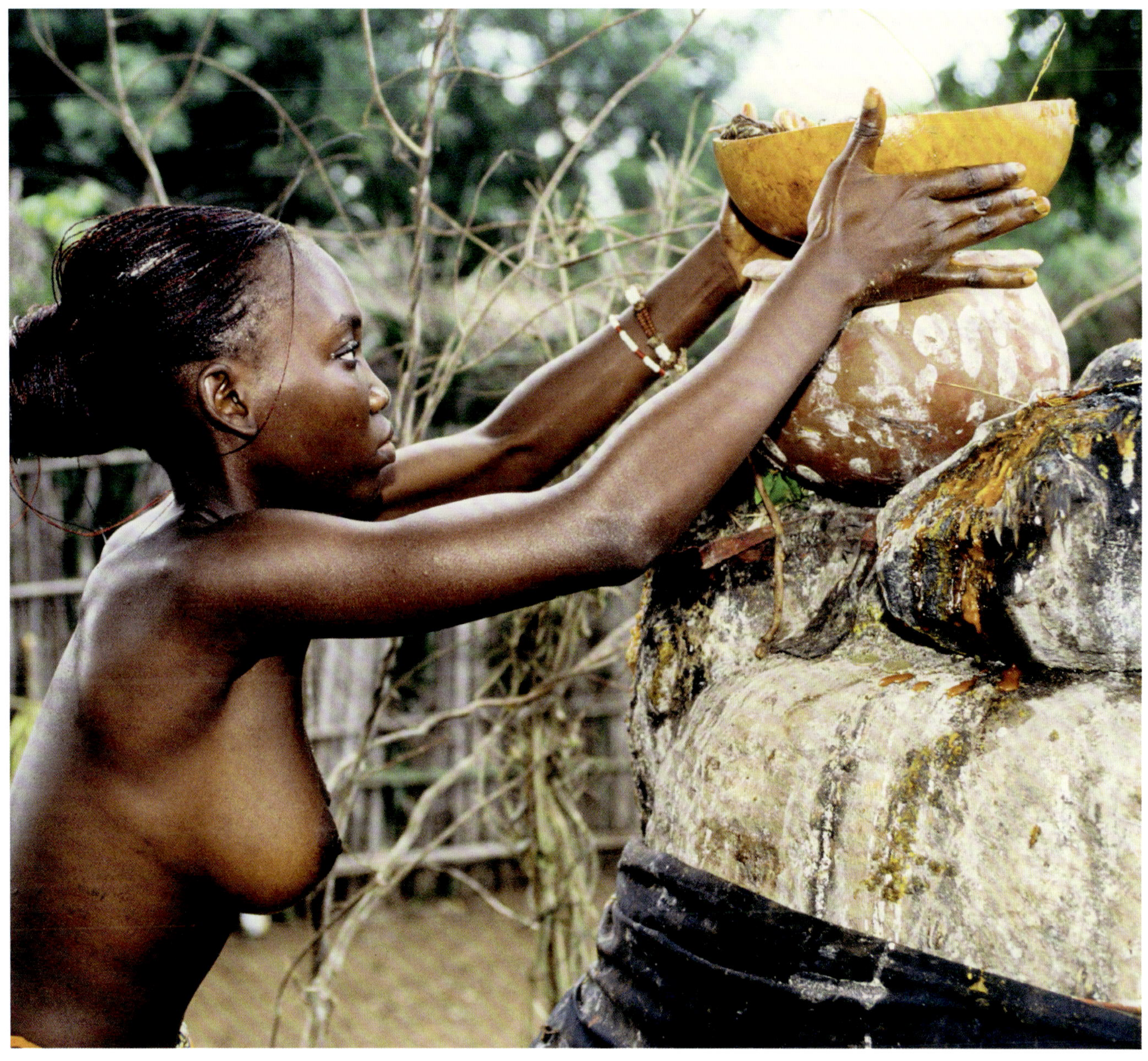

Sacrifice for Danou-Woto

Sacrifice pour Danou-Woto

Opfergabe für Danou-Woto

Ofrenda del sacrificio para Danou-Woto

Sacrifício para Danou-Woto

Offer voor Danou-Woto

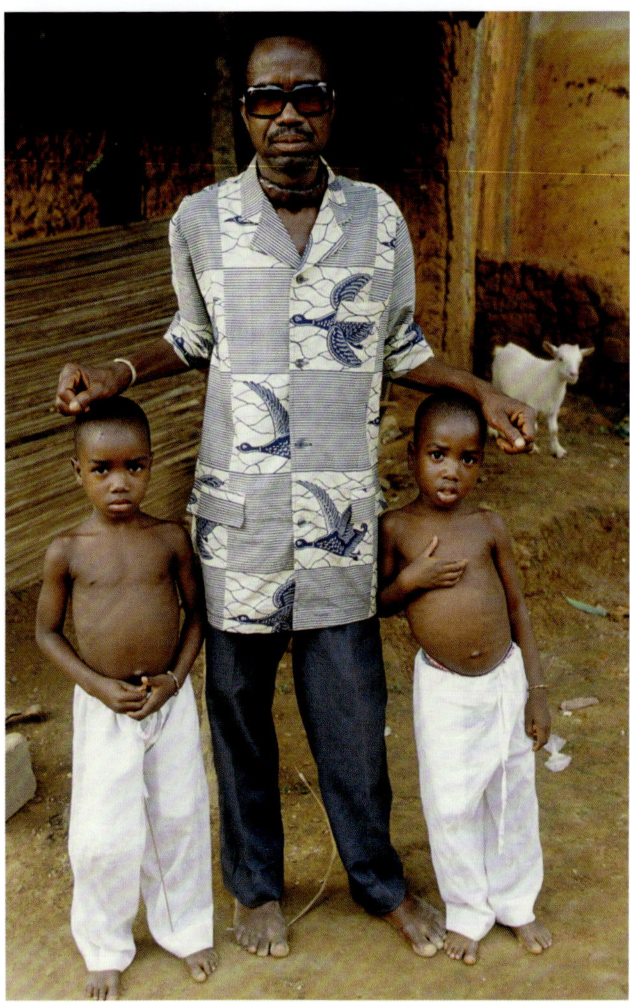

Father with twins
Un père avec ses jumeaux
Vater mit Zwillingen
Padre con gemelos
Pai com gêmeos
Vader met een tweeling

Local inhabitants with twin dolls
Autochtone avec poupées jumelles
Einheimische mit Zwillingspuppen
Locales con muñecas gemelas
Locais com bonecas gêmeas
Inheemse vrouw met tweelingpoppen

Twins—Remembrance in reverence

In West Africa, twins have a quite special meaning with many peoples. One reason for this is that twins are not born so frequently anywhere else for reasons that have hardly been investigated so far. Togo, Benin and Nigeria have long held top positions in the birth rate.

Because of the high infant mortality rate, especially in earlier times, often only one child survived, the deceased twin is honored in Benin in a special way. Small, wooden dolls, also called *Venavis,* serve as

Jumeaux, mémoire respectueuse

En Afrique de l'Ouest, les jumeaux revêtent une importance particulière pour de nombreuses ethnies. L'une des raisons tient au taux important de naissances gémellaires dans cette région, dont les causes ont peu été étudiées. Ainsi s'explique en partie le taux de natalité exceptionnel du Togo, du Bénin et du Nigeria.

À cause d'un taux de mortalité infantile élevé, en particulier par le passé, seulement un de ces deux enfants pouvait survivre. Au Bénin, le jumeau décédé jouit encore

Zwillinge – Gedenken in Ehrfurcht

In Westafrika haben Zwillinge bei vielen Völkern ganz besondere Bedeutung. Ein Grund dafür ist, dass aus bislang kaum untersuchten Ursachen nirgendwo häufiger Zwillinge zur Welt kommen. So nehmen auch Togo, Benin und Nigeria seit langer Zeit Spitzenpositionen bei der Geburtenrate ein.

Da wegen der hohen Kindersterblichkeit besonders in früheren Zeiten oft nur ein Kind überlebte, wird der verstorbene Zwilling in Benin in besonderer Weise

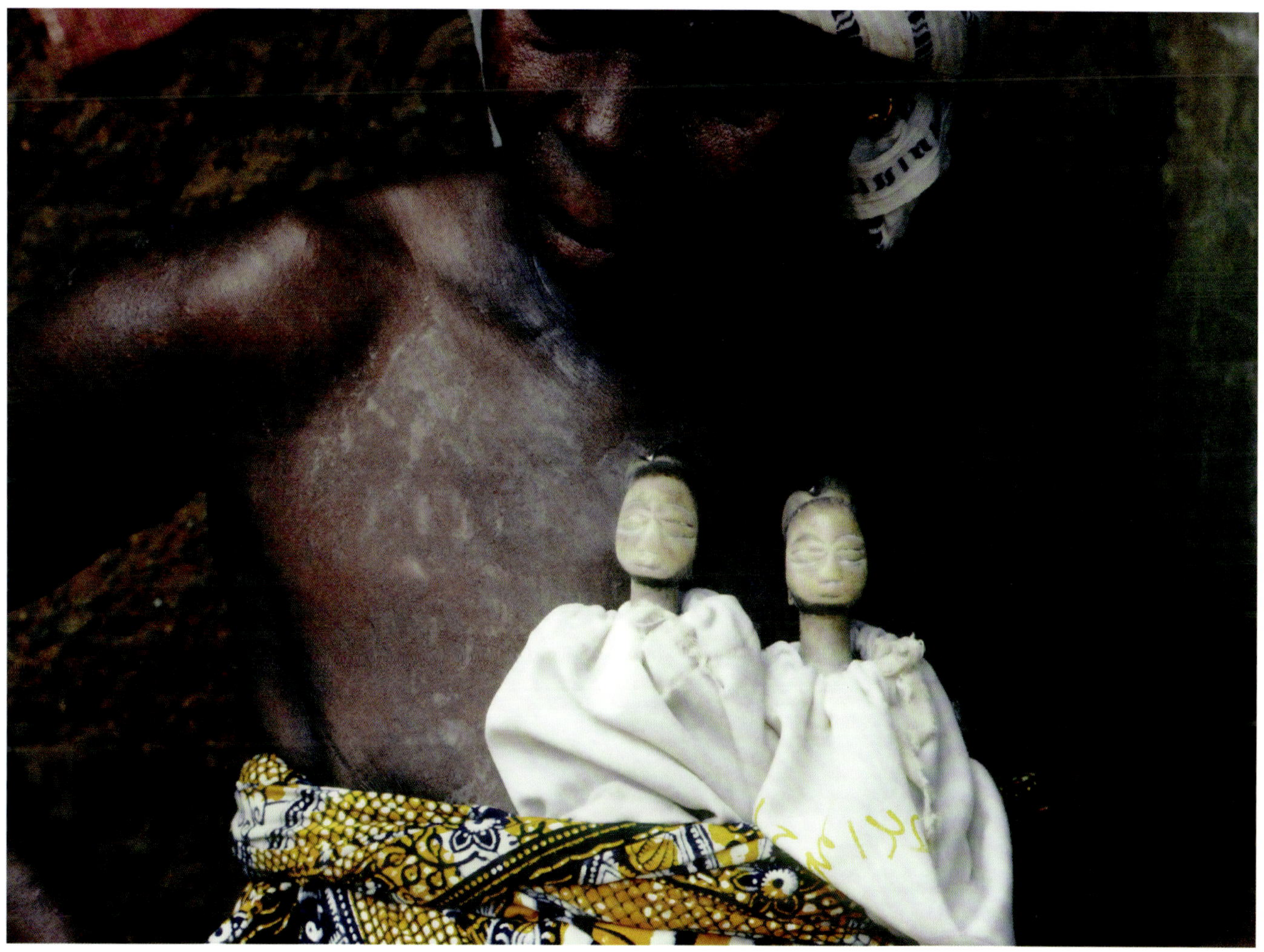

Los gemelos– Recuerdos en reverencia

En África Occidental, los gemelos tienen un significado muy especial para muchos pueblos. Una de las razones es que los gemelos no nacen en ningún otro lugar con tanta frecuencia como aquí,por causas que apenas se han investigado hasta el momento. Togo, Benin y Nigeria, por ejemplo, han ocupado desde hace mucho tiempo los primeros puestos en la tasa de natalidad.

Debido a la alta tasa de mortalidad infantil, especialmente en épocas anteriores en que sólo sobrevivía un niño, el gemelo

Gêmeos – Memória em reverência

Na África Ocidental, os gémeos têm um significado muito especial para muitos povos. Uma das razões para isso é que os gémeos não nascem mais frequentemente em lado nenhum por razões que até agora não foram investigadas. Togo, Benin e Nigéria, por exemplo, há muito ocupam posições de destaque na taxa de natalidade.

Devido à elevada taxa de mortalidade infantil, especialmente nos primeiros tempos, apenas uma criança sobreviveu frequentemente, o gémeo falecido é

Tweelingen – herdenken met eerbied

In West-Afrika heeft een tweeling voor veel mensen een bijzondere betekenis. Een reden daarvoor is dat tweelingen door tot nu toe nauwelijks onderzochte oorzaken nergens vaker worden geboren dan hier. Togo, Benin en Nigeria staan bijvoorbeeld allang in de top wat betreft geboortecijfers van tweelingen.

Door de hoge kindersterfte, vooral in het verleden, waarbij vaak slechts één kind het overleefde, wordt de overleden tweeling in Benin op bijzondere manieren geëerd.

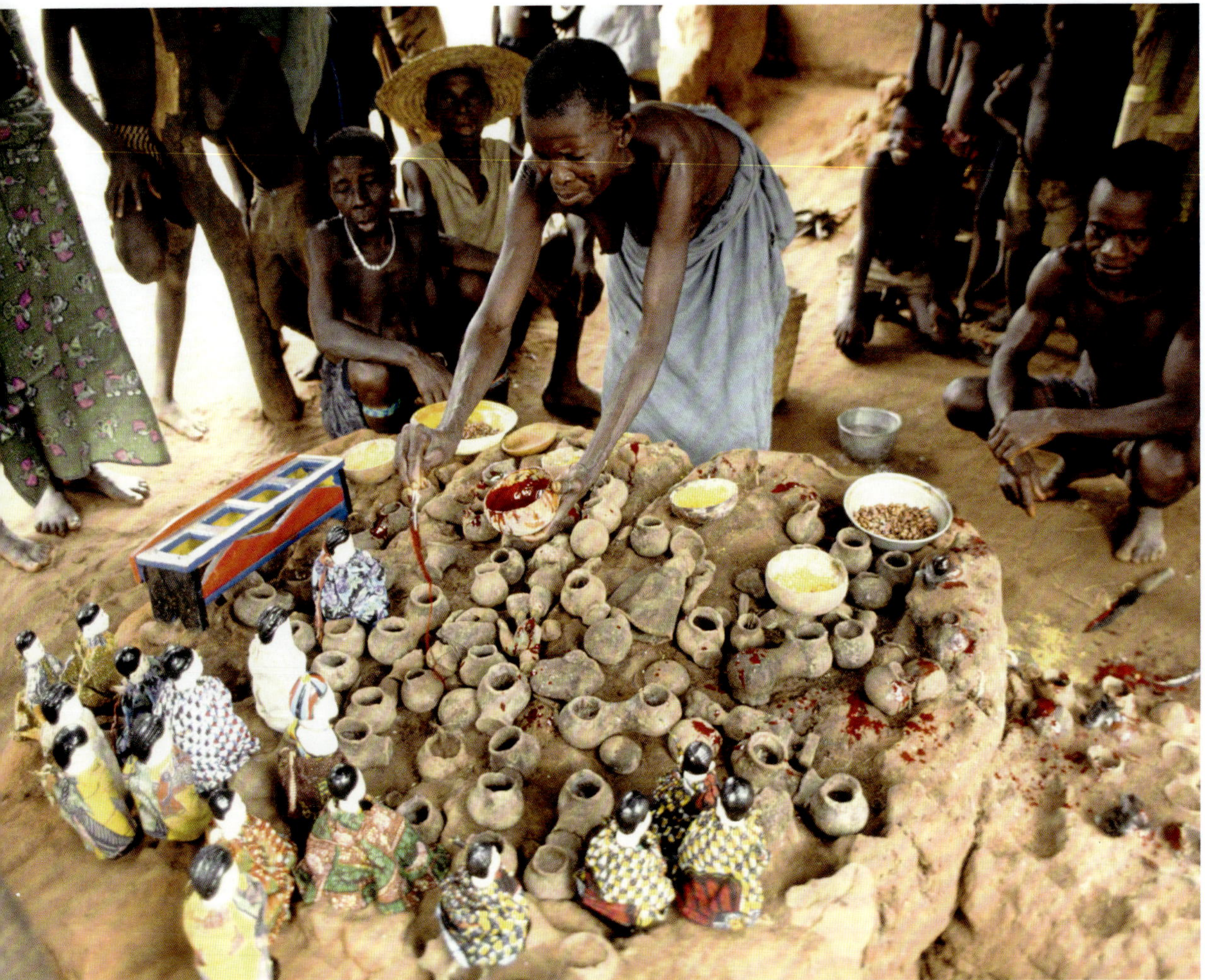

soul carriers for the different siblings and are cared for like a living child.

There are many meanings and rituals around these dolls, which represent a direct connection to the world beyond, for those still living. They therefore always endeavor to keep them benevolent, since their influence is considered powerful and they are closer to the gods than humans.

aujourd'hui d'une considération particulière. De petites poupées mortuaires en bois, également appelées *venavis,* servent à transporter l'âme des disparus et sont traitées et soignées comme des enfants vivants.

Ces poupées mortuaires possèdent de nombreuses significations et participent à de nombreux rituels, car, pour les vivants, elles représentent un lien direct avec l'autre monde. Influentes et plus proches des dieux que les hommes, on se doit d'être toujours bon avec elles.

gewürdigt. Kleine, hölzerne Totenpuppen, auch *Venavis* genannt, dienen als Seelenträger für das verschiedene Geschwisterchen und werden umsorgt und gepflegt wie ein lebendes Kind.

Es gibt viele Bedeutungen und Rituale rund um diese Totenpuppen, die für die noch Lebenden eine direkte Verbindung zur jenseitigen Welt darstellen. Man ist daher stets bemüht, sie gütig zu stimmen, da ihr Einfluss als mächtig gilt und sie den Göttern näher stehen als die Menschen.

Shaving the head. During a ceremony for her deceased twins, this woman is shorn. This is an outward sign of her great loss.

Rasage de tête. Au cours de la cérémonie en l'honneur des jumeaux décédés, cette femme est rasée. Elle témoigne ainsi par un signe extérieur de la perte immense qu'elle éprouve.

Rasur des Haupthaars. Während einer Zeremonie für ihre verstorbenen Zwillinge wird diese Frau geschoren. Damit wird ein äußerliches Zeichen für ihren großen Verlust gesetzt.

Afeitado del pelo de la cabeza. Esta mujer deja que le afeiten la cabeza durante una ceremonia para sus gemelos fallecidos. Esta es una muestra externa de su gran pérdida.

Depilação dos pêlos da cabeça. Esta mulher é tosquiada durante uma cerimónia para os seus gémeos falecidos. Isto é um sinal exterior da sua grande perda.

Het afscheren van het hoofdhaar. Deze vrouw wordt geschoren tijdens een ceremonie voor haar overleden tweeling. Hiermee krijgt ze een uiterlijk teken van haar grote verlies.

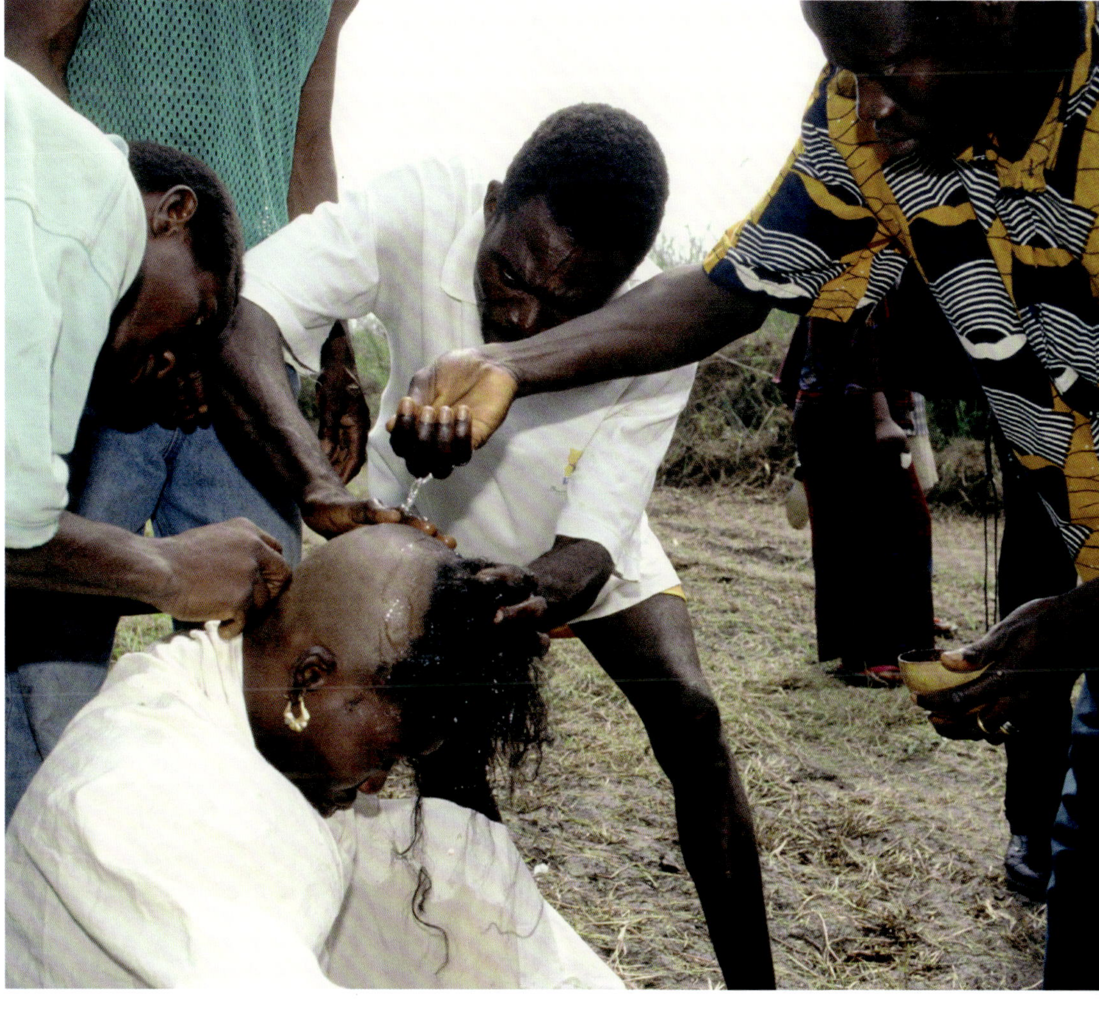

fallecido es especialmente apreciado en Benin. Pequeños muñecos muertos de madera, también llamados *Venavis,* sirven como portadores de alma para los diversos hermanos y son cuidados y tratados como si de un niño vivo se tratase.

Hay muchos significados y rituales alrededor de estos muñecos muertos, que representan una conexión directa con el mundo del más allá para los que aún viven. Por lo tanto, uno siempre se esfuerza por hacerlos sentir bien, ya que su influencia se considera poderosa y están más cerca de los dioses que los humanos.

especialmente apreciado no Benim. Pequenas bonecas de madeira mortas, também chamadas Venavis, servem como portadoras de almas para os vários irmãos e são cuidadas e cuidadas como uma criança viva.

Há muitos significados e rituais em torno dessas bonecas mortas, que representam uma conexão direta com o mundo além para os ainda vivos. Por isso, estamos sempre ansiosos para fazê-los bons, pois sua influência é considerada poderosa e eles estão mais próximos dos deuses do que os humanos.

Kleine, houten dodenpoppen, ook wel *venavi* genoemd, dienen als zielendrager voor de overleden broertjes en zusjes en worden verzorgd als een levend kind.

Er zijn allerlei betekenissen en rituelen rond deze dodenpoppen, die voor de overlevenden een directe verbinding vormen met de wereld aan gene zijde. Men doet daarom altijd zijn best ze gunstig te stemmen, omdat hun invloed als krachtig wordt beschouwd en ze dichter bij de goden staan dan de mensen.

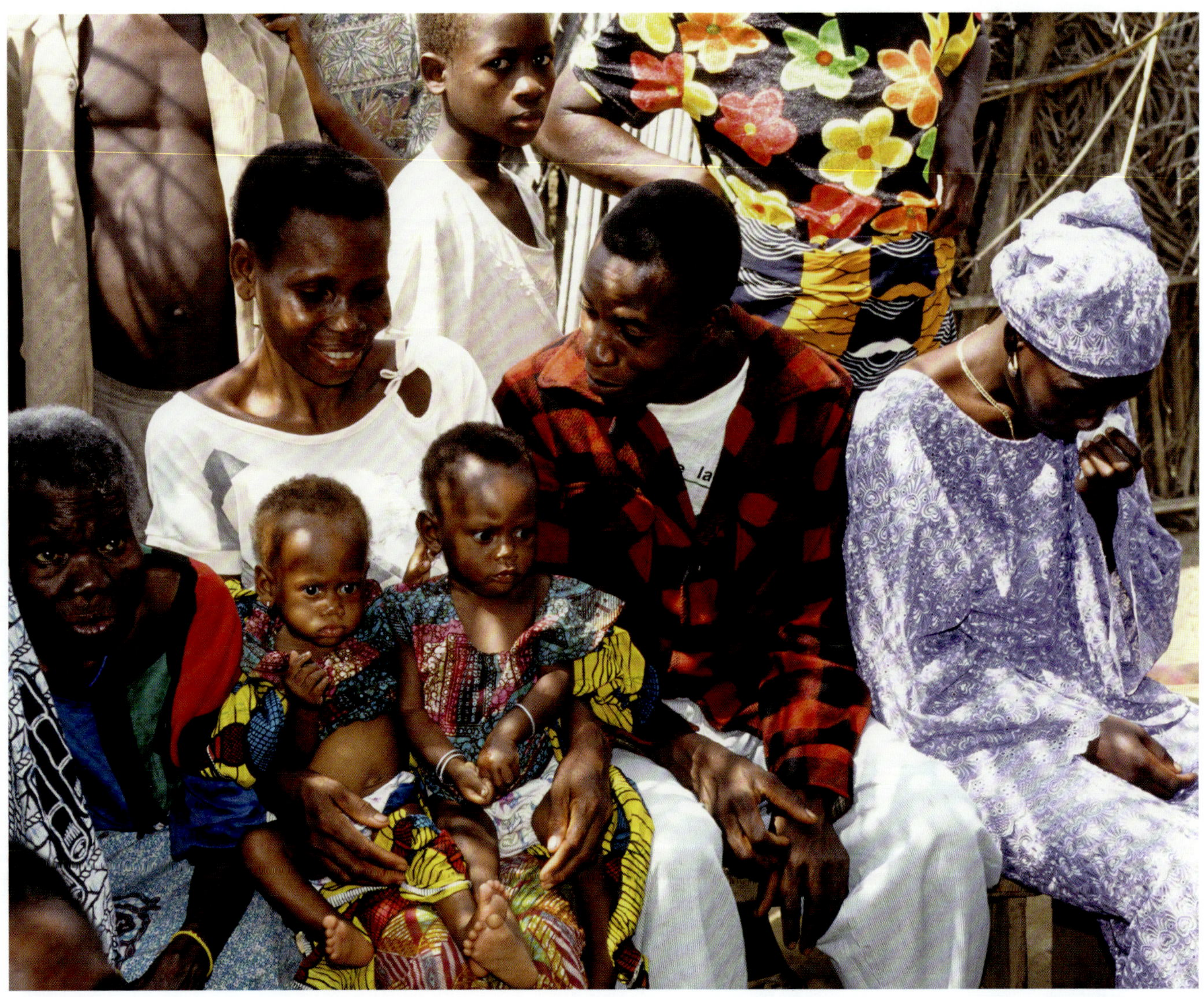

Shared grief

Deuil partagé

Gemeinsame Trauer

Dolor compartido

Luto partilhado

Gezamenlijke rouw

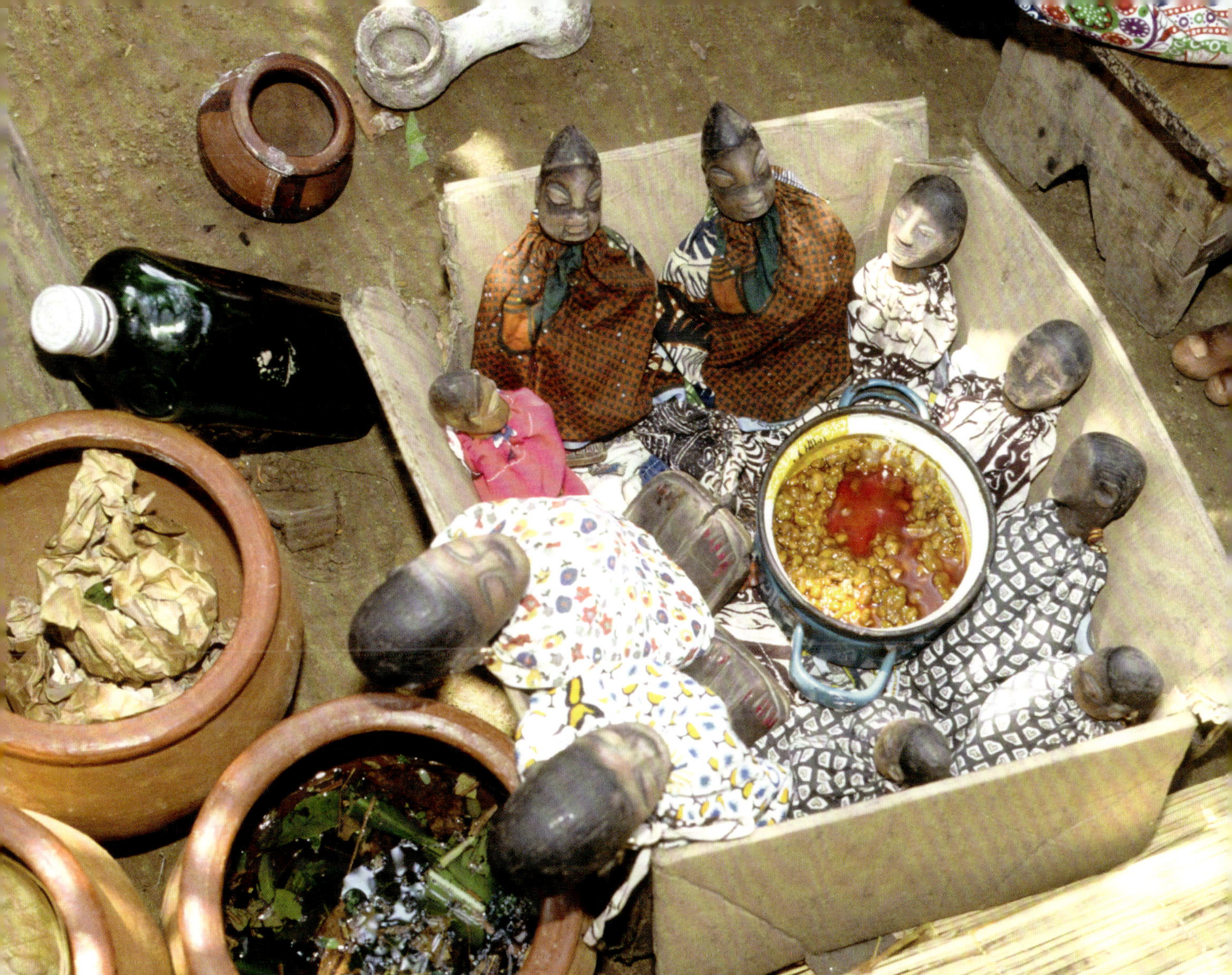

Sacrifice for the twins

Offrande pour les jumeaux

Opfer für die Zwillinge

Ofrenda ara los gemelos

Vítima dos gémeos

Offer voor de tweeling

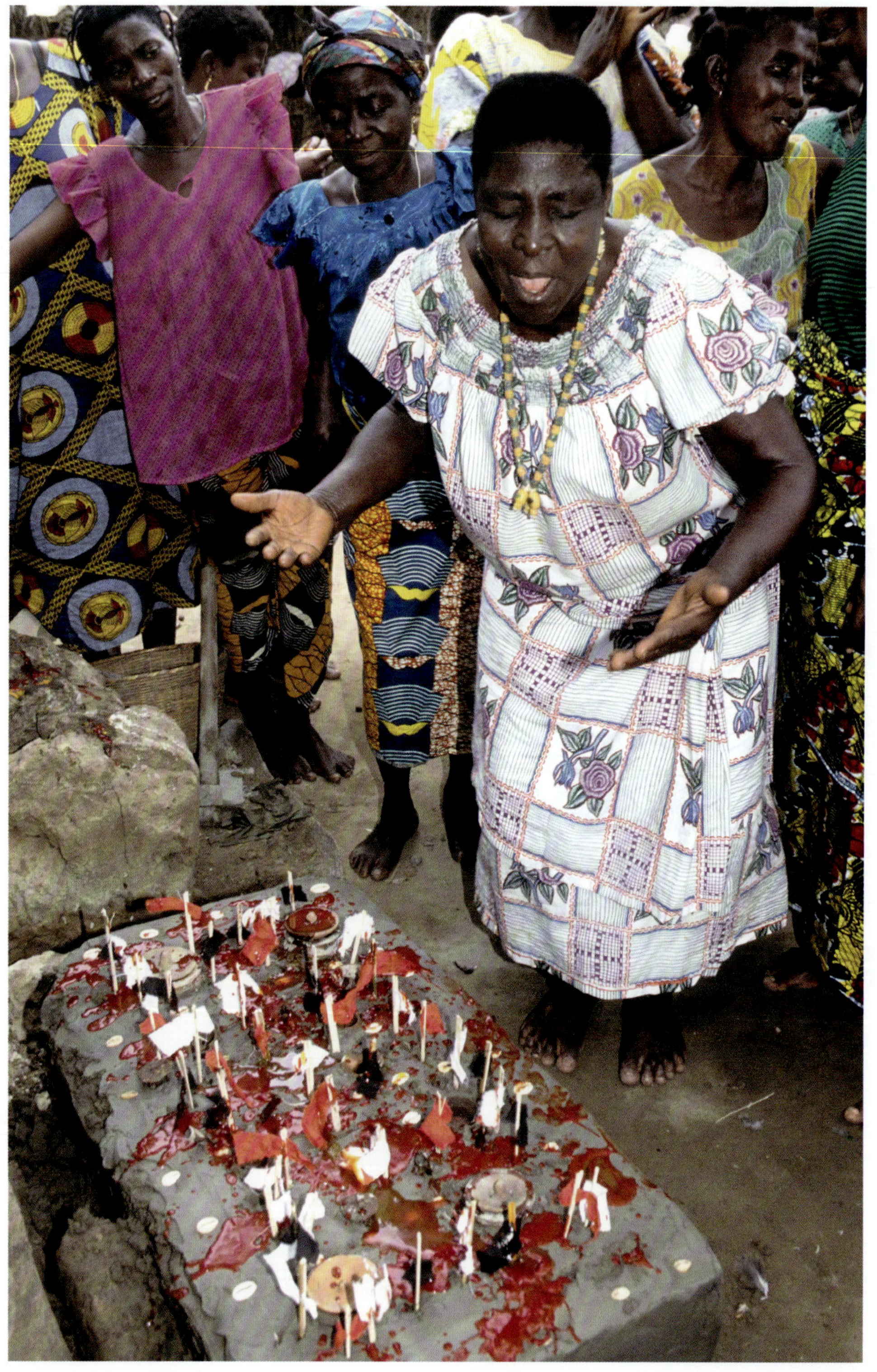

A newly erected twin altar. Nowhere in the world is the birth rate of twins as high as in West Africa. There has been insufficient research so far into why this is so.

Autel aux jumeaux nouvellement érigé. L'Afrique de l'Ouest est la région du monde où naissent le plus grand nombre de jumeaux. Aucune étude suffisamment poussée n'a permis d'en déterminer la cause.

Ein neu errichteter Zwillingsaltar. Nirgendwo in der Welt ist die Geburtenrate von Zwillingen so hoch wie in Westafrika. Bislang ist nicht ausreichend erforscht worden, woran dies liegt.

Un altar de gemelos recién erigido. En ninguna parte del mundo la tasa de natalidad de gemelos es tan alta como en África Occidental. Todavía no se ha investigado lo suficiente el porqué.

Um altar gêmeo recém erigido. Em nenhum lugar do mundo a taxa de natalidade dos gémeos é tão elevada como na África Ocidental. Ainda não houve investigação suficiente sobre o porquê.

Een nieuw tweelingenaltaar. Nergens ter wereld is het geboortecijfer van tweelingen zo hoog als in West-Afrika. Er is nog lang niet genoeg onderzoek gedaan naar de reden hiervoor.

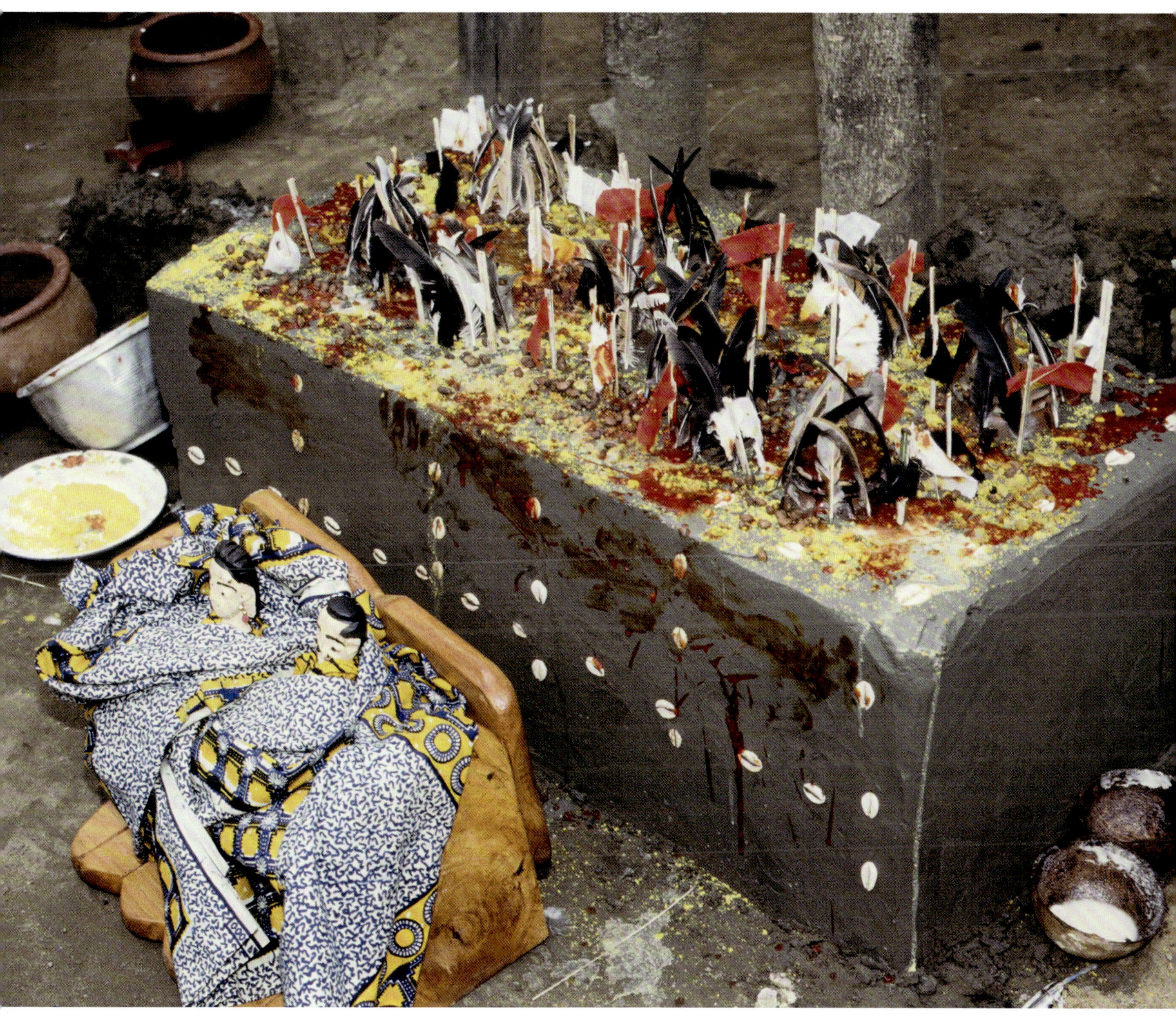

A newly erected twin altar

Autel aux jumeaux nouvellement érigé

Ein neu errichteter Zwillingsaltar

Un altar de gemelos recién erigido

Um altar gêmeo recém erigido

Een nieuw tweelingenaltaar

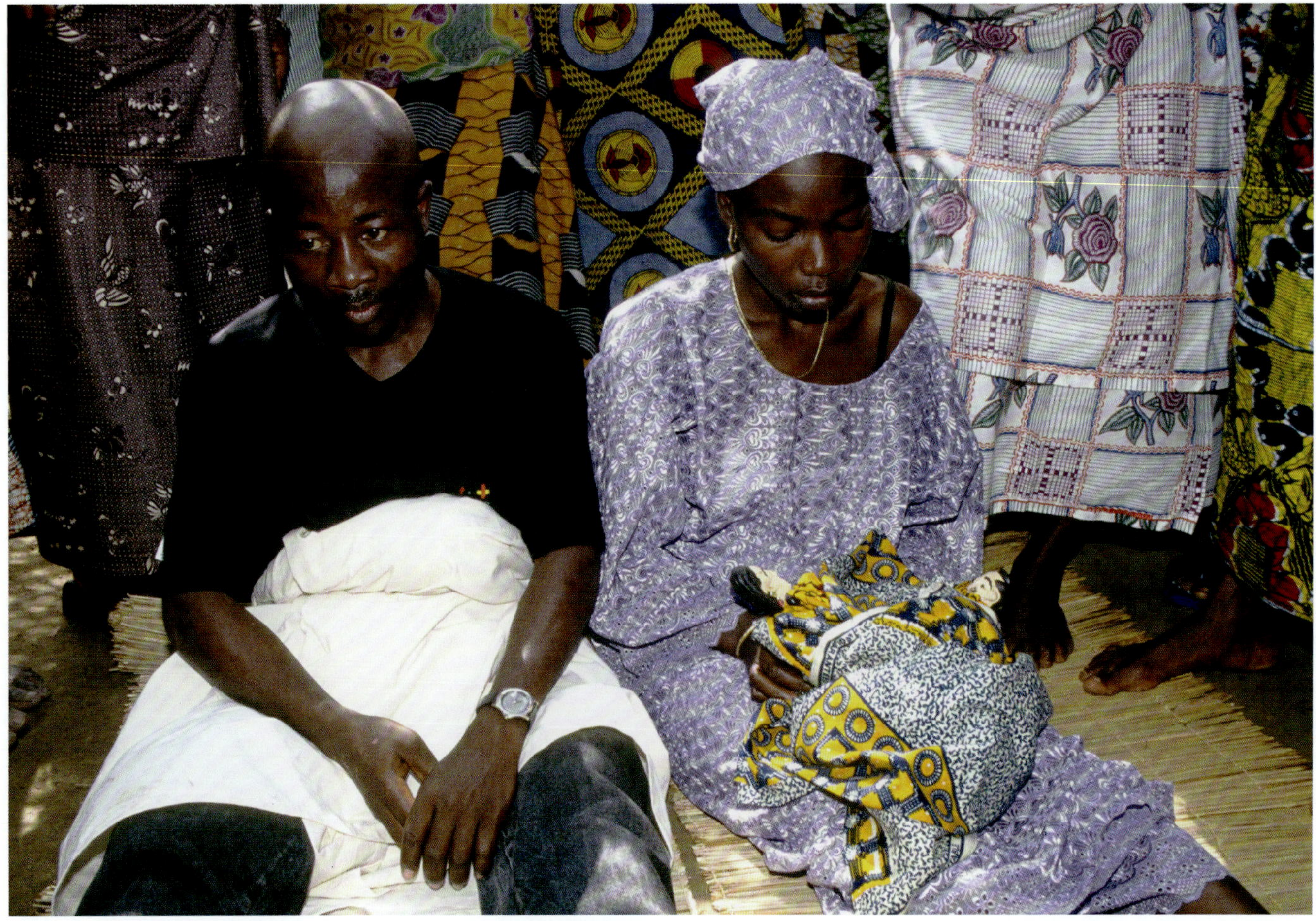

Back together. The father and mother of the dead twins are reunited. The ritual has caused the curse to be taken from them and their future children to live.

Réunis. Le père et la mère des jumeaux décédés sont à nouveau réunis. Le rituel a servi à chasser leur malédiction et permettra de garder en vie leurs enfants à venir.

Zusammengeführt. Der Vater und die Mutter der toten Zwillinge sind wieder vereint. Das Ritual hat bewirkt, dass der Fluch von ihnen genommen wurde und ihre künftigen Kinder am Leben bleiben werden.

Culto a los gemelos. El padre y la madre de los gemelos muertos se reúnen. El ritual ha funcionado y ha eliminado la maldición que recaía sobre ellos y sobre sus futuros hijos, para que así permanezcan en vida.

Fusão. O pai e a mãe dos gémeos mortos estão reunidos. O ritual fez com que a maldição fosse tirada deles e que seus futuros filhos vivessem.

Samengebracht. De vader en moeder van de dode tweeling zijn herenigd. Het ritueel heeft ertoe geleid dat de vloek op hen en hun toekomstige kinderen is weggenomen.

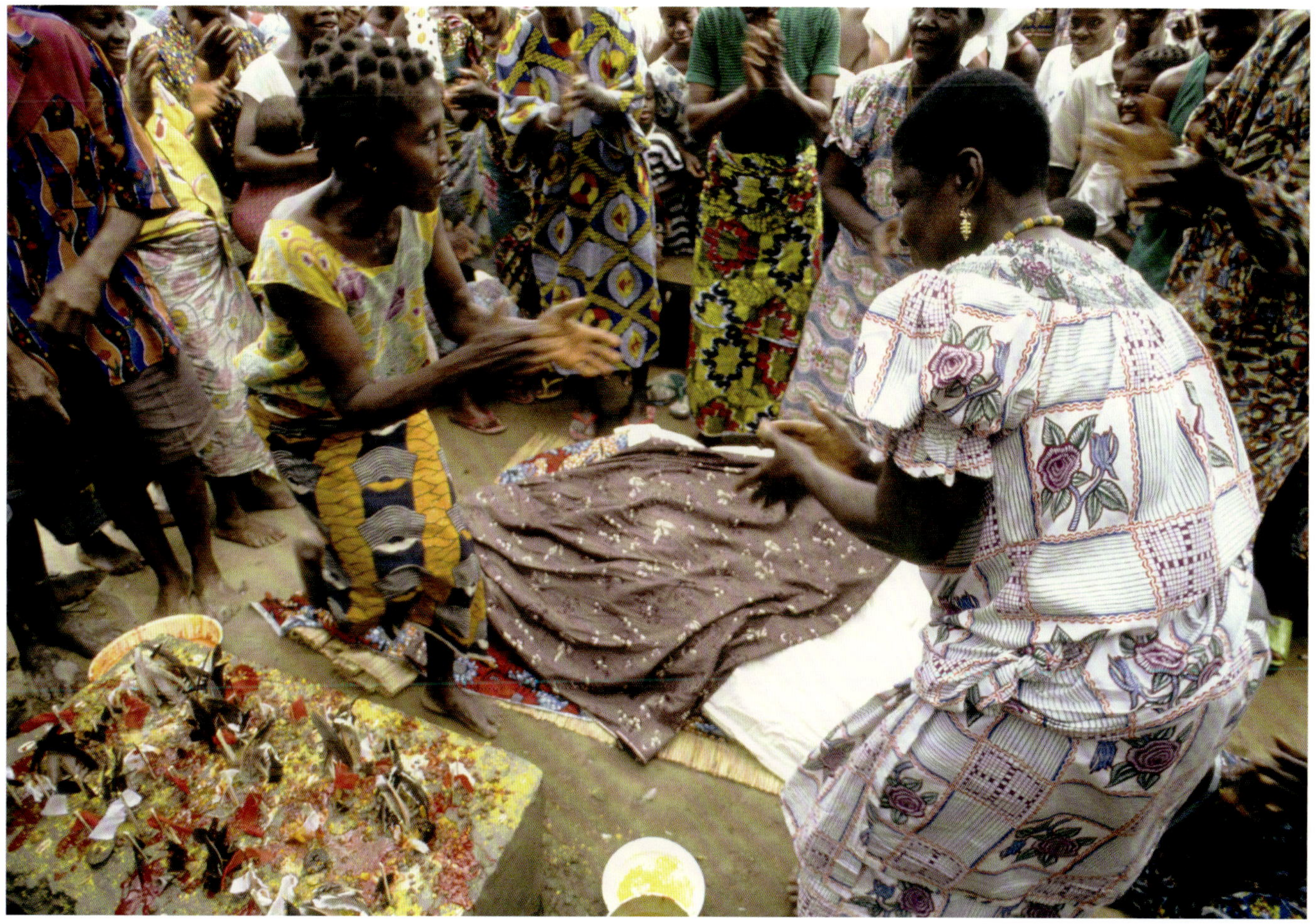

Encouragement from all sides. The couple is playfully challenged to immediately perform the coitus. Blankets that are hastily obtained should guarantee a minimum of discretion.

De toutes parts, des encouragements. Le couple est invité par les participants enjoués à procréer immédiatement. Un abri leur est rapidement fourni pour leur assurer un minimum d'intimité.

Ermunterung von allen Seiten. Das Paar wird spielerisch aufgefordert, umgehend den Beischlaf zu vollziehen. Eilig herbeigeschaffte Decken sollen ein Minimum an Diskretion gewährleisten.

Estímulo de todas las partes. A la pareja se le pide de forma divertida que realice el coito de inmediato. Las mantas que se traen apresuradamente deben garantizar un mínimo de discreción.

Encorajamento de todos os lados. O casal é convidado a realizar o coito imediatamente. Os cobertores que são introduzidos à pressa devem garantir um mínimo de discrição.

Van alle kanten aangemoedigd. Het echtpaar wordt speels gesommeerd meteen gemeenschap te hebben met elkaar. Dekens die haastig worden binnengebracht, moeten een minimum aan discretie garanderen.

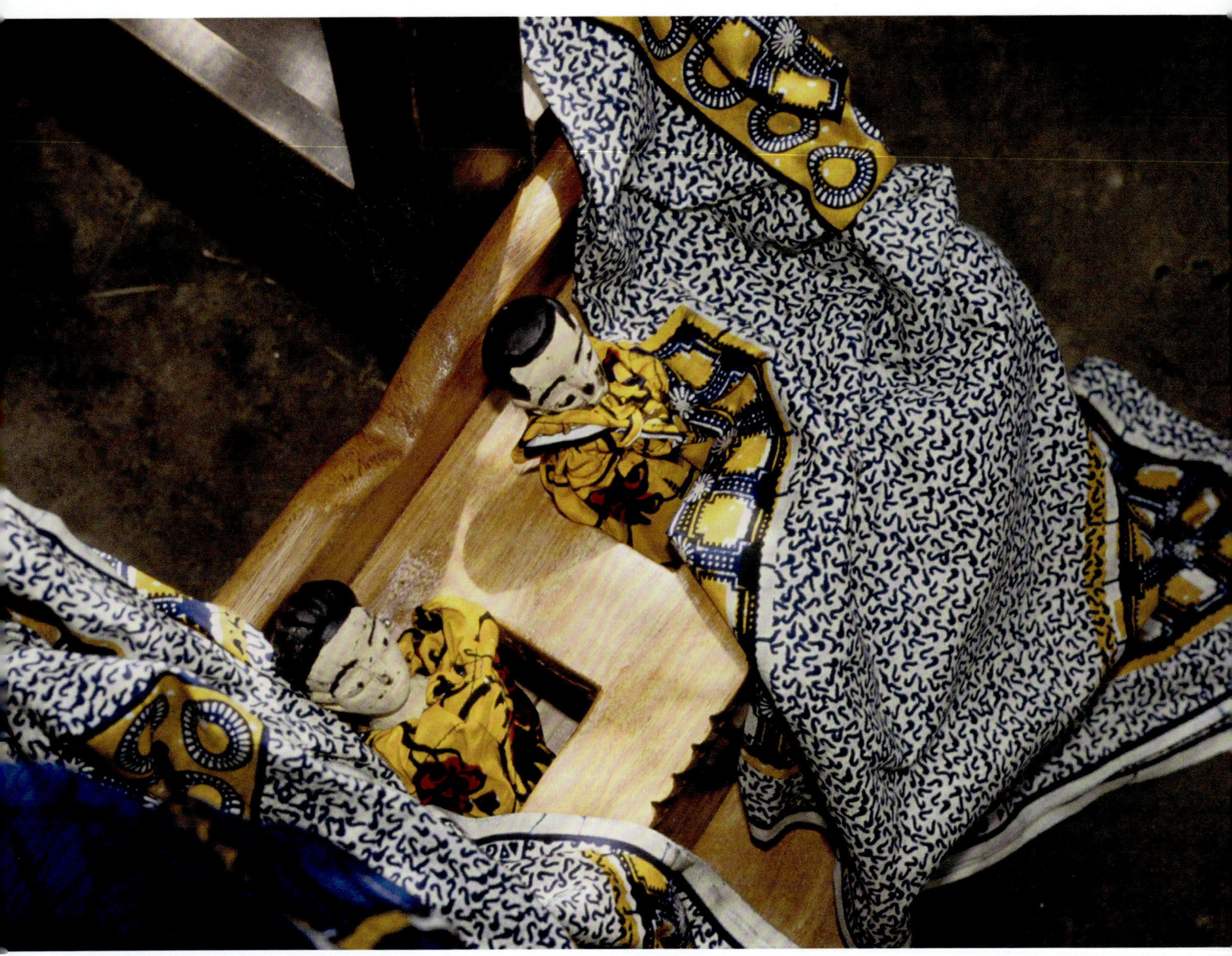

The twin dolls are always present

Les poupées jumelles sont toujours présentes

Die Zwillingspuppen sind immer dabei

Los muñecos gemelos están siempre presentes

As bonecas gêmeas estão sempre presentes

De tweelingpoppen zijn er altijd bij

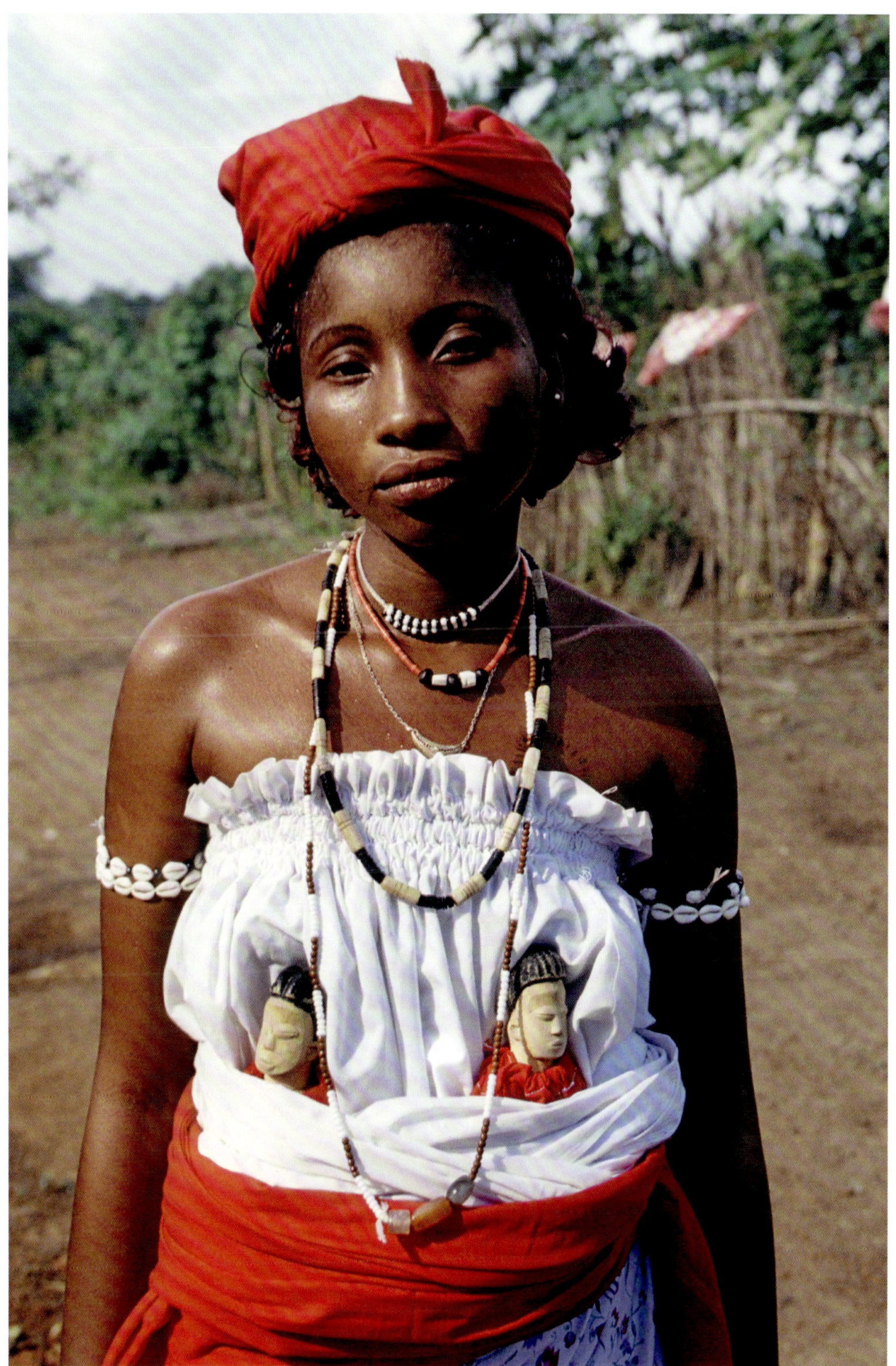

Vodun follower with twin dolls

Adepte vodun avec poupées jumelles

Vodunanhängerin mit Zwillingspuppen

Adepta Vodou con muñecos gemelos

Vodunanhängerin com bonecas gêmeas

Vodunaanhangster met tweelingpoppen

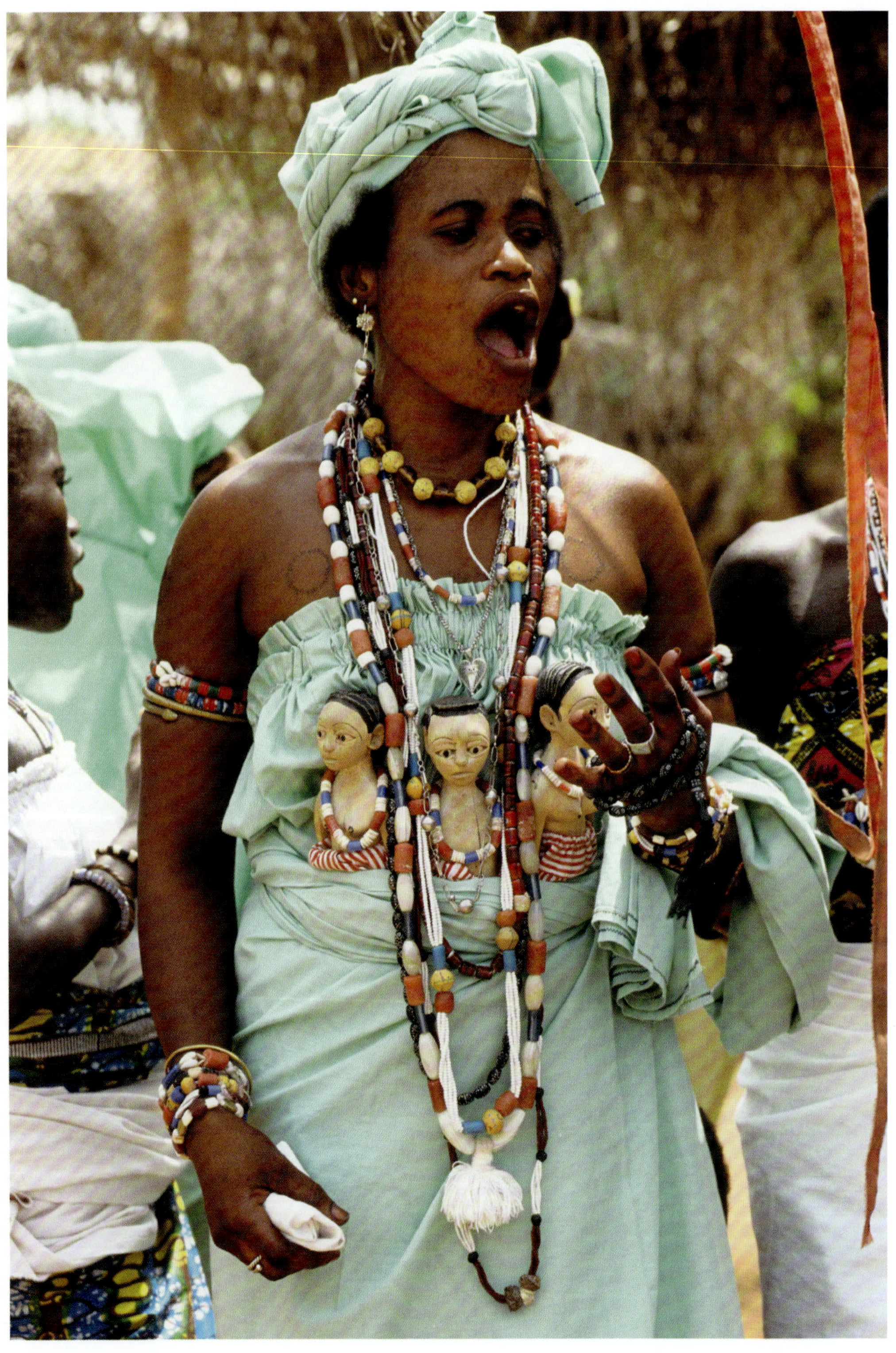

Vodun priestess with twin dolls

Prêtresse vodun avec poupées jumelles

Vodunpriesterin mit Zwillingspuppen

Sacerdotisa vudú con muñecas gemelas

Sacerdotisa vodu com bonecas gêmeas

Vodunpriesteres met tweelingpoppen

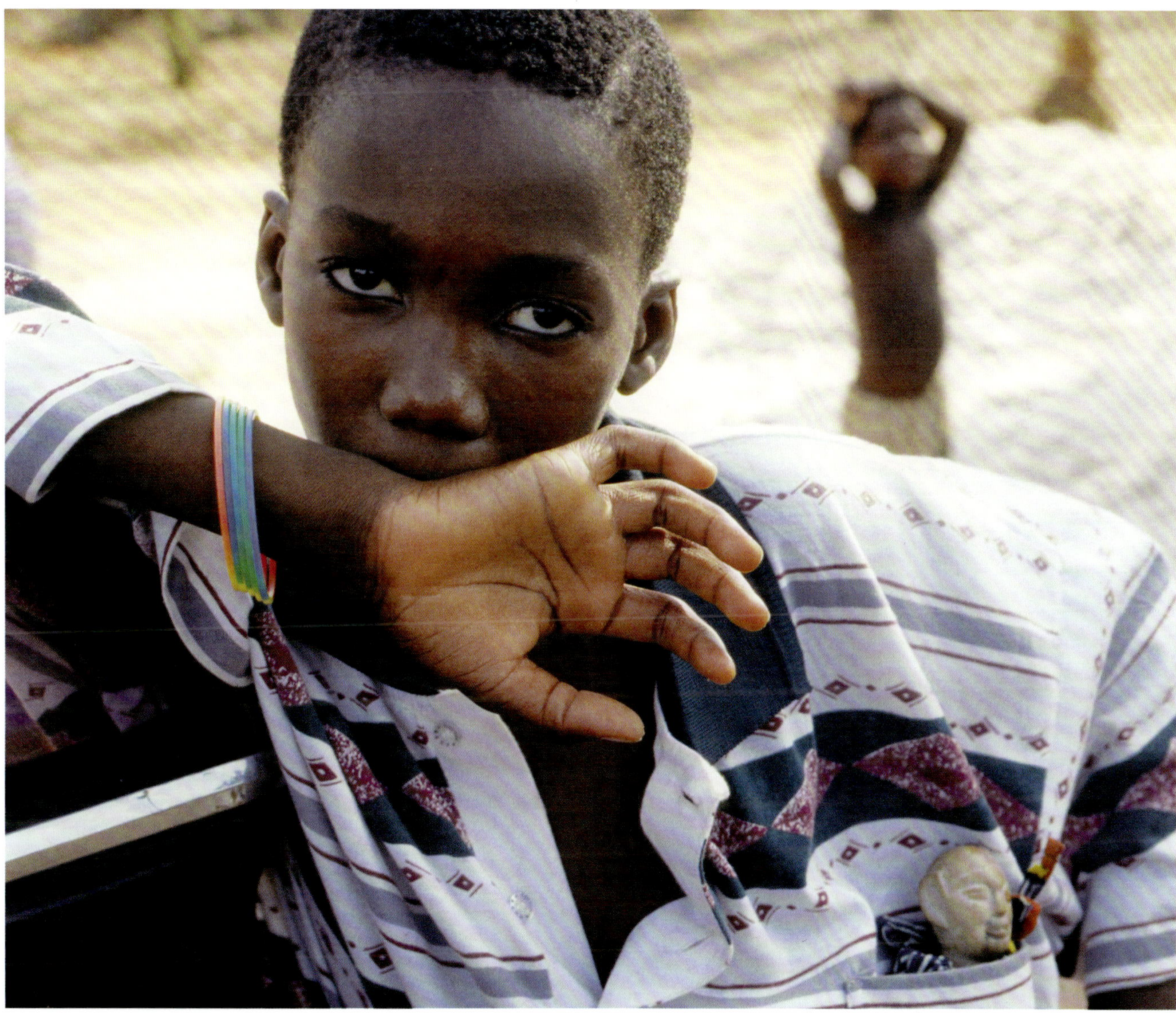

The brother is unforgotten. A schoolboy carries the doll for his deceased twin brother in his breast pocket. So he always takes part in the life of the boy and his family.

On n'oublie pas le frère. Un écolier porte dans la poche de sa chemise la figurine représentant son jumeau décédé. Celui-ci participe ainsi à la vie de ce jeune garçon et de sa famille.

Der Bruder ist unvergessen. Ein Schuljunge trägt in seiner Brusttasche die Puppe für seinen verstorbenen Zwillingsbruder. So nimmt dieser stets am Leben des Jungen und seiner Familie teil.

El hermano es inolvidable. Un estudiante lleva la muñeca de su hermano gemelo fallecido en el bolsillo de su pecho. Así que siempre participa en la vida del niño y de su familia.

O irmão não é esquecido. Um estudante carrega a boneca para o seu irmão gémeo falecido no bolso do peito. Por isso, ele participa sempre na vida do rapaz e da sua família.

De broer wordt niet vergeten. Een schooljongen draagt de pop voor zijn overleden tweelingbroer in zijn borstzak. Zo neemt die altijd deel aan het leven van de jongen en zijn familie.

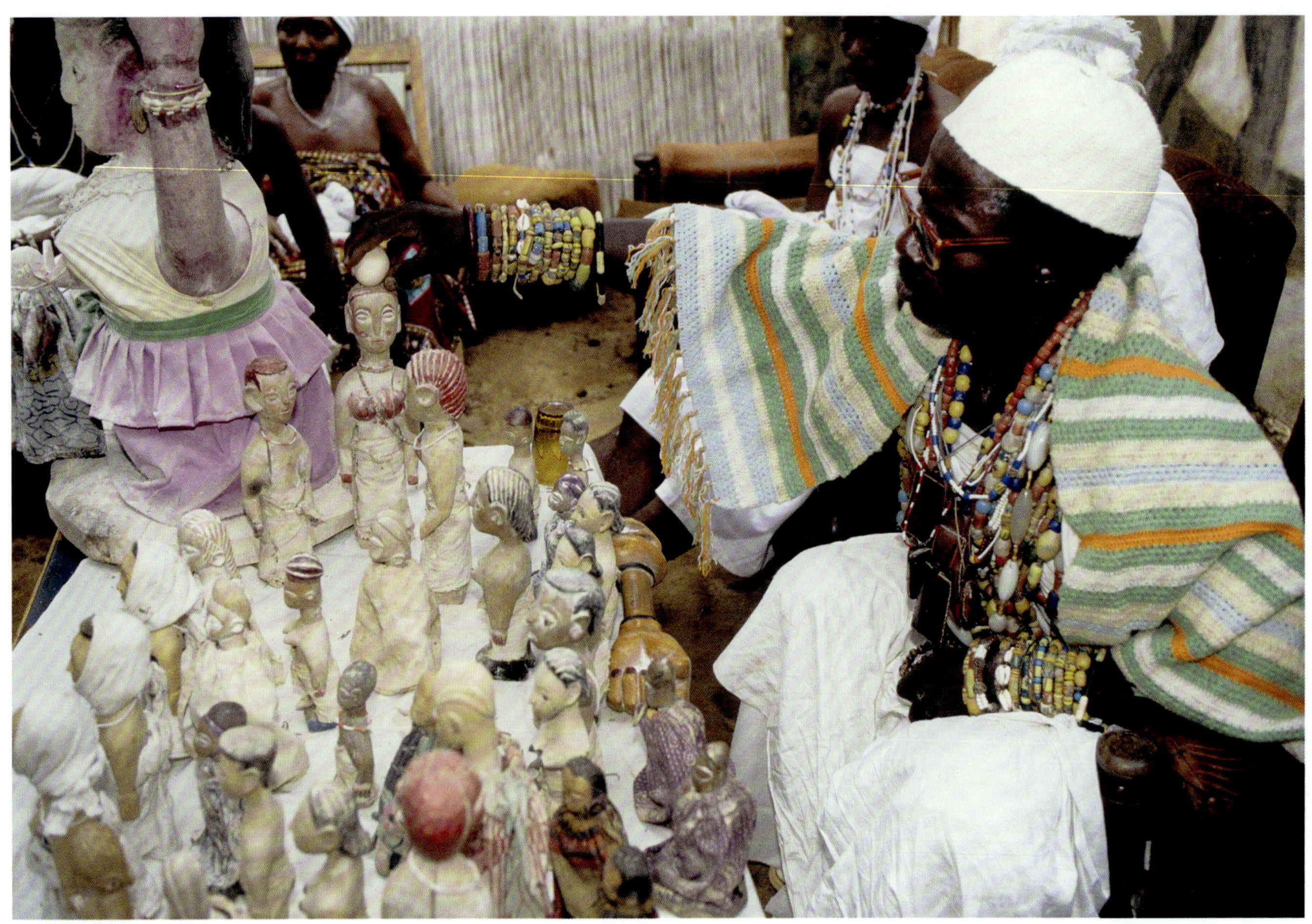

The priest blesses the twins

Le prêtre bénit les jumeaux

Der Priester segnet die Zwillinge

El sacerdote bendice a los gemelos

O padre abençoa os gémeos

De priester zegent de tweeling

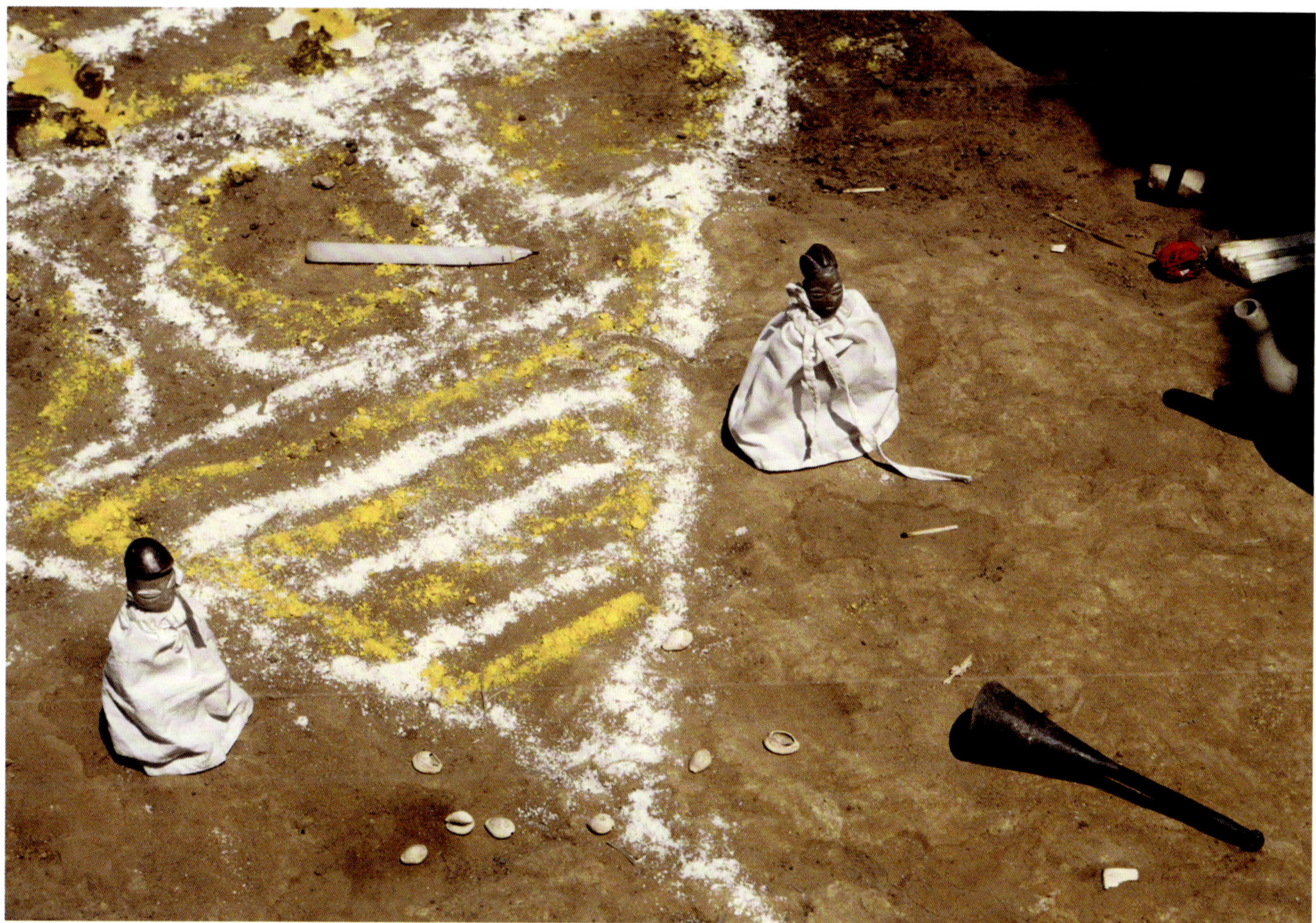

Twins as guardians. The twin figures can also take over the function of guardians. Here, on a metaphysical level, they secure the path that a woman in need will later walk along.

Les jumeaux en tant que gardiens. Les figurines de jumeaux peuvent également prendre la fonction de gardiens. Ici, elles sécurisent d'un point de vue métaphysique le chemin que devra emprunter une femme en détresse.

Zwillinge als Wächter. Die Zwillingsfiguren können auch die Funktion von Wächtern übernehmen. Hier sichern sie auf metaphysischer Ebene den Weg, den später eine notleidende Frau entlanglaufen wird.

Gemelos como guardianes. Las figuras de gemelos también pueden asumir la función de guardianes. Aquí, en un nivel metafísico, aseguran el camino que más tarde seguirá una mujer necesitada.

Gêmeos como guardiões. As figuras gêmeas também podem assumir a função de guardiões. Aqui, em nível metafísico, eles asseguram o caminho que mais tarde será seguido por uma mulher necessitada.

Tweelingen als wachters. De tweeling kan ook de functie van bewaker krijgen. Hier beveiligen ze op metafysisch niveau de weg die later gevolgd zal worden door een noodlijdende vrouw.

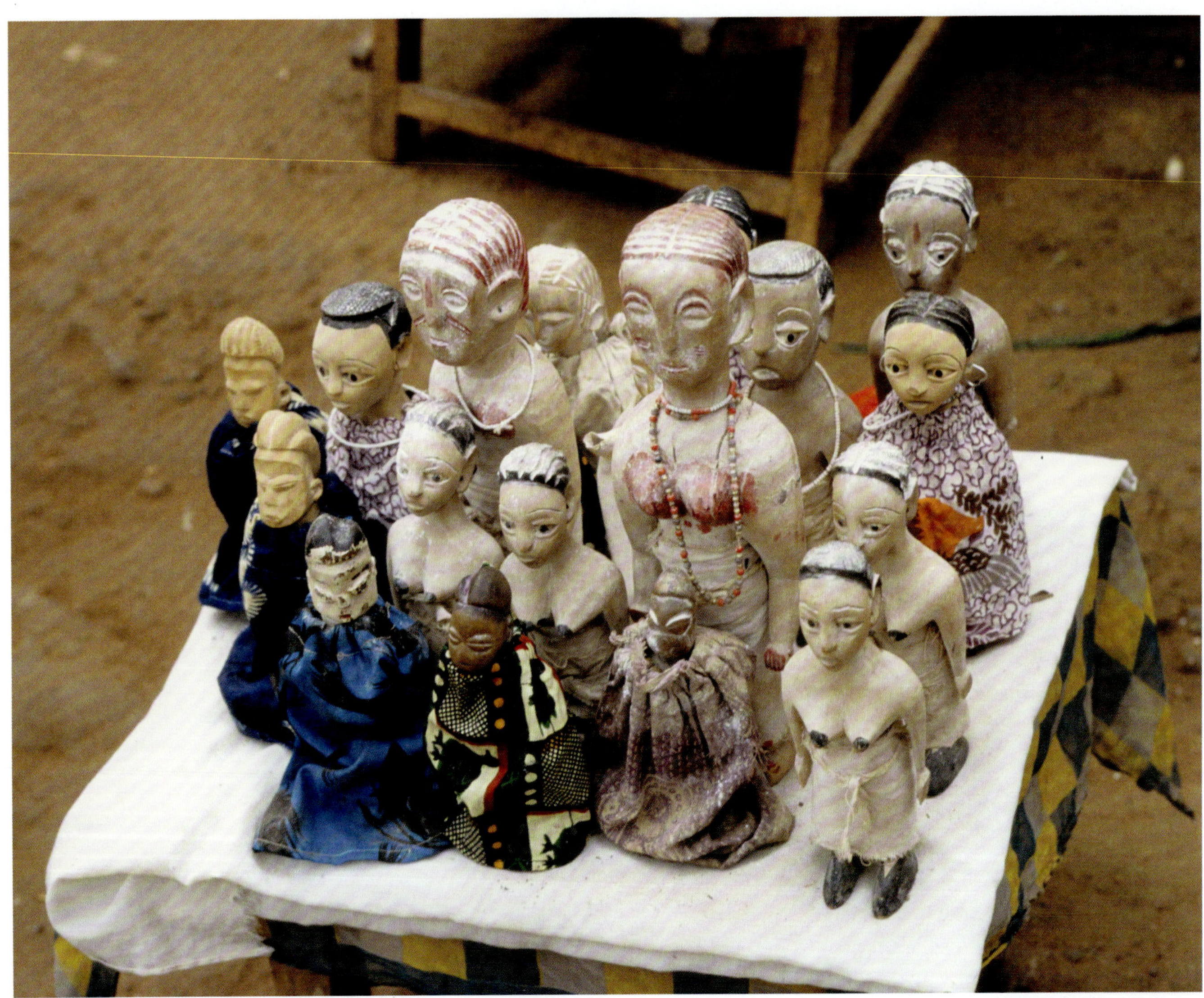

Honored guests

Invités de marque

Ehrengäste

Invitados de honor

Ilustres convidados

Eregasten

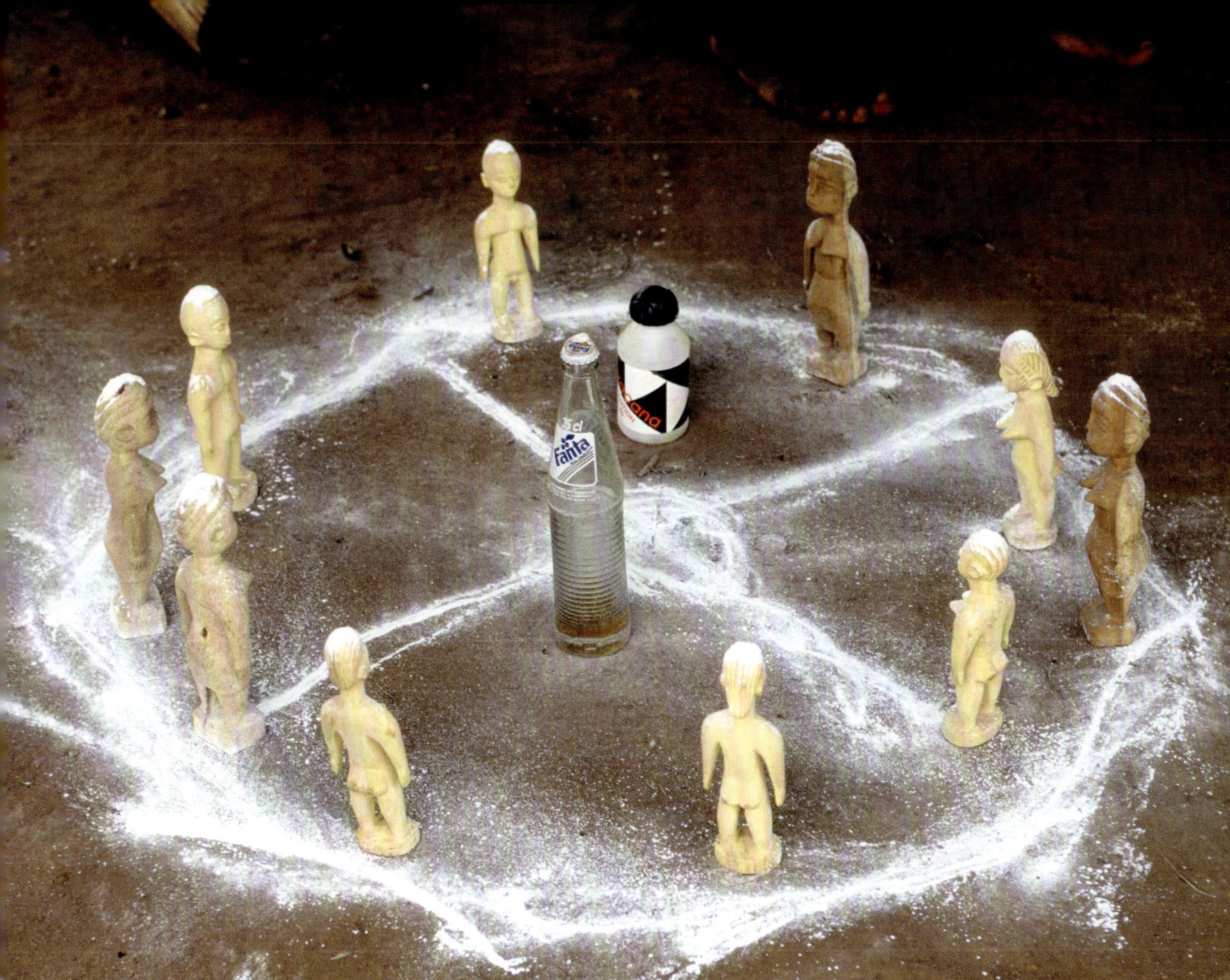

Protection ritual. Newly carved dolls for recently deceased twin siblings are subjected to a protective ceremony. The white circle cordons off the event.

Rituel de protection. Une cérémonie de protection est organisée autour de figurines sculptées pour des jumeaux récemment décédés. Le cercle blanc garantit la sécurité de l'événement.

Schutzritual. Neu geschnitzte Puppen für kürzlich verstorbene Zwillingsgeschwister werden einer Schutzzeremonie unterzogen. Der weiße Kreis sichert das Geschehen ab.

Ritual de protección. Los muñecos recién tallados para los hermanos gemelos recientemente fallecidos son sometidos a una ceremonia de protección. El círculo blanco asegura el evento.

Ritual de proteção. As bonecas recém-esculpidas para irmãos gêmeos recentemente falecidos são submetidas a uma cerimônia de proteção. O círculo branco assegura o evento.

Beschermingsritueel. Nieuw gesneden poppen voor pas overleden tweelingbroers en -zussen ondergaan een beschermende ceremonie. De witte cirkel beveiligt het evenement.

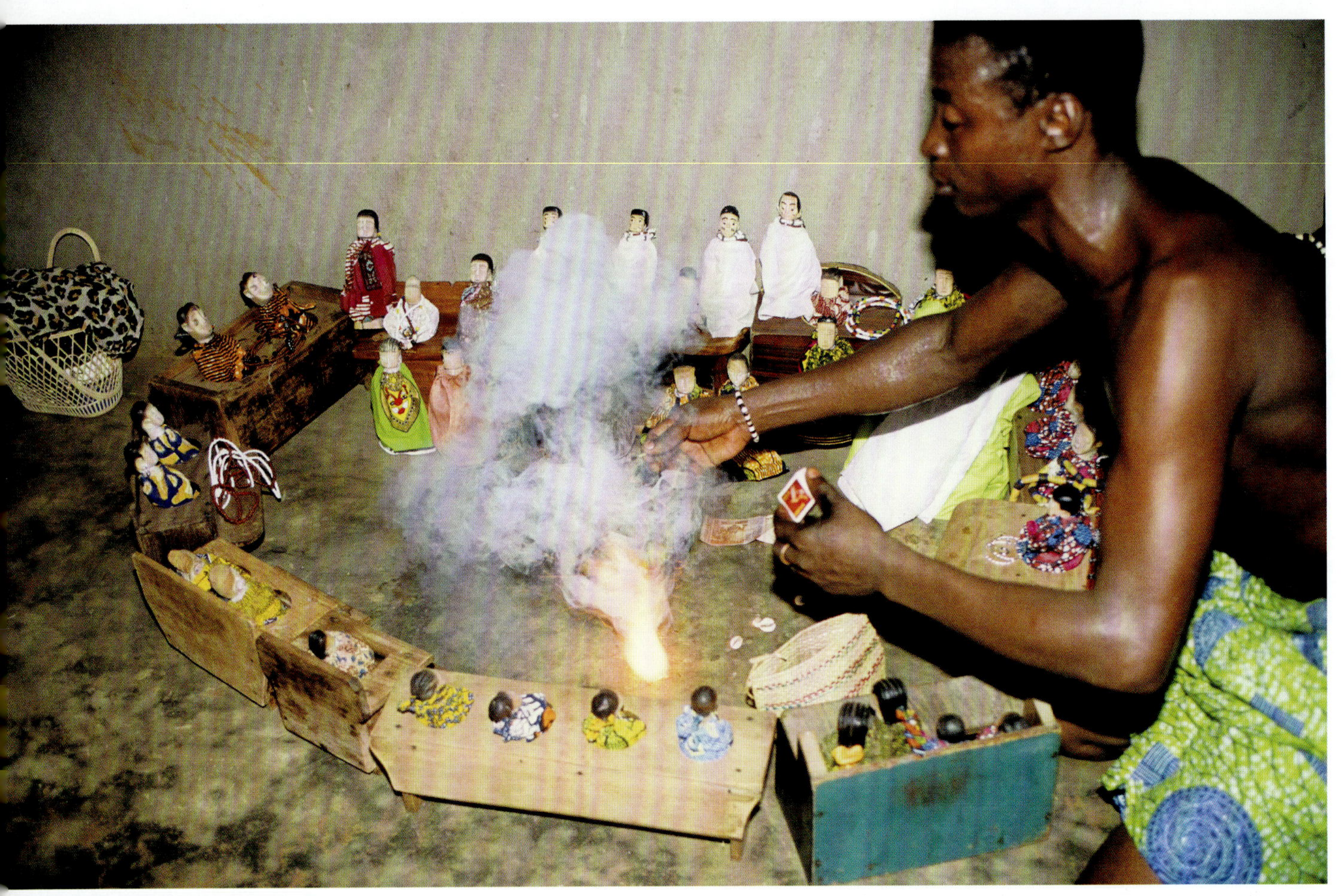

Protection ritual for the twins

Rituel de protection pour les jumeaux

Schutzritual für die Zwillinge

Ritual de protección para los gemelos

Ritual de protecção para os gémeos

Beschermingsritueel voor de tweeling

Place of honor at the table

Place d'honneur à table

Ehrenplatz an der Tafel

Puesto de honor en la pizarra

Lugar de honra no quadro-negro

Ereplaats aan tafel

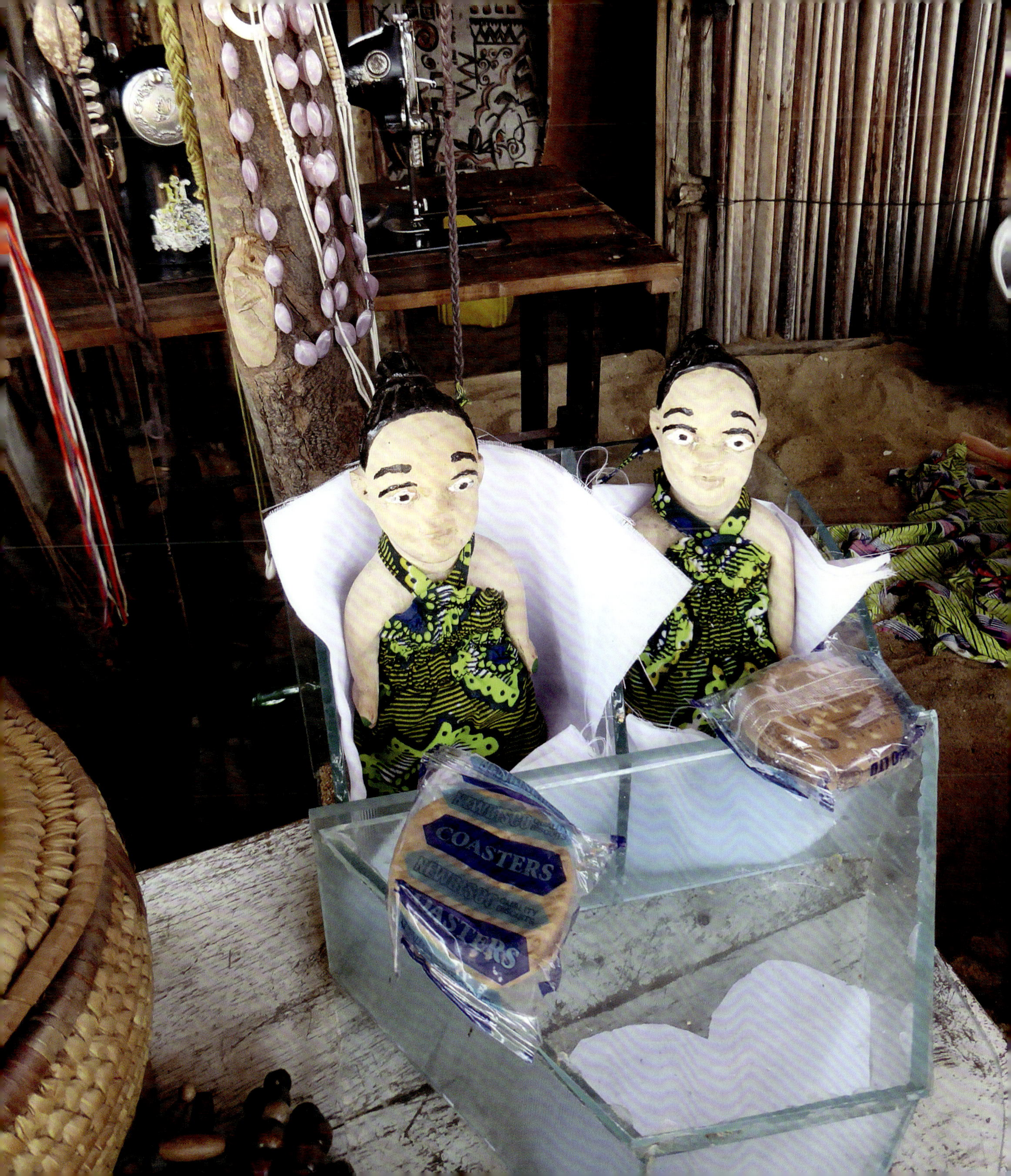
COASTERS
COASTERS

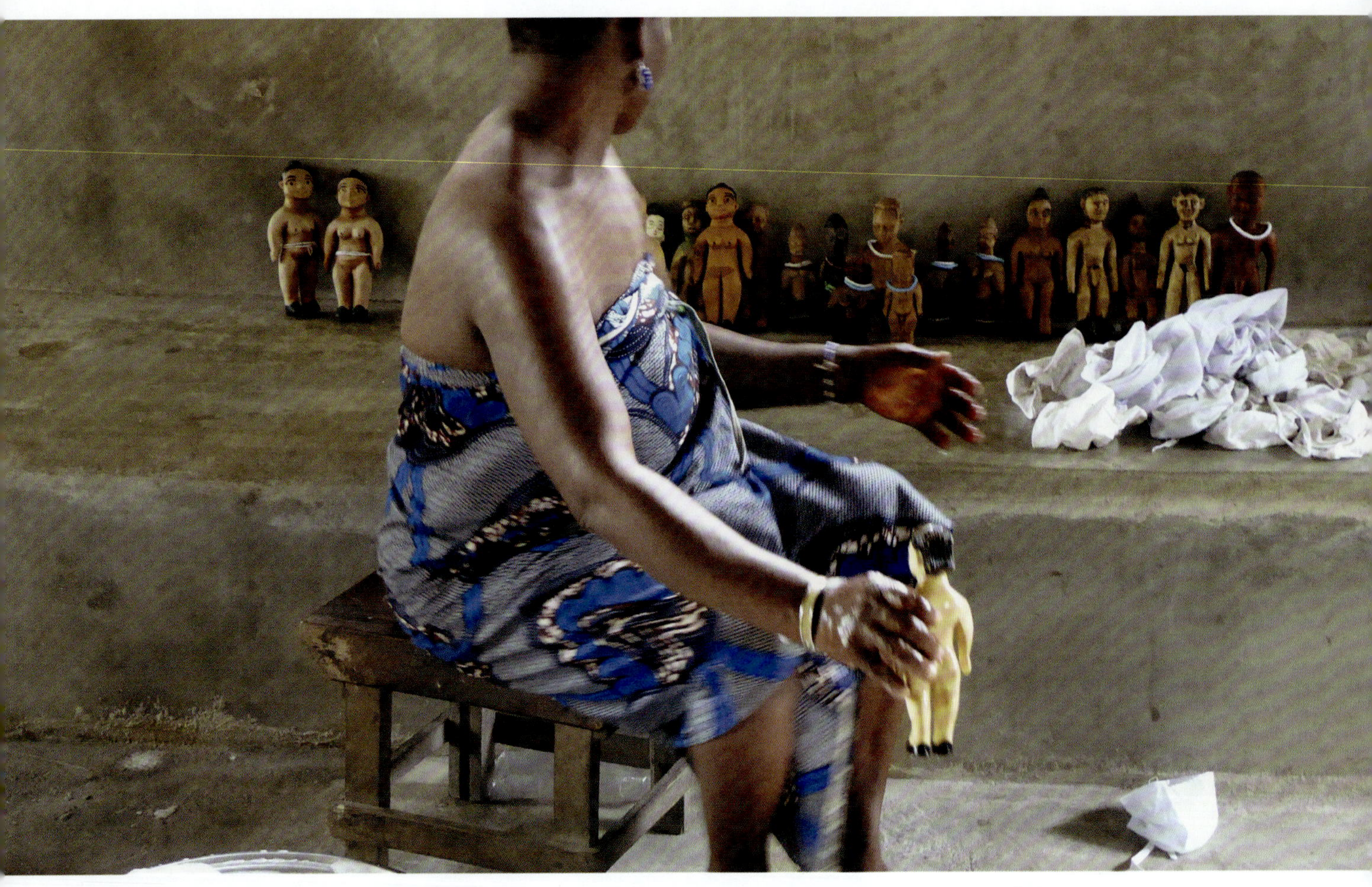

Washing the twin dolls

Ablutions des poupées jumelles

Waschung der Zwillingspuppen

Lavado de los muñecos gemelos

Lavagem das bonecas gémeas

Het wassen van de tweelingpoppen

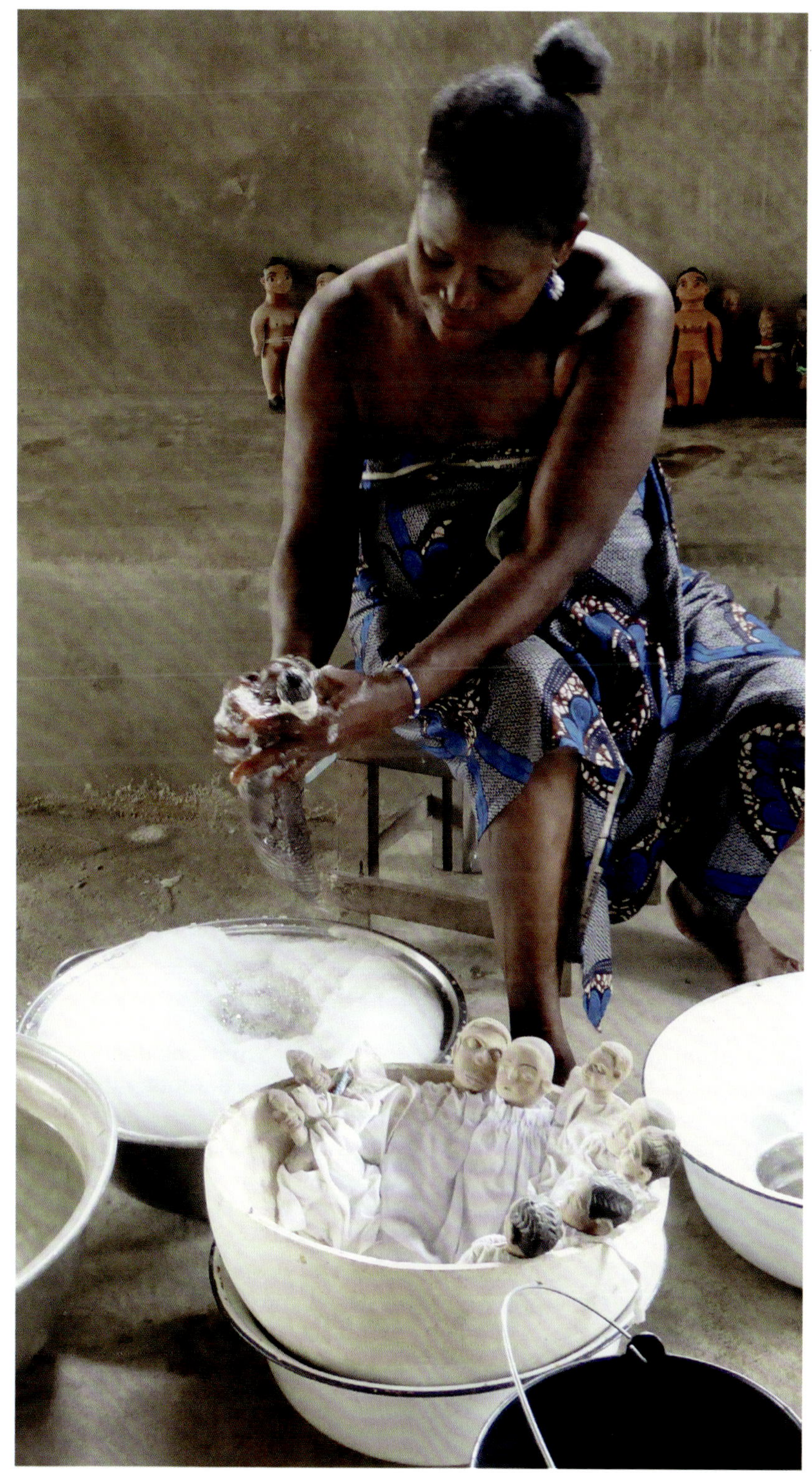

Freshly swaddled twin dolls. With motherly love the spirits of the deceased are given all that was not granted them in life.

Poupées jumelles fraîchement préparées. On apporte aux esprits des jumeaux décédés tous les soins et l'attention maternelle dont ils ne peuvent profiter en tant qu'êtres vivants.

Frisch gewickelte Zwillingspuppen. Mit mütterlicher Liebe lässt man den Geistern der Verstorbenen all das zuteil werden, was ihnen im Leben nicht vergönnt war.

Muñecos gemelos recién vestidos. Con amor maternal, los espíritus de los difuntos reciben todo lo que no les fue concedido en vida.

Bonecas gêmeas recém feridas. Com amor materno, os espíritos do falecido recebem tudo o que não lhes foi concedido na vida.

Net ingezwachtelde tweelingpoppen. Met moederlijke liefde krijgen de geesten van de overledenen alles wat ze in hun leven niet gegund was.

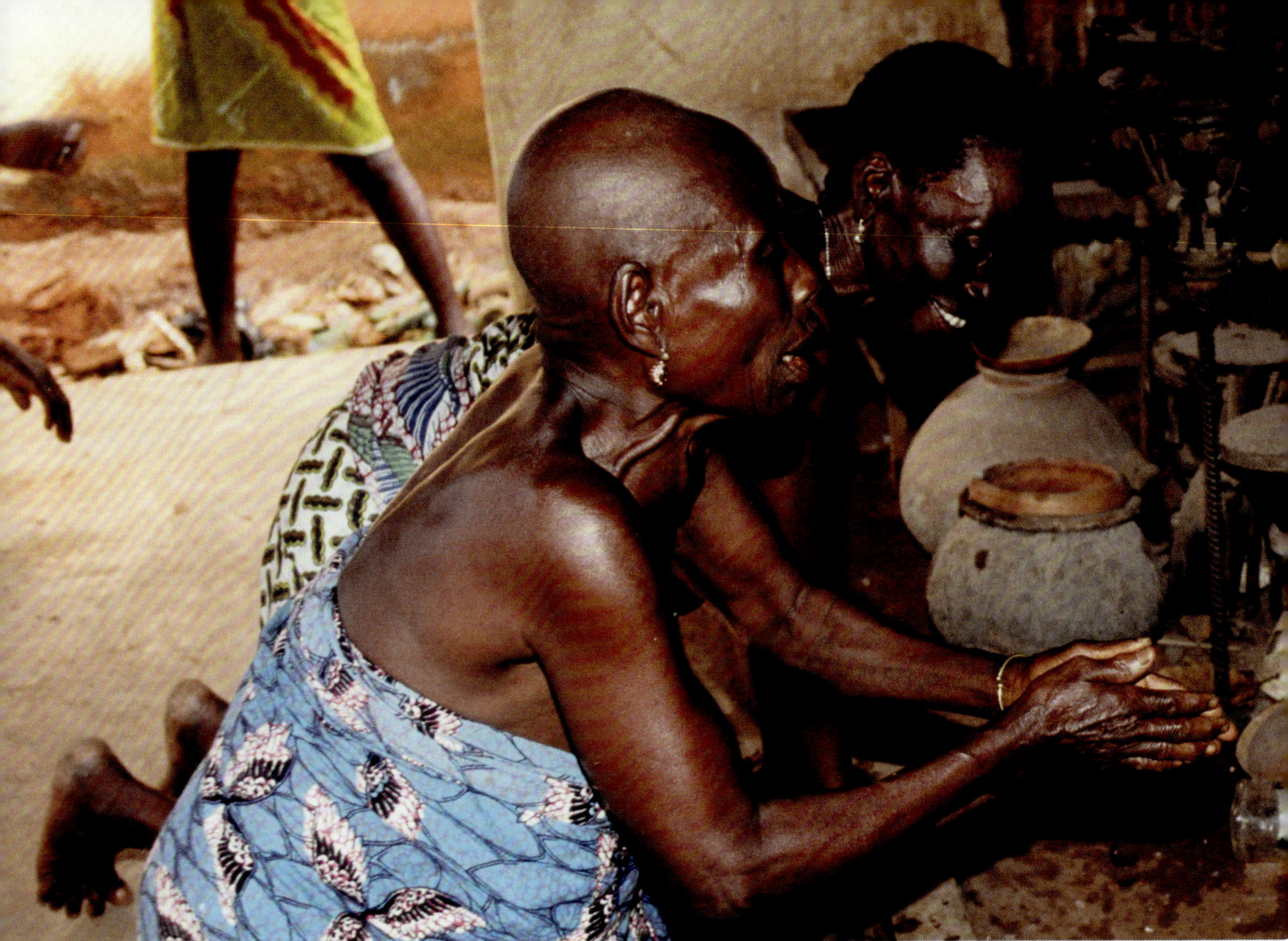

Asen—dwelling place for the spirits of the dead

Asen is the name given to the ancestral altars made by the Fon people, which serve as a home for the spirits of the dead on certain occasions. A specialty are the examples, in which forged figures, which are made with the "technique of the lost form" and are always unique, recreate individual scenes of the life and status of the deceased person.

As a rule, only dignitaries are awarded this honor, as both the forging work and the accompanying rites involve high costs. For example, strict traditional rules must be

Asen, les maisons des esprits des défunts

Le terme *asen* désigne les autels érigés pour les ancêtres par le peuple Fon, qui, parfois, servent de refuge à l'esprit des défunts. Certains exemplaires sont particulièrement singuliers, car ils comportent des figurines en fonte, fabriquées en un seul exemplaire selon la technique de la cire perdue. Elles représentent des scènes personnelles évoquant la vie et le statut de la personne décédée.

Cette technique de la cire perdue est en général réservée aux dignitaires, car

Asen – Wohnstätte für die Totengeister

Als *Asen* bezeichnet man die vom Volk der Fon angefertigten Ahnenaltäre, die den Geistern der Toten bei bestimmten Anlässen als Heimstatt dienen. Eine Besonderheit sind die Exemplare, bei denen Gussfiguren, die mit der „Technik der verlorenen Form" angefertigt werden und immer Unikate sind, individuelle Szenen vom Leben und Status der verstorbenen Person nachstellen.

Diese Ehrung wird in der Regel nur Würdenträgern zuteil, da sowohl die Schmiedearbeit als auch die begleitenden

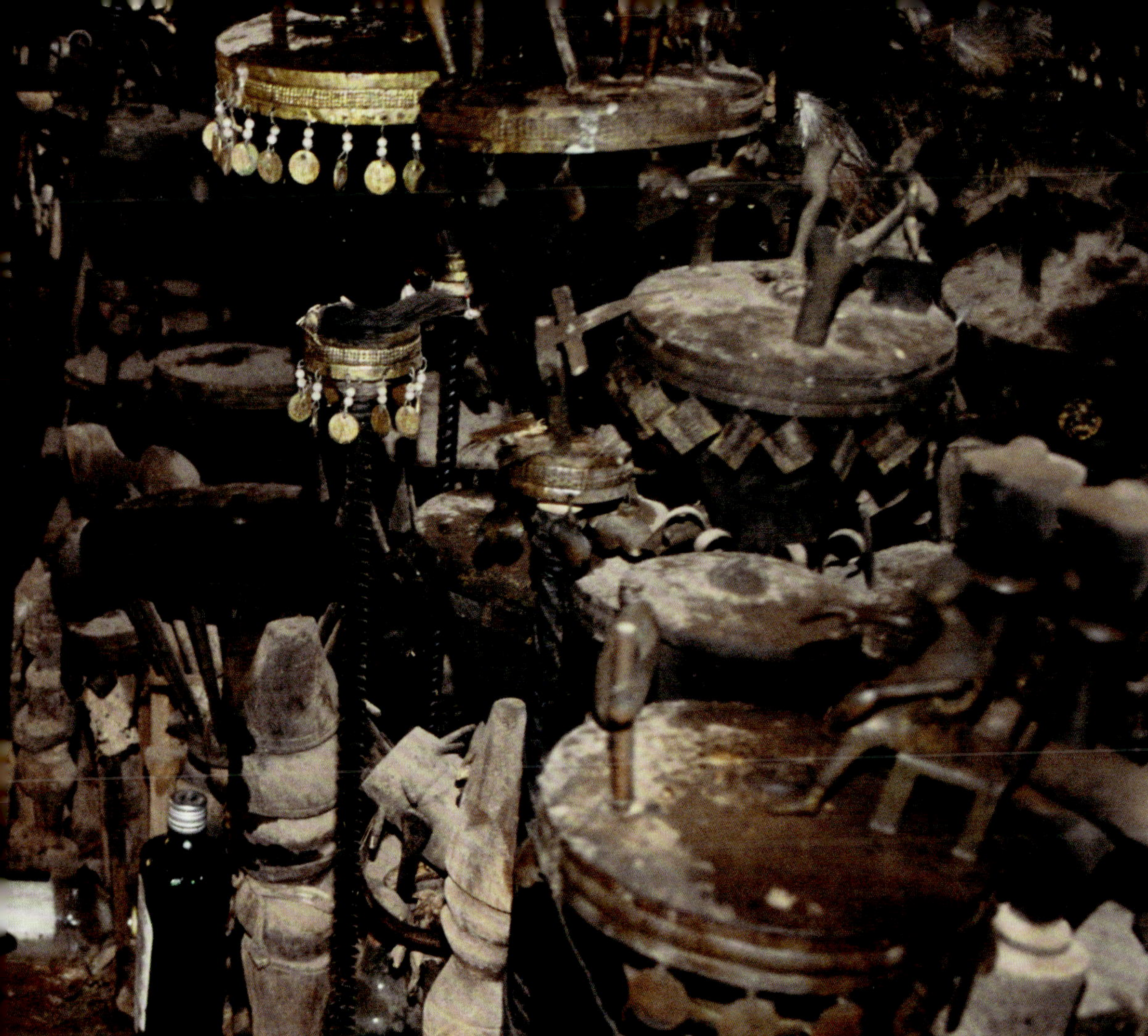

Asen– Morada para los espíritus de los muertos

Asen es el nombre dado a los altares ancestrales de los Fon, que sirven de hogar a los espíritus de los muertos en ciertas ocasiones. Una característica especial son las figuras fundidas, que están hechas con la "técnica de la forma perdida" y son siempre únicas. Estas figuras recrean escenas individuales de la vida y el estado de la persona fallecida.

Por regla general, sólo los dignatarios reciben este honor, ya que tanto el trabajo de forja como los ritos que lo acompañan

Asen – Lugar de morada para os espíritos dos mortos

Asen é o nome dado aos altares ancestrais feitos pelo povo Fon, que servem de lar para os espíritos dos mortos em certas ocasiões. Uma característica especial são as figuras de elenco, que são feitas com a "técnica da forma perdida" e são sempre únicas, que recriam cenas individuais da vida e status da pessoa falecida.

Em regra, só os dignitários recebem esta distinção, uma vez que tanto o trabalho de forjamento como os ritos que o acompanham implicam custos elevados.

Asen – thuis voor de geesten van de doden

Asen is de naam van de voorouderaltaren van het Fon-volk, die bij bepaalde gelegenheden dienen als thuis voor de geesten van de doden. Bijzonder zijn de altaren waarbij gegoten beeldjes, die met de 'techniek van de verloren was' zijn gemaakt en altijd uniek zijn, losse scènes uit het leven en de status van de overledene nabootscn.

Deze eer valt in de regel alleen hoogwaardigheidsbekleders ten deel, omdat zowel het smeedwerk als de bijbehorende riten hoge kosten met zich meedragen. Zo

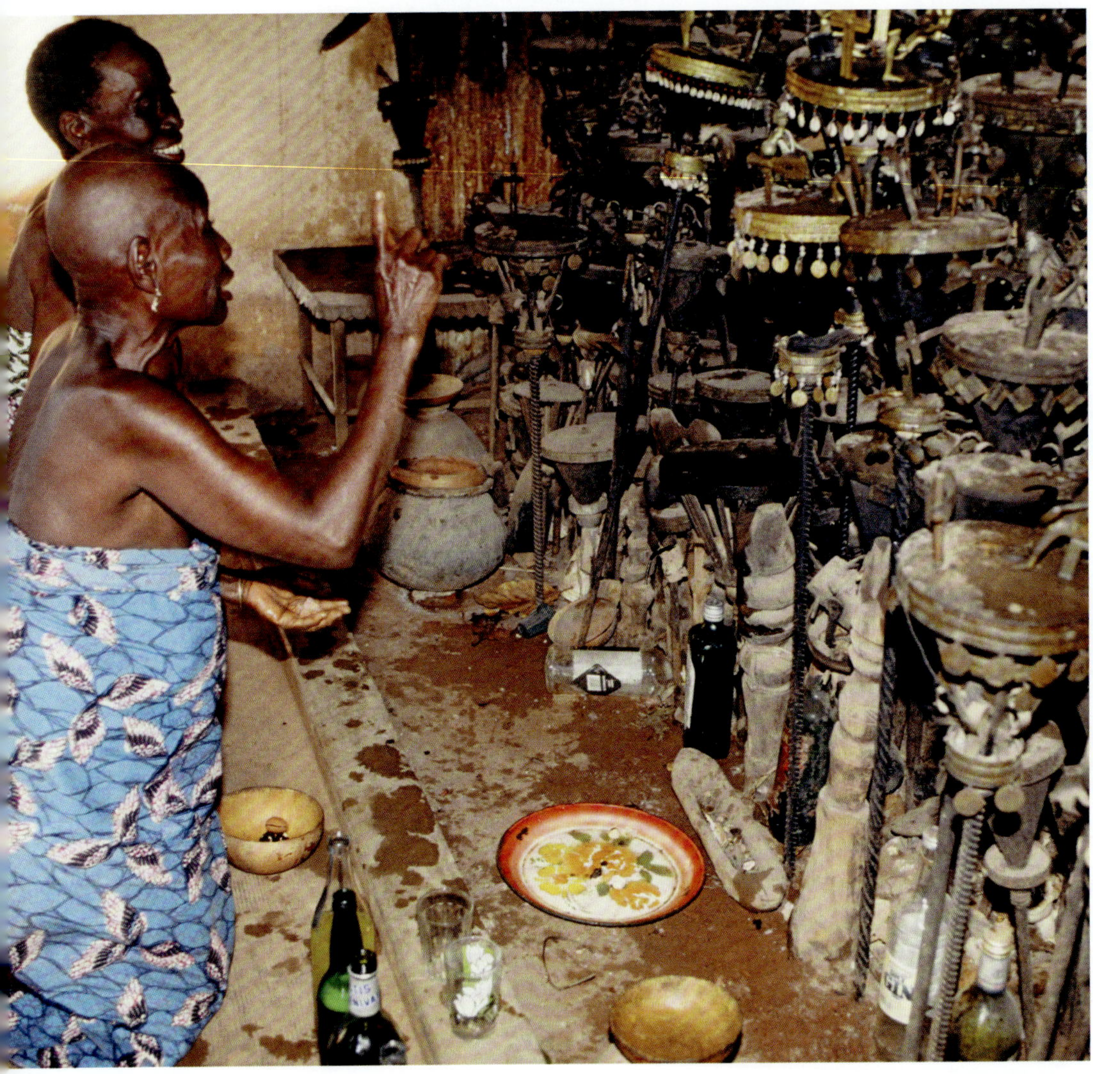

observed so that only the spirit of death that is intended to penetrate the Asen can do so.

For the living, the Asen are an important intersection between this world and the other, and food and drink sacrifices are offered at their shrine to seek the help, advice or blessing of the ancestors.

le travail de fonderie ainsi que les rites associés engendrent des frais importants. Des instructions traditionnelles très strictes doivent être respectées afin que seul l'esprit du défunt pénètre dans l'*asen* conçu pour lui.

Pour les vivants, les *asen* constituent des points de rencontre significatifs entre notre monde et celui de l'au-delà. Ils déposent devant les coffrets des mets et des boissons pour demander des conseils, un soutien ou la bénédiction des ancêtres.

Riten hohe Kosten verursachen. Beispielsweise müssen strenge traditionelle Vorschriften beachtet werden, damit einzig und allein der Totengeist in den Asen eindringt, dem dieser auch zugedacht ist.

Für die Lebenden sind die Asen ein bedeutender Schnittpunkt zwischen dies- und jenseitiger Welt.Ihrem Schrein werden Speise- und Trankopfer dargebracht, um Beistand, Rat oder Segen der Ahnen zu erbitten.

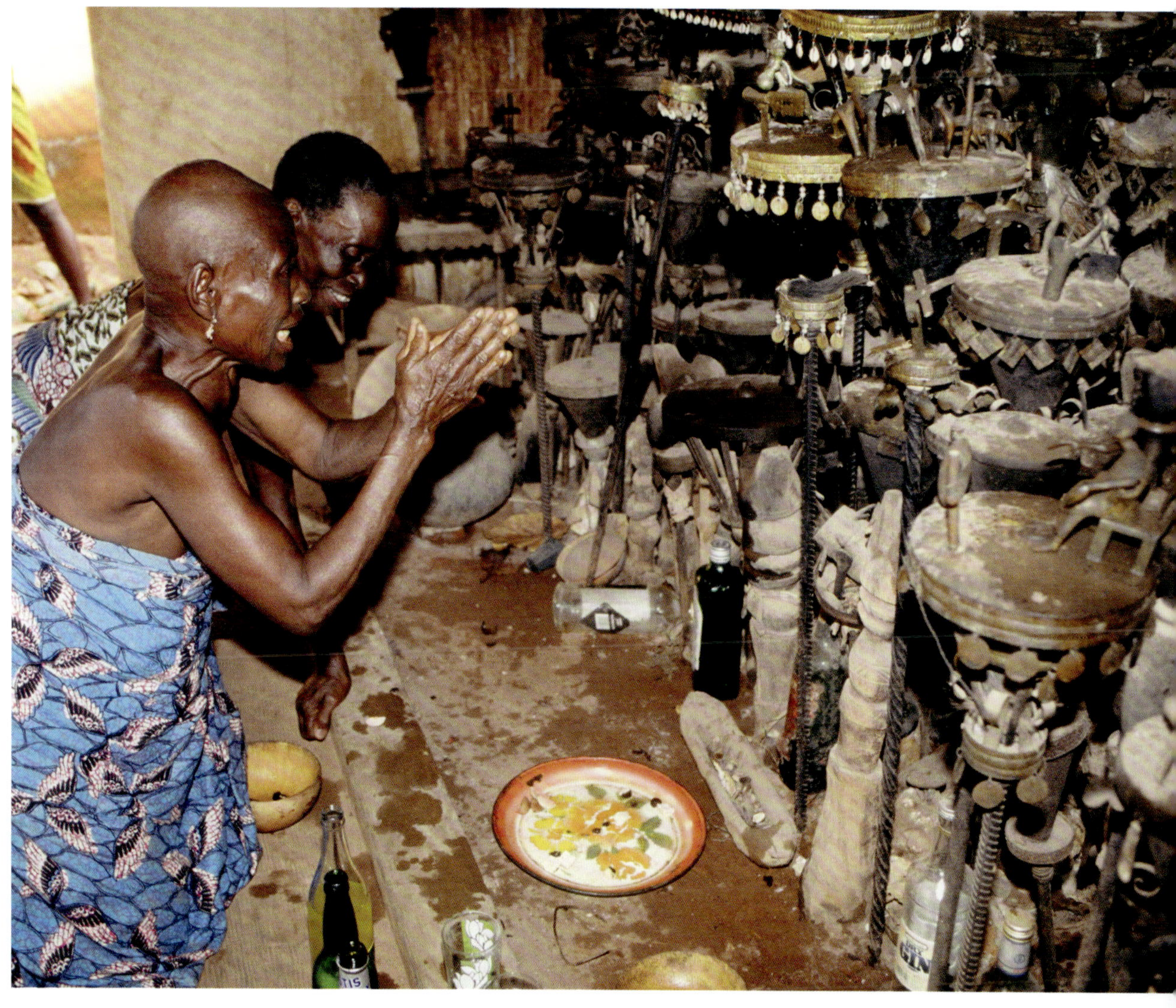

tienen un coste elevado. Por ejemplo, deben tenerse en cuentaestrictas normas tradicionales para que sólo el espíritu de los muertos pueda penetrar en el Asen, ya que está pensado para éste.

Para los vivos, los Asen son una importante intersección entre este mundo y el otro, y realizan ofrendas, tales como comida y bebida a su santuario para recibir ayuda, consejo o bendición de sus ancestros.

Por exemplo, devem ser observadas as rígidas regras tradicionais, de modo que só o Espírito dos mortos possa penetrar na Asen, o que é o seu propósito.

Para os vivos, os Asen são uma importante encruzilhada entre este e o outro mundo, e ofertas de comida e bebida são oferecidas ao seu santuário em busca da ajuda, conselho ou bênção de seus antepassados.

moeten bijvoorbeeld strikte traditionele voorschriften in acht worden genomen, zodat alleen de bedoelde geest van de doden in de *asen* kan doordringen.

Voor de levenden zijn de *asen* een belangrijk kruispunt tussen onze wereld en die aan gene zijde. De schrijn krijgt voedsel- en drankoffers aangeboden om de hulp, raad of zegen van de voorouders in te roepen.

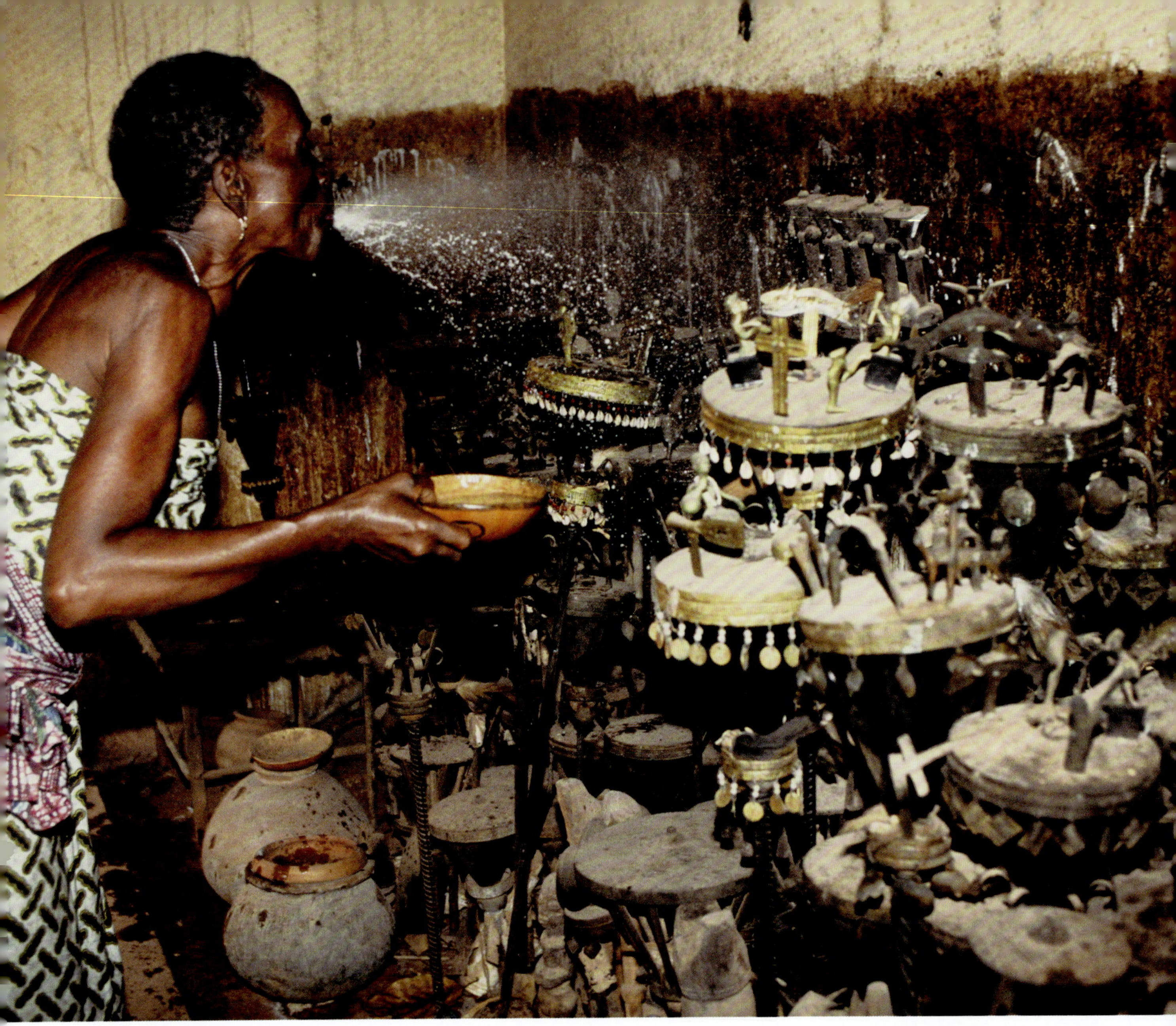

A farewell sip of beer. After offering food sacrifices and talking to the ancestors, the oldest woman in the family sprays a sip of beer over the Asen to complete the process.

Une gorgée de bière en guise d'au revoir. Après avoir apporté des mets en offrande et s'être entretenue avec les ancêtres, la plus vieille femme de la famille vaporise une gorgée de bière sur les *asen* pour clore le processus.

Ein Schluck Bier zum Abschied. Nach der Vorbringung von Speiseopfern und der Unterredung mit den Vorfahren versprüht die älteste Frau der Familie einen Schluck Bier über die Asen, um den Vorgang abzuschließen.

Un sorbo de cerveza para despedirse. Después de entregar ofrendas de comida y hablar con los antepasados, la mujer mayor de la familia rocía un sorbo de cerveza sobre el Asen para completar el proceso.

Um gole de cerveja para dizer adeus. Depois de oferecer ofertas de alimentos e conversar com os antepassados, a mulher mais velha da família bebe um gole de cerveja sobre o Asen para completar o processo.

Een slokje bier bij het afscheid. Na het aanbieden van een voedseloffer en een onderhoud met de voorouders sproeit de oudste vrouw van de familie een slokje bier over de asen om de procedure af te sluiten.

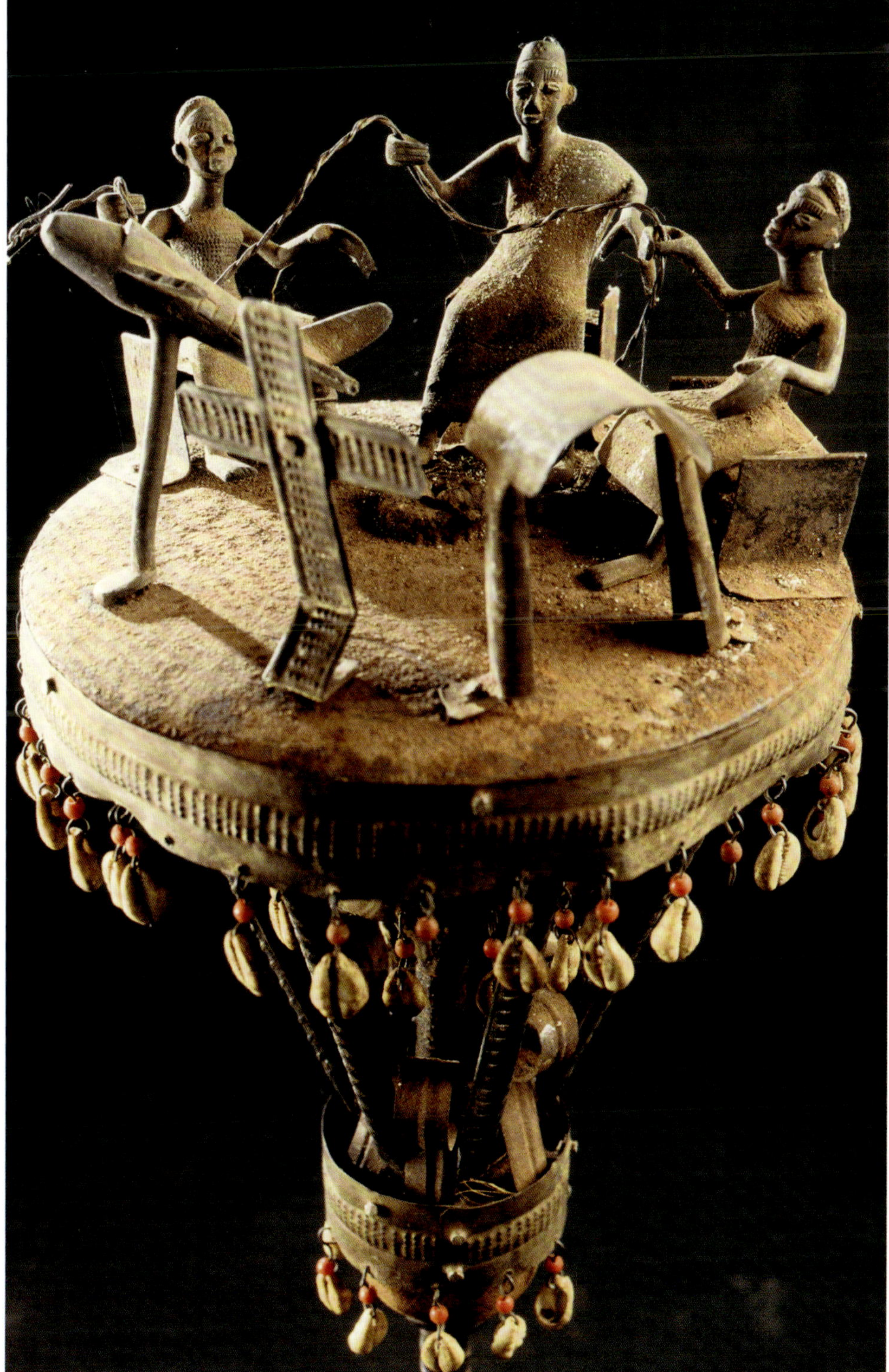

The Asen are witnesses. Newborn babies are also presented to the ancestors. In addition, marriages must be blessed by them and seeds before they are sown.

Les *asen* sont des témoins. Les nouveau-nés sont présentés aux ancêtres, dont la bénédiction est également nécessaire lorsqu'un mariage est scellé et avant de semer les cultures.

Die Asen sind Zeugen. Auch Neugeborene werden den Ahnen präsentiert. Ebenso bedarf es ihrer Segnung bei Eheschließungen und bei Saatgut vor dessen Ausbringung.

Los Asen son testigos. Los recién nacidos también se presentan a los antepasados. También deben ser bendecidos en el caso de matrimonios y semillas antes de ser sembrados.

Os Asen são testemunhas. Os recém-nascidos também são apresentados aos antepassados. Eles também devem ser abençoados no caso de casamentos e sementes antes de serem semeados.

De asen zijn getuigen. Ook pasgeborenen worden aan de voorouders voorgesteld. Verder heeft men hun zegen nodig voor huwelijken en voor zaad voordat het gezaaid wordt.

Bronze, sheet metal, steel/Bronze, tôle, acier, 95 × 20 cm

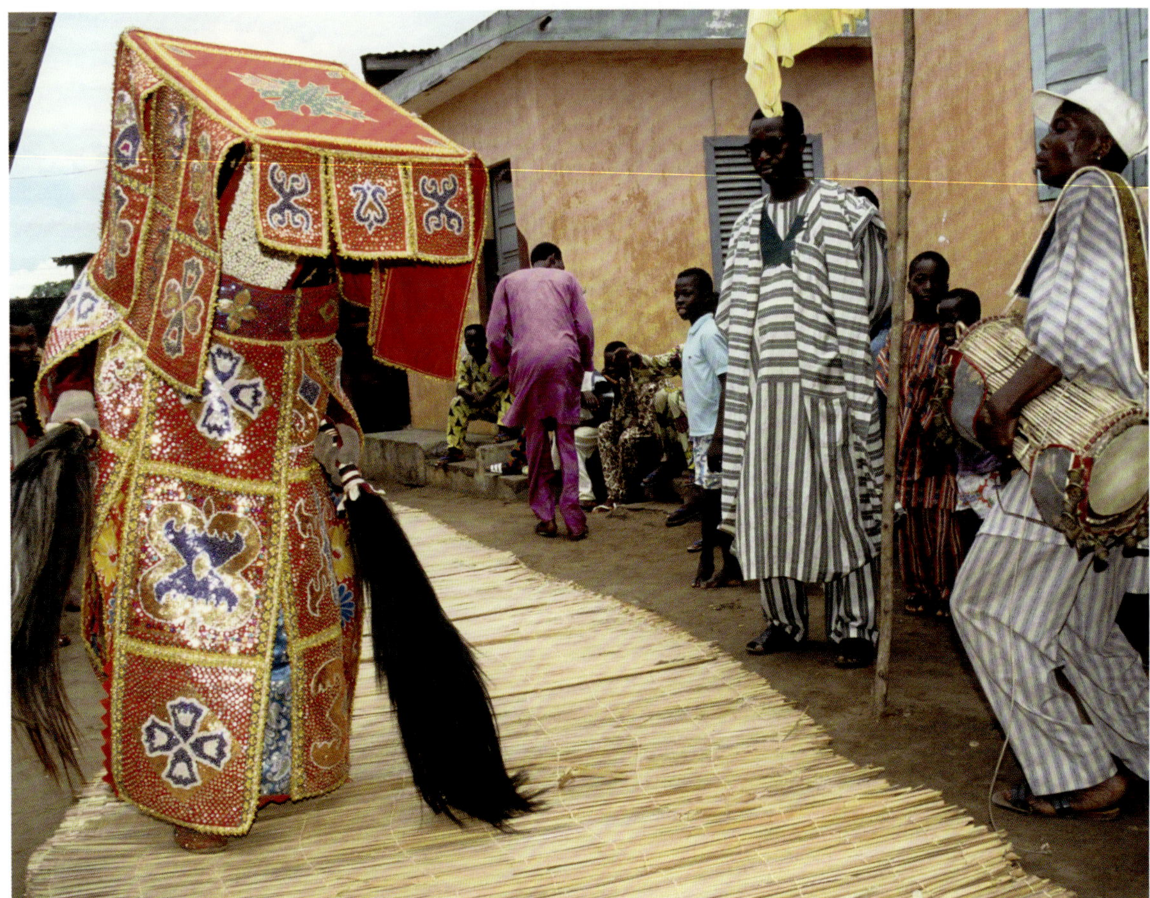

Egungun, the representatives of the ancestors

The secret society of the Egungun, which is found among the Yoruba people in Nigeria and Benin, is a mediator between the ancestors and the living. The society is always present at funerals, but its main appearance only takes place once a year, shortly before the fields are cultivated. Then one asks the ancestors in a traditional ceremony for a good harvest and the blessing for the community.

Part of the multi-layered rituals are dances in which the participants, dressed in sumptuous and impressive masks, are possessed by the spirits of the deceased. In a strangely elderly voice, they then issue

Egungun, les représentants des ancêtres

La société secrète d'Egungun, originaire de l'ethnie des Yoruba et présente au Nigeria et au Bénin, joue le rôle d'intermédiaire entre les ancêtres et les vivants. La confrérie est toujours présente aux inhumations, et une grande apparition est organisée une fois par an, juste avant le début des travaux agricoles. Au cours de cette cérémonie, on demande aux ancêtres de bonnes récoltes et la bénédiction des cultures.

Parmi les nombreux rituels, il existe des danses pendant lesquelles les participants, aux costumes et aux masques exubérants et impressionnants, sont possédés par les esprits des défunts. Empruntant une

Egungun, die Vertreter der Ahnen

Der Geheimbund der Egungun, der zum Volk der Yoruba gehört und sich in Nigeria und Benin findet, ist ein Mittler zwischen den Ahnen und den Lebenden. Bei Bestattungen ist der Bund stets zugegen, aber sein großer Hauptauftritt findet nur einmal jährlich statt, kurz bevor die Felder bestellt werden. Dann bittet man die Ahnen in einer traditionellen Zeremonie um gute Ernte und den Segen für die Gemeinde.

Teil der vielschichtigen Rituale sind Tänze, bei denen die mit üppigen und eindrucksvollen Masken eingekleideten Teilnehmer von den Geistern Verstorbener besessen werden. Mit

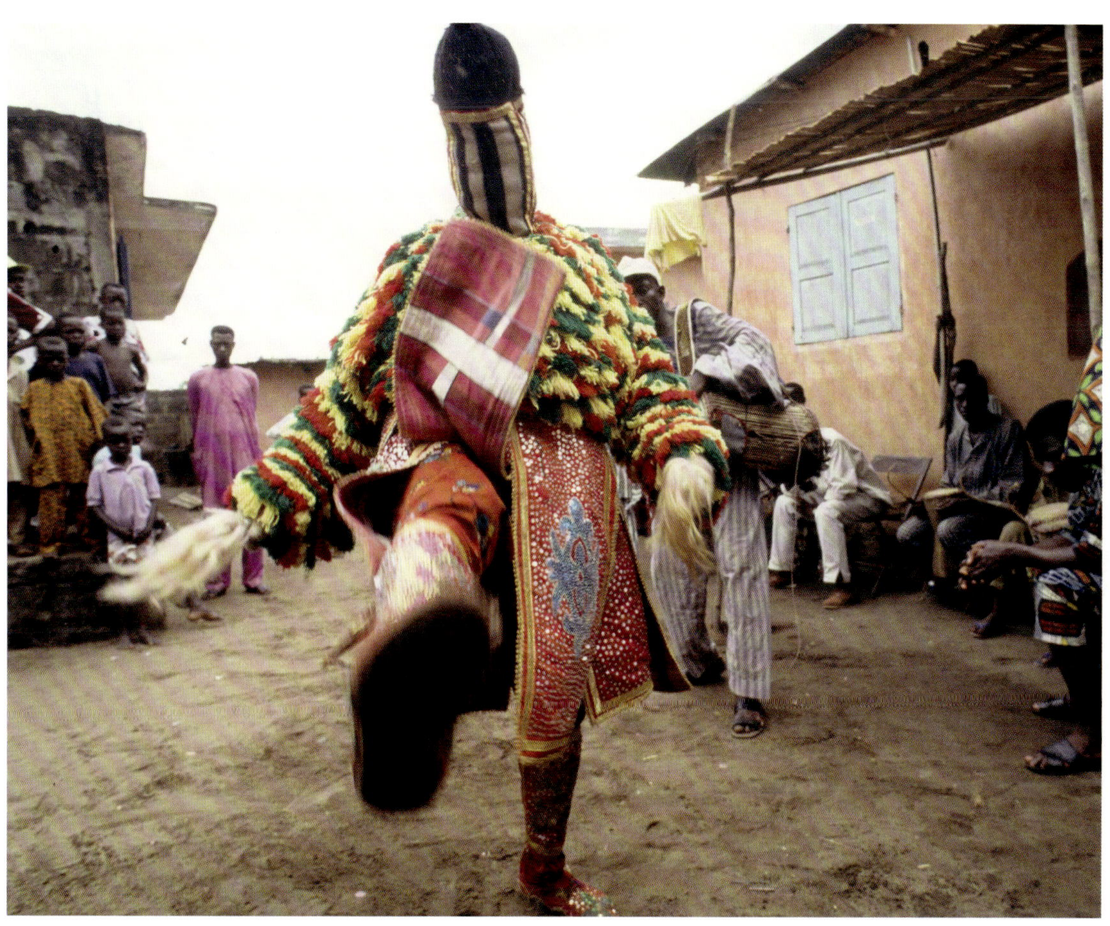

Egungun, los representantes de los ancestros

La sociedad secreta de los Egungun, que pertenece al pueblo Yoruba y se encuentra en Nigeria y Benin, es una mediadora entre los ancestros y los vivos. La alianza está siempre presente en los entierros, pero su mayor aparición sólo se produce una vez al año, poco antes de que se cultiven los campos. Luego, en una ceremonia tradicional, se les pide a los ancestros una buena cosecha y bendición para la comunidad.

Parte de los rituales son danzas en las que los participantes, vestidos con máscaras suntuosas e impresionantes, son poseídos por los espíritus de los difuntos. Con una

Egungun, Os representantes dos antepassados

A sociedade secreta dos Egungun, que pertence ao povo iorubá e se encontra na Nigéria e no Benim, é um mediador entre os antepassados e os vivos. A aliança está sempre presente nos enterros, mas o seu aspecto mais importante só ocorre uma vez por ano, pouco antes de os campos serem cultivados. Então, em uma cerimônia tradicional, os antepassados são convidados para uma boa colheita e bênção para a comunidade.

Parte dos rituais multicamadas são danças em que os participantes, vestidos com máscaras sumptuosas e impressionantes, são possuídos

Egungun, de vertegenwoordigers van de voorouders

Het geheime genootschap van de Egungun, dat bij het Yoruba-volk hoort en in Nigeria en Benin voorkomt, bemiddelt tussen de voorouders en de levenden. Het genootschap is altijd aanwezig bij begrafenissen, maar het belangrijkste optreden ervan vindt slechts één keer per jaar plaats, kort voordat de akkers worden bewerkt. Dan vraagt men de voorouders in een traditionele ceremonie om een goede oogst en zegen voor de gemeenschap.

Onderdeel van de veelgelaagde rituelen zijn dansen waarbij de deelnemers, verkleed en met uitbundige en indrukwekkende maskers, bezeten zijn door de geesten van

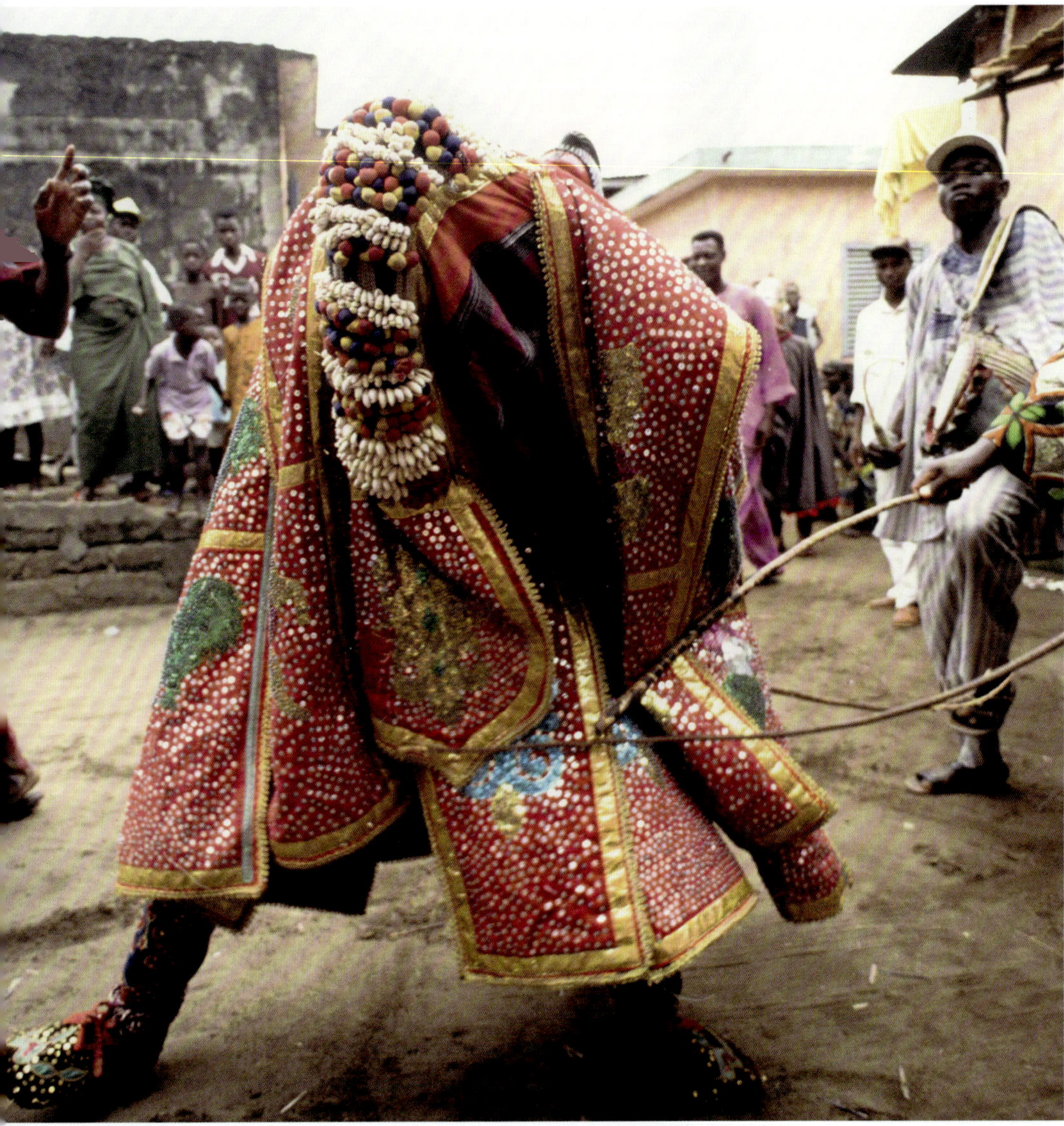

warnings and reprimand those involved in social quarrels, so that harmony may return to the village in view of the forthcoming work in the fields.

The spectacular events are always well attended and popular and respected by young and old.

voix étrange d'un autre âge, ils font des remontrances, en particulier à ceux qui prennent part à des disputes, et les exhortent à restaurer l'harmonie au sein du village pour accomplir ensemble les travaux agricoles imminents.

Ces manifestations spectaculaires attirent toujours beaucoup de monde et sont appréciées et suivies par les jeunes autant que par les plus âgés.

seltsam ältlicher Stimme sprechen sie dann Ermahnungen aus und weisen die an sozialen Zerwürfnissen Beteiligten zurecht, auf dass im Dorf angesichts der bevorstehenden Feldarbeit wieder Harmonie einkehren möge.

Die spektakulären Veranstaltungen sind stets gut besucht und bei Jung und Alt beliebt und geachtet.

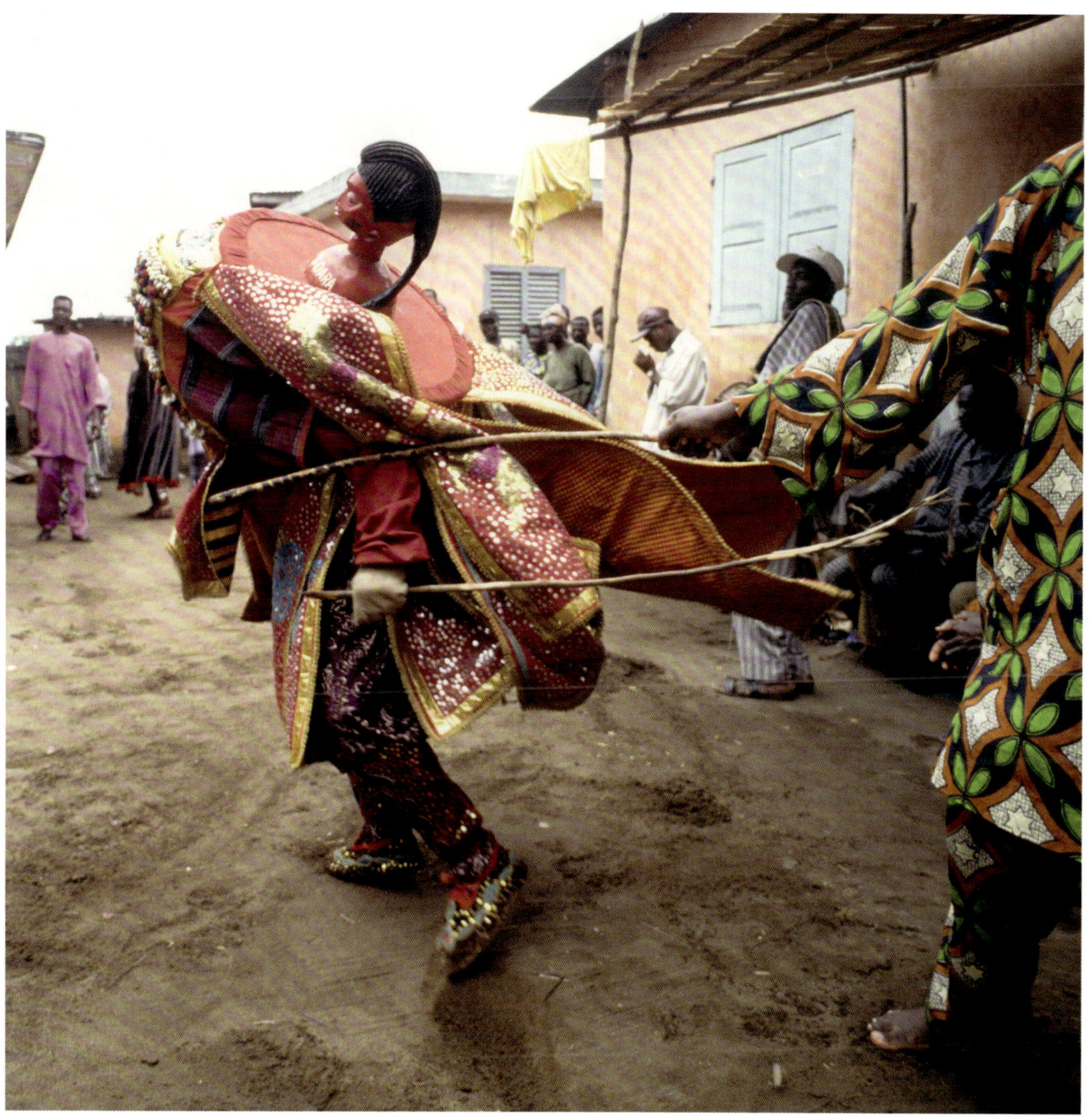

voz extrañamente anciana, exhortan y reprenden a los que participan en disputas sociales, para que la armonía pueda volver a la aldea ante el trabajo que se avecina en el campo.

Los espectaculares eventos son siempre muy concurridos y populares y respetados por jóvenes y mayores.

pelos espíritos do falecido. Numa voz estranhamente idosa, eles então exortam e repreendem os envolvidos em disputas sociais, para que a harmonia possa voltar à aldeia em face do trabalho futuro nos campos.

Os espectaculares eventos são sempre bem frequentados e populares e respeitados por jovens e idosos.

de overledenen. Met een vreemd ouwelijk stem spreken ze vermaningen uit en wijzen vervolgens degenen terecht die betrokken zijn bij maatschappelijk onmin, zodat met het oog op de komende werkzaamheden op het land de harmonie in het dorp kan erugkeren.

De spectaculaire vertoningen worden altijd goed bezocht en zijn populair bij jong en oud.

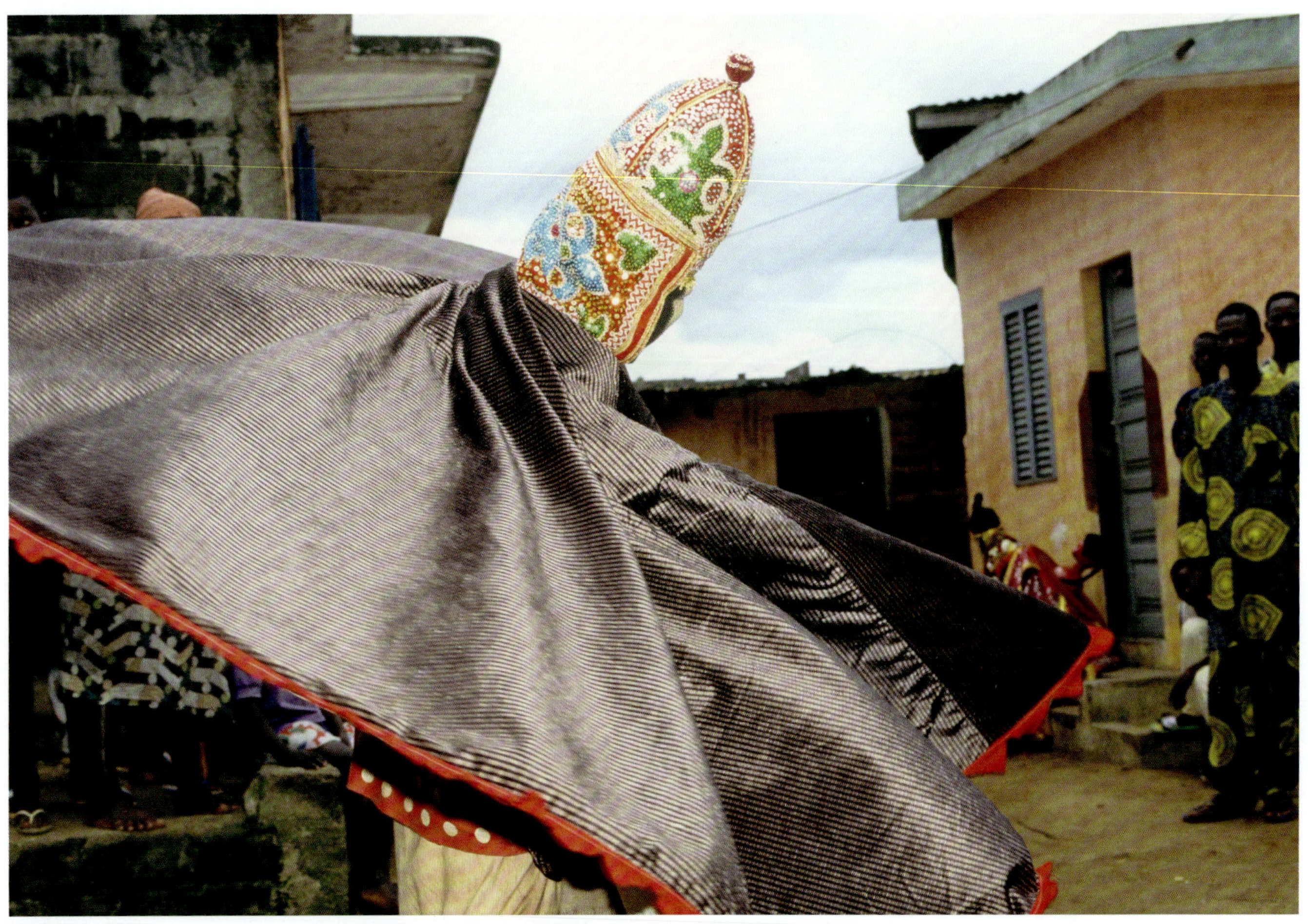

The Egungun whirl wildly across the village square

L'Egungun tourbillonne sauvagement sur la place du village

Wild wirbeln die Egungun über den Dorfplatz

Los Egúngún se arremolinan salvajemente por la plaza del pueblo

O Egungun gira selvagemmente através da praça da aldeia

De Egungun draaien wild rond over het dorpsplein

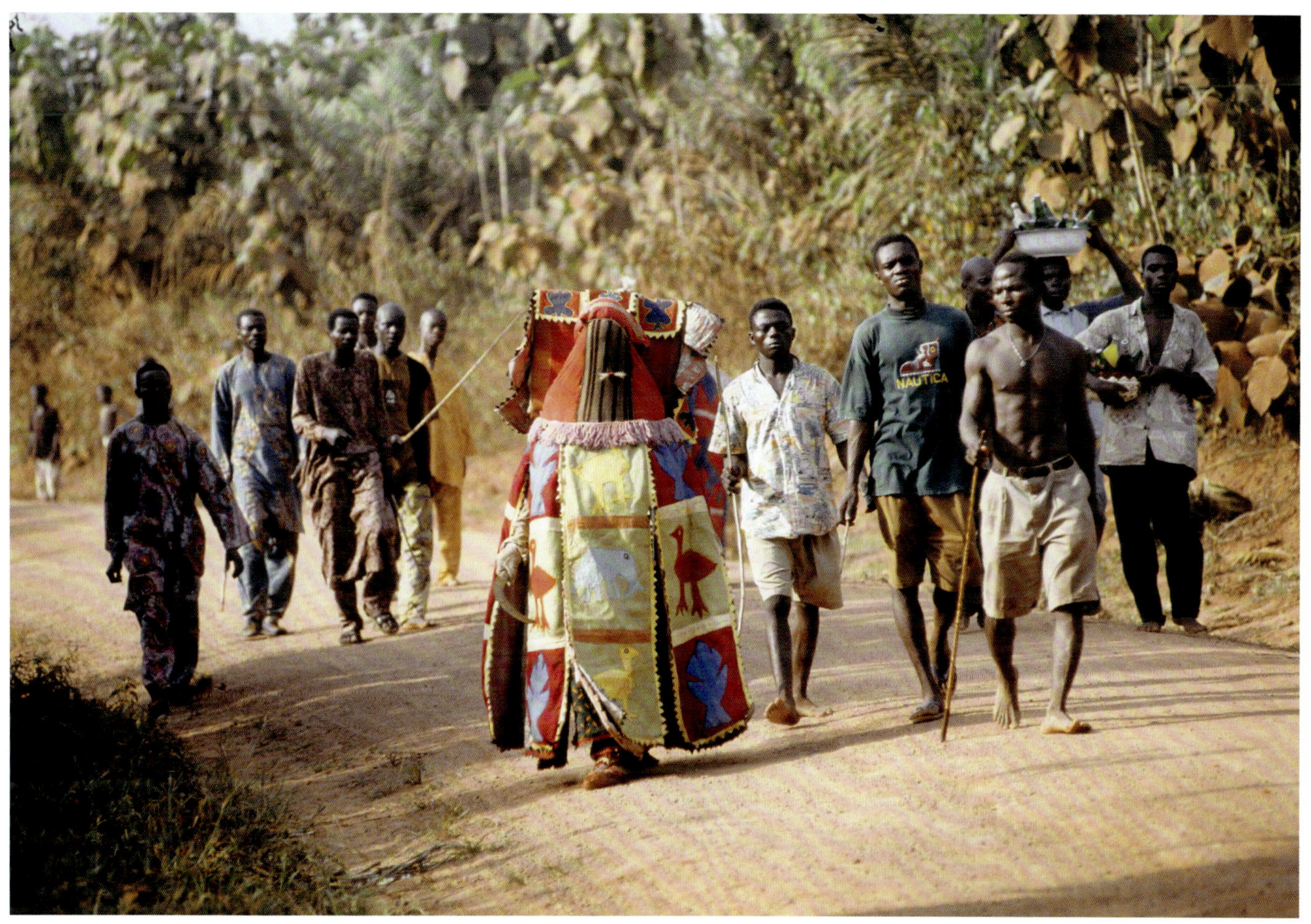

Collection for the Ancestor Festival

Collecte pour le festival des ancêtres

Kollekte für das Ahnenfest

Colección para la Fiesta de los Antepasados

Coleção para o Festival Ancestral

Geld inzamelen voor het voorouderfeest

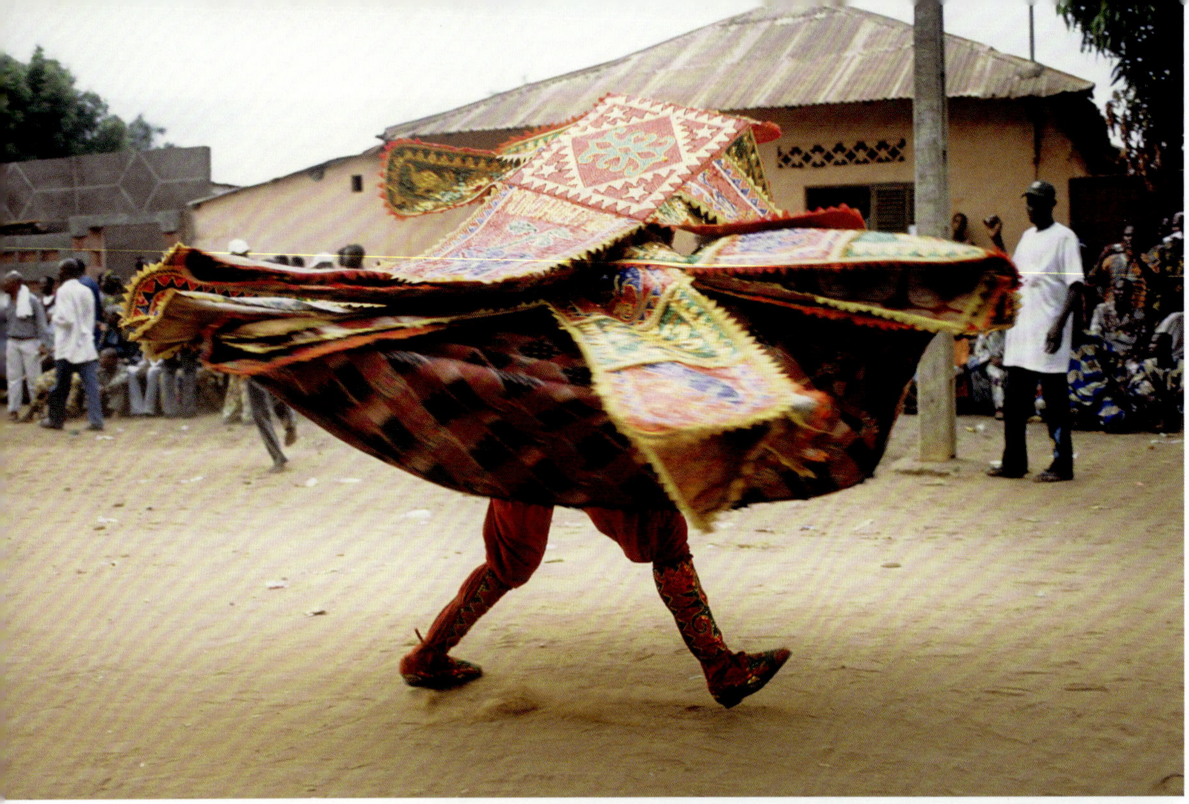

Spectacular scenes
are the rule

Les scènes
spectaculaires sont
de mise

Spektakuläre Szenen
sind die Regel

Las escenas
espectaculares son
la regla

Cenas espectaculares
são a regra

Spectaculaire scènes
zijn de regel

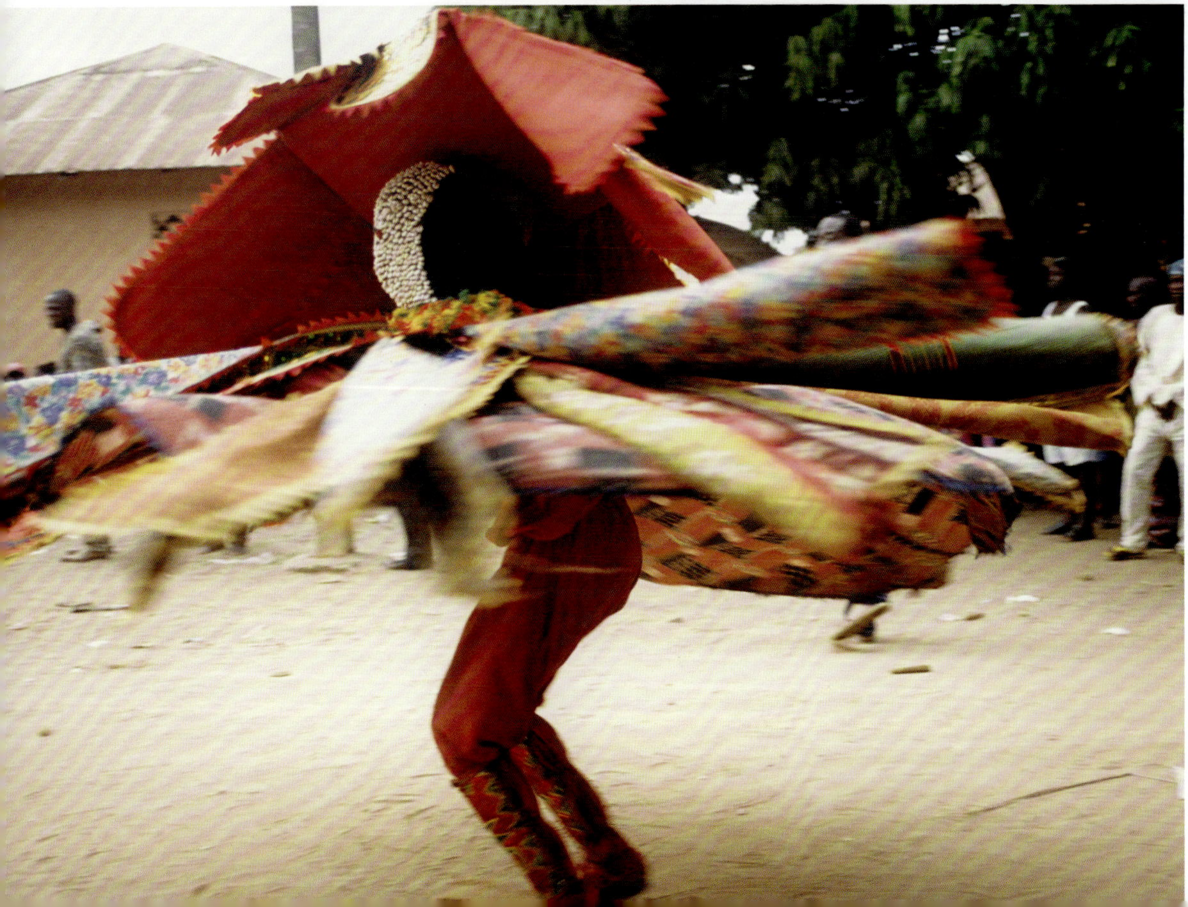

The people attending
respectfully keep
their distance

Les gens
rassemblés gardent
respectueusement
leurs distances

Die Versammelten
halten respektvoll
Abstand

La gente reunida
respetuosamente
mantiene su distancia

As pessoas
reunidas mantêm
respeitosamente a
distância

De verzamelde
mensen houden
respectvol afstand

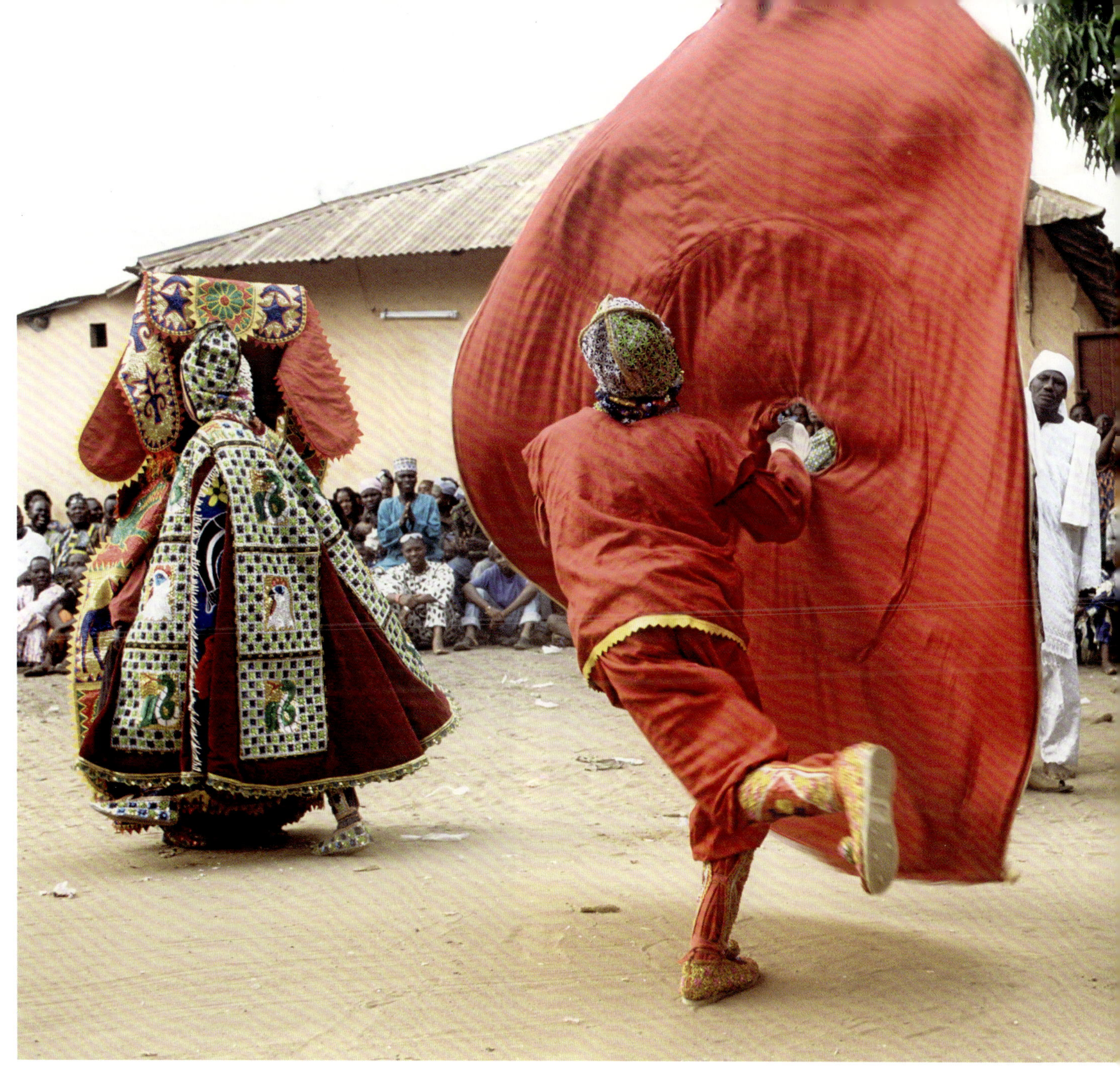

Spectacular scenes are the rule

Les scènes spectaculaires sont de mise

Spektakuläre Szenen sind die Regel

Las escenas espectaculares son la regla

Cenas espectaculares são a regra

Spectaculaire scènes zijn de regel

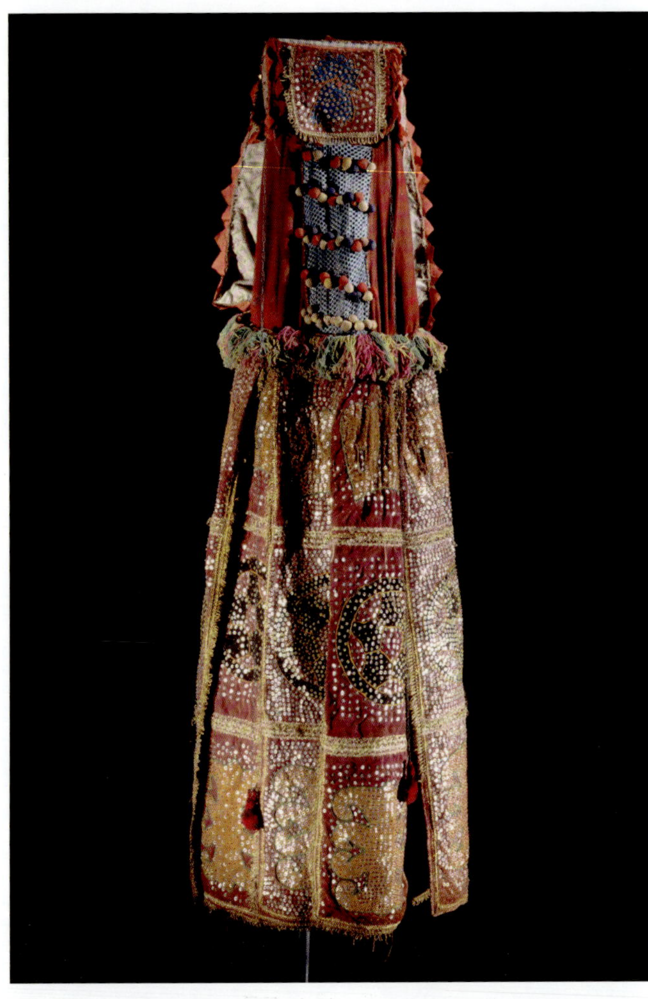

Egungun costume. They represent the deceased who have returned from Kutome, the realm of the dead, to offer help and advice to the people—or to judge them.

Costume Egungun. Les costumes représentent les défunts revenus du royaume des morts Kutome pour prodiguer aide et conseil aux humains, mais également pour les juger.

Egungun Kostüm. Sie repräsentieren die Verstorbenen, die aus dem Totenreich Kutome zurückgekehrt sind, um den Menschen Hilfe und Rat zu bieten – oder aber zu richten.

Traje de Egúngún. Representan a los difuntos que han regresado del reino de los muertos Kutome, para ofrecer ayuda y consejo a la gente– o para juzgarlos.

Fato de Egungun. Eles representam os mortos que voltaram do reino dos mortos, Kutome, para oferecer ajuda e conselhos ao povo – ou para julgá-los.

Egungun-kostuum. Zij vertegenwoordigen de overledenen die uit het rijk der doden, Kutome, zijn teruggekeerd om de mensen hulp en advies te bieden – of om ze te berechten.

Various textiles/Différents textiles, 175 × 35 cm

Egungun costume

Costume Egungun

Egungun Kostüm

Traje de Egúngún

Fato de Egungun

Egungun-kostuum

Various textiles, wooden figure/Différents textiles, figurine en bois, 175 × 40 cm

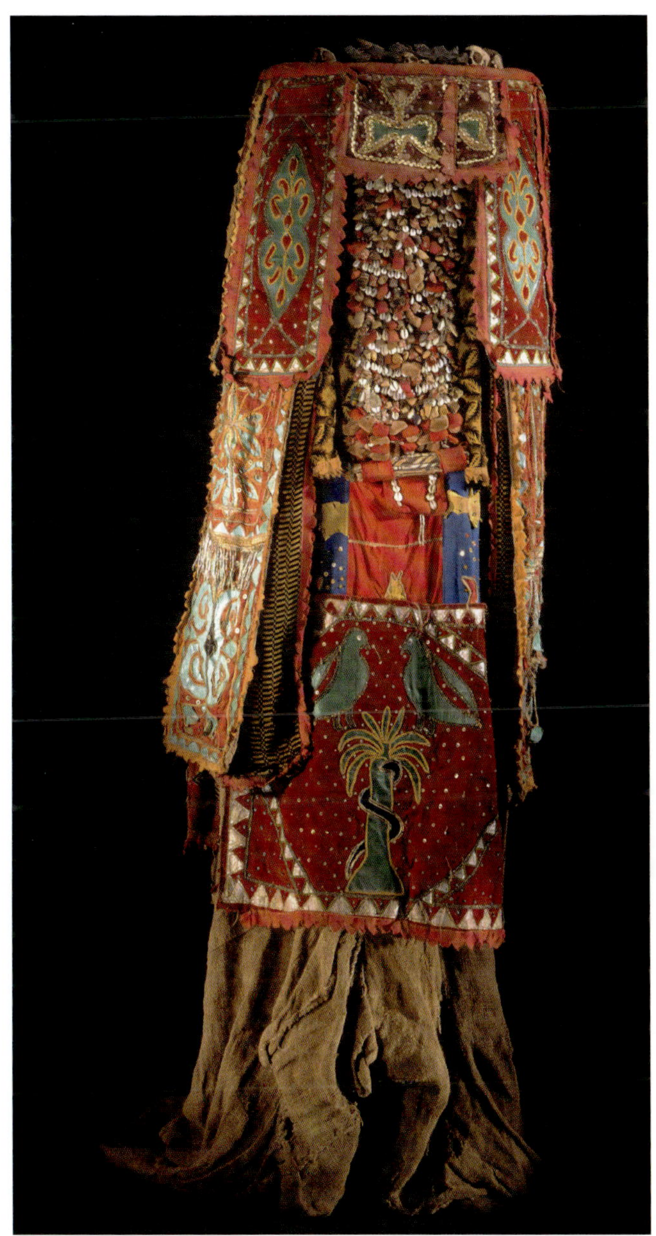

Egungun costume
Costume Egungun
Egungun Kostüm
Traje de Egúngún
Fato de Egungun
Egungun-kostuum

Various textiles, monkey skulls/Différents textiles, crânes de singe, 175 × 45 cm

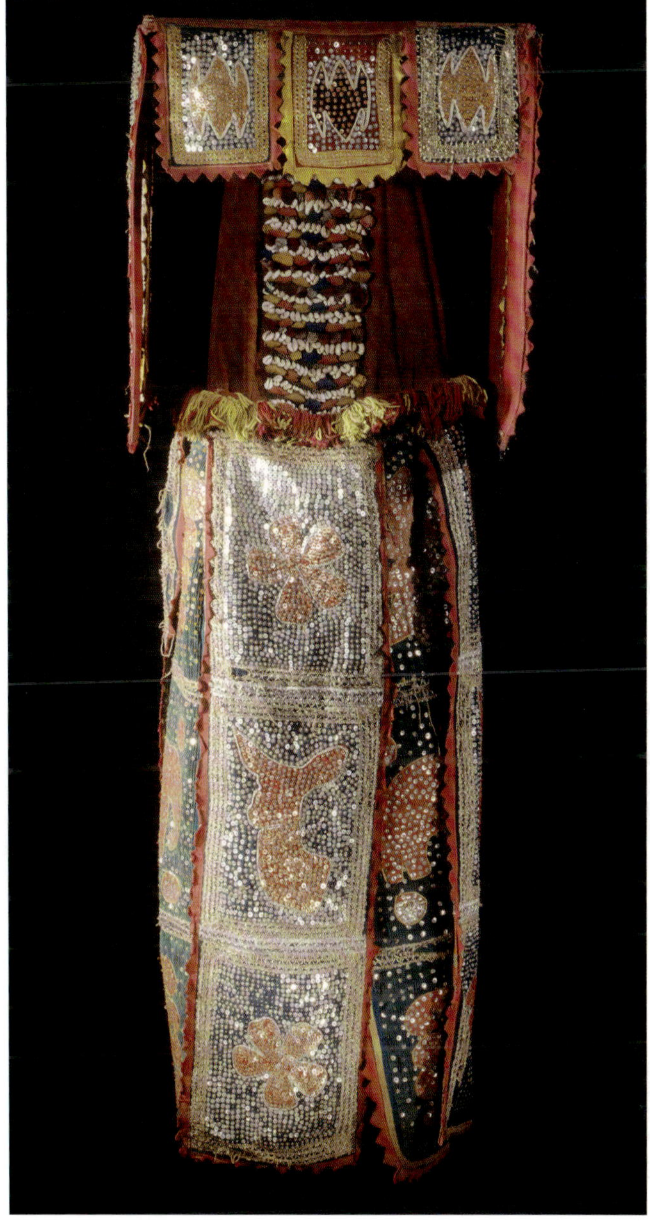

Egungun costume
Costume Egungun
Egungun Kostüm
Traje de Egúngún
Fato de Egungun
Egungun-kostuum

Various textiles/Différents textiles, 180 × 50 cm

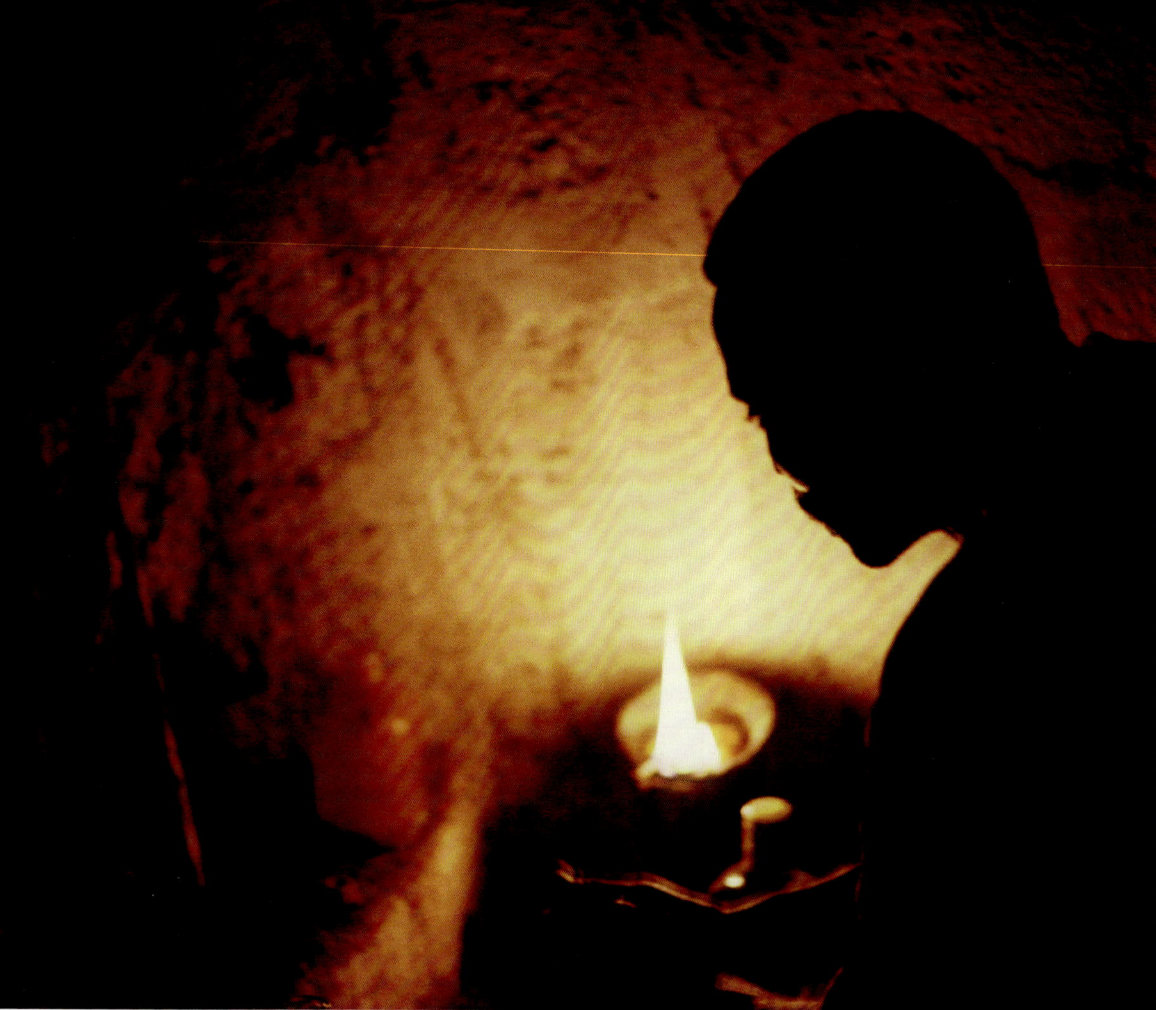

Egungun - The executioner

He is called a "jujuman", which means that he can both praise and punish—the Egungun executioner.

Egungun, a secret society that represents the deceased ancestors and can be found among the Yoruba in Nigeria and in neighbouring Benin, takes on the role of guardian of order and defender of morals in the traditional community. The "enforcer" wears a characteristic costume with a red fabric mask and a gorilla paw as a frightening attribute.

Those convicted of serious crimes are brought before him, and he holds court: The delinquents must kneel before a skull

Egungun, le bourreau

On le qualifie de *jujuman*. Cette expression indique qu'il peut complimenter mais également punir, il est le bourreau d'Egungun.

Egungun, société secrète représentant les ancêtres défunts, est présente chez les Yoruba du Nigeria et du Bénin voisin. Au sein de la communauté traditionnelle, elle joue le rôle de garant de la paix et de la moralité. Son «exécuteur» porte un costume caractéristique comprenant un masque en tissu rouge et, en guise d'ustensile effrayant, une patte de gorille.

Ceux qui ont été reconnus coupables de crimes capitaux sont amenés au *jujuman*

Egungun – Der Scharfrichter

Man bezeichnet ihn als „Jujuman", was zum Ausdruck bringt, dass er sowohl loben als auch strafen kann – der Egungun-Scharfrichter.

Egungun, ein Geheimbund, der die verstorbenen Ahnen vertritt und sich bei den Yoruba in Nigeria und im angrenzenden Benin findet, nimmt in der traditionellen Lebensgemeinschaft die Rolle eines Ordnungshüters und Moralwächters ein. Ihr „Vollstrecker" trägt ein charakteristisches Kostüm mit einer roten Stoffmaske und als schreckenerregendes Utensil eine Gorillapfote bei sich.

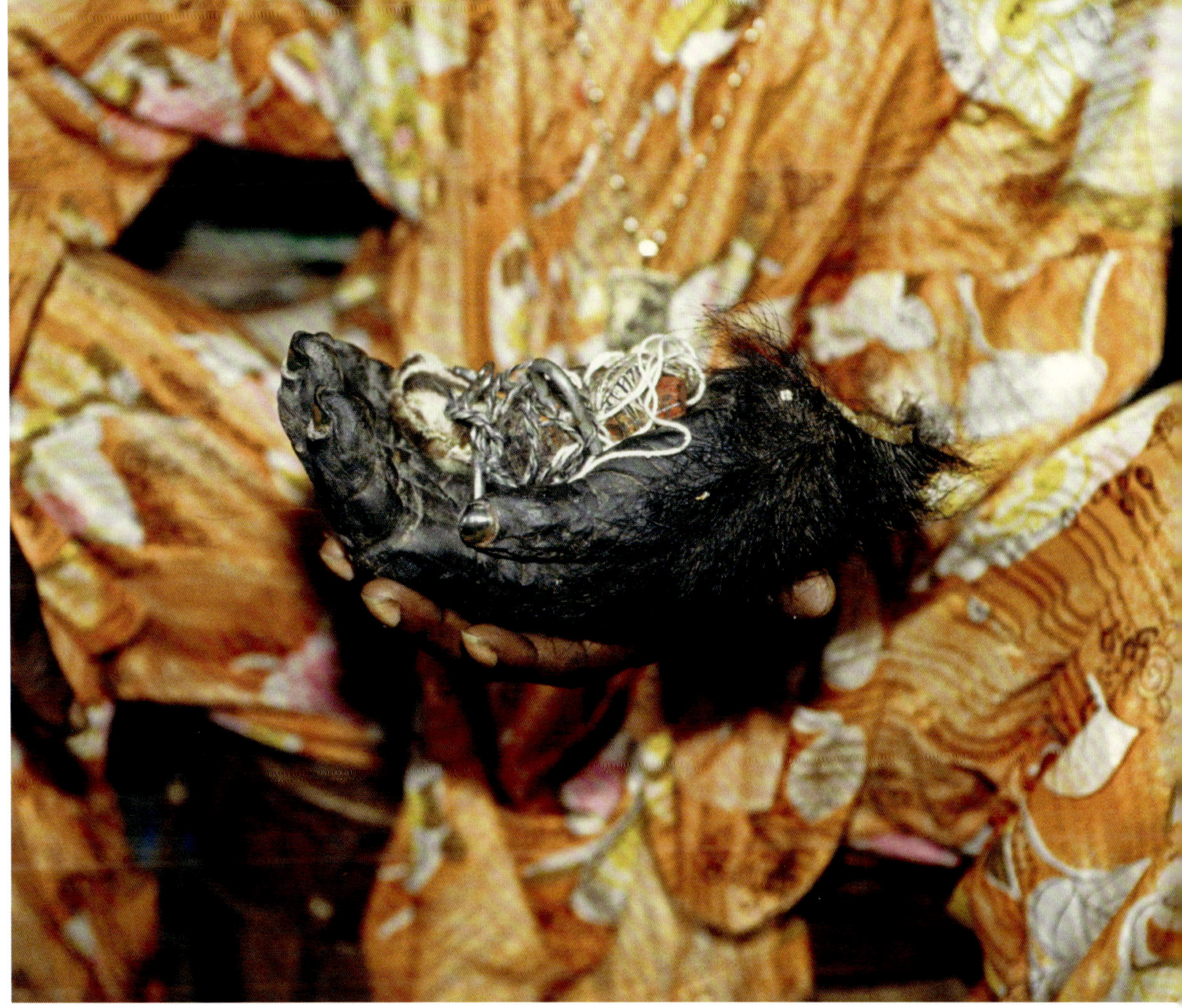

Egungun– El verdugo

Se le llama "jujumano", lo que
significa que puede alabar y castigar–
el verdugo Egungun.

Egungun, una sociedad secreta que
representa a los antepasados fallecidos y que
se encuentra entre los yoruba en Nigeria
y en el vecino Benin, desempeña el papel
de guardián del orden y de la moral en la
comunidad tradicional. Su "albacea" lleva
un traje característico con una máscara
de tela roja y una pata de gorila como
utensilio aterrador.

Es extraditado con criminales de
capital convictos, y tiene un tribunal: los
delincuentes tienen que arrodillarse frente a

Egungun – O carrasco

Ele é chamado de "jujuman", o que significa
que ele pode elogiar e punir – o carrasco
Egungun.

Egungun, uma sociedade secreta que
representa os antepassados falecidos e
pode ser encontrada entre os iorubás na
Nigéria e no vizinho Benin, desempenha
o papel de guardião da ordem e da moral
na comunidade tradicional. Seu "executor"
usa uma fantasia característica com uma
máscara de tecido vermelha e uma pata de
gorila como um utensílio assustador.

Ele é extraditado com criminosos
capitalistas condenados, e ele mantém o
tribunal: os delinqüentes têm que se ajoelhar

Egungun – de beul

Hij wordt een 'jujuman' genoemd, wat
betekent dat hij zowel kan prijzen als
straffen: de Egungun-beul.

Egungun, een geheim genootschap dat
de overleden voorouders vertegenwoordigt
en te vinden is bij de Yoruba in Nigeria
en het naburige Benin, speelt de rol van
wetshandhaver en moraalridder in de
traditionele gemeenschap. De beul, de
'uitvoerder', draagt een karakteristiek
kostuum met een rood stoffen masker en
een gorillapoot als angstaanjagende staf.

Aan hem worden veroordeelde
fraudeurs uitgeleverd, en hij spreekt recht:
de misdadigers moeten knielen voor

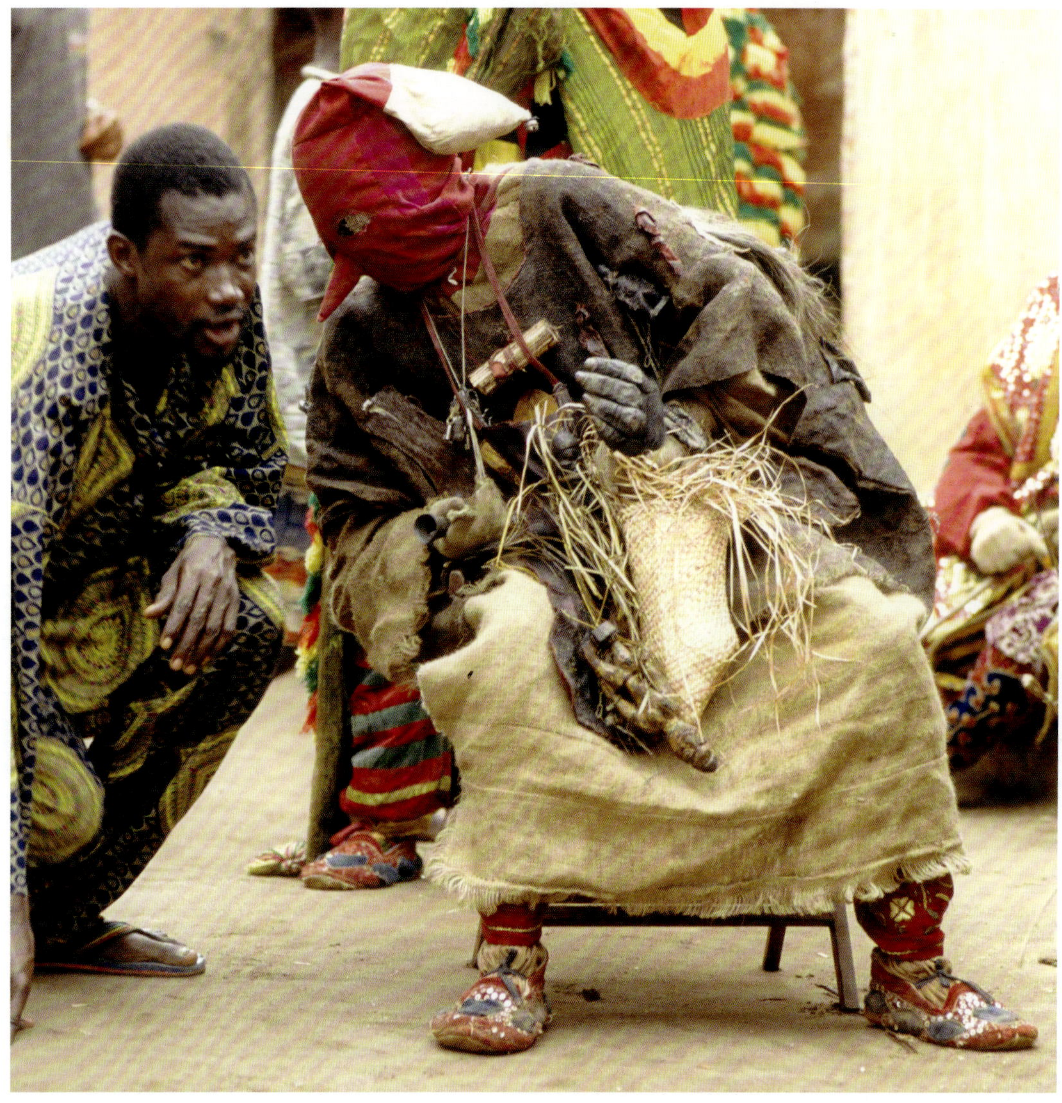

The Egungun judge. His red mask is reminiscent of the executioner, the robe of coarse sackcloth of the bush spirits—he is feared and respected equally.

Le bourreau d'Egungun. Son masque rouge évoque le bourreau et le costume en toile de sac figure l'esprit de la forêt, le *jujuman* est autant craint que respecté.

Der Scharfrichter der Egungun. Seine rote Maske erinnert an den Henker, das Gewand aus grobem Sackleinen an die Buschgeister – er ist gefürchtet und respektiert gleichermaßen.

El verdugo de los Egúngún. Su máscara roja recuerda al verdugo, la túnica de saco grueso de los espíritus del monte; es temido y respetado por igual.

O carrasco do Egungun. Sua máscara vermelha lembra o carrasco, o manto do saco grosseiro dos espíritos dos arbustos – ele é temido e respeitado igualmente.

De Egungun-beul. Zijn rode masker doet denken aan de beul, het gewaad van grove zakken aan de bushgeesten – hij wordt evenzeer gevreesd als gerespecteerd.

oracle and look into the mirrors there. The Jujuman follows every small eye movement attentively. In the worst case, his staff then touches the right shoulder of the villain, who then dies within ten days.

pour qu'il rende la justice : les délinquants doivent s'agenouiller devant un oracle-crâne et plonger leur regard dans des miroirs. Le *jujuman* scrute attentivement les moindres mouvements de leurs yeux. Dans les cas les plus graves, son bâton touche l'épaule droite du coupable, provoquant sa mort au cours des dix jours suivants.

Ihm werden überführte Kapitalverbrecher ausgeliefert, und er hält Gericht: Die Delinquenten müssen vor einem Schädelorakel niederknien und den Blick auf dort befindliche Spiegel richten. Jede noch so kleine Augenbewegung verfolgt der Jujuman dabei aufmerksam. Im schlimmsten Fall berührt sein Stab anschließend die rechte Schulter des Bösewichts, der daraufhin binnen zehn Tagen stirbt.

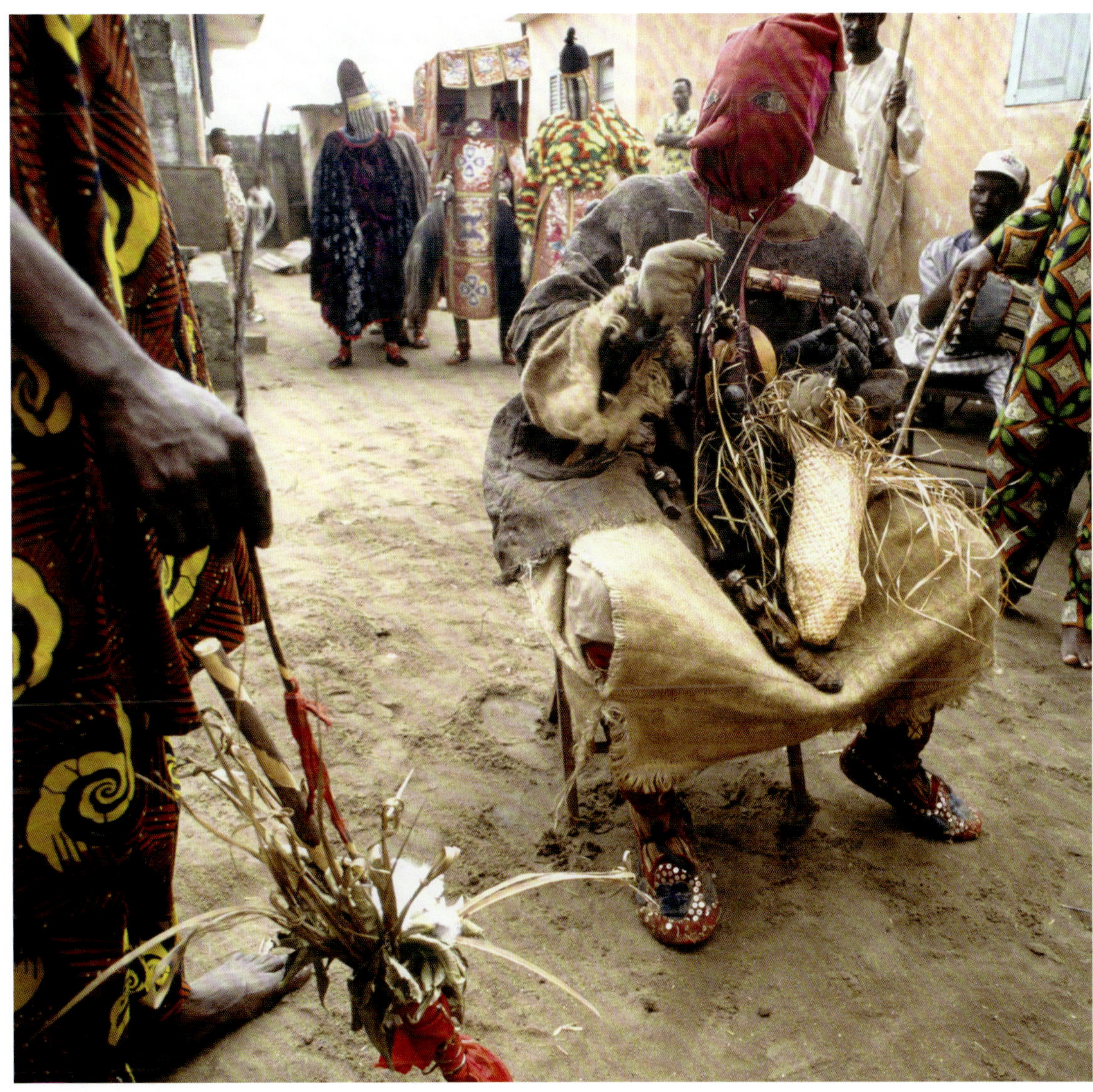

un cráneo oráculo y mirarse en los espejos. El Jujuman sigue cada movimiento de sus ojos, no importa cuán pequeño sea. En el peor de los casos, su bastón toca el hombro derecho del villano, que muere en un plazo de diez días.

na frente de uma doctora de crânio e olhar para os espelhos lá. O Jujuman segue cada movimento dos seus olhos, não importa quão pequeno seja. Na pior das hipóteses, a sua equipa toca no ombro direito do vilão, que morre dentro de dez dias.

een schedelorakel en een blik in de daar liggende spiegel werpen. De jujuman volgt daarbij elke oogbeweging, hoe klein ook. In het ergste geval raakt zijn staf dan de rechterschouder van de schurk aan, die vervolgens binnen tien dagen overlijdt.

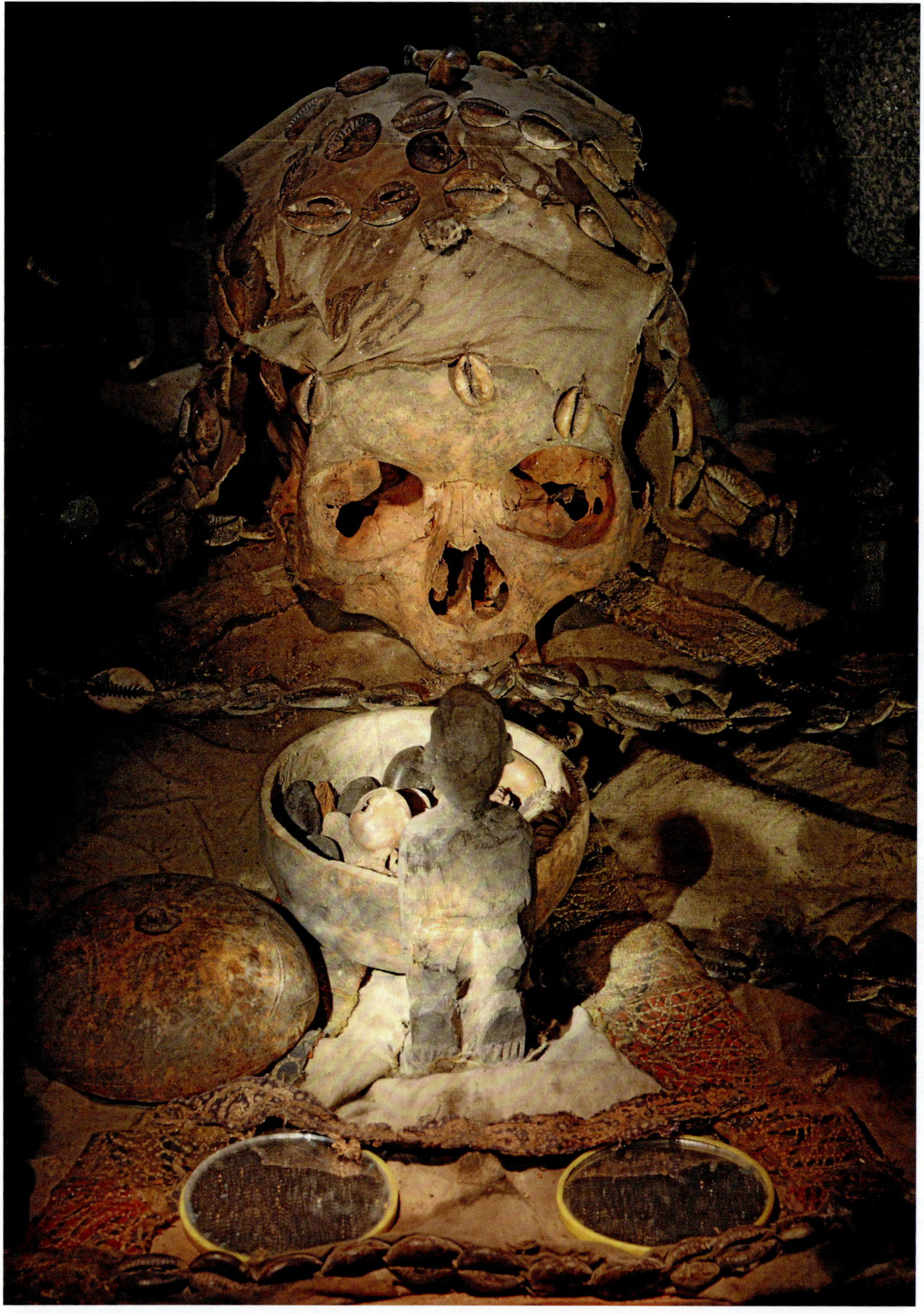

The oracle of the judge. With the help of the two mirrors, the suspects are convicted—their gaze begins to flutter and betrays them. They're unable to keep up their lies.

L'oracle du bourreau. Les suspects sont confondus à l'aide de deux miroirs, leur regard commence à vaciller et les trahit. Il leur est impossible de continuer à entretenir leurs mensonges.

Das Orakel des Scharfrichters. Mit Hilfe der beiden Spiegel werden die Verdächtigen überführt– ihr Blick beginnt zu flattern und verrät sie. Sie sind außerstande, ihre Lügen aufrecht zu erhalten.

El oráculo del verdugo. Con la ayuda de los dos espejos, los sospechosos son condenados – su mirada comienza a agitarse y los traiciona. Son incapaces de mantener sus mentiras.

O oráculo do carrasco. Com a ajuda dos dois espelhos, os suspeitos são condenados - seu olhar começa a tremular e os trai. Eles são incapazes de manter as suas mentiras.

Het orakel van de beul. Met behulp van twee spiegels worden de verdachten veroordeeld – hun blik begint te dwalen en verraadt hen. Ze zijn niet in staat om hun leugens overeind te houden.

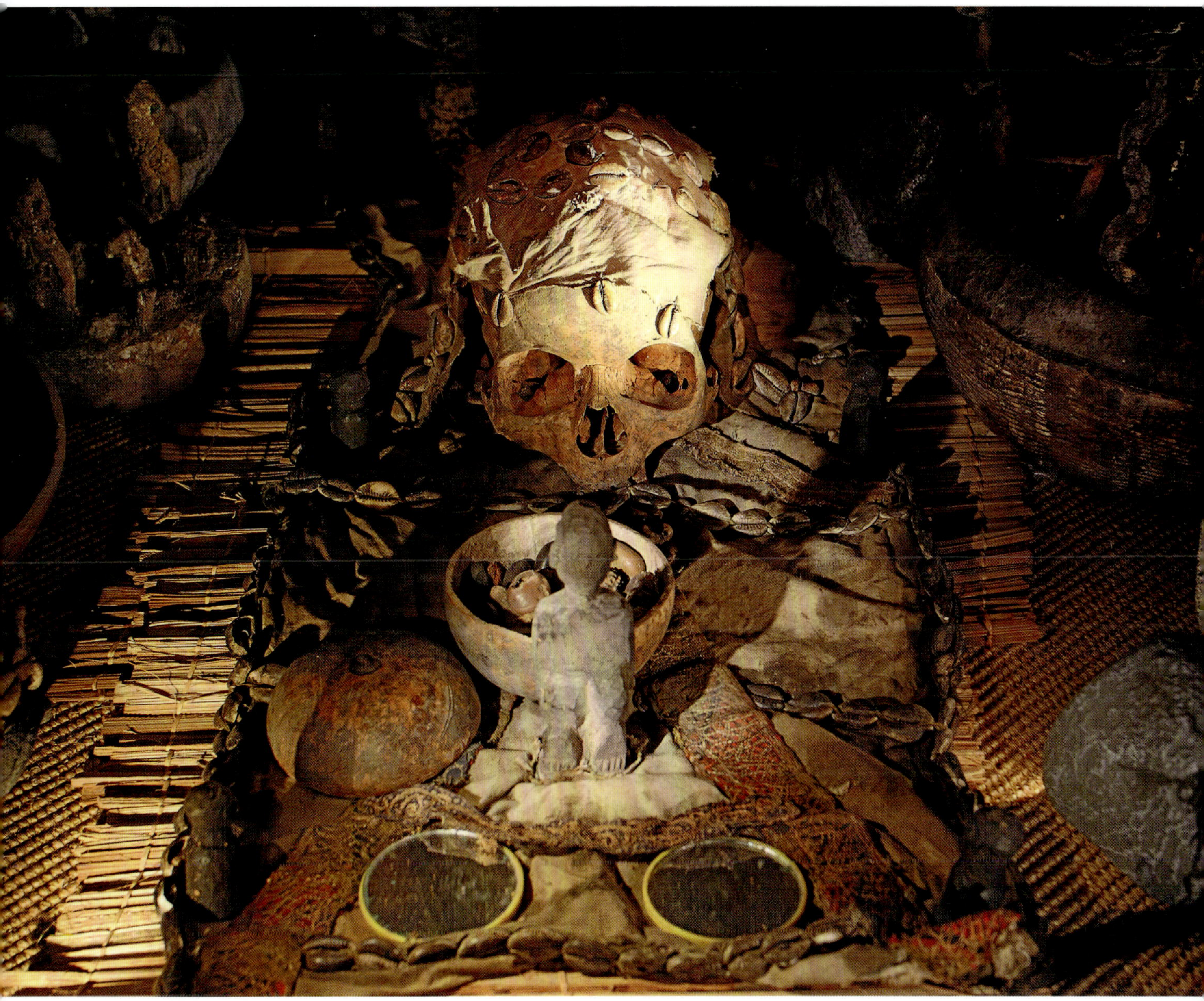

The oracle of the judge

L'oracle du bourreau

Das Orakel des Scharfrichters

El oráculo del verdugo

O oráculo do carrasco

Het orakel van de beul

Human skull, wooden figure, textiles, calabash/Crâne d'homme, figurine en bois, textiles, calebasses

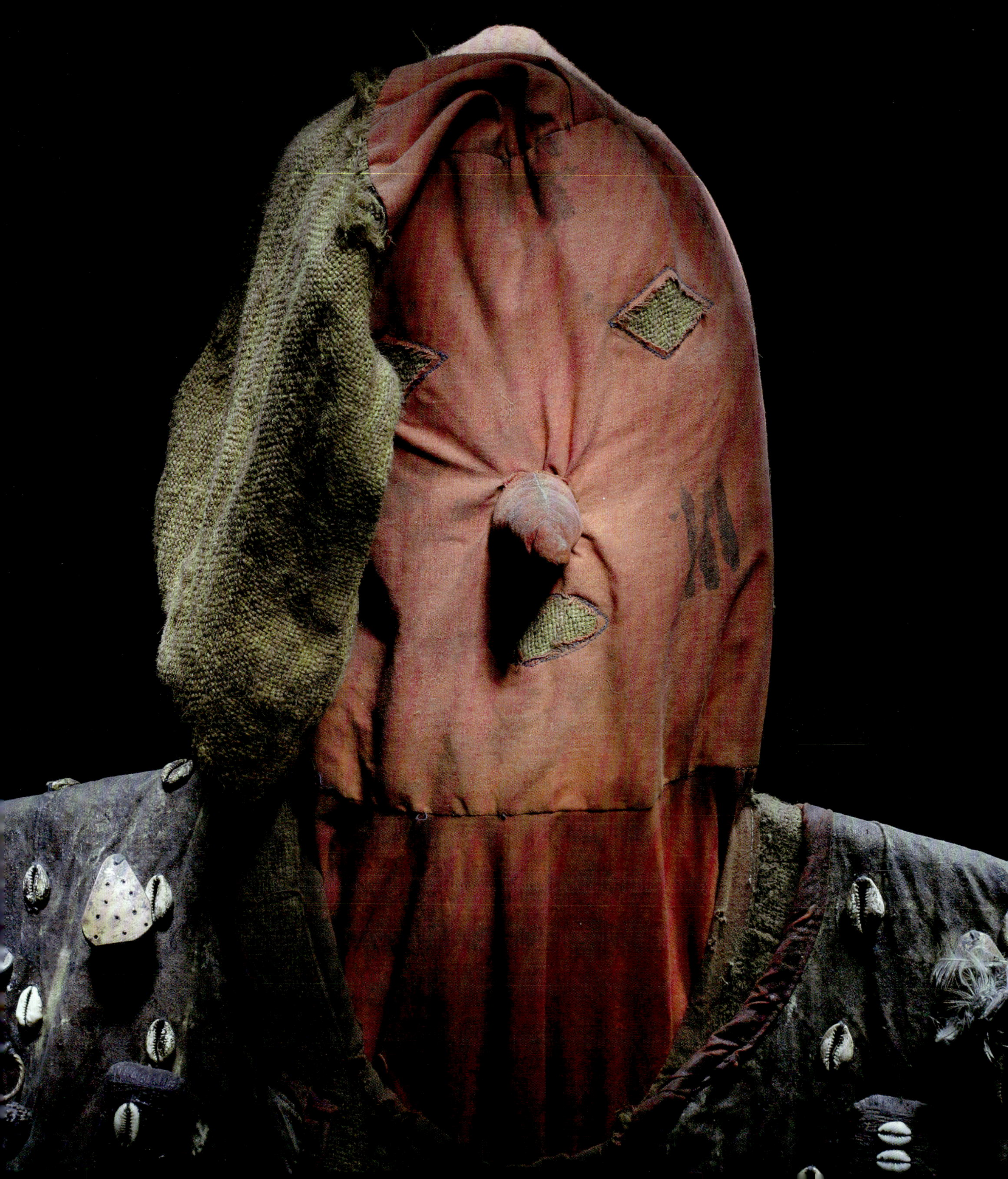

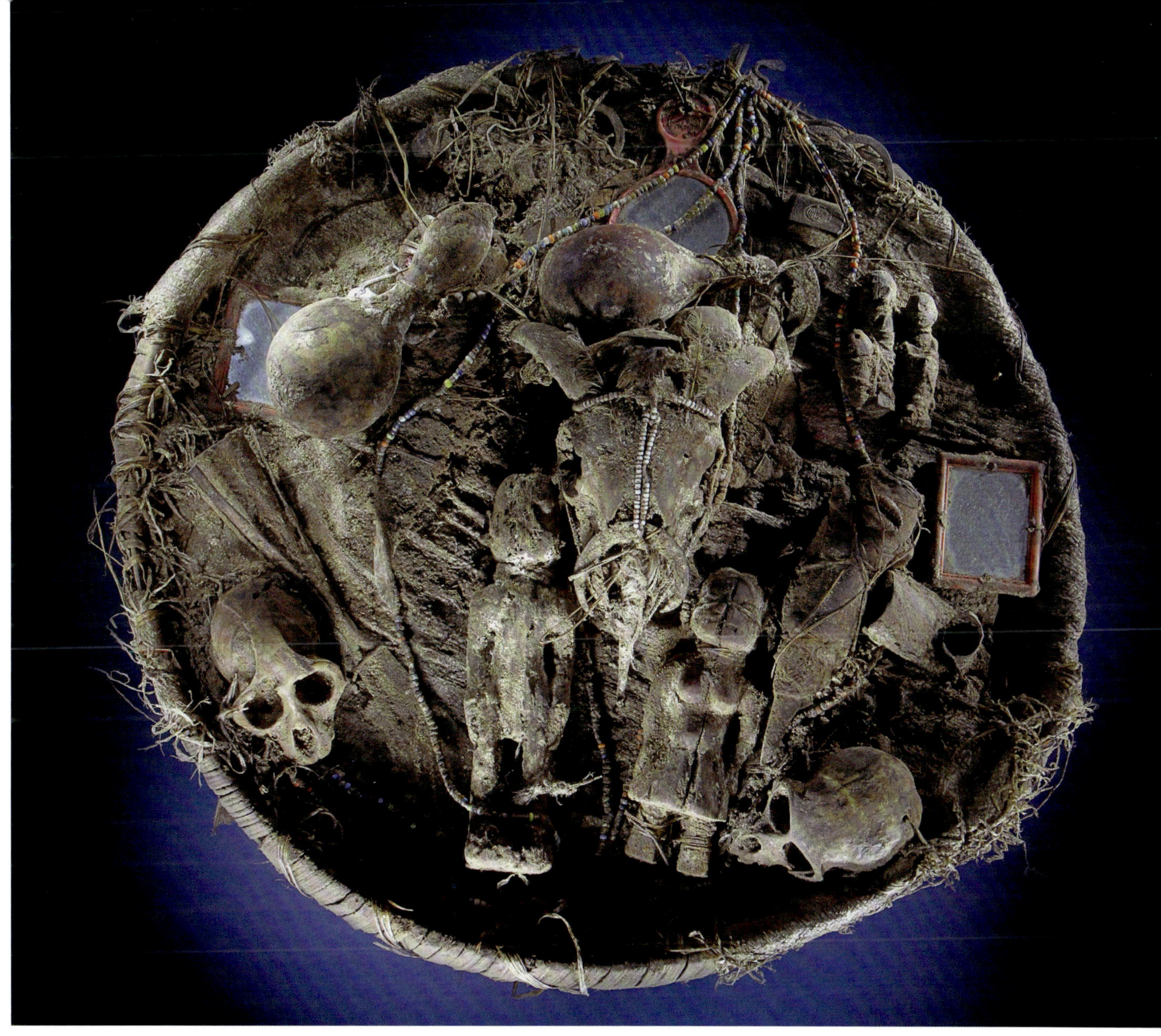

The Mask of the Jujuman

Le masque du *jujuman*

Die Maske des Jujuman

La Máscara del Jujumano

A Máscara da Jujuman

Het masker van de jujuman

Textiles/Textiles, 50 × 20 cm

Egungun oracle dish

Plat d'oracle Egungun

Orakelschale der Egungun

Oráculo del plato de Egúngún

Prato Oracle de Egungun

Orakelkom van de Egungun

Basketwork, animal skull, organic materials/Panier, crâne d'animal, matières organiques, 54 × 54 cm, Korb

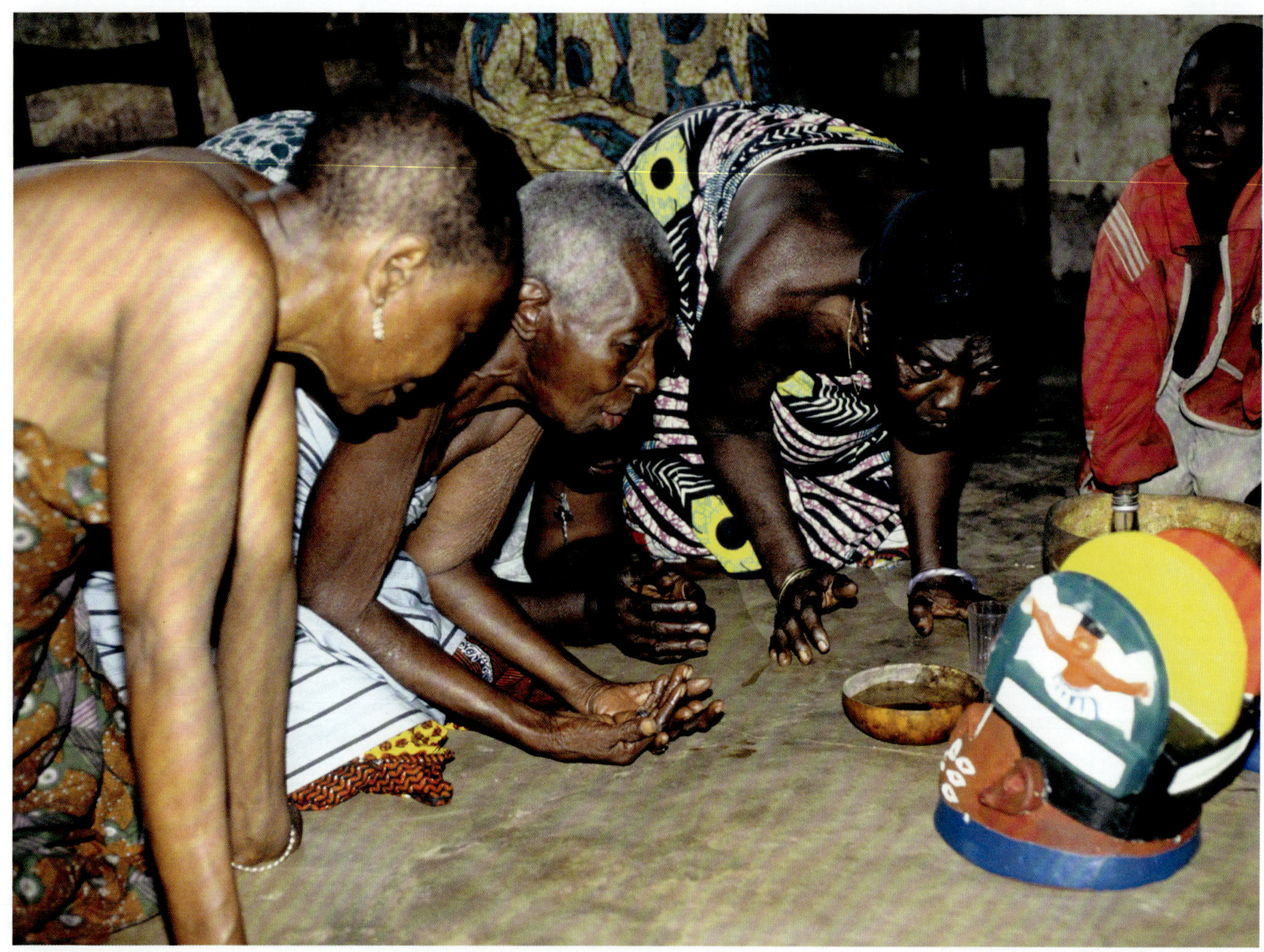

Gelede, the traditional theatre

The Gelede communities appear with rattles on their feet and colorful masquerades, their societies can be seen in many places once a year among the Yoruba in southwest Nigeria and in neighboring Benin. Their performances combine theatre, dance, music and traditional customs. In addition, reference is always made to regional events of the past year.

The artistic carvings on the masks tell stories. With representational scenes a special event as well as its moral meaning is presented here. Accordingly, the fun that all

Gèlèdé, le théâtre traditionnel

Les membres des communautés Gèlèdé se produisent au cours de mascarades multicolores, les chevilles enserrées de hochets. Ils apparaissent une fois par an dans de nombreuses localités Yoruba du sud-ouest du Nigeria et au Bénin. Leurs représentations allient théâtre, danse, musique et transmission traditionnelle des connaissances. Elles se réfèrent en outre toujours aux événements locaux de l'année passée.

Les magnifiques décorations sculptées des masques racontent des histoires.

Gelede, das traditionelle Theater

Mit Fußrasseln und farbenfroher Maskerade zeigen sich die Gelede-Gemeinschaften, deren Bünde vielerorts einmal jährlich bei den Yorubas im Südwesten Nigerias und im angrenzenden Benin auftreten. Ihre Vorstellungen vereinen Theater, Tanz, Musik und traditionelle Überlieferung. Außerdem wird stets Bezug auf regionale Vorkommnisse des vergangenen Jahres genommen.

Die kunstvollen Schnitzereien der Masken erzählen Geschichten. Mit gegenständlichen Szenen wird hier

Old women greet the Gelede masks
in the courtyard of the Yoruba King of
Sakete, Benin

Femmes âgées saluant les masques
Gèlèdé dans la cour du roi Yoruba de
Sakété, Bénin

Alte Frauen grüßen die Geledemasken im
Hof des Yorubakönigs von Sakete, Benin

Ancianas saludan a las máscaras de cuero
en el patio del rey yoruba de Sakete, Benin

Velhas mulheres cumprimentam as
máscaras de couro no pátio do rei iorubá
de Sakete, Benin

Oude vrouwen begroeten de Gelede-
maskers op de binnenplaats van de
Yoruba-koning van Sakete, Benin

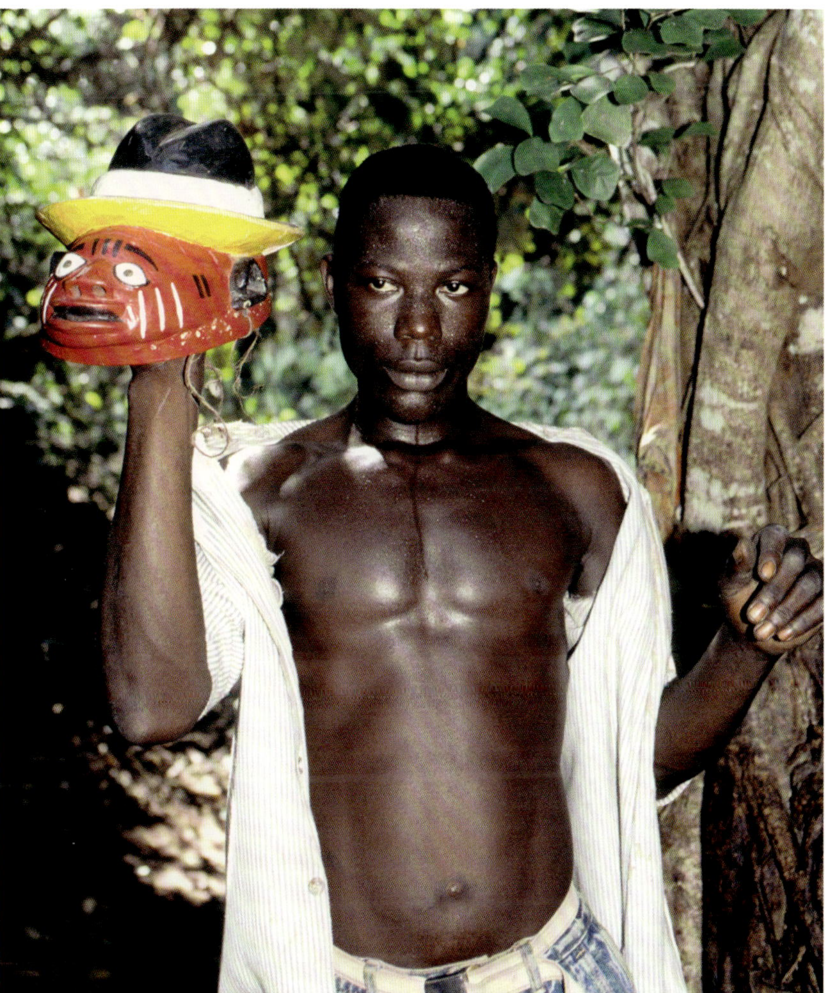

A young dancer presents his Gelede mask

Un jeune danseur présente son masque Gèlèdé

Ein junger Tänzer präsentiert seine Geledemaske

Un joven bailarín presenta su máscara de cuero

Um jovem dançarino apresenta sua máscara de couro

Een jonge danser presenteert zijn Gelede-masker

Gelede, el teatro tradicional

Con sus pies temblorosos y sus coloridas
máscaras, las comunidades Gelede, cuyas
federaciones aparecen en muchos lugares
una vez al año en los Yorubas, en el suroeste
de Nigeria, y en el vecino Benín, son un
escaparate. Sus actuaciones combinan teatro,
danza, música y tradiciones tradicionales.
Además, siempre se hace referencia a los
eventos regionales del año pasado.

Las formas artísticos de las máscaras
cuentan historias. Con escenas
representativas se anuncia aquí un
acontecimiento especial, así como su

Gelede, O teatro tradicional

As comunidades de Gelede, cujas federações
aparecem em muitos lugares uma vez por
ano nos Yorubas, no sudoeste da Nigéria
e no vizinho Benin, são uma vitrine. Os
seus espectáculos combinam teatro, dança,
música e tradições tradicionais. Além
disso, é sempre feita referência aos eventos
regionais do ano passado.

As esculturas artísticas das
máscaras contam histórias. Com cenas
representativas, um evento especial e seu
significado moral são anunciados aqui. A
diversão que todos os participantes das

Gelede, het traditionele theater

Met voetratels en kleurrijke maskers
vertonen de Gelede-gemeenschappen
zich, waarvan de verbanden bij de Yoruba
in Zuidwest-Nigeria en in het naburige
Benin op veel plaatsen één keer per jaar
optreden. Hun voorstellingen verenigen
theater, dans, muziek en traditionele
overleveringen. Bovendien wordt altijd
verwezen naar regionale gebeurtenissen uit
het afgelopen jaar.

Het kunstzinnige snijwerk van de
maskers vertelt verhalen. Met figuratieve
scènes wordt hier zowel een speciale

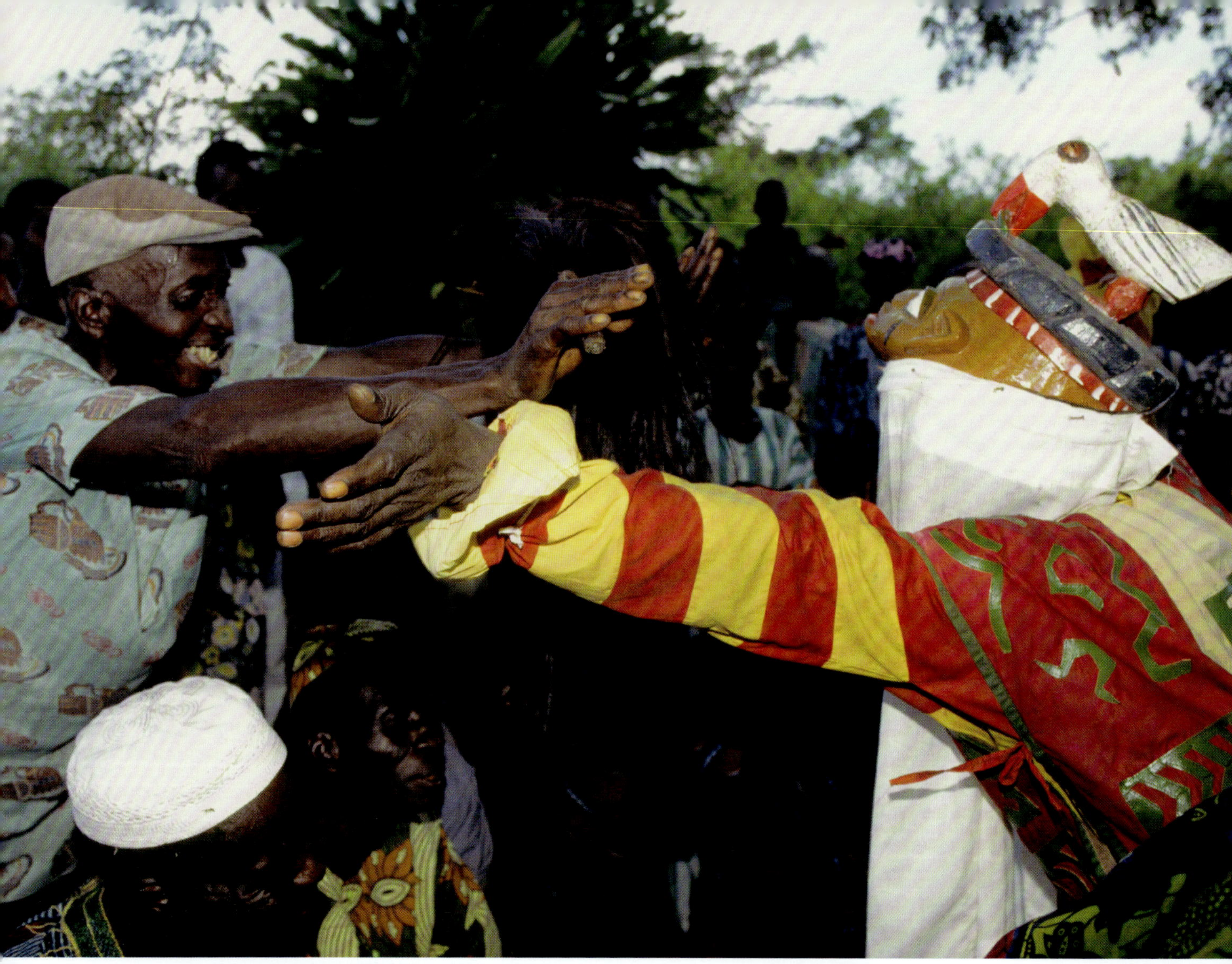

participants of the ceremonies have is great, because Gelede always has a conciliatory, humorous touch.

Even witches are more likely to be appealed to than threatened. Gelede sees them as a part of the community who also suffer from tensions and would rather be free of conflict than in disagreement with the people.

Au cours de cérénomies figuratives, des événements spécifiques et leur signification morale sont présentés. Tous les participants s'amusent énormément car la Gèlèdé possède toujours un aspect réjouissant, empreint d'humour.

À cette occasion, on en appelle aux sorciers plutôt qu'on ne les menace. Gèlèdé considère qu'ils font partie de la communauté, qu'ils souffrent eux aussi de ces tensions et qu'ils préféreraient vivre en paix plutôt qu'en conflit avec les hommes.

sowohl ein spezielles Ereignis als auch dessen moralische Bedeutung kundgetan. Entsprechend groß ist der Spaß, den alle Teilnehmer der Zeremonien haben, denn Gelede hat immer eine versöhnliche, humorvolle Note.

Selbst an Hexen wird eher appelliert, als dass man ihnen droht. Gelede sieht sie als einen Teil der Gemeinschaft, der seinerseits unter Spannungen leidet und lieber konfliktfrei wäre als im Streit mit den Menschen.

A public performance. In a mocking, instructive or even ironic form, the Gelede events comment on all topics related to human existence. Everyone involved has fun.

Représentation publique. La cérémonie Gèlèdé commente sur un ton humoristique, moralisateur ou ironique tous les thèmes de l'existence humaine, pour le grand plaisir de tous.

Ein öffentlicher Auftritt. In spöttischer, belehrender oder auch ironischer Form kommentieren die Geledeveranstaltungen alle Themen rund um das menschliche Dasein. Alle Beteiligten haben dabei Spaß.

Una actuación pública. De forma burlona, instructiva o incluso irónica, los eventos de Gelede comentan sobre todos los temas relacionados con la existencia humana. Todos los involucrados se divierten.

Um desempenho público. De forma zombeteira, instrutiva ou mesmo irônica, os eventos gelede comentam todos os tópicos relacionados à existência humana. Todos os envolvidos se divertem.

Een publiek optreden. In een spottende, leerzame of zelfs ironische vorm geven de Gelede-manifestaties commentaar op alle onderwerpen die verband houden met het menselijk bestaan. Alle deelnemers hebben plezier.

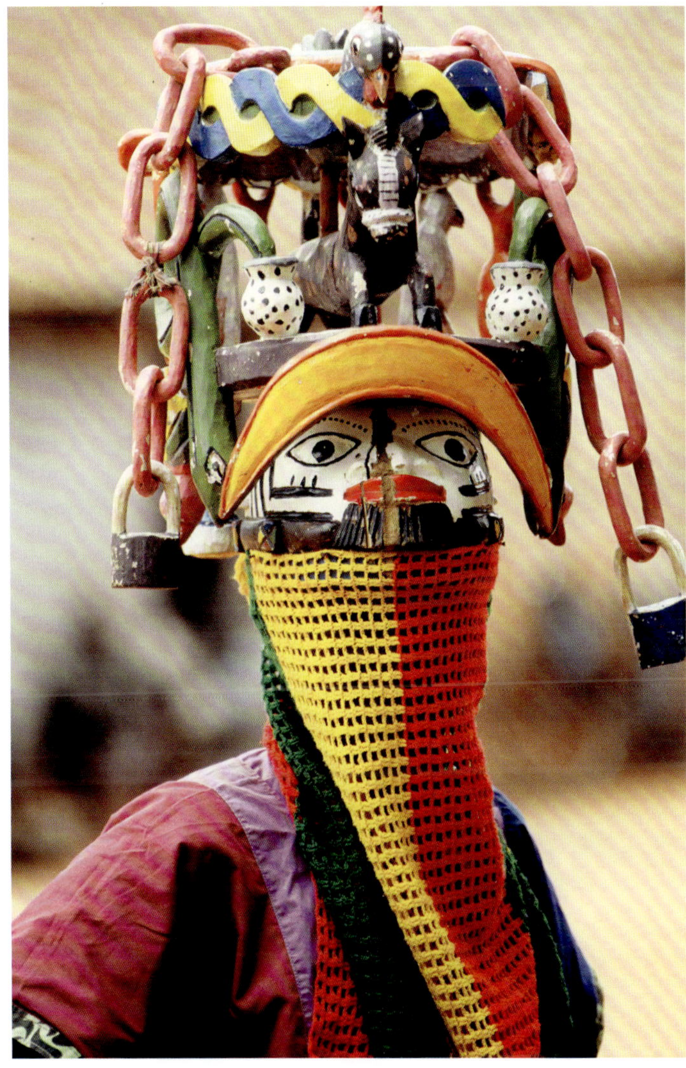

Magnificent construction on a Gelede mask

Magnifique structure sur un masque Gèlèdé

Prachtvoller Aufbau auf einer Geledemaske

Magnífica construcción sobre una máscara de cuero

Magnífica construção sobre uma máscara de couro

Prachtige opbouw op een Gelede-masker

significado moral. La diversión de todos los participantes de las ceremoniasestá asegurada, ya que Gelede siempre tiene una nota conciliadora y humorística.

Incluso las brujas son apeladas en lugar de amenazadas. Gelede las ve como parte de la comunidad, que a su vez sufre de tensión y prefiere estar libre de conflictos que en conflicto con la gente.

cerimônias têm é correspondentemente grande, porque Gelede sempre tem uma nota conciliatória, humorística.

Até as bruxas são apeladas em vez de ameaçadas. Gelede os vê como parte da comunidade, que por sua vez sofre de tensão e preferiria estar livre de conflitos do que em conflito com as pessoas.

gebeurtenis als de morele betekenis ervan verkondigd. Het plezier dat alle deelnemers aan de ceremoniën beleven is dan ook groot, want Gelede heeft altijd een verzoenende, humoristische noot.

Zelfs heksen worden eerder aangesproken dan bedreigd. Gelede ziet ze als onderdeel van de gemeenschap, die op zijn beurt lijdt onder spanningen en liever vrij is van conflicten dan ruzie heeft met mensen.

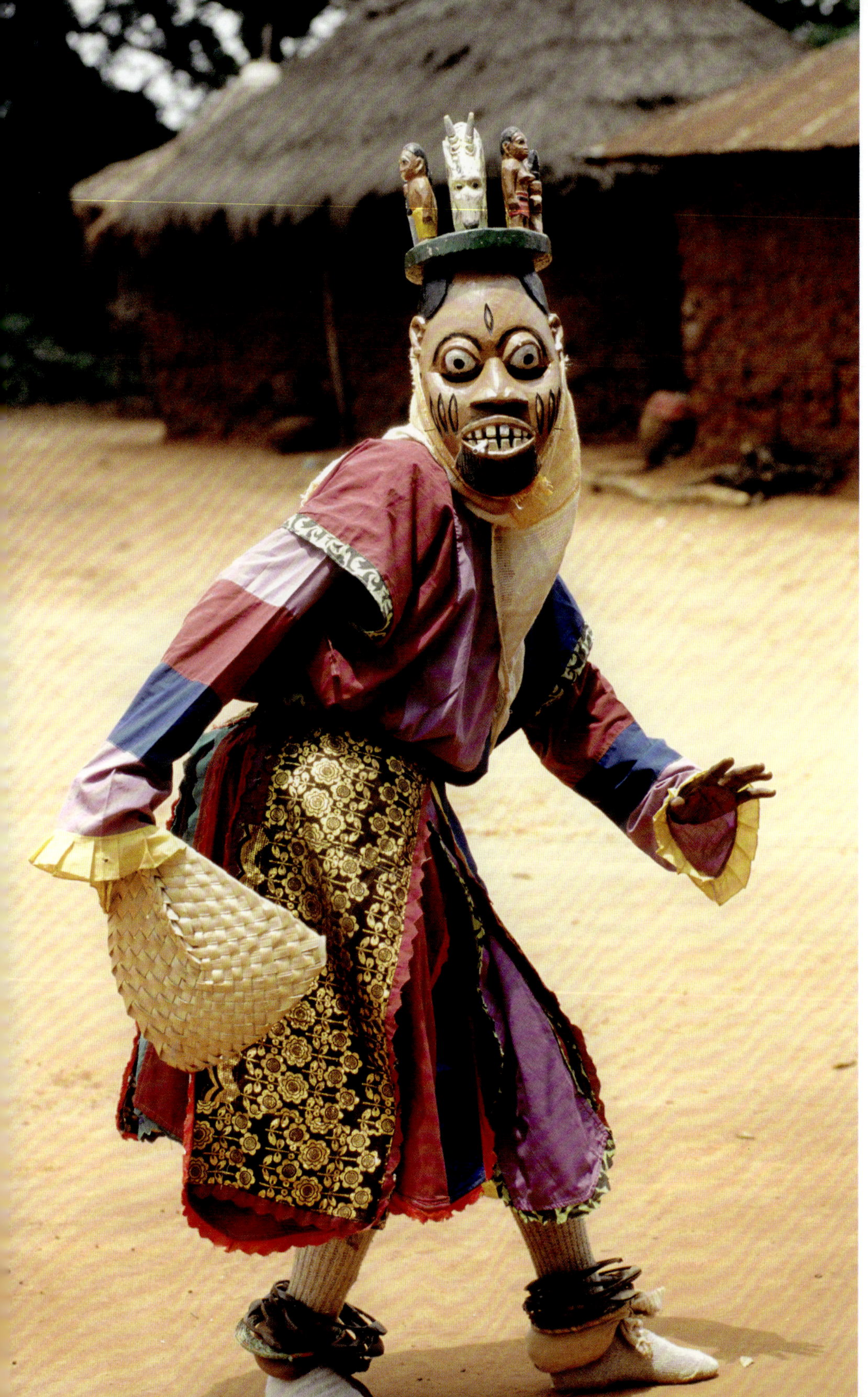

Gelede in action
Gèlèdé en action
Gelede in Aktion
Gelede en acción
Gelede em ação
Gelede in actie

Each mask tells a story
Chaque masque raconte une histoire
Jede Maske erzählt eine Geschichte
Cada máscara cuenta una historia
Cada máscara conta uma história
Elk masker vertelt een verhaal

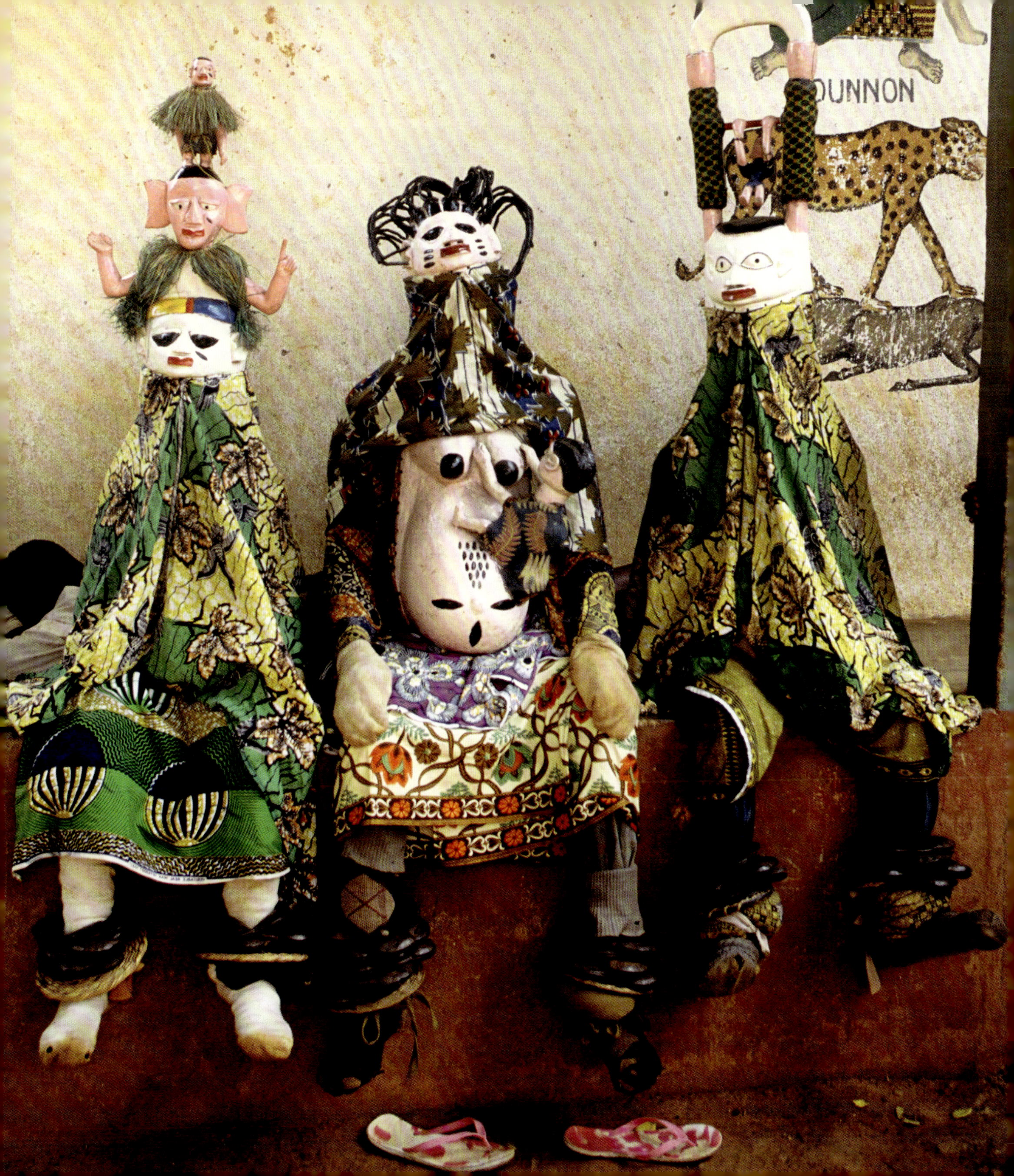
OUNNON

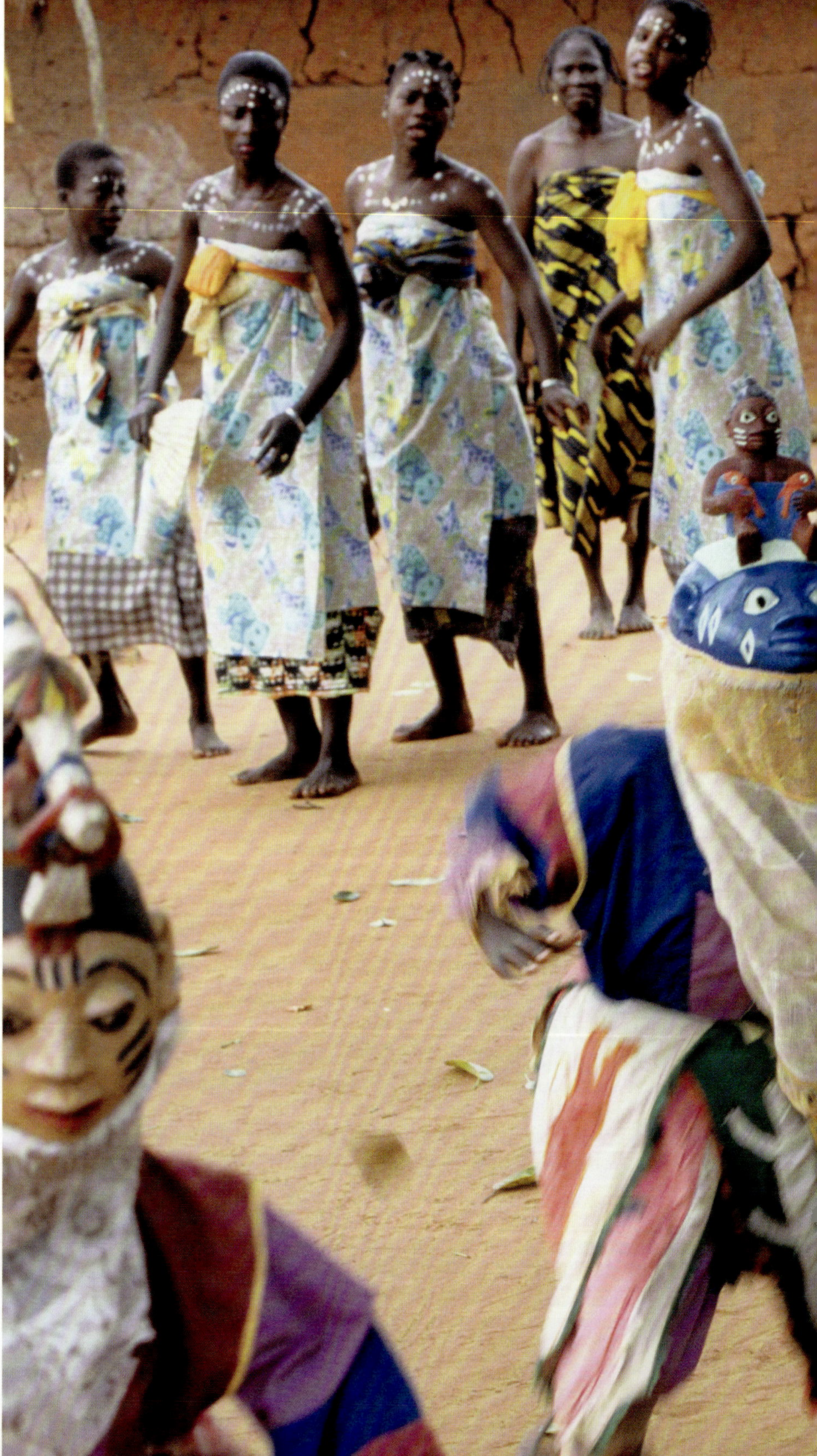

Common final chord. Before the joint march back into the holy grove, the dancers once again appear together to delight the audience with a spectacular last figure.

Dernière scène ensemble. Avant la marche de clôture qui les ramènera dans le bois sacré, les danseurs se réunissent une dernière fois, afin d'offrir aux spectateurs une ultime pièce spectaculaire.

Gemeinsamer Schlussakkord. Vor dem geschlossenen Abmarsch zurück in den heiligen Hain treten die Tänzer noch einmal gemeinsam an, um mit einer spektakulären letzten Figur die Zuschauer zu erfreuen.

Acorde final común. Antes de la marcha cerrada de vuelta a la arboleda sagrada, los bailarines compiten de nuevo para deleitar al público con una espectacular última figura.

Acorde final comum. Antes da marcha fechada de volta ao bosque sagrado, os dançarinos mais uma vez competem juntos para encantar o público com uma última figura espetacular.

Gezamenlijk slotakkoord. Voor de gesloten aftocht terug naar het heilige bosje treden de dansers nog een keer samen aan om het publiek te verrukken met een spectaculaire laatste figuur.

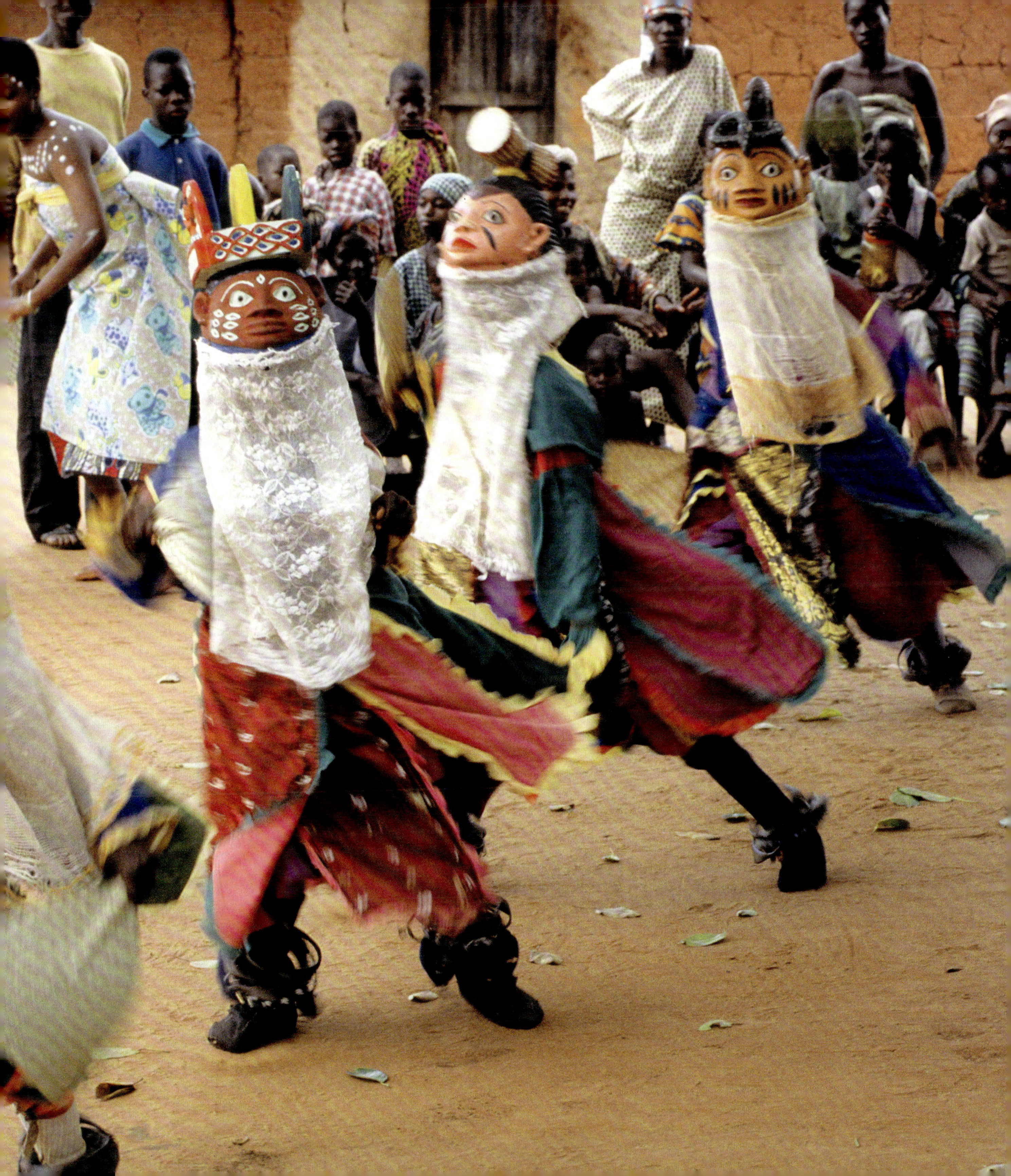

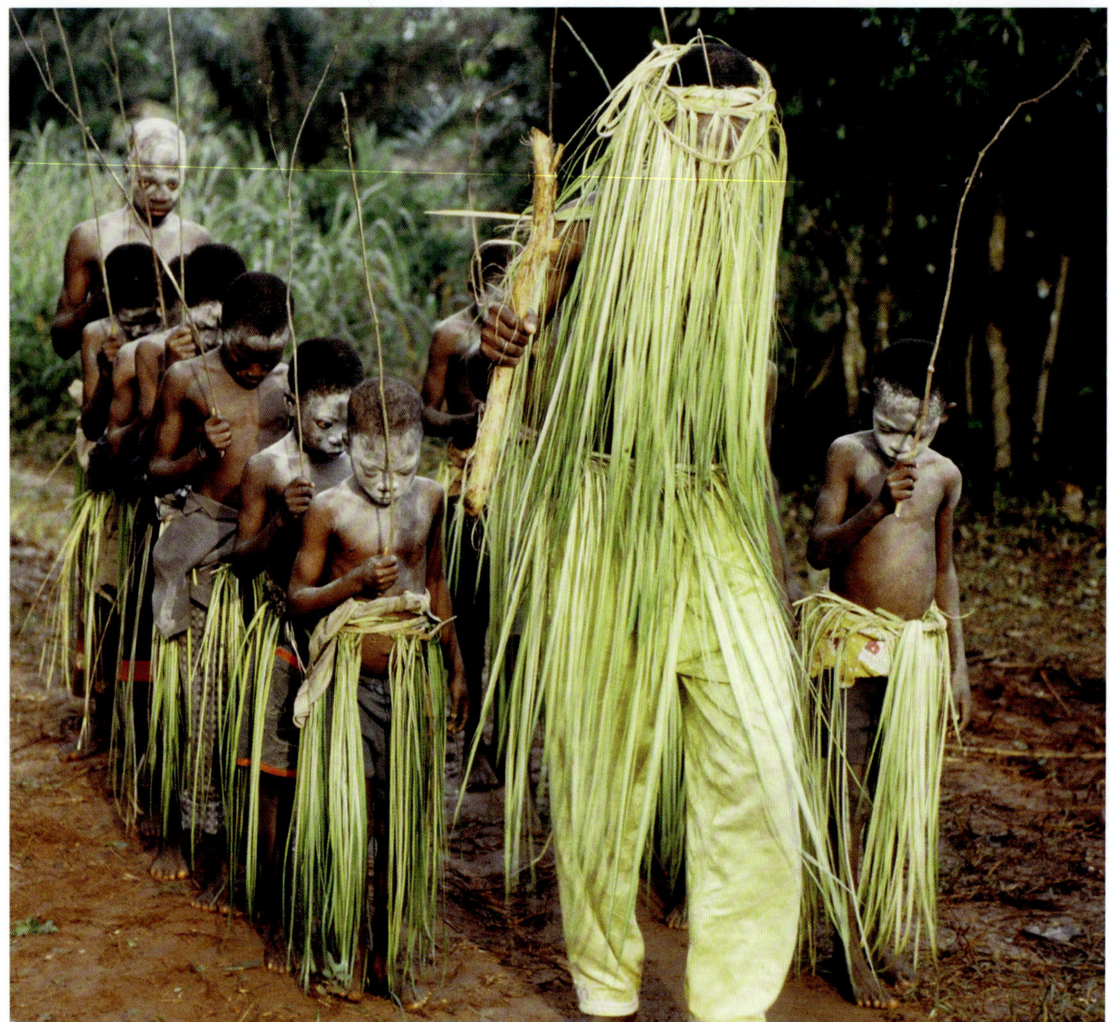

Oro, the buzzing woods guardian

An important secret society among the
Yoruba people is Oro. This association,
in which only men are initiated, has a
multitude of social functions. One of the
most important is Oro's activity around
burials, in which special rituals are used to
ensure that the spirits of the deceased are
safely transferred to the realm of the dead.

This society is also responsible for
maintaining social order and enforcing
moral rules. This extends to the imposition
and execution of penalties. In pre-colonial

Oro, les gardiens aux rhombes

Oro est une société secrète importante pour
l'ethnie des Yoruba. Cette confrérie, dont
tous les initiés sont des hommes, occupe de
très nombreuses fonctions sociales. L'une
de ses principales activités concerne les
inhumations, au cours desquelles elle veille,
à travers des rituels spéciaux, à ce que l'esprit
des défunts soit conduit sans encombre au
royaume des morts.

La confrérie est également responsable de
la préservation de l'ordre social et du respect
des principes moraux. Cette mission englobe

Oro, die Schwirrholzwächter

Eine wichtige Geheimgesellschaft beim
Volk der Yoruba ist Oro. Dieser Bund, in
den ausschließlich Männer initiiert werden,
hat eine Vielzahl sozialer Funktionen. Eine
der bedeutendsten ist Oros Aktivität rund
um Bestattungen, bei denen mit speziellen
Ritualen Sorge dafür getragen wird, dass die
Geister der Verstorbenen sicher ins Reich
der Toten überführt werden.

Auch die Wahrung der gesellschaftlichen
Ordnung und die Durchsetzung moralischer
Vorschriften ist Aufgabe dieser Gesellschaft.

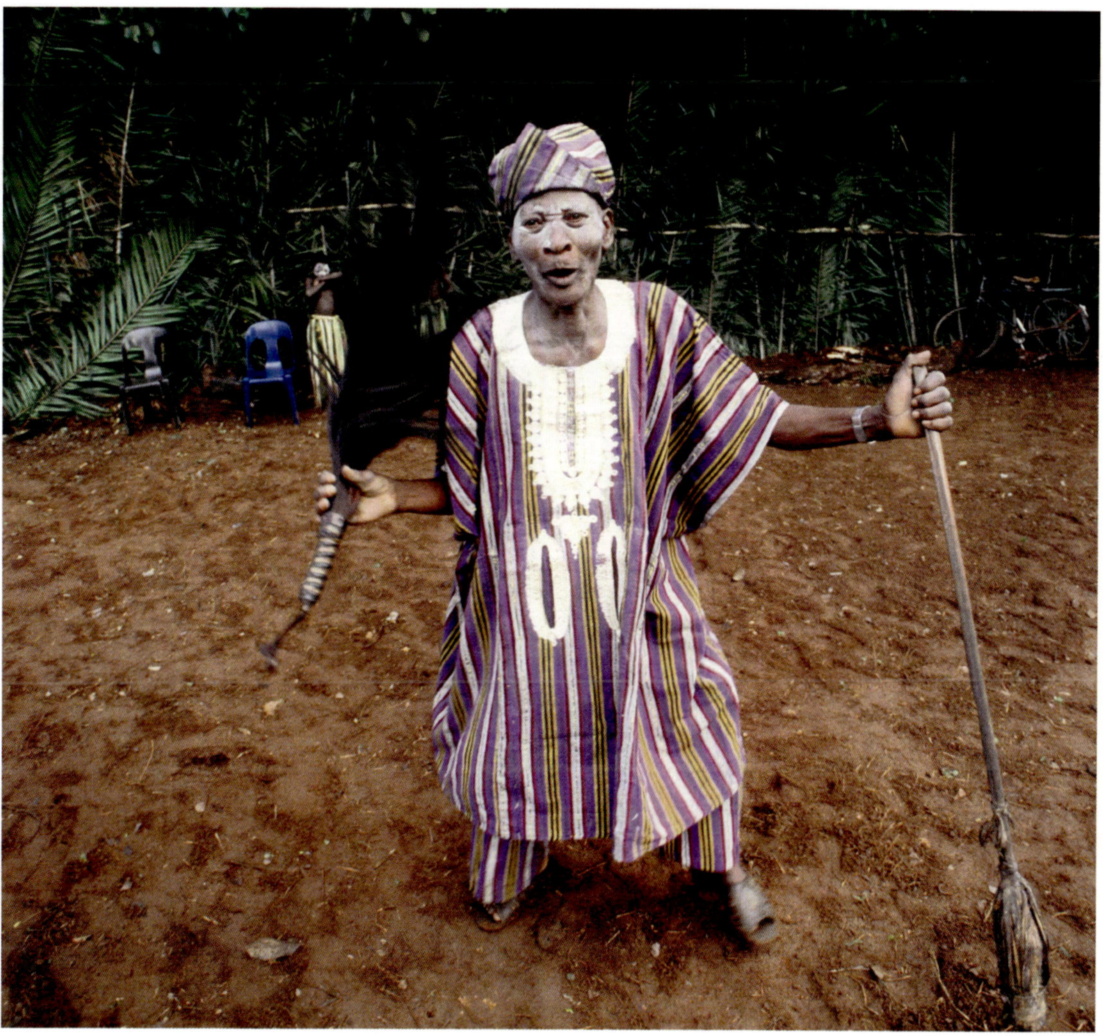

Oro, el guardián churinga

Una importante sociedad secreta entre el pueblo yoruba es Oro. Esta unión, en la que sólo los hombres son iniciados, tiene una multitud de funciones sociales. Una de las más importantes es la actividad de Oro en torno a los entierros, en los que se utilizan rituales especiales para garantizar que los espíritus de los fallecidos sean transferidos de forma segura al reino de los muertos.

También es tarea de esta sociedad mantener el orden social y hacer cumplir las normas morales. Esto se extiende a

Oro, O Guardião dos trovões

Uma importante sociedade secreta entre o povo iorubá é o Oro. Esta união, na qual somente os homens são iniciados, tem uma infinidade de funções sociais. Um dos mais importantes é a actividade de Oro em torno dos enterros, em que rituais especiais são usados para assegurar que os espíritos dos mortos são transferidos com segurança para o reino dos mortos.

É também tarefa desta sociedade manter a ordem social e impor regras morais. Isso se estende à imposição e execução de punições.

Oro, de bromhoutwachter

Een belangrijk geheim genootschap bij de Yoruba is Oro. Dit verbond bond, waarin alleen mannen worden geïnitieerd, heeft allerlei maatschappelijke functies. Tot de belangrijkste behoren Oro's werkzaamheden op begrafenissen, waarbij speciale rituelen ervoor moeten zorgen dat de geesten van de overledenen veilig naar het rijk van de doden worden overgebracht.

Ook het handhaven van de maatschappelijk orde en het afdwingen van morele voorschriften zijn taken van

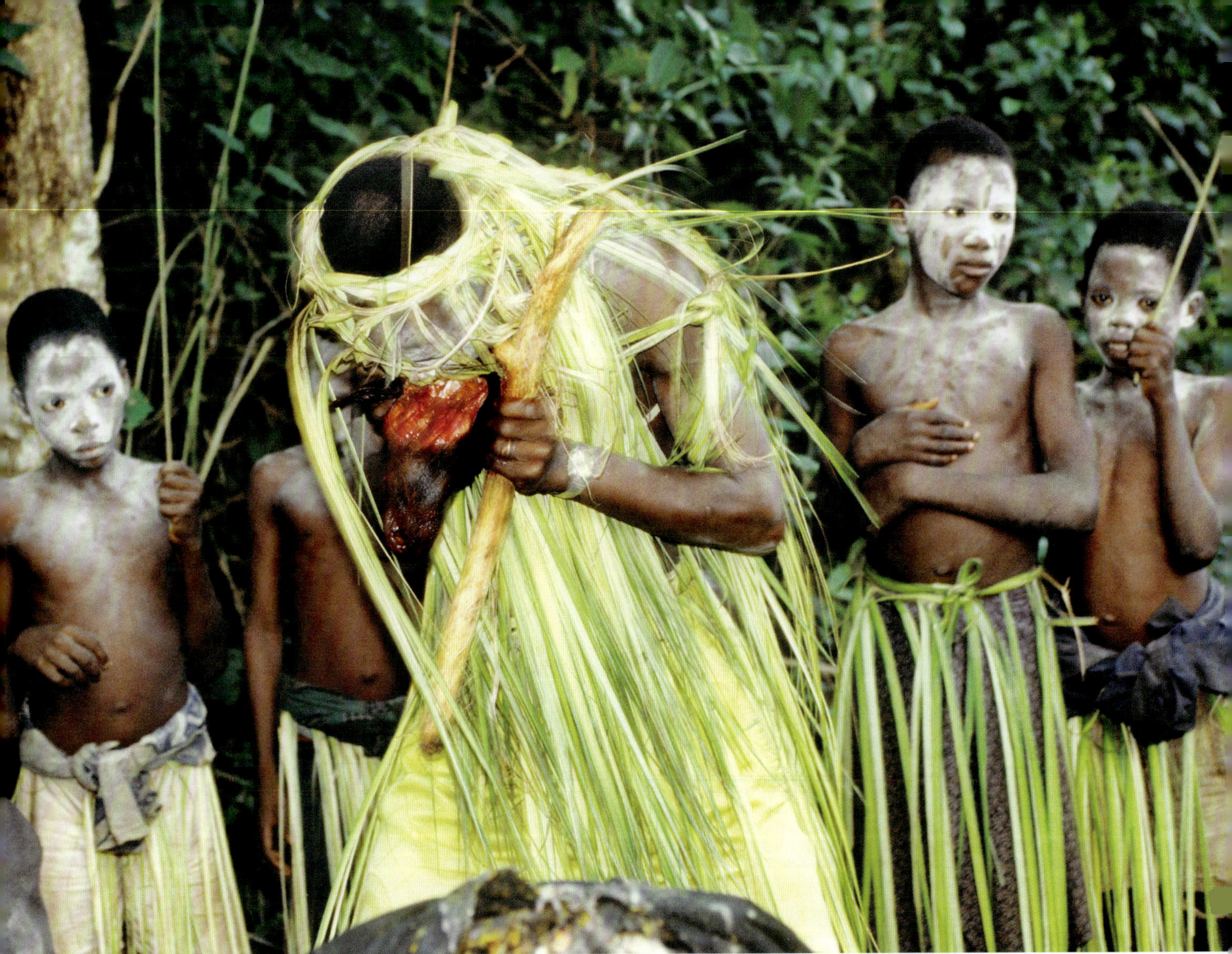

times the latter could also mean the death penalty.

Oro is also responsible for protection against witches and defending against them. With their repertoire of different buzzing woods, whose singing tone is considered the voice of the dead, Oro makes witches harmless and also announces in the community when someone is threatened with death.

la proclamation et l'exécution des sanctions. Ces dernières pouvaient aller jusqu'à la peine de mort à l'époque précoloniale.

Oro est également responsable de la protection et de la lutte contre les sorciers. Grâce à un répertoire joué par différents rhombes, dont le bourdonnement chantant traduit la voix des morts, Oro met hors d'état de nuire les sorciers ; elle annonce également à la société lorsqu'un individu est menacé de mort.

Dies reicht bis zur Verhängung und Durchführung von Strafen. Letzteres konnte in vorkolonialer Zeit auch die Todesstrafe bedeuten.

Oro ist außerdem für den Schutz vor Hexen und für deren Abwehr zuständig. Mit ihrem Repertoire unterschiedlicher Schwirrhölzer, deren singender Ton als Stimme der Toten gilt, macht Oro Hexen unschädlich und kündigt außerdem in der Gemeinschaft an, wenn jemand vom Tode bedroht ist.

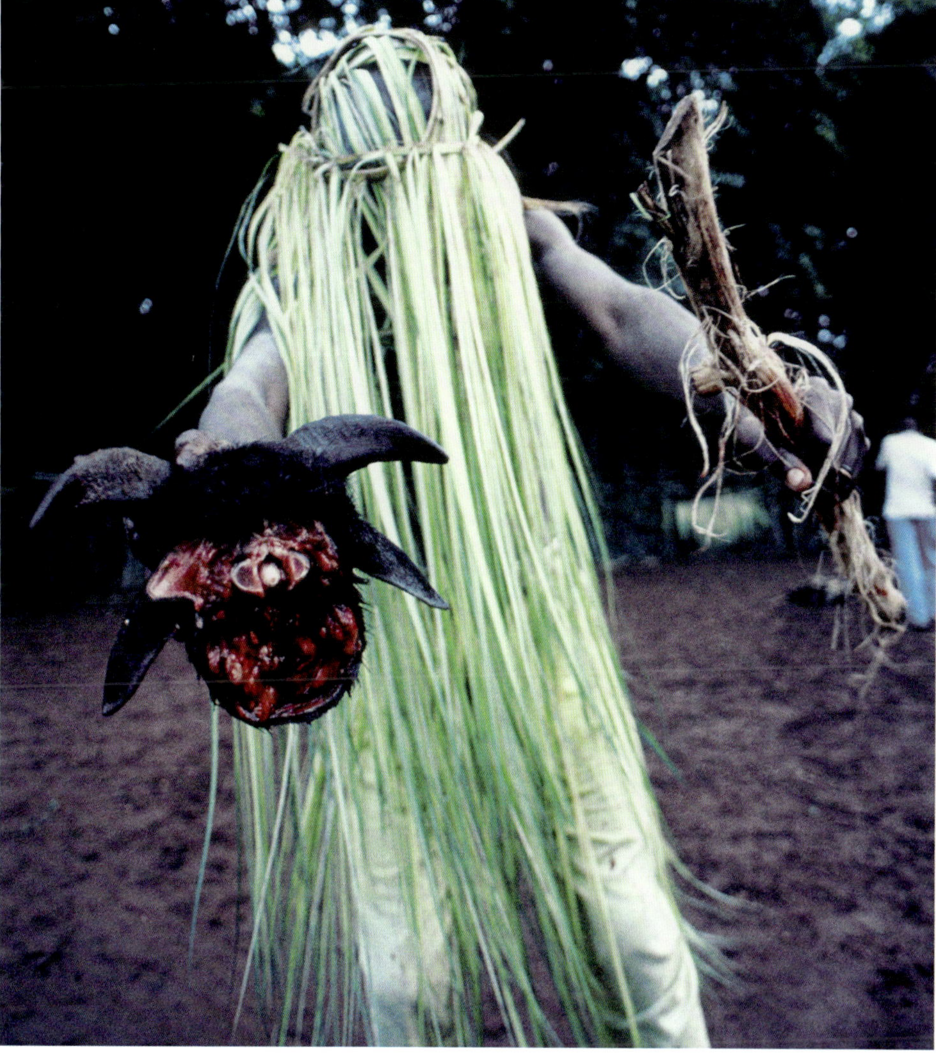

la imposición y ejecución de penas. Esto último podría significar también la pena de muerte en la época precolonial.

Oro también es responsable de la protección contra las brujas y de su defensa. Con su repertorio de diferenteschuringas, cuyo tono de canto es considerado como la voz de los muertos, Oro convierte a las brujas en inofensivas y también anuncia en la comunidad si alguien está amenazado de muerte.

Este último também pode significar a pena de morte em tempos pré-coloniais.

O Oro é também responsável pela protecção contra as bruxas e pela sua defesa. Com seu repertório de diferentes bosques zumbindo, cujo tom de canto é considerado como a voz dos mortos, Oro torna as bruxas inofensivas e também anuncia na comunidade se alguém é ameaçado de morte.

dit genootschap. Die reiken zelfs tot het opleggen en uitvoeren van straffen. Dat laatste kon in de prekoloniale tijd ook de doodstraf betekenen.

Oro is bovendien verantwoordelijk voor de bescherming tegen heksen en het afweren daarvan. Met zijn repertoire van diverse bromhouten, waarvan de zingende toon wordt beschouwd als de stem van de doden, maakt Oro heksen onschadelijk en verkondigt hij in de gemeenschap wanneer iemand met de dood wordt bedreigd.

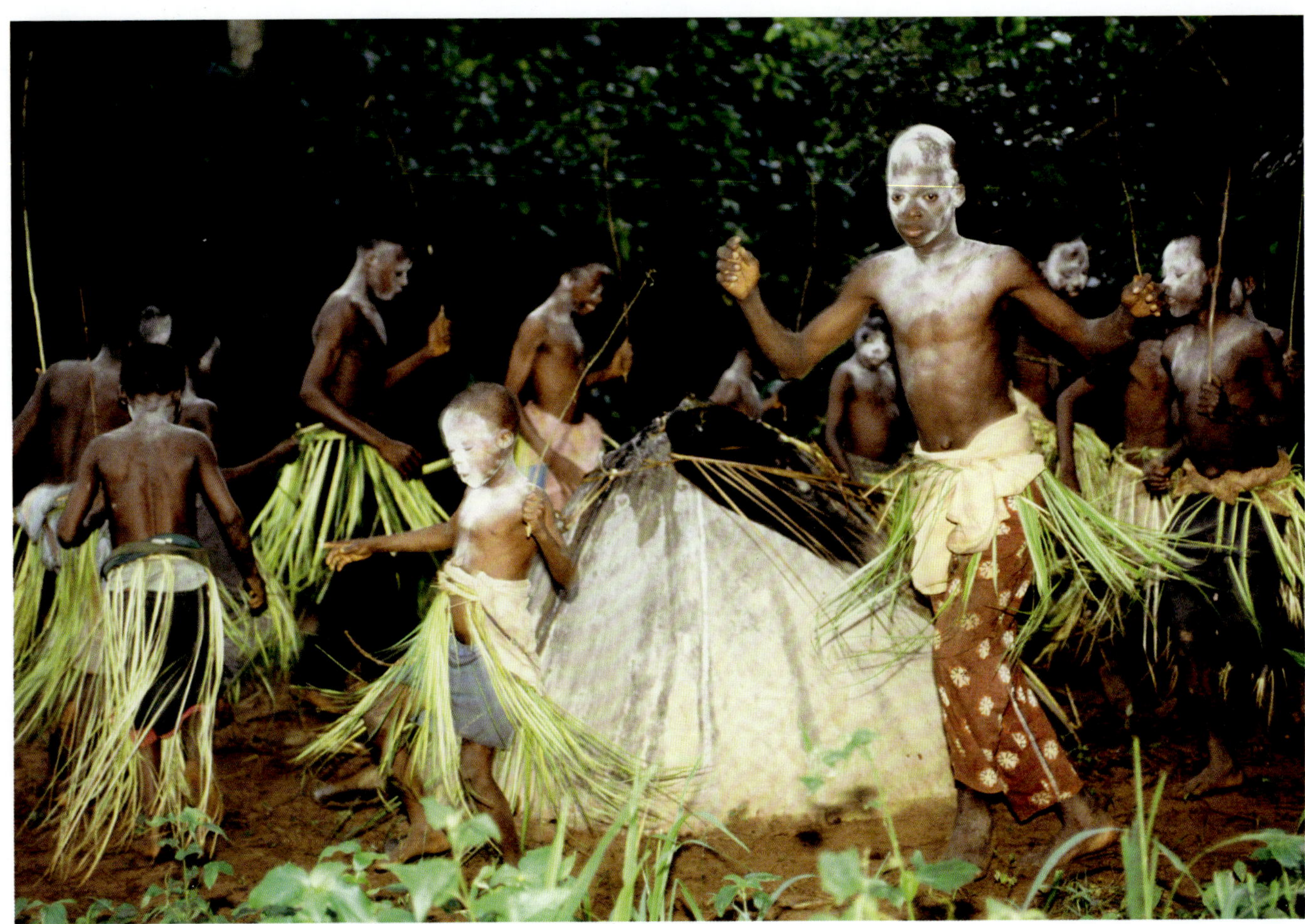

Ecstatic Dance

Danse extatique

Ekstatischer Tanz

Danza extática

Dança Eufórica

Extatische dans

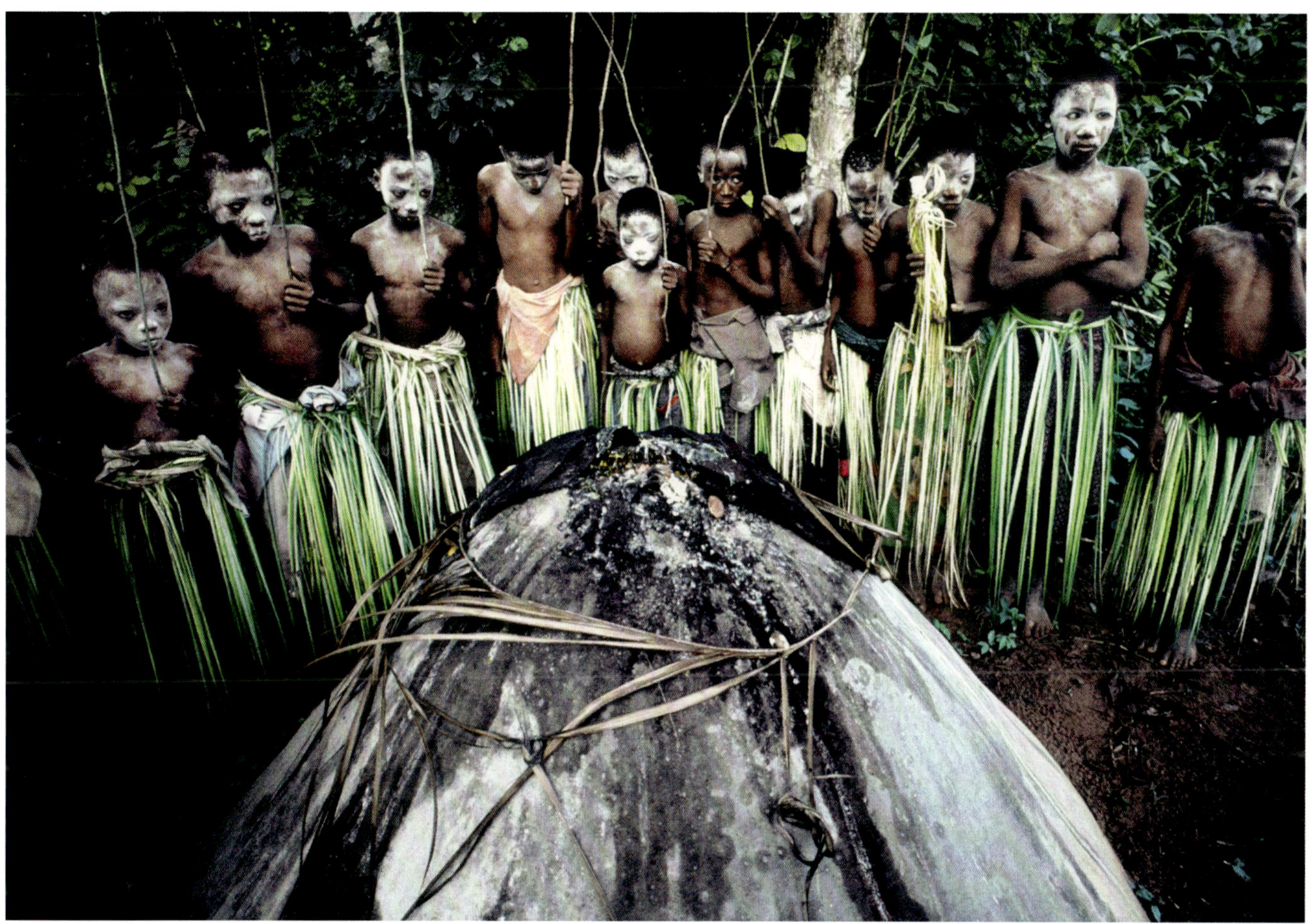

At the Oro sanctuary. Humble and awe-inspiring, the initiates stand before Oro's shrine. Oro is central in the service of the spirits of the dead. These speak through buzzing woods, which are a sign of Oro.

Au sanctuaire d'Oro. Humbles et marquant un profond respect, les initiés se tiennent devant l'autel d'Oro. Celui ci est essentiellement au service des esprits des défunts qui s'expriment par des rhombes. Ces instruments comptent parmi les insignes de la société secrète.

Am Heiligtum Oros. Demütig und voller Ehrfurcht stehen die Initianden vor dem Schrein Oros. Oro steht wesentlich im Dienst der Totengeister. Diese sprechen durch Schwirrhölzer, die ein Zeichen Oros sind.

En el santuario de Oro. Humildes y llenos de reverencia, los iniciados se paran ante el santuario de Oro. Oro está esencialmente al servicio de los espíritus de los muertos. Los espíritus hablan a través de los zumbidos de los bosques, que son un signo de Oro.

No santuário de Oros. Humilde e cheio de reverência, os iniciados estão diante do santuário de Oros. Oro está essencialmente ao serviço dos espíritos dos mortos. Os espíritos falam através de bosques zumbindo, que são um sinal de Oros.

In het heiligdom van Oro. De inwijdelingen staan deemoedig en vol eerbied voor het heiligdom van Oro. Oro is in wezen in dienst van de geesten van de doden. Die spreken door bromhouten, die een teken van Oro zijn.

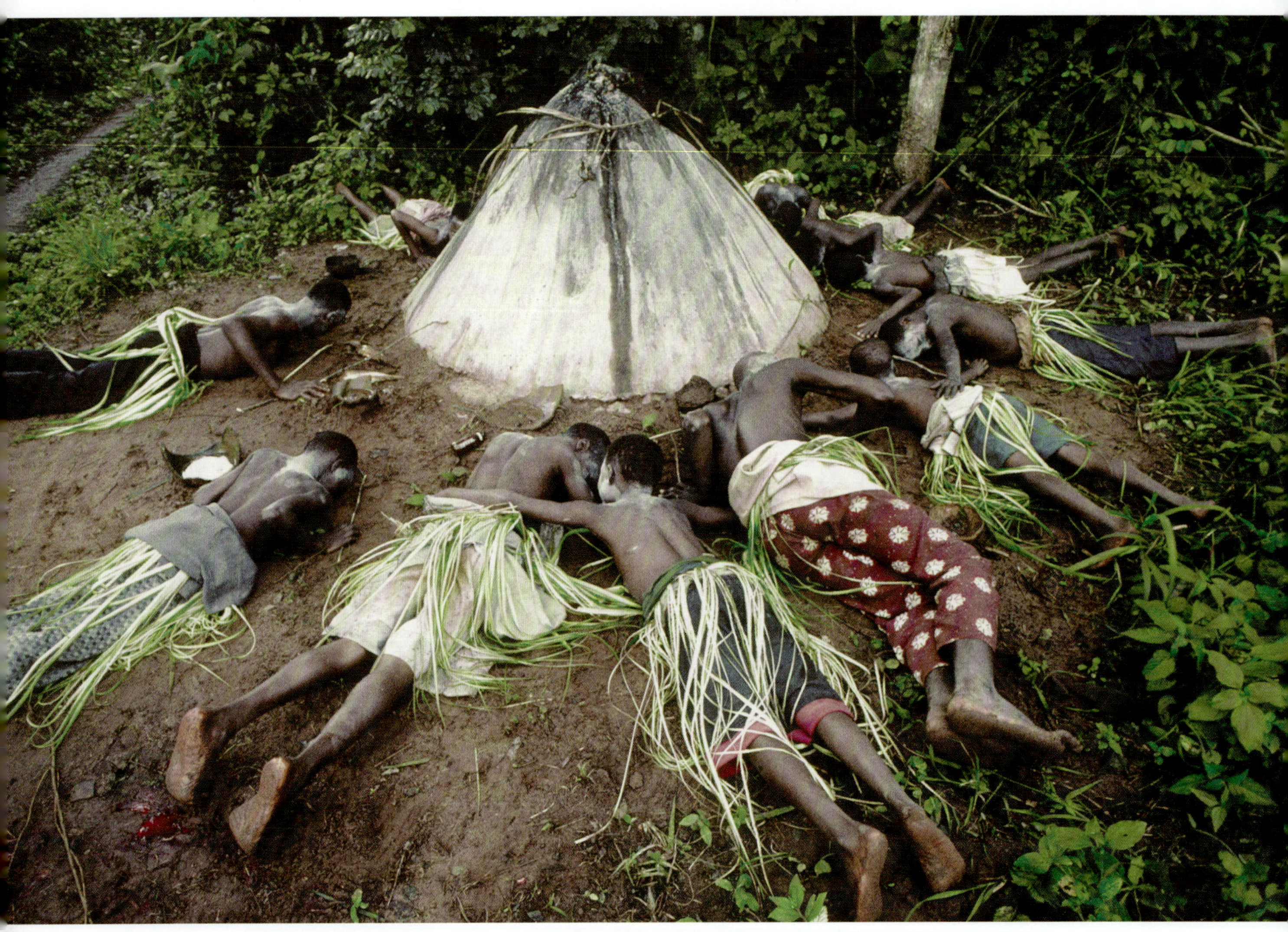

Exhausted from the dance at the Oro Shrine

Épuisement après la danse au sanctuaire d'Oro

Erschöpft vom Tanz an Oros Schrein

Exhausto del baile en el Santuario de Oro

Exausto da dança no Santuário de Oros

Uitgeput van de dans bij het heiligdom van Oro

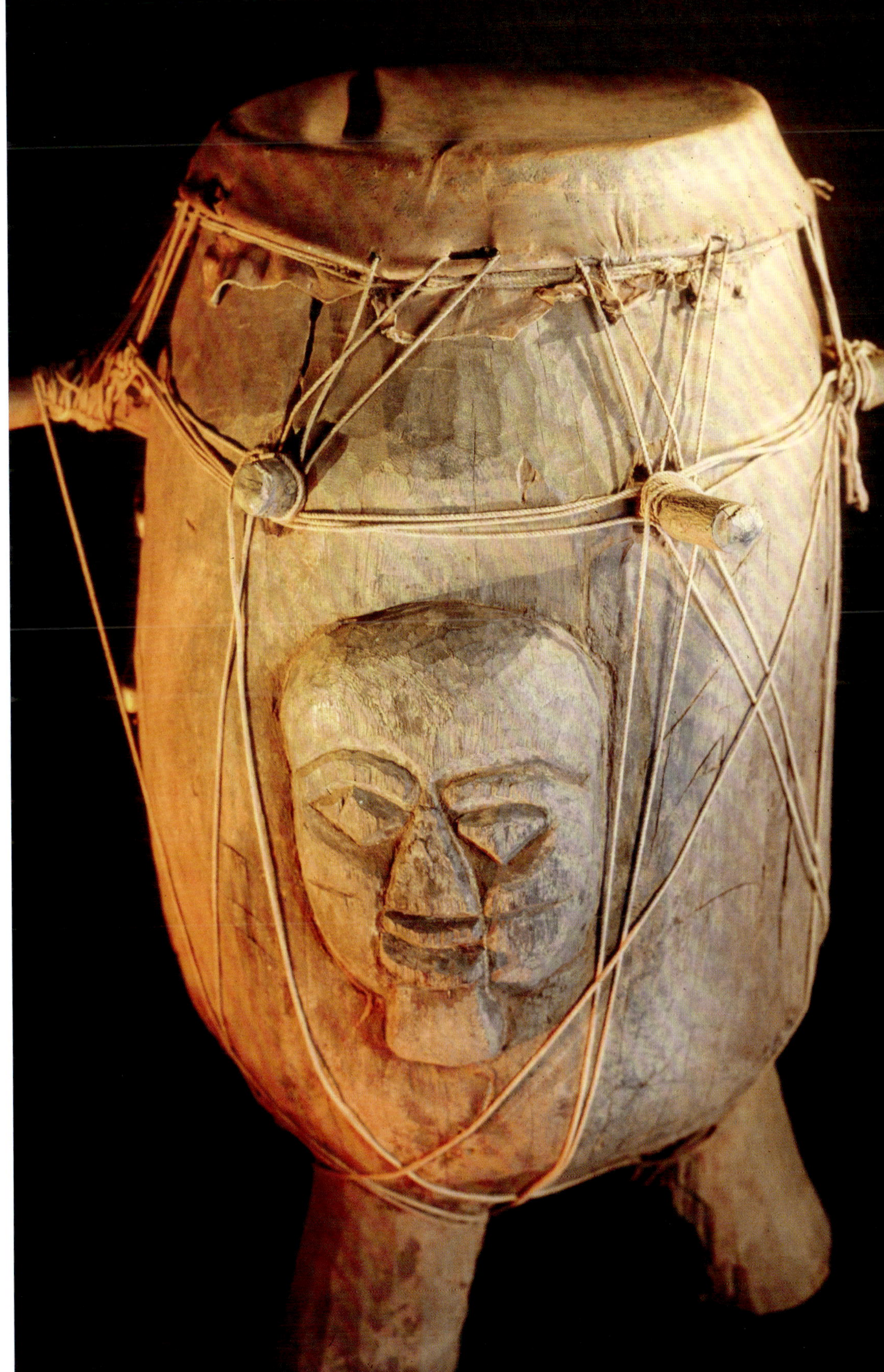

Ritual drum of the Oro
secret society

Tambour rituel de la société
secrète d'Oro

Ritualtrommel des Oro-
Geheimbundes

Tambor ritual de la sociedad
secreta Oro

Tambor ritual da sociedade
secreta Oro

Rituele trommel van het
geheime Oro-genootschap

Wood, leather/Bois, cuir,
90 × 36 cm

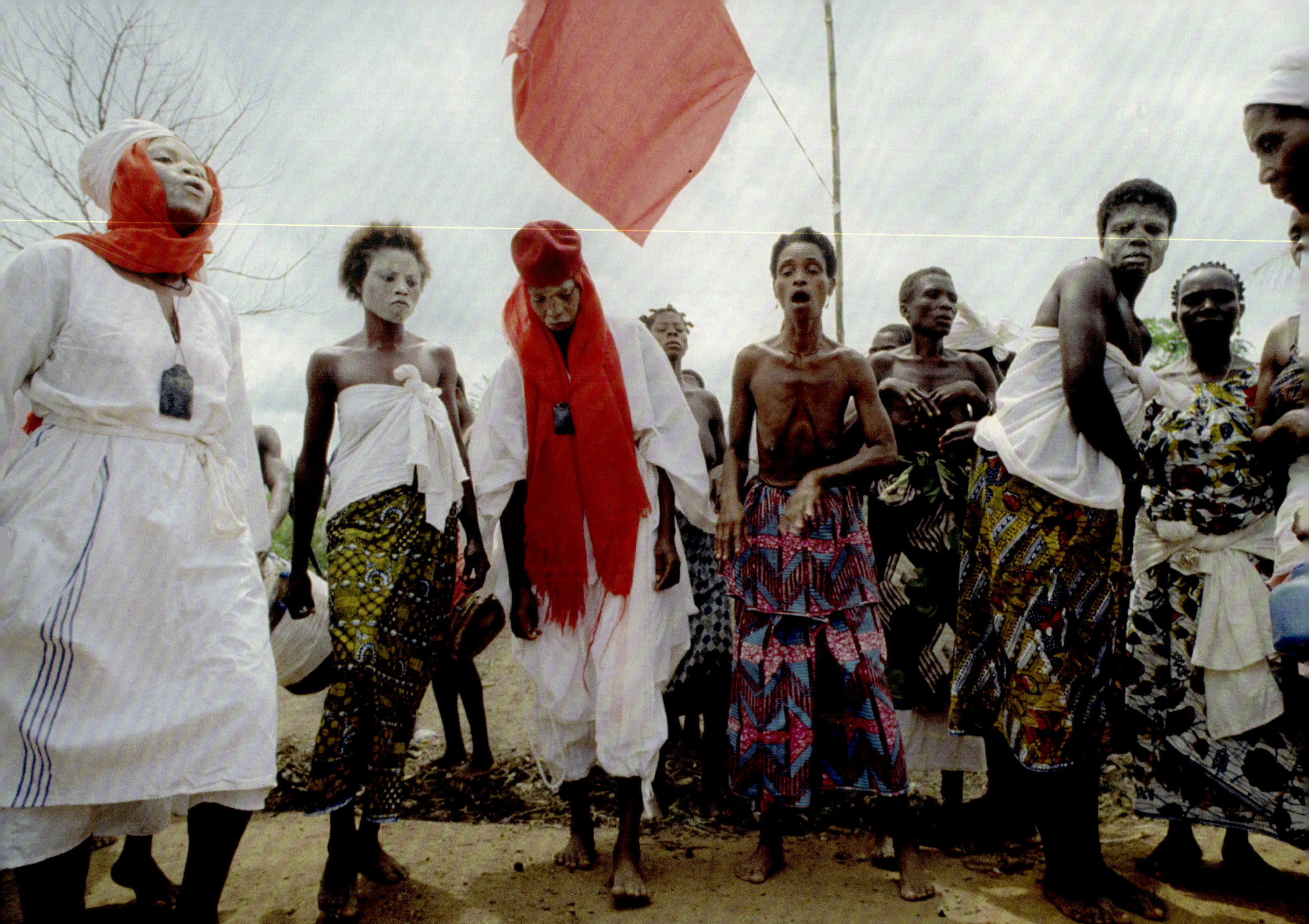

Tron—Warrior power against witchcraft

Many of the younger cults that turn against harmful magic were imported from the Muslim north, including Tron. This deity, whose followers fall into wild possessive trances, came via northern Ghana to the south coast. Typical are the Tron insignia worn at ceremonies, which can range from traditional weapons to animal fur attachements to turbans.

"The spirits of the Muslims," says the Tron priest Ajo Akone proudly, "are very powerful, for their followers in the north are mounted warriors who fear little else.

Tron, la force des guerriers contre la sorcellerie

Nombre de cultes récents, consacrés à la lutte contre la magie maléfique, ont été importés des régions du nord imprégnées de religion musulmane ; tel est le cas de Tron. Cette divinité, dont les adeptes tombent dans des transes de possession exaltées, est arrivée sur la côte sud, via le nord du Ghana. Les insignes portés par Tron au cours des cérémonies sont caractéristiques : armes traditionnelles, turbans et ornementations en fourrure animale notamment.

« Les esprits des musulmans, explique fièrement le prêtre Tron Ajo Akone, sont

Tron – Kriegerkraft gegen Hexerei

Viele der jüngeren Kulte, die sich gegen Schadenmagie wenden, wurden aus dem muslimisch geprägten Norden importiert, so auch Tron. Diese Gottheit, deren Anhänger in wilde Besessenheitstrancen fallen, kam über Nordghana zur Südküste. Typisch sind die bei Zeremonien getragenen Insignien Trons, die von traditionellen Waffen über Tierfellapplikationen bis hin zu Turbanen reichen können.

„Die Geister der Moslems", so sagt der Tron-Priester Ajo Akone stolz, „sind sehr mächtig, denn ihre Anhänger im Norden

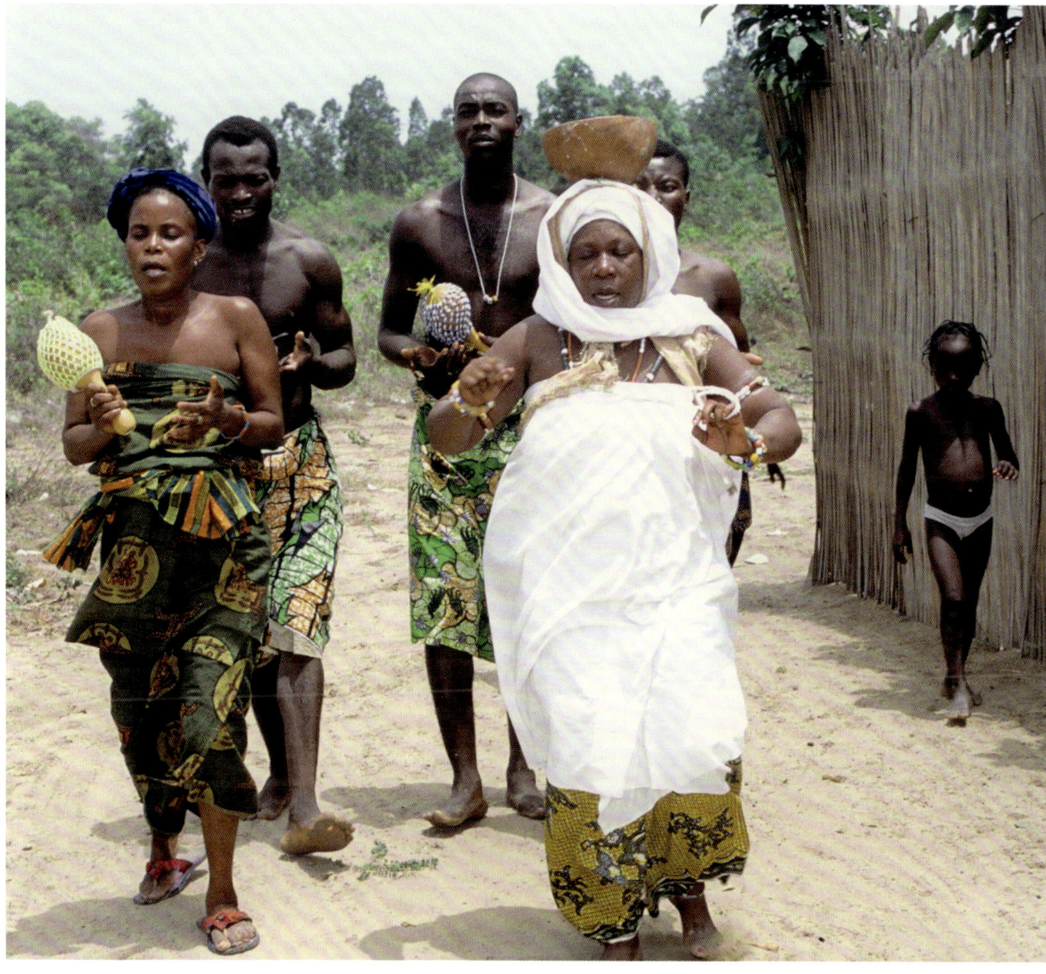

Mami Wata priestess at a
ritual for Tron

Prêtresse de Mami Wata
assistant à un rituel
pour Tron

Mami Wata Priesterin bei
Ritual für Tron

Sacerdotisa Mami Wata en
el ritual para Tron

Mami Wata sacerdotisa no
ritual de Tron

Priesteres van Mami Wata
bij het ritueel voor Tron

Tron– Poder guerrero contra la brujería

Muchos de los cultos más recientes que van en contra de la magia negra fueron importados del norte musulmán, incluyendo a Tron. Esta deidad, cuyos seguidores caen en salvajes trances de obsesión, llegó por el norte de Ghana hasta la costa sur. Típicas son las insignias de los Tron que se usan en las ceremonias, las cuales pueden variar desde armas tradicionales hasta el uso de pieles de animales y turbantes.

"Los espíritus de los musulmanes, dice con orgullo el sacerdote tronista Ajo Akone, son muy poderosos, pues sus seguidores

Tron – Poder guerreiro contra a bruxaria

Muitos dos cultos mais jovens que se voltam contra a magia do mal foram importados do norte muçulmano, incluindo Tron. Essa divindade, cujos seguidores caem em transe de obsessão selvagem, veio através do norte de Gana até a costa sul. Típicas são as insígnias dos Trons usadas em cerimônias, que podem variar de armas tradicionais a aplicações de peles de animais e turbantes.

"Os espíritos dos muçulmanos", diz orgulhosamente o sacerdote Tron Ajo Akone, "são muito poderosos, pois seus seguidores no norte são guerreiros

Tron – krijgersmacht tegen hekserij

Veel van de nieuwere culten die zich tegen schadelijke magie keren, werden geïmporteerd uit het islamitische noorden, waaronder Tron. Deze godheid, wiens volgelingen in een wilde, bezeten trance raakten, kwam via Noord-Ghana naar de zuidkust. Kenmerkend zijn de insignes van Tron die bij ceremoniën worden gedragen en die kunnen variëren van traditioncle wapens, applicaties van dierenhuiden tot tulbanden.

"De geesten van de moslims", zegt Tron-priester Ajo Akone trots, "zijn erg machtig,

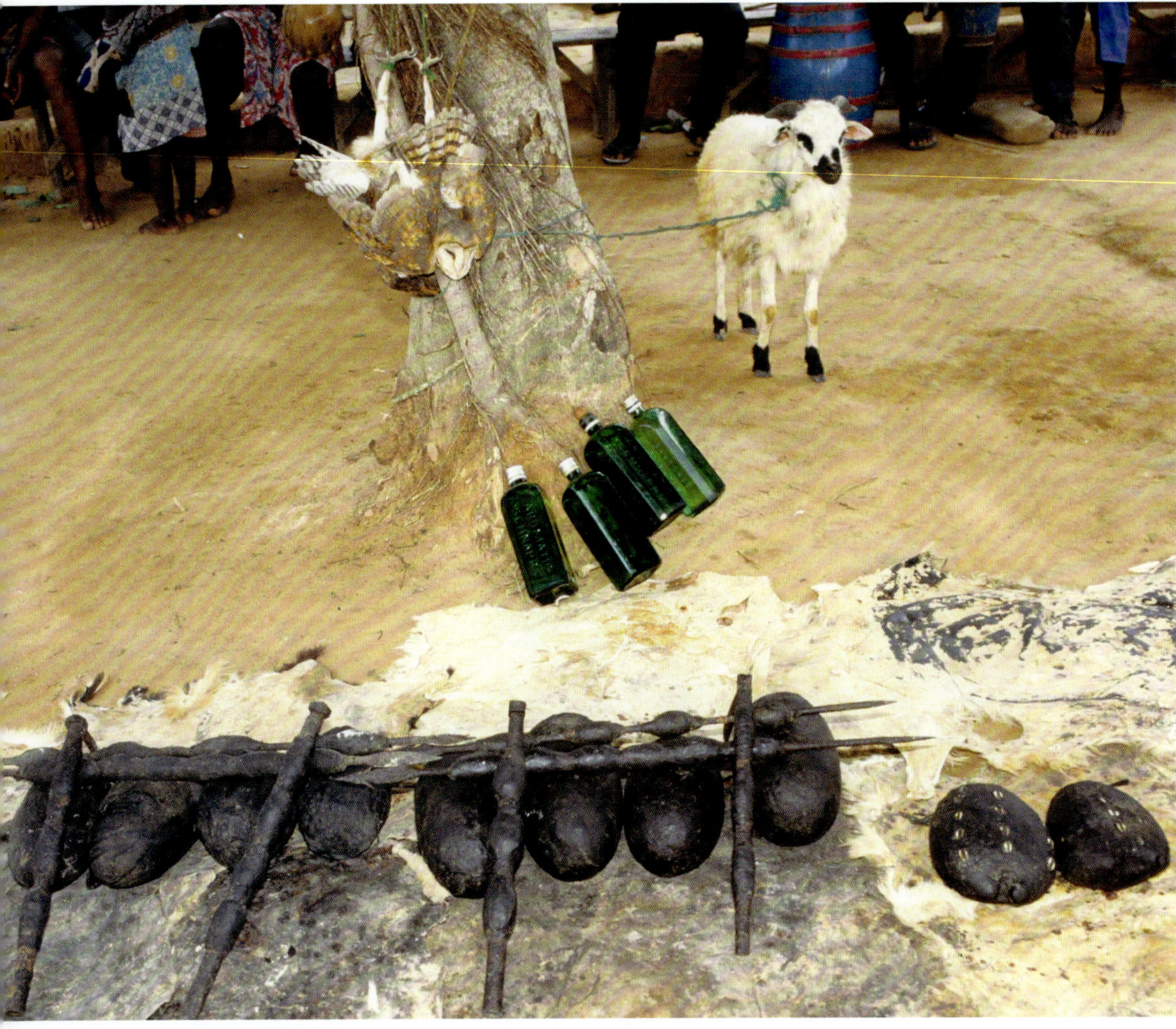

The adaptation and assimilation of foreign gods is not uncommon and serves to defend against witchcraft, which in turn can also gain strength.

Tron is frequently practiced by women, and often in Mami Wata temples there is also a small altar for Tron, which acts as a special insurance against evil for the believers.

très puissants, car leurs adeptes dans le nord sont des guerriers à cheval qui ne craignent pratiquement rien. » L'adaptation et l'assimilation de divinités étrangères ne sont pas rares et participent à la lutte contre la sorcellerie qui, de son côté, peut également s'adjoindre de nouvelles forces.

Le culte de Tron est pratiqué par de nombreuses femmes et il n'est pas rare de trouver dans les temples de Mami Wata un petit autel pour Tron, considéré par les croyantes comme une assurance supplémentaire contre les forces du mal.

sind berittene Krieger, die sonst kaum etwas fürchten". Die Adaption und Assimilierung von Fremdgöttern ist keine Seltenheit und dient der Abwehr von Hexerei, die ihrerseits ebenfalls an Stärke gewinnen kann.

Tron wird viel von Frauen praktiziert, und häufig findet man in Mami-Wata-Tempeln auch einen kleinen Altar für Tron, der für die Gläubigen wie eine Sonderversicherung gegen Böses wirkt.

Blood sacrifice for Tron. A massive medicine pack from the Tron Vodun is covered with fresh sacrificial blood. All around there are cola nuts, which play a role in many rituals in West Africa.

Sacrifice sanglant pour Tron. Paquet de remède du culte vodun de Tron, sur lequel vient d'être versé le sang frais d'une victime sacrificielle. Il est entouré de noix de cola qui jouent un rôle essentiel dans de nombreux rituels d'Afrique de l'Ouest.

Blutopfer für Tron. Eine von frischem Opferblut bedeckte, massive Medizinpackung des Tron-Voduns. Ringsum liegen Kolanüsse, die bei vielen Ritualen in Westafrika eine Rolle spielen.

Sacrificio de sangre para Tron. Un paquete de medicinas masivo del vudú Tron cubierto con sangre fresca de sacrificio. Alrededor hay nueces de cola, que juegan un papel en muchos rituales en África Occidental.

Sacrifício de sangue por Tron. Um enorme pacote de medicamentos de Tron Vodun coberto com sangue fresco de sacrifício. Por toda a parte há nozes de cola, que desempenham um papel em muitos rituais na África Ocidental.

Bloedoffer voor Tron. Een enorm, met met vers offerbloed bedekt medicijnenpakket van de Tron-vodun. Eromheen liggen kolanoten, die bij veel rituelen in West-Afrika een rol spelen.

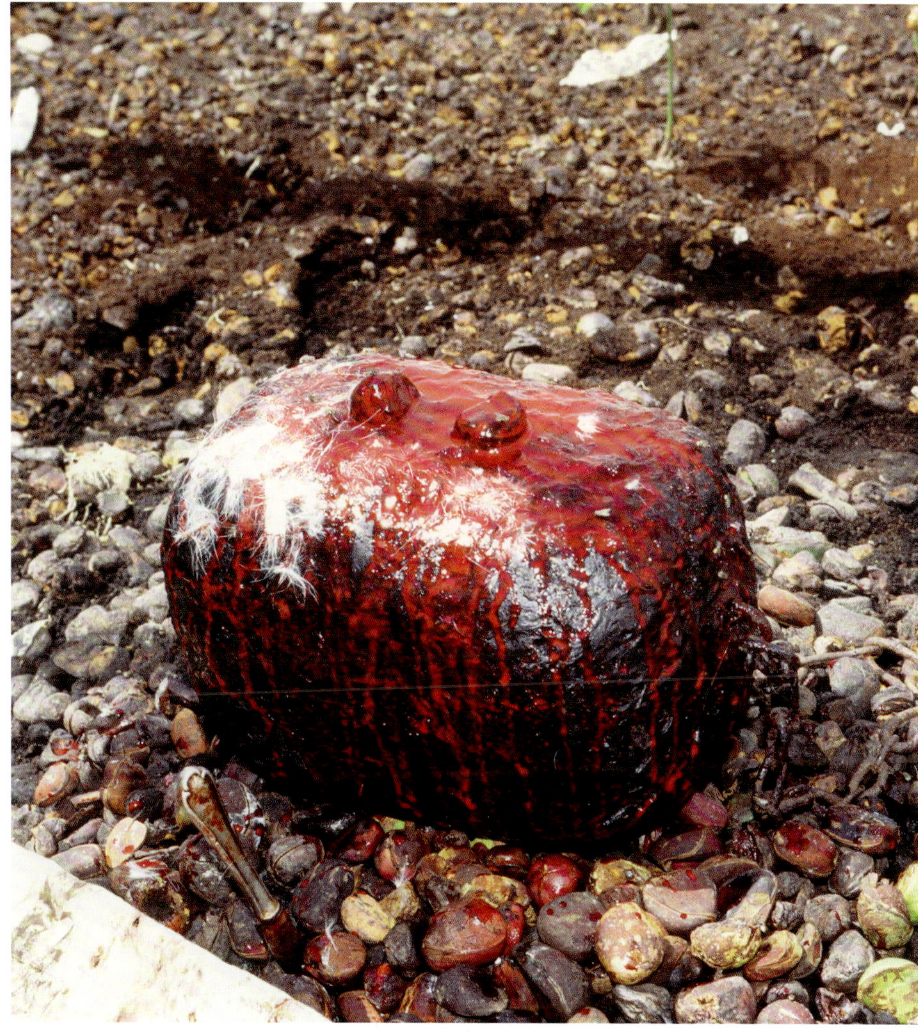

en el norte son guerreros a caballo que no le temen a casi nada". La adaptación y asimilación de dioses extranjeros es algo común, y sirve para protegerse de la brujería, que a su vez también puede ganar fuerza.

Tron es a menudo practicado por mujeres, y en los templos de Mami Wata a menudo se encuentra un pequeño altar para Tron, que sirve a los creyentes como un seguro especial contra el mal.

montados que pouco mais temem. A adaptação e assimilação de deuses estrangeiros não é incomum e serve para afastar a bruxaria, que por sua vez também pode ganhar força.

Tron é frequentemente praticado por mulheres, e nos templos de Mami Wata você frequentemente encontra um pequeno altar para Tron, que trabalha para os crentes como um seguro especial contra o mal.

want hun volgelingen in het noorden zijn bereden krijgers die weinig anders vrezen." De adaptatie en assimilatie van buitenlandse goden is niet ongewoon en dient om hekserij af te weren, die op haar beurt net zo goed aan kracht kan winnen.

Tron wordt vaak door vrouwen beoefend, en in de tempels van Mami Wata vind je vaak ook een klein altaar voor Tron, dat de gelovigen een speciale verzekering tegen het kwaad biedt.

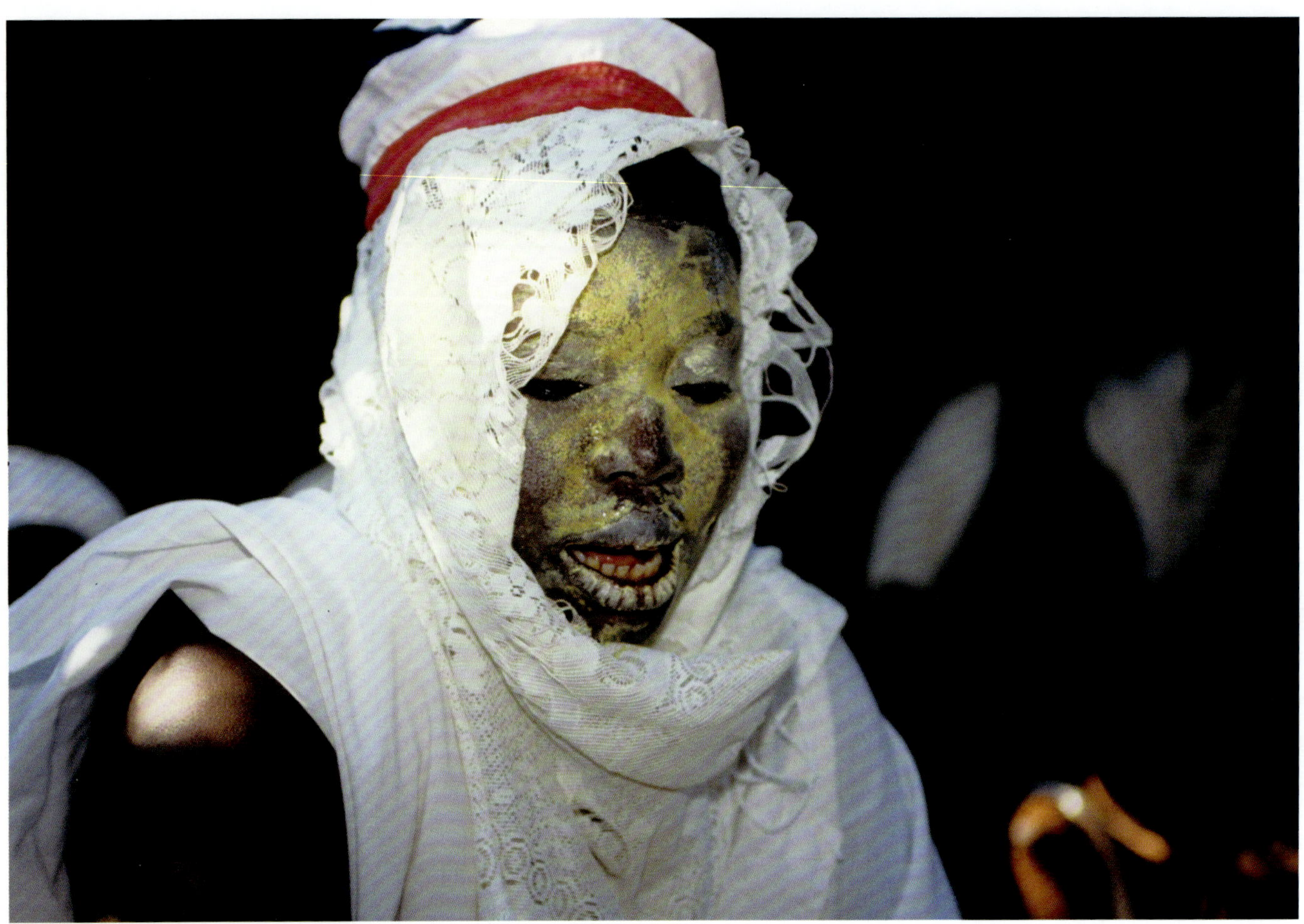

A Tron devotee in trance

Adepte de Tron en transe

Eine Tron-Anhängerin in Trance

Un devoto de Tron en trance

Um devoto Tron em transe

Een aanhangster van Tron in trance

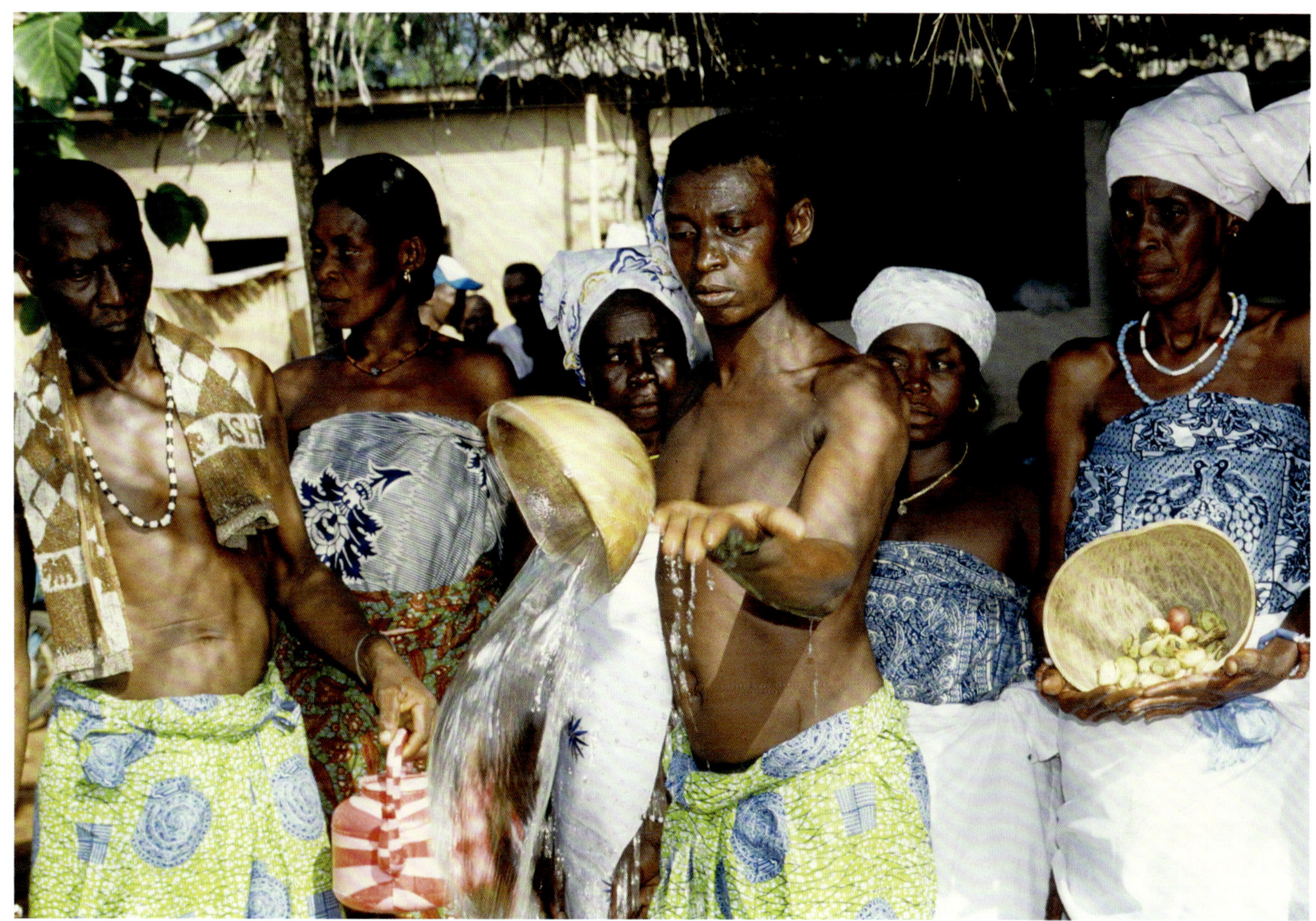

Tron Vodun Ceremony

Cérémonie pour le vodun Tron

Tron Vodun Zeremonie

Ceremonia de Tron vudú

Cerimônia de Vodu Tron

Ceremonie voor Tron

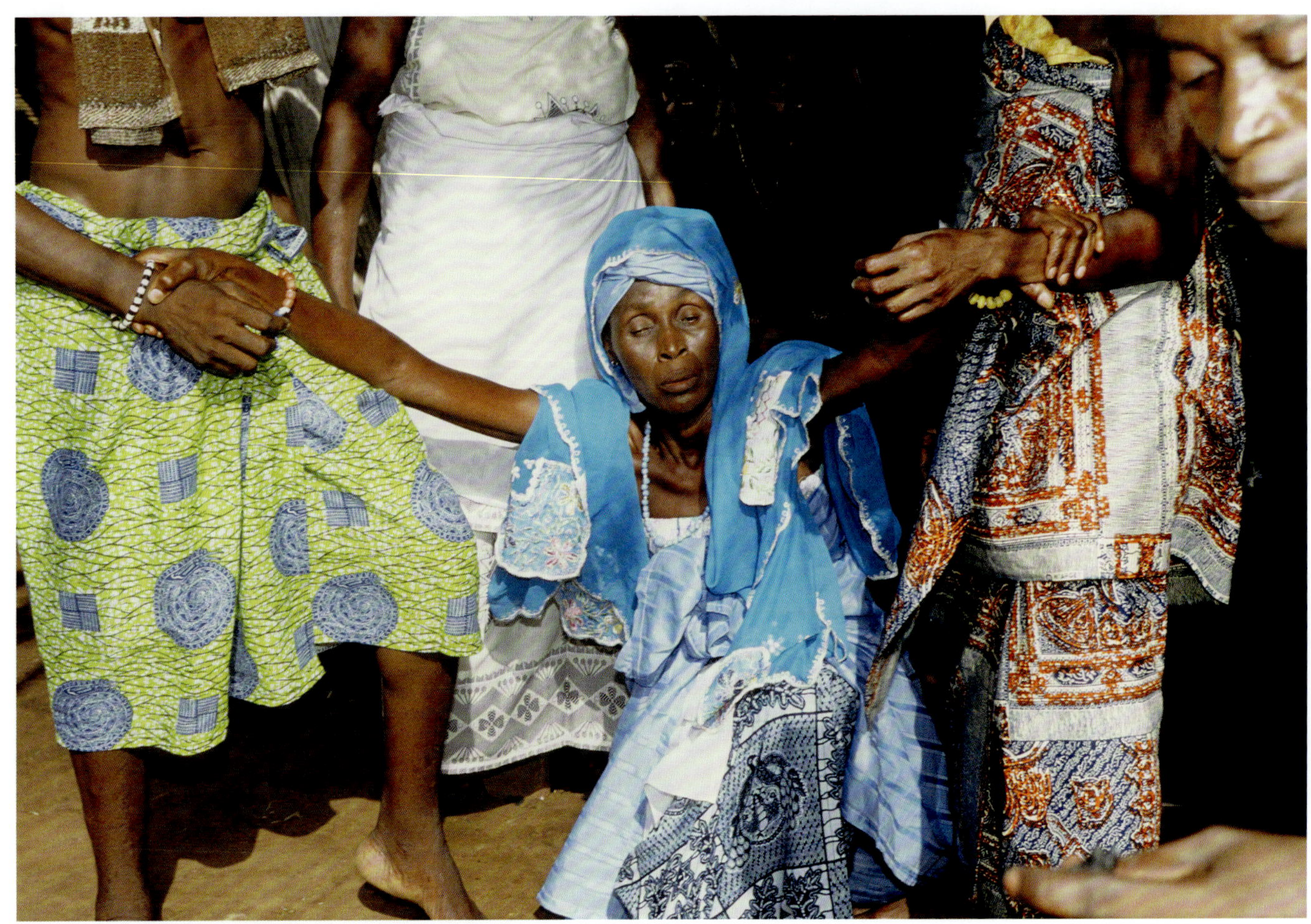

The trance is proof of the presence of Tron

La transe est la preuve de la présence de Tron

Die Trance ist der Beweis für die Anwesenheit Trons

El trance es prueba de la presencia de Tron

O transe é a prova da presença de Trons.

De trance is het bewijs van de aanwezigheid van Tron

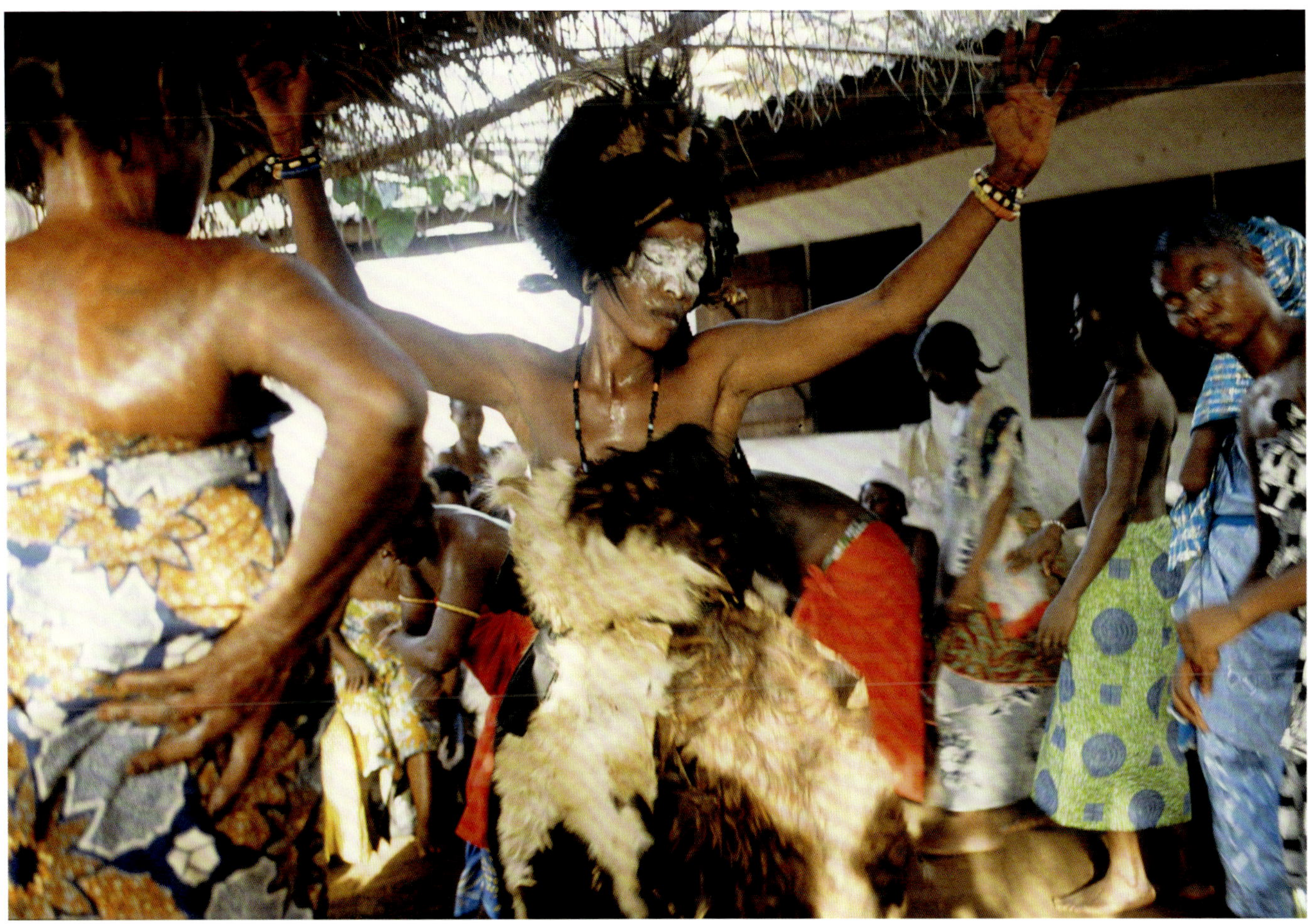

Tron is a savage god. Tron is a reliable partner in the Pantheon of the Vodun when it comes to fighting damage spells, especially those from witches. Ecstatic dances are part of it.

Tron est une divinité sauvage. Dans la lutte contre la magie maléfique, notamment contre les sorciers, Tron est un partenaire fiable dans le panthéon vodun. L'exécution de danses effrénées s'inscrit dans ce rituel.

Tron ist ein wilder Gott. Beim Kampf gegen Schadenzauberei, insbesondere der von Hexen, ist Tron ein verlässlicher Partner im Pantheon der Vodun. Entfesselte Tänze gehören dazu.

Tron es un dios salvaje. Tron es un socio fiable en el panteón del vudú cuando se trata de combatir la magia negra, especialmente la brujería. Los bailes desencadenados son parte de ello.

Tron é um deus selvagem. Tron é um parceiro confiável no Pantheon do Vodun quando se trata de lutar contra a magia dos danos, especialmente a bruxaria. Danças desenfreadas fazem parte dela.

Tron is een woeste god. Tron is een betrouwbare partner in het vodunpantheon bij het bestrijden van schadelijke tovenarij, vooral hekserij. Ontketende dansen horen erbij.

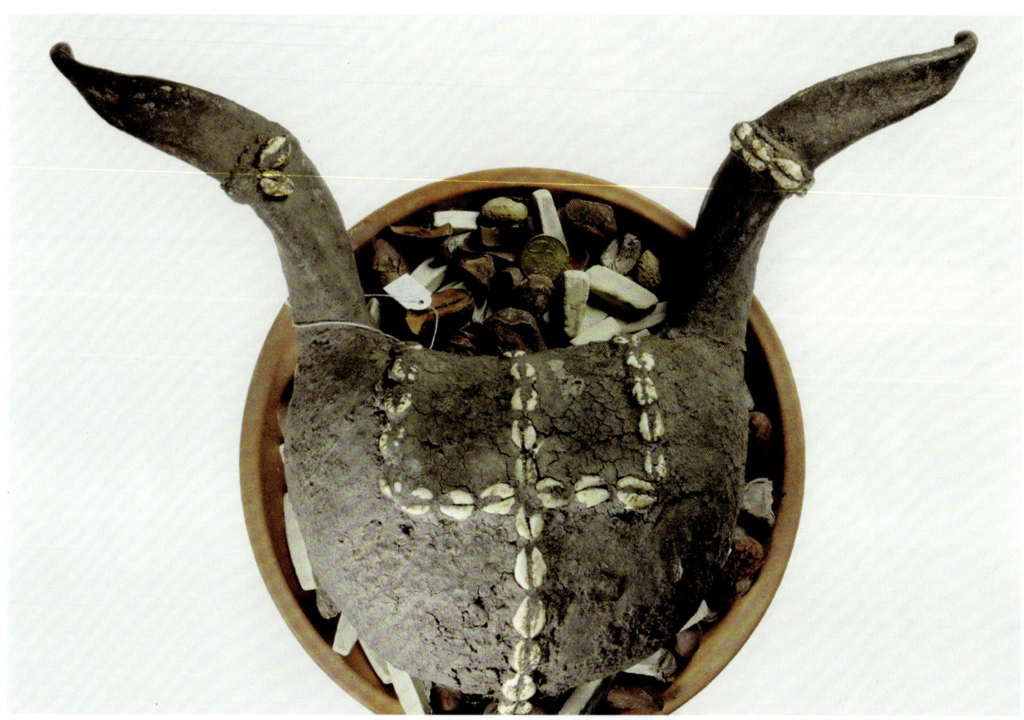

**Ritual item to
strengthen warriors**

**Objet rituel pour renforcer
les guerriers**

**Ritualgegenstand zur Stärkung
der Krieger**

**Ritual para fortalecer a
los guerreros**

**Ritual para fortalecer
os guerreiros**

**Ritueel voorwerp om krijgers
te versterken**

Horns, cowrie shell, package with
plants and organic materials/
Corne, coquillages, paquets avec
plantes et matières organiques,
23 × 42 cm

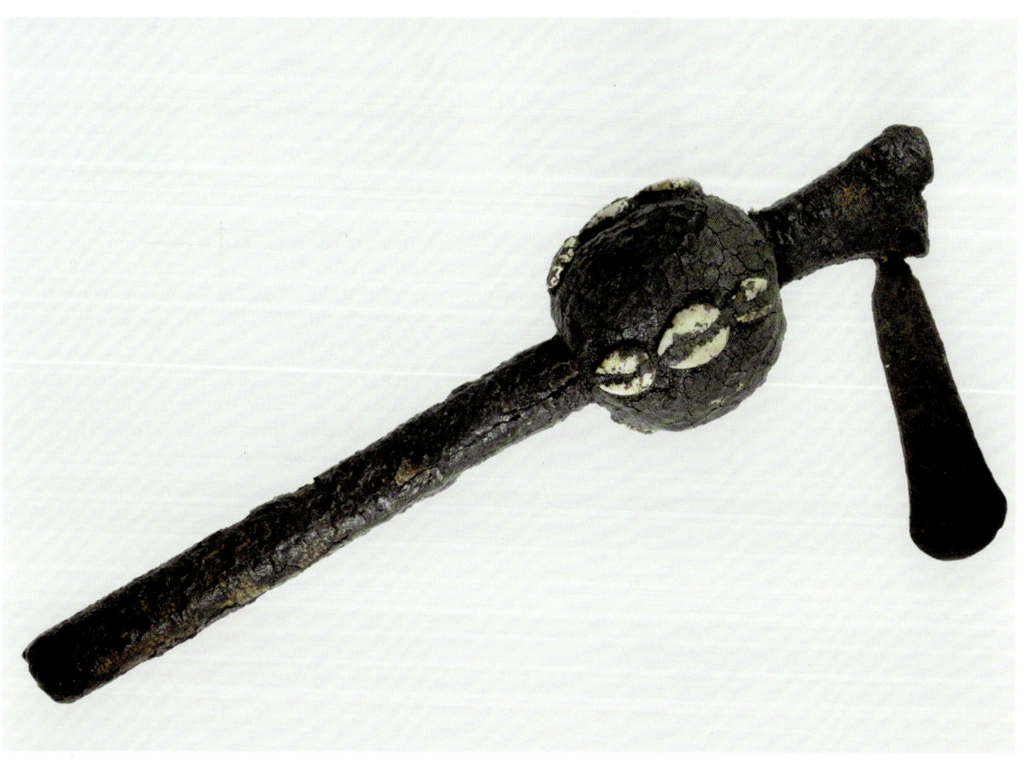

**Ritual item to strengthen
warriors**

**Objet rituel pour renforcer les
guerriers**

**Ritualgegenstand zur Stärkung
der Krieger**

**Ritual para fortalecer a
los guerreros**

**Ritual para fortalecer
os guerreiros**

**Ritueel voorwerp om krijgers te
versterken**

Wood, steel, organic material/
Bois, acier, matières organiques,
35 × 8 cm

Oracle package for divination

Paquet d'oracle pour la divination

Orakelpaket für die Divination

Paquete oráculo para adivinación

Pacote Oracle para Divinação

Orakelpakket voor de divinatie

Mirror, package with organic material/
Miroir, paquets avec matières
organiques, 16 × 18 cm

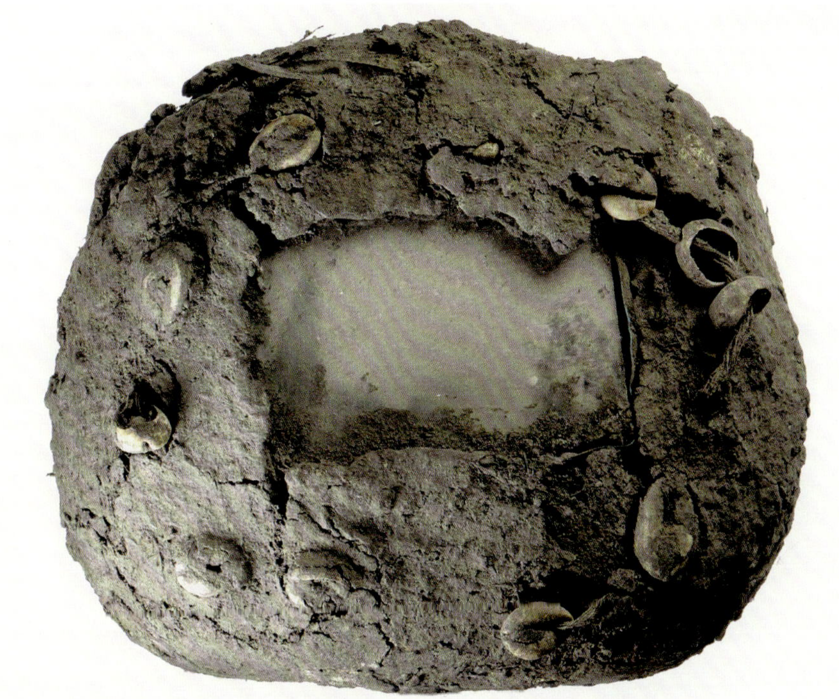

Ritual object for the protection
of followers

Objet rituel pour la protection
des adeptes

**Ritualgegenstand zum Schutz
der Anhänger**

Objeto ritual para la protección de
los colgantes

Objecto ritual para a protecção
de pingentes

**Ritueel voorwerp ter bescherming van
de aanhangers**

Package with organic material, iron
chain/Matières organiques, chaîne,
17 × 23 cm

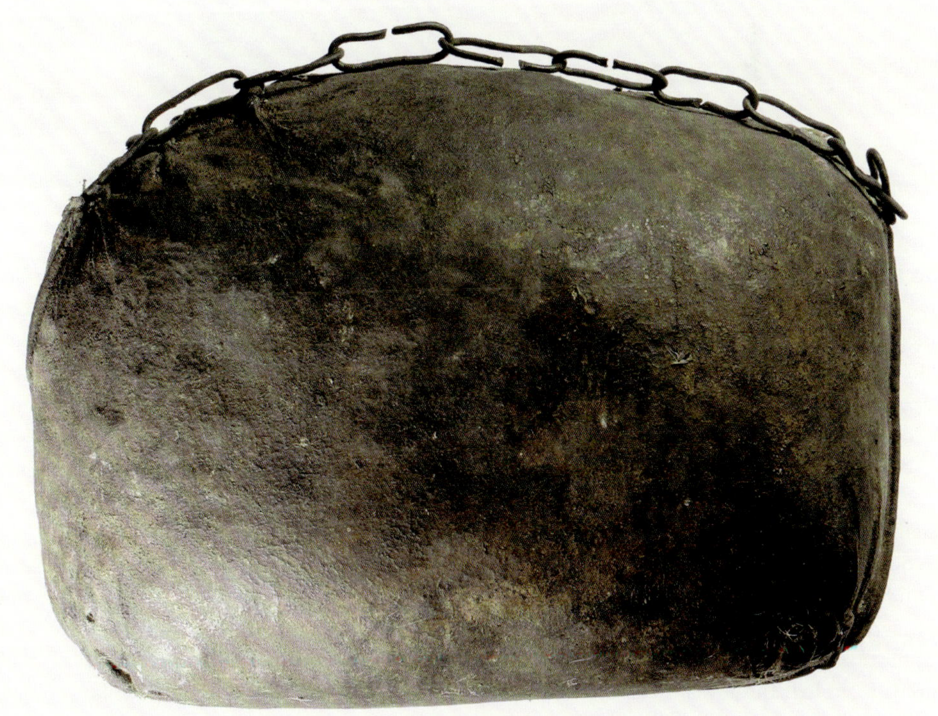

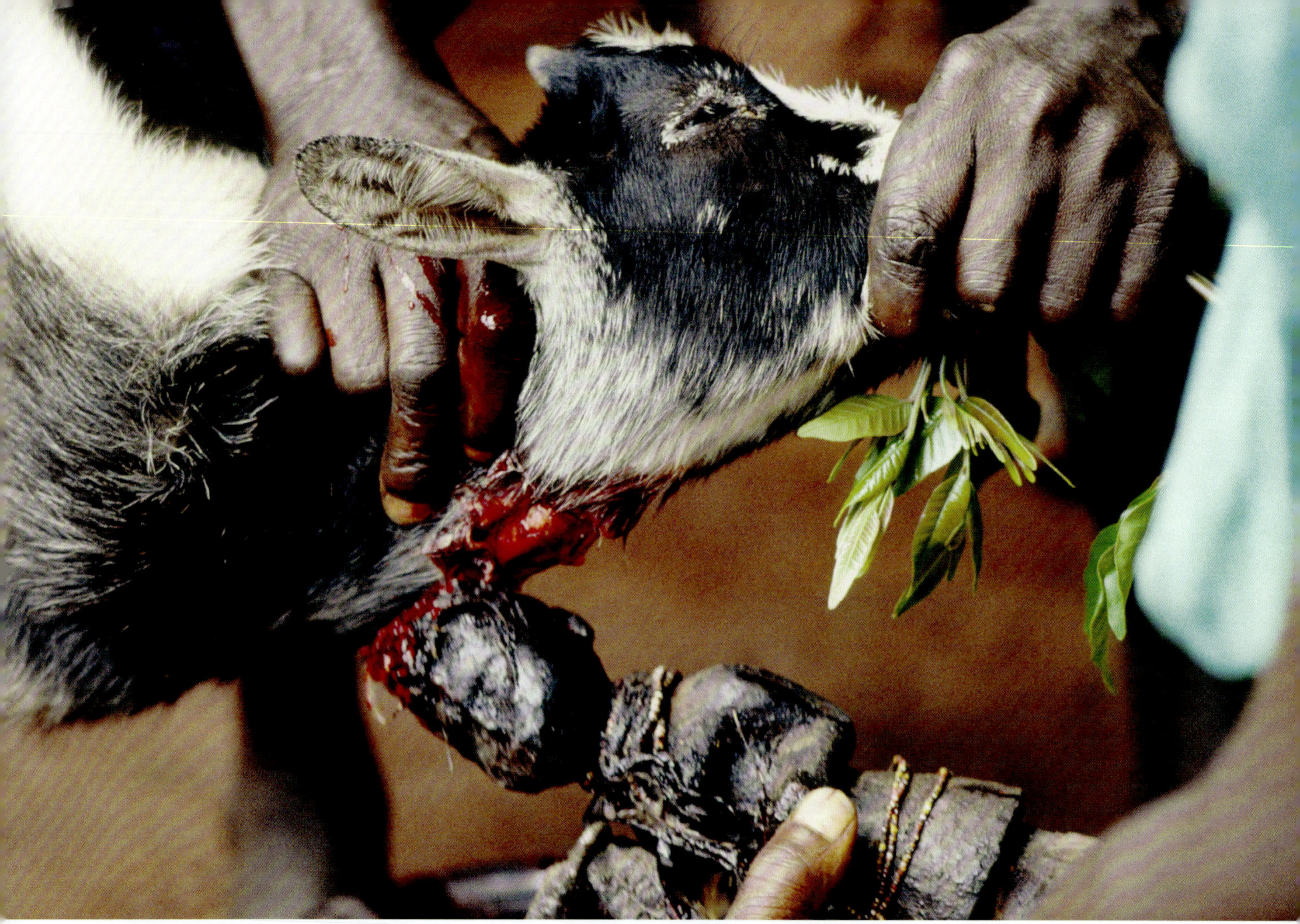

Bo and Bocio—Magic Objects

The word "Bocio" comes from the language area of the Fon in Benin and is composed of "Bo" (power) and "Cio" (body). Bocios are carriers of magical powers and are widely recognized and respected in West Africa.

A Bocio is made when the local priest of a community considers it necessary. For example, if a client's illness requires this for recovery. Also commissioned works and harmful spells are possible. The material that serves the medicine man as a carrier for the magical charge is the body—it is always a carving. The power that is applied usually consists of certain medicinal

Bo et *bocio*, objets magiques

Le mot *bocio* provient de la langue de l'ethnie Fon du Bénin et est constitué de *bo* (« force ») et de *cio* (« corps »). Les bocio sont donc des porteurs de puissance magique largement reconnus et respectés en Afrique de l'Ouest.

Le bocio est fabriqué à la demande du prêtre local d'une communauté, qui en éprouve le besoin. Par exemple, il peut être nécessaire à la guérison d'un client malade. Le bocio remplit également d'autres missions ou sert à la magie maléfique. Le matériau, que le guérisseur utilise pour transporter la charge magique, en constitue le « corps »,

Bo und Bocio – Magische Objekte

Das Wort *bocio* stammt aus dem Sprachraum der Fon in Benin und setzt sich aus *bo* (Kraft) und *cio* (Körper) zusammen. Bocios sind Träger magischer Kräfte und in Westafrika weithin anerkannt und respektiert.

Ein Bocio wird hergestellt, wenn der lokale Priester einer Gemeinschaft seine Anfertigung für nötig hält. Zum Beispiel wenn die Erkrankung eines Klienten dies zu seiner Genesung erfordert. Auch Auftragsarbeiten und Schadenzauber sind möglich. Die Materie, die dem Medizinmann als Träger für die magische

A Bocio is charged with the blood of the animal sacrifice
Bocio chargé du sang de l'animal sacrifié
Ein Bocio wird mit dem Blut des Tieropfers aufgeladen
Rellenando un bocio con la sangre del sacrificio animal
Um Bocio é carregado com o sangue do sacrifício animal
Een bocio wordt opgeladen met het bloed van het offerdier

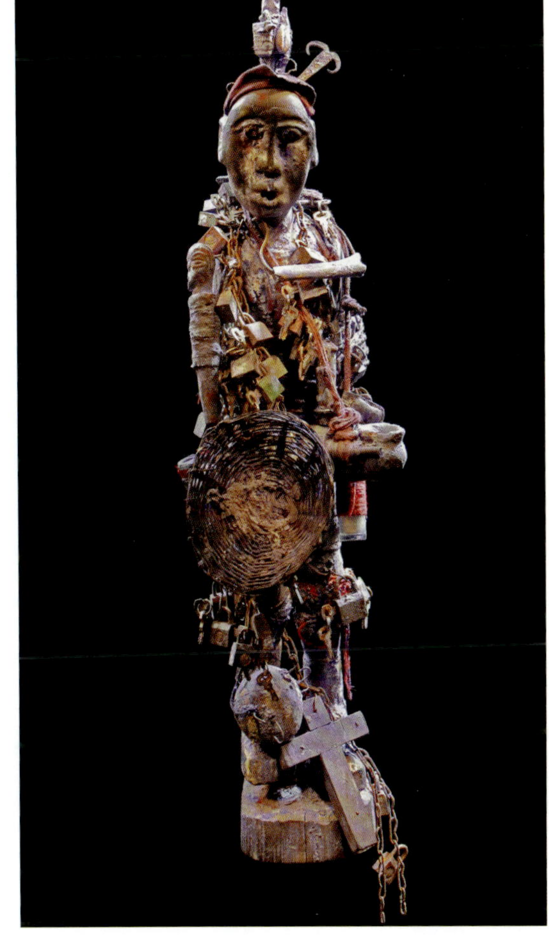

With this Football-Bocio players can be suspended, weakened and activated
Avec ce bocio-football, les joueurs peuvent être bloqués, affaiblis ou énergisés
Mit diesem Fußball-Bocio können Spieler gesperrt, geschwächt und aktiviert werden
Con este bocio de fútbol los jugadores pueden ser bloqueados, debilitados y activados
Com este Football-Bocio os jogadores podem ser bloqueados, enfraquecidos e activados
Met deze voetbal-bocio kunnen spelers versperd, verzwakt en geactiveerd worden
Wood, wickerwork, wire, metal/Bois, osier, fil métallique, métal, 70 × 20 cm

Bo y Bocio– Objetos mágicos

La palabra "Bocio" proviene del área lingüística del Fon en Benín y está compuesta por "Bo" (poder) y "Cio" (cuerpo). Los bocios son portadores de poderes mágicos y son ampliamente reconocidos y respetados en África Occidental.

Un Bocio se hace cuando el sacerdote local de una comunidad considera necesaria su producción. Por ejemplo, cuando la enfermedad de un cliente lo requiere para su recuperación. También es posible realizar trabajos por encargo y hechizos malignos. La materia que sirve al curandero como

Bo e Bocio – Objetos Mágicos

A palavra "Bocio" vem da área de linguagem do Fon em Benin e é composta por "Bo" (poder) e "Cio" (corpo). Os bocios são portadores de poderes mágicos e são amplamente reconhecidos e respeitados na África Ocidental.

Um Bocio é feito quando o sacerdote local de uma comunidade considera necessária a sua produção. Por exemplo, quando a doença de um cliente o requer para recuperação. O trabalho da Comissão e os feitiços de dano também são possíveis. A matéria que serve ao curandeiro como portador da carga mágica é o corpo – é

Bo en bocio, magische objecten

Het woord *bocio* komt uit het taalgebied van de Fon in Benin en bestaat uit *bo* (macht) en *cio* (lichaam). Bocio's zijn dragers van magische krachten en worden in West-Afrika algemeen erkend en gerespecteerd.

Een bocio wordt gemaakt wanneer de plaatselijke priester van een gemeenschap de productie ervan noodzakelijk acht. Bijvoorbeeld, wanneer de ziekte van een klant dat vereist voor de genezing. Ook werken in opdracht en schadelijke tovenarij zijn mogelijk. De materie die de medicijnman gebruikt als drager van de magische lading, is het lichaam – het gaat

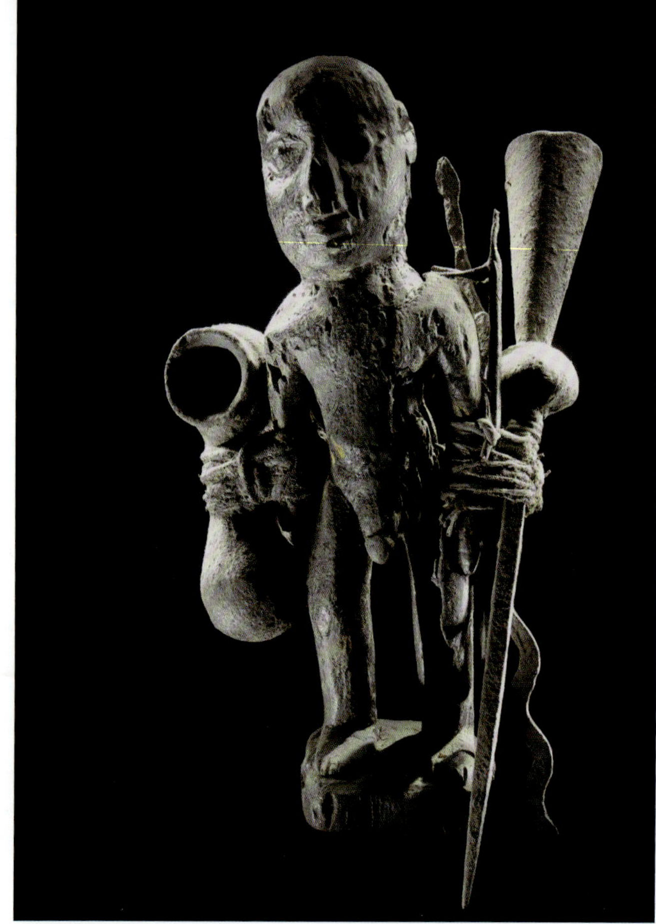

Triple-charged Bocio with the power of Sakpata, Dan and the twins
Bocio triplement chargé du pouvoir de Sakpata, de Dan et des jumeaux
Dreifach geladener Bocio mit der Kraft Sakpatas, Dans und der Zwillinge
Bocio de triple carga con el poder de Sakpata, Dan y los gemelos
O Triplo carregou Bocio com o poder de Sakpatas, Dans e os gémeos
Drievoudig geladen bocio met de kracht van Sakpata, Dan en de tweeling

Wood, metal/Bois, métal, 33 × 20 cm

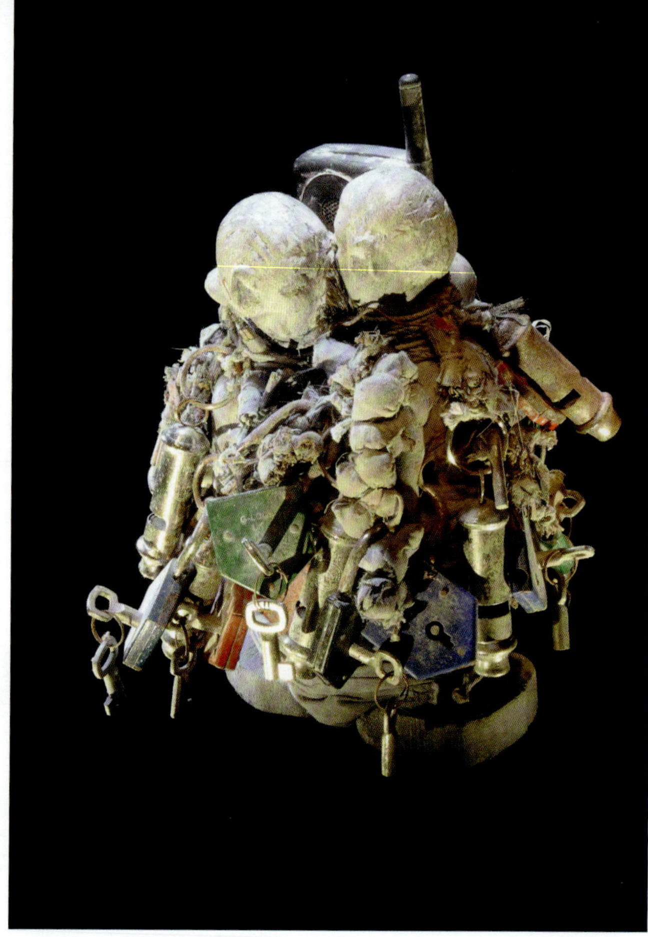

Telephone Bocio for a fast connection to the gods
Bocio-téléphone pour une connexion rapide aux dieux
Telefon-Bocio für die schnelle Verbindung zu den Göttern
Teléfono bocio para la conexión rápida con los dioses
Telefone Bocio para a conexão rápida com os deuses
Telefoon-bocio voor een snelle verbinding met de goden

Mobile phone, wood, locks, whistles/Téléphone mobile, bois, cadenas, sifflets, 23 × 16 cm

plants or animal components and its exact composition is kept strictly secret.

Whether the situation of the needy requires a Bocio or a Bo is decided individually by the priest.

qui prend toujours la forme d'une sculpture en bois. La « force » qui lui est appliquée est le plus souvent matérialisée par l'ajout de plantes médicinales spécifiques ou de parties d'animaux, mais sa composition exacte reste totalement secrète.

C'est au prêtre de déterminer pour chaque cas si la situation de la personne nécessite l'emploi d'un bocio ou d'un bo.

Ladung dient, ist hierbei der *Körper* – dabei handelt es sich immer um eine Schnitzerei. Die *Kraft*, die appliziert wird, besteht meist aus bestimmten Heilpflanzen oder tierischen Bestandteilen und wird in ihrer exakten Zusammensetzung streng geheimgehalten.

Ob die Situation der Hilfebedürftigen einen Bocio oder ein Bo erfordert, wird vom Priester individuell entschieden.

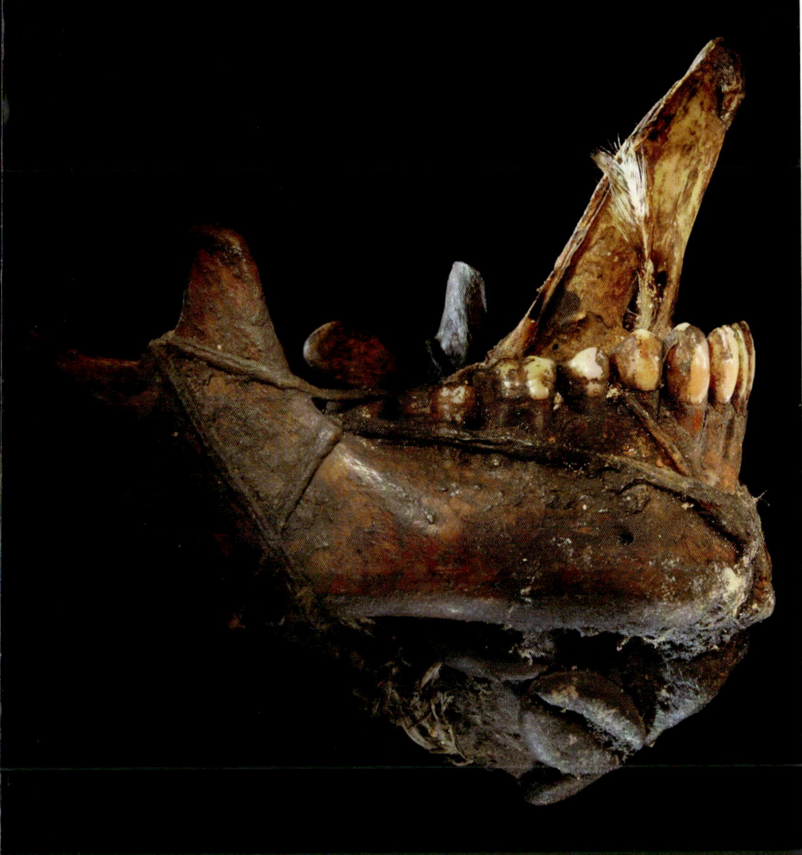

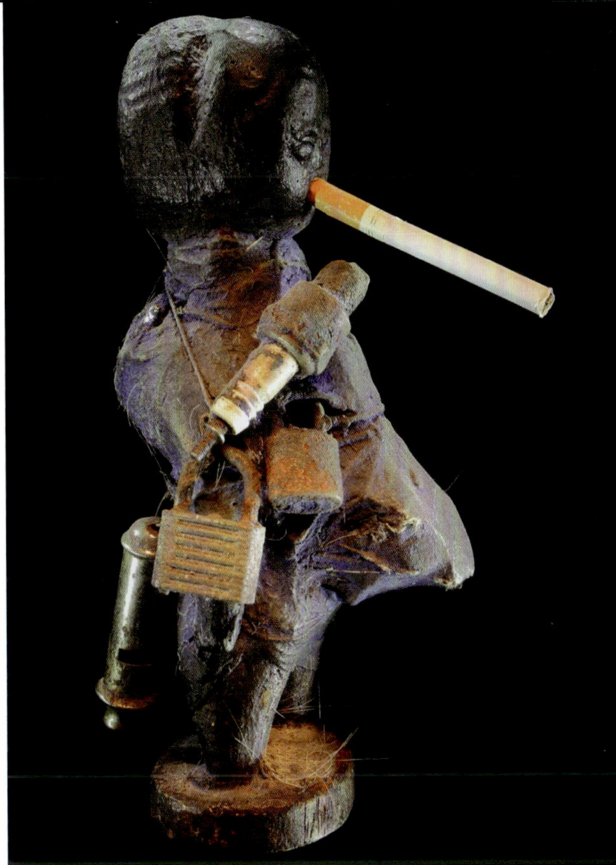

Bo (force object) against slander

Bo (objet de puissance) contre la calomnie

Bo (Kraftobjekt) gegen üble Nachrede

Bo (objeto de fuerza) contra la calumnia

Bo (objeto de força) contra a calúnia

Bo (krachtobject) tegen kwaadsprekerij

Human lower jaw, duckbill, packet of plants/Machoire humaine, bec de canard, plantes, 10 × 10 cm

Bocio for a football fan to strengthen his favorite team

Bocio pour un fan de football afin de renforcer son équipe favorite

Bocio für einen Fußballfan zur Stärkung seiner Lieblingsmannschaft

Bocio para un aficionado al fútbol para fortalecer a su equipo favorito

Bocio para um torcedor de futebol para fortalecer seu time favorito

Bocio voor een voetbalfan om zijn favoriete team te versterken

Wood, spark plug, steel locks, whistle/Bois, bougie d'allumage, cadenas en acier, sifflet, 26 × 20 cm

portador de la carga mágica es el cuerpo, en este caso se trata siempre de una escultura. El poder que se aplica suele consistir en ciertas plantas medicinales o componentes animales y su composición exacta se mantiene estrictamente en secreto.

El hecho de si la situación de los necesitados requiere un Bocio o un Bo es algo que decidide individualmente el sacerdote.

sempre uma escultura. O poder que é aplicado geralmente consiste em certas plantas medicinais ou componentes animais e é mantido estritamente secreto em sua composição exata.

Se a situação dos necessitados requer um Bocio ou um Bo é decidido individualmente pelo padre.

hierbij altijd om houtsnijwerk. De kracht die wordt aangebracht, geappliceerd, bestaat meestal uit bepaalde geneeskrachtige planten of dierlijke bestanddelen. De exacte samenstelling wordt strikt geheim gehouden.

Of de situatie van de hulpbehoevenden een bocio of een bo vereist, wordt per geval bepaald door de priester.

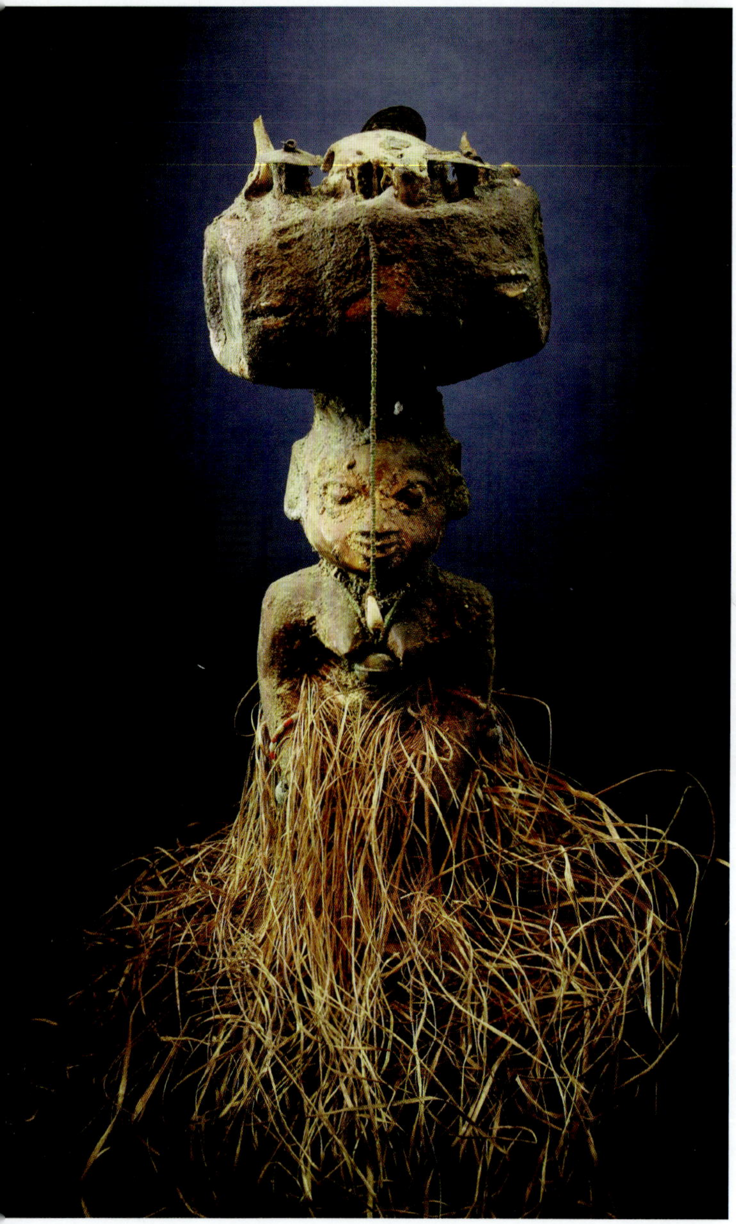

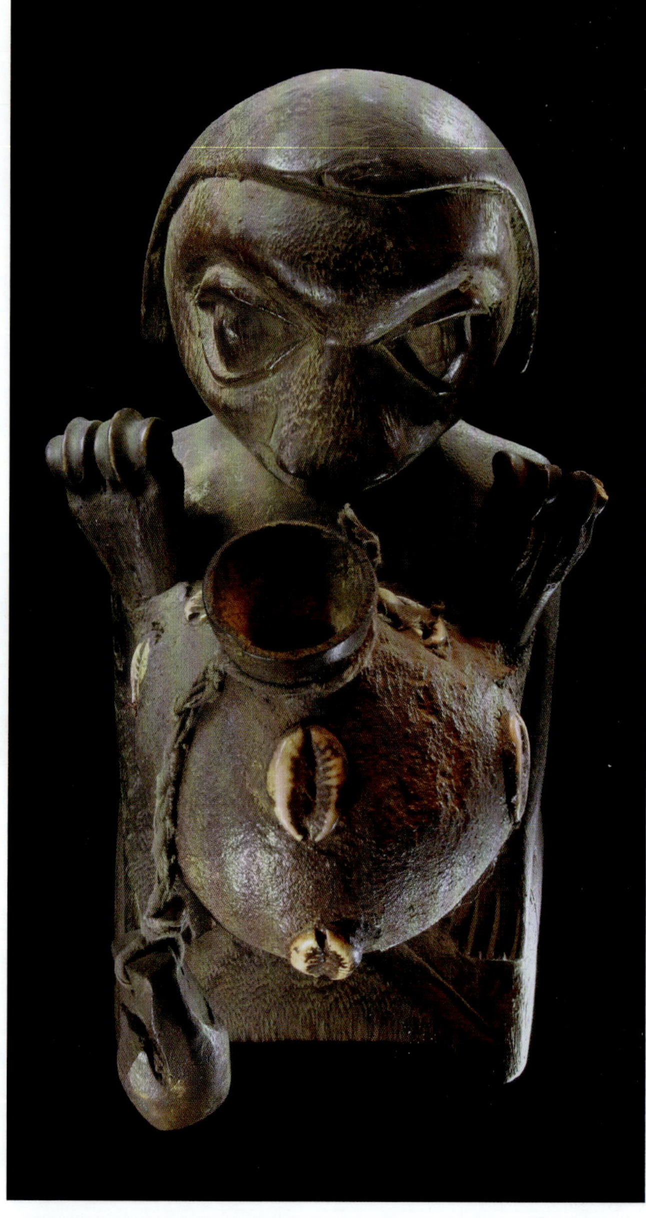

Bocio to protect against damaging spells

Bocio pour se protéger des mauvais sorts

Bocio zum Schutz vor Schadenzauber

Bocio para proteger contra los hechizos malignos

Bocio para proteger contra feitiços de dano

Bocio om te beschermen tegen boze tovenarij

Wood, raffia, bone/Bois, raphia, os, 44 × 16 cm

Bocio with medicine pack for healing

Bocio contenant des médicaments

Bocio mit Medizinpackung für Heilung

Bocio con botiquín para la curación

Bocio com pacote de medicamentos para a cura

Bocio met medicijnenpakket voor genezing

Wood, calabash, textiles/Bois, calebasses, textiles, 24 × 12 cm

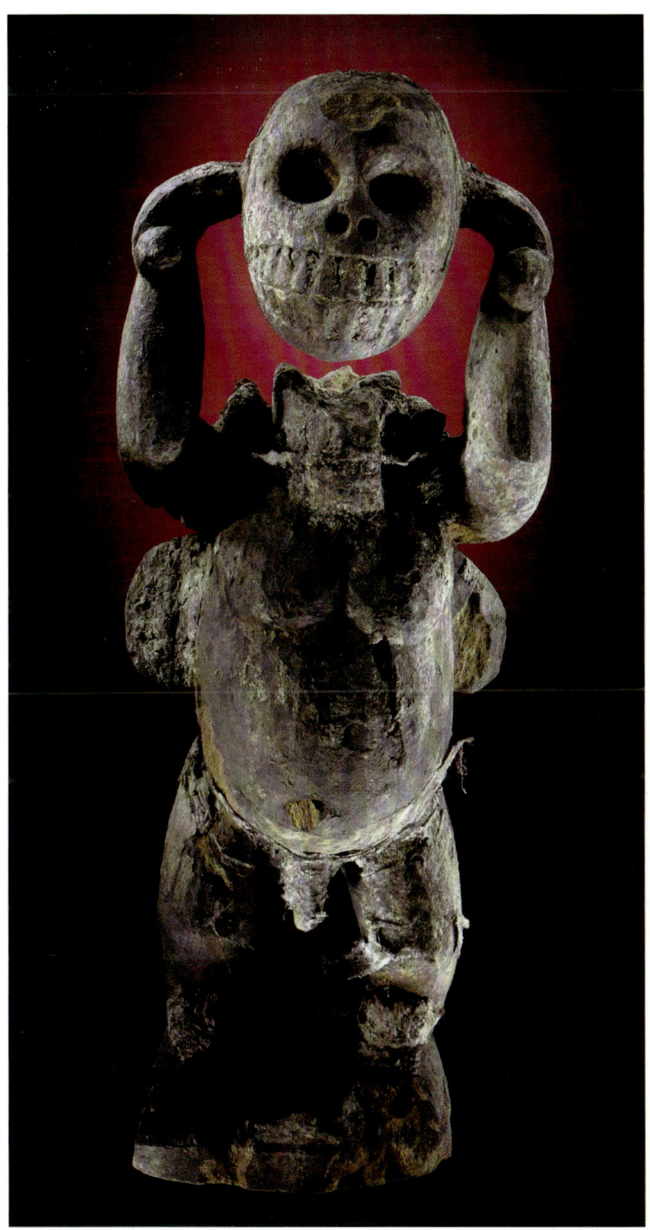

Bo (force object) for damage magic

Bo (objet de puissance) pour la magie maléfique

Bo (Kraftobjekt) für Schadenmagie

Bo (objeto de fuerza) para magia negra

Bo (objeto de força) para magia de dano

Bo (krachtobject) voor schadelijke tovenarij

Wood/Bois, 50 × 20 cm

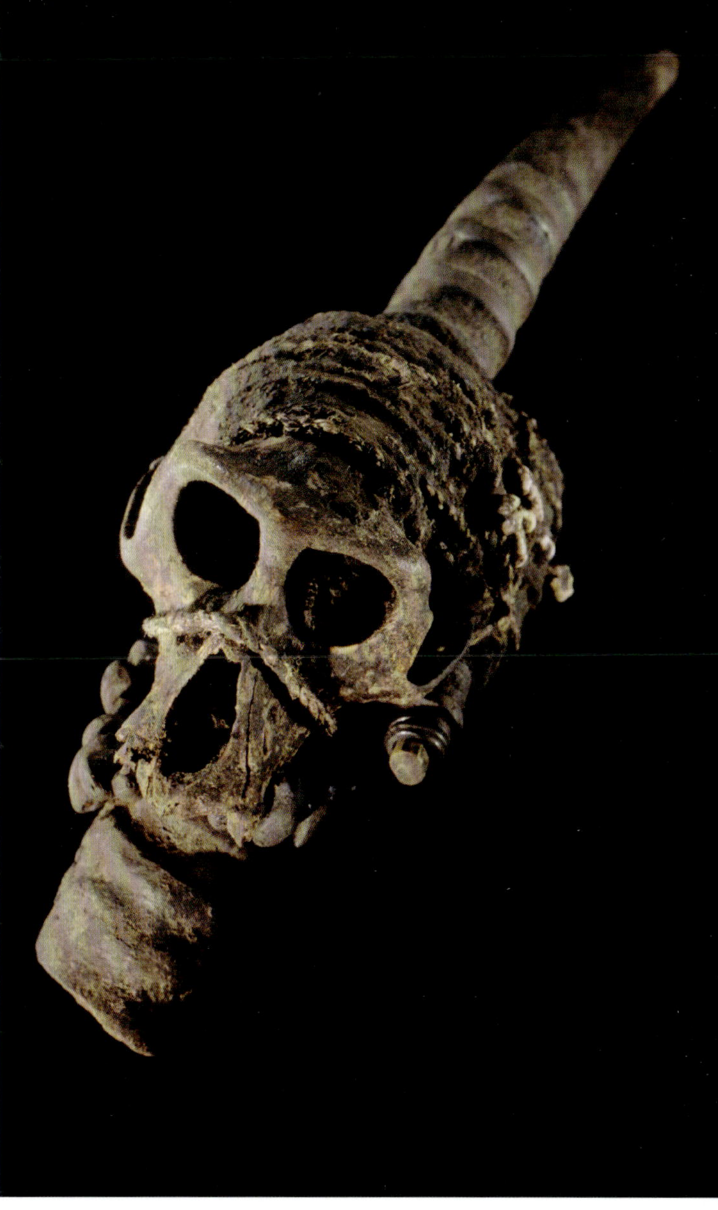

Magic horn for healing from witchcraft

Corne magique pour guérir de la sorcellerie

Magisches Horn zur Heilung von Hexereien

Cuerno mágico para curar la brujería

Chifre mágico para feitiçaria de cura

Toverhoorn voor het genezen van hekserij

Horn, monkey skull/Bois, crâne de singe, 20 × 40 cm

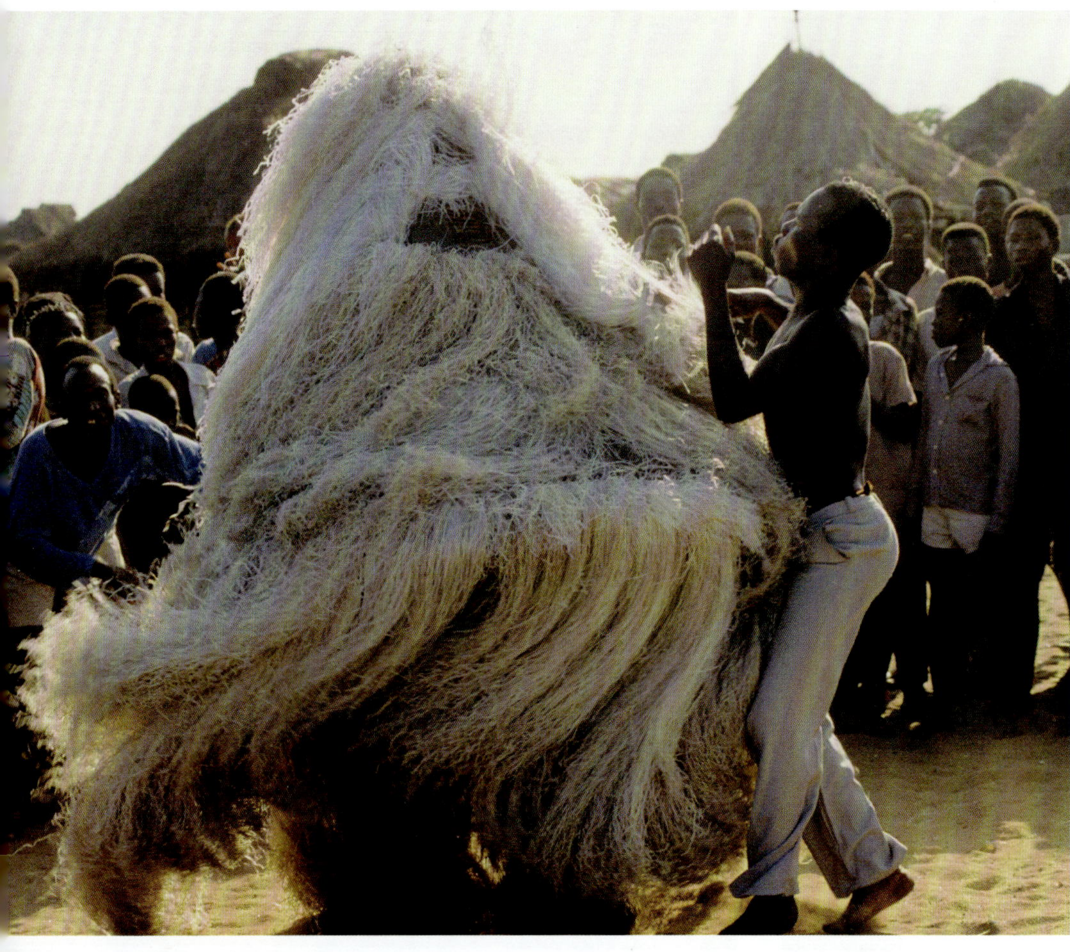

Zangbeto ceremony in a village near Grand Popo, Benin

Cérémonie Zangbeto dans un village près de Grand Popo, Bénin

Zangbeto-Zeremonie in einem Dorf bei Grand Popo, Benin

Ceremonia de Zangbeto en una aldea cerca de Grand Popo, Benin

Cerimônia de Zangbeto em uma vila perto de Grand Popo, Benin

Zangbeto-ceremonie in een dorp in de buurt van Grand Popo, Benin

Zangbeto Ceremony

Cérémonie Zangbeto

Zangbeto-Zeremonie

Ceremonia de Zangbeto

Cerimônia de Zangbeto

Zangbeto-ceremonie

Zangbeto—the Police of the night

According to a Yoruba legend, what enlivens the haystack-like costumes of the Zangbeto secret society is by no means the power of the dancers, but rather that of the night spirits.

In the social community of traditional Benin, the members of this society have the function of guardians of order, but are also regarded as guardians of old wisdoms. The appearance of Zangbeto, which takes place almost exclusively at night, is accordingly respected and feared at the same time.

In a state of trance, Zangbeto has insights into areas that people like to hide and therefore poses a serious danger to witches

Zangbeto, la police de la nuit

Selon une légende Yoruba, ce n'est pas la force des danseurs qui anime les costumes en forme de meules de foin de la société secrète Zangbeto, mais plutôt les esprits de la nuit.

Les membres de cette communauté occupent dans la société du Bénin traditionnel une fonction de gardiens de l'ordre et sont également considérés comme des protecteurs des savoirs anciens. L'apparition de Zangbeto, pratiquement exclusivement la nuit, est ainsi hautement estimée et redoutée.

En état de transe, Zangbeto acquiert la capacité d'examiner des domaines que les

Zangbeto – die Polizei der Nacht

Einer Legende der Yorubas zufolge ist das, was die Heuhaufen ähnelnden Kostüme des Zangbeto-Geheimbundes belebt, keineswegs die Kraft der Tänzer, sondern vielmehr die der Nachtgeister.

Die Mitglieder dieser Gesellschaft haben in der Sozialgemeinschaft des traditionellen Benins die Funktion von Ordnungswächtern, gelten aber auch als Bewahrer von alten Weisheiten. Das Erscheinen Zangbetos, das nahezu ausschließlich nachts erfolgt, ist dementsprechend geachtet und gefürchtet zugleich.

Im Zustand der Trance hat Zangbeto Einsichten in Bereiche, die Menschen gerne

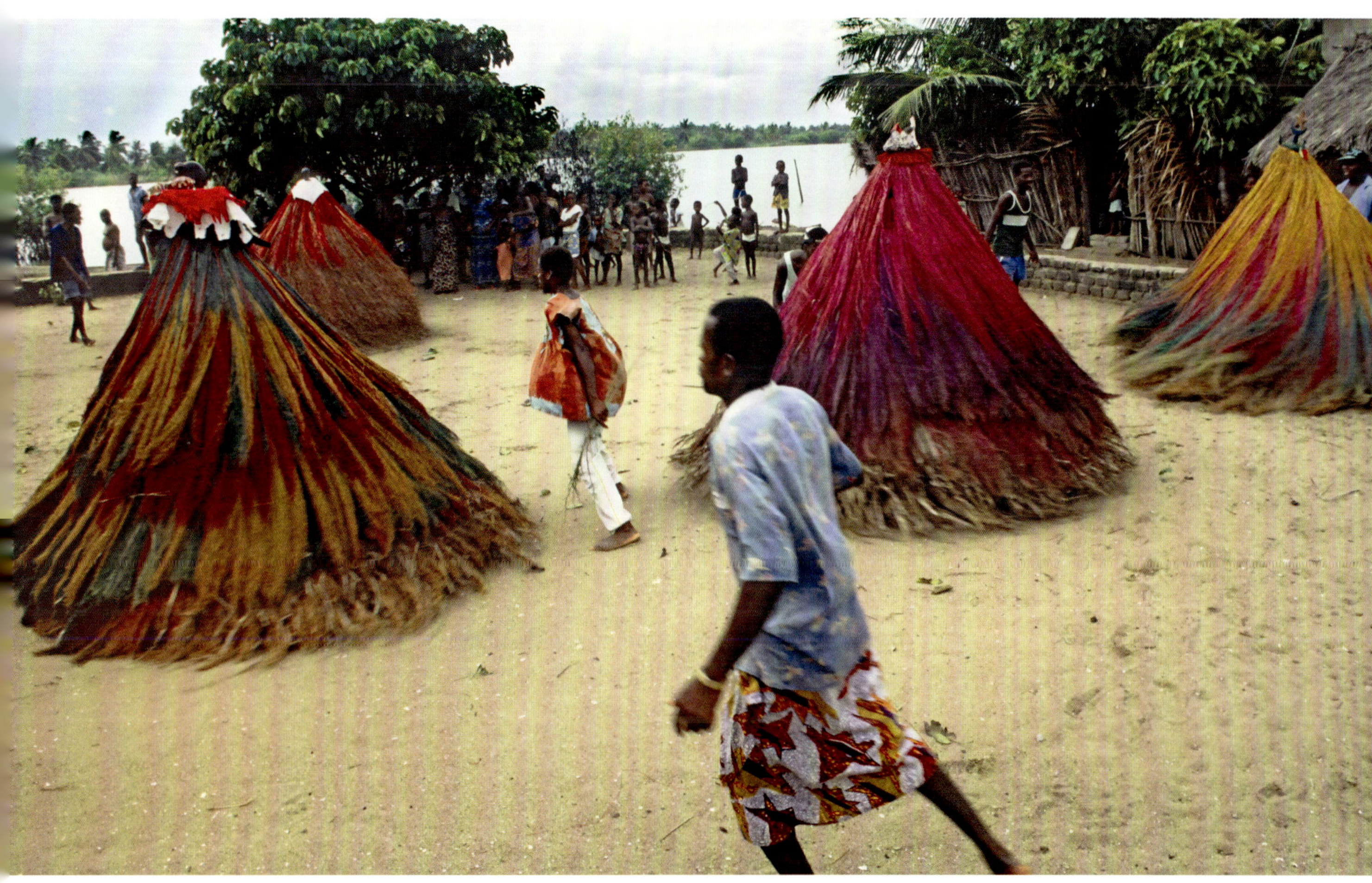

Zangbeto– La policía de la noche

Según una leyenda de Yoruba, lo que anima
los trajes de la sociedad secreta de Zangbeto,
que parecen pajares, no es en absoluto
el poder de los bailarines, sino el de los
espíritus nocturnos.

En la comunidad social del Benin
tradicional, los miembros de esta sociedad
tienen la función de guardianes del
orden, pero también son considerados
guardianes de la sabiduría antigua. La
aparición de Zangbeto, que tiene lugar casi
exclusivamente de noche, se respeta y teme
al mismo tiempo.

En un estado de trance, Zangbeto tiene
conocimiento de áreas que a la gente le gusta

Zangbeto – A polícia da noite

De acordo com uma lenda iorubá, o que
anima os trajes de palheiro da sociedade
secreta do Zangbeto não é de modo algum
o poder dos dançarinos, mas sim o dos
espíritos da noite.

Na comunidade social do Benin
tradicional, os membros dessa sociedade
têm a função de guardiães da ordem, mas
também são considerados como guardiães
da sabedoria antiga. O aparecimento
do Zangbeto, que acontece quase
exclusivamente à noite, é respeitado e
temido ao mesmo tempo.

Em estado de transe, o Zangbeto tem
insights sobre áreas que as pessoas gostam

Zangbeto – de politie van de nacht

Volgens een Yoruba-legende is dat wat de
hooibergachtige kostuums van het geheime
genootschap van Zangbeto verlevendigt
geenszins de kracht van de dansers, maar
eerder die van de nachtgeesten.

In de sociale gemeenschap van het
traditionele Benin hebben de leden van dit
genootschap de functie van ordehandhavers,
maar gelden ze ook als bewakers van
oude wijsheden. De verschijning van
Zangbeto, die bijna uitsluitend 's nachts
plaatsvindt, wordt dan ook gerespecteerd en
gevreesd tegelijk.

In trance heeft Zangbeto inzicht in
gebieden die mensen graag verbergen. Hij

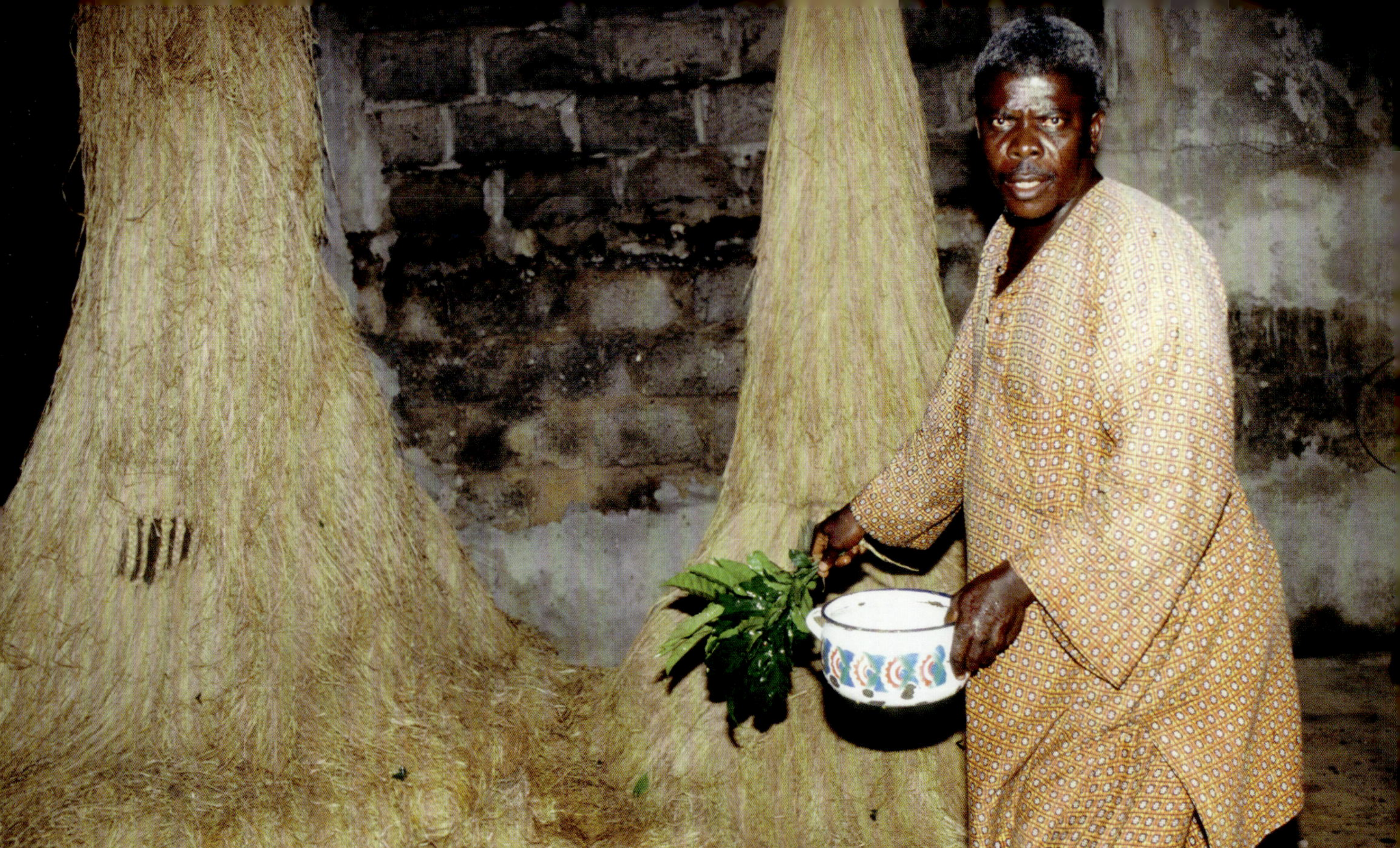

Secret Zangbeto Temple. The Zangbeto priest brings the "haystacks" to life by spraying holy water over them. For outsiders the access to the temple is forbidden, this was a great exception.

Temple secret Zangbeto. Le prêtre de Zangbeto éveille les « meules de foin » à la vie en jetant sur elles un peu d'eau bénite. L'accès au temple étant interdit aux non-initiés, la présence du photographe constitue une rare exception.

Geheimer Zangbeto-Tempel. Der Zangbeto-Priester erweckt die „Heuhaufen" zum Leben, indem er geweihtes Wasser über sie spritzt. Für Außenstehende ist der Zugang zum Tempel verboten, dies war eine große Ausnahme.

Templo secreto de Zangbeto. El sacerdote de Zangbeto da vida a los "pajares" rociándolos con agua consagrada. El acceso al templo está prohibido para los extranjeros, esta fue una gran excepción.

Templo Secreto do Zangbeto. O padre Zangbeto dá vida aos "palheiros" com a pulverização de água consagrada. O acesso ao templo é proibido para forasteiros, esta foi uma grande excepção.

Geheime Zangbeto-tempel. De Zangbeto-priester brengt de 'hooibergen' tot leven door ze te besproeien met gewijd water. De toegang tot de tempel is verboden voor buitenstaanders, dit was een grote uitzondering.

and evildoers. If these are convicted, the secret society also has the authority to determine and pronounce the sentence. It is said that Zangbeto was the country's most important force for order before regular governments established themselves. The society's influence is still considerable.

humains préfèrent dissimuler et représente ainsi un sérieux danger pour les sorciers et les malfaiteurs. Lorsque la société est convaincue qu'un individu a commis un crime, Zangbeto a également autorité pour juger le méfait et condamner le coupable. Elle était ainsi la principale autorité policière du pays avant l'établissement des gouvernements réguliers. L'influence de cette société reste considérable.

verbergen und stellt daher für Hexen und Übeltäter eine ernste Gefahr dar. Werden diese überführt, besitzt der Bund auch die Autoriät, das Strafmaß zu bestimmen und zu richten. Es heisst, Zangbeto war im Land die wichtigste Ordnungsmacht, bevor sich reguläre Regierungen etablierten. Der Einfluss des Bundes ist noch immer beträchtlich.

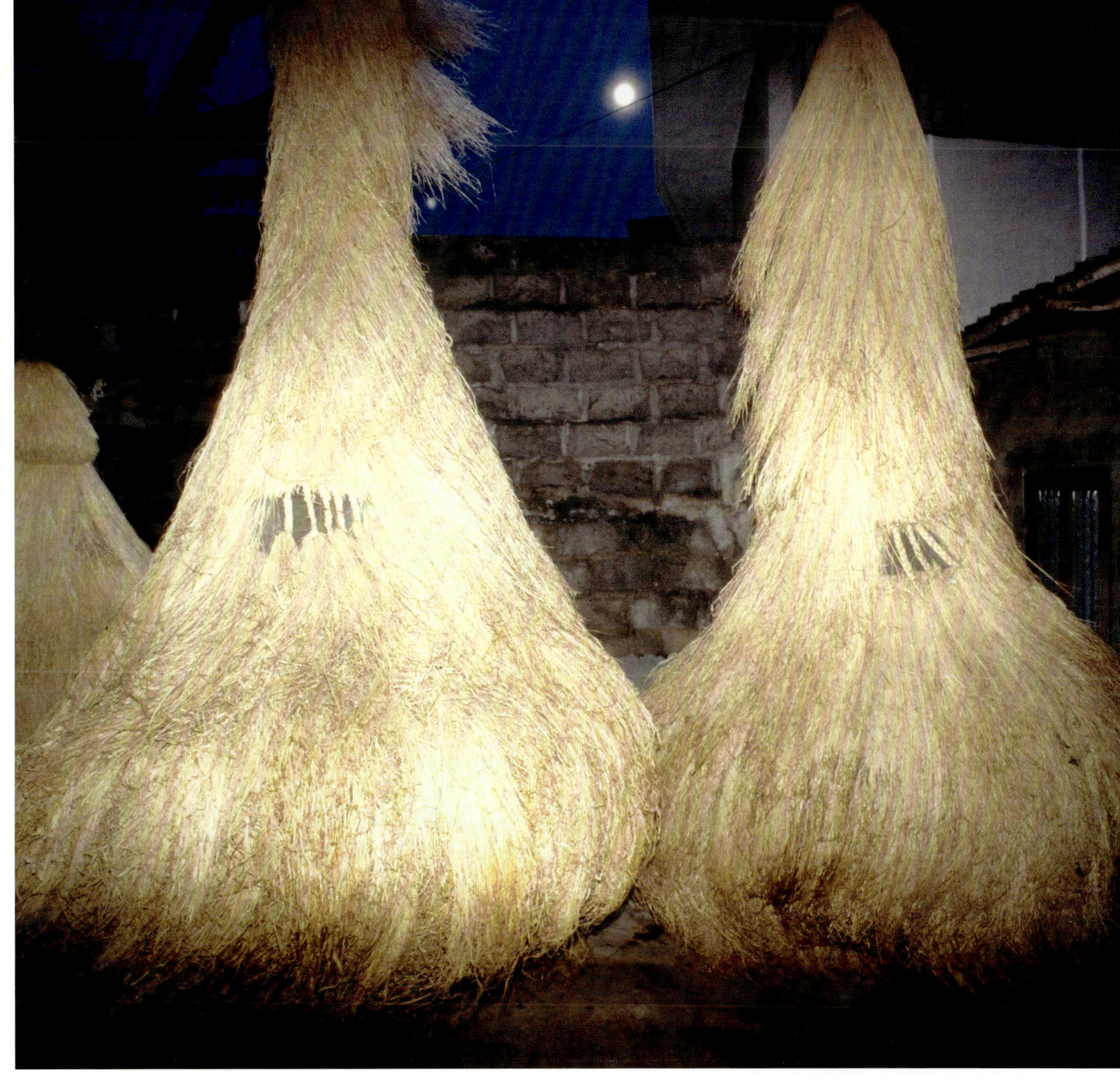

esconder y por lo tanto representa un serio peligro para las brujas y los malhechores. Si estos son condenados, la sociedad también tiene la autoridad para determinar y juzgar la sentencia. Se dice que Zangbeto era la fuerza de orden más importante del país antes de que se establecieran los gobiernos regulares. La influencia de la sociedad sigue siendo considerable.

de esconder e, portanto, representa um sério perigo para bruxas e malfeitores. Se estes forem condenados, o pacto também tem autoridade para determinar e julgar a sentença. Diz-se que o Zangbeto era a força de ordem mais importante do país antes do estabelecimento de governos regulares. A influência da Confederação é ainda considerável.

vormt daarom een ernstig gevaar voor heksen en boosdoeners. Als iemand schuldig wordt bevonden, heeft het genootschap ook de bevoegdheid om het vonnis te vellen en recht te spreken. Naar verluidt was Zangbeto de belangrijkste ordehandhaver van het land voordat de reguliere regeringen werden opgericht. De invloed van het genootschap is nog altijd aanzienlijk.

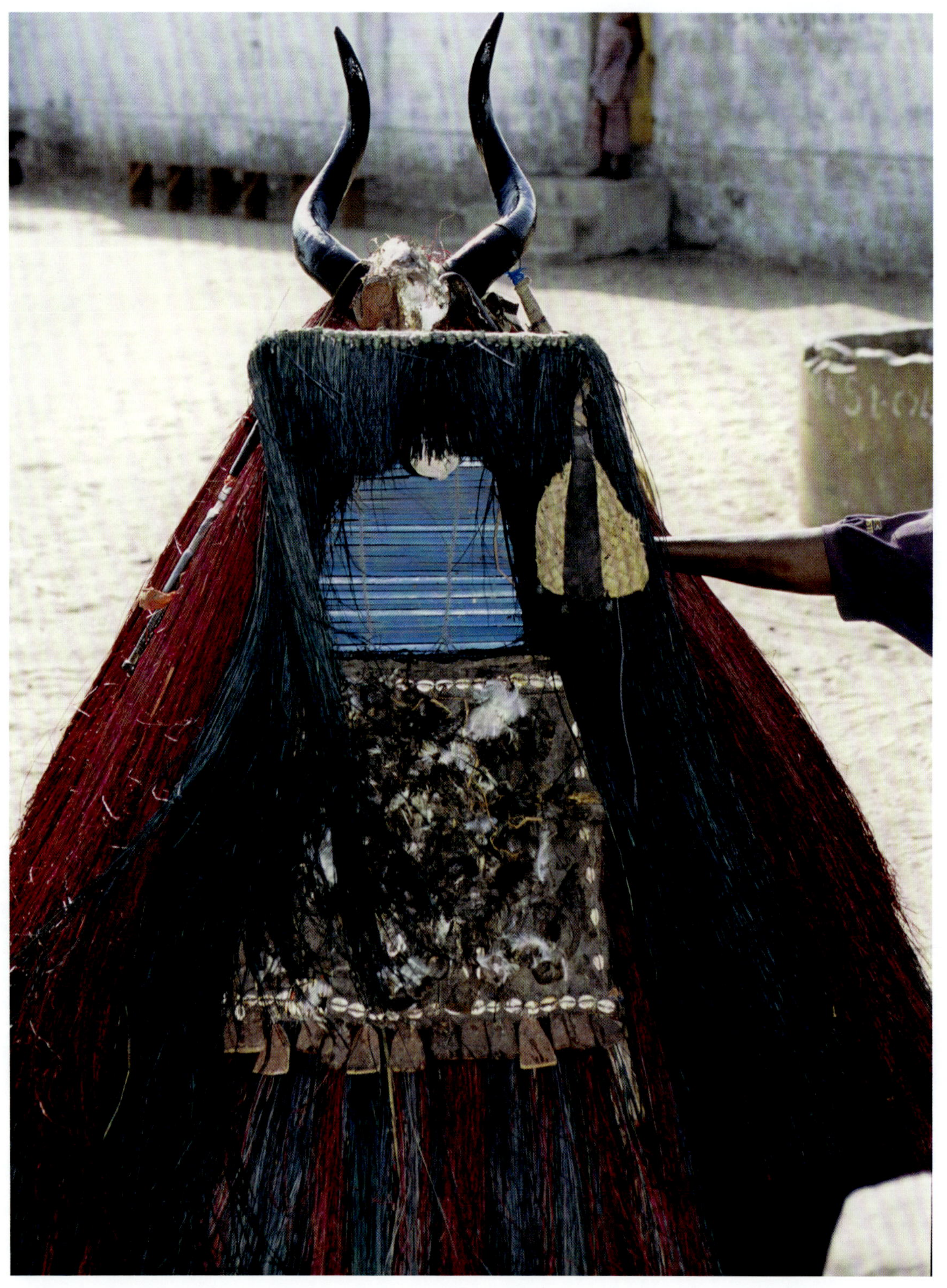

Zangbeto is on the
trail of the culprits

Zangbeto est sur la
piste des coupables

Zangbeto ist den
Übeltätern auf der
Spur

Zangbeto tras
las huellas de los
culpables

Zangbeto está no
rasto dos culpados

Zangbeto is de
boosdoeners op het
spoor

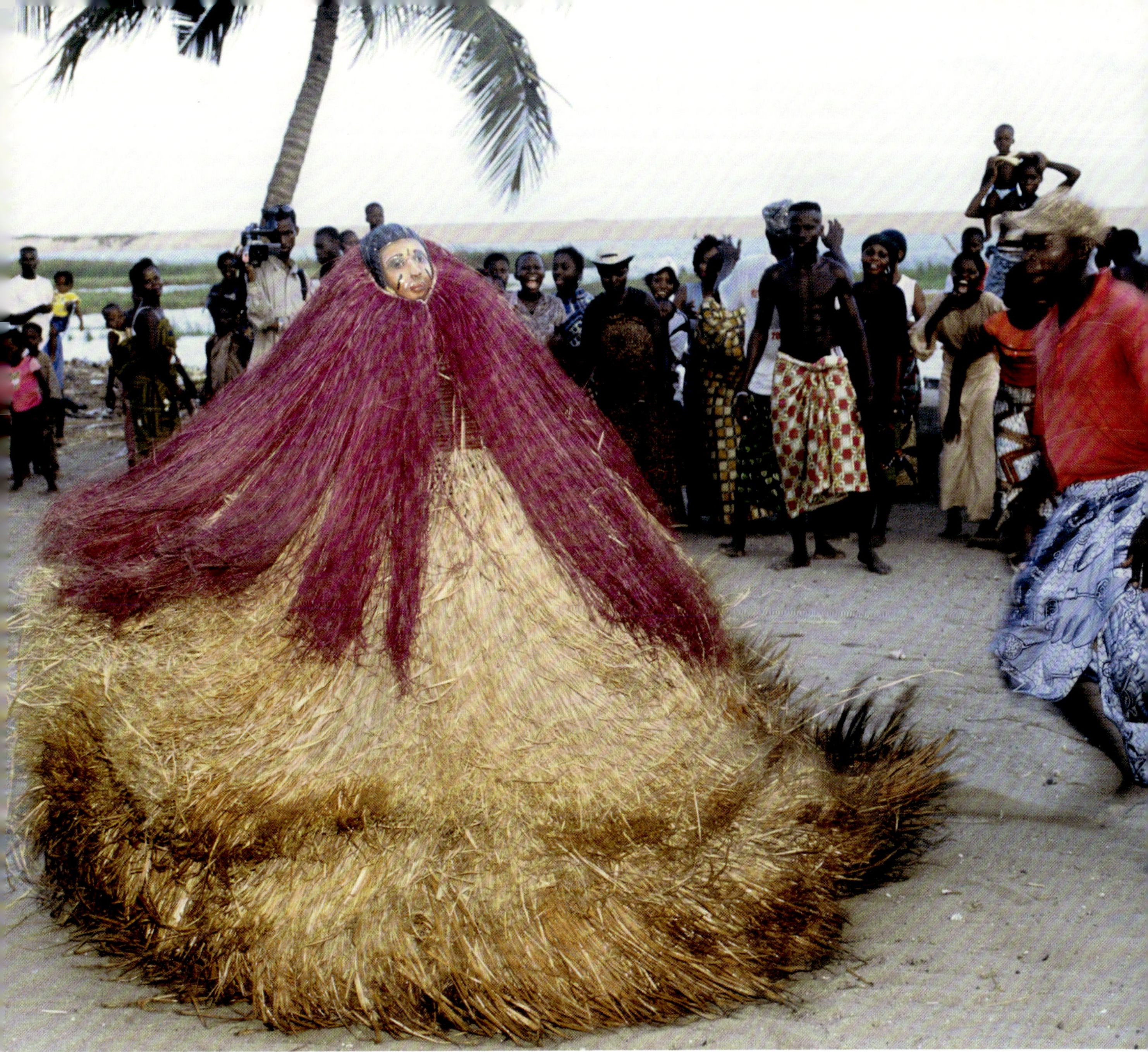

Zangbeto ceremony at Grand Popo, Benin
Cérémonie Zangbeto près de Grand Popo, Bénin
Zangbeto-Zeremonie bei Grand Popo, Benin
Ceremonia de Zangbeto en Grand Popo, Benin
Cerimônia de Zangbeto em Grand Popo, Benin
Zangbeto-ceremonie in Grand Popo, Benin

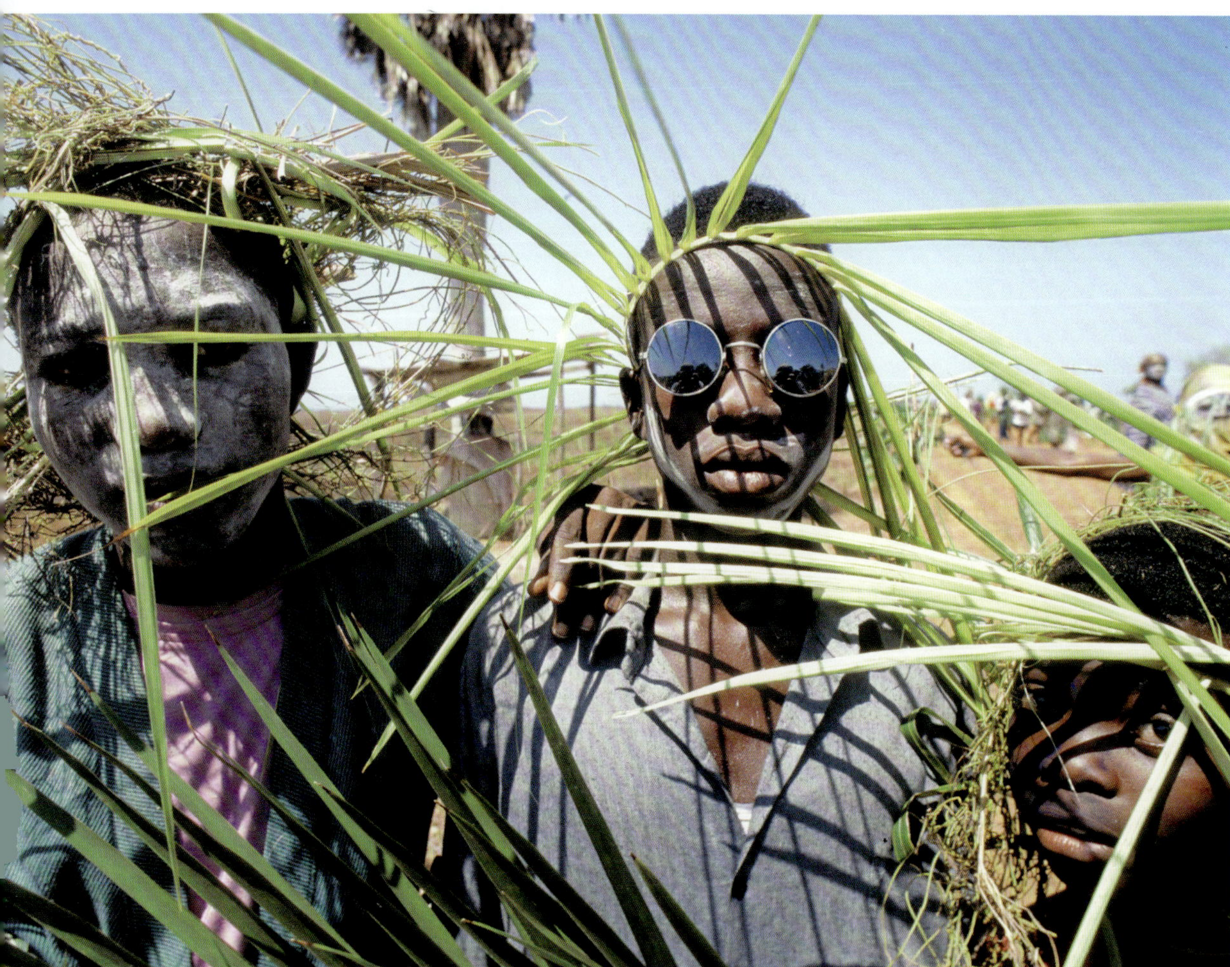

The Bush Spirits—Inhabitants of the Wild land

The wild, vast land of West Africa is home not only to the animals that the community needs to hunt, but also to a myriad of bush spirits. Some are very hostile to man, others neutral and some even friendly.

The experienced hunter, who can fall back on his own experiences and the traditions of his ancestors, succeeds in outwitting both bush spirits and animals and returning home with a good catch. Often such a expert of the wilderness also has a protective being in the realm of the bush spirits, which once revealed itself to him.

Les génies de brousse, habitants des terres sauvages

Les vastes régions sauvages d'Afrique de l'Ouest n'hébergent pas que des animaux dont la chasse est vitale pour la communauté, mais également d'innombrables génies de brousse. Nombre d'entre eux sont extrêmement hostiles aux hommes, certains sont neutres, mais beaucoup sont également sympathiques.

Le chasseur expérimenté, qui peut s'appuyer sur sa propre expérience mais aussi sur les savoirs transmis par ses prédécesseurs, parvient à tromper les génies de brousse et les animaux et à rentrer avec

Die Buschgeister – Bewohner des Wildlandes

Das wilde, weite Land Westafrikas beherbergt nicht nur die Tiere, die zu erjagen für die Gemeinschaft lebensnotwendig ist, sondern auch eine Unzahl von Buschgeistern. Manche sind dem Menschen sehr feindlich gesinnt, andere neutral und manche sogar freundlich.

Dem erfahrenen Jäger, der auf eigene Erfahrungen und die Überlieferungen seiner Vorfahren zurückgreifen kann, gelingt es, sowohl Buschgeister als auch Tiere zu überlisten und mit guter Beute

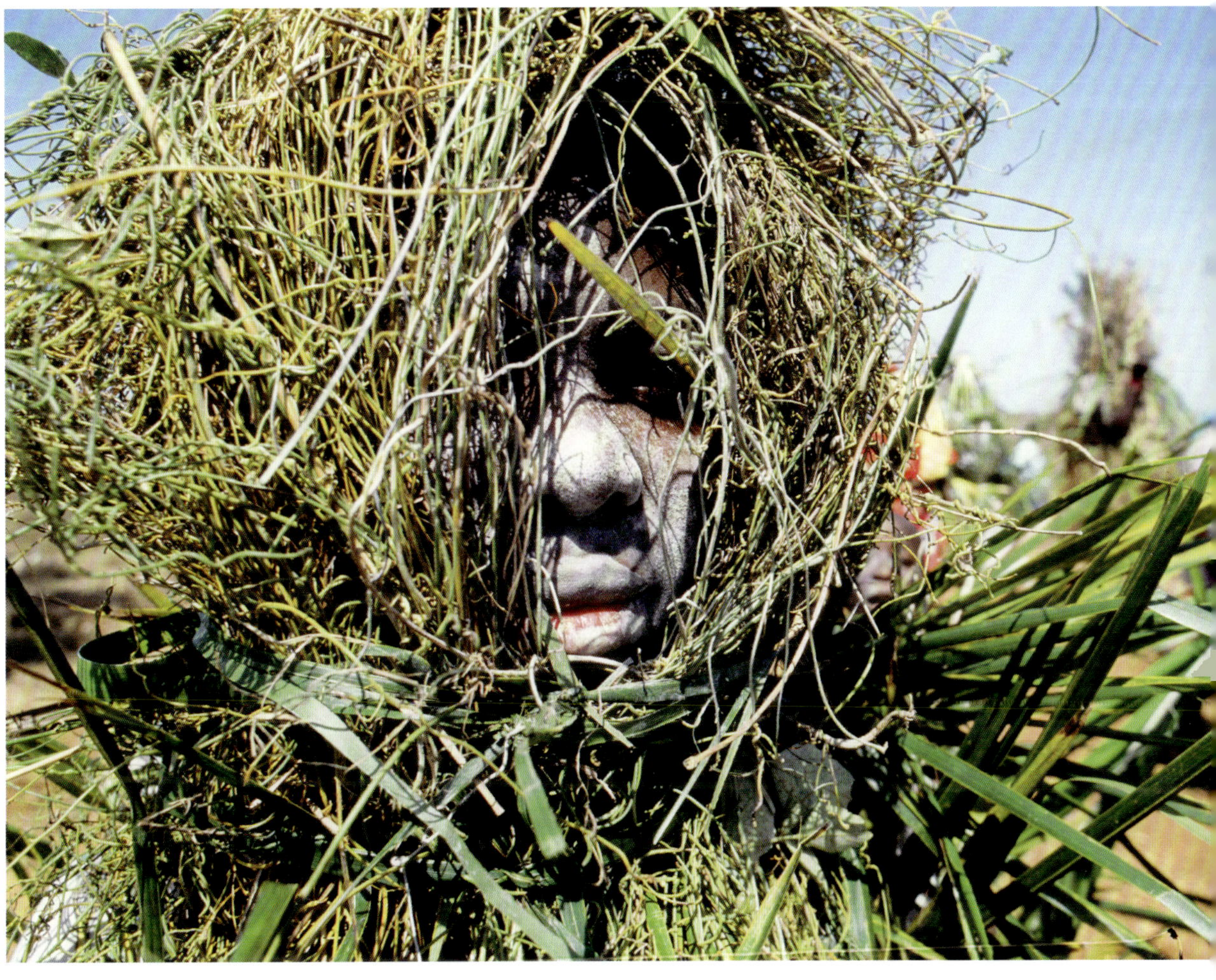

Los espíritus de Bush– Habitantes de la tierra salvaje

La vasta y salvaje tierra de África Occidental es el hogar no sólo de los animales que la comunidad necesita cazar, sino también de una miríada de espíritus arbustivos. Algunos son muy hostiles a los humanos, otros neutrales y otros incluso amistosos.

El cazador experimentado, que puede recurrir a sus propias experiencias y a las tradiciones de sus antepasados, logra burlar tanto a los espíritus de la selva como a los animales y regresar a casa con una buena presa. A menudo, tal conocedor del desierto también tiene un ser protector en el reino

Os Espíritos Bush – Habitantes da Terra Selvagem

A vasta e selvagem terra da África Ocidental é o lar não só dos animais que a comunidade precisa para caçar, mas também de uma miríade de espíritos do mato. Alguns são muito hostis aos humanos, outros são neutros e outros até amigos.

O caçador experiente, que pode recorrer às suas próprias experiências e às tradições dos seus antepassados, consegue enganar os espíritos dos arbustos e os animais e regressar a casa com uma boa presa. Muitas vezes, um tal conhecedor do deserto também tem um ser protetor no reino

De bushgeesten – bewoners van het wilde land

Het wilde, uitgestrekte land van West-Afrika herbergt niet alleen de dieren die van levensbelang zijn voor de gemeenschap, maar ook een groot aantal bushgeesten. Sommige daarvan zijn mensen erg vijandig gezind, andere zijn neutraal en sommige zijn zelfs vriendelijk te noemen.

De ervaren jager, die kan terugvallen op zijn eigen ervaringen en de tradities van zijn voorouders, slaagt erin om zowel de geesten als de dieren te slim af te zijn en met een goede prooi naar huis terug te keren. Vaak heeft zo'n kenner van de wildernis

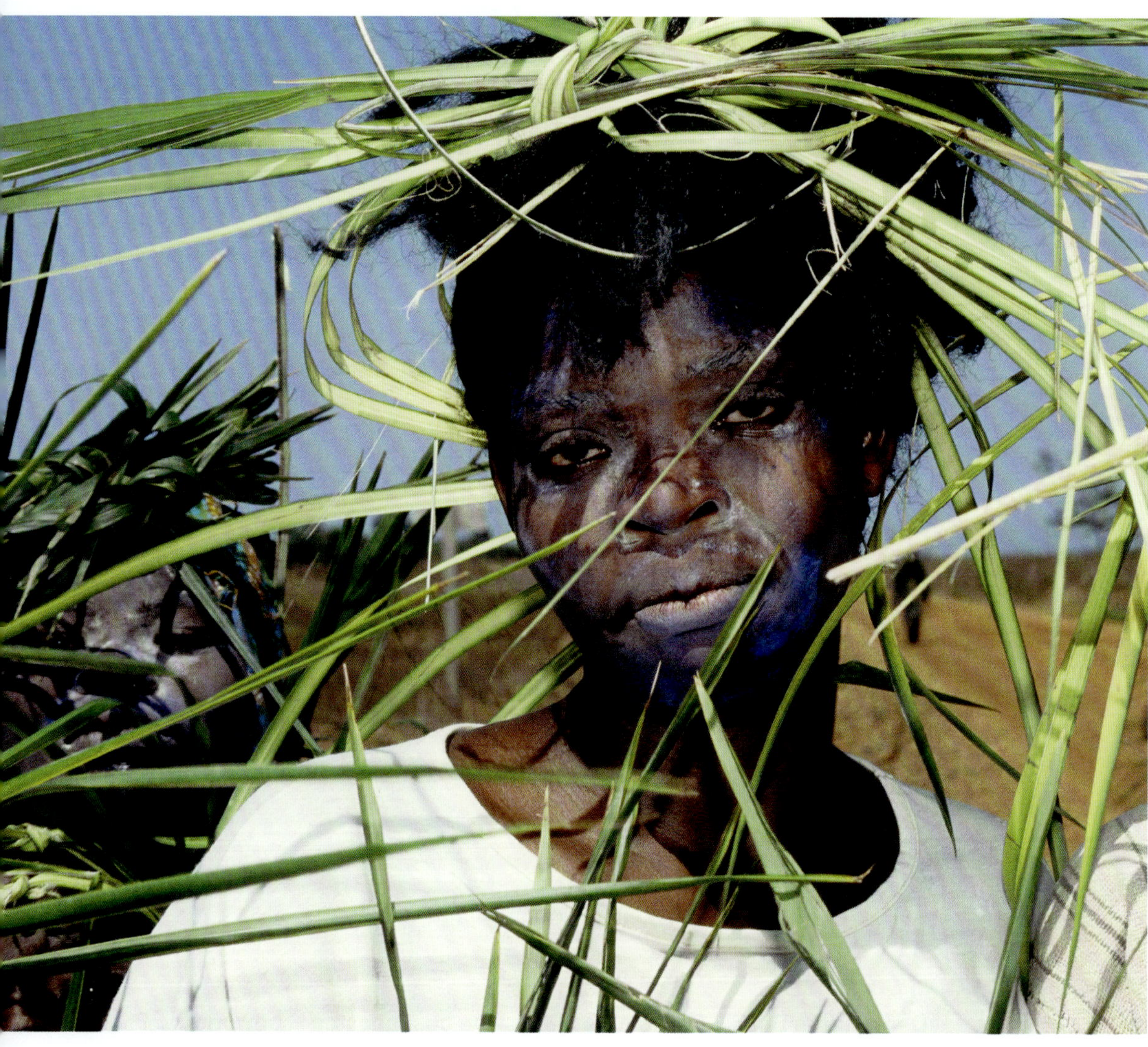

Accordingly revered, this connection can bring fertility, health and prosperity to the hunter and his family.

Many peoples therefore dedicate masks, dances and ceremonies to both the bush spirits and the spirits of the animals living in the bush.

un beau butin. Souvent, un tel spécialiste des terres sauvages possède une entité protectrice dans le royaume des génies de brousse qui s'est une fois manifestée à lui. Vénéré comme il se doit, ce personnage peut apporter fertilité, santé et prospérité au guerrier et à sa famille.

De nombreux masques, danses et cérémonies populaires sont dédiés aux génies de brousse et aux esprits des animaux qui y vivent et permettent à la population de marquer leur déférence.

heimzukehren. Oft hat ein solcher Kenner des Wildlandes auch ein Schutzwesen im Reich der Buschgeister, das sich ihm einst offenbarte. Entsprechend verehrt, kann diese Verbindung dem Jäger und seiner Familie Fruchtbarkeit, Gesundheit und Wohlstand bringen.

Sowohl den Buschgeistern als auch den Geistern der im Busch beheimateten Tiere werden daher bei vielen Völkern Masken, Tänze und Zeremonien gewidmet, mit denen man ihrer ehrfurchtsvoll gedenkt.

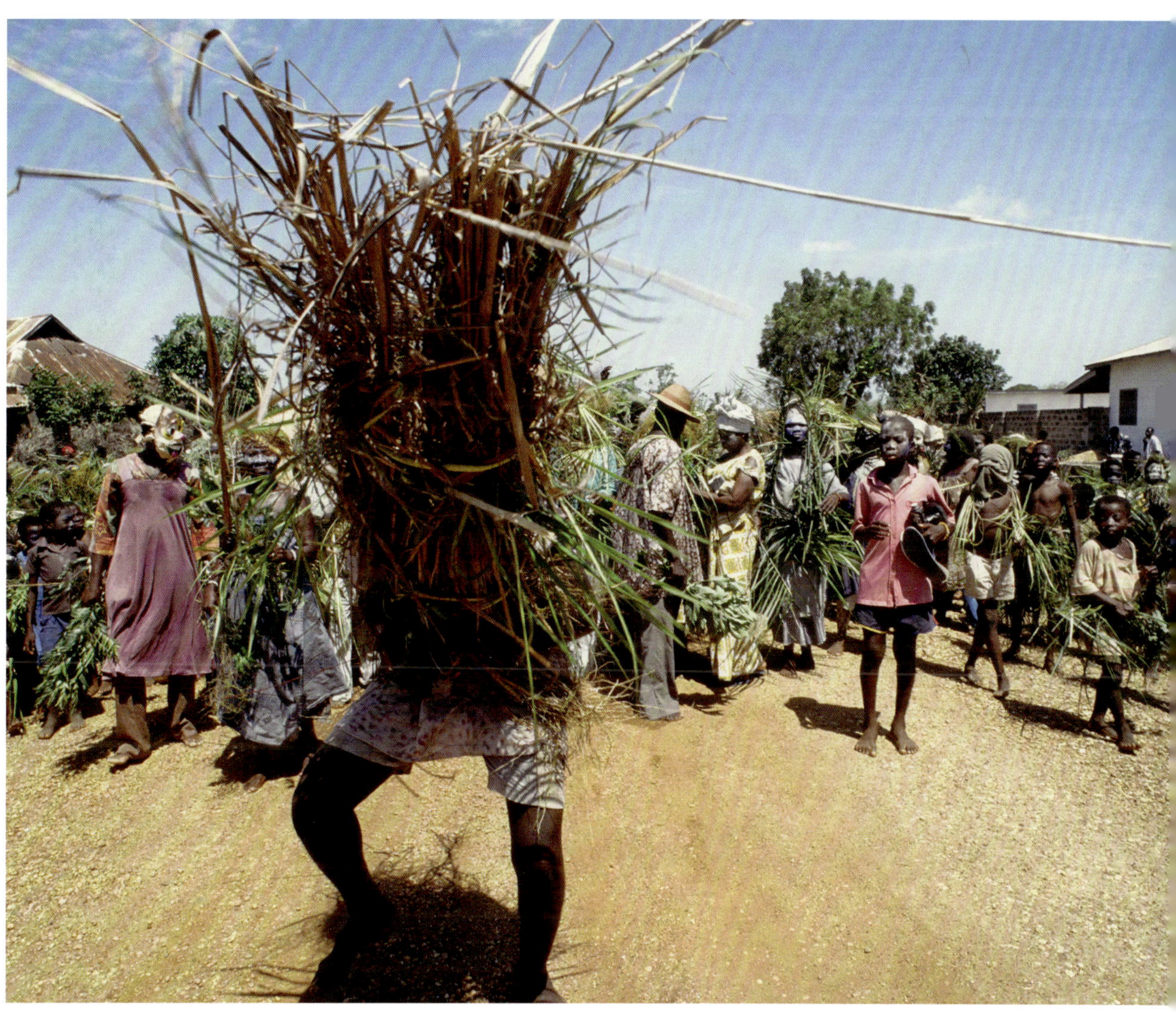

de los espíritus de los arbustos, que una vez se le reveló. Esta conexión puede traer fertilidad, salud y prosperidad al cazador y a su familia.

Muchos pueblos dedican máscaras, danzas y ceremonias a los espíritus de la selva, así como a los espíritus de los animales que viven en la selva.

dos espíritos dos arbustos, que uma vez se revelou a ele. Essa conexão pode trazer fertilidade, saúde e prosperidade para o caçador e sua família.

Muitos povos dedicam máscaras, danças e cerimônias aos espíritos do mato, bem como aos espíritos dos animais que vivem no mato.

ook een beschermend wezen in het rijk van de bushgeesten, dat zich ooit aan hem openbaarde. Deze relatie kan de jager en zijn familie vruchtbaarheid, gezondheid en welvaart brengen.

Veel mensen wijden maskers, dansen en ceremoniën aan de bushgeesten, maar ook aan de geesten van de dieren die in de rimboe leven.

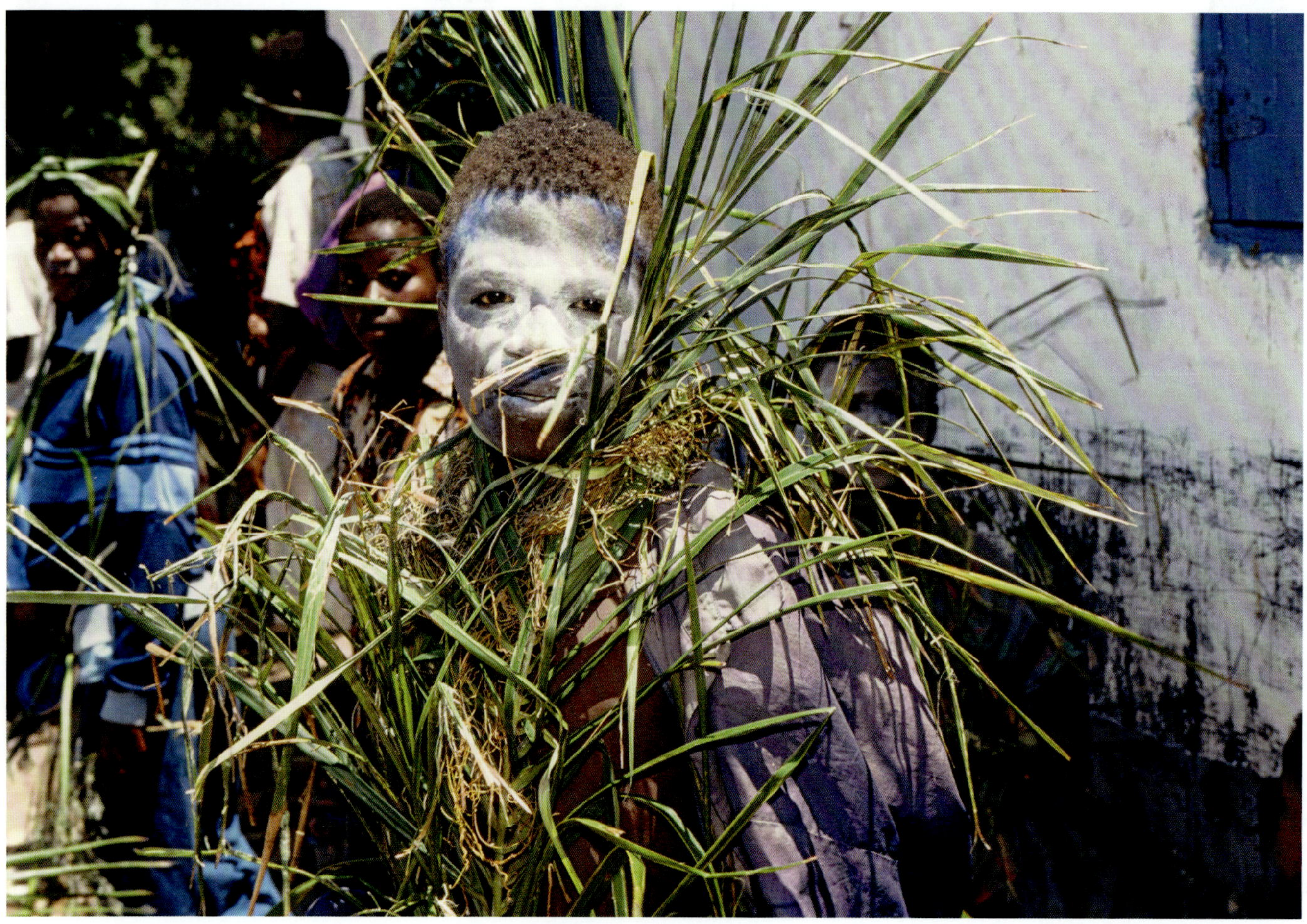

Appearance of a bush spirit. Painting their faces white is part of the masking. White is the color of death and symbolizes deceased hunters of rank among other things.

Apparition d'un génie de la brousse. Le visage entièrement enduit de blanc fait partie de la tradition. Le blanc est la couleur de la mort et symbolise notamment ici les grands chasseurs décédés.

Auftritt eines Buschgeistes. Teil der Maskierung ist die weiße Bemalung der Gesichter. Weiß ist die Farbe des Todes und symbolisiert hier unter anderem verstorbene Jäger von Rang.

Aparición de un fantasma de arbusto. Parte del enmascaramiento es la pintura blanca de las caras. El blanco es el color de la muerte y simboliza entre otras cosas a los cazadores de rango fallecidos.

Aparecimento de um fantasma arbustivo. Parte do mascaramento é a pintura branca das faces. Branco é a cor da morte e simboliza, entre outras coisas, caçadores mortos de categoria.

Het optreden van een bushgeest. Onderdeel van de maskerade is het wit schilderen van de gezichten. Wit is de kleur van de dood en symboliseert hier onder andere overleden jagers van aanzien.

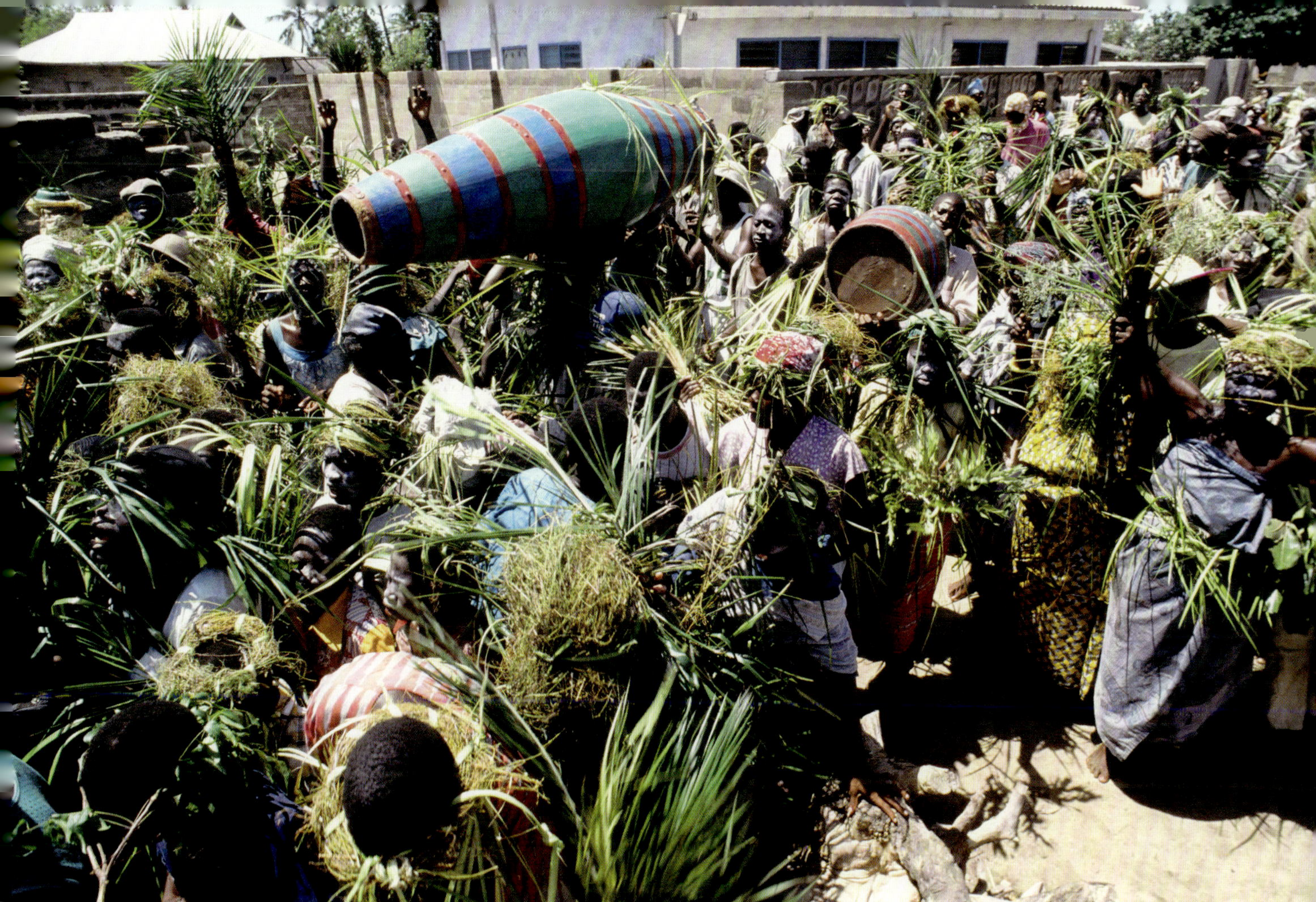

To the rhythm of the drum

Au rythme des tambours

Im Rhythmus der Trommel

Al ritmo del tambor

Ao ritmo do tambor

Op het ritme van de trommel

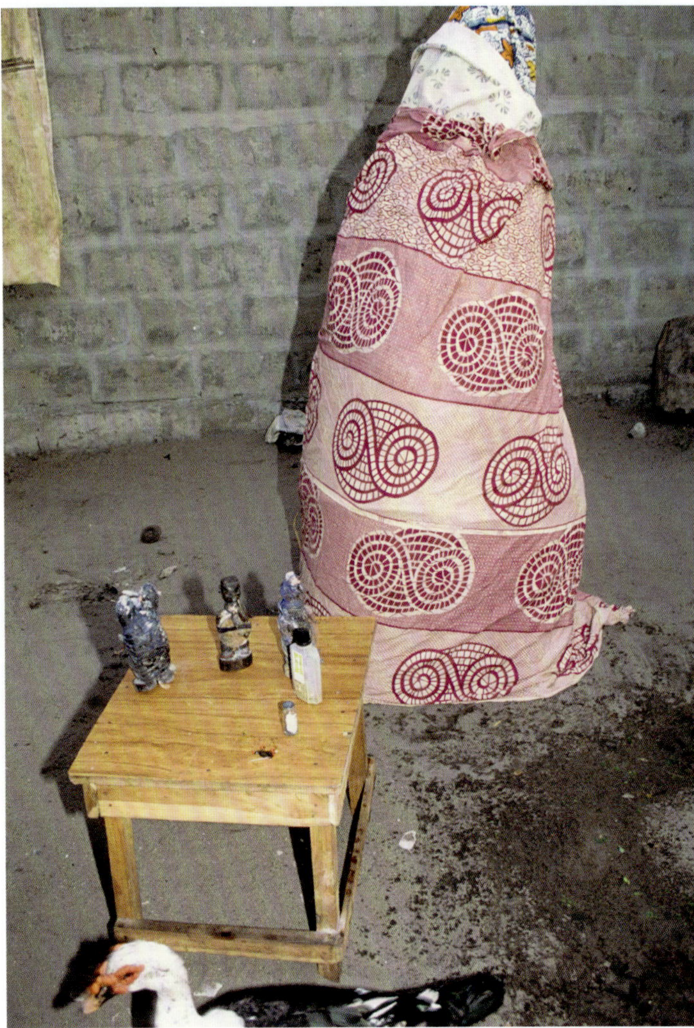

Tzakatou—healing from the African pistol

It can be found in many African countries, and it is considered a highly dangerous damaging spell. The "African pistol", the *Tzakatou,* is a powerful object with which projectiles of various kinds can be magically fired into human bodies—nails, blades, splinters, etc.—in a variety of ways.

Some Tzakatous are flat bowls whose edges show carved representations of possible ammunition, others are small pots in which parrot feathers, pieces of iron and

Le *tzakatou,* guérison contre le pistolet africain

Présent dans de nombreux pays d'Afrique, le *tzakatou* est considéré comme une magie maléfique dangereuse. Surnommé le « pistolet africain », il s'agit d'un objet occulte capable de faire pénétrer de manière magique dans le corps humain des projectiles de diverses sortes, clou, lame ou éclat notamment.

Beaucoup de *tzakatou* sont des récipients plats, dont les bords portent des représentations sculptées des munitions

Tzakatou – Heilung von der afrikanischen Pistole

Es gibt sie in vielen Ländern Afrikas, und sie gilt als brandgefährlicher Schadenzauber. Bei der „afrikanischen Pistole", der *Tzakatou,* handelt es sich um ein mächtiges Objekt, mit dem auf magische Weise Projektile unterschiedlichster Art in menschliche Körper geschossen werden können – Nägel, Klingen, Splitter et cetera.

Manche Tzakatous sind flache Schalen, deren Ränder geschnitzte Darstellungen der möglichen Munition

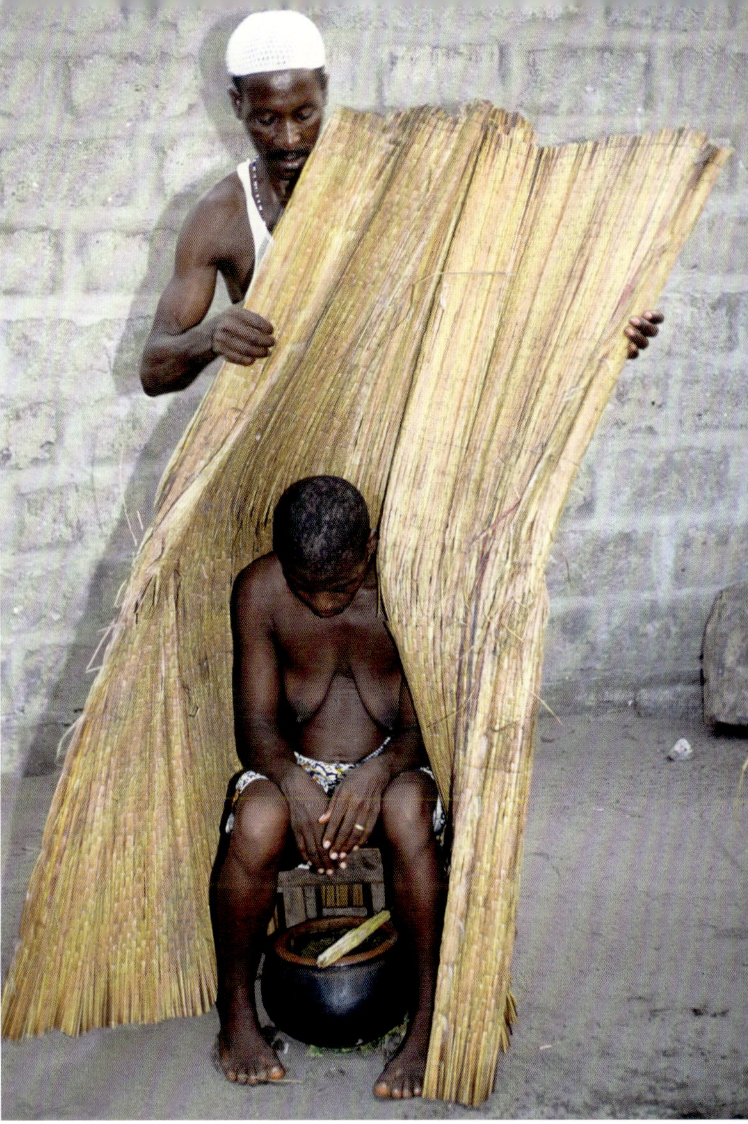

Tzakatou– La curación de la pistola africana

Se puede encontrar en muchos países africanos, y se considera un hechizo maligno muy peligroso. La "pistola africana", el *Tzakatou,* es un objeto poderoso que puede ser utilizado para disparar proyectiles de todo tipo en el cuerpo humano –clavos, espadas, astillas, etc.– de diversas maneras.

Algunos tzakatous son cuencos planos cuyos bordes muestran representaciones talladas de posibles municiones, otros son pequeñas ollas en las que se mezclan plumas

Tzakatou – A cura da pistola africana

Pode ser encontrada em muitos países africanos e é considerada um feitiço de danos altamente perigoso. A "Pistola Africana", a Tzakatou, é um objecto poderoso que pode ser usado para disparar magicamente projécteis de todos os tipos em corpos humanos – pregos, lâminas, lascas, etc. – de várias formas.

Alguns Tzakatous são tigelas planas cujas bordas mostram representações esculpidas de possíveis munições, outros são pequenos

Tzakatou – genezing van het Afrikaanse pistool

Het komt in veel Afrikaanse landen voor en wordt beschouwd als een brandgevaarlijke boze tovenarij. Het 'Afrikaanse pistool', de tzakatou, is een krachtig voorwerp waarmee op magische wijze allerlei projectielen in het menselijk lichaam kunnen worden geschoten: spijkers, messen, splinters, enzovoort.

Sommige tzakatou's zijn ondiepe kommen in de randen waarvan afbeeldingen van mogelijke munitie zijn

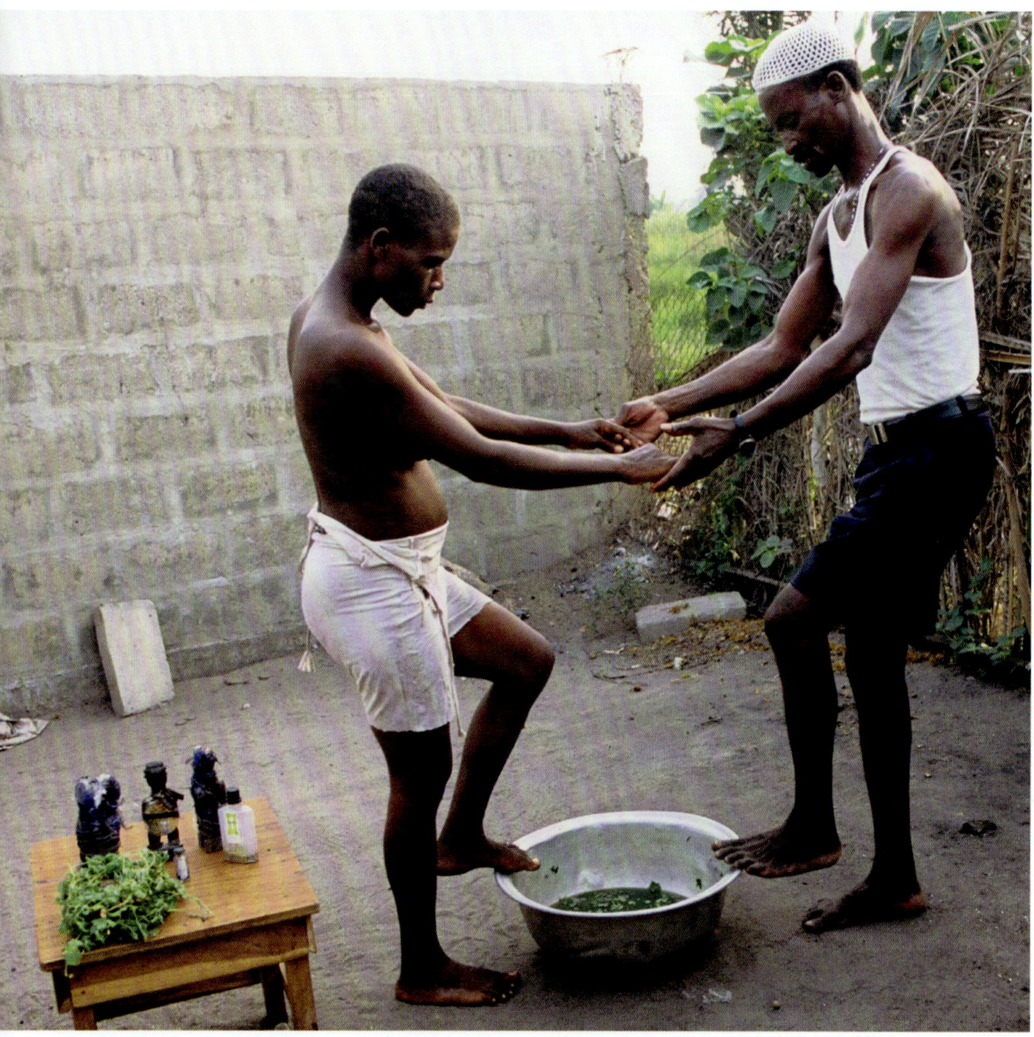

cowrie shells are combined together with secret substances.

Every Tuesday the Tzakatou is ready for use with the help of certain formulas in combination with a blood sacrifice. Few specialists understand how to cure their victims. This is accompanied by a sweat lodge ritual lasting several days in which the projectiles leave the body again.

possibles, d'autres sont de petits pots dans lesquels sont préparés des mélanges constitués de plumes de perroquets, de morceaux de fer, de cauris et de substances secrètes.

Le *tzakatou* est toujours prêt à entrer en action le mardi avec l'aide de formules spécifiques associées à un sacrifice. Rares sont les spécialistes capables de guérir ses victimes. Le processus implique un rituel de plusieurs jours dans une hutte de sudation, au cours duquel les projectiles vont quitter le corps.

zeigen, andere wiederum kleine Töpfe, in denen Papageienfedern, Eisenstücke und Kaurischnecken zusammen mit geheimen Substanzen verarbeitet sind.

Immer dienstags ist die Tzakatou mit Hilfe von bestimmten Formeln in Kombination mit einem Blutopfer einsatzbereit. Nur wenige Spezialisten verstehen sich auf die Heilung ihrer Opfer. Diese geht mit einem mehrtägigen Schwitzhüttenritual einher, in welchem die Projektile den Körper wieder verlassen.

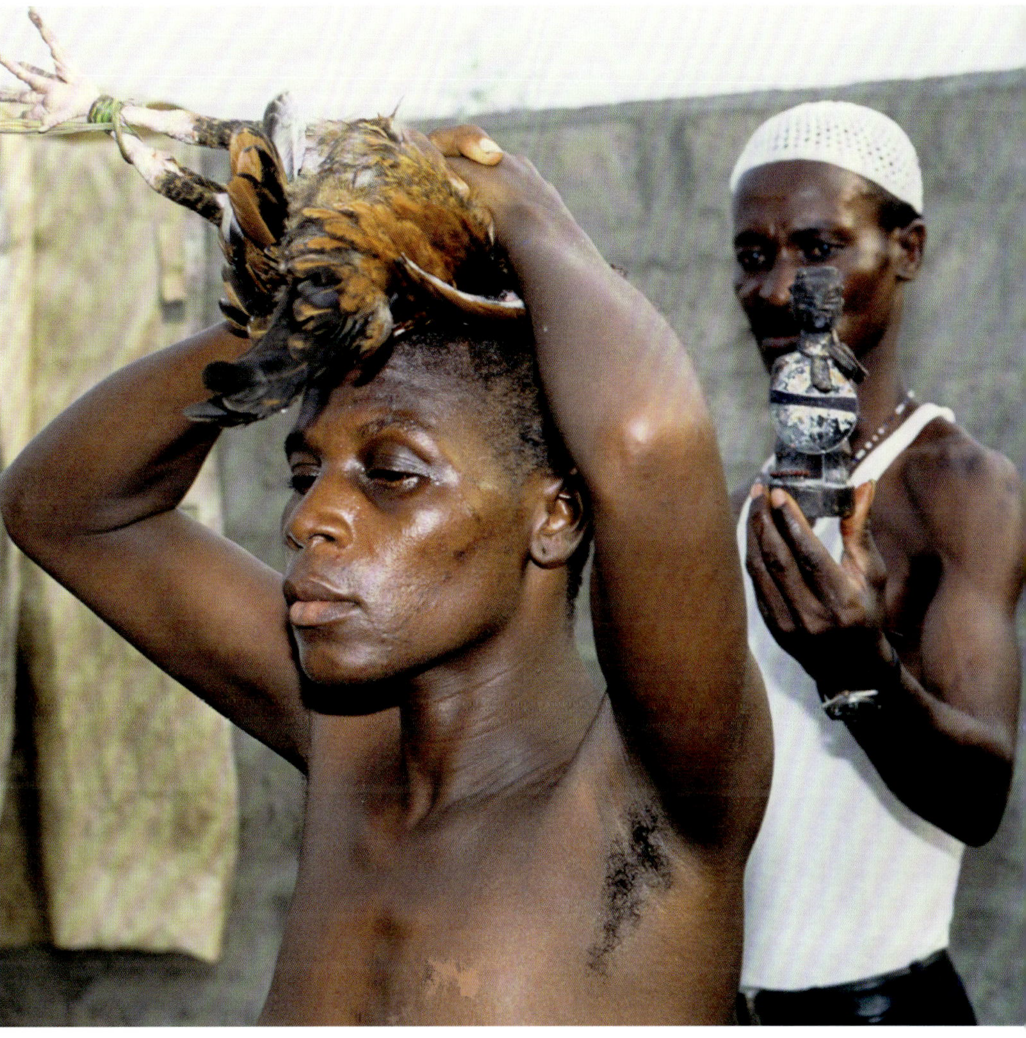

Treatment of a Tzakatou victim. The red cock on the head of the patient is for the Vodun Shango and is supposed to draw evil out of her body before it is sacrificed. Parallel to this, the priest uses a protective Bocio.

Traitement d'une victime de *tzakatou*. La poule rousse placée sur la tête du patient est destinée au vodun Shangô et doit, avant d'être sacrifiée, extirper le mal du corps. Le prêtre fait également intervenir un bocio protecteur.

Behandlung eines Tzakatou-Opfers. Der rote Hahn auf dem Kopf der Patientin ist für den Vodun Shango und soll, bevor er geopfert wird, das Böse aus ihrem Körper ziehen. Der Priester setzt parallel dazu einen Schutzbocio ein.

Tratamiento de una víctima de Tzakatou. El pollo rojo en la cabeza de la paciente es para el vudú Shango y se supone que saca el mal de su cuerpo antes de que sea sacrificado. Al mismo tiempo, el sacerdote utiliza un Bocio protector.

Tratamento de uma vítima de Tzakatou. O galo vermelho na cabeça do paciente é para o Vodun Shango e é suposto tirar o mal do seu corpo antes que ele seja sacrificado. Ao mesmo tempo, o padre usa um Bocio protector.

Behandeling van een tzakatou-slachtoffer. De rode haan op het hoofd van de patiënte is voor de vodun Shango en zou het kwaad uit haar lichaam trekken voordat hij wordt geofferd. Tegelijkertijd gebruikt de priester een beschermende bocio.

de loro, piezas de hierro y caracoles de santo junto con sustancias secretas.

Cada martes el Tzakatou está listo para ser utilizado con la ayuda de ciertas fórmulas en combinación con un sacrificio de sangre. Sólo unos pocos especialistas saben cómo curar a sus víctimas. Esto se acompaña de un ritual de cámara de sudación de varios días en el que los proyectiles vuelven a salir del cuerpo.

vasos em que penas de papagaio, pedaços de ferro e caracóis cowrie são trabalhados em conjunto com substâncias secretas.

Todas as terças-feiras o Tzakatou está pronto para ser usado com a ajuda de certas fórmulas em combinação com um sacrifício de sangue. Apenas alguns especialistas sabem como curar as suas vítimas. Este é acompanhado por um ritual de sweat lodge que dura vários dias, em que os projécteis deixam o corpo novamente.

uitgesneden, bij andere gaat het om potjes waarin papegaaienveren, stukjes ijzer en kaurischelpen met andere geheime bestanddelen worden verwerkt.

Elke dinsdag is de tzakatou met behulp van bepaalde formules in combinatie met een bloedoffer klaar voor gebruik. Slechts enkele specialisten weten hoe ze hun slachtoffers kunnen genezen. Dit gaat gepaard met een meerdaags zweethutritueel waarbij de projectielen het lichaam weer verlaten.

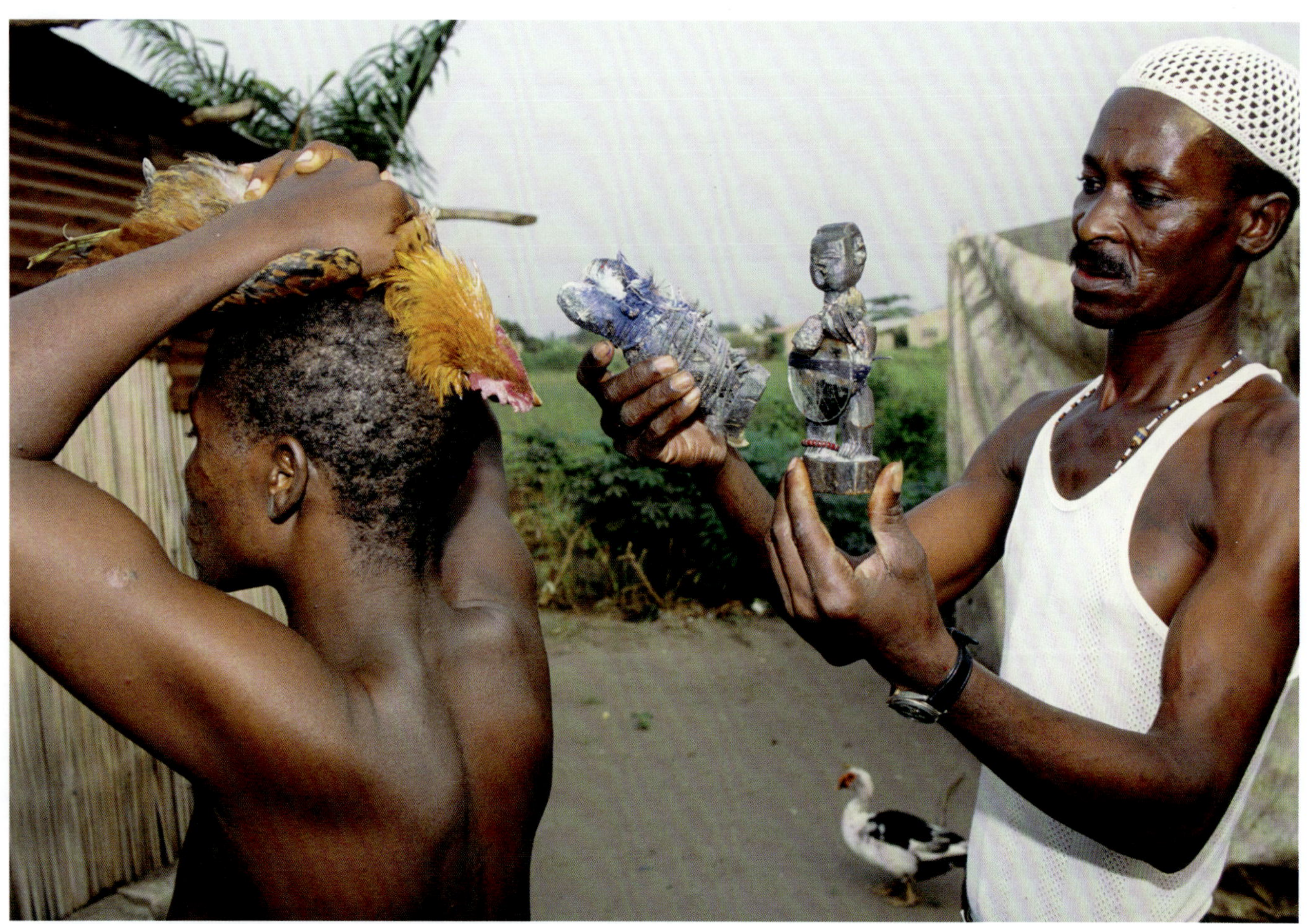

The goal is the removal of projectiles

L'objectif est de retirer les projectiles

Das Ziel ist die Entfernung der Projektile

El objetivo es la eliminación de proyectiles

O objectivo é a remoção de projécteis

Het doel is de projectielen te verwijderen

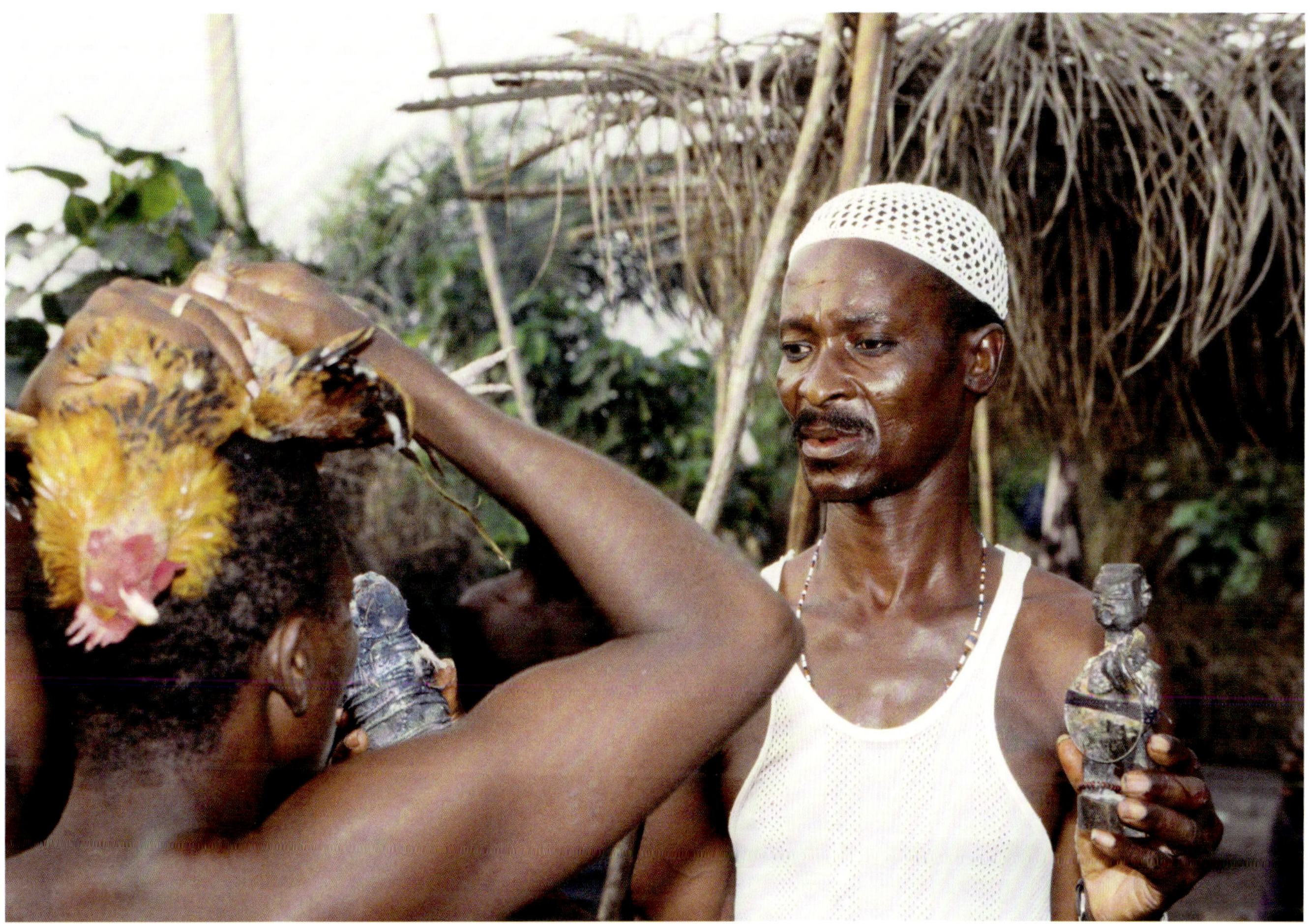

Treatment of a Tzakatou victim. The aim is to magically remove the projectiles shot into the victim such as glass splinters, nails, blades and screws. It's the only way the patient can survive the harmful spell.

Traitement d'une victime de *tzakatou*.
La victime doit être débarrassée des projectiles, éclats de verre, clous, lames ou vis, qui ont magiquement pénétré dans son corps. Telle est l'unique solution pour qu'elle survive à la magie maléfique.

Behandlung eines Tzakatou-Opfers. Es gilt, die auf magische Weise in das Opfer geschossenen Projektile wie Glassplitter, Nägel, Klingen und Schrauben wieder zu entfernen. Nur so kann der Patient den Schadenzauber überleben.

Tratamiento de una víctima de Tzakatou.
El objetivo es retirar por arte de magia los proyectiles disparados a la víctima, como fragmentos de vidrio, clavos, cuchillas y tornillos. Esta es la única forma en que el paciente puede sobrevivir al hechizo maligno.

Tratamento de uma vítima de Tzakatou.
O objectivo é remover magicamente os projécteis disparados contra a vítima, tais como fragmentos de vidro, pregos, lâminas e parafusos. Esta é a única forma de o paciente sobreviver ao feitiço de danos.

Behandeling van een tzakatou-slachtoffer. Het doel is om op magische wijze de projectielen te verwijderen die in het slachtoffer zijn geschoten, zoals glasscherven, spijkers, messen en schroeven. Dit is de enige manier waarop de patiënt de tovenarij kan overleven.

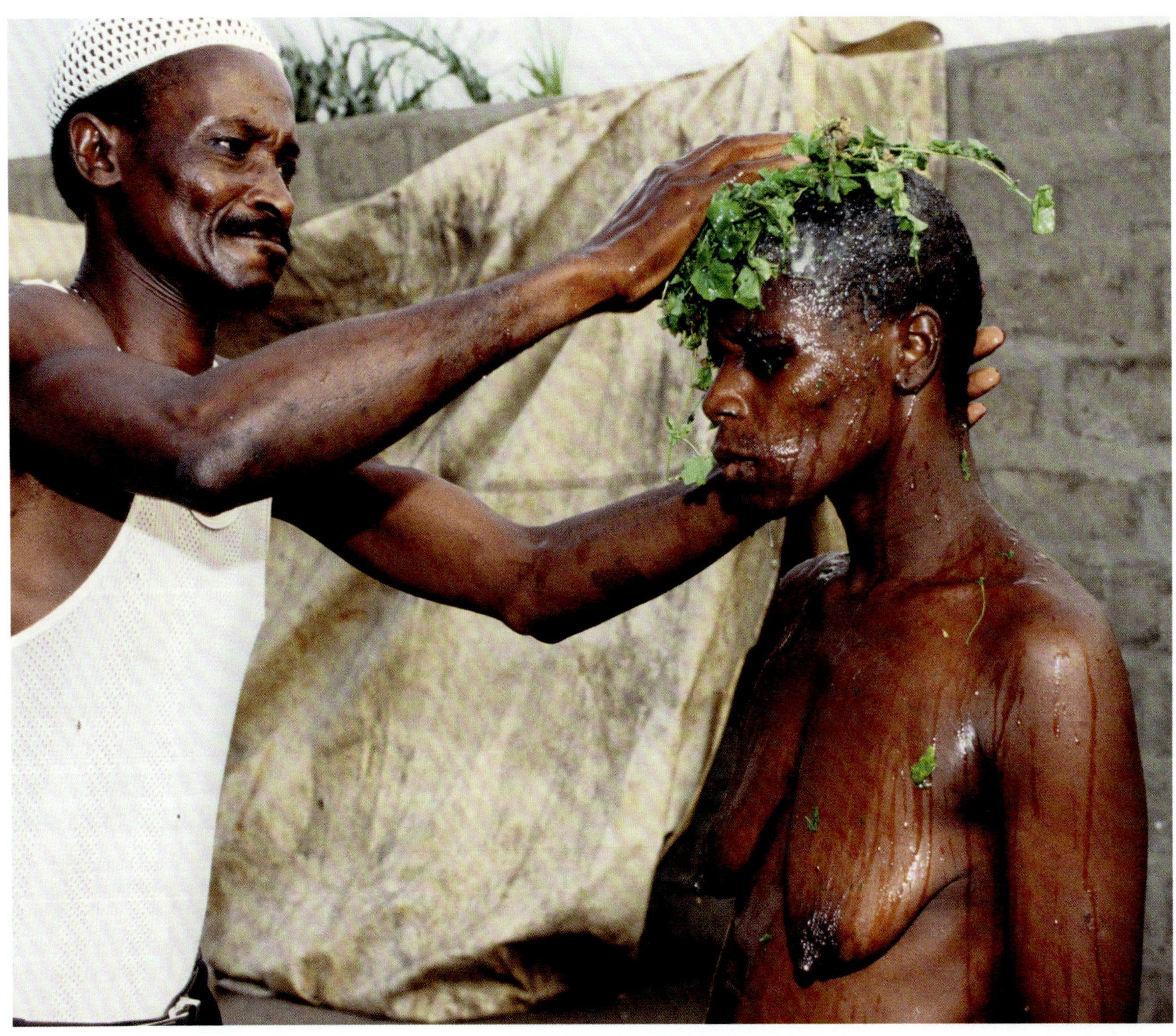

Treatment of a Tzakatou victim

Traitement d'une victime de *tzakatou*

Behandlung eines Tzakatou-Opfers

Tratamiento de una víctima de Tzakatou

Tratamento de uma vítima de Tzakatou

Behandeling van een tzakatou-slachtoffer

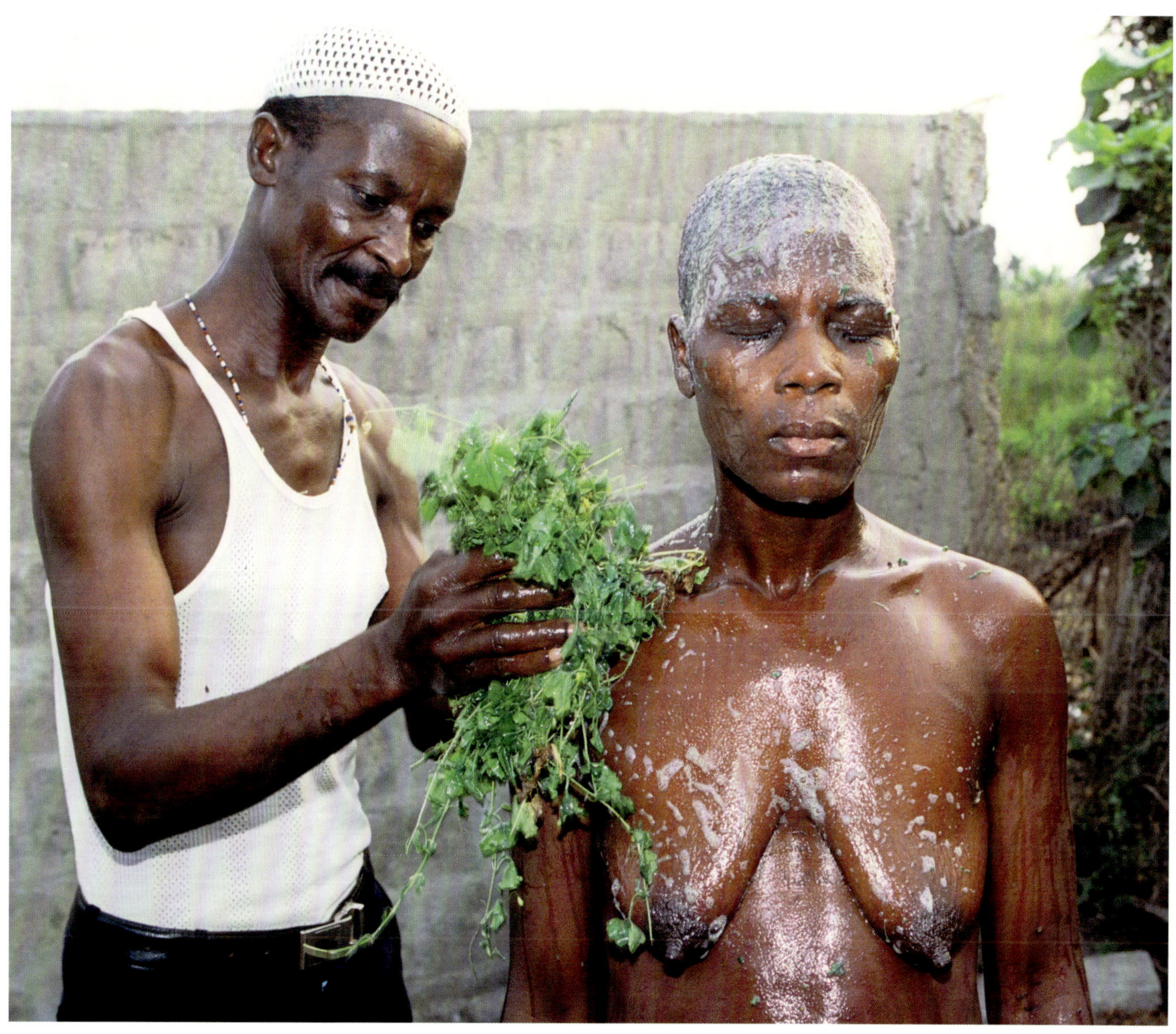

Medicinal plants are always present

Les plantes médicinales sont toujours présentes

Heilpflanzen sind immer dabei

Las plantas medicinales están siempre presentes

As plantas medicinais estão sempre presentes

Geneeskrachtige planten zijn altijd aanwezig

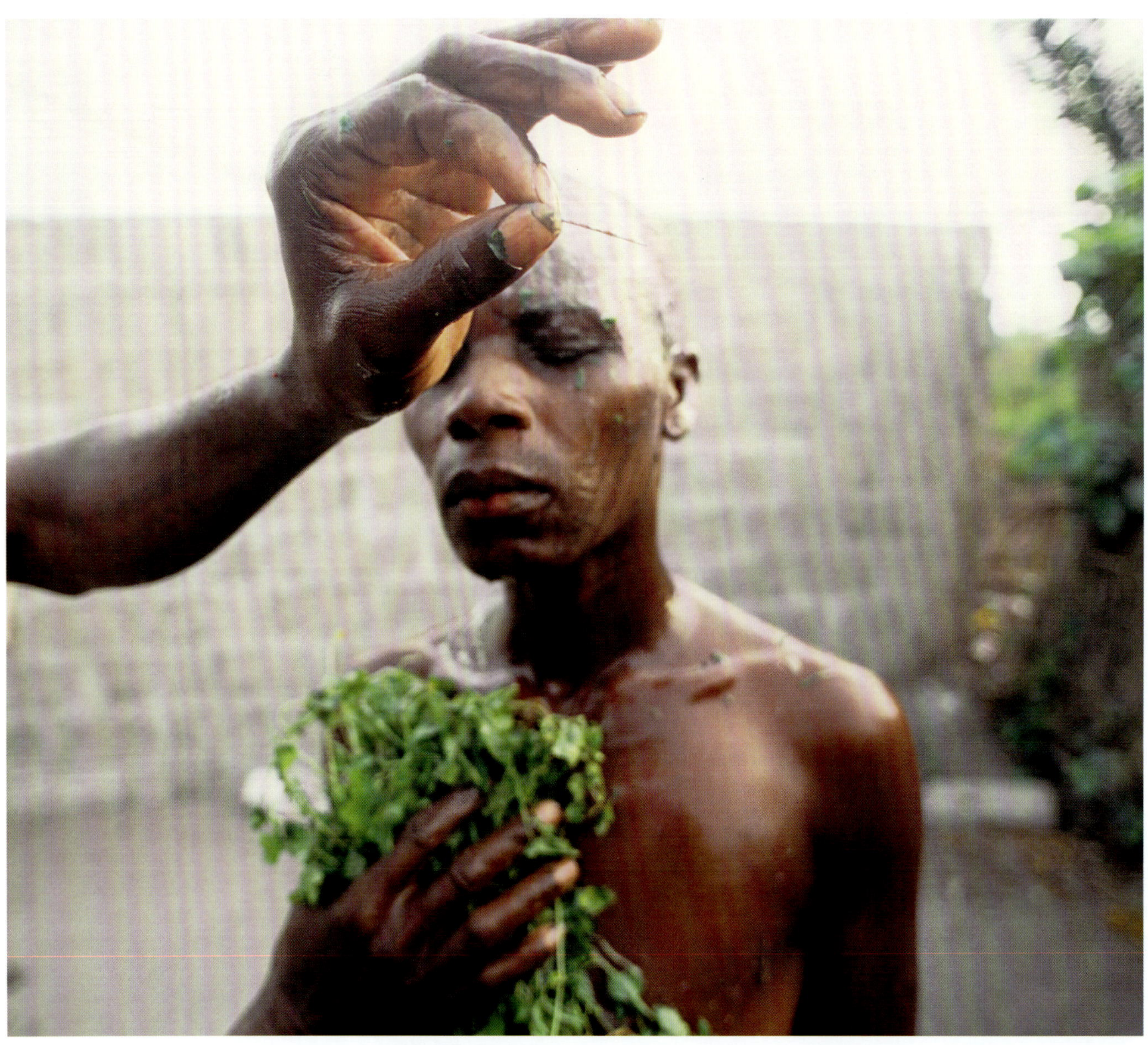

When the projectiles leave the body. After advanced treatment, pustules and purulent blisters form on the patient's body. From these places the projectiles—here a needle—emerge again.

Quand les projectiles quittent le corps. Au terme d'un traitement complexe, des pustules et des cloques purulentes se forment sur le corps de la patiente. C'est par ce biais que les projectiles, dans ce cas une aiguille, sortent du corps.

Wenn die Projektile den Körper verlassen. Nach fortgeschrittener Behandlung bilden sich Pusteln und eitrige Blasen am Körper der Patientin. An diesen Stellen treten die Projektile – hier eine Nadel – wieder aus.

Cuando los proyectiles abandonan el cuerpo. Después de un tratamiento avanzado, se forman pústulas y ampollas purulentas en el cuerpo del paciente. En estos lugares los proyectiles –aquí una aguja– emergen de nuevo.

Quando os projécteis deixam o corpo.. Após tratamento avançado, formam-se pústulas e bolhas purulentas no corpo do paciente. Nesses lugares os projécteis – aqui uma agulha – emergem novamente.

Wanneer de projectielen het lichaam verlaten. Na een gevorderde behandeling ontstaan er puisten en etterige blaren op het lichaam van de patiënte. Op deze plekken komen de projectielen (hier een naald) weer tevoorschijn.

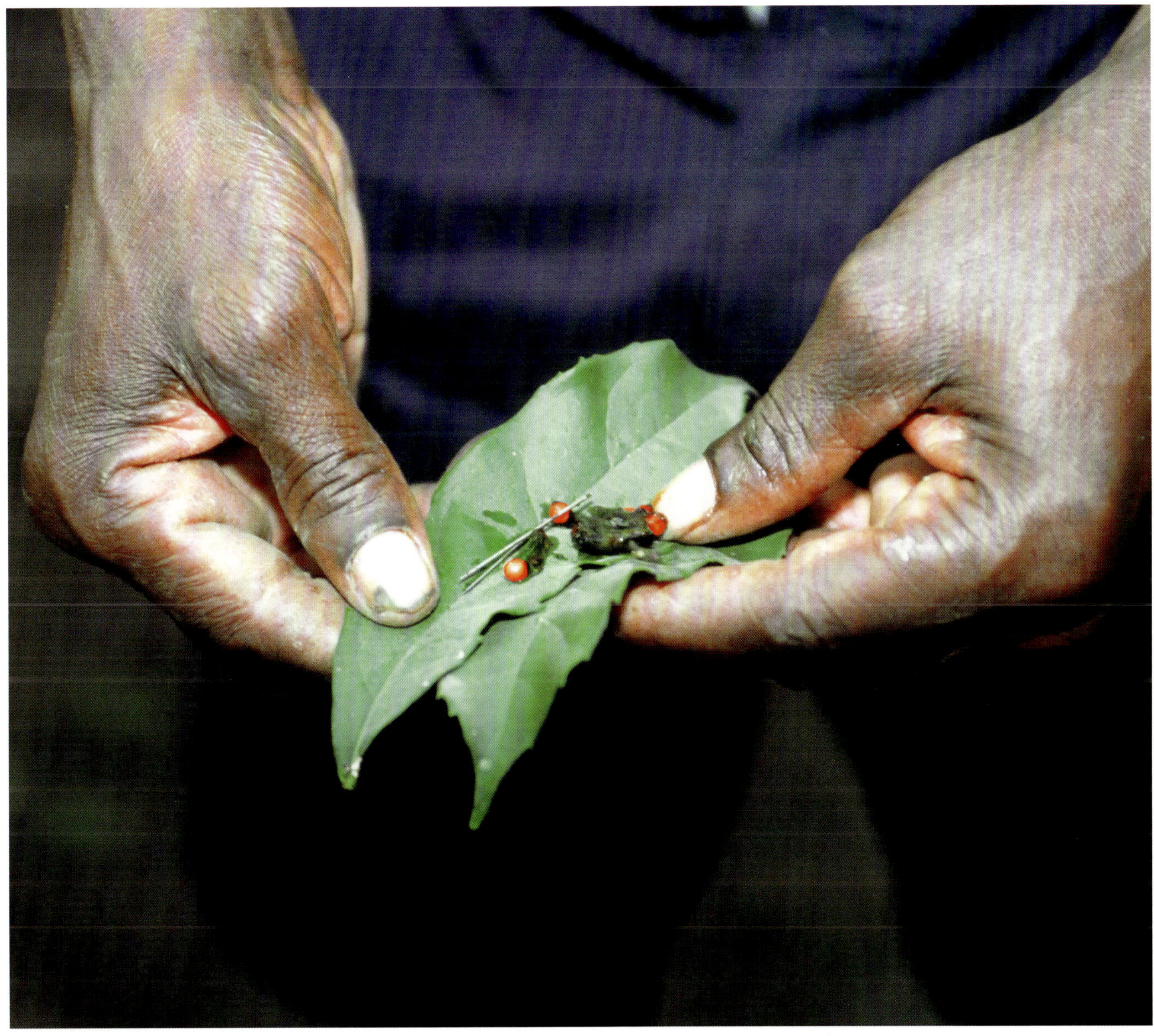

Escape from death. After removing the foreign bodies, the worst is over and the danger of death is averted. Various projectiles have left the body and remain with the priest for safety's sake.

Échapper à la mort. Après expulsion du corps étranger, le pire a été évité et la victime n'est plus en danger de mort. Divers projectiles sont sortis du corps et sont conservés par le prêtre pour plus de sécurité.

Dem Tode entronnen. Nach der Entfernung der Fremdkörper ist das Schlimmste überstanden und die Todesgefahr abgewendet. Diverse Projektile haben den Körper verlassen und verbleiben sicherheitshalber beim Priester.

Escapar de la muerte. Después de retirar los cuerpos extraños, lo peor ha pasado y se evita el peligro de muerte. Varios proyectiles han abandonado el cuerpo y permanecen con el sacerdote por seguridad.

Fugir da morte. Após a remoção dos corpos estranhos, o pior já passou e o perigo de morte foi evitado. Vários projécteis deixaram o corpo e permanecem com o padre por segurança.

Ontsnapt aan de dood. Na het verwijderen van de vreemde voorwerpen is het ergste leed geleden en wordt het doodsgevaar afgewend. Diverse projectielen hebben het lichaam verlaten en blijven veiligheidshalve bij de priester.

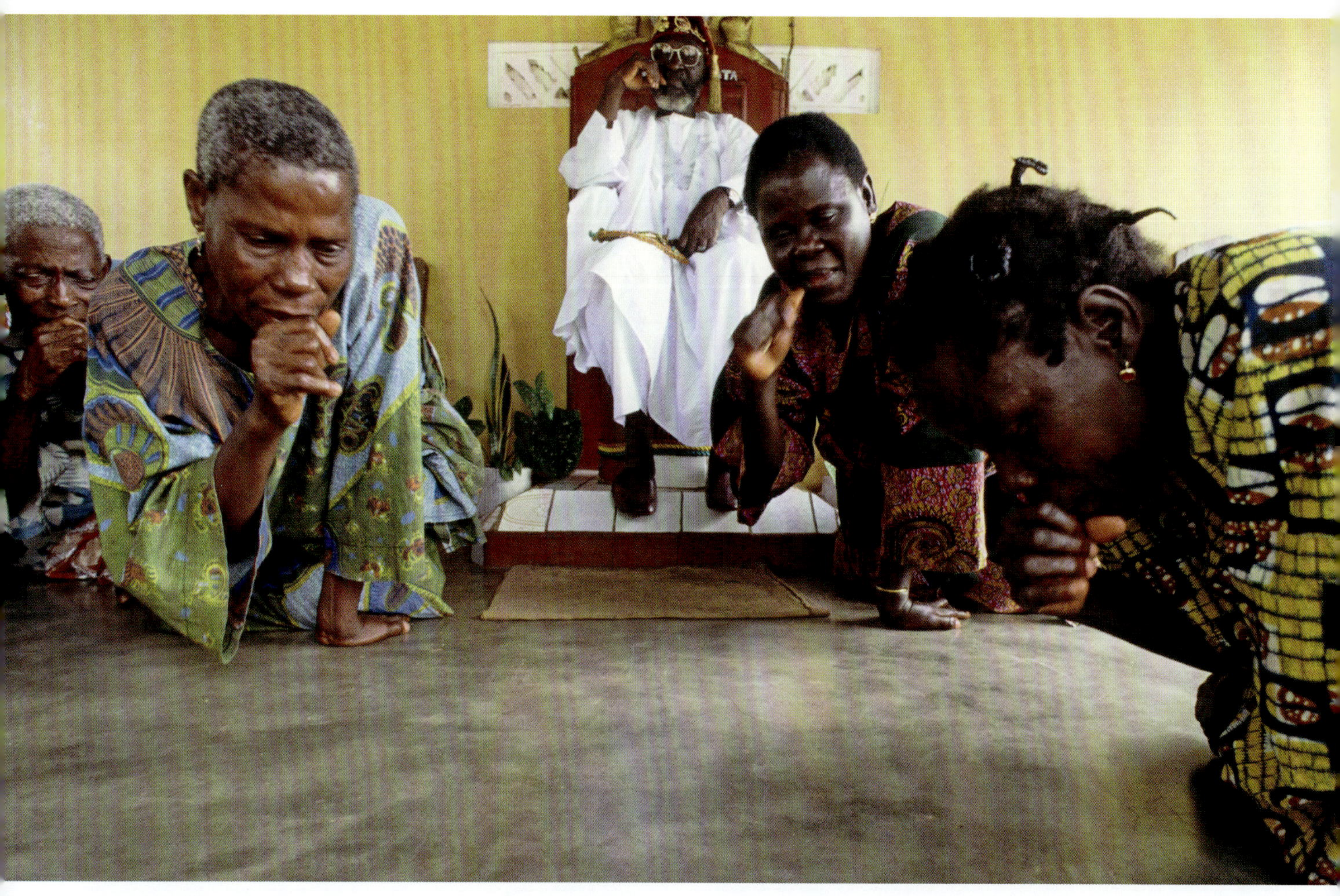

Sergent Kiki—at the gods' command

Sergent Kiki is an extraordinary personality in the world of the Vodun priests. He never gave up his title, which he received under Charles de Gaulle. The virtues that are at best attributed to members of the army - such as punctuality, order, discipline—were applied and adhered to by him throughout his life in all areas, including in his capacity as a Vodun priest.

His temple, in which the family god Abessan is worshipped, is characterized by extreme accuracy and order. The surrounding stones are as white as pearls,

Sergent Kiki, aux ordres des dieux

Sergent Kiki est une personnalité extraordinaire dans le monde des prêtres vodun. Son titre, obtenu sous l'autorité de Charles de Gaulle, lui est toujours resté. Les vertus que l'on attribue à l'armée, dans le meilleur des cas, telles que la ponctualité, l'ordre et la discipline, ont toujours été appliquées à tous les domaines de sa vie, y compris dans sa pratique vodun.

Son temple, dans lequel est vénéré le dieu de la famille Abessan, se caractérise par un ordonnancement impeccable. Les pierres qui l'entourent sont d'un blanc perle, les sols impeccables et le fétiche central,

Sergent Kiki – den Göttern zu Befehl

Eine außergewöhnliche Persönlichkeit in der Welt der Vodunpriester ist Sergent Kiki, der seinen unter Charles de Gaulle erhaltenen Titel nie abgelegt hat. Die Tugenden, die man Angehörigen der Armee im besten Fall zuschreibt – wie etwa Pünktlichkeit, Ordnung, Disziplin – wurden von ihm zeitlebens in allen Bereichen angewandt und fortgeführt, so auch in seiner Eigenschaft als Vodunpriester.

Sein Tempel, in dem der Familiengott Abessan verehrt wird, zeichnet sich durch äußerste Akkuratesse aus. Die ihn

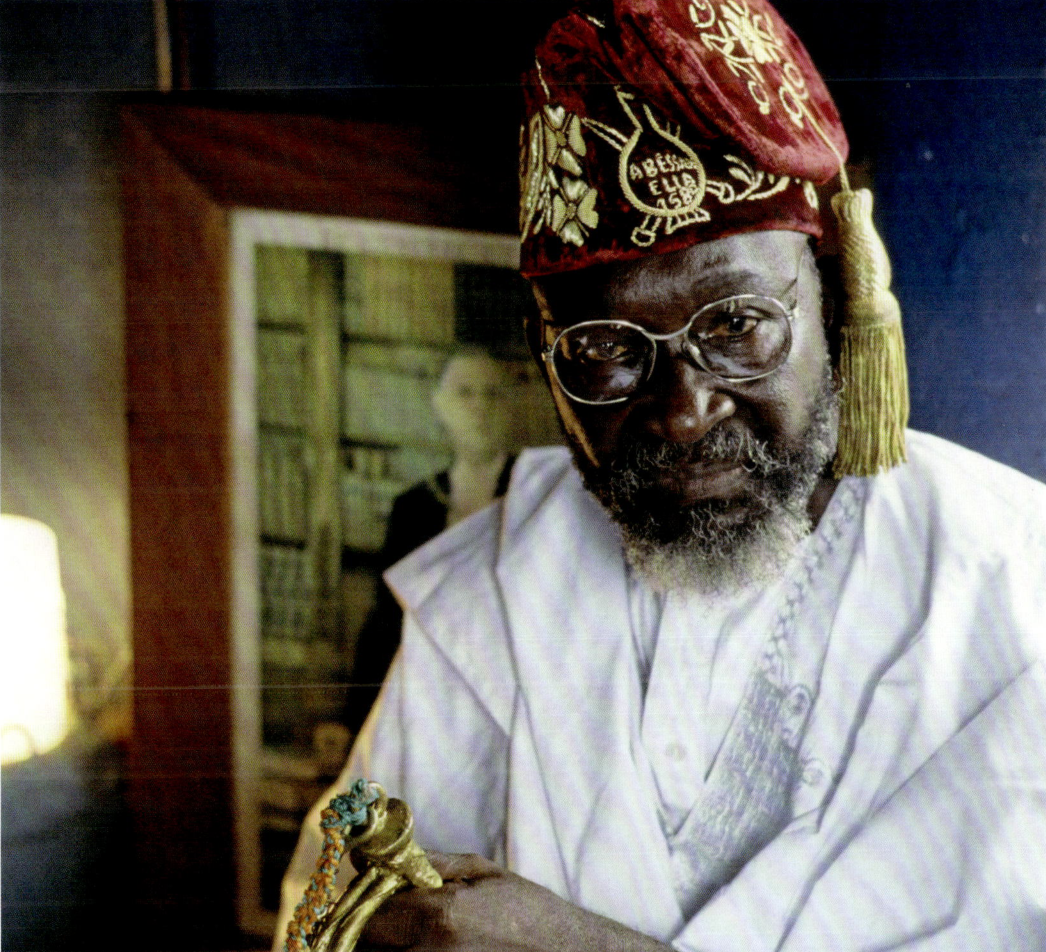

Sargento Kiki, a las órdenes de los dioses

El Sargento Kiki es una personalidad extraordinaria en el mundo de los sacerdotes vudúes, nunca renunció a su título, que fue conservado bajo la dirección de Charles de Gaulle. Las virtudes atribuidas a los miembros del ejército, tales como la puntualidad, el orden y la disciplina, fueron aplicadas y continuadas por él a lo largo de su vida en todos los ámbitos, incluso en su calidad de vudú.

Su templo, en el que se adora al dios de la familia Abessan, se caracteriza por su extrema precisión. Las piedras circundantes

Sergent Kiki – Ao comando dos deuses

Sergent Kiki é uma personalidade extraordinária no mundo dos padres Vodun. Ele nunca desistiu de seu título, que foi preservado sob Charles de Gaulle. As virtudes atribuídas aos membros do exército, na melhor das hipóteses - tais como pontualidade, ordem, disciplina - foram aplicadas e continuadas por ele durante toda a sua vida, em todas as áreas, inclusive na sua qualidade de vodo-sacerdote.

Seu templo, no qual o deus da família Abessan é adorado, é caracterizado pela extrema precisão. As pedras circundantes

Sergeant Kiki – op bevel van de goden

Sergeant Kiki is een buitengewone persoonlijkheid in de wereld van de vodunpriesters. Hij heeft zijn titel, die bewaard is gebleven onder Charles de Gaulle, nooit opgegeven. De deugden die aan soldaten van het leger werden toegeschreven – zoals stiptheid, orde, discipline – zijn door hem zijn hele leven op alle gebieden toegepast en doorgevoerd, ook in zijn hoedanigheid als vodunpriester.

Zijn tempel, waarin de familiegod Abessan wordt vereerd, wordt gekenmerkt door extreme accuratesse. De stenen die

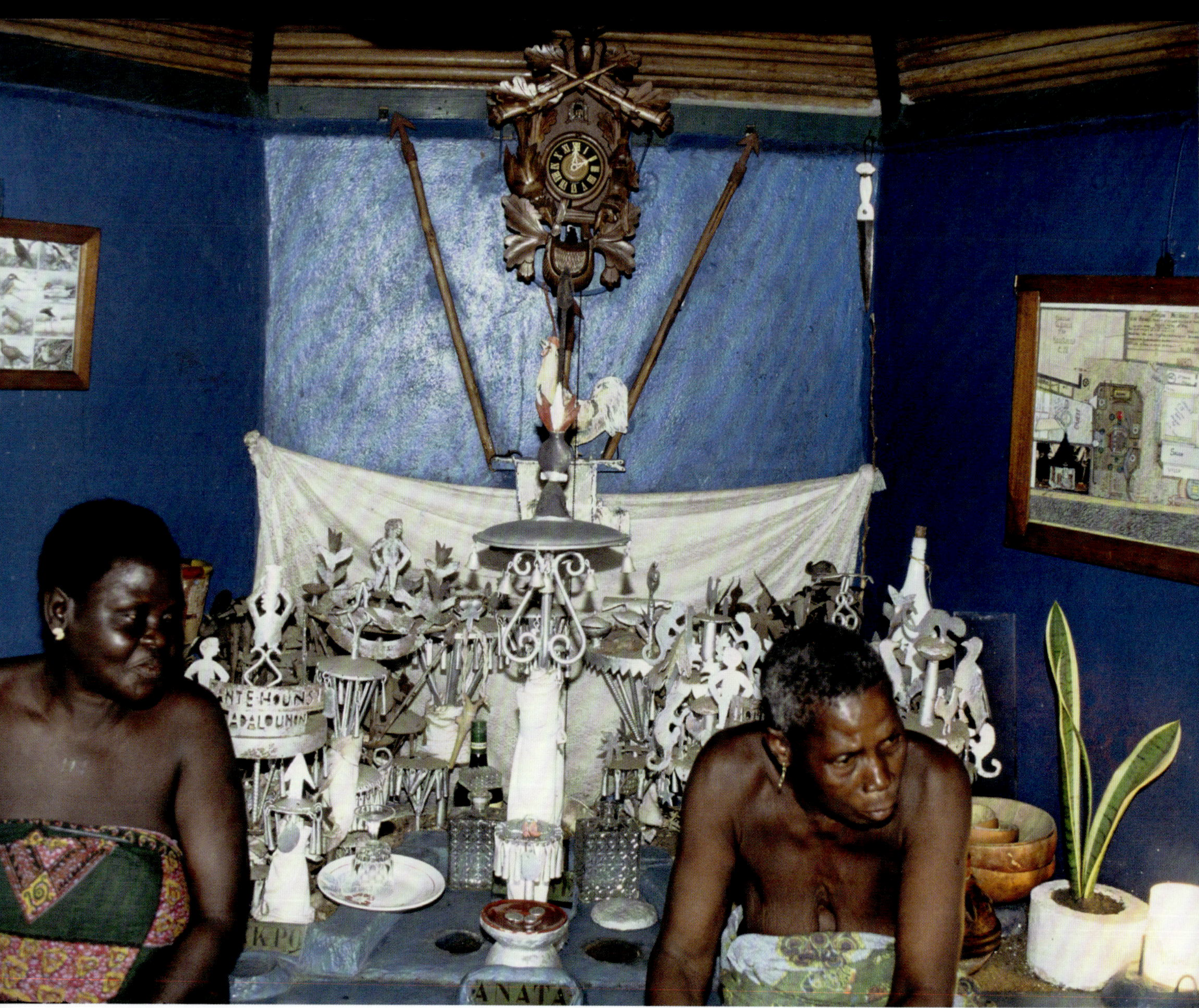

the floors are clean and the central fetish,
an accumulated mass of palm oil, blood and
other components, grows straight upwards
to the top.

Because of these signs of crystal-clear
conditions and divine command, but also
because of his biblical age, Sergent Kiki
is highly esteemed in his hometown of
Porto Novo.

mélange d'huile de palme, de sang et d'autres
composants, s'élève toujours plus haut.

Ces marques de discipline et d'autorité
divine, ainsi que son âge canonique, valent à
Sergent Kiki une grande renommée dans sa
ville natale de Porto-Novo.

umgebenden Steine sind perlweiß gehalten,
die Böden sauber und der zentrale Fetisch,
eine gewachsene Masse aus Palmöl, Blut und
anderen Bestandteilen, wächst kerzengerade
in die Höhe.

Aufgrund dieser Zeichen für glasklare
Verhältnisse und göttliche Befehlsgewalt,
aber auch wegen seines biblischen Alters,
wird Sergent Kiki in seiner Heimatstadt
Porto-Novo hoch geschätzt.

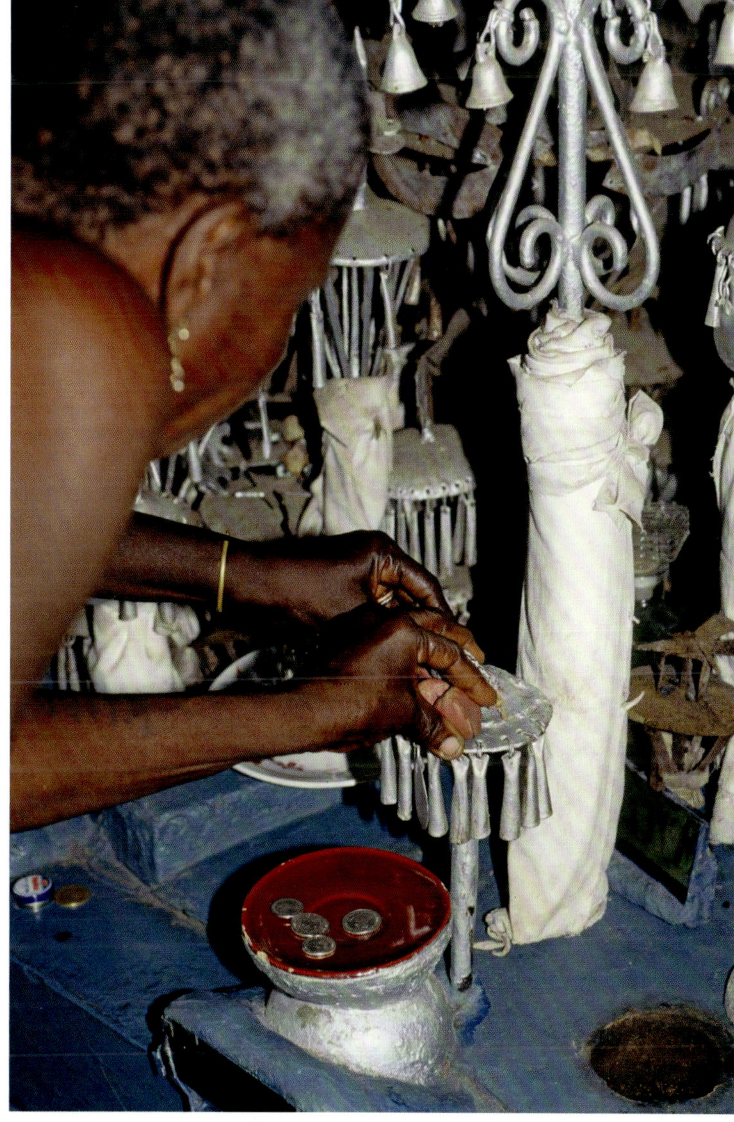

Money for the ancestors
De l'argent pour les ancêtres
Geldstücke für die Ahnen
Dinero para los antepasados
Dinheiro para os antepassados
Munten voor de voorouders

son de color blanco perla, los suelos limpios
y el fetiche central, una masa de aceite de
palma, sangre y otros componentes, crece en
línea recta.

El Sargento Kiki es muy apreciado en
su ciudad natal de Porto-Novo, no solo
por estas muestras de comportamientos
transparentes y su mandato divino, sino
también por su edad bíblica.

são de cor branca pérola, o chão está limpo
e o fetiche central, uma massa adulta de óleo
de palma, sangue e outros componentes,
cresce a direito.

Por causa desses sinais de condições
cristalinas e comando divino, mas também
por causa de sua idade bíblica, Sergent
Kiki é muito estimado em sua cidade natal,
Porto-Novo.

eromheen liggen zijn hagelwit, de vloeren
schoon en de centrale fetisj, een groeiende
massa van palmolie, bloed en andere
bestanddelen, groeit kaarsrecht omhoog.

Door deze tekenen van glasheldere
verhoudingen en goddelijk gezag, maar
ook vanwege zijn bijbelse ouderdom, wordt
Sergeant Kiki zeer gewaardeerd in zijn
geboorteplaats Porto-Novo.

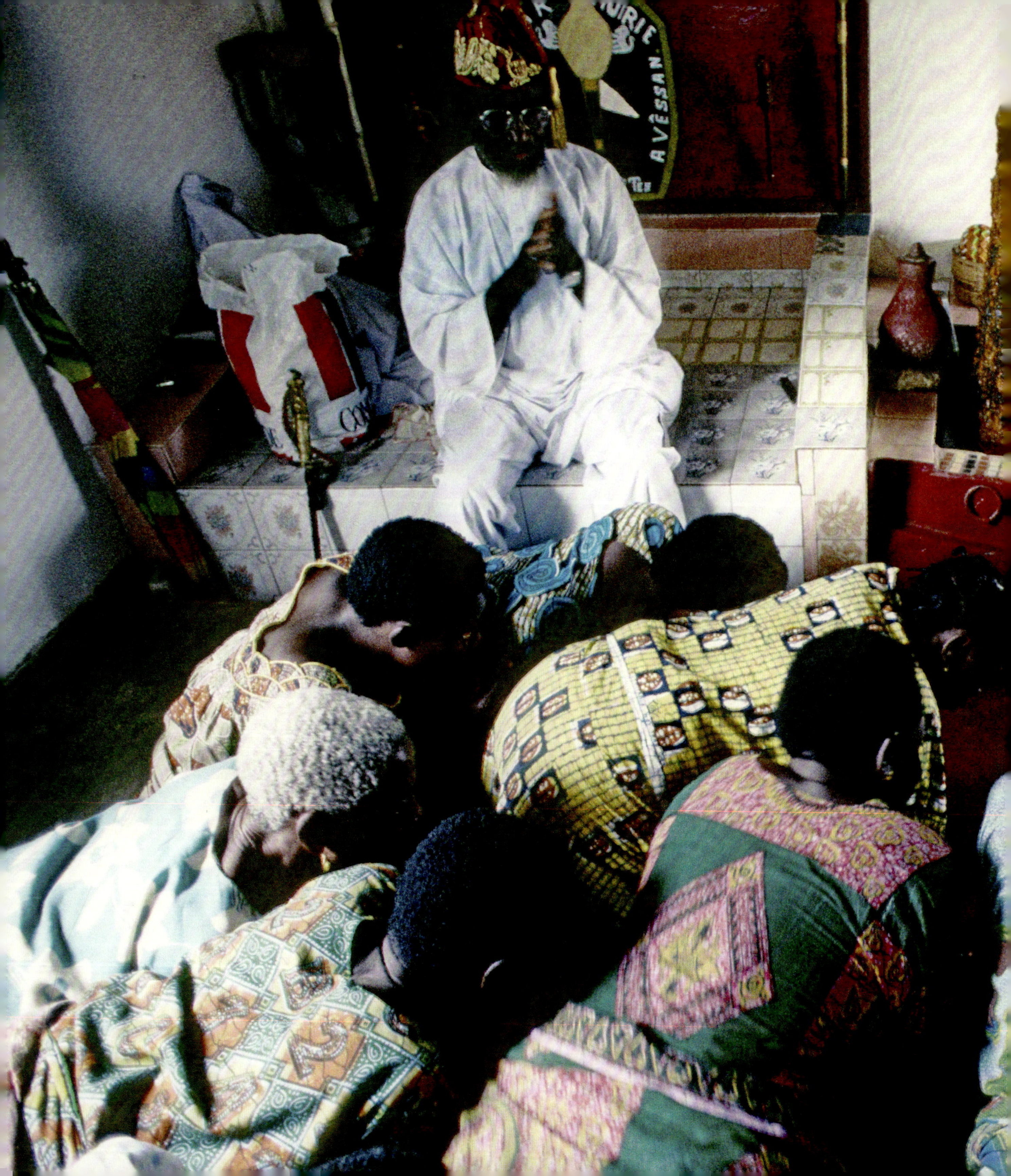

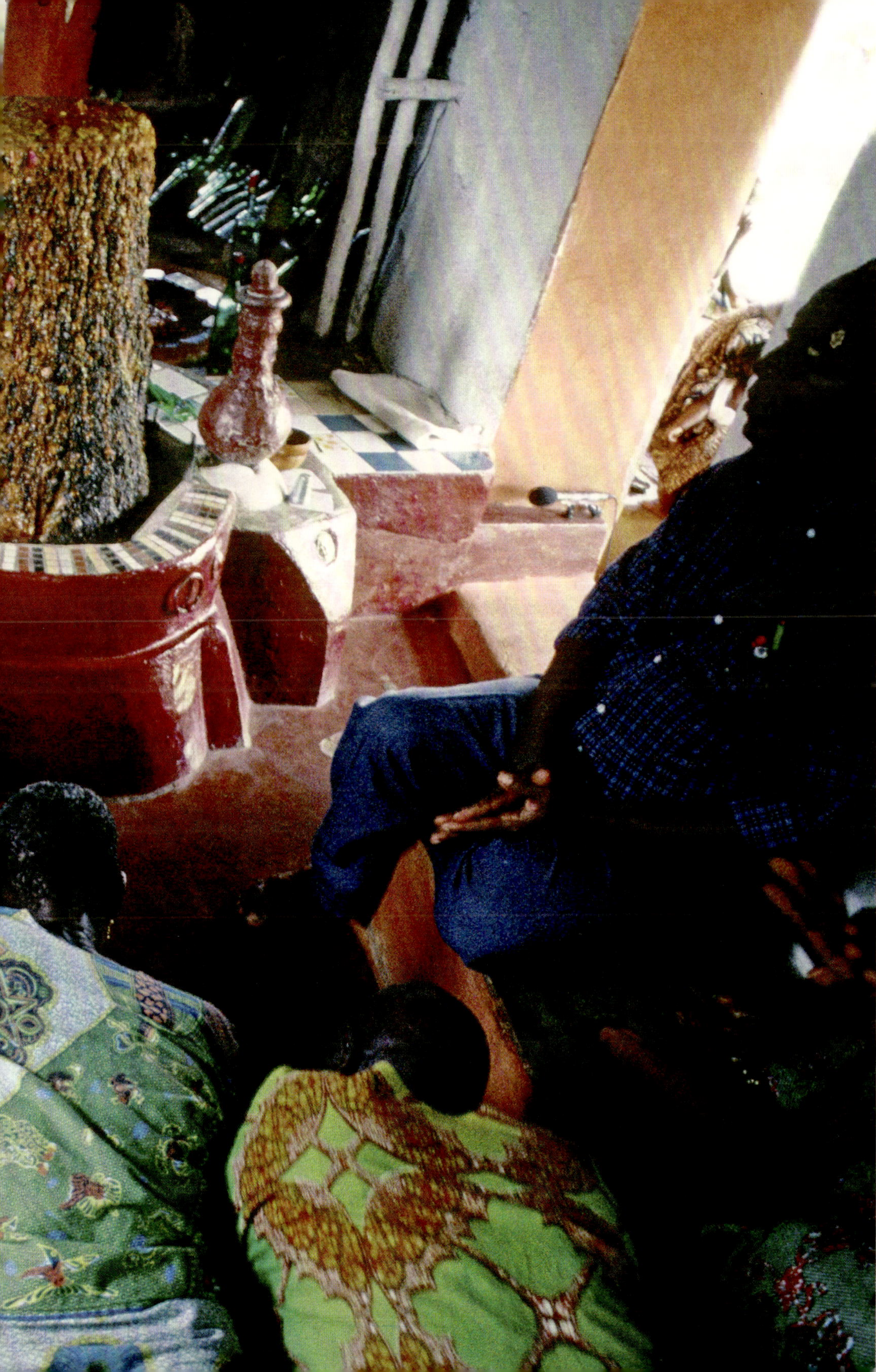

Homage is paid to the
house god Abessan. It is
not necessary to belong to
a family, it is also possible
for strangers to ask Abessan
for help. However, it is
important to ensure that
your shoes are clean.

**L'hommage est rendu au
dieu de la maison Abessan.**
Il n'est pas nécessaire de
faire partie de la famille
pour venir demander de
l'aide à Abessan, cette
possibilité est également
ouverte aux étrangers.
Toute personne pénétrant
le lieu doit en revanche
veiller à la propreté de ses
chaussures.

**Dem Hausgott Abessan
wird gehuldigt.** Es braucht
nicht zwingend die
Familienzugehörigkeit,
auch Fremden steht es
offen, Abessan um Hilfe
zu bitten. Auf sauberes
Schuhwerk ist aber zu
achten.

**Se rinde homenaje al dios
de la casa Abessan.** No
necesariamente hay que
pertenecer a una familia,
también los extraños
pueden pedir ayuda a
Abessan. Sin embargo,
es importante asegurarse
de que los zapatos estén
limpios.

**Homenagem é prestada
ao deus da casa
Abyssan.** Ela não precisa
necessariamente pertencer
a uma família, ela também
está aberta a estranhos
para pedir ajuda a Abyssan.
No entanto, é importante
garantir que os sapatos
estão limpos.

**Men brengt hulde aan de
huisgod Abyssan.** Het hoeft
niet per se de familie te
zijn, het staat vreemden
ook vrij om Abyssan om
hulp te vragen. Het is wel
belangrijk dat je schoenen
schoon zijn.

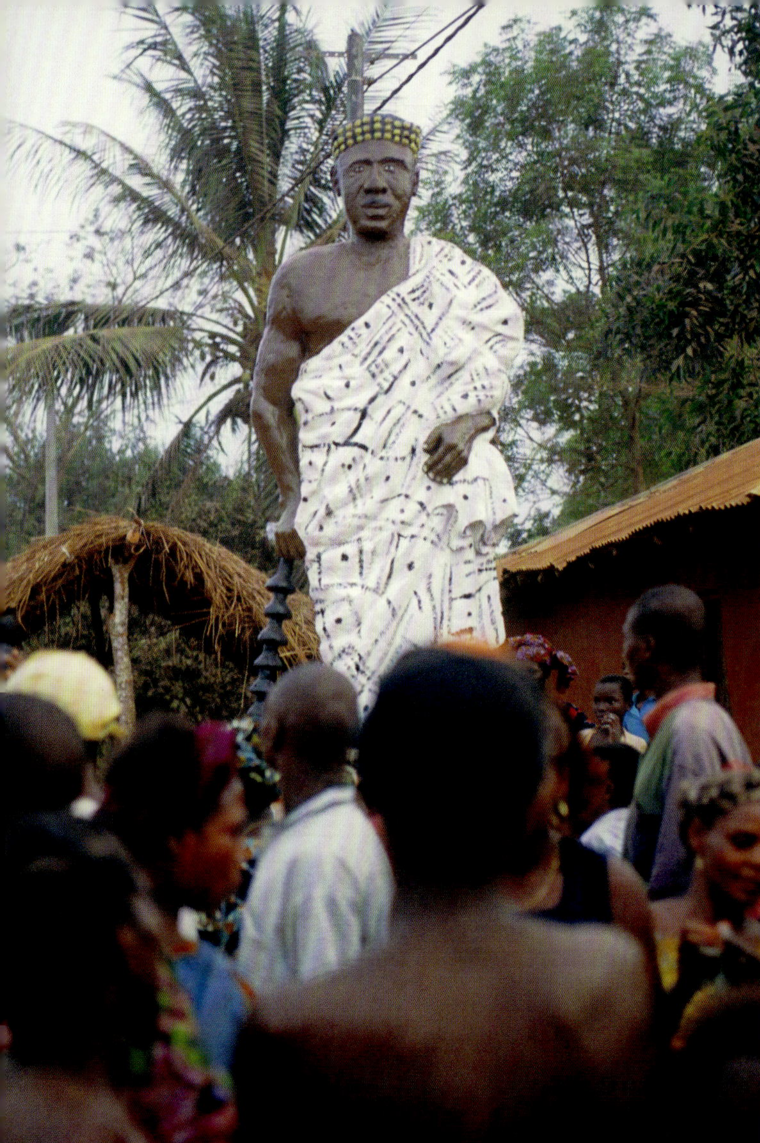

Cement statue of Sossa Guédéhoungué
Statue en ciment de Sossa Guédéhoungué
Zementstatue von Sossa Guédéhoungué
Estatua de cemento de Sossa Guédéhoungué
Estátua de cimento de Sossa Guédéhoungué
Cementen beeld van Sossa Guédéhoungué

Laying out of the coffin in the Sports Palace of Cotonou
Exposition du cercueil au palais des sports de Cotonou
Aufbahrung des Sarges im Sportpalast von Cotonou
Colocación del ataúd en el Palacio de los Deportes de Cotonú
Deitado fora do caixão no Palácio dos Desportos de Cotonou
Het opbaren van de kist in de sporthal van Cotonou

Last Honor for the
Vodun Pope

Sossa Guédéhoungué, who during his
lifetime was the president of the society in
which the Benin Vodun priests organized
themselves, was considered by many as
the "Pope of Vodun". Guests from all over
the world came to his funeral, and the
ceremonies went on for days.

Guédéhoungué, who grew up in Doutou
in the Mono District, came from an old
dynasty of priests and was initiated into the

Derniers honneurs pour
le pape du vodun

Sossa Guédéhoungué, ancien président
de l'organisation regroupant l'ensemble les
prêtres vodun béninois, était considéré par
beaucoup comme « le pape du vodun ».
Des personnalités du monde entier se sont
pressées à ses funérailles et les cérémonies
ont duré plusieurs jours.

Guédéhoungué avait grandi à Doutou
dans le département du Mono. Issu d'une
longue dynastie de prêtres, il fut initié très

Letzte Ehre für den
Vodun-Papst

Sossa Guédéhoungué, der zu Lebzeiten der
Präsident jener Gesellschaft war, in der sich
die Beniner Vodunpriester organisierten,
galt vielen als der „Papst des Vodun". Zu
seiner Beerdigung reisten Gäste aus aller
Welt an, und die Zeremonien gingen
über Tage.

Guédéhoungué, der in Doutou im
Mono-Distrikt aufgewachsen war, stammte
aus einer alten Priesterdynastie und wurde

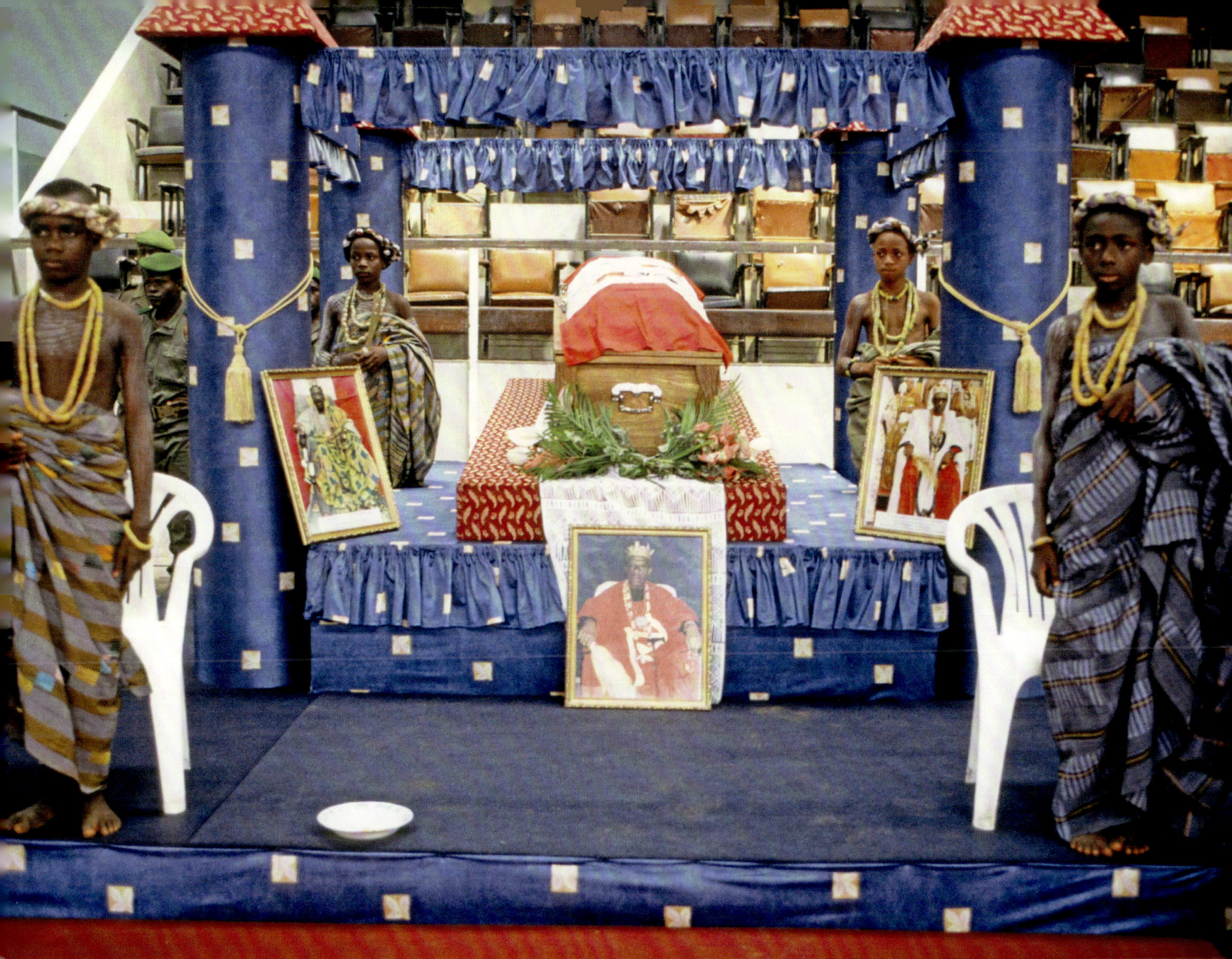

Última gloria al
Papa Vudú

Sossa Guédéhoungué, que durante su vida
fue presidente de la sociedad en la que
se organizaron los sacerdotes benineses
vudúistas, fue considerado por muchos
como el "*Papa de* Vudú". Invitados de todo
el mundo acudieron a su funeral, y las
ceremonias duraron días.

Guédéhoungué, que había crecido en
Doutou, en el distrito de Mono, provenía
de una antigua dinastía de sacerdotes y se

Última Glória ao
Papa Vodu

Sossa Guédéhoungué, que durante a sua
vida foi o presidente da sociedade na qual os
padres vodun beninenses se organizaram,
foi considerado por muitos como o "Papa
do vodu". Convidados de todo o mundo
vieram ao seu funeral, e as cerimónias
prolongaram-se por dias.

Guédéhoungué, que tinha crescido em
Doutou, no distrito de Mono, provinha
de uma antiga dinastia de sacerdotes e foi

Laatste eer voor
de vodunpaus

Sossa Guédéhoungué, die bij leven
voorzitter was van het genootschap waarin
de vodunpriesters van Benin waren
georganiseerd, werd door velen beschouwd
als de 'vodunpaus'. Gasten van over de hele
wereld kwamen naar zijn begrafenis, en de
ceremoniën gingen dagenlang door.

Guédéhoungué, die opgroeide in Doutou
in het departement Mono, kwam uit een
oude priesterdynastie en werd op zeer

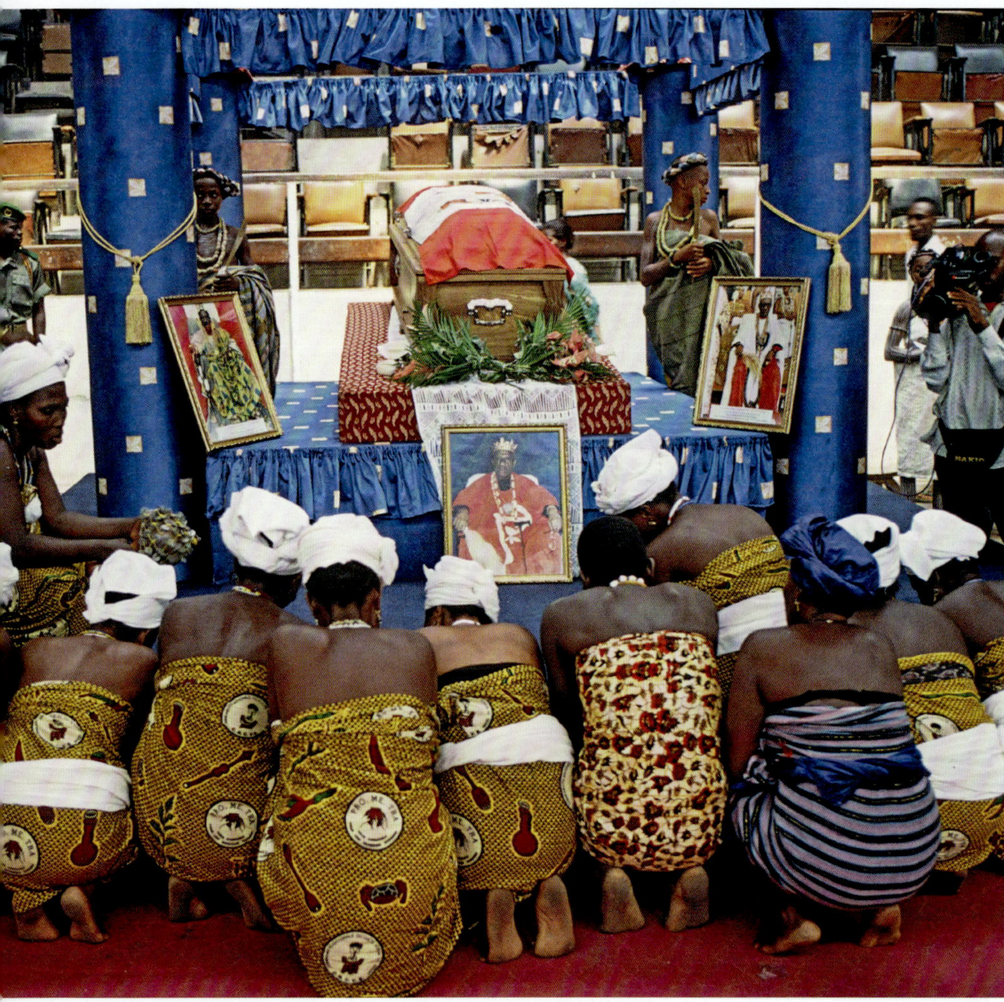

mysteries of Vodun at a very young age. His
abilities as a magician and healer earned
him supra-regional recognition, which even
included consulting for West African heads
of state. Inquiries from Europe, for example,
came from French football clubs ordering
magical services to influence the outcome of
important matches.

Guédéhoungué, who died at the age of
88, left 33 widows and 145 children. The
youngest child was three, the oldest son was
56 years old.

jeune au secret du vodun. Ses capacités de
magicien et de guérisseur lui valurent une
reconnaissance au-delà de sa seule région
et l'ont même amené à tenir des fonctions
de conseiller auprès de chefs d'État ouest-
africains. Des demandes lui étaient en outre
adressées depuis l'Europe, notamment en
provenance d'un club de football français
qui faisait appel à ses services de magie afin
de favoriser l'issue des matches importants.

Guédéhoungué mourut à l'âge de 88 ans
laissant derrière lui 33 veuves et 145 enfants.
Le dernier était âgé de 3 ans et le plus
vieux de 56.

schon sehr jung in die Geheimnisse des
Vodun eingeweiht. Seine Fähigkeiten
als Magier und Heiler verschafften ihm
überregionale Anerkennung, die bis hin zu
Beratertätigkeiten bei westafrikanischen
Staatschefs reichte. Anfragen aus Europa
kamen beispielsweise von französischen
Fußballclubs, die magische Dienstleistungen
orderten, um den Ausgang wichtiger Spiele
zu beeinflussen.

Guédéhoungué, der im Alter von 88
Jahren verstarb, hinterließ 33 Witwen und
145 Kinder. Das jüngste Kind war drei, der
älteste Sohn war 56 Jahre alt.

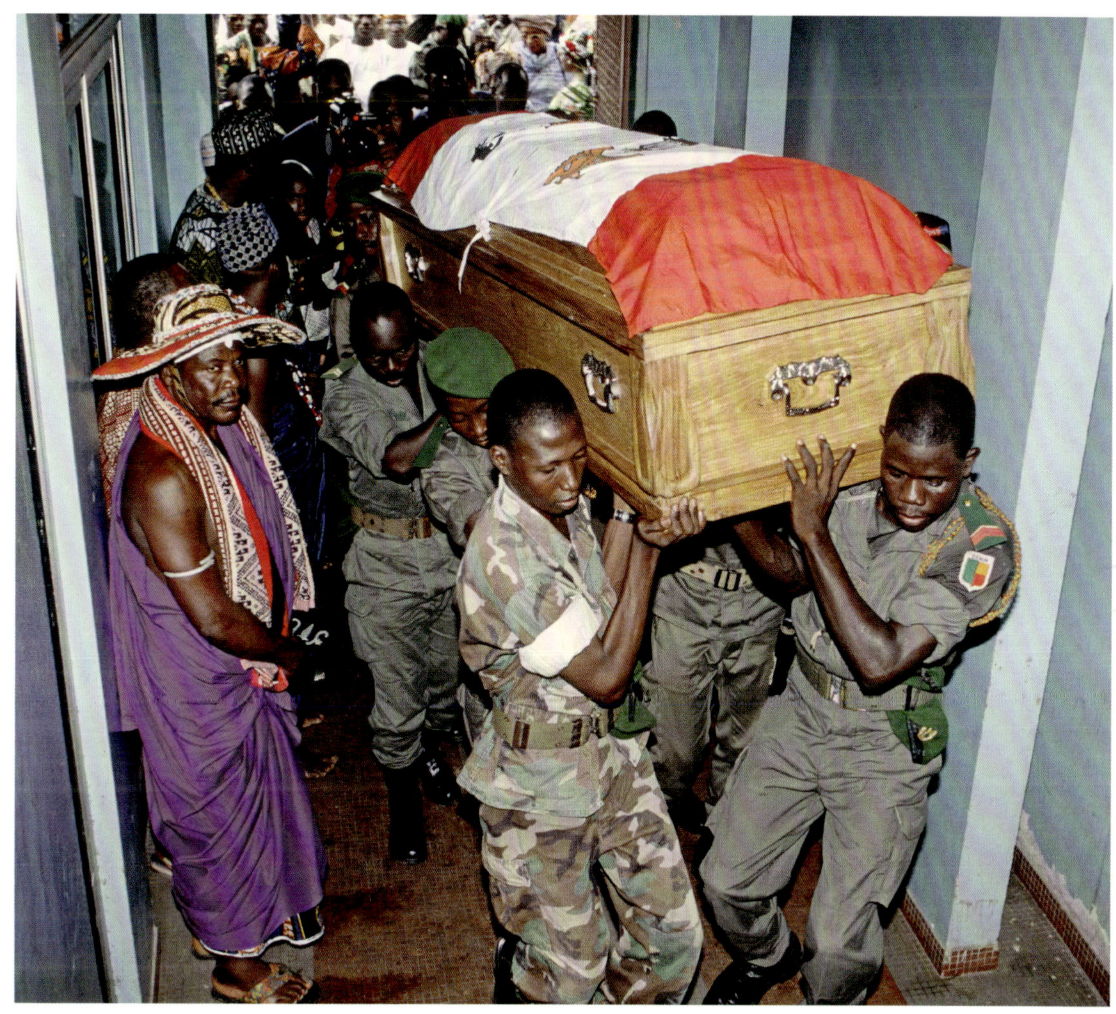

inició en los misterios del Vudú a una edad muy temprana. Sus habilidades como mago y curandero le valieron el reconocimiento suprarregional, que incluso se extendió a la consulta de los jefes de Estado de África Occidental. Las consultas procedentes de Europa, por ejemplo, procedían de clubes de fútbol franceses que encargaron servicios mágicos para influir en el resultado de partidos importantes.

Guédéhoungué, que murió a los 88 años, dejó 33 viudas y 145 hijos. El menor tenía tres años, el mayor 56.

iniciado nos mistérios do Vodu ainda muito jovem. Suas habilidades como mágico e curandeiro lhe renderam reconhecimento supra-regional, que se estendeu até mesmo à consulta de chefes de estado da África Ocidental. Os inquéritos da Europa, por exemplo, vieram de clubes de futebol franceses que encomendaram serviços mágicos para influenciar o resultado de jogos importantes.

Guédéhoungué, falecido aos 88 anos, deixou 33 viúvas e 145 crianças. A criança mais nova tinha três anos, o filho mais velho tinha 56 anos.

jonge leeftijd ingewijd in de geheimen van vodun. Zijn vaardigheden als magiër en genezer leverden hem landelijke erkenning op, zozeer zelfs dat West-Afrikaanse staatshoofden hem raadpleegden. Aanvragen uit Europa kwamen bijvoorbeeld van Franse voetbalclubs die magische dienstverlening bestelden om de uitkomst van belangrijke wedstrijden te beïnvloeden.

Guédéhoungué, die op 88-jarige leeftijd overleed, liet 33 weduwen en 145 kinderen na. Het jongste kind was drie, de oudste zoon 56 jaar.

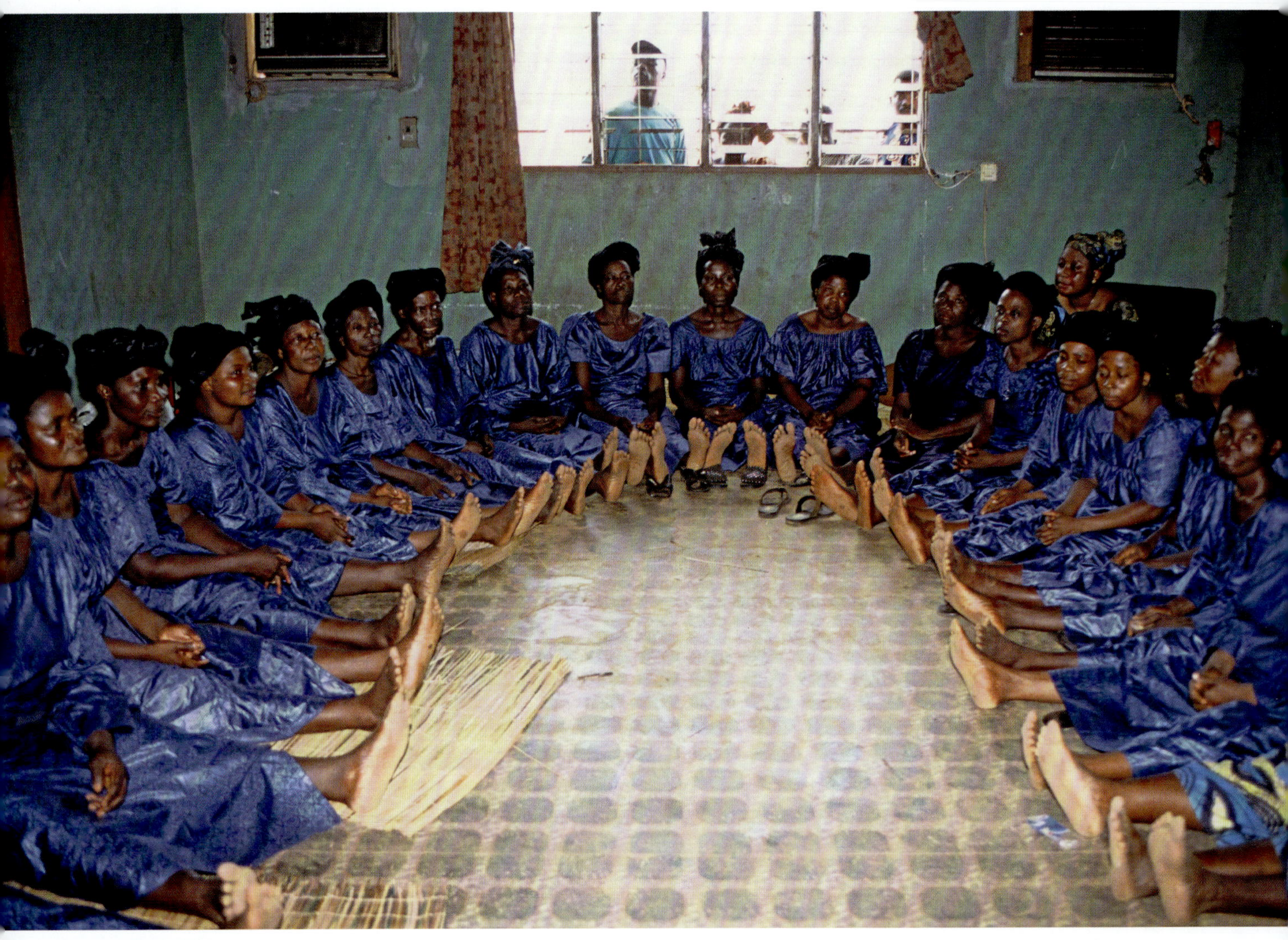

A hundred days of mourning. The widows of Guédéhoungué have to mourn for one hundred days and are not allowed to wash or leave the house during this time.

Cent jours de deuil. Les veuves de Guédéhoungué doivent pleurer sa mort pendant 100 jours et ne doivent ni se laver ni quitter la maison au cours de cette période.

Hundert Tage Trauer. Die Witwen Guédéhoungués müssen einhundert Tage lang trauern und dürfen sich in dieser Zeit nicht waschen und auch das Haus nicht verlassen.

Cien días de luto. Las viudas de Guédéhoungué tienen que llorar durante cien días y no se les permite lavarse o salir de la casa durante ese wtiempo.

Cem dias de luto. As viúvas de Guédéhoungué têm de chorar durante cem dias e não podem lavar ou sair de casa durante esse tempo.

Honderd dagen van rouw. De weduwen van Guédéhoungué moeten honderd dagen rouwen en mogen zich in deze periode niet wassen of het huis verlaten.

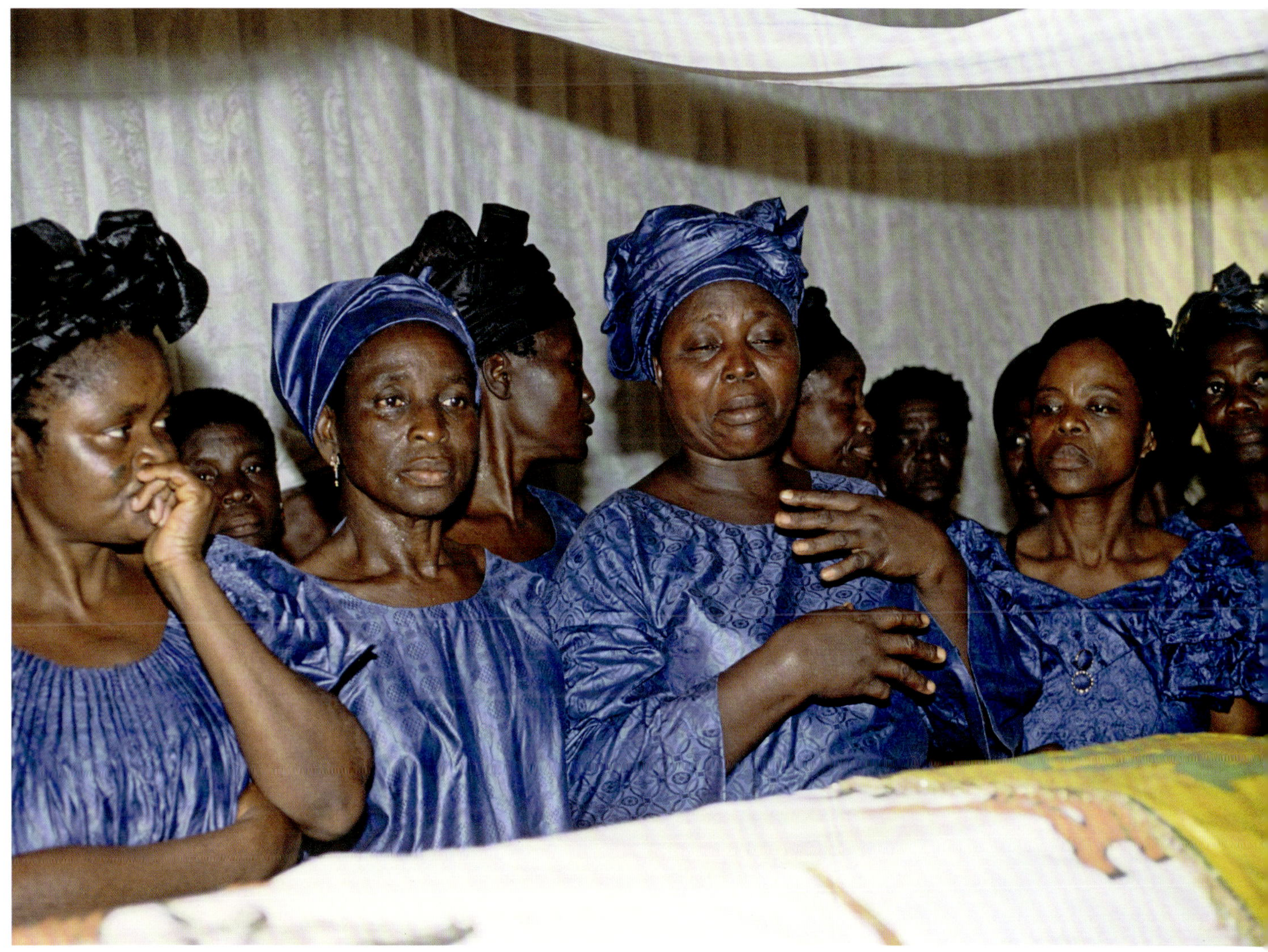

The widows say goodbye

L'au-revoir des veuves

Die Witwen nehmen Abschied

Las viudas se despiden

As viúvas dizem adeus

De weduwen nemen afscheid

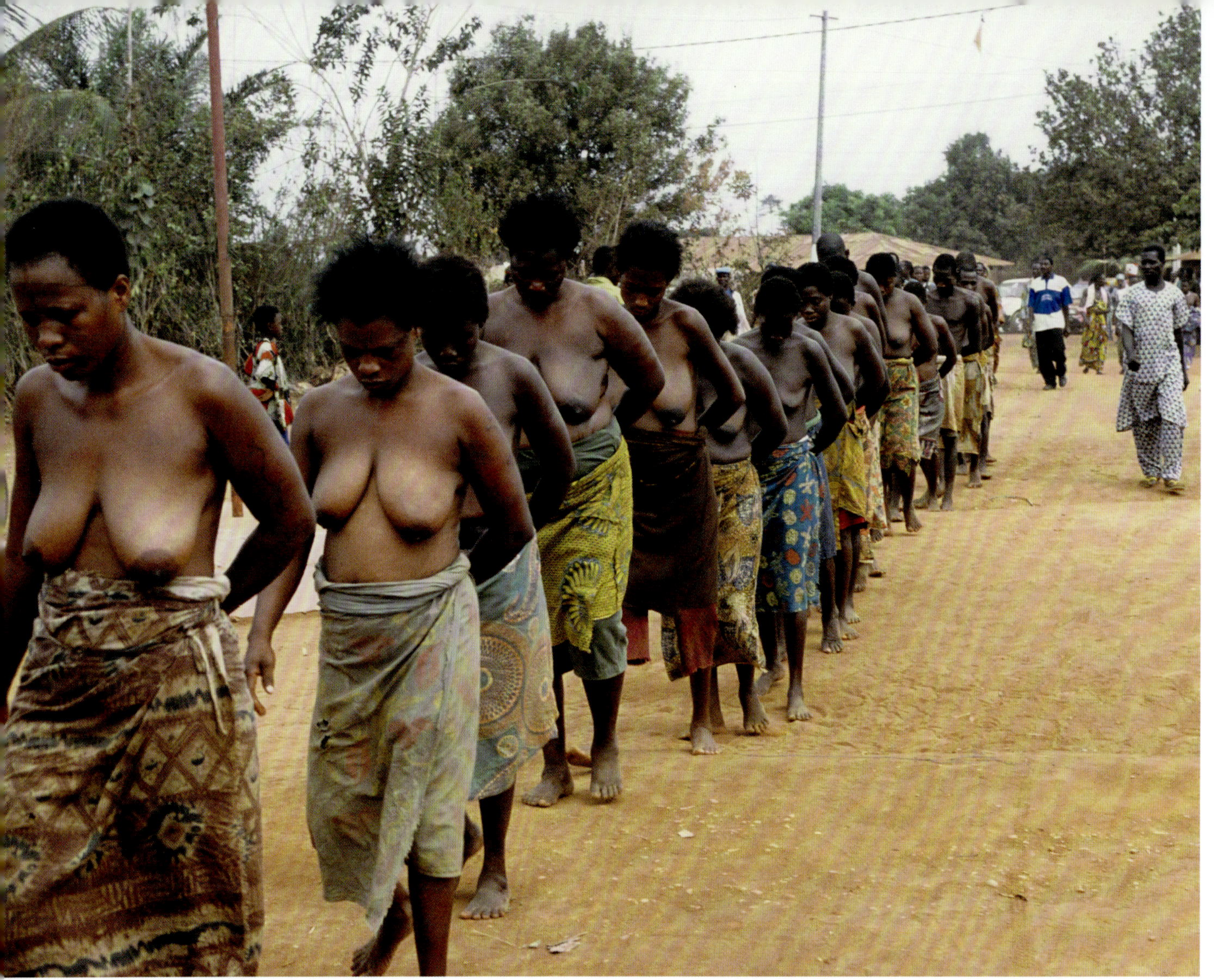

Mourning Vodun followers on their way to the grave in Doutou, Benin

Adeptes vodun endeuillées sur la route vers le tombeau à Doutou au Bénin

Trauernde Vodunanhänger auf dem Weg zum Grab in Doutou, Benin

Luto por los remolques de vudú en su camino a la tumba en Doutou, Benin

Trailers Vodun de luto a caminho da sepultura em Doutou, Benin

Rouwende vodunaanhangers op weg naar het graf in Doutou, Benin

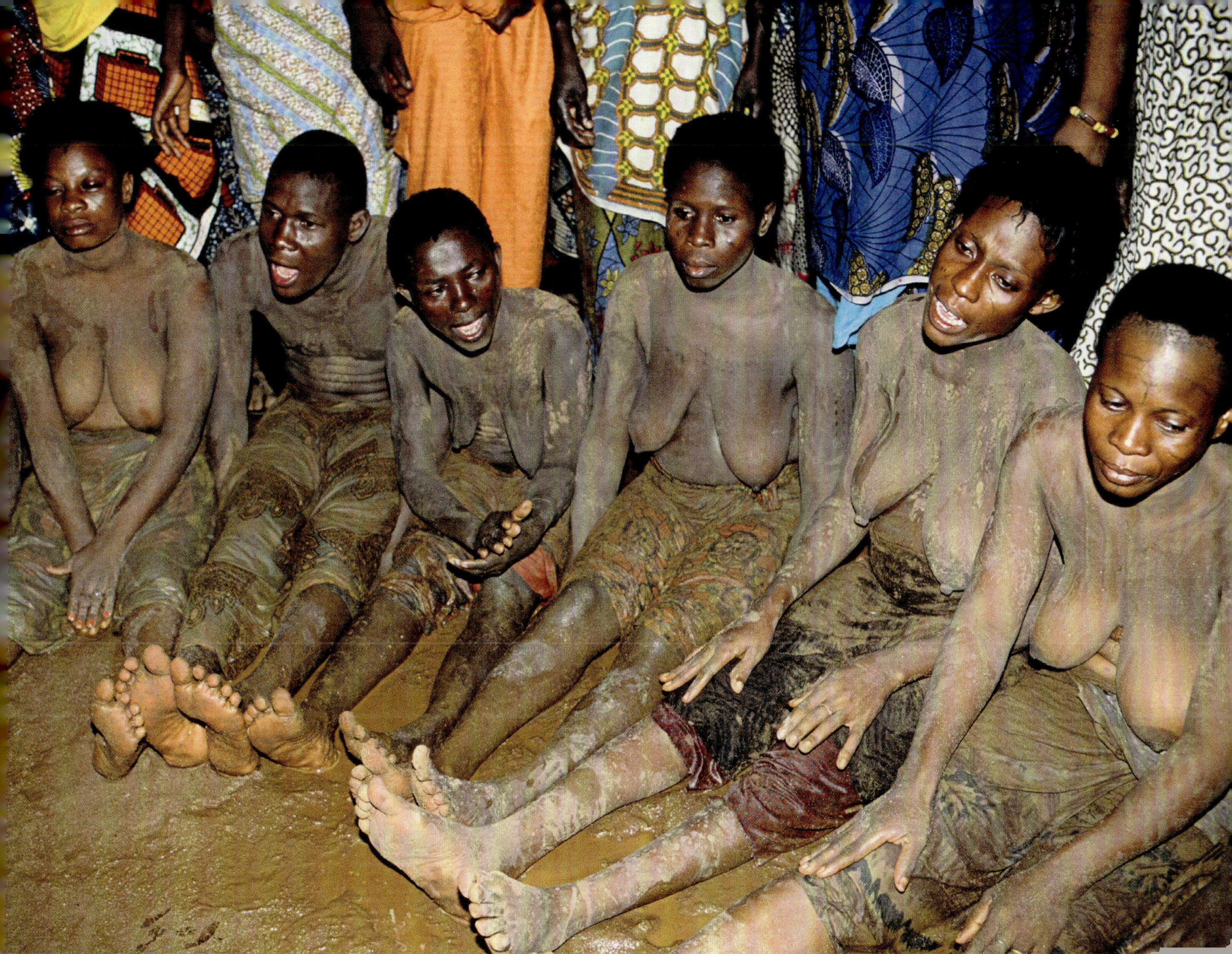

Mourning Vodun followers

Adeptes vodun en deuil

Trauernde Vodunanhänger

Adeptas de vudú de luto

Pendentes de Vodu de Luto

Rouwende vodunaanhangers

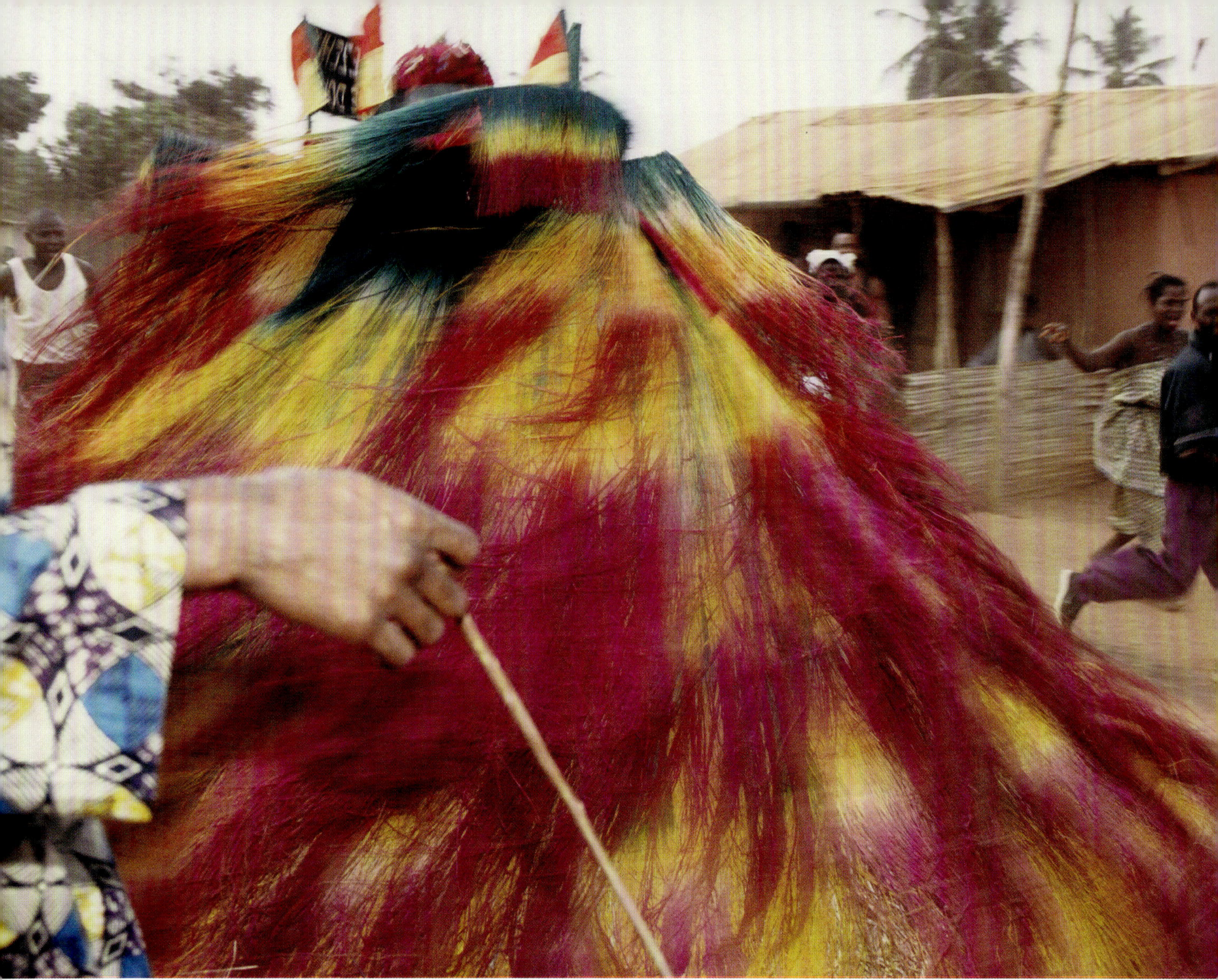

Zangbeto must not be missing. On the occasion of the funeral the Zangbeto secret society is also present and part of the procession.

Zangbeto ne doit pas manquer. La confrérie secrète de Zangbeto participe à la procession des funérailles.

Zangbeto darf nicht fehlen. Anlässlich der Beerdigung ist auch der Zangbeto-Geheimbund vor Ort und Teil der Prozession.

Zangbeto no debe estar ausente. Con motivo del funeral, la sociedad secreta de Zangbeto también está presente y forma parte de la procesión.

Zangbeto não deve estar ausente. Por ocasião do funeral, a sociedade secreta Zangbeto também está presente e faz parte da procissão.

Zangbeto mag niet ontbreken. Ter gelegenheid van de begrafenis is ook het geheime Zangbeto-genootschap aanwezig en maakt het deel uit van de stoet.

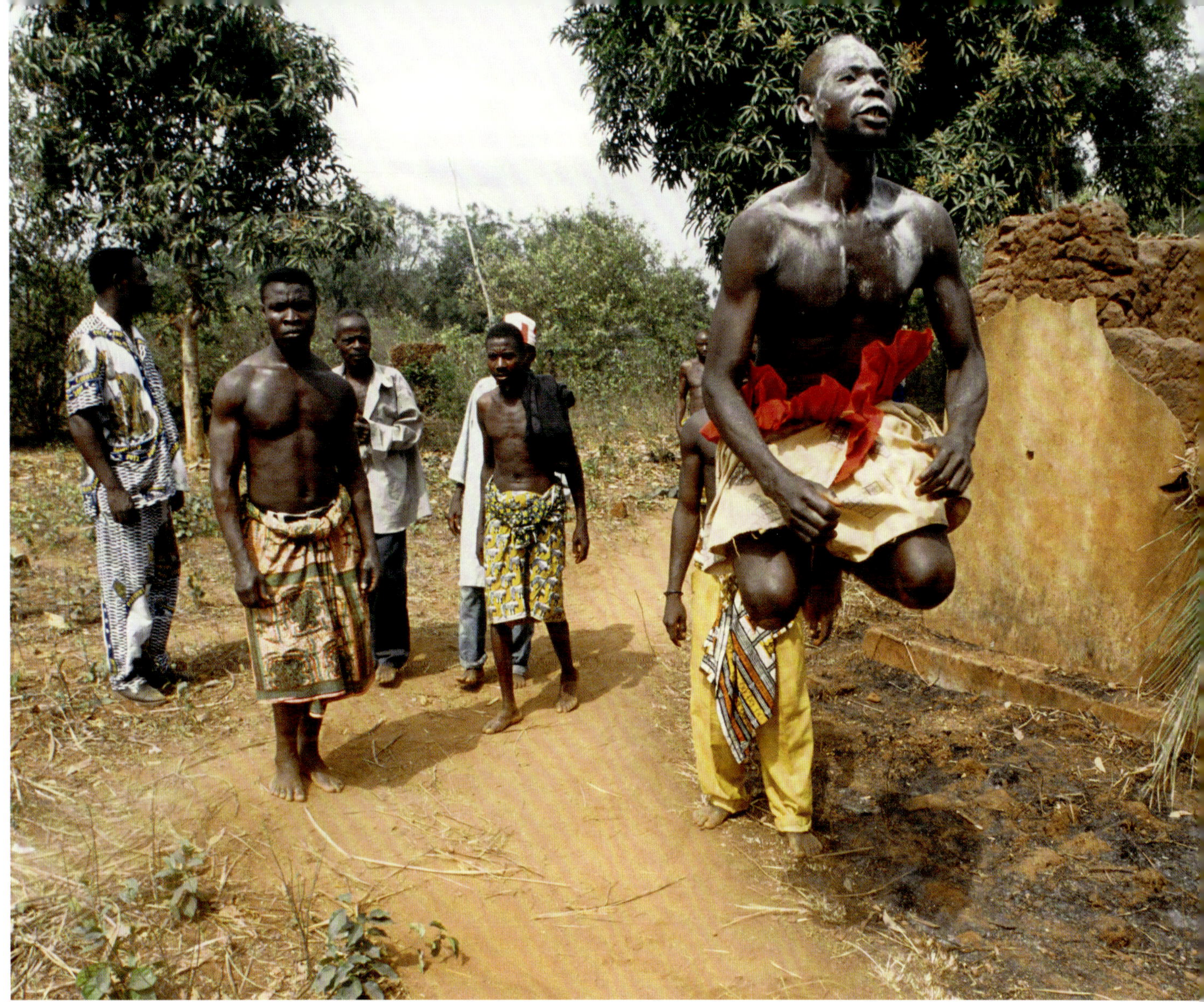

Mourning and Trance. A follower of the warrior Vodun Ganbada falls into a trance on his way to the last resting place of the Vodun Pope. In this state, Ganbada adepts are capable of artistic excellence.

Deuil et transe. Un adepte du dieu guerrier vodun Ganbada entre en transe sur le chemin menant à la dernière demeure du pape du vodun. Lorsqu'ils atteignent cet état, les adeptes de Ganbada sont capables de formidables performances artistiques.

Trauer und Trance. Ein Anhänger des Kriegervoduns Ganbada fällt auf dem Weg zur letzten Ruhestätte des Vodunpapstes in Trance. In diesem Zustand sind Ganbada-Adepten zu artistischen Höchstleistungen fähig.

Luto y trance. Un seguidor del guerrero vudú Ganbada entra en transe en su camino hacia el último lugar de descanso del Papa vudú. En este estado, los adeptos de Ganbada son capaces de alcanzar la excelencia artística.

Luto e Transe. Um seguidor do guerreiro vodu Ganbada entra em transe a caminho do último local de descanso do vodupope. Neste estado, os adeptos de Ganbada são capazes de excelência artística.

Rouw en trance. Een aanhanger van de krijgergod Ganbada raakt op weg naar de laatste rustplaats van de vodunpaus in trance. In deze staat zijn Ganbada-adepten in staat tot grootse artistieke prestaties.

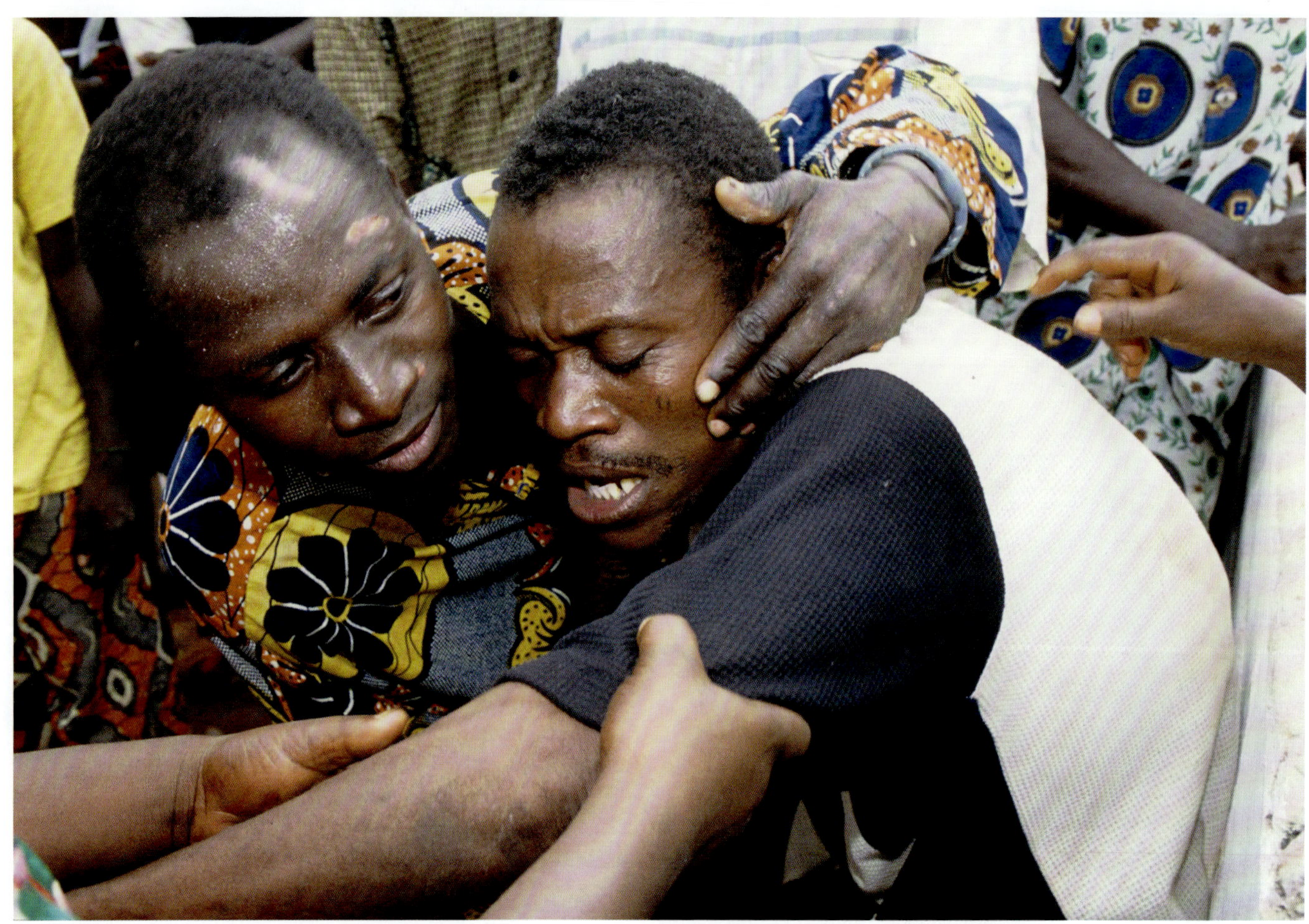

Mourning Vodun follower in a trance

Adepte vodun endeuillé et en transe

Trauernder Vodunanhänger in Trance

Adeptas de vudú de luto en trance

Pingente de Vodu de Luto em Trance

Rouwende vodunaanhangers in trance

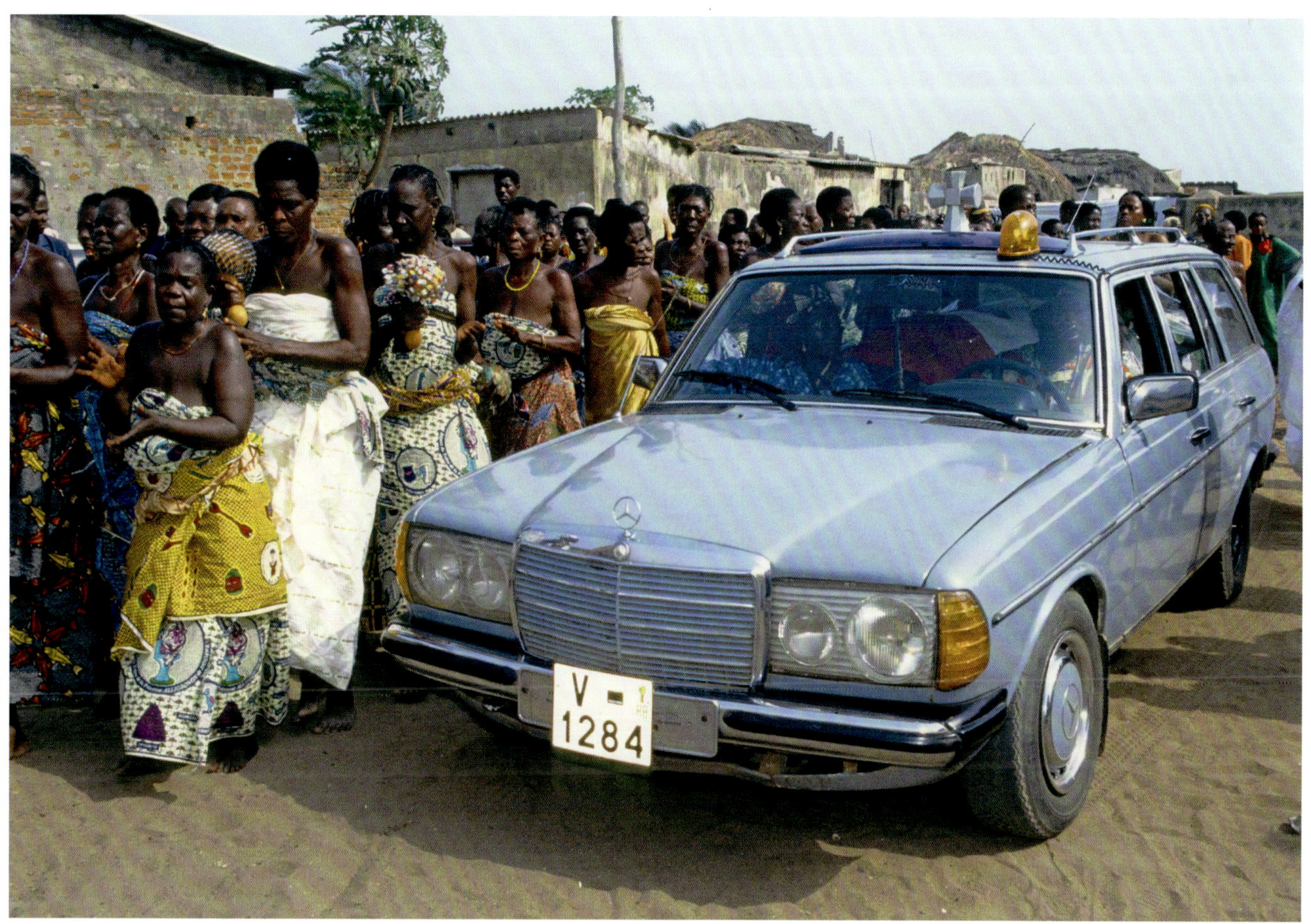

The hearse passes the procession of the mourners

Le corbillard passe devant la procession des pleureurs

Der Leichenwagen passiert die Prozession der Trauernden

El coche fúnebre pasa por la procesión de los dolientes

O carro funerário passa a procissão dos enlutados

De lijkwagen passeert de stoet van rouwenden

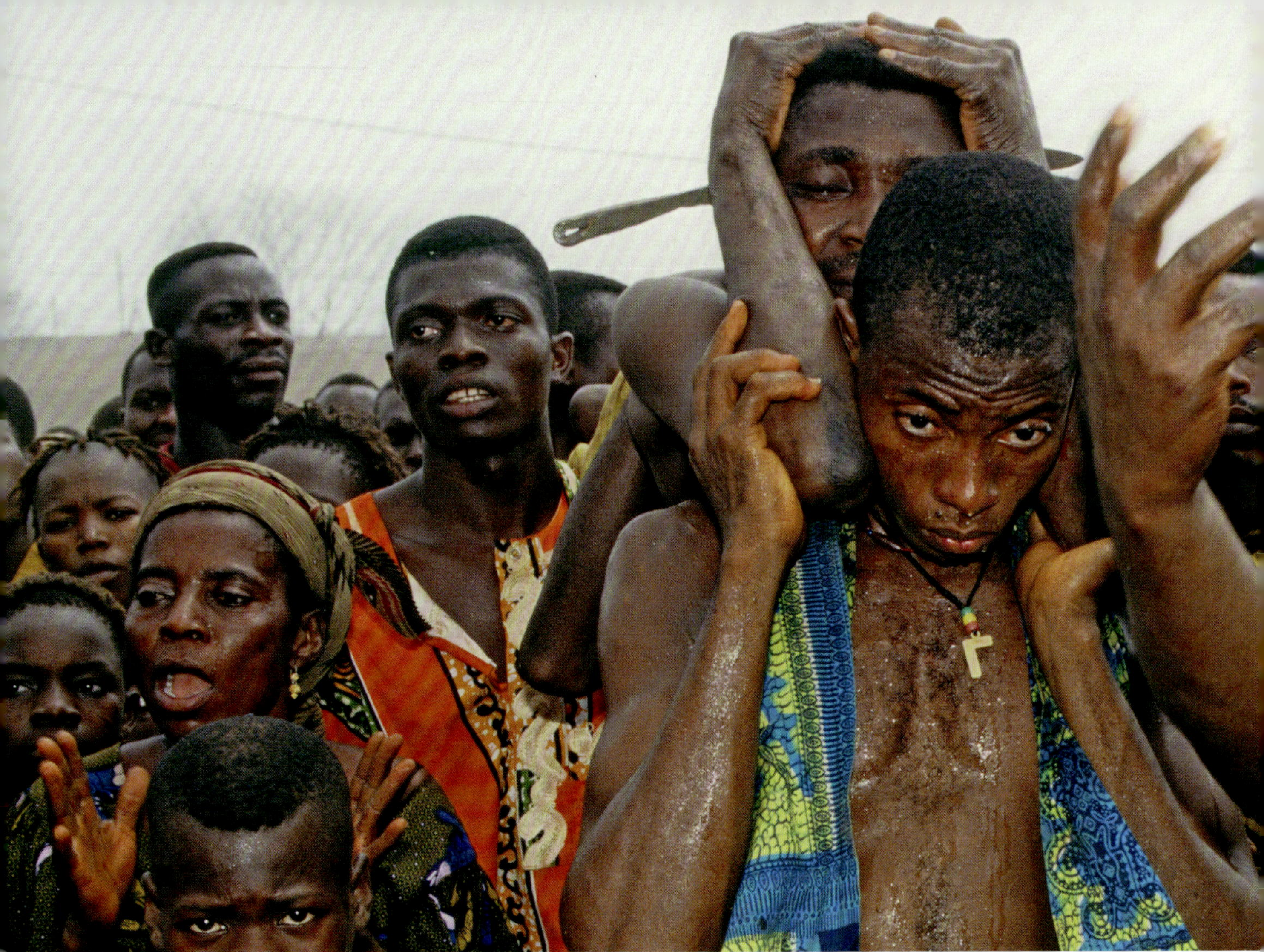

Martial Witch Defense:
Ganbada and Kokou

The precautions taken by Vodun followers
to recognize and avert damaging spells
are considerable. This was impressively
demonstrated at the funeral of Sossa
Guédéhoungué, the "Pope of Vodun".

Members of the cult communities around
the warrior gods Ganbada and Kokou took
extreme action to ensure that no witch dared
to enter Sossa's open grave. Shortly before
the coffin was lowered, people danced more
and more wildly and demonstrated their

Défense martiale contre les
sorciers, Ganbada et Kokou

Lorsqu'il s'agit de reconnaître et de lutter
contre la magie maléfique, les adeptes du
vodun sont prêts à prendre des mesures
radicales. Les funérailles de Sossa
Guédéhoungué, « pape du vodun » en
ont apporté une démonstration des plus
impressionnantes.

Les membres de la communauté
constituée autour des dieux guerriers
Ganbada et Kokou ont entrepris des
actions extrêmes afin de s'assurer qu'aucun

Martialische Hexenabwehr:
Ganbada und Kokou

Die Vorkehrungen, die von den
Vodunanhängern getroffen werden, wenn
es darum geht, Schadenzauber zu erkennen
und abzuwenden, sind beträchtlich. Beim
Begräbnis von Sossa Guédéhoungué, dem
„Papst des Vodun", wurde dies eindrucksvoll
unter Beweis gestellt.

Mitglieder der Kultgemeinschaften
um die Kriegergötter Ganbada und
Kokou trugen mit extremen Aktionen
Sorge dafür, dass keine Hexe es wagt, in

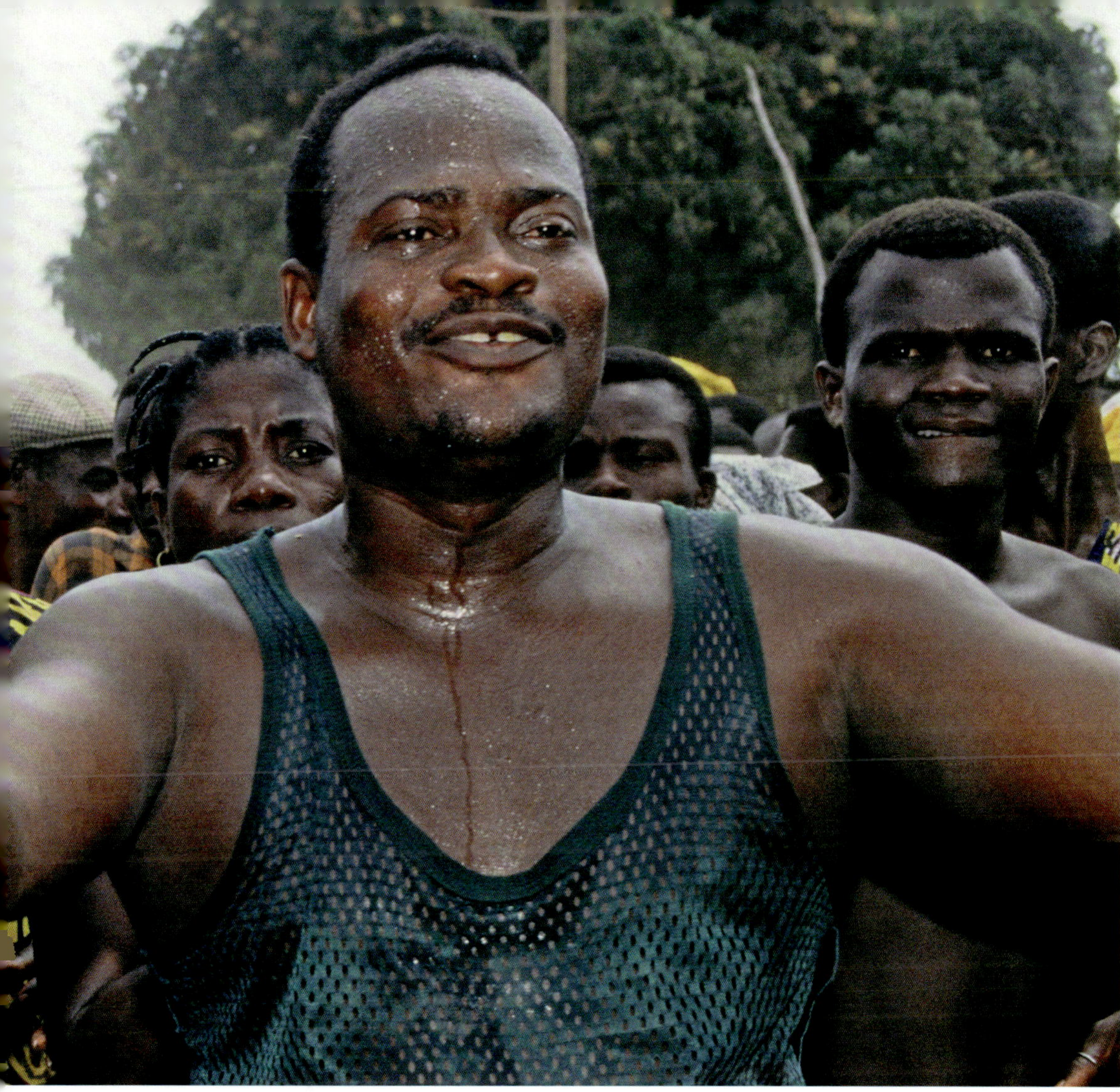

Defensa de la bruja marcial: Ganbada y Kokou

Las precauciones tomadas por los seguidores del Vudú para reconocer y evitar los hechizos malignos son considerables. El funeral de Sossa Guédéhoungué, el *"Papa del Vudú"*, fue una demostración impresionante de ello.

Los miembros de las comunidades de culto alrededor de los dioses guerreros *Ganbada y Kokou* tomaron medidas extremas para asegurar que ninguna bruja se atreviera a entrar en la tumba

Defesa das bruxas marciais: Ganbada e Kokou

As precauções tomadas pelos seguidores da Voduna para reconhecer e evitar feitiços de dano são consideráveis. O funeral de Sossa Guédéhoungué, o "Papa do Vodu", foi uma demonstração impressionante disso mesmo.

Membros das comunidades cult em torno dos deuses guerreiros Ganbada e Kokou tomaram medidas extremas para garantir que nenhuma bruxa ousasse entrar na sepultura aberta de Sossa. Pouco antes do caixão ser libertado, mais e mais pessoas

Krijgshaftige heksenafweer: Ganbada en Kokou

De voorzorgsmaatregelen die vodunaanhangers nemen om schadelijke magie te herkennen en af te weren zijn aanzienlijk. Dit werd indrukwekkend gedemonstreerd bij de begrafenis van Sossa Guédéhoungué, de 'vodunpaus'.

Leden van de cultusgemeenschappen rond de krijgersgoden Ganbada en Kokou namen extreme maatregelen om ervoor te zorgen dat geen enkele heks het aandurfde om Sossa's open graf te betreden. Kort voor

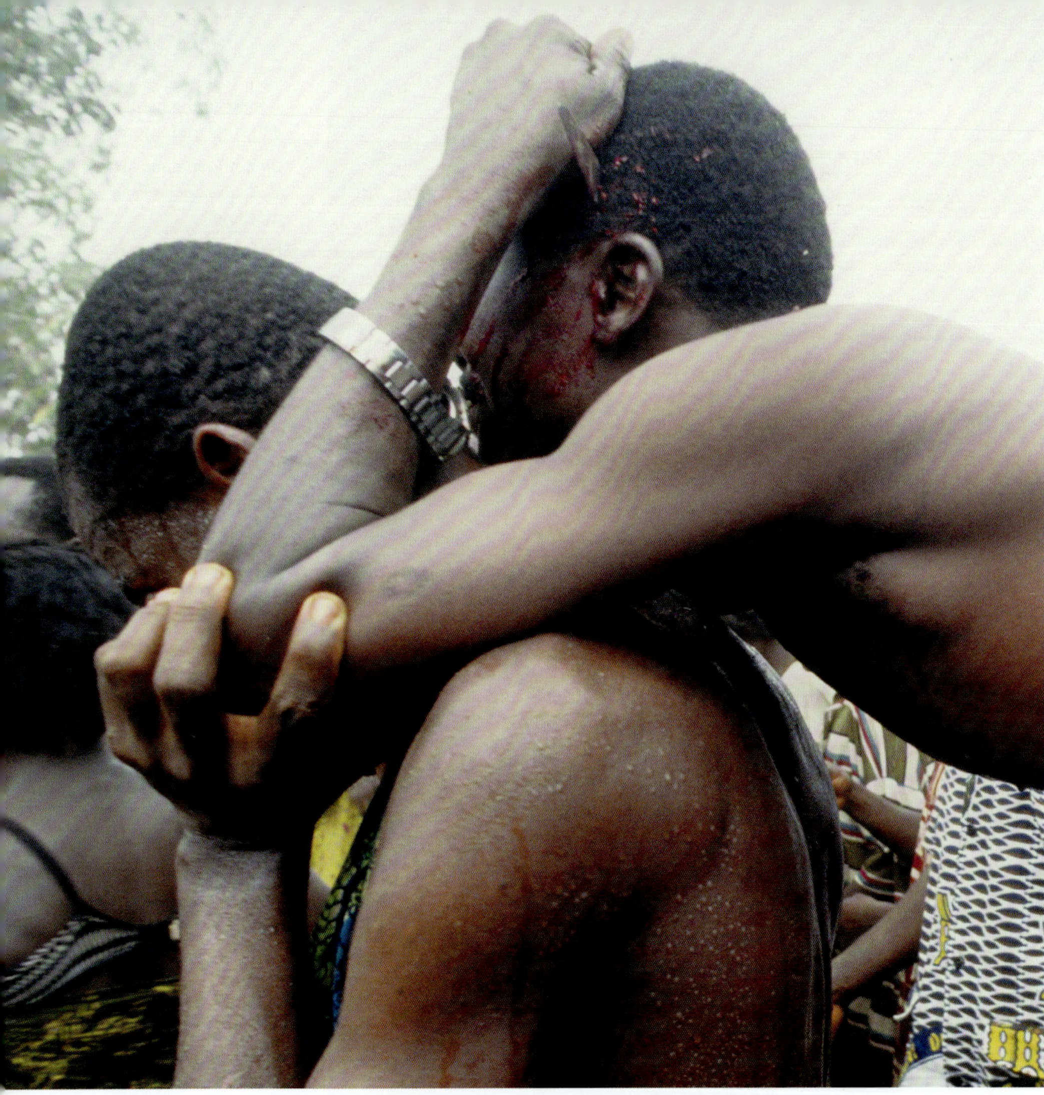

own painlessness and invulnerability with martial acts.

A man in a violent trance finally pulled out a long, rusty knife and stuck it into his head. The bystanders lifted him onto their shoulders and danced with him around Sossa's grave for over an hour. Such drastic defensive measures are rare, but they do occur.

sorcier n'oserait pénétrer dans la tombe ouverte de Sossa. Peu avant la mise en terre du cercueil, les danses ont redoublé alors que des démonstrations martiales visaient à démontrer l'absence de douleur et l'invincibilité.

Au plus fort de la transe, un homme s'est emparé d'un long couteau rouillé et se l'est planté en travers de la tête. Les hommes qui l'entouraient l'ont hissé sur leurs épaules et ont dansé avec lui plus d'une heure autour de la tombe de Sossa. De telles mesures de défense drastiques sont rares mais existent pourtant.

Sossas offenes Grab einzusteigen. Kurz vor der Sargeinlassung wurde immer wilder getanzt und mit martialischen Handlungen die eigene Schmerzlosigkeit und Unverwundbarkeit demonstriert.

Ein Mann in einer heftigen Trance zog schließlich ein langes, rostiges Messer und stieß es sich quer durch den Kopf. Die Umstehenden hievten ihn auf die Schultern und tanzten mit ihm über eine Stunde um Sossas Grab herum. Derart drastische Abwehrmaßnahmen sind zwar selten, aber sie kommen vor.

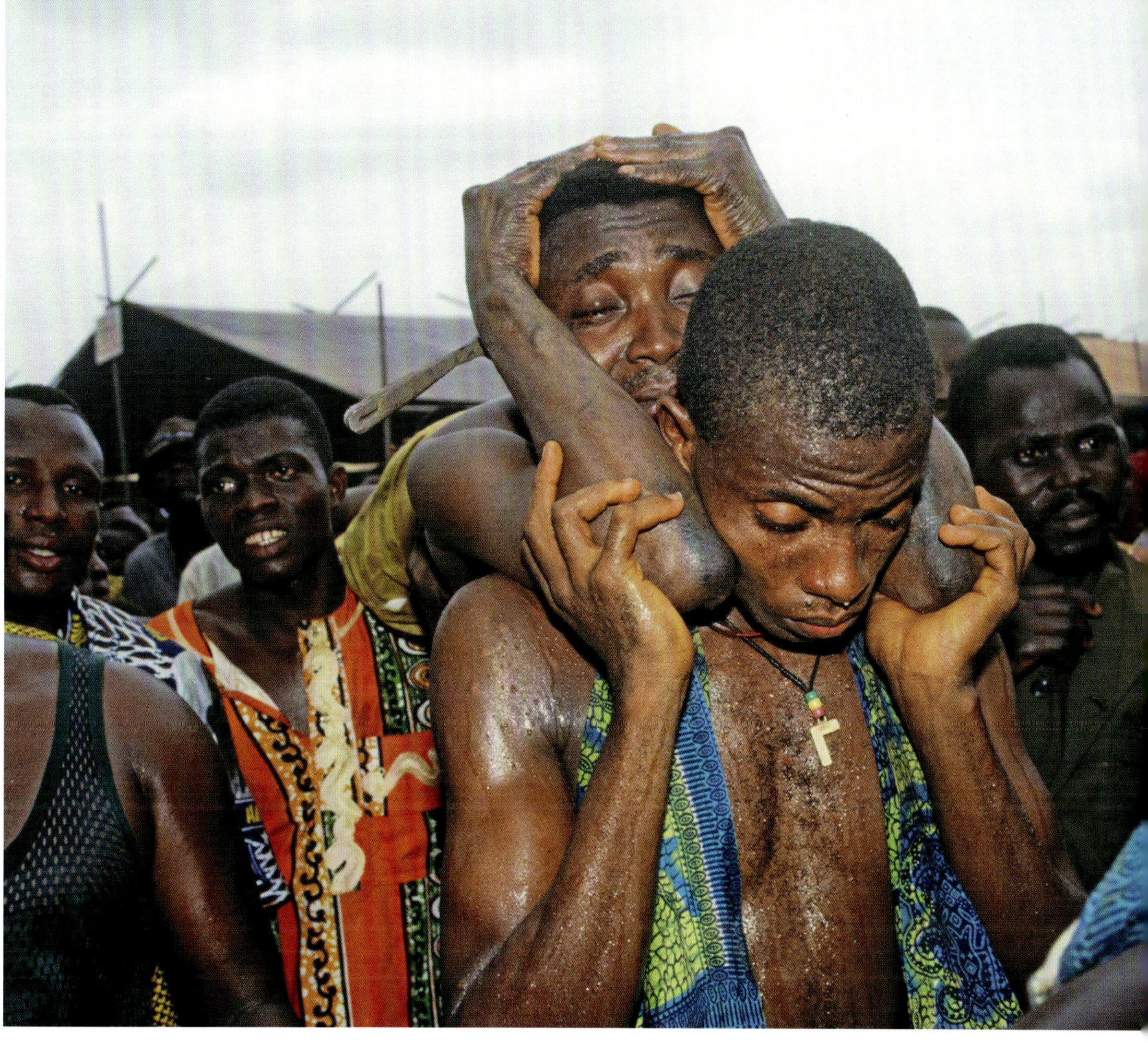

abierta de Sossa. Poco antes de que el ataúd fuera liberado, más y más gente bailaba salvajemente y demostraba su propia indolencia e invulnerabilidad con actos marciales.

Un hombre en trance violento finalmente sacó un cuchillo largo y oxidado y se lo clavó en la cabeza. Los transeúntes lo alzaron sobre sus hombros y bailaron con él alrededor de la tumba de Sossa durante más de una hora. Tales medidas defensivas drásticas son raras, pero ocurren.

dançavam loucamente e demonstravam a sua própria dor e invulnerabilidade com actos marciais.

Um homem em transe violento finalmente puxou uma longa faca enferrujada e empurrou-a pela cabeça. Os espectadores ergueram-no nos ombros e dançaram com ele à volta da campa de Sossa durante mais de uma hora. Tais medidas defensivas drásticas são raras, mas ocorrem.

de kist werd vrijgegeven, werd er steeds wilder gedanst en toonden mensen met krijgshandelingen hun eigen ongevoeligheid voor pijn en onkwetsbaarheid.

Een man in een heftige trance trok uiteindelijk een lang, roestig mes en stak het dwars door zijn hoofd. De omstanders hesen hem op hun schouders en hebben meer dan een uur met hem rond het graf van Sossa gedanst. Zulke drastische afweermaatregelen zijn zeldzaam, maar ze komen wel voor.

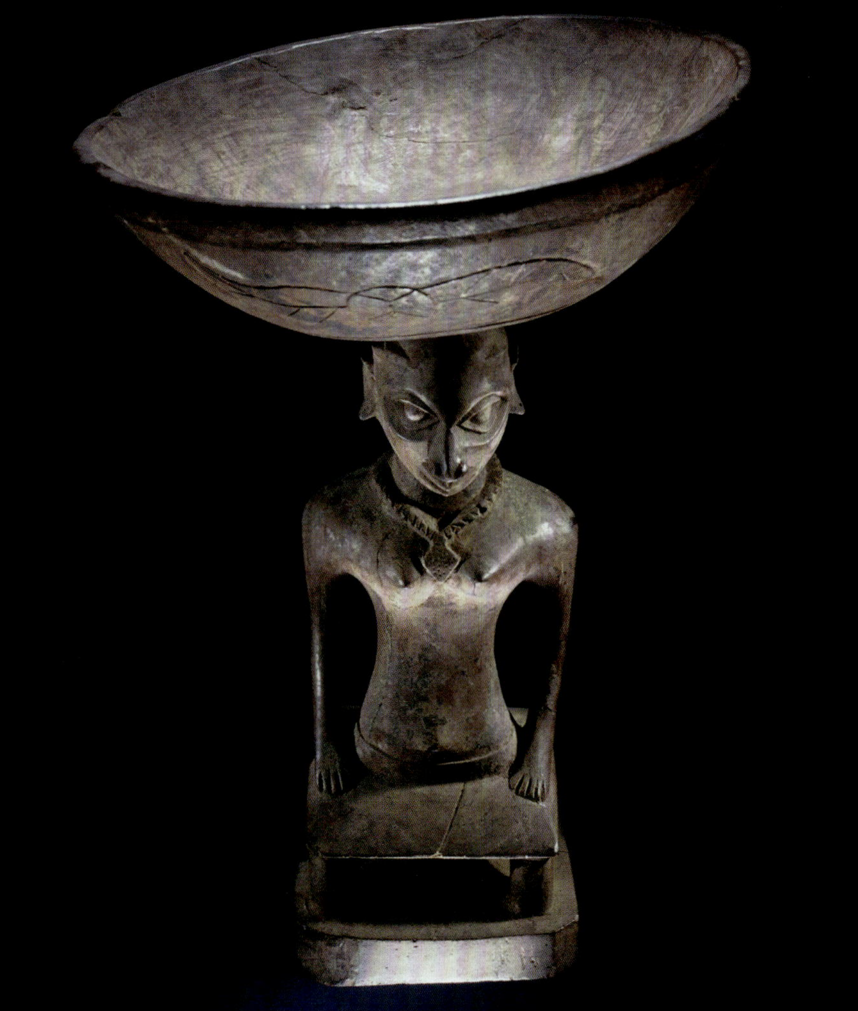

Fon witch bowl. This object served as a witch's bowl for the Fon people in Benin. As a symbol for the meat of the person involved, animal parts were eaten out of this bowl by witches.

Bol de sorcier Fon. Coupelle de sorcier du peuple Fon du Bénin. La viande animale déposée dans cette coupelle et consommée par les sorciers symbolise la chair de leur victime.

Fon-Hexenschale. Beim Volk der Fon in Benin diente dieses Objekt als Hexenschale. Symbolisch für das Fleisch der Zielperson wurden Tierteile aus dieser Schale heraus von Hexen verspeist.

Tazón de brujas Fon. Para el pueblo Fon de Benin, este objeto servía como cuenco de brujas. Las brujas se comieron partes de animales de este cuenco, símbolo de la carne de la persona objetivo.

Tigela de bruxa Fon. Para o povo Fon em Benin, este objecto serviu de taça de bruxa. Partes de animais foram comidas desta tigela por bruxas, símbolo da carne do alvo.

Heksenkom van de Fon. Voor het Fon-volk in Benin diende dit object als heksenkom. Uit deze kom aten heksen dierlijke delen, die het vlees van het mikpunt symboliseerden.

Wood/Bois, 60 × 45 cm

Magic, sorcery and witchcraft

In West Africa you can find countless stories about sorcery, magic and witchcraft. Just as the positive effects of the gods can be seen in medicinal plants, in food, in health and prosperity, so accidents, poisonings and diseases represent the other side of the coin.

In the worldview of the traditional community, cause and effect are not separated from the rest of existence. Whatever happens in life does not happen without reason, it is directly related to the world that surrounds the individual affected by an event.

Enchantement, magie et sorcellerie

Les histoires d'enchantement, de magie et de sorcellerie sont innombrables en Afrique de l'Ouest. Si la puissance bienveillante des dieux se matérialise à travers les vertus des plantes médicinales, les aliments, la prospérité et la santé, les accidents, empoisonnements et autres maladies constituent le revers de la médaille.

Selon la conception du monde de la société traditionnelle, causes et conséquences ne sont pas isolées du reste de l'existence. Tout ce qui se produit dans la vie n'arrive pas sans raison, mais est directement lié au monde qui entoure l'individu concerné.

Zauberei, Magie und Hexenwerk

In Westafrika findet man zahllose Geschichten über Zauberei, Magie und Hexenwerk. Ebenso, wie sich in den Heilpflanzen, in den Lebensmitteln, in Gesundheit und Wohlstand die positiven Wirkkräfte der Götter zeigen, so bilden Unglücksfälle, Vergiftungen und Krankheiten die Kehrseite der Medaille ab.

In der Weltanschauung der traditionellen Lebensgemeinschaft werden Ursache und Wirkung nicht vom Rest des Daseins entkoppelt. Was auch im Leben geschieht, es passiert nicht ohne Grund, es steht in einem direkten Zusammenhang mit der Welt, die das von einem Ereignis betroffene Individuum umgibt.

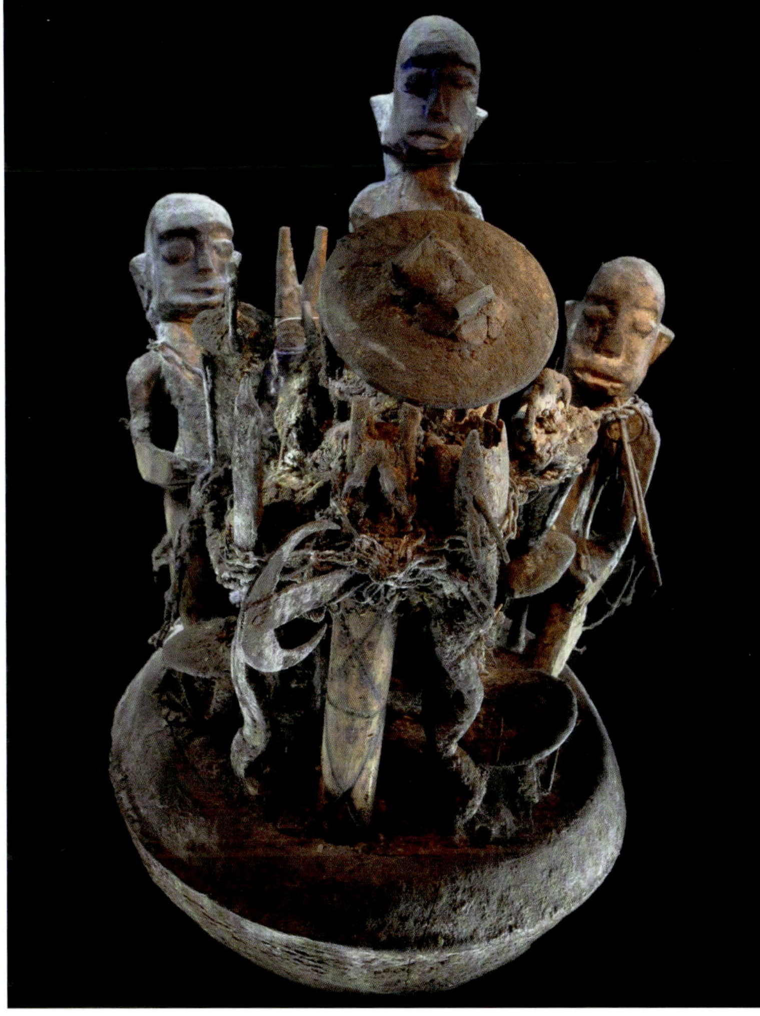

Black magic object
Objet de magie noire
Schwarzmagisches Objekt
Objeto de magia negra
Objeto de magia negra
Object van zwarte magie

Wood, various organic materials, metal, bone/Bois, matières organiques, métal, os, 45 × 26 cm

Magia, hechicería y brujería

En África Occidental se pueden encontrar innumerables historias sobre magia, hechicería y brujería. Así como las plantas curativas, la comida, la salud y la prosperidad muestran los efectos positivos de los dioses, los accidentes, los envenenamientos y las enfermedades muestran la otra cara de la moneda.

En la cosmovisión de la comunidad tradicional, la causa y el efecto no están desvinculados del resto de la existencia. Lo que sucede en la vida, no sucede sin razón, está directamente relacionado con el mundo que rodea al individuo afectado por un evento.

Magia, Feitiçaria e bruxaria

Na África Ocidental você pode encontrar inúmeras histórias sobre magia, magia e bruxaria. Assim como as plantas de cura, a comida, a saúde ea prosperidade mostrar os efeitos positivos dos deuses, assim os acidentes, envenenamentos e doenças mostram o outro lado da moeda.

Na visão de mundo da comunidade tradicional, causa e efeito não são dissociados do resto da existência. O que quer que aconteça na vida, não acontece sem razão, está directamente relacionado com o mundo que rodeia o indivíduo afectado por um acontecimento.

Magie, tovenarij en hekserij

In West-Afrika zijn er talloze verhalen over magie, tovenarij en hekserij. Net zoals de positieve invloeden van de goden te zien zijn in geneeskrachtige planten, voedsel, gezondheid en welvaart tonen ongelukken, vergiftigingen en ziekten de andere kant van de medaille.

In het wereldbeeld van traditionele levensgemeenschappen zijn oorzaak en gevolg niet losgekoppeld van de rest van het bestaan. Wat er ook gebeurt in het leven, het gebeurt niet zonder reden. Het is direct gerelateerd aan de wereld die het door een gebeurtenis getroffen individu omringt.

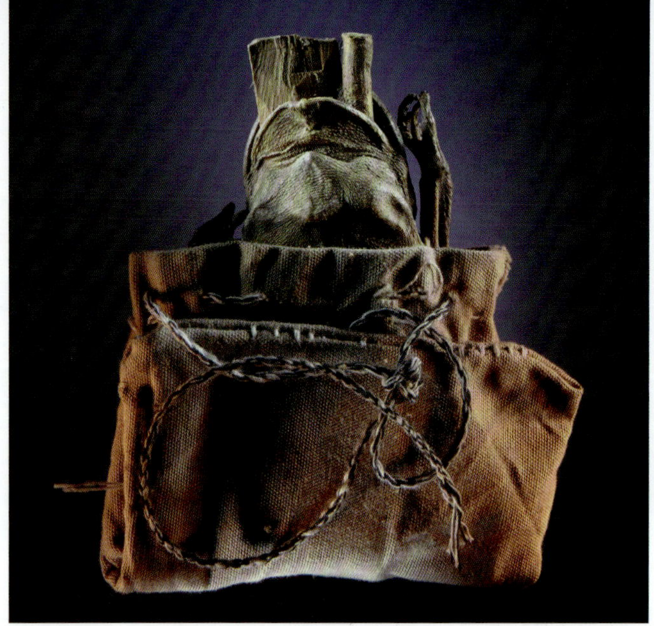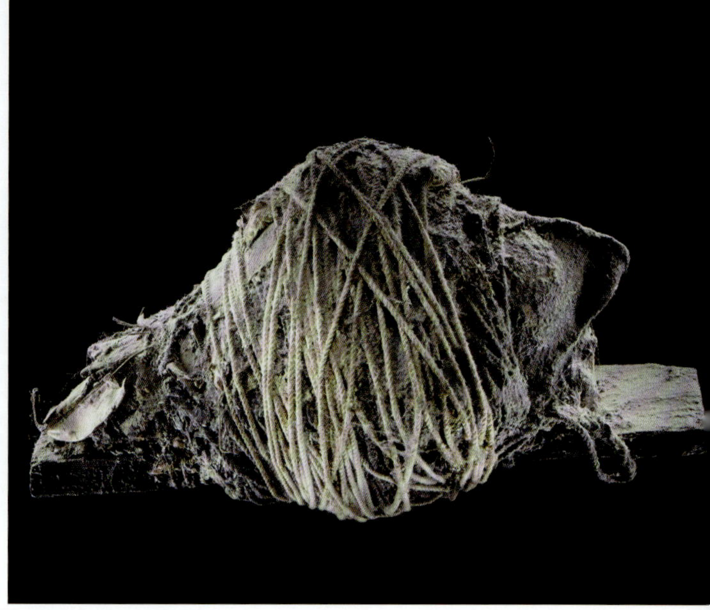

Black magic object. A dried frog in cloth with two wooden pegs in its mouth. If one pulls them out and penetrates the body of the frog with them, diseases are sent to the person intended.

Objet de magie noire. Grenouille séchée enveloppée de tissu. De sa bouche dépassent deux bâtonnets de bois. En les retirant pour les enfoncer dans le corps de la grenouille, on déclenche des maladies chez la personne que l'on cible.

Schwarzmagisches Objekt. Ein getrockneter Frosch in Stoff, in dessen Mund zwei Holzpflöcke stecken. Zieht man diese heraus und penetriert mit ihnen den Körper des Frosches, schickt man Krankheiten an die Zielperson.

Objeto de magia negra. Una rana seca en tela con dos clavijas de madera en la boca. Si uno las saca y penetra con ellas en el cuerpo de la rana, envía enfermedades a la persona objetivo.

Objeto de magia negra. Um sapo seco em tecido com duas cavilhas de madeira na boca. Se um puxa estes para fora e penetra com eles o corpo do sapo, um envia doenças para a pessoa alvo.

Object van zwarte magie. Een gedroogde kikker in een doek met twee houten pinnen in de mond. Als je deze eruit trekt en ze in het lichaam van de kikker steekt, stuur je ziekten naar het mikpunt.

Frog, wood, textiles/Grenouille, bois, textiles, 12 × 8 cm

Black magic object

Objet de magie noire

Schwarzmagisches Objekt

Objeto de magia negra

Objeto de magia negra

Object van zwarte magie

Dog skull, wood, plants, string/Crâne de chien, bois, plantes, ficelle, 10 × 20 cm

For example, the oracle consultation in the broader sense serves to show the deeper connections of existing problems in the social community. With the involvement of the gods, it offers solutions that have a holistic approach and take care of everyone involved.

Ainsi, la consultation des oracles vise par extension à mettre en évidence les corrélations profondes entre les problèmes existants au sein de la société. En association avec les dieux, les oracles proposent des solutions qui présentent une approche globale et prennent soin de toutes les personnes concernées.

So dient beispielsweise die Orakelbefragung im weiteren Sinne dazu, die tieferen Zusammenhänge bestehender Probleme in der Sozialgemeinschaft aufzuzeigen. Unter Einbindung der Götter bietet sie Lösungen an, die einen ganzheitlichen Ansatz haben und für alle Beteiligten Sorge tragen.

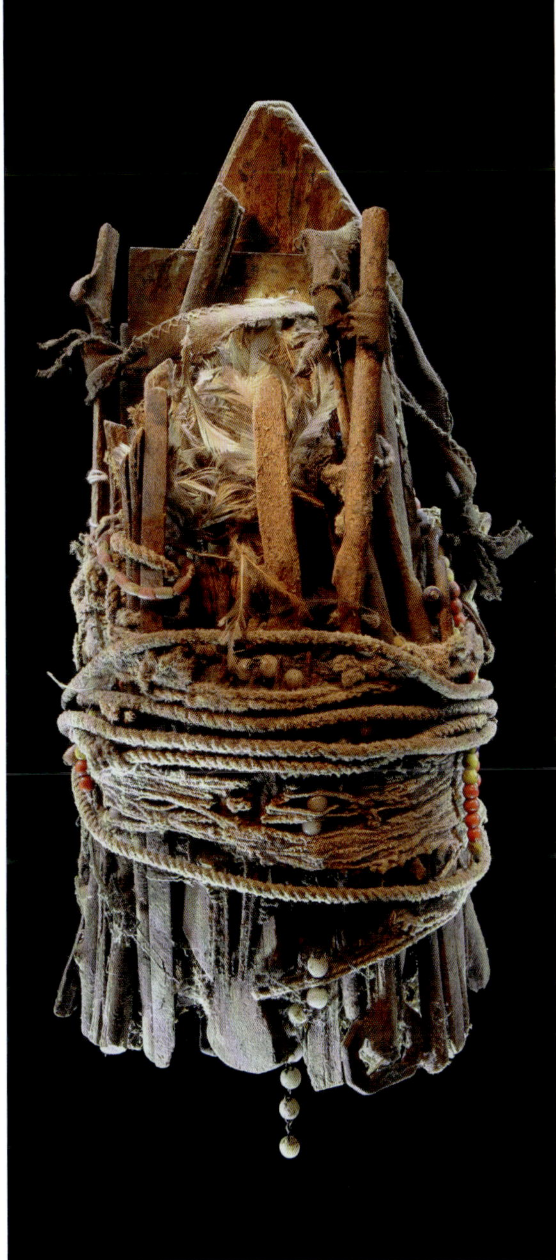

Black magic object. The object serves to capture a person in the figurative sense. They become helpless, can no longer do anything, their life force dwindles and they fall into a state of semi-consciousness.

Objet de magie noire. Cet objet permet de « clouer » au sens figuré une personne. Elle se retrouve alors sans défense, plus rien ne lui réussit, sa vigueur diminue et elle tombe dans un état de torpeur.

Schwarzmagisches Objekt. Das Objekt dient der Fesselung einer Person im übertragenen Sinne. Sie wird hilflos, nichts gelingt ihr mehr, die Lebenskraft schwindet, und sie fällt in einen Dämmerzustand.

Objeto de magia negra. El objeto sirve a la esclavitud de una persona en el sentido figurado. Se vuelve indefensa, nada tiene éxito, su vitalidad se desvanece y entra en un estado de crepúsculo.

Objeto de magia negra. O objeto serve a escravidão de uma pessoa no sentido figurativo. Ela fica desamparada, nada acontece, sua vitalidade desaparece e ela cai em um estado de crepúsculo.

Object van zwarte magie. Het object dient de ketening van een persoon in figuurlijke zin. Die wordt hulpeloos, niets lukt, zijn levenskracht verdwijnt en hij raakt in een staat tussen waken en slapen.

Wood/Bois, 24 × 12 cm

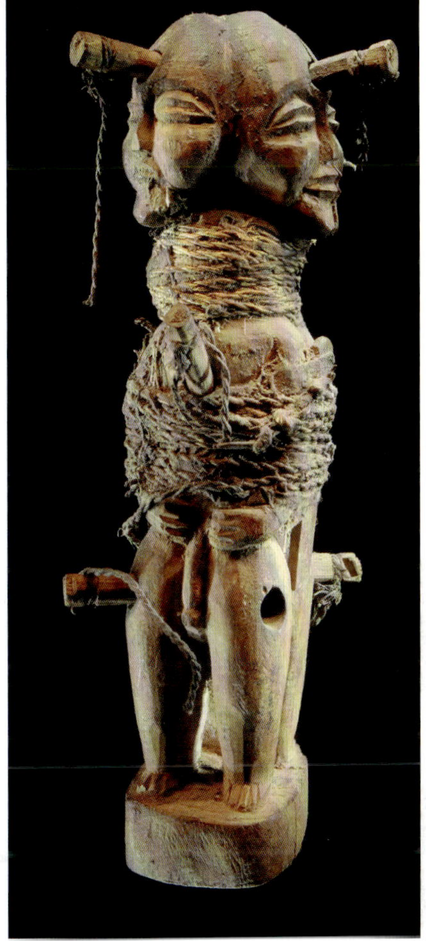

Black magic object

Objet de magie noire

Schwarzmagisches Objekt

Objeto de magia negra

Objeto de magia negra

Object van zwarte magie

Wood/Bois, 30 × 8 cm

Por ejemplo, la consulta al oráculo en el sentido más amplio sirve para mostrar las conexiones más profundas de los problemas existentes en la comunidad social. Con la participación de los dioses, ofrece soluciones que adoptan un enfoque holístico y se ocupan de todos los involucrados.

Por exemplo, a pesquisa do oráculo no sentido mais amplo serve para mostrar as conexões mais profundas dos problemas existentes na comunidade social. Com o envolvimento dos deuses, oferece soluções que tomam uma abordagem holística e cuidam de todos os envolvidos.

De orakelraadpleging in bredere zin dient bijvoorbeeld om de diepere verbanden van bestaande problemen in de sociale gemeenschap aan te tonen. Door het inpakken van de goden biedt ze oplossingen die een holistisch uitgangspunt hebben en voor alle betrokkenen zorgen.

Black magic object. This object can cause mental illness in the targeted person. They go insane and talk nonsense.

Objet de magie noire. Cet objet peut provoquer des maladies mentales chez la personne ciblée. Elle perd une partie de ses capacités psychiques et tient des discours incohérents.

Schwarzmagisches Objekt. Dieses Objekt kann Geisteskrankheiten bei der Zielperson verursachen. Sie wird unzurechnungsfähig und wirres Zeug reden.

Objeto de magia negra. Este objeto puede causar enfermedad mental en la persona objetivo. Se vuelve loca y confusa.

Objeto de magia negra

Este objeto pode causar doença mental no alvo.. Ela fica louca e confusa.

Object van zwarte magie. Dit object kan tot geesteziekten leiden bij het mikpunt. Die wordt ontoerekeningsvatbaar en zal wartaal spreken.

Human lower jaw, monkey skull/Machoire humaine, crâne de singe, 8 × 10 cm

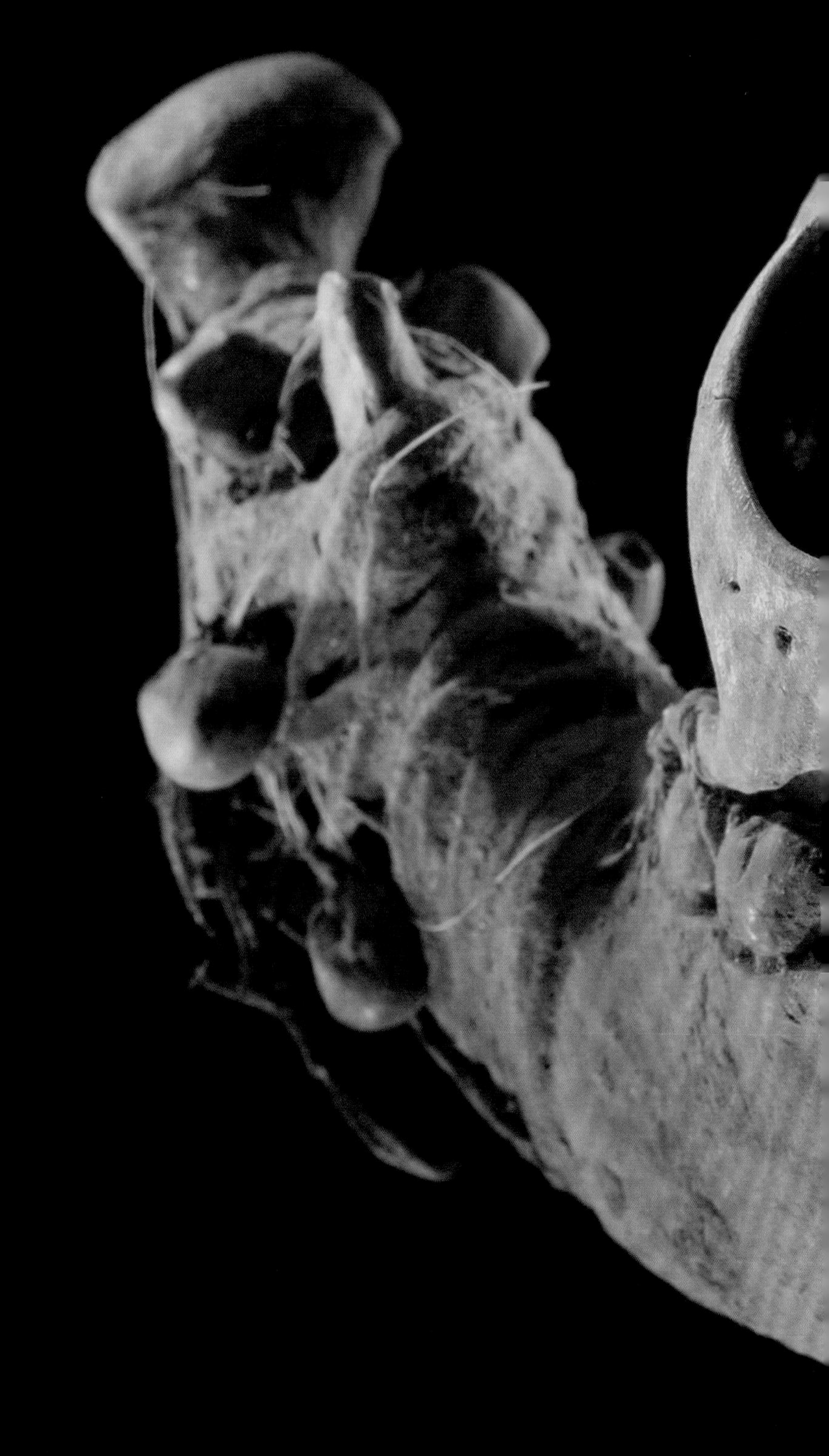

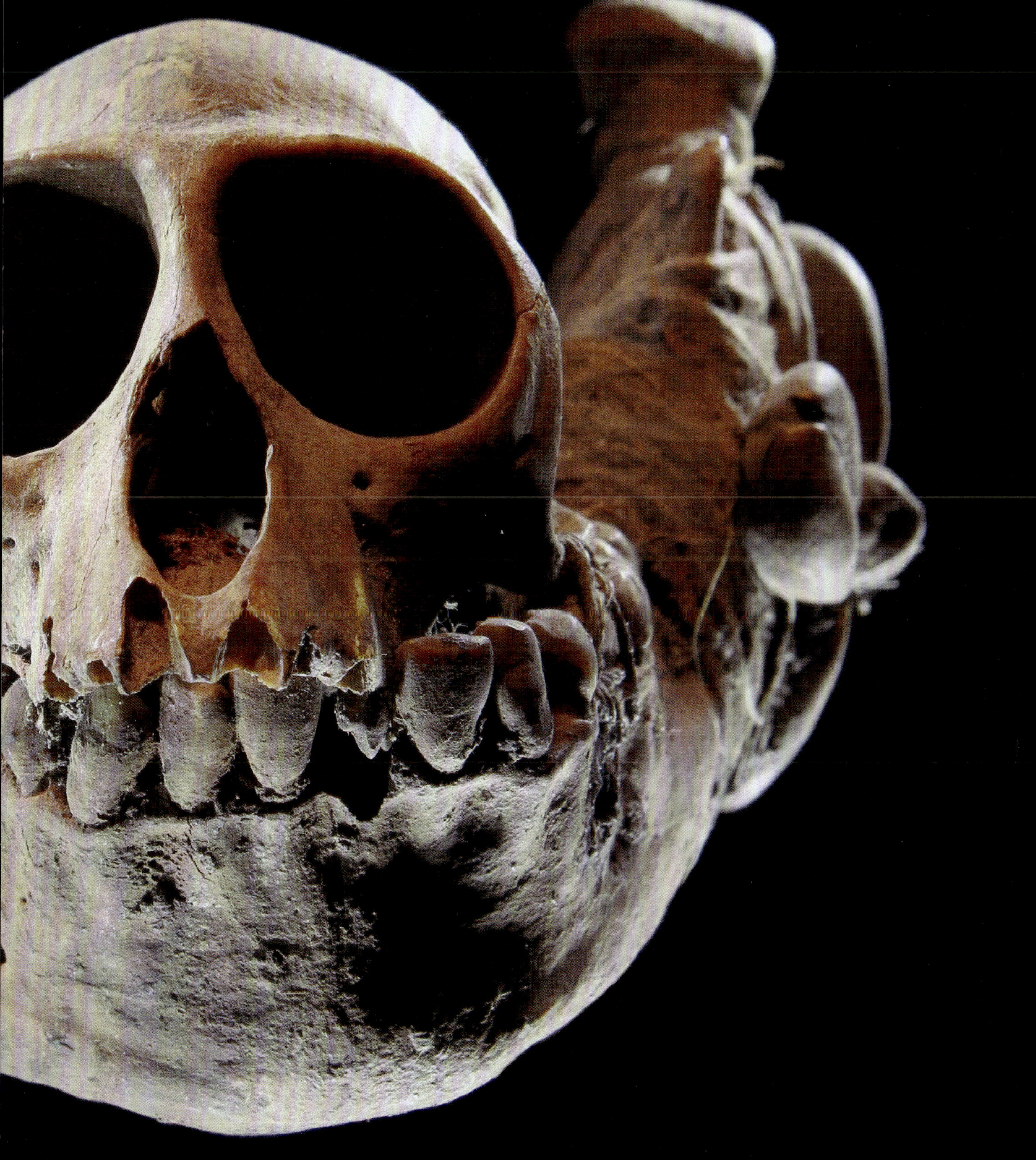

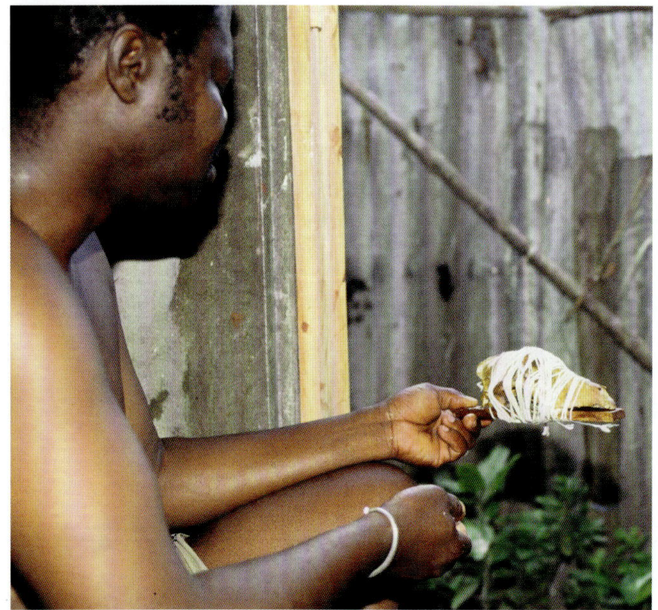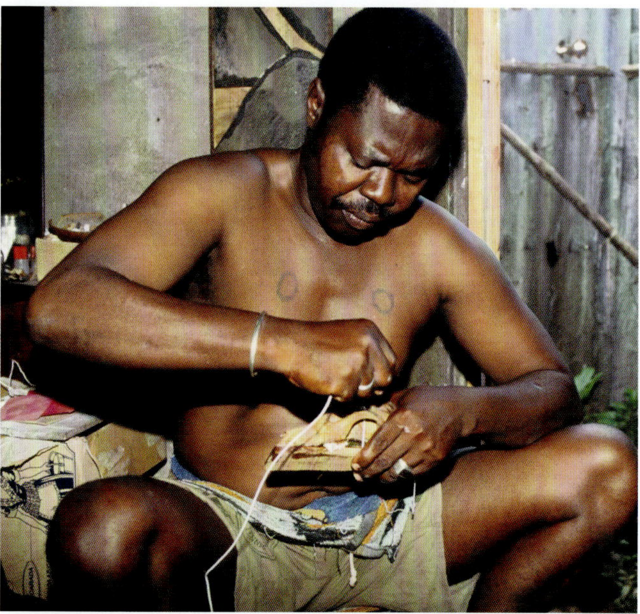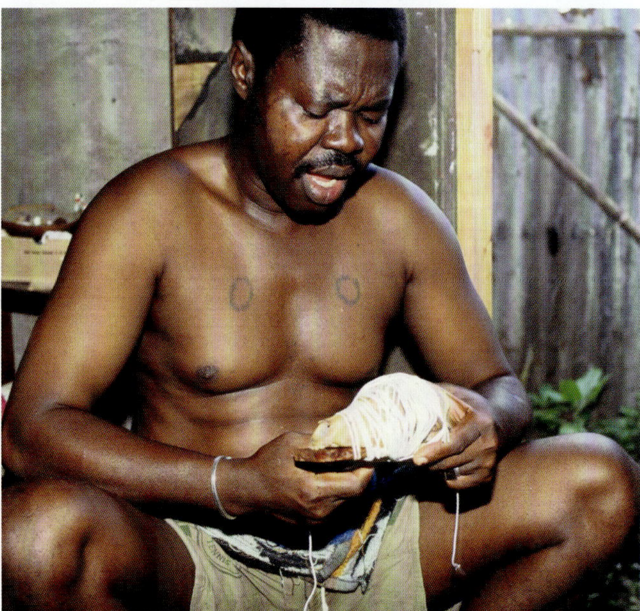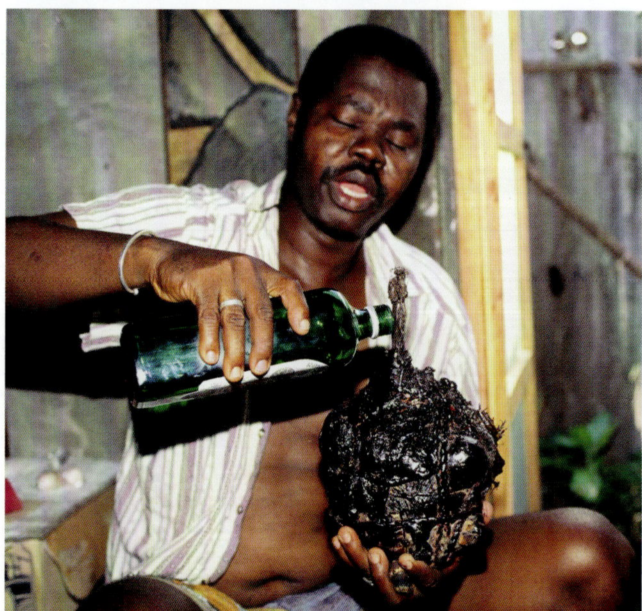

Witchcraft with binding of a dog's skull and invoking the forces of harm

Sorcellerie où l'on bande le crâne d'un chien en invoquant les forces maléfiques

Hexerei mit Fesselung eines Hundeschädels unter Anrufung der Schadenkräfte

Brujería con esclavitud del cráneo de un perro invocando las fuerzas del daño

Feitiçaria com escravidão do crânio de um cão invocando as forças do dano

Hekserij met het vastbinden van een hondenschedel onder aanroeping van de schadelijke krachten

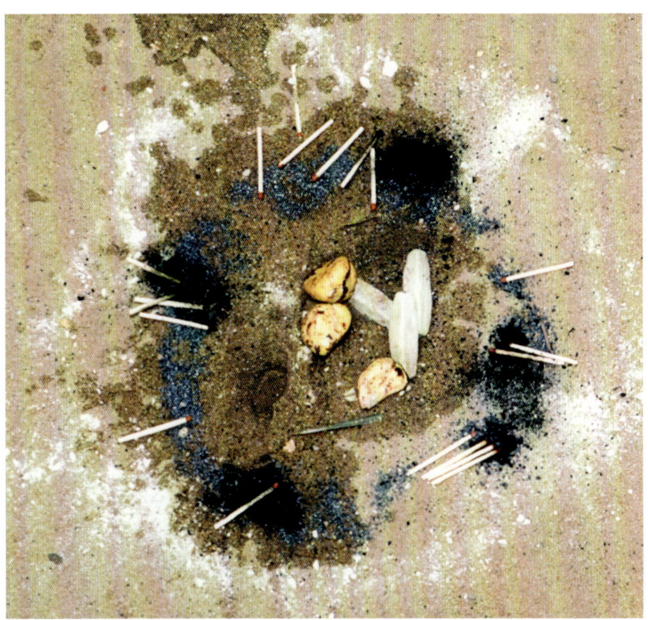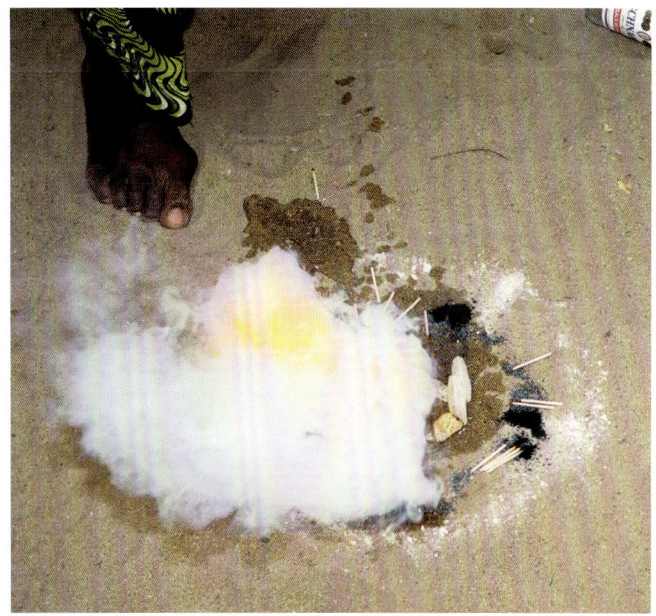
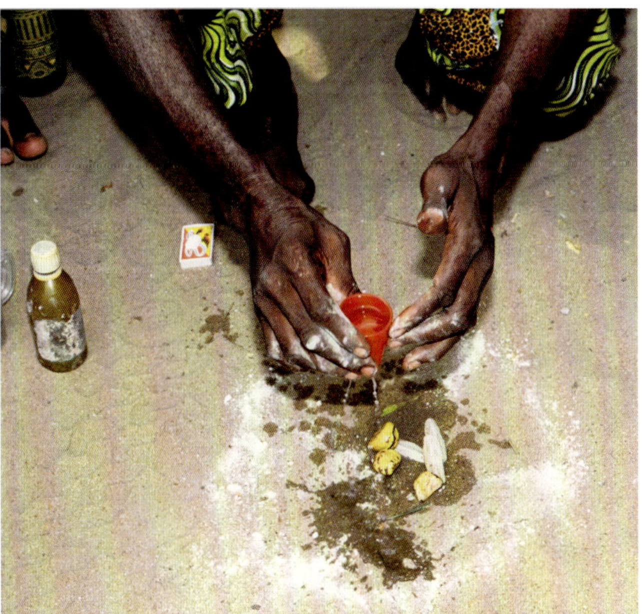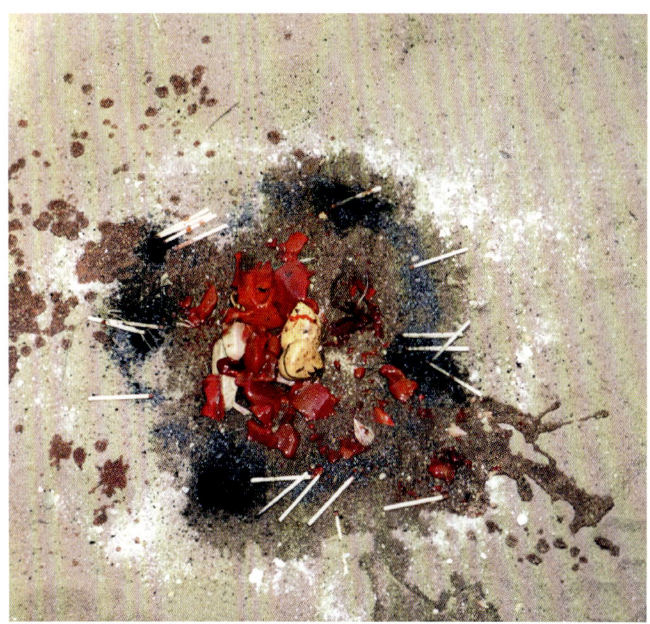

Against witchcraft with blood, liquor and gunpowder for the Vodun Sakla

Contre la sorcellerie avec du sang, de l'alcool et de la poudre à canon pour le vodun Sakla

Gegen die Hexerei mit Blut, Schnaps und Schießpulver für den Vodun Sakla

Contra la brujería con sangre, licor y pólvora para el vudú Sakla

Contra a bruxaria com sangue, licor e pólvora para o Vodun Sakla

Tegen hekserij met bloed, drank en buskruit voor de vodun Sakla

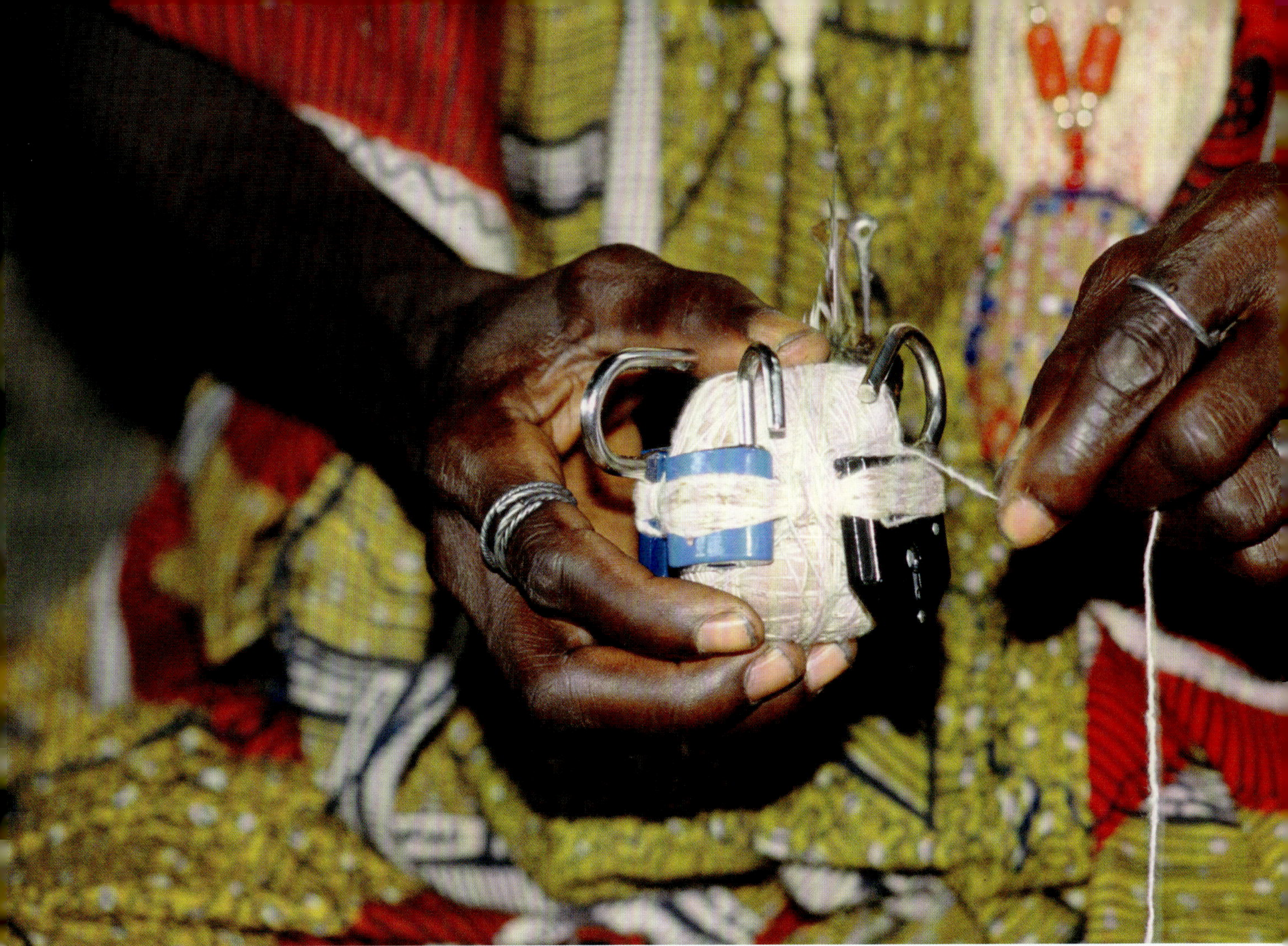

The Holi, the dreaded people

In Benin, the Holi people live secluded in the woods south of the small town of Kétou. This ethnic group, which comprises only about 6000 people, is feared throughout the country for its damaging magic.

It is not known exactly where the Holi came from, and many legends have sprung up around their descent. Some Holi bear eye-catching and for the region completely untypical decorative scars on their faces.

The famous Holi priest Alulu Zangu was initiated into the secrets by his mother and has inherited her post. When a client

Les Holi, peuple redouté

Le peuple Holi vit au Bénin, dans les forêts retirées au sud du petit village de Kétou. Cette ethnie d'environ 6 000 individus est redoutée dans le pays entier pour sa magie maléfique.

On ne sait pas exactement d'où viennent les Holi et de nombreuses légendes ont été rapportées autour de leurs origines. Beaucoup de Holi possèdent sur le visage des stigmates ornementaux impressionnants et totalement inhabituels pour la région.

Le célèbre prêtre Holi Alulu Zangu a été initié au secret par sa mère, puis a repris

Die Holi, das gefürchtete Volk

In Benin lebt abgeschieden in den Wäldern südlich des kleinen Ortes Kétou das Volk der Holi. Diese Ethnie, die nur etwa 6000 Personen umfasst, ist im ganzen Land gefürchtet für ihre Schadenmagie.

Man weiß nicht genau, wo die Holi herkommen, und viele Legenden ranken sich um ihre Abstammung. Manche Holi tragen auffällige und für die Region völlig atypische Schmucknarben im Gesicht.

Der bekannte Holi-Priester Alulu Zangu ist durch seine Mutter in die Geheimnisse eingeweiht worden und hat ihren Posten

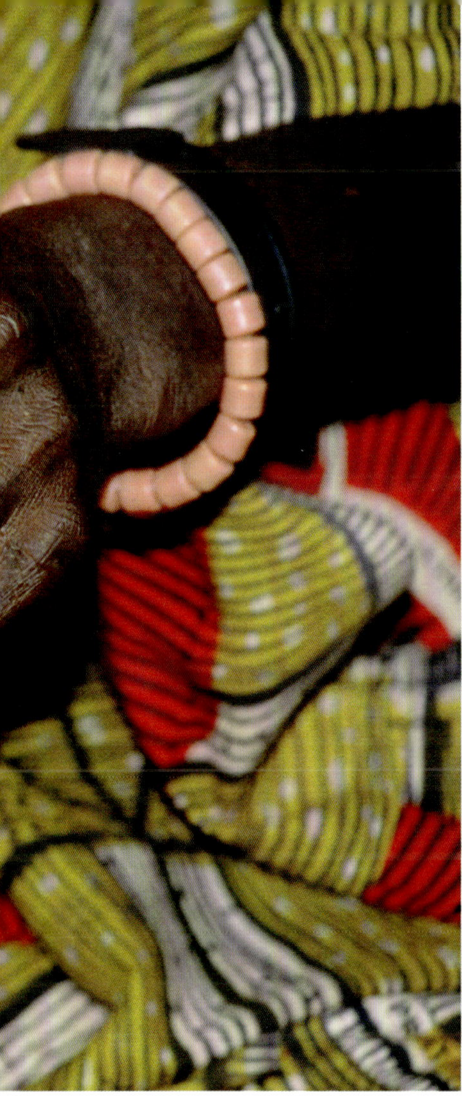

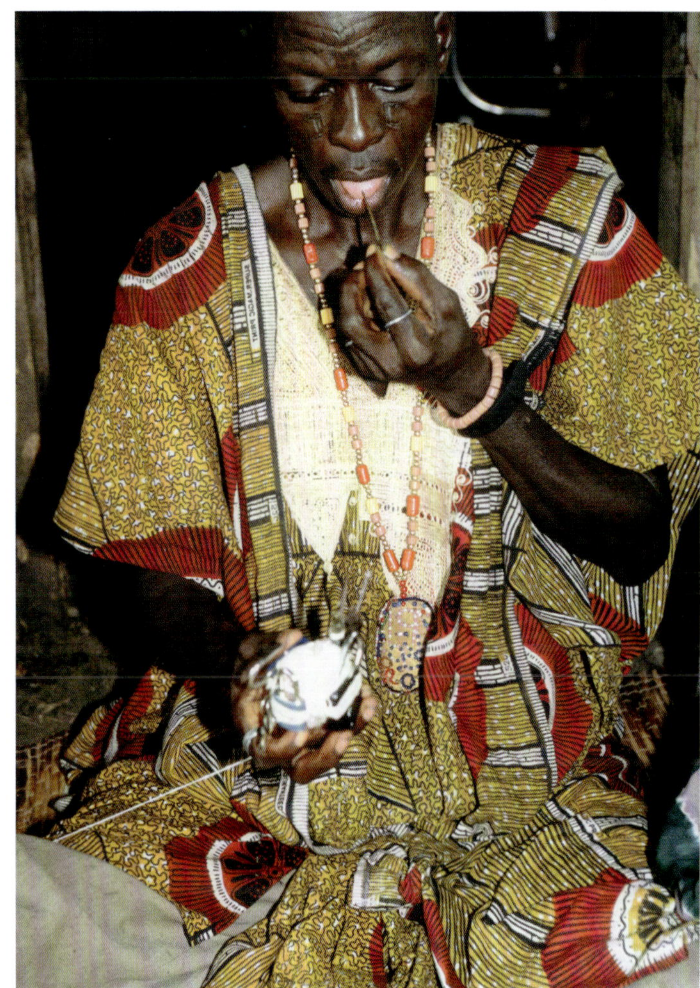

A sorcerer of the Holi prepares a Bo (power object) to kill someone

Un magicien Holi prépare un bo (objet de puissance) pour tuer quelqu'un

Ein Magier der Holi bereitet ein Bo (Kraftobjekt), um jemanden zu töten

Un mago Holi prepara un Bo (objeto de poder) para matar a alguien

Um mágico do Holi prepara um Bo (objeto de poder) para matar alguém

Een tovenaar van de Holi bereidt een bo (machtsobject) voor om iemand te doden

Los Holi, el pueblo temido

En Benin, el pueblo Holi vive aislado en los bosques al sur de la pequeña ciudad de Kétou. Este grupo étnico, que consta de sólo unas 6000 personas, es temido en todo el país por su magia negra.

No se sabe exactamente de dónde vienen los Holi, y muchas leyendas se entrelazan alrededor de sus ancestros. Algunos Holi tienen en sus rostros cicatrices decorativas llamativas y completamente atípicas para la región.

El famoso sacerdote Holi Alulu Zangu fue iniciado en los secretos por su madre

O Holi, As pessoas temidas

No Benim, o povo Holi vive isolado nos bosques ao sul da pequena cidade de Kétou. Este grupo étnico, composto por apenas cerca de 6000 pessoas, é temido em todo o país pela sua magia prejudicial.

Não se sabe exatamente de onde vem o Holi, e muitas lendas se entrelaçam em torno de seus ancestrais. Alguns Holi têm cicatrizes decorativas impressionantes e atípicas nos rostos.

O famoso sacerdote Holi Alulu Zangu foi iniciado nos segredos pela sua mãe e herdou o seu cargo. Quando um cliente das

De Holi, het gevreesde volk

In Benin woont het volk van de Holi in de bossen ten zuiden van het plaatsje Kétou. Deze etnische groep, die uit slechts zo'n 6000 mensen bestaat, is in het hele land gevreesd vanwege zijn schadelijke magie.

Het is niet precies bekend waar de Holi vandaan komen en veel legenden zijn verweven rond hun afstamming. Sommige Holi hebben opvallende en voor de regio volledig atypische sierlittekens op hun gezicht.

De beroemde Holi-priester Alulu Zangu werd door zijn moeder in de geheimen

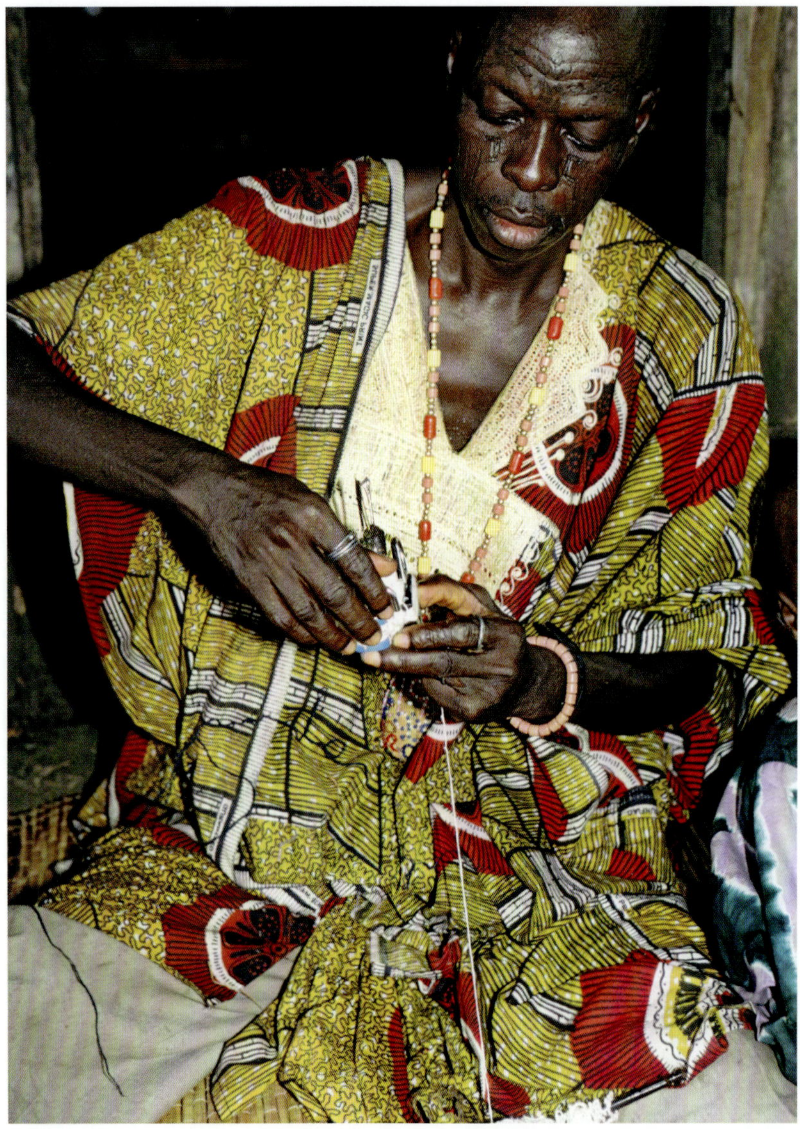

The ingredients of these magical objects are kept strictly secret. Animal parts, plant poisons and bondage are often used.

Les composants de cet objet magique sont gardés secrets. Il s'agit notamment souvent de fragments animaliers, de poisons végétaux et de liens.

Die Zutaten dieser magischen Arbeiten werden streng geheimgehalten. Oft kommen Tierteile, Pflanzengifte und Fesselungen zum Einsatz.

Los ingredientes de este mágico trabajo se mantienen estrictamente en secreto. A menudo se utilizan partes de animales, venenos de plantas y ataduras.

Os ingredientes deste trabalho mágico são mantidos estritamente secretos. Muitas vezes são usadas partes de animais, venenos de plantas e bondage.

De ingrediënten van dit magische werk worden strikt geheim gehouden. Vaak worden delen van dieren, plantengif en bondage gebruikt.

from the surrounding area comes to him, and commissions some harmful magic, the power of the women flows into his work. Zangu prepares the spell with special ingredients, and in the end the women get together, gather around the magical object and potentiate its effect with rites and chants whose contents are kept strictly secret.

sa fonction. Lorsqu'un client des environs le rencontre pour une mission de magie maléfique, la force des femmes s'infiltre au plus profond de sa pratique. Zangu prépare l'enchantement avec des ingrédients spécifiques, puis à la fin, les femmes interviennent, se réunissant autour de l'objet magique et augmentant son effet au moyen de rites et de chants dont le contenu est gardé strictement secret.

geerbt. Wenn aus dem Umland ein Klient zu ihm kommt, der eine Schadenmagie in Auftrag gibt, fließt die Kraft der Frauen grundsätzlich in seine Arbeit mit ein. Zangu bereitet den Zauber mit speziellen Ingredienzien vor, und am Ende kommen die Frauen zusammen, scharen sich um das magische Objekt und potenzieren seine Wirkung mit Riten und Gesängen, deren Inhalt streng geheim gehalten wird.

Dangerous bottles. Both materials and magical processes can be concentrated in bottles. They then become power objects, often used for damage spells.

Dangereuses bouteilles. Les bouteilles peuvent contenir différentes matières mais également des procédés magiques concentrés. Ce sont des objets actifs souvent utilisés en magie noire.

Gefährliche Flaschen. In Flaschen können sowohl Materialien als auch magische Vorgänge konzentriert werden. Sie werden dann zu Kraftobjekten, die oft für Schadenzauber herhalten.

Botellas peligrosas. Tanto los materiales como los procesos mágicos se pueden concentrar en botellas. Luego se convierten en objetos de poder, a menudo usados para hechizos malignos.

Garrafas perigosas. Tanto os materiais como os processos mágicos podem ser concentrados em garrafas. Depois tornam-se objetos de poder, muitas vezes usados para feitiços de dano.

Gevaarlijke flessen. Zowel materialen als magische processen kunnen worden geconcentreerd in flessen. Ze worden dan krachtobjecten, die vaak worden gebruikt voor kwade tovenarij.

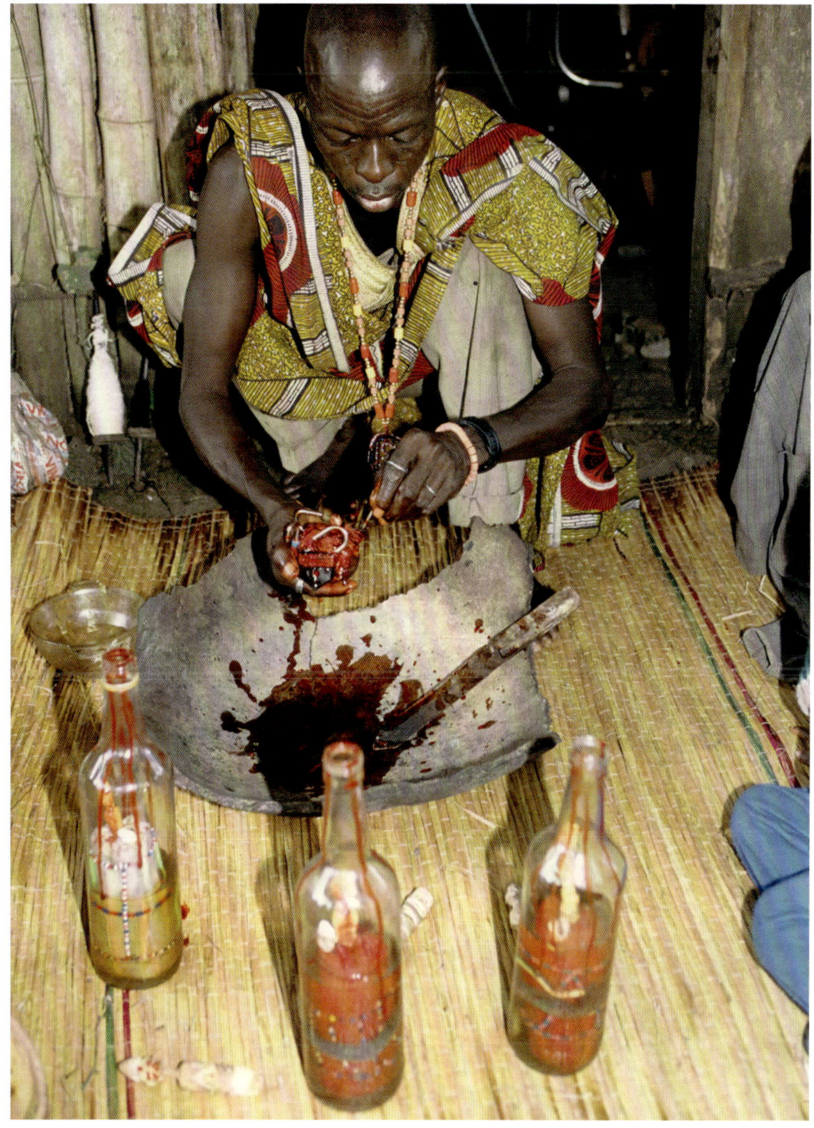

y heredó su puesto. Cuando un cliente de los alrededores se acerca a él para encargarle un hechizo maligno, el poder de las mujeresconfluye para realizar su trabajo. Zangu prepara el hechizo con ingredientes especiales, y al final las mujeres se reúnen, forman un grupo alrededor del objeto mágico, cuyo contenido se mantiene estrictamente en secreto, y potencian su efecto con ritos y canciones.

redondezas se aproxima dele, que comete uma magia de dano, o poder das mulheres flui para o seu trabalho. Zangu prepara o feitiço com ingredientes especiais, e no final as mulheres juntam-se, reúnem-se em torno do objecto mágico e potenciam o seu efeito com ritos e canções, cujos conteúdos são mantidos estritamente secretos.

ingewijd en erfde haar post. Wanneer een klant uit de omgeving naar hem toekomt om schadelijke magie te laten uitvoeren, vloeit de kracht van de vrouwcn in principe in zijn werk. Zangu bereidt de betovering voor met speciale ingrediënten, en uiteindelijk komen de vrouwen samen, scharen zich om het magische object heen en versterken het effect ervan met riten en gezangen, waarvan de inhoud strikt geheim wordt gehouden.

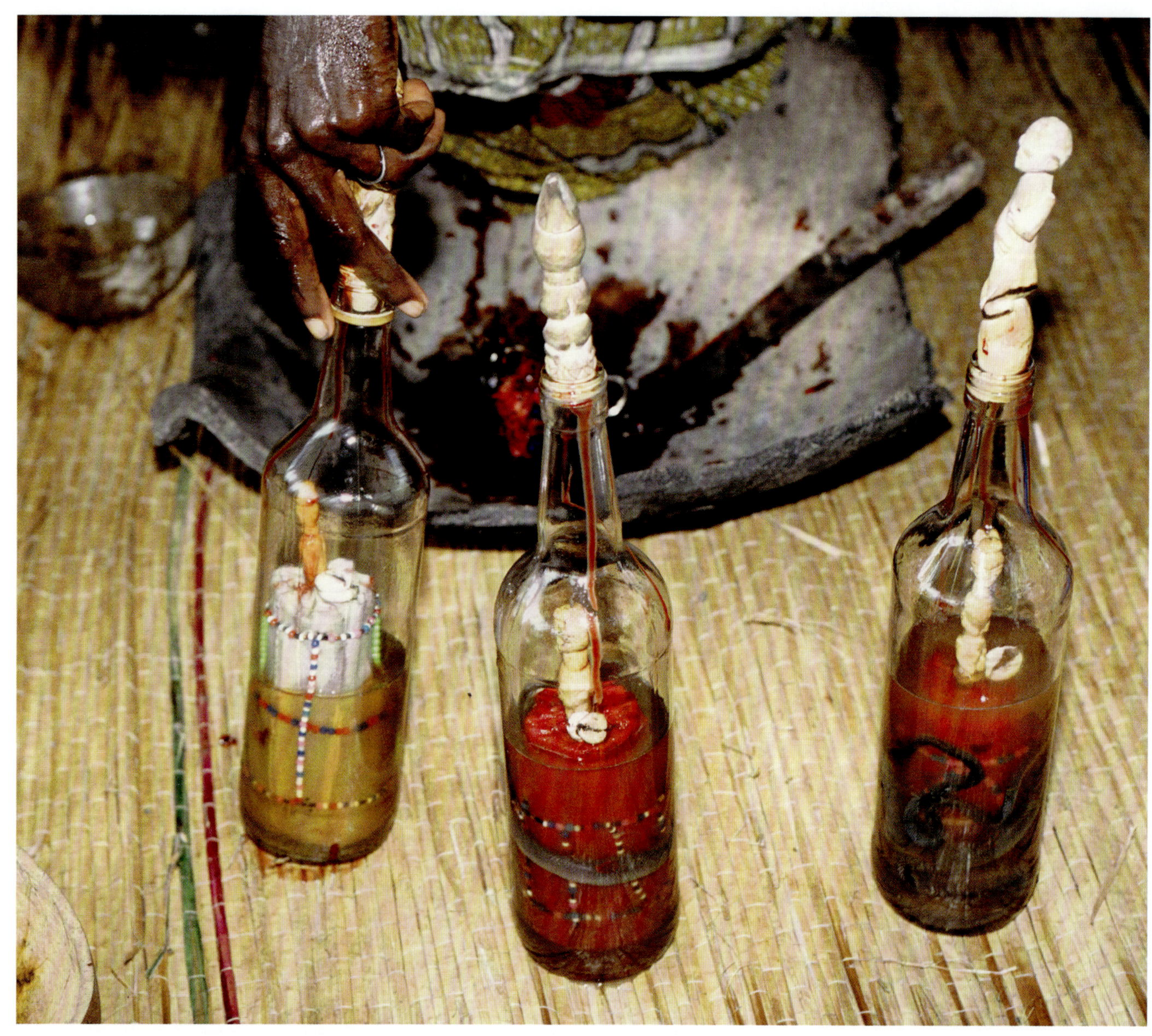

Bottle-Bos (power objects) with the people of the Holi

Bo-bouteilles (objets de puissance) auprès du peuple Holi

Flaschen-Bos (Kraftobjekte) beim Volk der Holi

Botellas Bo (objetos de poder) con la gente de Holi

Garrafa-Bos (objetos de poder) com as pessoas do Holi

Fles-bo's (machtsobjecten) van de Holi

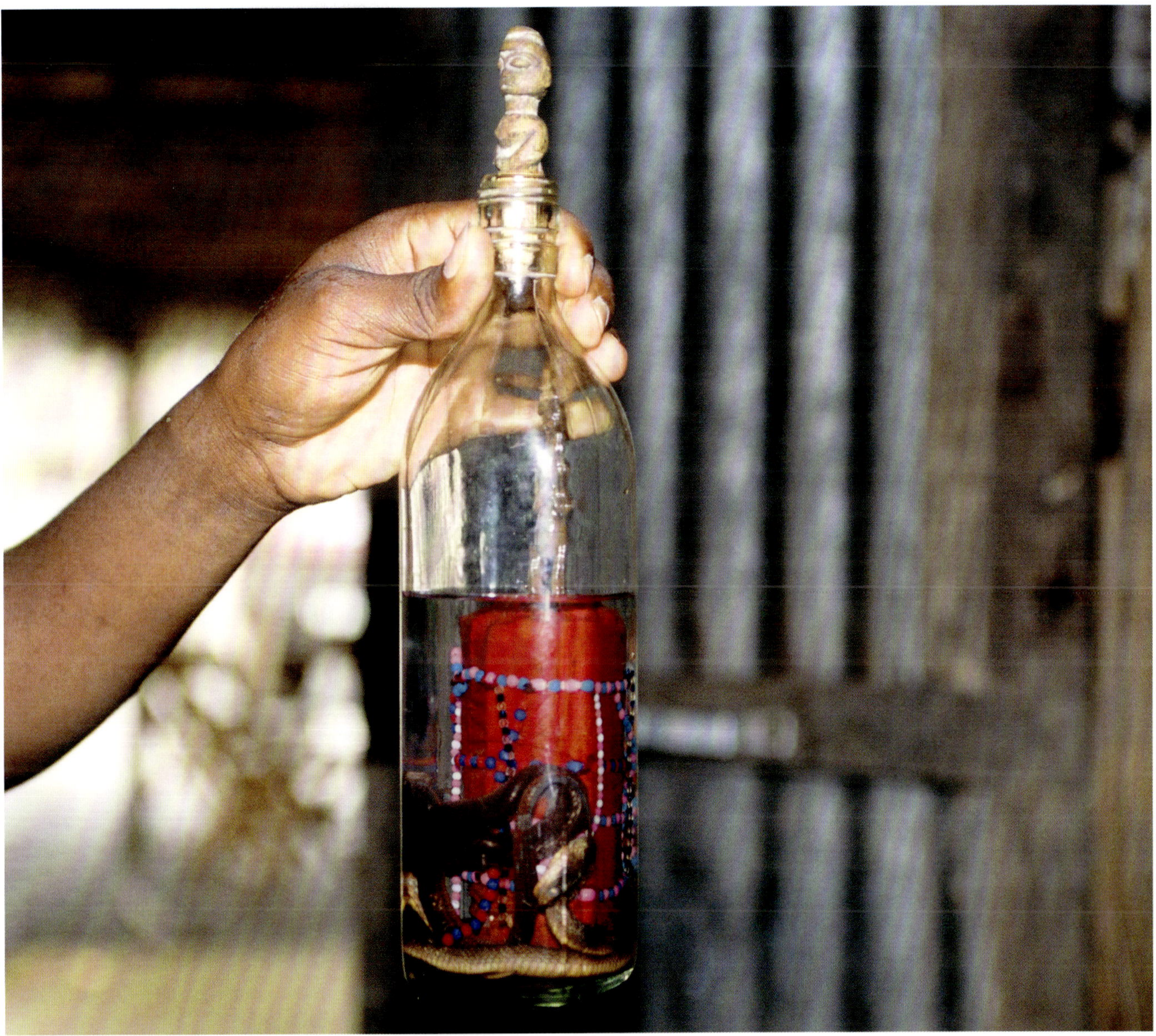

The test of fire and proof of trust. To seal the pact with a Holi Azeto, the client must drink from a bottle in which poisonous snakes are mixed with magical substances and alcohol.

Épreuve du feu et preuve de confiance. Pour sceller un pacte avec un azeto Holi, le client doit boire la préparation d'une bouteille contenant des serpents venimeux, des substances magiques et de l'alcool.

Feuerprobe und Vertrauensbeweis. Um den Pakt mit einem Holi-Azeto zu besiegeln, muss der Klient aus einer Flasche trinken, in der giftige Schlangen mit magischen Substanzen und Schnaps vermischt sind.

La prueba de fuego y la prueba de confianza. Para sellar el pacto con un Holi Azeto, el cliente debe beber de una botella en la que se mezclan serpientes venenosas con sustancias mágicas y licor.

O teste de fogo e a prova de confiança. Para selar o pacto com um Holi Azeto, o cliente deve beber de uma garrafa em que as cobras venenosas são misturadas com substâncias mágicas e licor.

Vuurproef en bewijs van vertrouwen. Om een pact met een Holi-azeto te sluiten, moet de klant drinken uit een fles waarin giftige slangen zijn vermengd met magische stoffen en sterkedrank.

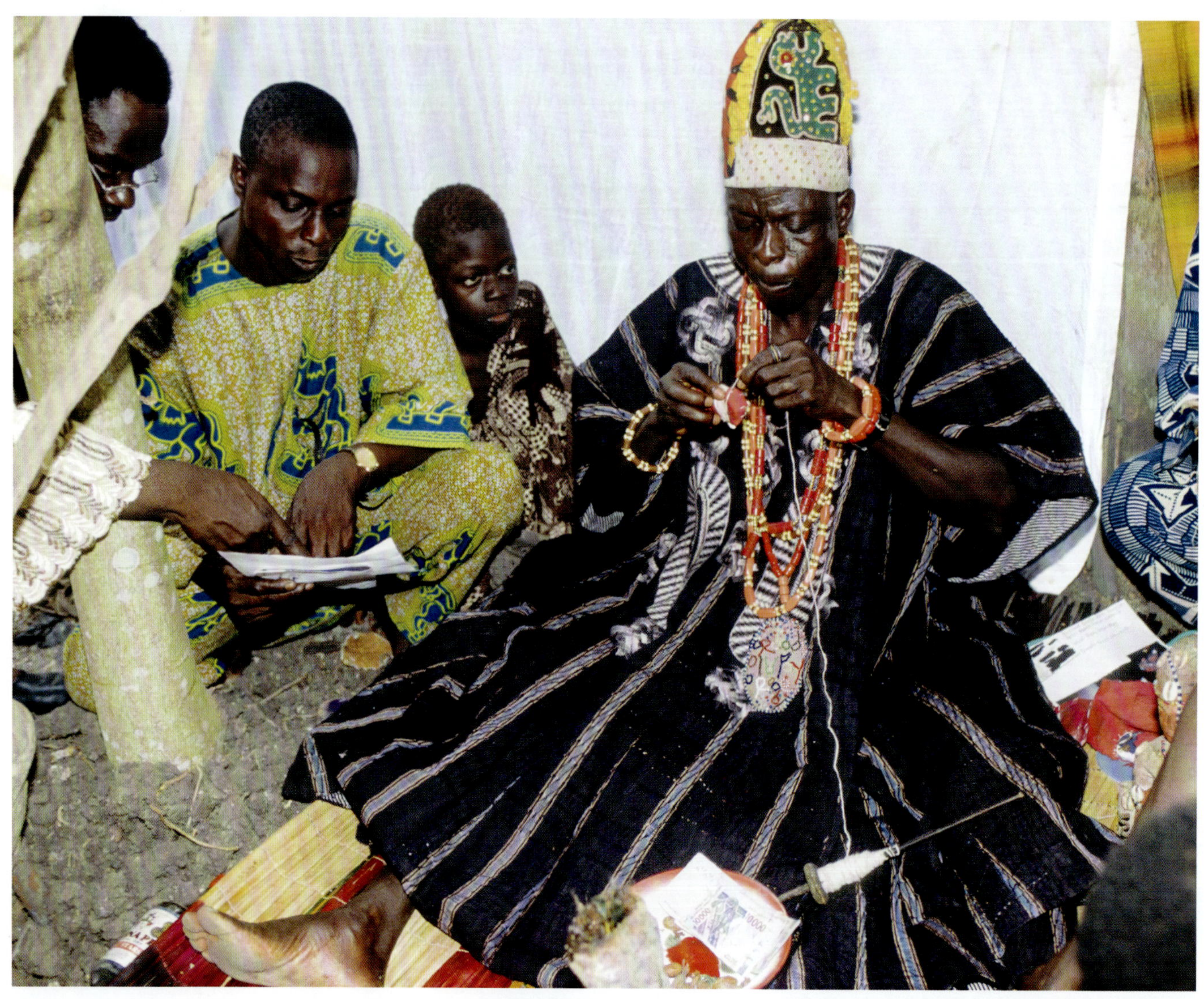

Origin of a damage spell

Début d'un rituel magique de mauvais sort

Entstehung eines Schadenzaubers

Realización de un hechizo maligno

Origem de um feitiço de dano

Boze tovenarij in de maak

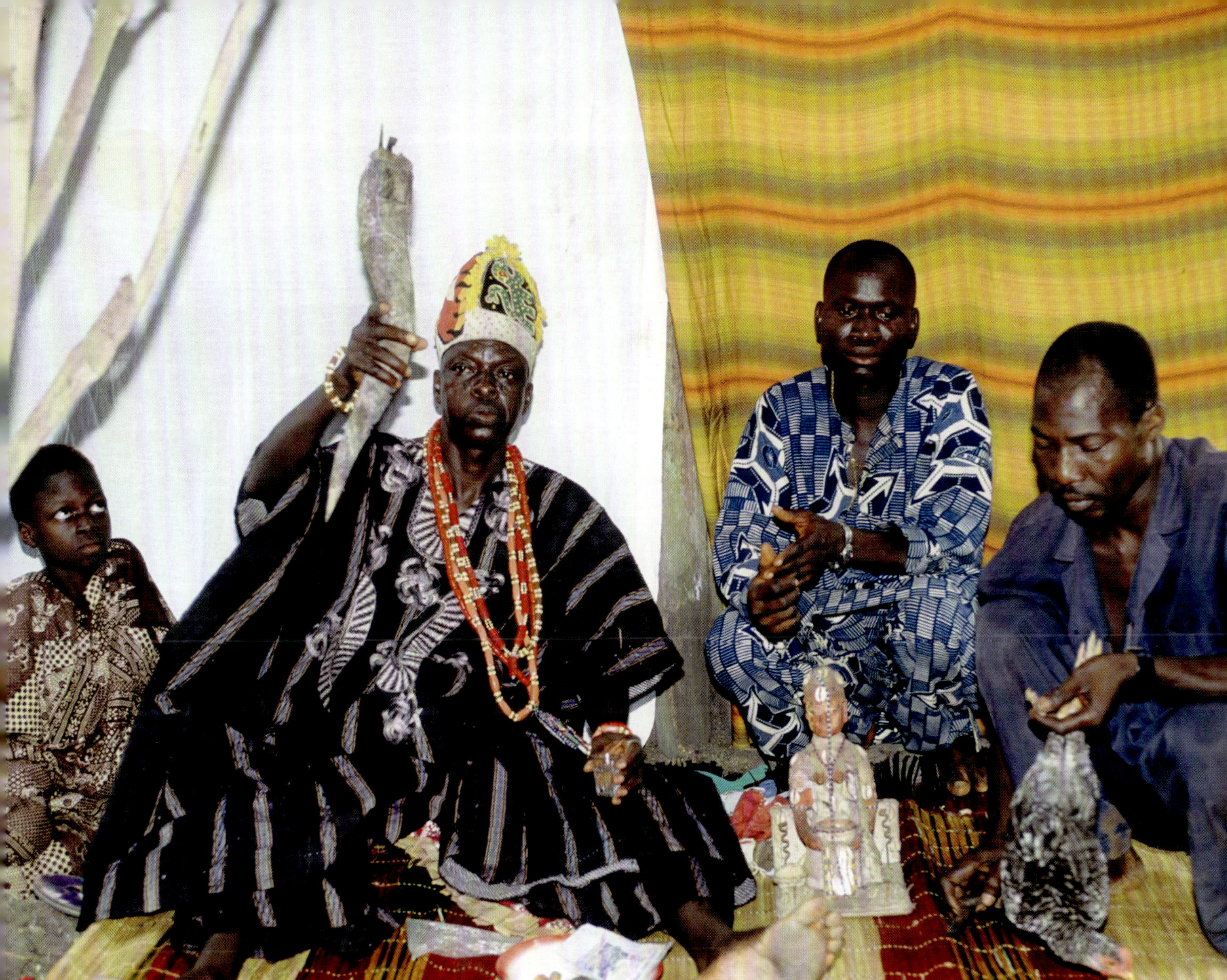

The magic horn calls the spirits

La corne magique appelle les esprits

Das magische Horn ruft die Geister

El cuerno mágico llama a los espíritus

O chifre mágico chama os espíritos

De toverhoorn roept de geesten

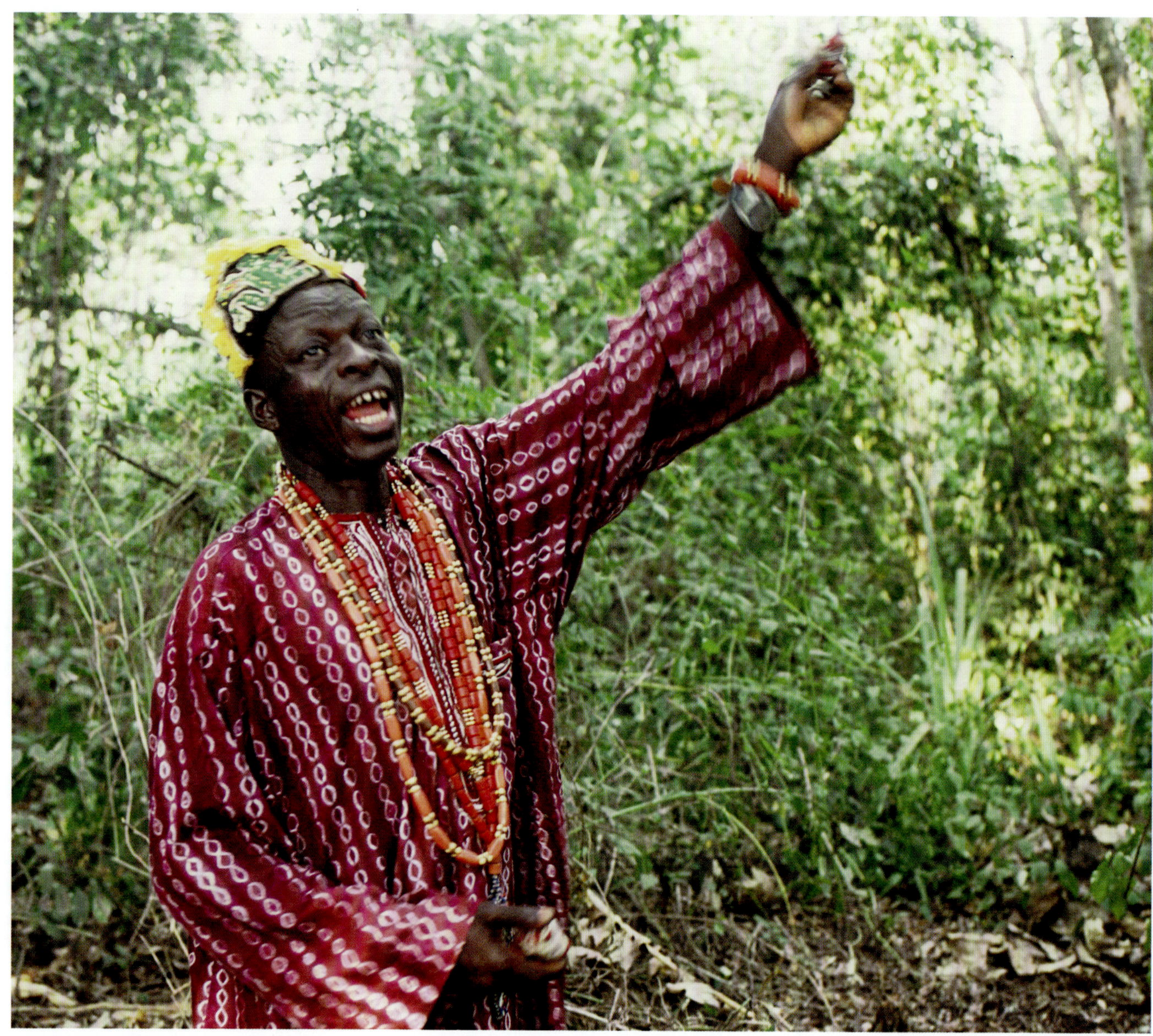

The cursed lock. In his holy grove, the Holi priest pronounces a curse through which the previously worked lock begins its work. Now the spell works actively on a metaphysical level.

Cadenas maudit. Dans son bois sacré, le prêtre Holi prononce une malédiction grâce à laquelle le cadenas préalablement préparé entre en action. À partir de ce moment-là, la magie agit sur le plan métaphysique.

Das verfluchte Schloss. In seinem heiligen Hain spricht der Holipriester einen Fluch aus, durch den das vorher bearbeitete Schloss seinen Dienst aufnimmt. Jetzt arbeitet der Zauber aktiv auf einer metaphysischen Ebene.

El candado maldito. En su santa arboleda, el sacerdote Holi pronuncia una maldición a través de la cual la cerradura previamente trabajada comienza su servicio. Ahora el hechizo trabaja activamente en un nivel metafísico.

O fechadura amaldiçoado. No seu santo bosque, o sacerdote Holi pronuncia uma maldição através da qual a fechadura previamente trabalhada começa o seu serviço. Agora o feitiço funciona ativamente em um nível metafísico.

Het vervloekte slot. In zijn heilige bosje spreekt de Holi-priester een vloek uit waardoor het eerder bewerkte slot aan zijn werk begint. Nu werkt de betovering actief op metafysisch niveau.

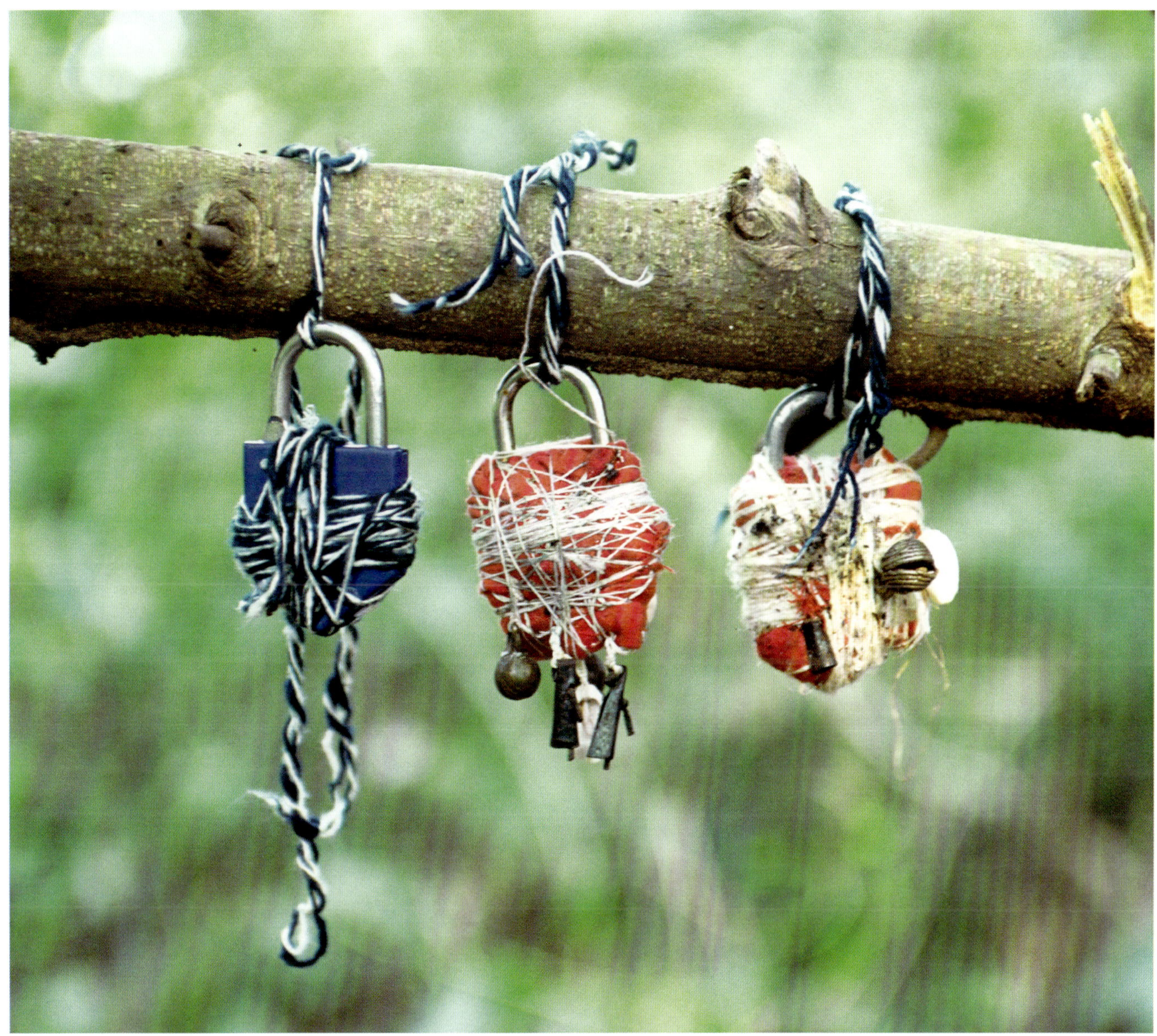

Caught in the lock. The victims are literally trapped in the lock. The black magic object is hung in the holy grove on a branch from which other target objects already suffer.

Piégées dans les cadenas. Les victimes sont cadenassées au sens figuré. Dans le bois magique, l'objet est suspendu à une branche, sur laquelle d'autres porteurs de magie sont déjà accrochés.

Im Schloss gefangen. Die Opfer sind im Schloss sprichwörtlich eingeschlossen. Das schwarzmagische Objekt kommt im heiligen Hain an einem Ast zu hängen, an dem bereits andere Zielobjekte leiden.

Atrapado en el candado. Las víctimas están literalmente atrapadas en el candado. El objeto de magia negra cuelga de una rama en la arboleda sagrada, de la que ya cuelgan otros objetos con diferentes objetivos.

Apanhado no fechadura. As vítimas estão literalmente presas no fechadura. O objeto de magia negra vem pendurado em um galho no bosque sagrado, do qual outros objetos-alvo já sofrem.

Gevangen in het slot. De slachtoffers zitten letterlijk gevangen in het slot. Het voorwerp van zwarte magie komt aan een tak in het heilige bosje te hangen, waar ook andere mikpunten al aan lijden.

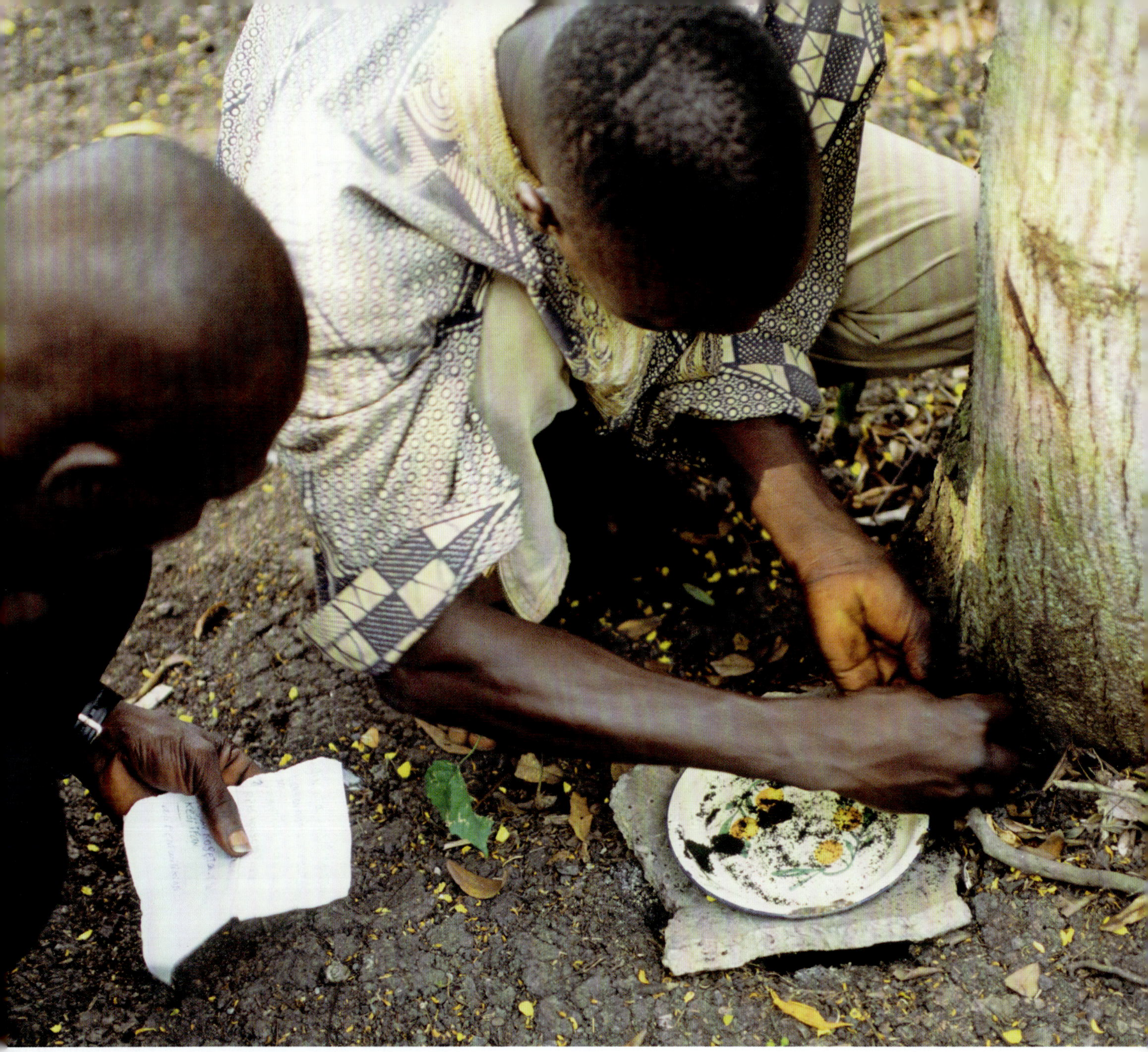

An assistant buries secret substances at a witch tree

Un assistant enterre des substances secrètes sous un arbre de sorcier

Ein Assistent begräbt geheime Substanzen am Hexenbaum

Un asistente entierra sustancias secretas en un árbol de brujas

Um assistente enterra substâncias secretas numa bruxa

Een assistent begraaft geheime substanties bij een heksenboom

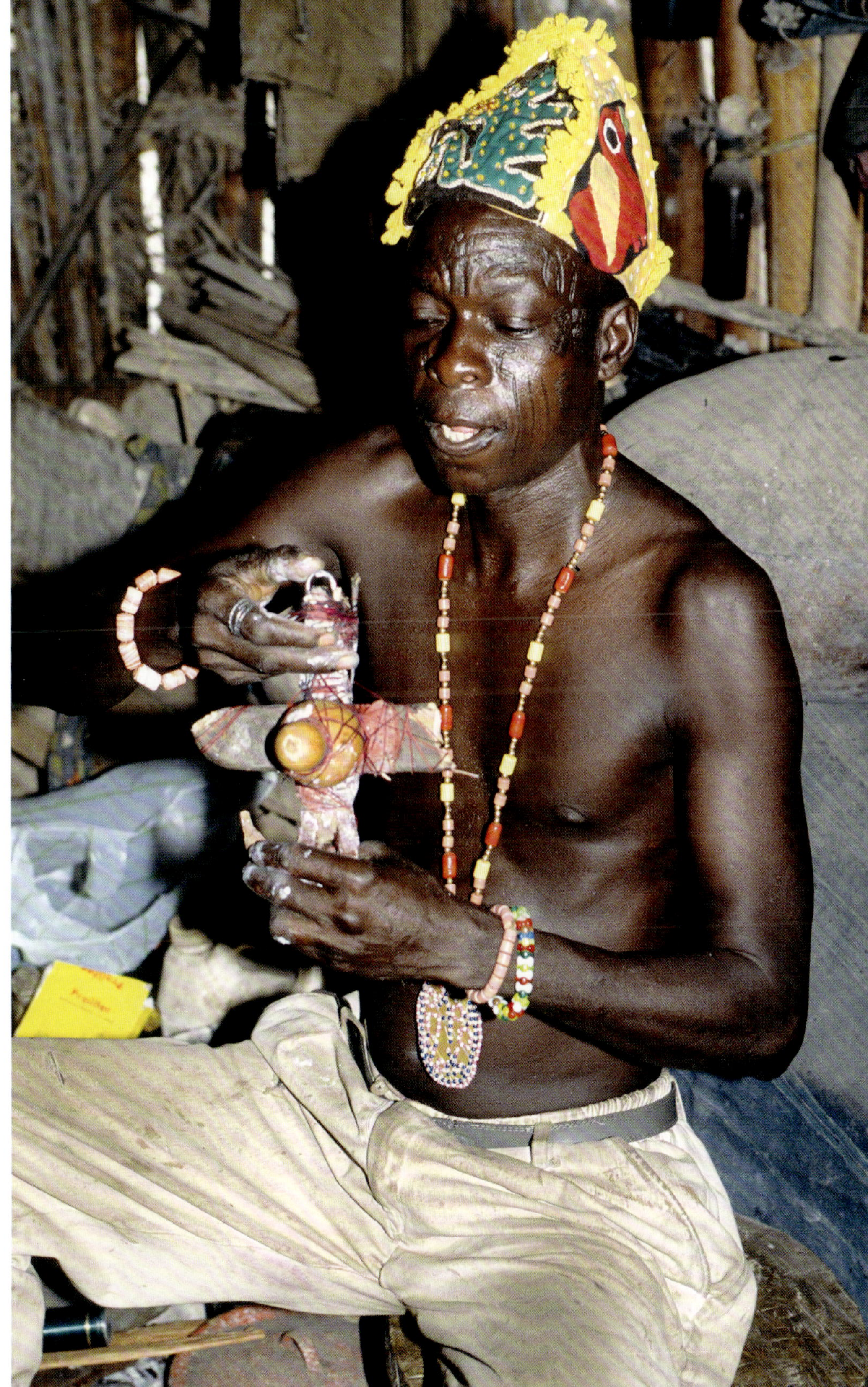

The spell that leads to arrest. The Holi Azeto builds a Bocio, with whose help the target person is to be arrested by the police. The lock used here is supposed to enclose the curse in the Bocio.

Le sort qui mène à l'arrestation. Le prêtre azeto Holi utilise un bocio qui aidera la police à arrêter la personne incriminée. Le cadenas utilisé ici doit enfermer la malédiction dans le bocio.

Der Zauber, der zur Festnahme führt. Der Holi-Azeto baut einen Bocio, mit dessen Hilfe die Zielperson von der Polizei festgenommen werden soll. Das hier zur Verwendung kommende Schloss soll den Fluch im Bocio verschließen.

El hechizo que lleva al arresto. El Holi-Azeto construye un Bocio, cuyo objetivo es que ayude a ser arrestado por la policía. El candado que se usa aquí se supone que encierra la maldición en el Bocio.

O fechadura que leva à prisão. O Holi-Azeto constrói um Bocio, com cuja ajuda o alvo será preso pela polícia. O castelo usado aqui é suposto fechar a maldição no Bocio.

De betovering die tot arrestatie leidt. De Holi-azeto maakt een bocio waarmee de politie het mikpunt kan arresteren. Het hier gebruikte slot moet de vloek insluiten in de bocio.

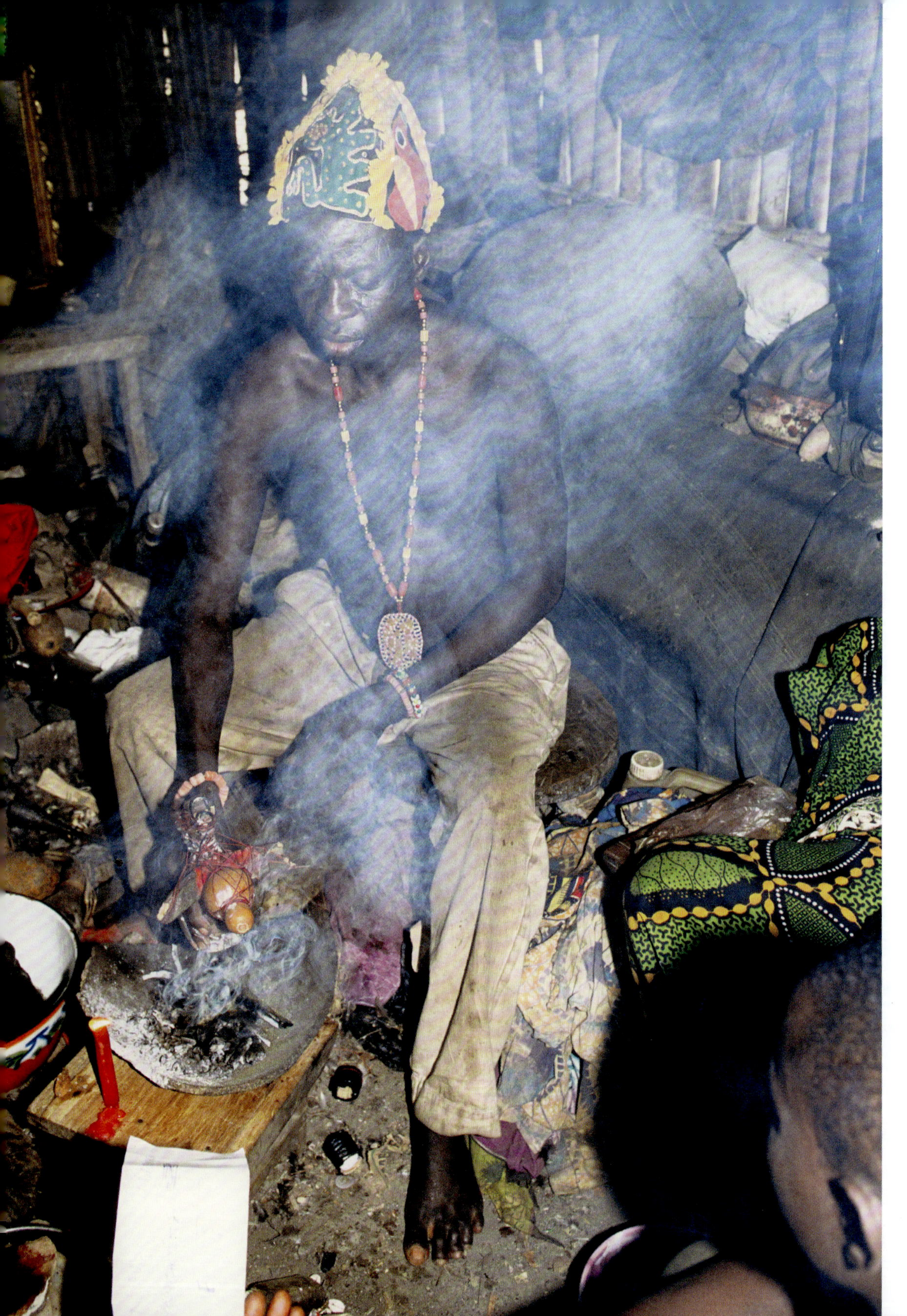

The smoke of special
herbs is part of the ritual

La fumée des herbes
spéciales fait partie
du rituel

Der Rauch spezieller
Kräuter gehört zum Ritual

El humo de hierbas
especiales es parte
del ritual

O fumo de ervas
especiais faz parte
do ritual

De rook van speciale
kruiden maakt deel uit
van het ritueel

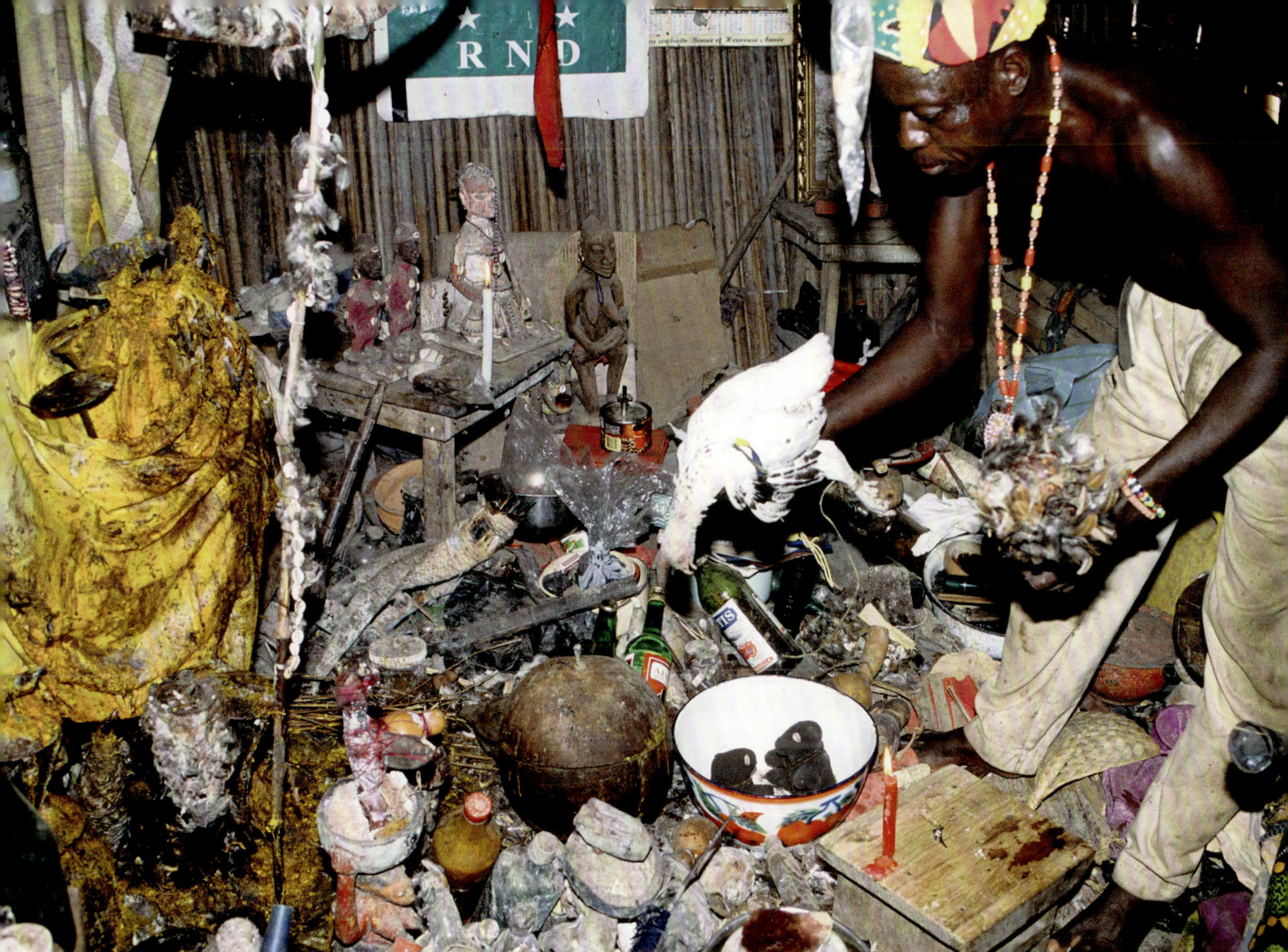

The blood of the animal sacrifice on the Bocio activates its magical power

Le sang de l'animal sacrifié sur le bocio active son pouvoir magique

Das Blut des Tieropfers auf dem Bocio aktiviert dessen magische Kraft

La sangre del sacrificio animal en el Bocio activa su poder mágico

O sangue do sacrifício animal no Bocio activa o seu poder mágico

Het bloed van het offerdier op de bocio activeert de magische kracht ervan

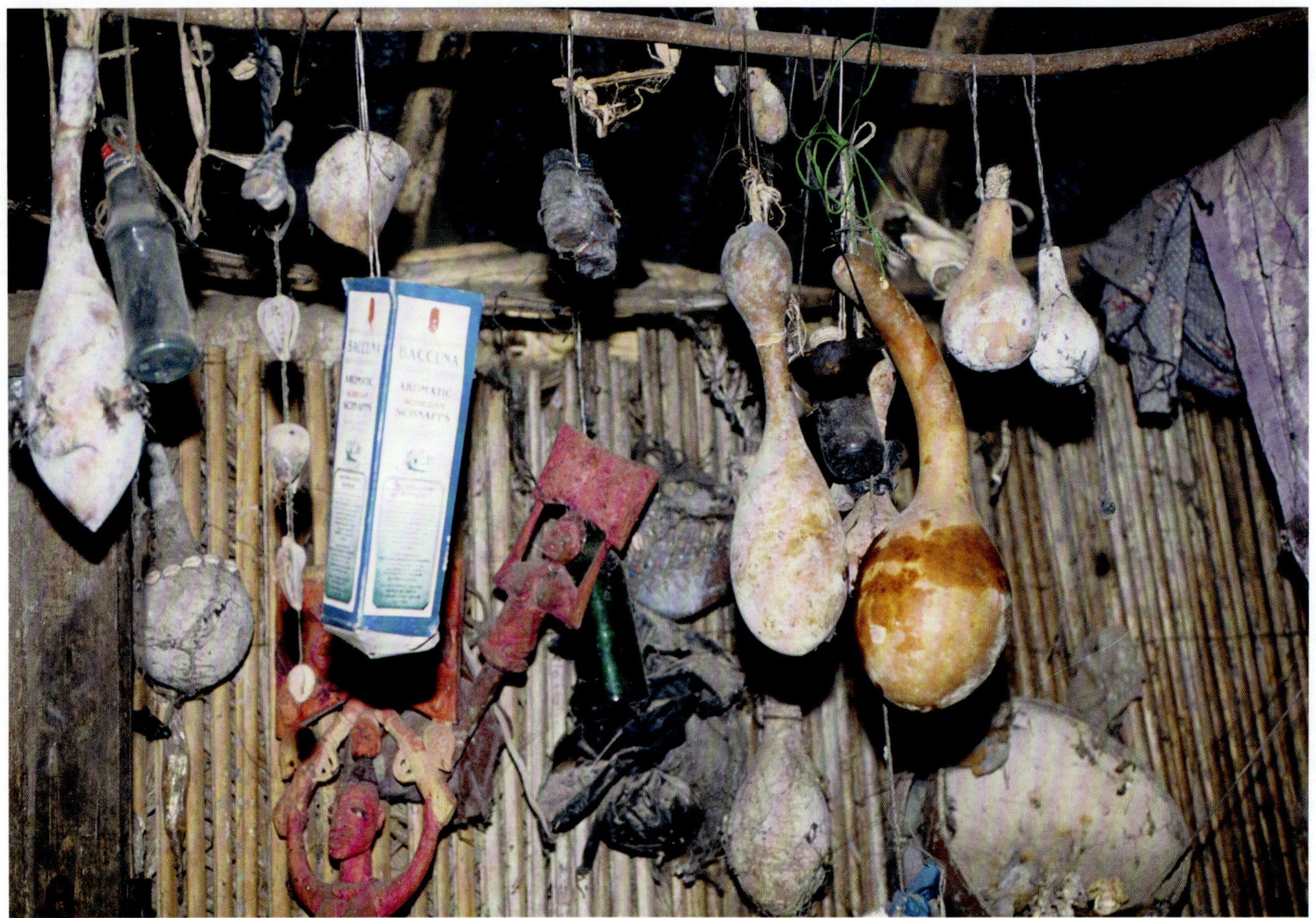

In the workshop of the Holi sorcerer. Calabashes with secret substances, magical objects and those directly related to certain Vodun gods —for example the red Shango figure in the middle—hang in the room.

Dans l'atelier du magicien Holi. Des calebasses renfermant des substances secrètes, des objets magiques et d'autres directement associés aux dieux vodun concernés sont suspendues dans la pièce. Remarquez la figurine de Shangô au centre.

In der Werkstatt des Holi-Magiers. Kalebassen mit geheimen Substanzen, magische Gegenstände und solche mit direktem Bezug zu bestimmten Vodungöttern – siehe die rote Shangofigur in der Mitte – hängen im Raum.

En el taller del mago Holi. Calabazas con sustancias secretas, objetos mágicos y aquellos directamente relacionados con ciertos dioses vudú –como la figura roja de Shango en el centro– cuelgan en la habitación.

Na oficina do mágico Holi.. Calabashes com substâncias secretas, objetos mágicos e aqueles diretamente relacionados a certos vodungods – ver o Shangofigure vermelho no meio – pendurar na sala.

In de werkplaats van de Holi-tovenaar. Kalebassen met geheime stoffen, magische voorwerpen en objecten die direct verbonden zijn met bepaalde goden (zie het rode Shango-beeldje in het midden) hangen in de ruimte.

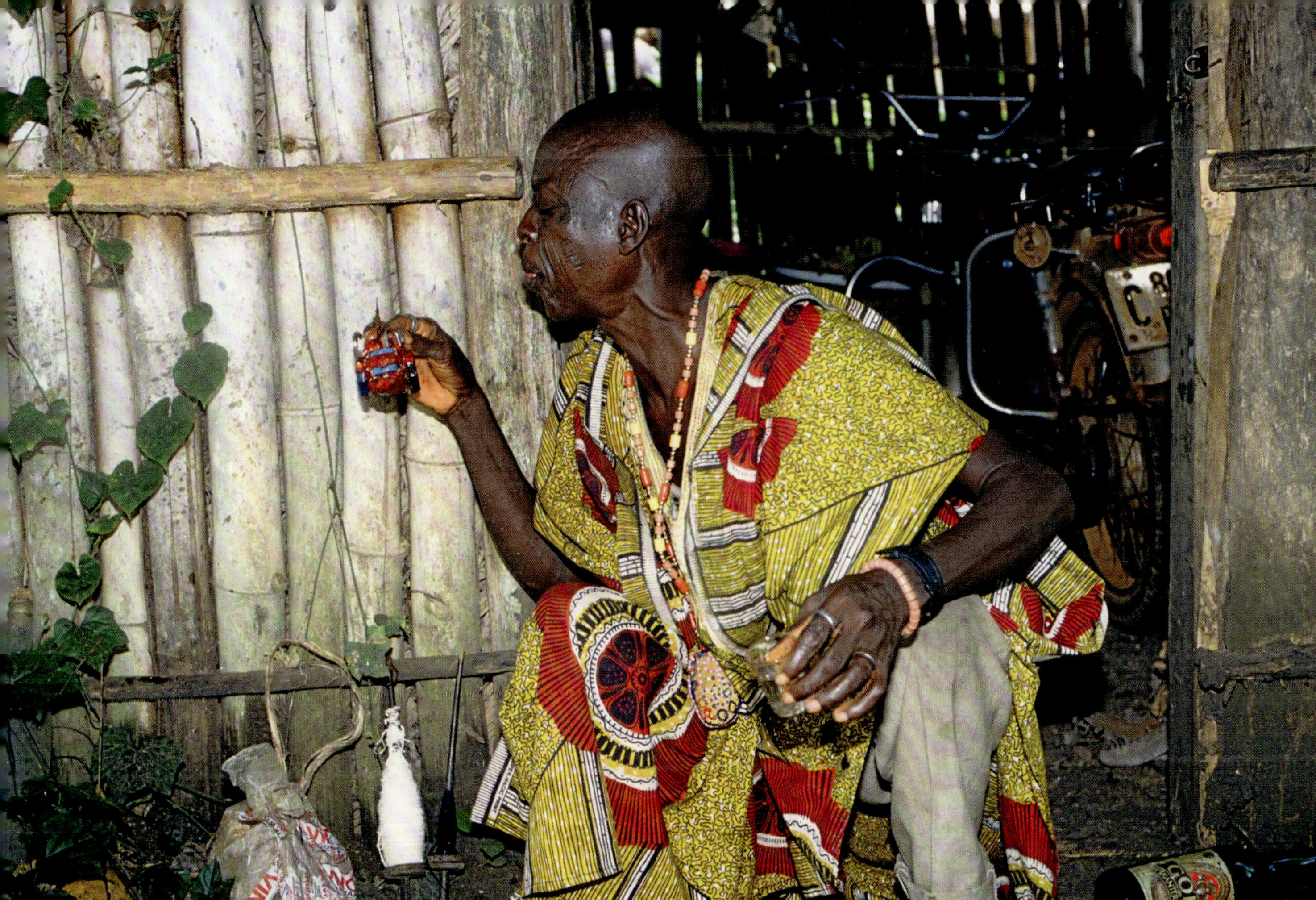

Holi priest in the preparation of a harmful magic
Prêtre Holi en pleine préparation d'une magie néfaste
Holi-Priester bei der Zubereitung einer Schadenmagie
Sacerdote Holi en la preparación de una magia negra
Holi sacerdote na preparação de uma magia prejudicial
Holi-priester bij de voorbereiding van schadelijke magie

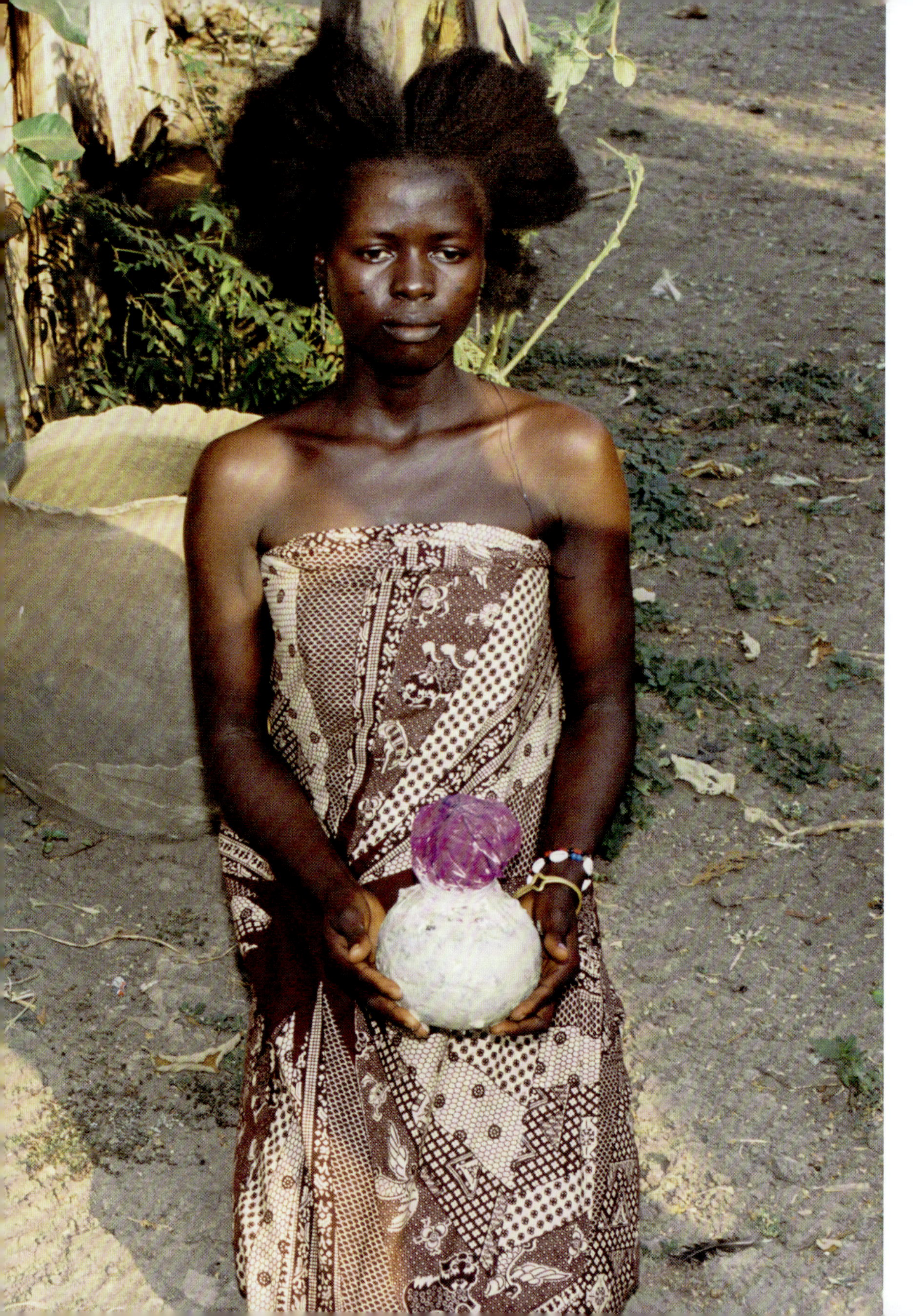

Handover of the magic
potion

Remise de la potion
magique

Übergabe des
Zaubertranks

Entrega de la poción
mágica

Entrega da poção mágica

Overdracht van het
toverdrankje

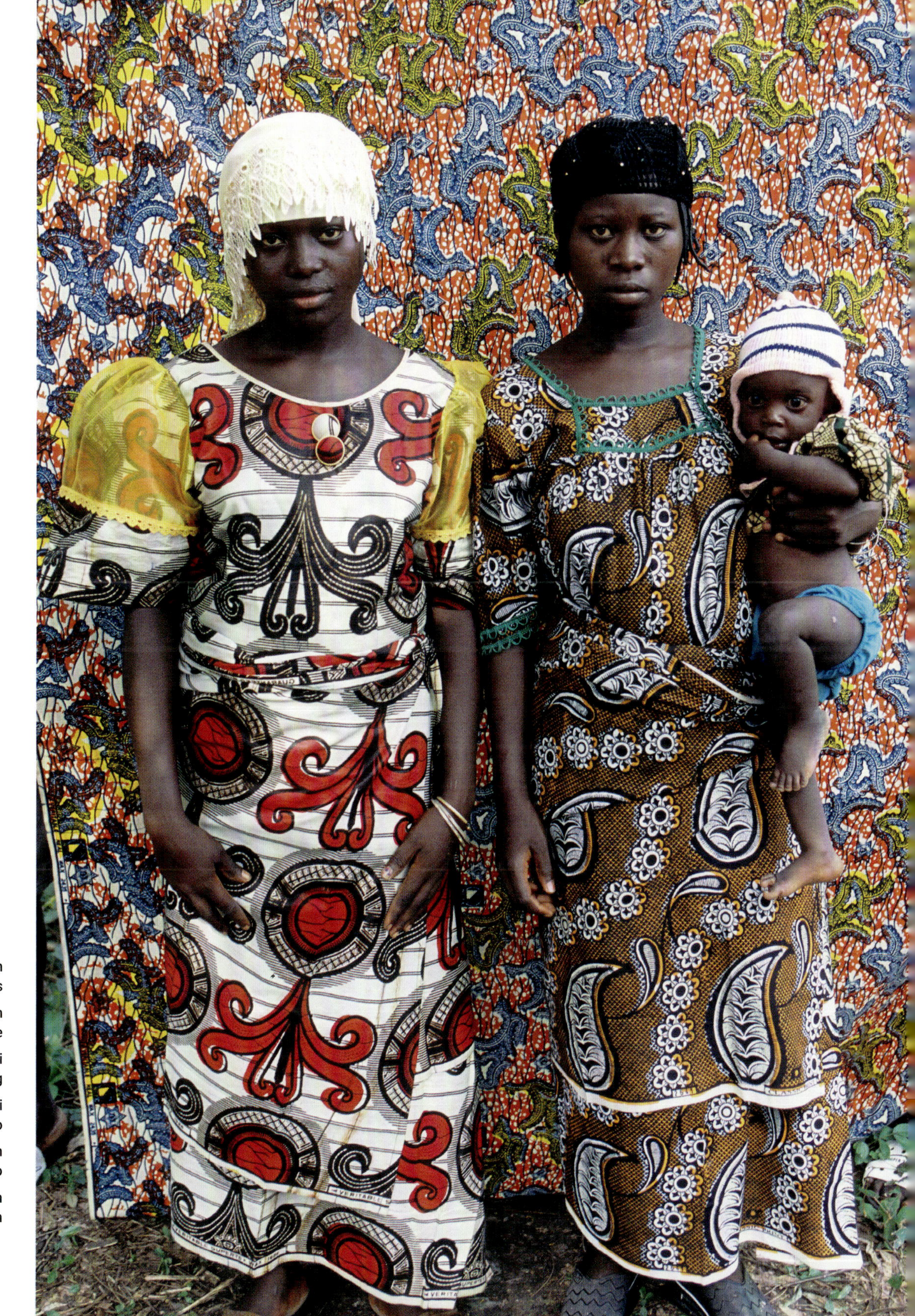

People of the Holi tribe in
Sunday dress

Membres du peuple Holi en
habits du dimanche

Menschen vom Volk der Holi
in Sonntagskleidung

Gente del pueblo Holi
vestida de domingo

Povo do povo Holi em
roupas de domingo

Mensen van het Holi-volk in
zondagse kleren

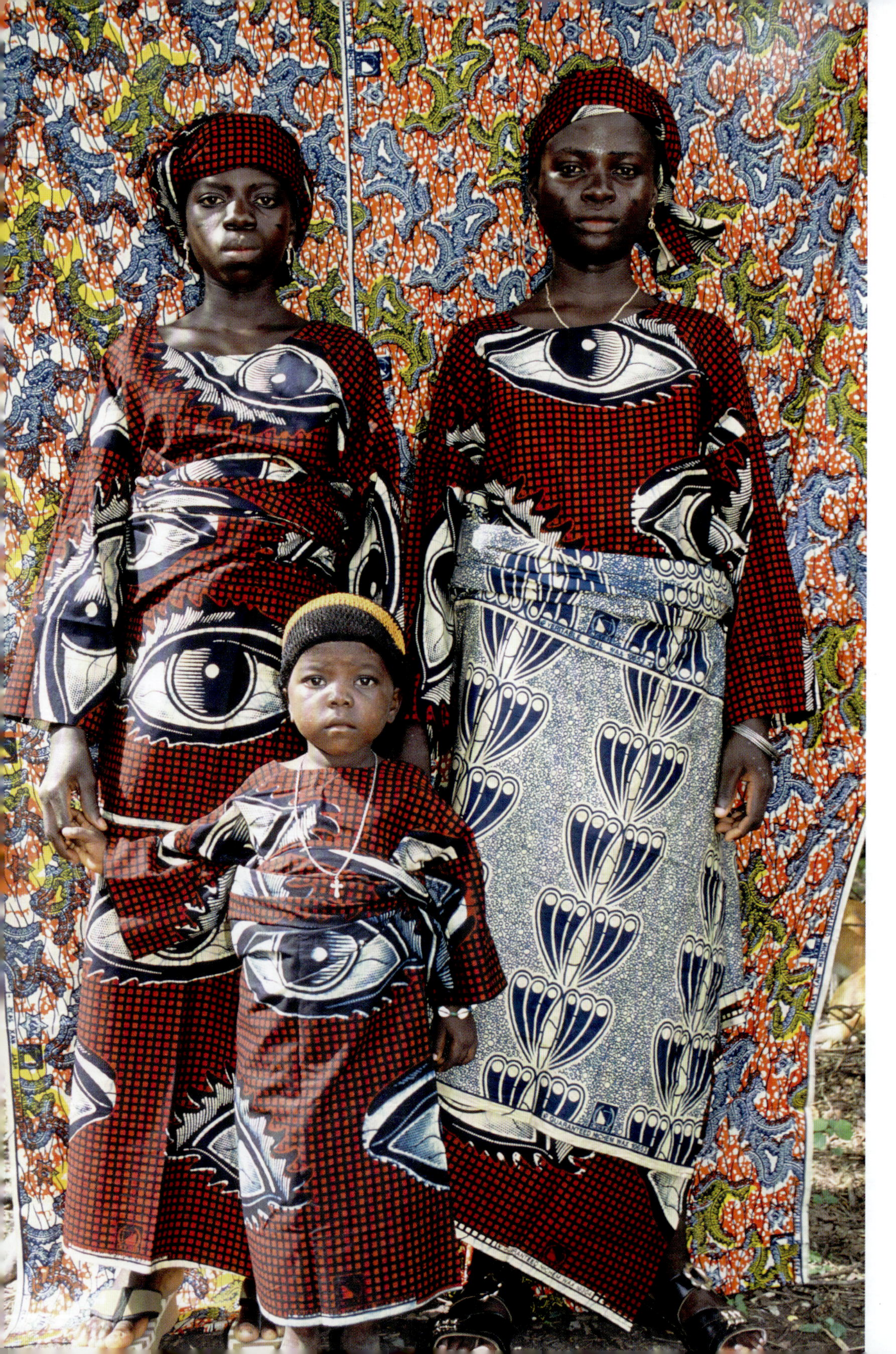

People of the Holi tribe in
Sunday dress

Membres du peuple Holi en
habits du dimanche

Menschen vom Volk der Holi
in Sonntagskleidung

Gente del pueblo Holi vestida
de domingo

Povo do povo Holi em roupas
de domingo

Mensen van het Holi-volk in
zondagse kleren

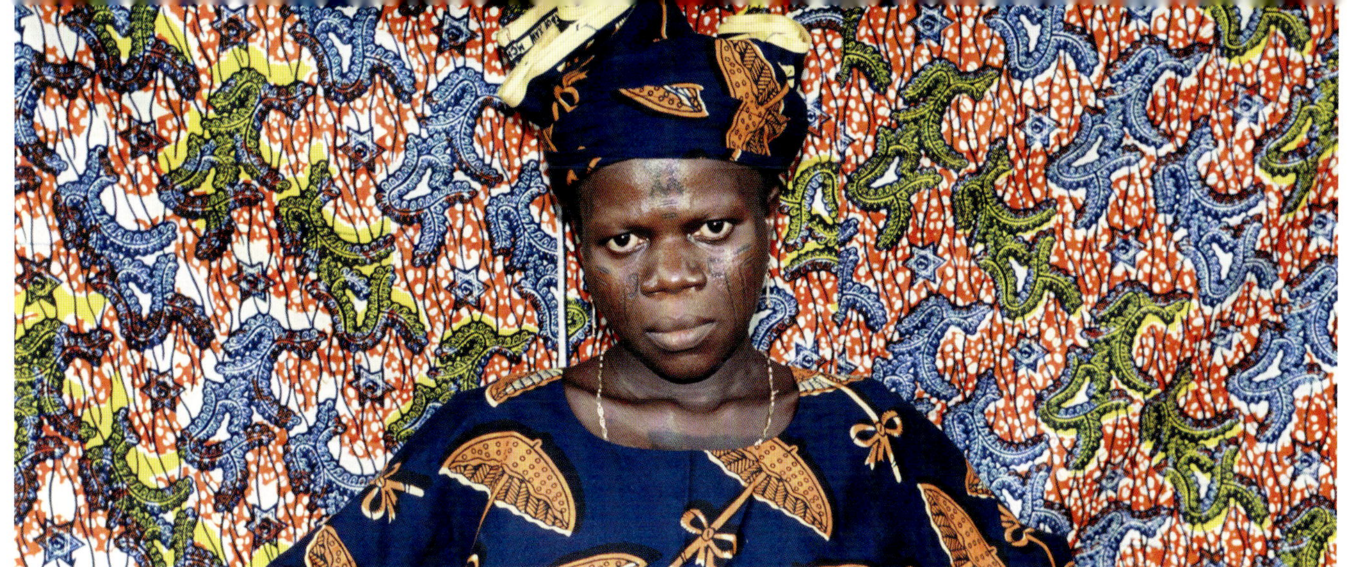

A woman of the Holi tribe in Sunday dress
Femme du peuple Holi en habits du dimanche
Eine Frau vom Volk der Holi in Sonntagskleidung
Una mujer del pueblo Holi vestida de domingo
Uma mulher do povo Holi com roupas de domingo
Een vrouw van het Holi-volk in zondagse kleren

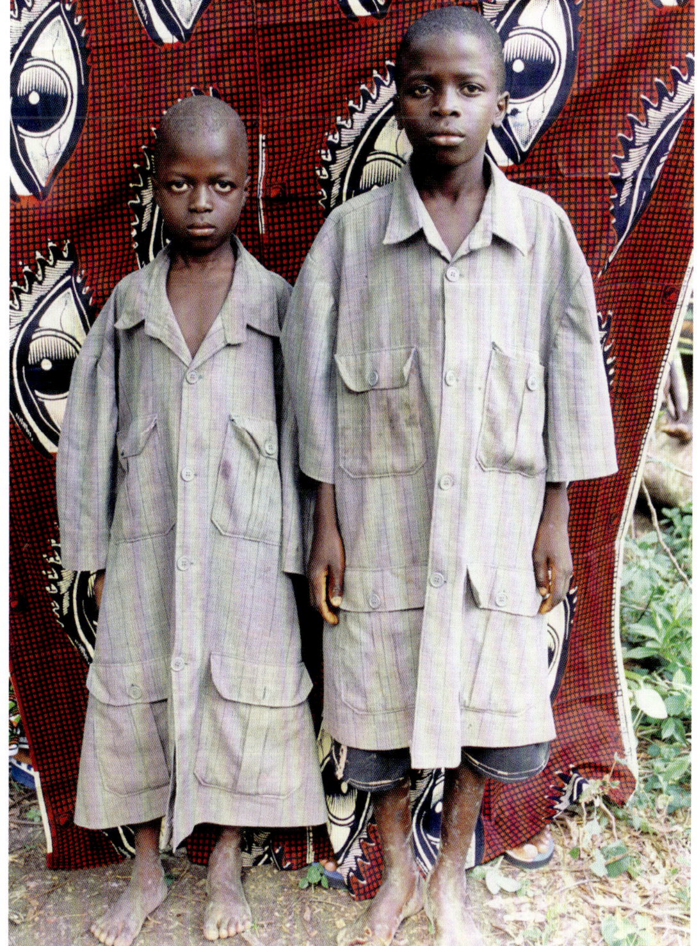

Youth of the Holi tribe
Des jeunes du peuple Holi
Die Jugend vom Volk der Holi
La juventud del pueblo Holi
Juventude do povo Holi
De jeugd van het Holi-volk

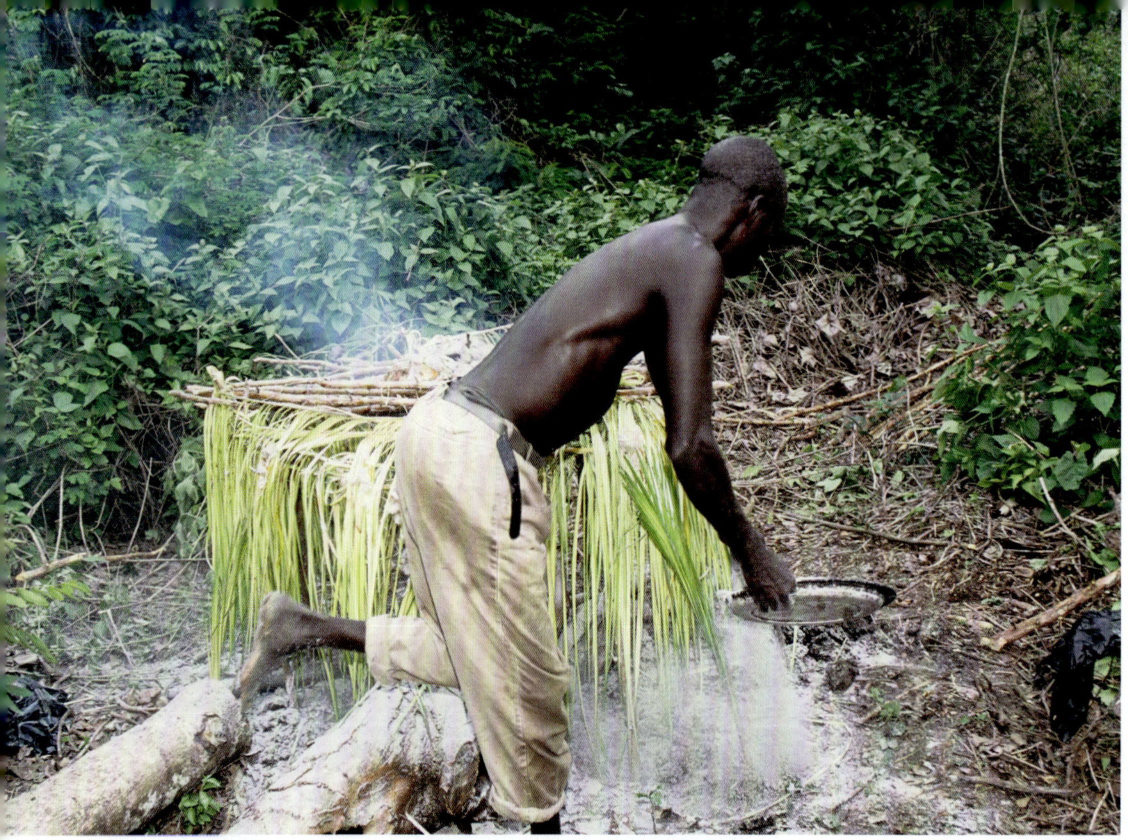

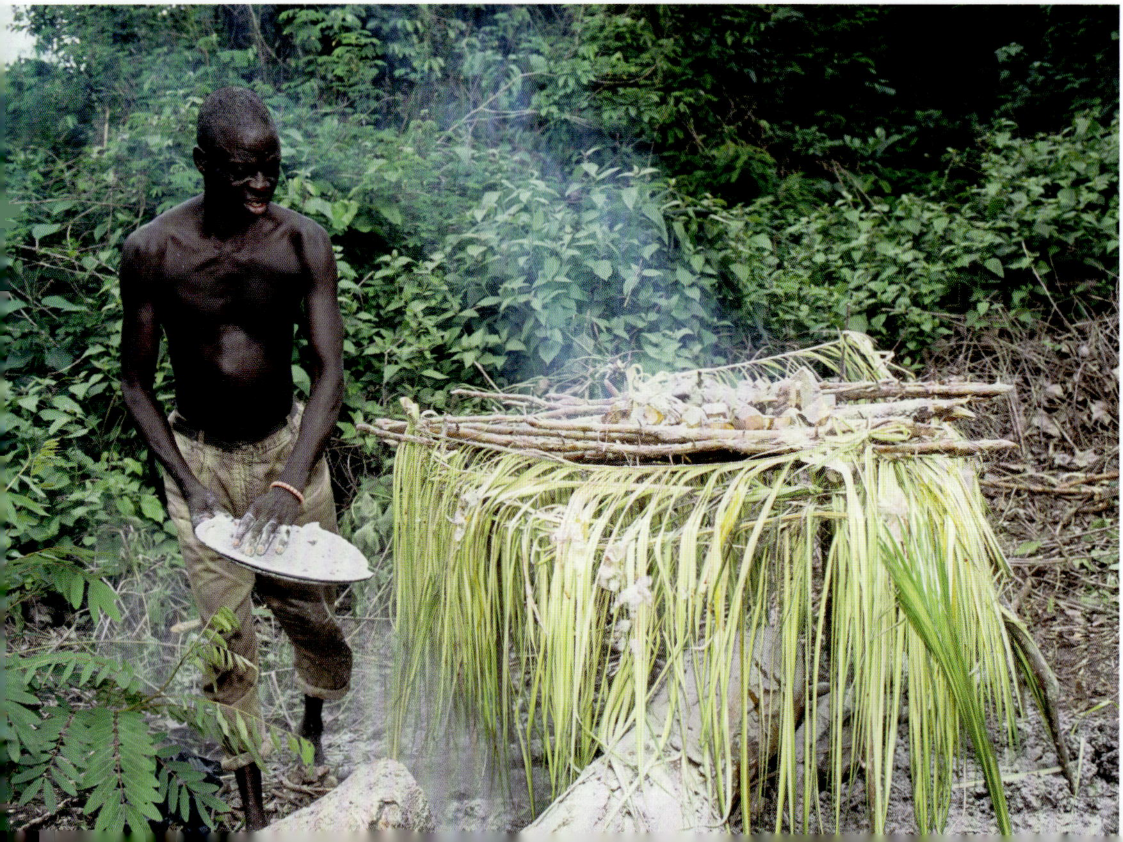

Ritual for influencing the weather. The Holi sorcerer has built an altar in the forest on which he has stacked special plants. He sprinkles them with magic powder. The ritual is to stop the rain that has been going on for days.

Rituel pour influencer le temps. Le magicien Holi a construit un autel dans la forêt sur lequel il a empilé des plantes spéciales. Il le saupoudre de poudre magique. Ce rituel a pour objectif de faire cesser la pluie qui persiste depuis plusieurs jours.

Ritual zur Beeinflussung des Wetters. Der Holi-Zauberer hat im Wald einen Altar aufgebaut, auf dem er spezielle Pflanzen aufgeschichtet hat. Diese bestäubt er mit magischem Puder. Das Ritual soll den seit Tagen währenden Regen stoppen.

Ritual para influir en el tiempo. El mago Holi ha construido un altar en el bosque, sobre el que ha apilado plantas especiales. Las espolvorea con polvo mágico. Se supone que el ritual debe detener la lluvia que ha estado cayendo durante días.

Ritual para influenciar o clima. O feiticeiro de Holi construiu um altar na floresta, sobre o qual empilhou plantas especiais. Ele polvilha-as com pó mágico. O ritual é suposto parar a chuva que dura há dias.

Ritueel ter beïnvloeding van het weer. De Holi-tovenaar heeft een altaar gebouwd in het bos, waarop hij speciale planten heeft gestapeld. Hij bestuift ze met magisch poeder. Het ritueel zou de regen stoppen die al dagen aanhoudt.

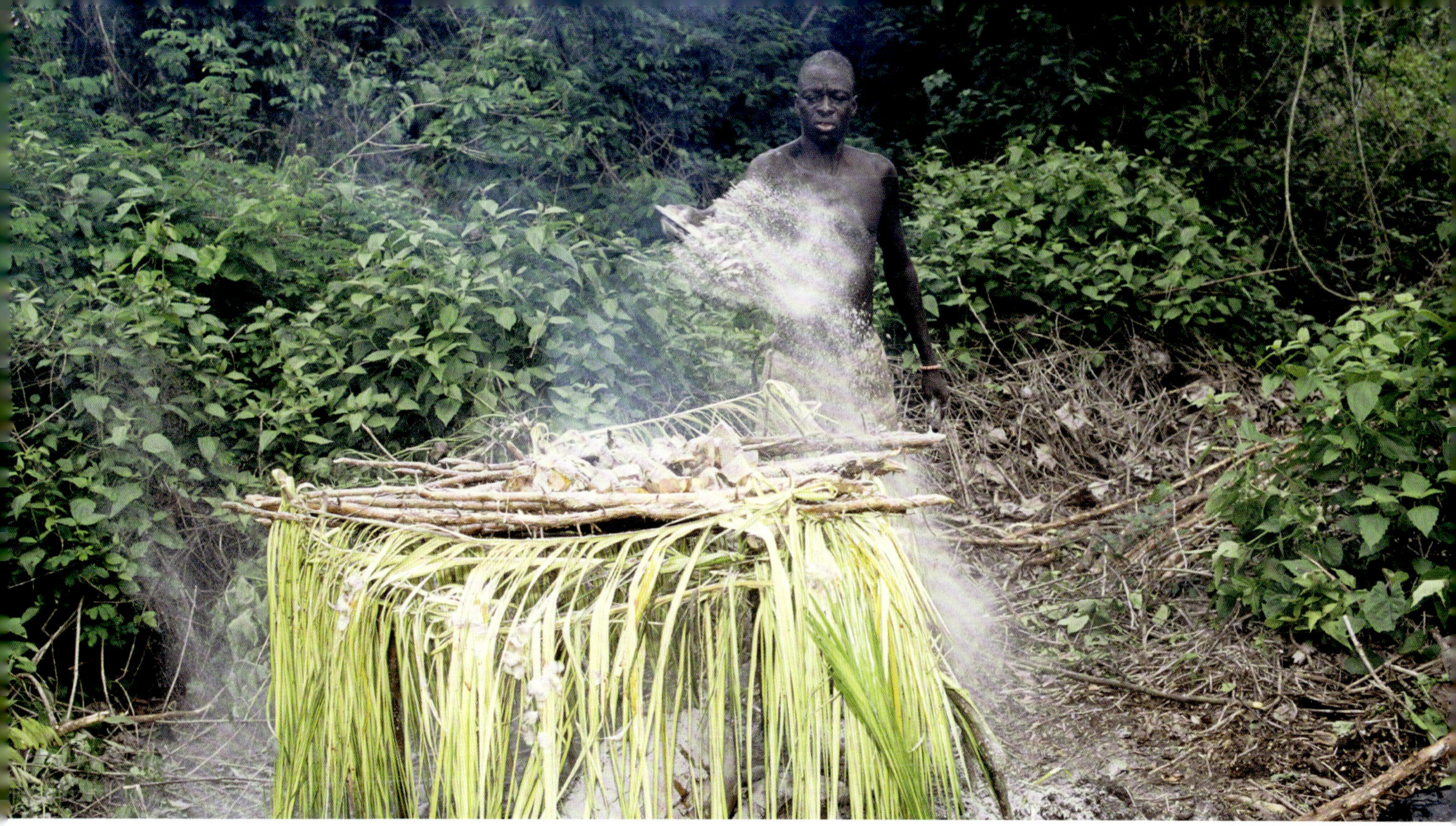

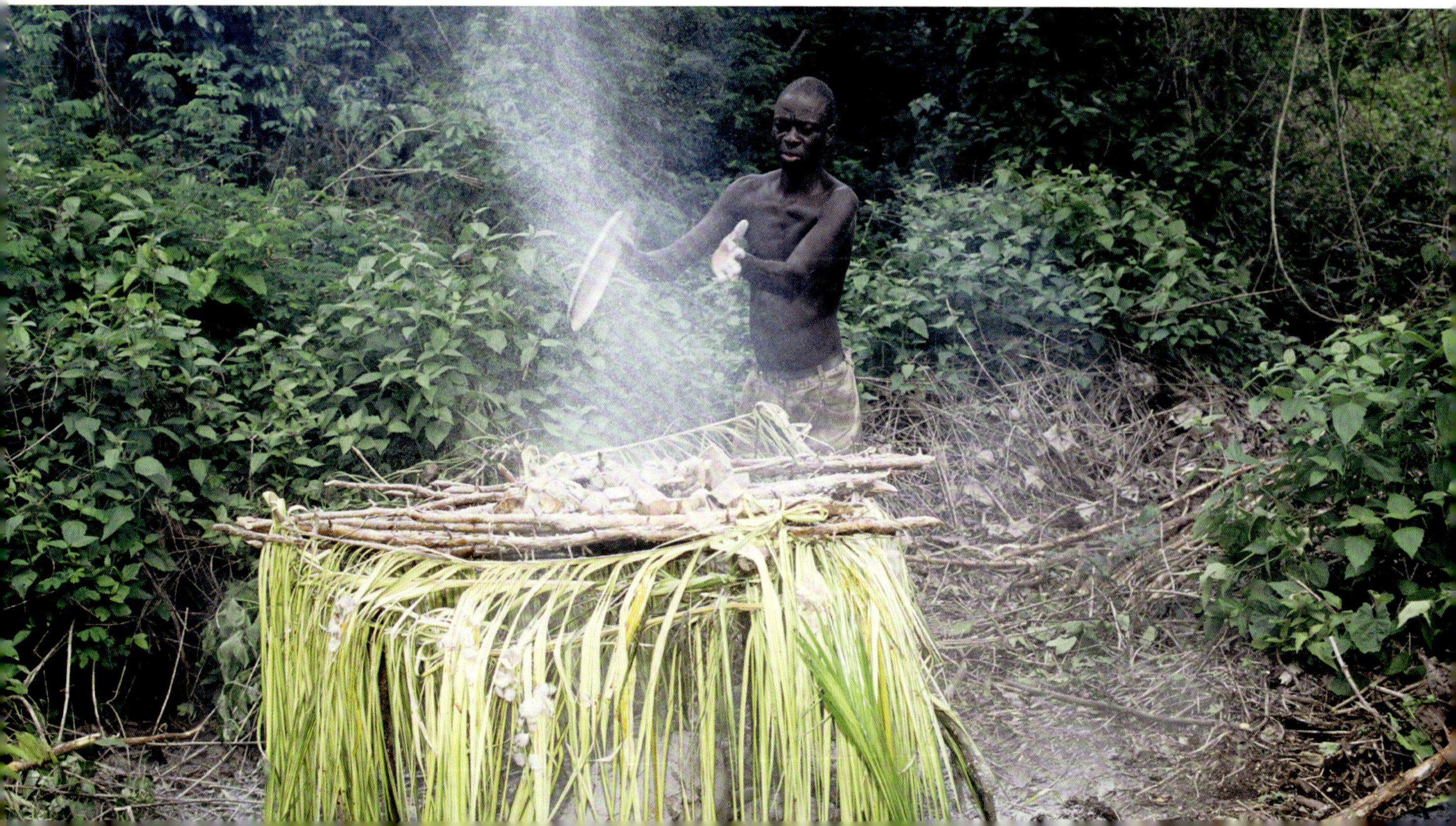

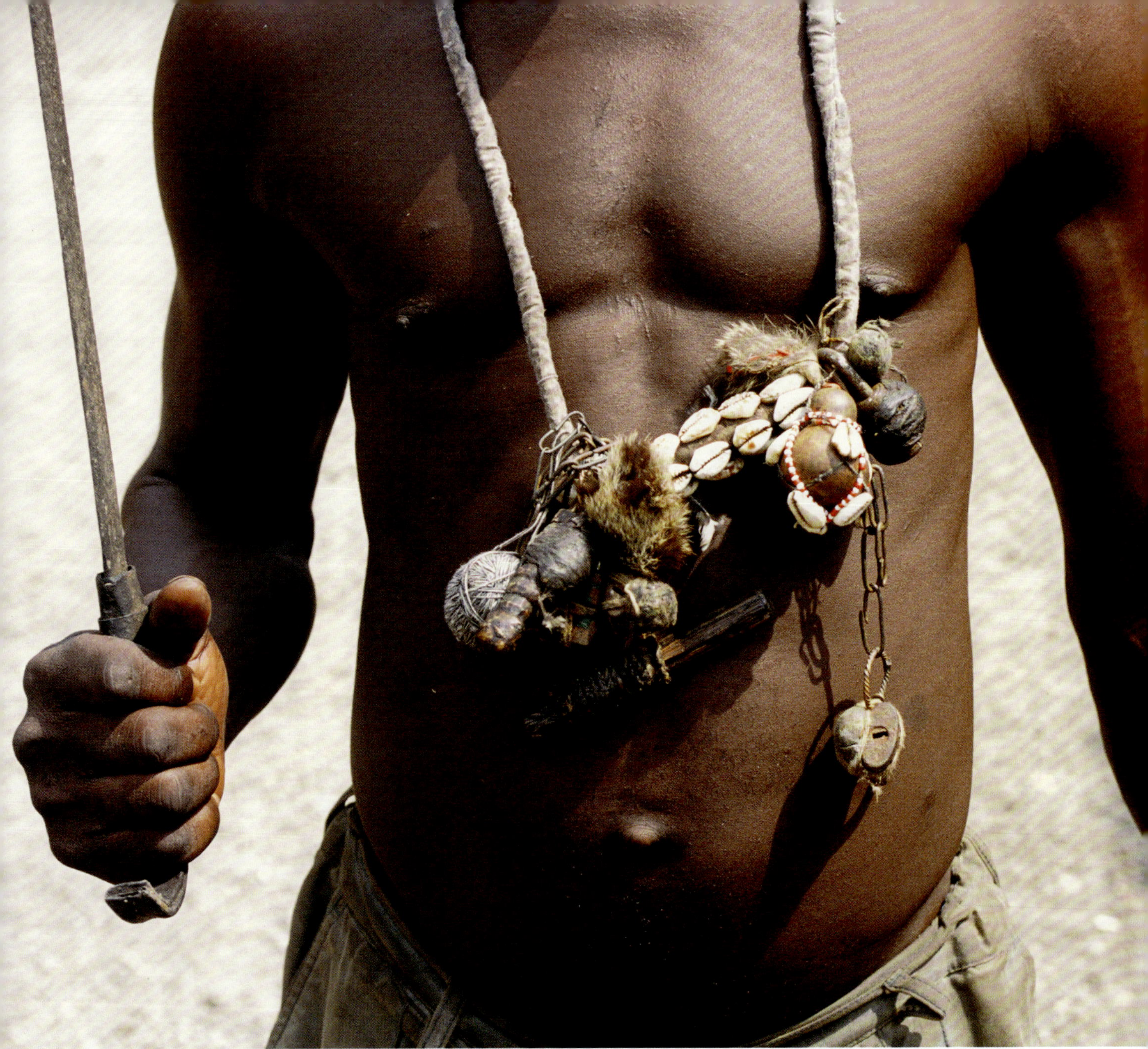

A Holi warrior with a protective force object (Bo)

Un guerrier Holi avec un objet de force protectrice (bo)

Ein Holi-Krieger mit einem Schutz-Kraftobjekt (Bo)

Un guerrero Holi con un objeto de fuerza protectora (Bo)

Um guerreiro Holi com um objeto de força protetora (Bo)

Een Holi-krijger met een beschermend krachtobject (bo)

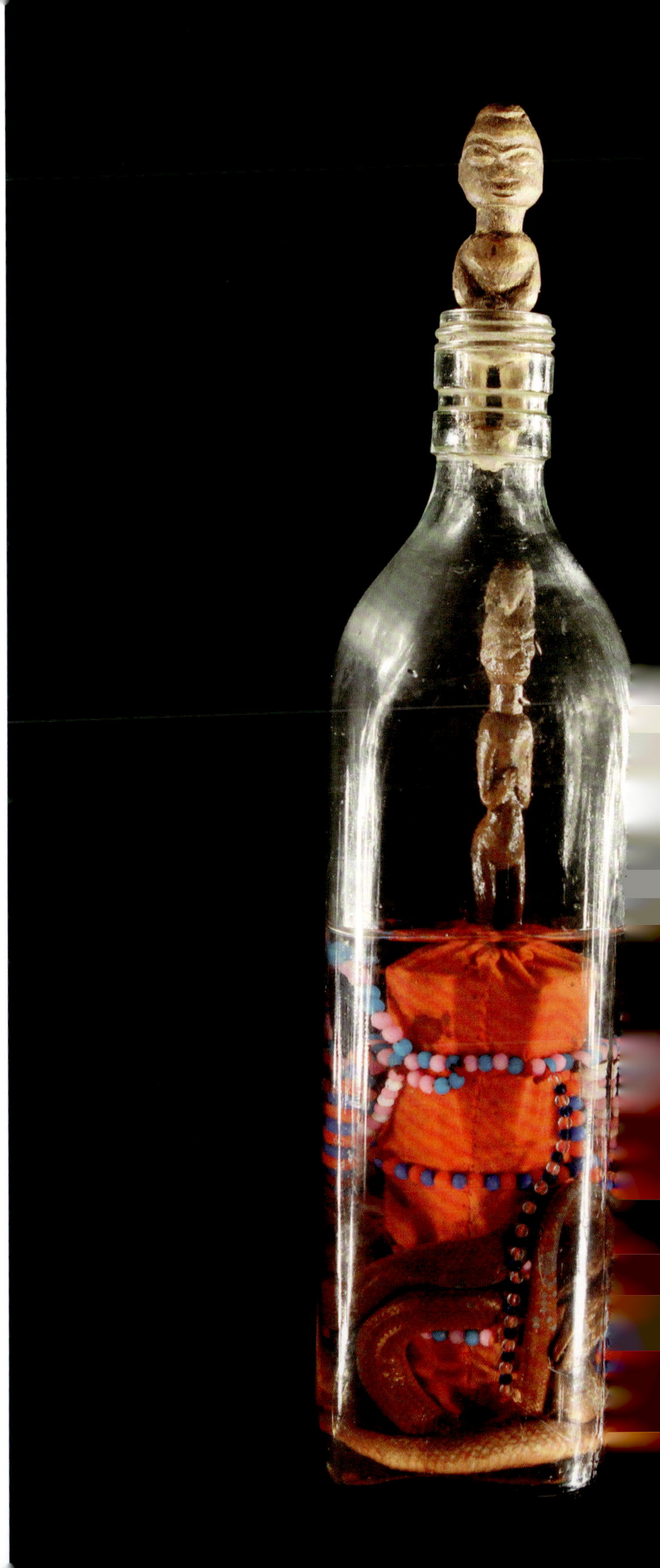

Snake bottle with truth serum.
This power object contains a
potion to convict liars.

**Bouteille serpent avec sérum
de vérité.** Cet objet actif
contient une boisson qui doit
permettre de percer à jour un
menteur.

**Schlangenflasche mit
Wahrheitsserum.** Dieses
Kraftobjekt enthält einen
Trank, der Lügner überführen
soll.

**Botella de serpiente con suero
de la verdad.** Este objeto de
poder contiene una poción,
que es para condenar a los
mentirosos.

**Garrafa de cobra com soro da
verdade.** Este objeto de poder
contém uma poção, que é
condenar mentirosos.

**Slangenfles met
waarheidsserum.** Dit
krachtobject bevat een drankje
dat leugenaars schuldig moet
verklaren.

Glass, wood, snakes, textiles,
glass beads, organic material,
palm schnapps/Verre, bois,
serpents, textiles, perles de verre,
matières organiques, vin de
palme, 30 × 8 cm

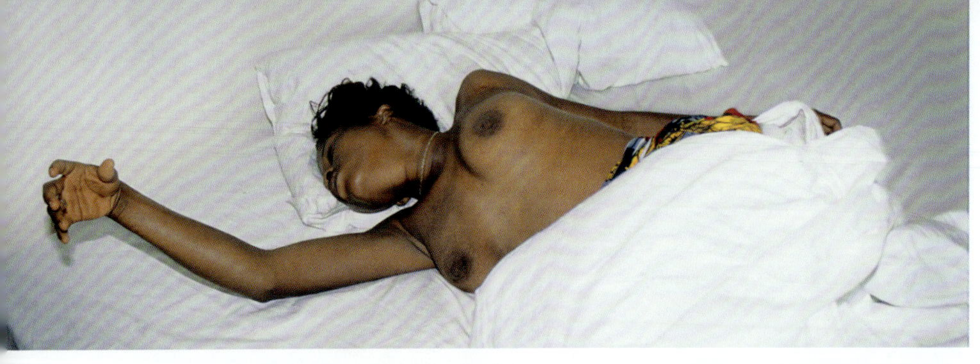

Rosalyn suffered from a curse
Rosalyn souffrait d'une malédiction
Rosalyn litt unter einem Fluch
Rosalyn sufrió una maldición
A Rosalyn sofria de uma maldição
Rosalyn leed onder een vloek

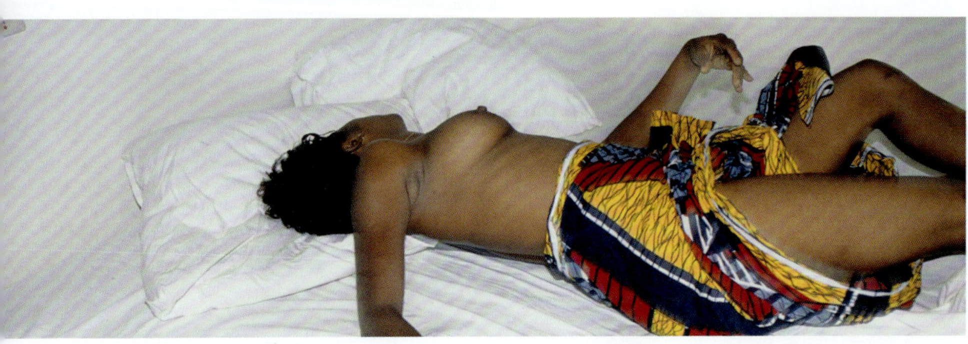

Her dreams were a symptom of witchcraft
Ses rêves étaient un symptôme de sorcellerie
Ihre Träume waren ein Symptom von Hexerei
Sus sueños eran un síntoma de brujería
Os seus sonhos eram um sintoma de bruxaria
Haar dromen waren een symptoom van hekserij

Nightmares—Witches come at night

Rosalyn lived in a small village in the Mono region of Benin. She couldn't say exactly when the nightmares had started, she just knew that they were getting worse and worse. Horrible creatures with claws and horns were stalking her night after night, and the distance between Rosalyn and them was decreasing all the time. She started to lose weight. Her condition deteriorated noticeably.

When the suspicion arose that she could be a victim of witchcraft, everything happened very quickly. She was taken out of the suffocating atmosphere of the village and to Cotonou, where the questioning of the oracle by an experienced priest confirmed the fears: one of Rosalyn's aunts was jealous of her and had exerted a strong harmful spell against her.

This would have been fatal if untreated and unrecognized, but Rosalyn had luck in her misfortune: She was able to recover.

Cauchemars, les sorciers viennent la nuit

Rosalyn vivait dans un petit village du département de Mono au Bénin. Elle ne se rappelait plus quand exactement les cauchemars avaient commencé, mais elle savait qu'ils empiraient. Des entités épouvantables, griffues et cornues, la poursuivaient chaque nuit et la distance les séparant d'elle ne cessait de se réduire. Elle commença à maigrir et son état se dégrada à vue d'œil.

Dès que ses proches soupçonnèrent qu'elle était victime de sorcellerie, tout se passa très vite. On lui fit quitter le village à l'atmosphère délétère. Elle se rendit à Cotonou où l'oracle fut interrogé par l'intermédiaire d'un prêtre célèbre qui confirma les soupçons : une tante de Rosalyn, jalouse d'elle, lui avait jeté un sortilège puissant de magie maléfique.

S'il n'avait pas été pris à temps, il aurait pu la tuer sans que personne ne comprenne, mais Rosalyn a eu de la chance, elle a pu être guérie.

Albträume – Nachts kommen die Hexen

Rosalyn lebte in einem kleinen Dorf in der Monoregion von Benin. Sie konnte nicht mehr genau sagen, wann die Albträume begonnen hatten, sie wusste nur, dass sie zunehmend schlimmer wurden. Grauenhafte Wesen mit Klauen und Hörnern stellten ihr Nacht für Nacht nach, und der Abstand zwischen Rosalyn und ihnen verringerte sich unaufhörlich. Sie begann, abzumagern. Ihr Zustand verschlechterte sich zusehends.

Als der Verdacht aufkam, dass sie ein Opfer von Hexerei sein könnte, ging alles ganz schnell. Man brachte sie heraus aus der erstickenden Atmosphäre des Dorfes und nach Cotonou, wo die Befragung des Orakels durch einen erfahrenen Priester die Befürchtungen bestätigte: Eine Tante Rosalyns war eifersüchtig auf sie gewesen und hatte einen starken Schadenzauber gegen sie angestrengt.

Dieser wäre unbehandelt und unerkannt tödlich gewesen, aber so hatte Rosalyn Glück im Unglück: Sie fand Genesung.

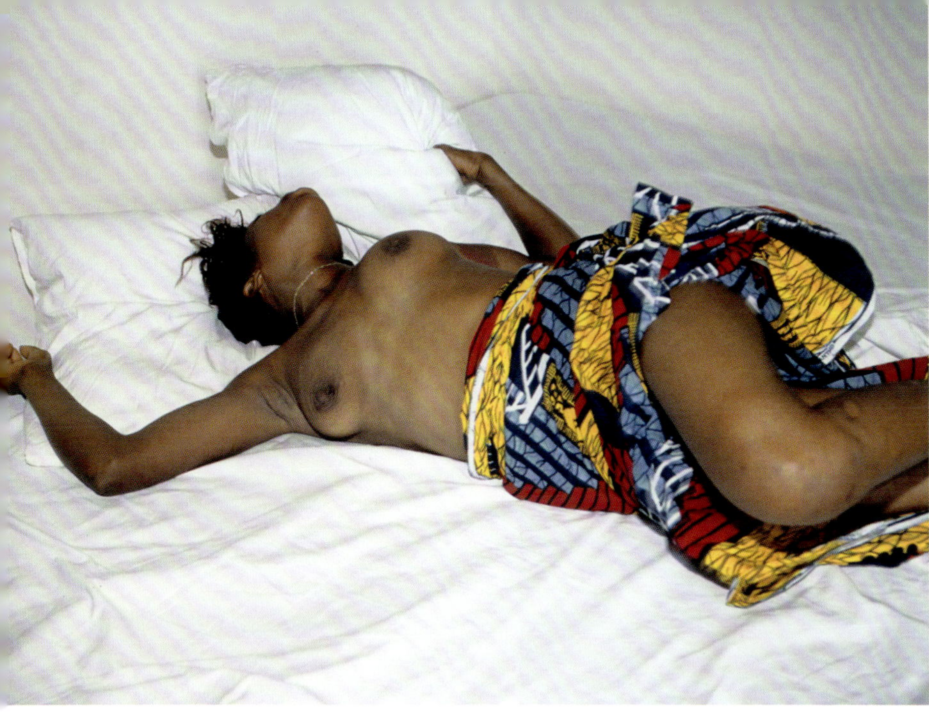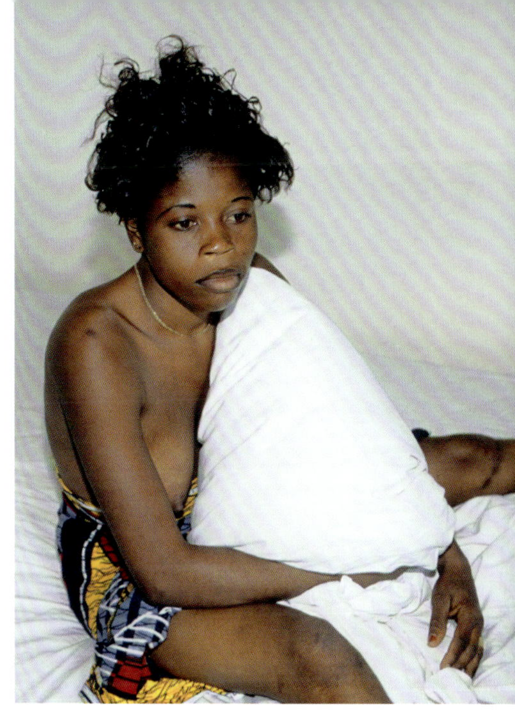

Pesadillas– Las brujas vienen de noche

Rosalyn vivía en un pequeño pueblo de la monoregión de Benin. No podía decir exactamente cuándo habían empezado las pesadillas, sólo sabía que estaban empeorando. Horribles criaturas con garras y cuernos la acechaban noche tras noche, y la distancia entre Rosalyn y ellos se estrechaba de forma incesante. Comenzó a perder peso. Su estado se deterioró notablemente.
Cuando surgió la sospecha de que podía ser víctima de la brujería, todo fue muy rápido. La sacaron de la sofocante atmósfera del pueblo y la llevaron a Cotonou, donde la consulta al oráculo por parte de un sacerdote experimentado confirmó sus temores: una tía de Rosalyn estaba celosa de ella y la había hechizado con un fuerte hechizo maligno.

Esto habría sido mortal de no haber sido diagnosticado y tratado, pero Rosalyn tuvo suerte dentro de lo malo: se recuperó.

Pesadelos – As bruxas vêm à noite

Rosalyn vivia numa pequena aldeia na monorregião de Benin. Ela não podia dizer exatamente quando os pesadelos começaram, só sabia que eles estavam piorando. Criaturas horríveis com garras e chifres perseguiam-na noite após noite, e a distância entre Rosalyn e eles era cada vez menor. Ela começou a perder peso. O seu estado deteriorou-se visivelmente.

Quando surgiu a suspeita de que ela poderia ser vítima de bruxaria, tudo foi muito rápido. Foi levada para fora da atmosfera sufocante da aldeia e para Cotonou, onde o interrogatório do oráculo por um sacerdote experiente confirmou os seus receios: uma tia Rosalyns tinha ciúmes dela e tinha-lhe lançado um forte feitiço de dano.

Isto não teria sido tratado e não teria sido reconhecido como mortal, mas assim, Rosalyn teve sorte no infortúnio: ela encontrou a recuperação.

Nachtmerries – 's nachts komen de heksen

Rosalyn woonde in een dorpje in het departement Mono in Benin. Ze kon niet precies zeggen wanneer de nachtmerries waren begonnen, ze wist gewoon dat het erger werd. Vreselijke wezens met klauwen en hoorns achtervolgden haar elke nacht, en hun afstand tot Rosalyn werd steeds kleiner. Ze begon af te vallen. Haar toestand verslechterde zienderogen.

Toen de verdenking opkwam dat ze het slachtoffer kon zijn van hekserij, ging alles heel snel. Ze werd uit de verstikkende sfeer van het dorp gehaald en naar Cotonou gebracht, waar de ondervraging van het orakel door een ervaren priester haar angsten bevestigde: een tante van Rosalyn was jaloers op haar geweest en had schadelijke tovenarij op haar laten uitoefenen.

Dit zou zonder behandeling en herkenning dodelijk zijn geweest, maar Rosalyn had geluk bij een ongeluk: ze werd genezen.

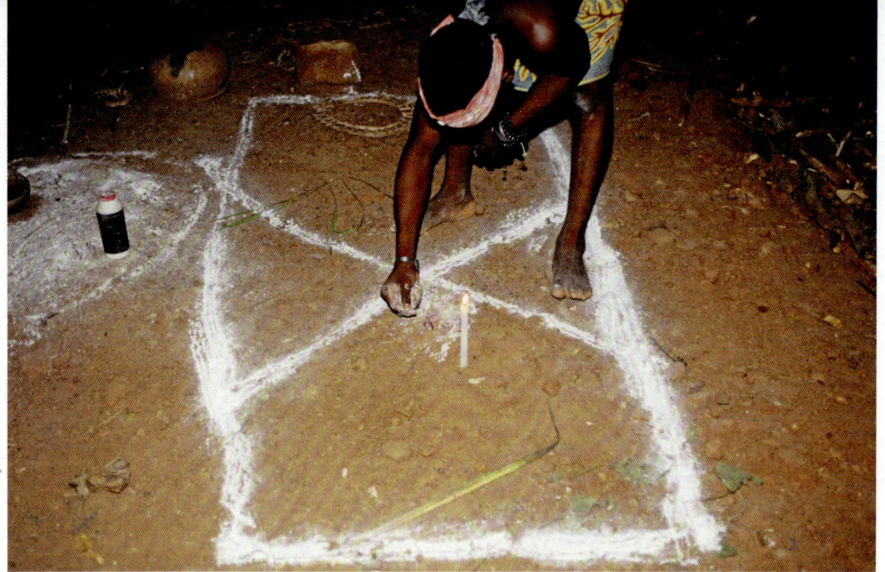

During the ceremony, all those uninvolved hide

Pendant la cérémonie, toutes les personnes non concernées se cachent

Während der Zeremonie verstecken sich alle Unbeteiligten

Durante la ceremonia, se esconden todos los que no están involucrados

Durante a cerimónia, todos os esconderijos não envolvidos.

Tijdens de ceremonie verstoppen alle buitenstaanders zich

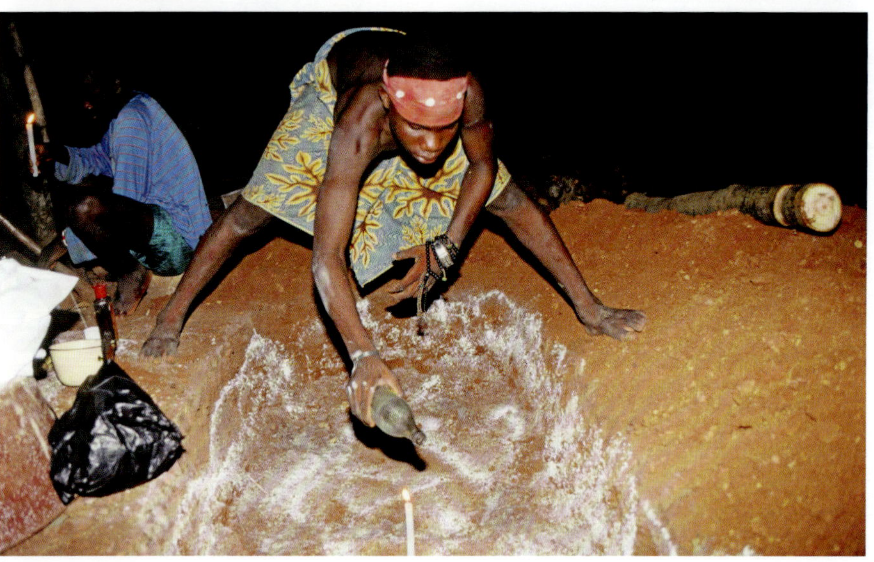

A sacrifice of schnapps to appease the earth

De l'alcool en sacrifice pour apaiser la terre

Ein Schnaps-Trankopfer zur Besänftigung der Erde

Un sacrificio de aguardiente para apaciguar la tierra

Um sacrifício de bebida de schnapps para apaziguar a terra

Een sterkedrankoffer om de aarde te sussen

Harmful spells—draconian defense against the greatest suffering

In the area of natural religions, there are damaging spells that inevitably lead to death. Some of them are so strong that draconian measures are needed to ward off the aggressive forces or to make them benevolent. In the case of a young woman of the Adja people in the Mono region of Benin, the healer recognized such a threat during the oracle questioning.

Magie maléfique, méthodes draconiennes en cas d'urgence

Dans le domaine du vodun, certains sortilèges maléfiques mènent inévitablement à la mort. Beaucoup sont tellement puissants que seules des mesures draconiennes permettent les repousser ou les inverser. Pour une jeune femme de l'ethnie Adja, vivant dans le département de Mono au Bénin, le guérisseur interrogea l'oracle et reconnut un danger de mort.

Schadenzauber – drakonische Abwehr in höchster Not

Im Bereich der Naturreligionen gibt es Schadenzauber, die unweigerlich zum Tode führen. Manche von ihnen sind so stark, dass es drakonischer Maßnahmen bedarf, um die aggressiven Kräfte abzuwehren oder gütig zu stimmen. Im Fall einer jungen Frau vom Volk der Adja in der Monoregion Benins erkannte der Heiler während der Orakelbefragung eine solche Bedrohung.

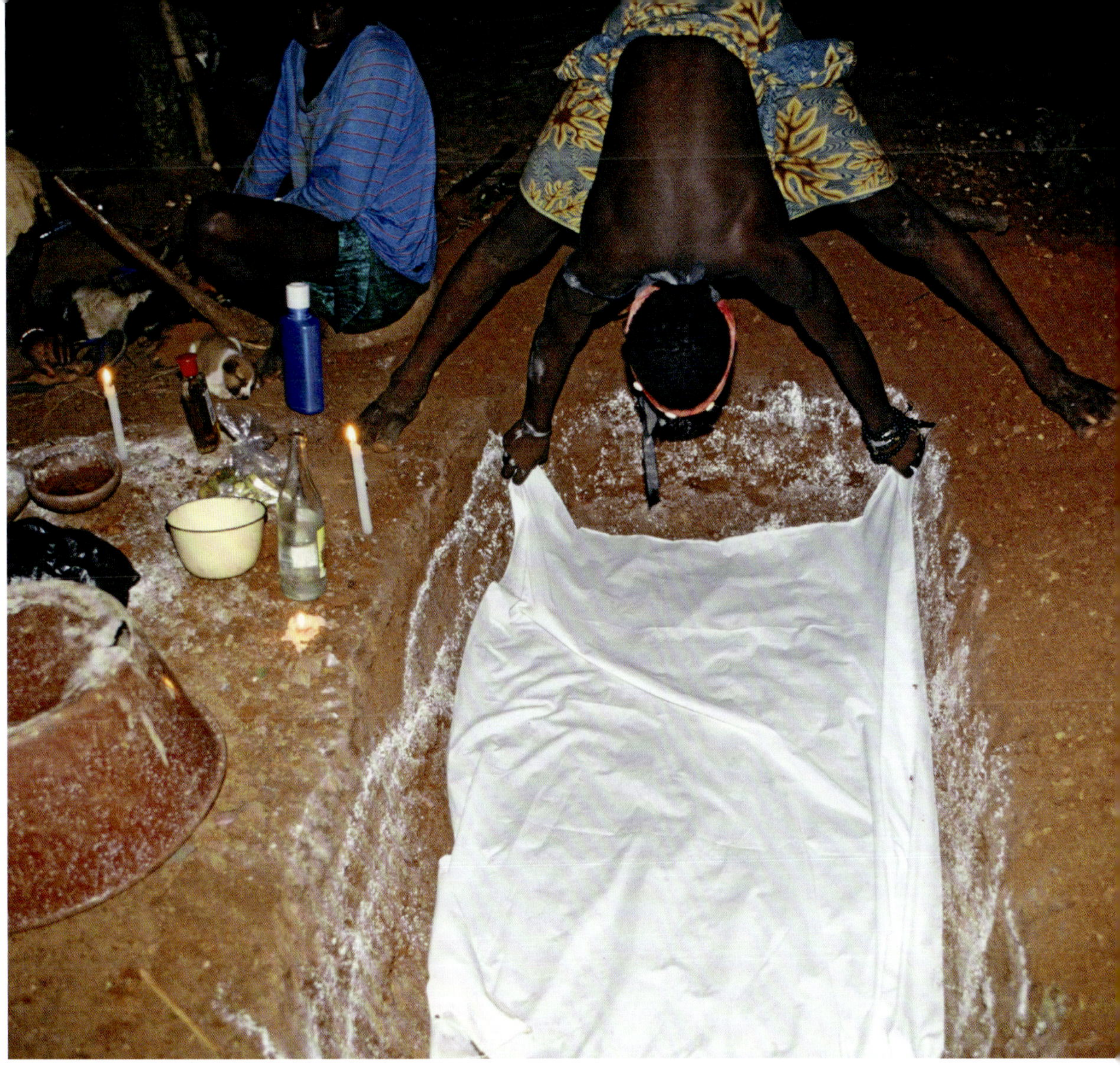

Hechizo maligno– Defensa draconiana en los casos de máxima emergencia

En el área de las religiones naturales, hay hechizos malignos que inevitablemente conducen a la muerte. Algunos de ellos son tan fuertes que se necesitan medidas draconianas para protegerse de las fuerzas agresivas o hacerlas benignas. En el caso de una joven del pueblo Adja en la monoregión de Benin, el curandero reconoció tal amenaza durante la consulta al oráculo.

Feitiço de dano – Defesa draconiana no mais alto nível de perigo

Na área das religiões naturais, há feitiços de dano que inevitavelmente levam à morte. Alguns deles são tão fortes que são necessárias medidas draconianas para afastar as forças agressivas ou torná-las benignas. No caso de uma jovem mulher do povo Adja na monoregião de Benin, o curandeiro reconheceu tal ameaça durante o interrogatório do oráculo.

Zwarte magie – draconische verdediging in hoge nood

Op het terrein van natuurreligies zijn er boze betoveringen die onvermijdelijk tot de dood leiden. Sommige zijn zo sterk dat er draconische maatregelen nodig zijn om de agressieve krachten af te weren of goedaardig te maken. In het geval van een jonge vrouw uit het Adja-volk in het departement Mono in Benin herkende de genezer een dergelijke bedreiging tijdens het orakelverhoor.

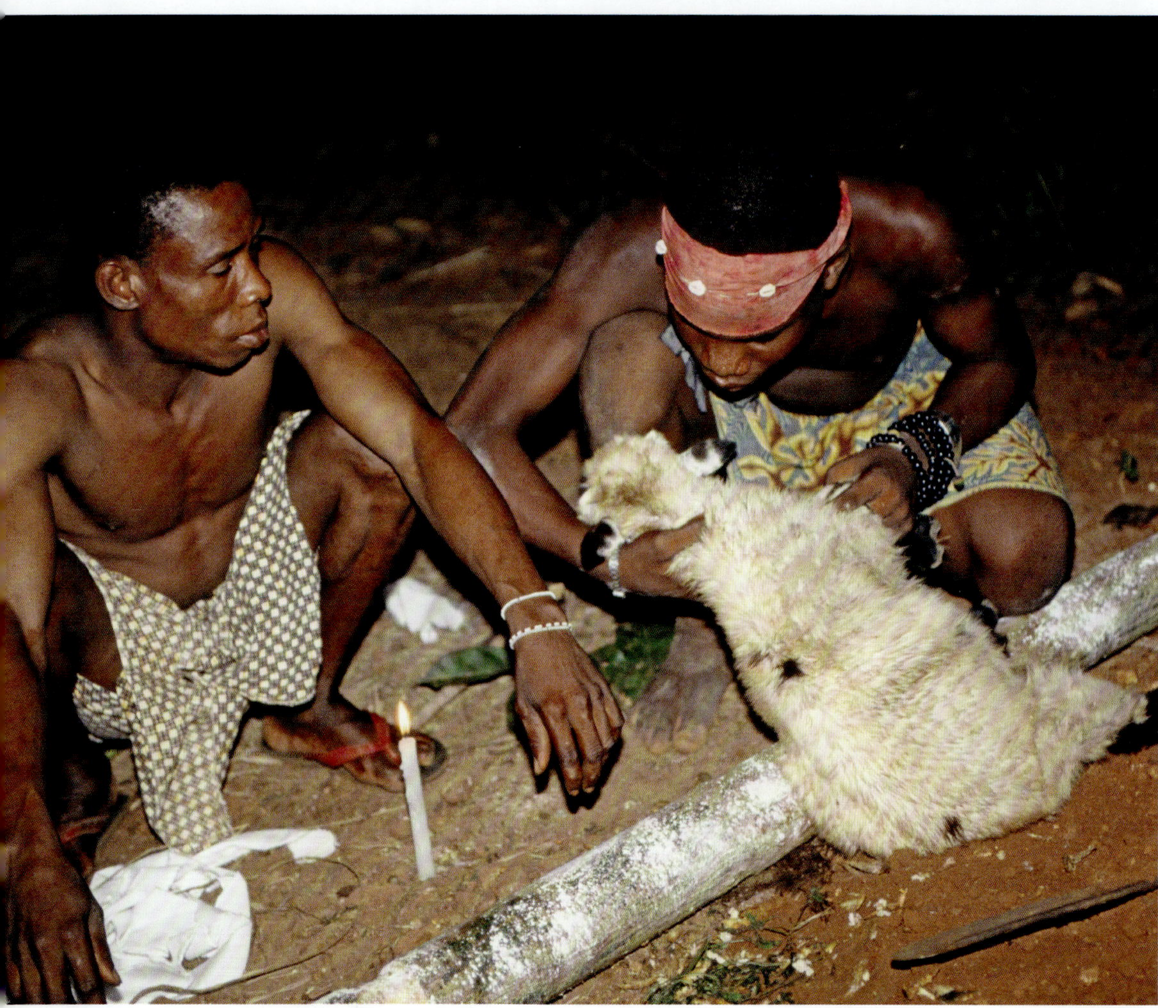

A ram is the first animal. The trunk of a bush, the same size as the young woman, will symbolize her in her current, sick condition.

Un bélier est le premier animal. Un tronc de la taille de la patiente symbolise la jeune femme dans son état actuel de malade.

Ein Widder ist das erste Tier. Der Staudenstamm von der Größe der jungen Frau wird sie in ihrem aktuellen, kranken Zustand symbolisieren.

Un carnero es el primer animal. El tronco del tamaño de la joven simbolizará su estado actual de enfermedad.

Um carneiro é o primeiro animal. O tronco perene do tamanho da jovem mulher vai simbolizá-la em seu atual estado de doença.

Een ram is het eerste dier. De plantenstam ter grootte van de jonge vrouw moet haar symboliseren in haar huidige, zieke toestand.

The measure necessary was the strongest defensive spell known to the priest and required a neutral executor, since the priest himself threatened to become a victim of witchcraft during its execution. Subsequently, a banana tree was pruned to the size of the sick person. Young animals, whose task was to send cries for help to the gods as sacrificial voices, were tied to it.

This montage of offerings was finally buried by the priest's son to satisfy the witches' greed for blood.

Ce cas nécessitait l'acte de magie défensive le plus puissant connu du prêtre, ainsi qu'un exécuteur neutre car, au cours du processus, le prêtre pouvait lui aussi risquer d'être victime du sorcier. On prépara un tronc de bananier de la taille de la jeune femme. De jeunes animaux furent attachés au tronc afin que leur voix adresse aux dieux des appels au secours.

Les bêtes sacrifiées furent finalement enterrées par le fils du prêtre afin de calmer la soif de sang des sorciers

Die erforderliche Maßnahme war der stärkste dem Priester bekannte Abwehrzauber und erforderte einen neutralen Vollstrecker, da der Priester bei ihrer Ausführung selbst Opfer der Hexerei zu werden drohte. Im Folgenden wurde eine Bananenstaude auf die Größe der Kranken zurechtgestutzt. An diese fesselte man junge Tiere, deren Aufgabe es war, als Opferstimme Hilferufe an die Götter zu schicken.

Diese Montage aus Opfergaben wurde schließlich vom Sohn des Priesters beerdigt, um die Gier der Hexen nach Blut zu stillen.

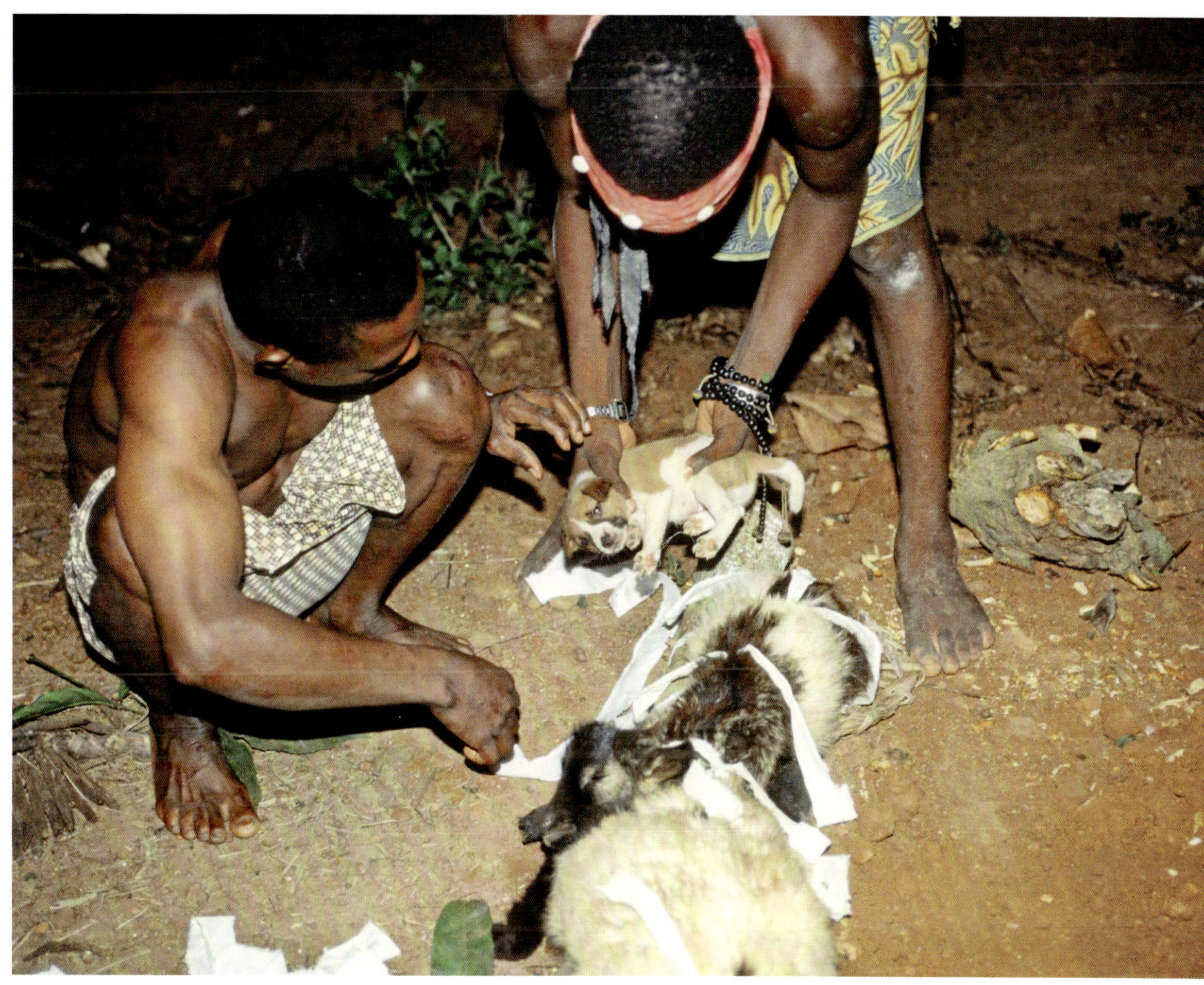

La medida necesaria consistía en el hechizo defensivo más fuerte conocido por el sacerdote y requería un ejecutor neutral, ya que el propio sacerdote sufría el peligro de convertirse en víctima de la brujería durante su ejecución. A continuación, se podó una planta de banana del tamaño de los enfermos. A ésta iban atados los animales jóvenes, cuya tarea era enviar gritos de ayuda a los dioses como voces de sacrificio.

Este montaje de ofrendas fue finalmente enterrado por el hijo del sacerdote para satisfacer la codicia de sangre de las brujas.

A medida necessária era o feitiço defensivo mais forte conhecido pelo padre e exigia um executor neutro, uma vez que o próprio padre ameaçava tornar-se vítima de bruxaria durante a sua execução. A seguir foi aparada uma bananeira do tamanho dos doentes. Animais jovens eram amarrados a estes, cuja tarefa era enviar gritos de socorro aos deuses como vozes de sacrifício.

Esta montagem de oferendas foi finalmente enterrada pelo filho do padre para satisfazer a ganância das bruxas por sangue.

De noodzakelijke maatregel was de sterkste verdedigende spreuk die de priester kende en vereiste een neutrale uitvoerder, aangezien de priester zelf het slachtoffer dreigde te worden van hekserij tijdens de uitvoering ervan. Vervolgens werd de stam van een bananenplant gesnoeid ter grootte van de zieke. Daaraan werden jonge dieren vastgebonden, die de opdracht hadden om als offerstem de goden om hulp te vragen.

Deze montage van offergaven werd uiteindelijk door de zoon van de priester begraven om de bloeddorst van de heksen te bevredigen.

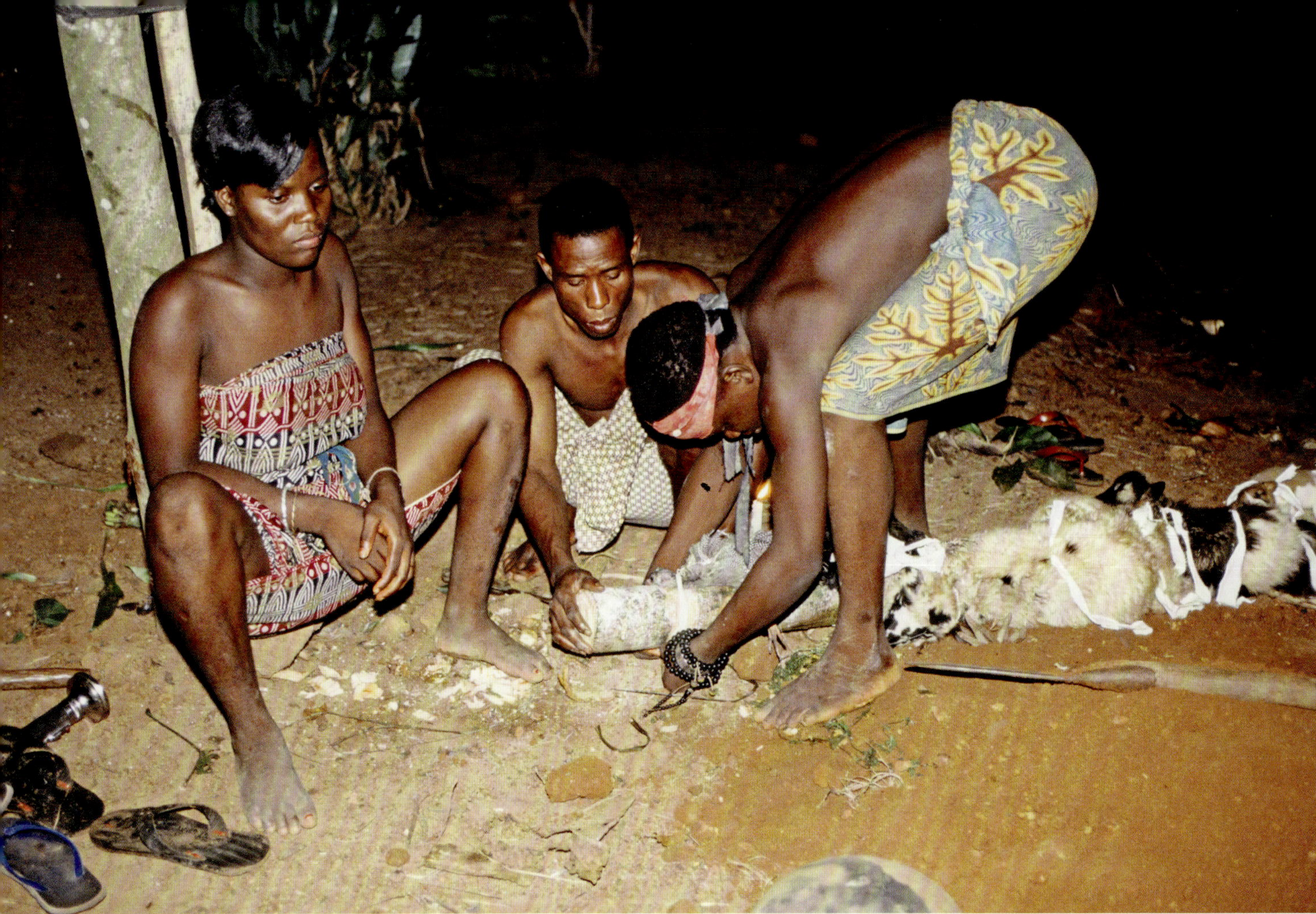

All the villagers are hiding. Those who are not involved have hidden in their huts and avoid going outside - as long as the curse is not banished, this can have fatal consequences for everyone.

Tous les villageois se sont cachés. Toutes les personnes non concernées se sont retirées chez elles et évitent de sortir. Tant que la malédiction n'est pas conjurée, le risque de mort peut toucher tout le monde.

Alle Dorfbewohner haben sich versteckt. Wer nicht beteiligt ist, hat sich in seiner Hütte versteckt und vermeidet es, nach draußen zu gehen – solange der Fluch nicht gebannt ist, kann das für jeden tödliche Folgen haben.

Todos los aldeanos se están escondiendo. Cualquiera que no esté involucrado se ha escondido en su cabaña y evita salir - mientras no se destierre la maldición, esto puede tener consecuencias fatales para todos.

Todos os aldeões estão escondidos. Qualquer pessoa que não esteja envolvida escondeu-se na sua cabana e evita sair - enquanto a maldição não for banida, isso pode ter consequências fatais para todos.

Alle dorpelingen verbergen zich. Wie er niet bij betrokken is, heeft zich in zijn hut verstopt en komt niet naar buiten – zolang de vloek niet opgeheven is, kan die fatale gevolgen hebben voor iedereen.

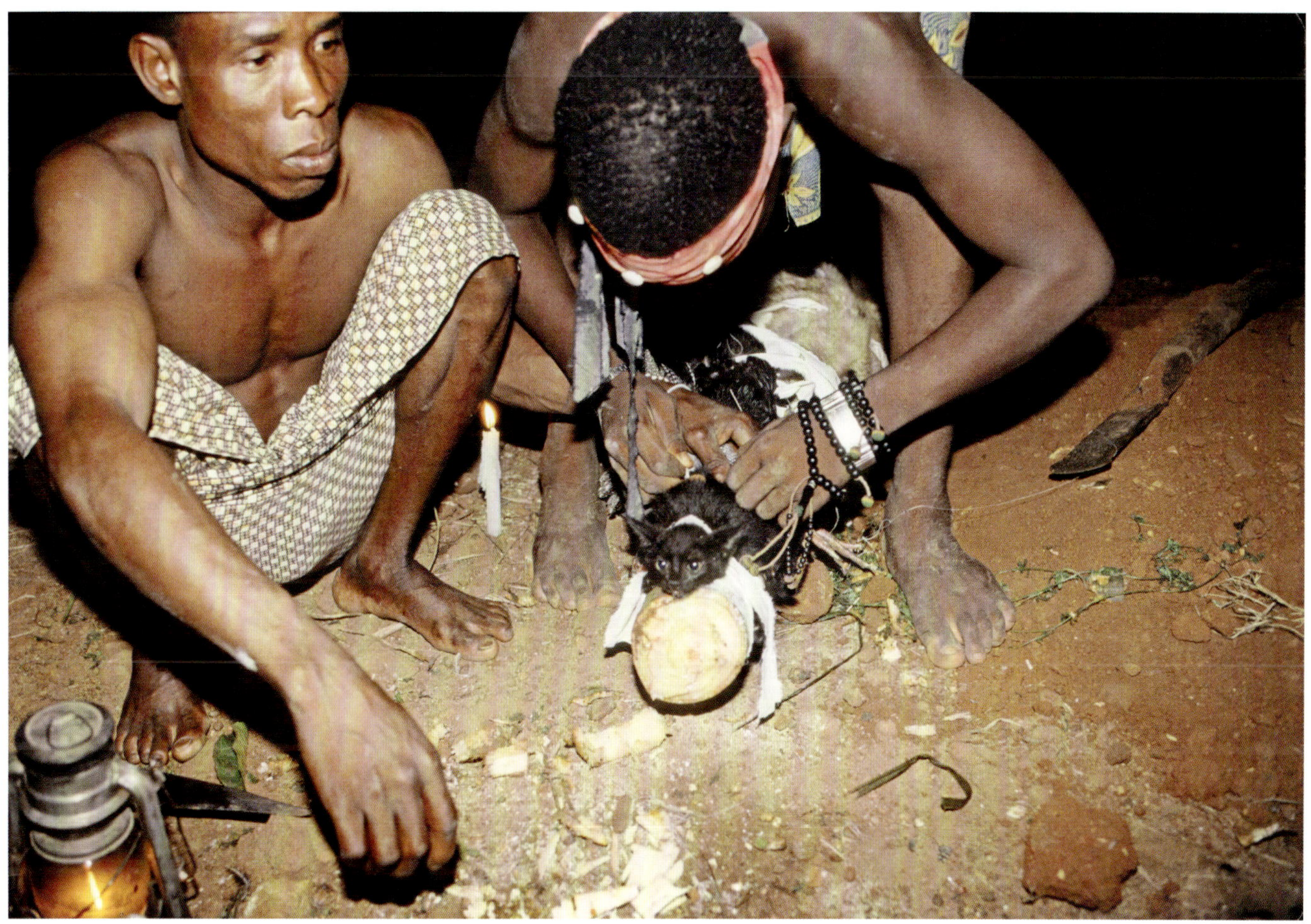

The oracle says it's the bewitched girl's only chance

D'après l'oracle, c'est la seule chance de la jeune fille ensorcelée

Das Orakel sagt, es sei die einzige Chance des verhexten Mädchens

El oráculo dice que es la única oportunidad de la chica hechizada

O oráculo diz que é a única hipótese da rapariga enfeitiçada

Het orakel zegt dat dit de enige kans is voor het behekste meisje

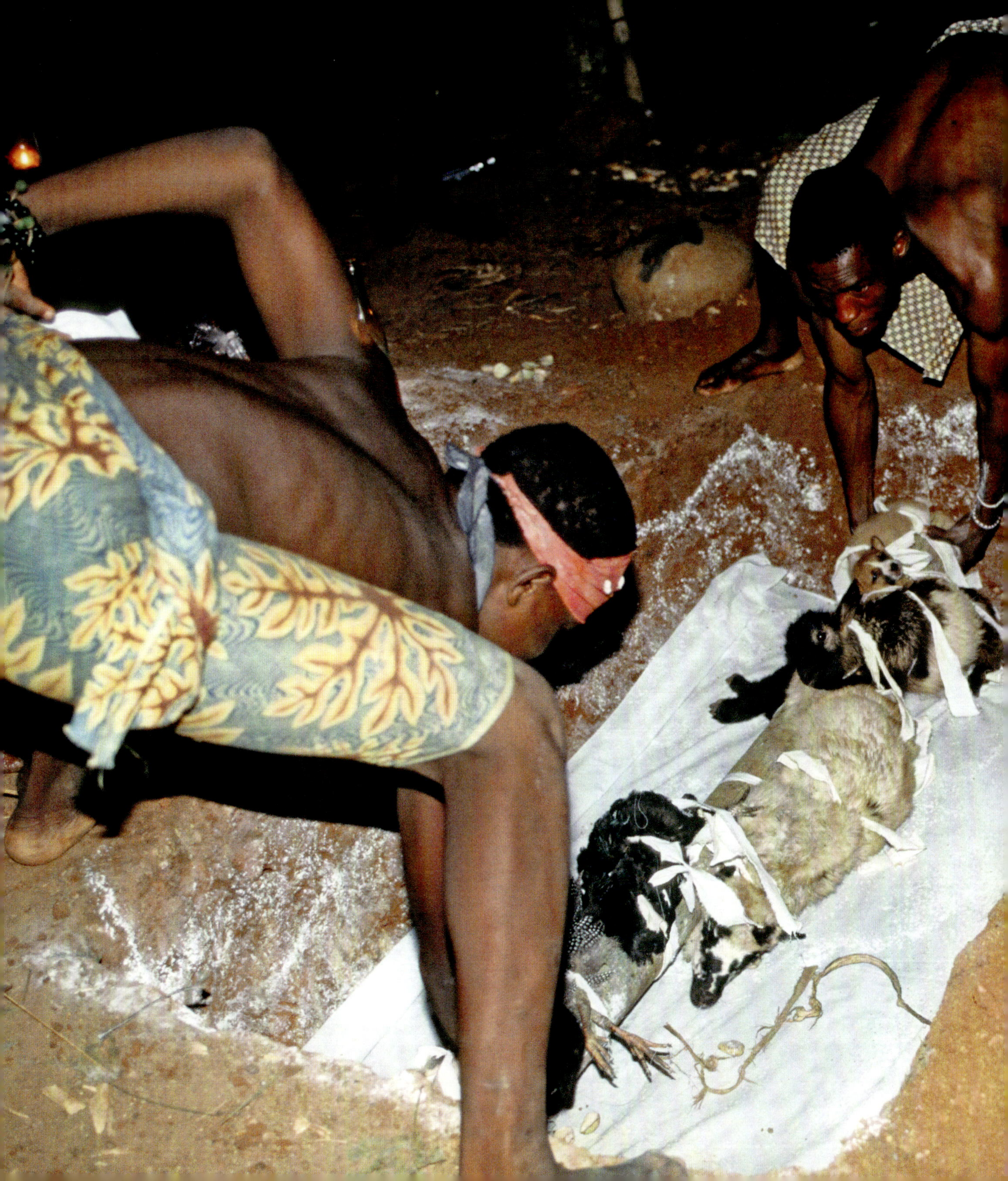

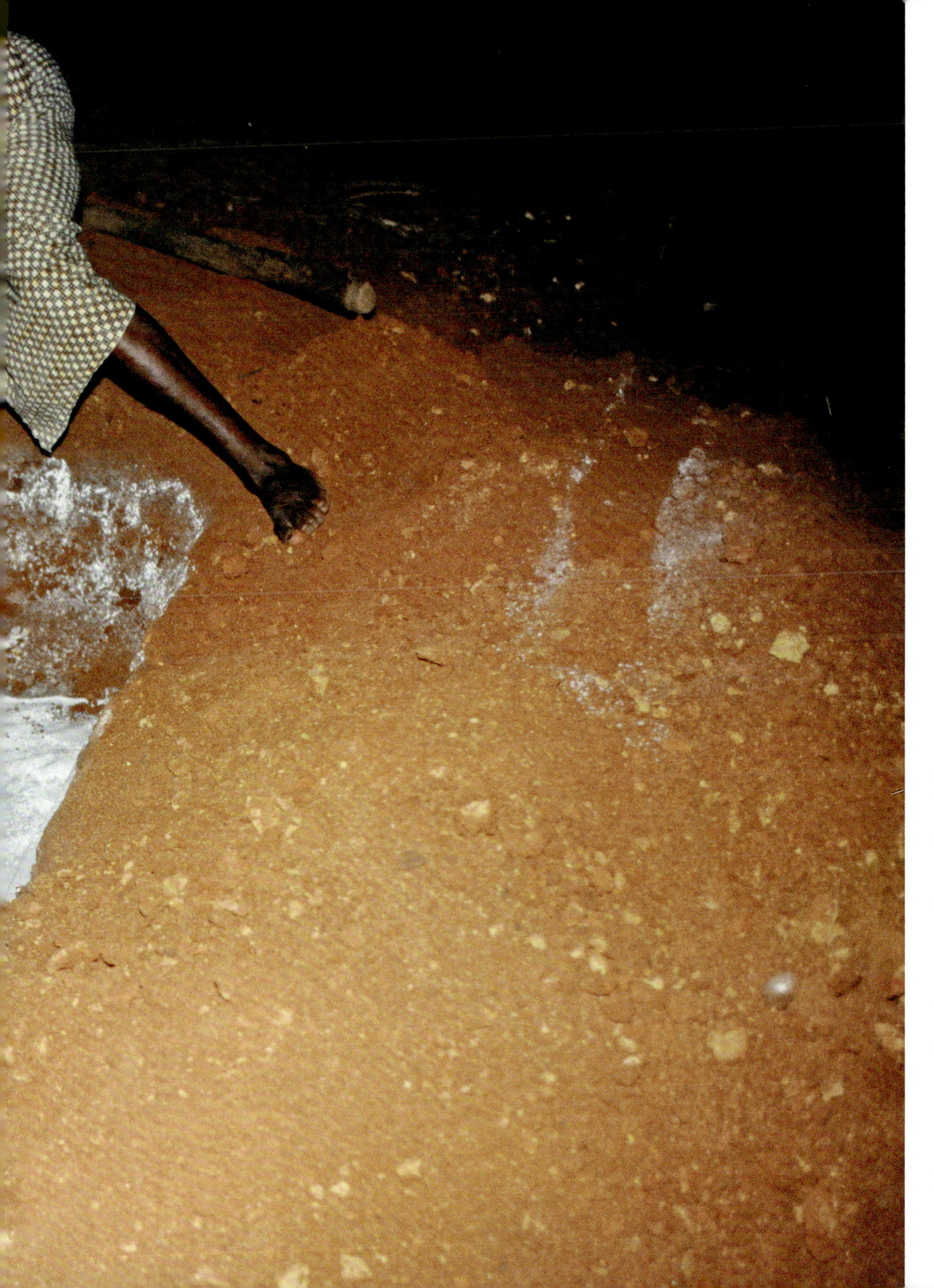

The tribe with
the animals is
let into the grave

Les animaux
sont déposés
dans la fosse

Der Stamm
mit den Tieren
wird ins Grab
eingelassen

Se deja entrar a
la tribu con los
animales en la
tumba

A tribo com
os animais
é deixada na
sepultura

De stam met
dieren wordt in
het graf gelaten

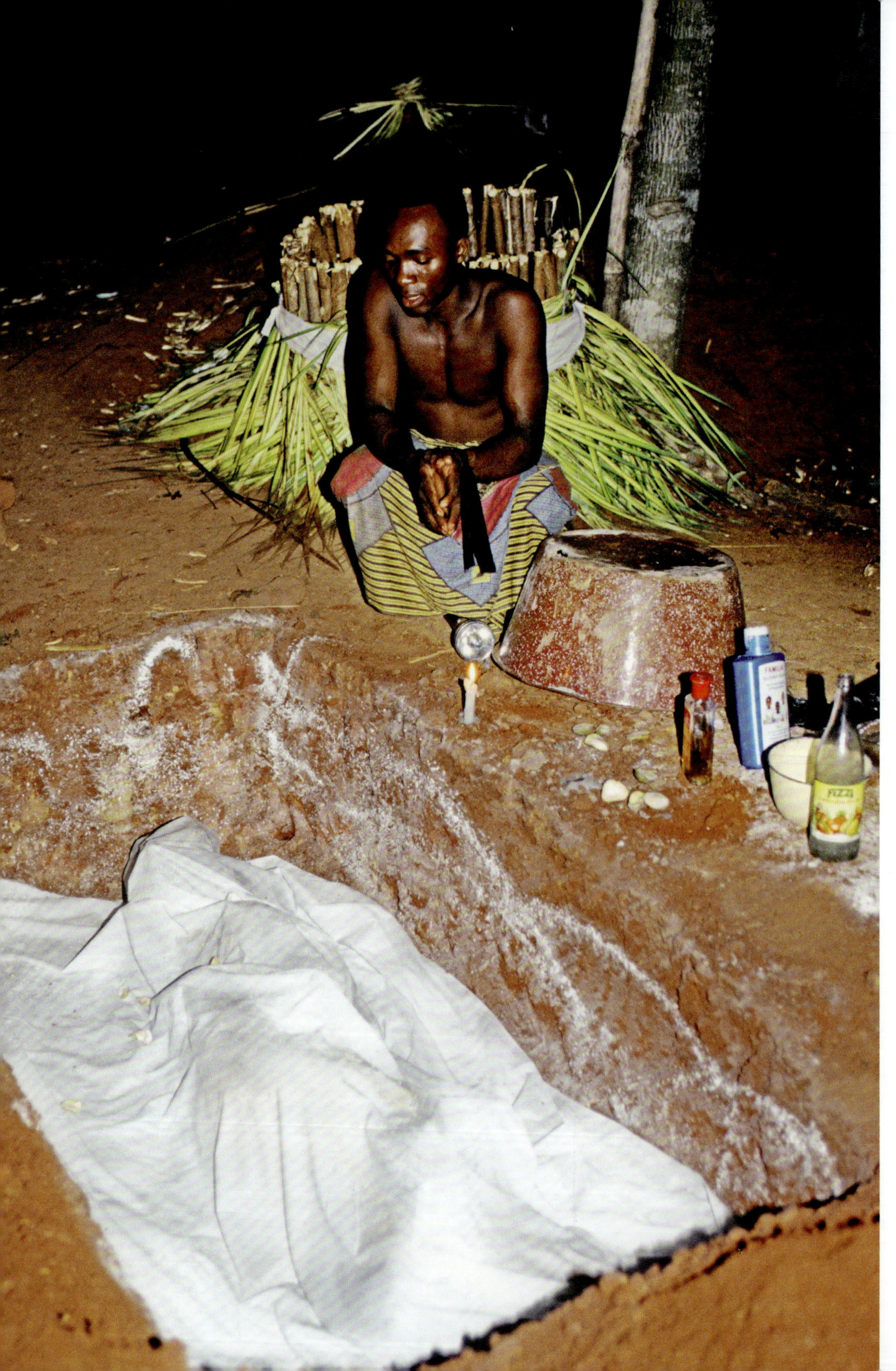

They squirm like a human being. The frightened animals desperately try to free themselves. Covered by the sheet, it looks as if their movement comes from a single body—that of a human being.

Ils convulsent comme un être humain. Les animaux effrayés tentent bien évidemment de s'échapper. Sous le drap dont ils ont été recouverts, leurs mouvements semblent provenir d'un unique corps, celui d'une jeune femme.

Sie winden sich wie ein Mensch. Die verängstigten Tiere versuchen verzweifelt, sich zu befreien. Vom Leintuch bedeckt sieht es aus, als stamme ihre Bewegung von einem einzigen Körper – dem eines Menschen.

Te retuerces como un ser humano. Los animales asustados intentan desesperadamente liberarse. Cubiertos por la sábana, parece que sus movimiento proviene de un solo cuerpo, el de un ser humano.

Você se contorce como um ser humano. Os animais assustados tentam desesperadamente libertar-se. Coberto pelo lençol, parece que o seu movimento vem de um único corpo – o de um ser humano.

Ze kronkelen als een mens. De angstige dieren proberen zich wanhopig te bevrijden. Bedekt door het laken lijkt het alsof hun bewegingen afkomstig zijn van één lichaam – dat van een mens.

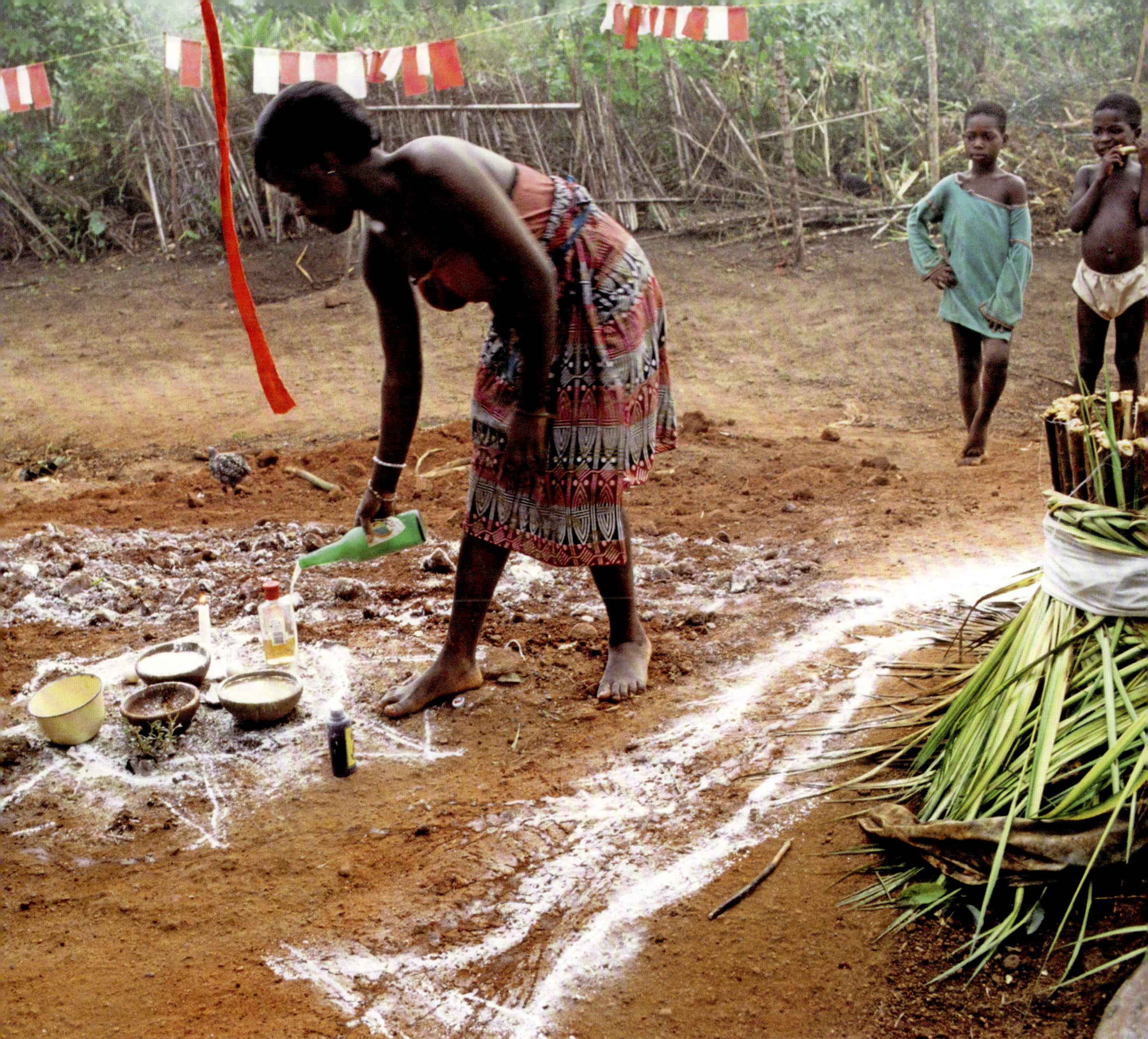

The next morning. The rescued girl pours out a libation. The villagers dare to leave their dwellings again because the priest has given the all-clear.

Le lendemain matin. La jeune femme sauvée répand une boisson en offrande. Les villageois s'autorisent à nouveau à quitter leur logement car le prêtre a annoncé la fin de l'alerte.

Am nächsten Morgen. Das gerettete Mädchen vergießt ein Trankopfer. Die Dorfbewohner trauen sich wieder aus ihren Behausungen heraus, da der Priester Entwarnung gegeben hat.

A la mañana siguiente. La chica rescatada realiza una libación. Los aldeanos se atreven a dejar sus casas de nuevo porque el sacerdote ha dado el visto bueno.

Na manhã seguinte. A rapariga resgatada derrama uma libação. Os aldeões se atrevem a deixar suas casas novamente porque o padre deu tudo certo.

De volgende ochtend. Het geredde meisje werpt een plengoffer. De dorpelingen durven hun huizen weer te verlaten, omdat de priester heeft aangegeven dat alles veilig is.

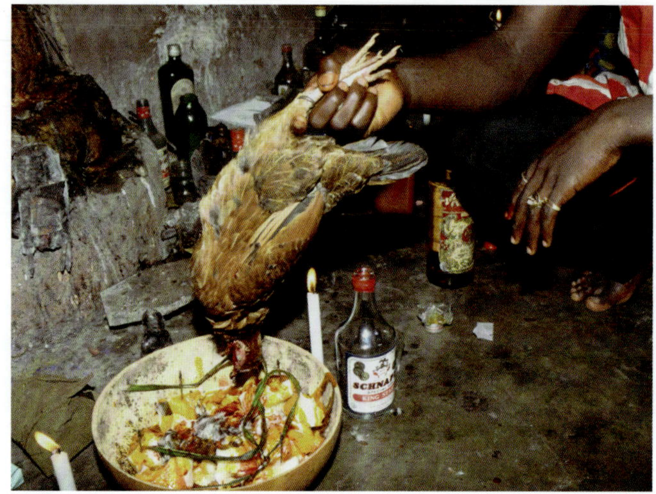

An animal sacrifice completes the offering

Un sacrifice animal complète l'offrande

Ein Tieropfer komplettiert die Opfergabe

Un sacrificio de animales completa la ofrenda

Um sacrifício animal completa o sacrifício

Een dierenoffer maakt het offer compleet

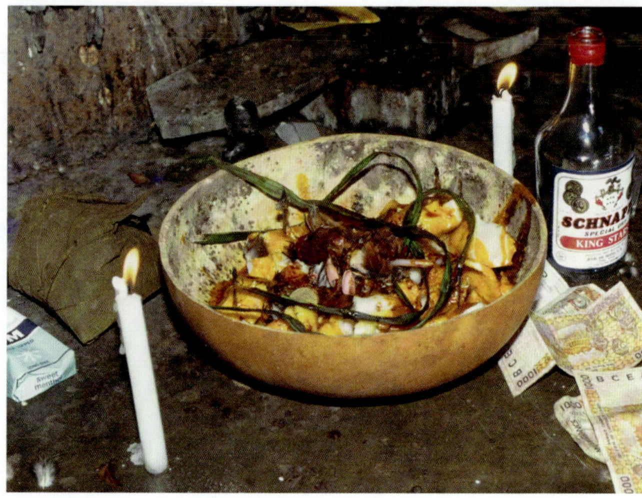

The Sacrifice prepared by the healer

Le sacrifice préparé par le guérisseur

Das vom Heiler fertig zubereitete Opfer

El sacrificio preparado por el curandero

O sacrifício preparado pelo curandeiro

Het door de genezer bereide offer

Crossroads—The sacrifice at the crossroads

In addition to the numerous secret societies and rituals that serve to ward off and combat damaging spells and witchcraft, there is also the inclusive approach in the world of Vodun. Here the witches are honored and pacified, they are asked to stay away, so to speak, and are offered a sacrifice prophylactically.

In the present case, after the diagnosis, the oracle provided the answer to the question of what should be sacrificed and where. The desired setting was a crossroads, a classic place in that the destiny of the event was illustrated by the various possibilities of the route.

The client was instructed to offer the sacrifice, which the priest had previously compiled in the temple, during the day—a typical event in Benin.

Sacrifices au croisement

Outre les nombreuses sociétés secrètes et rituelles servant à repousser et combattre les envoûtements et la magie noire, il existe dans le monde du vodun une approche inclusive. Dans celle-ci, les sorciers sont respectés et apaisés, on leur demande en quelque sorte de rester éloignés et on leur présente une offrande dans un esprit quasi prophylactique.

Dans le cas présenté ici, le diagnostic a d'abord été suivi d'une consultation de l'oracle afin de savoir quels devaient être l'objet et le lieu de l'offrande. La scène souhaitée était un croisement, lieu classique, dans la mesure où il illustre, à travers les différentes voies possibles, l'aspect fataliste de l'univers.

Le client devait ensuite déposer audit lieu l'offrande préparée au temple par le prêtre, en plein jour, pratique tout à fait typique du Bénin.

Crossroads – Das Opfer an der Kreuzung

Neben den zahlreichen Geheimgesellschaften und Ritualen, die zur Abwehr und Bekämpfung von Schadenzauber und Hexerei dienen, gibt es in der Welt des Vodun auch den inklusiven Ansatz. Hierbei werden die Hexen geehrt und beschwichtigt, man bittet sie gewissermaßen um ihr Fernbleiben und bringt ihnen prophylaktisch ein Opfer dar.

Im vorliegenden Fall erbrachte nach der Diagnose zunächst eine Orakelbefragung die Antwort auf die Frage, was und wo geopfert werden sollte. Der gewünschte Schauplatz war eine Kreuzung, ein klassischer Ort insofern, als dass die Schicksalhaftigkeit des Ganzen durch die verschiedenen Möglichkeiten des Wegverlaufs illustriert wurde.

Der Klient wurde angewiesen, die zuvor vom Priester im Tempel zusammengestellte Opfergabe tagsüber darzubringen – in Benin ein durchaus typisches Ereignis.

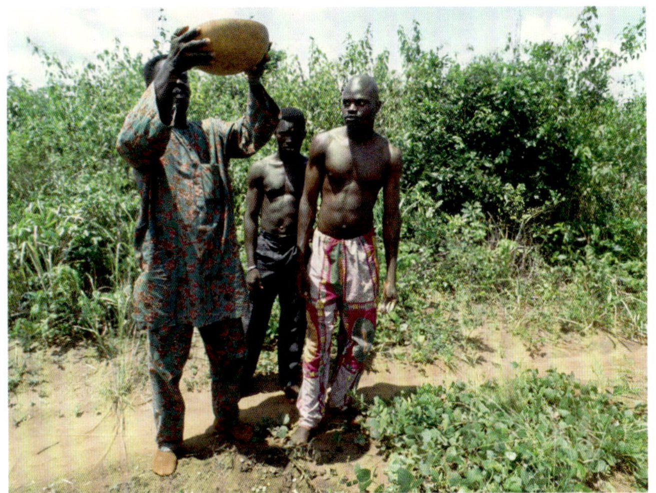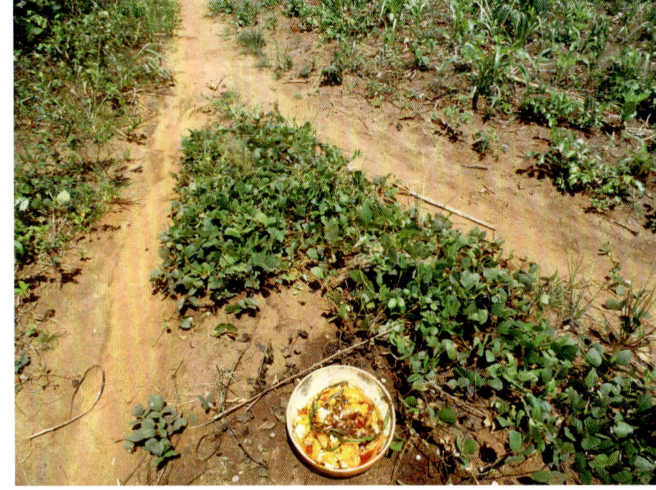

The patient offers the sacrifice
Le patient apporte l'offrande
Der Patient bringt das Opfer dar
El paciente ofrece a la víctima
O paciente oferece à vítima
De patiënt biedt het offer aan

The fork in the road is a symbolic place
Le croisement est un lieu symbolique
Die Weggabelung ist ein symbolträchtiger Ort
La bifurcación de la carretera es un lugar simbólico
O garfo na estrada é um lugar simbólico
De wegsplitsing is een symbolische plaats

Crossroads– La víctima en el cruce

Además de las numerosas sociedades secretas y rituales que sirven para protegerse y combatir los hechizos y la brujería, también existe el enfoque inclusivo en el mundo del Vudú. Las brujas son honradas y apaciguadas, se les pide que se alejen y se les ofrece un sacrificio profiláctico.

En el presente caso, después del diagnóstico, una consulta al oráculo dio la respuesta a la pregunta de qué y dónde se debía sacrificar. El escenario deseado era un cruce, un lugar clásico en el que el destino del conjunto quedaba ilustrado por las diversas posibilidades del camino.

El cliente fue instruido para ofrecer el sacrificio, que había sido previamente compilado durante el día por el sacerdote - un evento típico en Benin.

Crossroads – A vítima na encruzilhada

Além das inúmeras sociedades secretas e rituais que servem para afastar e combater feitiços de dano e bruxaria, há também a abordagem inclusiva no mundo do Vodun. As bruxas são honrados e apaziguados, eles são convidados a ficar longe e são oferecidos um sacrifício profilaticamente.

No caso em apreço, após o diagnóstico, um oráculo questionador deu resposta à questão de saber o que e onde deve ser sacrificado. O cenário desejado era uma encruzilhada, um lugar clássico em que o destino do todo era ilustrado pelas várias possibilidades do caminho.

O cliente foi instruído a oferecer o sacrifício, que havia sido previamente compilado pelo sacerdote no templo, durante o dia – um evento típico em Benin.

Crossroads – het offer op het kruispunt

Naast de vele geheime genootschappen en rituelen die zwarte magie en hekserij moeten afweren en bestrijden, is er in de vodunwereld ook een inclusieve aanpak. Hierbij worden de heksen geëerd en gepaaid, krijgen ze preventief een offer aangeboden en wordt ze in zekere zin gevraagd om ver weg te blijven.

In het onderhavige geval, na de diagnose, kwam bij een orakelraadpleging het antwoord op de vraag wat en waar er moest worden geofferd. De gewenste plek was een kruispunt, in zoverre een klassieke offerplaats omdat de noodlottigheid van het geheel werd geïllustreerd door de verschillende mogelijkheden van de wegrichtingen.

De cliënt kreeg de opdracht het offer, dat eerder door de priester in de tempel was samengesteld, overdag te brengen – een heel normale gebeurtenis in Benin.

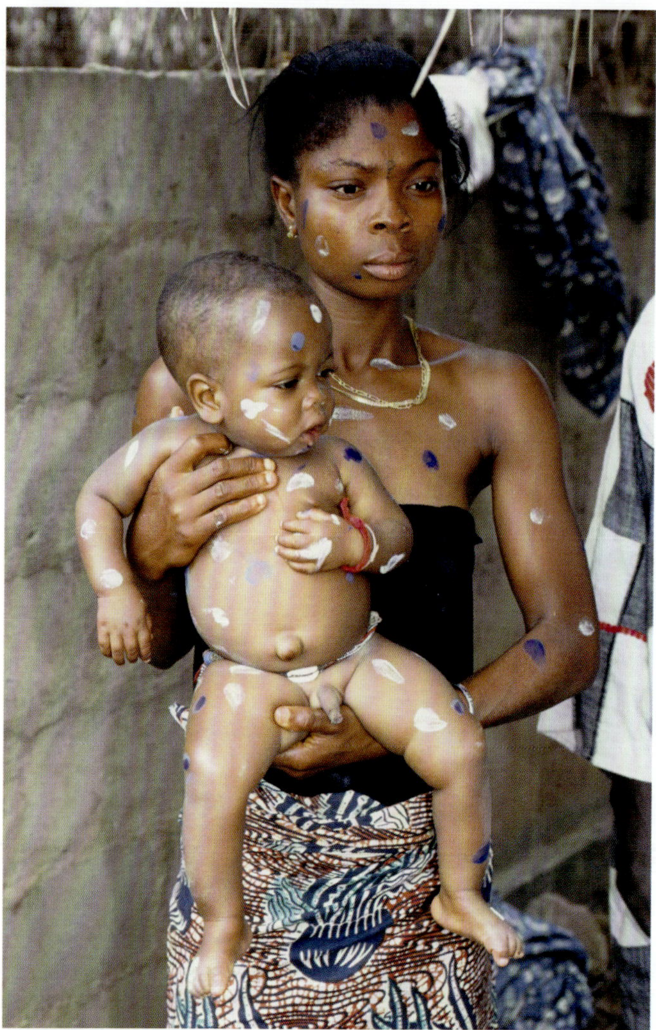

Witch protection for a baby

In Bopa in the Mono district of Benin lives a family that has been a victim of witchcraft for generations. Members were plagued by insidious metaphysical attacks, and many times over the years healing ceremonies and protective rituals were required. In order to prevent this curse in general, it has become established within the family to protect even the youngest against the impending disaster.

Here an anti-witchcraft treatment is successfully carried out on a baby. The Vodun called upon and involved in this case

Protection d'un bébé contre les sorciers

À Bopa, dans le département de Mono, vit une famille victime depuis des générations de sorcellerie. Ses membres sont tourmentés par des attaques métaphysiques sournoises. De nombreux rituels de protection et des cérémonies de guérison ont été nécessaires au fil des ans. Pour prévenir cette malédiction, il a été établi que les membres de la famille devaient être protégés dès leur plus jeune âge contre le malheur latent.

Hexenschutz für ein Baby

In Bopa am Monodistrikt Benins lebt eine Familie, die seit Generationen immer wieder Opfer von Hexerei wird. Die Mitglieder wurden von heimtückischen metaphysischen Angriffen geplagt, und viele Male waren im Laufe der Jahre Heilzeremonien und Schutzrituale erforderlich. Um diesem Fluch generell vorzubeugen, hat es sich innerhalb der Familie etabliert, schon die Jüngsten gegen das drohende Unheil zu schützen.

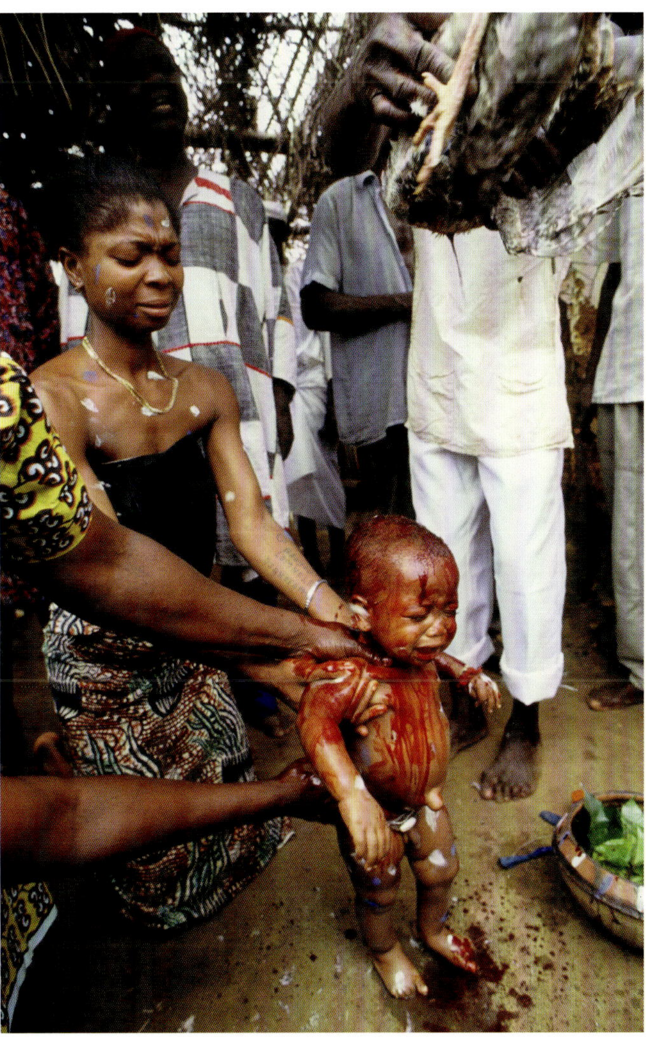

Protección de las brujas para un bebé

En Bopa, en el monodistrito de Benin, vive una familia que ha sido víctima de la brujería durante generaciones. Los miembros estaban plagados de ataques metafísicos traicioneros, y las ceremonias de sanación y los rituales de protección eran necesarios muchas veces a lo largo de los años. Para prevenir esta maldición en general, se ha establecido dentro de la familia, proteger incluso a los más pequeños contra la amenaza del desastre.

Protecção de bruxas para um bebé

Em Bopa, no monodistrito de Benin, vive uma família que foi vítima de bruxaria durante gerações. Os membros foram atormentados por ataques metafísicos traiçoeiros, e cerimónias de cura e rituais protetores foram necessários muitas vezes ao longo dos anos. A fim de evitar esta maldição em geral, estabeleceu-se no seio da família para proteger até os mais jovens contra a ameaça da catástrofe.

Aqui tal tratamento anti-feitiçaria é realizado com sucesso em um bebê.

Bescherming tegen heksen voor baby's

In Bopa, in het departement Mono in Benin, woont een familie die al generaties lang het slachtoffer is van hekserij. De leden worden geplaagd door achterbakse metafysische aanvallen en in de loop der jaren zijn er al veel genezingsceremoniën en beschermende rituelen nodig geweest. Om deze vloek in het algemeen te voorkomen, is het in de familie gemeengoed geworden om zelfs de allerjongsten te beschermen tegen het dreigende onheil.

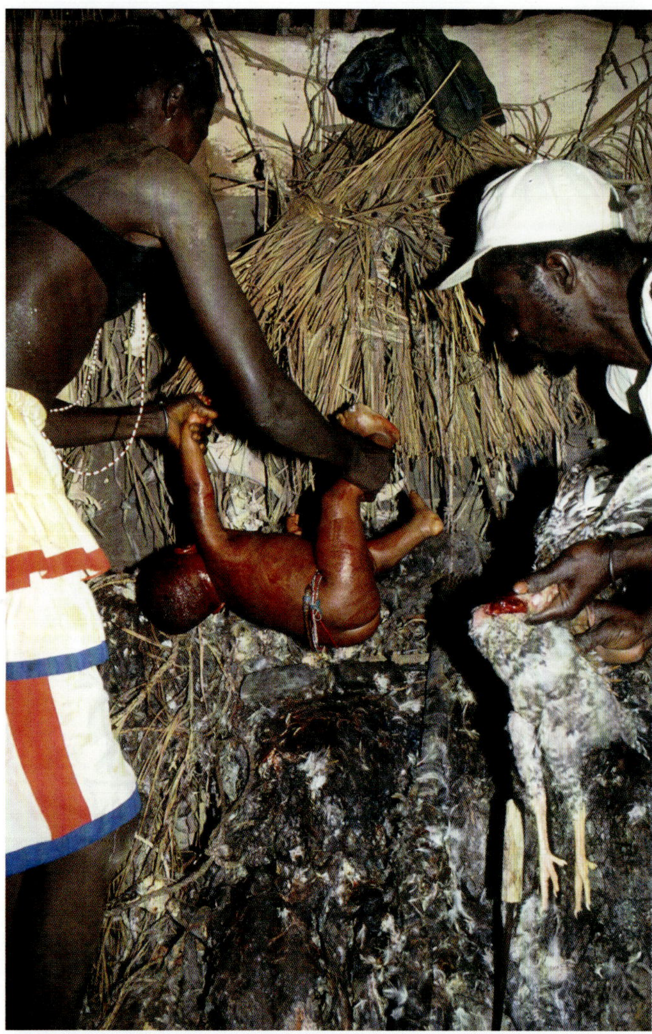

to strengthen the family is Ganbada, one of the younger, extremely warlike gods. These are particularly successful in combating damaging spells.

At the end of the ceremony the baby, generously anointed with the blood of a sacrificial animal, is allowed to sit on the Ganbada fetish.

Ce type de traitement contre la sorcellerie a été prodigué avec succès à un bébé. Le vodun appelé dans ce cas pour soutenir la famille est Ganbada, l'un des jeunes dieux les plus guerriers. Ceux-ci sont particulièrement efficaces dans la lutte contre la magie maléfique.

À la fin de la cérémonie, le bébé devait être recouvert du sang d'un animal sacrifié et prendre place sur le fétiche de Ganbada.

Hier wird eine solche Anti-Hexereibehandlung erfolgreich bei einem Baby durchgeführt. Der Vodun, der in diesem Fall zur Verstärkung der Familie angerufen und eingebunden wird, ist Ganbada, einer der jüngeren, äußerst kriegerischen Götter. Diese sind insbesondere bei der Bekämpfung von Schadenzaubern sehr erfolgreich.

Am Ende der Zeremonie darf das Baby, großzügig mit dem Blut eines Opfertieres eingerieben, auf dem Ganbadafetisch Platz nehmen.

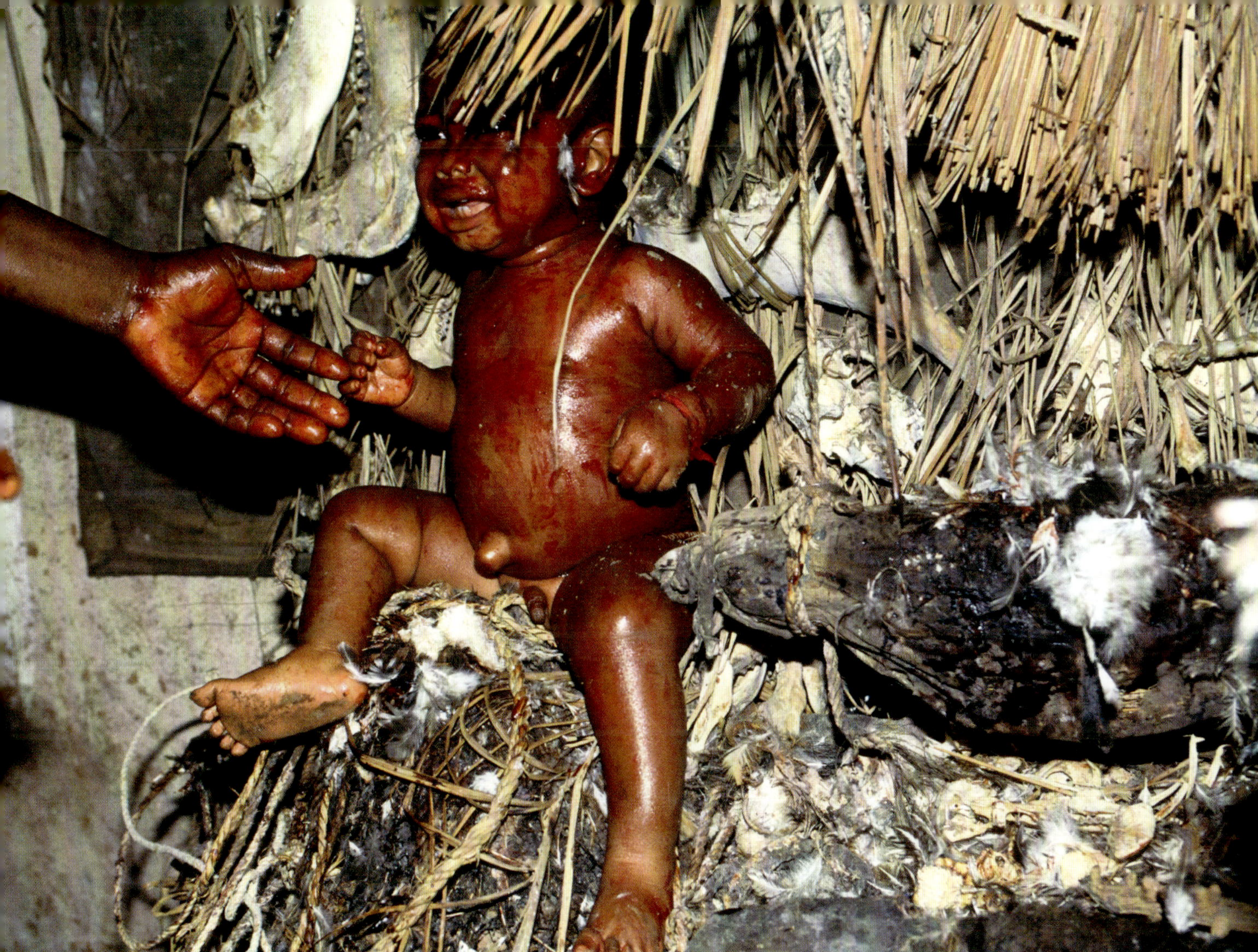

Aquí se lleva a cabo con éxito un tratamiento contra la brujería en un bebé. El Vudú, que en este caso es llamado e involucrado para fortalecer a la familia, es Ganbada, uno de los dioses más jóvenes y extremadamente belicosos. Estos son particularmente exitosos en la lucha contra los hechizos malignos.

Al final de la ceremonia, el bebé, generosamente frotado con la sangre de un animal de sacrificio, puede sentarse en la mesa fetiche ganbada.

O Vodun, que neste caso é chamado e envolvido para fortalecer a família, é Ganbada, um dos deuses mais jovens e extremamente guerreiros. Estes são particularmente bem sucedidos no combate aos feitiços de dano.

No final da cerimônia, o bebê, generosamente esfregado com o sangue de um animal de sacrifício, pode sentar-se na mesa de fetiche da ganbada.

Hier wordt met succes een antihekserijbehandeling uitgevoerd op een baby. De vodun, die in dit geval ter versterking van de familie wordt opgeroepen, is Ganbada, een van de nieuwere, extreem oorlogszuchtige goden. Deze zijn met name succesvol in de strijd tegen schadelijke tovenarij.

Aan het einde van de ceremonie mag de baby, royaal ingewreven met het bloed van een offerdier, op de Ganbada-fetisj plaatsnemen.

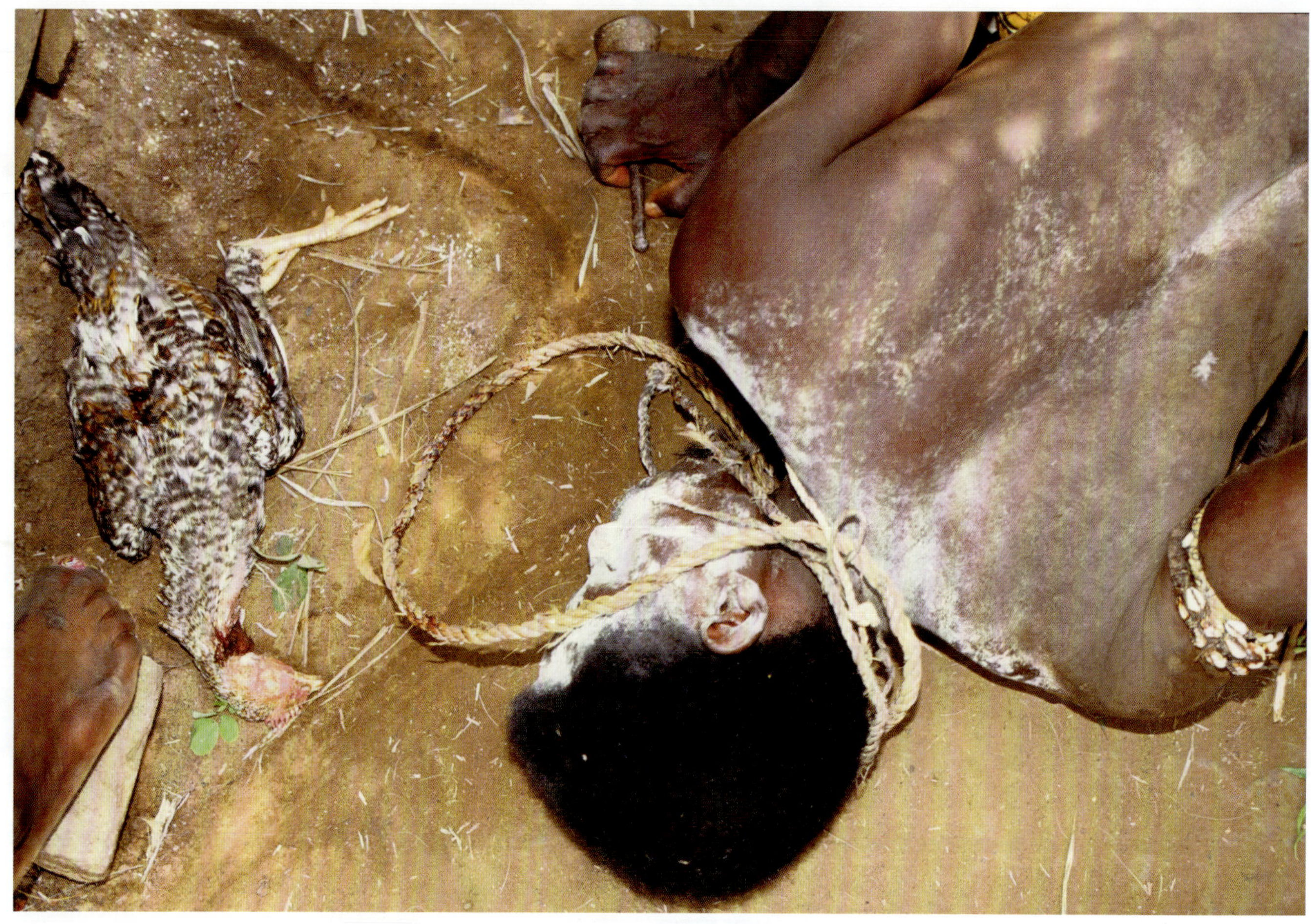

In a heavy trance, the devotee receives Ganbada's instructions.
Dans une transe profonde, l'adepte reçoit les directives de Ganbada
In schwerer Trance empfängt der Anhänger Ganbadas Weisungen
En un trance pesado, el devoto recibe las instrucciones de Ganbada
Num transe pesado, o devoto recebe as instruções de Ganbada
In diepe trance ontvangt de Ganbada-adept instructies

A final sacrifice for the family Vodun
Un dernier sacrifice pour le vodun de la famille
Ein Abschlussopfer für den Familienvodun
Un sacrificio final por el vudú de la familia
Um sacrifício final para o vodu da família
Een laatste offer voor de familievodun

The adept passes on the advice of Ganbada
to the mother

L'adepte transmet le conseil de
Ganbada à la mère

Der Adept gibt der Mutter die Ratschläge
Ganbadas weiter

El adepto transmite el consejo de Ganbada
a la madre

O adepto passa o conselho de
Ganbada à mãe

De adept geeft de adviezen van Ganbada
door aan de moeder

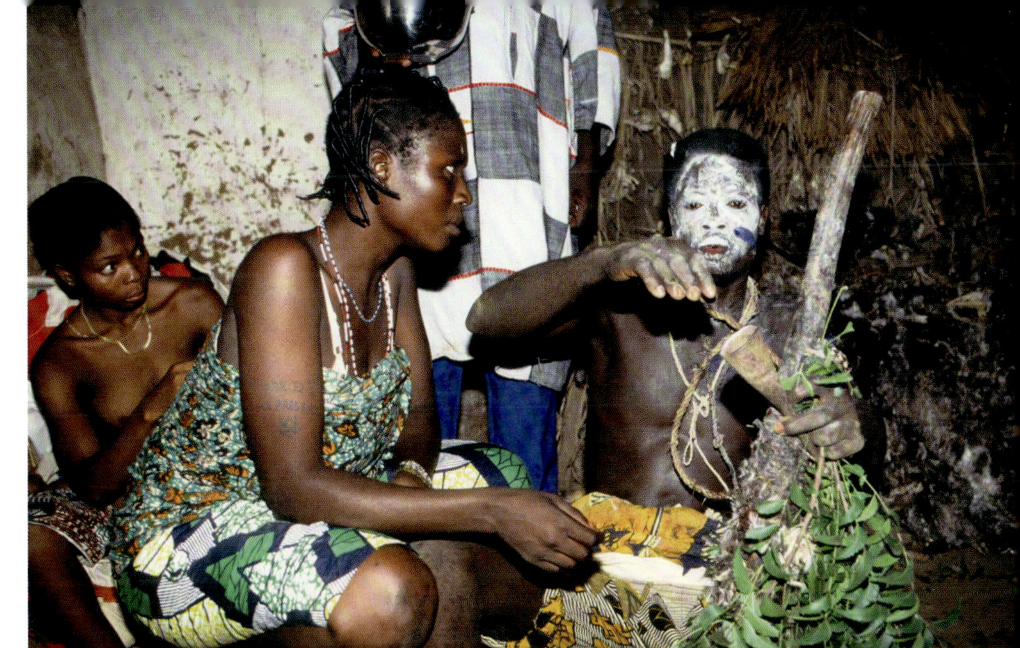

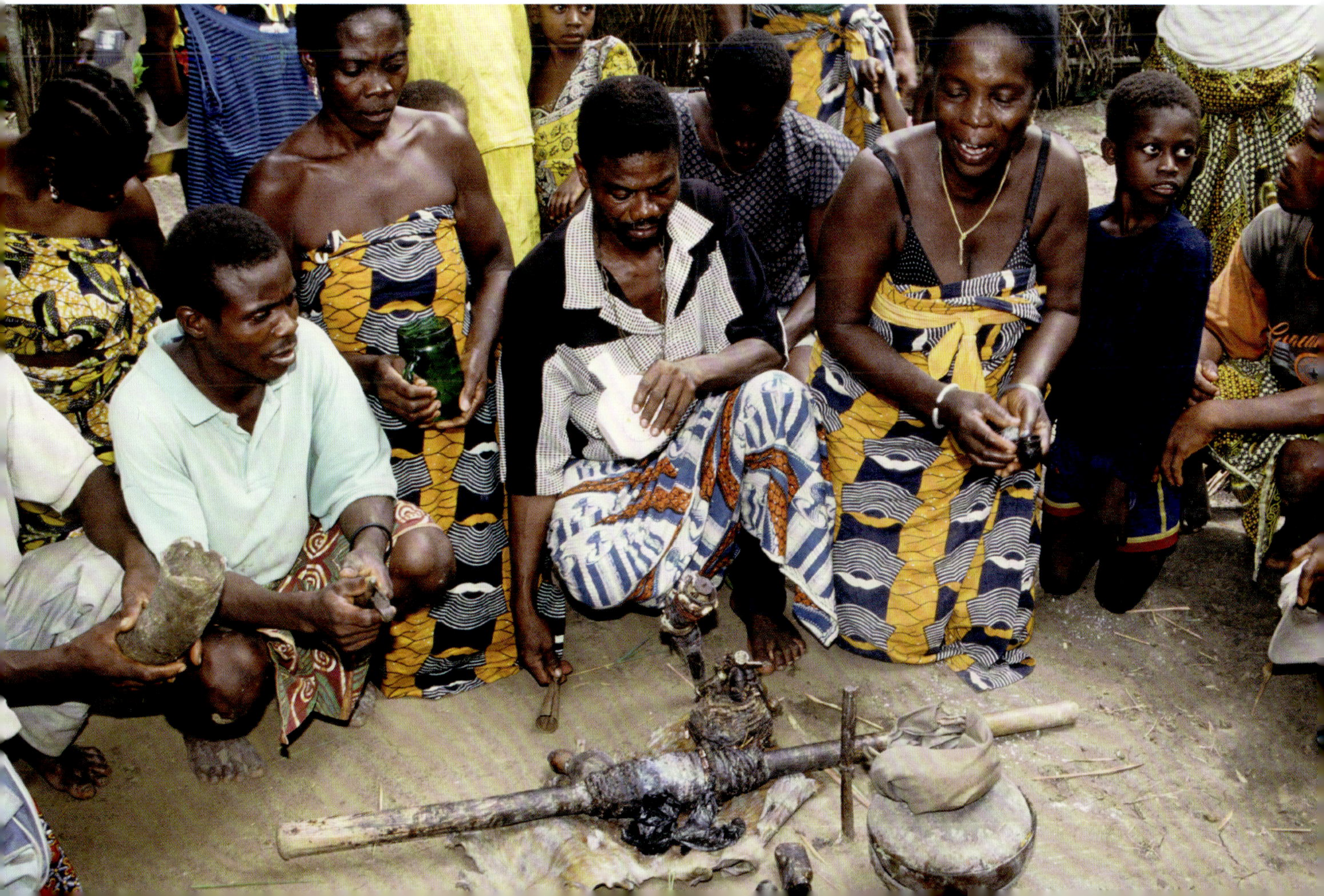

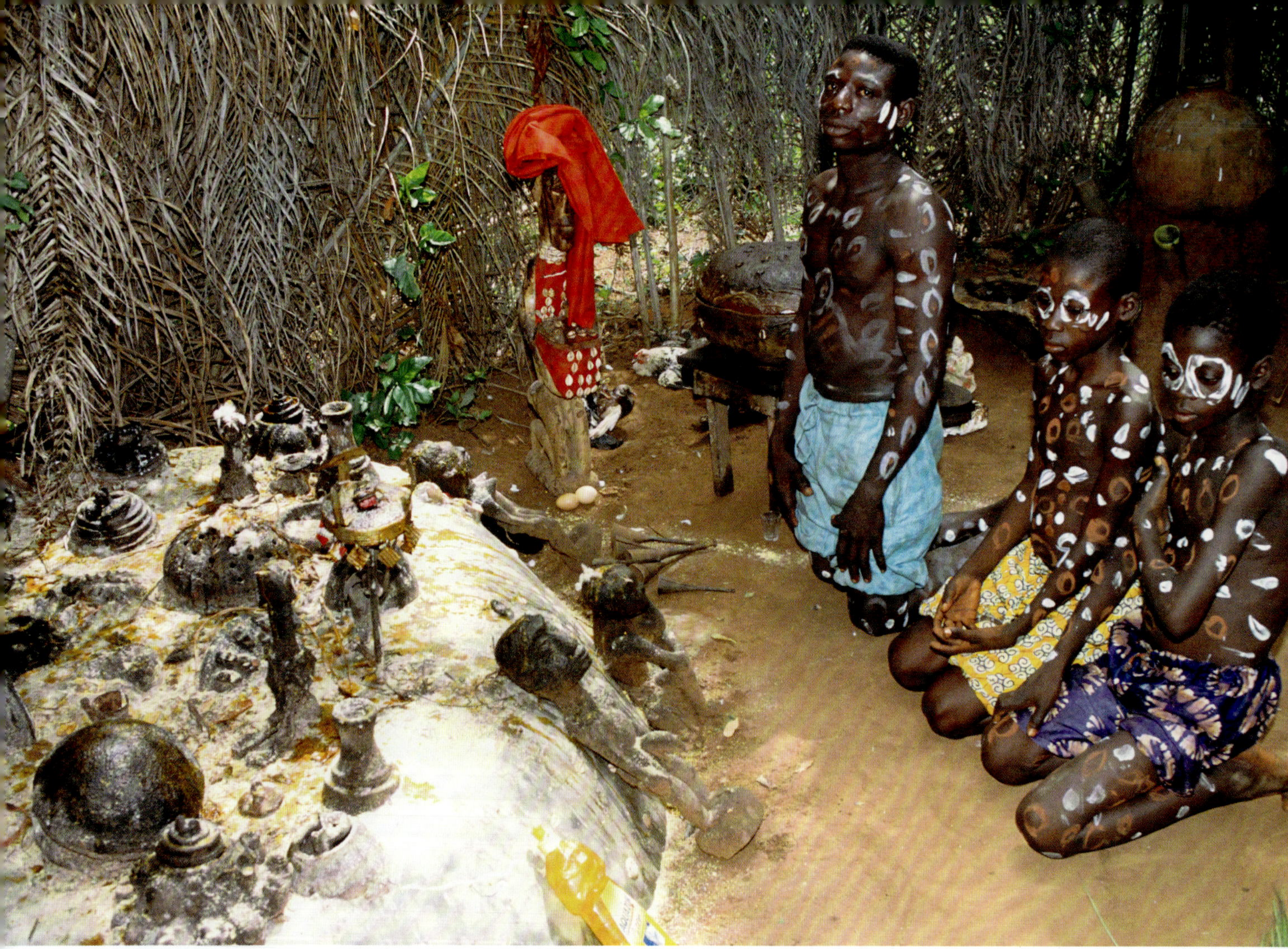

Healing three bewitched brothers

The oracle's response clearly demonstrated what there had been signs of before. The three young Benin brothers, who had been suffering from severe symptoms of witchcraft for weeks, had been cursed by their own mother. After the mother had been chased away, the children's condition worsened again and they were taken to Abomey to the *Azeto*.

Azetos are sorcerers who are masters of witchcraft and, unlike witches, are the only ones who can not only cause such a spell to do damage, but also undo it. This led to a

Guérison de trois frères envoûtés

La réponse de l'oracle confirma clairement la cause des signes avant-coureurs repérés : trois jeunes frères béninois, qui souffraient depuis plusieurs semaines de violents symptômes de sorcellerie, étaient victimes d'une malédiction jetée par leur propre mère. La mère chassée, l'état des trois frères a pourtant empiré, on les a donc adressés à un *azeto* d'Abomey.

Les *azeto* sont des magiciens qui maîtrisent l'art de la sorcellerie. Cependant, contrairement aux sorciers, eux seuls sont capables d'annuler les envoûtements en

Heilung drei verhexter Brüder

Die Antwort des Orakels belegte eindeutig, wofür es bereits im Vorfeld Anzeichen gegeben hatte. Die drei jungen Beniner Brüder, die seit Wochen unter schweren Symptomen von Hexerei litten, waren von ihrer eigenen Mutter mit einem Fluch belegt worden. Nachdem man die Mutter verjagt hatte, verschlimmerte sich der Zustand der Kinder abermals, woraufhin man sie nach Abomey zum *Azeto* brachte.

Azetos sind Magier, die das Hexenhandwerk beherrschen und im Gegensatz zu den Hexen die einzigen sind,

Young patients in front of the shrine of the healer

Jeunes patients devant l'autel du guérisseur

Die jungen Patienten vor dem Schrein des Heilers

Pacientes jóvenes frente al santuario del curandero

Jovens pacientes em frente ao santuário do curandeiro

Jonge patiënten voor het heiligdom van de genezer

They will be dripped with the blood of the animal victim

Ils seront aspergés du sang de l'animal sacrifié

Sie werden mit dem Blut des Tieropfers betropft

Son impregnados con la sangre de la víctima animal

Eles serão gotejados com o sangue da vítima animal

Ze worden bedruppeld met het bloed van het offerdier

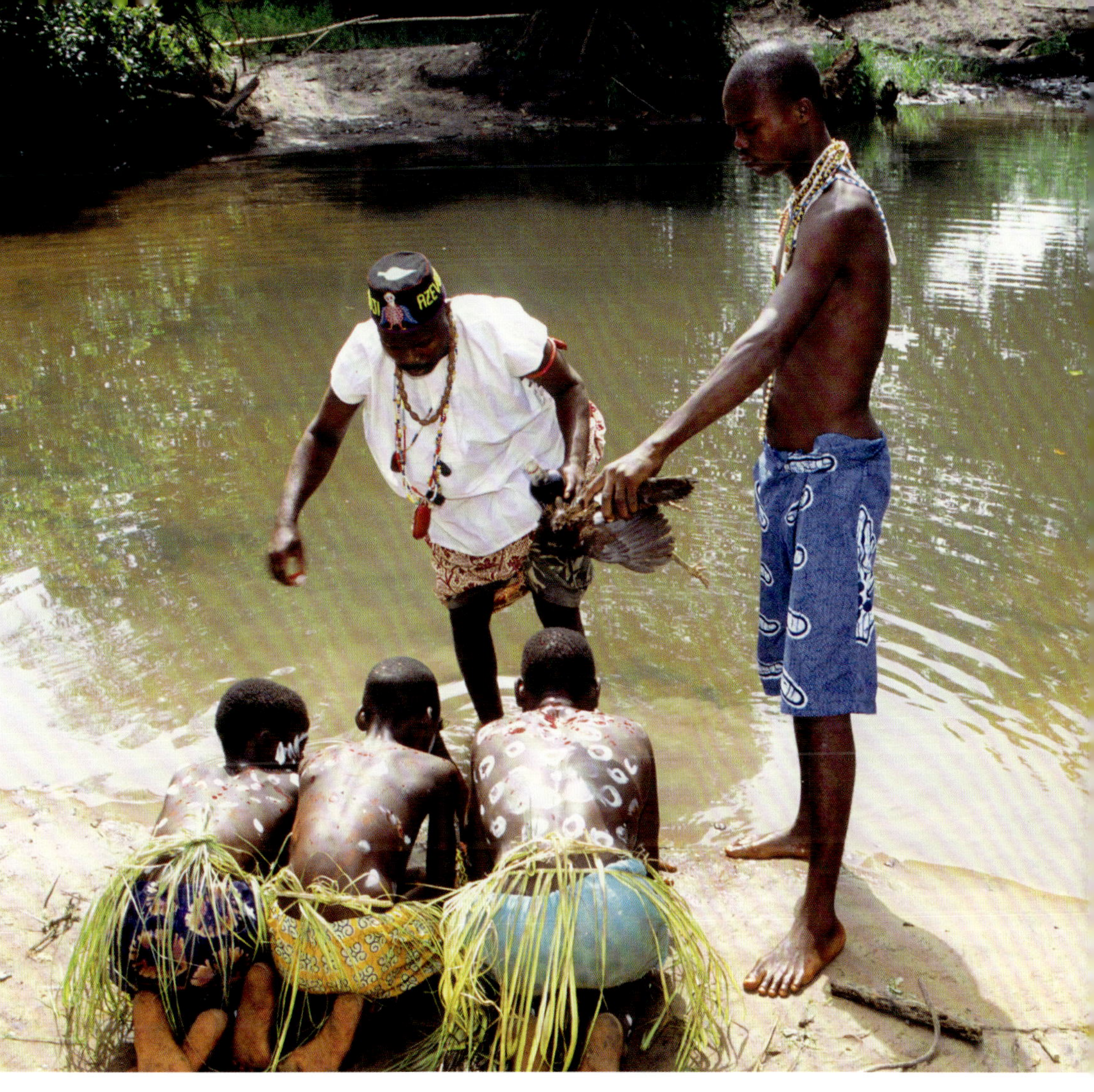

Sanando a tres hermanos maldecidos

La respuesta del oráculo corroboró claramentelas evidencias que se habían ido manifestado hasta el momento. Los tres hermanos jóvenes de Benin, que habían estado sufriendo graves síntomas de brujería durante semanas, habían sido maldecidos por su propia madre. Después de que la madre fue expulsada, la condición de los niños empeoró de nuevo y fueron llevados a Abomey, a un *azeto*.

Los *azetos* son magos que dominan el arte de la brujería y, a diferencia de las

Curando três irmãos enfeitiçados

A resposta do oráculo demonstrou claramente do que havia sinais antes. Os três jovens irmãos Benin, que há semanas sofriam de graves sintomas de bruxaria, tinham sido amaldiçoados pela própria mãe. Depois que a mãe foi expulsa, a condição das crianças piorou novamente e elas foram levadas para Abomey, para o Azeto.

Os azetos são magos que dominam a arte da bruxaria e, ao contrário das bruxas, são os únicos que podem não só causar tais danos, mas também revertê-los. Isto levou a um ritual que durou vários dias,

Genezing van drie behekste broers

De reactie van het orakel toonde duidelijk aan waarvoor er al eerder tekenen waren. De drie jonge broers uit Benin, die al weken leden aan ernstige symptomen van hekserij, waren door hun eigen moeder vervloekt. Nadat de moeder was verjaagd, verslechterde de toestand van de kinderen weer en werden ze naar Abomey gebracht, naar de *azeto*.

Azeto's zijn magiërs die het vak van hekserij beheersen. Zij zijn, in tegenstelling tot heksen, de enigen die een schadelijke betovering kunnen bewerkstelligen en ook

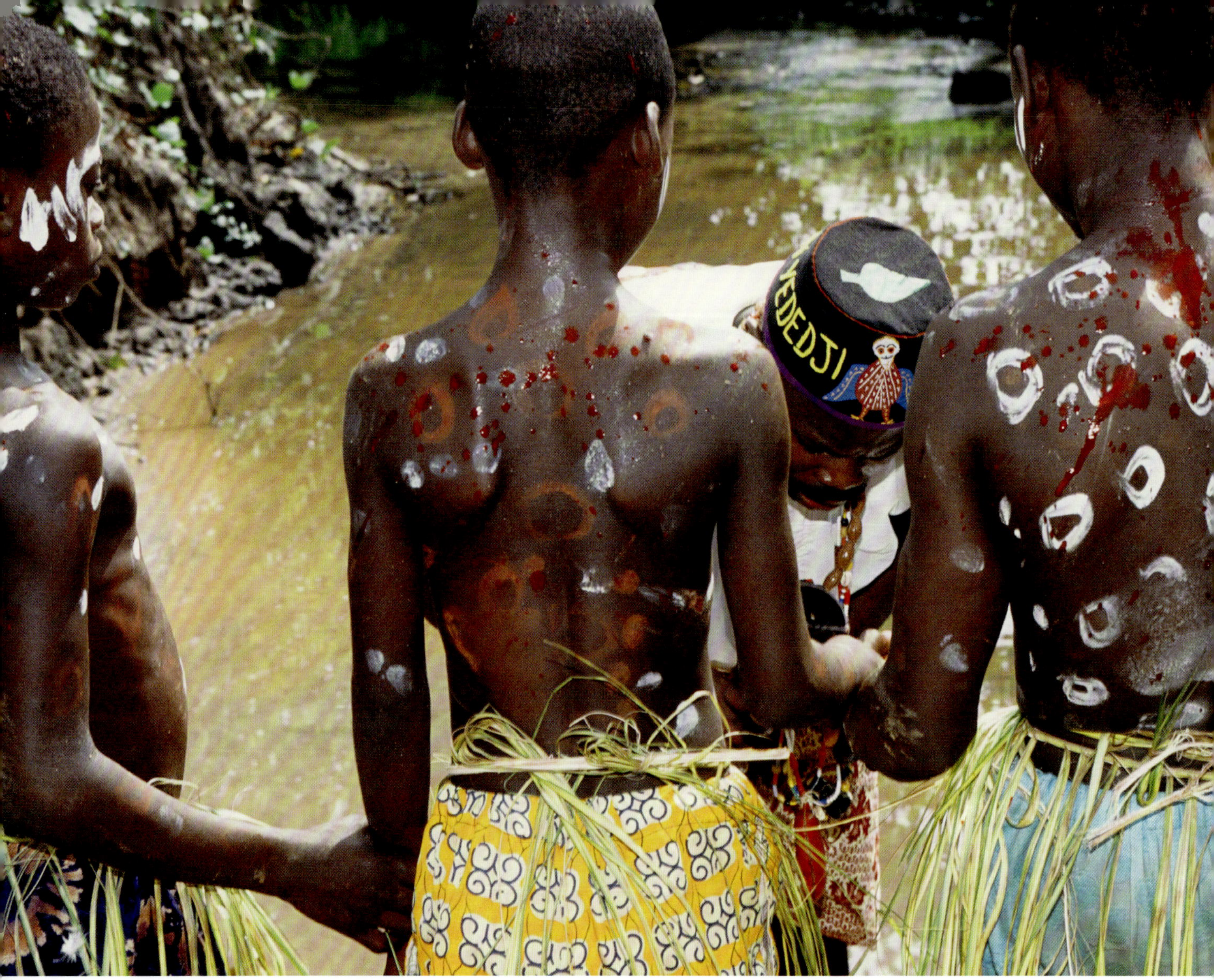

ritual lasting several days, during which the brothers underwent extensive treatments. These included ritual purification ceremonies, animal sacrifices and several baths in river water.

Afterwards the brothers recovered within a few days and lived in peace with an aunt.

plus de pouvoir les décider. Un rituel de plusieurs jours fut donc organisé, au cours duquel la fratrie fit l'objet de multiples manipulations, impliquant notamment des cérémonies rituelles de purification, des sacrifices d'animaux et plusieurs bains dans l'eau du fleuve.

Quelques jours plus tard, les trois frères se sentirent mieux et vécurent ensuite en paix chez leur tante.

die einen solchen Schadenzauber nicht nur veranlassen, sondern auch rückgängig machen können. So kam es zu einem mehrtägigen Ritual, in dessen Verlauf die Brüder umfangreichen Behandlungen unterzogen wurden. Dazu zählten rituelle Reinigungszeremonien, Tieropfer und mehrere Bäder im Flusswasser.

Im Anschluss daran erholten sich die Brüder binnen weniger Tage und lebten fortan in Frieden bei einer Tante.

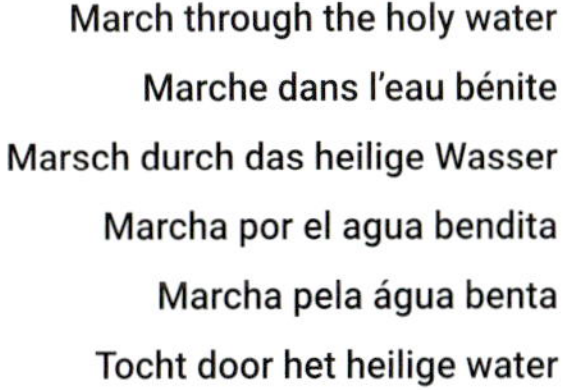

brujas, son los únicos que no sólo pueden causar ese daño, sino también revertirlo. Esto condujo a un ritual que duró varios días, durante los cuales los hermanos se sometieron a extensos tratamientos. Éstos incluyeron ceremonias rituales de limpieza, sacrificios de animales y varios baños en el agua del río.

Finalmente, los hermanos se recuperaron en pocos días y vivieron en paz en casa de su tía.

durante o qual os irmãos foram submetidos a tratamentos extensivos. Estas incluíam cerimónias rituais de limpeza, sacrifícios de animais e vários banhos na água do rio.

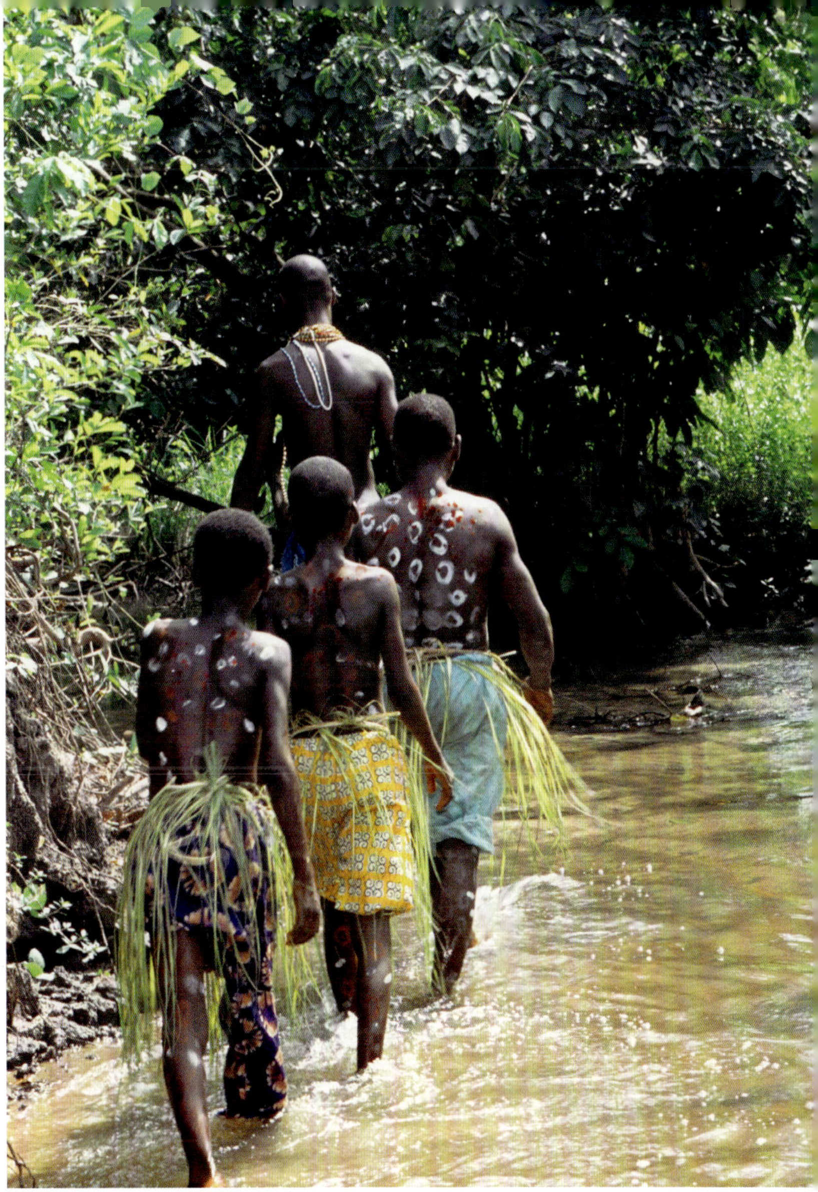

Depois, os irmãos se recuperaram em poucos dias e viveram em paz com uma tia.

weer ongedaan kunnen maken. Zo kwam het tot een meerdaags ritueel, waarbij de broers uitgebreide behandelingen ondergingen. Deze omvatten rituele reinigingsceremoniën, dierenoffers en verschillende baden in het rivierwater.

Daarna herstelden de broers binnen enkele dagen en konden ze in alle rust bij een tante gaan wonen.

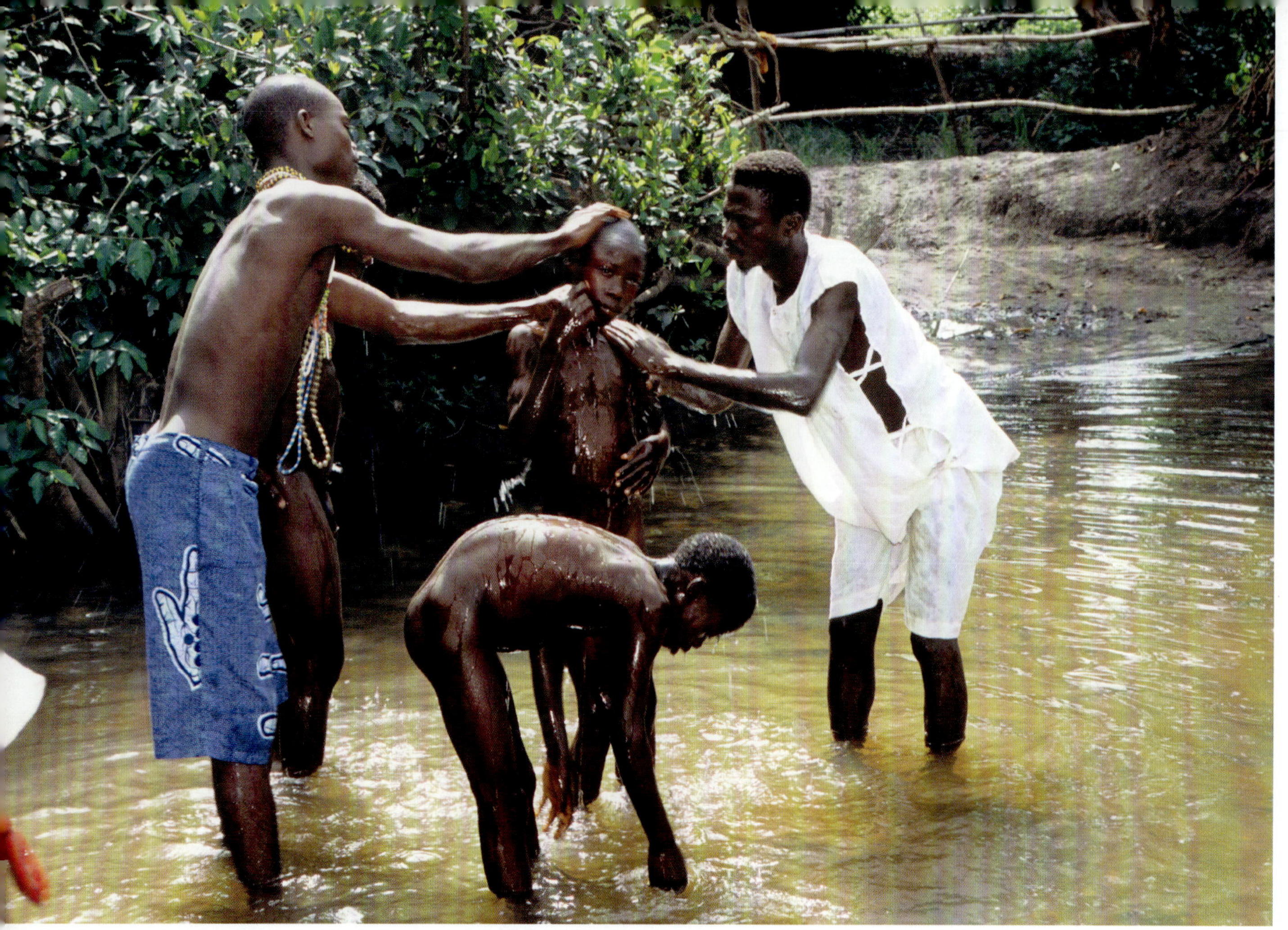

Bath in holy water

Bain dans l'eau bénite

Bad im heiligen Wasser

Baño en agua bendita

Banho em água benta

Bad in het heilige water

After the bath the brothers are dressed in red wrap skirts

Après le bain, on revêt les frères de jupes rouges

Nach dem Bad werden die Brüder in rote Wickelröcke gekleidet

Después del baño, los hermanos se visten con faldas de envoltura roja

Depois do banho, os irmãos estão vestidos com saias vermelhas

Na het bad worden de broers gekleed in rode wikkelrokken

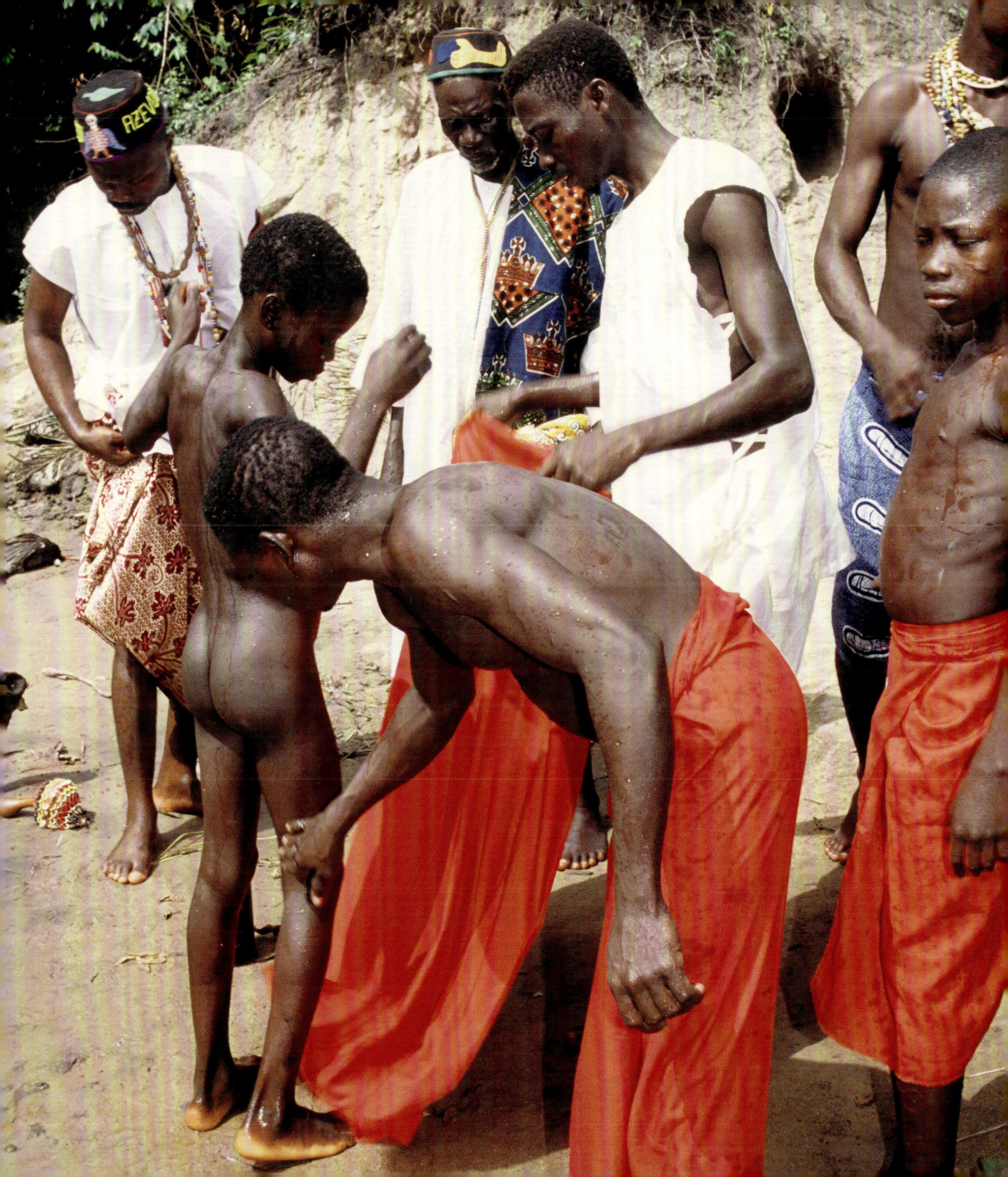

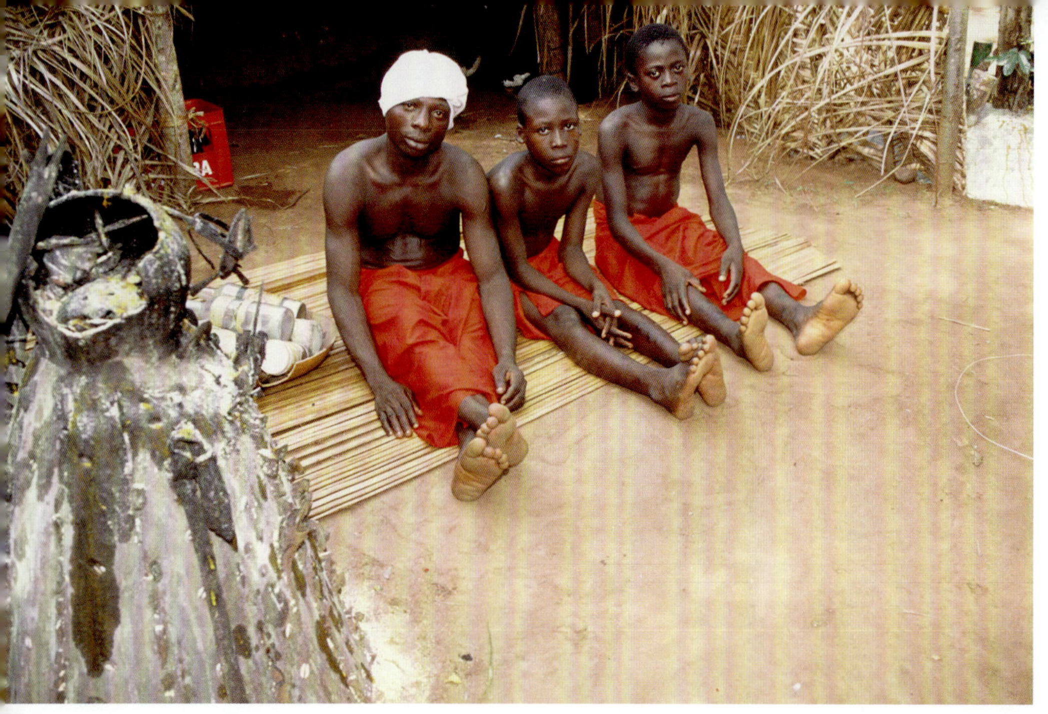

The patients have to wait in front of the temple

Les patients doivent attendre devant le temple

Die Patienten sollen vor dem Tempel warten

Dile a los pacientes que esperen frente al templo

Diz aos pacientes para esperarem em frente ao templo

De patiënten moeten voor de tempel wachten

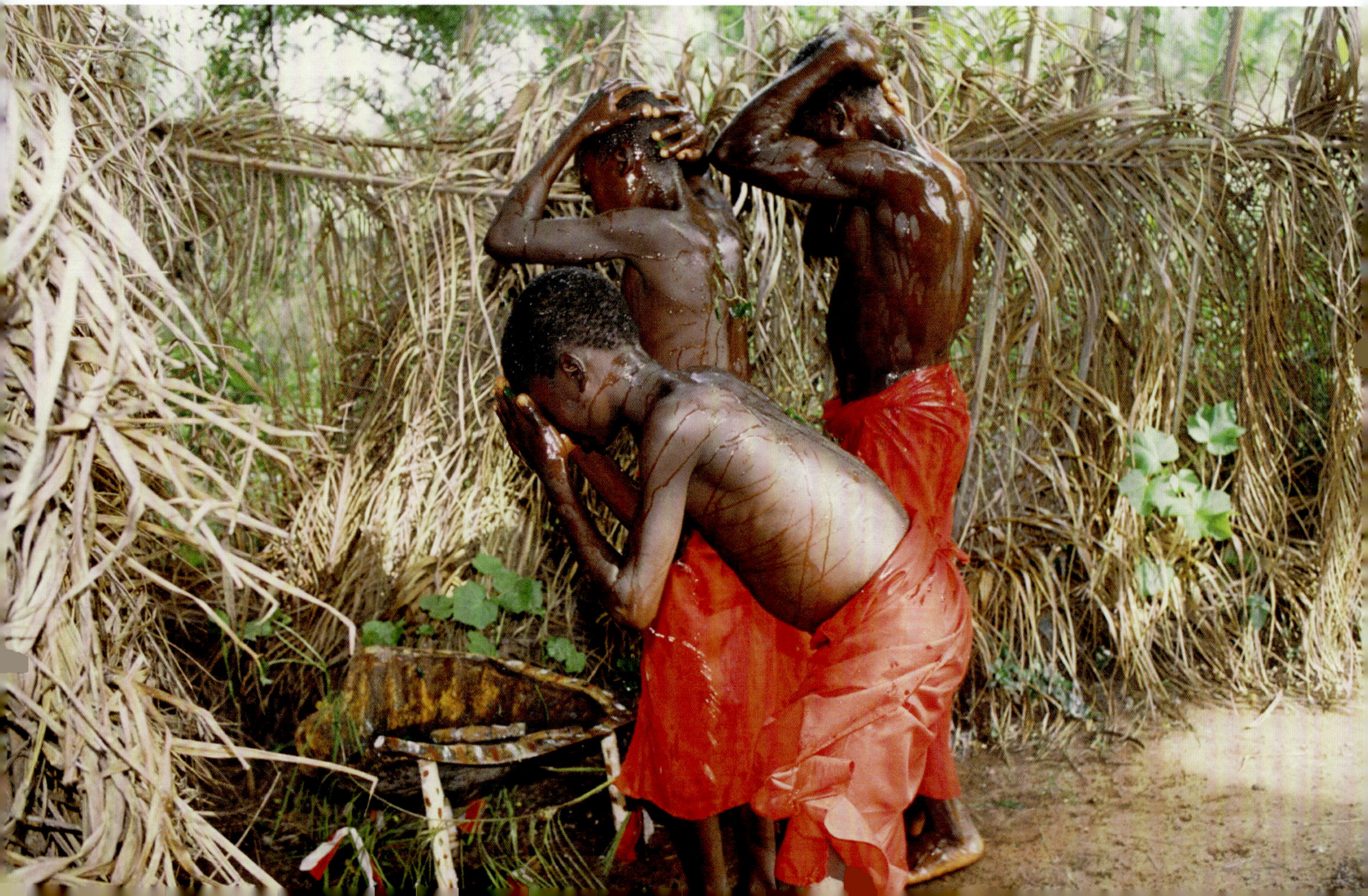

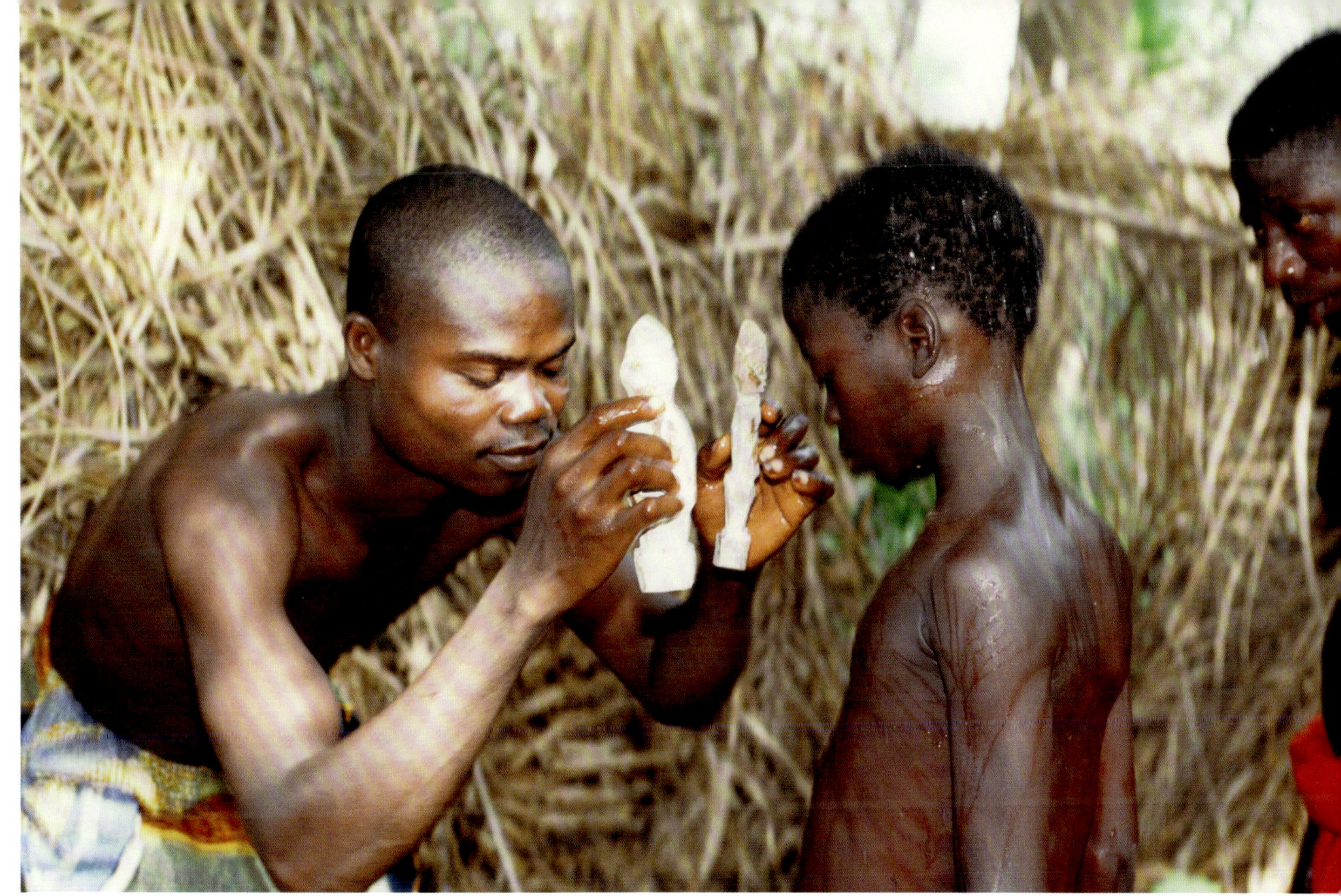

The Expulsion of the Evil Spirits. Now various purification rituals follow, with which the brothers are to be rescued from the bad spirits, which seek to kill them.

Purification des mauvais esprits. Plusieurs rituels de purification sont ensuite pratiqués. Ils doivent permettre aux frères de se libérer des mauvais esprits qui ont essayé d'attenter à leurs jours.

Die Austreibung der bösen Geister. Nun folgen diverse Reinigungsrituale, mit denen die Brüder von den bösen Geistern, die ihnen nach dem Leben trachten, gelöst werden sollen.

La expulsión de los espíritus malignos. Ahora sigue varios rituales de limpieza para liberar a los hermanos de los espíritus malignos que buscan sus vidas.

A Expulsão dos Espíritos Malignos. Agora siga vários rituais de limpeza para libertar os irmãos dos maus espíritos que buscam suas vidas.

De verdrijving van de boze geesten. Nu volgen verschillende reinigingsrituelen om de broeders te bevrijden van de boze geesten die hen naar het leven staan.

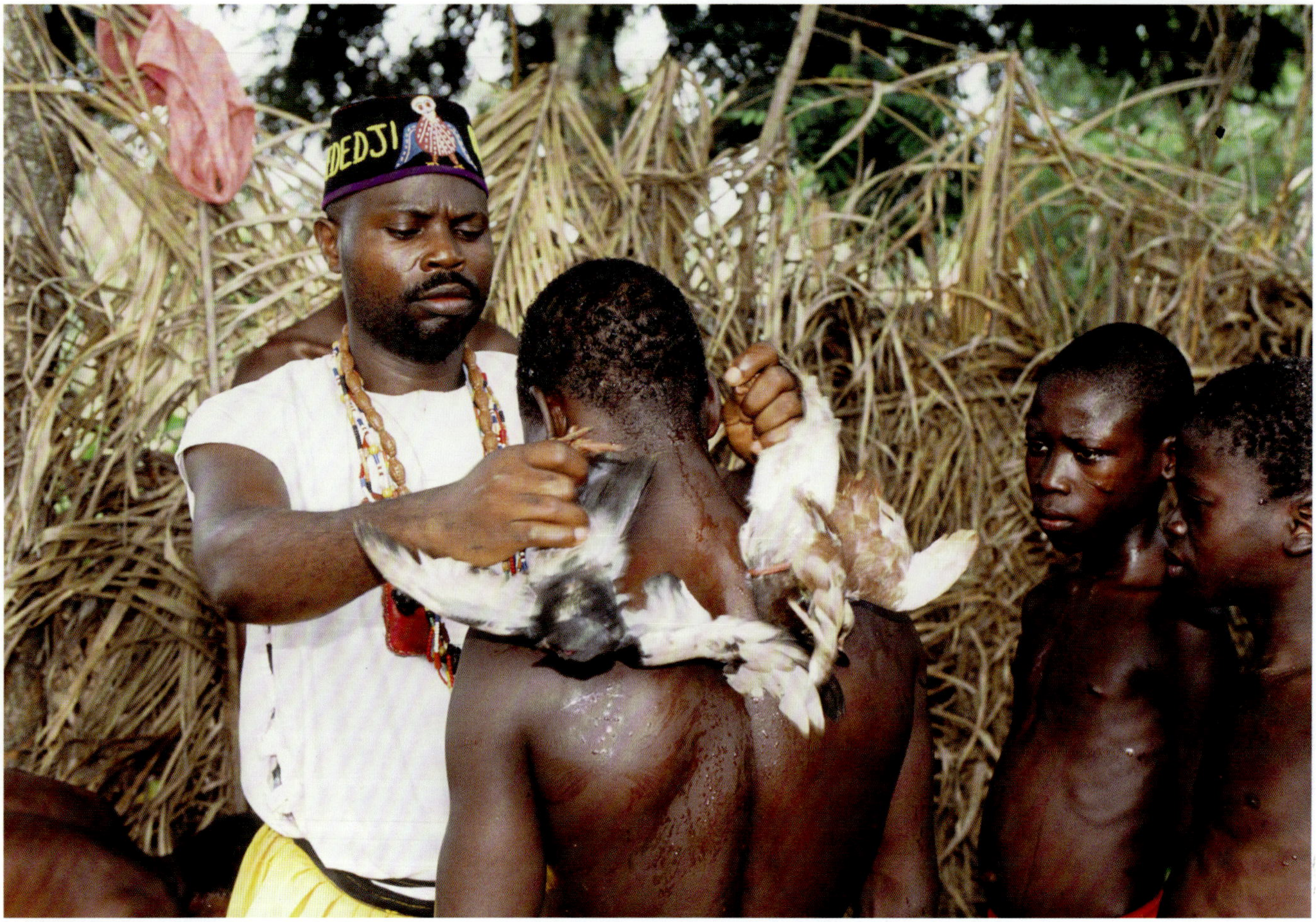

Nestor Azeto offers a sacrifice for protection
Nestor Azeto offre une protection aux victimes
Nestor Azeto bringt Opfer zum Schutz dar
Néstor Azeto ofrece protección a las víctimas
Nestor Azeto oferece proteção às vítimas
Nestor Azeto brengt offers ter bescherming

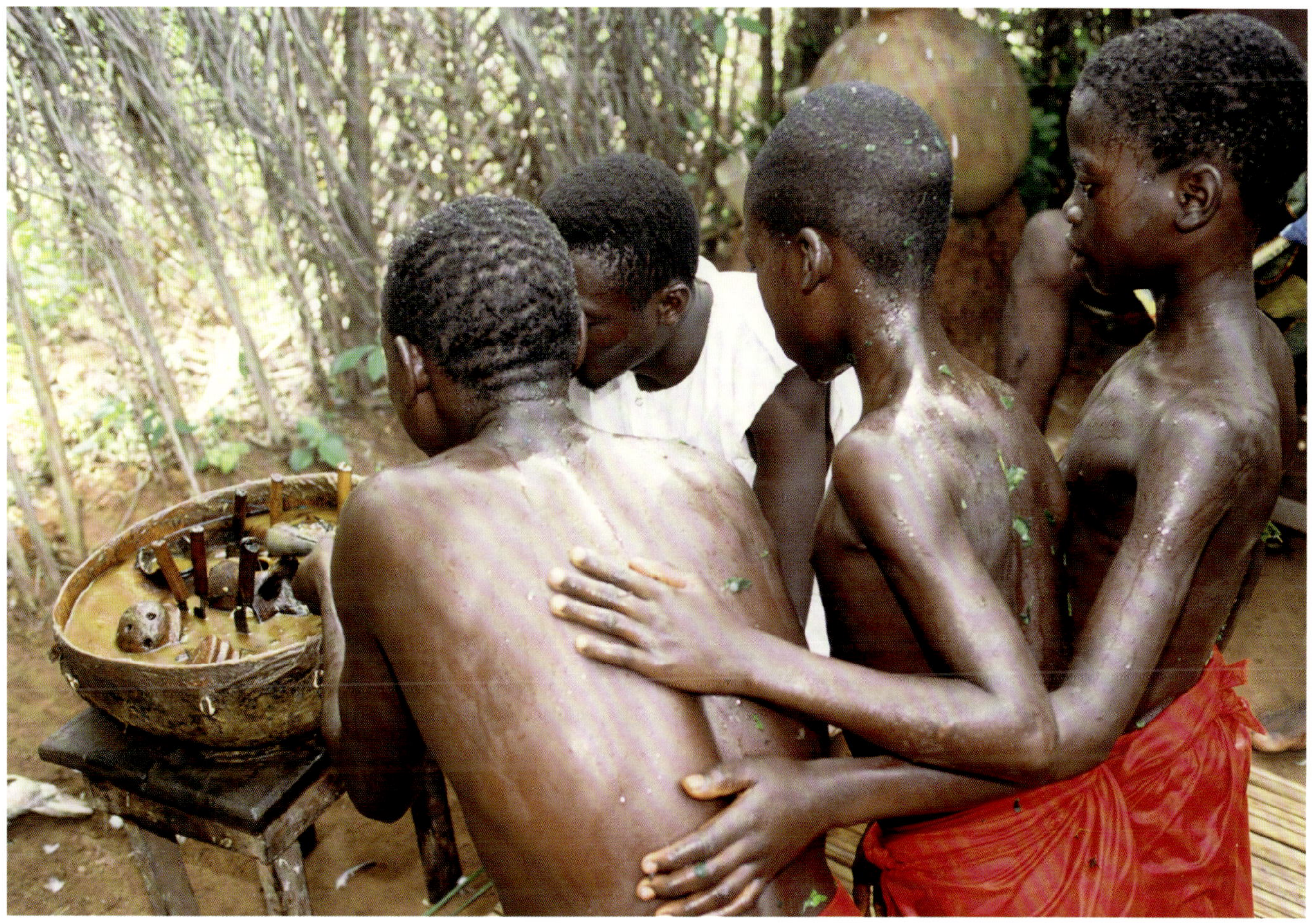

With secret formulas. In the presence of the patients, Nestor Azeto casts a spell with his magic bowl to give the brothers the necessary protection from now on.

Formules secrètes. En présence des patients, Nestor Azeto supplie sa coupe magique d'accorder dorénavant à la fratrie la protection nécessaire

Mit geheimen Formeln. In der Gegenwart der Patienten beschwört Nestor Azeto seine magische Schale, den Brüdern fortan den nötigen Schutz zukommen zu lassen.

Con fórmulas secretas. En presencia de los pacientes, Néstor Azeto conjura su cuenco mágico para dar a los hermanos la protección necesaria.

Com fórmulas secretas. Na presença dos pacientes, Nestor Azeto conjura sua tigela mágica para dar aos irmãos a proteção necessária.

Met geheime formules. In het bijzijn van de patiënten bezweert Nestor Azeto zijn magische kom om de broers de nodige bescherming te geven.

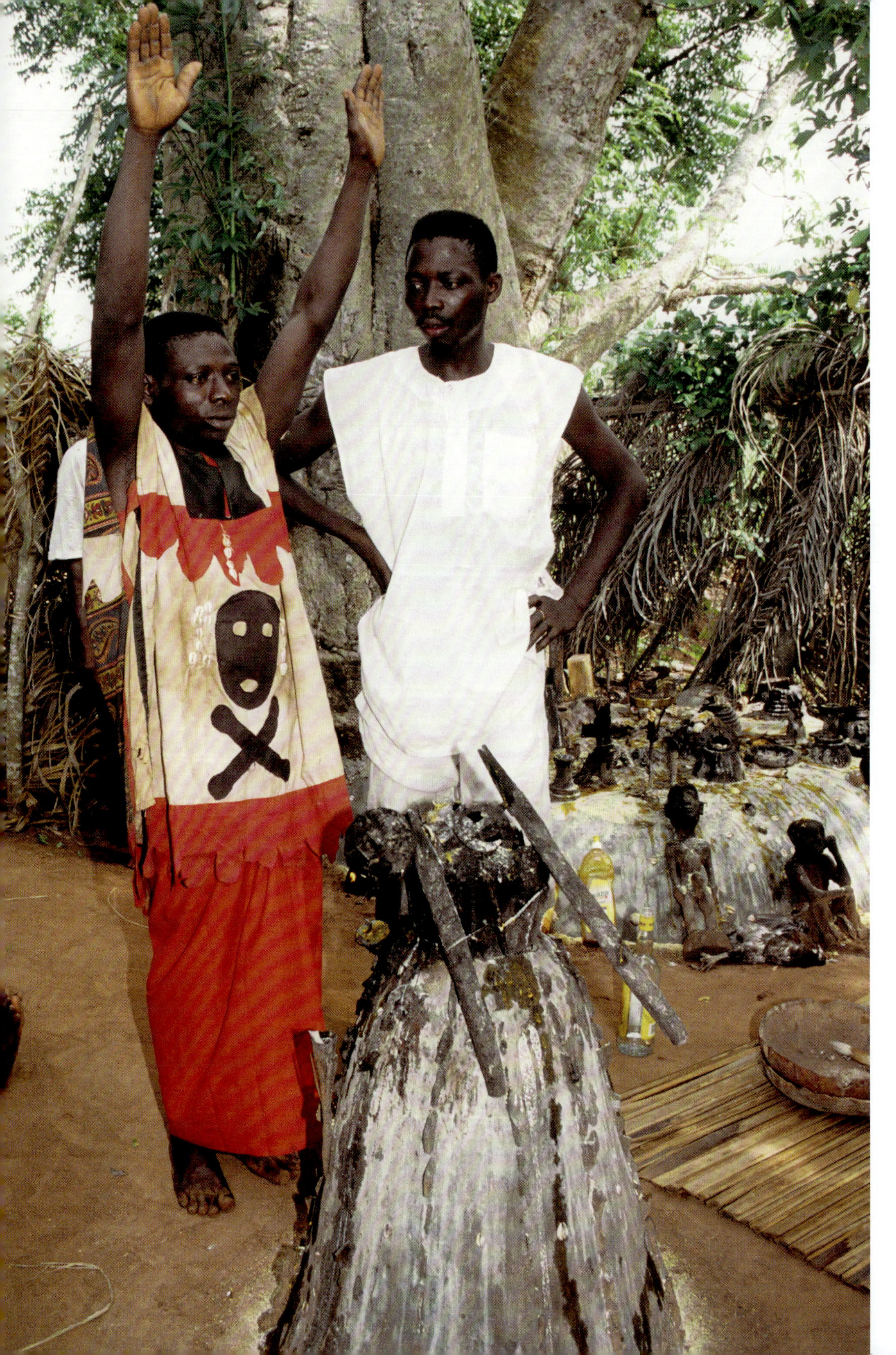

A change of clothes just before
the end

Des vêtements de rechange
juste avant la fin

Ein Kleiderwechsel kurz
vor Schluss

Una muda de ropa justo antes
del final

Uma mudança de roupa mesmo
antes do fim

Andere kleren net voor
het einde

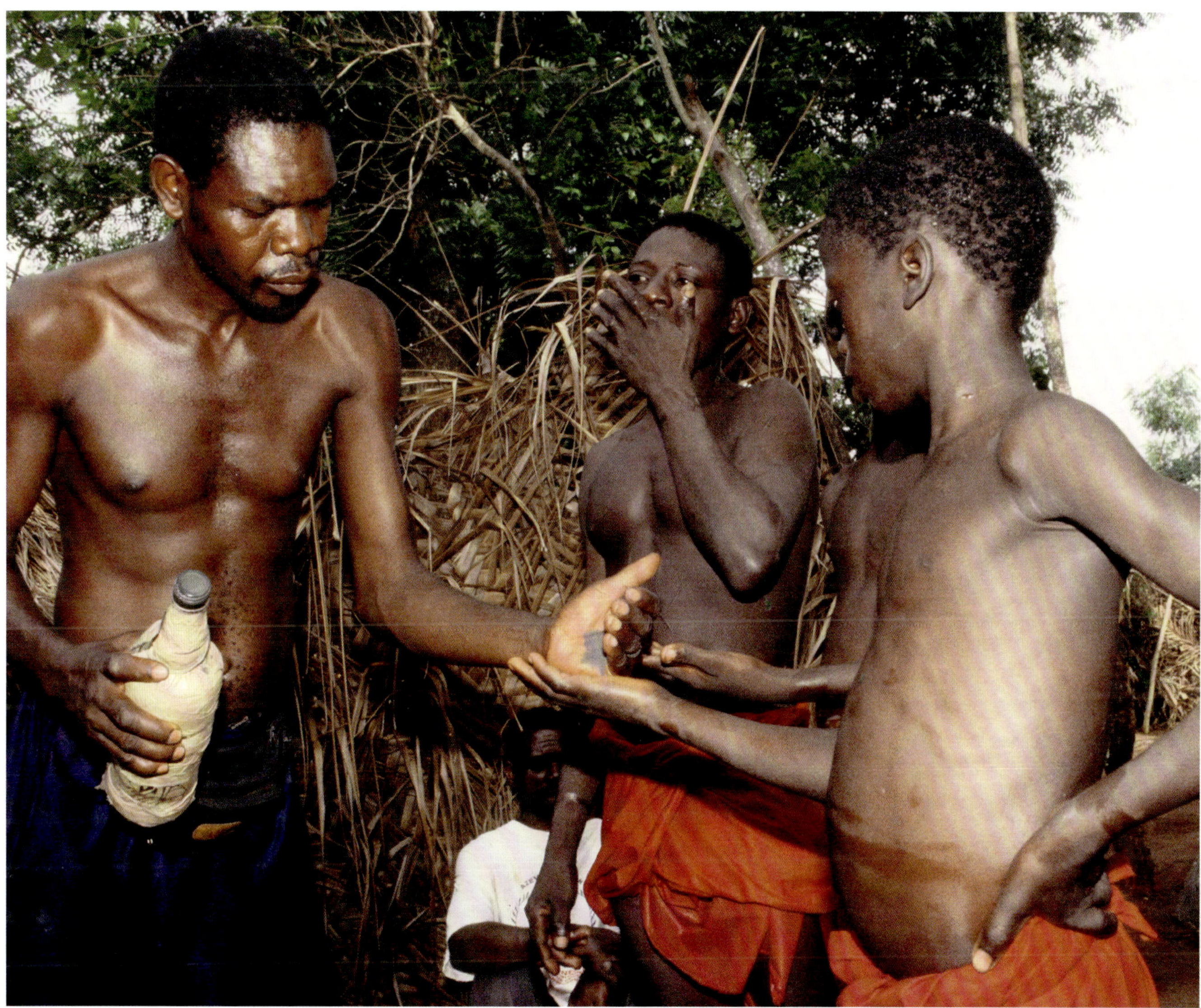

Medication and vaccination. Finally, the three brothers are given various drinks and powders that are similar in effect to specific medicines and vaccines.

Médicaments et vaccination. Pour clôturer le rituel, les trois frères se voient administrer plusieurs boissons et poudres dont l'action se rapproche de celle de médicaments et vaccins.

Medikation und Impfung. Zum Schluss erhalten die drei Brüder verschiedene Getränke und Pulver, die in ihrer Wirkung spezifischen Medikamenten und Impfstoffen ähneln.

Medicamentos y vacuna. Al final, los tres hermanos reciben diversas bebidas y polvos cuyos efectos se asemejan a los de medicamentos y vacunas específicas.

Medicação e vacinação. No final, os três irmãos recebem várias bebidas e pós cujos efeitos se assemelham aos de medicamentos e vacinas específicos.

Geneesmiddelen en vaccinatie. Tot slot krijgen de drie broers verschillende dranken en poeders waarvan de werking lijkt op die van specifieke medicijnen en vaccins.

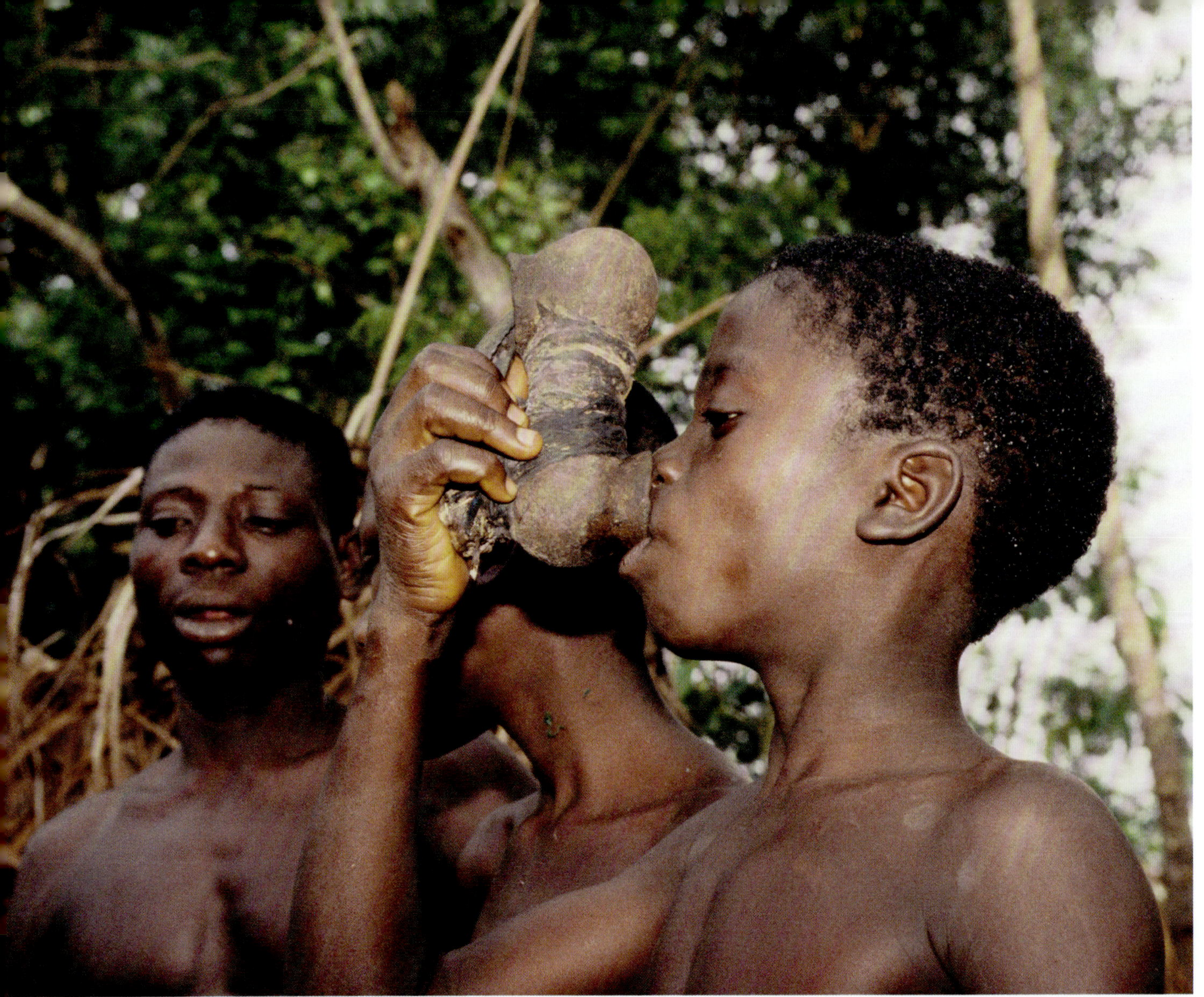

Medication against witchcraft is the final step

Le remède contre la sorcellerie est la dernière étape

Medikamente gegen die Hexerei bilden den Abschluss

La medicación contra la brujería es el paso final

A medicação contra a feitiçaria é a etapa final

Medicatie tegen hekserij vormt de afsluiting

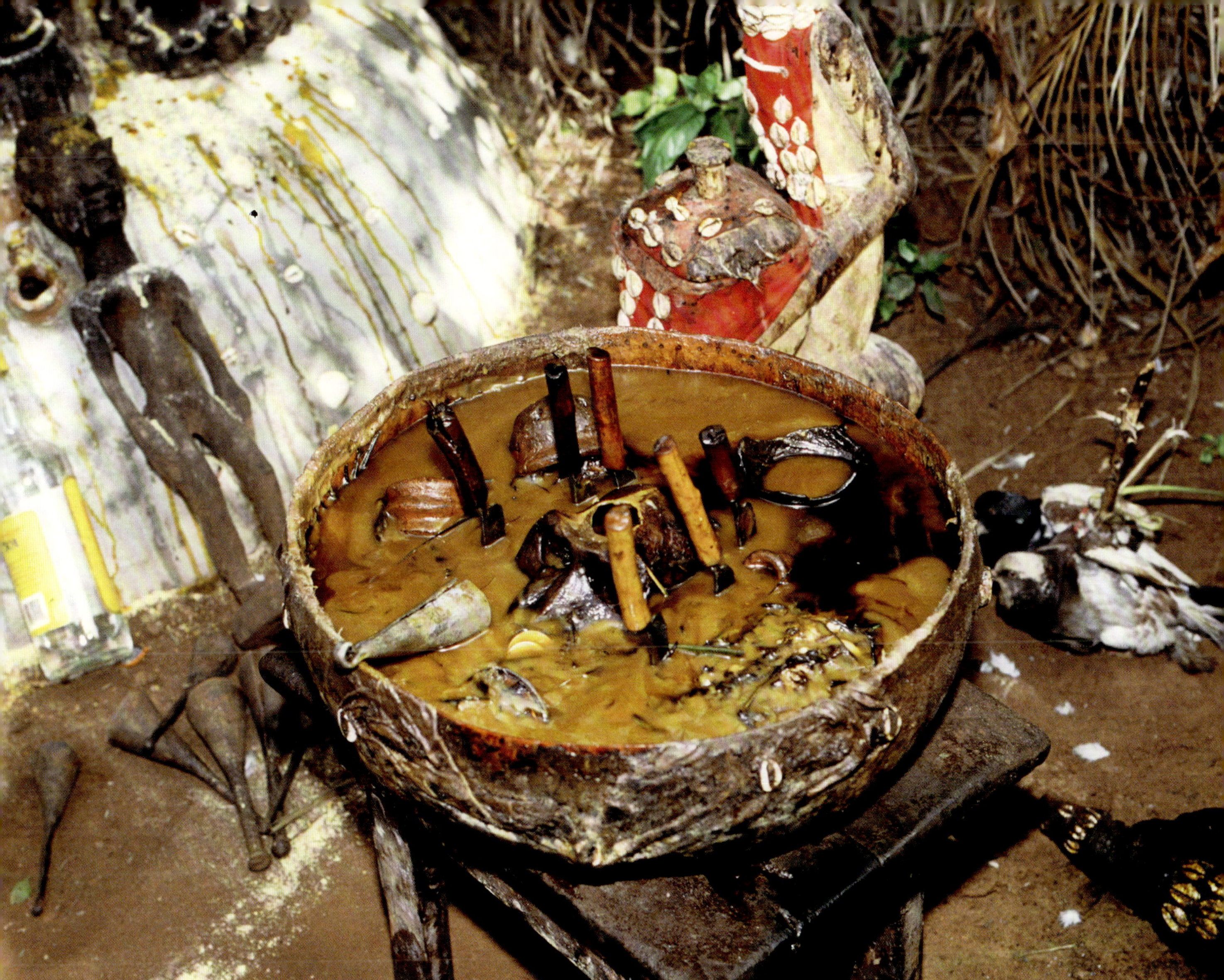

Nestor Acetos magic Osanyin bowl.
The substances contained in these bowls are regarded as bearers of magical powers. In their combination, which can vary with each healer, they are highly potent metaphysical medicines.

Bol Osanyin magique de Nestor Azeto.
Les ingrédients contenus dans cette vasque sont considérés comme des porteurs de puissances magiques. C'est dans leur combinaison, qui peut varier en fonction de chaque guérisseur, que réside leur potentiel de guérison métaphysique.

Nestor Azetos magische Osanyin-Schale. Die in diesen Schalen enthaltenen Substanzen gelten als Träger magischer Kräfte. In ihrer Kombination, die bei jedem Heiler variieren kann, sind sie hochpotente metaphysische Medizin.

Cuenco Osanyin mágico de Nestor Acetos.
Las sustancias contenidas en estos cuencos son consideradas como portadoras de poderes mágicos. En su combinación, que puede variar con cada curandero, son medicina metafísica altamente potente.

Nestor Acetos tigela mágica Osanyin.
As substâncias contidas nestes recipientes são consideradas como portadores de poderes mágicos. Em sua combinação, que pode variar com cada curandeiro, eles são medicina metafísica altamente potente.

De magische kom (osanyin) van Nestor Azeto.
De stoffen in deze kom gelden als dragers van magische krachten. In hun combinatie, die per genezer kan verschillen, zijn het zeer krachtige metafysische geneesmiddelen.

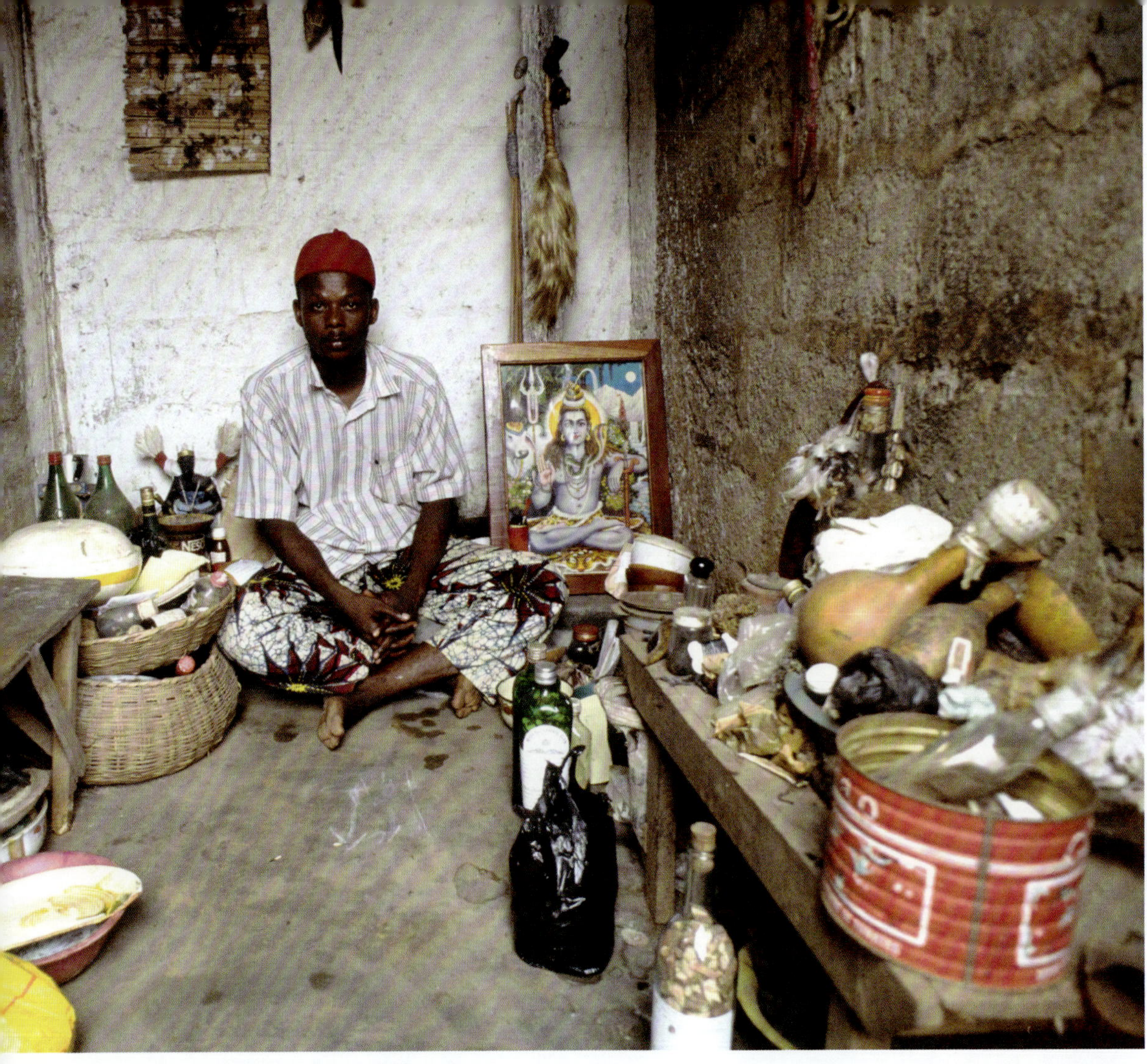

The youngest healer of Porto-Novo

Casimir Dah-Moussa is an Egungun priest in Porto-Novo and thus maintains close ties to his ancestors. But this is by no means his only competence.

Because of his origin—Dah-Moussa comes from a respected family of extremely successful healers—he was allowed to acquire secret first-hand knowledge about the gods and their correspondences in the realm of medicinal and poisonous plants, even as an adolescent. Being the eldest son, his father always took him into the bush as a helper when collecting roots, flowers,

Le plus jeune guérisseur de Porto-Novo

Casimir Dah-Moussa est un prêtre Egungun de Porto-Novo qui entretient des relations étroites avec les ancêtres. Toutefois, telle n'est pas son unique compétence.

Dah-Moussa est issu d'une famille estimée de guérisseurs extrêmement efficaces. Du fait de ses origines, il était à bonne école, dès l'adolescence, pour assimiler les savoirs secrets relatifs aux divinités et leur correspondance dans le royaume des plantes tant bienfaitrices que vénéneuses. Grâce à son père, à qui il a

Der jüngste Heiler von Porto-Novo

Casimir Dah-Moussa ist Egungun-Priester in Porto-Novo und pflegt somit enge Verbindungen zu den Ahnen. Doch das ist längst nicht seine einzige Kompetenz.

Aufgrund seiner Herkunft – Dah-Moussa entstammt einer angesehenen Familie äußerst erfolgreicher Heiler – durfte er sich schon als Heranwachsender aus erster Hand geheimes Wissen über die Gottheiten und ihre Entsprechungen im Reich der Heil- und Giftpflanzen aneignen. Durch seinen Vater, der ihn als ältesten Sohn beim Sammeln der Wurzeln, Blüten, Knollen und Lianen stets

Medicine with dog skull against Aids
Médicament avec crâne de chien contre le sida
Medizin mit Hundeschädel gegen Aids
Medicina con cráneo de perro contra el sida
Medicamentos com crânio de cão contra SIDA
Medicijn met hondenschedel tegen aids

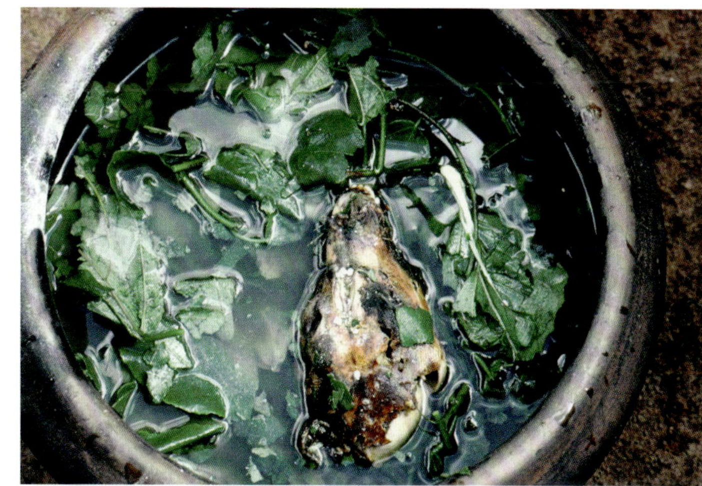

Fetish with freshly sacrificed feathers and blood
Fétiche fraîchement sacrifié avec des plumes et du sang
Frisch mit Federn und Blut beopferter Fetisch
Fetiche recién sacrificado con plumas y sangre
Fetiche recentemente sacrificado com penas e sangue
Fetisj waaraan net geofferd is met veren en bloed

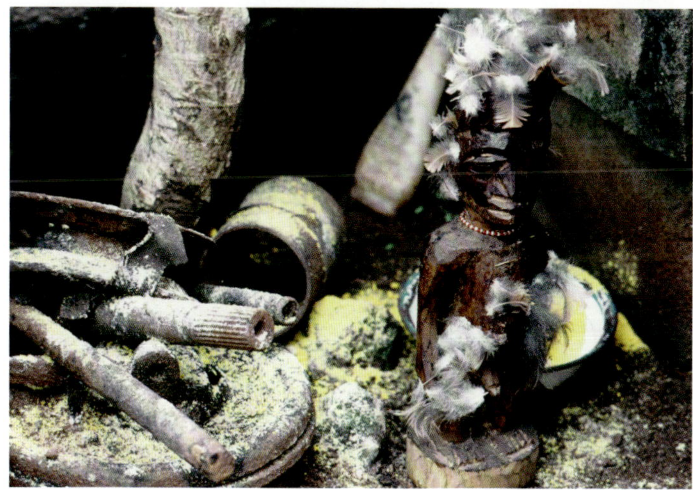

El curandero más joven de Porto-Novo

Casimir Dah-Moussa es un sacerdote *Egungun* en Porto-Novo y por lo tanto mantiene estrechos lazos con sus antepasados. Pero esta no es su única competencia.

Debido a su origen–Dah-Moussa proviene de una respetada familia de curanderos extremadamente exitosos– se le permitió adquirir ya en su adolescencia, conocimientos secretos de primera mano sobre las deidades y sus correspondencias en el reino de las plantas medicinales y

O mais jovem curandeiro de Porto-Novo

Casimir Dah-Moussa é um padre Egungun em Porto-Novo, mantendo assim laços estreitos com os seus antepassados. Mas esta não é, de modo algum, a sua única competência.

Devido à sua origem – Dah-Moussa vem de uma família respeitada de curandeiros extremamente bem sucedidos – foi-lhe permitido adquirir conhecimento secreto em primeira mão sobre as divindades e suas correspondências no domínio das plantas medicinais e venenosas, mesmo quando

De jongste genezer van Porto-Novo

Casimir Dah-Moussa is een Egungun-priester in Porto-Novo die nauwe banden met zijn voorouders onderhoudt. Maar dit is wbeslist niet zijn enige vaardigheid.

Vanwege zijn afkomst (Dah-Moussa komt uit een gerespecteerde familie van zeer succesvolle genezers) mocht hij als adolescent al uit de eerste hand geheime kennis opdoen over de goden en hun tegenhangers in de wereld van geneeskrachtige en giftige planten. Via zijn vader, die hem als oudste zoon altijd als hulpje bij het verzamelen van wortels,

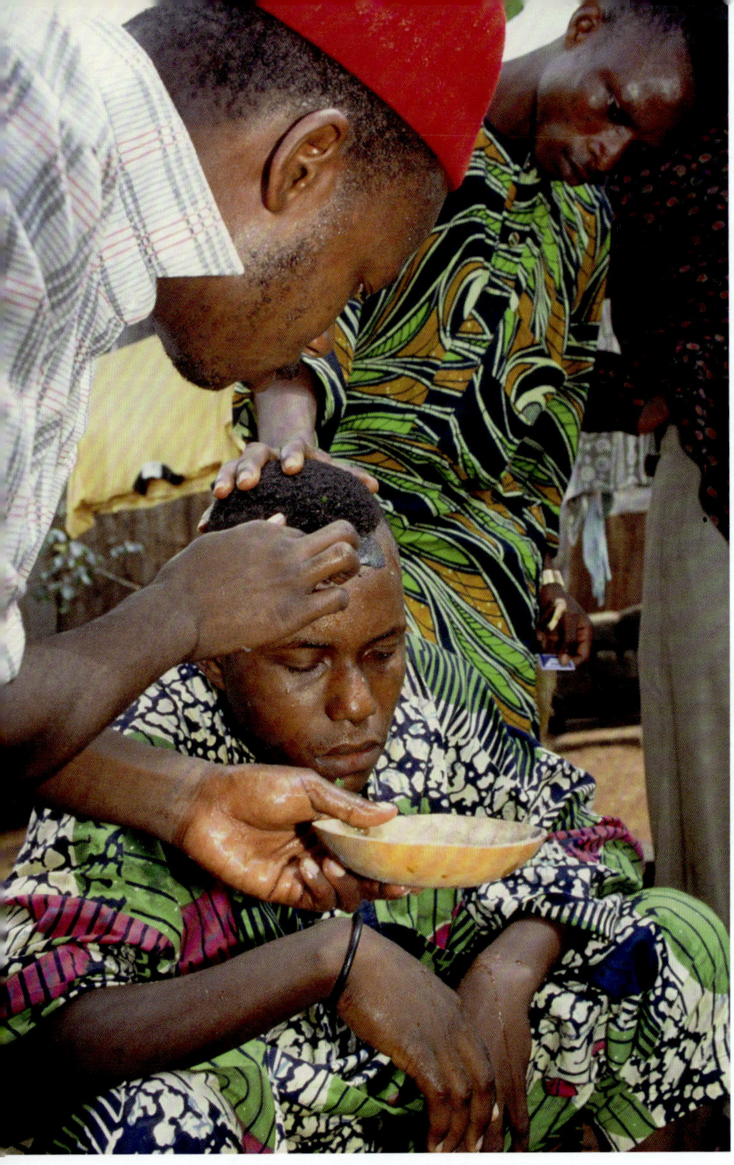

Headache treatment. The healer rubs a powder specially made for headaches into a small incision on the patient's head. Soon the client will be better.

Traitement des maux de tête. Le guérisseur frictionne une petite entaille sur le crâne du patient avec la poudre qu'il a préparée contre les maux de tête. Son patient se sentira rapidement mieux.

Behandlung von Kopfschmerzen. In eine kleine Schnittwunde am Kopf des Patienten reibt der Heiler einen eigens gegen Kopfschmerzen hergestellten Puder. Bald wird es dem Klienten besser gehen.

Tratamiento del dolor de cabeza. El curandero frota un polvo especialmente producido para los dolores de cabeza en un pequeño corte en la cabeza del paciente. Pronto el cliente se sentirá mejor.

Tratamento das dores de cabeça. O curandeiro esfrega um pó especialmente produzido para dores de cabeça num pequeno corte na cabeça do paciente. Em breve o cliente vai sentir-se melhor.

Behandeling tegen hoofdpijn. De genezer wrijft een speciaal voor hoofdpijn gemaakt poeder in een sneetje op het hoofd van de patiënt. Binnenkort zal hij zich beter voelen.

tubers and lianas. In this way he became probably the youngest expert of his guild in Porto Novo.

His unique characteristic is above all the breadth of his knowledge, which makes him a well-known expert and in demand far beyond the city limits, especially in the prevention of and fight against witchcraft and other harmful spells.

servi d'assistant en tant que fils aîné pour la cueillette des racines, fleurs, bulbes et autres lianes, il est devenu probablement le plus jeune de sa corporation à Porto-Novo.

Il se distingue en particulier par l'étendue de ses connaissances. Expert reconnu et demandé bien au-delà des limites de la ville, on le consulte pour tout ce qui concerne la lutte et la défense contre la sorcellerie et les sortilèges maléfiques.

als Helfer mit in den Busch nahm, wurde er in Porto-Novo zum vermutlich jüngsten Experten seiner Zunft.

Sein Alleinstellungsmerkmal ist dabei vor allem die Bandbreite seines Wissens, das ihn besonders bei der Abwehr und Bekämpfung von Hexerei und sonstigem Schadenzauber zu einem bis weit über die Stadtgrenzen hinaus bekannten und gefragten Experten macht.

The Lord of medicinal plants. The "Amam", so-called "leaves with power", are indispensable when it comes to the preparation of medicine. Dah-Moussa knows many tinctures, powders and ointments against diseases and curses.

Le seigneur des plantes médicinales. La plante amam, ou « feuilles puissantes », est indispensable à la préparation de remèdes. Dah-Moussa connaît de nombreuses teintures, poudres et onguents contre divers sortilèges et maladies.

Der Herr der Heilpflanzen. Die „Amam", sogenannte „Blätter mit Macht", sind unverzichtbar, wenn es um die Zubereitung von Medizin geht. Dah-Moussa kennt viele Tinkturen, Pulver und Salben gegen Krankheiten und Flüche.

El Señor de las plantas medicinales. El "Amam", llamado "hojas con poder", es indispensable cuando se trata de la preparación de la medicina. Dah-Moussa conoce muchas tinturas, polvos y ungüentos contra enfermedades y maldiciones.

O Senhor das Plantas Medicinais. O "Amam", chamado "folhas com poder", é indispensável quando se trata da preparação da medicina. Dah-Moussa conhece muitas tinturas, pós e pomadas contra doenças e maldições.

Heer van de geneeskrachtige planten. De amam, de zogenaamde 'bladeren met kracht', zijn onmisbaar bij de bereiding van medicijnen. Dah-Moussa kent veel tincturen, poeders en zalven tegen ziekten en vloeken.

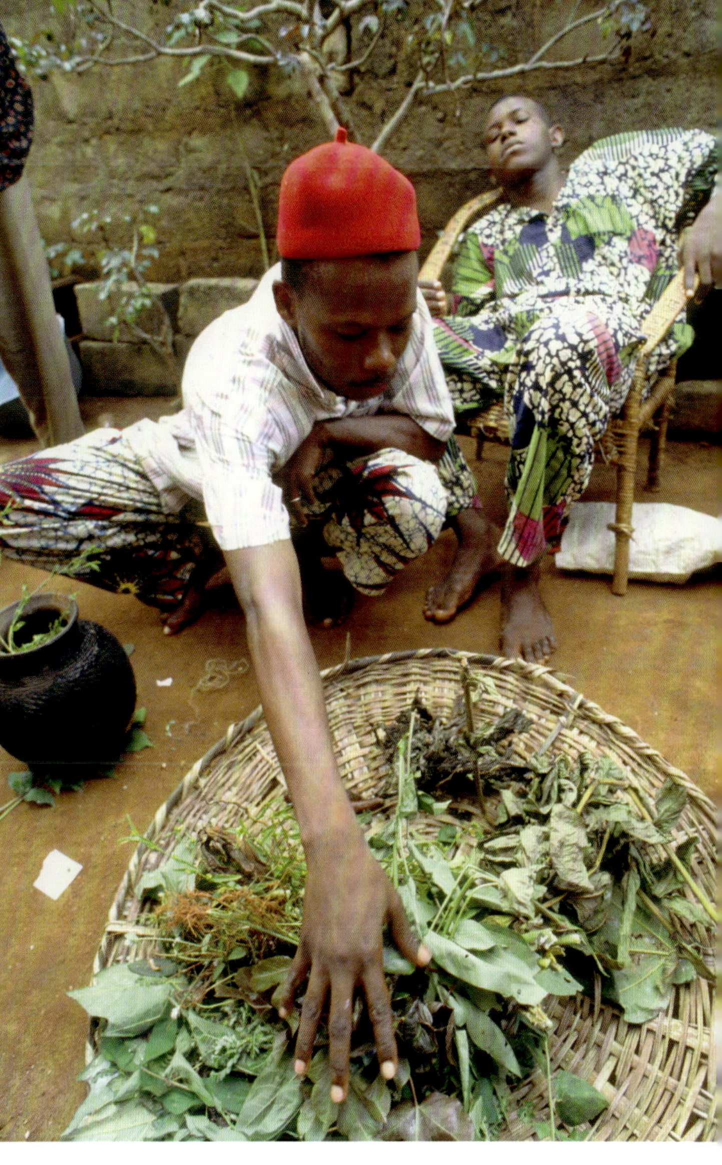

venenosas. A través de su padre, que como hijo mayor siempre lo llevaba al monte como ayudante en la recolección de raíces, flores, tubérculos y lianas, se convirtió probablemente en el experto más joven de su gremio en Porto Novo.

Su característica distintiva es sobre todo la amplitud de sus conocimientos, lo que le convierte en un experto conocido y solicitado mucho más allá de las fronterasde la ciudad, especialmente en la defensa y la lucha contra la brujería y otros hechizos.

adolescente. Através de seu pai, que como filho mais velho sempre o levou para o mato como ajudante na coleta de raízes, flores, tubérculos e cipós, ele se tornou provavelmente o mais jovem especialista de sua guilda em Porto-Novo.

Seu único ponto de venda é, acima de tudo, a amplitude de seu conhecimento, o que o torna um especialista conhecido e em demanda muito além dos limites da cidade, especialmente na defesa e luta contra a bruxaria e outros feitiços de dano.

bloemen, knollen en lianen meenam naar de bush, werd hij in Porto-Novo waarschijnlijk de jongste expert van zijn gilde.

Zijn belangrijkste pluspunt daarbij is vooral de breedte van zijn kennis, die hem tot ver buiten de stadsgrenzen tot een alombekende en veelgevraagde expert maakt, vooral bij de verdediging en strijd tegen hekserij en andere vormen van zwarte magie.

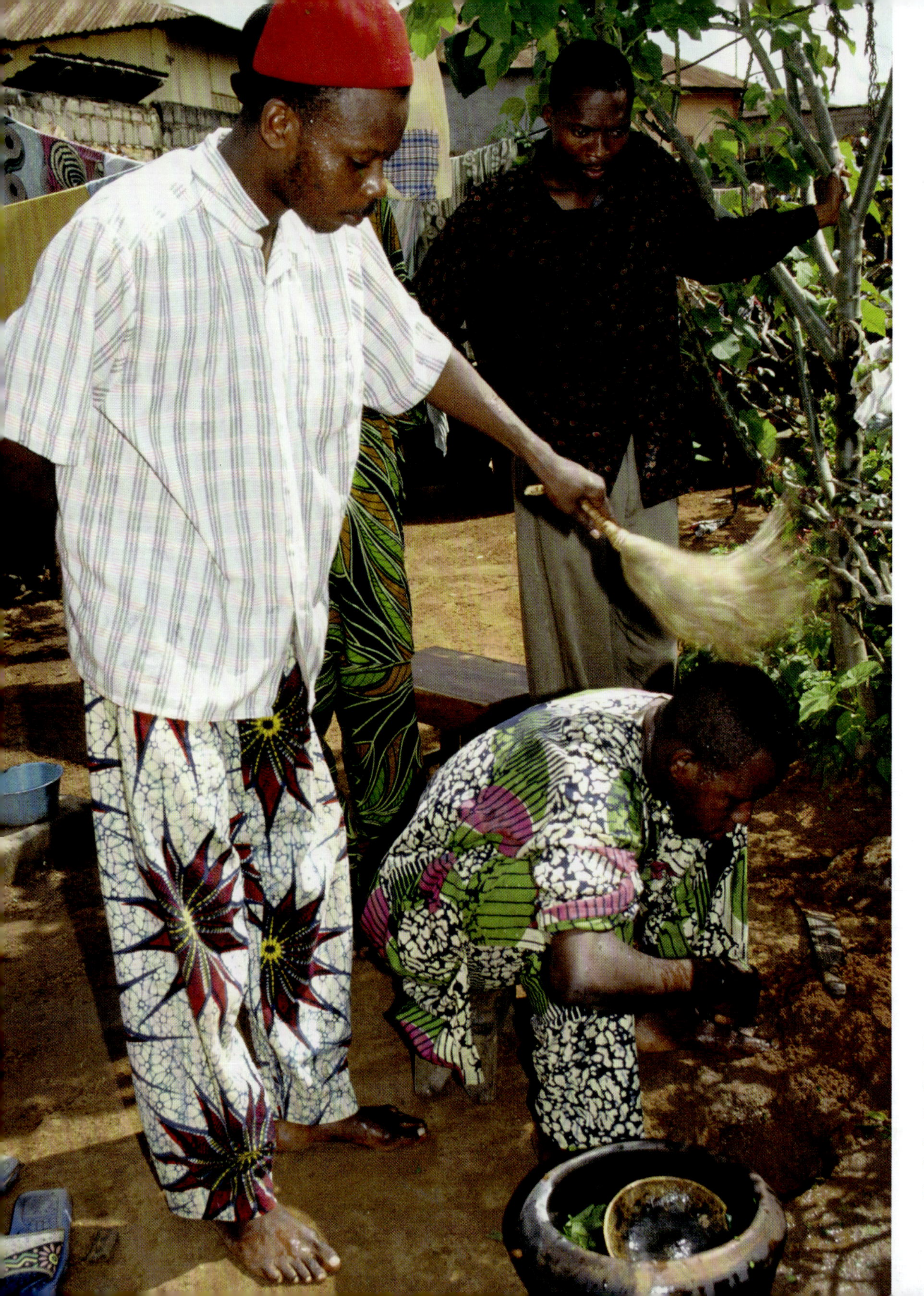

Medical treatment

Traitement thérapeutique

Krankenbehandlung

Atención médica

Tratamento médico

Ziekenbehandeling

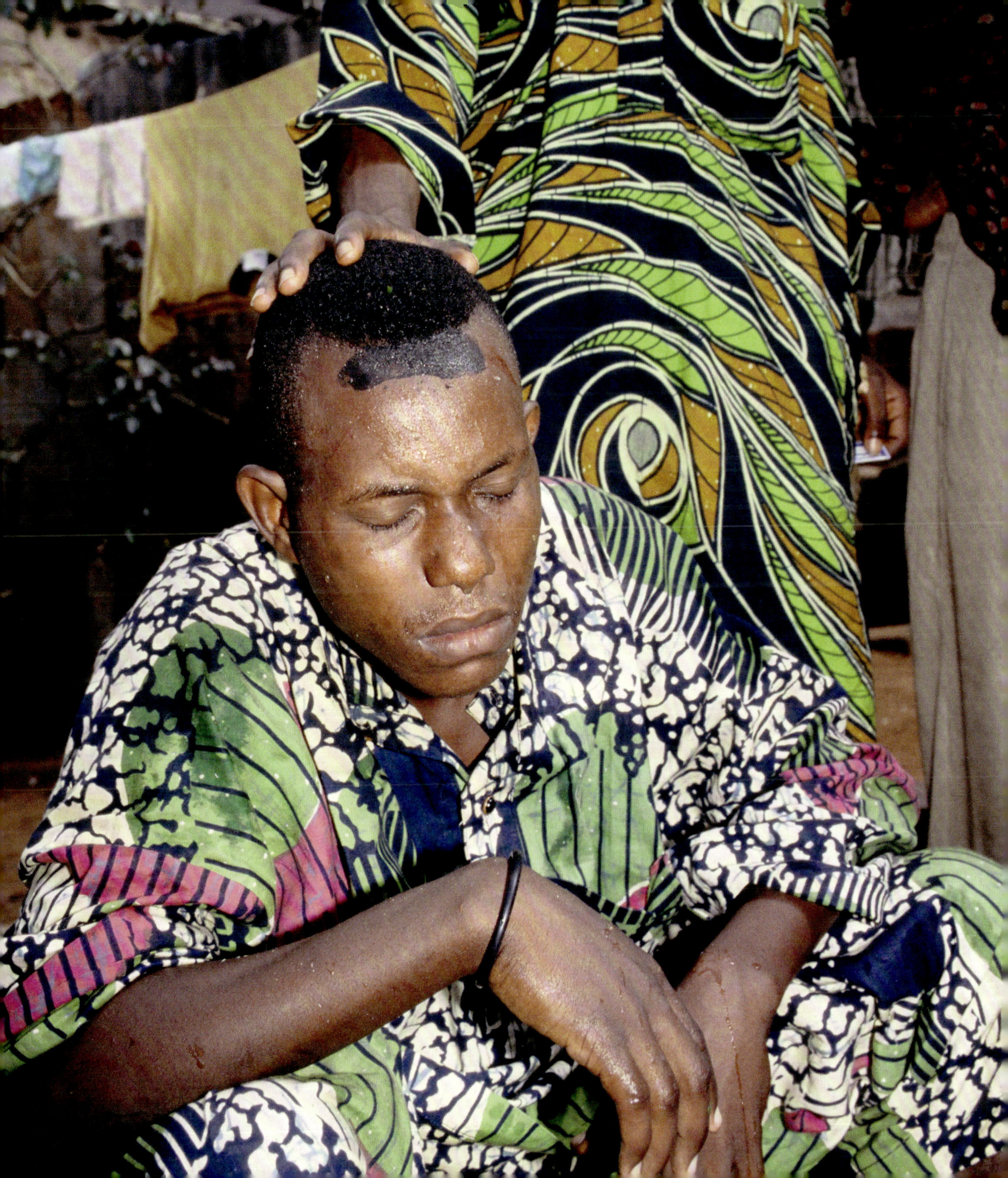

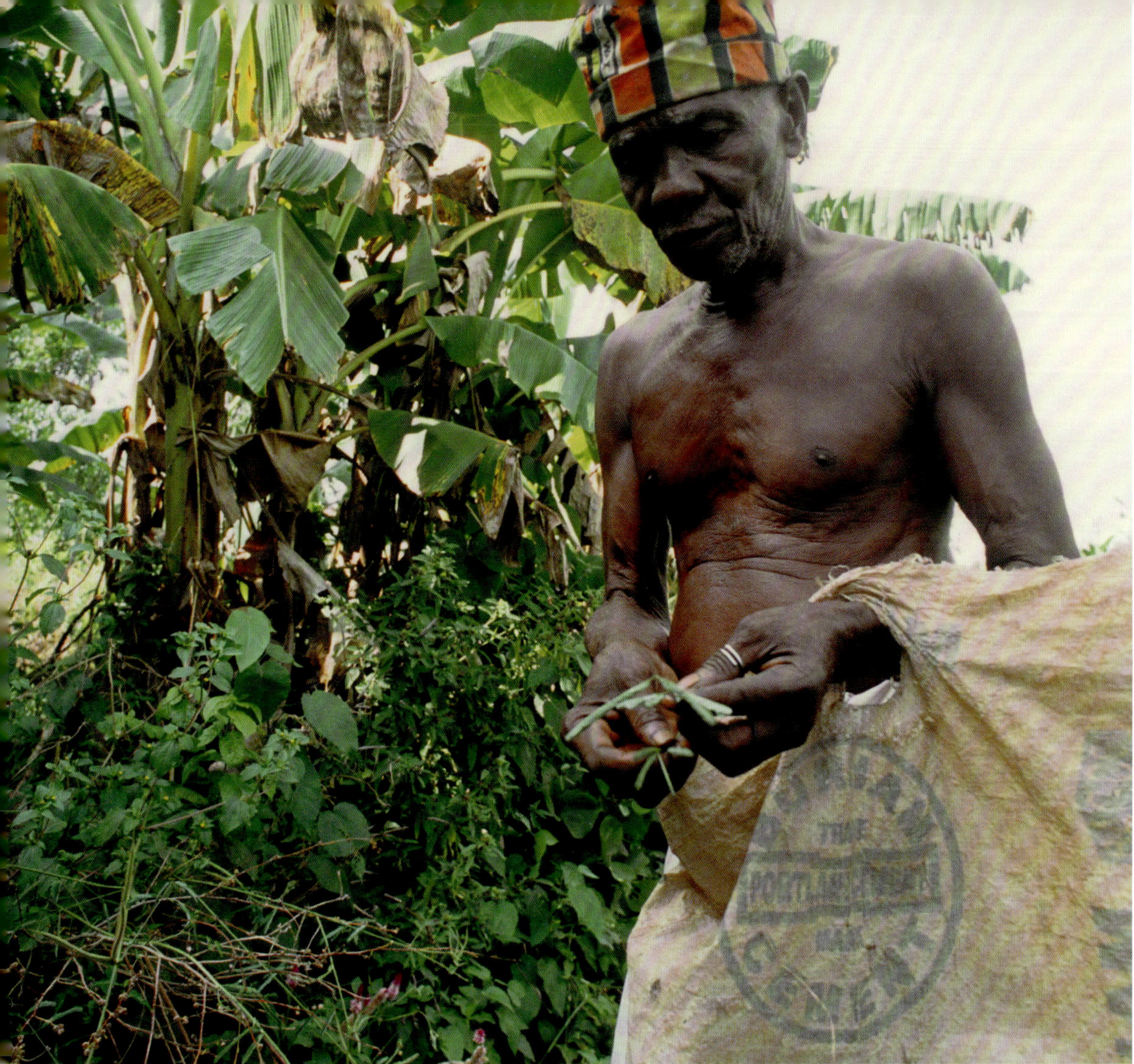

Medicine—image of divine powers

In Africa, the knowledge of medicinal plants and their use is a major component of cultural identity. The connection with religious and spiritual ideas has always existed, for nature is experienced as divine activity per se. The gods and their qualities manifest themselves in the forces of nature and the entire outside world, they are the ones who give plants and animals their individual power and meaning.

This is very well illustrated by the information that the famous ethnologist

Médecine, à l'image de la puissance des dieux

En Afrique, la connaissance des plantes médicinales et de leur emploi constitue une pièce maîtresse de l'identité culturelle. Le lien entre les plantes et les concepts religieux et spirituels existe depuis toujours, puisque la nature est vécue comme un bienfait divin. Les dieux et leurs attributs se manifestent dans les éléments naturels et dans l'ensemble du monde extérieur, ce sont eux qui donnent aux plantes et aux animaux leurs pouvoirs et leurs significations.

Medizin – Abbild göttlicher Kräfte

In Afrika ist das Wissen um Heilpflanzen und deren Verwendung ein Hauptbestandteil der kulturellen Identität. Die Verbindung mit religiösen und spirituellen Vorstellungen ist seit jeher gegeben, denn die Natur wird als göttliches Wirken per se erlebt. Die Götter und ihre Eigenschaften manifestieren sich in den Naturgewalten und der gesamten Außenwelt, sie sind es, die den Pflanzen und Tieren ihre individuelle Macht und Bedeutung geben.

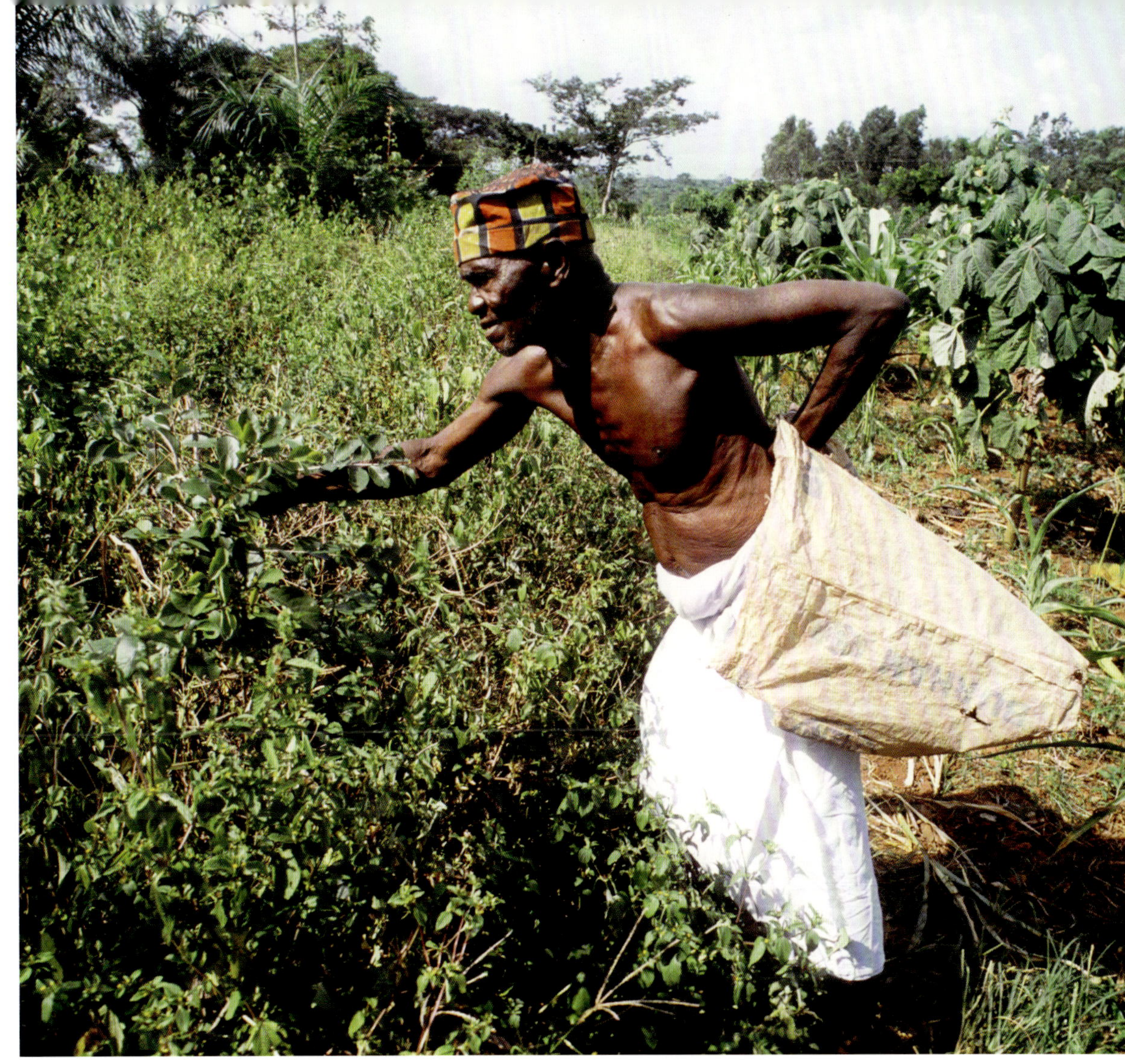

Medicina– Imagen de los poderes divinos

En África, el conocimiento de las plantas medicinales y su uso es un componente importante de la identidad cultural. La conexión con las ideas religiosas y espirituales siempre ha existido, porque la naturaleza se experimenta como actividad divina. Los dioses y sus cualidades se manifiestan en las fuerzas de la naturaleza y en todo el mundo exterior, ellos son los que conceden a las plantas y a los animales su propio poder y significado.

Medicina – Imagem dos poderes divinos

Na África, o conhecimento das plantas medicinais e seu uso é um componente importante da identidade cultural. A conexão com as idéias religiosas e espirituais sempre existiu, porque a natureza é experimentada como atividade divina per se. Os deuses e as suas qualidades manifestam-se nas forças da natureza e em todo o mundo exterior, são eles que dão às plantas e aos animais o seu poder e significado individual.

Geneeskunde – beeld van goddelijke krachten

In Afrika is de kennis van medicinale planten en het gebruik ervan een belangrijk onderdeel van de culturele identiteit. De verbinding met religieuze en spirituele ideeën heeft altijd al bestaan, omdat de natuur als een goddelijk werk op zich wordt ervaren. De goden en hun eigenschappen manifesteren zich in de krachten van de natuur en de hele buitenwereld. Die geven planten en dieren hun geheel eigen kracht en betekenis.

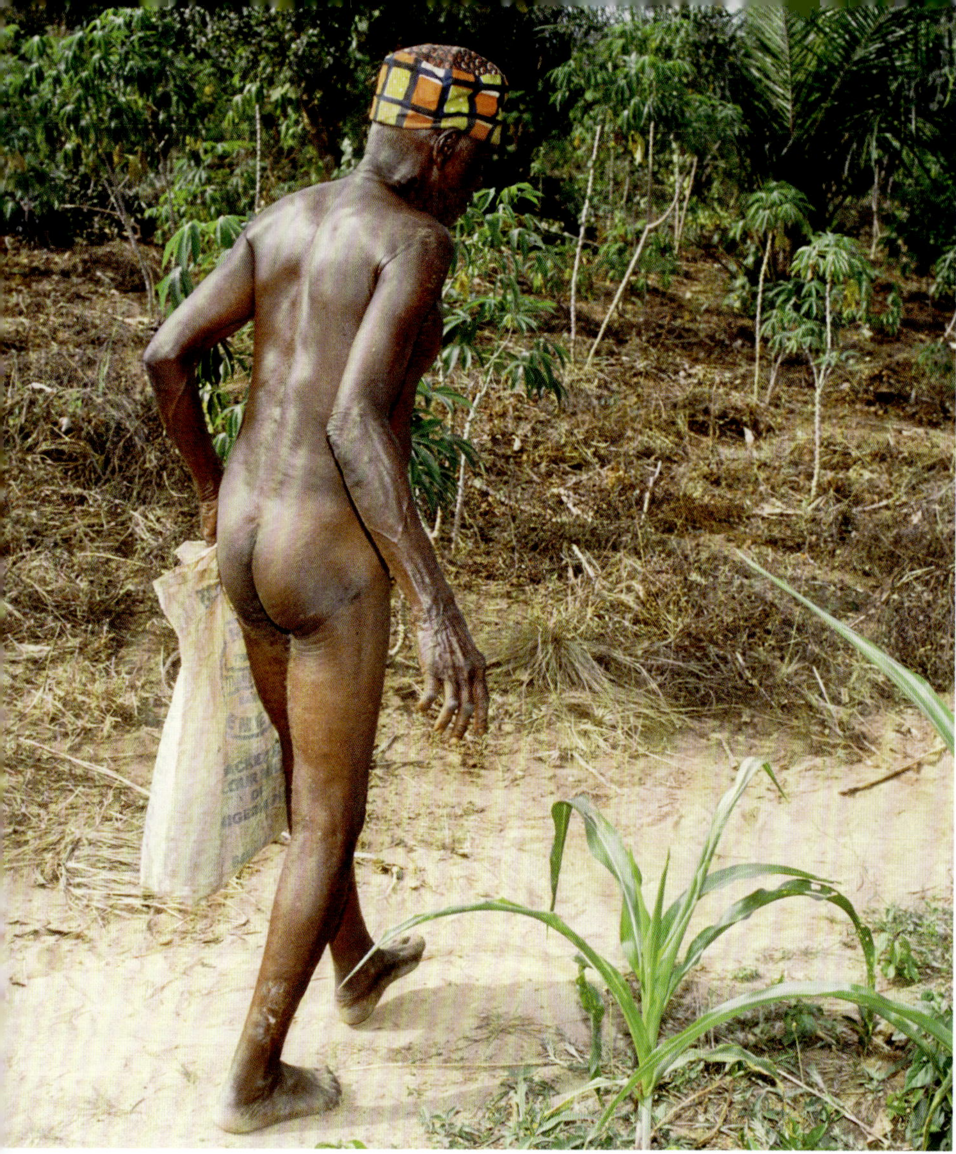

The process of collecting is regulated. He picks some plants only naked, because their power is then greater, others he invokes with secret formulas, still others may only be collected at night. Everything according to the rules.

Le processus de collecte est réglementé. Beaucoup de plantes doivent de préférence être cueillies nu, car cela renforce leur puissance, d'autres sont révélées par des formules secrètes et d'autres encore ne doivent être récoltées que la nuit. Chaque action s'effectue selon des règles précises.

Der Vorgang des Sammelns ist reglementiert. Manche Pflanzen pflückt er nur nackt, weil ihre Kraft dann größer ist, andere bespricht er mit geheimen Formeln, wieder andere dürfen nur nachts gesammelt werden. Alles hat seine Ordnung.

El proceso de recolección está regulado. Algunas plantas las recoge desnudo, porque su fuerza es entonces mayor, con otras va diciendo fórmulas secretas, y otras sólo las recoge de noche. Todo tiene su orden.

O processo de coleta é regulado. Algumas plantas ele escolhe apenas nuas, porque a sua força é então maior, outras ele discute com fórmulas secretas, outras ainda podem ser coletadas apenas à noite. Tudo tem a sua ordem.

De plukprocedure is gebonden aan regels. Sommige planten plukt hij alleen naakt, omdat hun kracht dan groter is, andere bezweert hij met geheime formules, weer andere mogen alleen 's nachts worden verzameld. Alles heeft zijn orde.

Melville Herskovits received about 1935 from a Fon medicine man during his research in Dahomey (today Benin): *If he knew the names and stories of all the leaves of the forest,* the healer told Herskovits, *then he knew everything there was to know about Dahomey's religion.*

The oral transmission and secrecy of this knowledge has a long tradition in Africa.

Cette relation est parfaitement illustrée par les propos d'un guérisseur Fon, consignés par le célèbre ethnologue Melville Herskovits vers 1935, au cours de ses recherches au Dahomey : « *Celui qui connaîtrait le nom et l'histoire de toutes les feuilles de la forêt saurait tout ce qu'il y a à savoir de la religion du Dahomey.* »

La transmission orale et la conservation du secret des connaissances jouissent également en Afrique d'une longue tradition.

Sehr gut wird dies illustriert durch die Info, die der berühmte Ethnologe Melville Herskovits circa 1935 bei seinen Recherchen in Dahomey (heute Benin) von einem Fon-Medizinmann erhielt: *Wenn er die Namen und Geschichten aller Blätter des Waldes wüsste,* so der Heiler zu Herskovits, *dann wüsste er auch alles über die Religion Dahomeys, was es zu wissen gibt.*

Die mündliche Weitergabe und die Geheimhaltung dieses Wissen hat in Afrika eine lange Tradition.

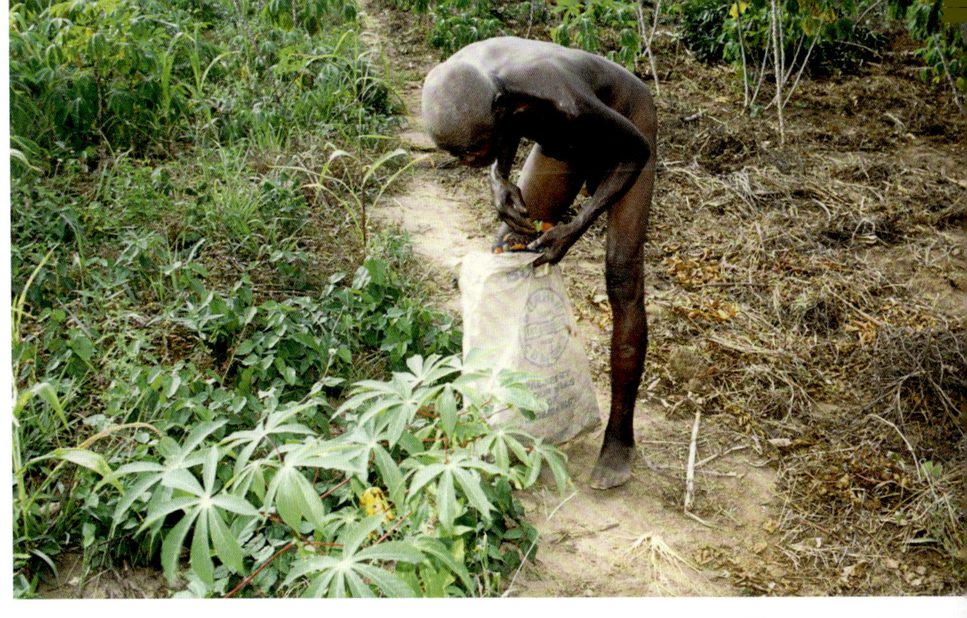

The Old Healer collecting medicinal plants

Le vieux guérisseur récoltant des plantes médicinales

Der alte Heiler beim Sammeln von Heilpflanzen

El viejo curandero que colecciona plantas medicinales

O curandeiro velho que coleta plantas medicinais

De oude genezer bij het plukken van geneeskrachtige planten

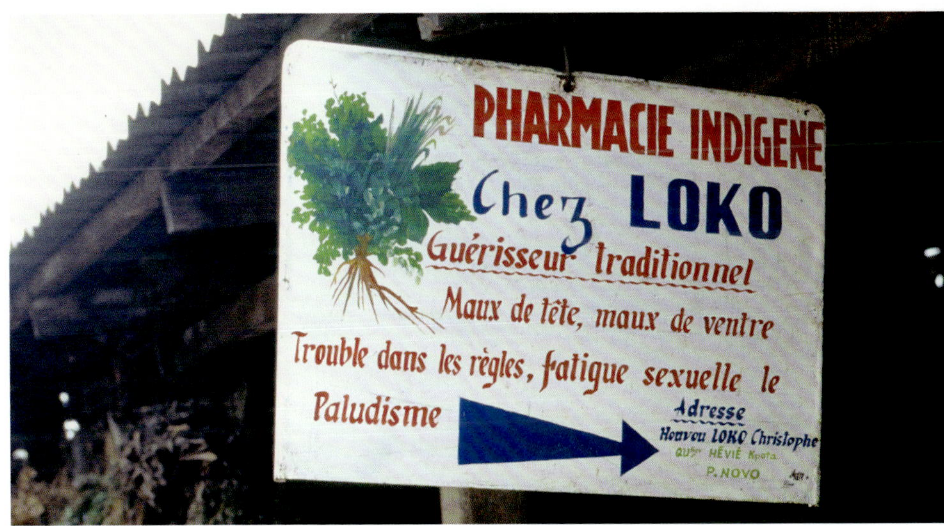

Advertising sign of a plant pharmacy in Porto Novo, Benin

Affiche publicitaire d'une pharmacie de plantes à Porto Novo, Bénin

Werbeschild einer Pflanzenapotheke in Porto Novo, Benin

Cartel publicitario de una farmacia en Porto Novo, Benin

Sinal publicitário de uma farmácia em Porto Novo, Benim

Uithangbord van een plantenapotheek in Porto Novo, Benin

Esto viene muy bien ilustrado en la información que el famoso etnólogo Melville Herskovits recibió alrededor de 1935 de un curandero Fon durante su investigación en Dahomey (hoy Benin): *si conoces los nombres y las historias de todas las hojas del bosque,* así le decía el curanderoa Herskovits, *entonces sabrás todo lo que hay que saber sobre la religión de Dahomey.*

La transmisión oral y el secreto de este conocimiento tiene una larga tradición en África.

Isto é muito bem ilustrado pela informação que o famoso etnólogo Melville Herskovits recebeu cerca de 1935 de um curandeiro Fon durante a sua pesquisa em Dahomey (hoje Benin): Se ele sabia os nomes e histórias de todas as folhas da floresta, o curandeiro contou a Herskovits, então ele sabia tudo o que havia para saber sobre a religião de Dahomey.

A transmissão oral e o secretismo deste conhecimento têm uma longa tradição em África.

Dit wordt zeer goed geïllustreerd door de informatie die de beroemde etnoloog Melville Herskovits rond 1935 tijdens zijn onderzoek in Dahomey (nu Benin) kreeg van een Fon-medicijnman: *als hij de namen en verhalen van alle bladeren van het bos kende,* vertelde de medicijnman aan Herskovits, *wist hij alles wat er te weten viel over het geloof van Dahomey.*

De mondelinge overdracht en geheimhouding van deze kennis heeft een lange traditie in Afrika.

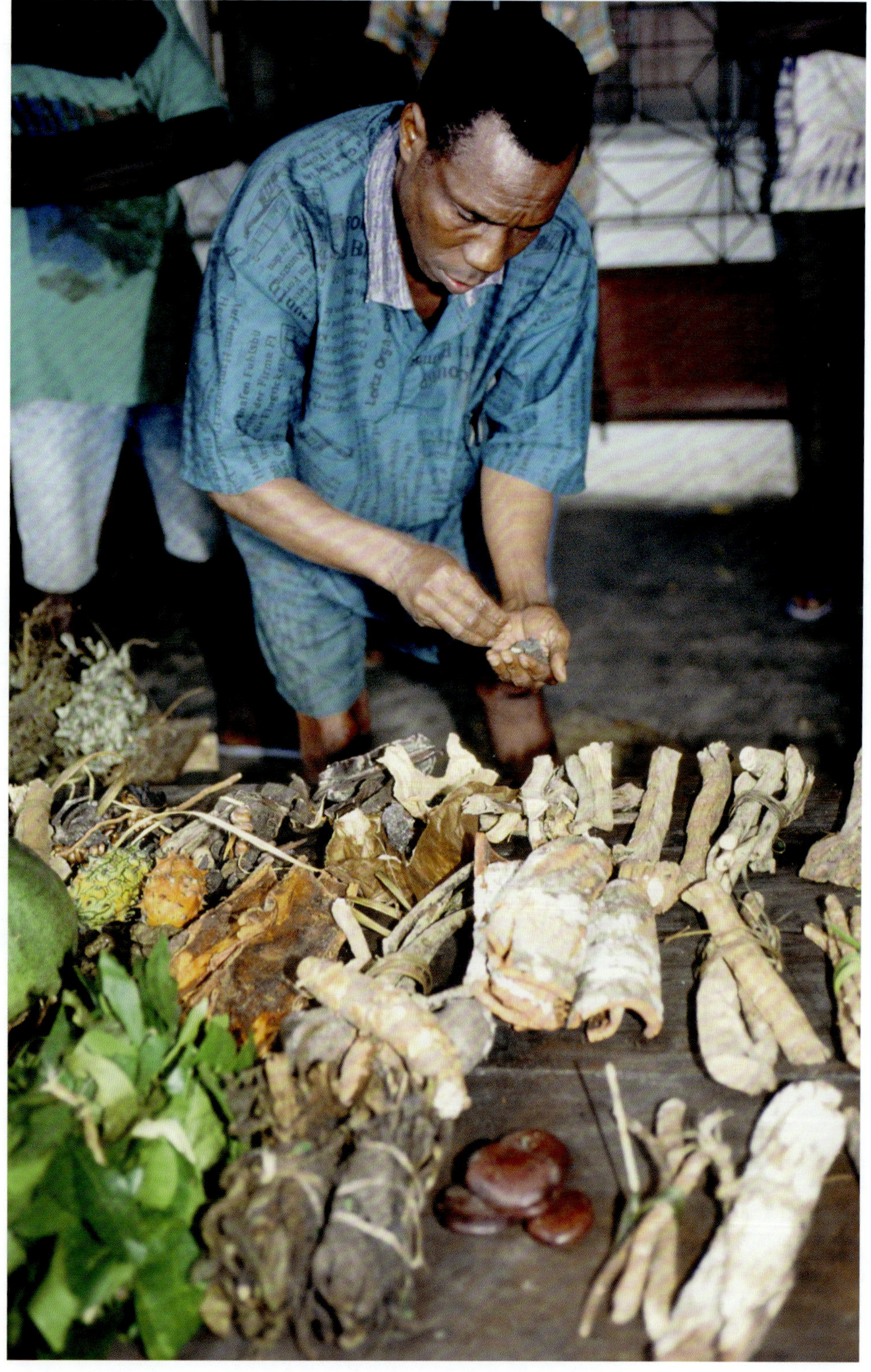

The Healer Antoine Tottin from Cotonou, **Benin**. With his expertise in medicinal plants, he feeds 13 women and 60 children. A special aphrodisiac he has developed is one of bestsellers.

Le guérisseur Antoine Tottin à Cotonou, **Bénin**. Grâce à ses connaissances sur les plantes médicinales, il subvient aux besoins de 13 femmes et 60 enfants. Un aphrodisiaque de sa composition compte parmi ses produits les plus vendus.

Der Heiler Antoine Tottin aus Cotonou, **Benin**. Mit seinem Fachwissen um die Heilpflanzen ernährt er 13 Frauen und 60 Kinder. Besonders ein von ihm entwickeltes Aphrodisiakum gehört zu den Verkaufsschlagern.

El curandero Antoine Tottin de Cotonou, **Benin**. Con sus conocimientos de plantas medicinales alimenta a 13 mujeres y 60 niños. Un afrodisíaco especialmente desarrollado por él pertenece a los productos más vendidos.

O curandeiro Antoine Tottin de Cotonou, **Benin**. Com o seu conhecimento de plantas medicinais, alimenta 13 mulheres e 60 crianças. Especialmente um afrodisíaco desenvolvido por ele pertence aos mais vendidos.

De genezer Antoine Tottin uit Cotonou, **Benin**. Met zijn kennis van medicinale planten voedt hij dertien vrouwen en zestig kinderen. Vooral een door hem ontwikkeld afrodisiacum is een verkoopsucces.

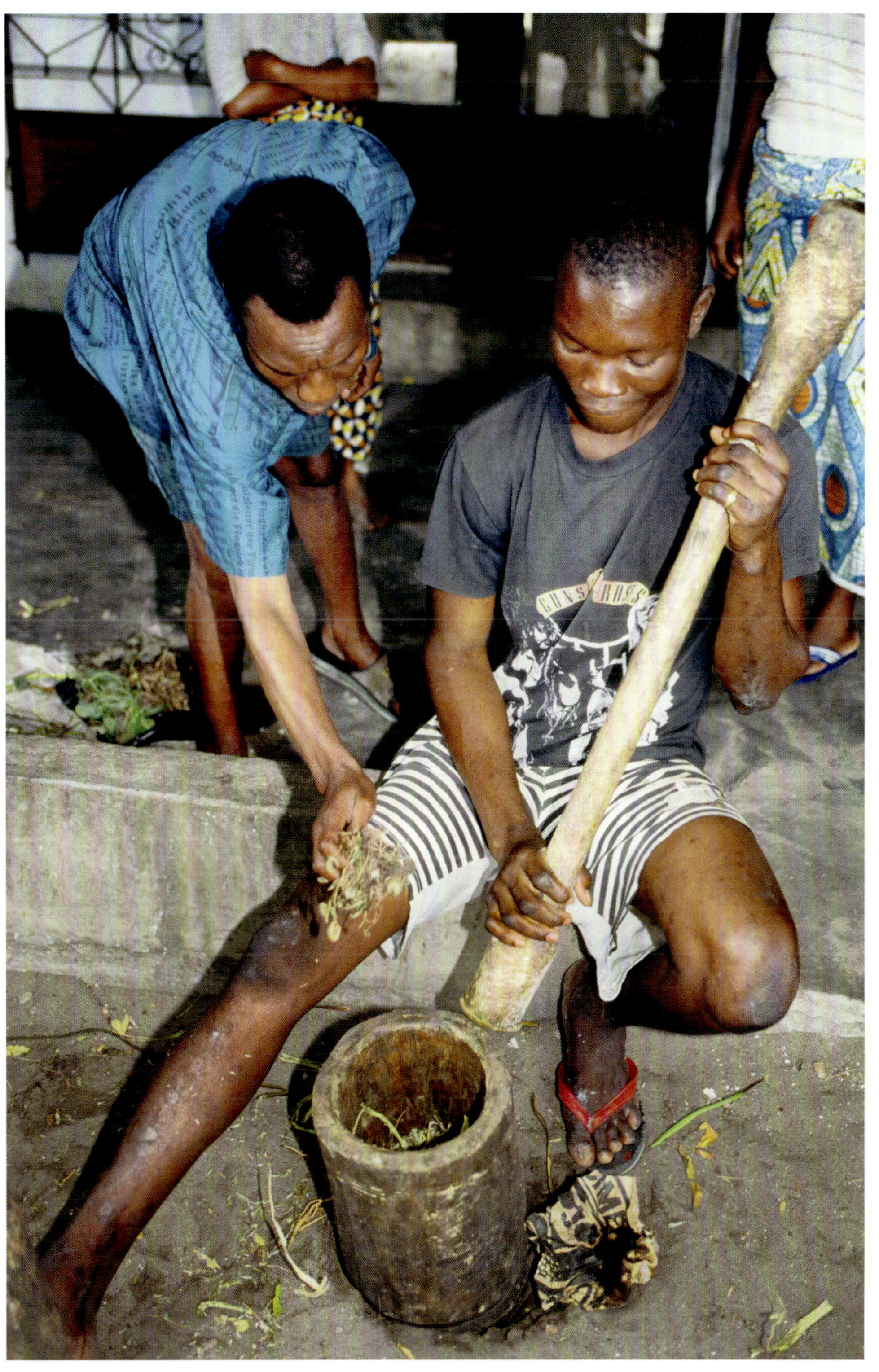

The mortar is used to pound
the plants.

Le mortier est utilisé pour piler
les plantes

Mit dem Mörser werden die
Pflanzen zerstampft

El mortero se utiliza para machacar
las plantas

O almofariz é usado para triturar
as plantas

In de vijzel worden de
planten vermalen

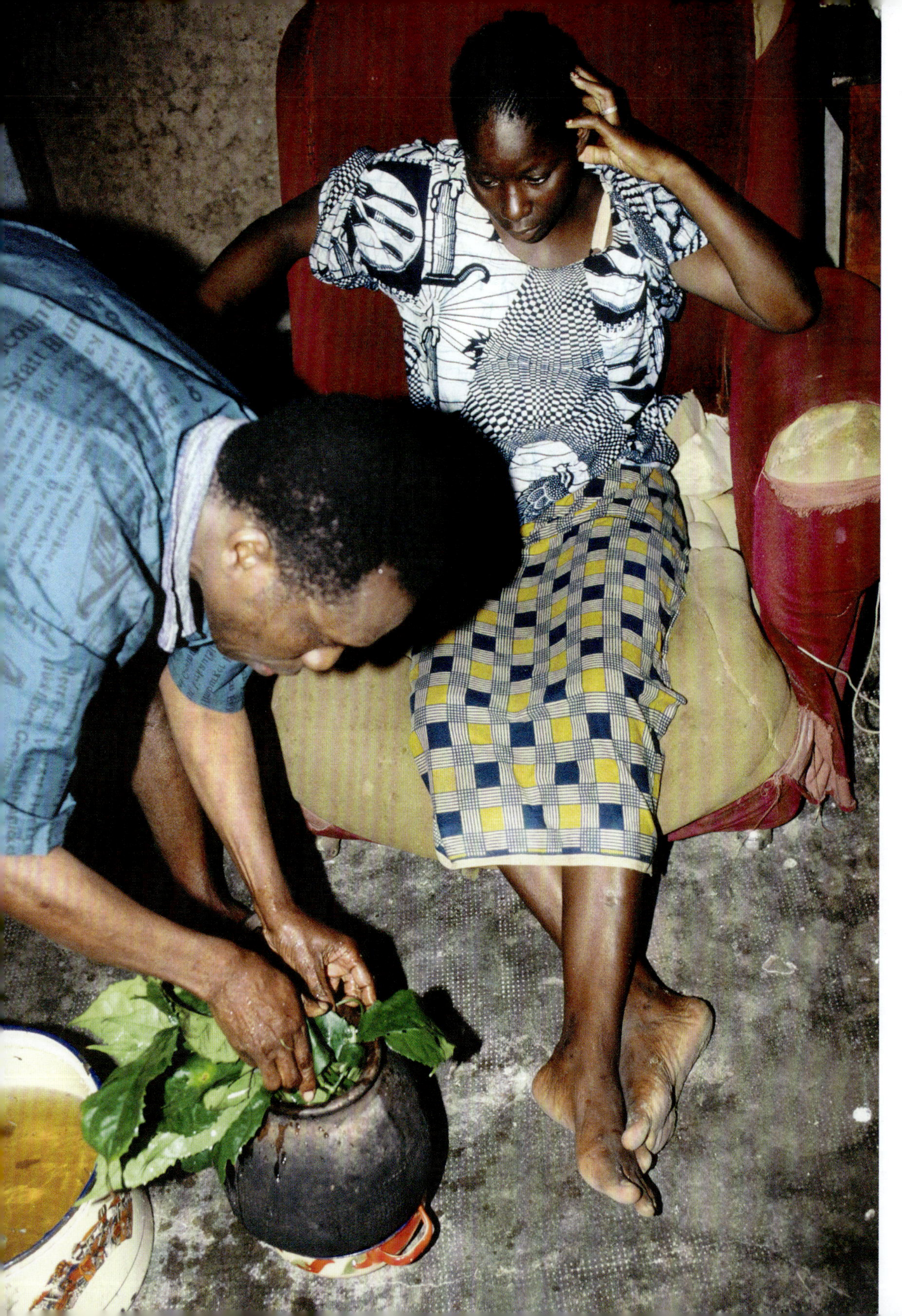

Treatment of a patient

Traitement d'une patiente

Behandlung einer Patientin

Tratamiento de un paciente

Tratamento de um paciente

Behandeling van een patiënte

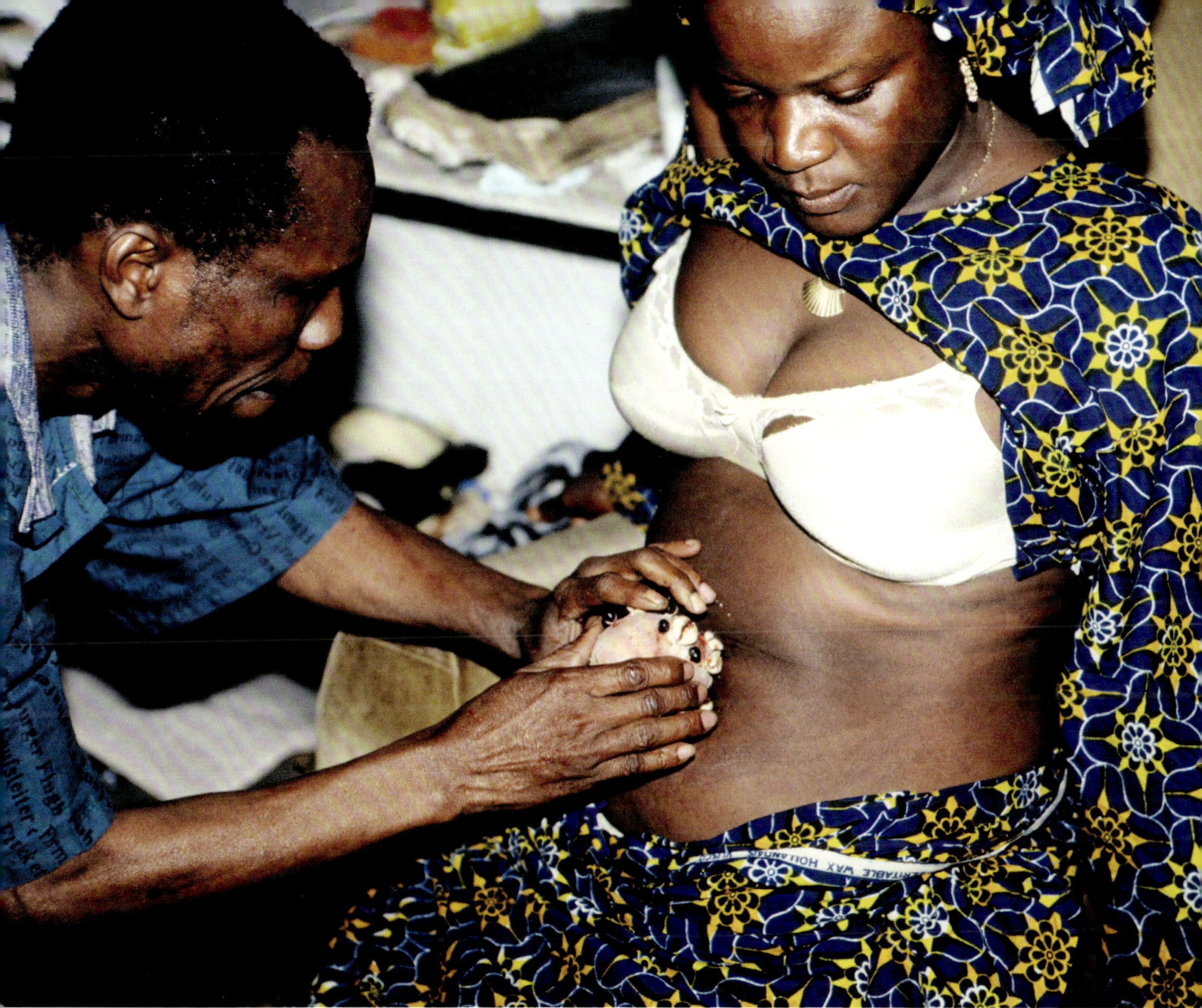

Antoine Tottin is a practical healer. When it comes to healing, he is an all-rounder, similar to the general practitioner in the West. Here he treats the abdominal pain of a client with crushed Yam roots and a magic bottle.

Antoine Tottin est un praticien. En matière de guérison, cet homme est un praticien complet, à la manière d'un généraliste en Occident. Sur cette photographie, on le voit traiter les maux de ventre d'une patiente à l'aide de tubercules d'igname et d'une bouteille magique.

Antoine Tottin ist ein praktischer Heiler. In Sachen Heilung ist er ein Allrounder, ähnlich dem praktischen Arzt im Westen. Hier behandelt er die Bauchschmerzen einer Klientin mit zerstoßenen Yamsknollen und einer magischen Flasche.

Antoine Tottin es un curandero práctico. En lo que se refiere a la curación, es un hombre polifacético, similar al médico general de Occidente. Aquí trata el dolor abdominal de un cliente con Yamsknollen aplastado y una botella mágica.

Antoine Tottin é um curandeiro prático. Quando se trata de cura, ele é um "all-rounder", semelhante ao médico de clínica geral no Ocidente. Aqui ele trata a dor abdominal de um cliente com Yamsknollen esmagado e uma garrafa mágica.

Antoine Tottin is een praktiserende genezer. Op het gebied van genezing is hij een specialist, vergelijkbaar met de westerse huisarts. Hier behandelt hij de buikpijn van een patiënte met fijngestampte yams en een magische fles.

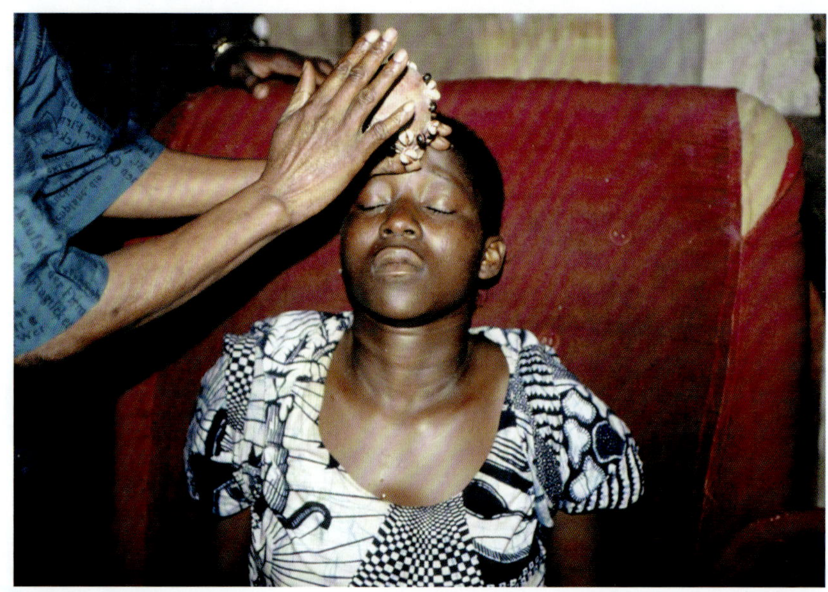

Antoine Tottin at work
Antoine Tottin en plein travail
Antoine Tottin bei der Arbeit
Antoine Tottin trabajando
Antoine Tottin no trabalho
Antoine Tottin aan het werk

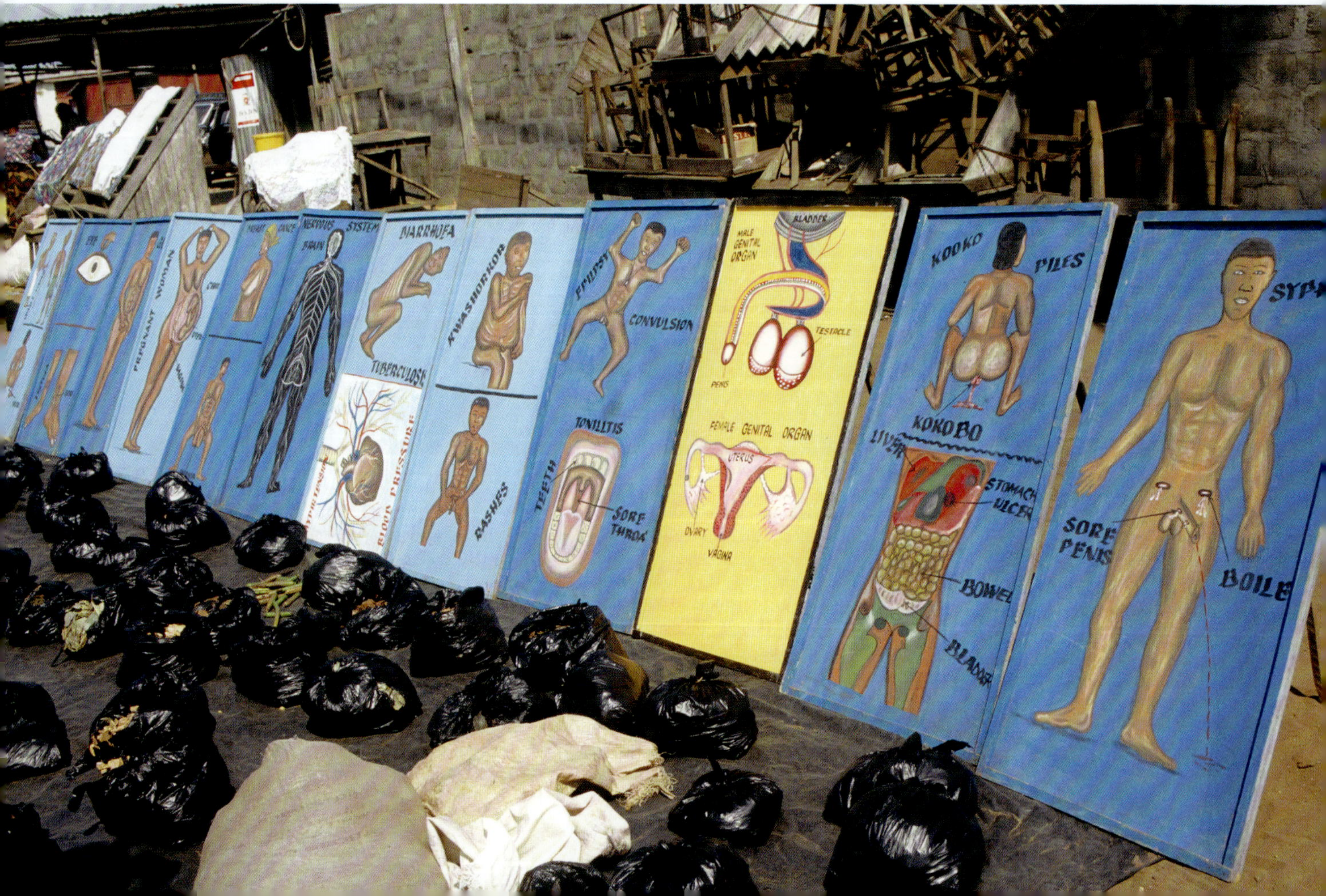

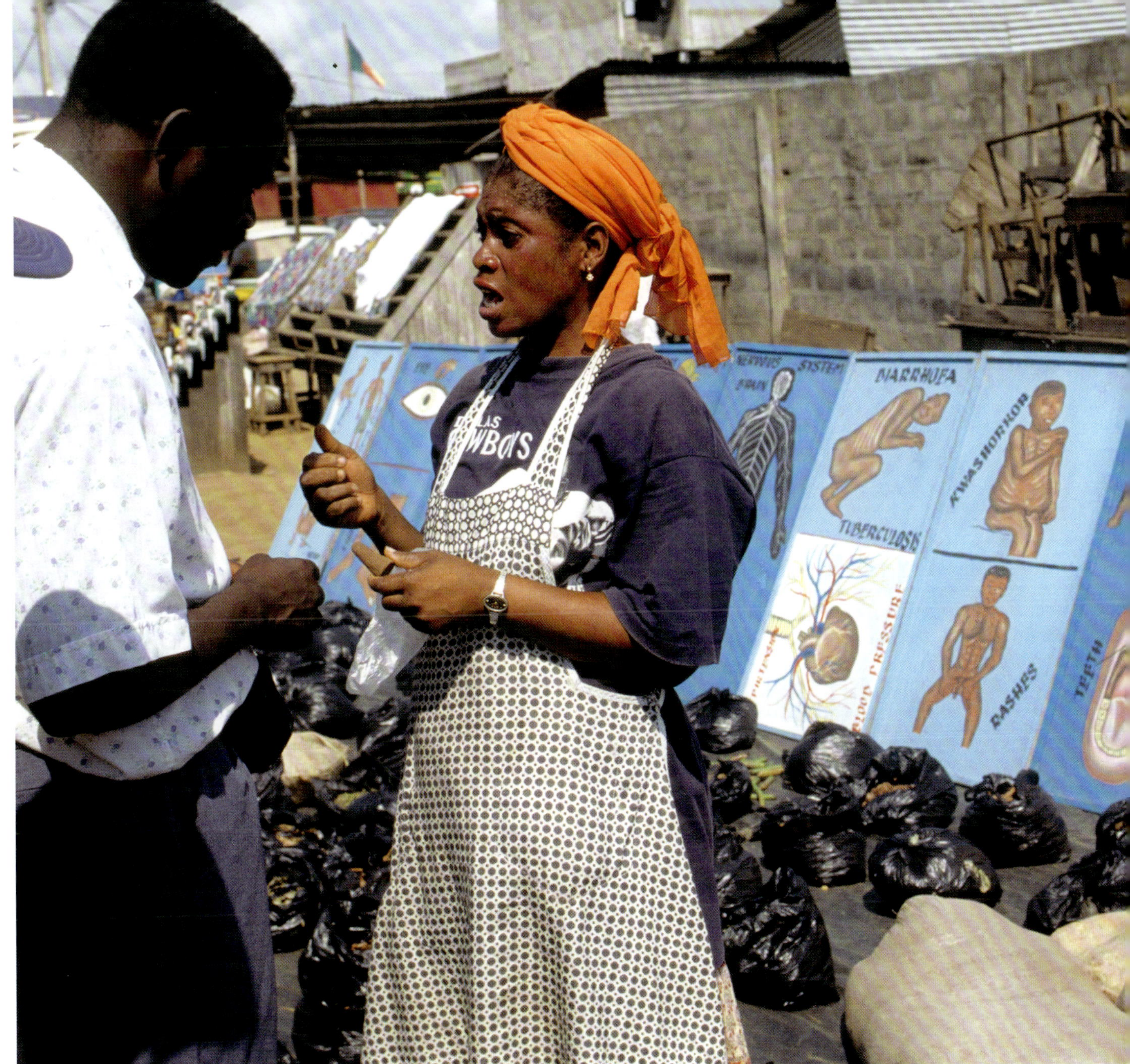

Street pharmacy in Ghana

Pharmacie de rue au Ghana

Straßenapotheke in Ghana

Farmacia en la calle en Ghana

Farmácia de rua em Gana

Straatapotheek in Ghana

Dealer of herbal medicine

Marchande de remèdes à base de plantes

Händlerin für pflanzliche Arzneien

Distribuidor de hierbas

Negociante de ervas

Handelaarster in plantaardige medicijnen

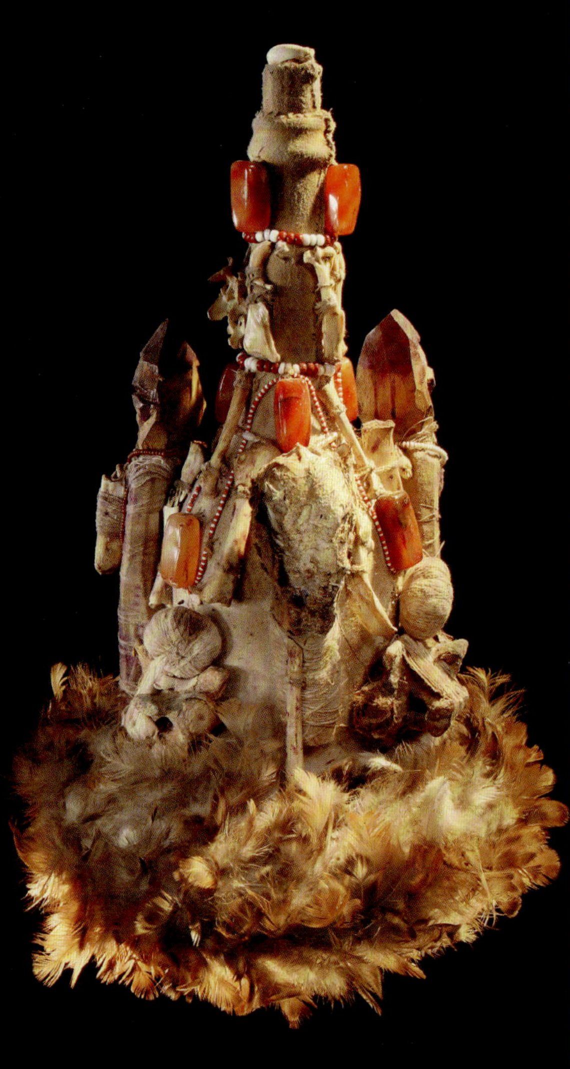

Witch bottle with owl feathers

Bouteille de sorcier avec plumes de hibou

Hexenflasche mit Eulenfedern

Botella de brujo con plumas de búho

Frasco de bruxa com penas de coruja

Heksenfles met uilenveren

Glass bottle, owl feather, bone, duckbill and other organic materials/ Flacon de verre, plumes de hiboux, os, bec de canard, matières organiques, 34 × 20 cm

Witch bottle with human lower jaw

Bouteille de sorcier avec mâchoire inférieure humaine

Hexenflasche mit menschlichem Unterkiefer

Botella de brujo con mandíbula humana

Frasco de bruxa com maxilar inferior humano

Heksenfles met menselijke onderkaak

Glass bottle, human lower jaw/Flacon de verre, machoire humaine, 32 × 10 cm

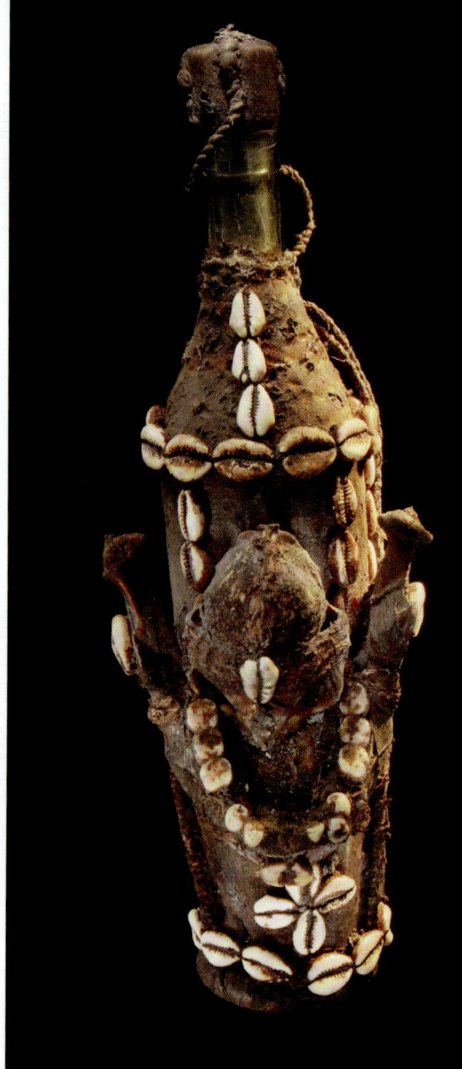

Bottles—objects of power

In Benin, bottles are used for all kinds of magic. You can find these differently decorated objects in healing and protection ceremonies as well as in damage magic. They are often filled with Sodabi, a palm schnapps mixed with secret ingredients during bottling, which unfolds its magical effect after consumption in precisely defined doses. However, other contents can also be used, and the externally applied medicines do the rest.

Animal parts are attached to some bottles, roots and plant mixtures are

Les bouteilles, objets de puissance

Au Bénin, les bouteilles possèdent de multiples utilités en magie. Ces objets, décorés de façon extrêmement variés, sont présents dans les cérémonies de guérison et de protection, mais également dans la magie maléfique. Elles sont généralement remplies de *sodabi*, une liqueur à base de vin de palme mélangée à divers ingrédients secrets directement dans la bouteille, qui étend son action magique lorsqu'elle est consommée à des doses strictement prescrites. D'autres contenus peuvent cependant être utilisés,

Flaschen – Objekte der Kraft

In Benin werden Flaschen für Zaubereien aller Art verwendet. Man findet diese sehr unterschiedlich ausstaffierten Objekte sowohl in Heilungs- und Schutzzeremonien als auch in der Schadenmagie. Oft sind sie mit Sodabi, einem Palmschnaps gefüllt, der im Zuge der Flaschenbearbeitung mit geheimen Ingredienzien gemischt wurde und seine magische Wirkung nach dem Genuss genau festgelegter Dosierungen entfaltet. Es können aber auch andere Inhalte zum Einsatz kommen, und die

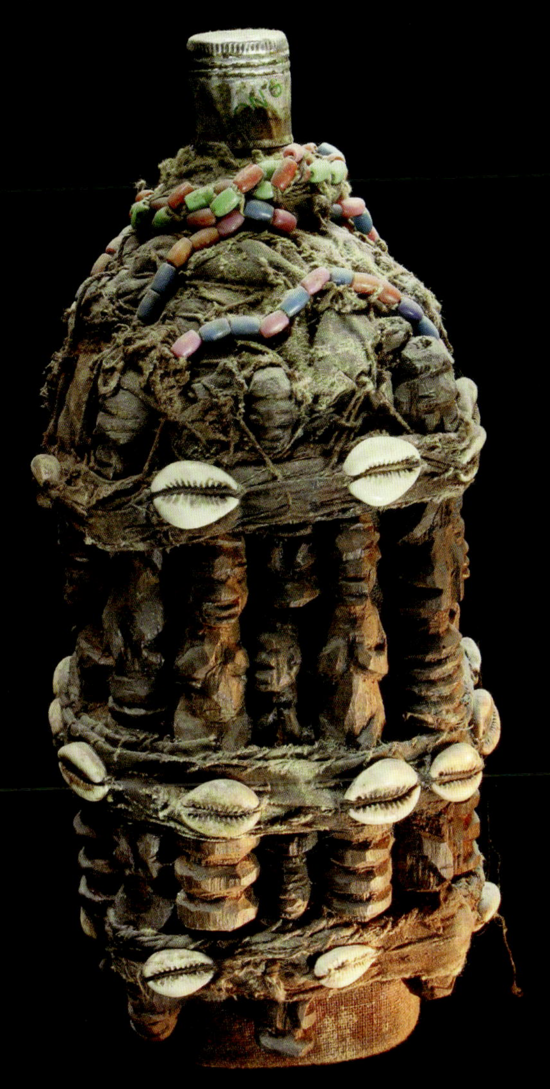

Protective bottle against
damage spells

Bouteille de protection contre
les mauvais sorts

Schutzflasche vor Schadenzauber

Botella protectora contra
hechizos malignos

Frasco protector contra feitiços
danificados

Beschermende fles tegen
boze tovenarij

Glass bottle, wooden figures/Flacon
de verre, figurines en bois, 29 × 12 cm

Bottle with the power of the warrior
Vodun Kokou

Bouteille renfermant le pouvoir du
vodun guerrier Kokou

Flasche mit der Kraft des
Kriegervoduns Kokou

Botella con el poder del guerrero
vudú Kokou

Garrafa com o poder do vodu
guerreiro Kokou

Fles met de kracht van de
krijgergod Kokou

Glass bottle, wooden figure/Flacon de
verre, bois, 29 × 8 cm

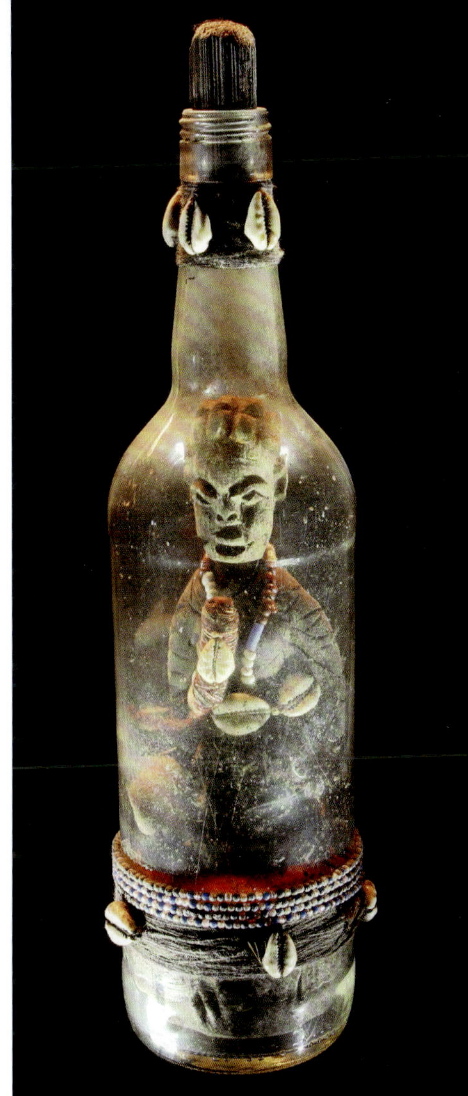

Botellas– Objetos de poder

En Benin, las botellas se utilizan para
todo tipo de magia. En las ceremonias
de curación y protección, así como en la
magianegra, se pueden encontrar estos
objetos decorados de forma diferente.
A menudo se llenan con Sodabi, un
aguardiente de palma que ha sido mezclado
con ingredientes secretos durante el proceso
de elaboración de la botella y despliega
su efecto mágico después del consumo de
dosis definidas con precisión. Sin embargo,
también se pueden utilizar otros contenidos,

Garrafas – Objetos de poder

No Benin, as garrafas são usadas para
todos os tipos de magia. Você pode
encontrar estes objetos decorados de forma
diferente em cerimônias de cura e proteção,
bem como em magia de dano. Eles são
frequentemente enchidos com Sodabi,
um schnapps de palma que foi misturado
com ingredientes secretos no decurso do
processamento de garrafas e desdobra o
seu efeito mágico após o consumo de doses
definidas com precisão. No entanto, outros
conteúdos também podem ser usados, e

Flessen – objecten van macht

In Benin worden flessen gebruikt
voor allerlei soorten tovenarij. Je kunt
deze zeer uiteenlopend versierde
voorwerpen aantreffen in genezings- en
beschermingsceremoniën en eveneens
in de schadelijke magie. Ze worden vaak
gevuld met sodabi, een sterkedrank
van palmbomen, die in de loop van de
flesbewerking wordt vermengd met
geheime ingrediënten en zijn magische
werking ontwikkelt na de consumptie van
nauwkeurig vastgelegde doses. Er kan echter

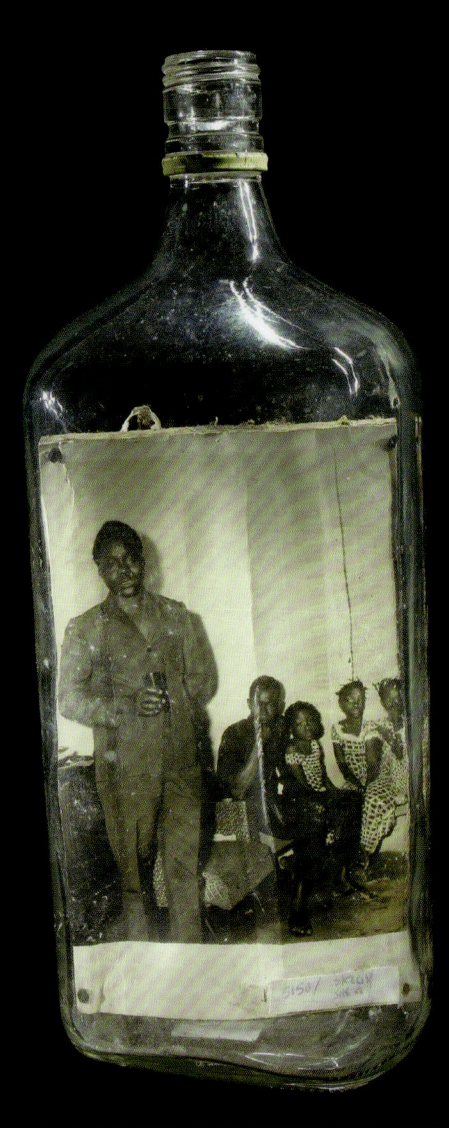

Protective bottle by Simon Soha. The artist, the offspring of a Vodun family of priests, once made this bottle as protection for President Kérékou.

Bouteille protectrice de Simon Soha. Cette bouteille avait été fabriquée pour le président Kérékou par un artiste issu d'une famille de prêtres vodun, en guise de protection.

Schutzflasche von Simon Soha. Der Künstler, Sproß einer Vodun-Priesterfamilie, fertigte diese Flasche einst als Schutz für den Präsidenten Kérékou.

Botella protectora de Simon Soha. El artista, descendiente de una família de sacerdotes vudúes, fabricó una vez esta botella como protección para el Presidente Kérékou.

Garrafa protectora de Simon Soha. O artista, descendente de uma família de padres vodun, fez uma vez esta garrafa como protecção para o Presidente Kérékou.

Beschermende fles van Simon Soha. De kunstenaar, spruit van een vodunpriestersfamilie, maakte deze beschermende fles ooit voor president Kérékou.

Glass bottle, photo, wood, glass beads/Flacon de verre, photo, bois, perles de verre, 29 × 12 cm

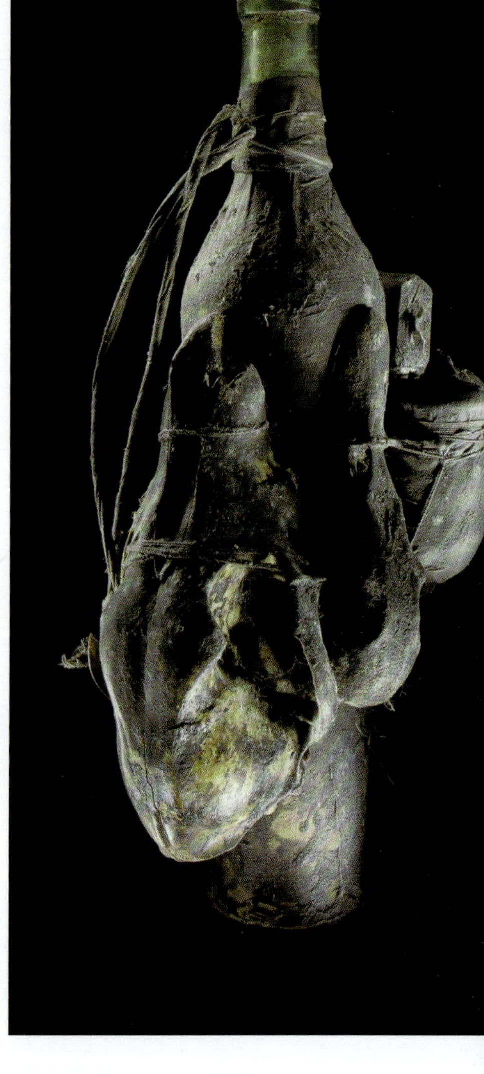

Witch bottle

Bouteille de sorcier

Hexenflasche

Botella de brujo

Garrafa de bruxa

Heksenfles

Glass bottle, dog skull/Flacon de verre, crâne de chien, 29 × 15 cm

attached to others, and sometimes human bones or small bocios are attached.

These seemingly arbitrarily chosen ingredients are components of partly century-old recipes, which the traditional medicine man took over from his ancestors during a lengthy training.

et les traitements appliqués à l'extérieur augmentent encore les possibilités.

Des morceaux d'animaux sont souvent accrochés aux bouteilles, pour d'autres ce sont des racines et des mélanges de plantes, ou encore des os humains ou de petits bocio.

Ces ingrédients qui semblent choisis arbitrairement entrent en réalité dans la composition de recettes multiséculaires que le guérisseur traditionnel a appris auprès de ses prédécesseurs au cours d'une longue formation.

äußerlich applizierten Medizinen tun ein Übriges.

An manchen Flaschen sind tierische Teile befestigt, an anderen Wurzeln und pflanzliche Mixturen und manchmal sind es auch Menschenknochen oder kleine Bocios.

Diese willkürlich gewählt scheinenden Zutaten sind Bestandteile teils jahrhundertealter Rezepturen, die der traditionelle Medizinmann während einer langwierigen Ausbildung seinerseits von den Vorfahren übernommen hat.

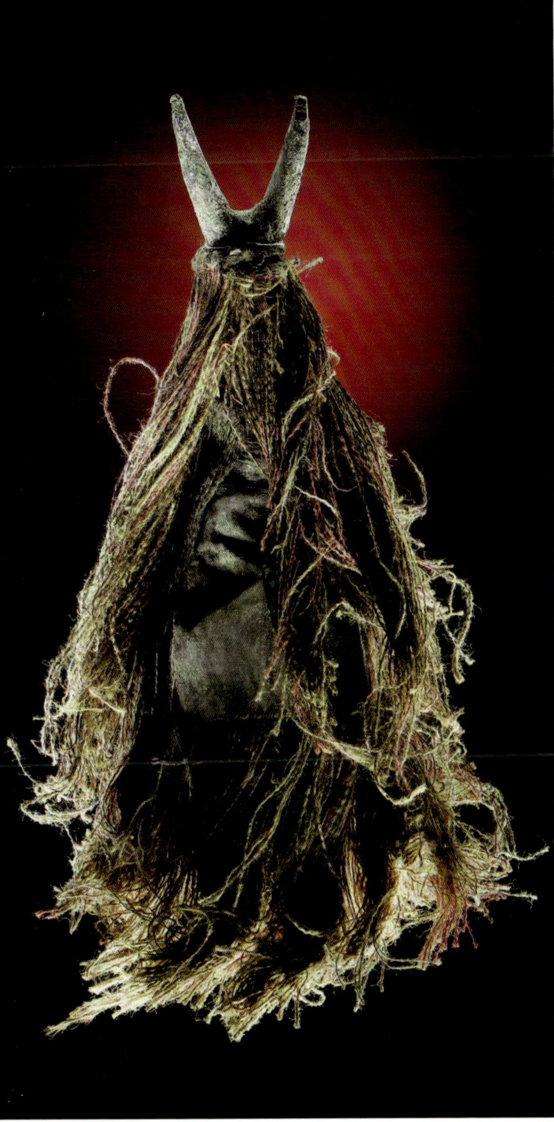

Zangbeto bottle. Externally similar to the Zangbeto costumes, this bottle contains the power of the secret society. The helpers drink from it at ceremonies to fortify themselves.

Bouteille de Zangbeto. Présentant une apparence proche des costumes de Zangbeto, cette bouteille renferme la puissance de la confrérie secrète. Au cours des cérémonies, ses membres en boivent le contenu pour augmenter leur force.

Zangbetoflasche. Äußerlich den Zangbeto-Kostümen ähnlich, enthält diese Flasche die Kraft des Geheimbundes. Seine Helfer trinken bei Zeremonien aus ihr, um sich zu stärken.

Botella de Zangbeto. Externamente similar a los trajes de Zangbeto, esta botella contiene el poder de la sociedad secreta. Sus ayudantes beben de ella durante las ceremonias para fortalecerse.

Garrafa de Zangbeto. Externamente semelhante aos trajes do Zangbeto, esta garrafa contém o poder da sociedade secreta. Os seus ajudantes bebem dela durante as cerimónias para se fortalecerem.

Zangbeto-fles. Qua uiterlijk vergelijkbaar met de Zangbeto-kostuums bevat deze fles de kracht van het geheime genootschap. De helpers drinken er tijdens ceremoniën van om zich te sterken.

Glass bottle, threads, wood/Flacon de verre, ficelles, bois, 43 × 18 cm

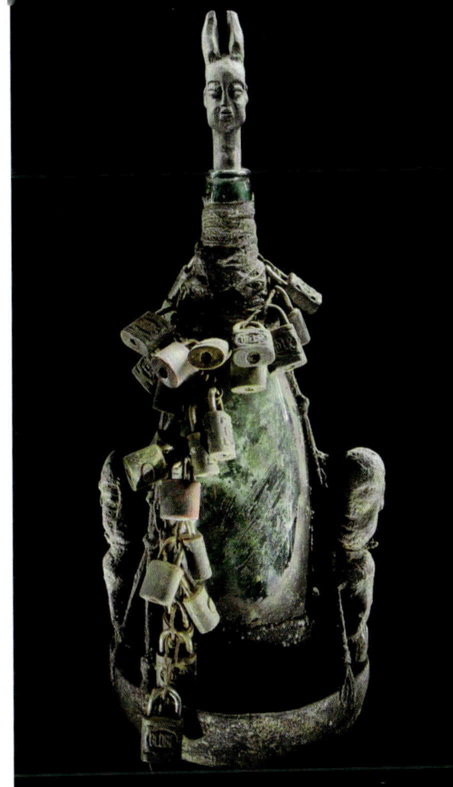

Bottle with the power of Legba

Bouteille contenant la puissance de Legba

Flasche mit der Kraft Legbas

Botella con el poder de Legbas

Garrafa com o poder Legbas

Fles met de kracht van Legba

Glass bottle, wooden figure, locks, calabash/Flacon de verre, figurines en bois, cadenas, calebasses, 40 × 20 cm

y los medicamentos aplicados externamente hacen el resto.

En algunas botellas se adhieren partes de animales, en otras raíces y mezclas vegetales y a veces también huesos humanos o pequeños bocios.

Estos ingredientes aparentemente elegidos de forma arbitraria son componentes de recetas en parte centenarias, que el curandero tradicional tomó de sus antepasados durante un largo entrenamiento.

os medicamentos aplicados externamente fazem o resto.

Em algumas garrafas são anexadas partes de animais, em outras raízes e misturas vegetais e às vezes são também ossos humanos ou pequenos bocios.

Estes ingredientes aparentemente arbitrariamente escolhidos são componentes de receitas parcialmente centenárias, que o homem da medicina tradicional assumiu de seus antepassados durante um longo treinamento.

ook een andere inhoud worden gebruikt, en de aan de buitenkant aangebrachte geneesmiddelen doen de rest.

Op sommige flessen zitten dierlijke onderdelen vast, op andere wortels en plantaardige mengsels en soms zitten er ook menselijke botten of kleine bocio's op.

Deze schijnbaar willekeurig gekozen ingrediënten zijn bestanddelen van deels eeuwenoude recepten, die de traditionele medicijnman tijdens een lange opleiding van zijn voorouders heeft overgenomen.

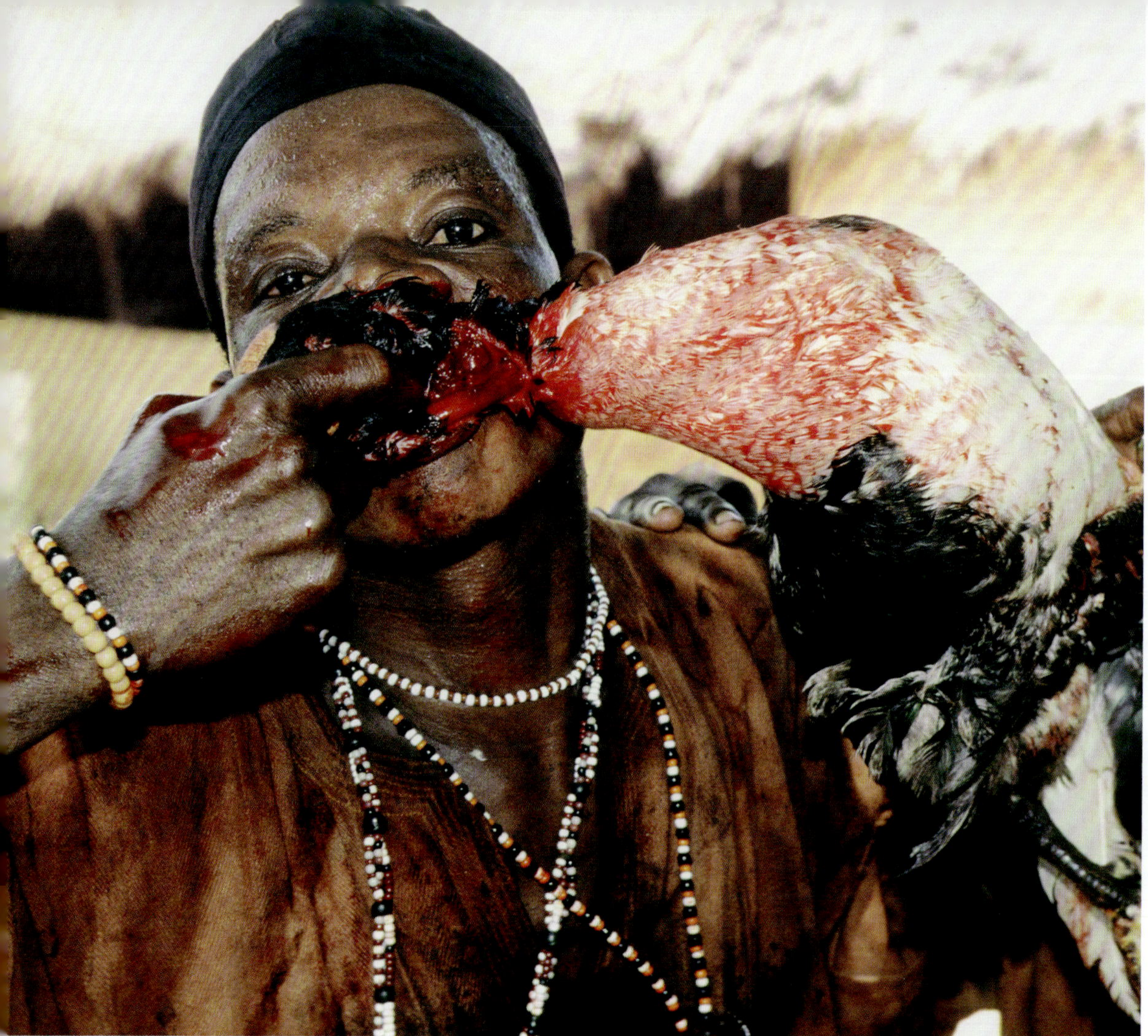

Nana Tongo, the god from the north

Nana Tongo is a god whose responsibilities have varied greatly over time. In the 1920s his popularity had penetrated from the Tong region on the border between Ghana and Burkina Faso to the south coast.

In the north, the god known as "Ton-nab" (Chief of Tongo) had mostly been sacrificed to for good harvests and sufficient rainfall, whereas in the areas of his later distribution Ton-nab's qualities were highly valued in the persecution of witches. In the Volta region a shrine was therefore erected by the priest Charles Adowo around 1995.

Nana Tongo, le dieu venu du nord

Nana Tongo est un dieu dont les domaines de compétences ont énormément varié au fil du temps. Dans les années 1920, sa popularité s'est étendue depuis la région de l'ethnie Tong, située à la frontière entre le Ghana et le Burkina Faso, jusqu'à la côte sud.

Dans le nord, ce dieu, connu sous le nom de Ton-nab (chef de Tongo), était surtout sollicité pour donner des récoltes abondantes et une pluie suffisante, alors que dans les régions où il s'est diffusé ultérieurement, ses qualités dans la lutte contre les sorciers étaient particulièrement

Nana Tongo, der Gott aus dem Norden

Nana Tongo ist ein Gott, dessen Zuständigkeitsbereiche im Laufe der Zeit stark variierten. In den Zwanzigerjahren des 20. Jahrhunderts war seine Popularität von der Tong-Region im Grenzbereich zwischen Ghana und Burkina Faso bis an die Südküste gedrungen.

Im Norden hatte man den als „Ton-nab" (Chief von Tongo) bekannten Gott vor allem für gute Ernten und ausreichende Regenfälle beopfert, wohingegen in den Gebieten seiner späteren Verbreitung Ton-nabs Qualitäten bei

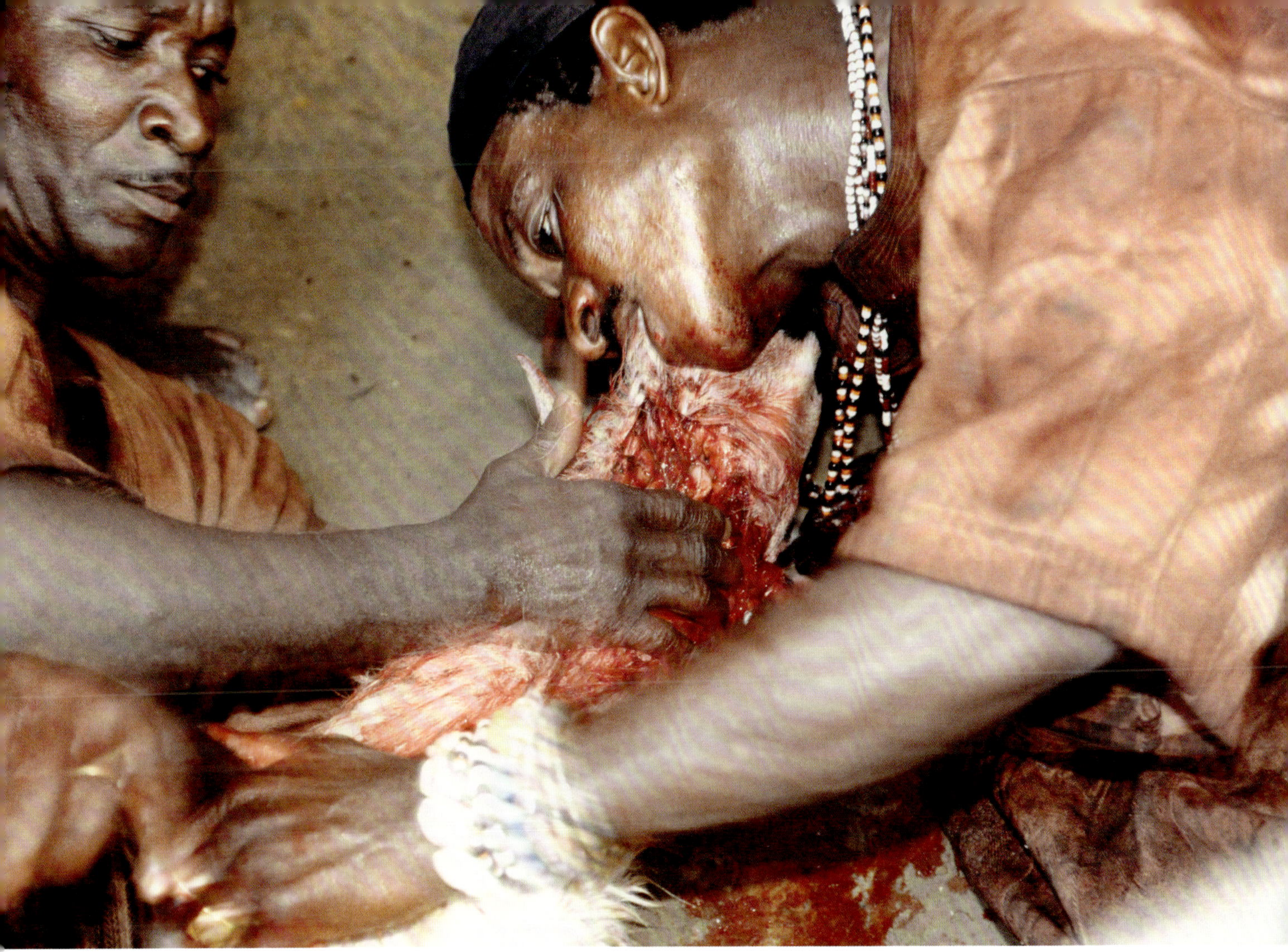

Nana Tongo, el Dios del Norte

Nana Tongo es un dios cuyas responsabilidades han variado mucho a lo largo del tiempo. En los años veinte del siglo XX su popularidad había penetrado desde la región de Tong, en la frontera entre Ghana y Burkina Faso, hasta la costa sur.

En el norte, el dios conocido como "Ton-nab" (Jefe de Tongo) se el ofrecían sacrificios sobre todo por buenas cosechas y abundantes lluvias, mientras que en las zonas de su posterior expansion, las cualidades de Ton-nab eran muy valoradas en la persecución de brujas. En la región del

Nana Tongo, o deus do norte

Nana Tongo é um deus cujas responsabilidades têm variado muito ao longo do tempo. Nos anos vinte do século XX, a sua popularidade tinha penetrado desde a região de Tong, na fronteira entre o Gana e o Burkina Faso, até à costa sul.

No norte, o deus conhecido como "Ton-nab" (Chefe do Tongo) tinha sido sacrificado acima de tudo por boas colheitas e chuva suficiente, enquanto que nas áreas de sua distribuição posterior as qualidades de Ton-nab eram altamente valorizadas

Nana Tongo, de god uit het noorden

Nana Tongo is een god wiens bevoegdheden in de loop der tijd sterk uiteenliepen. In de jaren twintig van de 20e eeuw was zijn populariteit doorgedrongen van de Tong-regio op de grens tussen Ghana en Burkina Faso tot aan de zuidkust.

In het noorden offerde men de als 'Ton-nab' (hoofdman van Tongo) bekendstaande god vooral voor goede oogsten en voldoende regenval, terwijl in de gebieden waar Ton-nab later verspreid raakte zijn eigenschappen om heksen te vervolgen zeer gewaardeerd werden. In de regio Volta

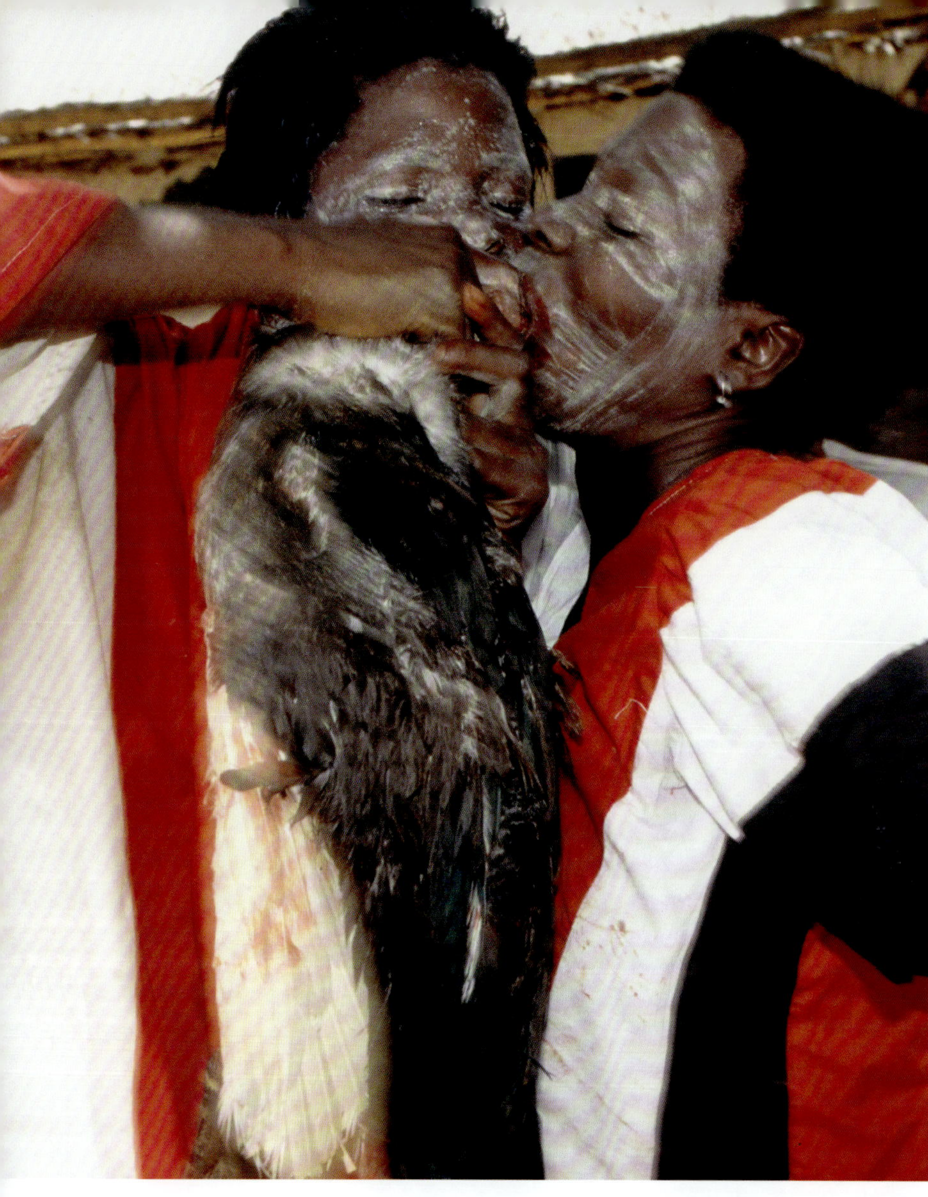

With the ram's carcass between his teeth. After the cult objects of Nana Tongo have been soaked with the blood of the sacrificed ram, the priest and his helpers, all in a deep trance, bite into the dead wanimal.

Avec la carcasse du bélier entre les dents. Après que les objets du culte de Nana Tongo ont été arrosés du sang du bélier sacrifié, le prêtre et ses assistants mordent eux-mêmes dans l'animal mort au cours d'une transe intense.

Mit dem Kadaver des Widders zwischen den Zähnen. Nachdem die Kultobjekte Nana Tongos mit dem Blut des geopferten Widders getränkt wurden, beißen der Priester und seine Helfer, alle in schwerer Trance, selbst in das tote Tier.

Con el cuerpo del carnero entre los dientes. Después de que los objetos de culto de Nana Tongo han sido empapados con la sangre del carnero sacrificado, el sacerdote y sus ayudantes, todos en un fuerte trance, muerden incluso al animal muerto.

Com a carcaça do carneiro entre os dentes. Depois que os objetos de culto de Nana Tongo foram embebidos com o sangue do carneiro sacrificado, o sacerdote e seus ajudantes, todos em um transe pesado, mordem até o animal morto.

Met het kadaver van de ram tussen zijn tanden. Nadat de cultusobjecten van Nana Tongo zijn doordrenkt met het bloed van de geofferde ram, bijten de priester en zijn helpers, allemaal in een zware trance, zelf in het dode dier.

Adowo had completed his three years of apprenticeship as a medicine man in the north in the Zuarungu area and had been strongly impressed by the power of Nana Tongo during this time.

Animal sacrifices and possessive trances are the order of the day at the feasts in honor of this god.

appréciées. Dans la région de la Volta, un reliquaire lui a été érigé vers 1995 par le prêtre Charles Adowo. Adowo venait de terminer trois années de formation de guérisseur dans le nord, dans la région de Zuarungu, et était à l'époque fortement impressionné par le pouvoir de Nana Tongo.

Au cours des fêtes organisées en l'honneur du dieu, sacrifices d'animaux et transes de possession sont à l'ordre du jour.

der Hexenverfolgung hoch geschätzt wurden. In der Voltaregion wurde ihm deshalb um 1995 von dem Priester Charles Adowo ein Schrein errichtet. Adowo hatte seine drei Lehrjahre zum Medizinmann im Norden in der Gegend um Zuarungu absolviert und war in dieser Zeit von der Macht Nana Tongos stark beeindruckt worden.

Bei den Festen zu Ehren des Gottes sind Tieropfer und Besessenheitstrancen an der Tagesordnung.

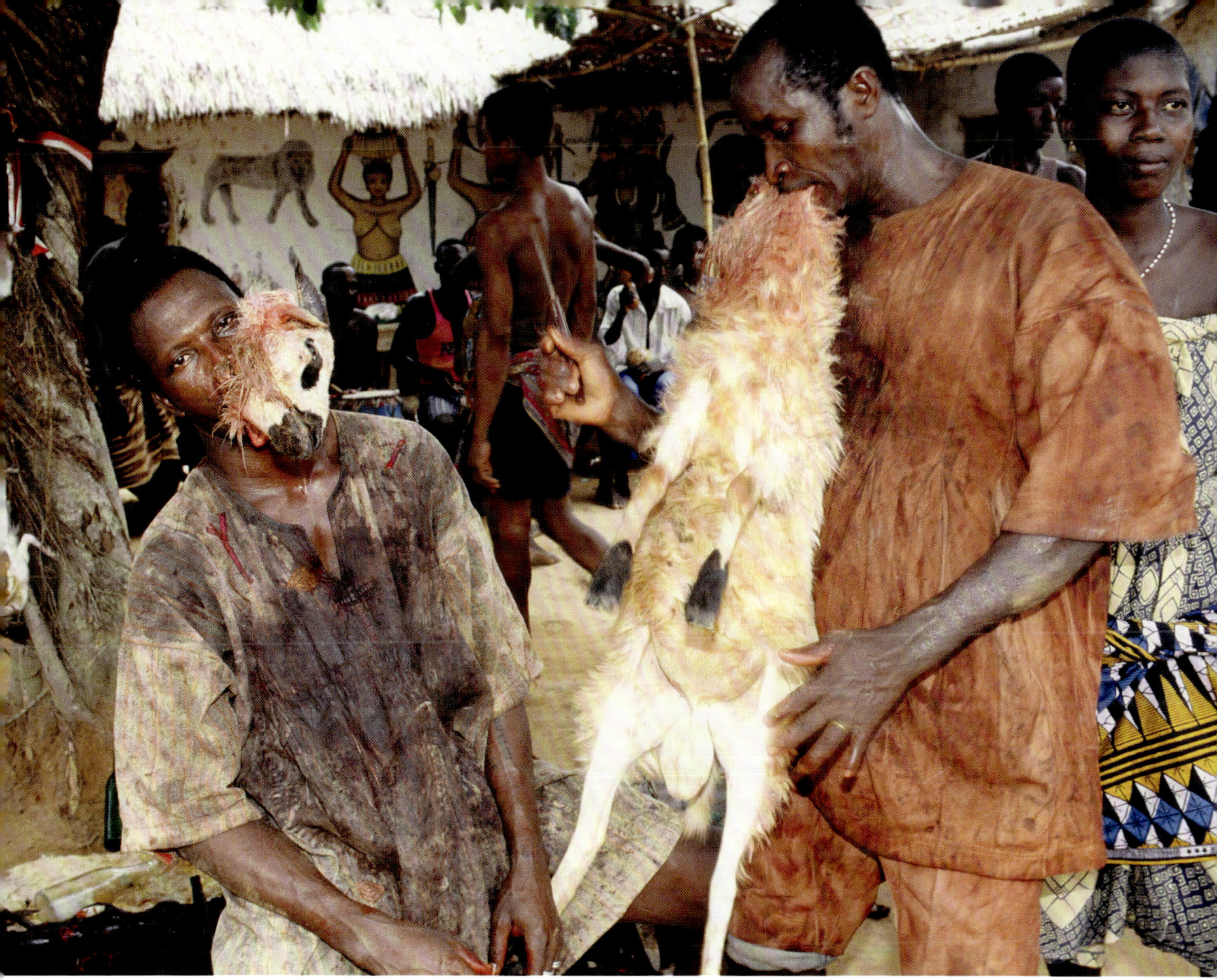

Volta, el sacerdote Charles Adowo erigió un santuario alrededor de 1995. Adowo había completado sus tres años como curandero en el norte, en la zona de Zuarungu, y había quedado muy impresionado por el poder de Nana Tongo durante ese tiempo.

Los sacrificios de animales y los trances en los que son poseídos están a la orden del día en las celebraciones en honor al dios.

na perseguição de bruxas. Na região do Volta, um santuário foi erigido por volta de 1995 pelo padre Charles Adowo. Adowo completou seus três anos como curandeiro no norte da área ao redor de Zuarungu e ficou fortemente impressionado com o poder de Nana Tongo durante esse tempo.

Os sacrifícios animais e os transe de possessão são a ordem do dia das celebrações em honra do deus.

richtte de priester Charles Adowo om die reden rond 1995 een heiligdom voor hem op. Adowo had zijn driejarige opleiding als medicijnman in het noorden in de omgeving van Zuarungu voltooid en was in deze tijd sterk onder de indruk geraakt van de kracht van Nana Tongo.

Dierenoffers en bezeten trances zijn aan de orde van de dag bij de feesten ter ere van de god.

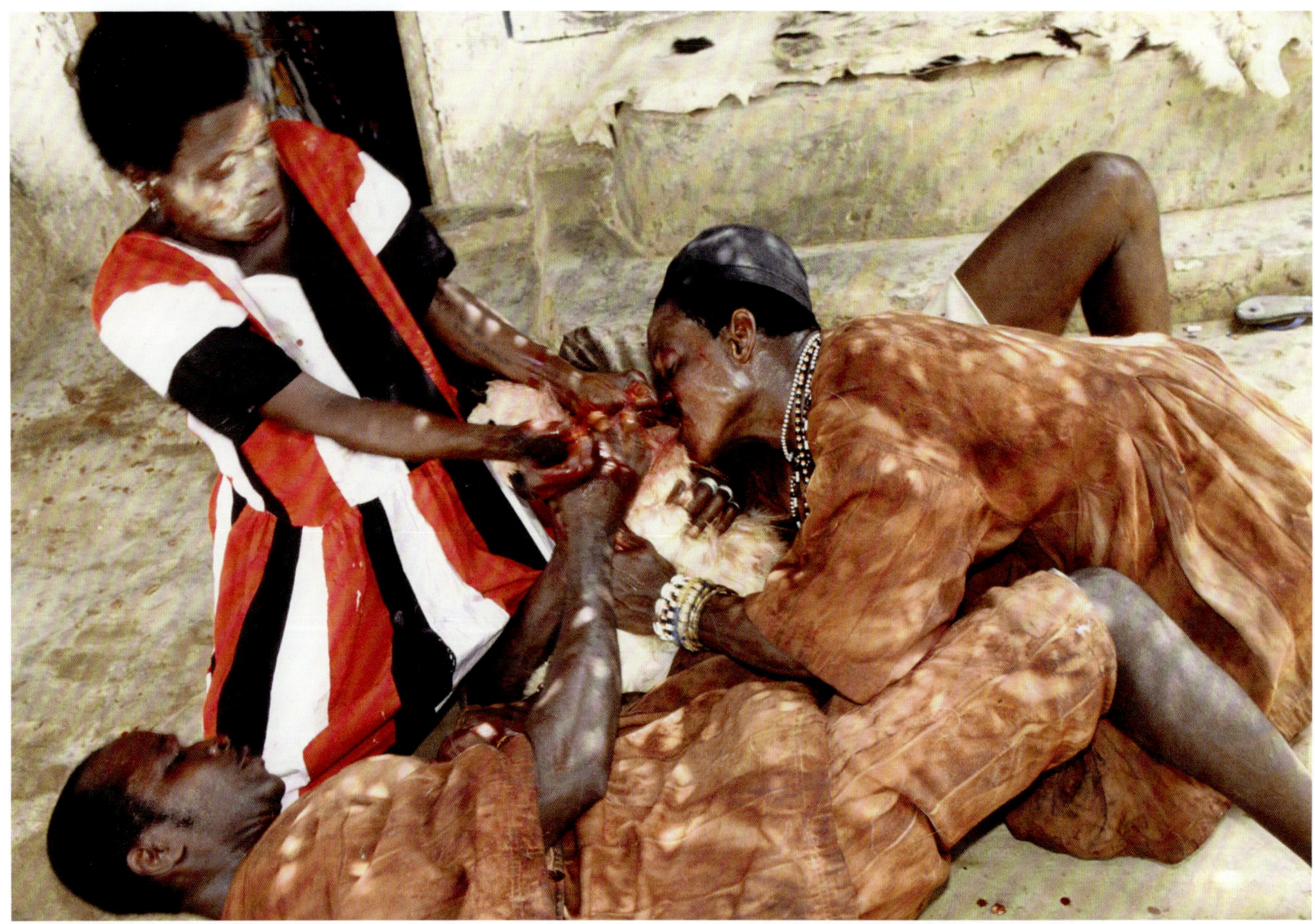

Blood frenzy in a trance. Between the priest and his helpers there is a real battle for the sacrificial animal, in which everyone tries to obtain as much of the blood as possible.

Frénésie sanguinaire en transe. Un combat dans les règles s'engage entre le prêtre et ses assistants autour de l'animal sacrifié, chacun essayant de boire le maximum de sang, par tous les moyens possibles.

Blutrausch in Trance. Zwischen dem Priester und seinen Helfern entbrennt ein regelrechter Kampf um das Opfertier, bei dem jeder soviel von dem Blut zu erlangen sucht wie nur irgend möglich.

Frenesí sangriento en transe. Entre el sacerdote y sus ayudantes hay una verdadera batalla por el animal del sacrificio, en la que todos tratan de obtener la mayor cantidad de sangre posible.

Frenesi de sangue em transe. Entre o sacerdote e seus ajudantes há uma batalha real pelo animal de sacrifício, na qual todos tentam obter o máximo de sangue possível.

Bloedige roes in trance. Tussen de priester en zijn helpers is een echte strijd om het offerdier ontbrand, waarbij iedereen probeert zoveel mogelijk van het bloed te krijgen.

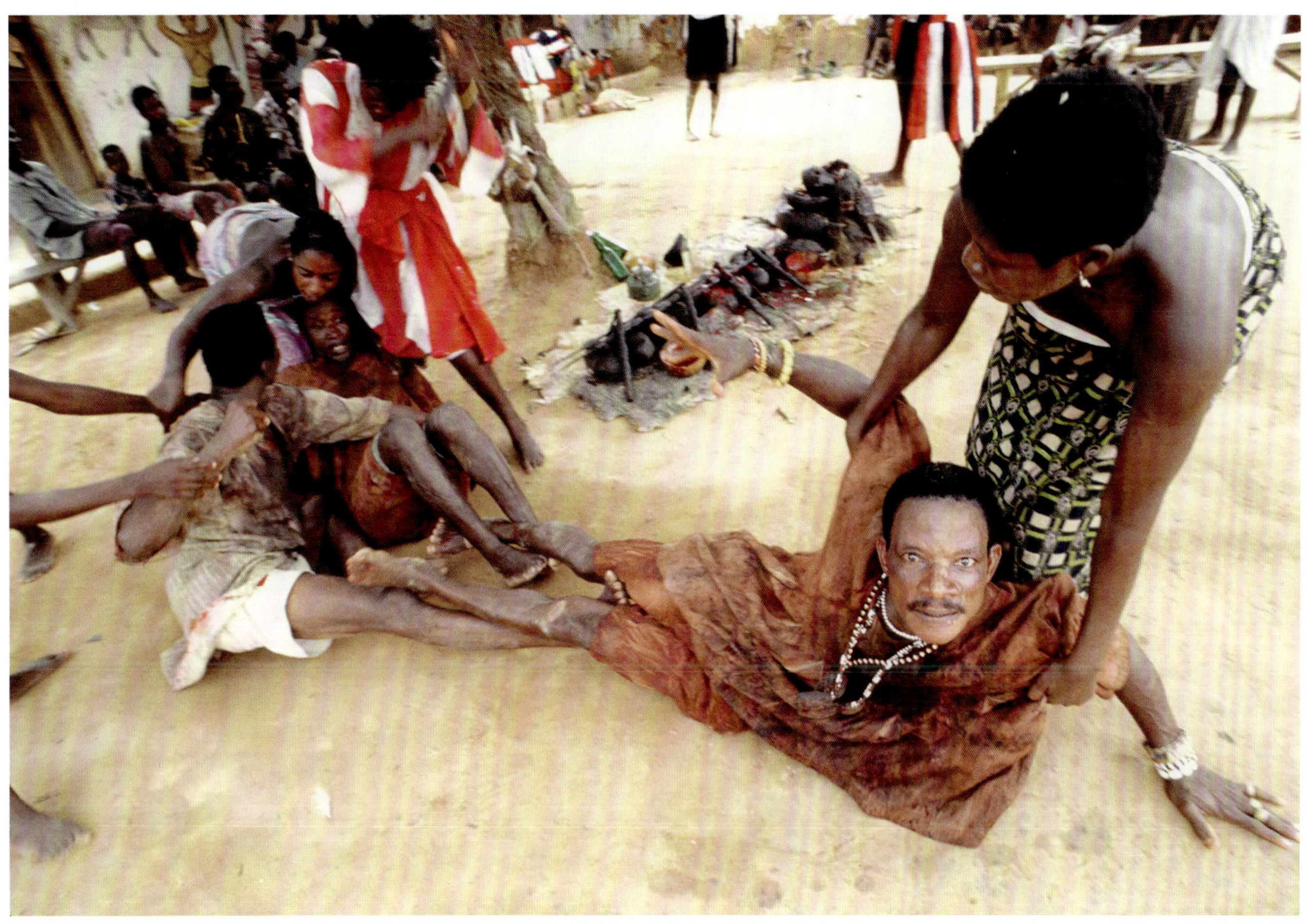

An assistant supports the man marked by the trance

Un assistant soutient l'homme en transe

Ein Assistent stützt den von der Trance Gezeichneten

Un asistente apoya al hombre en trance

Um assistente apoia o homem marcado pelo transe

Een assistent ondersteunt een door trance getekende man

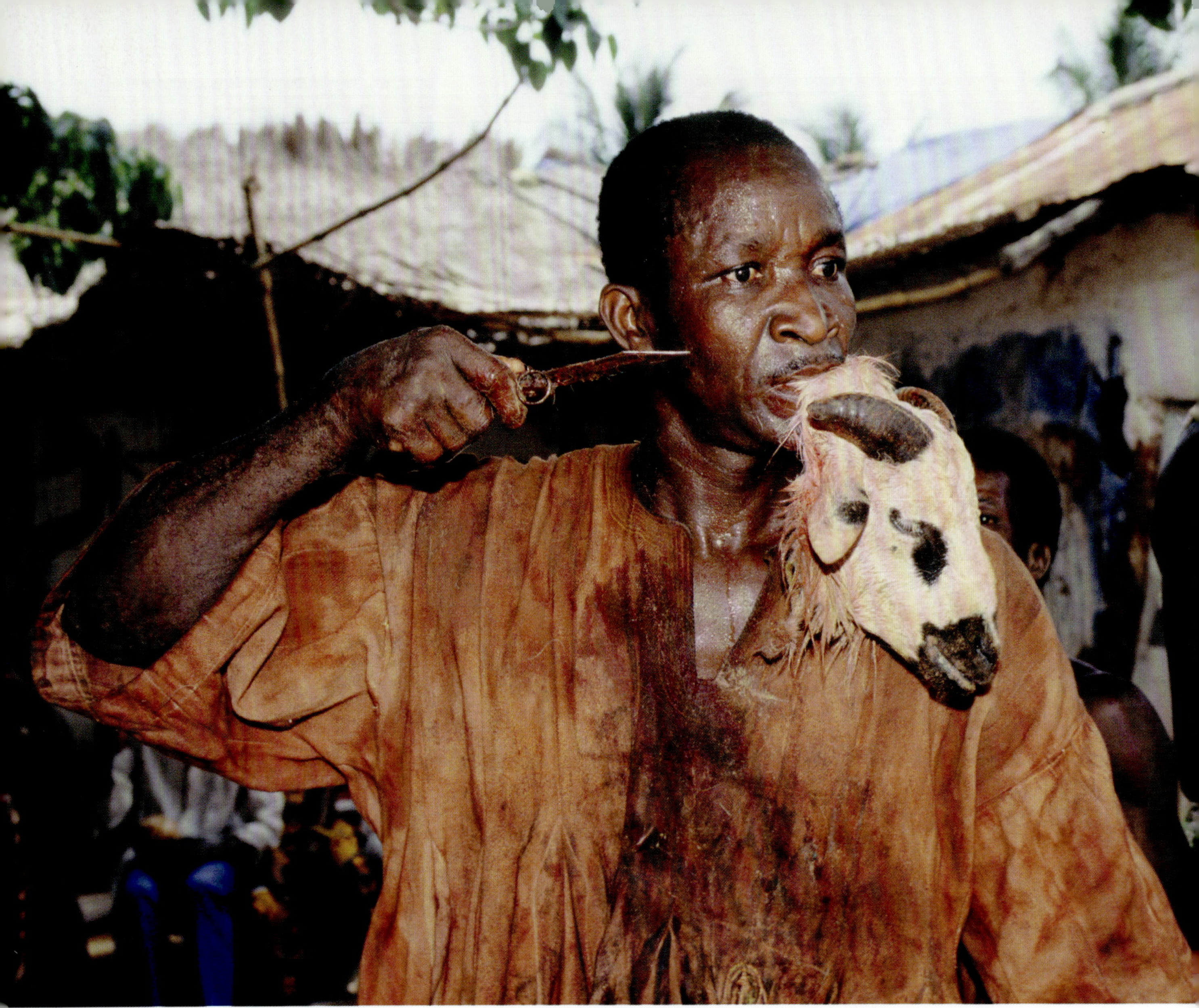

The wild spectacle is not in vain. Witchcraft and harmful spells of all kinds are the declared enemy of the wild Vodun imported from the warlike north. Therefore violence is needed to put a stop to it.

Ce spectacle sauvage n'est pas en vain. Sorcellerie et magie noire de tout ordre sont les ennemis déclarés du vodun tumultueux importé des régions guerrières du nord. Ce combat nécessite des mesures radicales.

Das wilde Spektakel ist nicht umsonst. Hexerei und Schadenzauber aller Art sind der erklärte Feind der aus dem kriegerischen Norden importierten, wilden Vodun. Entsprechend martialisch gilt es, dem Einhalt zu gebieten.

El espectáculo salvaje no es en vano. La brujería y los hechizos malignos de todo tipo son el enemigo declarado del vudú salvaje importado del guerrero norte. Por lo tanto, es necesario poner fin a esto.

O espetáculo selvagem não é em vão. Bruxaria e feitiços de dano de todos os tipos são o inimigo declarado do Vodun selvagem importado do norte guerreiro. Por conseguinte, é necessário pôr fim a isto.

Het woeste spektakel is niet tevergeefs. Hekserij en alle soorten boze magie zijn tot vijand verklaard door de woeste, uit het oorlogszuchtige noorden geïmporteerde god. Daarom is het noodzakelijk hier een eind aan te maken.

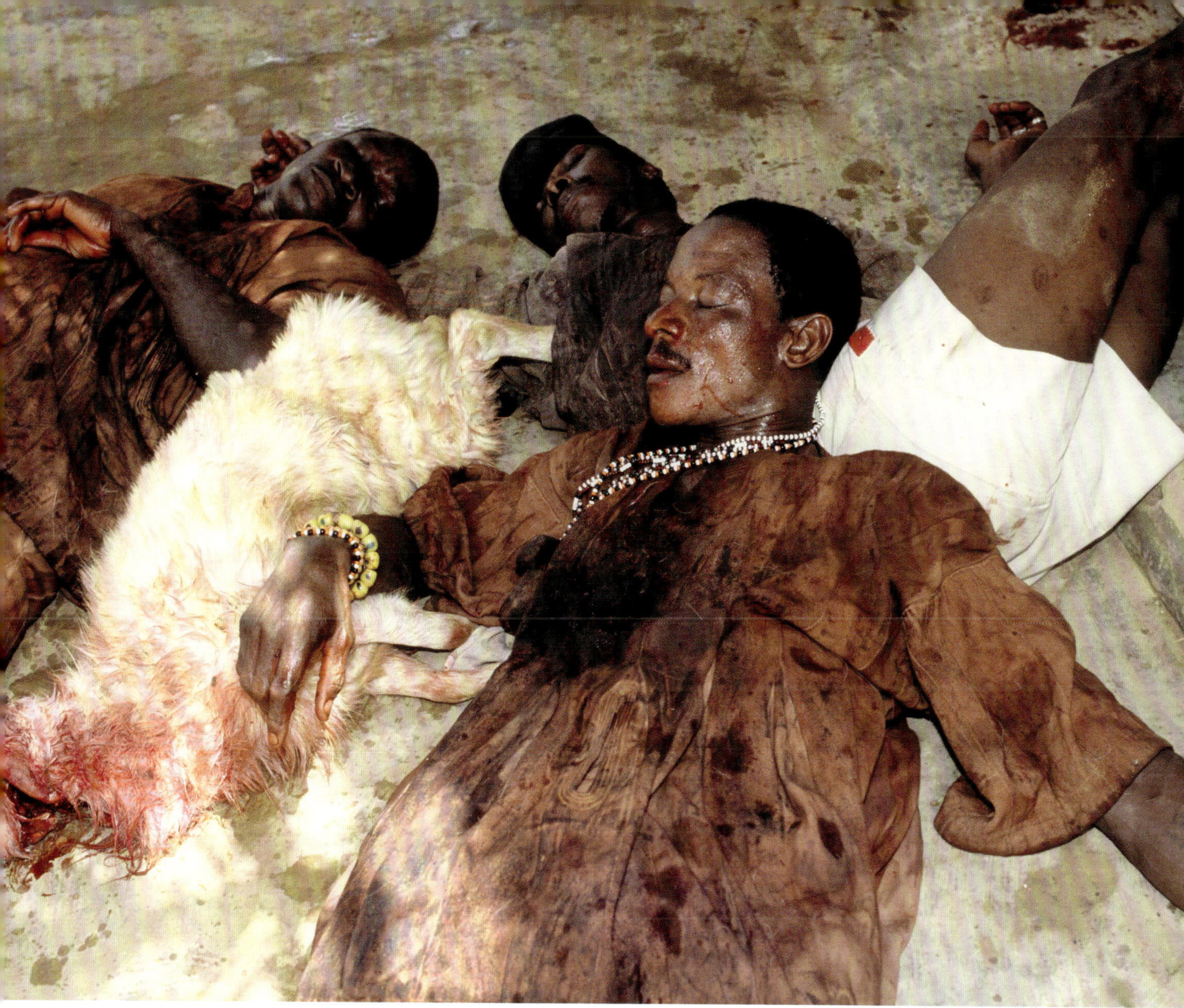

At the end of the ceremony

À la fin de la cérémonie

Am Ende der Zeremonie

Al final de la ceremonia

No final da cerimónia

Aan het eind van de ceremonie

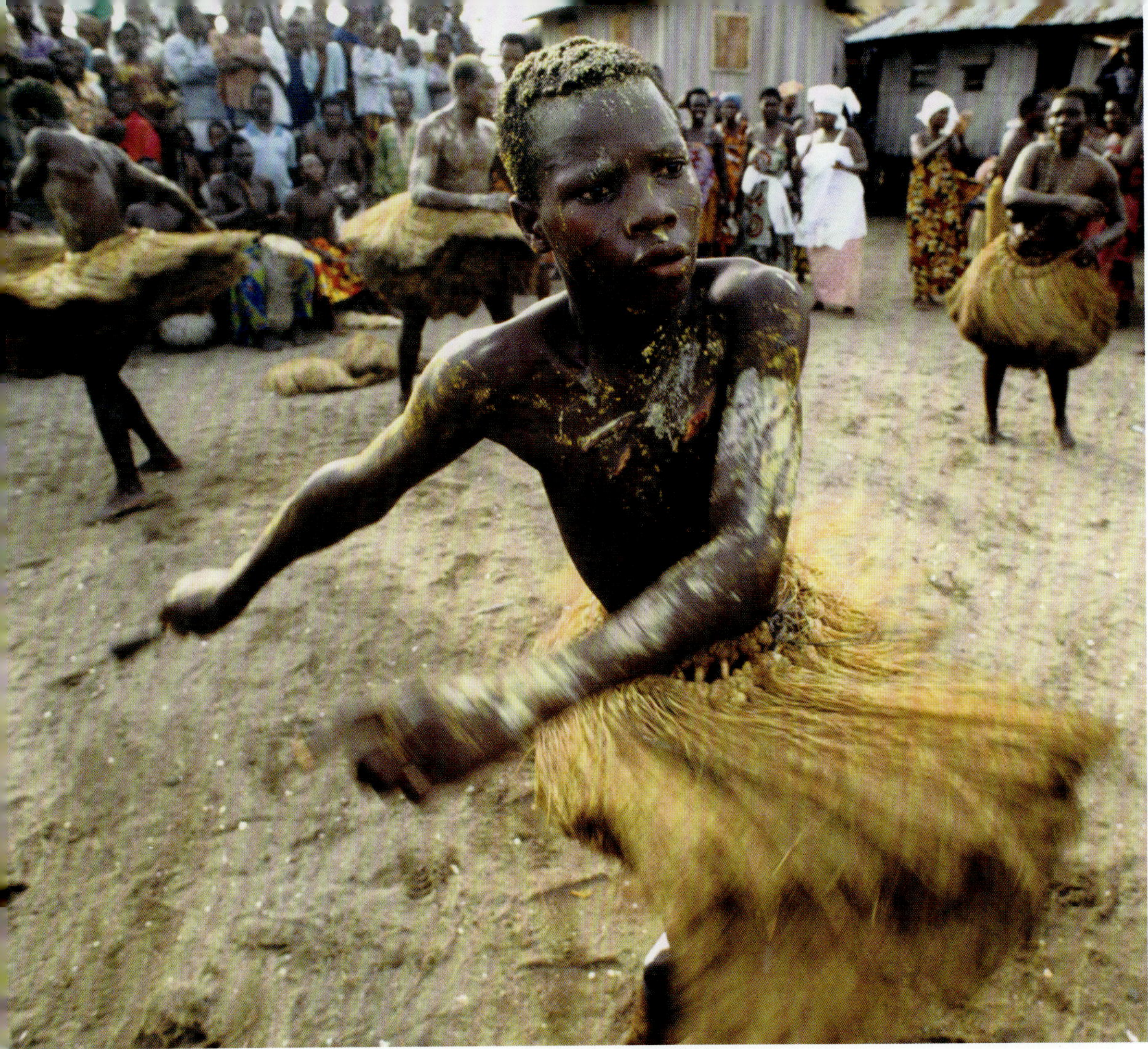

Kokou ceremony on
the village square

Cérémonie dédiée à
Kokou sur la place du
village

Kokou-Zeremonie auf
dem Dorfplatz

Ceremonia Kokou en
la plaza del pueblo

Cerimônia Kokou na
praça da aldeia

Kokou-ceremonie op
het dorpsplein

Martial acts
demonstrate Kokous
intrepidity

Les arts martiaux
illustrent l'intrépidité
de Kokou

Martialische
Handlungen
demonstrieren
Kokous
Unerschrockenheit

Los actos marciales
demuestran la
intrepidez de Kokou

Os actos marciais
demonstram a
intrepidez de Kokous

Krijgshandelingen
demonstreren Kokou's
onverschrokkenheid

Kokou—unleashed against the witches

The warlike god Kokou, who is mainly worshipped in parts of Ghana, Togo and Benin, is master of secret medicines to ward off witches and harmful spells. He belongs to the pantheon of the younger Goro Vodun cults (*Goro* means "cola nut" among the Hausa people).

These gods, mostly imported from the Islamic-influenced north, are characterized by their ferocity, which is expressed by the followers in extreme possession trances. Also ritual performances, in which their

Kokou, déchaîné contre les sorciers

Le dieu guerrier Kokou, tout particulièrement vénéré dans certaines régions du Ghana, du Togo et du Bénin, est le maître des médecines secrètes contre les sorciers et la magie noire. Il fait partie du panthéon des cultes goro-vodun récents (*goro* signifiant « noix de cola » en langue hausa).

Ces dieux importés des régions nord fortement imprégnées d'islam se distinguent par leur fougue, qui s'exprime chez leurs adeptes à travers des transes de possession

Kokou – entfesselt gegen die Hexen

Der kriegerische Gott Kokou, der vornehmlich in Teilen Ghanas, Togos und Benins verehrt wird, ist Herr über geheime Medizinen zur Abwehr von Hexen und Schadenzauber. Er gehört zum Pantheon der jüngeren Goro-Vodunkulte (*Goro* bedeutet „Kolanuss" beim Volk der Hausa).

Diese meist aus dem islamisch geprägten Norden importierten Götter zeichnen sich durch ihre Wildheit aus, die bei den Anhängern in extremen Besessenheitstrancen zum Ausdruck

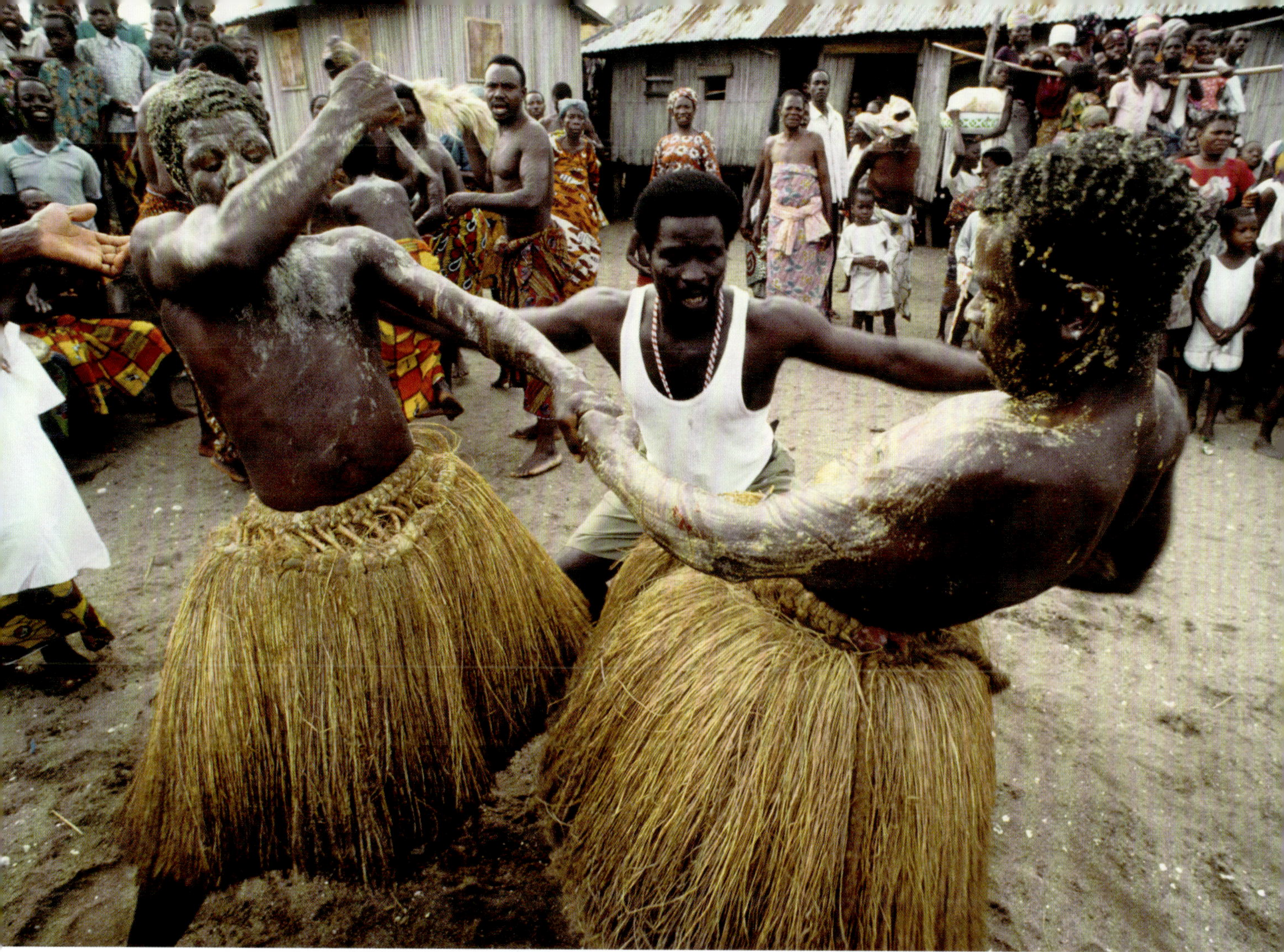

Kokou– desatado contra las brujas

El dios guerrero Kokou, que se adora
principalmente en algunas partes de Ghana,
Togo y Benin, es el maestro de las medicinas
secretas para protegerse de las brujas y de
los hechizosmalignos. Pertenece al panteón
de los cultos vudú más jóvenes de Goro
(Goro significa "nuez de cola" entre el
pueblo Hausa).

Estos dioses, en su mayoría importados
del norte islámico, se caracterizan por
su ferocidad, que es expresada por los
seguidores en extremos trancesen los

Kokou – Libertado contra as bruxas

O deus guerreiro Kokou, que é adorado
principalmente em algumas partes de Gana,
Togo e Benin, é mestre em remédios secretos
para afastar bruxas e feitiços de dano. Ele
pertence ao panteão dos vodunkults Goro
mais jovens (Goro significa "Kolanuss" entre
o povo Hausa).

Estes deuses, na sua maioria importados
do norte islâmico, são caracterizados
pela sua ferocidade, que é expressa pelos
seguidores em transe de extrema obsessão.
Também as exposições rituais, nas quais

Kokou – ontketend tegen de heksen

De oorlogszuchtige god Kokou, die vooral
in delen van Ghana, Togo en Benin wordt
aanbeden, is meester van de geheime
medicijnen om heksen en schadelijke
tovenarij af te weren. Hij behoort tot
het pantheon van de nieuwere goro-
voduncultus (*goro* betekent 'kolanoot' bij het
Hausa-volk).

Deze meestal uit het islamitische
noorden geïmporteerde goden worden
gekenmerkt door hun woestheid, die tot
uitdrukking komt in extreem bezeten

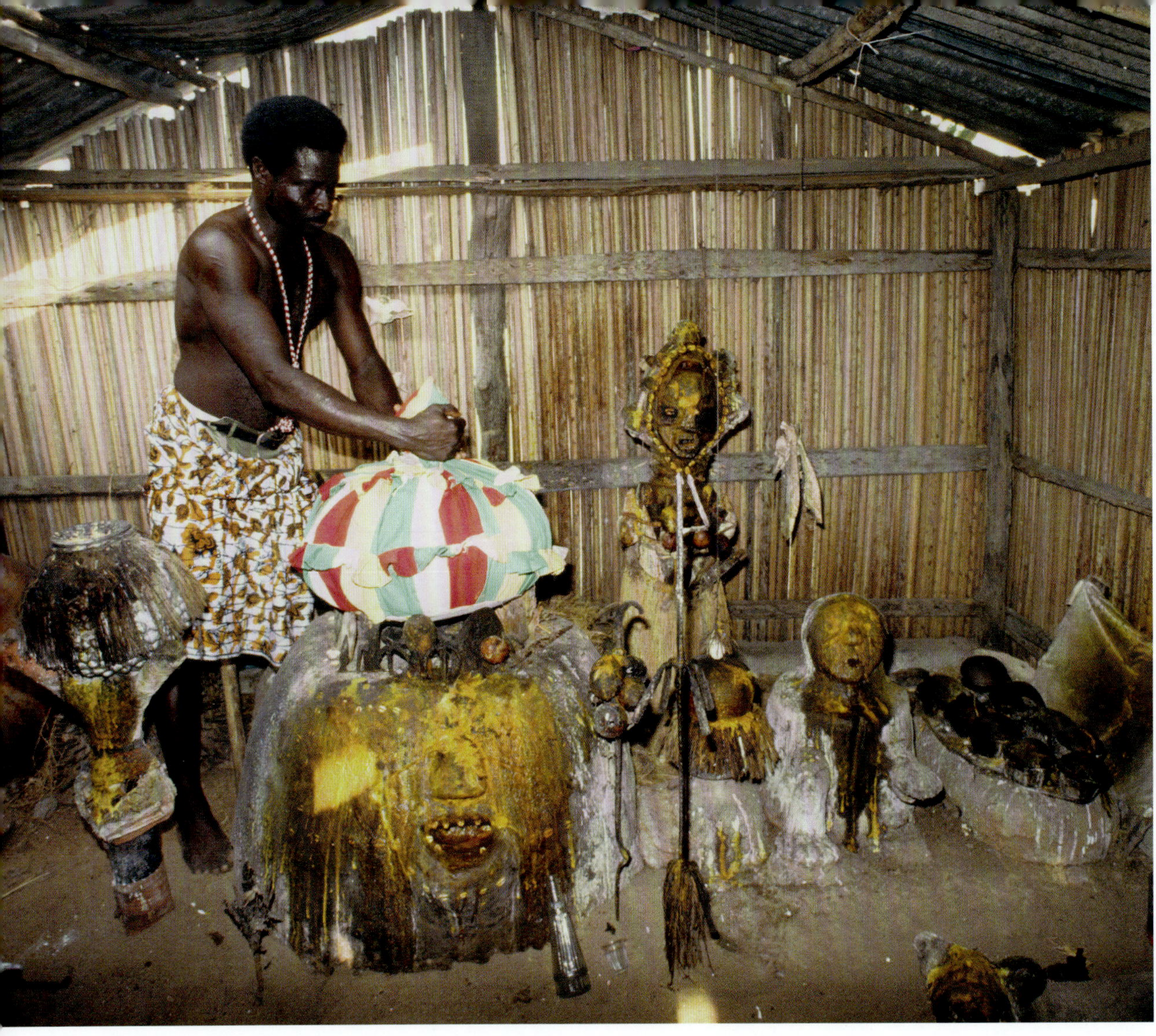

own immunity against witchcraft is demonstrated by autoaggressive actions, are not uncommon.

With white faces and skirts made of raffia, the fibres of a palm tree, the Kokou followers dance to drum rhythms that change abruptly and vary greatly in speed. A trance-inducing effect is attributed to the characteristics of the accompanying music.

extrêmes. De même, il n'est pas rare d'assister à des exhibitions rituelles au cours desquelles les adeptes démontrent leur immunité contre la sorcellerie au moyen de comportements auto-agressifs.

Avec leur visage peint en blanc, les adeptes de Kokou sont vêtus d'une robe en raffia, fibres issues d'une espèce de palmier. Ils dansent au son des tambours, dont le rythme s'interrompt brusquement et le tempo marque d'importantes variations. On prête à ces particularités de la musique un effet stimulant sur la transe.

kommt. Auch rituelle Zurschaustellungen, bei denen die eigene Immunität gegen Hexenkräfte durch autoaggressive Handlungen demonstriert wird, sind keine Seltenheit.

Mit weißgefärbten Gesichtern und in Röcken aus Raffia, den Fasern eines Palmengewächses, tanzen die Gläubigen Kokous zu Trommelrhythmen, die sich abrupt ändern und in ihrer Geschwindigkeit stark variieren. Diesen Merkmalen der Begleitmusik schreibt man tranceinduzierende Wirkung zu.

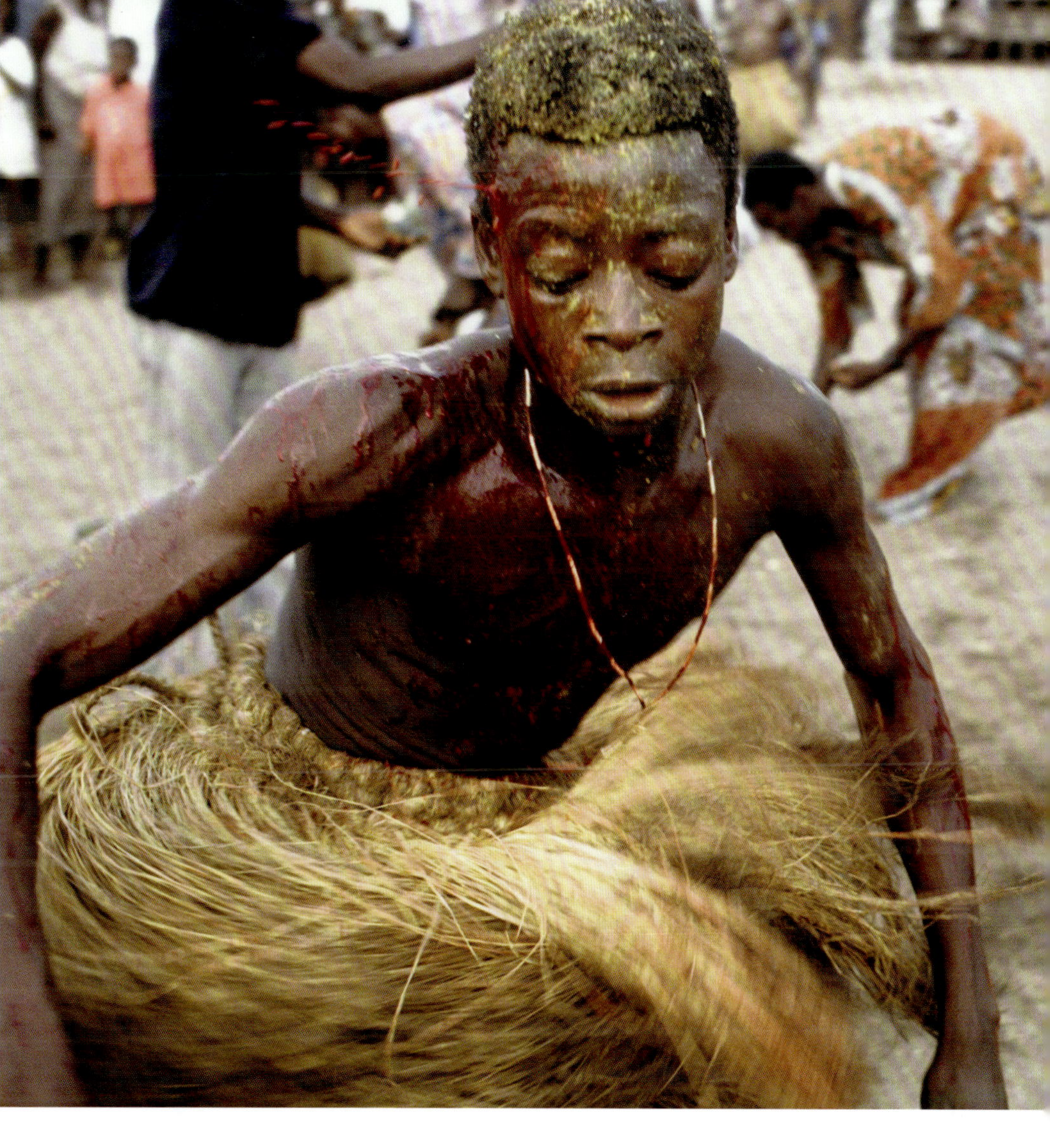

Kokou follower in a trance. He's bleeding from a head wound, but that doesn't matter in the state of trance. They have undreamt-of powers and do not feel any pain, especially with Kokou.

Adepte de Kokou en transe. Du sang s'écoule d'une blessure à la tête, mais cet homme en état de transe n'y prête aucune attention. Les participants jouissent d'une force inattendue et ne ressentent aucune douleur, surtout dans une cérémonie pour Kokou.

Kokous Anhänger in Trance. Er blutet aus einer Kopfwunde, aber das spielt im Zustand der Trance keinerlei Rolle. Die Betreffenden verfügen über ungeahnte Kräfte und verspüren keinerlei Schmerz, vor allem nicht bei Kokou.

Adepto de Kokou en trance. Sangra por una herida en la cabeza, pero eso no importa en el estado de trance. Tienen poderes inimaginables y no sienten dolor, especialmente con Kokou.

Pingente Kokous em transe. Ele sangra de uma ferida na cabeça, mas isso não importa no estado de transe. Eles têm poderes inimagináveis e não sentem dor, especialmente com Kokou.

Aanhangers van Kokou in trance. Hij bloedt uit een hoofdwond, maar dat maakt niet uit in trance. De betrokkenen bezitten ongekende krachten en voelen geen pijn, zeker niet bij Kokou.

que son poseídos. Tampoco son raras las exhibiciones rituales, en las que la propia inmunidad contra los poderes de las brujas se demuestra mediante acciones autoagresivas.

Con rostros blancos y faldas de rafia, fibras de una palmera, los creyentes de Kokou bailan a ritmos de tambor que cambian bruscamente y varían mucho en velocidad. La música de acompañamiento produce un efecto inductor de trance.

a própria imunidade contra os poderes das bruxas é demonstrada por acções autoagressivas, não são raras.

Com rostos brancos e saias feitas de ráfia, as fibras de uma palmeira, os crentes dançam em ritmo de tambor que mudam abruptamente e variam muito em velocidade. Estas características da música que a acompanha são atribuídas com um efeito indutor de transe.

trances bij de aanhangers. Ook rituele uitingen waarmee de eigen immuniteit tegen heksenkrachten wordt gedemonstreerd door handelingen van zelfagressie, zijn geen zeldzaamheid.

Met wit geschilderde gezichten en rokken van raffia, de vezels van een palmplant, dansen de aanhangers van Kokou op trommelritmes die abrupt veranderen en sterk kunnen variëren in snelheid. Aan deze kenmerken van de begeleidingsmuziek wordt een trance-opwekkend effect toegeschreven.

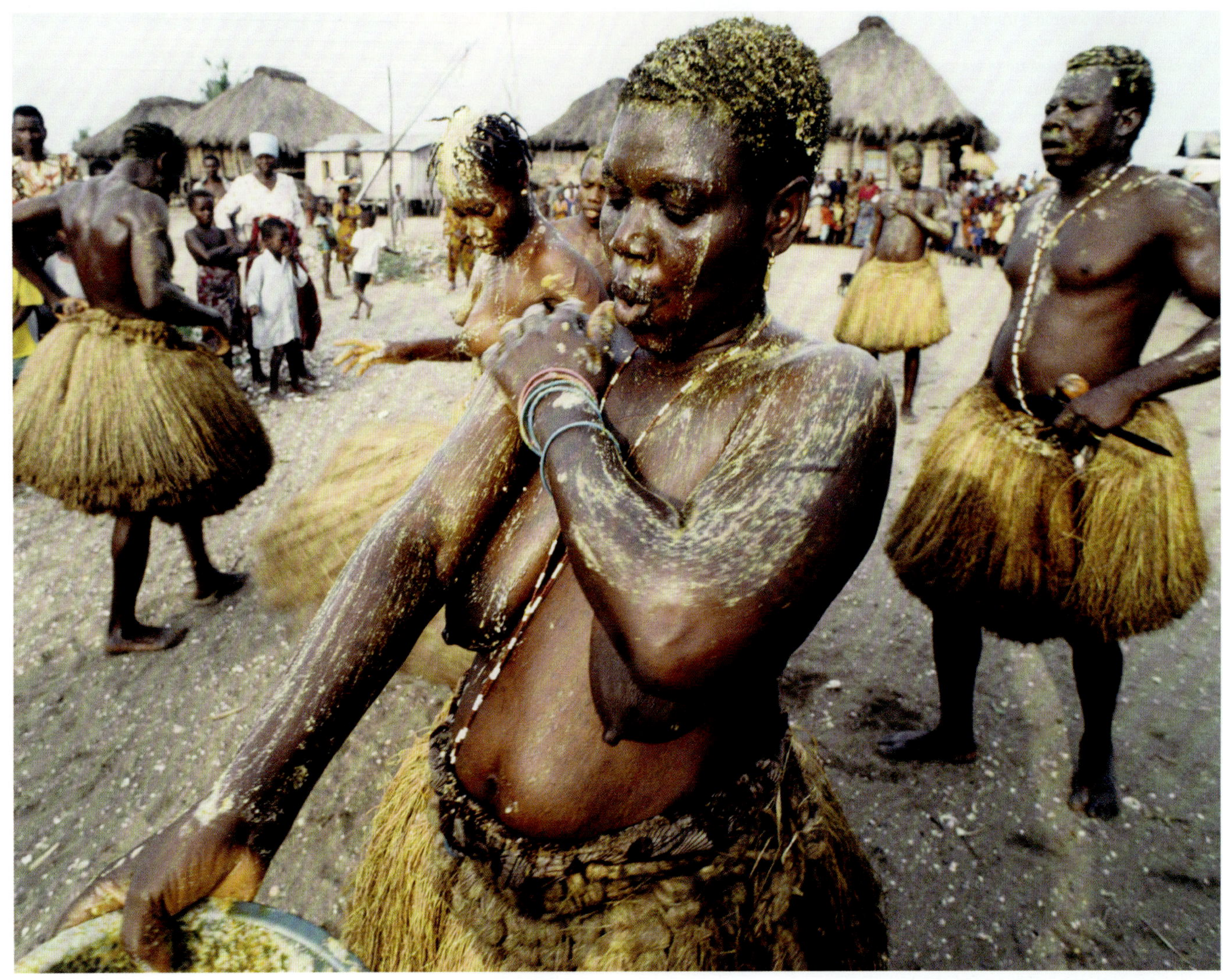

Building up strength. Anointment with Djassi, a paste of palm oil, corn flour and other ingredients, is supposed to strengthen the powers of this Kokou devotee for the upcoming ritual.

Renforcement des énergies. L'onction avec la pâte djassi, constituée d'huile de palme, de farine de maïs et d'autres ingrédients, doit augmenter les forces de cette adepte de Kokou pour le rituel à venir.

Stärkung der Kräfte. Die Salbung mit Djassi, einer Paste aus Palmöl, Maismehl und weiteren Zutaten, soll die Kräfte dieser Kokou-Anhängerin für das bevorstehende Ritual stärken.

Fortalecimiento de las fuerzas. La unción con Djassi, una pasta de aceite de palma, harina de maíz y otros ingredientes, se supone que fortalece los poderes de este devoto Kokou para el próximo ritual.

Forças de reforço. A unção com Djassi, uma pasta de óleo de palma, farinha de milho e outros ingredientes, é suposto fortalecer os poderes deste devoto Kokou para o próximo ritual.

Versterking van de krachten. De zalving met djassi, een pasta van palmolie, maïsmeel en andere ingrediënten, zou de kracht van deze Kokou-aanhangster voor het komende ritueel moeten vergroten.

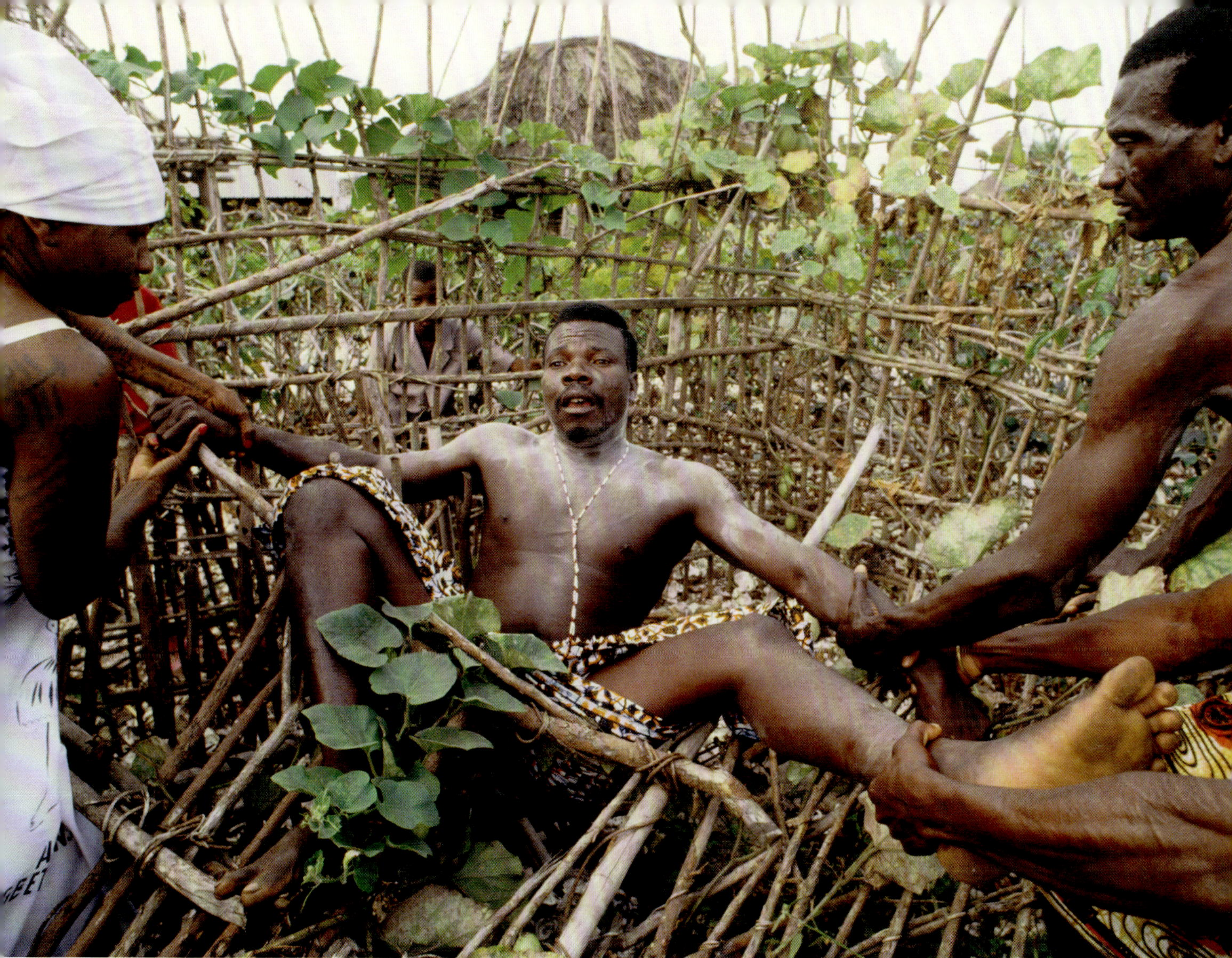

Help after falling into a trance

De l'aide après une chute en transe

Hilfe nach Sturz in Trance

Ayuda después de caer en trance

Ajuda depois de cair em transe

Hulp na een val in trance

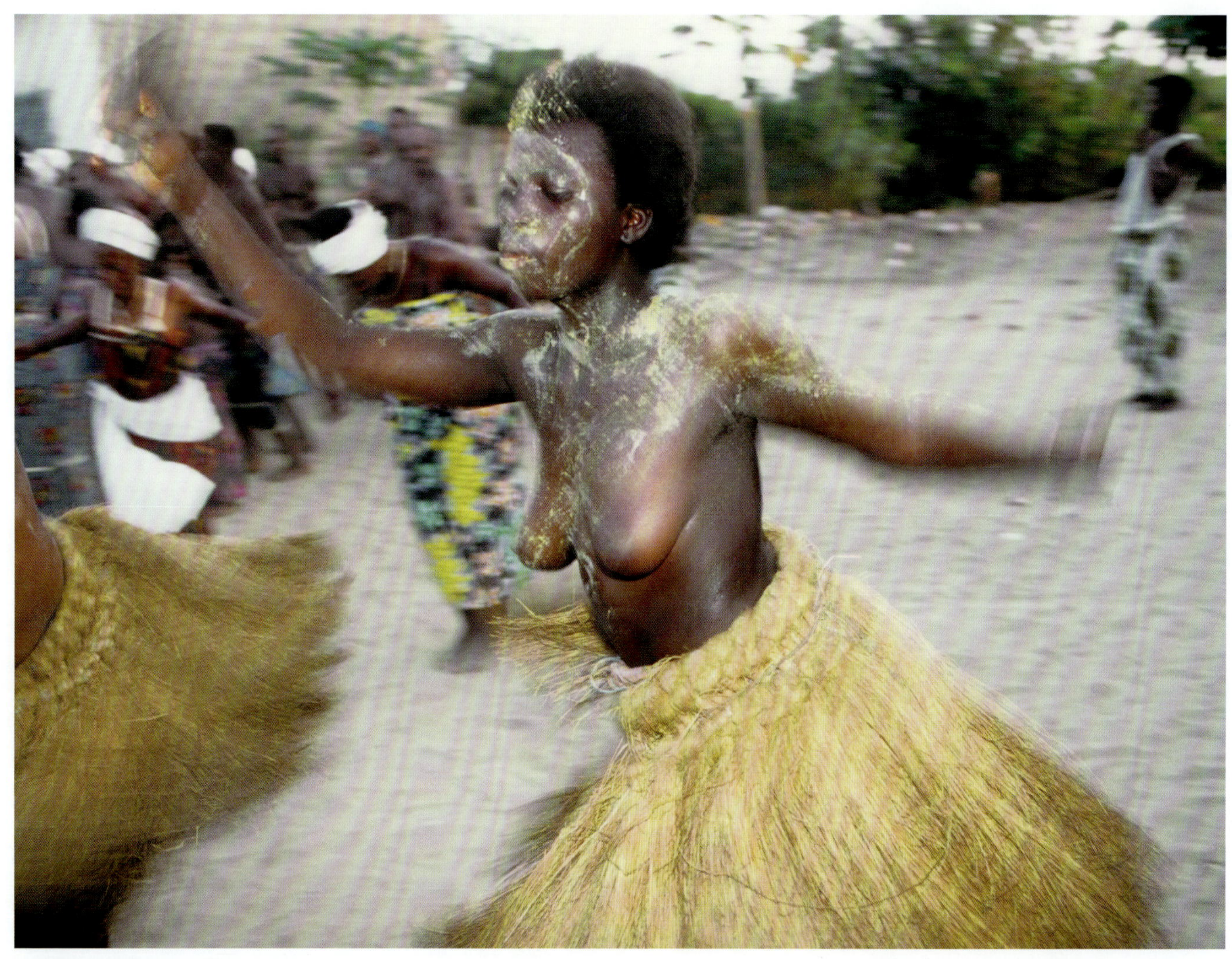

Kokou ceremony at Cotonou, Benin

Cérémonie dédiée à Kokou à Cotonou, Bénin

Kokou-Zeremonie bei Cotonou, Benin

Ceremonia Kokou en Cotonou, Benin

Cerimónia de Kokou em Cotonou, Benim

Kokou-ceremonie in Cotonou, Benin

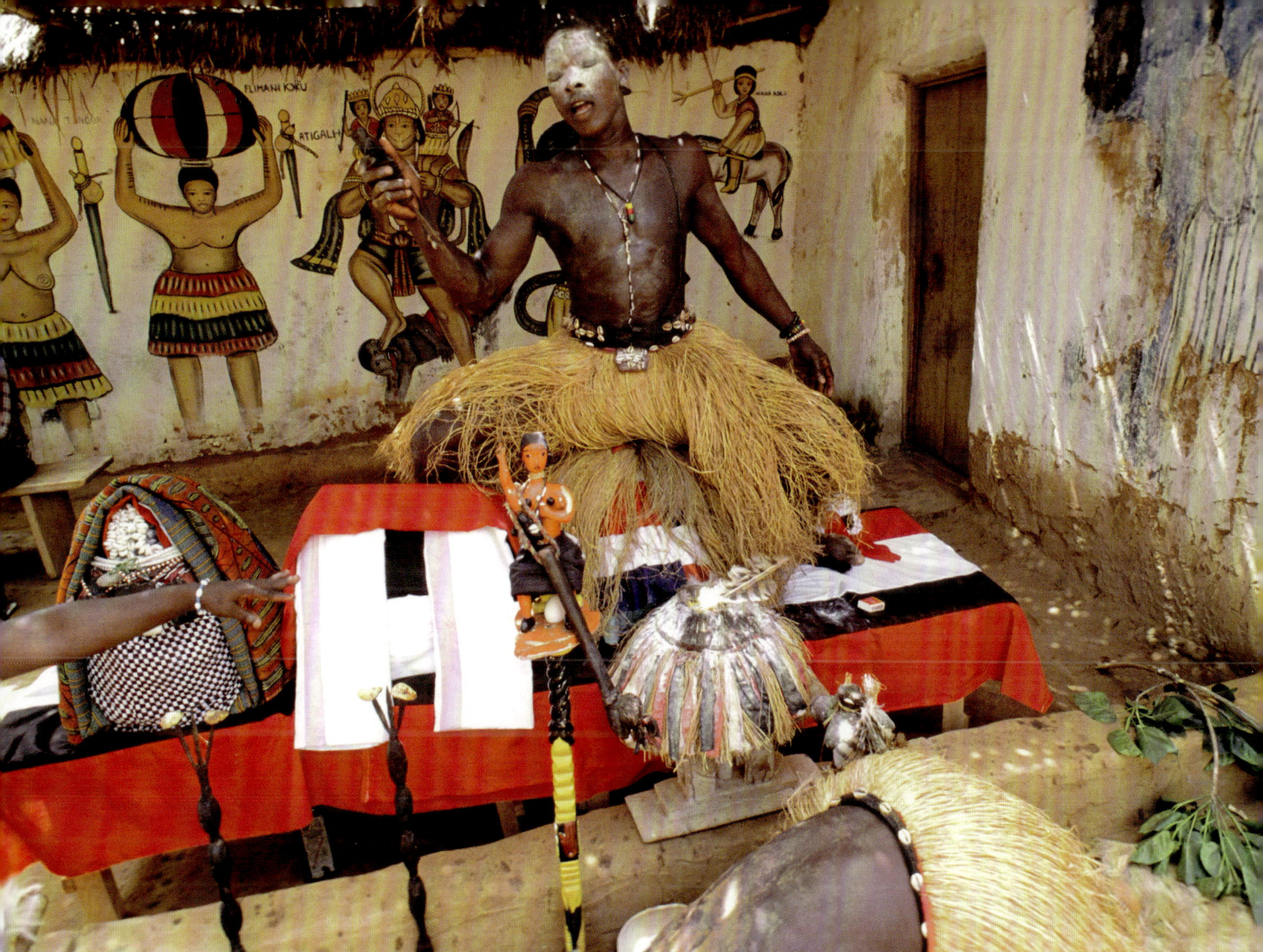

Kokou's magic in calabashes. Calabashes wrapped in cloths, in which the potencies of the deity are stored in the form of secret plant preparations, are kept in this shrine for Kokou.

La magie de Kokou dans des calebasses. Dans ce sanctuaire consacré à Kokou sont conservées des calebasses enveloppées de linges. Elles referment la puissance de la déité sous forme de préparations végétales secrètes.

Kokous Magie in Kalebassen. In diesem Schrein Kokous werden von Tüchern umwickelte Kalebassen aufbewahrt, in denen die Potenzen der Gottheit in Form von geheimen Pflanzenzubereitungen lagern.

Magia Kokou en calabazas. En este santuario se guardan calabazas Kokou envueltas en telas, en las que se almacenan las potencias de la deidad en forma de preparaciones secretas de plantas.

Coco mágico em calabashes. Neste santuário Kokous são mantidos calabashes envolto em panos, em que as potências da divindade são armazenados sob a forma de preparações vegetais secretas.

De magie van Kokou in kalebassen. In dit heiligdom van Kokou worden de kalebassen met doeken omwikkeld. Hierin worden de potenties van de godheid in de vorm van geheime plantenpreparaten bewaard.

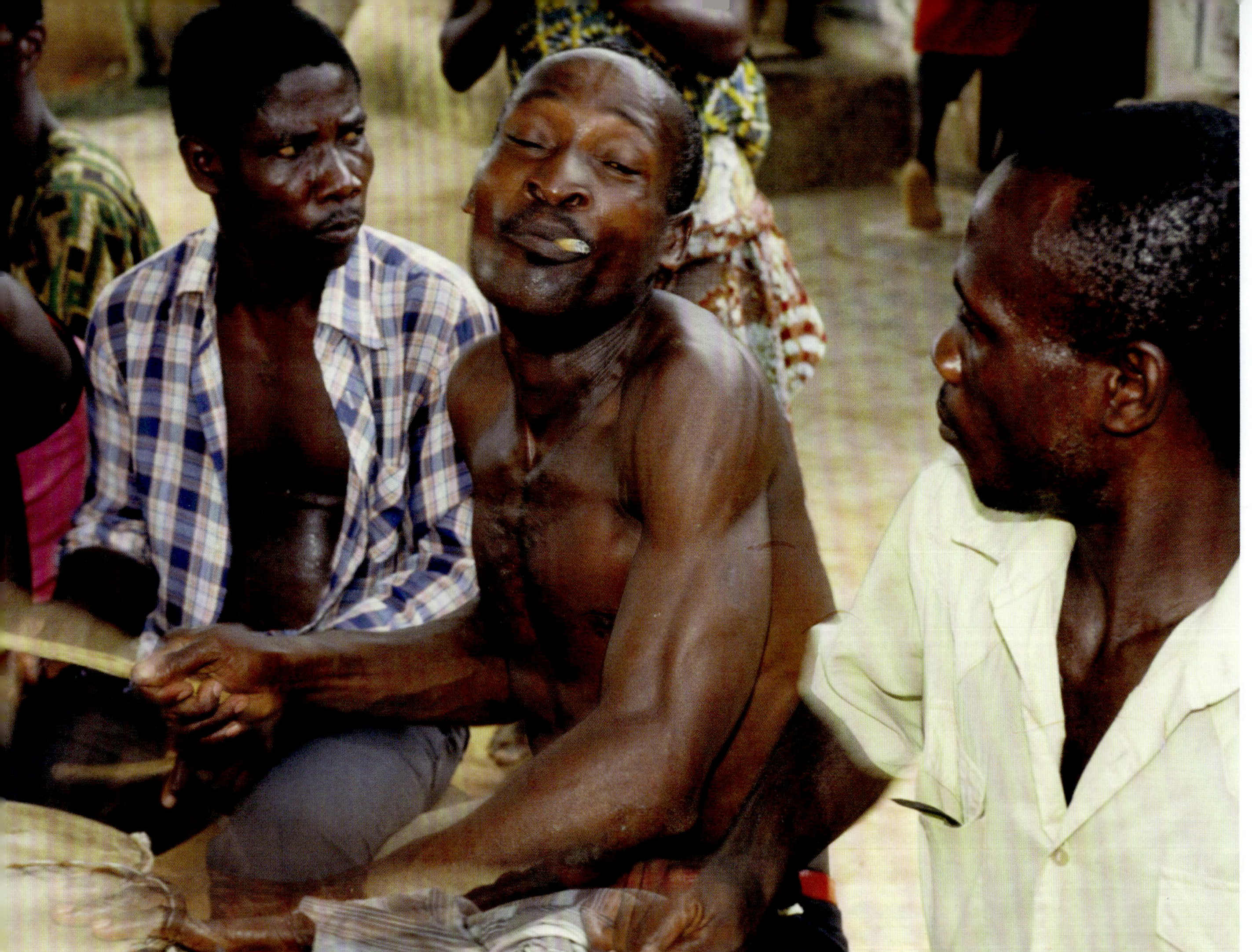

Drummers are always present

Les percussionnistes sont toujours présents

Trommler sind immer dabei

Los tamborileros están siempre presentes

Os bateristas estão sempre presentes

Trommelaars zijn altijd aanwezig

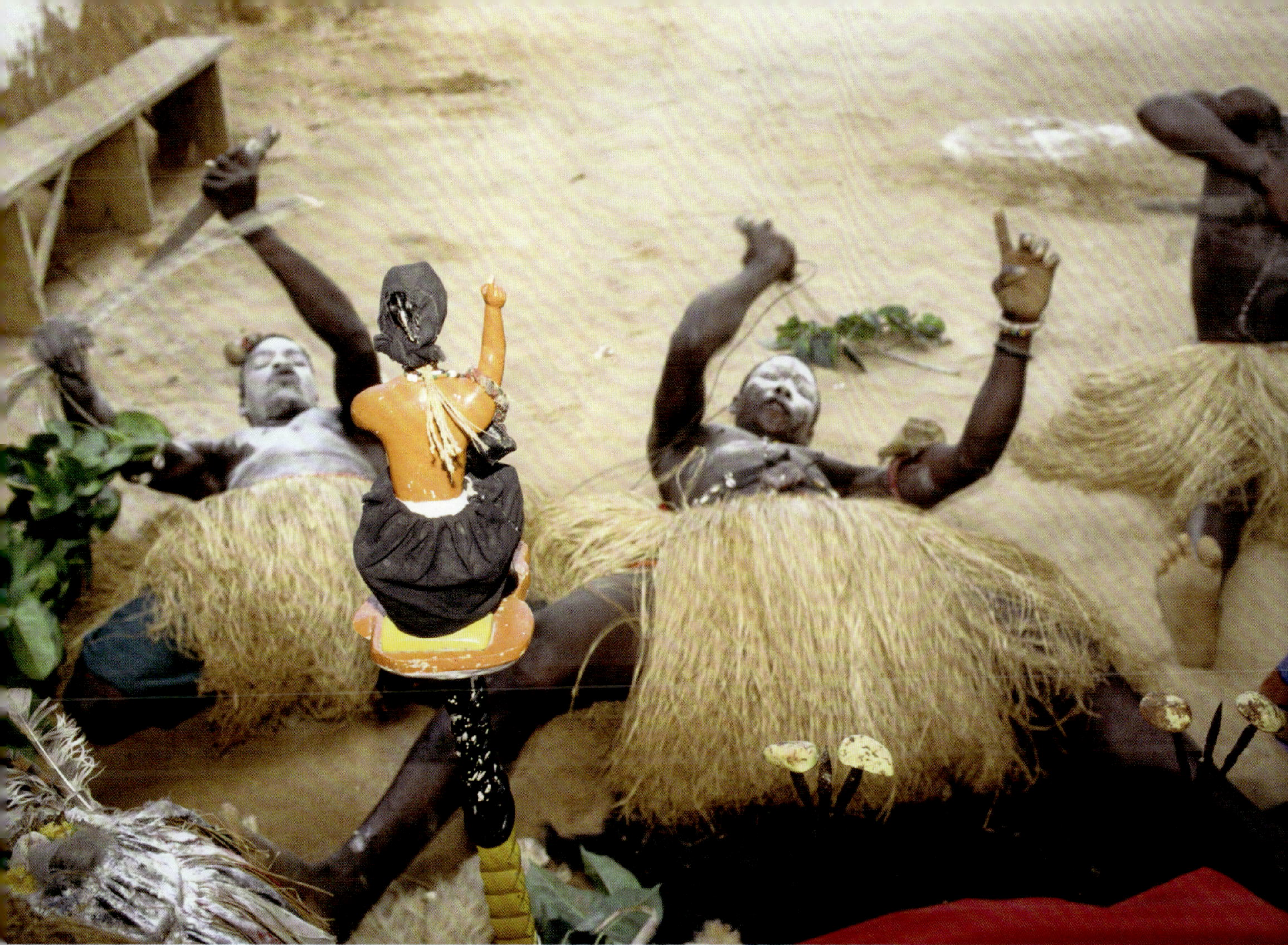

The skirts of raffia are typical for Kokou adepts

Les jupes de raphia sont typiques des adeptes de Kokou

Die Röcke aus Raffiastroh sind typisch für Kokou-Adepten

Las faldas de tiras de raffia son típicas de los adeptos de Kokou

As saias de Raffiastroh são típicas de Kokou-Adepts

De rokken van raffia zijn typerend voor Kokou-adepten

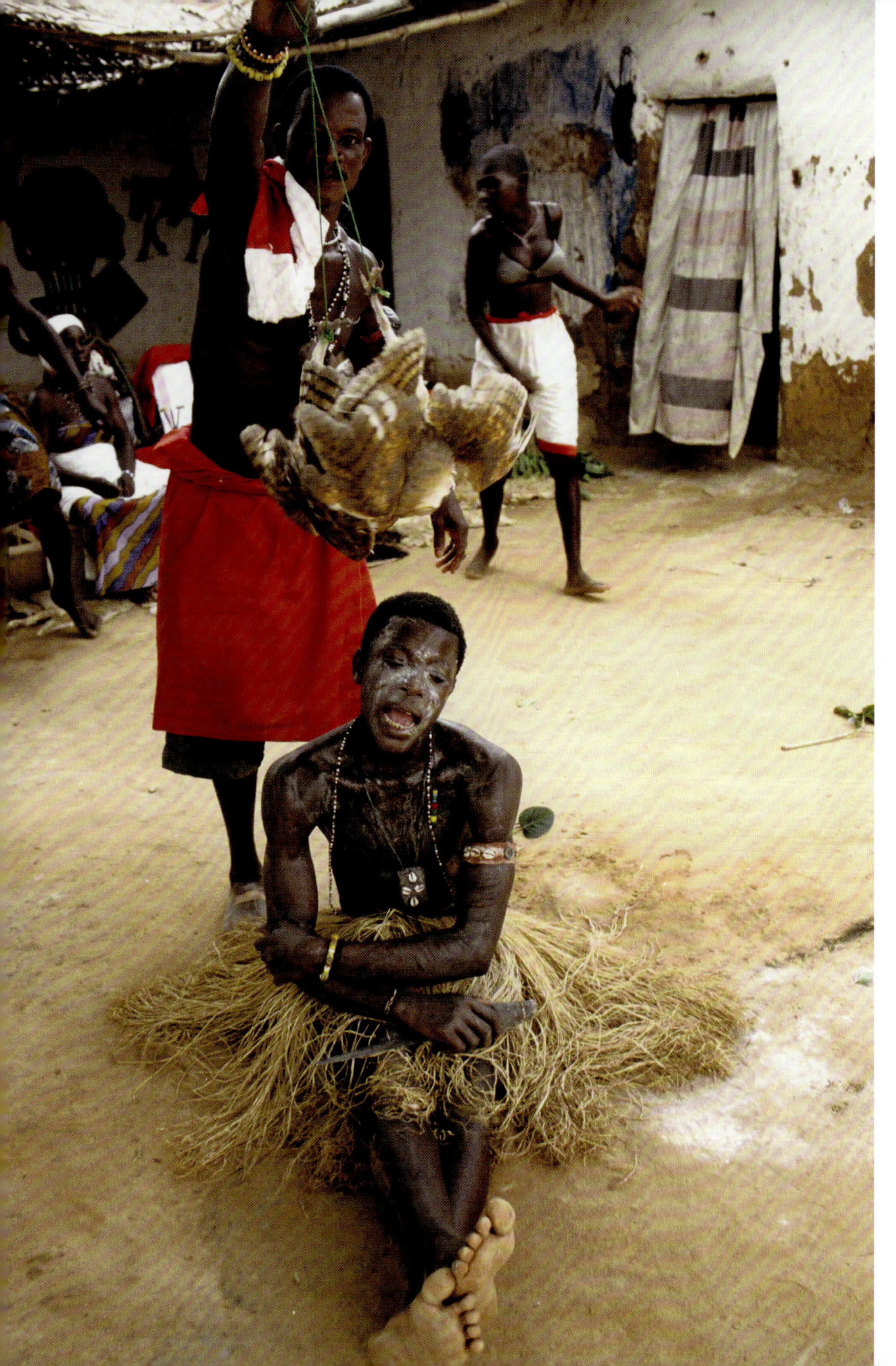

The priest holds a witch-bird
over the adept

Le prêtre tient un oiseau
sorcier au dessus de l'adepte

Der Priester hält einen
Hexenvogel über den Adepten

El sacerdote sostiene un pájaro
brujo sobre el adepto

O padre tem uma bruxa sobre
o adepto

De priester houdt een
heksenvogel boven de adept

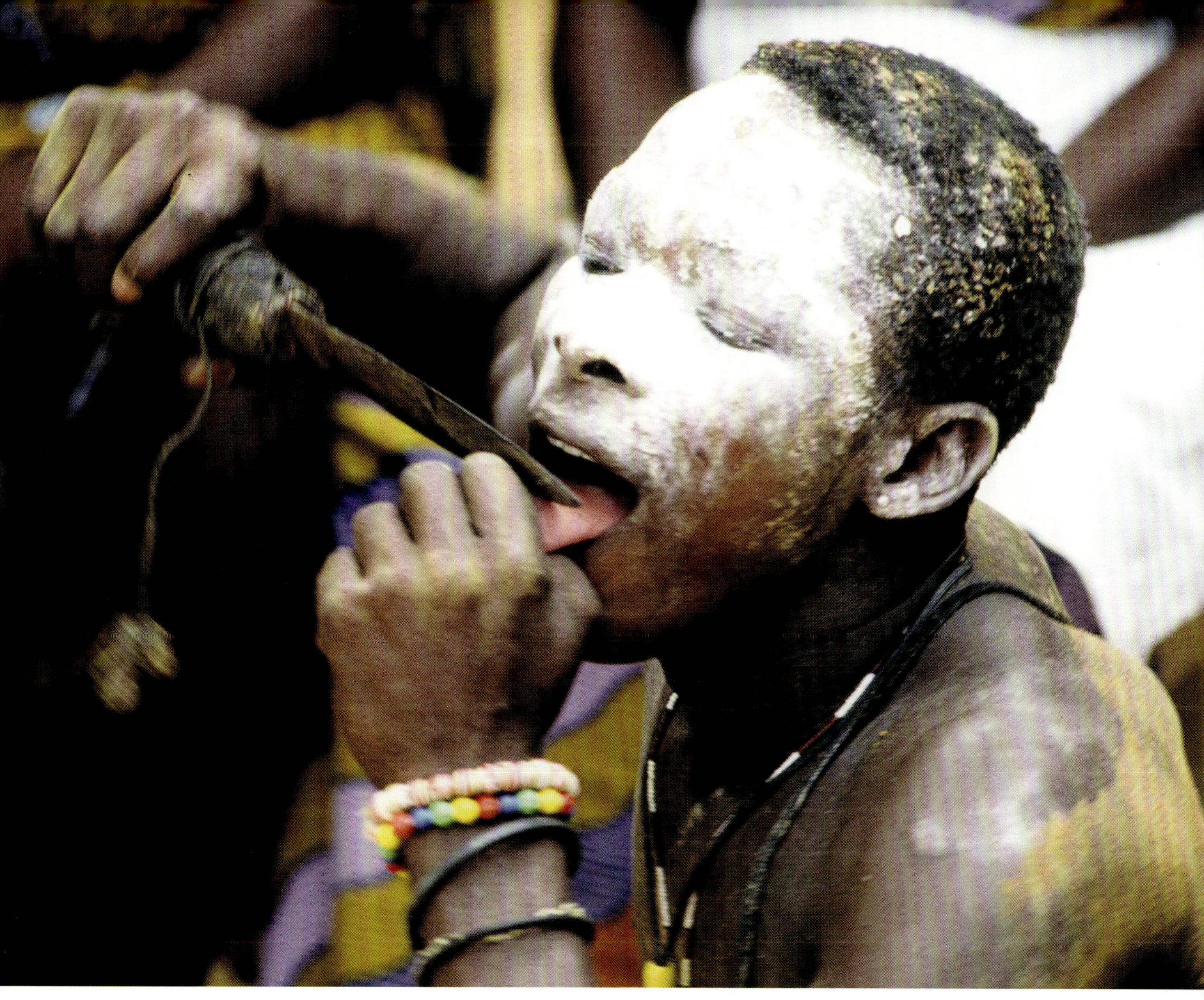

Cuts as a sign of power. The followers cut themselves and each other with knives to show their strength, painlessness and fearlessness towards the evil forces.

Les coupures, signes de pouvoir. Les adeptes s'entaillent eux-mêmes et mutuellement avec des couteaux. Ils démontrent ainsi leur force et indiquent aux puissances maléfiques qu'ils ne ressentent ni douleur ni peur.

Schnitte zum Zeichen der Kraft. Die Anhänger schneiden sich selbst und gegenseitig mit Messern, um ihre Kraft, Schmerzlosigkeit und Unerschrockenheit gegenüber den bösen Mächten zu zeigen.

Cortes como signo de fuerza. Los seguidores se cortan a sí mismos y a los demás con cuchillos para mostrar su fuerza, indolencia e intrepidez hacia los poderes del mal.

Cortes como sinal de poder. Os seguidores se cortaram e se cortaram com facas para mostrar sua força, indolência e destemor para com as forças malignas.

Snee als teken van macht. De volgelingen snijden zichzelf en elkaar met messen om hun kracht, ongevoeligheid voor pijn en onverschrokkenheid tegenover de boze machten te tonen.

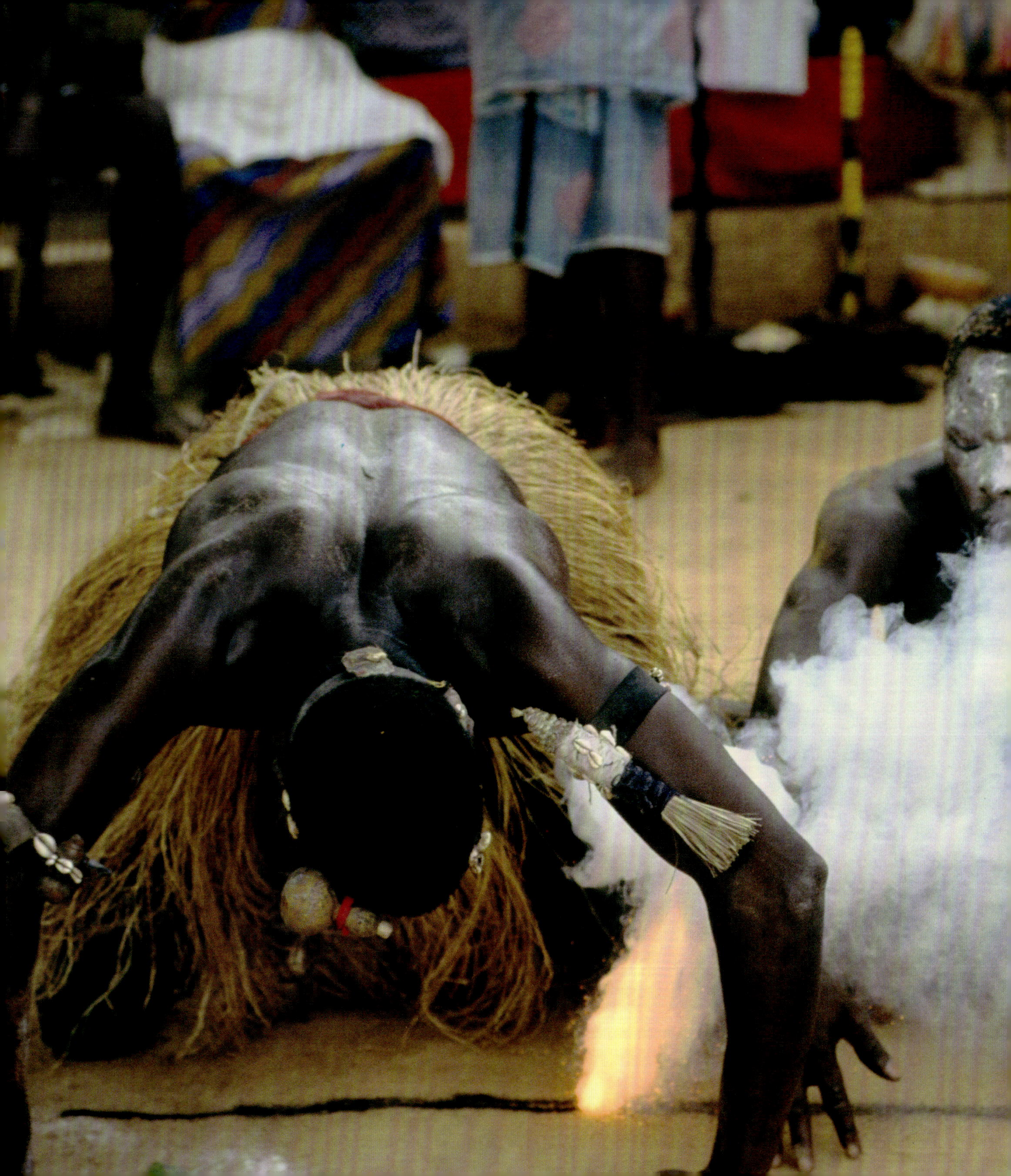

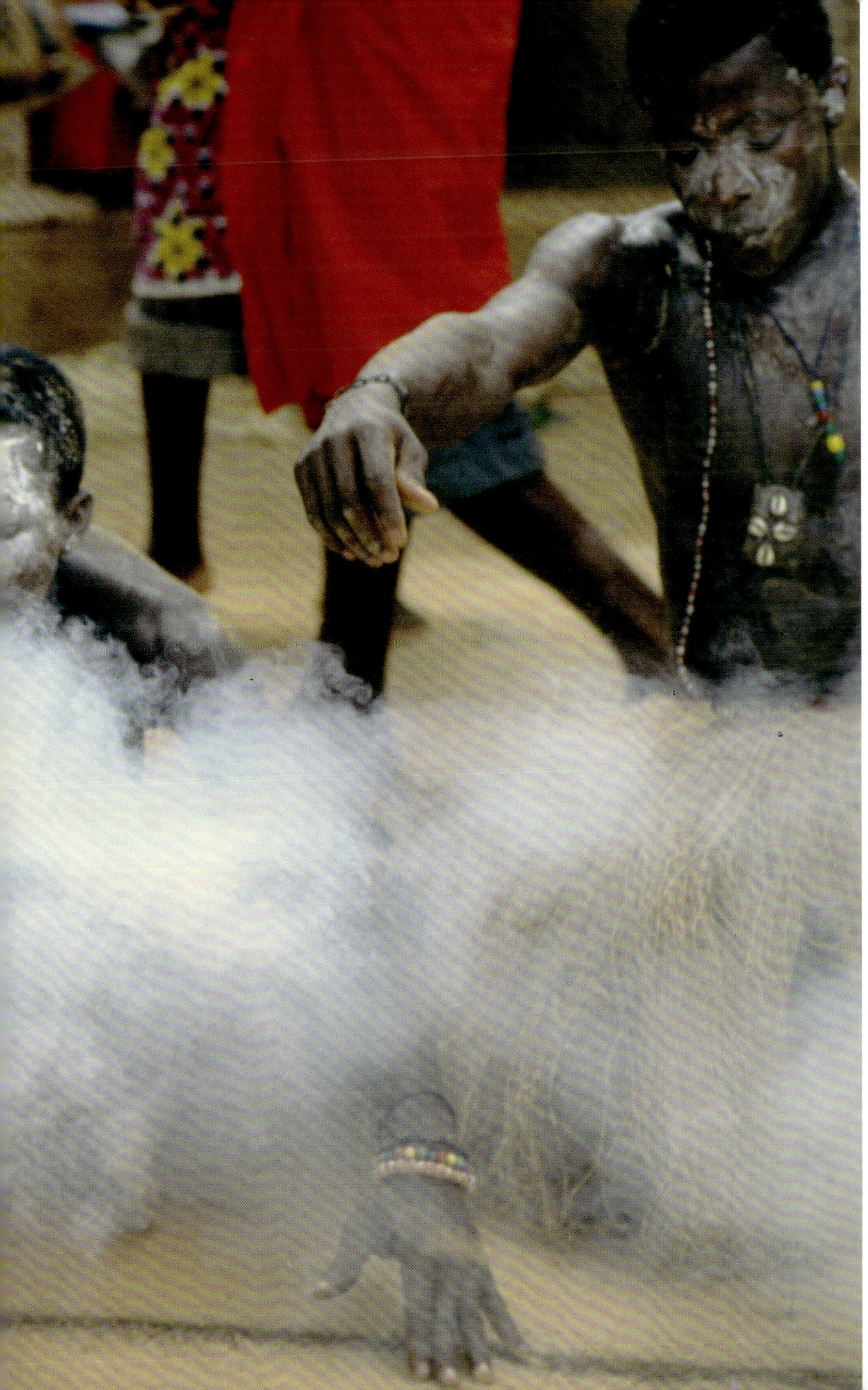

Inhalation for strength. Here the smoke of ignited gunpowder is being inhaled. This will stir up the blood of the Kokou adepts and provide new strength for the ongoing ceremony.

Inhaler pour se renforcer. Les hommes aspirent la fumée de la poudre à canon enflammée. Elle échauffe le sang des adeptes de Kokou et renouvelle leur force pour la suite de la cérémonie.

Inhalation zur Stärkung. Hier wird der Rauch von entzündetem Schießpulver inhaliert. Dies bringt das Blut der Kokou-Adepten in Wallung und sorgt für neue Kraft bei der laufenden Zeremonie.

Inhalación para el fortalecimiento. Aquí el humo es inhalado por la pólvora encendida. Esto hace que la sangre de los adeptos de Kokou se ruborice y proporciona una nueva fuerza en la ceremonia en curso.

Inalação para reforço. Aqui o fumo é inalado pela pólvora inflamada. Isto traz o sangue dos adeptos de Kokou para o flush e proporciona uma nova força na cerimónia em curso.

Inhalatie ter versterking. Hier wordt de rook van ontstoken buskruit ingeademd. Dit brengt het bloed van de Kokou-adepten aan de kook en geeft nieuwe kracht in de lopende ceremonie.

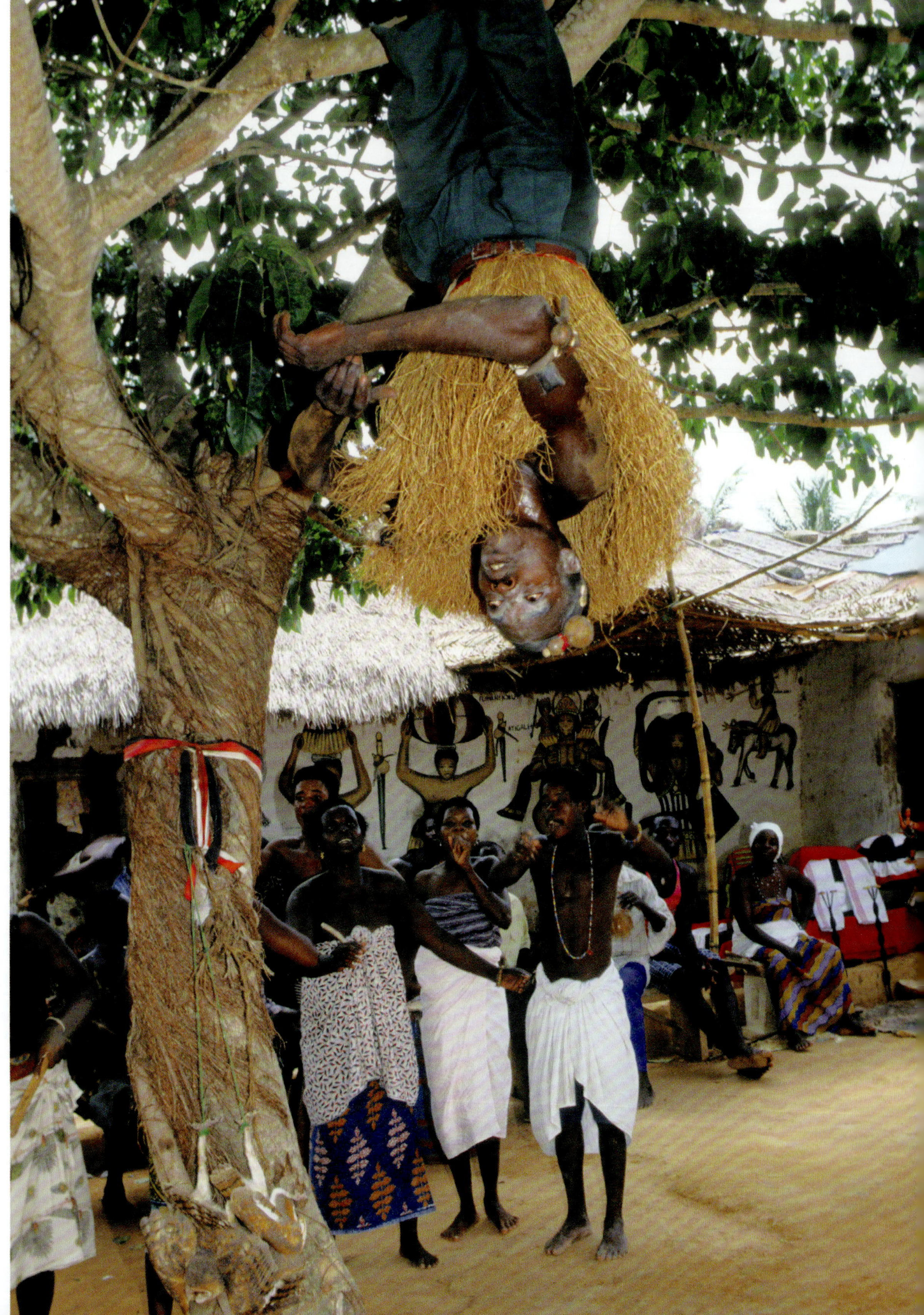

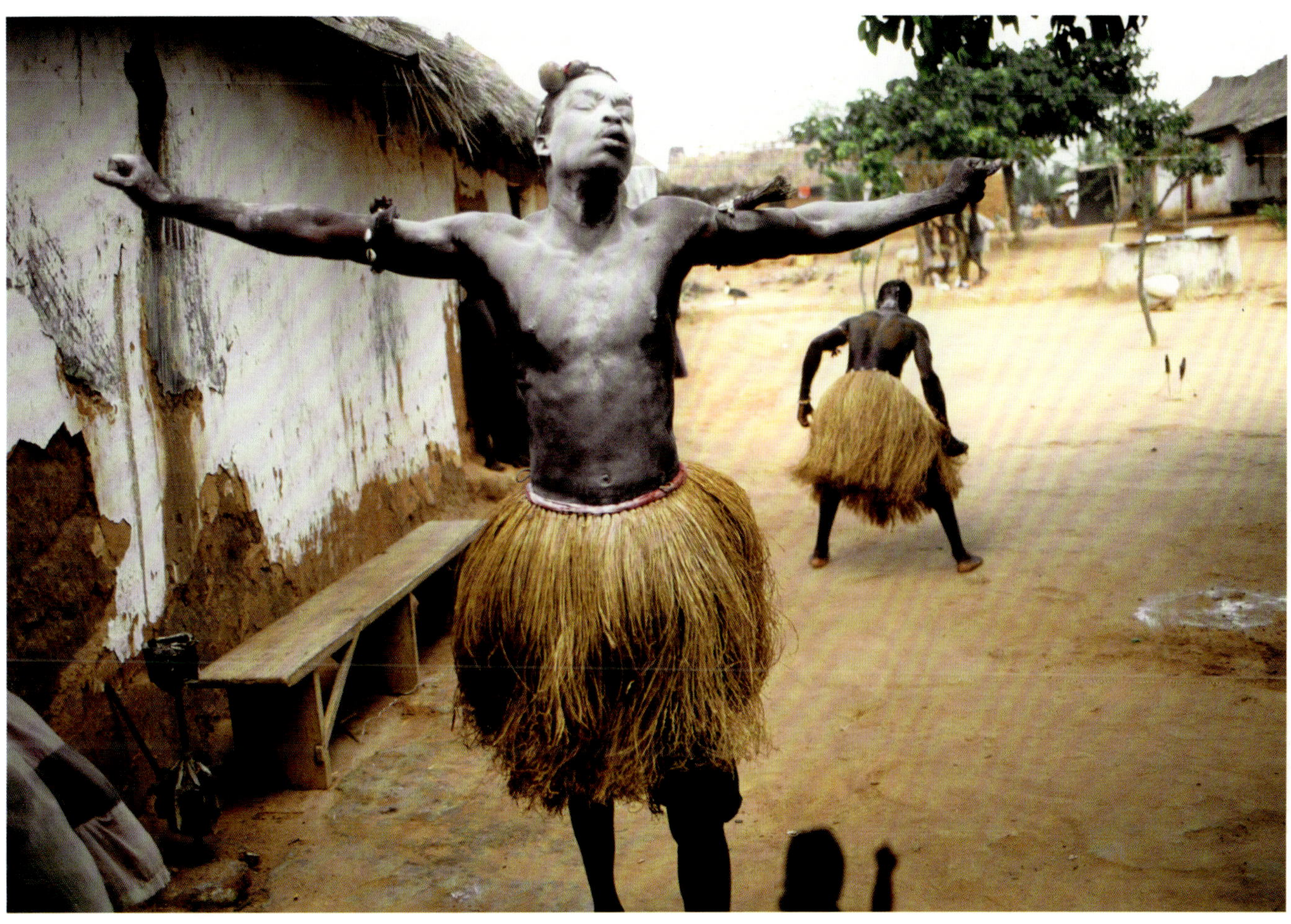

Head over heels like witches. The Kokou adept hangs upside down from the tree, imitating the witches who "have turned their nature upside down". Two owls hang on the tree (witch-birds) in the same position.

Tête en bas, comme les sorciers. Ce disciple de Kokou s'est suspendu à un arbre la tête en bas pour imiter les sorciers qui ont « mis leur nature à l'envers ». Deux chouettes (oiseaux des sorciers) sont également suspendues à l'arbre dans cette position.

Kopfüber wie die Hexen. Der Kokou-Adept hängt kopfüber vom Baum und imitiert so die Hexen, die „ihre Natur auf den Kopf gestellt haben". Am Baum hängen zwei Eulen (Hexenvögel) in derselben Position.

Boca abajo como las brujas. El adepto Kokou cuelga al revés del árbol, imitando a las brujas que "han dado la vuelta a su naturaleza". Dos búhos (brujas) cuelgan del árbol en la misma posición.

Cabeça sobre calcanhares como bruxas. O Adepto Kokou pende de cabeça para baixo da árvore, imitando as bruxas que "viraram a sua natureza de cabeça para baixo". Duas corujas (bruxas) penduradas na árvore na mesma posição.

Met het hoofd omlaag, net als heksen. De Kokou-aanhanger hangt ondersteboven aan de boom en imiteert zo de heksen die 'hun aard op de kop hebben gezet'. Twee uilen (heksen) hangen in dezelfde positie aan de boom.

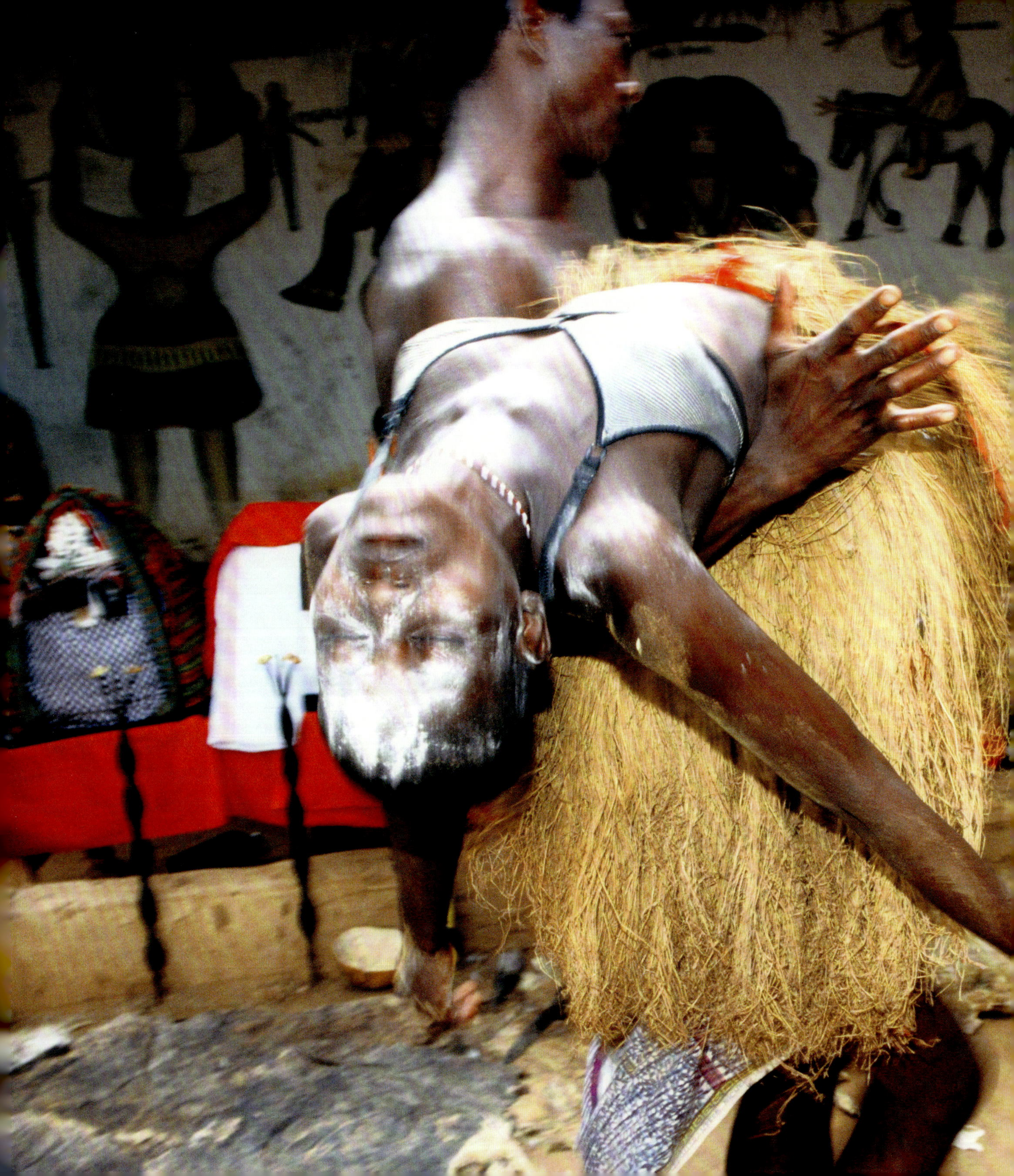

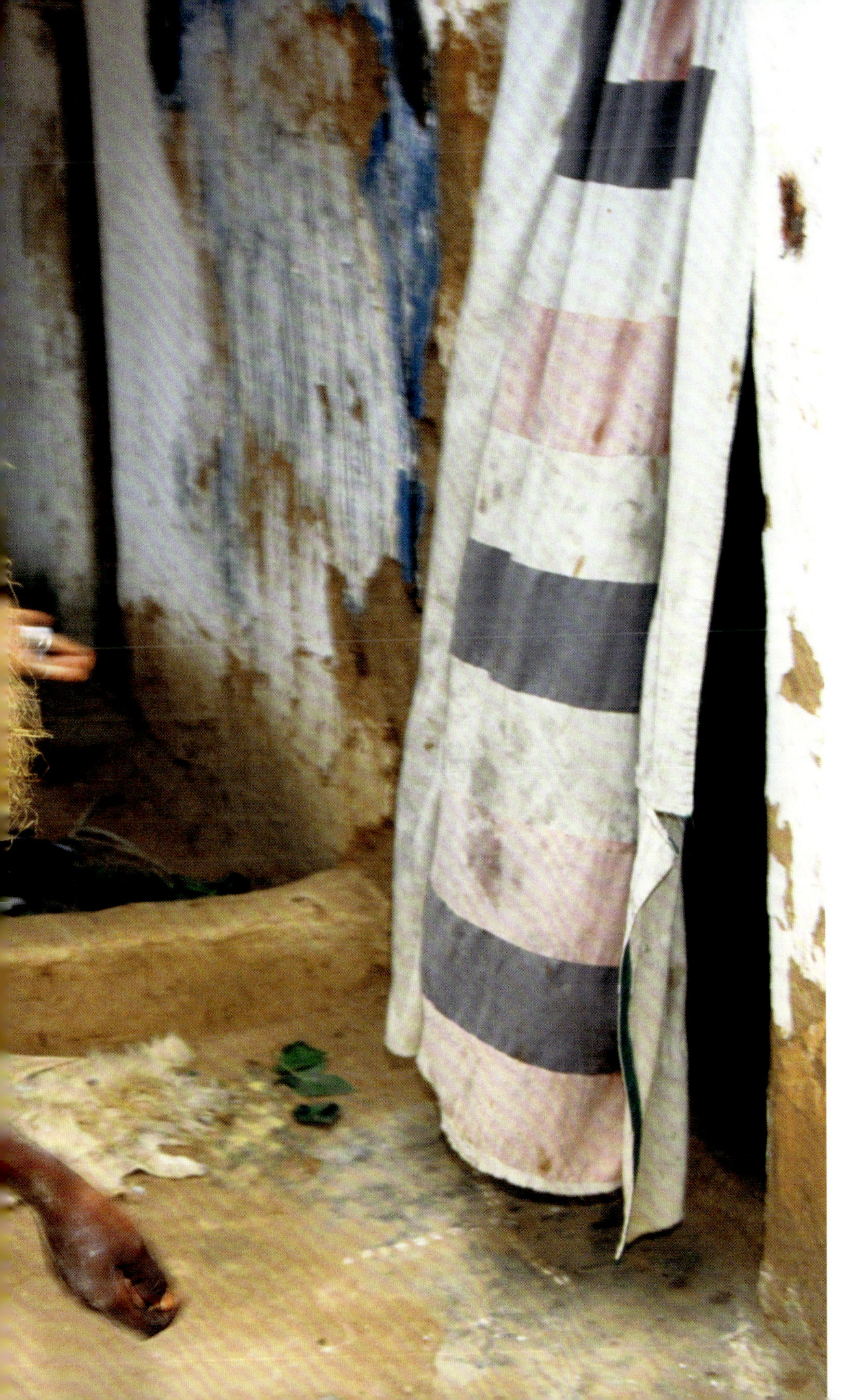

Women are in the minority
Les femmes sont minoritaires
Frauen sind in der Minderheit
Las mujeres son minoría
As mulheres estão em minoria
Vrouwen zijn in de minderheid

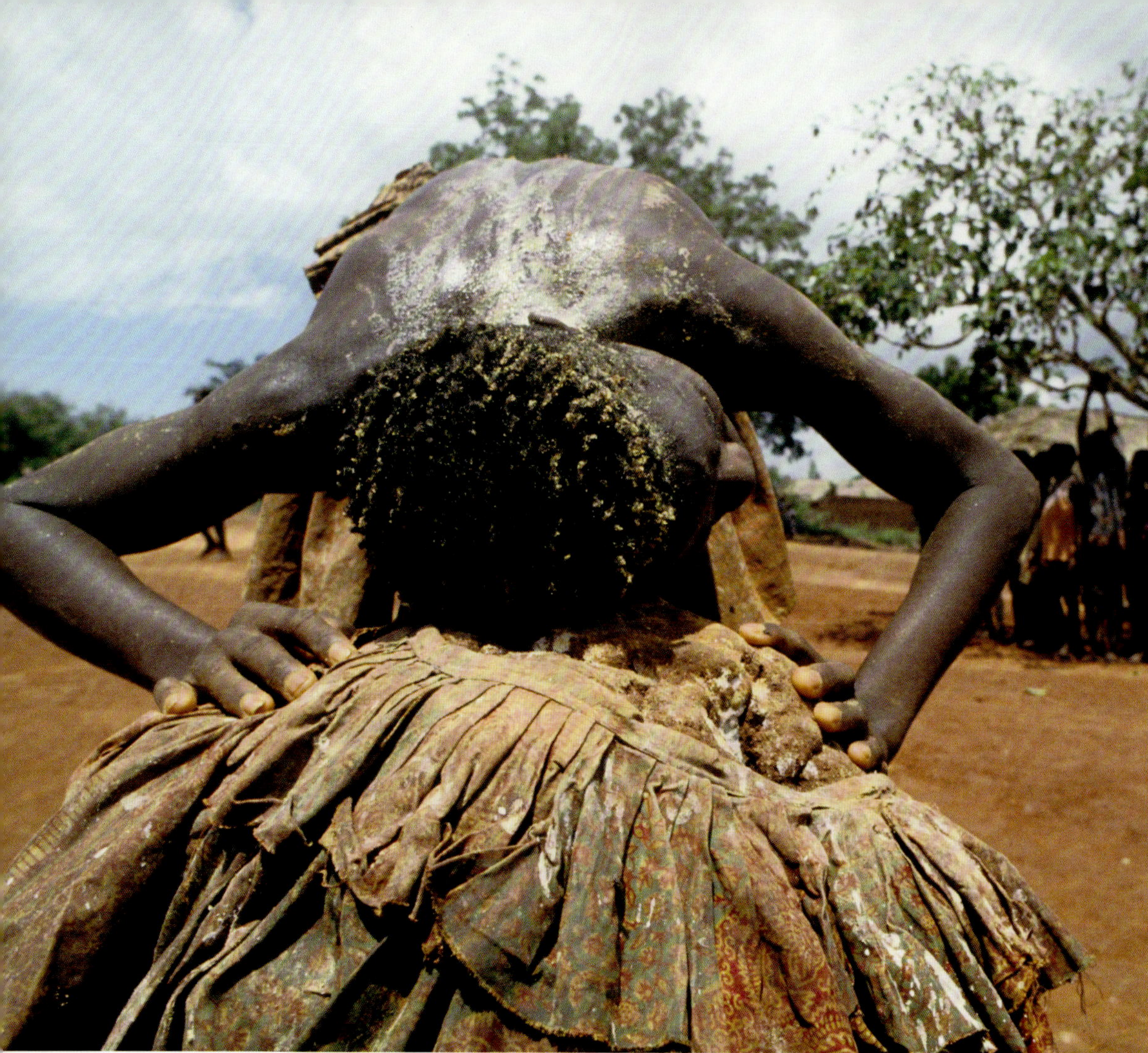

Djagli—Wild as a bird

In the Mono region of Benin a Vodun has established itself, whose energetic ceremonies have become known far beyond the region. It concerns *Djagli,* which means "bird" in the language of the Adja people.

The name says it all, because in the course of wild obsessive trances the god Djagli lets his followers dance for hours with elaborate jumps and steps that resemble those of various birds. Djagli belongs to the newer cults, which are often summarized under the name Goro-Vodun. Many of these younger gods have been imported from

Djagli, sauvage comme un oiseau

Au Bénin, dans le département de Mono, s'est établi un vodun dont les cérémonies empreintes d'une forte énergie sont aujourd'hui connues bien au-delà de la région. Il s'agit de Djagli qui, dans la langue de l'ethnie Adja, signifie « oiseau ».

Son nom est très parlant : au cours de transes de possession intenses, le dieu Djagli fait danser ses adeptes pendant des heures. Ils exécutent des sauts et des pas désordonnés qui les font ressembler à différents oiseaux. Djagli fait partie des nouveaux cultes, souvent regroupés sous

Djagli – Wild wie ein Vogel

In der Monoregion von Benin hat sich ein Vodun etabliert, dessen energetische Zeremonien bis weit über das Gebiet hinaus bekannt geworden sind. Es handelt sich um *Djagli,* was in der Sprache des Volkes der Adja soviel bedeutet wie „Vogel".

Der Name ist Programm, denn im Zuge wilder Besessenheitstrancen lässt der Gott Djagli seine Anhänger stundenlang tanzen und dabei entfessel Sprünge und Schritte vollführen, die denen verschiedener Vögel ähneln. Djagli gehört zu den neueren Kulten, die oft unter dem Namen Goro-

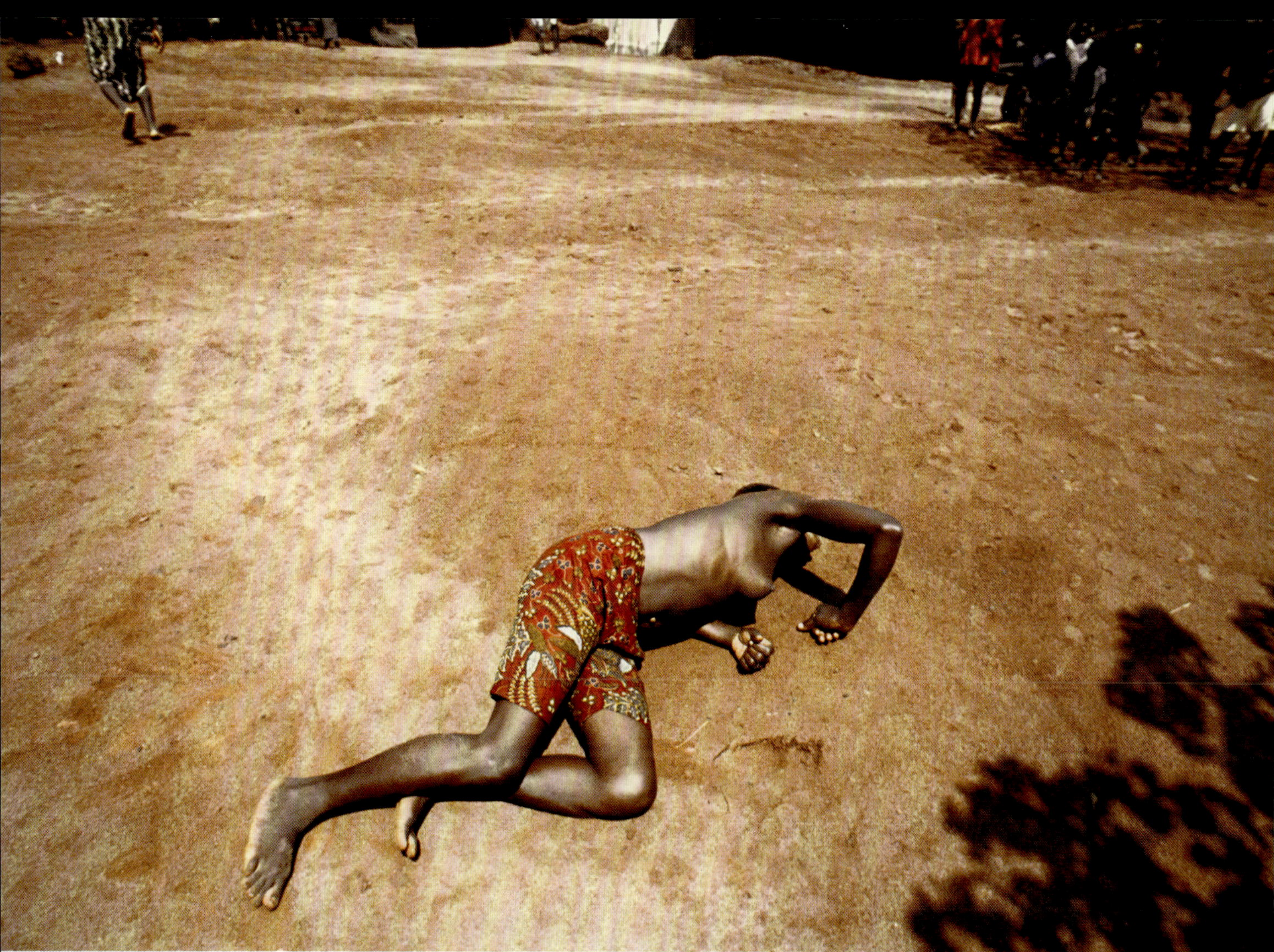

Djagli – Salvaje como un pájaro

En la monoregión de Benin se ha establecido un Vudú, cuyas enérgicas ceremonias se han dado a conocer mucho más allá de la región. Es *Djagli,* que significa "pájaro" en el idioma del pueblo *Adja*.

El nombre es programa, porque en el curso de los salvajes trances en los que son poseídos, el dios Djagli deja que sus seguidores bailen durante horas dando saltos y pasos, que se asemejan a los de diferentes pájaros. Djagli pertenece a los cultos más recientes, que a menudo se resumen bajo el nombre de Vudú Goro.

Djagli – Jogo como um pássaro

Na monorregião de Benin um Vodun se estabeleceu, cujas cerimônias energéticas se tornaram conhecidas muito além da região. É Djagli, que significa "pássaro" na língua do povo Adja.

O nome é programa, porque no curso de trances de obsessão selvagem o deus Djagli deixa seus seguidores dançarem durante horas e desencadear saltos e passos, que se assemelham aos de aves diferentes. Djagli pertence aos cultos mais recentes, que são frequentemente resumidos sob o nome de Goro-Vodun. Muitos desses deuses

Djagli – wild als een vogel

In het departement Mono in Benin heeft zich een vodun gevestigd waarvan de energetische ceremoniën tot ver buiten het gebied bekend zijn geworden. Het gaat hierbij om Djagli, wat in de taal van het Adja-volk zoveel als 'vogel' betekent.

De naam geeft het programma aan, want met woeste, bezeten trances laat de god Djagli zijn volgelingen urenlang dansen. Hij laat ze daarbij sprongen en passen maken die lijken op die van diverse vogels. Djagli behoort tot de nieuwere cultussen, die vaak op één hoop worden gegooid onder de naam

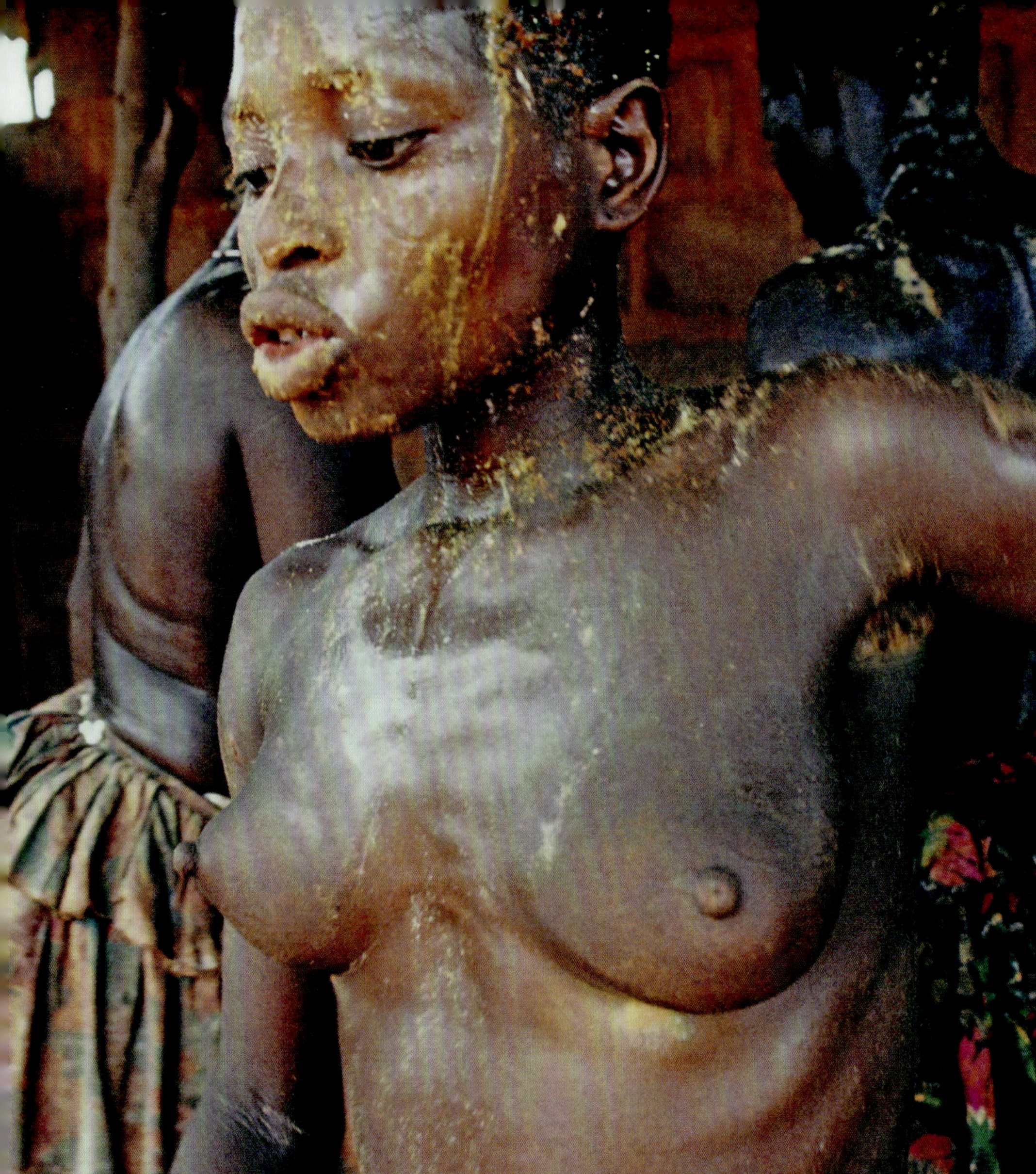

An adept of Djagli during the ceremony. Because witches love to slip into the shape of birds, the followers of Djagli imitate them in order to become equal to them and defeat the evil powers.

Adepte de Djagli pendant la cérémonie. Les sorciers se matérialisant de préférence sous la forme d'oiseaux, les adeptes de Djagli les imitent pour se mettre à leur niveau et parvenir à vaincre les forces maléfiques.

Adeptin Djaglis während der Zeremonie. Weil Hexen mit Vorliebe in die. Gestalt von Vögeln schlüpfen, ahmen die Anhänger Djaglis diese nach, um ihnen ebenbürtig zu werden und die bösen Mächte zu bezwingen.

Adepta de Djagli durante la ceremonia. Como a las brujas les gusta deslizarse como los pájaros, los seguidores de Djagli las imitan para llegar a ser iguales a ellas y derrotar a los poderes del mal.

Adeptin Djaglis durante a cerimônia. Porque as bruxas gostam de deslizar em forma de pássaros, os seguidores de Djagli imitam-nos para se igualarem a eles e derrotarem os poderes malignos.

Aanhangster van Djagli tijdens de ceremonie. Omdat heksen bij voorkeur uitkomen in de vorm van vogels, imiteren de volgelingen van Djagli ze om ertegen opgewassen te zijn en de boze machten te bedwingen.

northern regions, as it were, and all have in common the declared fight against damage spells and witchcraft.

A further characteristic is the warlike aspect of these communities; apart from extreme trance states, the gods usually demand many animal or blood sacrifices.

l'appellation *goro*-vodun. Beaucoup de ces dieux récents ont été importés des régions du nord et ont tous pour point commun la lutte déclarée contre la magie maléfique et la sorcellerie.

L'autre grande caractéristique de ce type de culte concerne son aspect guerrier ; outre les états de transe extrême, les dieux exigent en général d'importantes offrandes d'animaux sacrifiés ou de sang.

Vodun zusammengefasst werden. Viele dieser jüngeren Götter sind aus nördlichen Regionen gewissermaßen importiert worden, und allen gemein ist der erklärte Kampf gegen Schadenzauber und Hexerei.

Ein weiteres Merkmal ist der kriegerische Aspekt dieser Gemeinschaften; neben extremen Trancezuständen verlangen die Götter in der Regel viele Tier- beziehungsweise Blutopfer.

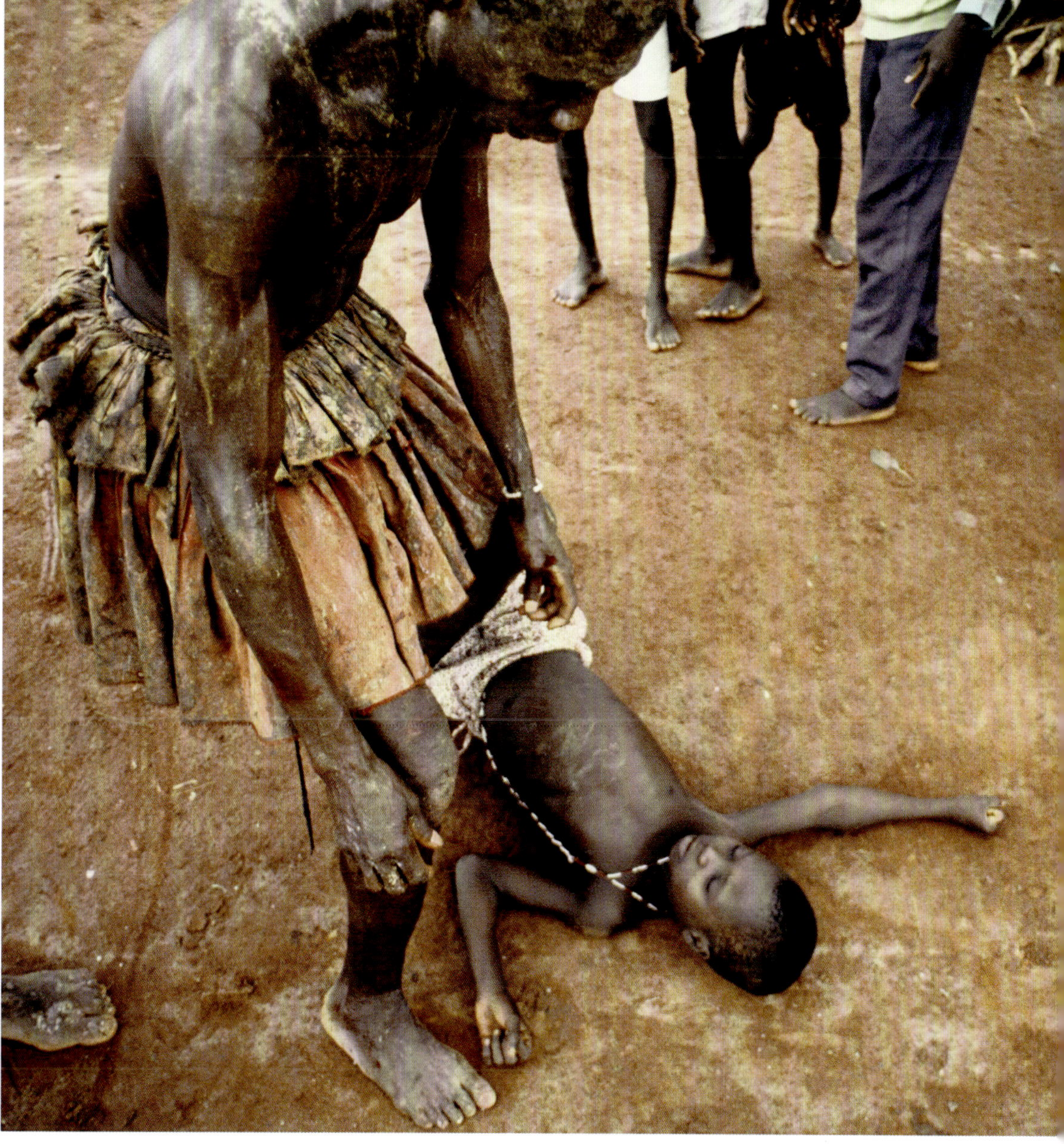

In the crosshairs of the gods. The gods themselves determine which body they take possession of—here it is a little boy who just came out of school. Now he's writhing in a trance.

Dans la ligne de mire des dieux. Les dieux choisissent eux-mêmes le corps qu'ils vont occuper. Ici, il s'agit d'un jeune garçon qui, tout juste revenu de l'école, est entré en transe.

Im Fadenkreuz der Götter. Die Götter bestimmen selbst, von welchem Körper sie Besitz ergreifen – hier ist es ein kleiner Junge, der gerade aus der Schule kam. Jetzt windet er sich in Trance.

En la mira de los dioses. Los propios dioses determinan de qué cuerpo se apoderan: aquí se trata de un niño que acaba de salir de la escuela. Ahora entra en trance.

Na mira dos deuses. Os próprios deuses determinam de que corpo tomam posse - aqui está um menino que acabou de sair da escola. Agora ele transforma-se num transe.

In het vizier van de goden. De goden bepalen zelf van welk lichaam ze bezit nemen. Hier is het een jongetje dat net uit school kwam. Nu kronkelt hij in trance.

Muchos de estos dioses más jóvenes han sido importados de las regiones del norte, y todos tienen en común la lucha declarada contra los hechizos y la brujería.

Otra característica es el aspecto guerrero de estas comunidades; aparte de los estados de trance extremos, los dioses suelen exigir muchos sacrificios de animales o de sangre.

mais jovens foram importados das regiões do norte, e todos têm em comum a luta declarada contra feitiços de dano e feitiçaria.

Uma outra característica é o aspecto bélico dessas comunidades; além de estados de transe extremos, os deuses geralmente exigem muitos sacrifícios de animais ou sangue.

goro-vodun. Veel van deze nieuwere goden zijn tot op zekere hoogte geïmporteerd uit de noordelijke regio's en hebben de uitgesproken strijd tegen zwarte magie en hekserij gemeen.

Een ander kenmerk is het oorlogszuchtige aspect van deze gemeenschappen; afgezien van extreme trancetoestanden eisen de goden meestal veel dieren- of bloedoffers.

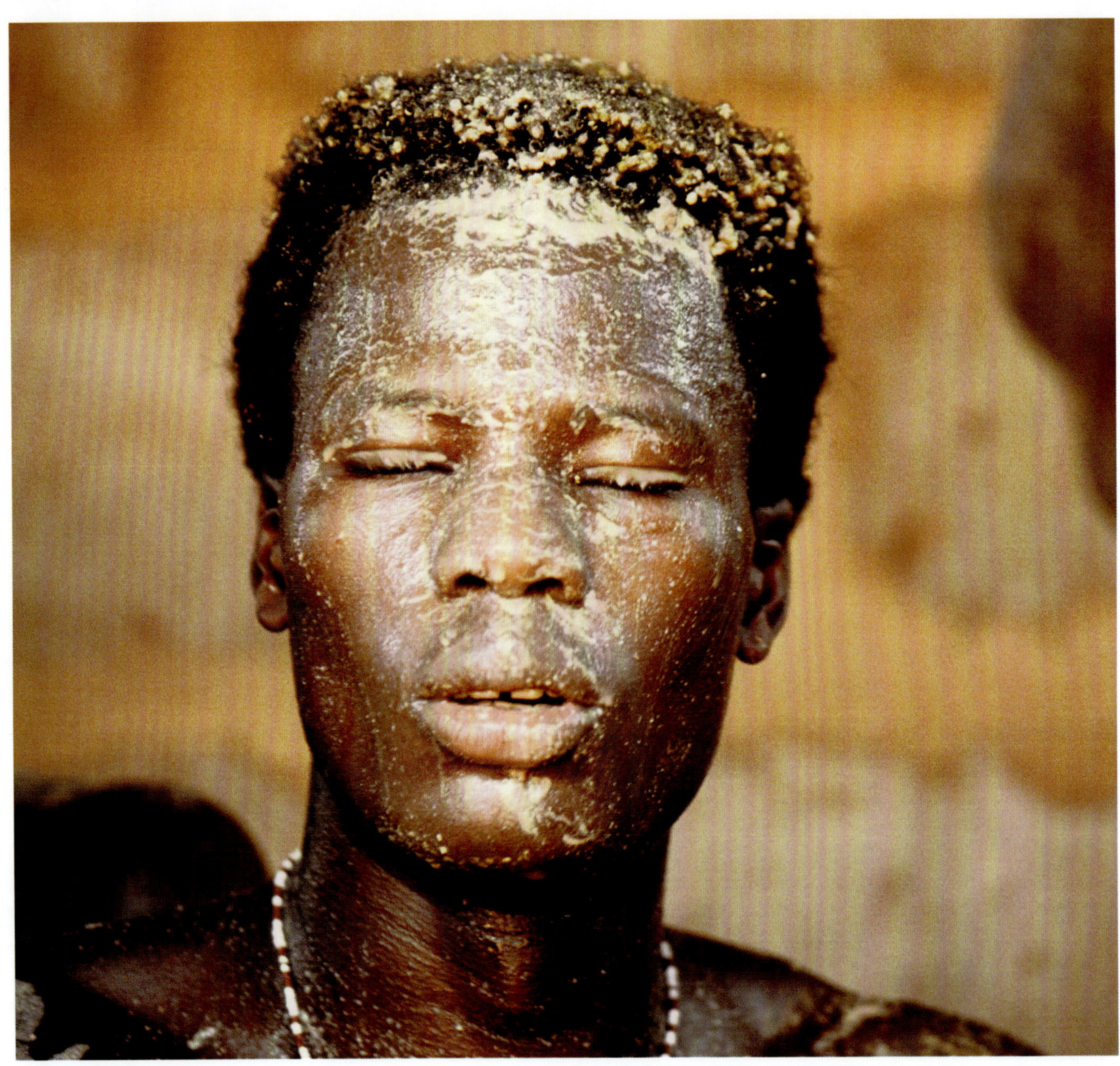

A follower of Djagli in a trance

Adepte de Djagli en transe

Ein Anhänger Djaglis in Trance

Un adepto de Djagli en trance

Um pingente de Djagli em transe

Een aanhangster van Djagli in trance

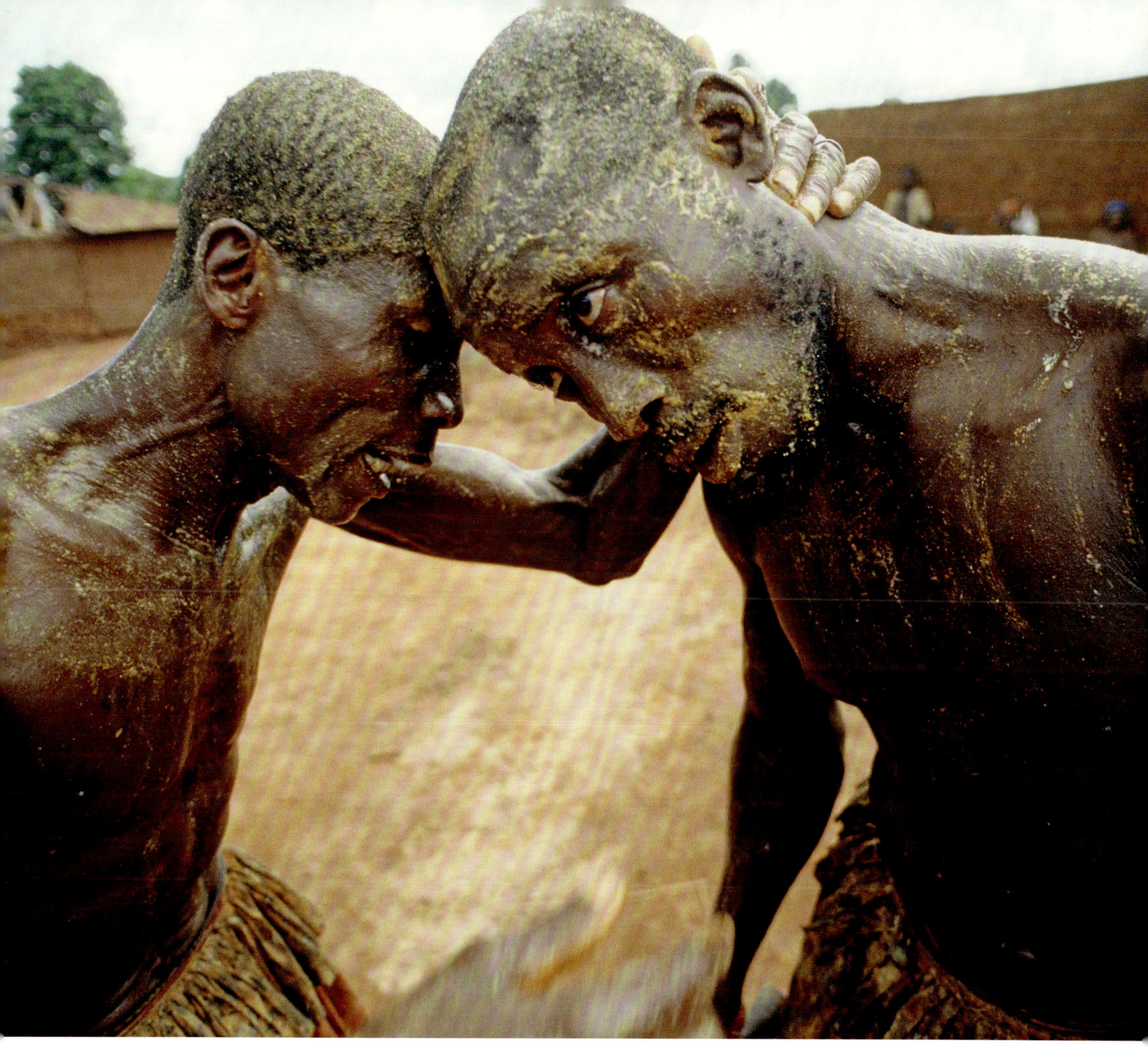

Follower of Djagli in a trance

Adepte de Djagli en transe

Anhänger Djaglis in Trance

Adepto de Djagli en trance

Pingente Djaglis em transe

Aanhangers van Djagli in trance

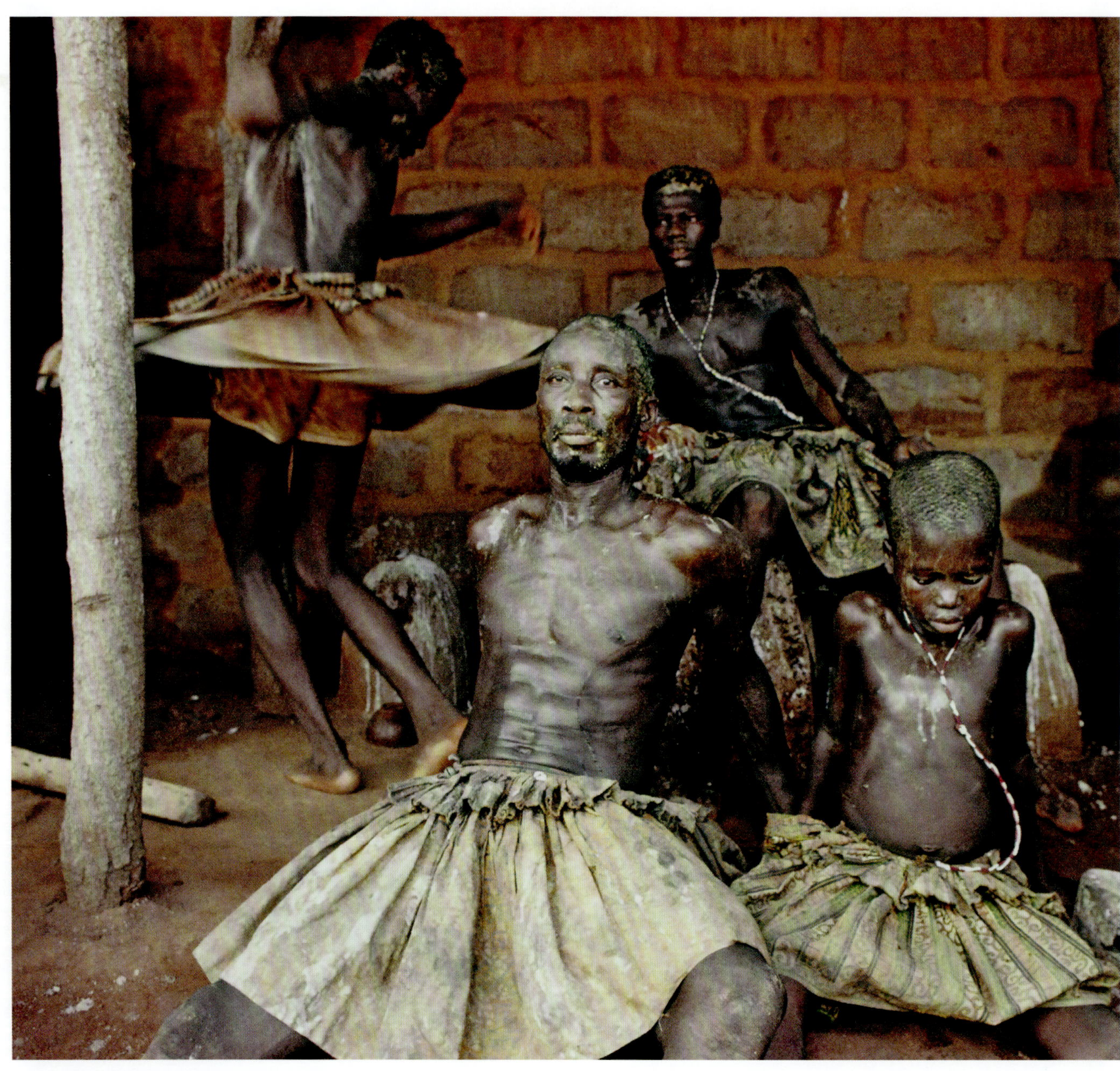

The dances go on for many hours

Les danses durent de nombreuses heures

Die Tänze gehen über viele Stunden

Los bailes duran muchas horas

As danças continuam por muitas horas

De dansen gaan urenlang door

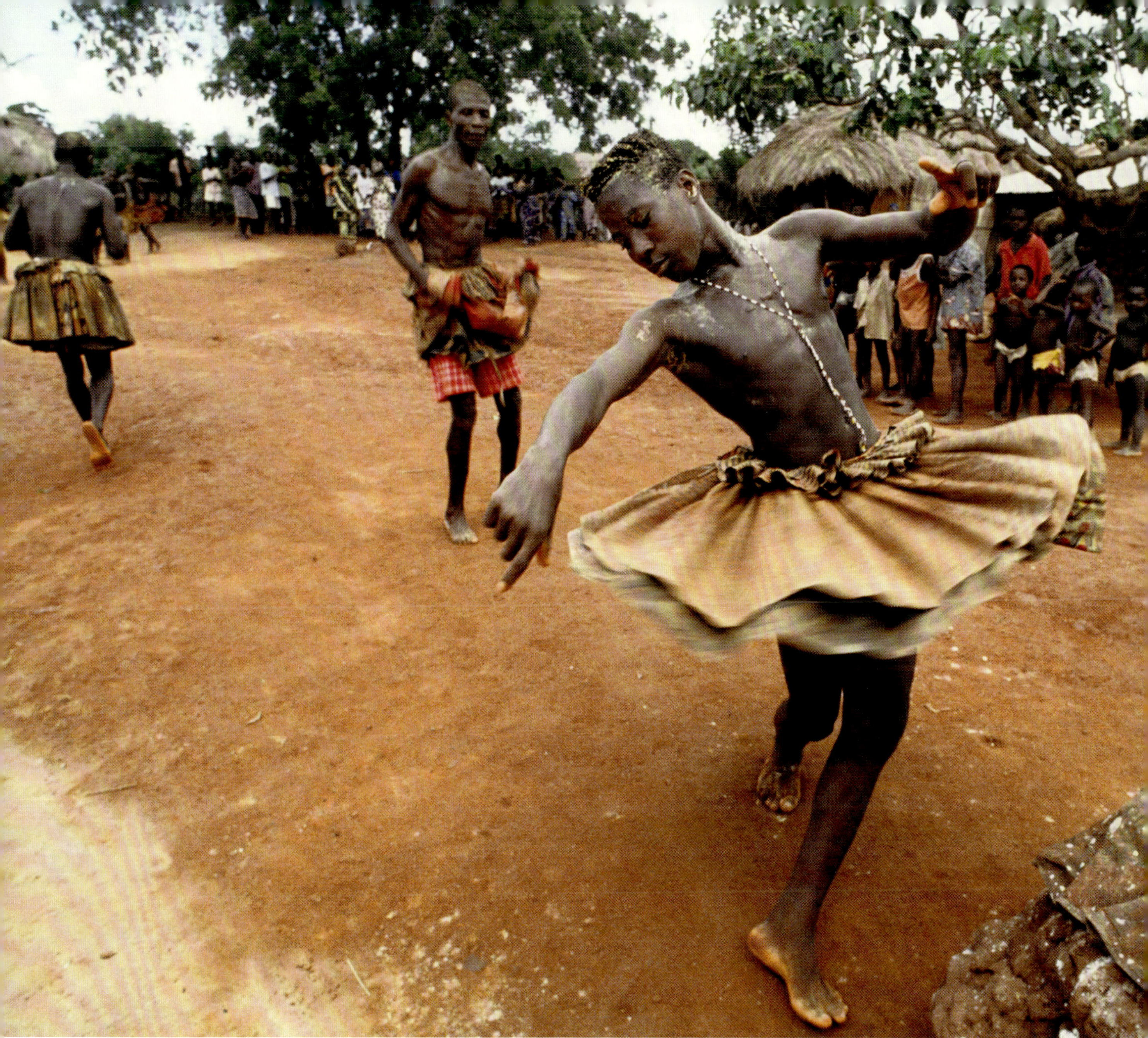

Djagli adepts at the dance

Adepte de Djagli dansant

Djagli-Adepten beim Tanz

Los adeptos de Djagli en el baile

Djagli adeptos da dança

Dansende Djagli-adepten

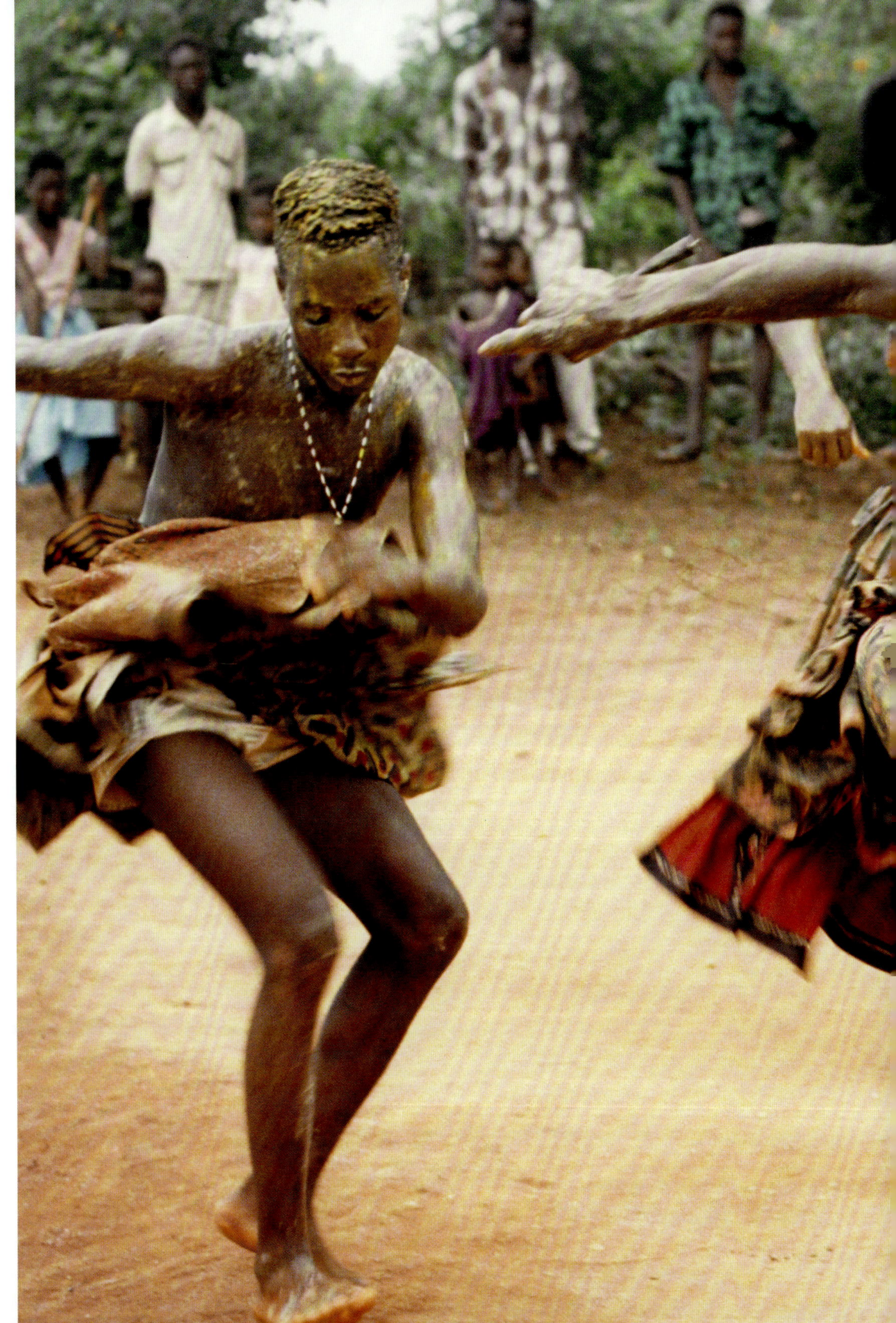

Djagli adepts at the dance
Adeptes de Djagli dansant
Djagli-Adepten beim Tanz
Los adeptos de Djagli en
el baile
Djagli adeptos da dança
Dansende Djagli adepten

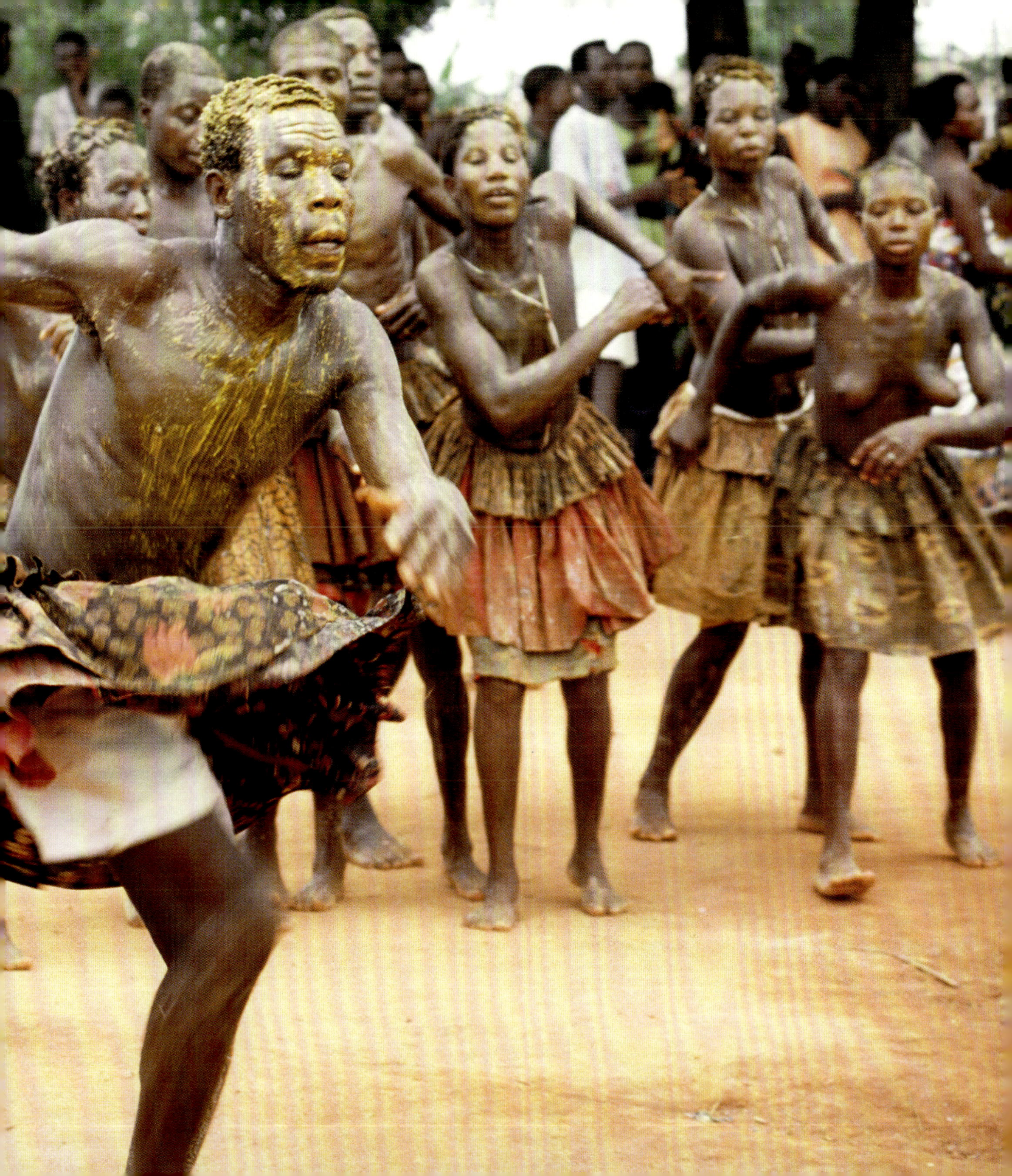

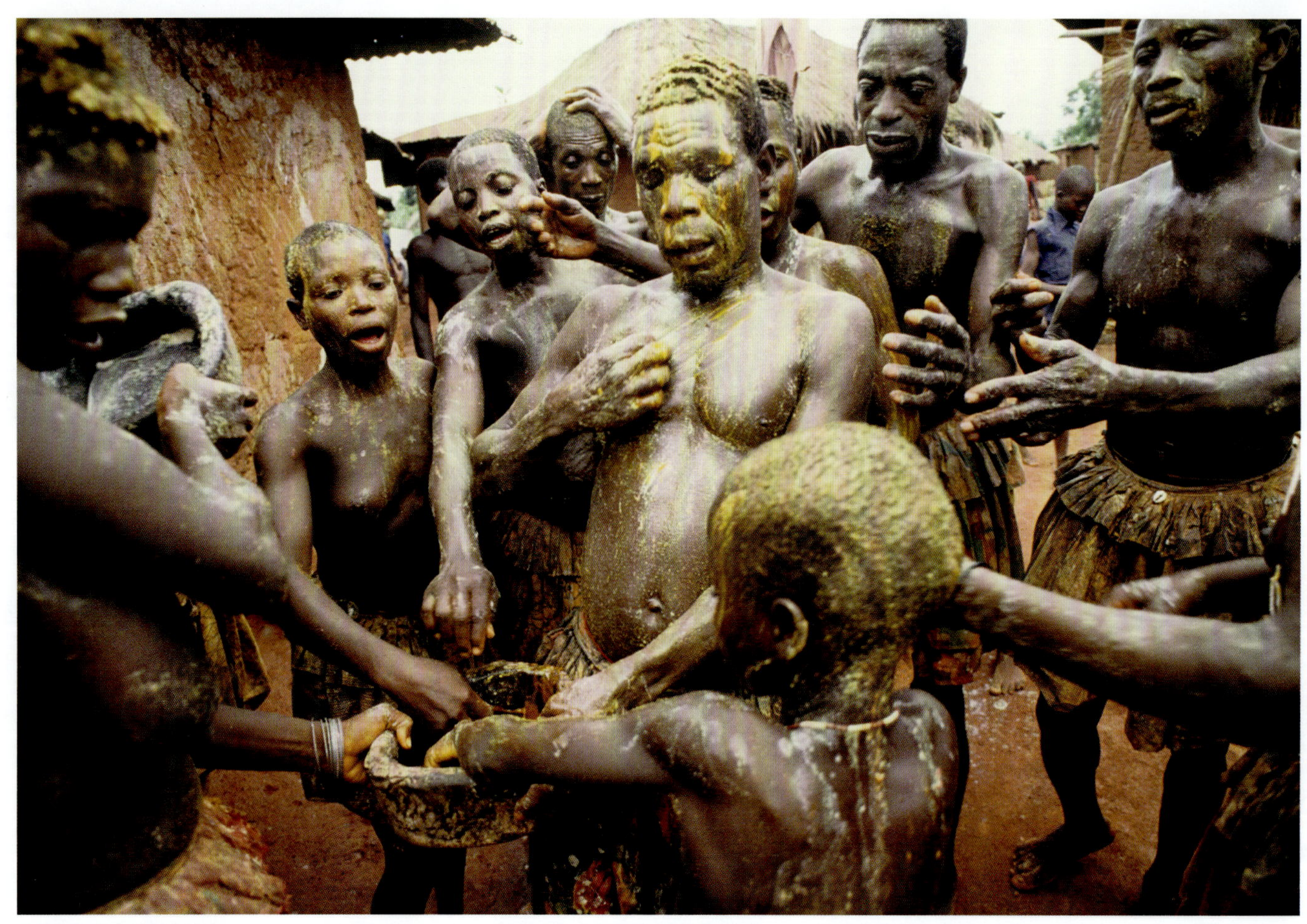

Additional Djassi for everyone

Supplément de djassi pour tous

Djassi-Nachschlag für alle

Djassi para todos

Acompanhamento de Djassi para todos

Extra djassi voor iedereen

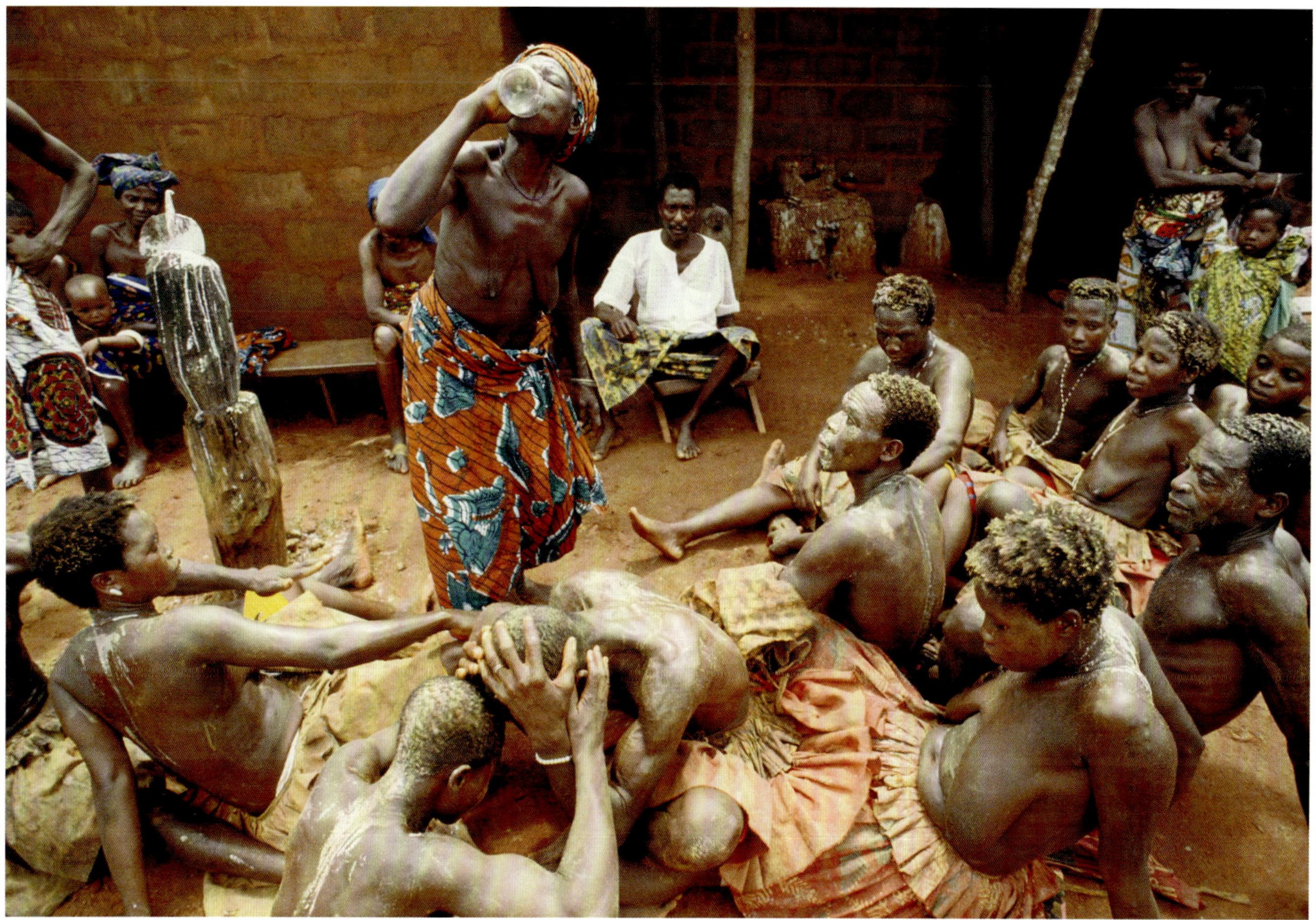

Blessing by the old priestess. The experienced priestess repeatedly takes a mouthful of gin and blows it out in the mist over the Djagli adept. This gesture means blessing and increase of power at the same time.

Bénédiction de la vieille prêtresse. La prêtresse expérimentée remplit à nouveau sa bouche de gin et le crache sur les adeptes de Djagli. Ce geste est un signe de bénédiction et augmente la force.

Segnung durch die alte Priesterin. Die erfahrene Priesterin nimmt wiederholt einen Mund voll Gin und prustet ihn im Sprühnebel über den Djagli-Adepten aus. Diese Geste bedeutet Segnung und Kraftzuwachs zugleich.

Bendición de la vieja sacerdotisa. La experimentada sacerdotisa se llena repetidamente la boca de ginebra y la expulsa en la neblina sobre los adeptos de Djagli. Este gesto es tanto una bendición como un aumento de fuerza.

Bênção da velha sacerdotisa. A sacerdotisa experiente toma repetidamente uma boca cheia de gin e esguicha-a na névoa de pulverização sobre os adeptos de Djagli. Este gesto é simultaneamente uma bênção e um aumento de força.

Zegening door de oude priesteres. De ervaren priesteres neemt herhaaldelijk een mondvol sterkedrank en spuugt die uit over de Djagli-adepten. Dit gebaar is zowel een zegen als krachtversterker.

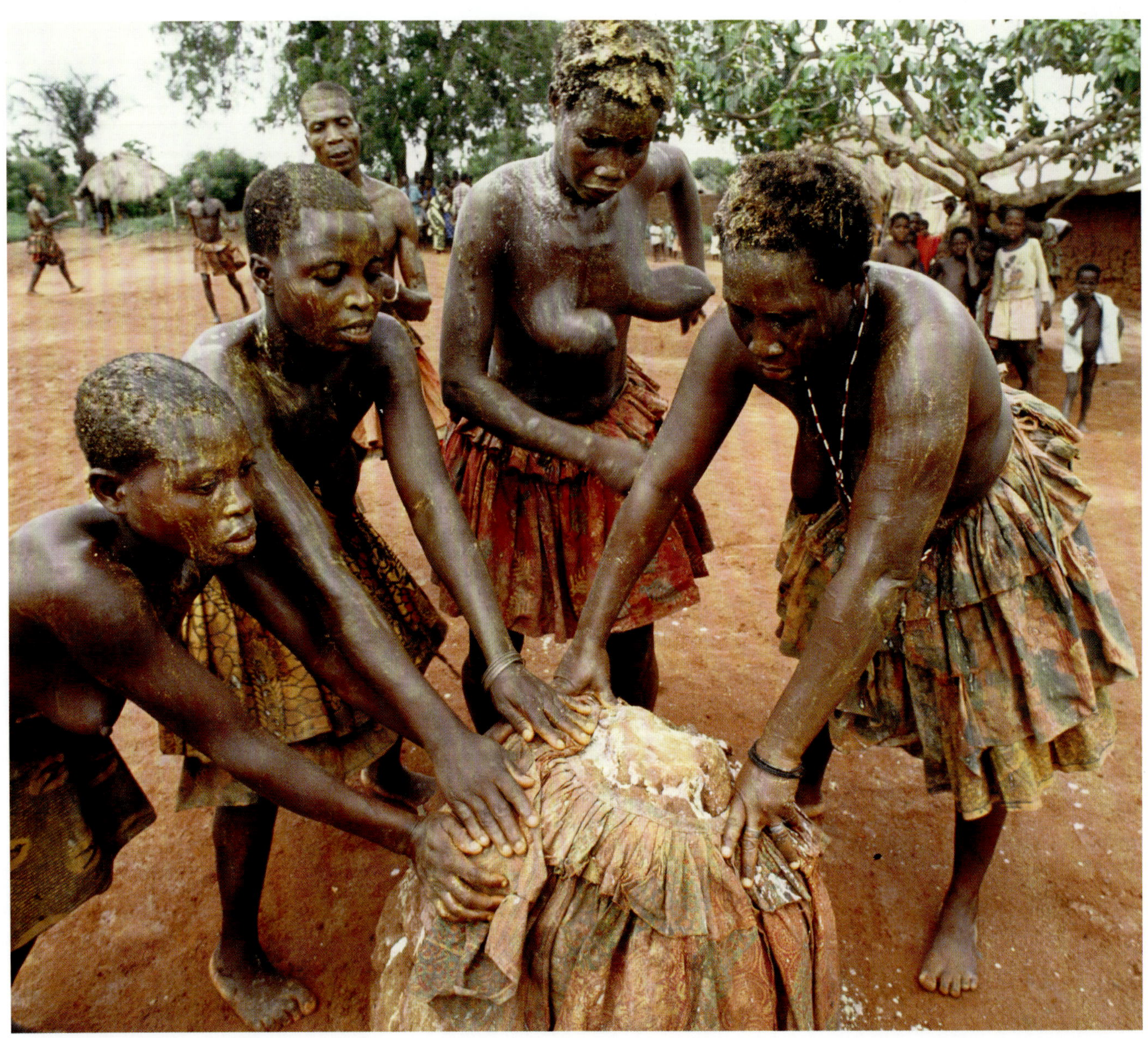

Legba makes the contact. Legba, who is a Vodun and mediator between humans and the other gods, is repeatedly the target of the adepts. At his shrine they ask for contact with Djagli.

Legba établit le contact. Legba, vodun et intermédiaire entre les hommes et les autres dieux, reçoit régulièrement l'attention des adeptes. Son autel leur permet d'entrer en contact avec Djagli.

Legba stellt den Kontakt her. Legba, seinerseits ein Vodun und Mittelsmann zwischen den Menschen und den übrigen Göttern, ist wiederholt das Ziel der Adepten. An seinem Schrein erbitten sie den Kontakt zu Djagli.

Legba toma contacto. Legba, por su parte vudú y mediador entre los humanos y los otros dioses, es repetidamente el blanco de los adeptos. En su santuario piden contacto con Djagli.

Legba faz o contato. Legba, por sua vez um vodu e mediador entre os humanos e os outros deuses, é repetidamente o alvo dos adeptos. No seu santuário pedem contacto com Djagli.

Legba legt het contact. Legba, van zijn kant een vodun en bemiddelaar tussen mensen en de andere goden, is herhaaldelijk het doel van de adepten. Bij zijn heiligdom vragen ze om contact met Djagli.

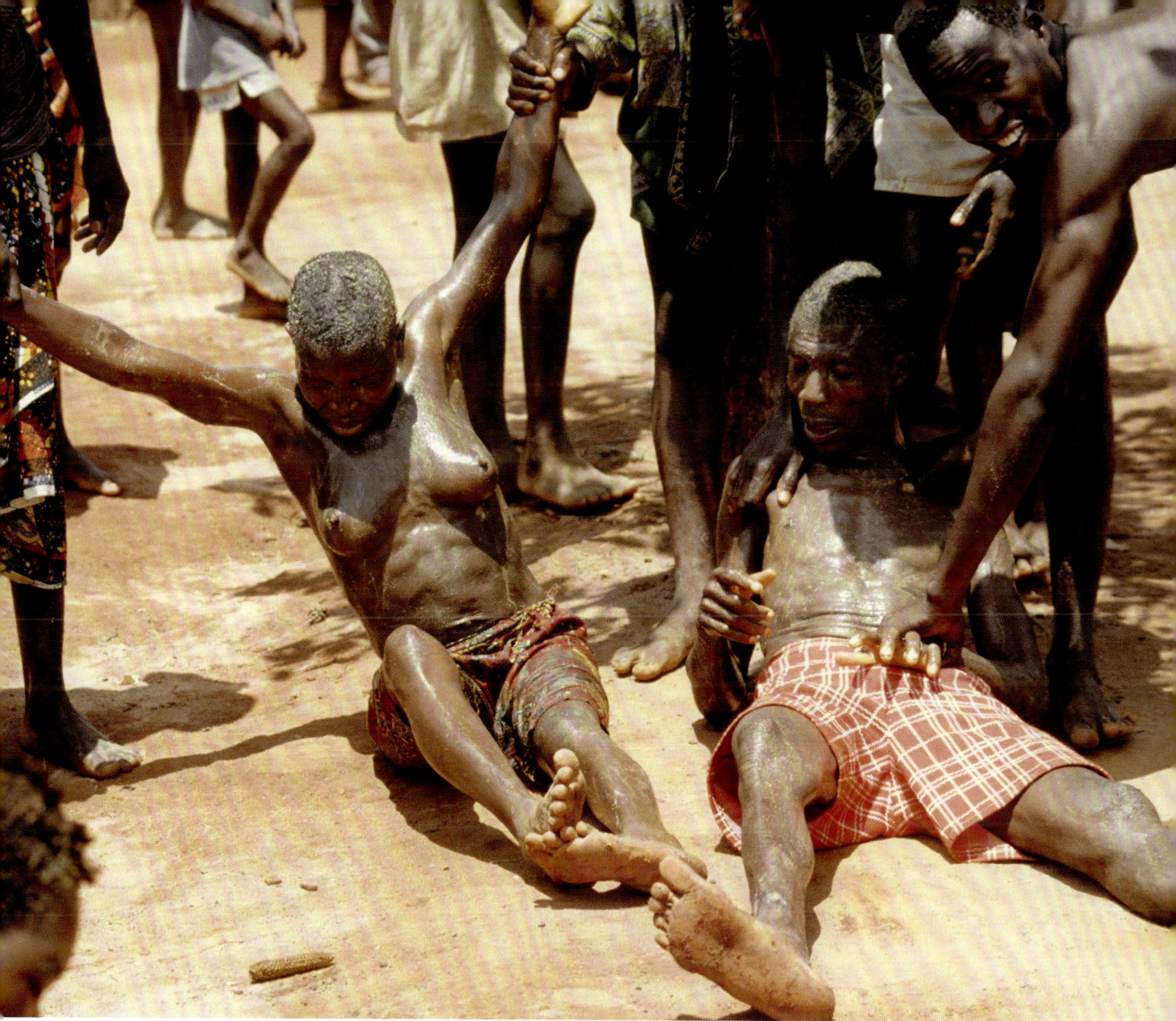

Exhausted Djagli adepts at the end of the ceremony

Adeptes de Djagli épuisés à la fin de la cérémonie

Erschöpfte Djagli-Adepten am Ende der Zeremonie

Los adeptos de Djagli agotados al final de la ceremonia

Adeptos de Djagli exaustos no final da cerimónia

Uitgeputte Djagli-adepten aan het eind van de ceremonie

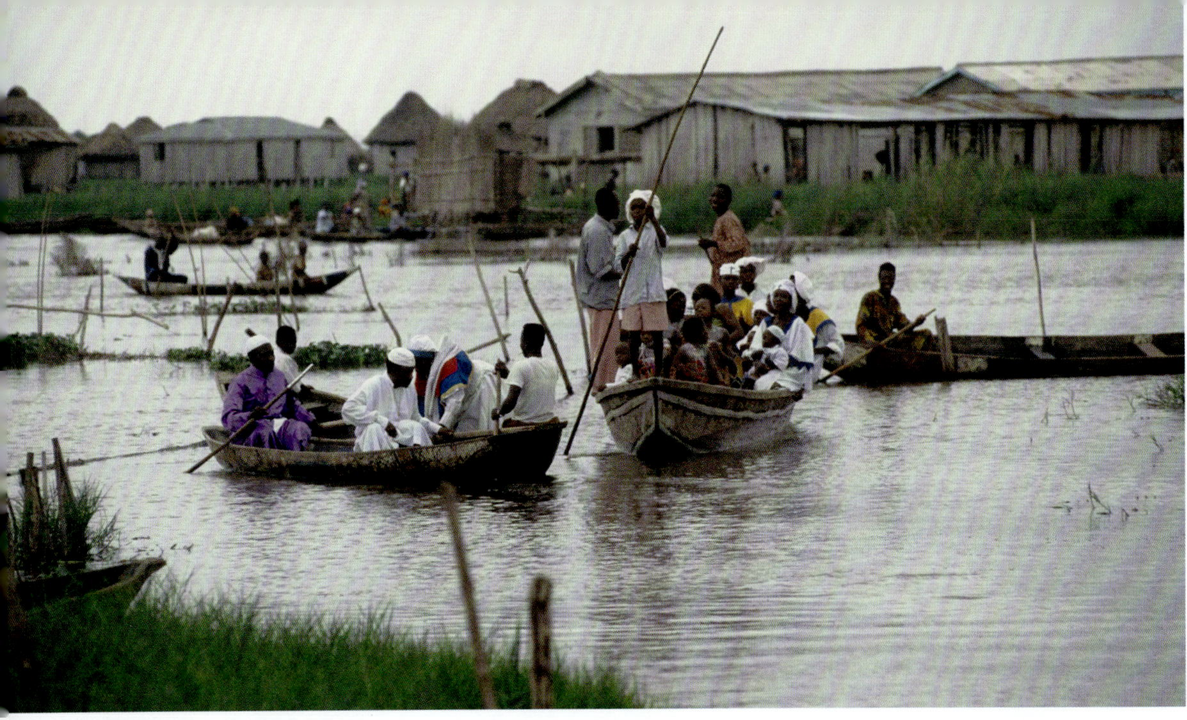

Attigali followers on Lac Nokoué paddle to ceremony

Les adeptes d'Attigali sur le lac Nokoué pagayent vers la cérémonie

Attigali-Anhänger auf dem Lac Nokoué paddeln zur Zeremonie

Adeptos de Attigali en el lago Nokoué para la ceremonia

Attigali pingentes sobre Lac Nokoué remar para a cerimônia

Attigali-aanhangers op het Lac Nokoué peddelen naar de plechtigheid

Attigali—Wild mixture against witches

A new Vodun is Attigali, which occurs in southern Benin, Togo and Ghana. This is a syncretistic cult, which mixes elements of Catholicism with beliefs of the Celestial Christians, but has also adopted Mami Wata and other influences.

At the ceremonies that take place in Ganvié at Lac Nokoué in Benin in honor of Attigali, for example, witchcraft is fought first and foremost. In the course of this, energetic dances take place, in which the dancers appear with wide skirts and faces whitened with kaolin. Trance states are desired and evidence that Attigali has descended and is among the followers.

The cult objects on the altar, encrusted in black with the coagulated blood of old offerings, are sacrificed with a white dove at the ceremony, in addition the priest ignites gunpowder.

Attigali, mélange sauvage contre les sorciers

Attigali est un vodun récent, présent au sud du Bénin, du Togo et du Ghana. C'est un culte syncrétique qui emprunte des éléments au catholicisme, avec des représentations du christianisme céleste, mais également à Mami Wata et à d'autres influences.

Les cérémonies organisées en l'honneur d'Attigali, à Ganvié sur la rive du lac Nokoué, sont principalement dédiées à la lutte contre la sorcellerie. Elles comprennent des danses impétueuses, auxquelles participent des danseuses vêtues d'une robe blanche et au visage blanchi de kaolin. L'état de transe est recherché et apporte la preuve qu'Attigali est descendu pour être présent parmi les adeptes.

Une colombe blanche est offerte en sacrifice sur l'autel. Celui-ci est chargé d'objets de culte recouverts d'une croûte noire constituée du sang séché des sacrifices antérieurs. Le prêtre enflamme également de la poudre à canon.

Attigali – Wilde Mischung gegen Hexen

Ein neuer Vodun ist Attigali, der im Süden Benins, Togos und Ghanas vorkommt. Hierbei handelt es sich um einen synkretistischen Kult, der Elemente aus dem Katholizismus mit Glaubensvorstellungen der Himmlischen Christen vermengt, aber auch Mami Wata und weitere Einflüsse aufgenommen hat.

Bei den Zeremonien, die beispielsweise in Ganvié am Lac Nokoué in Benin zu Ehren Attigalis stattfinden, wird in erster Linie die Hexerei bekämpft. Im Zuge dessen finden energetische Tänze statt, bei denen die Tänzerinnen mit weiten Röcken und von Kaolin geweißten Gesichtern auftreten. Trancezustände sind erwünscht und Beleg dafür, dass Attigali herabgestiegen und unter den Anhängern ist.

Den vom geronnenen Blut alter Opfergaben schwarz verkrusteten Kultgegenständen auf dem Altar wird bei der Zeremonie eine weiße Taube als Opfer gebracht, außerdem entzündet der Priester Schießpulver.

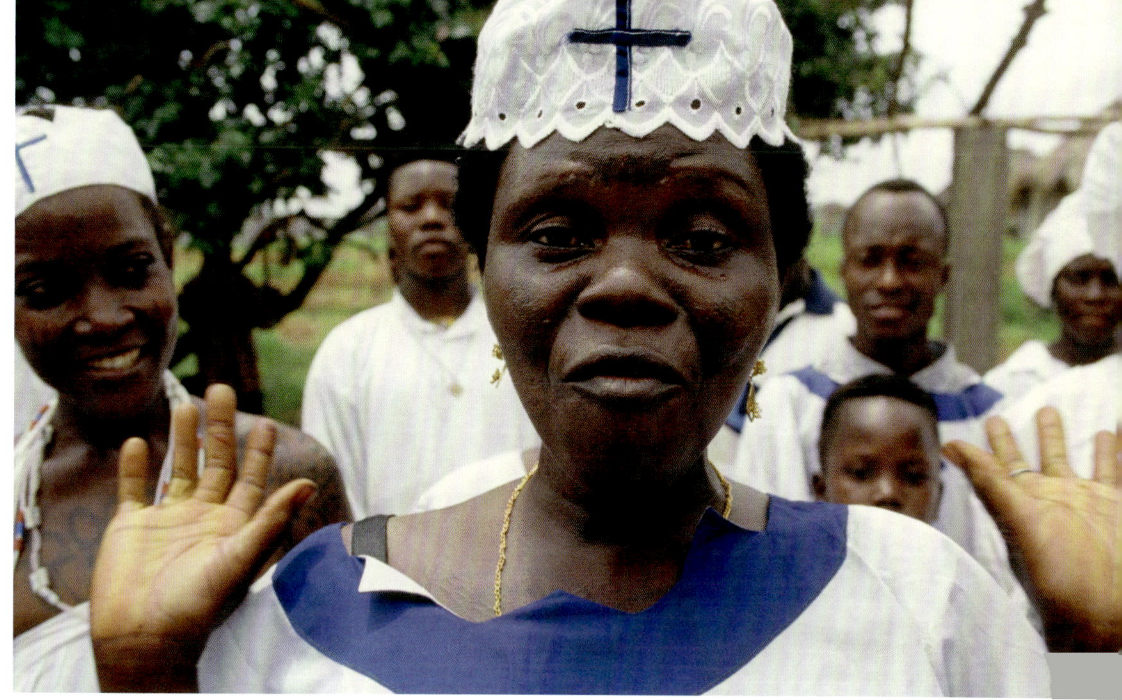

Attigali– Mezcla salvaje contra las brujas

Un nuevo vudú es Attigali, que se encuentra en el sur de Benin, Togo y Ghana. Se trata de un culto sincretista que mezcla elementos del catolicismo con las creencias de los cristianos celestiales, pero que también ha adoptado a Mami Wata y otras influencias.

En las ceremonias que tienen lugar en Ganvié am Lac Nokoué, en Benín, en honor de Attigali, por ejemplo, se combate en primer lugar la brujería. En los desfiles de estas ceremonias se realizan energéticos bailes, en los que los bailarines aparecen con faldas anchas y rostros blanqueados con caolín. Los estados de trance son deseados y prueban que Attigali ha descendido y está entre los seguidores.

En la ceremonia se sacrifica una paloma blanca junto con los objetos de culto sobre el altar, incrustados en negro por la sangre coagulada de viejas ofrendas. Además, el sacerdote enciende la pólvora.

Attigali – Mistura selvagem contra bruxas

Um novo vodu é o Attigali, que ocorre no sul do Benin, Togo e Gana. Este é um culto sincretista que mistura elementos do catolicismo com crenças dos cristãos celestes, mas também adotou Mami Wata e outras influências.

Nas cerimónias que se realizam em Ganvié am Lac Nokoué, no Benim, em honra de Attigali, por exemplo, a feitiçaria é combatida antes de mais nada. No decorrer destas danças enérgicas acontecem, nas quais os dançarinos aparecem com saias largas e rostos branqueados com caulim. Os estados de transe são desejados e provam que Attigali desceu e está entre os seguidores.

Os objetos de culto sobre o altar, incrustados de preto pelo sangue coagulado das ofertas antigas, são sacrificados com uma pomba branca na cerimónia, e o sacerdote também acende a pólvora.

Attigali – wilde mix tegen heksen

Een nieuwe vodun is Attigali, die voorkomt in Zuid-Benin, Togo en Ghana. Het gaat hier om een syncretistische cultus die elementen van het katholicisme vermengt met de overtuigingen van de wedergeboren christenen, maar die ook Mami Wata en andere invloeden heeft overgenomen.

Bij de plechtigheden ter ere van Attigali in bijvoorbeeld Ganvié aan het Lac Nokoué in Benin wordt in de eerste plaats de hekserij bestreden. In het kader hiervan vinden energetische dansen plaats, waarbij danseressen met wijde rokken en met kaolien gebleekte gezichten verschijnen. Een staat van trance is gewenst en bewijst dat Attigali is neergedaald en onder de volgelingen is.

Bij de door het gestolde bloed van oude offers zwart geworden cultusvoorwerpen op het altaar wordt tijdens de ceremonie een witte duif geofferd en de priester steekt ook buskruit aan.

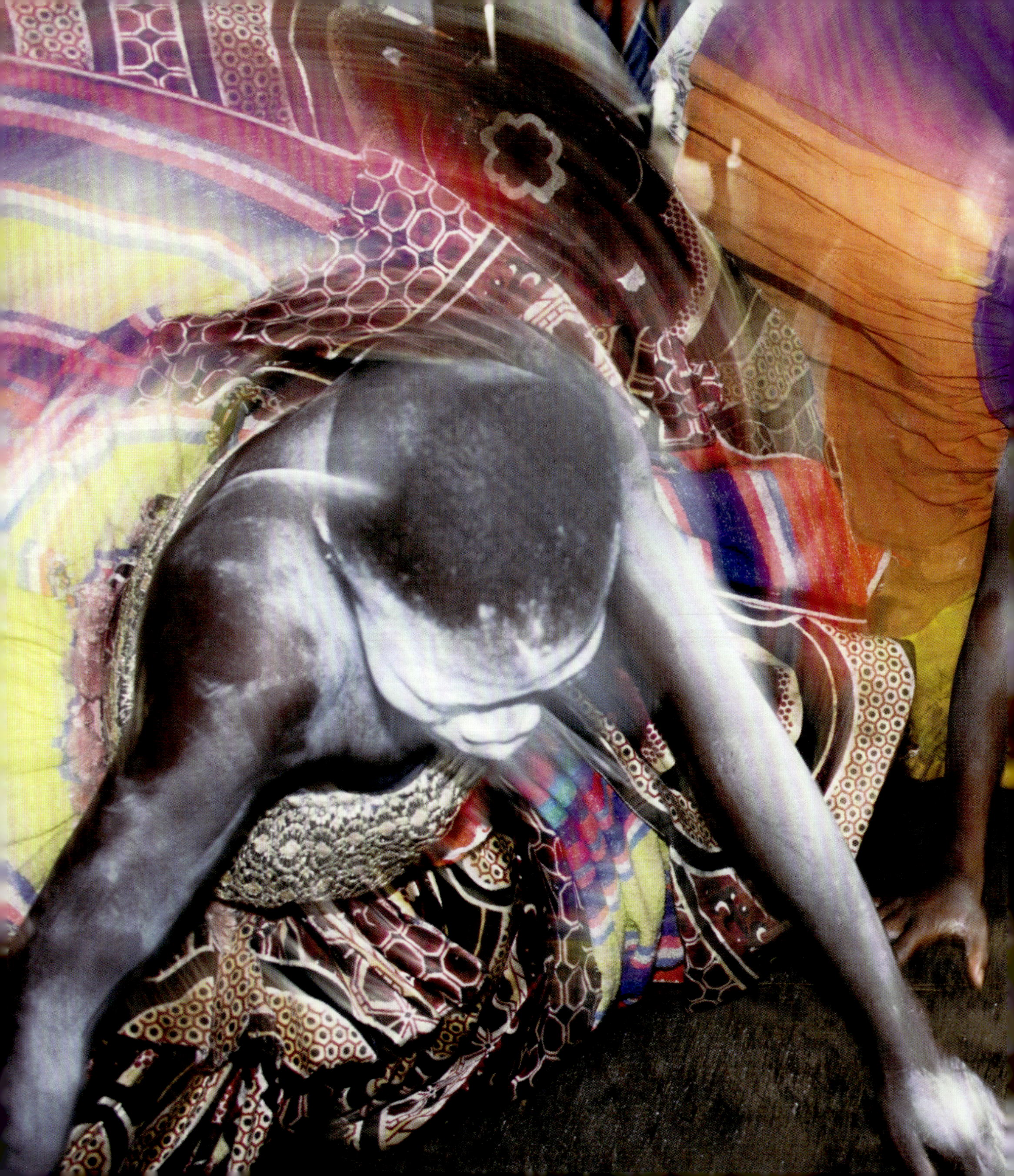

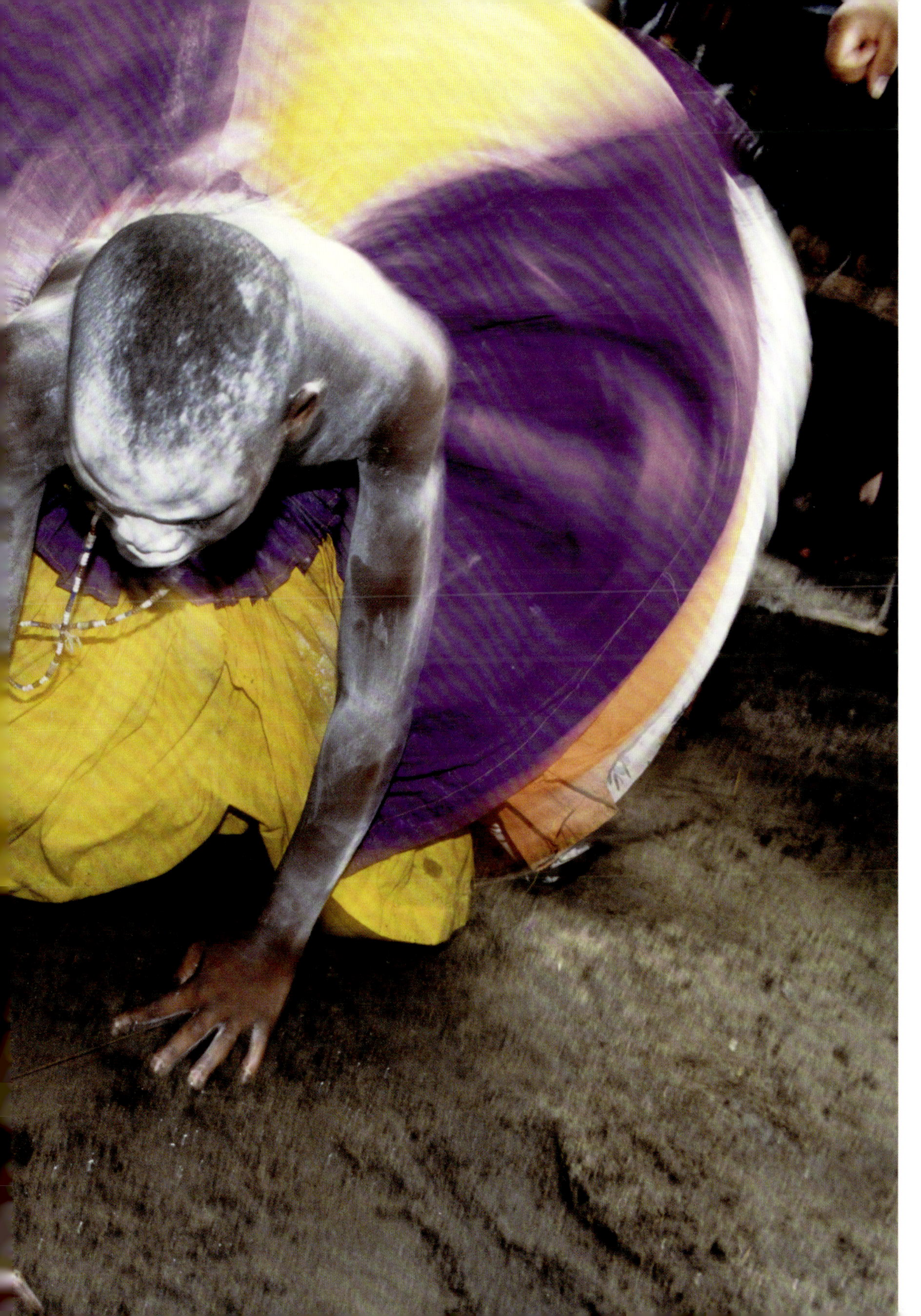

Two boys possessed
by Attigali dancing

Deux garçons
possédés par Attigali
pendant la danse

Zwei von Attigali
besessene Jungen
beim Tanz

Dos chicos poseídos
por Attigali en el baile

Dois rapazes
possuídos por Attigali
no baile

Twee dansende
jongens die bezeten
zijn door Attigali

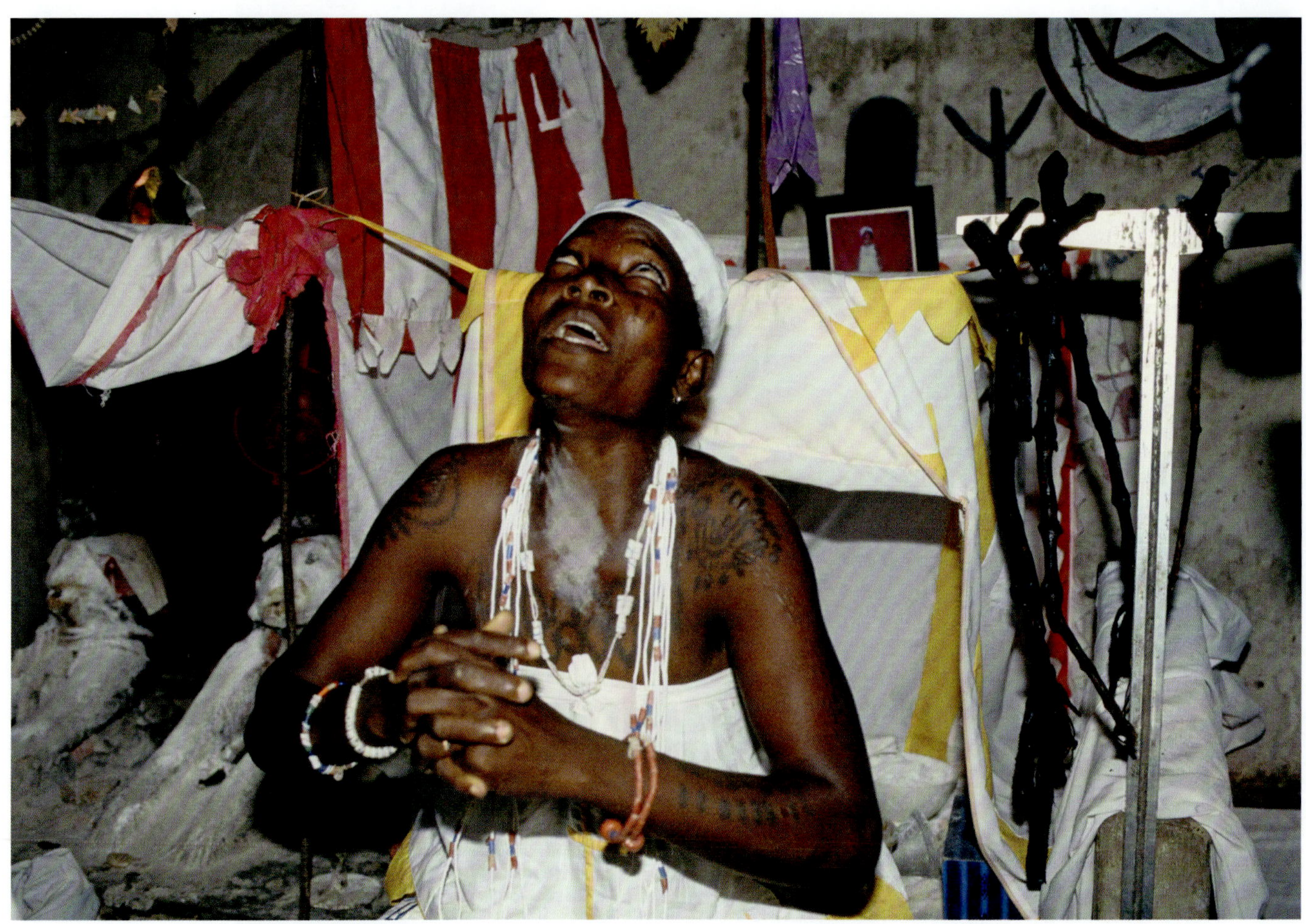

An adept in a trance at Attigali's shrine

Adepte en transe au sanctuaire d'Attigali

Eine Adeptin in Trance an Attigalis Schrein

Un adepto en trance en el santuario de Attigali

Um adepto em transe no santuário de Attigali

Een aanhangster in trance bij Attigali's heiligdom

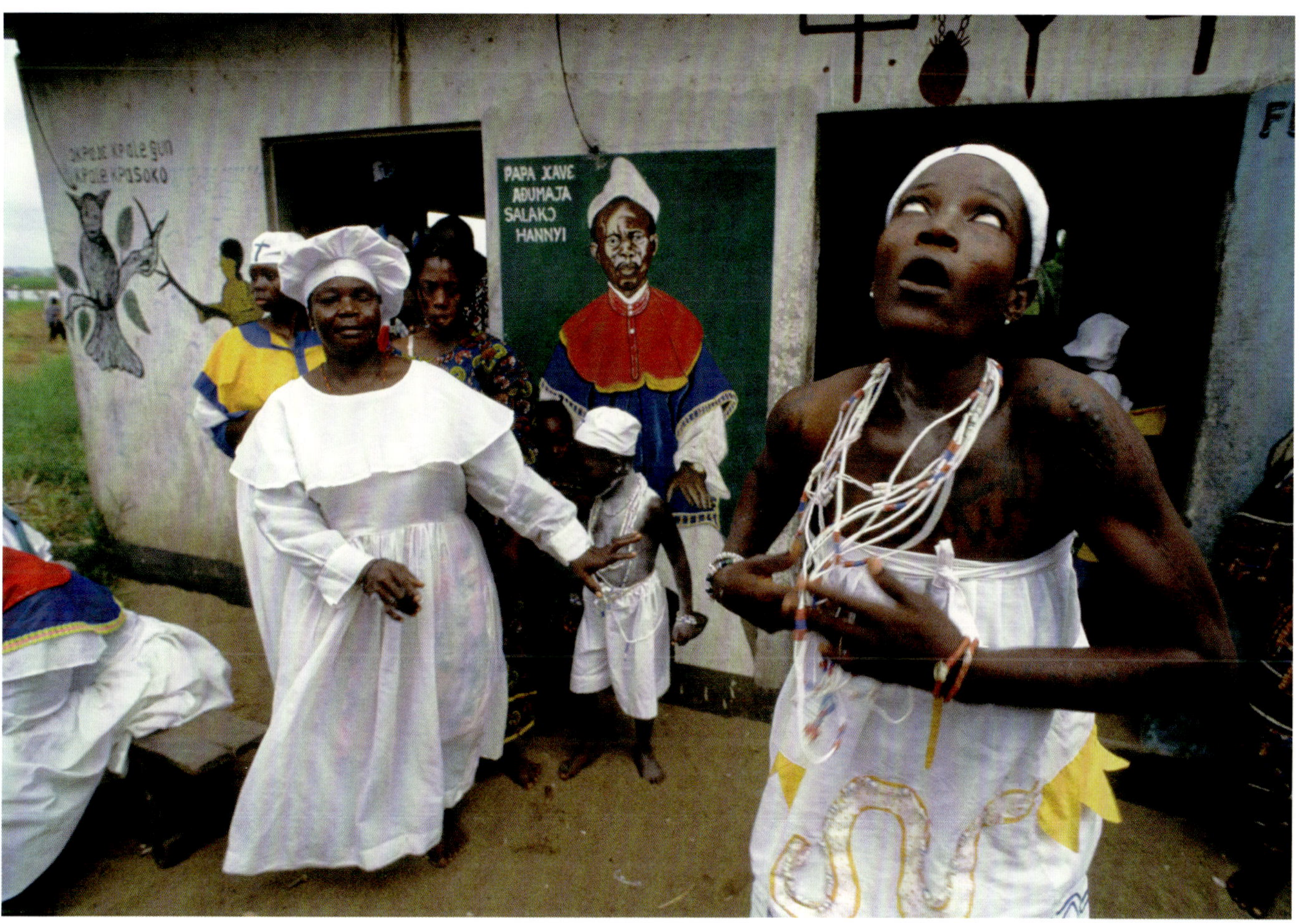

Follower of Attigali in a trance

Adepte d'Attigali en transe

Anhänger Attigalis in Trance

Adepto de Attigali en trance

Pingente Attigalis em transe

Aanhangster van Attigali in trance

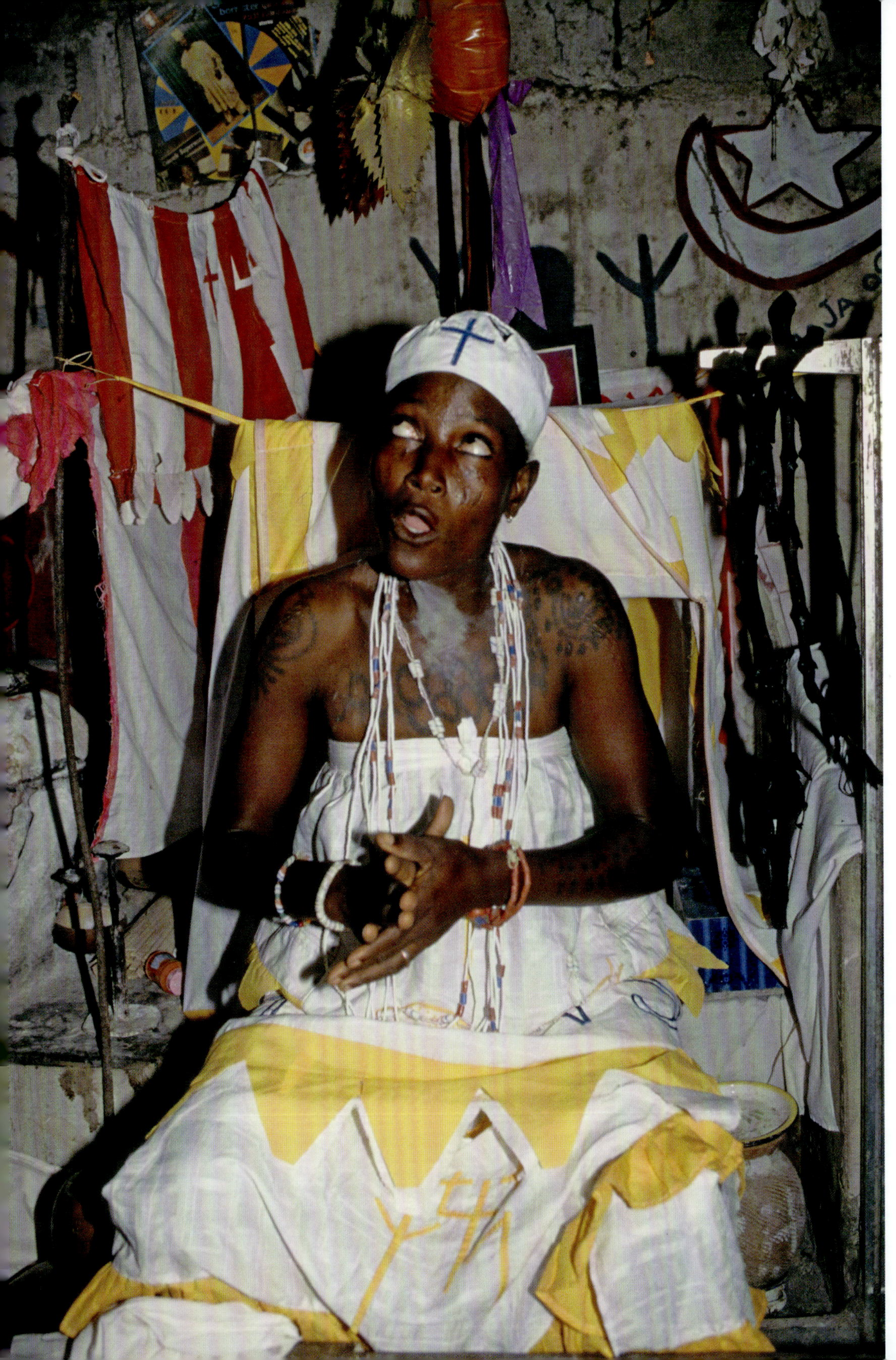

At the shrine of Attigali. The blue cross does not stand for Christ, but for the highest Vodun god. Nevertheless, Attigali has also adopted rites of the Catholic Church and of born-again Christians.

Au sanctuaire d'Attigali. La croix bleue ne fait pas référence au Christ mais à la plus haute divinité vodun. Cependant, Attigali a repris certains rites provenant de l'Église catholique et associés au Christ ressuscité.

Am Schrein Attigalis. Das blaue Kreuz steht nicht für Christus, sondern für die höchste Vodungottheit. Dennoch hat Attigali auch Riten der katholischen Kirche und der Wiedergeborenen Christen übernommen.

En el santuario de Attigali. La cruz azul no representa a Cristo, sino a la deidad más elevada de vudú. Sin embargo, Attigali también ha adoptado ritos de la iglesia católica y de los cristianos nacidos de nuevo.

No Santuário Attigalis. A cruz azul não significa Cristo, mas sim a mais alta divindade Vodung. No entanto, Attigali também adotou ritos da Igreja Católica e dos cristãos nascidos de novo.

Bij het heiligdom van Attigali. Het blauwe kruis staat niet voor Christus, maar voor de hoogste vodungod. Toch heeft Attigali ook rituelen van de katholieke kerk en de wedergeboren christenen overgenomen.

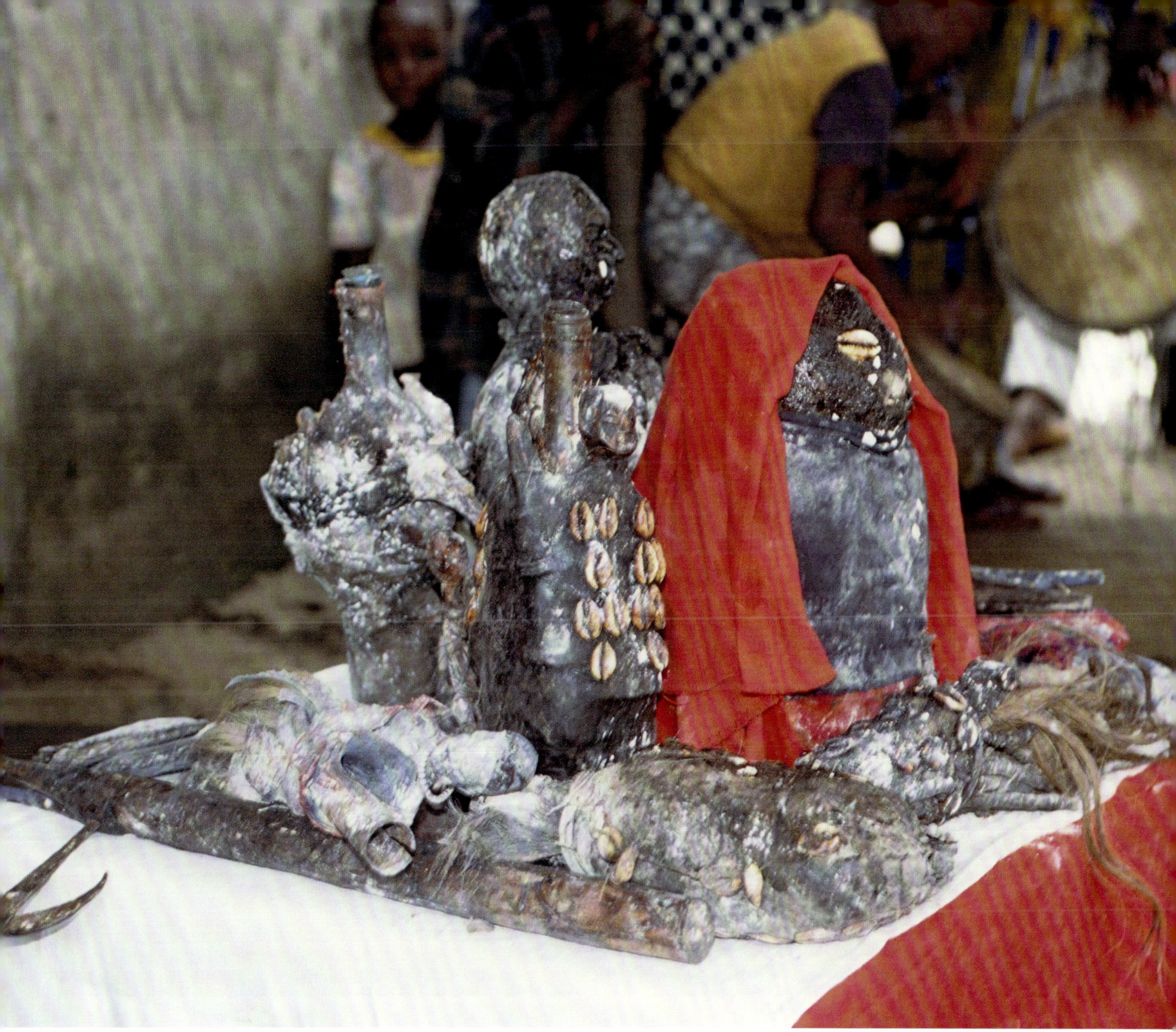

Attigali cult objects on an altar. Encrusted with the black coagulated blood of previous offerings, Attigali's cult objects witness another energetic ritual against the powers of witchcraft.

Objets du culte d'Attigali sur un autel. Recouverts d'une croûte noire constituée du sang versé au cours des sacrifices, les objets de culte d'Attigali témoignent d'un autre rituel énergétique contre les forces de la sorcellerie.

Kultobjekte Attigalis auf einem Altar. Vom schwarz geronnenen Blut vorheriger Opfergaben überkrustet, werden die Kultobjekte Attigalis Zeugen eines weiteren, energetischen Rituals gegen die Kräfte der Hexerei.

Objetos de culto de Attigali sobre un altar. Cubiertos con la sangre negra coagulada de las ofrendas anteriores, los objetos de culto de Attigali son testigos de otro ritual energético contra los poderes de la brujería.

Objetos de culto Attigalis sobre um altar. Incrustados com o sangue negro coagulado das oferendas anteriores, os objectos de culto de Attigali testemunham outro ritual energético contra os poderes da feitiçaria.

Cultusobjecten van Attigali op een altaar. Met zwart gestold bloed van eerdere offers bedekte cultusobjecten voor Attigali getuigen van nog een energetisch ritueel tegen de krachten van hekserij.

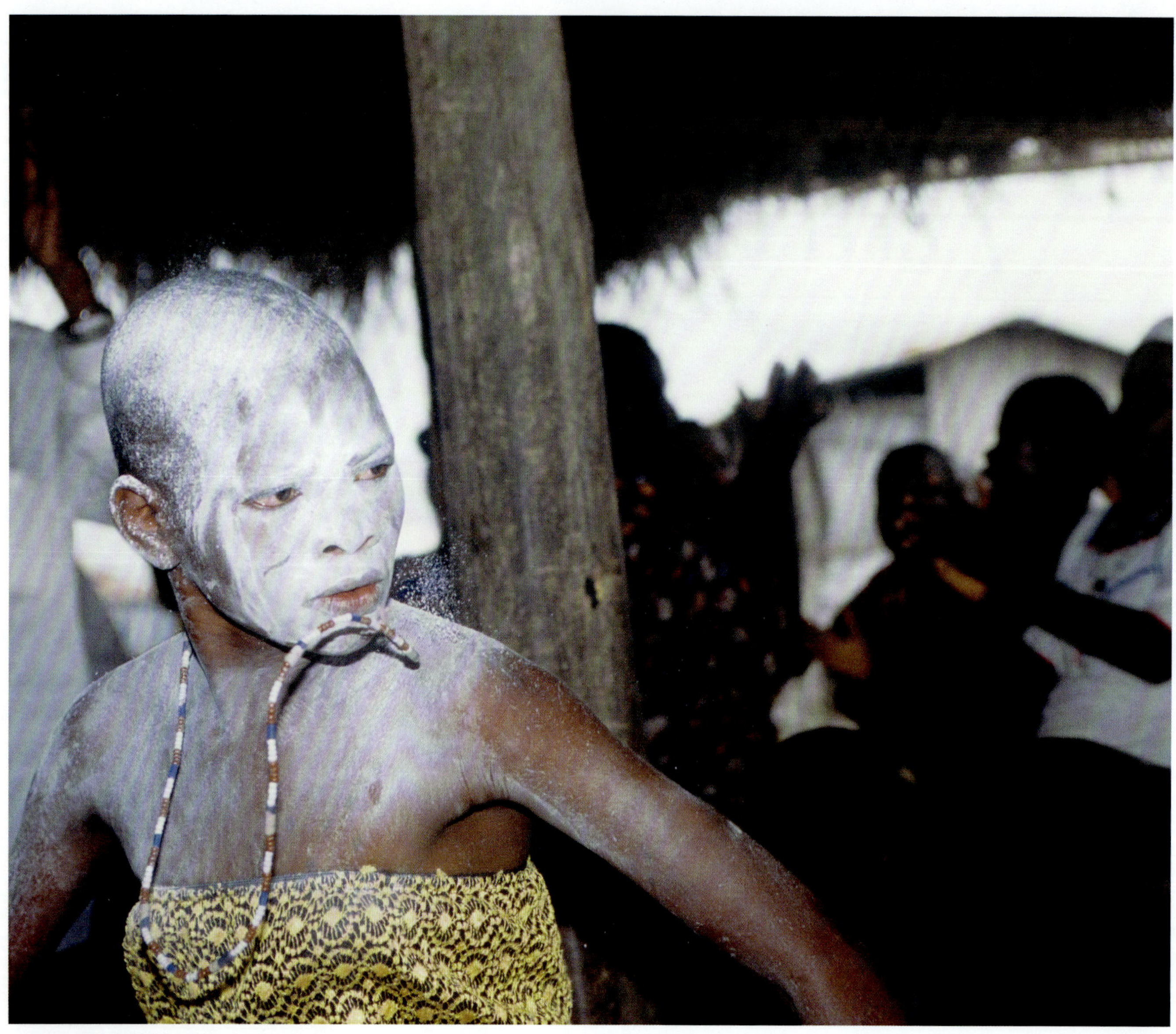

A young Attigali adept dances in a trance

Une jeune adepte d'Attigali danse en transe

Eine junge Attigali-Adeptin tanzt in Trance

Un joven adepto de Attigali baila en trance

Um jovem Átigali adepto das danças em transe

Een jonge Attigali-aanhangster danst in trance

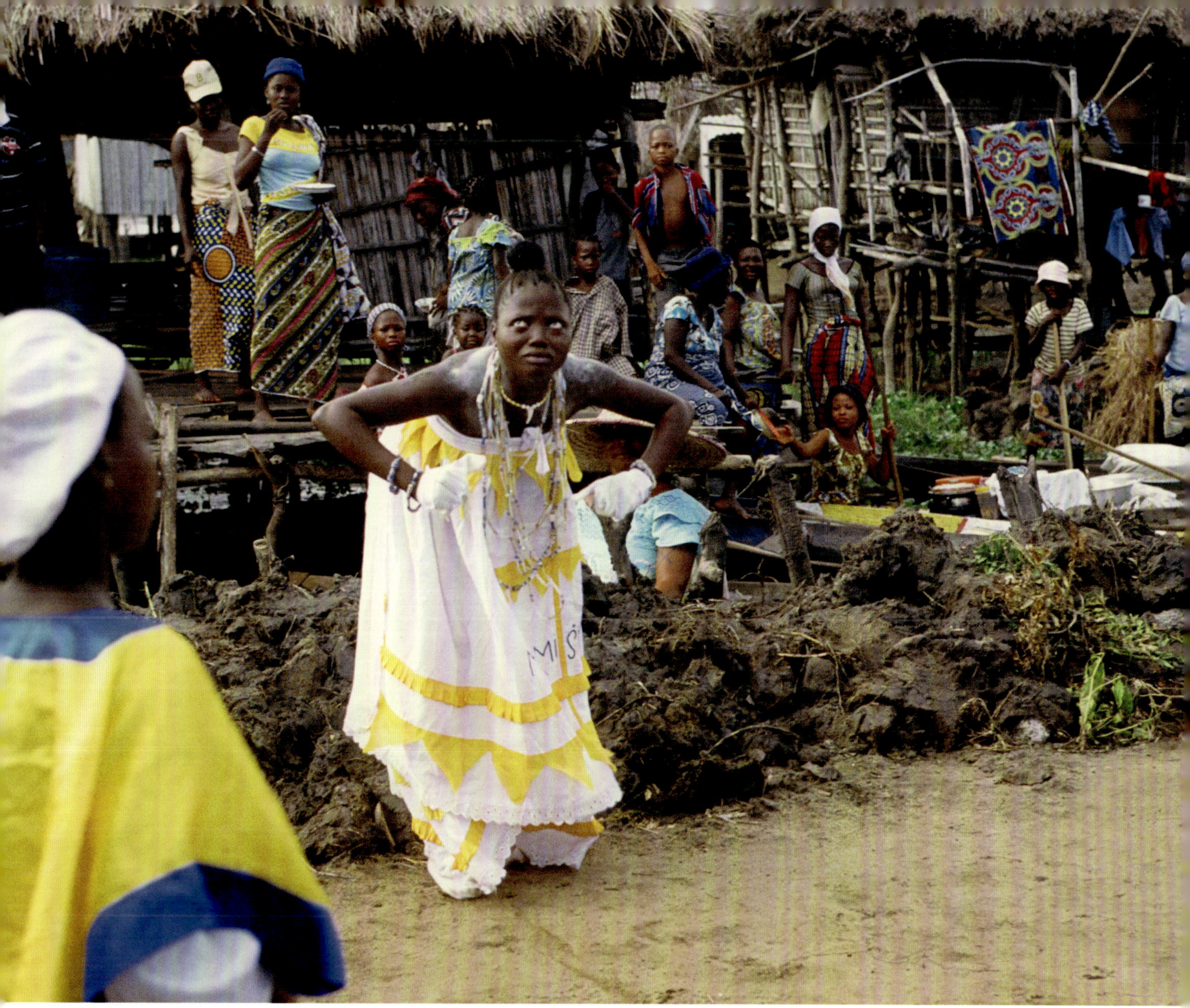

Ceremony on the Lac Nokoué, Benin. It is one of many tiny islands with accumulations of pile dwellings where the Attigali ceremony takes place. Attigali is a Vodun who fights against damaging magic.

Cérémonie sur le lac Nokoué, Bénin. Sur le lac, de nombreuses et minuscules îles aménagées avec des constructions sur pilotis accueillent une cérémonie pour Attigali. Ce vodun lutte principalement contre la magie maléfique.

Zeremonie auf dem Lac Nokoué, Benin. Es ist eine von vielen winzigen Inseln mit Ansammlungen von Pfahlbauten, auf dem die Attigali-Zeremonie stattfindet. Im Kern ist Attigali ein Vodun, der gegen Schadenmagie kämpft.

Ceremonia en el lago Nokoué, Benin. Es una de las muchas islas diminutas con acumulaciones de viviendas en pilas en las que se celebra la ceremonia de Attigali, un vudú que lucha contra la magia negra.

Cerimônia no Lac Nokoué, Benin. É uma das muitas ilhas minúsculas com acumulações de moradias em pilha sobre as quais se realiza a cerimónia Attigali. Attigali é um vodu que luta contra a magia do mal.

Ceremonie op het Lac Nokoué, Benin. Op een van de vele kleine eilandjes met groepjes paalwoningen vindt de Attigali-ceremonie plaats. Attigali is een vodun die vecht tegen schadelijke magie.

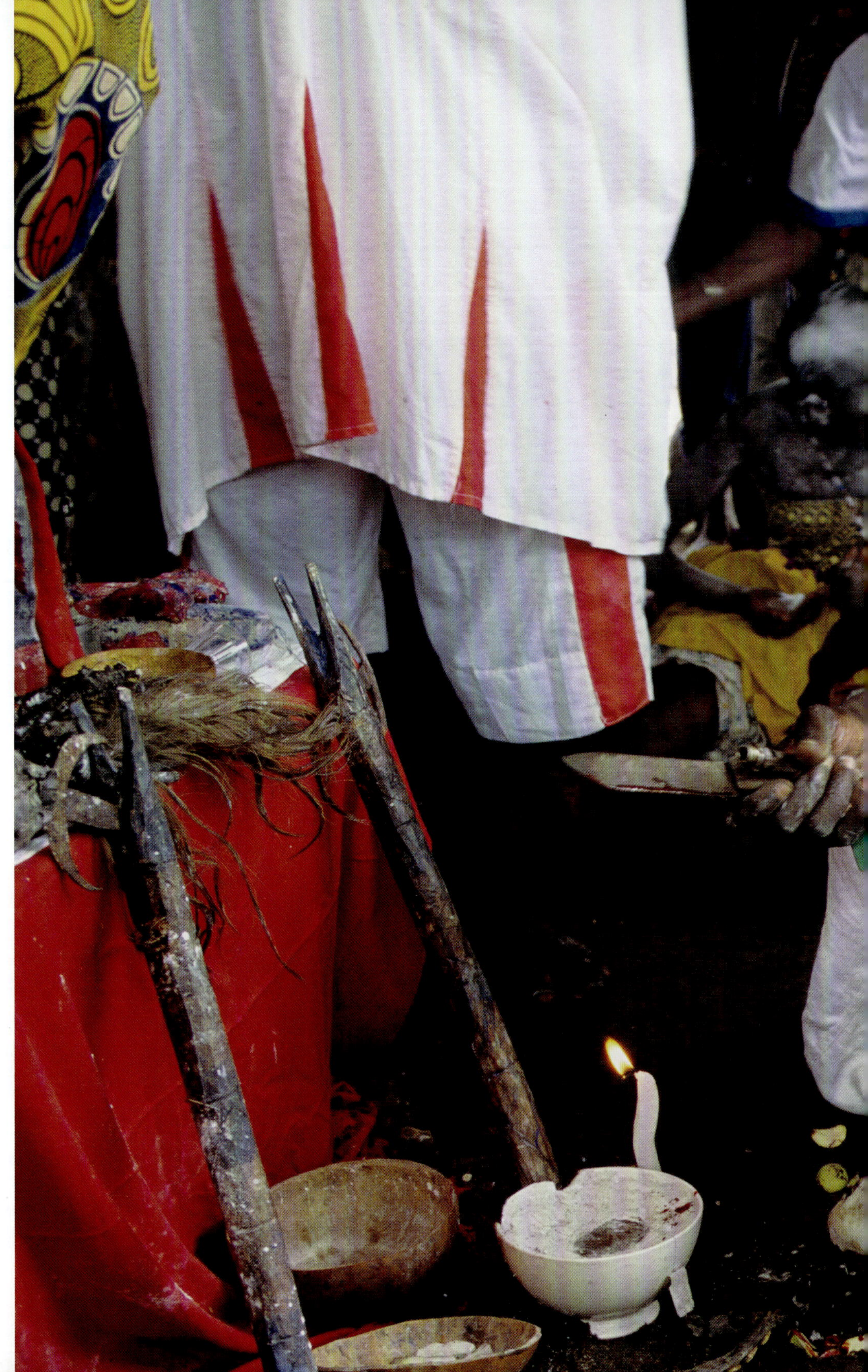

The Attigali priest sacrifices a
chicken for the gods

Le prêtre d'Attigali sacrifie un
poulet aux dieux

Der Attigali-Priester opfert ein
Huhn für die Götter

El sacerdote Attigali sacrifica un
pollo para los dioses

O padre Átigali sacrifica uma
galinha pelos deuses

De Attigali-priester offert een kip
voor de goden

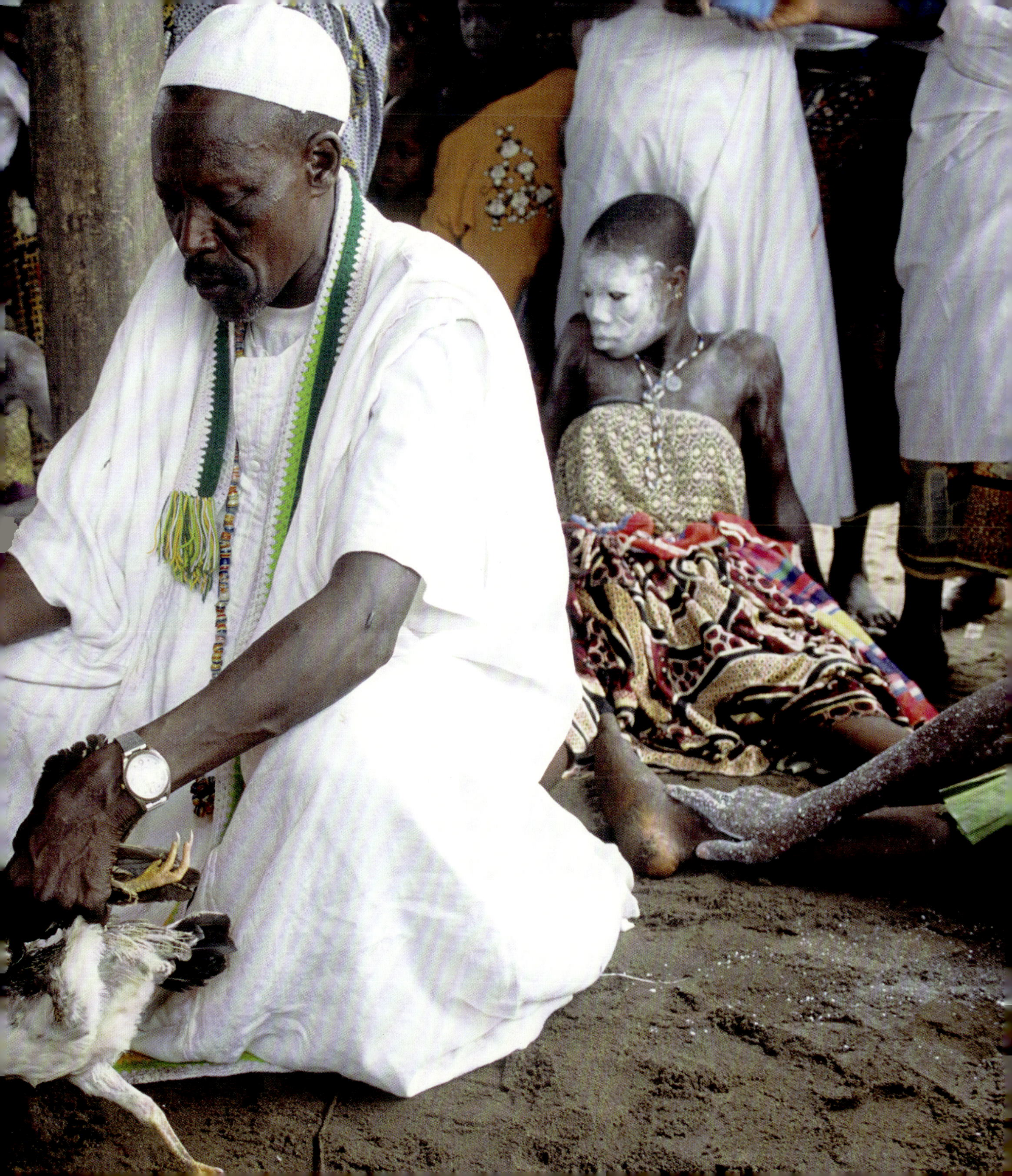

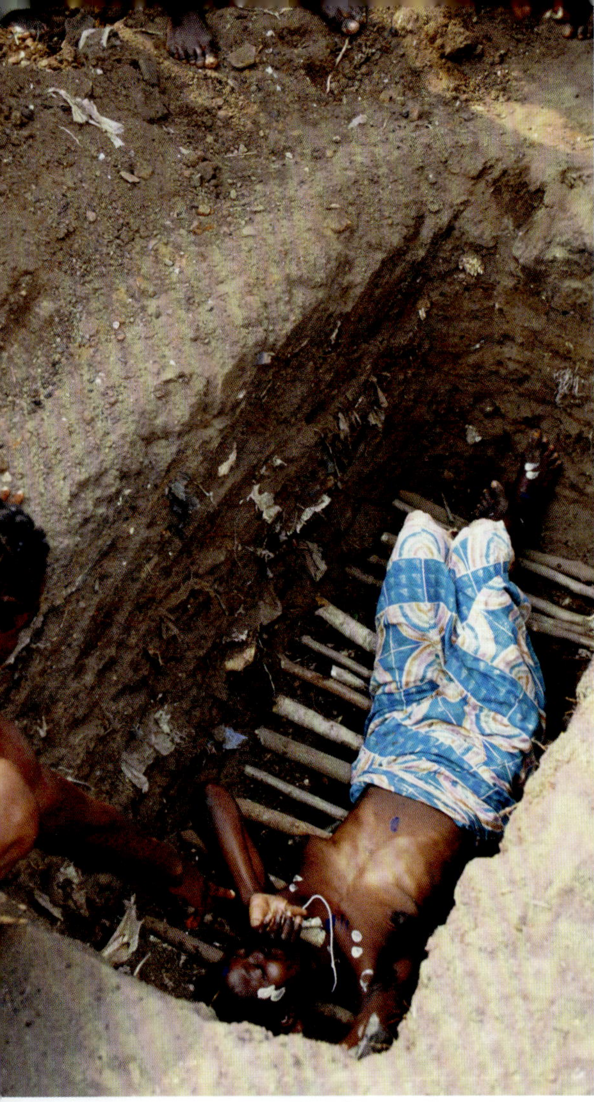

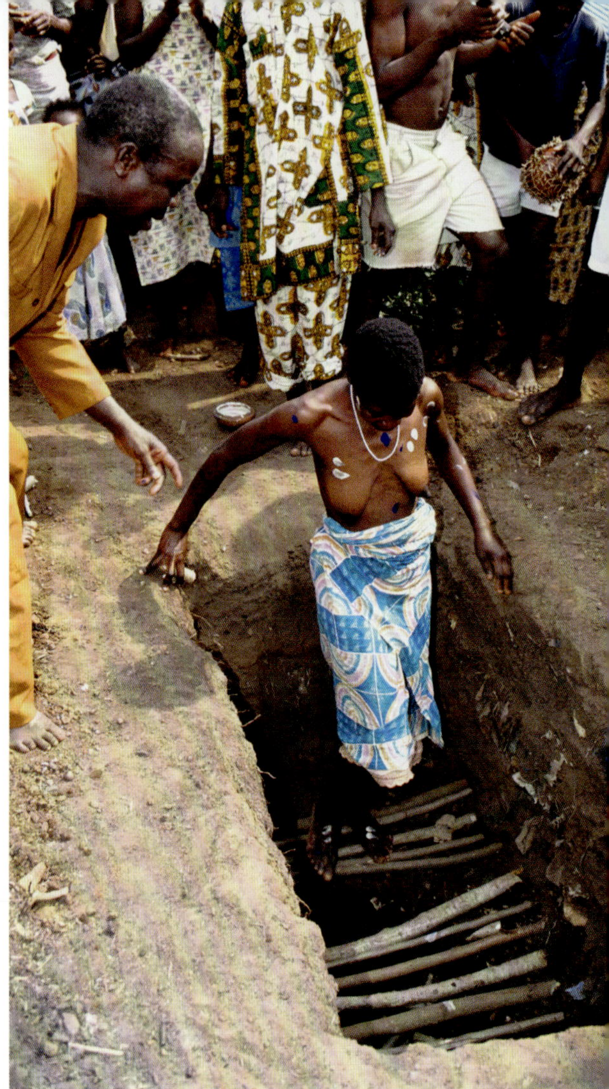

New Year—Funeral of Sin and Rebirth

The Ewe people have a special ceremony in the Benin Mono district, which is traditionally attended by all the villagers on New Year's Day.

First, like a funeral, a great grave is dug. In the course of the festivity all those present then climb into the pit one after the other and lie down flat in it. They hold a stick specially prepared by the medicine man, the *kpantin*, to whom they whisper the misdeeds of the past year. After confession, the person is sprinkled with white powder and then,

Nouvelle année, enterrement des péchés et renaissance

Pour l'ethnie Éwé, dans le département du Mono, il existe une cérémonie spécifique pour la nouvelle année à laquelle tous les villageois prennent traditionnellement part.

Dans un premier temps, une grande tombe est creusée, comme pour un enterrement. Au cours des festivités, tous les participants sautent à tour de rôle dans la tombe et s'allongent au fond. On leur remet un bâton spécial, préparé par le guérisseur et appelé *kpantin,* auquel ils chuchotent les forfaits qu'ils ont commis au cours de l'année

Neujahr – Sündenbegräbnis und Wiedergeburt

Beim Volk der Ewe gibt es in der Region des Beniner Monodistriktes eine besondere Zeremonie, an der zu Neujahr alle Dorfbewohner traditionell teilnehmen.

Zuerst wird, einer Beerdigung gleich, ein großes Grab ausgehoben. Im Laufe der Festivität steigen dann alle Anwesenden nacheinander in die Grube und legen sich flach hinein. Dabei halten sie einen vom Medizinmann speziell präparierten Stock, den *kpantin,* dem sie flüsternd die Missetaten des vergangenen Jahres

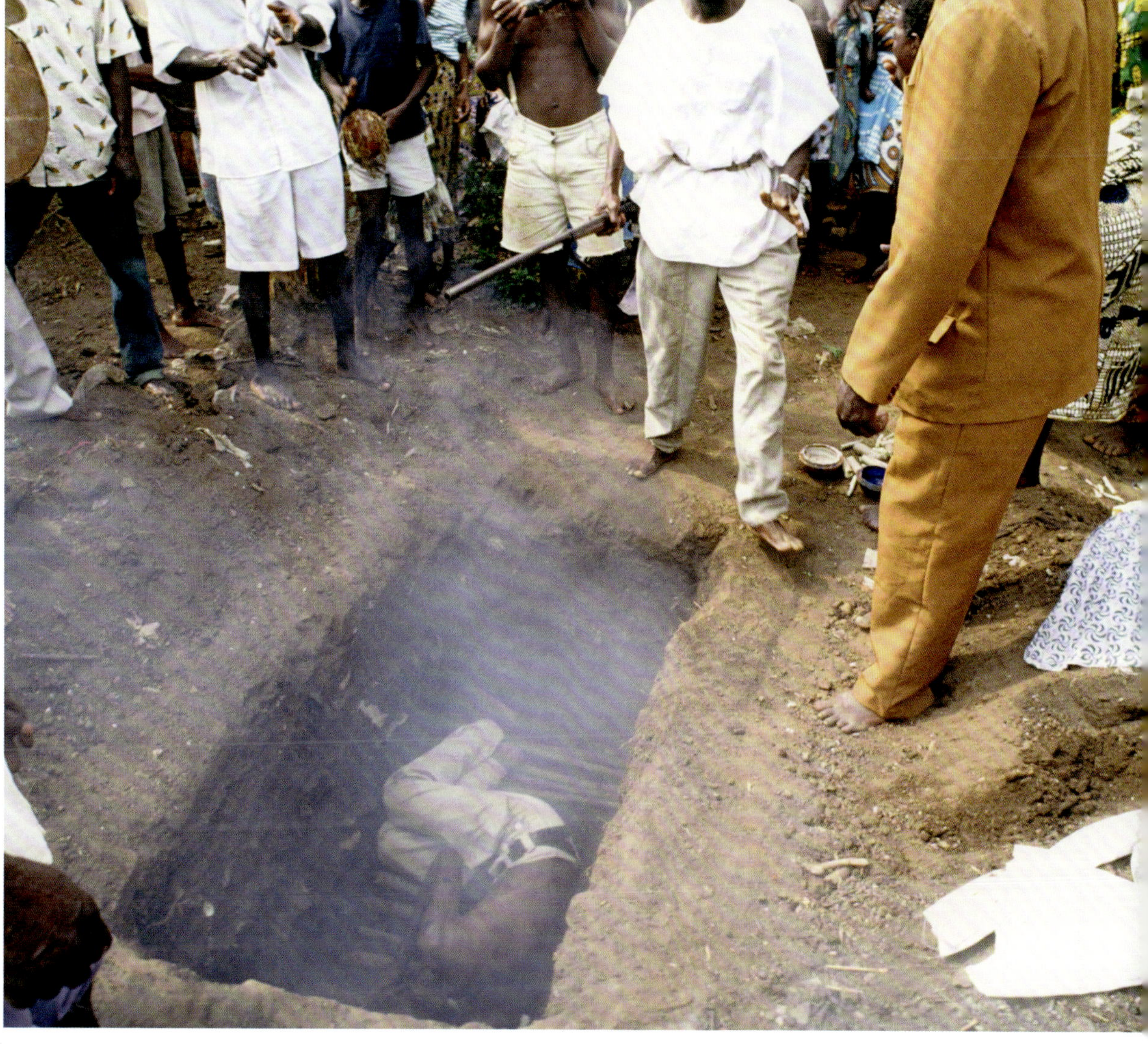

Año Nuevo– El entierro del pecado y el renacimiento

El pueblo de Ewe celebra una ceremonia especial en la región del monodistrito de Benin, a la que tradicionalmente asisten todos los aldeanos el día de Año Nuevo.

Primero, como en un funeral, se excava una gran tumba. En el transcurso de la fiesta, todos los presentes se meten uno tras otro en el foso y se acuestan. Una vez allí, cogen un palo especialmente preparado por el curandero, el *kpantin,* a quien le susurran las fechorías del año pasado. Después de la confesión, la persona en cuestión es

Ano Novo – Funeral do Pecado e Renascimento

O povo Ewe tem uma cerimônia especial na região monodistrital de Benin, que é tradicionalmente frequentada por todos os aldeões no Dia de Ano Novo.

Primeiro, como um funeral, uma grande sepultura é cavada. No decorrer da festa, todos os presentes sobem um após o outro para o poço e deitam-se no chão. Eles seguram um bastão especialmente preparado pelo curandeiro, o *kpantin,* a quem sussurram os erros do ano passado. Após a confissão, a pessoa em questão

Nieuwjaar – begrafenis van zonden en wedergeboorte

Het Ewe-volk in het departement Mono in Benin heeft een speciale ceremonie die traditioneel op nieuwjaarsdag door alle dorpelingen wordt bijgewoond.

Eerst wordt er, net als bij een begrafenis, een groot graf gegraven. In de loop van het feest klimmen alle aanwezigen na elkaar het gat in en gaan plat liggen. Ze houden een speciaal door de medicijnman geprepareerde stok vast, de *kpantin*, die ze hun wandaden van het afgelopen jaar toefluisteren. Aansluitend op de biecht

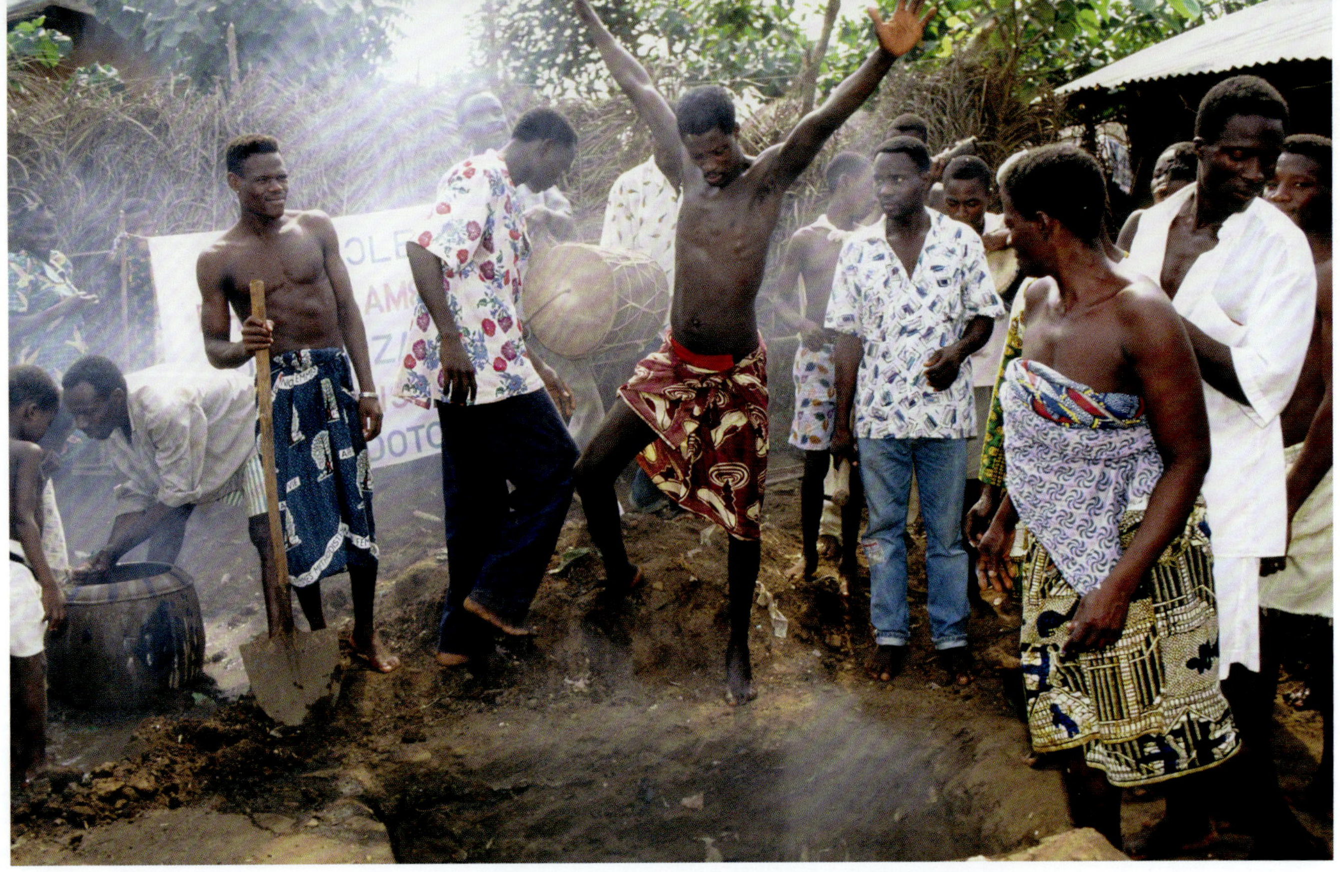

The joy of some is great. The ritual, which gives everyone in the social community a new beginning for their own path in life and for their relationships with one another, causes leaps of joy.

Certains sont en liesse. Le rituel déclenche des sauts de joie : il permet à tous les membres de la communauté de prendre un nouveau départ pour eux-mêmes et dans leurs relations avec les autres.

Die Freude bei manchen ist groß. Das Ritual, das allen in der Sozialgemeinschaft einen neuen Anfang für den eigenen Weg und die Beziehungen untereinander ermöglicht, sorgt für Freudensprünge.

La alegría de algunos es grande. El ritual, que proporciona a cada uno en la comunidad social un nuevo comienzo para su propio camino y para sus relaciones con los demás, hace que todos den saltos de alegría.

A alegria de alguns é grande. O ritual, que dá a cada um na comunidade social um novo começo para o seu próprio caminho e para as suas relações mútuas, proporciona saltos de alegria.

De vreugde van sommigen is groot. Het ritueel, dat iedereen in de gemeenschap een nieuw begin geeft voor zijn eigen weg en voor de relaties met elkaar, leidt tot vreugdesprongen.

symbolically purified, resurrected from the grave. Now they share with the community the good intentions for the time ahead.

A washing with holy water seals the project. The confessional wood charged with negative energy, on the other hand, is buried in a ritual setting, as is the past evil.

passée. À la fin de la confession, l'adepte est recouvert de poudre blanche puis ressorti de la tombe, symboliquement purifié. Il annonce alors à la société ses bonnes intentions pour l'année à venir.

Un lavage à l'eau bénite scelle la cérémonie. Le bâton confessionnel chargé d'énergie négative ainsi que les torts de l'année écoulée sont enterrés rituellement.

mitteilen. Im Anschluss an die Beichte wird die betreffende Person mit weißem Puder bestäubt, um danach, symbolisch gereinigt, aus dem Grab wiederaufzuerstehen. Jetzt teilt sie der Gemeinschaft die guten Vorsätze für die bevorstehende Zeit mit.

Eine Waschung mit gesegnetem Wasser besiegelt das Vorhaben. Das mit der negativen Energie aufgeladene Beichtholz hingegen wird, ebenso wie das vergangene Böse, im rituellen Rahmen beerdigt.

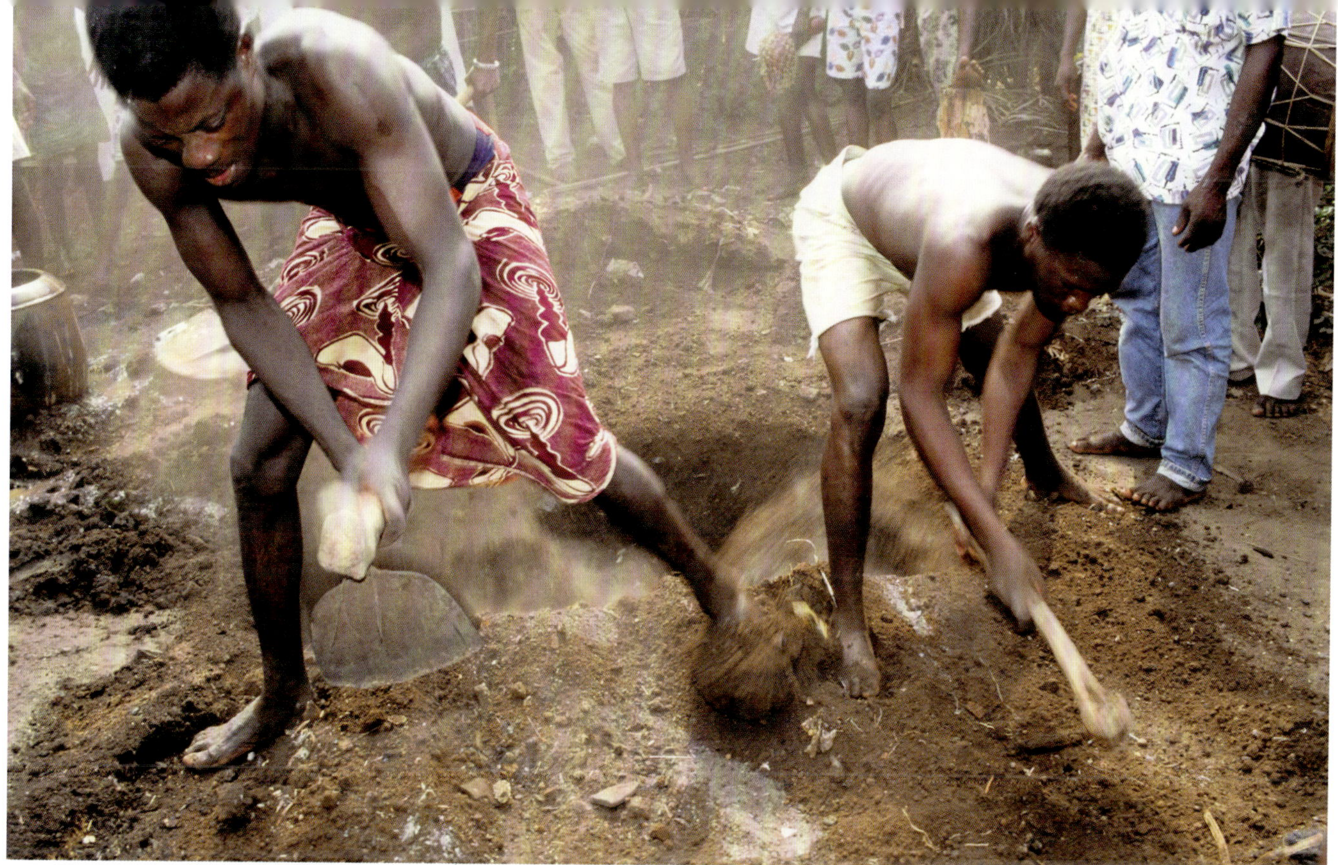

In the end, the contaminated soils will be buried
À la fin, les sites contaminés seront ensevelis
Am Ende werden die Altlasten begraben
Al final, se entierran las antiguas cargas
No final, os locais contaminados serão enterrados
Aan het eind worden de oude zorgen begraven

espolvoreada con polvo blanco y luego, simbólicamente limpiada y resucitada de la tumba. Ahora comunica a la comunidad las buenas intenciones para el futuro.

Un lavado con agua bendita sellael propósito. La madera confesional cargada de energía negativa, por otro lado, queda enterrada en un ambiente ritual, al igual que el mal del pasado.

é polvilhada com pó branco e depois, simbolicamente limpa, ressuscitada da sepultura. Agora ela comunica à comunidade as boas intenções para o futuro.

Uma lavagem com água abençoada sela o projeto. A madeira de confissão carregada de energia negativa, por outro lado, é enterrada num ambiente ritual, como o mal do passado.

wordt de persoon in kwestie bestrooid met wit poeder, waarna hij, symbolisch gereinigd, opstaat uit het graf. Nu deelt hij de gemeenschap zijn goede bedoelingen voor de komende tijd mee.

Een wassing met gezegend water bezegelt het voornemen. Het met negatieve energie geladen biechthout wordt daarentegen begraven, net als het kwaad uit het verleden.

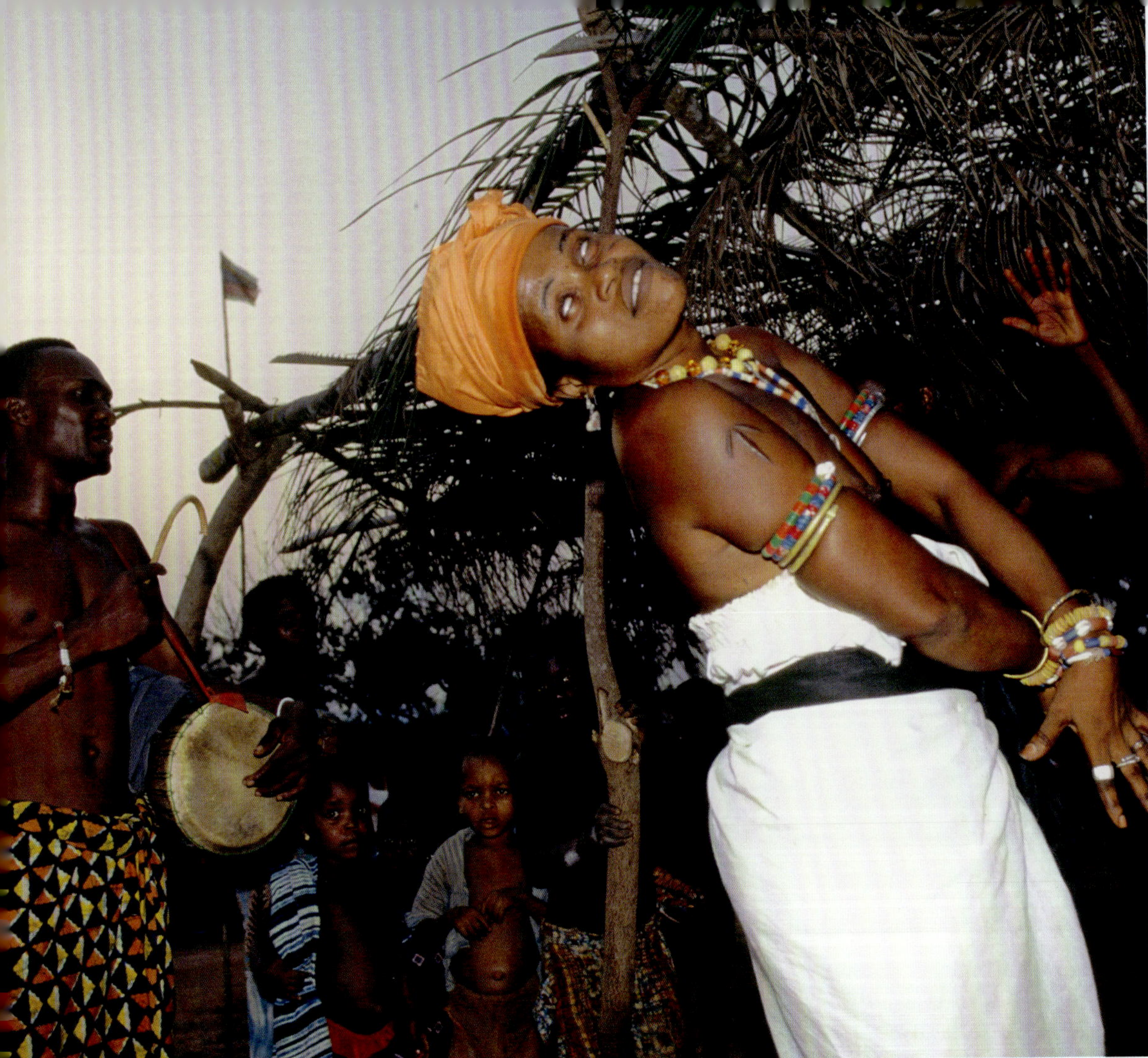

Delassi—unleashing par excellence

The Benin priestess Delassi is an esteemed luminary in her field - the number of clients who have come to her with large and small problems and gone back on their way healthy and satisfied is very high.

Only a few of them know that Delassi herself once belonged to the sick who could only recover through initiation into a Vodun faith community. She is therefore very familiar with the suffering of the patients and her ability to empathize is correspondingly pronounced. However,

Delassi, déchaînement par excellence

La prêtresse béninoise Delassi est une sommité estimée dans sa région : elle reçoit énormément de clients qui la consultent pour des problèmes plus ou moins importants, puis repartent, guéris et satisfaits.

Peu d'entre eux savent que Delassi était elle-même autrefois malade et que seule une initiation dans une communauté religieuse vodun a pu la guérir. Les malheurs de ses patients lui sont donc familiers et son attitude en est d'autant plus nourrie

Delassi – Entfesselung par excellence

Die Beniner Priesterin Delassi ist eine geschätzte Koryphäe auf ihrem Gebiet – die Zahl der Klienten, die mit großen und kleinen Problemen zu ihr kamen und gesund und zufrieden wieder ihres Weges gingen, liegt sehr hoch.

Nur wenige von ihnen wissen, dass Delassi einst selbst zu den Kranken gehörte, die nur durch die Initiation in eine Vodun-Glaubensgemeinschaft genesen konnten. Das Leid der Patienten ist ihr also sehr geläufig und entsprechend ausgeprägt ist

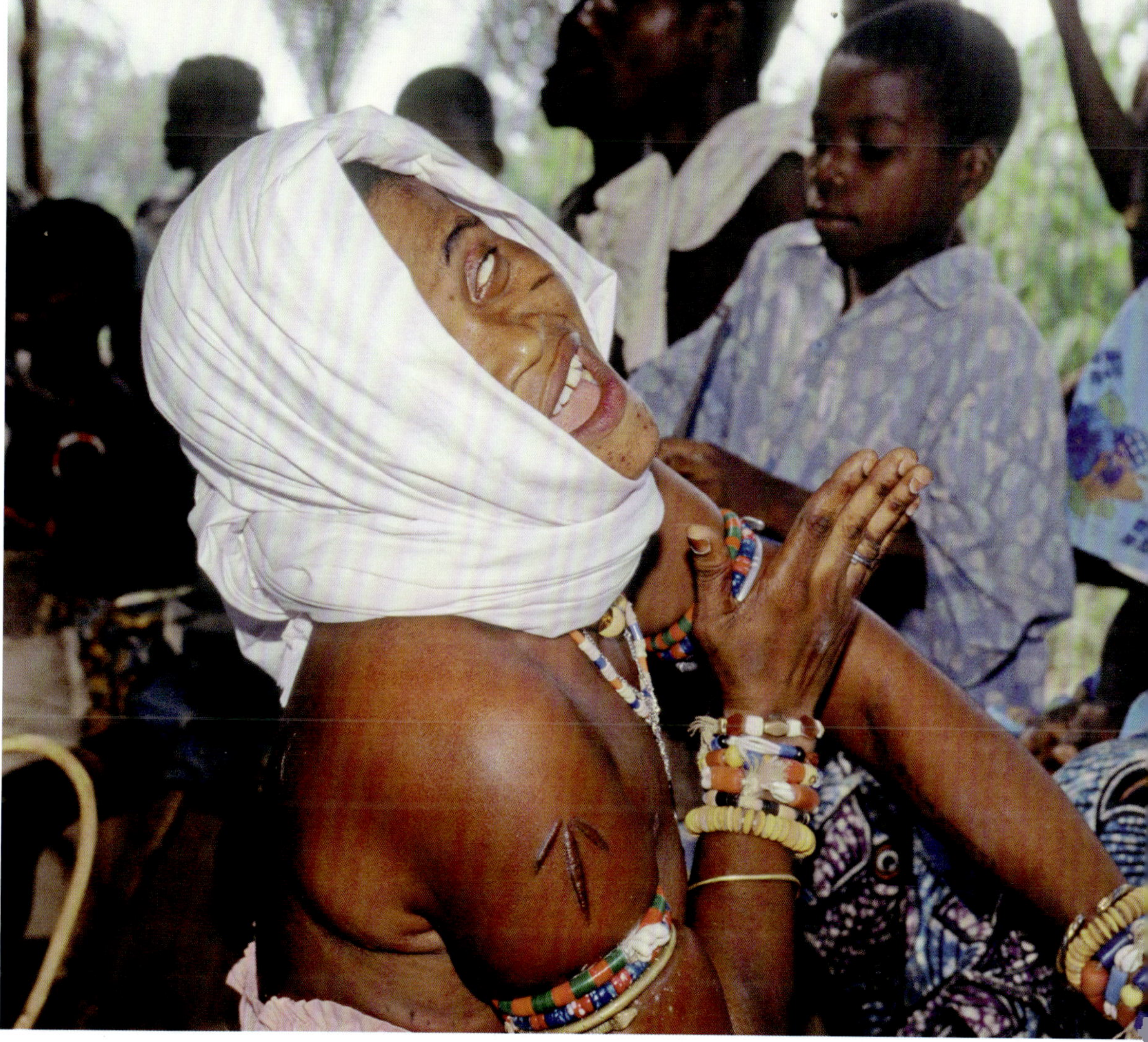

Delassi– La liberación por excelencia

La sacerdotisa beninesa Delassi es una eminencia en su campo– el número de clientes que acudieron a ella con problemas grandes y pequeños y que volvieron a su camino sanos y satisfechos es muy alto.

Sólo unos pocos saben que la misma Delassi perteneció alguna vez a los enfermos que sólo podían recuperarse mediante la iniciación en una comunidad de fe vudú. Por lo tanto, está muy familiarizada con el sufrimiento de los pacientes y su capacidad de empatizar esta, por lo tanto,

Delassi – Libertando por excelência

A sacerdotisa beninense Delassi é uma figura muito apreciada no seu campo – o número de clientes que vieram ter com ela com grandes e pequenos problemas e voltaram para o seu caminho saudável e satisfeito é muito elevado.

Apenas alguns deles sabem que a própria Delassi já pertenceu aos doentes que só puderam se recuperar através da iniciação em uma comunidade de fé vodu. Ela está, portanto, muito familiarizada com o sofrimento dos doentes e a sua capacidade de empatizar é consequentemente

Delassi – ontketening bij uitstek

De priesteres Delassi uit Benin is een gerespecteerde coryfee in haar vakgebied – het aantal klanten dat met grote en kleine problemen naar haar toekwam en gezond en tevreden weer naar huis ging, is erg groot.

Slechts weinigen van hen weten dat Delassi zelf ooit tot de zieken behoorde die alleen konden herstellen door inwijding in een vodungeloofsgemeenschap. Ze is dus zeer vertrouwd met het leed van de patiënten en heeft daardoor ook een uitgesproken inlevingsvermogen. Naast deze zachte kant bezit ze echter ook het tegendeel.

403

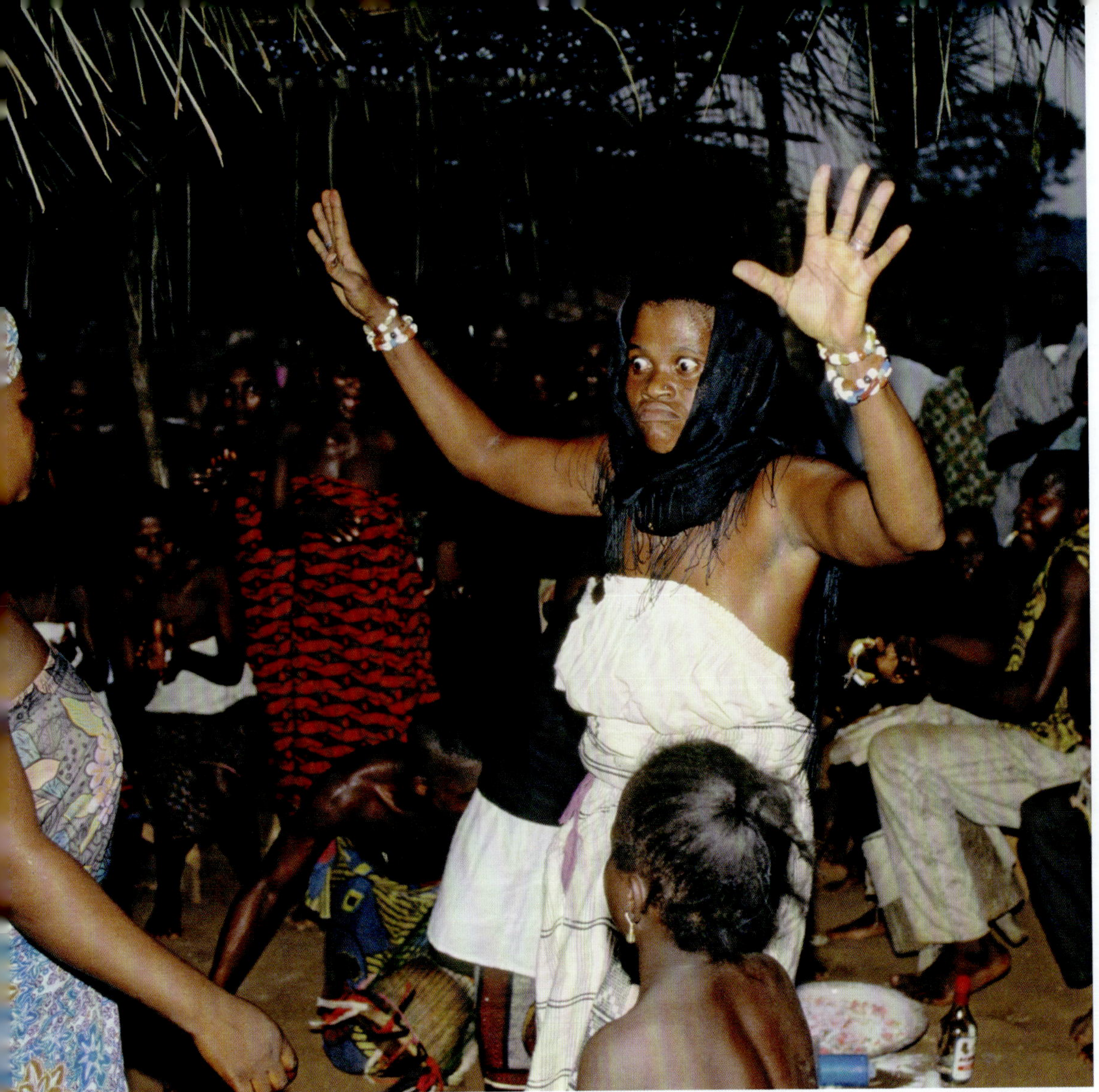

besides this gentle side you also have the opposite.

Then as now, when Delassi falls into a trance, things get out of hand. The petite woman then slips into a state of ecstasy that goes far beyond what is the norm in this area. For those present, however, this is a good sign because the gods are definitely present.

d'empathie. Elle renferme cependant en elle, à côté de cette facette délicate, un antagonisme.

Aujourd'hui comme hier, l'adage prévaut : lorsque Delassi entre en transe, plus rien n'est sous contrôle. Cette femme charmante tombe dans un état de déchaînement absolument hors normes. Pour ses adeptes, cette situation est bon signe car cela indique que les dieux sont bien présents.

ihre Fähigkeit zur Empathie. Neben dieser sanften Seite wohnt ihr aber auch das Gegenteil inne.

Damals wie heute gilt: Wenn Delassi in Trance fällt, geraten die Dinge außer Kontrolle. Die zierliche Frau rutscht dann in einen Zustand der Entfesselung, der weit über das Maß dessen hinausgeht, was in diesem Bereich Norm ist. Für die Anwesenden ist das allerdings ein gutes Zeichen, denn die Götter sind somit definitiv anwesend.

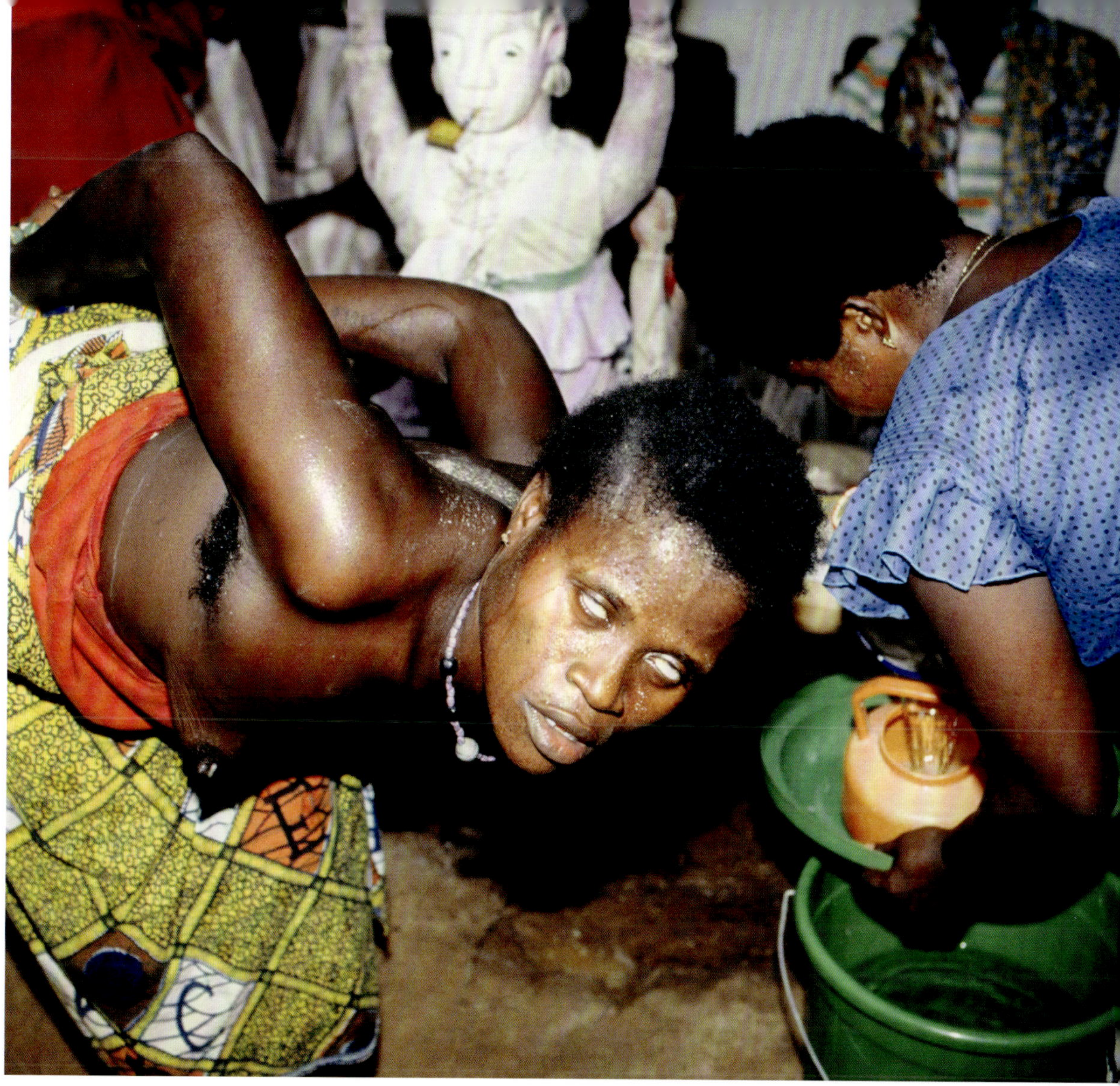

muydesarrollada. Además de este lado suave, sin embargo, también presenta el lado opuesto.

Tanto en el pasado como en la actualidad, cuando Delassi entra en trance, las cosas pierden el control. La pequeña mujer entra en un estado de liberación que va mucho más allá de lo normal. Para los presentes, sin embargo, esto es una buena señal, porque los dioses están definitivamente presentes.

pronunciada. Além deste lado gentil, porém, você também tem o oposto.

Então, como agora, quando Delassi cai em transe, as coisas ficam fora de controle. A mulher petite então escorrega em um estado de liberação que vai muito além do que é a norma nesta área. Para os presentes, porém, isso é um bom sinal, pois os deuses estão definitivamente presentes.

Toen gold net als nu: als Delassi in trance raakt, loopt het uit de hand. De tengere vrouw glijdt dan in een staat van ontketening die veel verder gaat dan wat op dit gebied de norm is. Voor de aanwezigen is dit echter een goed teken, want dan zijn de goden zeker aanwezig.

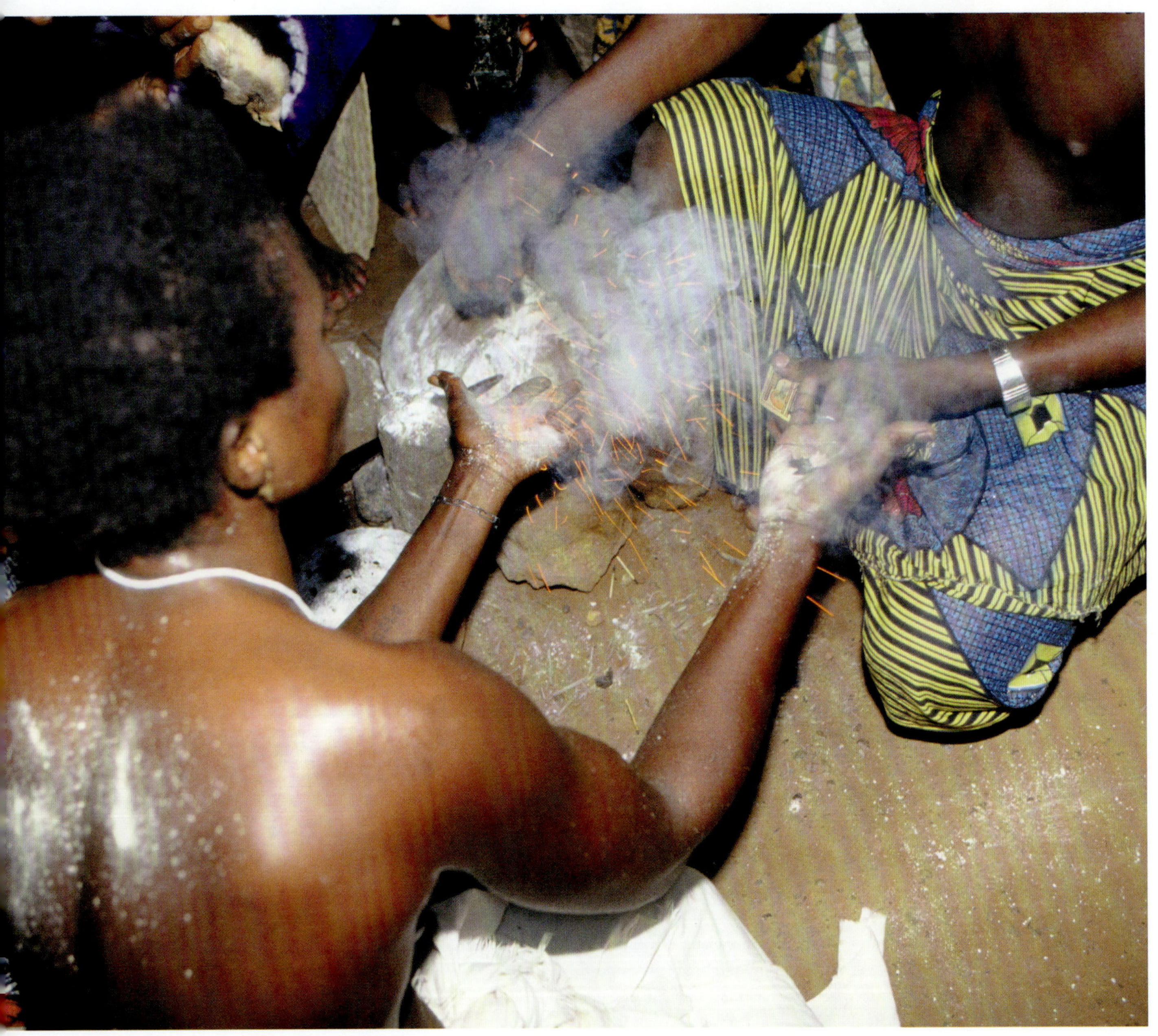

An adept receives Mami Wata's sign

Une adepte reçoit le signe de Mami Wata

Eine Adeptin erhält Mami Watas Zeichen

Un adepto recibe el signo de Mami Wata

Um adepto recebe o sinal de Mami Wata

Een aanhangster ontvangt Mami Wata's teken

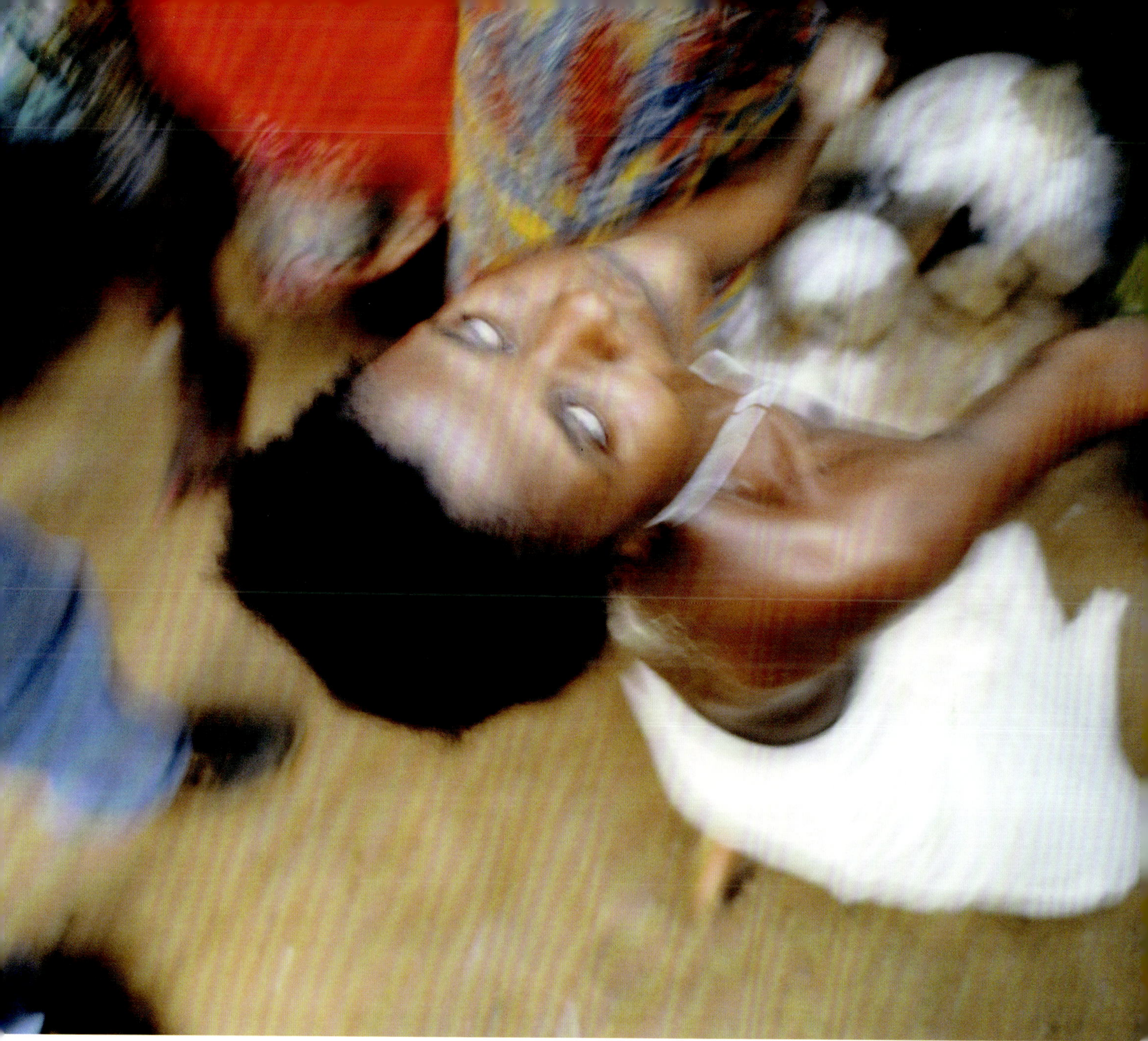

Mami Wata adept in a wild trance

Adepte de Mami Wata dans une transe sauvage

Mami Wata-Adeptin in wilder Trance

Adepta de Mami Wata en un trance salvaje

Mami Wata-Adeptin em transe selvagem

Mami Wata-aanhangster in woeste trance

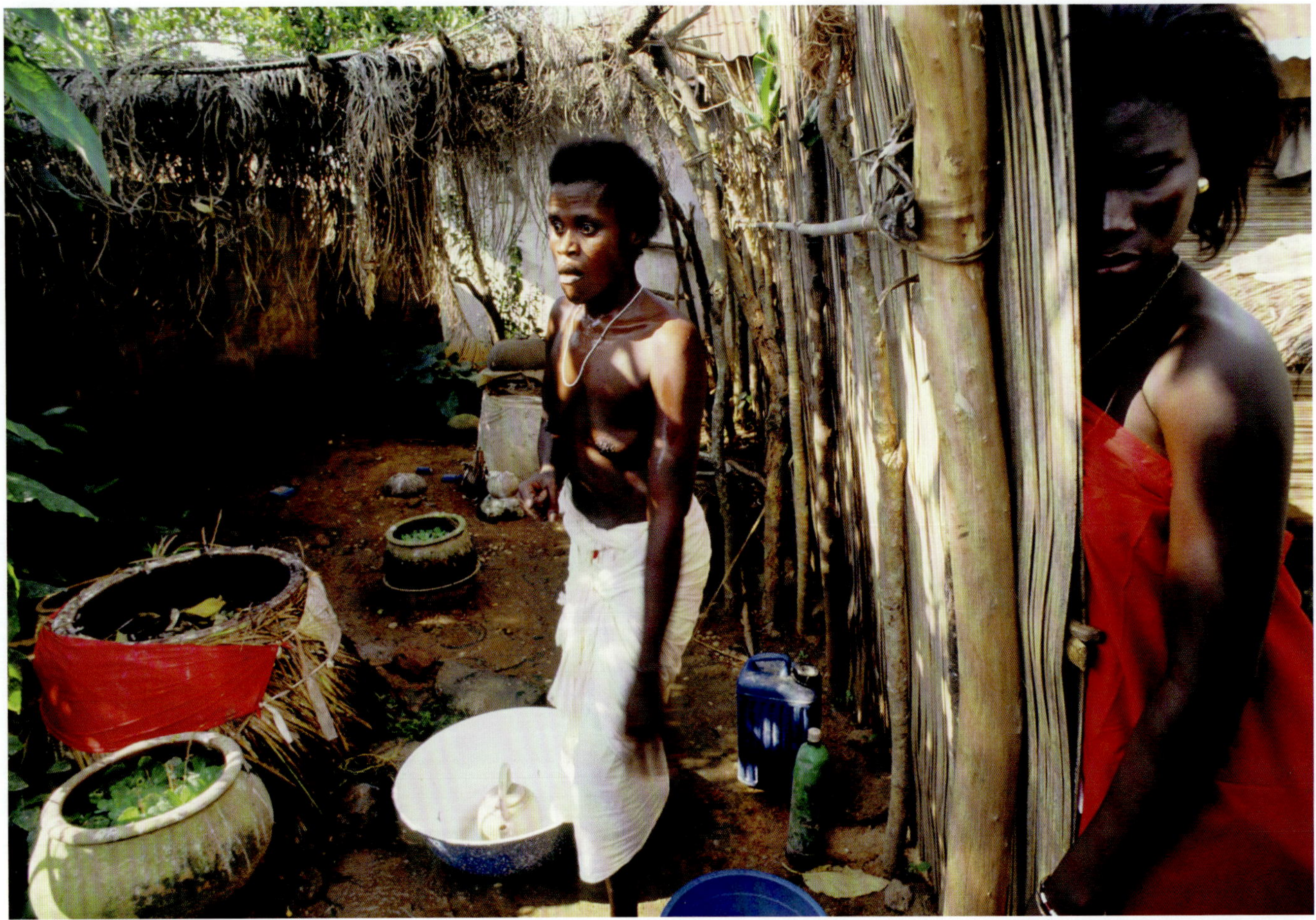

After the trance. The priestess has gently taken her adept out of the trance, which, depending on the deity, is possible at any time through the use of various means. Usually the trance ends by itself.

Après la transe. La prêtresse a délicatement mis fin à la transe de cette adepte. Ce processus est toujours possible par différents moyens, en fonction de chaque divinité. En règle générale, la transe s'arrête d'elle-même.

Nach der Trance. Die Priesterin hat ihre Adeptin sanft aus der Trance herausgeholt, was, je nach Gottheit, durch den Einsatz verschiedener Mittel jederzeit möglich ist. In der Regel endet die Trance von selbst.

Después del trance. La sacerdotisa ha sacado suavemente a su adepto del trance, lo cual, dependiendo de la deidad, es posible en cualquier momento a través del uso de varios medios. Normalmente el trance termina por sí solo.

Depois do transe. A sacerdotisa tirou suavemente seu adepto do transe, o que, dependendo da divindade, é possível a qualquer momento através do uso de vários meios. Normalmente, o transe termina por si só.

Na de trance. De priesteres heeft de adept zachtjes uit haar trance gehaald, wat, afhankelijk van de godheid, op elk moment mogelijk is door het gebruik van verschillende middelen. Meestal eindigt de trance vanzelf.

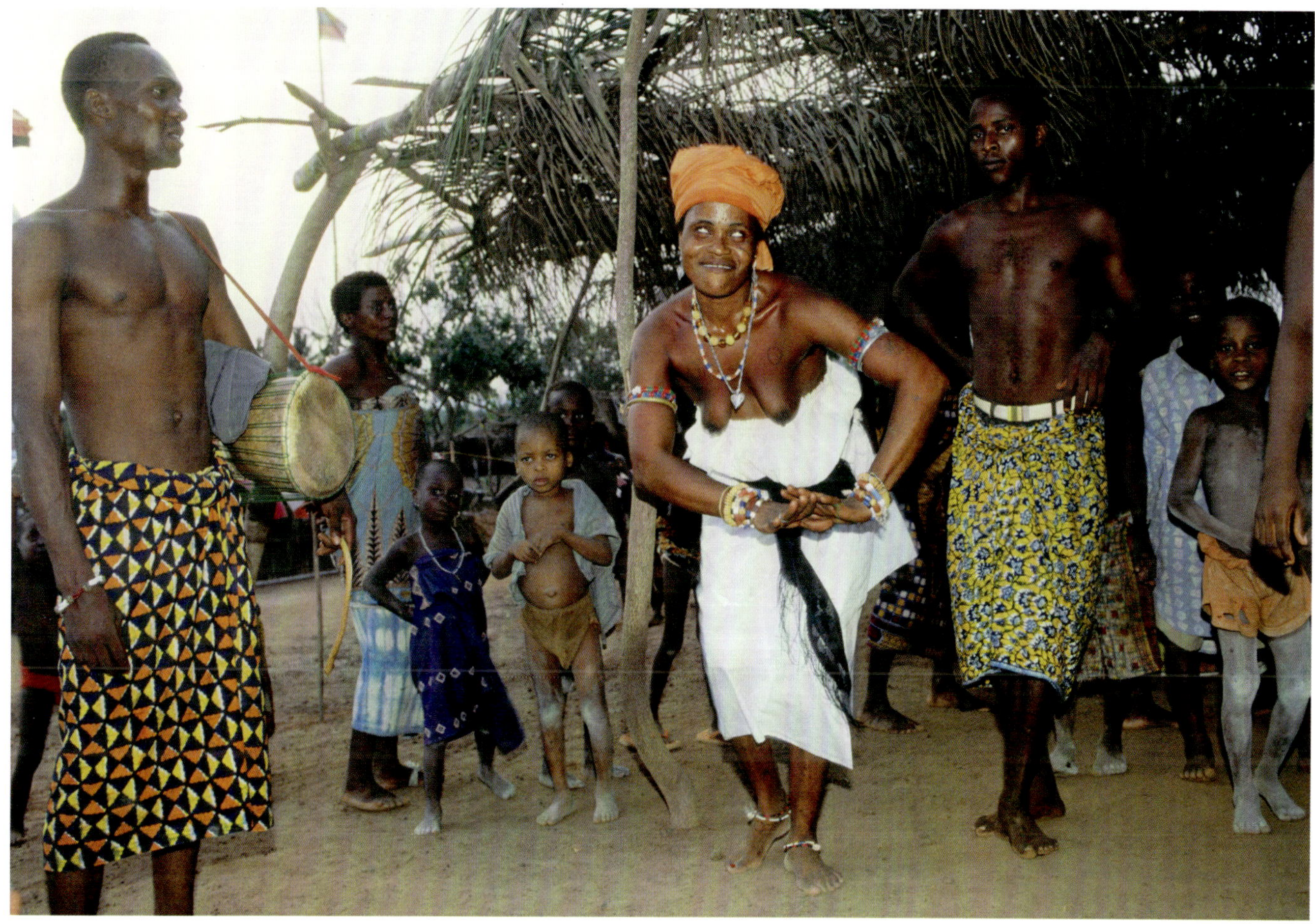

The priestess Delassi in a trance. Delassi, priestess for Mami Wata and the warrior Vodun Tron, is known for her particularly wild trance states.

La prêtresse Delassi en transe. Delassi, prêtresse de Mami Wata et du vodun guerrier Tron, est célèbre pour ses états de transe particulièrement tumultueux.

Die Priesterin Delassi in Trance. Delassi, Priesterin für Mami Wata und den Kriegervodun Tron, ist bekannt für ihre besonders wilden Trancezustände.

La sacerdotisa Delassi en trance. Delassi, sacerdotisa de Mami Wata y del guerrero vudú Tron, es conocida por sus estados de trance particularmente salvajes.

A sacerdotisa Delassi em transe. Delassi, sacerdotisa de Mami Wata e do vodu guerreiro Tron, é conhecida por seus estados de transe particularmente selvagens.

Priesteres Delassi in trance. Delassi, priesteres voor Mami Wata en de krijgergod Tron, staat bekend om haar extreem woeste trances.

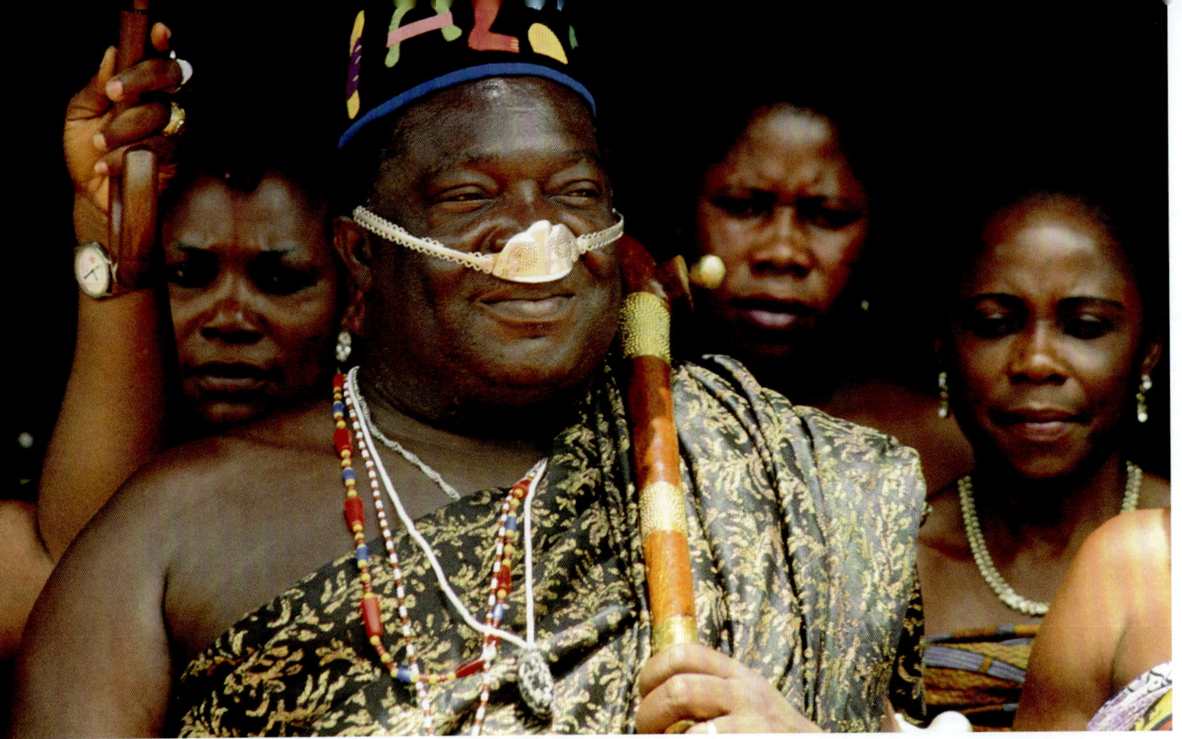

The King of Abomey

The history of the kings in Dahomey, today's Benin, is marked by many legends and upheavals. Many cruel events are recorded in the country's annals, for under some rulers human sacrifice and tyranny were the order of the day.

Modern times are much more peaceful, which can be shown in the restrained work of King Dedjralagni. He was a member of the royal family and was required to take on the position, even though he was not particularly interested in the post. At work, he was a satisfied, respected cop. But now he should leave all this behind him and take responsibility for complicated royal affairs and seven wives.

It is also said that the silver strainer that kings traditionally have to wear on their noses to filter the air has got on his nerves.

Le roi d'Abomey

L'histoire des rois du Dahomey se distingue par ses légendes et bouleversements nombreux. Le pays compte dans ses annales des événements atroces, car plusieurs de ses dirigeants pratiquaient couramment sacrifices humains et actes de tyrannie.

Les temps modernes marquent un apaisement incontestable, comme l'illustrent les actions modérées du roi Dédjralagni. Descendant de la famille royale, il fut appelé à gouverner, bien qu'il reconnut honnêtement ne pas être particulièrement intéressé par le poste. Au cours de sa vie professionnelle, il a été un politicien paisible et respecté. Il dut cependant laisser tout cela derrière lui lorsqu'il endossa la responsabilité des affaires du royaume, tout en s'occupant de sept femmes.

On dit en outre qu'il était fortement excédé par le crible d'argent, filtre pour l'air traditionnel des rois, qu'il était obligé de porter devant le nez.

Der König von Abomey

Die Geschichte der Könige ist in Dahomey, dem heutigen Benin, von vielen Legenden und Umbrüchen gezeichnet. Grausame Begebenheiten stehen in den Annalen des Landes, denn unter manchen Herrschern waren Menschenopfer und Tyrannei an der Tagesordnung.

In der Neuzeit ging es wesentlich friedlicher zu, was anhand des gemäßigten Wirkens von König Dedjralagni belegt werden kann. Dieser stammte gebürtig aus der Königsfamilie und wurde in die Pflicht genommen, obwohl er an dem Posten erklärtermaßen nicht sonderlich interessiert war. Im Berufsleben war er ein zufriedener, respektierter Polizist. Nun aber sollte er das alles hinter sich lassen und die Verantwortung für komplizierte Königsangelegenheiten und sieben Frauen übernehmen.

Es heißt zudem, dass ihm das Silbersieb, das die Könige traditionell zur Luftfilterung auf der Nase tragen müssen, sehr auf den Nerv gegangen sei.

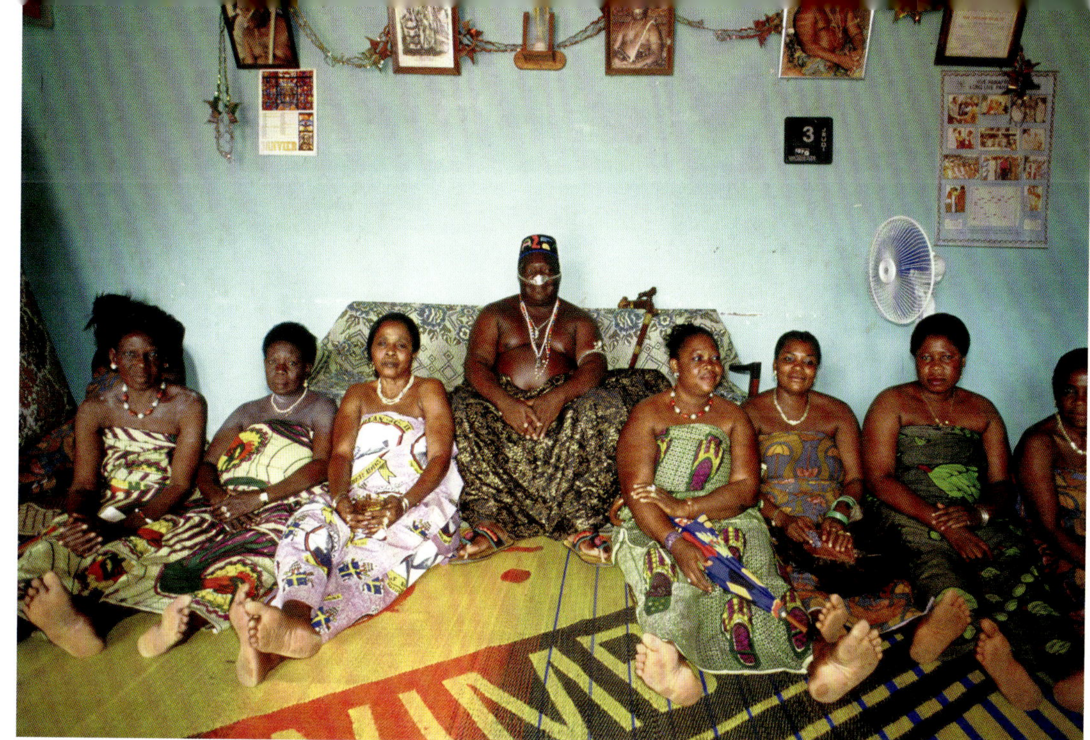

With the princesses
in the audience hall of
the palace

Avec les princesses
dans la salle d'audience
du palais

Mit den Prinzessinnen im
Audienzsaal des Palastes

Con las princesas en
el salón de audiencias
del palacio

Com as princesas na sala
de audiências do palácio

Met de prinsessen in
de audiëntiezaal van
het paleis

El Rey de Abomey

La historia de los reyes de Dahomey, el
Benín actual, está marcada por muchas
leyendas y trastornos. Los acontecimientos
crueles se encuentran en los anales del país,
ya que bajo algunos gobernantes el sacrificio
humano y la tiranía estaban a la orden
del día.

Los tiempos modernos eran mucho más
pacíficos, lo que se puede comprobar por
el moderado trabajo del rey Dedjralagni.
Era nativo de la familia real y fue llamado
a rendir cuentas, aunque no estaba
particularmente interesado en el cargo. En
su vida profesional fue un policía satisfecho
y respetado. Pero ahora debería dejar todo
eso atrás y asumir la responsabilidad de
complicados asuntos reales y siete mujeres.

También se dice que el tamiz de plata que
los reyes tradicionalmente tienen que llevar
en la nariz para filtrar el aire, le saltó de los
nervios.

O Rei de Abomey

A história dos reis em Dahomey, o atual
Benin, é marcada por muitas lendas e
convulsões. Acontecimentos cruéis podem
ser encontrados nos anais do país, pois sob
alguns governantes o sacrifício humano e a
tirania estavam na ordem do dia.

Os tempos modernos foram muito mais
pacíficos, o que pode ser comprovado pelo
trabalho moderado do Rei Dedjralagni.
Ele era um nativo da família real e foi
chamado a prestar contas, embora ele não
estava particularmente interessado no
cargo. Em sua vida profissional ele era um
policial satisfeito e respeitado. Mas agora
ele deve deixar tudo isso para trás e assumir
a responsabilidade por assuntos reais
complicados e sete mulheres.

Diz-se também que a peneira prateada
que os reis tradicionalmente têm de usar no
nariz para filtrar o ar tem nos seus nervos.

De koning van Abomey

De geschiedenis van de koningen in
Dahomey, het huidige Benin, staat bol van
de legenden en omwentelingen. Wrede
voorvallen zijn te vinden in de annalen van
het land, want onder sommige heersers
waren mensenoffers en tirannie aan de orde
van de dag.

In de moderne tijd ging het er veel
vrediger aan toe, wat kan worden
aangetoond door het gematigde werk van
koning Dedjralagni. Hij was afkomstig
uit de koninklijke familie en werd op zijn
verantwoordelijkheden aangesproken,
hoewel hij niet bijzonder geïnteresseerd
was in de functie. In zijn beroepsleven
was hij een tevreden en gerespecteerd
politieman. Maar nu moet hij dat allemaal
achter zich laten en de verantwoordelijkheid
nemen voor ingewikkelde koninklijke
aangelegenheden en zeven vrouwen.

De zilveren zeef die koningen
traditiegetrouw op de neus moeten dragen
om de lucht te filteren, zou hem zwaar op
zijn zenuwen werken.

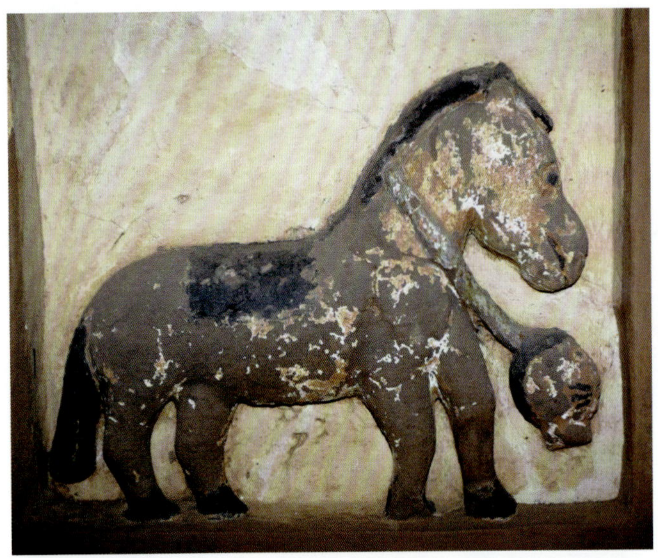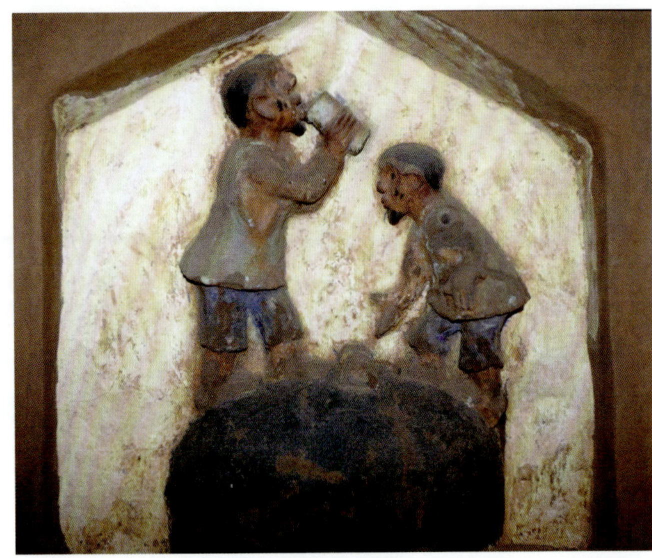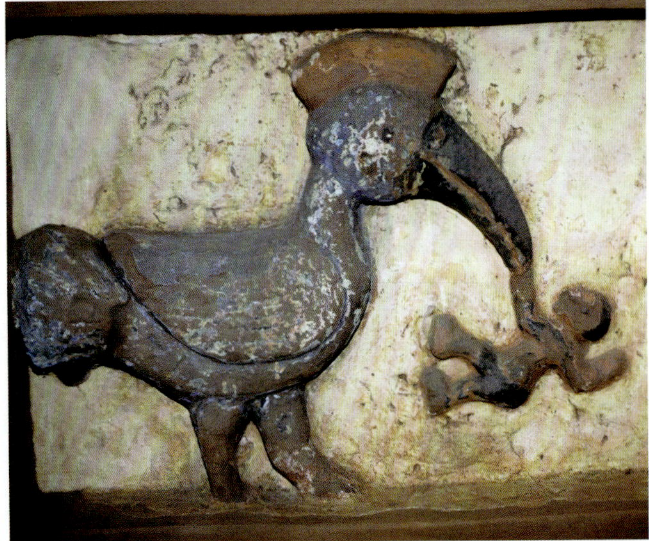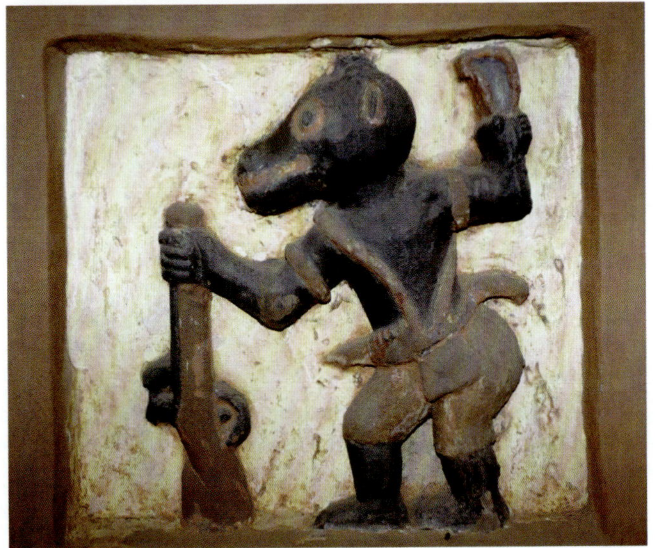

Palace sculptures from Abomey. In iconographic representations, the reliefs in the architectural complex of the Palace of Abomey in Benin show the history of the Fon people and some of their kings.

Sculptures du palais d'Abomey. Ces bas-reliefs ornant le complexe architectural du palais d'Abomey racontent, à travers des représentations iconographiques, l'histoire du peuple Fon et de quelques-uns de ses rois.

Palastskulpturen von Abomey.
In ikonografischen Darstellungen zeigen die Reliefs in dem Architekturkomplex des Palastes von Abomey in Benin die Geschichte des Fon-Volkes und einiger seiner Könige.

Esculturas de palacio de Abomey.
En representaciones iconográficas, los relieves del complejo arquitectónico del Palacio de Abomey en Benin muestran la historia del pueblo Fon y de algunos de sus reyes.

Esculturas de Palácio de Abomey.
Em representações iconográficas, os relevos do complexo arquitectónico do Palácio de Abomey, no Benim, mostram a história do povo Fon e de alguns dos seus reis.

Sculpturen uit het paleis van Abomey.
In iconografische voorstellingen tonen de reliëfs in het paleizencomplex van Abomey in Benin de geschiedenis van de Fon en enkele van hun koningen.

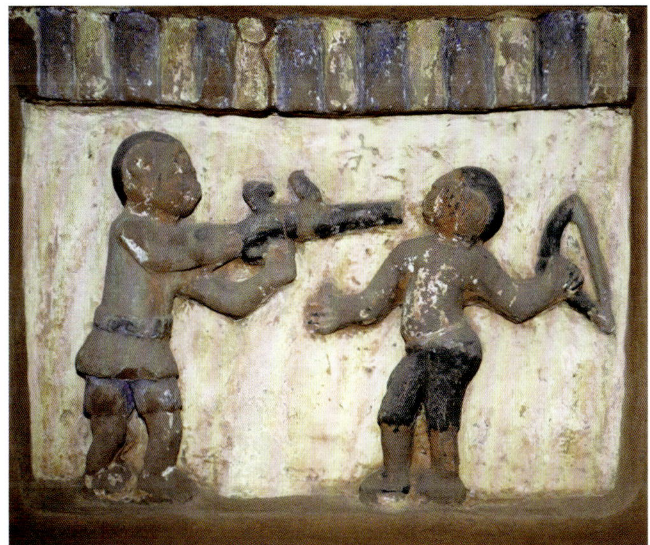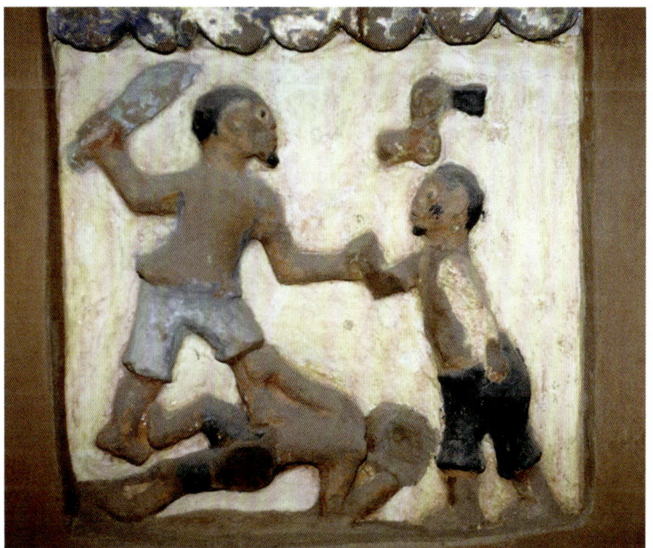

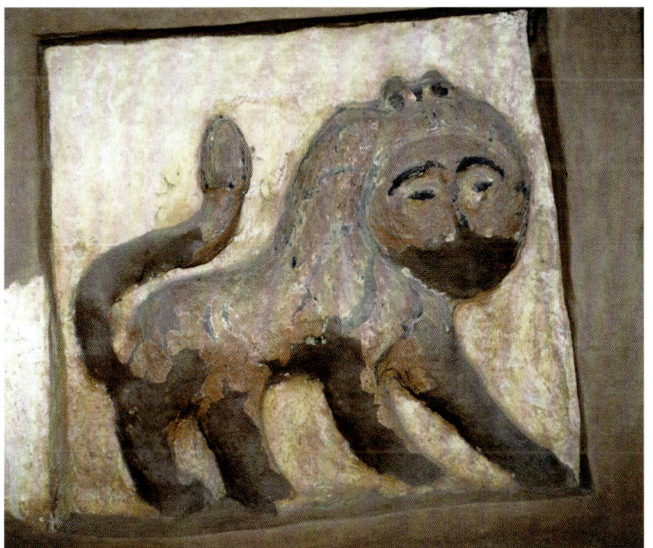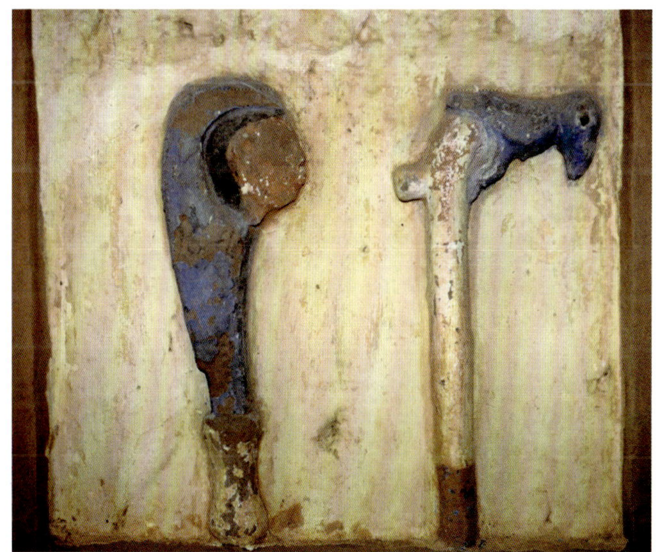

Palace sculptures by Abomey. Among other things, the heroes of traditional myths, the symbols of the rulers and references to some of the most famous Vodun gods are depicted. Altogether there are about 50 reliefs.

Sculptures du palais d'Abomey. Parmi les représentations, on remarque notamment les héros des mythes traditionnels, les symboles des souverains et des références aux dieux vodun les plus connus. Ce bâtiment compte une cinquantaine de bas-reliefs

Palastskulpturen von Abomey. Dargestellt sind unter anderem die Helden traditioneller Mythen, die Symbole der Herrscher und Verweise auf einige der bekanntesten Vodungötter. Insgesamt existieren etwa 50 Reliefs.

Esculturas de palacio de Abomey. Describe, entre otras cosas, los héroes de los mitos tradicionales, los símbolos de los gobernantes y las referencias a algunos de los dioses vudú más famosos. En total hay unos 50 relieves.

Esculturas de Palácio de Abomey. Ele retrata, entre outras coisas, os heróis dos mitos tradicionais, os símbolos dos governantes e as referências a alguns dos vodungods mais famosos. No total, há cerca de 50 relevos.

Sculpturen uit het paleis van Abomey. Afgebeeld zijn onder andere de helden uit traditionele mythen, symbolen van de heersers en verwijzingen naar enkele van de beroemdste vodungoden. In totaal zijn er zo'n vijftig reliëfs.

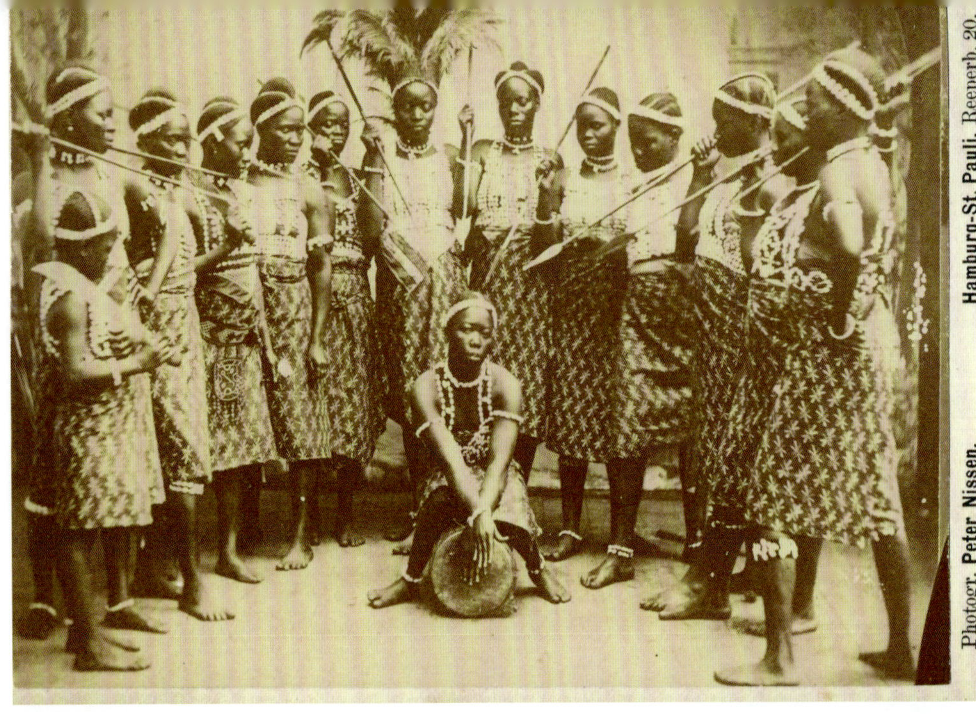

Historical illustration of the Amazons of Dahomey

Illustration historique des Amazones du Dahomey

Historische Abbildung der Amazonen von Dahomey

Ilustración histórica de las Amazonas de Dahomey

Ilustração histórica das Amazonas de Dahomey

Historische foto van de Amazones van Dahomey

The Amazons—Dahomey's fearless women's army

They were regarded as a merciless female troop and were the bodyguards of the king in old Dahomey.

An Amazon myth tells of King Gézo (1818–1858) who wanted to pave a road with the skulls of his enemies from the Nago people. Every day his dearest favorite Amazon delivered him two heads, obligated to do so. At some point the Nagos managed to decapitate her in turn. The Nago Chief was aggrieved that he had lost countless men to her and therefore mounted her skull on a male figure in a wooden box during a magical ceremony. This guardian figure served to warn the Nagos in the event of another Amazon attack.

When, out of nowhere, three bloodstains appeared in front of the box, it was immediately placed at the entrance to the village with the curtain raised—and the attack was fended off. The Nagos used the box for 160 years.

Les Amazones, l'armée de femmes intrépides du Dahomey

Cette troupe de femmes impitoyables était la garde du roi de l'ancien Dahomey.

L'un des mythes des Amazones relate l'histoire du roi Ghézo (qui régna de 1818 à 1858). Il avait décidé de paver une route avec les crânes de ses ennemis de l'ethnie Nago. Chaque jour, l'une de ses Amazones préférées lui apportait consciencieusement deux têtes. Un jour cependant, les Nago réussirent à la capturer et la décapitèrent. Leur chef, ulcéré par l'important nombre d'hommes qu'elle avait réussi à lui ravir, fit, au cours d'une cérémonie magique, placer sa tête sur un corps masculin mis dans une boîte en bois. Ce gardien servit alors à avertir les Nago des nouvelles attaques des Amazones.

Lorsque trois tâches de sang apparaissaient soudainement sur la caisse, on l'installait immédiatement, rideau soulevé, sur le chemin d'accès au village, ce qui suffisait à repousser l'attaque. Les Nago l'utilisèrent pendant 160 ans.

Die Amazonen – Dahomeys furchtlose Frauenarmee

Sie galten als unerbittliche Frauentruppe und waren die Leibwachen des Königs im alten Dahomey.

Ein Amazonenmythos berichtet von König Gézo (amtierte 1818–1858), der mit den Schädeldecken seiner Feinde vom Volk der Nago eine Straße pflastern wollte. Täglich servierte ihm seine liebste Amazone dazu pflichtschuldig zwei Köpfe. Irgendwann gelang es den Nagos wiederum, sie zu enthaupten. Der Nago-Chief war gekränkt, zahllose Männer an sie verloren zu haben und montierte ihren Schädel deshalb während einer magischen Zeremonie auf eine männliche Figur in einem Holzkasten. Diese Wächterfigur diente dazu, die Nagos bei einem erneuten Amazonenangriff zu warnen.

Wenn wie aus dem Nichts drei Blutflecke vor der Kiste auftauchten, stellte man sie umgehend mit erhobenem Vorhang an den Dorfeingang – und der Angriff war abgewehrt. Die Nagos nutzten die Kiste 160 Jahre lang.

Wood, human skull, metal/Bois, crâne humain, métal, 58 × 36 cm

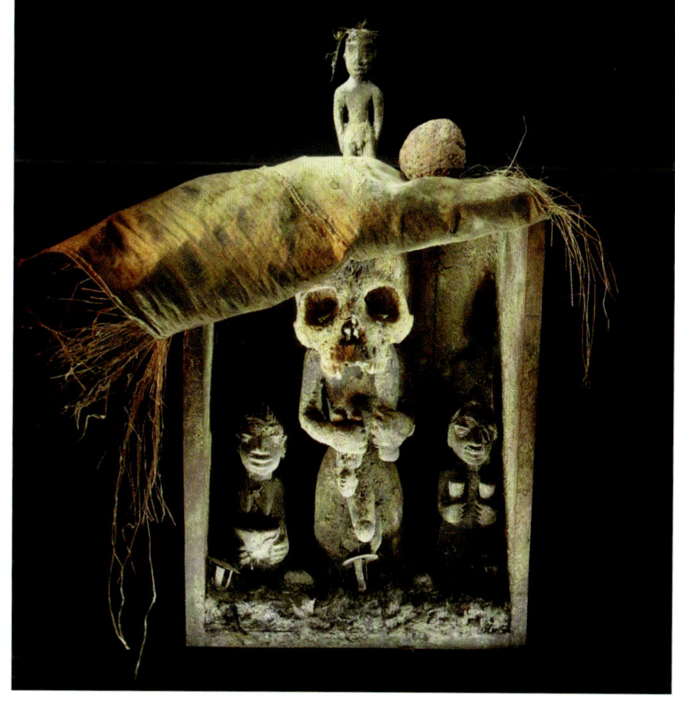

Las Amazonas– El ejército de mujeres intrépidas de Dahomey

Eran consideradas como una tropa femenina implacable y eran las guardaespaldas del rey en la antigua Dahomey.

Un mito amazónico habla del rey Gézo (1818–1858) que quiso pavimentar un camino con las calaveras de sus enemigos del pueblo nago. Cada día, su querida Amazona, obligada a ello, le servía dos cabezas. Hasta que un día los Nagos lograron decapitarla. El Jefe de los Nagos estaba enfadado por haber perdido innumerables hombres y por eso colocó su cráneo sobre una figura masculina en una caja de madera durante una ceremonia mágica. Esta figura guardiana sirvió para advertir a los Nagos de otro ataque amazónico.

Cuando, de la nada, aparecieron tres manchas de sangre delante de la caja, la colocaron inmediatamente en la entrada de la aldea con la cortina levantada, y así se defendieron del ataque. Los Nagos usaron la caja durante 160 años.

As Amazonas – Dahomeys destemido exército de mulheres

Eles eram considerados como uma tropa feminina implacável e eram os guarda-costas do rei no velho Dahomey.

Um mito amazónico fala do rei Gézo (1818–1858) que queria pavimentar uma estrada com as caveiras de seus inimigos do povo Nago. Todos os dias, a sua querida Amazónia servia-lhe duas cabeças, obrigadas a fazê-lo. A certa altura, os Nagos conseguiram decapitá-los novamente. O chefe Nago ficou ofendido por ter perdido inúmeros homens para eles e, portanto, montou seu crânio em uma figura masculina em uma caixa de madeira durante uma cerimônia mágica. Esta figura guardiã serviu para avisar os Nagos de outro ataque amazónico.

Quando, do nada, três manchas de sangue apareceram na frente da caixa, elas foram imediatamente colocadas na entrada da aldeia com a cortina levantada – e o ataque foi evitado. Os Nagos usaram a caixa durante 160 anos.

De Amazones – het onverschrokken vrouwenleger van Dahomey

Zij werden beschouwd als een meedogenloos vrouwenleger en waren de lijfwachten van de koning in het oude Dahomey.

Een mythe over de Amazones gaat over koning Gézo (regerend van 1818-1858) die een weg wilde plaveien met de schedeldaken van zijn vijanden van het Nago-volk. Zijn favoriete Amazone bracht hem daarom plichtsgetrouw elke dag twee afgehakte hoofden. Op een dag werd zij op haar beurt onthoofd door de Nago. Het Nago-opperhoofd monteerde een houten kistje met haar schedel erin op een mannenfiguur omdat hij gekrenkt was door het feit dat hij zoveel mannen aan haar had verloren. Het wachterbeeld waarschuwde de Nago voortaan voor alle nieuwe Amazone-aanvallen.

Als er vanuit het niets drie bloedvlekken voor het kistje verschenen, moest men het met opgetrokken gordijn bij de ingang van het dorp zetten – de aanval werd zo afgeweerd. De Nago gebruikten het kistje 160 jaar lang.

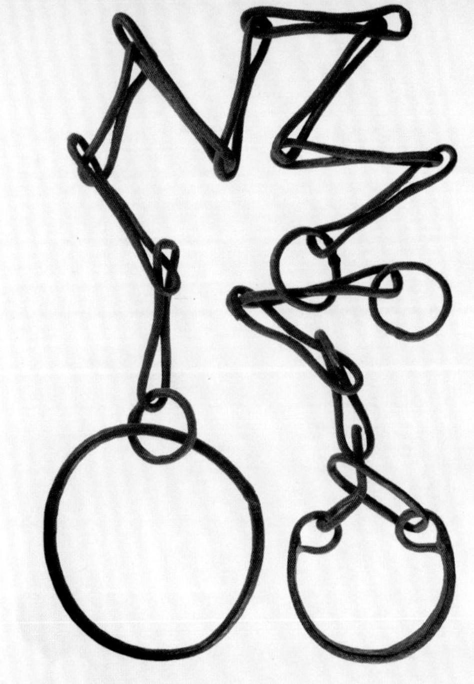

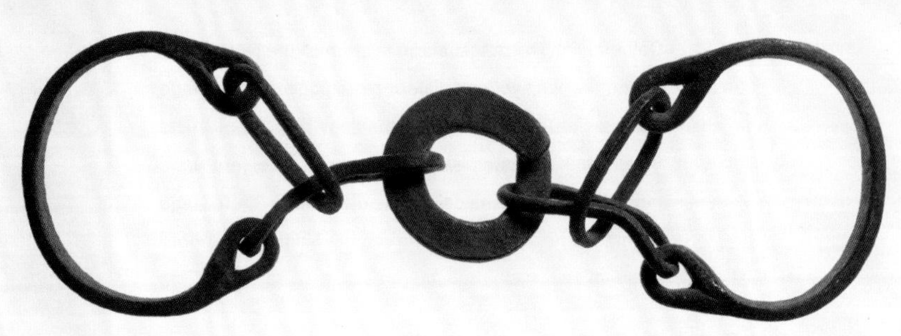

Iron shackles from the colonial period
Chaînes de fer de l'époque coloniale
Eisenfesseln aus der Kolonialzeit
Grilletes de hierro de la época colonial
Grilhões de ferro do período colonial
IJzeren ketenen uit de koloniale tijd

150 × 15 cm
10 × 34 cm

Slavery—The unpunished injustice

Transatlantic slavery, which began in the middle of the 15th century as a result of the Portuguese activities on the coast of West Africa, is one of the darkest chapters in human history.

This largest ever displacement of peoples was soon carried out by all European naval powers and was actively supported by human traffickers and rulers in the countries of origin of the slaves. Along with goods like alcohol, cloth, cowrie shells, gold and much more, one acquired the disenfranchised unfortunates. Many of them died miserably under horrible conditions long before reaching the New World. The slave ships weren't escorted by shark swarms for no reason.

Over almost four centuries, an estimated 40 million Africans were enslaved in the course of triangular trade between Europe, West Africa and the Caribbean, taking into account the estimated number of unreported cases.

Esclavage, violente oppression

Le commerce transatlantique des esclaves, qui fut instauré par les Portugais au milieu du XVe siècle le long des côtes d'Afrique de l'Ouest, compte parmi les chapitres les plus sombres de l'histoire de l'humanité.

Toutes les puissances maritimes européennes participèrent bientôt à la plus importante déportation de populations de tous les temps, activement soutenue par les marchands d'esclaves et les dirigeants des pays d'origine des esclaves. On pouvait acquérir ces malheureux dépourvus de tout droit contre divers biens, alcool, tissus, cauris ou or notamment. Nombre d'entre eux périrent dans des conditions atroces bien avant d'atteindre le Nouveau Monde. Les bateaux négriers n'étaient pas escortés par des requins sans raison…

En pratiquement quatre siècles, le commerce triangulaire entre l'Europe, l'Afrique de l'Ouest et les Caraïbes réduisit en esclavage environ 40 millions d'Africains, selon des estimations officieuses.

Sklaverei – Das ungesühnte Unrecht

Die transatlantische Sklaverei, die Mitte des 15. Jahrhunderts durch das Wirken der Portugiesen an der Küste Westafrikas begann, gehört zu den dunkelsten Kapiteln der Menschheitsgeschichte.

Diese größte Völkerverschleppung aller Zeiten wurde bald von allen europäischen Seemächten betrieben und von Menschenhändlern wie Machthabern in den Herkunftsländern der Sklaven tatkräftig unterstützt. Mit Gütern wie Alkohol, Stoffen, Kaurischnecken, Gold und vielem mehr erwarb man die entrechteten Unglücklichen. Viele von ihnen gingen unter grauenhaften Bedingungen lange vor dem Erreichen der Neuen Welt jämmerlich zugrunde. Die Sklavenschiffe wurden nicht grundlos von Haischwärmen eskortiert.

Im Laufe von fast vier Jahrhunderten sind im Zuge des Dreieckshandels zwischen Europa, Westafrika und der Karibik – wenn man die Dunkelziffer berücksichtigt – schätzungsweise 40 Millionen Afrikaner versklavt worden.

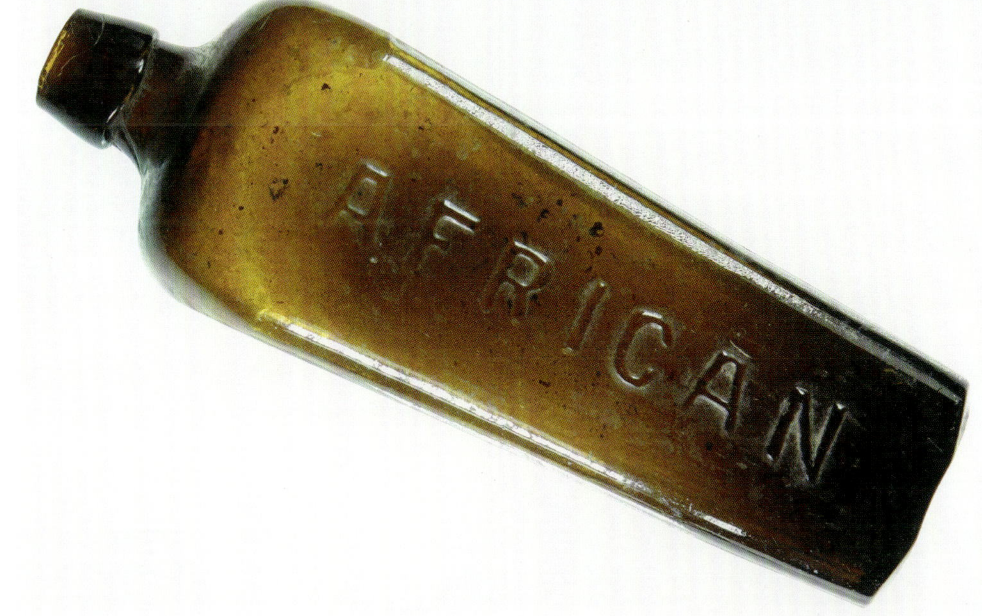

Colonial schnapps bottle
Flasque d'alcool de l'époque coloniale
Schnapsflasche aus der Kolonialzeit
Botella de aguardiente de la época colonial
Garrafa de aguardente colonial
Drankfles uit de koloniale tijd
Glass bottle/Flacon de verre, 23 × 8 cm

Esclavitud – La injusticia impune

La esclavitud transatlántica, que comenzó a mediados del siglo XV como resultado de las actividades portuguesas en la costa de África Occidental, es uno de los capítulos más oscuros de la historia de la humanidad.

Este mayor arrastre de pueblos de la historia fue llevado a cabo muy pronto por todas las potencias marítimas europeas y apoyado activamente por los traficantes de seres humanos y los gobernantes de los países de origen de los esclavos. Con bienes como el alcohol, las telas, los caracolesde santo, el oro y mucho más, se adquirían a los desafortunados, los cuales quedaban privados de sus derechos. Muchos de ellos murieron miserablemente en condiciones horribles mucho antes de llegar al Nuevo Mundo. Los barcos de esclavos no fueron escoltados por enjambres de tiburones porque sí.

Durante casi cuatro siglos, se estima que 40 millones de africanos han sido esclavizados en el curso del comercio triangular entre Europa, África occidental y el Caribe, teniendo en cuenta el número estimado de casos no denunciados.

Escravidão – A injustiça impune

A escravatura transatlântica, que começou em meados do século XV como resultado das atividades portuguesas na costa da África Ocidental, é um dos capítulos mais negros da história humana.

Este maior arrastamento de povos de sempre foi rapidamente levado a cabo por todas as potências marítimas europeias e activamente apoiado por traficantes e governantes de seres humanos nos países de origem dos escravos. Com mercadorias como álcool, tecidos, caracóis cowrie, ouro e muito mais se adquiriu os deserdados desafortunados. Muitos deles morreram miseravelmente em condições horríveis muito antes de chegarem ao Novo Mundo. Os navios de escravos não eram, sem razão, escoltados por enxames de tubarões.

Ao longo de quase quatro séculos, cerca de 40 milhões de africanos foram escravizados no decurso do comércio triangular entre a Europa, a África Ocidental e as Caraíbas, tendo em conta o número estimado de casos não comunicados.

Slavernij – ongewroken onrecht

De trans-Atlantische slavernij, die halverwege de 15e eeuw begon door Portugese activiteiten aan de kust van West-Afrika, vormt een van de donkerste hoofdstukken in de menselijke geschiedenis.

Deze grootste deportatie aller tijden werd al snel uitgevoerd door alle Europese zeemachten en actief ondersteund door mensensmokkelaars en heersers in de landen van herkomst van de slaven. Met ruilmiddelen als alcohol, stoffen, kaurischelpen, goud en nog veel meer verwierf men de rechteloze ongelukkigen. Velen van hen stierven onder erbarmelijke omstandigheden, lang voordat ze de Nieuwe Wereld bereikten. De slavenschepen werden niet zonder reden begeleid door zwermen haaien.

In de loop van bijna vier eeuwen zijn naar schatting 40 miljoen Afrikanen in het kader van de driehoekshandel tussen Europa, West-Afrika en het Caribisch gebied tot slaaf gemaakt – het geschatte aantal niet officieel geregistreerde gevallen in aanmerking genomen.

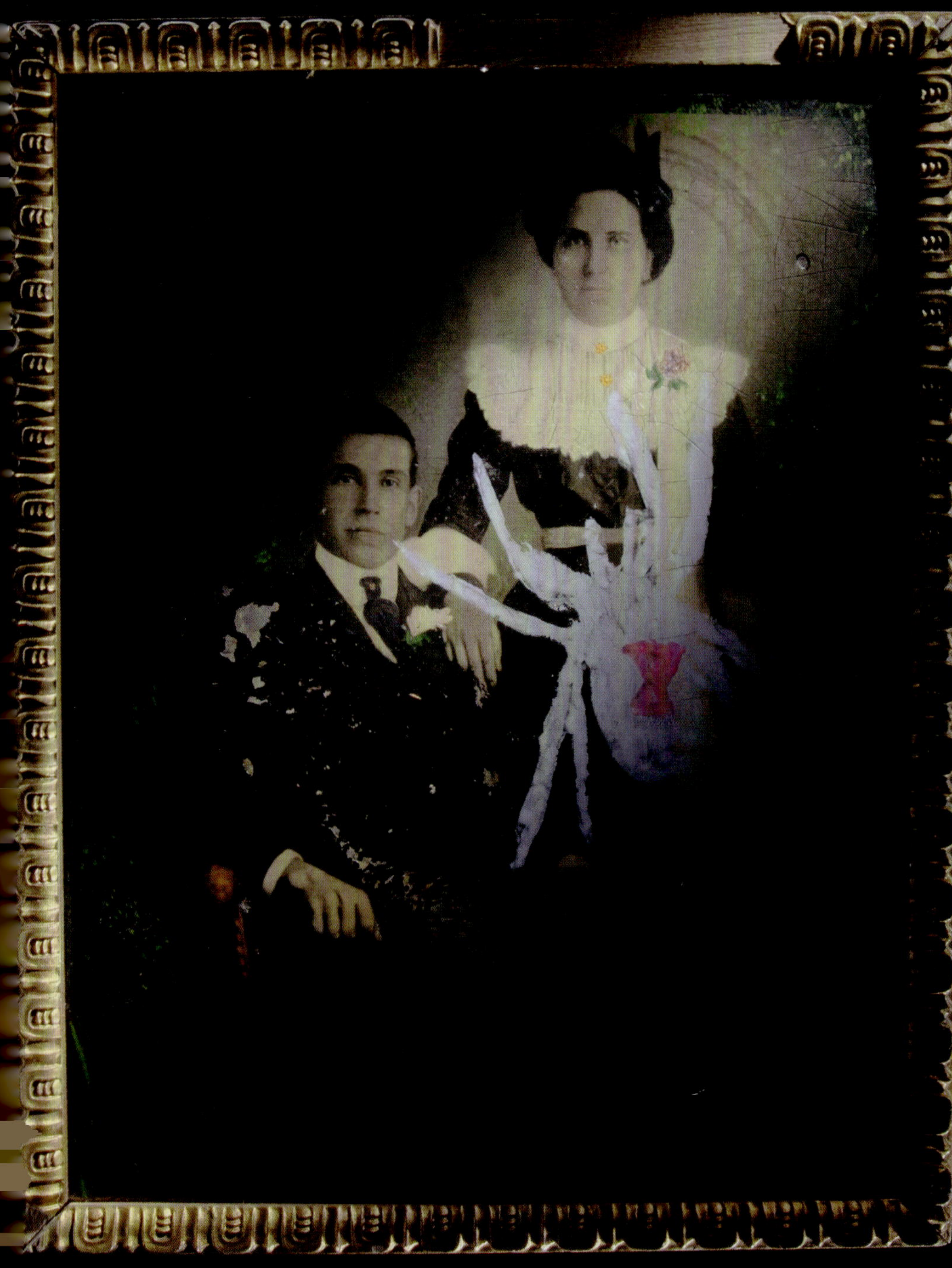

Cursed image of a plantation owner couple. This painting was once stolen by slaves from a manor house and cursed, as shown by the black widow in the painting. The plantation owners were supposed to die.

Portrait maudit d'un couple propriétaire d'une plantation. Cette photographie a été dérobée par des esclaves dans la maison de leurs maîtres et frappée d'un sort comme en témoigne la veuve noire apposée sur l'image. Les propriétaires de la plantation devaient mourir.

Verfluchtes Bildnis eines Plantagenbesitzerpaares. Dieses Bild wurde einst von Sklaven aus einem Herrenhaus entwendet und mit einem Fluch belegt, von dem die schwarze Witwe auf dem Bild kündet. Die Plantagenbesitzer sollten sterben.

Imagen maldita de una pareja de dueños de una plantación. Esta foto fue robada una vez por los esclavos de una casa señorial y fue maldecida por la viuda negra de la foto. Los dueños de las plantaciones iban a morir.

Imagem amaldiçoada de um casal de proprietários de plantações. Este quadro foi uma vez roubado pelos escravos de uma casa senhorial e foi amaldiçoado pela viúva negra no quadro. Os donos das plantações iam morrer.

Vervloekte foto van plantagebezitters. Deze foto werd ooit door slaven gestolen uit een landhuis en vervloekt. Daarvan getuigt de zwarte weduwe op de foto. De plantagebezitters zouden sterven.

24 × 20 cm

Various Manillas. aManillas were pre-coin currency, which were also used as exchange currency in the slave trade.

Manilles diverses. Les manilles étaient des monnaies primitives, notamment utilisées comme valeur d'échange dans le commerce des esclaves.

Verschiedene Manillen. Manillen waren vormünzliche Zahlungsmittel, die auch als Tauschwährung im Sklavenhandel zum Einsatz kamen.

Varias manillas. Las manillas eran moneda corriente, que también se utilizaban como moneda de cambio en la trata de esclavos.

Vários Manillas. Manillas eram moeda pré-moeda, que também eram usadas como moeda de troca no comércio de escravos.

Diverse manillen. Manillen waren betaalmiddelen voor de komst van munten. Ze werden ook als ruilmiddel in de slavenhandel gebruikt.

Bronze

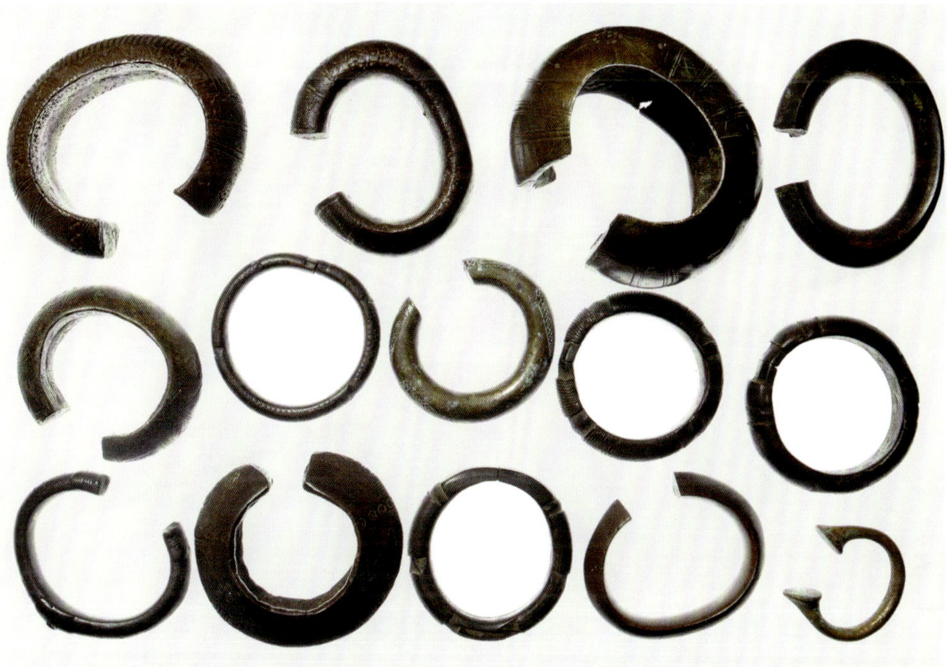

Model of a French slave ship from the 17th century

Maquette d'un navire négrier français du XVIIᵉ siècle

Modell eines französischen Sklavenschiffes aus dem 17. Jahrhundert

Maqueta de un barco de esclavos francés del siglo XVII

Modelo de um navio de escravos francês do século XVII

Model van een Frans slavenschip uit de 17e eeuw

Wood, linen, twine/bois, lin, ficelle,,
40 × 60 cm

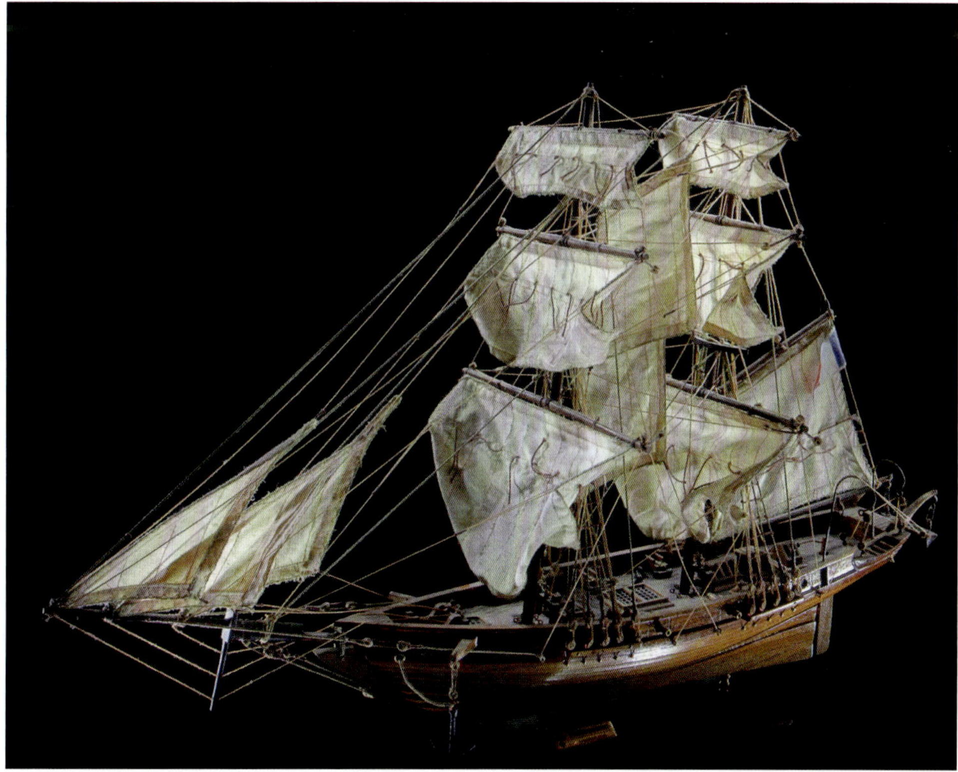

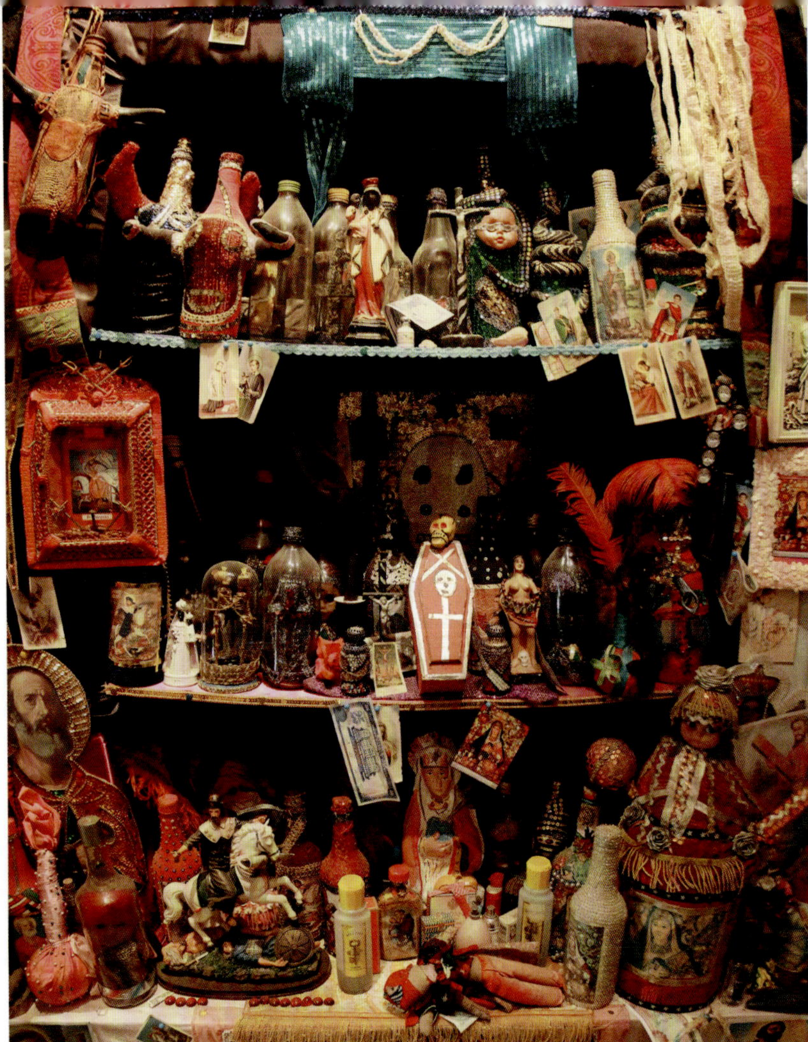

Haiti—Rada and Petro

The Haitian Vodou can be roughly divided into the directions *Rada* and *Petro.* The Rada side includes more West African influences and is considered gentler, whereas the Petro side has the rather hot-blooded forces of Central African origin.

There is *Bondye* (Creole "Good God") a creator deity, whose enormous dimension does not allow a direct contact by humans. For this the *Loas* are available, divine spirit beings, which often have correspondences with the Catholic patron saints.

The image of Vodou in Haiti has suffered a lot due to numerous horror stories. In the

Haïti, Rada et Petro

Le vaudou haïtien se divise schématiquement en deux « directions » : Rada et Petro. Le côté Rada est plus imprégné des influences ouest-africaines et est considéré comme plus doux, alors que l'on retrouve dans le Petro les forces impétueuses de ses origines centrafricaines.

Bondyé (« Bon Dieu » en créole) est une divinité créatrice, mais son immense puissance ne permet pas aux humains d'entrer directement en contact avec elle. Pour cela des *loas* sont à disposition. Ces êtres divins présentent souvent des correspondances avec les saints catholiques.

Haiti – Rada und Petro

Der haitianische Vodou lässt sich grob in die Richtungen *Rada* und *Petro* unterteilen. Die Radaseite hat mehr westafrikanische Einflüsse und gilt als sanfter, wohingegen sich im Petro eher heißblütige Kräfte zentralafrikanischer Herkunft finden.

Es gibt mit *Bondye* (kreolisch „Guter Gott") eine Schöpfergottheit, deren gewaltige Dimension einen direkten Kontakt durch die Menschen nicht zulässt. Für diesen stehen die *Loas* zur Verfügung, göttliche Geistwesen, die oft Entsprechungen bei den katholischen Schutzheiligen haben.

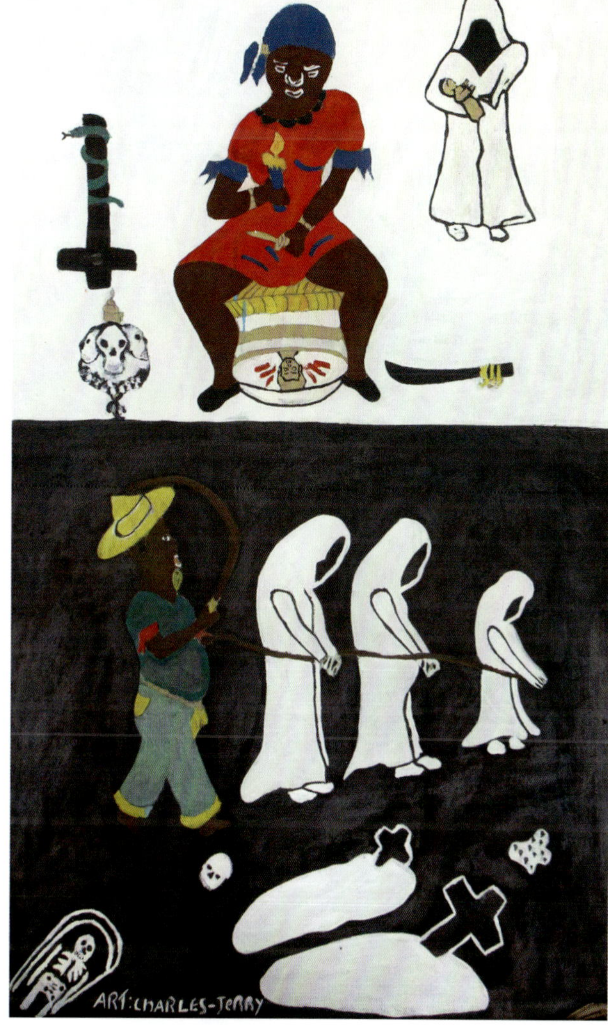

Haití– Rada y Petro

El Vodou haitiano se puede dividir más
o menos en las direcciones Rada y Petro.
El lado de Rada tiene más influencias
de África Occidental y se considera más
suave, mientras que el lado de Petro
tiene fuerzas de sangre caliente de origen
centroafricano.

Con *Bondye* (criollo "Buen Dios")
existe una deidad creadora, cuya enorme
dimensión no permite el contacto directo
de los humanos. Para ello, están disponibles
los *Loas,* seres espirituales divinos que a
menudo tienen correspondencias con los
santos patrones católicos.

Haiti – Rada e Petro

O Vodu haitiano pode ser dividido
aproximadamente nas direções Rada e
Petro. O lado Rada tem mais influências
da África Ocidental e é considerado
mais brando, enquanto o lado Petro
tem forças de sangue quente de origem
centro africana.

Há com Bondye (crioulo "Bom Deus")
uma divindade criadora, cuja enorme
dimensão não permite um contato direto
com os humanos. Para isso estão disponíveis
os Loas, seres espirituais divinos, que muitas
vezes têm correspondências com os santos
padroeiros católicos.

Haïti – rada en petro

De Haïtiaanse vodou kan grofweg
worden onderverdeeld in de richtingen
rada en petro. De rada-kant heeft meer
West-Afrikaanse invloeden en wordt als
zachter beschouwd, terwijl in petro eerder
warmbloedige krachten van Centraal-
Afrikaanse afkomst te vinden zijn.

Met Bondye (de Creoolse 'goede
god') is er een schepper-god, waarvan
de enorme omvang geen direct contact
door mensen toestaat. Hiervoor zijn de
loa's beschikbaar, goddelijke geesten die
vaak overeenkomsten vertonen met de
katholieke beschermheiligen.

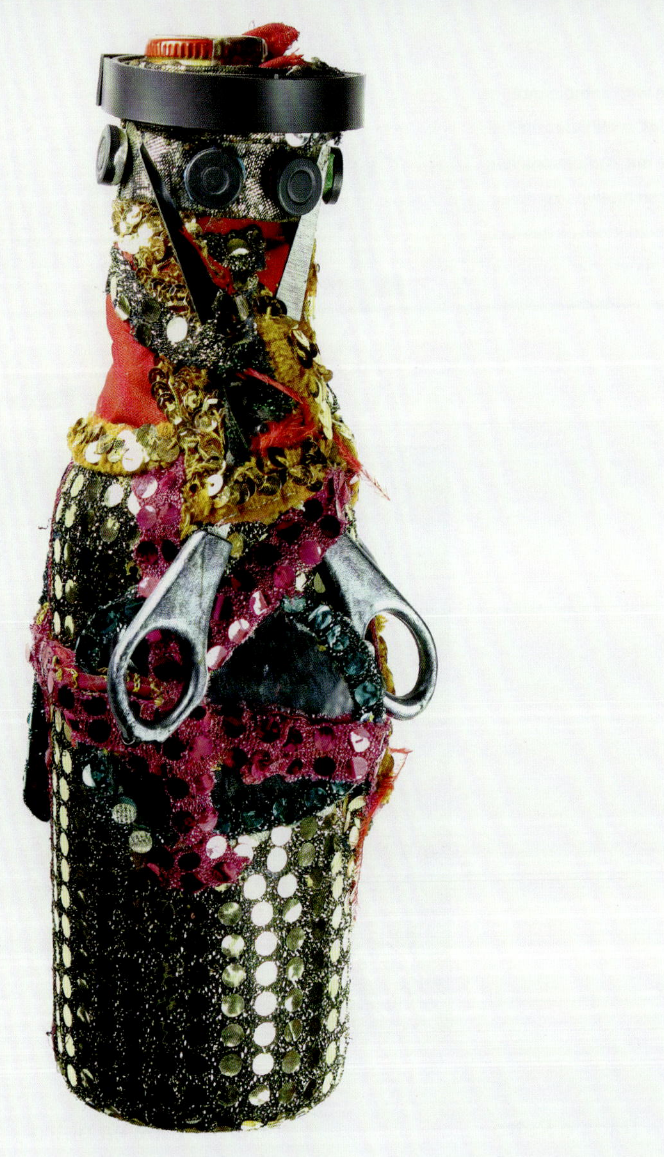

Zombie bottle. The bottle works on an astral level with the power of a dead man. Organic substances from this person are part of the magic mixture in the bottle.

Bouteille zombi. Les bouteilles possèdent une influence sur les astres quand elles utilisent la force d'un défunt. En règle générale, le mélange magique que renferme la bouteille comprend certaines substances organiques de cette personne.

Zombie-Flasche. Die Flasche arbeitet auf astraler Ebene mit der Kraft eines Toten. In der Regel gehören organische Substanzen dieser Person zu der in der Flasche befindlichen magischen Mischung.

Botella zombie. La botella funciona a nivel astral con el poder de un hombre muerto. Normalmente, la mezcla mágica de la botella está compuesta por sustancias orgánicas de esta persona.

Garrafa de zumbi. A garrafa funciona a um nível astral com o poder de um homem morto. Normalmente, as substâncias orgânicas desta pessoa pertencem à mistura mágica na garrafa.

Zombiefles. De fles werkt op astraal niveau met de kracht van een dode. Meestal behoren organische stoffen van deze persoon tot het magische mengsel in de fles.

Bottle, textiles, magnets/Bouteille, textiles, aimants, 26 × 10 cm

end, they have only adapted the massive fears that had long before arisen among slave traders in the face of African beliefs. As the last piece of original black identity, African faith has never allowed itself to be put in chains and has fertilized every religion that came into contact with it.

L'image du vaudou haïtien a beaucoup souffert d'innombrables récits horribles. Ils n'étaient en réalité que la traduction des formidables craintes qu'inspiraient les croyances africaines aux marchands d'esclaves. Dernier lambeau de l'identité noire originelle, la croyance africaine n'a jamais pu être étouffée et a enrichi toutes les religions avec lesquelles elle est entrée en contact.

Das Image des Vodou in Haiti hat sehr unter den Gruselgeschichten gelitten. Diese haben letztlich nur die massiven Ängste adaptiert, die lange vorher bei den Sklavenhändlern angesichts der afrikanischen Glaubensvorstellungen aufkamen. Als letztes Stück ursprünglicher schwarzer Identität hat sich der afrikanische Glaube nie in Ketten legen lassen und jede Religion befruchtet, die mit ihm in Berührung kam.

Damballah bottle (equivalent to Vodun "Dan" in Benin)

Bouteille de Damballah (équivalent du vodun "Dan" au Bénin)

Damballah Flasche (entspricht Vodun „Dan" in Benin)

Botella Damballah (equivalente al vudú "Dan" en Benin)

Garrafa de Damballah (equivalente a Vodun "Dan" no Benin)

Damballah-fles (komt overeen met de vodun Dan in Benin)

Bottle, doll head, textiles/Bouteille, tête de poupée, textiles, 30 × 14 cm

La imagen del Vodou en Haití ha sufrido mucho por las historias de horror. Al final, sólo adaptaron los temores masivos que habían surgido mucho antes entre los traficantes de esclavos en vista de las creencias africanas. Como última pieza de la identidad negra original, la fe africana nunca se ha dejado encadenar y ha fecundado a todas las religiones que han entrado en contacto con ella.

A imagem de Vodu no Haiti sofreu muito com as histórias de terror. No final, eles apenas adaptaram os medos massivos que tinham surgido muito antes entre os comerciantes de escravos, tendo em conta as crenças africanas. Como a última peça de identidade negra original, a fé africana nunca se deixou acorrentar e fertilizar todas as religiões que entraram em contacto com ela.

Het imago van vodou in Haïti heeft ernstig te lijden gehad van alle gruwelverhalen. Deze namen uiteindelijk alleen de enorme angsten over die lang daarvoor onder de slavenhandelaren waren ontstaan bij de aanblik van de Afrikaanse geloofsopvattingen. Als laatste stukje van de oorspronkelijke zwarte identiteit heeft het Afrikaanse geloof zich nooit laten ketenen en elke religie bevrucht die ermee in contact kwam.

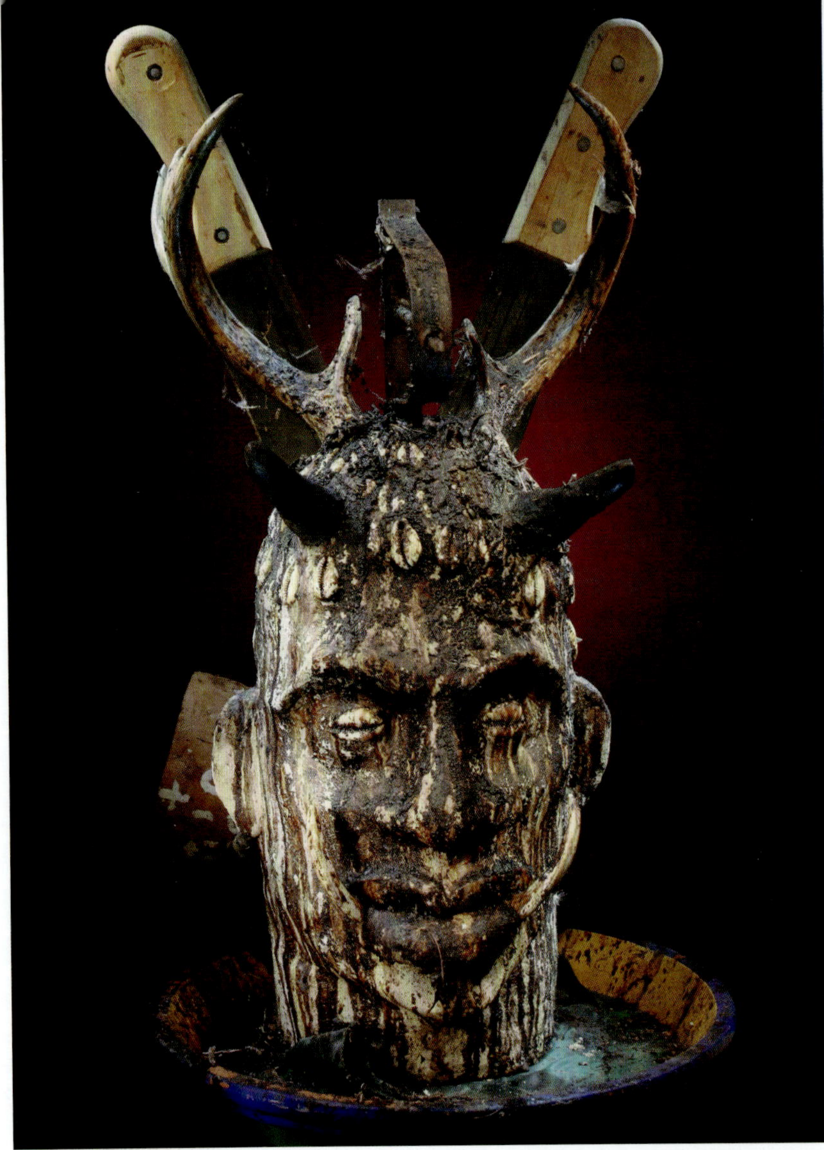

Palo—Congo in Cuba

Palo is also called "Las Reglas de Congo", because mainly the religious ideas of Bantu slaves, who came from Central Africa, have gone into this Afro-Cuban religion. There are also Christian Catholic elements and a wealth of other influences.

There is a creator deity called *Nzambi*, but it is too powerful to be addressed directly by the people. For them the *Kimpungulu* are responsible, spirits, who

Palo, Congo de Cuba

Ce n'est pas par hasard si le Palo s'appelle également « Las Reglas de Congo ». Les concepts religieux des esclaves Bantou venus d'Afrique centrale ont fusionné dans cette religion afro-cubaine. Elle synthétise également des éléments chrétiens et catholiques et une multitude d'autres influences.

La divinité créatrice, Nzambi, paraît trop puissante aux hommes pour qu'ils osent s'adresser directement à elle. Les

Palo – Kongo in Kuba

Man nennt Palo auch „Las Reglas de Congo", weil vornehmlich die religiösen Vorstellungen von Bantu-Sklaven, die aus Zentralafrika stammten, in diese afrokubanische Religion eingegangen sind. Zudem finden sich christlich katholische Elemente und eine Fülle weiterer Einflüsse.

Es gibt eine Schöpfergottheit mit dem Namen *Nzambi*, die jedoch für die Menschen zu gewaltig ist, um von ihnen direkt angesprochen zu werden. Für sie

424

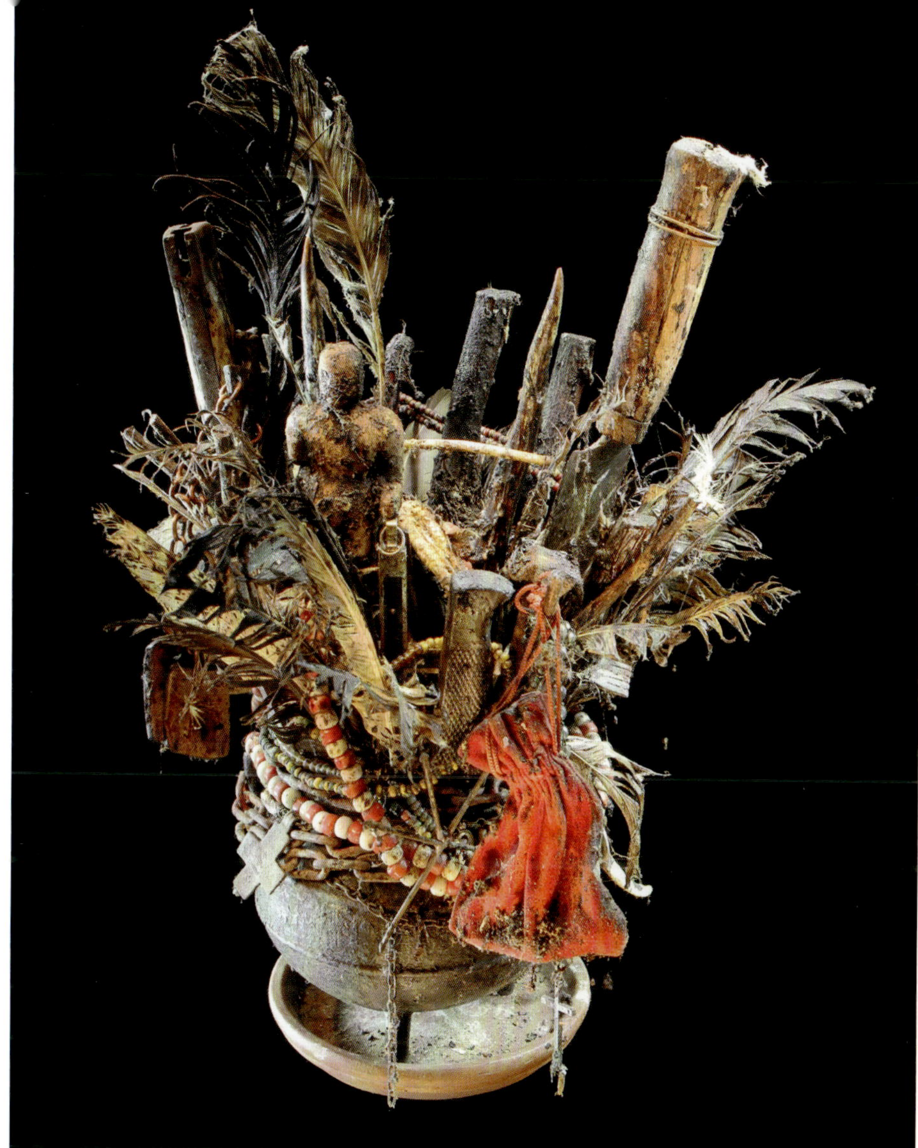

Palo– El Congo en Cuba

Palo también es conocido como "Las Reglas
de El Congo", porque en esta religion
afrocubana, principalmente han entrado
las ideas religiosas de los esclavos bantúes,
que vinieron de África Central También hay
elementos católicos cristianos y una gran
cantidad de otras influencias.

Hay una deidad creadora llamada
Nzambi, pero es demasiado poderosa para
que la gente se dirija directamente a ella. Los
Kimpungulu, espíritus que se encuentran

Palo – Congo em Cuba

Palo também é chamado de "Las Reglas de
Congo", porque principalmente as idéias
religiosas dos escravos bantu, que vieram da
África Central, entraram nesta religião afrocubana. Há também elementos católicos
cristãos e uma riqueza de outras influências.

Existe uma divindade criadora chamada
Nzambi, mas é demasiado poderosa
para que as pessoas sejam abordadas
directamente. Para eles os Kimpungulu são
responsáveis, espíritos, que estão em um

Palo – Congo in Cuba

Palo wordt ook wel 'las reglas de Congo'
genoemd, omdat vooral de religieuze ideeën
van de uit Centraal-Afrika afkomstige
Bantoe-slaven ingang vonden in deze Afro-
Cubaanse religie. Palo bevat ook christelijke
katholieke elementen en een schat aan
andere invloeden.

Er is een schepper-god die Nzambi heet,
die echter te krachtig is voor mensen om
hem direct te kunnen aanspreken. Hiertoe
zijn de *kimpungulu* bevoegd, geesten die op

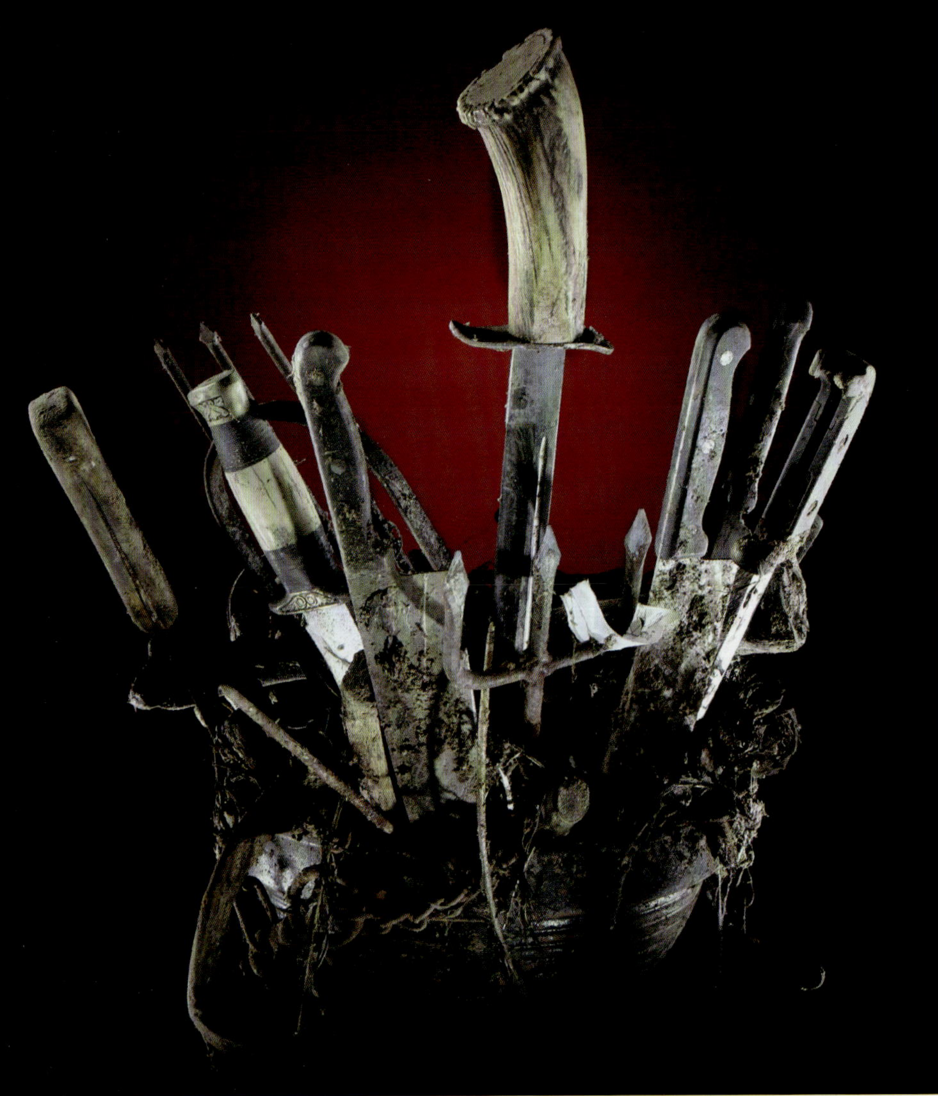

The Jewish Nganga. The nature of this pot is black magic nature and protects against damage spells. It is made on Good Friday and can be used for all kinds of magic.

La nganga juive. Ce pot est un accessoire de magie noire et protège des sortilèges maléfiques. Il a été fabriqué un vendredi saint et peut être utilisé pour les ensorcellements de toutes sortes.

Der „jüdische Nganga". Dieser Topf ist schwarzmagischer Natur und schützt vor Schadenzauber. Er wird am Karfreitag hergestellt und lässt sich für Zauberei aller Art verwenden.

El Nganga judío. Este bote es de naturaleza de magia negra y protege contra los hechizos malignos. Se hace el Viernes Santo y se puede usar para todo tipo de magia.

O Nganga Judeu. Este pote é de magia negra e protege contra feitiços de dano. É feito na Sexta-feira Santa e pode ser usado para todos os tipos de magia.

De 'joodse' nganga. Deze pot is van zwart magische aard en beschermt tegen boze tovenarij. Hij is gemaakt op Goede Vrijdag en kan gebruikt worden voor allerlei soorten magie.

stand on a lower level and are closer to the people and their interests.

Protracted initiations are necessary to obtain priestly status with Palo. The preparations are considerable. They include, for example, learning the secrets of certain medicinal plants, the gods associated with them, dances, chants, ritual sequences and much more. The knowledge is passed on exclusively verbally.

Kimpungulu sont des esprits prévus à cet effet car ils sont d'un niveau inférieur et plus proches des intérêts des hommes. L'obtention du statut de prêtre de Palo nécessite une longue initiation. Les préparations sont considérables et impliquent notamment la connaissance des secrets relatifs aux plantes médicinales spécifiques, aux dieux qui leur sont associés, aux danses, chants et processions rituelles. Ces savoirs font essentiellement l'objet d'une transmission orale.

sind die *Kimpungulu* zuständig, Geister, die auf einer niedrigeren Stufe stehen und den Menschen und ihren Belangen näher sind.

Langwierige Initiationen sind erforderlich, um bei Palo den Priesterstatus zu erlangen. Die Vorbereitungen sind beträchtlich. Sie beinhalten beispielsweise das Erlernen der Geheimnisse um bestimmte Heilpflanzen, die mit ihnen assoziierten Götter, Tänze, Gesänge, Ritualabfolgen und vieles mehr. Das Wissen wird ausschließlich mündlich weitergegeben.

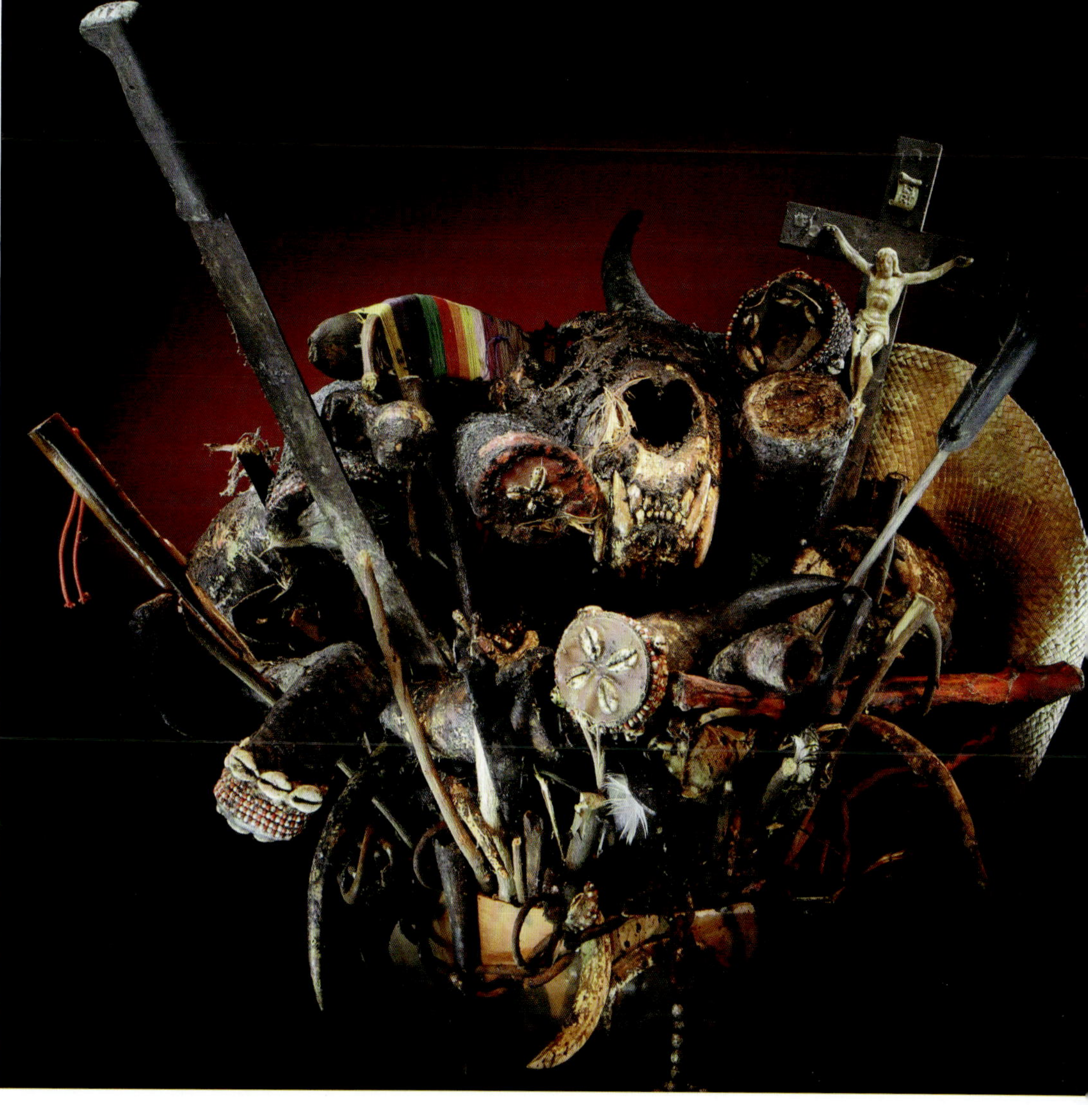

Nganga of a high Congo deity. This Nganga from the Palo Mayombe is dedicated to Nsasi Siete Rayos, the Congolese god of thunderstorms, lightning and thunder.

Nganga d'une haute divinité du Congo. Cette nganga de Palo Mayombe est dédiée à Nsasi Siete Rayo, dieu congolais de l'orage, des éclairs et du tonnerre.

Nganga einer hohen Kongo-Gottheit. Dieser Nganga aus dem Palo Mayombe ist Nsasi Siete Rayos, dem kongolesischen Gott des Gewitters, Blitzes und Donners geweiht.

Nganga de una alta deidad del Congo. Este Nganga del Palo Mayombe está dedicado a Nsasi Siete Rayos, el dios congolés de las tormentas, relámpagos y truenos.

Nganga de uma alta divindade do Congo. Este Nganga do Palo Mayombe é dedicado a Nsasi Siete Rayos, o deus congolês das trovoadas, relâmpagos e trovões.

Nganga van een hoge Congolese godheid. Deze nganga uit de palo mayombe is gewijd aan Nsasi Siete Rayos, de Congolese god van onweer, bliksem en donder.

en un nivel inferior y están más cerca de los humanos y de sus intereses, son los encargados de representarla.

Se necesitan iniciaciones prolongadas para obtener el estatus sacerdotal con Palo. Los preparativos son considerables. Incluyen, por ejemplo, aprender los secretos de ciertas plantas medicinales, los dioses asociados con ellas, danzas, cantos, secuencias rituales y mucho más. El conocimiento sólo se transmite oralmente.

nível mais baixo e estão mais próximos dos humanos e seus interesses.

As iniciações prolongadas são necessárias para obter o estatuto sacerdotal com Palo. Os preparativos são consideráveis. Eles incluem, por exemplo, aprender os segredos de certas plantas medicinais, os deuses associados a elas, danças, cantos, seqüências rituais e muito mais. O conhecimento só é transmitido oralmente.

een lager niveau staan en dichter bij de mens en zijn belangen staan.

Langdurige initiaties zijn nodig om de status van priester bij palo te krijgen. De voorbereidingen zijn aanzienlijk. Ze behelzen bijvoorbeeld het leren van de geheimen van bepaalde geneeskrachtige planten, de hiermee geassocieerde goden, dansen, gezangen, rituele sequenties en nog veel meer. De kennis wordt alleen mondeling overgedragen.

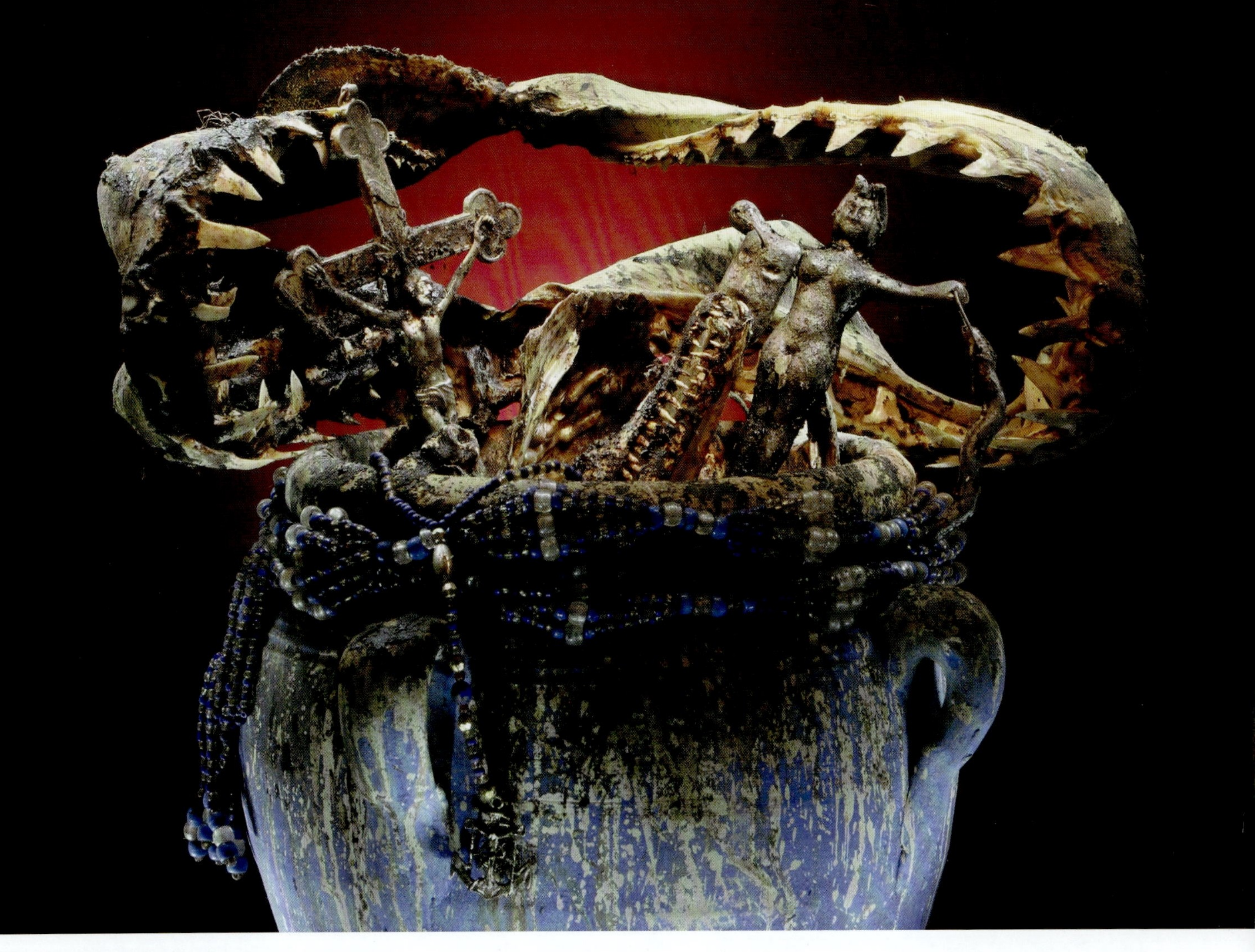

Nganga for Madre Agua
Nganga pour Madre Agua
Nganga für Madre Agua
Nganga para Madre Agua
Nganga para Madre Agua
Nganga voor Madre Agua

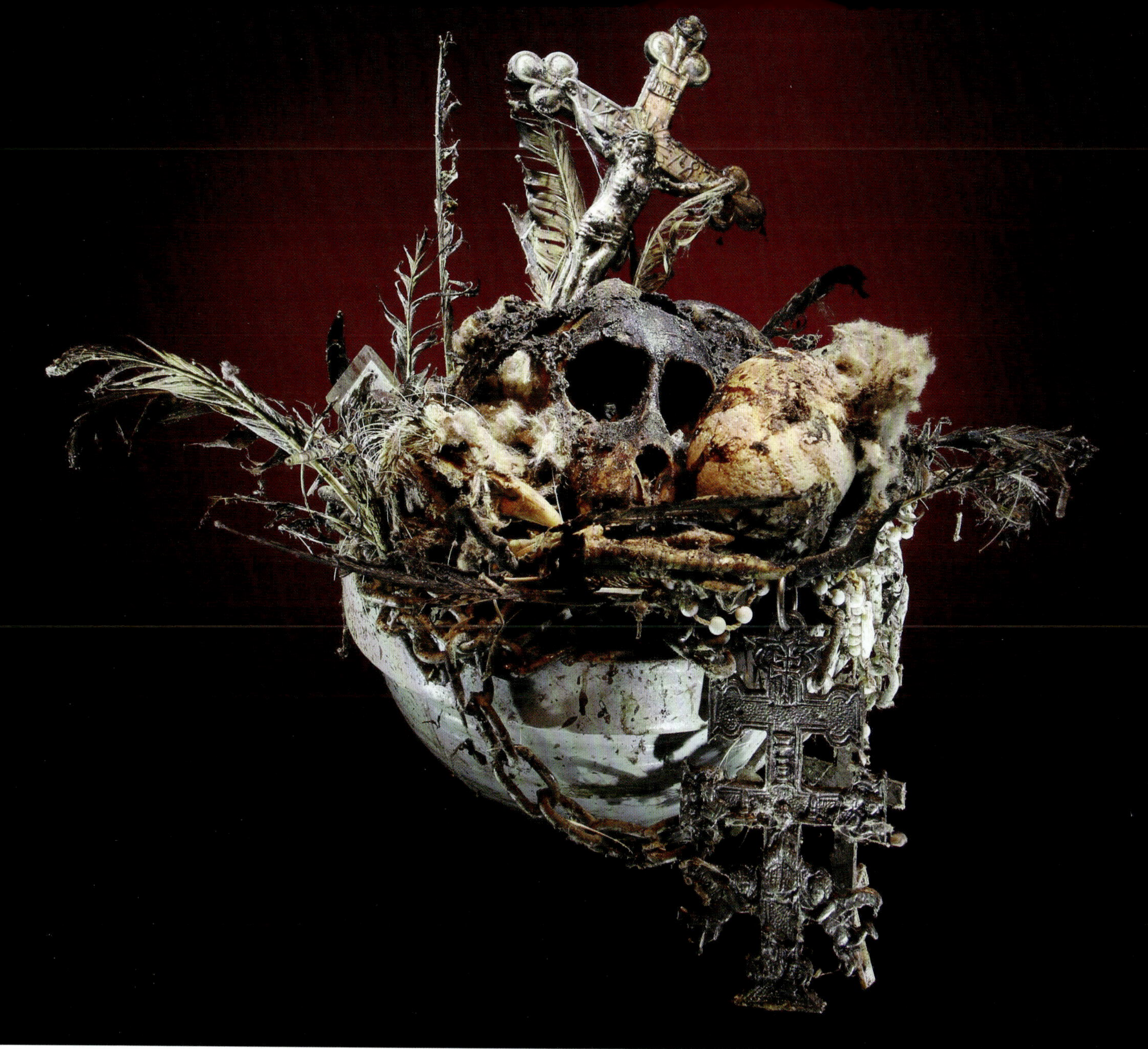

Kunankisi cult object. Kunankisi is also described as the Holy Sacrament and is the heart of the Christian oriented Kimbisa Order, a line of the Palo.

Objet de culte Kunanski. Kunankisi, considéré comme le Sacrement saint, est la pièce centrale de l'ordre Kimbisa d'inspiration chrétienne, qui constitue l'une des lignées du Palo.

Kultobjekt Kunankisi. Kunankisi wird auch als das Heilige Sakrament beschrieben und ist das Herzstück des christlich orientierten Kimbisa-Ordens, einer Linie des Palo.

Objeto de culto Kunankisi. Kunankisi también se describe como el Santísimo Sacramento y es el corazón de la orden c ristiana Kimbisa, una línea del Palo.

Objeto de culto Kunankisi. Kunankisi também é descrita como o Santo Sacramento e é o coração da Ordem Cristã Kimbisa, uma linha do Palo.

Cultusobject Kunankisi. Kunankisi wordt ook wel het Heilig Sacrament genoemd en is het hart van de christelijke Kimbisa-orde, een lijn van de palo.

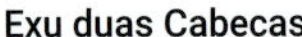

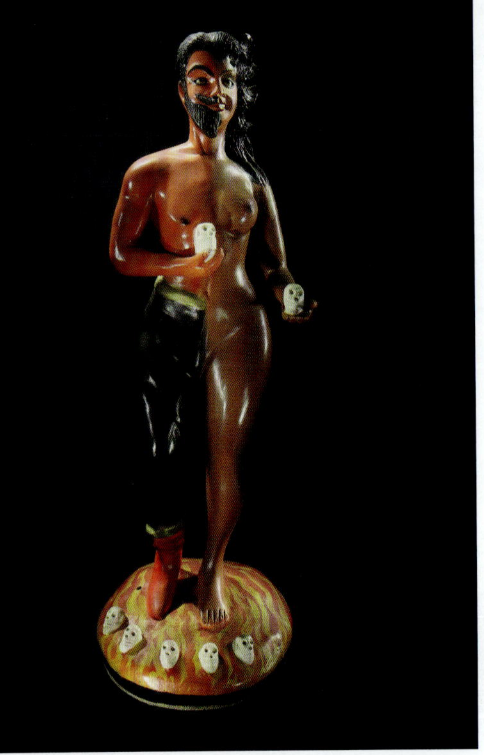

Quimbanda, a child of Macumba

Originally it belonged to the tradition of the Afro-Brazilian religion Macumba, but then broke away from it and today plays an important role mainly in the underground of the Brazilian cities.

What we are talking about here is *Quimbanda,* a faith that has absorbed many influences from the Angolan and Congolese bantu religions. For the layman, the altars with their often wild mixtures of devotional objects give the impression of shrill, bizarre pop art, but beneath this surface everything has its strict order.

To the deities—*Exus* (masculine) and *Pomba giras* (feminine)—the sacrifices are gladly offered at night at crossroads. Mostly schnapps, tobacco, flowers, perfume or food preparations are used. The gods, known as morally demanding, are considered strict, but helpful and reliable towards their followers.

Quimbanda, enfant de Macumba

Intégrée originellement à la tradition de la religion afro-brésilienne Macumba, la Quimbanda s'est ensuite détachée d'elle et joue aujourd'hui essentiellement un rôle dans la clandestinité des grandes villes brésiliennes.

Cette tendance religieuse regroupe de nombreuses influences issues des religions Bantou de l'Angola et du Congo. Pour le profane, ses autels et leur assortiment débridé d'articles de piété produisent l'effet d'une étrange sculpture Pop Art tape à l'œil, mais malgré les apparences, chaque chose est à sa place.

Les adeptes déposent souvent des offrandes aux croisements des voies de circulation, de nuit, à l'attention des déités Exus (masculin) et Pomba giras (féminin). Alcool, tabac, fleurs, parfum ou mets cuisinés sont ainsi mis à disposition. Réputés pour leur haute exigence morale, les dieux sont forts, serviables et fiables.

Quimbanda, ein Kind Macumbas

Ursprünglich gehörte sie zur Tradition der afrobrasilianischen Religion Macumba, löste sich dann aber von ihr und spielt heute vorwiegend im Untergrund der brasilianischen Großstädte eine wichtige Rolle.

Die Rede ist von *Quimbanda,* einer Glaubensrichtung, die viele Einflüsse aus den angolanischen und kongolesischen Banturreligionen in sich aufgenommen hat. Für den Laien erwecken die Altäre mit ihren oft wilden Mischungen von Devotionalien den Eindruck schriller, bizarrer Pop-Art, aber unter dieser Oberfläche hat alles seine strenge Ordnung.

Den Gottheiten – *Exus* (maskulin) und *Pomba giras* (feminin) – werden die Opfer (meist Schnaps, Tabak, Blumen, Parfüm oder Speisezubereitungen) gern nachts an Wegkreuzungen dargebracht. Die als moralisch anspruchsvoll bekannten Götter gelten ihren Anhängern gegenüber als streng, aber hilfsbereit und zuverlässig.

Exu Cobra

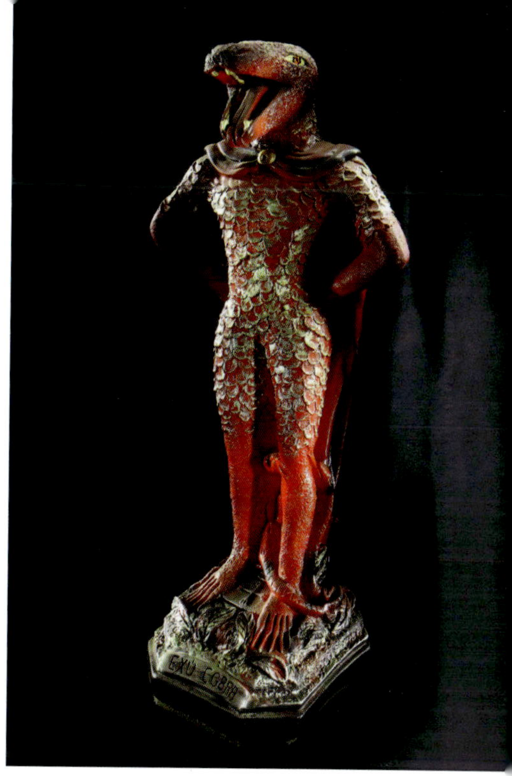

Quimbanda, un hijo de Macumba

Originalmente pertenecía a la tradición de la religión afro-brasileña Macumba, pero luego se separó de ella y hoy juega un papel importante principalmente en el subsuelo de las ciudades brasileñas.

Estamos hablando de *Quimbanda,* una fe que ha absorbido muchas influencias de las religiones angoleñas y congoleñas prohibidas. Para el profano, los altares con sus mezclas a menudo salvajes de objetos devocionales dan la impresión de un arte pop estridente y bizarro, pero bajo esta superficie todo tiene su orden estricto.

A las deidades –*Exus* (masculino) y *Pomba giras* (femenino)– a menudo se les ofrecen sacrificios por la noche en las encrucijadas. Se utilizan principalmente aguardiente, tabaco, flores, perfumes o preparaciones alimenticias. Los dioses, conocidos como moralmente exigentes, se consideran estrictos con sus seguidores, pero serviciales y confiables.

Quimbanda, uma criança de Macumba

Originalmente pertencia à tradição da religião afro-brasileira Macumba, mas depois rompeu com ela e hoje desempenha um papel importante principalmente no metrô das cidades brasileiras.

Estamos a falar da Quimbanda, uma fé que tem absorvido muitas influências das religiões banidas angolana e congolesa. Para o leigo, os altares com suas misturas muitas vezes selvagens de objetos devocionais dão a impressão de arte pop estridente e bizarra, mas sob essa superfície tudo tem sua ordem estrita.

As divindades - Exus (masculina) e Pomba giras (feminina) - são frequentemente sacrificadas à noite em encruzilhadas. Principalmente schnapps, tabaco, flores, perfumes ou preparações alimentares são utilizados. Os deuses, conhecidos como moralmente exigentes, são considerados rígidos para com os seus seguidores, mas úteis e confiáveis.

Quimbanda, een kind van Macumba

Quimbanda stond oorspronkelijk in de traditie van de Afro-Braziliaanse religie macumba, maar maakte zich daar los van en speelt tegenwoordig vooral ondergronds een belangrijke rol in Braziliaanse steden.

We hebben het over quimbanda, een geloof dat veel invloeden uit de Angolese en Congolese Bantoe-godsdiensten heeft overgenomen. Voor de leek wekken de altaren met hun vaak wilde mengelingen van devotionalia de indruk van schrille, bizarre popart, maar onder dit oppervlak heeft alles een strikte orde.

Aan de godheden – Exus (mannelijk) en Pomba giras (vrouwelijk) – wordt vaak 's nachts op een kruispunt geofferd. Meestal worden hiervoor sterkedrank, tabak, bloemen, parfum of bereide etenswaren gebruikt. De als moreel veeleisend bekendstaande goden worden tegenover hun volgelingen beschouwd als streng, maar behulpzaam en betrouwbaar.

KÖNEMANN

© 2019 koenemann.com GmbH

www.koenemann.com

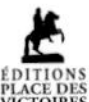

© Éditions Place des Victoires
6, rue du Mail – 75002 Paris
www.victoires.com
ISBN : 978-2-8099-1741-3
Dépôt légal : 1er trimestre 2020

Concept, Project Management: koenemann.com GmbH

Text: Philipp Schiemann

Translation into French (text) : Véronique Valentin

Translations into English, Spanish, Portuguese and Dutch by koenemann.com GmbH

Layout: Regine Ermert

Picture credits: Henning Christoph, Markus Matzel; p. 421 Charles Art Jerry

Alle abgebildeten Objekte auf den Studioaufnahmen stammen aus der Sammlung Henning Christoph / Soul of Africa Museum, Essen.

All objects depicted on the studio pictures come from the Henning Christoph Collection / Soul of Africa Museum, Essen, Germany.

ISBN: 978-3-7419-2478-1

Printed in China by Shyft Publishing / Hunan Tianwen Xinhua Printing Co., Ltd.